Fodor's

THE COMPLETE GUIDE TO
THE NATIONAL PARKS
OF THE WEST

2nd Edition

Fodor's Travel Publications   New York, Toronto, London, Sydney, Auckland
www.fodors.com

Be a Fodor's Correspondent

Share your trip with Fodor's

Our latest guidebook to the National Parks of the West owes its success to travelers like you. Throughout, you'll find photographs submitted by members of Fodors.com to our "Show Us Your ... National Parks" photo contest. Facing this page is one of the contest's winning photographs taken by Christina Colluci of her 6-year-old daughter "gliding" along the boardwalk around Grand Prismatic Spring in Yellowstone National Park. All winners received a copy of *The National Parks* by Dayton Duncan and Ken Burns published by Knopf Publishing Group, which sponsored the contest.

We are especially proud of this color edition. No other guide to the National Parks of the West is as up to date or has as much practical planning information, along with hundreds of color photographs and illustrated maps. We've also included "Word of Mouth" quotes from travelers who shared their experiences with others on our forums. If you're inspired and can plan a better trip because of this guide, we've done our job.

We invite you to join the travel conversation: Your opinion matters to us and to your fellow travelers. Come to Fodors.com to plan your trip, share an experience, ask a question, submit a photograph, post a review, or write a trip report. Tell our editors about your trip. They want to know what went well and how we can make this guide even better. Share your opinions at our feedback center at fodors.com/feedback, or email us at editors@fodors.com with the subject line "National Parks Editor." You might find your comments published in a future Fodor's guide. We look forward to hearing from you.

Happy Traveling!

Tim Jarrell, Publisher

FODOR'S THE COMPLETE GUIDE TO THE NATIONAL PARKS OF THE WEST

Editor: Debbie Harmsen, Michael Nalepa

Editorial Contributors: Linda Cabasin, Maria Hart, Salwa Jabado, Shannon M. Kelly, Matt Lombardi, Jess Moss, Cate Starmer

Writers: John Blodgett, Barbara Colligan, Cheryl Crabtree, Patrick Dearen, Jennifer Edwards, Jane Gendron, Carrie Frasure, Cara LaBrie, Mara Levin, Tom Griffith, Brian Kevin, Debbie Olsen, Steve Pastorino, Gary Peterson, Marge Peterson, Reed Parsell, Martha Schindler Connors, Swain Scheps, Holly S. Smith, Christine Vovakes, Bobbi Zane

Production Editor: Carrie Parker

Maps & Illustrations: Mark Stroud and Henry Colomb, Moon Street Cartography; Tom Patterson, *cartographers;* Bob Blake, Rebecca Baer, *map editors;* William Wu, *information graphics*

Design: Fabrizio La Rocca, *creative director;* Guido Caroti, *art directors;* Tina Malaney, Chie Ushio, Jessica Walsh, *designers;* Melanie Marin, *senior picture editor*

Cover Photo: (Thor's Hammer, Bryce Canyon National Park, Utah): Jeff Vanuga

Production Manager: Steve Slawsky

SPECIAL SALES

This book is available at special discounts for bulk purchases for sales promotions or premiums. Special editions, including personalized covers, excerpts of existing books, and corporate imprints, can be created in large quantities for special needs. For more information, write to Special Markets/Premium Sales, 1745 Broadway, MD 6-2, New York, New York 10019, or e-mail specialmarkets@randomhouse.com.

AN IMPORTANT TIP & AN INVITATION

Although all prices, opening times, and other details in this book are based on information supplied to us at press time, changes occur all the time in the travel world, and Fodor's cannot accept responsibility for facts that become outdated or for inadvertent errors or omissions. So **always confirm information when it matters,** especially if you're making a detour to visit a specific place. Your experiences—positive and negative— matter to us. If we have missed or misstated something, **please write to us.** We follow up on all suggestions. Contact the The Complete Guide to the National Parks of the West editor at editors@fodors.com or c/o Fodor's at 1745 Broadway, New York, NY 10019.

PRINTED IN SINGAPORE

10 9 8 7 6 5 4 3 2 1

CONTENTS

Fodor's Features

MAPS

ABOUT THIS BOOK

What's Inside

For each of the 37 national parks of the West, our writers have gathered comprehensive information on everything within the park and on the towns and attractions nearby. We have included as many sights, activities, lodging and dining options, and practical details as space allows, focusing on delivering the kind of in-depth, first-hand knowledge that you won't get elsewhere. Our first three chapters introduce you to the national parks of the West and provide tips on how to make the most of your visits to these national treasures. Following these insightful chapters is our suggested Driving Tours, a mix of itineraries that help you match parks together for regional road-trips. The bulk of the book are the chapters for each national park, listed alphabetically. For those who love to camp, we've also included a campground chart at the back of the book to help you quickly see what camping is like at national park campgrounds.

Our Ratings

Sometimes you find terrific travel experiences and sometimes they just find you. But usually the burden is on you to select the right combination of experiences. That's where our ratings come in.

As travelers we've all discovered a place so wonderful that its worthiness is obvious. And sometimes that place is so experiential that superlatives don't do it justice: you just have to be there to know. These sights, properties, and experiences get our highest rating, **Fodor's Choice,** indicated by orange stars throughout this book.

Black stars highlight sights and properties we deem **Highly Recommended,** places that our writers, editors, and readers praise again and again for consistency and excellence.

By default, there's another category: Any place we include in this book is by definition worth your time, unless we say otherwise. And we will.

Disagree with any of our choices? Care to nominate a place or suggest that we rate one more highly? Visit our feedback center at www.fodors.com/feedback.

Budget Well

Hotel and restaurant price categories from ¢ to $$$$ are defined in the opening pages of each chapter. For attractions, we always give standard adult admission fees; reductions are usually available for children, students, and senior citizens. Want to pay with plastic? **AE, D, DC, MC, V** following restaurant and hotel listings indicate whether American Express, Discover, Diners

Listings

★	Fodor's Choice
★	Highly recommended
⊠	Physical address
⊹	Directions or Map coordinates
⑤	Mailing address
☎	Telephone
🖷	Fax
⊕	On the Web
✉	E-mail
🎫	Admission fee
⊙	Open/closed times
Ⓜ	Metro stations
⊟	Credit cards

Hotels & Restaurants

🏨	Hotel
⇆	Number of rooms
⟁	Facilities
❑	Meal plans
✕	Restaurant
⟁	Reservations
🏛	Dress code
⊠	Smoking
🍷	BYOB

Outdoors

♣	Golf
⟁	Camping

Other

♨	Family-friendly
⇨	See also
⊠	Branch address
☞	Take note

Club, MasterCard, and Visa are accepted.Restaurants

Unless we state otherwise, restaurants are open for lunch and dinner daily. We mention dress only when there's a specific requirement and reservations only when they're essential or not accepted—it's always best to book ahead.

Hotels

Hotels have private bath, phone, TV, and air-conditioning and operate on the European Plan (*aka* EP, meaning without meals), unless we specify that they use the Continental Plan (CP, with a continental breakfast), Breakfast Plan (BP, with a full breakfast), or Modified American Plan (MAP, with breakfast and dinner), or are all-inclusive (including all meals and most activities). We always list facilities but not whether you'll be charged an extra fee to use them, so always when pricing accommodations, find out what's included.

Campgrounds

For many visitors, camping is a central part of the national park experience. In our Where to Stay sections, we list most of the developed, frontcountry campgrounds in a park, as well as often primitive and backcountry options, plus some of the best camping outside the parks. We also have a section in the back of the book, "Campgrounds at a Glance," with campground charts for all 37 parks in this book. You can see what each campground has to offer, including such facilities as showers and fire rings, seasonal closings, and how much a campsite costs. When applicable, we also explain the park's backcountry camping opportunities and policies for permits and fire safety.

WHAT IT COSTS					
	¢	$	$$	$$$	$$$$
Restaurants	under $8	$8–$12	$13–$20	$21–$30	over $30
Hotels	under $70	$70–$100	$101–$150	$151–$200	over $200
Camping	under $10	$10–$17	$18–$35	$36–$50	over $50

Restaurant prices are per person for a main course at dinner. Hotel prices are per night for two people in a standard double room in high season, excluding taxes and services charges. Camping prices are for a standard (no hookups, pit toilets, fire grates, picnic tables) campsite per night. Prices and price categories are in U.S. dollars except for the three Canadian parks in this book—Banff, Jasper, Waterton—in which the dollars represent Canadian dollars.

Welcome to
the Parks

NATIONAL TREASURES

"I went to the woods because I wished to live deliberately," wrote Henry David Thoreau, ". . . to front only the essential facts of life, and see if I could learn what it had to teach, and not, when I came to die, discover that I had not lived . . . I wanted to live deep and suck out all the marrow of life."

For many, a trip to the national parks is just that: a deliberate departure from measured daily life; an escape to a place where one can breathe life in deeply—a "seize the day," if you will. In a society overwrought with constant man-made stimulation—billboards, sound bites, a flood of unsolicited mail—something deep within the human spirit cries out for tranquility, for a place where the stimulation is not an intrusion that distracts and drains us, but a delightful diversion that invigorates us and fills us with wonder.

With their bigger-than-life panoramas, the more than three-dozen western national parks covered in this guide are particularly good at awakening the senses and igniting the imagination. Whether it's the bubbling mud pots and steaming fumaroles at Yellowstone, the raging Colorado River pushing through the Grand Canyon, or the quiet nibblings and ambulations of mule deer, black bears, and bighorn sheep at Yosemite, the stirrings of creation remind us that there is a refreshing alternate reality outside our brick-and-mortar-confined existences.

A visit to a western national park is more than a retreat. It is a great adventure. You can explore new terrain, encounter creatures great and small—think hungry grizzly, scrappy marmot—and add more knowledge to your noggin through naturalist talks and ranger walks.

If you, or your family, want mega action, the parks offer that, too. Float the Rio Grande at Big Bend, rock climb at Joshua Tree, wheel around in your 4X4 at Capitol Reef, or strap on some snowshoes or cross-country skis and tackle the powder at Grand Teton.

Any way you look at it, you can definitely live deliberately.

—The Editors

NATIONAL PARK SERVICE THEN AND NOW

1

Go West, Young Man

A romantic image of the West has gripped the American psyche since the nation's birth. As the frontier shifted from the Ohio River Valley to the Great Plains to the Rocky Mountains and finally to the Pacific, the land just over the horizon promised freedom, open space, self-sufficiency, and adventure. Manifest Destiny, gold rushes, and the Homestead Act of 1862—which offered 160-acre parcels of land to anyone 21 years or older with $18—spurred settlers, prospectors, soldiers, and laborers to tame the American West.

Vocal Pioneers

During this unprecedented landgrab, interest in preserving scenic western lands and archaeological sites emerged, as well as a national sense of responsibility for the wilderness. While exploring the Dakotas in 1832, painter George Catlin noted the potential for loss of wildlife and wilderness. He wrote that it could be preserved "by some great protecting policy of government . . . in a magnificent park."

The tipping point came three decades later. In 1864, in the midst of the Civil War, President Lincoln set aside Yosemite Valley and the Mariposa Grove of giant sequoias as a public trust to preserve the land for future generations. This revolutionary federal preservation concept was just the beginning. When a handful of would-be entrepreneurs explored Yellowstone in 1870, dreaming up the possibilities for development of this fairyland they'd found, a lawyer, Cornelius Hedges, made the bold suggestion that they preserve this geologically astounding land rather than capitalize on it.

Whatever persuasive prose Hedges used is not certain, but persuade them he did. A year later, one of these explorers was in

WHAT'S NEW AT THE PARKS

New Trails and Parks Connections. In March 2009, the National Park Service announced it would be making $333,000 worth of improvements to several places where the NPS intersects with the National Trails System. The Connect Trails to Parks project will include a new trail connecting the Old Spanish National Historic Trail and Slickrock National Recreational Trail to Arches National Park in Moab, Utah.

NPS in Transition. In January 2009, Mary Bomar resigned as director of the National Park Service. Dan Wenk served as acting NPS Director, until late September of that year, when the Senate approved NPS veteran Jonathan Jarvis to be the new director.

Centennial Challenge Charges Ahead. As part of the national parks' Centennial Challenge, designed to get the parks into shape for their 100th anniversary in 2016, the NPS plans to put $27 million—$10.5 million from the federal government, the rest matching gifts from private companies and individuals—toward improving structures, managing natural assets, and increasing educational programs.

Economic Stimulus Money Going to the Parks. In April 2009, Secretary of the Interior Ken Salazar announced that the $787 billion economic stimulus package passed by Congress would provide more than $750 million to the NPS, restoring and protecting resources and creating jobs in more than 750 national parks.

the House of Representatives promoting the park plan. Also lobbying for Yellowstone were artist Thomas Moran, photographer William Henry Jackson, and U.S. Geological Survey director Ferdinand Hayden, who'd been appointed by Congress to lead an expedition to Yellowstone to validate the rumors of its otherworldly features. Congress was more than convinced of its merits to be preserved, and in early 1872, President Ulysses S. Grant signed into law the bill creating Yellowstone National Park.

The 1890s saw the creation of several more national parks, as well as the Forest Reserve Act of 1891, which led to our first national forests. In 1906 the Antiquities Act passed, which allowed presidents to name national monuments. That same year, President Theodore Roosevelt established Devils Tower as the first such site, making Wyoming the home of both the first national park and first national monument.

Pioneering conservationists like Robert Underwood Johnson and John Muir advocated for further preservation of Western treasures. Muir, who founded the Sierra Club in 1892 and is often called the father of the National Park System, greatly influenced Theodore Roosevelt, who went on to establish five national parks.

The Birth of the National Park System

By 1916 the Interior Department oversaw 14 national parks. In order to streamline the management of the national parks and monuments, President Woodrow Wilson approved legislation creating the National Park Service, or NPS. The mission of the new agency under the Interior Department was "to conserve the scenery and the natural and historic objects and the wildlife therein and to provide for the enjoyment of the same in such manner and by such means as will leave them unimpaired for the enjoyment of future generations."

While Washington made these lands protected, railroads made visiting them a reality. Thousands traveled west to such national parks as Grand Canyon, Glacier, Yosemite Valley, and Crater Lake, and stayed in the extravagant lodges constructed by the railroad companies.

Growing Pains

The parks initially had operated on the premise of preservation and visitor enjoyment, but by 1932, the park concept had expanded to include educational components with the formation of the NPS's Naturalist Division. The naturalists were

NATIONAL PARKS TIMELINE

1872	Yellowstone National Park becomes the world's first national park.
1890	Sequoia, Yosemite, and General Grant (later part of Kings Canyon) become national parks.
1902	President Theodore Roosevelt establishes his first of five parks, Crater Lake.

assigned to interpret park features to the public through educational outreaches. The park system had also begun to rethink its wildlife management practices.

The 1930s brought a core of hardy workers to the nation's parks and forests through the Civilian Conservation Corps (CCC), part of President Franklin Delano Roosevelt's Works Progress Administration during the Great Depression. A total of 41 work camps were set up within the national parks.

As the country's population continued to grow, and society learned more about the environment and the effects of the Industrial Revolution, there was a need to take additional steps to retain pristine wilderness and historic areas. Congress addressed this in the 1960s and early '70s with a host of legislative measures: the Wilderness Act (1964), National Historic Preservation Act (1966), Clean Air Act (1967), Wild and Scenic Rivers Act (1968), National Environmental Policy Act (1969), and the Endangered Species Act (1973).

The NPS Today

The National Park Service now manages nearly 400 natural, cultural, and recreational sites on some 84 million acres. These sites include national parks as well as monuments, memorials, historic parks, and national preserves. The NPS defines these lands as follows:

National Park: A natural place, generally large in size, that possesses an array of attributes, including an outstanding example of a particular type of resource and great opportunities for public use and enjoyment (or for scientific study). It may also be historically significant. National parks are protected from hunting, mining, logging, and other consumptive activities.

National Historic Park: A historic site that extends beyond single properties.

National Historic Site: Usually containing a single historical feature directly associated with its subject. Derived from the Historic Sites Act of 1935, a number of historic sites were established by secretaries of the Interior, but most have been authorized by acts of Congress. They appear on the National Register of Historic Places.

National Monument: A landmark, structure, or other object of historic or scientific interest situated on lands owned or controlled by the rnment.

National Memorial: Commemorative of a historic person or episode.

National Preserve: An area having characteristics associated with national parks, but in

1903	Theodore Roosevelt makes Wind Cave the country's seventh national park, and the first dedicated to preserving a cave.
1906	Congress selects Mesa Verde as a national park. It is the first cultural park in the system.
1916	President Woodrow Wilson signs the Organic Act, creating the National Park Service.
1919	The Grand Canyon goes from a national monument to a national park.

1933	Franklin Delano Roosevelt develops the Civilian Conservation Corps, which works in national parks and forests, planting three billion trees in nine years.
1951	After much debate, the National Park Service adopts its official emblem: the outline of an arrowhead surrounding a mountain, a sequoia tree, a river, and a bison. The arrowhead represents historical and archaeological values, the tree and bison represent vegetation and wildlife, and the mountains and water represent scenic and recreational values.

which oil and gas exploration and extraction, hunting, and trapping are allowed. Many existing national preserves, without sport hunting, would qualify for national park designation.

National Recreation Area: Places with this designation include reservoirs used for water-based activities and urban parks that combine outdoor recreation with the preservation of significant historic resources and important natural areas.

Hot Issues

More than a century ago, conservationists were instrumental in establishing the national parks as preserved areas; their efforts continue today, as these set-aside areas face a host of challenges, including overcrowding, noise and light pollution, and wildlife management. And of course, funding is consistently a concern.

Here are a few of the issues facing the National Park Service today:

Attendance. Although the parks must compete with an ever-expanding range of entertainment options, attendance has been holding steady for the past several years, with close to 275 million recreational visits each year. A major challenge for the coming century will be attracting an increasingly busy, plugged-in population to visit the wilderness. Paradoxically, the most popular parks are facing the opposite problem—making sure huge seasonal crowds don't negatively impact the parks.

Funding. Tight budgets force the parks to consider alternative revenue sources, including corporate sponsorships. But you won't be seeing "McDonald's Grand Canyon" or "Half Dome, brought to you by Coca-Cola" anytime soon. In fact, 2009 was the second year that the NPS, through its Centennial Challenge program, was able to more than double its federal dollars with matching donations made by private companies and individuals.

Migration Patterns. Managing wildlife is an increasingly complex responsibility. The parks' animal inhabitants don't recognize political boundaries: for example, elk stray into unprotected areas around Rocky Mountain National Park, and wolves hunt beyond the confines of Yellowstone, sometimes killing animals on nearby ranches.

Pollution. Standing in a pristine natural paradise like Yellowstone or the Grand Canyon, you're not likely to think about pollution—but the problem encompasses more than just visible smog. As development encroaches on the parks, it brings

1967	Congress establishes the National Park Foundation as a separate, fund-raising arm for the parks.
1984	The fossils of one of the oldest dinosaurs ever unearthed are found in Petrified Forest National Park.
1987	Annual recreational visitors to the parks hits an all time high: 287,244,998.
1988	Devastating fires rage through Yellowstone, spreading to 793,000 of the park's 2.2 million acres. One of the fires, which

	consumed over 410,000 acres, was caused by a discarded cigarette.
1994	Death Valley and Joshua Tree national monuments each become national parks.
2001	The George W. Bush administration establishes the National Parks Legacy Project to provide funds to restore and improve park facilities and landscapes, increase park trails, and uphold existing initiatives to protect parkland from fires as well as mining and drilling operatives.

the bright lights of the city one step closer to the wilderness. The resulting light pollution causes overly illuminated skies with fewer visible stars, which can be disappointing for visitors and deadly for disoriented birds and other animals.

Meanwhile, noise pollution, much of it from aircraft, threatens to break the silence that many visitors seek in the parks. This is especially troublesome at the Grand Canyon. There are also other factors putting the parks' air, water, and land at risk. High ozone levels in Sequoia National Park, for example, can cause respiratory irritation and are damaging Jeffrey pines.

What's Next for the NPS

Currently underway is a multimillion-dollar program called the Centennial Initiative, launched under the George W. Bush administration, designed to get the parks ready for another 100 years of service in time for their centennial anniversary in 2016. In 2008, the NPS established the Centennial Challenge hoping to match an equal or greater amount in philanthropic donations with federal dollars. Under the Initiative, the NPS spent $52 million on 111 projects in 2008, including an extensive rehabilitation of the Tunnel View Overlook at Yosemite National Park in California.

In 2009, the park service announced plans for several more new projects, including the completion of a comprehensive inventory of the myriad plants and animals in Yellowstone National Park. Also in 2009, Congress passed the Omnibus Public Lands Act, which designated 2 million acres as wilderness, including the backcountry of Rocky Mountain National Park.

Acknowledgments: We thank the Department of the Interior for their helpful resources, including *A Brief History of the National Park Service.*

2004	Great Sand Dunes in Colorado gains national park designation; it is the newest national park.
2007	Congress is presented with a record $2.4-billion budget for the parks, plus a $100-million donation match program as part of the Centennial Initiative.
2009	President Barack Obama signs the American Recovery and Reinvestment Act, which allocates $3 billion to the Interior Department, including $750 million to restore and protect America's National Parks.

THE ROOSEVELT TOUCH

Without Theodore Roosevelt and Franklin Roosevelt, many of America's natural treasures would have ceased to exist. A generation apart, the two men were moved by the dire state of their nation to ramrod monumental changes in how the country preserved its outdoor wonders.

For Theodore, it was the disappearance of the bison and rampant misuse of the land in the western United States. For Franklin, it was the needs of an unemployed population—and the need to save the country's ravaged forestland. Both men, through sheer force of will, drove their ideals into law.

Theodore, who believed America had an almost divine responsibility for proper stewardship of its ample resources, brought his conservationist leanings to the presidency in 1901. As part of his revolutionary administration, he established the U.S. Forest Service, along with 150 national forests; the first national wildlife refuge; 51 bird preserves; four game preserves; five national parks; and 18 national monuments, including four that became national parks— Grand Canyon, Petrified Forest, Lassen Peak, and Mount Olympus (Olympic). His efforts accounted for more than half of the lands to be managed by the National Park Service when it was created in 1916—seven years after his presidency ended.

Franklin, who believed the president was called to lead with character and morality (and to rescue the country from the throes of the Great Depression), created millions of jobs on public works projects—including many in the national parks. Almost immediately after his inauguration in 1933, he developed the Civilian Conservation Corps. Over nine years, it employed 5% of American males and

> ### DYNAMIC DUO
>
> **TEDDY**
> **Lifespan:** 1858–1919
> **Saying:** Speak softly and carry a big stick.
> **Regulated:** Railroads
> **Unique qualities:** Youngest president (age 42); won Nobel Peace Prize (for mediating the Russo-Japanese War)
>
> **FDR**
> **Lifespan:** 1882–1945
> **Saying:** The only thing we have to fear is fear itself.
> **Regulated:** Wall Street
> **Unique qualities:** Only president with polio; only four-term president; established the WPA (Works Progress Administration)

planted about 3 billion trees. The corps was instrumental in suppressing forest fires, clearing campgrounds, constructing roads and trails, controlling floods and soil erosion, and eradicating undesirable plants. The CCC also enabled the NPS to improve existing public lands, establish new national parks, and guide the development of a system of state parks. Seven states gained their first state parks through the CCC's efforts, and at the project's end in 1942, a total of 711 state parks had been established. Additionally, Franklin added to the NPS holdings his Hyde Park, NY, home.

Though the inspiration for each differed, their contributions were similar, as are their legacies. They stand as giants among American presidents and as standard-bearers for government-aided conservation.

—Gary Peterson

WILDLIFE IN THE PARKS

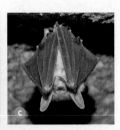

Bats (C): Caves within the national parks teem with bats, the only mammals that can fly. Although not threatening to humans, bats do carry and can transmit dangerous diseases such as rabies. Enormous bat colonies can be observed whirling and flying out of caves en masse at dusk for feeding time, returning around sunrise. You also can observe bats when they roost in snags—dead, hollowed-out trees still standing in the forest after lightning strikes and wildfires.

Big Horn Sheep (A): Clambering along rocky ledges, muscular bighorn sheep fascinate with their ability to travel so easily where the rest of us can't. In winter the docile herd animals descend to lower elevations. Like their fellow park residents, the mule deer, bighorns rut in autumn, when antlered males fight each other dramatically over mates. Rams have heavy, curled horns, while ewes' horns are short and slightly bent. From afar it's easy to spot

both sexes' white rumps, which stand out brightly against their furry brown coats.

Bison (D): The nappy, dispassionate American bison may not be the western frontier's most charismatic ungulate, but it's certainly the most iconic. Yellowstone has the country's only continuously wild herd numbers (hovering around 4,000), though you also can see the large creatures in other national parks. A hefty bull can reach six feet at the shoulder and weigh a ton. Bulls and cows alike sport short, curved horns, which they'll use to gore tourists who invade their space.

Black Bear (B): Don't kid yourself: these excellent sniffers can smell your freeze-dried dinner from a mile away. Though they naturally forage for acorns and berries, black bears are omnivores and can be aggressive, especially if they're protecting their cubs. Unlike grizzlies, black bears don't have a shoulder hump. They're also smaller than grizzlies, measuring about

the same height as a human adult–but weighing much more (averaging up to 600 pounds), depending on their age and sex. They also have larger ears than their grizzly cousins. They hibernate for up to seven months in the winter, and at lower elevations that see more moderate winters they may not sleep much at all. Most have inky black fur, but a golden-tan or cinnamon color is not uncommon.

Great Horned Owl (E): Residing in forests, this large owl has prominent ear tufts and a white throat with barred markings preys. It preys on squirrels, hares, grouse, and other birds.

Coyote (F): Imagine having food on your mind all the time. That's life for this sniffing, fretting, foraging omnivore. Coyotes' indiscriminate diets include carrion, small mammals, insects, and grasses. They're about 30 pounds or more, distinguishing them from much larger wolves. The gray-tan canines travel alone or in small packs and, with rare exceptions, pose little threat to humans.

Eagles (G): With a wingspan of 6 to 8 feet, bald eagles are primarily fish eaters, but they will also take birds or small mammals when the opportunity presents itself. Their broad nests top trees like oversized, tangled crowns. Bald eagles' unmistakable white heads distinguish them from uniformly dark-brown golden eagles, which nest on cliffs and prey on small mammals and ptarmigan. With a wingspan of up to 7½ feet, the adult golden eagle has plumage that is entirely dark, except for a golden head.

Elk (H): A bull's antlers can weigh 40 pounds and, in summer, shed a soft fur known as antler velvet. Elk congregate where forest meets meadows, summering at high elevations before migrating lower in winter. In September and October, bulls attract a "harem" of mating partners by bugling, a loud and surreal whistling.

Grizzly Bear (D): These furry bogeymen alternately fascinate and frighten. A mature male grizzly can weigh 700 pounds and stand 8 feet tall. Whitish shoulder hairs give grizzlies their name and help distinguish them from black bears, as do a distinctive muscle mass on their back and the convex curve of their snout. High meadows are their prime habitat, especially at dawn and dusk. Hibernation generally lasts from November to March, after which they emerge hungry, sometimes prompting trail and campground closures. Grand Teton National Park is seeing rising populations of grizzlies as Yellowstone bears migrate south.

Jack Rabbit (A): Unmistakable for its mule-like ears and swift, bounding gait, the jackrabbit can induce a brief case of heart failure if you happen upon one and startle it into an explosive escape. It is extremely common in the Southwest.

Marmot (C): Yellow-bellied marmots like to live high up among granite rock piles of talus slopes and along riverbanks, so if you see them, it's likely to be along high-country trails. The rocky strongholds help protect these furry ground squirrels—one of the largest rodents in North America—from such natural predators as eagles and hawks. Marmots have an unusual addiction: they've developed a taste for anti-freeze coolant, and they'll go to great lengths to get it!

Moose (B): Feeding on fir, willows, and aspens, the moose is the largest member of the deer family: the largest bulls stand 7 feet tall at the shoulders and weigh up to 1,600 pounds. Distinctive characteristics include its antlers, which lay flat like palmate satellite dishes. The peak of breeding occurs in late September. Females give birth to calves in late May and early June; twins are the norm.

Mountain Lion (J): Although the mountain lion is an occasional predator, chances are you won't see him at most of the parks. That doesn't mean he isn't there, closely watching and wondering if you'll notice him. Also called cougars, these enormous carnivores live throughout the Southwest desert and in the Sierra Nevada, too. They're tawny colored, can be 8 feet long, and weigh up to 200 pounds. They're capable of taking down a mule deer or elk.

Mule Deer (G): Often seen grazing in meadows and forests are mule deer, with their black-tipped tails and pronounced antlers. Their name comes from the shape of their ears, which resemble mules' ears. Their unusual gait—all four feet can hit the ground at once—gives them an advantage over predators, as they move faster over scrubby terrain and can change directions instantly. They rut in autumn, when males clash antlers over mates.

Prairie Dog (I): Called "petit chien" (little dog) by French explorers, the prairie dog is a delightful little member of the squirrel family. The short blacktailed, buff-colored ones found in the Dakotas have small ears and can be seen digging burrows. They get their name from the way they make noise: it sounds like a bark.

Pronghorn Antelope (H): The tan-brown creatures have excellent vision, hearing, and smell, and they can run up to 60 MPH. Antelopes shed their antlers every year. Antelope can engage in brutal behavior during the mating season.

Wolf (F): These impressive canines form close-knit family packs, which may range from a few animals to more than 30. Packs hunt a variety of prey, from small mammals and birds to caribou and moose. They communicate with each other through body language, barks, and howls. Grey wolves tend to be 70 to 120 pounds, larger than a coyote.

GREAT LODGES
OF THE NATIONAL PARKS

by Marge Peterson

"IF YOU BUILD IT, THEY WILL COME" could apply to the railroad companies who laid track in the early 1900s to lure wealthy Easterners westward. But these scrappy companies took the declaration an inspired step further by building luxury hotels at the end of the line.

The Atchison, Topeka, and Santa Fe Railway finished a 65-mi railroad spur from Williams, Arizona, to the South Rim of the Grand Canyon and built the spectacular Arizona lodge El Tovar. Union Pacific helped finance lodges at Bryce and Zion, Northern Pacific was behind the hotels in Yellowstone, and the Great Northern Railway built Glacier Park Lodge, many Glacier Hotels, and the Prince of Wales Hotel. Today, the rails don't drive tourism to the parks all that much. But the lodges still do. And you don't have to be wealthy to stay in one.

What makes them great? Unlike previous wilderness accommodations that were built like city hotels so guests would feel safe, these new lodges incorporated materials from the environment like the lodgepole pines and Rhyolite stone used in building Old Faithful Inn. As long as these nature-inspired structures had creature comforts—which then, and in some cases now, doesn't include in-room televisions—architects felt guests would be happy.

> Architects felt guests would be happy as long as the lodges had creature comforts.

Opposite: Balconies claw skyward in the Old Faithful Inn's 76-foot high lobby. *Above:* Bringing the outside in at the Prince of Wales Hotel at Waterton Lakes National Park in Alberta, Canada.

TOP LODGES

EL TOVAR, GRAND CANYON

"In the Grand Canyon, Arizona has a natural wonder, which, so far as I know, is in kind unparalleled throughout the rest of the world," said Teddy Roosevelt in 1903, speaking from the area where the El Tovar would open two years later. "What you can do is to keep it for your children, your children's children, and for all who come after you, as one of the great sights which every American if he can travel at all should see."

Set atop the South Rim of the Grand Canyon, El Tovar so blends into the landscape, with its stone, wood, and earthy tones, that it looks almost like another tier of the multilayered, multi-hued canyon. With the elegance of a European villa and warm atmosphere of a rustic log cabin, it is arguably the most luxurious of the lodges.

Opened in 1905, El Tovar was named for Spanish explorer Don Pedro de Tobar (the "b" was changed to "v" to avoid people saying "to the bar") and was designed by architect Charles Whittlesey. Built for $250,000, it had 95 rooms, electricity, indoor plumbing, steam heat, solariums, and lounges. Originally, Jersey cows and poultry grazed on site, and greenhouses provided fresh herbs and flowers for guests feasting in the dining room. One of its most famous diners and overnight guests was **Teddy Roosevelt**, who came to dinner in muddy boots and dusty riding gear—or so says local lore. In addition to Roosevelt, seven other presidents have stayed here. For its 100th birthday, the hotel received a $4.6 million restoration.

Ahwahnee Lodge

AHWAHNEE, YOSEMITE

Blending into a backdrop of granite cliffs, the elegant Ahwahnee Lodge, which opened in 1927, is six stories tall with three wings in a "Y" layout. Then-NPS Director Stephen Mather believed that attracting wealthy, influential folks into Yosemite would lend support and congressional funding to the national parks system.

Architect Gilbert Stanley Underwood was commissioned to build a first-class fireproof hotel that blended in with the landscape. In order to resist fire, concrete was formed within timbers and then dyed to resemble redwood. The motifs and patterns found in the basketry of the local Indian tribes were used on the ceiling beams, stained-glass windows, and concrete floors. Luminaries who have signed the lodge guest book include Franklin and Eleanor Roosevelt, John F. Kennedy, Queen Elizabeth, and Clark Gable.

Right, president Teddy Roosevelt.

OLD FAITHFUL, YELLOWSTONE

Shock and awe may best describe the reaction of people entering the lobby of Old Faithful Inn in Yellowstone Park. Its 76-foot high lobby has four levels of balconies with supports created with gnarled branches from a tangle of trees reaching the ceiling. Construction costs of $140,000 were financed by the Northern Pacific Railroad and the Yellowstone Park Association. Wings were added to the hotel in 1915 and 1927—it would be difficult to duplicate the inn's construction today, since cutting down trees, gathering wood, and quarrying rock inside the park are now illegal.

The park's most famous geyser, Old Faithful is less than 100 yards from the inn. Approximate times for its eruptions are posted in the lobby.

WHAT TO EXPECT

Some lodges were built more than 100 years ago, when rooms and beds were smaller. However, the difference in room size is more than offset by the huge amount of public space offered on the properties. The availability of television and Internet access varies from lodge to lodge.

BRYCE CANYON LODGE

Bryce Canyon Lodge was the second structure built in the Union Pacific's Loop Tours building program, which included Cedar Breaks, Zion, the North Rim of the Grand Canyon, and a stop at Kaibab National Forest. In a grove of ponderosa pines within walking distance of the rim, the lodge opened in 1925 with 70 guest rooms, three deluxe suites, one studio room, and 40 log cabins. The property was known for its sing-aways, where employees lined up in front of the lodge and sang a farewell to departing guests. When plans to build another lodge on the rim didn't materialize, a gift shop, soda fountain, barbershop, and auditorium were added.

Above, Old Faithful Inn. Top, Bryce Canyon Lodge.

Crater Lake Lodge

CRATER LAKE LODGE

When Crater Lake Lodge opened in 1915, it was anything but grand: the exterior was covered in tarpaper, fiberboard separated the guest rooms, bathrooms were shared, and the electricity seldom worked. But visitors loved it anyway because of the lake view. Due to its structural defects, the $30,000 building was closed to the public in 1989. Public admiration swayed Congress to grant $15 million for renovations, and the lodge was completely rebuilt and reopened in May 1995. Perched on the rim of a defunct caldera filled with cobalt blue water, the lodge has a fantastic deck, as well as an architectural trademark, a massive stone fireplace.

GLACIER PARK LODGE

An eclectic interior design with towering tree trunks highlights Glacier Park Lodge. Samuel L. Bartlett was the architect of record, but Louis Hill, president of the Great Northern Railway, controlled every aspect of the design. Hill patterned the lodge, which opened in 1913, after the Oregon Forestry Building he saw at the Lewis & Clark Exposition in Portland.

He had 60 Douglas firs (40 feet high and 40 inches in diameter) shipped in from the Northwest for the colonnade.

When rail passengers arrived at Glacier Park Station, they saw Indian teepees scattered across the lawn as part of a show presented to visitors, colorful banks of flowers, and the majestic lodge.

The park and lodge were heavily promoted. On top of the half a million dollars it took to build and furnish Glacier Park Lodge, Hill spent $300,000 on artists, filmmakers, calendars, playing cards, and a special train car with a public exhibit. *The New York Times* said, "Next to Col. Roosevelt, L.W. Hill is about the best advertising man in the United States."

Glacier Park Lodge

LAKE LOUISE & BANFF SPRINGS

In the late 1800s, William Cornelius Van Horne, general manager of the Canadian Pacific Railway, said, "Since we can't export the scenery, we will have to import the tourists." And so they did. The railroad developed Fairmont Banff Springs Hotel and the Fairmont Chateau Lake Louise, both of which opened their doors in 1890.

While the great lodges of America's national parks have a comfortable hunting-lodge aura, Canada's Banff and Lake Louise accommodations have a stately, opulent ambience.

Banff Springs Hotel

Fairmont Banff Springs, a mile walk from downtown Banff, is styled after a Scottish baronial castle. Combining the best of the past with the amenities sought by modern-day travelers, the hotel offers tennis, golf, bowling, horseback rides, indoor and outdoor swimming, and one of the largest spas in Canada.

Surrounded by snow-tipped mountain peaks and the majestic Victorian Glacier, Chateau Lake Louise is on the shore of pristine Lake Louise, where you can hike, downhill or cross-country ski, cycle, and canoe.

TO RESERVE A ROOM

Reservations at historic lodges should be made six months to a year in advance (for Yellowstone, definitely 12 months in advance) directly with the lodge's Internet sites; however, you can always check for last-minute cancellations. Be wary of other Internet reservation services that charge a non-refundable fee of up to 12 percent to book the lodging. ■ TIP→ Dining reservations at lodge restaurants often can be made when you book your room.

OTHER GREAT LODGES

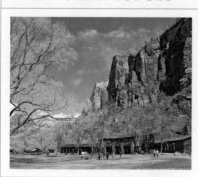

GLACIER NATIONAL PARK
Belton Chalet, Lake McDonald Lodge, Many Glacier Hotel, Sperry & Granite Park Chalets

GRAND CANYON NATIONAL PARK
Grand Canyon Lodge—North Rim

MOUNT RAINIER NATIONAL PARK
Paradise Inn

WATERTON LAKES NATIONAL PARK
Prince of Wales Hotel

ZION NATIONAL PARK
Zion Park Lodge

Zion Park Lodge.

Choosing a Park

WHAT'S WHERE

ARCHES UTAH	**Location:** Eastern Utah **Known for:** The world's largest concentration of natural sandstone arches—more than 2,000 at last count. **Biggest crowds:** April through October **Accessibility:** Many arches can be viewed from your car. **Why kids like it:** Walking through rock windows and playing on sand dunes is like taking a trip to Mars. **What hikers say:** Awe-inspiring scenery and thrilling walks on the tops of sandstone fins make this place hard to forget. Only four hours (235 mi) from Salt Lake City, this 77,000-acre park is easy to visit. Nearby is Moab, an adventure hotspot, with world-class white-water rafting on the Colorado River, rock climbing, four-wheeling, and mountain biking.
BADLANDS SOUTH DAKOTA	**Location:** Southwestern South Dakota **Known for:** Eroded buttes and spires that cast amazing shades of red and yellow across the South Dakota prairie. **Biggest crowds:** July and August **Accessibility:** Just off Interstate 90, the park has a breathtaking loop driving tour with scenic overlooks and picnic areas. **Why kids like it:** Seeing a fossil for a three-toed horse is cool! **What hikers say:** The best way to view this unworldly area is on the solitary 10-mi loop of the Castle Trail. Badlands is big—244,000 acres. It's about 80 mi east of Rapid City, but it feels like another planet. In addition to scenery even the world's greatest artists would struggle to recreate, it has some of the world's richest mammal fossil beds.
BANFF  ALBERTA	**Location:** Alberta, Canada **Known for:** Stunning mountain scenery and wildlife. **Biggest crowds:** July and August **Accessibility:** An extensive road network allows access to hiking trails, ski resorts, glaciers, lakes, and other attractions. **Why kids like it:** Interpretive programs help kids learn about bears, wolves, fire, photography, and human history. **What hikers say:** Great trails for beginners and experienced hikers lead to spectacular scenic vistas and natural wonders. Canada's first national park, 80 mi west of Calgary, Alberta, comprises 1.6 million acres of mountains, glaciers, forests, and more. In winter it has some of the world's best skiing.

BIG BEND TEXAS	**Location:** Southwestern Texas **Known for:** Diverse landscape and wildlife. **Biggest crowds:** Thanksgiving, Christmas, and spring break **Accessibility:** Some of the prettiest sites, such as the Chisos Mountains, are accessible by road. **Why kids like it:** Rangers routinely throw star-viewing parties. **What hikers say:** Solitude-seekers find bliss here, where 200 mi of hiking trails begged to be explored. About 430 mi west of San Antonio and 300 mi south of El Paso, the 800,000-acre park is in a remote location, with the Rio Grande River along its southern border. Its limitless skies and ample space are two of its strongest selling points.
BLACK CANYON OF THE GUNNISON COLORADO	**Location:** Western Colorado **Known for:** A steep and narrow river gorge with sheer cliffs and a drop twice as high as the Empire State Building. **Biggest crowds:** Summer (especially July and August) **Accessibility:** Numerous overlooks can be reached via South Rim and North Rim roads. **Why kids like it:** A hike on either side of the canyon offers dizzying views of sheer rock walls and the rushing river below. **What hikers say:** Trails to the inner canyon are unmarked and unmaintained—but their beauty is unmatched. About 250 mi southwest of Denver and set between Curecanti National Recreation Area and Gunnison Gorge National Conservation Area, Black Canyon of the Gunnison is more than 30,000 acres of drama, especially rock climbers.
BRYCE CANYON UTAH	**Location:** Southern Utah **Known for:** Bright, red-orange rocks in bizarre shapes. **Biggest crowds:** June through September **Accessibility:** You can see a lot from roadside overlooks. **Why kids like it:** Exploring the hoodoos (spectacular columns of rock) is like wandering through a giant maze. **What hikers say:** You see amazing colors at sunrise and sunset. Full-moon hikes in the hoodoos aren't to be missed. Just 4½ hours (270 mi) from either Las Vegas or Salt Lake City, 36,000-acre Bryce Canyon is within a few hours of Utah's other national parks. It's also near Kodachrome Basin State Park and Grand Staircase-Escalante National Monument.

CANYONLANDS 	**Location:** Southeastern Utah **Known for:** Biking on White Rim Road, white-water rafting in Cataract Canyon—plus spires, pinnacles, cliffs, and mesas as far as the eye can see. **Biggest crowds:** Spring and early fall **Accessibility:** It's easy to see three mountain ranges and countless canyons from the many overlooks throughout the park. **Why kids like it:** They can almost see home from here—no matter where home is! **What hikers say:** Some of the best hikes in the world are here, particularly in the remote Maze area of the park. Beyond its spectacular scenery and top-notch outdoor activities, Canyonlands is also a place to find solitary reflections—with 527 square mi of space surrounding you and bald eagles and red-tail hawks floating above you. About an hour (68 mi) southwest of Moab and four hours (about 250 mi) southeast of Salt Lake City, the park offers peaceful canoeing on the Colorado and Green rivers, as well as great mountain biking, four-wheeling, rock-climbing, and hiking.
CAPITOL REEF 	**Location:** South-central Utah **Known for:** The 100-mi-long Waterpocket Fold, a monocline (or "wrinkle" in the Earth's crust). **Biggest crowds:** May through September **Accessibility:** You can see many of Capitol Reef's geological wonders from Scenic Drive. **Why kids like it:** They get to pick fruit in the orchards at the historic Fruita settlement and see mule deer, coyotes, desert bighorn sheep—and bats!—up close. **What hikers say:** A huge backcountry with light traffic is perfect for a quiet retreat, especially if you like geology, archeology, or strolls along the river. Seven times larger than nearby Bryce Canyon and much less crowded than either Bryce Canyon or Zion national parks, Capitol Reef provides 240,000 acres of peace and quiet—and exceptional colors, especially at sunset. The park has many options for day hikes as well as backcountry trips into slot canyons, arches, cliffs, domes, and slickrock. It's about 220 mi south of Salt Lake City and 340 mi northeast of Las Vegas.

CARLSBAD CAVERNS NEW MEXICO	**Location:** Southeastern New Mexico **Known for:** 113 caves, bizarre underground rock formations, and 300,000 diving, dipping, sonar-blipping bats. **Biggest crowds:** Spring and summer vacations **Accessibility:** You'll need to head underground to see the park's true highlights—three of Carlsbad's largest caverns are fully lit and inset with audio guides, and several guided tours are available to less-visited portions. **Why kids like it:** Bat Flights showcase thousands of bats on their nightly commute. Older kids can join their parents on cave tours that range from an easy stroll through vast underground chambers to a crawl-on-your-belly adventure. **What hikers say:** While most of the hiking is underground, the aboveground sights—such as rocks shaped like bones, straws, mushrooms, and faces—are spectacular, too. The park is 47,000 acres, with more than 8 acres taken up by its biggest cave, aptly called the Big Room. Visitors reach the caverns via an elevator that sinks 75 stories below the surface. The park is about 23 mi from the town of Carlsbad, 150 mi east of El Paso, and 305 mi southeast of Albuquerque.
CHANNEL ISLANDS CALIFORNIA	**Location:** Southern California **Known for:** Pristine land- and seascapes with an exceptional variety of marine and terrestrial plants and animals—145 species here are found nowhere else on the planet. **Biggest crowds:** Holidays and summer weekends **Accessibility:** You must take boat or plane to reach the islands. **Why kids like it:** They get to see lots of California critters, like dolphins, sea lions, whales, eagles, and pelicans. **What hikers say:** You can trek into blissfully uncrowded and serene wilderness areas—with miles of trails and spectacular views from nearly every vantage point. Although just 60 mi northwest of Los Angeles, the Channel Islands are worlds away from the urban sprawl and tangled freeways on the mainland, making this five-island, 250,000-acre park the ultimate destination for nature lovers aiming to "get away from it all." The park is accessible by boat from harbors in Ventura and Oxnard (about an hour north of L.A.) and Santa Barbara (about 1½ hours north of L.A.); trips take from 45 minutes to three hours plus.

CRATER LAKE	**Location:** Southern Oregon **Known for:** Being the seventh deepest lake in the world. **Biggest crowds:** July and August **Accessibility:** The park has a short summer; access during most other times is contingent upon road conditions. Several scenic overlooks lie along the 33-mi-long Rim Drive. **Why kids like it:** You can take a cool boat ride in the middle of the caldera. **What hikers say:** So many trails, so little time. Crater Lake is a geologic marvel and a hiker's paradise. The park itself is more than 183,000 acres, and includes about 90 mi of trails. The star of the park is the 21-square-mi sapphire blue expanse of the nation's deepest lake, which draws visitors from around the world. The area's volcanic past is apparent everywhere, and the park is filled with the unhurried, untamed, and untouched essence of solitude. Eugene, Oregon, is 133 mi away, and Portland is 244 mi to the north.
DEATH VALLEY 	**Location:** Southeastern California, Southwestern Nevada **Known for:** Breathtaking vistas, blasting 120-degree heat, mysterious moving rocks. **Biggest crowds:** Late fall through early spring **Accessibility:** You'll need a vehicle to get around the vast park; 4X4s are required on some backcountry roads. **Why kids like it:** The park has a *Star Wars* feel to it—which makes sense, since this was the location for the film's Tatooine (Luke Skywalker's home planet) scenes. Nighttime desert walks often include kangaroo rats and kit fox. **What hikers say:** The Titus and Fall Canyons offer spectacular narrows, washes, and dryfall (a rock chute that becomes a waterfall during thunderstorms). Just don't venture out into this park without adequate clothing, sun protection, food, and water—even in the winter. The desert is very unforgiving. The largest national park in the contiguous United States and the lowest point in the Western hemisphere, 3.4 million-acre Death Valley is a vast, lonely, beautiful place. This desert landscape is surrounded by majestic mountains, dry lake beds, and other geological wonders. From Furnace Creek Visitors Center, Baker is about 113 mi to the southeast, Las Vegas is about 141 mi to the east, and Los Angeles is roughly 294 mi to the southwest.

GLACIER-WATERTON LAKES 	**Location:** Northwest Montana/Southwest Alberta, Canada **Known for:** Great hiking and inspiring vistas. **Biggest crowds:** Early July through mid-September **Accessibility:** Glacier's Going-to-the-Sun-Road has unparalleled views of both sides of the Continental Divide. **Why kids like it:** The multitude of short hikes to scenic spots, fun boat trips, and excellent interpretive programs. **What hikers say:** Million-acre Glacier National Park is world-renowned for its backcountry trails and wilderness areas. The rugged mountains that weave their way through the parks seem to have glaciers in every hollow, melting into tiny streams, raging rivers, and ice-cold mountain lakes. The U.S. entrance is 156 mi north of Missoula.
GRAND CANYON 	**Location:** Northwestern Arizona **Known for:** Unsurpassed natural wonder that's 277 river mi long, up to 18 mi wide, and a mile deep. **Biggest crowds:** Summer and spring break **Accessibility:** The popular Rim Trail and all the viewpoints along the South Rim are easily accessible. **Why kids like it:** The mule rides, river rafting . . . and watching Grandma scream when she sees a snake or scorpion. **What hikers say:** Make the trek down: camping at the bottom under the stars is a once-in-a-lifetime experience. Encompassing 1.2 million acres, the Grand Canyon both exalts and humbles the human spirit. View the spectacle from the South Rim, 230 mi north of Phoenix and 280 mi east of Las Vegas, or the less-traveled North Rim.
GRAND TETON 	**Location:** Northwestern Wyoming **Known for:** Jagged peaks, pristine lakes, and diverse wildlife. **Biggest crowds:** July and August **Accessibility:** View much of it from roadside overlooks. **Why kids like it:** Wild animals, oh my! **What hikers say:** Grand Teton has trails for every skill level, from simple strolls around mountain lakes to steep treks. About 275 mi northeast of Salt Lake City and 550 mi northwest of Denver, 310,000-acre Grand Teton National Park is near Yellowstone, but it's its own impressive destination, highlighted by the regal Tetons rising out of Jackson Hole.

GREAT BASIN 	**Location:** Eastern Nevada **Known for:** The Lehman Caves and ancient bristlecone pines. **Biggest crowds:** Summer **Accessibility:** The scenic drive leads to Lehman Caves and 13,063-foot Wheeler Peak. **Why kids like it:** The stalactites, stalagmites, and popcorn in Lehman Caves are unlike anything they've ever seen. **What hikers say:** It's great for solitary backcountry treks. Roughly 4 hours from both Las Vegas (234 mi) and Salt Lake City (286 mi), Great Basin is one of the nation's least-visited national parks (there isn't even an entrance fee). Its 77,000 acres hold more than 40 caves and 60 mi of marked trails.
GREAT SAND DUNES 	**Location:** South-central Colorado **Known for:** Its towering, land-locked sand dunes **Biggest crowds:** June through August **Accessibility:** The road only goes to the visitor center. Access the dunes via a paved path and viewing platform. **Why kids like it:** Kids love to throw themselves over sandy precipices or roll down the dunes (all in perfect safety). Splashing in the perennially ice-cold Medano Creek is also a hit. **What hikers say:** For fabulous views of the Sangre de Cristo mountains, take the Mosca Pass or Music Pass trail. The Great Sand Dunes National Park and Preserve encompass 150,000 acres of unique hydrological and geological systems, including 30 square mi of dune fields. It's about five hours (200 mi) southwest of Denver via I–25.
GUADALUPE MOUNTAINS 	**Location:** West Texas **Known for:** Several lofty peaks, including 8,749-foot Guadalupe Peak; plus the world's finest fossilized reef. **Biggest crowds:** Spring break and fall **Accessibility:** It's easy to access the park from the highway. **Why kids like it:** It's home to more than 300 types of birds. **What hikers say:** Trails lead up and down rocky terrain and through lush foliage. This remote 86,000-acre park, 110 mi northeast of El Paso and 40 mi south of Carlsbad Caverns, draws thousands of visitors every fall, when the hardwoods of McKittrick Canyon burst into flaming color.

JASPER 	**Location:** Southwestern Alberta, Canada **Known for:** Being the largest of the Canadian Rocky Mountain national parks, at 2.7 million acres. **Biggest crowds:** July and August **Accessibility:** Wildlife and scenery can be easily viewed from roads and viewpoints. **Why kids like it:** Modern amusements pale in comparison to spotting elk, bighorn sheep, and black bears. **What hikers say:** The park's 746 mi of hiking trails take you to scenic viewpoints, past raging waterfalls, through wildflower-carpeted meadows, and to the Columbia Icefield, one of the world's largest accumulations of snow and ice. One of the largest protected mountain ecosystems in the world, 42,000-acre Jasper National Park woos visitors with its lakes, glaciers, waterfalls, and mountains. The park is 192 mi west of Edmonton and 256 mi northwest of Calgary.
JOSHUA TREE	**Location:** South-central California **Known for:** World-class rock climbing, desert scenery. **Biggest crowds:** October through May **Accessibility:** Much of the park can be seen from the roads. **Why kids like it:** Giant piles of rocks are great places to play hide-and-seek—and encounter some strange critters. The park's eponymous Joshua trees—twisted and prickly, with clumps of spiny leaves—are straight out of a Dr. Seuss book. **What hikers say:** Great views lurk around almost every bend. The 794,000-acre park attracts more than a million visitors a year, who come to enjoy brilliant wildflower displays and starry nights. It lies 140 mi east of Los Angeles, 175 mi north-east of San Diego, and 215 mi southwest of Las Vegas.
LASSEN VOLCANIC	**Location:** Northeastern California **Known for:** Mt. Lassen, a dormant volcano that last erupted in 1915—plus every other type of known volcano, roiling mud pots, and hissing steam vents. **Biggest crowds:** Mid-July through mid-September **Accessibility:** You can take in stunning views of many of the park's geological features from the road. Mellow hiking trails lead to waterfalls and meadows. **Why kids like it:** Anything that simultaneously belches and emits a sulphury "rotten egg" smell is very, very cool.

What hikers say: Whether you hike Mt. Lassen on a clear day or scale it with a guide under a full moon, the experience is unforgettable.

About 250 mi northeast of San Francisco, Lassen Volcanic has 106,000 acres of spectacular geologic wonders plus more than 150 mi of hiking trails, countless mountain lakes and streams, and canyon overlooks, plus wildlife and wildflowers galore.

MESA VERDE

COLORADO

Location: Southwestern Colorado
Known for: Hundreds of ancestral Puebloan cliff dwellings.
Biggest crowds: Mid-June through August
Accessibility: You can see much of the park from the Mesa Top Loop Road, but a guided hike is your best bet.
Why kids like it: They get to climb on ladders up cliffs.
What hikers say: See ancient stone artwork on the Petroglyph Point Trail.

Located in the Four Corners region—the junction of Utah, Colorado, New Mexico, and Arizona—52,000-acre Mesa Verde is far enough away from major cities that the night skies blaze with stars. Denver is 400 mi to the northeast; Phoenix is 450 mi to the southwest; Salt Lake City is 372 mi to the northwest; and Albuquerque is 267 mi to the south.

MOUNT RAINIER

WASHINGTON

Location: West-central Washington
Known for: America's (some say) most magical mountain.
Biggest crowds: July through early September
Accessibility: Massive glaciers and dozens of thundering water-falls are accessible from the road or via short hikes.
Why kids like it: Hikes cover lush temperate rainforest, old-growth forests of hemlock and fir, high meadows, and tundra—not to mention hot springs, glaciers, lakes, and waterfalls.
What hikers say: Enjoy more than 240 mi of maintained trails—or seek real adventure by summiting Mt. Rainier or encircling it via the 93-mi-long Wonderland Trail.

The fifth highest mountain in the Lower 48, Mt. Rainier is so massive that the summit is rarely visible—but when conditions are right, the image of the entire mountain is unforgettable. Skirted around the base of Rainier are cathedral-like groves of Douglas fir, western hemlock, and western red cedar. The 236,000-acrepark is roughly 80 mi south of Seattle and 60 mi southeast of Olympia.

NORTH CASCADES	**Location:** Northwestern Washington **Known for:** Snow-covered mountain panoramas and glaciers. **Biggest crowds:** Late June through early September **Accessibility:** Highway 20 covers some pretty ground, but you need a boat or floatplane to reach Lake Chelan towns. **Why kids like it:** Hiking on a real glacier is unforgettable—especially if you add in marmots, golden eagles, and coyotes. **What hikers say:** Each season brings visual thrills: summer waterfalls, autumn leaves, winter snows, and spring flowers. This 505,000-acre expanse of montane wilderness is part of a 684,000-acre complex with more than half of the glaciers in America. The park's about 75 mi north of Seattle.
OLYMPIC	**Location:** Northwestern Washington **Known for:** Temperate rainforests, rugged coastal expanses, Sol Duc hot springs, and hiking (or skiing) at Hurricane Ridge. **Biggest crowds:** June through September **Accessibility:** Most attractions are found far off Highway 101 or down hills that require hikes of 15 minutes or more. **Why kids like it:** The Hoh Rainforest trails are lined with ideal climbing sites at massive fallen logs and knotted stumps; beaches are playgrounds with sea stacks and tide pools. **What hikers say:** With rainforest, mountain, beach tracks, and even hot springs—every trail brings a new adventure. Be on the lookout for elk, deer, bears, and bald eagles. Centered on Mount Olympus and framed on three sides by water, this 922,651-acre park covers much of Washington's forest-clad Olympic Peninsula. The park is about 1½ hours west of Seattle and two hours northwest of Olympia.
PETRIFIED FOREST	**Location:** Northeastern Arizona **Known for:** Fallen and fossilized trees. **Biggest crowds:** June through August **Accessibility:** Much of the park is viewable from scenic road overlooks and short, paved hikes. **Why kids like it:** Fossilized trees look like colored rock. **What hikers say:** Go into the backcountry if you want more strenuous trails, but watch for rattlesnakes. This 218,533-acre park is 200 mi west of Albuquerque and 240 mi northeast of Phoenix.

REDWOOD CALIFORNIA	**Location:** Northern California **Known for:** The world's tallest trees: giant coast redwoods. **Biggest crowds:** Mid-June through early September **Accessibility:** You can get great views from your car along Highway 101, which traverses the park north to south. **Why kids like it:** Parts of the park feel positively prehistoric, the kind of place where kids imagine dinosaurs coming to life. **What hikers say:** More than 200 mi of trails let you see redwoods in their primitive environments. About 300 mi north of San Francisco and 330 mi south of Portland, Redwood encompasses three state parks spanning 132,000 acres. Roosevelt elk are a common sight.
ROCKY MOUNTAIN COLORADO	**Location:** North-central Colorado **Known for:** Alpine lakes and scenic peaks. **Biggest crowds:** Summer **Accessibility:** The park's shuttle takes you to the main sites. **Why kids like it:** Elk are everywhere. **What hikers say:** There are more than 350 mi of trails, some through high-alpine terrain with lake views. The 265,828 acres of wildlands and alpine tundra of Rocky Mountain National Park are just 70 mi northwest of Denver. Inhabited by black bears, elk, and bighorn sheep, the park has scads of peaks to climb (including 14,259-foot Long's Peak). Touristy Estes Park abuts the park's eastern entrance.
SAGUARO ARIZONA	**Location:** Southeastern Arizona **Known for:** Its dense stand of saguaro cacti. **Biggest crowds:** December through April **Accessibility:** Two scenic loop drives wind through desert lowlands and saguaro forests. **Why kids like it:** Towering saguaros, crazy-looking critters, and indecipherable rock art equal adventures in an alien world. **What hikers say:** Short day hikes in both districts of the park give visitors a chance to spot the desert's elusive wildlife. The 91,000-acre park is split into two districts bookending Tucson (about 30 mi apart); the better collection of cacti is found in the west district. The east district has a paved road popular with cyclists, as well as extensive backcountry trails.

SEQUOIA AND KINGS CANYON CALIFORNIA	**Location:** Central California **Known for:** Groves of giant sequoias and Kings River Canyon. **Biggest crowds:** Summer (especially weekends) **Accessibility:** By road you can reach one-fifth of the park, including the General Sherman Tree and Grant Grove. **Why kids like it:** Look, Mom, a treehouse! They can run around really big trees still standing, and barrel through hollowed out ones, such as Fallen Monarch in Grant Grove. **What hikers say:** The park has more than 800 mi of trails, including stunning and secluded backcountry trails that meander into the hills from the floor of Kings River Canyon. Sequoia and Kings Canyon are perched on the western face of the southern Sierra Nevada, where ancient evergreens tower above the jagged mountain slopes. South of Yosemite and east of Death Valley, these two parks are administered as one. Together, they cover about 865,000 acres; they're about a five-hour drive from either Los Angeles (210 mi) or San Francisco (267 mi).
THEODORE ROOSEVELT NORTH DAKOTA	**Location:** Western North Dakota **Known for:** Chunks of badlands on the Little Missouri River and the 26th president's beloved Elkhorn Ranch. **Biggest crowds:** July and August **Accessibility:** Scenic drives wind through the North and South units, taking you past prairie dog towns, turn-outs with interpretive signs, and panoramic views. **Why kids like it:** There are lots of animals to see, including wild horses, elk, and bison. **What hikers say:** The park's South Unit is known for its unique hiking trails, including the super-steep Painted Canyon. Theodore Roosevelt National Park's South Unit is the more commonly visited of the park's two sections, which together span more than 70,000 acres. The park is about 134 mi west of Bismarck; its southern entrance is off I–94 in Medora, a walkable town with museums, gift shops, and a beautiful and challenging golf course; it's also home to the world-famous Medora Musical.

WIND CAVE 	**Location:** Southwestern South Dakota **Known for:** Having one of the largest caves in the world, with approximately 95 percent of the world's known boxwork formations (3-D calcite honeycomb patterns on cave walls and ceilings). **Biggest crowds:** July and August **Accessibility:** You can easily view the beautiful Black Hills and the grassland prairie from the road, but to get the park's full effect, you'll need to head into the cave (where there are easily accessible tours and other programs). **Why kids like it:** Exploring a huge underground cave! **What hikers say:** There's great hiking here—both above and below ground. Bounded by Black Hills National Forest to the West and wind-swept prairie to the east, Wind Cave National Park comprises 28,295 acres and two distinct ecosystems—mountain forest and mixed grass prairie—plus a 125-mi-long cave. The park is 58 mi south of Rapid City and 250 mi northeast of Cheyenne.
YELLOWSTONE 	**Location:** Northwestern Wyoming (and parts of Idaho and Montana) **Known for:** Extreme and consistent seismic activity, resulting in the world's most extraordinary geysers and hot springs. **Biggest crowds:** Mid-July through mid-August **Accessibility:** Driving in and around Yellowstone will take you past snowcapped peaks and creek-carved canyons. You can view Old Faithful from easy access points. **Why kids like it:** Walking around belching and hissing hotspots are awesome! So is being in a buffalo traffic jam. **What hikers say:** You can explore geysers, hot springs, and boiling mud pots on easy, self-guided hikes. Yellowstone also has more than 2.2 million acresof wilderness on more than 1,100 mi of trails. Best known for its gushing geysers and flowing hot springs, Yellowstone National Park—the oldest national park in the world—is an eclectic mix of hydrothermal activity. The park is 350 mi northeast of Salt Lake City, 192 mi southeast of Butte, and 472 mi northwest of Cheyenne.

| YOSEMITE
CALIFORNIA | **Location:** Central California
Known for: The soaring granite monliths of Half Dome and El Capitan, and shimmering waterfalls.
Biggest crowds: June through September
Accessibility: Dozens of famed features lie along paved roads. A free (accessible) shuttle on the valley's flat floor links attractions and services.
Why kids like it: There are great ranger programs and campfires in the summer, and ice-skating in the winter.
What hikers say: With 800 mi of trails before you, leave the crowds behind and head for the high country trails around Tuolumne Meadows and along Tioga Road.

The 748,000-acre park is north of Sequoia and Kings Canyon National Parks and south of Lake Tahoe. Traffic arriving from San Francisco (four hours or 195 mi away), Los Angeles (six hours or 313 mi away), and other points west and south funnels in on three busy two-lane highways; from the east, only Highway 120 crosses the Sierra into the park, but it's closed late fall through spring. |
| ZION
UTAH | **Location:** Southwestern Utah
Known for: Sheer 2,000-foot cliffs and river-carved canyons.
Biggest crowds: May through September
Accessibility: Scenic drive leads to many features and easily accessible trails.
Why kids like it: Swimming and tubing the Virgin River really beat the summer heat.
What hikers say: Hiking the Narrows and the Subway are life-list activities.

Located 2½ hours (160 mi) northeast of Las Vegas and 5 hours (300 mi) south of Salt Lake City, Zion National Park is located right next to hospitable Springdale, which is full of amenities and charm. From here you can travel quickly to Red Canyon and Bryce Canyon National Park, as well as Kanab—known as Little Hollywood for all of the Westerns filmed there over the years. The park encompasses 147,000 acres. |

THE BEST OF THE NATIONAL PARKS

Best Parks for Accessibility

The best way to get an in-depth look at the parks is by exploring them on foot, horseback, or via some other mode of transportation, but sometimes physical conditioning or time prevents this from happening. The main sites at the following parks aren't too far off the beaten path—many are even visible from the comfort of your car.

■ **Badlands.** Drive slowly on the two-lane loop through the park, setting aside plenty of time for stopping at the overlooks. The view changes as you drive, moving from rocky formations to prairie.

■ **Bryce.** The 18-mi road along Plateau Rim has numerous overlooks and a handful of spurs and provides fabulous views of this park's famous red-orange hoodoos and points beyond. If you want to journey beyond the overlooks, several nearby trailheads offer quick escapes into the park's interior.

■ **Crater Lake.** View the lake from various perspectives along the 33-mi loop Rim Drive. Though you can see much without pulling over, take the time to stop at a few overlooks off the road. The drive will take two or more hours.

■ **Mesa Verde.** Once the main park road passes the Morefield Campground, it forks, and the two branches lead to the archaeological treasures of the Wetherill and Chapin Mesas, respectively. Most sites are close enough to be viewed from the road, but short trails lead in for a closer look (and a few sites are wheelchair accessible).

■ **Petrified Forest.** Whether you enter from the north or the south entrance, the 28-mi park road leads to both visitor centers and a handful of quick and easy trails that meander among petrified trees.

Best Parks for Burning Calories

The national parks are great places for a workout. Whether you walk, run, ski, paddle, or bike, you'll rarely have an excuse not to keep up with your exercise regimen while you're on vacation here. Hard-core fitness junkies should check out the following parks, which are particularly well suited for extreme exertion.

■ **Black Canyon of the Gunnison.** The Painted Wall, Colorado's tallest vertical wall at 2,250 feet, is just one of the major rock faces that attract the cream of the climbing crop to this rugged park, known for its dizzying heights. The vast majority of the climbs are for advanced and expert climbers only, and all are multi-pitch routes located in remote areas of the park. Bouldering enthusiasts should head to the Marmot Rocks area, which is a bit less demanding.

■ **Canyonlands.** Three distinct areas, or districts—Island in the Sky, The Maze, and The Needles—comprise this popular but spacious national park; each one offers plenty of opportunities to put boot (or mountain bike) to sandstone and become totally immersed in sun and solitude. The Maze is your best bet for getting away from it all—you can only reach it by driving at least 20 mi on lonely dirt roads.

■ **Mount Rainier.** Mt. Rainier is encircled by the aptly named Wonderland Trail—a whopping 93-mi trek that takes 10–14 days to complete. It's as rugged as it is long; elevation gains and losses of 3,500 feet in a day are not uncommon. Snow hangs around higher elevations into June and even July, and rain can appear at almost any time. The faint of heart and tender of sole should tramp elsewhere.

Best Parks for Cultural History

When you're surrounded by such overwhelming natural beauty, and so many opportunities to take part in outdoor activities, it's easy to overlook the parks' cultural attractions. But it would be a shame to miss out on a history lesson during your visit, whether it's touring an ancient dwelling, witnessing a historical reenactment, or visiting a great American icon.

■ **Mesa Verde.** Established in 1906, Mesa Verde was the first national park to "preserve the works of man," according to President Theodore Roosevelt. The ancestral Pueblo people lived here from AD 550 to AD 1300, and to date more than 4,000 archeological sites—including 600 cliff dwellings—have been unearthed. Today, researchers continue to discover and catalogue artifacts at Mesa Verde on a regular basis.

■ **Petrified Forest.** The roots at this park aren't just from its ancient trees: the area's human history and culture extend back more than 13,000 years, from prehistoric people to the more modern travelers of Route 66. You can still see petroglyphs scratched and carved into stone, as well as many other artifacts, from the ancestors of the Hopi, Zuni, and Navajo.

■ **Theodore Roosevelt.** It's fitting that Theodore Roosevelt—a major proponent of preservation who signed into law five national parks—should have a national park named in his honor. This North Dakota gem contains land that was once part of Roosevelt's Dakota Territory ranch. Visitors can step inside the former president's log cabin or peruse the visitor center's wide selection of books, posters, audio recordings, and videos dedicated to telling his many stories.

Best Parks for Day Trippers

Some urbanites are fortunate to live just a short drive away from a national park. For those who live elsewhere, these parks have large gateway cities nearby that are served by major airports with plenty of car rental agencies, making a trip to a park a surprisingly quick getaway.

■ **Joshua Tree.** A quick two- or three-hour drive east from the urban sprawl of Los Angeles brings you to the junction of the Mojave and Colorado deserts. Joshua Tree National Park, named for extensive stands of the gnarled tree, is home to one of the finest wildflower displays in Southern California each spring.

■ **Mt. Rainier.** Why just stare at the elusive, majestic mountain from afar? Seattle residents and visitors can easily make their way to Mt. Rainier National Park, just 60 mi away. You can pack a lot in a day: gawk at glaciers, hike one of the trails (the park has more than 240 mi of maintained trails), and poke around the Longmire historic district.

■ **Rocky Mountain.** It's about a two-hour drive from Denver up to one of the most visited national parks in the country, where you can view elk, enjoy alpine scenery, and myriad flora and fauna. Hiking and picnicking along its lakes makes a perfect activity for a day retreat.

■ **Saguaro.** You'll find the largest concentration of the towering saguaro cactus, famed emblem of the desert southwest, just minutes outside Tucson. The park is divided into two sections: the Rincon Mountain District to the east and the Tucson Mountain District to the west.

Best Parks for Fun and Funky Activities

All of the national parks exist for a reason: to protect something that was deemed worthy of recognition and preservation. Still, a few have such unusual and unique features, or unusual surroundings, that they stand out from the rest.

■ **Badlands.** The park and surrounding Black Hills are perfect for family getaways, and you can't get much funkier than Wall Drug on Main Street in nearby Wall, S.D. It even has an animated T-rex in the yard. In the park itself, visiting the prarie dog towns and seeing these creatures antics can bring laughter to your carload of people.

■ **Carlsbad Caverns.** From mid-May to mid-October, watch thousands of bats spiral up into the evening sky from deep within the earth as they set out on their nightly hunt. If possible, get in on the ranger-led discussion beforehand in the nearby amphitheater.

■ **Crater Lake.** Take a boat tour on the clearest, deepest lake in the United States (and the seventh deepest in the world). Formed by volcanic activity, Crater Lake's deepest point is 1,943 feet down, and the sapphire-blue water is so clear that sunlight can penetrate to a depth of 400 feet.

■ **Lassen Volcanic.** Though dormant since 1921, activity around volcanic Lassen Peak makes it clear that there's still a lot going on beneath the ground. Fumaroles, mud pots, and bubbling hot springs dot the landscape. It's a fun and sometimes smelly place to explore; but beware of the scalding water.

Best Parks for Getting a Taste of the Wild West

The American West isn't as wild as it once was, but you can find traces of its storied past. From small preserved towns to vast desert spaces, it's still possible to feel like you've stepped into a Western movie.

■ **Badlands.** Few words conjure up images of the old, Wild West better than the word "Badlands"—except maybe "Deadwood," a town 100 mi northwest of the park. Once an infamous gold camp, the entire town of Deadwood has been named a National Historic Landmark. A nearby cemetery is the final resting place of Wild Bill Hickok and Calamity Jane.

■ **Big Bend.** Far from civilization, this West Texas park can easily bring out the John Wayne or Clint Eastwood in you. The desert environs are exactly where a Hollywood cowboy would feel at home. Try a tour by horseback to complete the vibe.

■ **Death Valley.** Death Valley is not the most hospitable place—at least during certain times of the year—but the climate isn't as horrible as the park's reputation would suggest. Still, the name and the location have long epitomized the very idea of the desert in American literature, film, and television.

■ **Zion.** Thirty miles southeast of Zion's east entrance is the small city of Kanab, Utah, famously known as Little Hollywood for all the old westerns shot in its environs. Downtown hotels still highlight the rooms where John Wayne and other film stars slept. This area of southern Utah has also served as the backdrop for TV shows (including *Gunsmoke*) and many Jeep commercials.

Best Parks for Grinning and "Bearing" It

One of the parks' greatest attractions is their wildlife, and few animals attract as much attention as black and grizzly bears. Cubs are cute and playful, but they shouldn't be approached—Mama is often close and will view you as a threat to her little ones. Still, when seen from a safe distance, bears serve as great reminders of the wildness that the national parks are meant to preserve and protect.

■ **Black Canyon of the Gunnison.** Black bears inhabit this southwest Colorado park, though you aren't likely to see them. If you do, back away slowly and avert your eyes.

■ **Glacier.** There are so many black and grizzly bears in this part of Montana that they often come onto people's property, getting inside homes and causing general mayhem—though attacks on humans are rare. When hiking, make noise, especially when about to turn a corner or bend in the road. Say "Hey, bear!" and clap your hands.

■ **Yellowstone.** The inspiration for fictional Jellystone Park and its anthropomorphic bears Yogi and Boo-Boo, Yellowstone is home to the greatest concentration of grizzly bears in the Lower 48. Black bears are also present here. They can be blond, brown, cinnamon, or black. If you see a bear in the park, keep your distance and don't give it food.

■ **Yosemite.** American black bears are the only bruins left in Yosemite (the California grizzly was hunted to extinction in the early 20th century). Today, the park is home to between 300 and 500 black bears; most are brown. If a bear threatens you, make noise and look big.

Best Parks for Inspiration

It's hard to not be inspired when you're at a national park. Natural wonders, peace and quiet, and ancient sites will likely leave you awestruck, no matter where you visit. These five parks, however, have left their mark on some famous visitors, impacting their subsequent work.

■ **Glacier.** It took a lot to impress pioneering naturalist John Muir, who once called Glacier a "precious reserve" and "the best care-killing scenery on the continent." Take a boat ride on one of the lakes for particularly inspiring views.

■ **Great Basin.** Among America's least visited national parks, Great Basin is also one of the most beautiful. Tucked away on Nevada's eastern border, far from major population centers, the park is a great place to hide from life and work back home.

■ **North Cascades.** Jack Kerouac, Gary Snyder, and Philip Whalen, fixtures of the Beat scene, all worked as National Park Service fire lookouts in the 1950s at Desolation Peak in North Cascades. Portions of Kerouac's *Desolation Angels* and *The Dharma Bums* chronicle his experiences on the mountain.

■ **Rocky Mountain.** With more than 60 mountains 12,000 feet or higher, 355 mi of hiking trails, 150 lakes, 450 mi of streams, and countless far-reaching vistas, Rocky Mountain has plenty to keep you inspired (and off the phone).

■ **Yosemite.** Ansel Adams' repeated visits to Yosemite provided him with the intimate understanding necessary to previsualize many of the famous images he captured here. His exposures of Half Dome are particularly noteworthy, and are among his best-known works.

Best Parks to Pitch a Tent in

The national parks offer myriad options for sleeping close to nature, whether you rest your head on the plush bunks of an RV or beneath a tree separated from the stars by just a thin sheet of nylon. The facilities may vary, but many campers agree that the best way to see the parks is to get out into the undeveloped wilderness.

■ **Canyonlands.** The Maze, one of Canyonlands' three distinct districts, is a backcountry camper's heaven. Named for its labyrinthlike canyons, there's room to explore for days. Remote access via long dirt roads ensures that crowds are nonexistent.

■ **Capitol Reef.** Remote and wide-open Cathedral Valley, accessible by crossing the Fremont River in a high-clearance vehicle, is filled with stunning monoliths and silence. First-come, first-served primitive backcountry campsites provide a base for exploration.

■ **Olympic.** Don't be deterred by the very real threat of rain at this mossy, misty, and wonderfully undeveloped national park. With the Pacific Ocean and temperate rain forests to the west and craggy peaks scattered throughout its interior, Olympic is a backpacker's delight. Its designated campgrounds are popular, too. Several have water views and kid's activities.

■ **Yosemite.** Beyond the Yosemite Valley and iconic sites like Half Dome, this park has a huge, almost secret backcountry perfect for backpackers and horseback riders wishing to embark on extended trips. In fact, 94.5 percent of the park is undeveloped wilderness. If you choose instead one of the developed campgrounds, book early—at least three months in advance.

Best Parks for Romantics

One of the marks of a great relationship is the ability to travel together. And while getting there may induce some stress, once you're at a national park, your spirits should lighten. The beauty and serenity of the parks can help you focus on each other, not your Daytimer. Each of these national parks is a destination well suited for celebrating your bond with that special someone.

■ **Banff.** There is no shortage of escapist lodging at Banff, regardless of your budget or interests. There are more than 100 accommodation options around Lake Louise alone, from cozy little cottages to large, historic lodges. And when you're not gazing into each other's eyes, you can stare at the breathtaking mountain scenery. Any one of the scenic drives can also help you relax and unwind.

■ **Channel Islands.** The mountains that dot this park off the coast of California are often obscured by mists, and animals found nowhere else on earth add to the park's otherworldly feel. The Pacific Ocean is the main attraction here: play on its beaches, ply its waters on a kayak, or tour it by boat as you enjoy an island escape for two—albeit one totally different than a typical Caribbean trip.

■ **Grand Canyon.** For couples who don't mind sweating a little to get to a romantic destination, the depths of the Grand Canyon offers the quintessential Western camping experience. Sleeping at the base of this massive canyon under a clear black sky blazing with bright stars is something to add to your life's to-do list. (After a long hike—or mule ride—it is also the perfect occasion for a massage!)

Best Parks for Scenic Drives

Car-bound tourists often get a raw deal, but plenty of travelers without the ability (or desire) for strenuous hikes want to experience the national parks, too. And let's be honest—even if you're exploring a park on foot, you have to get to the trailhead first. And sometimes the road there is amazing in its own right.

■ **Glacier.** Even the hardiest hiker will admit that there's something special about speeding along a road named Going-to-the-Sun. Every year the local newspapers chronicle the road's opening for the season, when big snowplows finally clear its high passes. The 50-mi stretch of road crosses the Continental Divide at Logan Pass, and is one of America's most beautiful drives. There's even a tour you can sign up for so everyone in your group can ooh and aah without one of you having to focus on the driving.

■ **Redwood.** Keeping your eyes on the road can be a challenge when you're passing 300-foot-tall trees. The 8-mi Coastal Drive is especially wonderful, offering views of the Pacific Ocean, with glimpses of sea lions and pelicans likely, and access to a section of the Coastal Trail, with turnouts for picnicking and gawking in wonder at majestic redwoods.

■ **Rocky Mountain.** The 48-mi Trail Ridge Road is the world's highest continuously paved road, with a maximum elevation of 12,183 feet. Connecting the park's east and west entrances, the road crosses the Continental Divide at Milner Pass and can take up to two months to clear of snow for its Memorial Day opening. The entire drive can be done in a couple hours, but allow more time to stop and gaze out from the many turnouts.

Best Parks for Desert Solitaire

America's national parks run the gamut in terms of cultural, geographic, and geological attractions, but the desolate, arid environs offer a unique experience often colored by our nation's romantic notion of the desert. If you're seeking peace and quiet, you'll likely find it here.

■ **Arches.** Edward Abbey wrote his seminal *Desert Solitaire*, the book that defined the term, while stationed here as a park ranger in the 1960s. Though most often seen by car these days, Arches has an uncrowded backcountry that Abbey—were he alive—would argue is the best way to experience the place anyhow.

■ **Big Bend.** Even in West Texas—a region known for wide-open and silent spaces—Big Bend is quite remote. Among the least visited of the nation's national parks, it was dubbed El Despoblado (The Unpopulated Place), by early Spanish explorers, and has changed little since then. This is a great place to lose yourself among cacti and sprawling mountains.

■ **Death Valley.** With its inhospitable environment and forbidding name, Death Valley has come to epitomize the desert of the American Southwest. It attracts only one million visitors a year, mainly outside the scorching summer months—but even in the high season, the park's vast 3.4 million acres of space guarantee peace and solitude.

■ **Joshua Tree.** This south-central California park is prime hiking, rock climbing, and exploring country, where you can have a close-up encounter with coyotes, desert pack rats, golden eagles, rattlers, and exotic plants like the creamy white yucca, crimson-tipped ocotillo, and spiny cholla cactus.

Best Parks for Spotting Bald Eagles

It may sound clichéd, but you'll never forget the first time you see a bald eagle in person, soaring on the wing or diving into an icy stream to snatch up a fish with its talons. The national icon's white head and tail, set against a dark body, are not its only points of distinction—eagles are huge, far larger than even the biggest hawk. You can view these amazing birds at many of the national parks, but visit one of the following for your best chance at a sighting.

■ **North Cascades.** Bald eagles are so much a part of this region that an annual festival is held in their honor along the Upper Skagit River, where hundreds of the regal birds gather each winter. Highlights include American Indian music and dancing and bluegrass workshops. In the park itself, look for them along the Skagit River and various lakes.

■ **Olympic.** A coastal section of this park protects a stunning 65-mi stretch of Pacific Ocean coastline, providing an ideal environment for the fish-loving bald eagle. Another fish-lover, the osprey, is also commonly found here—and from a distance, these birds look a lot like bald eagles. Up close, there's is no resemblance whatsoever, so use your binoculars to be sure. You're most likely to spot an eagle on the Shi Shi or Rialto beaches or the Ozette Loop hiking trail.

■ **Yellowstone.** As much a part of Yellowstone as the grizzly bear and bison, bald eagles can usually be seen in the vicinity of Yellowstone Lake—though you may see them in the park's interior as well, especially around the Madison River or the Hayden Valley. Greater Yellowstone provides habitat for more than 100 breeding pairs of bald eagles.

Best Parks for Train Travel

Traveling by train to and from a national park is a rare treat, harkening back to the days when most visitors arrived by rail. Fortunately, two of the nation's grandest and most historic national parks are still fully accessible via trains coming from a handful of major metropolitan areas.

■ **Glacier.** Amtrak's Empire Builder stops at the east and west sides of Glacier on its way from Chicago to either Seattle or Portland. Shuttle service is available from either station to lodging in the park (with a prior reservation). The train also stops to the west in Whitefish, Montana, where there are additional lodging options.

■ **Grand Canyon.** Grand Canyon Railway offers a variety of daily train services from Williams, Arizona, to the park's South Rim. The adults-only Sunset Limited runs during weekends in the fall, allowing passengers to witness one of Grand Canyon's unmatched sunsets while enjoying appetizers and full bar service. From November through January, The Polar Express train reenacts the classic children's book (make sure to reserve far in advance). Amtrak's Southwest Chief stops in Williams on its Chicago to Los Angeles run, making Grand Canyon one of the few national parks fully accessible by rail transportation.

■ **Rocky Mountain.** Amtrak's California Zephyr line, running from San Francisco to Chicago, covers some of the West's most beautiful terrain, including the Rockies and Sierra Nevadas. It stops at Granby, Colorado, the western gateway to Rocky Mountain National Park. The local Avalanche Car Rentals (☎ 970/887–3908 ⊕ *www.avscars.com*) can meet you at the station.

IF YOU LIKE

2

BEACHES
Channel Islands
Olympic

BIRDS
Big Bend
Great Sand Dunes
Mount Rainier
Rocky Mountain
Theodore Roosevelt

BISON
Grand Teton
Great Sand Dunes
Rocky Mountain
Theodore Roosevelt

BOATING
Big Bend
Channel Islands
Glacier-Waterton
Grand Canyon
Grand Teton
Lassen Volcanic
North Cascades
Olympic
Redwood
Theodore Roosevelt
Yellowstone
Yosemite

**CAVES AND
CAVERNS**
Carlsbad Caverns
Great Basin
Sequoia and Kings
Canyon
Wind Cave

CLIMBING
Arches
Black Canyon of the
Gunnison
CanyonLands
Capitol Reef

Grand Teton
Joshua Tree
Mount Rainier
North Cascades
Olympic
Rocky Mountain
Sequoia and Kings
Canyon
Yosemite
Zion

FISHING
Big Bend
Black Canyon of the
Gunnison
Capitol Reef
Crater Lake
Glacier-Waterton
Grand Canyon
Grand Teton
Great Basin
Lassen Volcanic
Mount Rainier
North Cascades
Olympic
Redwood
Rocky Mountain
Sequoia and Kings
Canyon
Theodore Roosevelt
Yellowstone
Yosemite

**GEOLOGICAL
GREATS**
Arches
Bryce Canyon
Crater Lake
Grand Canyon
Petrified ForeSt
Yellowstone

**GLACIERS AND
ICEFIELDS**
Banff
Glacier-Waterton
Grand Teton
Jasper
Mount Rainier
North Cascades
Olympic

GRAND GEYSERS
Crater Lake
Death Valley
Lassen Volcanic
Mount Rainier
Olympic
Yellowstone

**HORSEBACK
RIDING**
Banff
Glacier
Lassen Volcanic
Mount Rainier
Olympic
Rocky Mountain
Theodore Roosevelt
Yosemite

**MAJESTIC
MOUNTAINS**
Big Bend
Capitol Reef
Glacier
Grand Teton
Guadalupe Mountains
North Cascades
Olympic
Rocky Mountain
Sequoia and Kings
Canyon
Yosemite

TERRIFIC TREES
Joshua Tree
North Cascades
Olympic
Petrified Forest
Redwood
Sequoia and Kings
Canyon
Yosemite

VOLCANOES
Crater Lake
Death Valley
Lassen Volcanic
Mount Rainier
Yellowstone

WATERFALLS
Banff
Crater Lake
Jasper
Great Sand Dunes
Lassen Volcanic
Mount Rainier
Olympic
Yellowstone
Yosemite

**WINTER
RECREATION**
Bryce Canyon
Mount Rainier
Olympic
Rocky Mountain
Yellowstone
Yosemite
Zion

Planning
Your Visit

PARK PASSES

Nation-wide Passes

If you're going to visit several American national parks in one vacation or over the course of a year, you may save money by investing in an annual pass. Each of these passes admits the cardholder and others in the vehicle (or up to three others at places that charge per person) to any national park in the United States and other designated federal recreational lands, such as national wildlife refuges, forests, and grasslands (find participating areas at ⊕ *store.usgs.gov/pass*).

You must have photo identification with you when presenting your pass at any park entrance. All passes are nontransferable and nonrefundable. If they are lost or stolen, they will need to be repurchased.

See ⊕ *www.nps.gov/fees_passes.htm* for additional information.

America the Beautiful Annual Pass. This $80 pass is valid for a year from the date of purchase. Buy the pass online (⊕ *store. usgs.gov/pass*), by phone (☎ *888/275–8747 Ext. 1*) or in person.

America the Beautiful Senior Pass. If you're 62 or older, you can purchase this pass for $10, and it is valid for a lifetime. You must purchase it in person.

America the Beautiful Access Pass. Those with disabilities may acquire a parks pass that is free of charge and valid for a lifetime. You must show documentation of your disability, and the pass can only be obtained in person.

America the Beautiful Volunteer Pass. Volunteer 500 or more service hours in national parks or other federal recreation lands and you'll be eligible for this free pass that is valid for one year from the date of acquisition.

Canadian Park Passes

Canada also offers annual passes to its parks. In Canada, an individual pass is only good for that person, not for everyone in the vehicle. For a carload of people to be admitted, you need the family/group pass. All passes must be purchased in person at one of the participating parks or historic sites.

The pass must be signed by the cardholder and is nontransferable. Retain your receipt/proof of purchase in case you lose your pass and need to have it replaced.

See ⊕ *www.pc.gc.ca* for details.

Discovery Package. Good for entrance to 27 of Canada's national parks and 78 national historic sites for a year, this pass cost $85 for individuals, $73 for those 65 and older, and $43 for youth up to age 16. A family/group package pass is $166.

National Parks of Canada Pass. The annual pass for Canada's national parks is $68 for individuals, $58 for those 65 and older, $34 for youth up to age 16, and $137 for a family/group pass.

Other Annual Passes

Most individual national parks also offer an annual pass for unlimited access for a year to that particular park. Prices vary, but hover around $30 to $50. In a few cases these passes include admission to two parks that are near each other, such as Grand Teton and Yellowstone. ■TIP➔ If you think you might be back to the park within a year, ask at the gate how much the annual pass is. Some parks, such as Bryce Canyon, charge $25 for the regular entrance fee but it's only $5 more for the annual pass—meaning a $20 savings if you return to the park within the year.

WHAT TO PACK

Everyone's Top 10

Packing lists for any trip vary according to the individual and his or her needs, of course, but here are 10 essential things for a national parks vacation to include in your luggage.

1. Binoculars. Many of the parks are a bird (and animal)-watcher's dream. A pair of binos will help you spot feathered friends as well as larger creatures. Binoculars are sold according to power, or how much the objects you're viewing are magnified (i.e., 7x, 10x, 12x, etc.) and the diameter of objective lens, which is the one on the fat end of the binoculars (the bigger the objective lens, the more light that gets in and the sharper your image should be). 10x is a good choice for magnification, field of view, and steadiness. If the magnification is higher, the field of view is smaller, and your hand movements will prevent you from seeing well, unless you use a tripod.

2. Clothes that layer. In the West, days can often be warm while nights turn chilly. The weather also can change quickly during the day, with things going from warm and sunny to windy and wet in a matter of minutes. This means you need to pack with both warm and cold (as well as wet and dry) weather in mind. The easiest is to dress in layers. Experts suggest synthetics such as polyester (used in Coolmax and other "wicking" fabrics that draw moisture away from your skin, and fleece, which is an insulator) and lightweight merino wool. Look for socks in wicking wool or polyester. Don't forget a waterproof poncho or jacket.

3. Long pants and long-sleeved shirts. It's wise to minimize exposed skin when hiking, especially in higher altitudes and areas with poison ivy and/or ticks.

4. Sturdy shoes or hiking boots. If you plan to do a lot of backcountry hiking, then also consider ankle support, which helps for unpaved trails. Be sure to break in your boots before the trip.

5. Insect repellant. If you're hiking or camping in an area with lots of mosquitoes, a good bug spray can help keep your trip from being a swatting marathon. A repellant also helps deter ticks. Most experts recommend repellants with DEET (N,N-diethyl-m-toulamide); the higher the level of DEET, the longer the product will be effective. Just be sure to use a separate sunscreen, not a single product with both ingredients (this is because you're supposed to reapply sunscreen every few hours, but doing so with DEET could deliver a dangerous dose of the chemical).

6. Skin moisturizer, sunscreen, and lip balm. In the parks you're likely to be outside for longer than you're used to at home and in higher altitudes and drier climates—all of which can leave your skin and lips parched, making you more vulnerable to sun- and windburn. Sunscreen should provide both UVA and UVB protection, with an SPF of at least 15; look for a lotion marked "sweatproof" or "sport."

7. Sunglasses and hat. Higher elevation means more ultraviolet radiation. Look for sunglasses that provide 100% UV protection.

8. Journal and Camera. When your jaw drops at the glorious vistas, and your head clears from all the fresh air, taking a picture may be your first instinct, but you also may find some thoughts of inspiration longing to be penned. Consider a journal that is weatherproof (sporting-goods stores often sell them). Journal entries may even help you later when it comes time to identify and write captions for your photographs.

9. Snacks and water. National parks by their nature are remote, and some are very lacking in services. Bring plenty of healthy snacks with you, as well as water. When hiking in hot weather, experts recommend ½ to 1 quart of water (or another fluid) per person, per hour, to prevent potentially dangerous dehydration. High elevation can increase your chances of dehydration, as well. Even if you're not hiking, have some food in the car for long drives through the park, where facilities might be scarce.

10. First-Aid Kit. A solid kit should contain a first-aid manual, aspirin (or ibuprofen), razor blades, tweezers, a needle, scissors, adhesive bandages, butterfly bandages, sterile gauze pads, one-inch wide adhesive tape, an elastic bandage, antibacterial ointment, antiseptic cream, antihistamines, calamine lotion, and moleskin for blisters.

Hiking Items

For vacations where you'll be going on hiking trips longer than an hour or two, consider investing in the following:

- **a compass and map** (⇨ *Maps box*)

- **a daypack** with enough room for everybody's essentials

- **energy bars** (they may not be five-star dining, but they do give you energy and keep your kids—and you—from being cranky)

- **a hiking stick or poles,** especially if you've got bad knees

- **a water filter** to treat water in the backcountry

- **bear bells** if you're in bear country

Camping Gear

Planning on saving money and roughing it on your national parks vacation? In addition to a working tent (check the zipper before you go!) and tent pegs, sleeping bags and pillows, and, of course, the

---

MAPS

If you plan to do a lot of hiking or mountaineering, especially in the backcountry, invest in detailed maps and a compass. Topographical maps are sold in well-equipped outdoor stores (REI and Cabela's, for example). Maps in different scales are available from the U.S. Geological Survey. To order, go to ⊕ www.usgs.gov/pubprod or call ☎ 303/202–4700 or 888/275–8747; you'll need to first request the free index and catalog, from which you can find and order the specific maps you need.

---

ingredients for s'mores (graham crackers, chocolate bars, and marshmallows), here are some things veteran campers recommend be among your gear:

- **camping chairs** (folding or collapsible)

- **camp stove**

- **cooking utensils and plates, cups, etc.**

- **duct tape** (great for covering tears)

- **flashlight or lantern**

- **matches**

- **paper towels, napkins**

- **a multipurpose knife**

- **a rope** (for laundry or to help tie things down; pack clothespins, too)

- **a sleeping pad or air mattress** (optional, but using one under your sleeping bag can make a big difference in a good night's sleep; another option is a cot)

- **a tarp** (will help keep the bottom of your tent—and subsequently you!—dry)

FAMILY FUN

Top 5 Tips

1. Plan ahead. Rooms and campsites fill up fast, so make your reservations as early as you can, says Kathy Kupper, a public affairs specialist with the National Park Service. Many parks will have every room and campsite booked several months in advance (weekends are especially popular). Kupper recommends booking at least six months ahead, and more if you plan to visit one of the more popular parks, such as Grand Canyon, Grand Teton, Rocky Mountain, Yellowstone, or Yosemite. If you plan on staying outside the park, check with the hotels you're considering as far ahead as you can, as these places can fill up fast as well. You also can go online. All of the National Parks have a Web site—links to all of them are at the National Park Service page, ⊕ *www.nps.gov*. Many of the parks' pages have a "For Kids" link.

2. Get the kids involved. It might seem easier to do the planning yourself, but you'll probably have a better time—and your kids definitely will—if you involve them, says Steve Zachary, a ranger and education specialist at Lassen Volcanic National Park in California. No matter how old they are, children ought to have a good idea of where you're going and what you're about to experience. "It builds excitement beforehand, and lets the kids feel as if they've got a say in what you're doing." Zachary, who has traveled extensively through the national parks with his two sons, recommends discussing the park's various attractions and giving your kids a few choices.

3. Know your children. Consider your child's interests, says Zachary. This will help you plan a vacation that's both safe and memorable (for all the right reasons). For starters, if you have kids under 4, be honest

with yourself about whether the national park itself is age appropriate. Parents are notorious for projecting their awe for majestic scenery and overall enthusiasm for sightseeing on their younger kids, who might be more interested in cataloging the snacks in the hotel room's minibar. Likewise, Zachary says, be realistic about your child's stamina and ability. "I've seen parents who want to climb up to the volcano with their 10-year-old, but they live at sea level and the kid has never been hiking. This is a 2½-mi hike at 7,000 feet. In the end, nobody has any fun and the kid now hates hiking."

4. Pack wisely. Be sure you're bringing kid-sized versions of the necessities you'll pack for yourself: Depending on the park you're visiting (and the activities you're planning), that might include sturdy hiking shoes, sunglasses, sunscreen, and insect repellant. You'll almost certainly need a few layers of clothing and plenty of water and snacks. Kids can be more susceptible to heat stress and dehydration than adults, meaning they need plenty of water when exercising. The American Academy of Pediatrics recommends giving your child about five ounces of water or another beverage every 20 minutes during strenuous exercise; studies show that kids are more willing to take flavored drinks than plain water.

5. Develop a Plan B. National parks are natural places, meaning they change dramatically with the seasons and the weather. So you should decide on alternate activities if Mother Nature isn't cooperative. And if you've already talked with your kids about your options, you can pick a new plan that appeals to everyone.

SAMPLE BUDGET FOR FAMILY OF FOUR

Here is an idea of what a family of four might spend on a three-day trip to Grand Canyon National Park, during which they stay and eat all their meals within the park. Depending on your accommodations and dining-out options, the total you spend can vary dramatically.

Admission: $25 per car; admission covers seven days in the park.

Lodging: Rooms in one of the in-park lodges on the popular South Rim range from approximately $50 to $320 a night. Total for three nights: $150 to $960, or more if you have older children in a separate room. Tent camping in one of the park's campgrounds averages $15 per night. Total: $45. Backpackers must pay $10 for a backcountry permit and $5 per person, per night to camp below the rim (or $5 per group, per night above the rim). Total: $25 to $70.

Meals: Dining options in the park range from no-frills snack bars to upscale restaurants. Per-meal costs run from $10 to $40 or more. Total (12 meals per day for three days): $360 to $1,440, or less, if cooking meals over your campfire or packing sack lunches.

Souvenirs: Budget $5 to $10 per person per day for souvenirs so each person can get something small each day, or one or two larger items per trip. Total: $60 to $120.

TOTAL COST: $470 to $2,545

Budgeting Your Trip

Like most vacations, a trip to a national park can be as frugal, or as fancy, as you like. Here are a few things to consider:

Getting In. Individual admission to the national parks ranges from free to $25, depending on the park (see our Essentials section at the beginning of each park chapter to learn individual rates). You also can buy an America the Beautiful Pass for $80, which will get you, and everyone in your group, into any national park (as well as other federal recreation areas) for one year.

Sleeping. Fewer than half of the parks charge for camping; the cost is typically under $20 per night. In many parks, you also can stay at a lodge, where prices run from $100 to $500 a night. There are also usually several accommodation options outside each park.

Eating. All of the in-park concessions are run by companies under contract with the National Park Service, meaning their prices are set by the government. Generally speaking, prices are a bit higher than what you'd pay outside the park, but not significantly so. You also can bring in your own food and eat at one of the park's picnic areas.

Entertainment. The wonders of the park are entertainment enough for many youngsters, but the many sports and outdoor activities—from hiking and bicycling to horseback riding and cave touring, depending on the park—help children stay active while exploring the park. Many park visitor centers also have films; some parks, such as Grand Canyon and Zion, even have IMAX movies. Cost for these offerings varies, ranging from free to a couple hundred dollars for something like a white-water rafting trip.

Souvenirs. All of the parks have gift shops, and many stock items that are actually useful. For example, you'll find things like kid-sized binoculars, fanny packs, and magnifying glasses, all of which can make your child's visit even more enjoyable (and valuable). You can call ahead to see what's available, or just budget a few dollars to cover one item (maybe something you might have bought for your child anyway, like a disposable camera).

Kids Programs

About half of the 390 U.S. national parks are part of the Junior Ranger Program, which offers school-age kids the opportunity to learn about the park by filling out a short workbook or participating in an activity such as taking a hike with a park ranger. After completing the program, kids get a badge (or a pin or patch, depending on the park). For availability, check with the ranger station or visitor center when you arrive; some parks also put their Junior Ranger booklets online.

In addition to the Junior Ranger Program, kids can find a variety of activities designed just for them. Some parks, such as Sequoia, loan "Discovery Packs," backpacks filled with kid-friendly tools like magnifying glasses. Call ahead for availability.

Many parks also have general-interest programs that kids love. For example, Rocky Mountain National Park offers "Skins and Skulls," where visitors can touch a bear's fur and a marmot's skull, among other things, says Kyle Patterson, Public Information Officer for the park. "It helps kids—and adults—understand and explore in a hands-on, yet totally safe, way."

When you're through with the organized activities and are ready to head off on your own, remember that kids often take

a shorter view of things than adults do, meaning they may need to be reminded once in awhile of why you're there and what lies ahead. A parent in Oregon recounts, "When I was hiking with my kids in Yosemite and they started to get whiny, I'd tell then, 'Hey guys, think of how much fun we're going to have at this swimming hole!' We'd also play games like I Spy." Other kids might like a scavenger hunt.

Camping Tips

A night in a tent under the stars is the highlight of many kids' trips to a national park. Making sure it's a pleasant experience, however, takes some preparation.

A Cub Scouts pack leader advises that you **check the weather forecast—and your tent—before you go.** "We actually had a family who brought a brand-new tent that hadn't even been taken out of the box until they got to the campground, only to discover while trying to assemble it that the door was defective so it didn't zip closed. Imagine the mosquito bites they had in the morning!"

She also suggests that, if possible, **choose your tent site carefully.** "Trust me," she says, "you don't want to pitch your tent next to someone who snores all night!"

One item you "gotta have," she adds, is **toilet paper.** "No explanation necessary."

If your typical view of the night sky consists of a handful of stars dimly twinkling through a hazy, light-polluted sky, get ready for a treat. In the parks, the night sky blazes with starlight—and with a little practice, you can give your family a memorable astronomical tour.

Constellations

Constellations are stories in the sky—many depict animals or figures from Greek mythology. Brush up on a few of these tales before your trip, and you'll be an instant source of nighttime entertainment.

The stars in the Northern Hemisphere appear to rotate around Polaris, the North Star, in fixed positions relative to one another. To get your celestial bearings, first find the bright stars of the Big Dipper. An imaginary line drawn through the two stars that form the outside edge of the cup (away from the handle) will point straight to Polaris (Polaris also serves as the last star in the handle of the Little Dipper). Once you've identified Polaris, you should be able to find the other stars on our chart. Myriad astronomy books and Web sites have additional star charts; *National Geographic* has a cool interactive version with images from the Hubble Space Telescope (🌐 *www.nationalgeographic.com/stars*)

Planets

Stars twinkle, planets don't (because they're so much closer to Earth, the atmosphere doesn't distort their light as much). Planets are also bright, which makes them fairly easy to spot. Unfortunately, we can't show their positions on this star chart, because planets orbit the sun and move in relation to the stars.

The easiest planet to spot is Venus, the brightest object in the night sky besides the moon and the Earth's closest planetary neighbor. Look for it just before sunrise or just after sunset; it'll be near the point where the sun is rising or setting. (Venus and Earth orbit the sun at different speeds; when Venus is moving away from Earth, we see it in the morning, and when it's moving toward us, we see it in the evening.) Like the moon, Venus goes through phases—check it out through a pair of binoculars. You can also spot Mars, Jupiter, Saturn, and Mercury—with or without the aid of binoculars.

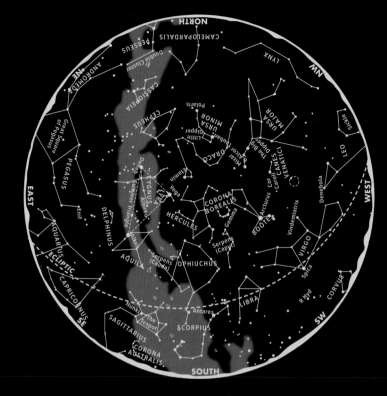

Meteors

It's hard to match the magic of a meteor shower, the natural fireworks display that occurs as Earth passes through a cloud of debris called meteoroids. These pieces of space junk—most the size of a pebble—hit our atmosphere at high speeds, and the intense friction produces brief but brilliant streaks of light. Single meteors are often called "shooting stars" or "falling stars."

Since our planet passes through the same patches of interstellar refuse each year, it's easy to roughly predict when the major meteor showers will occur. Notable ones include the Perseids (mid-August), the Orionids (late October), the Leonids (mid-November), and the Geminids (mid-December). Each shower is named after the point in the sky where meteors appear to originate. If you're not visiting during a shower, don't worry—you can spot individual meteors any time of the year.

Satellites

Right now, according to NASA, there are about 3,000 operative man-made satellites (along with 6,000 pieces of space junk) orbiting the Earth—and you can catch a glimpse of one with a little practice. Satellites look like fast-moving, non-blinking points of light; the best way to spot one is to lie on your back and scan the sky for movement. Be on the lookout for satellites an hour or two before or after sunset (though you may see them at other times as well).

You can take the guesswork out of the search with a few cool online tools (⊕ *www.nasa. gov* or *www.heavens-above.com*). Select your location, and these Web sites will help you predict—down to the minute—when certain objects will be streaking overhead. It's especially worthwhile to use these sites to look for the two brightest satellites: the International Space Station and the space shuttle.

ROCK CLIMBING Q&A

Curious about the sport of rock climbing? The national parks are prime venues for this adventurous, adrenaline-pumping pursuit. The best parks in the West for climbers are Yosemite, Joshua Tree, Grand Teton, Black Canyon of the Gunnison, Rocky Mountain, and Canyonlands (just outside the Needles district in Indian Creek).

Answering our questions about rock climbing is Jason Martin, a climbing guide and author and the program coordinator for the **American Alpine Institute (AAI)** (⊠ *1515 12th St., Bellingham, WA 98225* ☎ *360/671–1505* ⊕ *www.aai.cc*), one of the premier rock-climbing and mountaineering schools in the United States.

Is rock climbing safe?

Contrary to popular belief, rock climbing is remarkably safe. A greater number of accidents occur in skiing, river rafting, even hiking, than in rock climbing. The consequences for errors, mistakes, and a lack of adequate training in rock climbing are severe, and so most people consider the sport to be dangerous. That said, most people participating in the activity know what they are doing and know how to stay safe.

What's a safe age to begin?

To push one's physical and mental limits within the sport, it is best to start as young as possible in order to develop strength and technique during formative years. Those who wish to climb recreationally but aren't interested in making progressively harder and harder climbs can start any time. In our introductory programs, we see children from age 10 up to seniors well over 60, and every age in between. With indoor climbing walls, a generally safe and controlled environment, kids can start climbing (with some adult assistance) as soon as they are able to climb up ladders on the playground. However, types of climbing that require a better understanding of ropes and equipment should be saved for children who have more critical thinking skills, generally kids who are 10 to 14 years old. For outdoor lead climbing that involves complex anchor and rope-work scenarios, climbers tend to be 16 years and older. On the flip side, we work with folks in their 50s and even 60s who are getting into rock climbing and mountaineering for the first time, and they tend to learn quickly.

What shape should you be in?

Beginners don't need to have a high level of fitness. The myth is that climbing requires a massive amount of upper body strength. This isn't true at all. Instead, it requires good use of your feet, an economy of movement, and good technique, all of which can be learned.

This isn't to say that there is no value in good overall fitness. While a person who doesn't have a high level of fitness will be able to enjoy climbing, the person who is a little bit more fit will advance into harder and steeper climbs more quickly.

But, where are the nets?

Climbers don't use nets. Instead, they use special nylon ropes and protective gear and anchors to secure themselves and prevent any injury in the event of a fall. Beginners will have the ropes secured above them and attached to their harnesses. As they climb, the rope will remain snug. If they slip, the rope will immediately catch them. If they lose any altitude at all, it will be because the ropes stretch a little bit.

Experienced climbers aren't scared very often for two reasons. First, they trust their gear. They know that most of it has been rated to hold the weight of a small vehicle and simply won't break under the weight

of a human being. Second, they become used to the altitude and exposure.

Experienced climbing guides will do everything in their power to help their students understand the strength of their gear. They will also choose climbs that don't have a lot of exposure so that people have time to get used to the sensation of climbing and being off the ground.

Does it damage the rocks?

Climbing itself does not damage the rocks. However, there are times when a climber might require "fixed anchors," which are usually small bolts that are placed permanently in the rock. Most climbers are conscientious and try to camouflage the bolts so that people on the ground won't see them, but they're still a hot topic among climbers and land managers. In fact, the use of bolts as fixed anchors has been limited or even banned in many national parks.

What gear do you need?

If you work with an instructor or go out with experienced friends, you'll only need a few items. Once you learn the basics and are ready to climb on your own, you'll need to invest in a lot more equipment. But getting started is easy and not terribly expensive. The basics are:

- a harness
- a helmet
- rock shoes (special sticky, tight-fitting shoes)
- a locking carabiner
- a belay device

Anything else to add?

Rock climbing is a great sport. It provides for a wonderful outdoor adventure and it's an excellent excuse to visit new places. And when you learn to do it right, it's much easier than it looks, and the personal rewards are much greater than you might think. It's fun, it builds self-confidence, and it gives you an amazing sense of accomplishment.

TAKE A TOUR

Whether you want an experienced guide for an active-sport trip, or an educational but leisurely program that takes the planning out of your hands, tours can be ideal for all ages and life situations—families, outdoor enthusiasts, and retirees.

Adventure Trips

Many trip organizers specialize in only one type of activity; however, a few companies guide different kinds of active trips. (In some cases, these larger companies also act essentially as a clearinghouse or agent for smaller trip outfitters.) Be sure to sign on with a reliable outfitter; getting stuck with a shoddy operator can be disappointing, uncomfortable, and even dangerous. Some sports—white-water rafting and mountaineering, for example—have organizations that license or certify guides, and you should be sure that the guide you're with is properly accredited.

Tour Operators Backroads (⊠ 801 Cedar St., Berkeley, CA 94710 ☎ 510/527–1555 or 800/462–2848 ⊕ www.backroads.com). **Off the Beaten Path** (⊠ 7 E. Beall St., Bozeman, MT 59715 ☎ 800/445–2995 ⊕ www.offthebeatenpath.com). **REI Adventures** (⊠ P.O. Box 1938, Sumner, WA 98390 ☎ 253/437–1100 or 800/622–2236 ⊕ www.rei.com/adventures). **Trek America** (⊡ P.O. Box 189, Rockaway, NJ 07866 ☎ 973/983–1144 or 800/873–5872 ⊕ www.trekamerica.com). **The World Outdoors** (⊠ 2840 Wilderness Pl., Suite D, Boulder, CO 80301 ☎ 303/413–0938 or 800/488–8483 ⊕ www.theworldoutdoors.com).

Senior Tours

Those in their golden years can join special tours, some of which are quite adventurous, such as Elderhostel's grandparent-grandchild river rafting trip on the Grand Canyon's Colorado River.

Tour Operators Elderhostel (⊠ 11 Ave. de LafayetteBoston, MA 02111 ☎ 800/454–5768 ⊕ www.elderhostel.org). **Walking The World** (⊡ P.O. Box 1186, Fort Collins, CO 80522 ☎ 970/498–0500 ⊕ www.walkingtheworld.com).

Single-Park Tours

If you want to concentrate solely on one park, contact the park directly to learn about organized tours they may have. Or look into one of these organizations:

Tour Operators Glacier Park, Inc. (⊡ P.O. Box 2025, Columbia Falls, MT 59912 ☎ 406/892–2525 ⊕ www.glacierparkinc.com) offers weeklong excursions specifically in Glacier and Waterton that include meals, narration on rides in vintage Ford Jammers, and time for play away from the group. **Grand Canyon Tour Company** (⊠ 4343 N. Rancho Dr., Ste. 230, Las Vegas, NV 89130 ☎ 702/655–6060 or 800/222–6966 ⊕ www.grandcanyontourcompany.com) provides tours of the park from Las Vegas. **The Yellowstone Association Institute** (⊡ P.O. Box 117, Yellowstone National Park, WY 82190 ☎ 406/848–2400 ⊕ www.yellowstoneassociation.org) offers guided tours and trips in Yellowstone, ranging from backcountry expeditions to "Lodging and Learning" experiences.

Tours with Accessibility

Tour Operator Access Tours (⊡ P.O. Box 499, Victor, ID 83455 ☎ 800/929–4811 ⊕ www.accesstours.org) leads nine-day trips for people who use wheelchairs or have other mobility impairments and can customize trips for groups of five or more.

CAPTURING THE PARKS ON FILM

Today's digital cameras make it difficult to take a truly lousy picture, but there are still some things even the best models can't do without your expertise. The tips below (some of them classic photography techniques) won't turn you into the next Ansel Adams, but they might prevent you from being upstaged by your 5-year-old with her own digital camera.

The Golden Hours. The best photos are taken when most of us are either snoozing or eating dinner: about an hour before and after sunrise and sunset. When the light is gentle and golden, your photos are less likely to be over-exposed and filled with harsh shadows and squinting people.

Divide to Conquer. You can't go wrong with the Rule of Thirds: When you're setting up a shot, mentally divide your picture area into thirds, horizontally and vertically, which will give you nine squares. Any one of the four places where the squares intersect represents a good spot to place your primary subject. (If all this talk of imaginary lines makes your head spin, just remember not to automatically plop your primary focal point in the center of your photos).

Lock Your Focus. To get a properly focused photo using a camera with auto-focus, press the shutter button down halfway and wait a few seconds before pressing down completely. (On most cameras, a light or a cheery beep will indicate that you're good to go.)

Circumvent Auto Focus. If your camera isn't focusing on your desired focal point, center the primary subject smack in the middle of the frame and depress the shutter button halfway, allowing the camera to focus. Then compose your photo properly (moving your camera so the focal point isn't in the center of the shot), and press the shutter all the way down.

Jettison the Jitters. Shaky hands are among the most common cause of out-of-focus photos. If ice water doesn't run through your veins, invest in a tripod or put the camera on something steady—such as a wall, a bench, or a rock—when you shoot. If all else fails, lean against something sturdy to brace yourself.

Consider the Imagery. Before you press that shutter button, take a moment or two to consider *why* you're shooting what you're shooting. Once you've determined this, start setting up your photo. Look for interesting lines that curve into your image—such as a path, the shoreline, or a fence—and use them to create the impression of depth. You can also avoid flat images by photographing people with their bodies or faces positioned at an angle to the camera.

Ignore All the Rules. Sure, thoughtful contemplation and careful execution are likely to produce brilliant images—but there are times when you just need to capture the moment. If you see something wonderful, grab your camera and just get the picture. If the photo turns out to be blurry, off-center, or over- or under-exposed, you can always Photoshop it later.

Special Considerations. If you're going to any Indian reservations (many are located near national parks), check the rules before you take photographs. In many cases you must purchase a permit.

STAYING HEALTHY, PLAYING IT SAFE

Altitude Sickness

Altitude sickness can result when your body is thrown into high elevations without having time to adjust. When you're at a mile (5,280 feet) or more above sea level, and especially when you're higher than 8,500 feet, you may feel symptoms of altitude sickness: shortness of breath, light-headedness, nausea, fatigue, headache, and trouble sleeping. To help your body adjust to the new elevation, drink lots of water, avoid alcohol, and wait a day or two before attempting vigorous activity. If your conditions are severe, last several days, or worsen, seek medical attention. Altitude sickness can develop into serious conditions, and in extreme cases can even lead to death.

Animal Bites

Rangers will tell you that rattlesnakes are more scared of us than we are of them. But should a rattlesnake (or any other snake) decide to strike, stay calm and still (panic and a lot of movement can spread the poison). Have someone else get medical help for you right away. If you are bitten by any other wild animal—even a small one— seek medical attention immediately. You may need a rabies or tetanus shot.

Hypothermia

When your body gets too cold for too long, hypothermia can develop. Symptoms are chills, fatigue, shivering, and lack of mental clarity. If someone you're traveling with develops hypothermia seek shelter, remove any wet clothes from them, and wrap them in warm blankets. Warm their corse first, not their extremities. If you have hot packs, put them under the armpits. It also helps for you to get into the blankets with them so they can pull from your body heat. Hot (not cold!) beverages also help.

Safety Concerns

America's national parks have been set aside to preserve some of the most outstanding landscapes in the world. This is nature at its finest, and in raw form. This means that although parks are wonderful venues for families, providing experiences they'll remember for a lifetime, it's important that children realize that national parks are not theme parks or zoos. They need to respect and take caution with the surroundings. Here are some safety tips to keep in mind:

Don't feed the animals. Animals in some of the larger national parks are used to humans being around and may not flee at your presence. But this doesn't mean you should feed them. It is unhealthy for them to eat people food, and because it further acclimates them to humans, it can lead to them being more aggressive, and thus more dangerous, to future visitors.

Register at trailheads. If there's a notebook where you can write down your name and the time you're starting your hike, jot it down so park personnel know where you are should inclement weather or another danger occur. Also, don't hike alone, especially in bear country.

Practice fire safety. Check with the visitor center on campfire rules, and never build fires in the backcountry: One breath of wind can carry a cinder for miles and plant it on dry grasslands just ready to blaze. When cooking over your campfire, clear the ground around it first of dry leaves and grass, keep the fire inside the pit, throw used matches into the fire, and keep a pot of water or sand nearby. Don't start a fire when you're alone, and never leave it unattended. Lastly, it should go without saying: never cook in your tent or any poorly ventilated area.

MORE TIPS AND TIDBITS

Camera Care

If you're flying, don't pack camera equipment in checked luggage, where it is much more susceptible to damage. If you're using a traditional camera, keep the film out of the sun and heat.

Discounts for Seniors

To qualify for age-related discounts, don't wait until you've used a service. Mention your senior-citizen status up front when booking hotel reservations and before you're seated in restaurants. Have identification on hand to back up your claim.

Pets in the Park

Generally, pets are allowed only in developed areas of the national parks, including drive-in campgrounds and picnic areas. *They must be kept on a leash at all times.* With the exception of guide dogs, pets are not allowed inside buildings, on most trails, on beaches, or in the backcountry. They also may be prohibited in areas controlled by concessionaires, such as restaurants. Some national parks have kennels; call ahead to learn the details and to see if there's availability. Some of the national forests (⊕ *www.fs.fed.us*) surrounding the parks have camping and are more lenient with pets.

Traveling with Disabilities

Most national parks have some accessible visitor centers, restrooms, campsites, and trails. If you use a guide dog, check with the park ahead of time to see if they allow service animals.

PARK RESOURCES

ORGANIZATIONS

National Parks Conservation Association (⌐🏠 *1300 19th St. NW, Ste. 300, Washington, DC 20036* ☎ *800/628–7275* ⊕ *www.npca.org*) raises awareness of the parks through public, media, and government education.

National Park Foundation (⌐🏠 *1201 Eye St. NW, Ste. 550B, Washington, DC 20005* ☎ *202/354–6460* ⊕ *www.nationalparks.org*) is a non-profit, fund-raising arm of the National Park Service.

National Park Service (⌐🏠 *National Park Service/Department of Interior, 1849 C St. NW, Washington, DC 20240* ☎ *202/208–6843* ⊕ *www.nps.gov*).

Parks Canada (⌐🏠 *25 Eddy St., Gatineau, Quebec K1A 0M5* ☎ *888/773–8888* ⊕ *www.pc.gc.ca*).

PUBLICATIONS

National Park System: Map and Guide (⌐🏠 *Federal Citizen Information Center, P.O. Box 100, Pueblo, CO 81002* ☎ *888/878–3256* ☒ *$2.50* ⊕ *www.pueblo.gsa.gov*), published by the NPS, is a full-color map listing activities at more than 300 parks and other federal lands.

FIELD GUIDE: COMMON GEOLOGY AND TERRAIN TERMS

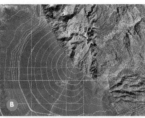

Some of the western national parks' greatest assets are the unique landscapes and bizarre geological features; many are found in only a handful of places on the planet. As you explore these national treasures, refer to this geological glossary for more information about the forces that shaped the awesome sites around you. By the end of your trip, you'll be able to tell the difference between a syncline, an anticline, and a monocline!

Alluvial Fans

(B) Cloudbursts in the desert cause water to rush down the faces of barren mountains and hills. Since it cannot be easily absorbed into the dry, packed soil, the water spreads out into rivulets and streams, leaving behind fan-shaped wedges of sediment. Look for these distinctive features in Death Valley and the Mojave Desert.

Anticline

Movements of the Earth's crust produce these upward-curving, convex folds when they push originally horizontal rock layers upward in one spot. The anticline slopes downward from the crest.

Arch

(A) This type of window in a rock wall forms either through erosion, when wind and sand wear away the rock face, or through the freezing action of water. When water enters spaces or joints in a rock and freezes there, the expansion of the ice can crack off chunks of rock. The parks of southern Utah contain many arches.

Badlands

(D) Much of the sedimentary rock that eroded from the Black Hills was deposited in South Dakota's Badlands, along with ash from the volcanoes in the Yellowstone area. The wind blew and water flowed over the landscape, carving out huge buttes and cliffs in a process that

continues to this day. In the relatively soft, half-hardened rocks, the elements also carved drainage channels with a distinctive V shape, creating a network of ravines and ridgelines. These formations are devoid of vegetation because erosion carries off seeds and roots. The amphitheater at Bryce Canyon National Park is another example of badlands.

Basin

(C) A basin is depression in the ground that collects sediment. Within a basin there are often smaller anticlines and synclines. The Great Basin is an example of a geologic basin.

Biological Soil Crusts

Also known as cryptobiotic soil crust or biocrust, this black, bumpy stuff covers the ground throughout the Colorado Plateau. It is composed of cyanobacteria, green algae, lichens, fungi, and mosses that form a living cover on the ground. The crust stabilizes the soil and allows plants to germinate and root. If it's destroyed or damaged, new plant life cannot grow. It can take an estimated 50 to 250 years for this living organism to completely repair itself.

The Black Hills

South Dakota's Black Hills began as a mountainous landscape covered with limestone and shale sedimentary rock, but this covering gradually eroded away, exposing a granite face. Much of the sedimentary rock that eroded from the Black Hills was deposited in the Badlands.

Bridge

(H) If a window through a rock has been created by (now-receded) water flowing beneath it, it is called a bridge. You can see many natural bridges in the Colorado Plateau, such as Hickman Bridge at Capitol Reef National Park.

Letters within parentheses refer to illustrations on pages 70 and 71.

Butte

A butte is what remains when a mesa erodes—a hill with a flat top and steep sides. You can see good examples of this formation in Glacier and Canyonlands national parks.

Caldera

Although it is the largest and deepest example, the bowl-shaped depression in which Crater Lake lies is only one of many calderas along the Pacific Rim. Created when volcanoes blow their tops, small caldera remnants lie atop Mount Rainier and Mount Baker, and a bigger one remains on Mount St. Helens, where its side blew out in 1980.

Canyon

(G) A canyon forms when water and wind erode soft layers of the Earth's rock crust. The hardness of the rock determines the shape of the canyon: a narrow, or slot, canyon generally results when the rock is the same composition all the way down and water runs through the crack. A step-like canyon such as the Grand Canyon forms when alternating soft and hard layers are eroded by wind and water, with a river cutting a narrow groove in the bottom of the canyon.

Caves

Caves—natural underground chambers—give you an opportunity to descend below the Earth's surface and learn about the forces of heat and water upon rocks and minerals. Crystal Cave in Sequoia National park has excellent examples of stalactites and stalagmites. In South Dakota, Jewel Cave and Wind Cave, each with more than 100 mi of mapped passageway, rank as second and fourth longest in the world, respectively, and each is home to incredibly rare rock formations. In New Mexico, Carlsbad Caverns' extensive cave system includes the Big Room, which has a 255-foot-high ceiling.

Colorado Plateau

The region of plateaus, mesas, and canyons encompassing much of Colorado, Utah, Arizona, and New Mexico, and eight national parks—Arches, Bryce Canyon, Canyonlands, Capitol Reef, Grand Canyon, Mesa Verde, Petrified Forest, and Zion)—is known as the Colorado Plateau.

The Continental Divide

The Continental Divide of North America is a ridge that crosses the continent from north to south, separating water flowing east and water flowing west. The divide follows the crest of the Rockies through Glacier, Yellowstone, and Rocky Mountain national parks.

Desert Pavement

High winds can scour away sand, silt, and other small particles of soil, leaving behind a densely packed layer of coarse pebbles and gravel known as desert pavement. You can see it in arid areas such as the plains of Big Bend National Park.

Desert Varnish

This reddish-brown or black coating seems to drip down canyon walls as if from a spilled can of paint. Windblown dust or rain containing iron and manganese, along with microorganisms living on the rock's surface, create the color. Ancestral Puebloans and other ancient American Indians scratched drawings called petroglyphs into the desert varnish.

Fault Zones

Shifting underground land masses such as those of California's famous San Andreas Fault have helped create many of Joshua Tree National Park's upper elevations,

including the Pinto Mountains on the northern border and the Little San Bernardino Mountains on the southwest side. This same geologic upheaval has shifted and cracked underground rocks, damming up the flow of groundwater and forcing it to the surface, making precious moisture available to wildlife and plants.

Fossil Reef

(F) Much of the desert region of Texas and New Mexico shares a common geologic past, when a warm, shallow inland sea covered a large area. As the sea evaporated, a nearly 400-mi-long limestone reef was deposited, made up of sediment, dead plants, and the skeletons of tiny sea creatures. Movement in the Earth's surface later thrust the reef upward, helping to shape the Guadalupe Mountains. One of the largest and most visible examples of fossil reef is Capitan Reef in Guadalupe Mountains National Park, which attracts geologists from around the world.

Geothermal Features

Hissing geysers, burbling mud pots, and boiling cauldrons have fascinated travelers ever since mountain man John Coulter described them to an unbelieving public in 1810. Today, these "freaks of a fiery nature," as Rudyard Kipling described them, are still clearly visible in Lassen Volcanic and Yellowstone national parks. Geysers, hot springs, and fumaroles are created when superheated water rises to the earth's surface from a magma chamber below. In the case of geysers, the water is trapped under the surface until the pressure is so great that it bursts through. Mud pots, also known as paint pots, are a combination of hot water, hydrogen sulfide gas, and dissolved volcanic rock. The mixture looks like a hot, smelly, burping pudding. ⇨ *In-focus feature in Yellowstone National Park (chapter 37) for more information.*

Glaciers

Heavy snow compacted by centuries of accumulation forms the distinctive blue, dense ice of a glacier. Incremental movement, usually inches a year, is what distinguishes a glacier from a snowfield; most of the glaciers in the contiguous United States are in Washington and Oregon, and most are receding due to global warming.

Hot Springs

Past the eastern escarpment of the Sierra, evidence of the region's volcanic history remains in the giant calderas of the high-mountain desert. In the area west of Death Valley National Park, countless hot springs issue from the earth and form small to medium-size pools in the ground, some of which are suitable for bathing. If you should stumble upon one, never jump in without first testing the water's temperature. The locals keep many of the springs secret, but in some places people have piped the hot waters into developed pools. While driving on U.S. 395, look for road signs pointing the way to numerous hot springs.

Laccolithic Mountains

Throughout the Colorado Plateau, many mountain ranges seem to rise suddenly out of the flat earth, with no transitional foothills. These ranges are generally located over faults in the earth's crust. They formed as molten rock, or magma, flowed up from below, and hardened under layers of sedimentary rock. Erosion and other geologic forces subsequently exposed the volcanic rock in the form of mountains. Among the region's laccolithic ranges are the La Sal Mountains near Moab, Utah; the Abajo Mountains near Canyonlands National Park's Needles District; and the La Plata and Ute mountains near Mesa Verde National Park.

Mesa

A hill with a smooth, flat, table-like top is a mesa, which means "table" in Spanish. It is a clear example of how hard rock stands higher and protects the soft rock beneath. A single mesa may cover hundreds of square miles of land. At the Island in the Sky District of Canyonlands National Park and at Mesa Verde you are standing on top of a mesa.

Monocline

The most notable geologic feature of the Colorado Plateau, a monocline is a bit like half an anticline (see above). The layers of rock on either side of a monocline are mostly level, but they bend downward like a step. Pioneers often called them "reefs" because the formations were a barrier to passage through the area. The Waterpocket Fold in Capitol Reef National Park is a most dramatic example of a monocline. Another example is the Monument Upwarp, which extends from Kayenta, Arizona, to the confluence of the Green and Colorado rivers in Canyonlands National Park. There are many smaller anticlines and synclines along the Upwarp.

Monument

This general term applies to geologic formations that are much taller than they are wide, or to formations that resemble man-made structures. You can see many examples of the first type of monument in Capitol Reef National Park's Cathedral Valley; in Monument Valley, Arizona; and in the White Rim Monument Basin area at Canyonlands National Park. Monuments that fall into the second category include the Sinking Ship in Bryce Canyon National Park and the Three Penguins at Arches National Park.

Petrified Wood

If you want to know what the desert Southwest used to look like, picture the Florida Everglades populated with giant dragonflies and smaller species of dinosaurs. Arizona's Petrified Forest offers a glimpse of the once lush, tropical world. Stumps and logs from the ancient woodland are now turned to rock because they were immersed in water and sealed away from the air, so normal decay did not occur. Instead, the preserved wood gradually hardened as silica, or sand, filtered into its porous spaces, almost like cement. Erosion was among the geological processes that exposed the wood.

Plains

Once home to vast herds of bison that blackened the prairie for miles, the grasslands across the nation's center today serve as America's breadbasket, supplying much of the nation and parts of the world with dairy products, grain, seeds, cattle, poultry, and pork.

Playa

Dry, salt-encrusted lake beds known as playas ("beaches" in Spanish) commonly lie in the low points of arid southwestern valleys. You can see examples in the Sonoran Desert near Tucson and in Death Valley National Park.

The Rocky Mountains

The Rocky Mountain chain reaches from northwestern Canada down through Washington, Idaho, Montana, Wyoming, Colorado, Utah, and into New Mexico. The huge mountains are thought to have been raised by massive tectonic plates colliding, pushing the Earth's crust upwards. The soft rocks eroded and were split by deep fault zones, exposing the harder granite for which the mountains are known.

Sand Dunes

The sand dunes that you occasionally come across in the Colorado Plateau have been deposited by winds. Wind blowing past rock formations will pick up grains of sand. If the wind then passes through a natural channel like a window or a slot canyon, it will lose speed when the channel ends and the sand will drop onto the ground. Plants cannot grow in these dry, windy spots, so the wind continues to deposit sand, and a dune forms. Two good examples in canyon country are at Coral Pink Sand Dunes State Park near Zion National Park, and on Route 24 near Capitol Reef National Park.

Sierra Nevada

The Sierra Nevada mountain range is marked by a gentle rise on the west side and a sharp drop-off on the east side. The land east of the crest sank dramatically by several thousand feet, resulting in the eastern escarpment having no foothills. Moisture from the Pacific cools as the air rises up the mountains, eventually condensing and falling as rain or snow. So little water is left in the air by the time it crosses the range that the giant valleys and deserts to the east remain dry much of the year. Gaps in the crest, like Donner Pass on I–80 near Lake Tahoe, hint that large rivers once flowed westward to the ocean. The Pacific Crest Trail, which travels from Mexico to Canada, follows the line of the Sierra crest.

Spheroidal Weathering

The desert's boulder gardens, such as Joshua Tree National Park's Wonderland of Rocks, as well as the dome monoliths like Yosemite's Half Dome, originated when molten rock seeped up from beneath the Earth's crust and into the fissures or joints of other types of rock. When the magma cooled and hardened, its expansion caused the rock around it to split apart. The rounded, stacked, and blocky boulders were then shaped by wind and rain into near-spheres.

Spire

As a butte erodes, it may become one or more spires. There are many buttes and spires in Utah's national park.

Syncline

A syncline is a trough-like, downward-curving fold in the rock layers of the earth's crust, with its sides dipping in toward the axis. You can see synclines and anticlines as you drive throughout the Colorado Plateau.

Volcanoes

The volcanoes of the Sierra Madres, such as Mount Rainier, Crater Lake, Mount Hood, and Mount Baker, are not, as commonly believed, dormant. Instead, most are described as "episodically active," as Mount St. Helens was in 1980. At one time, the Sierra was a much lower mountain range, with peaks of only about 3,000 feet. When volcanic activity began, the flow of lava thrust the mountains upward and spilled out over the surface, hardening into new top layers of igneous rock. Evidence of the region's volcanic history is most visible in the area around Mount Lassen, where you can see recent manifestations of the geological forces of volcanism.

Window

(E) One of the more intriguing landforms you will encounter while touring canyon country are large openings in solid rock walls. These are known as arches or bridges, depending on what created the opening. Together, the two types of forms are called windows.

Driving Tours

4

PACIFIC NORTHWEST DRIVING TOUR

NORTH CASCADES NATIONAL PARK

DAY 1   Start in ❶ **Sedro-Woolley,** where you can pick up information about ❷ **North Cascades National Park** at the park headquarters. From Sedro-Woolley, it's a 45-minute drive on Route 20 to the park entrance. Take your first stroll through an old-growth forest from the visitor center in Newhalem, then devote the rest of the day to driving through the **Cascades** on Route 20, stopping at various overlooks. Exit the park and continue through the **Methow Valley.** Head south on Route 20, then Route 153, then U.S. 97, then I–82 (just over 300 mi total) to ❸ **Yakima** to stay the night.

THE PLAN
DISTANCE: 1,450 mi
TIME: 10 days
BREAKS: Overnight in Yakima, Mount Rainier National Park, Port Angeles, and Olympic National Park, WA; and Florence, Crater Lake National Park, and Ashland, OR.

MOUNT RAINIER NATIONAL PARK

DAYS 2 AND 3   On the morning of Day 2, take U.S. 12 west from Yakima 102 mi to Ohanapecosh, the southern entrance to ❹ **Mount Rainier National Park.** When you arrive, take the 31-mi two-hour drive on Sunrise Road, which reveals the "back" (northeast) side of Rainier. A room at the **Paradise Inn** is your base for the next two nights. On Day 3, energetic hikers will want to tackle one of the four- to six-hour trails that lead up among the park's many peaks. Or try one of the ranger-led walks through wildflower meadows. Another option is to hike to Panorama Point near the foot of the **Muir Snowfield** for breathtaking views of the glaciers and high ridges of Rainier overhead. After dinner at the inn, watch the sunset's alpenglow on the peak from the back porch.

MOUNT ST. HELENS AND THE OLYMPIC FOOTHILLS

DAY 4   Today, follow Routes 706 and 7 to U.S. 12 from Paradise, heading west to I–5. When you reach the interstate, drive south to Route 504 to spend the day visiting the ❺ **Mount St. Helens National Volcanic Monument,** where you can see the destruction caused from the 1980 volcanic eruption. Return to I–5 the way you came in and head north to Olympia, where you should pick up U.S. 101 North. The highway winds through scenic

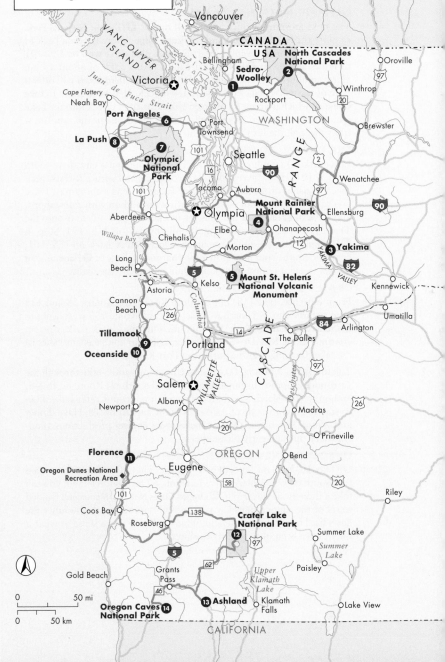

Pacific Northwest Driving Tour

BRITISH COLUMBIA

Vancouver

VANCOUVER ISLAND

CANADA
USA

Bellingham

Victoria

Cape Flattery
Neah Bay

Juan de Fuca Strait

Sedro-Woolley ①

North Cascades National Park ②

Oroville

97

Rockport

Winthrop

20

Brewster

WASHINGTON

RANGE

Port Angeles ⑥

La Push ⑧

⑦

Olympic National Park

Port Townsend

101

Seattle

2

Wenatchee

16

Tacoma

Auburn

90

97

Aberdeen

⭐ Olympia

Elbe

Mount Rainier National Park ④

Ellensburg

90

Willapa Bay

Chehalis

Morton

Ohanapecosh

12

Yakima ③

82

Long Beach

101

Astoria

5

Kelso

⑤ **Mount St. Helens National Volcanic Monument**

YAKIMA VALLEY

Kennewick

Cannon Beach

26

Columbia

14

The Dalles

84

Umatilla

Arlington

Tillamook

Oceanside ⑩

⑨

Portland

CASCADE

Deschutes

97

⭐ Salem

Albany

WILLAMETTE VALLEY

20

Madras

26

Newport

Prineville

Florence ⑪

OREGON

Eugene

Bend

20

Oregon Dunes National Recreation Area

58

101

Coos Bay

Roseburg

138

Crater Lake National Park ⑫

97

Summer Lake

Riley

5

62

Summer Lake

Paisley

Gold Beach

Grants Pass

Upper Klamath Lake

46

Oregon Caves National Park ⑭

⑬ **Ashland**

Klamath Falls

Lake View

CALIFORNIA

0   50 mi
0   50 km

Puget Sound countryside, skirting the Olympic foothills and periodically dipping down to the waterfront. Stop at ❻**Port Angeles,** 136 mi (three hours) from the junction of Route 504 and I–5, to have dinner and spend the night.

OLYMPIC NATIONAL PARK

DAYS 5 AND 6 The next morning, launch into a full day at ❼**Olympic National Park.** Explore the **Hoh Rain Forest** and **Hurricane Ridge** before heading back to Port Angeles for the evening. Start Day 6 with a drive west on U.S. 101 to Forks and on to ❽**La Push** via Route 110, a total of about 45 mi. Here, an hour-long lunchtime stroll to **Second or Third Beach** will offer a taste of the wild Pacific coastline. Back on U.S. 101, head south to **Lake Quinault,** which is about 98 mi from Lake Crescent. Check into the Lake Quinault Lodge, then drive up the river 6 mi to one of the rain-forest trails through the lush Quinault Valley.

THE PACIFIC COAST

DAY 7 Leave Lake Quinault early on Day 7 for the long but scenic drive south on U.S. 101. Here the road winds through coastal spruce forests, periodically rising on headlands to offer Pacific Ocean panoramas. Once you're in Oregon, small seaside resort towns beckon with cafés, shops, and inns. In ❾**Tillamook** (famous for its cheese), take a detour onto the Three Capes Loop, a stunning 35-mile byway off U.S. 101. Stop in ❿**Oceanside** (on the loop) for lunch. Once you're back on U.S. 101, continue south. Your final stop is the charming village of ⓫**Florence,** 290 mi (six to eight hours) from Lake Quinault; spend the night.

CRATER LAKE NATIONAL PARK

DAYS 8 AND 9 From Florence, take U.S. 101 south to Reedsport, Routes 38 and 138 west to Sutherlin, I–5 south to Roseburg, and Route 138 west again to ⓬**Crater Lake National Park,** 180 mi total. Once inside the park, you can continue along Rim Drive for another half hour for excellent views of the lake. Overnight in the park or in Fort Klamath.

The following morning, take the lake boat tour and a hike through the surrounding forest. In the afternoon, head south on Route 62 to I–5, and on to ⓭**Ashland,** 83 mi (about two hours) from Crater Lake. Plan to stay the night in one of Ashland's many superb B&Bs. Have dinner and attend one of the **Oregon Shakespeare Festival** productions (mid-February through early November).

OREGON CAVES NATIONAL MONUMENT

DAY 10 On Day 10, head back north on I–5 from Ashland to Grants Pass, then turn south on U.S. 199. At Cave Junction, 67 mi from Ashland, you can take a three-hour side trip to ⓮**Oregon Caves National Monument.** Guided tours of the unique marble caves last 90 minutes; in the summer the day's final tour is by candlelight, which will give you a sense of what it might have been like for early explorers.

CANADIAN ROCKIES DRIVING TOUR

Note: Watch for wildlife on the highways and roads as you are driving through the mountains.

THE PLAN

DISTANCE: 750–1,000 mi

TIME: 10 days

BREAKS: Overnight in Jasper, AB; Lake Louise, AB; Emerald Lake, BC; and Banff, AB; Fairmont or Kimberley, BC; Waterton National Park, AB; East Glacier, MT; and West Glacier, MT

JASPER NATIONAL PARK

DAYS 1 AND 2   From ❶ **Edmonton,** travel west on Yellowhead Highway 16 to ❷ **Jasper National Park.** You'll pass through some stunning scenery as you move from the prairies to the foothills and into the mountains. Watch for bighorn sheep, mountain goats, elk, and bears as you enter the park. Spend your afternoon exploring the shops and sites of the Jasper Townsite. Stop at the Jasper Information Centre to get trail maps and information about free park interpretive programs. Take a drive to ❸ **Disaster Point Animal Lick,** about 53 km (33 mi) northeast of the town of Jasper and watch for sheep and other wildlife. Then make a stop at nearby Miette Hot Springs and enjoy a swim in the hot mineral pools. If there is still time in the evening, take in an interpretive program at Whistlers Outdoor Theatre just outside Jasper Townsite.

Spend the next morning exploring ❹ **Mt. Edith Cavell** located off Highway 93 about 27 km (17 mi) south of Jasper. The 1-km (½) trail from the parking lot leads to the base of an imposing cliff, where you can see the stunning Angel Glacier. A steep 3-km (2-mi) trail climbs up the valley to Cavell Meadows, which are carpeted with wildflowers from mid-July to mid-August. There are many options for the afternoon: hiking in nearby ❺ **Maligne Canyon,** canoeing or horseback riding near the Jasper Park Lodge or Pyramid Lake, or swimming in Lake Edith.

ICEFIELDS PARKWAY

DAY 3   From Jasper Townsite, proceed west along Connaught Drive. At the intersection of the Yellowhead Highway 16, proceed through the lights straight ahead to reach Highway 93, the Icefields Parkway. Make a short stop at ❻ **Athabasca Falls,** just 31 km (19 mi) south of Jasper. The 75-foot falls are some of the most powerful falls in the mountain national parks. Continue driving along the Icefields Parkway until you reach the Athabasca Glacier, one of the eight major glaciers making up the ❼ **Columbia Icefield.** This incredible ice field covers an area of approximately 325 square km (125 square mi) and is one of the largest accumulations of ice and snow south of the Arctic Circle. Enjoy lunch at the Icefield Centre, and then experience an ice explorer bus tour or a guided hike of the Athabasca Glacier. *For safety reasons, do not venture onto the glacier without a guide.* Continue driving along the Icefields Parkway, passing the Weeping Wall and stopping to stretch your legs at the Saskatchewan River Crossing and at scenic Bow Lake, before stopping for the night at ❽ **Lake Louise.**

4

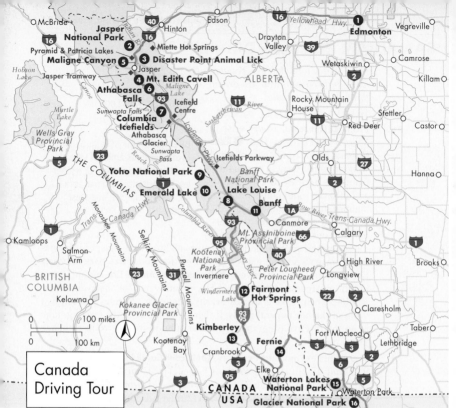

LAKE LOUISE

DAY 4 Spend the morning enjoying the scenery at the beautiful Lake Louise, snapping a few pictures of the impressive Victoria Glacier flowing off the mountain at the lake's end. You can enjoy morning tea at the classy Fairmont Chateau Lake Louise Hotel adjacent to the lake, then, from June through September, ride the Lake Louise Sightseeing Gondola to the Whitehorn Lodge, where you can participate in a guided hike or an interpretive presentation and enjoy lunch on an alpine plateau with a view of a dozen-plus glaciers. If time permits, take a drive 32 km (20 mi) west to ❾ Yoho National Park and visit ❿ Emerald Lake, where you can rent a canoe, have dinner at the teahouse, or take a stroll. You can overnight at Emerald Lake Lodge or stay 57 km (35 mi) away in Banff, your hub for the next two days.

BANFF NATIONAL PARK

Spend the morning of Day 5 exploring the quaint shops and restaurants crammed together on Banff Avenue in the ⓫ Banff Townsite. Visit Canada Place in the afternoon to participate in fun interactive activities and learn about Canada's history and culture. Stop at the Fairmont Banff Springs Hotel, a National Historic Site, and stroll the grounds or take an early evening guided horseback ride from the onsite stables. Finish your day with a late-night dip in the Banff Upper Hot Springs.

"I arose before dawn to capture the sunrise as it lit up Goat Mountain in crimson light towering above St. Mary Lake in Glacier National Park." —photo by Bart Edson, Fodors.com member

One your second day in Banff, take a short, early morning jaunt on Vermillion Lakes Drive, off the West Banff exit from Highway 1. Common wildlife sightings include elk, bighorn sheep, muskrat, and the occasional moose. When you return to town, visit the Banff Gondola to enjoy the view from the 7,500-foot summit of Sulfur Mountain. Try to take in an artistic performance at the Banff Centre in the evening, or experience the nightlife on Banff Avenue.

FAIRMONT OR KIMBERLEY, BC

DAY 7 This morning, head southwest from Banff into British Columbia on Highway 93. Stop and enjoy the hot springs in the small town of ⑫ Fairmont Hot Springs. Consider reserving a white-water rapids excursion or a voyageur canoe trip ahead of time with Kootenay River Runners in nearby Radium ☎ 250/347–9210 or 800/599–4399 ⊕ www.raftingtherockies.com. Or enjoy a round of golf at one of the championship courses in the area. Stay the night in Fairmont Hot Springs, or drive a little farther on Highway 83 to spend the evening in the Bavarian-style mountain town of ⑬ Kimberley.

WATERTON LAKES NATIONAL PARK
AND GLACIER NATIONAL PARK

DAYS 8–10 From Fairmont or Kimberley, continue driving south on Highway 93 to Jaffray. Just after Jaffray, turn east onto Highway 3 towards the ski resort town of ⑭ Fernie, which is a good place for a bite to eat. Continue driving east on Highway 3 through the scenic Crowsnest Pass into Alberta and stop at the Frank Slide Interpretive Centre to learn the history behind the 1903 rock slide that destroyed the tiny town of Frank. At Pincher Creek turn south onto Highway 6 and head toward

⑮ Waterton Lakes National Park. Explore the Waterton Townsite and enjoy dinner and a view from the Prince of Wales Hotel.

On the morning of Day 9, take a drive southwest on the Akamina Parkway to Cameron Lake, where you can enjoy the trails around the lake or rent a rowboat and a fishing rod to try catching trout. If time permits, take a drive on Red Rock Parkway, followed by a walk around Red Rock Canyon or a short 2.8-km (1.7-mi) hike from the visitor center to Bear's Hump, featuring a great view of the townsite.

Make your way from Waterton to Glacier by choosing one of two routes. From mid-May to mid-September you can take Provincial Road 5 to the Chief Mountain International Highway and across the border to State 17, and then U.S. 89, which leads to the eastern entrance of **⑯ Glacier National Park.** *Be sure to check border-crossing hours.* (When this route is closed, take Provincial Road 5 east to Cardston, then turn south on Provincial Road 2, which connects with U.S. 89.) Spend the night in East Glacier at Many Glacier Hotel or Glacier Park Lodge.

On Day 10, treat yourself to a drive up the Going-to-the-Sun Road from East Glacier to West Glacier. The road travels from the lowest elevations to the summit of the Continental Divide and is open from mid-June to mid-September. Stop at the Logan Pass Visitor Center to learn about the park's flora and fauna before taking a short hike along the scenic Skyline Trail. Snap a picture of Bird Woman Falls as you proceed toward West Glacier, and stop to take the short hike to McDonald Falls. The Lake Macdonald Lodge makes a good lunch or dinner stop, and from here you can also rent a canoe or take a guided cruise on the lake. Overnight in West Glacier.

GLACIER TO GRAND TETON DRIVING TOUR

GLACIER NATIONAL PARK AND MONTANA SCENIC BYWAYS

DAY 1　After visiting **❶ Glacier National Park,** with its 1,500 square mi of exquisite ice-carved terrain, plan to spend half a day (or more, depending on stops) driving on a scenic, 160-mi route through western Montana. Start off going southwest on U.S. 2 to **❷ Kalispell,** then south on Highway 206 and Highway 83, through

THE PLAN
DISTANCE: 850–1,000 mi
TIME: 7 days
BREAKS: Overnight in Glacier National Park, and Bozeman or Livingston, MT; and Yellowstone National Park, Grand Teton National Park, and Jackson, WY

the Seeley–Swan Valley, where you'll have a view of the Mission Range to the west and the Swan Range to the east. South of **❸ Seeley Lake** turn east on Route 200, and then take Route 141 to the small town of **❹ Avon,** about 36 mi west of Helena. From here, turn west on U.S. 12 to connect with I–90. Continue southeast 10 mi to **❺ Deer Lodge,** and 41 mi to the century-old mining town of **❻ Butte,** where the lavish Copper King Mansion reveals what you could buy with an unlimited household budget back in the 1880s, when it was built. From Butte, follow I–90 to

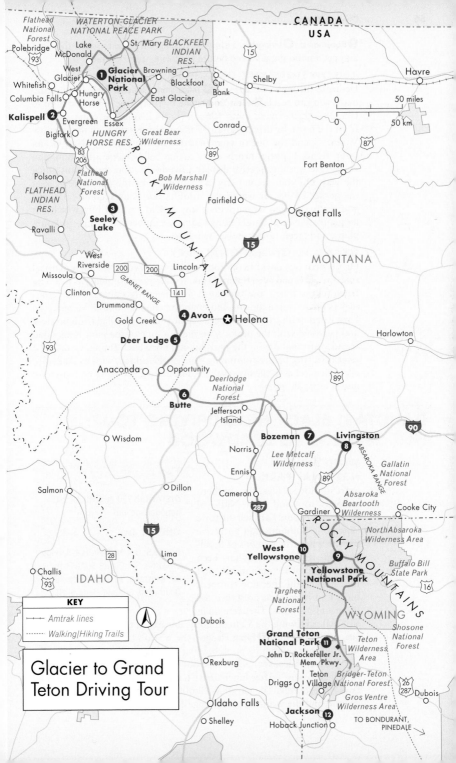

Glacier to Grand Teton Driving Tour

❼Bozeman or **❽Livingston.** Either town is a good place to spend the night and get a good night's sleep before exploring Yellowstone.

YELLOWSTONE NATIONAL PARK

DAYS 2 AND 3   Dedicate the next two days to **❾Yellowstone National Park.** From Bozeman, you can reach **❿West Yellowstone** by following I–90 west 8 mi to U.S. 287, then driving south 106 mi. (From Livingston, enter the park from the north by driving south 57 mi on U.S. 89 through the Paradise Valley.) Spend the rest of your first day on the park's 142-mi Grand Loop Road. It passes nearly every major Yellowstone attraction, and you'll discover interpretive displays, overlooks, and short trails along the way. On your second day in the park, hike the park's trails, visit the geyser basins, or watch the wildlife. For your accommodations, you really can't go wrong with a stay at Old Faithful Inn, which has lodgepole-pine walls and ceiling beams, an immense volcanic rock fireplace, and green-tinted, etched windows.

GRAND TETON NATIONAL PARK

DAYS 4 AND 5   On the final two days of your tour, experience Wyoming's other national treasure, **⓫Grand Teton National Park.** Its northern boundary is just 8 mi from Yellowstone's south entrance. The sheer ruggedness of the Tetons makes them seem imposing and unapproachable, but a drive on Teton Park Road, with frequent stops at scenic turnouts, will get you up close and personal with the peaks. Overnight in one of the park lodges and spend your final day in the park hiking, horseback riding, or taking a river float trip, before continuing south to **⓬Jackson,** with its landmark elk antler arches in the town square, fine dining, art galleries, museums, and eclectic shopping.

DAKOTAS' BLACK HILLS DRIVING TOUR: HOT SPRINGS TO DEADWOOD

WIND CAVE NATIONAL PARK

DAY 1   Start in Hot Springs, the southern gateway to Wind Cave National Park. Here you can see historic sandstone buildings and an active dig site where the remains of fossilized full-sized mammoths have been discovered. The mammoths fell into a sinkhole, became trapped, died, and have been preserved for thousands of years. They remain in

THE PLAN

DISTANCE: 120 mi (340 mi with optional add-on)

TIME: 5–7 days

BREAKS: Overnight in Hot Springs or Custer, SD; Custer State Park, SD; Keystone, SD; Rapid City, SD; Deadwood, SD; and Medora, ND.

situ. After viewing the 52 mammoths unearthed to date at **❶Mammoth Site,** take a dip into **❷Evans Plunge**—the world's largest natural warmwater indoor swimming pool, holding 1 million gallons. (You can also enjoy waterslides, swinging rings, hot tubs, arcades, and a full-service health club here.) After lunch, drive 6 mi north on U.S. 385 to **❸Wind Cave National Park.** The park has 28,000 acres of wildlife habitat above ground and the world's fourth-longest cave below. Take an afternoon

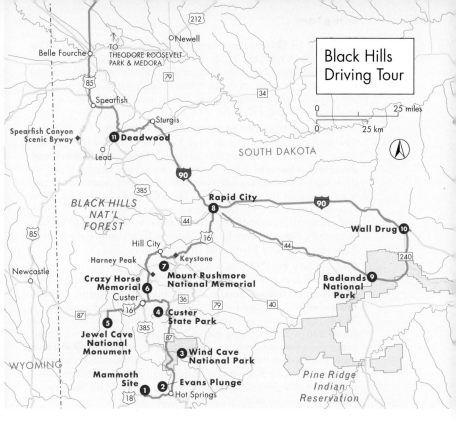

cave tour and a short drive through the park. Overnight at nearby Custer State Park or stay in one of the Custer Resort Lodges—or possibly stay in one of the B&Bs around Hot Springs or Custer.

CUSTER STATE PARK

DAY 2   Spend today at ④ **Custer State Park,** just 5 mi east of Custer on U.S. 16A. The 110-square-mi park has exceptional drives, lots of wildlife, and fingerlike granite spires rising from the forest floor. Relax on a hayride and enjoy a chuck wagon supper, or take a Jeep tour into the buffalo herds. Overnight in one of four enchanting mountain lodges.

JEWEL CAVE NATIONAL MONUMENT
AND CRAZY HORSE MEMORIAL

DAY 3   Today, venture down U.S. 16 to ⑤ **Jewel Cave National Monument,** where you can see the beautiful nailhead and dogtooth spar crystals lining its more than 100 mi of passageways. As you head from Custer State Park to Jewel Cave National Monument, you pass through the friendly community of Custer on U.S. 385. It's surrounded by some of the Black Hills' most striking scenery—picture towering rock formations spearing out of ponderosa pine forests. If you have extra time, explore Cathedral Spires, Harney Peak, and Needles Highway (Highway 87).

After visiting Jewel Cave, head back to Custer and take U.S. 16/385 toward the former gold and tin mining town of Hill City. Along the way you'll hit ❻ **Crazy Horse Memorial,** the colossal mountain carving of the legendary Lakota leader. The memorial's complex includes the Indian Museum of North America, which displays beautiful bead- and quillwork from many of the continent's native nations. Overnight at one of the hotels in and around Keystone, such as the K Bar S Lodge, or stay at a hotel in Hill City.

MOUNT RUSHMORE NATIONAL MEMORIAL

DAY 4   This morning, travel just 3 mi from Keystone (10 from Hill City) on Route 244 (the Gutzon Borglum Memorial Highway) to ❼ **Mount Rushmore National Memorial,** where you can view the huge, carved renderings of presidents Washington, Jefferson, Roosevelt, and Lincoln. Afterward, head northwest for 17 mi on U.S. 16 to ❽ **Rapid City,** western South Dakota's largest city and the eastern gateway to the Black Hills. Overnight here and enjoy visiting the many museums and touring the sites. Great family spots include Reptile Gardens, Bear Country, the Journey Museum, Storybook Island, and Dinosaur Hill.

BADLANDS NATIONAL PARK

DAY 5   Begin your day early and drive 55 mi on Route 44 to the North Unit of ❾ **Badlands National Park.** Badlands Loop Road wiggles through this moonlike landscape for 32 mi. When you've had enough of this 380-square-mi geologic wonderland, head back to the hills. Exit onto Route 240 at the northeast entrance to catch I–90. For a fun excursion, take a little detour east to Wall for its world-famous ❿ **Wall Drug Store.** Founded on the premise that free ice water would attract road-weary travelers, the huge emporium carries all manner of Westernalia— including 6,000 pairs of cowboy boots. Enjoy lunch at the Western Art Gallery Restaurant or the picnic area out back.

Spend this afternoon and tonight in ⓫ **Deadwood,** reached via U.S. 14 and 14A. This Old West mining town has 80 gaming halls, including Old Style Saloon No. 10, which bills itself as "the only museum in the world with a bar." Upstairs, at the Deadwood Social Club, you can discover outstanding food at reasonable prices and the best wine selection in the state. To view rare artifacts from the town's colorful past, such as items that once belonged to Wild Bill Hickok, visit Adams Memorial Museum. Overnight in Deadwood's Franklin Hotel (built in 1903), where past guests have included Theodore Roosevelt, Babe Ruth, John Wayne, and country duo Big & Rich.

THEODORE ROOSEVELT NATIONAL PARK

DAYS 6 AND   If you want to include Theodore Roosevelt in your tour, tack on two
7 OPTION   extra days. Begin Day 6 by traveling from the hills to the plains and then to North Dakota's badlands via U.S. 85. At the intersection with I–94, turn west. When grassy plains give way to tall ridges of fire-colored rock, you'll know you've hit Theodore Roosevelt National Park. Painted Canyon scenic overlook will give you a first tremendous view of the park. Spend the next day in the South Unit, where highlights include prairie dog towns, a petrified forest, and several overlooks. Overnight in the historic frontier town of **Medora.** It has wonderful golf, several good places to eat, and the Medora Musical, a good family activity.

NORTHERN CALIFORNIA DRIVING TOUR

California's North Coast and Far North are sparsely peopled and amply forested. Driving east and south, you'll see ragged shoreline, the lush Cascade Range, and mighty Sierra Nevada peaks. This tour takes you along curving, two-lane scenic routes where the going is sometimes slow—especially if you're following a logging truck. Distances between services can be long and lonely, and the weather is unpredictable, so keep your tank and cooler full. This tour is not recommended in winter due to wet and snowy conditions, road closures in the mountains, and park seasonality.

> **THE PLAN**
>
> **DISTANCE:** 750 mi
>
> **TIME:** 8 days
>
> **BREAKS:** Overnight in Eureka, Redding, Lassen Volcanic National Park, Tahoe City, and Yosemite National Park, CA.

4

REDWOOD NATIONAL PARK

DAY 1 Begin your journey in coastal Crescent City, 20 mi south of the Oregon state line, and drive south into ❶ **Redwood National Park** on Redwood Highway/U.S. 101. At the Lagoon Creek picnic area, hike the Hidden Beach section of the Coastal Trail to the Klamath Overlook. Continuing south on the highway, turn west onto Coastal Drive, a partially unpaved road that threads through the big trees and past ocean vistas. The road merges with Newton B. Drury Scenic Parkway in Prairie Creek Redwoods State Park; continue south to the visitor center at Orick. Get a free permit for Tall Trees Access Road, then backtrack north on the parkway to Bald Hills Road. The twisting route connects with the partly unpaved access road to Tall Trees Grove. After a look at some of the world's tallest redwoods, stop in Lady Bird Johnson Grove and return to the highway. Head down U.S. 101 to spend the night amid the Victorian architecture of ❷ **Eureka.**

EUREKA TO REDDING

DAY 2 The next morning, head a few miles north on U.S. 101 and pick up Route 299 east at Arcata. The mountain road winds along the canyon of the wild and scenic Trinity River to the gold-rush town of ❸ **Weaverville.** Take a stroll and take in some history, then continue east to Redding and north on I–5 to ❹ **Shasta Lake,** where you can take a tour of Lake Shasta Caverns and get out on the water. Finish the day back in ❺ **Redding** with a sunset walk across Santiago Calatrava's modernist Sundial Bridge.

LASSEN VOLCANIC NATIONAL PARK

DAYS 3 AND 4 On Day 3 (spring through fall), drive east on Route 44 to ❻ **Lassen Volcanic National Park.** When you arrive, start at the Loomis Museum and drive the park road (Route 89) south through lava fields and past geothermal springs, stopping for hikes at Kings Creek Falls, Lassen Peak, and Bumpass Hell. This is where the Sierra Nevada meets the Cascades; plant and animal species unique to each coexist here, and the area's winters are harsh and snowy. Take Route 89 south out of the park to Route 36 east, then head north on Warner Valley Road from Chester back into the park and check into the Drakesbad Guest Ranch for two

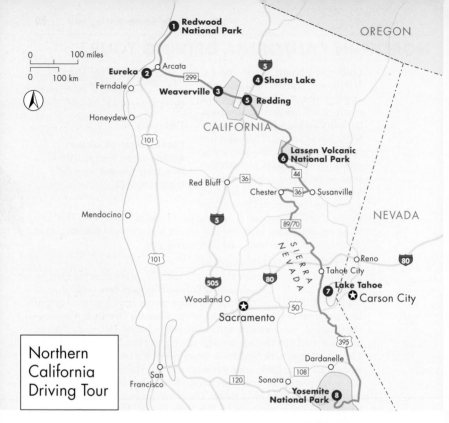

Northern California Driving Tour

nights (make reservations far in advance). Spend Day 4 horseback riding through Lassen or hiking to thermal features near the ranch.

In winter, roads into Lassen are closed. If you're touring then, drive straight from Redding to Lake Tahoe via I–5 south and Route 50 east.

LAKE TAHOE

DAY 5 AND 6 Start your fifth day by driving south on Route 89 for three hours (about 150 mi) to **❼ Lake Tahoe**, where you can spend the afternoon and the following day hiking, swimming, and gambling. Drive around the lake and take in the dazzling views, or if it's winter, hit the slopes and enjoy Tahoe's phenomenal skiing. The town of Tahoe City on the northwest shore has accommodations ranging from rustic vacation cottages to small hotel-style resorts.

YOSEMITE NATIONAL PARK

DAYS 7 AND 8 Early on the morning of Day 7 (spring through fall), take Route 89 southeast to U.S. 395, about 85 mi or 2½ hours from Tahoe City. Turn south on U.S. 395 and drive 60 mi through the high-mountain desert of the eastern Sierra to Route 120. Drive west on Route 120 and enter **❽ Yosemite National Park** through its eastern gate. The 60-mi crossing through the high country takes you over Tioga Pass (9,941 feet) and along the highest stretch of road in California. Stop for lunch in

Tuolumne Meadows and stretch your legs with a hike through alpine wildflowers (July and August).

Traffic through the park can move slowly in summer; plan on two full hours to reach the valley from the eastern gate. Take the hike to Yosemite Falls, and have a cocktail at the grand Ahwahnee Hotel. In the evening, attend one of the fascinating ranger programs or a presentation at Yosemite Theater. If you have secured an advance reservation, stay two nights in Yosemite Valley or Wawona (closed January and February). Otherwise, get a room in Mariposa, 40 mi west of the Valley on Route 140.

Ride the shuttle or rent a bike your last day in Yosemite so you don't have to fight for a parking space. Hike to Vernal Fall and to Mirror Lake, and drop in at the visitor center, museum, and Indian Village. Drive up to Glacier Point for a valley-wide view, timing your arrival for sunset. End your day with a relaxing dinner at the Wawona Hotel.

In winter, snow closes parts of Route 89 around Tahoe; Route 120 is closed east of Yosemite November through May (and sometimes into late June). To get from Lake Tahoe to Yosemite via an alternate route during these times, take U.S. 50 west to Route 49 south to Route 120 east. Route 49 takes you along the Mother Lode, through the heart of Gold Country.

SOUTHERN CALIFORNIA DRIVING TOUR

YOSEMITE, SEQUOIA, AND KINGS CANYON NATIONAL PARKS

DAYS 1 AND 2   After visiting ❶ **Yosemite National Park,** leave Yosemite Valley on Route 41 south and drive 100 mi, or about two hours, to Fresno and the turnoff for Route 180 east. Ahead 50 mi, you'll reach the entrance to ❷ **Kings Canyon National Park.** Follow Route 180 (summer only) along the Kings River and its giant granite canyon, well over a mile deep at some points. Stop along the way at pull-outs for long vistas of some of the highest mountains in the United States. (In winter, you'll have to head south on the Generals Highway.)

> **THE PLAN**
>
> **DISTANCE:** 1,200–1,600 mi
>
> **TIME:** 9–11 days
>
> **BREAKS:** Overnight in Yosemite National Park; Sequoia or Kings Canyon National Park; Death Valley National Park; and Palm Springs, Los Angeles, and Ventura, CA.

Double back to the Generals Highway and continue south to ❸ **Sequoia National Park,** where some of the world's oldest and largest trees stand. Driving the winding, 40-mi-long Generals Highway takes about two hours. Book in advance and stay for two nights in either of the two parks. Spend the intervening day further exploring the parks.

DEATH VALLEY NATIONAL PARK

DAYS 3 AND 4   On Day 5 leave Sequoia via the southern entrance and follow Route 198 about 23 mi to Route 65 south, where you'll turn left and head 60 mi toward Bakersfield. Route 65 ends at Route 99 south; get on

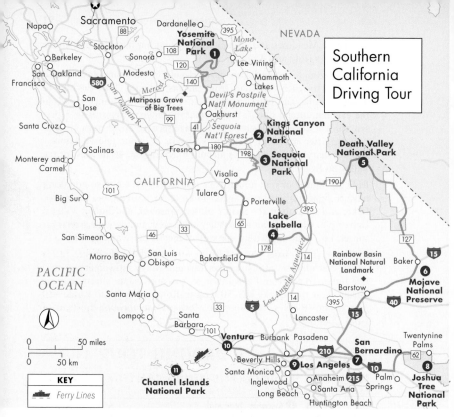

the freeway, go one exit to Route 204 (Golden State Avenue), and turn onto Route 178 east. Follow Route 178 through the southern tip of the Sequoia National Forest, and about 35 mi from Bakersfield, you'll reach ❹ **Lake Isabella**, the reservoir that catches the water from the Kern River, the major drainage for snow melting off the peaks in Sequoia National Park. The trip from Sequoia to the lake should take three hours.

Continue east on Route 178 for about 55 mi, where the road joins U.S. 395 north. Turn north on U.S. 395 and travel about 80 mi to Route 190 east, where you'll turn right and continue 60 mi to ❺ **Death Valley National Park.** Vast expanses of desert and mountain ranges extend as far as the eye can see, and you'll find the lowest point on the continent here, at 282 feet below sea level. Summer heat is brutal, and all safety precautions should be taken. Plan on spending the night here, but be sure to secure reservations in advance; this isolated area is not a place to wander around looking for a room. From Lake Isabella, the trip should take three to four hours, so expect an eight-hour, 400-mi day of driving from Sequoia National Park. Alternatively, stop in Bakersfield for the night, or camp at Lake Isabella, and make the trip the next day. If you make the trip in one shot, spend two nights in Death Valley and explore the park for a full day. If you stop for the night between Sequoia and

Death Valley, get an early start so you can spend most of the day in the park, then overnight there.

MOJAVE NATIONAL PRESERVE AND JOSHUA TREE NATIONAL PARK

DAY 5   Leave Death Valley early in the morning on Day 5. Travel east on Route 190 to Death Valley Junction and turn south onto Route 127, passing ❻ **Mojave National Preserve.** Drive 115 mi through the Mojave Desert to I–15, then travel south 60 mi on the interstate to **Barstow;** stop here for lunch. The town is nothing special, but you can take a short hike through a landscape of colored sedimentary rock 8 mi north of town. The trip from Death Valley to Barstow should take around four hours. From Barstow, head south for 70 mi on I–15 (follow I–215 at the split outside ❼ **San Bernardino**) until you hit I–10. Proceed east on I–10 for about 95 mi and turn at the exit to ❽ **Joshua Tree National Park** just north of the interstate. Spend a few hours exploring the numerous, easy short hikes through a landscape that transitions between the Mojave Desert and the more arid, sparsely vegetated Colorado Desert. Overnight in Palm Springs.

CHANNEL ISLANDS NATIONAL PARK

DAYS 6 AND 7   Spend the morning of Day 6 in Joshua Tree, and then hop onto I–10 and head west toward ❾ **Los Angeles,** which is about 95 mi away. Pay attention: Los Angeles's freeway system uses both names and numbers, and sometimes the route number changes but the name of the freeway does not.

Spend a day hanging out in the city, or skip L.A. and head straight to ❿ **Ventura,** by taking Route 57 (Orange Freeway) north from I–10 to I–210 (Foothill Freeway) and heading west for 19 mi to Route 134 (Ventura Freeway) west. Approximately 16 mi ahead, Route 134 merges with U.S. 101 north. Though the road numbers change, you will remain on the Ventura Freeway for about 50 mi until you're in seaside Ventura, one of the gateway cities to ⓫ **Channel Islands National Park** and home to the park's visitor center. Many folks stop here but don't actually make it out to the islands; if you're planning to visit the islands themselves, you'll need a reservation for the boat.

VENTURA TO SAN FRANCISCO

DAYS 8 AND 9 OPTION   If you continue on to San Francisco you have a delightful drive still ahead of you. Following U.S. 101 north you'll pass **San Luis Obispo,** home of Mission San Luis Obispo de Tolosa, the County Historical Museum, and the kitschy and garish Madonna Inn. From San Luis Obispo you can continue north either on scenic but slow Route 1 (Pacific Coast Highway) or on speedy but nondescript U.S. 101. Either way, it's about 230 mi to **San Francisco.** Along the way, stop in **Monterey and Carmel,** where you can have lunch and visit the Monterey Bay Aquarium or the Carmel Mission.

—by Mike Nalepa

4

CANYON COUNTRY DRIVING TOUR

ZION AND BRYCE CANYON

DAYS 1 AND 2 From Las Vegas, head up I–15, and take the Route 9 exit to **❶ Zion National Park.** Spend your afternoon in the park—if it's April to October, take the National Park Service bus down Zion Canyon Scenic Drive (in fact, when the bus is "in season," cars are not allowed in the canyon). Overnight in Springdale, the bustling town right next to the park. The Best Western Zion Park Inn is your best bet for getting a room in the high season. Its Switchback Grille is excellent and open for breakfast, lunch, and dinner.

> **THE PLAN**
>
> **DISTANCE:** 1,000–1,200 mi
>
> **TIME:** 10 days
>
> **BREAKS:** Overnight in Springdale, Bryce, Torrey, and Moab, UT; Cortez, CO; Monument Valley or Tuba City, AZ; Tusayan or South Rim, AZ

Spend the next morning in Zion. For a nice hike, try the short and easy (read: family-friendly) Canyon Overlook Trail, where you can gaze at the massive rock formations, such as East and West Temples. It won't take very long, even if you linger with your camera, so follow it with a stroll along the Emerald Pools Trail in Zion Canyon itself, where you might come across tame wild turkeys and ravens looking for handouts.

Depart the area via Route 9, the **❷ Zion–Mount Carmel Highway.** You'll pass through a 1.1-mi-long tunnel that is so narrow, RVs and towed vehicles must pay for an escort through. When you emerge, you are in slickrock country, where huge, petrified sandstone dunes are etched by ancient waters. Stay on Route 9 for 23 mi and then turn north onto U.S. 89. After 42 mi, you will reach Route 12, where you should turn east and drive 14 mi to the entrance of **❸ Bryce Canyon National Park.** The overall trip from Zion to Bryce Canyon is about 90 minutes.

Central to your tour of Bryce Canyon is the 18-mi main park road, from which numerous scenic turnouts reveal vistas of bright red-orange rock (we recommend starting with the view at Sunrise Point). You'll notice that the air is a little cooler here than it was at Zion, so get out and enjoy it. Trails most worth checking out include the Bristlecone Loop Trail and the Navajo Loop Trail, both of which you can easily fit into a day trip and will get you into the heart of the park with minimum effort. Listen for peregrine falcons deep in the side canyons, and keep an eye out for the species of prairie dog that only lives in these parts. Overnight in the park or at Ruby's Inn, near the junction of Routes 12 and 63.

CAPITOL REEF

DAY 3 Head out this morning on the spectacular **❹ Utah Scenic Byway–Route 12.** If the views don't take your breath away, the narrow, winding road with little margin for error will. Route 12 winds over and through **❺ Grand Staircase-Escalante National Monument.** The views from the narrow hogback are nothing short of incredible. About 14 mi past the town of Escalante on Route 12 you can stop at **❻ Calf Creek Recreation**

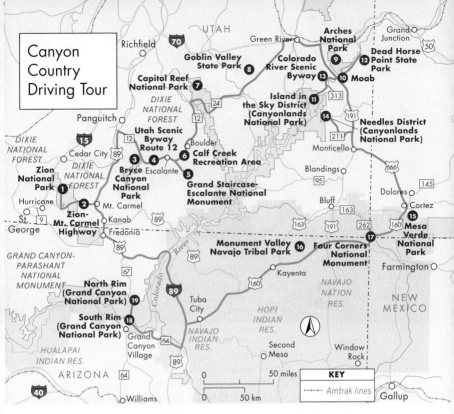

Area to stretch your legs or make a 5½-mi round-trip hike to a gorgeous backcountry waterfall. Route 12 continues to gain elevation as you pass over Boulder Mountain.

At the intersection of Routes 12 and 24, turn east onto Route 24. You have traveled 112 mi from Bryce Canyon to reach **❼ Capitol Reef National Park.** The crowds are smaller here than at other national parks in the state, and the scenery is stunning. Orchards in the small enclave of Fruita produce fruit—peaches, pears, and apples—in the late summer and early fall, and are close by ancient Indian rock art. If it's still daylight when you arrive, hike the 1-mi Hickman Bridge Trail if you want to explore a little, or stop in at the visitor center until 4:30 PM (later in the summer) and view pioneer and American Indian exhibits, talk with rangers about geography or geology, or watch a film. Nearby Torrey is your best bet for lodging, and be sure to eat at the seasonal Cafe Diablo, serving some of Utah's finest Southwest cuisine from late April to late October. Enjoy freshly brewed coffee and baked goods at Robber's Roost Books and Beverages while perusing a selection of regionally themed books, viewing local artisan jewelry, or even browsing the Internet.

"Every turn on the Fiery Furnace Trail in Arches brought views of unbelievable natural sculptures, including this double arch." —photo by CarlB9090, Fodors.com member

ARCHES AND CANYONLANDS

DAYS 4–6 Explore Capitol Reef more the next morning. When you leave, travel east and north for 75 mi on Route 24. If you want a break after about an hour, stop at the small ❽ **Goblin Valley State Park**, 12 mi west off Route 24. Youngsters love to run around the sandstone formations known as "goblins." Return to Route 24 and take it to I–70, turn east and continue your journey.

Twenty mi from Green River take exit 182 south onto U.S. 191, going about 27 mi toward ❾ **Arches National Park**, which holds the world's largest concentration of natural rock windows or "arches." Plan on spending three nights in ❿ **Moab** while you explore the area. Adventurous types, note that the Colorado River runs near Moab. If you can squeeze in a raft trip on this legendary Western waterway, do it. Otherwise, dedicate Day 5 to Arches, perhaps including a guided hike in the Fiery Furnace, a maze of sandstone canyons and fins that is considered one of the most spectacular hikes in the park. Then on Day 6, launch your ⓫ **Canyonlands National Park** experience with the Island in the Sky District—but first take a detour to the mesa top at ⓬ **Dead Horse Point State Park** for magnificent views of the Colorado River as it goosenecks through the canyons below. To reach the state park, go 10 mi north of Moab on U.S. 191 to Route 313. Drive west for 15 mi, then turn right onto the unnamed road; continue for 6 mi to the Dead Horse fee station. To get from Dead Horse to Islands in the Sky, return to Route 313 and drive 7 mi past the Dead Horse turnoff to reach the park visitor center.

On your way back to Moab, enjoy the natural scenery on the ⓭ **Colorado River Scenic Byway (Route 128)**, which runs for about 44 mi along the river, or view man-made art by traveling down Route 279 (Potash Road), where ancient American Indian rock-art panels pop up after 4.8 mi from the U.S. 191 turnoff.

MESA VERDE

DAYS 7 AND 8 On Day 7, travel 42 mi south of Moab on U.S. 191. At this point, you have a choice to make. Either turn onto Route 211 and drive 34 mi to ⓮ **Canyonlands' Needles District**, which is distinctly different from Island in the Sky, or skip this part of the park and drive straight to Monticello.

From Monticello, take U.S. 491 to Cortez, Colorado, and follow U.S. 160 to ⓯ **Mesa Verde National Park.** The overall trip from Monticello to Mesa Verde is about 90 not particularly impressive miles. The park, however, where ancient dwellings of the Ancestral Puebloan people are the highlight, is more than worth the drive. Overnight in Cortez tonight and tomorrow night while you take Day 8 to explore Mesa Verde.

THE FOUR CORNERS AND MONUMENT VALLEY

DAY 9 This morning, head southwest into Arizona on U.S. 160 for the spectacular, deep-red desert of ⓰ **Monument Valley Navajo Tribal Park**, whose buttes and spires you will recognize from countless movie westerns and television commercials—if you want to do the 17-mi self-guided drive here, give yourself a couple of hours, or take a tram tour. Long before you get here, though, stop for a fun photo-op at ⓱ **Four Corners National Monument**, which straddles Colorado, New Mexico, Arizona, and Utah. Call it a night at Gouldings Lodge in Monument Valley, or in Tuba City. You'll want to get a good night's sleep and start early for your finale at **Grand Canyon National Park.**

THE GRAND CANYON

DAY 10 From Tuba City, you can reach the park via U.S. 89 and Route 64 for the South Rim, or Alternate 89 and Route 67 for the North rim. If you have only one day, do the ⓲ **South Rim.** A good hike is the South Rim Trail, part of which is paved and wheelchair accessible. You can overnight just outside the park in Tusayan or stay on the edge of the canyon in El Tovar (reserve far in advance).

To complete the loop, you can reach Zion National Park from the ⓳ **North Rim** by taking Alternate 89 north through the mountains. The road is winding and steep, but oh so beautiful. If you're heading back to Las Vegas from the South Rim take Route 64 south to Williams and then pick up I–40 West to U.S. 93 North.

4

DINOSAUR NATIONAL MONUMENT TO GREAT SAND DUNES DRIVING TOUR

DINOSAUR NATIONAL MONUMENT

DAY 1 Start your weeklong driving tour at ❶ Dinosaur National Monument, which straddles the Utah–Colorado border, 200 mi from Salt Lake City and 300 mi from Denver. In the little town of ❷ Dinosaur, CO, a monument entrance and visitor center is located on the main drag, U.S. 40 (known as Brontosaurus Boulevard). Your best bets for lodging, unless you plan to camp in the monument, are in the town of ❸ Rangely, 20 mi south of Dinosaur via Route 64.

> ### THE PLAN
>
> DISTANCE: 650–670 mi
>
> TIME: 7 days
>
> BREAKS: Overnight in Dinosaur National Monument or Rangely; Grand Lake or Rocky Mountain National Park; Estes Park; Colorado Springs; Lake Pueblo State Park or Pueblo, CO.

The monument was named for its rich deposits of fossils, but there is more to do than play amateur archeologist. Here the Yampa River meets the famed Green River, so rafters, boaters, and floaters of all types have a wide selection of river-access points and riverside campgrounds from which to choose. Landlubbers can drive north from the visitor center along Harpers Corner Drive for an assortment of scenic overlooks. At road's end is the Harpers Corner Trail, an easy 2-mi round-trip stroll to a spectacular viewpoint of three canyons. *Be sure to watch where you step, for fossils of crinoids, a marine animal whose remains look plantlike, are embedded in the rock along the way.*

EN ROUTE TO THE ROCKIES

DAY 2 The journey on Day 2 takes you across northern Colorado's ranching communities to the heart of the Rockies. From Dinosaur National Monument, play hide-and-seek with the Yampa River as you travel 130 mi east across U.S. 40 to ❹ Steamboat Springs, best known for world-class skiing with a cowboy-chic ambience. Explore the historic downtown and have lunch at the kid-friendly Mahogany Ridge Brewery and Grill.

After lunch, continue east on U.S. 40 to ❺ Granby and U.S. 34. Turn north on U.S. 34 toward ❻ Grand Lake, the western gateway to Rocky Mountain National Park. Overnight in Grand Lake or the Timber Creek Campground inside the park.

ROCKY MOUNTAIN NATIONAL PARK

DAYS 3 AND 4 Spend the next two days in north-central Colorado's crown jewel, ❼ Rocky Mountain National Park. Begin by exploring Holzwarth Historic Site, a former guest ranch that once attracted trout fishers; then take a short hike on the paved, wheelchair-accessible Coyote Valley Trail for a chance view of elk or moose. Afterward, drive north on high-in-the-sky I–34, over the Continental Divide, and up to the Alpine Visitor Center, the only place in the park with dining services (a snack bar serves items such as chili, hot dogs, and kids' picks like PB and J). Get a park newspaper for times and locations of the ranger programs.

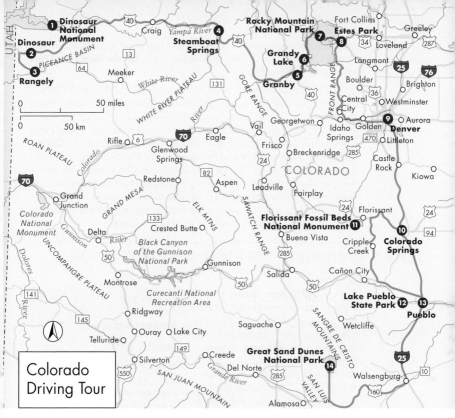

Colorado
Driving Tour

This afternoon, come down the east side of Trail Ridge Road, where several turnouts let you pull over and enjoy the vistas, including that of towering 14,259-foot Longs Peak. Overnight tonight and tomorrow night in one of the park's eastern campgrounds or in the town of **❽ Estes Park.** Spend Day 4 exploring the park's east side, including a hike around Bear Lake.

DENVER AND COLORADO SPRINGS

DAY 5 This morning, drive south via the Peak to Peak Scenic Byway, with views of the Continental Divide and its approaches, before catching I–25 at **❾ Denver.** (Note that the Peak to Peak route is 55 mi but will probably take 90 minutes.) If you have kids, a fun lunch stop in Denver is Casa Bonita's, in a strip mall and hard to miss with its pink facade.

After lunch, head south on I–25 for the hour drive to **❿ Colorado Springs;** overnight here in the shadow of 14,110-foot Pikes Peak.

FLORISSANT FOSSIL BEDS NATIONAL MONUMENT

DAY 6 Just west of Pikes Peak via U.S. 24, and about 50 mi west of Colorado Springs, is **⓫ Florissant Fossil Beds National Monument,** where you can spend the morning exploring petrified redwood stumps approaching 14 feet in diameter and fossil quarries filled with ancient plants and insects. Don't miss the "Big Stump"—once the base of a towering redwood, the ancient stump is 38 feet in circumference. After lunch in the picnic area near the visitor center, take the Gold Belt Tour Scenic and Historic Byway south to U.S. 50 and then overnight in **⑫ Lake Pueblo State Park** or in nearby **⑬ Pueblo.**

GREAT SAND DUNES NATIONAL PARK AND PRESERVE

DAY 7   Today's drive will take you to the San Luis Valley. From Pueblo, travel south on U.S. 50 and merge onto I–25 South. Continue on I–25 until you reach U.S. 160, then head due west toward Alamosa. About 14 mi east of Alamosa turn north at Highway 150 and go 20 mi to **⑭ Great Sand Dunes National Park and Preserve,** where North America's tallest dunes, reaching up to 750 feet, are surrounded by some of the tallest peaks in the United States (including the 14,000-foot Crestone Peaks to the north). Summer travelers are advised to avoid hiking on the dunes during midday, when the sand is hottest, but if your toes get toasty, dip them afterward in the cool waters of Medano Creek.

TEXAS AND NEW MEXICO DRIVING TOUR

EL PASO

DAY 1   Start in **❶ El Paso, Texas.** If you want to take a peek at Old Mexico just south of the border, take the "Border Jumper" trolley the next day and visit **❷ Juarez, Mexico**— however, caution is advised. Check the State Department's travel advisories first (⊕ *travel.state.gov*). If you go hop off at one of the shopping stops to pick up fine jewelry and leather goods, or barter for

> **THE PLAN**
>
> **DISTANCE:** 460–800 mi
>
> **TIME:** 5–7 days
>
> **BREAKS:** Overnight in El Paso and Lajitas, TX, and Carlsbad, NM, with a possible add-on in Albuquerque or Santa Fe, NM

bargains at the city's *mercado*. Spend the night in El Paso and search out one of the city's coveted Mexican restaurants—such as Leo's (⊠ *315 E. Mills Ave.* ☎ *915/544–1001*).

BIG BEND NATIONAL PARK

DAYS 2 AND 3   Head for the immense blue-sky country of West Texas by proceeding southeast on I–10 for about three hours or 120 mi, and dropping south at Kent onto Route 118. It takes about 2½ hours to travel about 150 mi to the west entrance of **❸ Big Bend National Park.** Before entering the park, spend the night in **❹ Lajitas,** on Route 170 about 20 mi west of the park entrance. The charming Lajitas Resort on the Rio Grande is a good alternative to the plainer lodgings closer to the park—although it's a bit more expensive. Another alternative is the park's Chisos Mountains Lodge. Accommodations here are bare-bones (you won't even find a room phone), but the peacefulness inside reflects the calm but rugged mountain beauty outside. Be sure to reserve several months in advance, especially for Spring Break stays. Pack a picnic lunch and spend the third day of your tour exploring the park via its mostly paved—though narrow and sometimes curving—roadways. Hike some of the trails and look for the succulent, thorny spikes of the lechuguilla, which is unique to the Chihuahuan Desert.

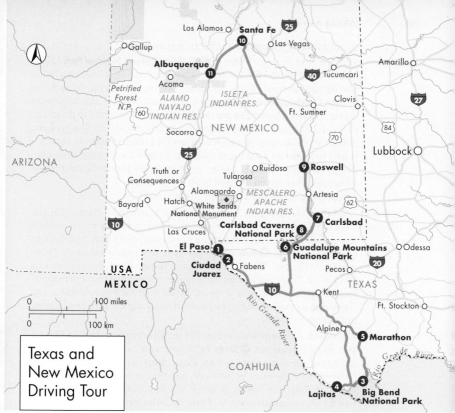

GUADALUPE MOUNTAINS NATIONAL PARK

DAY 4 On Day 4 head north from Big Bend on U.S. 385 about 40 mi to the tiny town of ⑤ **Marathon.** Take a peek at the tiled courtyards and cool gardens of the historic Gage Hotel, then dally in the nearby shops where you'll find landscapes by southwestern artists, Central American imports, and cured cowhides. If you're shopping on Sunday, be sure to go early—most shops close by mid-afternoon. Afterward, proceed west on U.S. 90 for about 30 mi to Alpine and north on Route 118 about 75 mi to I–10. Travel west on I–10 for about 40 mi or 30 minutes. Turn north onto Route 54, a slower, two-lane highway, for about 53 mi and then northeast onto U.S. 62/180 for about 2 mi to reach ⑥ **Guadalupe Mountains National Park.** Including a short stop in Marathon, the drive to Guadalupe from Big Bend should take about four to five hours. Orient yourself at the park visitor center, where displays and a video will introduce you to this northernmost region of the Chihuahuan Desert. Spend a few hours hiking some of the easier trails, and if you're lucky enough to visit in fall, don't miss the spectacular foliage of **McKittrick Canyon.** Stop off at the **Frijole Ranch Museum** for a healthy dose of history and ranching culture. The museum (Frijole means bean, by the way) is about 2 mi north of the park visitor center. Because of the dearth of lodging options nearby, plan on spending the night in ⑦ **Carlsbad, NM,** about 55 mi northeast of the park on U.S. 62/180.

CARLSBAD CAVERNS NATIONAL PARK

DAY 5   Start the next day with a visit to ❽ **Carlsbad Caverns National Park,** 27 mi southwest of town on U.S. 62/180. Plan on spending at least two hours touring the caverns. Fill the afternoon with a swim in the Pecos River at **Lake Carlsbad Recreation Area,** or visit the botanical and zoological displays at **Living Desert Zoo and Gardens State Park** (in order to do justice to the 1,200 acres, spectral wolves, and carrion-smelling flowers here, plan to set aside more than a few hours for Living Desert). In summer, return to Carlsbad Caverns at sunset to witness the swirling mass exodus of bats from the cave as they prepare to gorge on—literally—tons of insects. Then spend another night in Carlsbad.

SANTA FE AND ALBUQUERQUE

OPTIONAL   After the bats have gone home to roost, it's time to hit the road again.
ADD-ONS   Take U.S. 285 north on your way to the southwestern arts and cultural mecca that is Sante Fe, but be sure to cleanse your palate first with an eyeful of kitsch in ❾ **Roswell.** To get there from Carlsbad, drive 76 mi north on U.S. 285. There isn't much to this tiny town, but rumors of a UFO crash-landing and a government cover-up have made the desert-locked burgh famous. The shops are filled with alien memorabilia, and if you pop through in May, you might even see a giant alien head among the hot air balloons.

Afterward, a pleasant three-hour, 193-mi drive north on U.S. 285 brings you from Roswell to ❿ **Santa Fe,** where you can explore the adobe charms of the downtown central Plaza. Stop first at the Palace of the Governors on the Plaza's north side, and then investigate the crafts and wares of American Indian outdoor vendors. East of the Plaza, check out the Romanesque-style St. Francis Cathedral. The northern New Mexico city is sometimes referred to as a "holy place" for photographers because of the luminous quality of the light here; check out some examples at local museums such as the Museum of Fine Arts. Or, take in indigenous art at the Museum of Indian Arts and Culture, and homegrown art at the Museum of International Folk Art. Treat yourself to some fine New Mexican cuisine in the evening—we highly recommend the distinctive, regional Mexican fare served here.

If you're in the mood for more "old Southwest," spend an extra day in ⓫ **Albuquerque,** just an hour-long, 60-mi ride from Santa Fe. Start out by strolling through the shops of Old Town Plaza, then visit the New Mexico Museum of Natural History and Science. After lunch, head north to the Indian Pueblo Cultural Center and then west to Petroglyph National Monument. Return east for a sunset ride on the Sandia Peak Aerial Tramway.

Arches National Park

WORD OF MOUTH

"I always see the same photo of the delicate arch, where it's long, and thin, as seen from the side. I decided to get down below it, and found that it looked just like a curling wave in the ocean."
                    —photo by Evan Spiler, Fodors.com member

WELCOME TO ARCHES

TOP REASONS TO GO

★ **Unique terrain:** There's nowhere else on Earth that looks like this.

★ **Memorable snapshots:** You have to have a picture of Delicate Arch at sunset.

★ **Treasures hanging in the balance:** Landscape Arch is the longest open span in the world. Come quick! Due to its delicate nature, it could fall before you see it.

★ **Fiery Furnace:** A hike through this maze of rock walls and fins is sure to make you fall in love with the desert and appreciate nature at its most spectacular.

★ **Window to nature:** The park has the largest collection of natural arches in the world—more than 2,500. They make great frames through which to view moonrises, mountains, and more.

1 Devils Garden. About 18 mi from the visitor center, this is the end of the road in Arches. Trails lead to Landscape Arch and numerous other natural rock windows. This area also has picnic tables, the park's only campground, and an amphitheater.

2 Fiery Furnace. This forbiddingly named area is so labeled because its orange spires of rock look much like tongues of flame, especially in the late-afternoon sun. About 14 mi from the visitor center, it's the site for ranger-guided walks.

3 The Windows. Reached on a spur 9.2 mi from the visitor center, this area of the park is where visitors with little time stop. Here you can see many of the park's natural arches from your car or on an easy rolling trail.

4 Balanced Rock. Seemingly defying gravity, a giant rock teeters atop its pedestal, creating a 128-foot formation of red rock grandeur right along the roadside, 9.2 mi from the visitor center.

5 Petrified Dunes. Just a tiny pull-out about 5 mi from the visitor center, this scenic stop is where you can take pictures of acres and acres of petrified sand dunes.

6 Courthouse Towers. The Three Gossips, Sheep Rock, and Tower of Babel are the rock formations to see here. Enter this section of the park 3 mi past the visitor center. The Park Avenue Trail winds through the area, which was named for its steep walls and towers that look like buildings.

7 Moab. About 5 mi south of the park is this hub town for both Arches and Canyonlands.

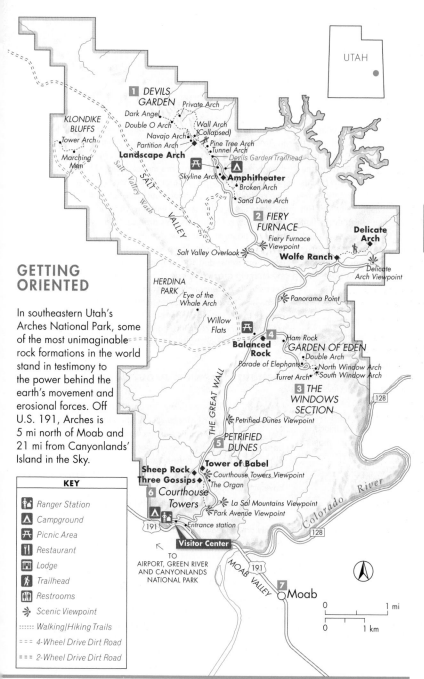

UTAH

1 DEVILS GARDEN

KLONDIKE BLUFFS

Private Arch

Dark Angel
Double O Arch
Tower Arch
Navajo Arch
Partition Arch
Landscape Arch

Marching Men

Wall Arch (Collapsed)
Pine Tree Arch
Tunnel Arch
Devils Garden Trailhead

SALT VALLEY WASH

SALT VALLEY

Skyline Arch ◆ **Amphitheater**
● Broken Arch
● Sand Dune Arch

2 FIERY FURNACE

5

Fiery Furnace Viewpoint

Delicate Arch

Salt Valley Overlook
Wolfe Ranch

Delicate Arch Viewpoint

GETTING ORIENTED

HERDINA PARK

Eye of the Whale Arch

Willow Flats

● Panorama Point

In southeastern Utah's Arches National Park, some of the most unimaginable rock formations in the world stand in testimony to the power behind the earth's movement and erosional forces. Off U.S. 191, Arches is 5 mi north of Moab and 21 mi from Canyonlands' Island in the Sky.

4
Balanced Rock

● Ham Rock
GARDEN OF EDEN
● Double Arch
North Window Arch
South Window Arch

Parade of Elephants
Turret Arch

3 THE WINDOWS SECTION

128

THE GREAT WALL

Petrified Dunes Viewpoint

5 PETRIFIED DUNES

● **Tower of Babel**

Sheep Rock
Three Gossips ◆
6 Courthouse Towers
The Organ

Courthouse Towers Viewpoint

La Sal Mountains Viewpoint
Park Avenue Viewpoint

Colorado River

191
● Entrance station

128

Visitor Center

TO AIRPORT, GREEN RIVER AND CANYONLANDS NATIONAL PARK

MOAB VALLEY

191

7 ○ Moab

KEY	
👫	*Ranger Station*
⛺	*Campground*
🔱	*Picnic Area*
🍴	*Restaurant*
🏨	*Lodge*
🚶	*Trailhead*
🚻	*Restrooms*
⚜	*Scenic Viewpoint*
┈┈	*Walking/Hiking Trails*
═ ═	*4-Wheel Drive Dirt Road*
═ ═	*2-Wheel Drive Dirt Road*

0 ———— 1 mi
0 ———— 1 km

ARCHES PLANNER

When to Go

The busiest times of year are spring and fall. In the spring, blooming wildflowers and temperatures in the 70s bring the year's largest crowds. The crowds remain steady in summer as the thermostat approaches 100°F in July and then soars beyond that for about four weeks. In August, sudden, dramatic cloudbursts create rainfalls over red rock walls and dramatic skies for a part of the day.

Fall weather is perfect—clear, warm days, and crisp, cool nights. The park almost clears out in winter, and from December through February you can hike any of the trails in relative solitude. Snow seldom falls in the valley beneath the La Sal Mountains, and when it does, Arches is a photographer's paradise, as snow drapes slickrock mounds and natural rock windows.

Avg. High/Low Temps.

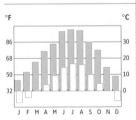

Note: Extreme highs often exceed 100°F in July and August.

Flora and Fauna

As in any desert environment, the best time to see wildlife in Arches is early morning or evening. Summer temperatures keep most animals tucked away in cool places, though ravens and lizards are the exceptions. If you happen to be in the right place at the right time, you may spot one of the beautiful, turquoise-necklace-collared lizards. It's more likely you'll see the western whiptail. Mule deer, jackrabbits, and small rodents are usually active in cool morning hours or near dusk. You may spot a lone coyote foraging day or night. The park protects a small herd of desert bighorns, and some of their tribe are seen early in the morning grazing beside U.S. 191 south of the Arches entrance. If you encounter bighorn sheep, do not approach them. They have been known to charge people who attempt to get too close. The park's mule deer and small mammals such as chipmunks are very used to seeing people and may allow you to get close—but don't feed them.

Getting Here and Around

Interstate 70 is the speedway that gets you across Utah. To dip southeast toward Moab, veer off the interstate onto U.S. 191, a main artery running all the way south to the Arizona border, skirting Arches' western border, Moab, and the Monti-La Sal National Forest along the way. Alternatively, you can take Route 128, Colorado River Scenic Byway, traveling just east of Arches.

The nearest airport is Canyonlands Field (aka Grand County Airport, ☎ 435/259–4849), 18 mi north of Moab. Flights are limited. The nearest train "station" is a solitary Amtrak (☎ 800/872–7245) stop in Green River, about 50 mi northwest of Moab.

Branching off the main, 18-mi park road are two spurs, a 2½-mi one to the Windows section and a 1.6-mi one to the Delicate Arch trailhead and viewpoint. There are several four-wheel-drive roads in the park; always check at the visitor center for conditions before attempting to drive them. U.S. 191 tends to back up mid-morning to early afternoon. There's likely to be less traffic at 8 AM or sunset.

Updated by
Jane Gendron

The red rock landscape of Arches National Park awakens the spirit and challenges the imagination: balanced rocks teeter unthinkably on pedestals; sandstone arches—of which there are more than 2,500—frame the sky with peekaboo windows; and formations like the Three Penguins greet you at points throughout the 73,379-acre park. Far from a stereotypical beige-tone palette with the occasional cactus, the desert here is adorned with a rich tapestry of colors: red, orange, purple, pink, creamy ivory, deep chocolate, and even shades of turquoise. The Fiery Furnace burns like a wildfire at sunset, and acres of petrified sand dunes rise across the horizon.

PARK ESSENTIALS

ACCESSIBILITY

Not all park facilities meet federally mandated accessibility standards, but as visitation to Arches climbs, the park is making efforts to increase accessibility. Visitors with mobility impairments can access the visitor center, all restrooms throughout the park, and one campsite (#7) at the Devils Garden Campground. The Park Avenue Viewpoint is a paved path with a slight decline near the end, and both Delicate Arch and Balanced Rock viewpoints are partially hard surfaced.

ADMISSION FEES AND PERMITS

Admission to the park is $10 per vehicle and $5 per person on foot, motorcycle, or bicycle, good for seven days. You must pay admission to Canyonlands separately. A $25 local park pass grants you admission to both the Arches and Canyonlands parks as well as the Natural Bridges and Hovenweep national monuments for one year.

ARCHES IN ONE DAY

Start early, while the day is still cool, with a 3-mi round-trip hike on the **Delicate Arch Trail**. The route is strenuous but quite rewarding. Pause for a healthy snack before heading for **Landscape Arch**, the second of the park's two must-see arches. To get there you must hike through **Devils Garden**, a great spot for morning photography.

If you're accustomed to hiking you might next hike out to **Double O**, a trip that is well worth the effort but that can be tough after the hike to Delicate Arch—especially in July or August. If you do hike to Double O,

take your lunch with you and have a picnic in the shade of a juniper or in a rock alcove. By the time you return you'll be ready to see the rest of the park by car, with some short strolls on easy paths.

In the mid- to late afternoon, drive to **Balanced Rock** for photos, then on to **the Windows**. Wander around on the easy gravel paths for more great photo ops. Depending on what time the sun is due to set, go into town for dinner before or after you drive out to Delicate Arch or the Fiery Furnace and watch the sun set the rocks on fire.

Permits are required for backcountry camping and for hiking without a park ranger in the Fiery Furnace. You can purchase a Fiery Furnace permit ($4 per adult, $2 per child ages 7–12) at the visitor center.

ADMISSION HOURS
Arches National Park is open year-round, seven days a week, around the clock. It's in the mountain time zone.

ATMS/BANKS
There are no ATMs in the park. The nearest ATM and full-service bank is in Moab.

CELL-PHONE RECEPTION
Cell-phone reception is available intermittently in the park. You can find a public telephone at the park's visitor center.

PARK CONTACT INFORMATION
Arches National Park ⊠ N. U.S. 191, Moab, UT ☎ 435/719–2299 ⊕ www.nps. gov/arch.

SCENIC DRIVES

Arches Main Park Road. Although they are not formally designated as such, the main park road and its two short spurs are scenic drives, and you can see much of the park from your car. The main road takes you through Courthouse Towers, where you can see Sheep Rock and the Three Gossips, then alongside the Great Wall, the Petrified Dunes and Balanced Rock. A drive to the Windows section takes you to attractions like Double Arch and you can see Skyline Arch along the roadside as you approach the campground. The road to Delicate Arch is not particularly scenic, but it allows you hiking access to one of the park's main features. Allow about two hours to drive the 36-mi round-trip, more if you explore the spurs and their features and stop at viewpoints along the way.

WHAT TO SEE

HISTORIC SITE

Wolfe Ranch. Built in 1906 out of Fremont cottonwoods, this rustic one-room cabin housed the Wolfe family after their first cabin was lost to a flash flood. In addition to the cabin you can see remains of a root cellar and a corral. Even older than these structures is the nearby Ute rock-art panel by the Delicate Arch trailhead. About 150 feet past the footbridge and before the trail starts to climb, you can see images of bighorn sheep, figures on horseback, as well as some smaller images believed to be dogs. To reach the panel, follow the narrow dirt trail along the rock escarpment until you see the interpretive sign. ⊠ *12.9 mi from park entrance, 1.2 mi off main road.*

SCENIC STOPS

The sky is big here, so it's easy to spot some of the arches from your car. But despite the endless horizon, you should really step outside and walk beneath the spans and giant walls of orange rock. This gives you a much better idea of their proportion. No doubt you will feel as writer Edward Abbey did when he awoke on his first day as a park ranger in Arches: that you're walking in the most beautiful place on Earth.

■ TIP➔ Visit as the sun goes down. At sunset, the rock formations in Arches glow like fire and you'll often find photographers behind their tripods waiting for the sweet light to descend upon Delicate Arch or other popular park sites. The Fiery Furnace earns its name as its narrow fins glow red just before the sun dips below the horizon. Full-moon nights are particularly dramatic in Arches as the creamy white Navajo sandstone reflects light, and eerie silhouettes are created by towering fins and formations.

Balanced Rock. One of the park's favorite sights, this rock has remained mysteriously balanced on its pedestal for who knows how long. The formation's total height is 128 feet, with the huge balanced rock rising 55 feet above the pedestal. A short loop (0.3 mi) around the base gives you an opportunity to stretch your legs and take photographs. ⊠ *9.2 mi from park entrance, off main road.*

Fodor's Choice ★ **Delicate Arch.** The familiar symbol of Arches National Park, if not for the entire state of Utah, Delicate Arch is tall enough to shelter a four-story building. The arch is a remnant of an Entrada Sandstone fin; the rest of the rock has eroded and now frames the La Sal Mountains in the background. You can drive a couple of miles off the main road to view the arch from a distance, or you can hike right up to it. The trail is a moderately strenuous 3-mi round-trip hike. ⊠ *13 mi from park entrance, 2.2 mi off main road.*

Double Arch. In the Windows section of the park, Double Arch has appeared in several Hollywood movies, including *Indiana Jones and the Last Crusade.* Less than ¼ mi from the parking lot, the spectacular rock formation can be reached in about 10 minutes. ⊠ *11.7 mi from park entrance off main road.*

★ **Landscape Arch.** This natural rock opening competes with Kolob Arch at Zion for the title of largest geologic span in the world. Measuring 306 feet from base to base, it appears as a delicate ribbon of rock bending over the horizon. In 1991, a slab of rock about 60 feet long, 11 feet wide, and 4 feet thick fell from the underside, leaving it even thinner. You can reach it by walking a rolling, gravel 1.4-mi-long trail. ⊠ *Devils Garden, 18 mi park entrance off main road.*

Skyline Arch. A quick walk from the parking lot gives you closer views and better photos of the arch. The short trail is 0.4-mi round-trip and only takes a few minutes to travel. ⊠ *16½ mi from park entrance off main road.*

☮ **The Windows.** Many people with limited time to spend in the park drive to this area. Here you can see a large concentration of natural windows and walk a path that winds beneath them. ⊠ *11.7 mi from park entrance, 2½ mi off main road.*

VISITOR CENTER

Arches Visitor Center. It's definitely worth stopping to see the interactive displays here; they'll make your sightseeing tour through the park more meaningful. Take time to view the 15-minute park film and shop the bookstore for trail guides, books, and maps to enhance your visit. Exhibits inform you about geology, natural history, and human presence (from Anglo ranchers to Ancestral Puebloan and Fremont) in the Arches area. There is water in vending machines outside the center. ⊠ *At the park entrance* ☏ *435/719–2299* ☉ *Hrs vary but generally 8* AM–*4:30* PM *daily, with extended hrs late spring through early fall.*

SPORTS AND THE OUTDOORS

Arches National Park lies in the middle of the adventure capital of the world. Deep canyons and towering walls are everywhere you look. Slick sandstone surfaces, known as slickrock, make for some of the world's best mountain biking. Thousand-foot sandstone walls draw rock climbers from across the globe. There's no better place for hiking; you can choose from shady canyons or feel like you are on top of the world as you traverse red rock fins that reach for the sky. The Colorado River runs parallel to the park, and can give you every kind of white-water adventure.

Moab-based outfitters can set you up for any sport you may have a desire to try: mountain biking, ATVs, dirt bikes, four-wheel-drive vehicles, kayaking, climbing, and even skydiving. Within the park, it's best to stick with basics such as hiking, sightseeing, and photography. Climbers and other adventure seekers should always inquire at the visitor center about restrictions.

BICYCLING

There's outstanding mountain biking all around Arches National Park, but the park proper is not the best place to explore on two wheels. Bicycles are only allowed on established roads and since there are no

GOOD READS

Operated by Canyonlands Natural History Association, **Arches Visitor Center Bookstore** (⊠ *At the park entrance* ☏ *435/259–6003*) is the place to buy maps, guidebooks, driving tours on CD, and material about the natural and cultural history of Arches National Park.

■ *A Naturalist's Guide to Canyon Country,* by David Williams and Gloria Brown, is an excellent, compact field guide for both Arches and Canyonlands national parks.

■ *Best Easy Day Hikes: Arches and Canyonlands,* by Bill Schneider, is a pocket-size trail guide that should boost your confidence as you hit the trails.

■ *Canyon Country Wildflowers,* by Damian Fagan, can help you name the colorful blossoms you see during wildflower season (spring and early summer).

■ *Desert Solitaire*—every visitor should read Edward Abbey's classic.

■ *Exploring Canyonlands and Arches National Parks,* by Bill Schneider, provides comprehensive advice on hiking trails, backcountry roads, and trip planning.

■ *Hiking Guide to Arches National Park,* by Damian Fagan, details all of the park's hiking trails.

■ *Road Guide to Arches National Park,* by Peter Anderson, has basic information about the geology and natural history in the park.

■ *Moab Classic Hikes,* by Damian Fagan, succinctly gives the skinny on 40 area hikes and includes maps and photos.

■ *Self-Guided Driving Tour CD,* by Canyonlands History Association, is like having a ranger in your car; CDs can be rented or purchased.

shoulders, cyclists share the roadway with drivers and pedestrians gawking at the scenery. If you do want to take a spin in the park, try Willow Flats Road, the old entrance to the park. The road is about 6½-mi long one way and starts directly across from the Balanced Rock parking lot. It's a pretty mountain bike ride on dirt and sand through slickrock, pinyon, and juniper country. You must stay on the road with your bicycle or you chance steep fines.

OUTFITTERS
AND
EXPEDITIONS
For bicycle rentals, repairs, and espresso, stop at **Chile Pepper Bikes** (⊠ *702 S. Main St., Moab* ☏ *435/259–4688 or 888/677–4688* ⊕ *www. chilebikes.com*) before you hit the trails. **Poison Spider Bicycles** (⊠ *497 N. Main St., Moab* ☏ *435/259–7882 or 800/635–1792*) is a fully loaded shop (with rental bikes, new equipments, and bike shuttle service) staffed by young, friendly bike experts. For full-suspension bike rentals and sales, solid advice on trails, and parts, equipment and gear, **Rim Cyclery** (⊠ *94 W. 100 South, Moab* ☏ *435/259–5333 or 888/304–8219* ⊕ *www. rimcyclery.com*) is the oldest bike shop in town. Reliable, friendly, and professional, **Rim Tours** (⊠ *1233 S. U.S. 191, Moab* ☏ *435/259–5223 or 800/626–7335* ⊕ *www.rimtours.com*) can take you on a great guided mountain-bike tour. Trips include Gemini Bridges, the Slickrock Trail, Klondike Bluffs, and many other locations—including the White Rim Trail in Canyonlands.

Western Spirit Cycling (✉ *478 Mill Creek Dr., Moab* ☎ *435/259–8732 or 800/845–2453* ⊕ *www.western-spirit.com*) offers fully supported, go-at-your-own-pace multiday bike tours throughout the region, including trips to Canyonlands, the 140-mi Kokopelli Trail, which runs from Grand Junction, Colorado, to Moab and other two-wheeled adventures. Guides versed in the geologic wonders of the area cook up meals worthy of the scenery each night. There's also the option to combine a Green River kayak trip with the three-night bike route. *For additional bike rentals and expeditions,* ⇨ *Multisport Outfitters and Expeditions box and Canyonlands National Park (chapter 11).*

> **NOTABLE QUOTE**
>
> "You can't see *anything* from a car; you've got to get out and walk, better yet crawl, on hands and knees, over the sandstone and through the thornbush and cactus. When traces of blood begin to mark your trail you'll see something, maybe."
>
> —Edward Abbey, *Desert Solitaire*

BIRD-WATCHING

Within the park you'll definitely see plenty of the big, black, beautiful raven. Look for them perched on top of a picturesque juniper branch or balancing on the bald knob of a rock. The noisy black-billed magpie populates the park, as do the more melodic canyon and rock wrens. Lucky visitors will spot a red-tailed hawk and hear its distinctive call.

Serious birders will have more fun visiting the **Scott M. Matheson Wetlands Preserve** (⇨ *What's Nearby*) just 5 mi south of the park. The wetlands is home to more than 225 species of birds including the wood duck, western screech owl, indigo bunting, and plumbeous vireo.

BOATING AND RIVER EXPEDITIONS

Although the Colorado River runs along the border of the park, there is no boating within the park proper. You can, however, enjoy a splashy ride nearby on the Fisher Towers stretch of the river near Moab, and there are plenty of fine outfitters in Moab that can set you up for expeditions. *For rafting outside the park,* ⇨ *Rafting, under Area Activities in the What's Nearby section.*

OUTFITTERS AND EXPEDITIONS An excellent choice for a guided day- or multiday trip on the Colorado or Green rivers, **Canyon Voyages Adventure Co.** (✉ *211 N. Main St., Moab* ☎ *435/259–6007 or 800/733–6007* ⊕ *www.canyonvoyages.com*) is a friendly, professional company. It's also the only company that operates a kayak school for those who want to learn how to run the rapids on their own, and you can rent rafts and kayaks here. Inside the booking office is a great shop that sells river gear, outdoor clothes, hats, sandals, and backpacks. You can rent a raft or book a raft trip on the Green and Colorado rivers (or venture to Canyonlands National Park) with **Holiday River Expeditions** (✉ *2075 E. Main St., Green River* ☎ *435/564–3276 or 800/624–6323* ⊕ *www.bikeraft.com*), a reliable company with decades of river experience. The folks at **Tex's Riverways** (✉ *691 N. 500 W, Moab* ☎ *435/259–5101 or 877/662–2839* ⊕ *www.texsriverways.com*) can shuttle you to and from the Green or Colorado River when you rent a canoe for exploring on your own (or even if you

MULTISPORT OUTFITTERS AND EXPEDITIONS

Adrift Adventures. This outfitter offers daylong or multiday raft trips on the Colorado or Green rivers, rock-art tours, sea kayaking, 4X4 excursions, a movie-set tour, and a combination horseback ride and river trip. ✉ *378 N. Main, Moab* ☎ *435/259–8594 or 800/874–4483* ⊕ *www.adrift.net.*

Coyote Shuttle. If you need a ride to or from your bicycle trailhead or river trip, call the Coyote. These folks also do shuttles to and from Green River for the train and bus service there. ✉ *55 W. 300 S, Moab* ☎ *435/260–2097 or 435/259–8656* ⊕ *www.coyoteshuttle.com.*

Moab Adventure Center. For a short trip on the Colorado River, a Hummer tour, scenic flight, national park tour, or rubber kayak rental, contact this reputable company. ✉ *225 S. Main St., Moab* ☎ *435/259–7019 or 888/622–4097* ⊕ *www.moabadventurecenter.com.*

NAVTEC. A fast little boat engineered by this outfit gets you down the Colorado River and through Cataract Canyon in one day. Take trips up to six days in length, or head out on 4X4 trips into nearby backcountry. ✉ *321 N. Main St., Moab* ☎ *435/259–7983 or 800/833–1278* ⊕ *www.navtec.com.*

Red Cliffs Adventure Lodge. Take a horseback ride near one of Moab's working cattle ranches. The lodge also arranges guided rafting, hiking, and biking trips through local outfitters. ✉ *Milepost 14, Rte. 128, Moab* ☎ *435/259–2002 or 866/812–2002* ⊕ *www.redcliffslodge.com.*

Roadrunner Shuttle. Call this company for ride to the airport or for a river or bike shuttle. If you happen to be into dirt biking, ask about the owner's other business, Dual Sport Utah, for dirt bike, off-road tours. ☎ *435/259–9402* ⊕ *www.roadrunnershuttle.com.*

have your own gear and just need a shuttle). *For additional boating outfitters, ⇨ Multisport Outfitters and Expeditions box.*

FISHING

There is no fishing in Arches National Park, and the Colorado River is too silty to offer good fishing. The nearby La Sal Mountains are dotted with small lakes that are stocked with small trout, but finding good native trout fishing in the area will take some effort.

FOUR-WHEELING

With thousands of acres of nearby Bureau of Land Management lands to enjoy, it's hardly necessary to use the park's limited trails for four-wheel adventures. You can, however, go backcountry in Arches on the Willow Flats Road and the Salt Valley Road—just don't set out for this expedition without first stopping at the visitor center to learn of current conditions. The Salt Valley road is very sandy and requires special driving skills.

OUTFITTERS AND EXPEDITIONS **Coyote Land Tours** (☎ *435/259–6649* ⊕ *www.coyoteshuttle.com*) can take you to backcountry where you could never wander on your own. The company's big Mercedes Unimog vehicles cover some rough terrain, while you sit back and enjoy the sites. Touring the backcountry near Moab in open-air Hummer vehicles, **Highpoint Hummer & ATV Tours &**

Rentals (✉ *281 N. Main St., Moab* ☎ *435/259–2972 or 877/486–6833* ⊕ *www.highpointhummer.com*) offers two- and four-hour "high" adventure trips as well as "low" adventure tours for the more timid traveler. Also available are ATVs, Jeeps, and dirt bikes for rent as well as guided ATV, hiking, and canyoneering tours.

For additional guided 4X4 trips, ⇨ Multisport Outfitters and Expeditions box.

HIKING

Getting out on any one of the park trails will surely cause you to fall in love with this Martian landscape. But remember, you are hiking in a desert environment. Many people succumb to heat and dehydration because they do not drink enough water. Park rangers recommend a gallon of water per day per person.

For guided hiking expeditions, ⇨ Multisport Outfitters and Expeditions box.

PAW PRINTS

If Fido is along for the Arches adventure, keep in mind that pooches aren't allowed on the national park trails and must be on-leash in the Devils Garden Campground. However, canines can join you on Bureau of Land Management trails, such as Negro Bill Canyon (named with little tact for one of the town's first non-native settler's, William Granstaff), which match the beauty of in-park hikes. The heat can be stifling, so remember to bring enough water for you and your four-legged friend, hit the trails in the early morning hours, and avoid mid-summer scorchers.

EASY

☾ **Balanced Rock Trail.** You'll want to stop at Balanced Rock for photo opportunities, so you may as well walk the easy, partially paved trail around the famous landmark. This is one of the most accessible trails in the park and is suitable for small children and folks who may have difficulty walking. The trail is only 0.3 mi round-trip; you should allow 15 minutes for the walk. ✉ *Trailhead approximately 9 mi from park entrance.*

Broken Arch Trail. An easy walk across open grassland, this loop trail passes Broken Arch, which is also visible from the road. The arch gets its name because it appears to be cracked in the middle, but it's not really broken. The trail is 1.3 mi round-trip, and you should allow about an hour for the walk. ✉ *Trailhead at end of Sand Dune Arch trail, 0.3 mi off main road, 11 mi from park entrance.*

Double Arch Trail. Near the trail to Windows, this relatively flat trail leads you to two massive arches that make for great photo opportunities. Although only 0.8 mi round-trip, it gives you a good taste of desert flora and fauna. ✉ *Trailhead 2½ mi from main road, on the Windows Section spur road.*

Park Avenue Trail. Walk under the gaze of Queen Nefertiti, a giant rock formation that some observers think has Egyptian-looking features. The nearby rock walls resemble a New York City skyline—hence the name Park Avenue. The trail is fairly easy, with only a short hill to navigate. It's 2 mi round-trip, or, if you are traveling with companions, you can

Devils Garden Trail

Dark Angel ◆

Double O Arch ◆

← TO VISITOR CENTER
AND CAMPGROUND

Navajo Arch ◆

Partition Arch ◆

Private Arch ◆

◆ Landscape Arch

KEY

Trailhead
Parking
◆
Tunnel
Arch

◆ Pine Tree
Arch

Primitive Loop

····· *Main Trails*

····· *Side Trails*

····· *Primitive Loop*

have one of them pick you up at the Courthouse Towers Viewpoint, making it a 1-mi trek downhill. Allow about 45 minutes for the one-way journey. ⊠ *Trailhead off main road, 2 mi from park entrance.*

♨ **Sand Dune Arch Trail.** Your kids will return to the car with shoes full of sand from this giant sandbox in the desert. A cautionary note: do not climb or jump off the arch; rangers have dealt with several accidents involving people who have done so. Set aside 15–30 minutes for this shady, 0.3-mi walk. The trail intersects with the Broken Arch Trail, so if you visit both arches, it's a 1½-mi round-trip. ⊠ *Trailhead off main road, about 15½ mi from park entrance.*

MODERATE

Fodor'sChoice **Devils Garden Trail.** If you want to take a longer hike in the park, head
★ out on this network of trails, where you can see a number of arches, including the remains of Wall Arch, which crumbled in 2008. You will reach Tunnel and Pine Tree arches after only 0.4 mi on the gravel trail, and Landscape Arch is 0.4 mi from the trailhead. Past Landscape Arch the trail changes dramatically, increasing in difficulty with many short, steep climbs. You will encounter some heights as you inch your way across a long rock fin. The trail is marked with rock cairns, and it's always a good idea to locate the next one before moving on. Along the way to Double O Arch, 2 mi from the trailhead, you can take short detours to Navajo and Partition arches. A round-trip hike to Double O takes from two to three hours. For a longer hike, include Dark Angel and/or return to the trailhead on the primitive loop. This is a difficult route through fins with a short side trip to Private Arch. If you hike all the way to Dark Angel and return on the primitive loop, the trail is 7.2 mi round-trip. Allow about five hours for this adventure, take plenty of water, and watch your route carefully. ⊠ *Trailhead off main road, 18 mi from park entrance.*

Tower Arch Trail. In a remote, seldom-visited area of the park, this trail takes you to a giant rock opening. If you look beneath the arch you will see a 1922 inscription left by Alex Ringhoffer, who "discovered" this section of the park. Reach the trail by driving to the Klondike Bluffs parking area via a dirt road that starts at the main park road across from Broken Arch. Check with park rangers for road conditions before attempting the drive. Allow from two to three hours for this hike. ⊠ *Trailhead 24½ mi from park entrance, 7.7 mi off main road.*

DIFFICULT

★ **Delicate Arch Trail.** To see the park's most famous freestanding arch up close takes some effort. The 3-mi round-trip trail ascends a steep slick-rock slope that offers no shade—it's very hot in summer. What you find at the end of the trail is, however, worth the hard work. You can walk under the arch and take advantage of abundant photo ops, especially at sunset. In spite of its difficulty, this is a very popular trail. Allow anywhere from one to three hours for this hike, depending on your fitness level and how long you plan to linger at the arch. If you go at sunset, bring a headlamp or flashlight for the hike down. The trail starts at Wolfe Ranch. ⊠ *Trailhead 13 mi from park entrance, 2.2 mi off main road.*

WORD OF MOUTH

"Delicate Arch is definitely the best bang for the buck. I also really enjoyed the 5-mi round-trip hike to Dark Angel. This hike goes right by Landscape Arch. Sometimes the easy ones (like Park Avenue and the Windows) are also really great."
—Utahtea

"Schedule your day so that you will be up at Delicate Arch at sunset for the best lighting for photos. This is one of the icons of the West along with Half Dome, El Capitan, and Toroweap."
—Supercilious

★ **Fiery Furnace Hiking.** Rangers strongly suggest taking the guided hike (⇨ *Ranger Programs*) through this area before you set out on your own, as there is no marked trail. A hike here is a challenging but fascinating trip through rugged terrain into the heart of Arches. The trek occasionally requires the use of hands and feet to scramble up and through narrow cracks and along narrow ledges above drop-offs. To hike this area on your own you must get a permit at the visitor center ($4). If you're not familiar with the Furnace you can easily get lost and cause resource damage, so watch your step and use great caution. ⊠ *Trailhead off main road, about 15 mi from visitor center.*

ROCK CLIMBING AND CANYONEERING

Rock climbers travel from across the country to scale the sheer red rock walls of Arches National Park and surrounding areas. Most climbing routes in the park require advanced techniques. Permits are not required, but you are responsible for knowing park regulations and restricted routes. Two popular routes ascend Owl Rock in the Garden of Eden (about 10 mi from the visitor center), the well-worn route has a difficulty of 5.8, while a more challenging option is 5.11 on a scale that goes up to 5.13+. Many climbing routes are available in the Park Avenue area, about 2.2 mi from the visitor center. These routes are also extremely difficult climbs. No commercial outfitters are allowed to lead rock-climbing excursions in the park, but guided canyoneering (which involves ropes, rappelling, and some basic climbing) is permitted. New climbing policies were put in place in 2006; before climbing, it's imperative that you stop at the visitor center and talk with a ranger.

OUTFITTERS
AND
EXPEDITIONS

Desert Highlights (✉ *50 E. Center St., Moab* ☎ *435/259–6649* ⊕ *www. deserthighlights.com*) has the park's blessing to take adventurous types off the Fiery Furnace ranger route for descents and ascents through canyons (with the help of ropes). The guides also lead other full-day and multiday canyoneering treks to destinations both inside and outside the national parks. Desert Highlights does not offer guided rock climbing. **Moab Cliffs & Canyons**

WORD OF MOUTH

"The ranger-led hike through Fiery Furnace is excellent. It can be tough to get a reservation at times since you have to make them in person and they can be booked for three to four days. Most of the other trails are within your time frame and all are amazing." —bee_man

(✉ *63 E. Cedar St., Moab* ☎ *435/259–6649* ⊕ *www.cliffsandcanyons. com*) leads half- and full-day canyoneering adventures (inside and outside the park) as well as outside-the-parks rock climbing trips for novices and seasoned climbers alike. Mount the spires of Castle Valley or ascend crack climbs, like Indian Creek.

EDUCATIONAL OFFERINGS

RANGER PROGRAMS

As you explore Arches, look for sandwich boards announcing RANGER SIGHTINGS and stop for a 3- to 10-minute program led by park staff. Topics range from geology and desert plants to mountain lions and the Colorado River. If you're lucky, more in-depth campfire programs or guided walks (in addition to the beloved Fiery Furnace walk) may be available during your visit. For information on current schedules and locations of park programs, contact the visitor center (☎ *435/719–2299*) or check the bulletin boards located throughout the park.

ℭ

Fodor'sChoice

★

Fiery Furnace Walk. Join a park ranger on a two- or three-hour walk through a mazelike labyrinth of rock fins and narrow sandstone canyons. You'll see arches that can't be viewed from the park road and spend time listening to the desert. You should be relatively fit and not afraid of heights if you plan to take this moderately strenuous walk. Wear sturdy hiking shoes, sunscreen, and a hat, and bring at least a quart of water. Walks into the Fiery Furnace are usually offered twice a day (hours vary) and leave from Fiery Furnace Viewpoint. Tickets may be purchased for this popular activity up to seven days in advance at the visitor center. Children ages 7–12 pay half–price. ■ TIP➔ **Book early as the program usually fills two to four days prior to each walk.** ✉ *Fiery Furnace trailhead, off the main road, about 15 mi from park visitor center* 🎫 *$10* ◷ *Mid-Mar.–Oct., daily (hrs vary)*.

ℭ

Junior Ranger Program. Kids 2 through 12 can pick up a Junior Ranger booklet at the visitor center. It's full of activities, word games, drawings, and educational material about the park and the wildlife. To earn your Junior Ranger badge, you must complete several activities in the booklet, attend a ranger program, watch the park film, or gather a bag of litter. For ranger program veterans, ages 8 and up, ask about the "extra credit" Red Rock Ranger Program. ☎ *435/719–2299* 🎫 *Free*.

LEARNING RESOURCES

Red Rock Explorer Pack. Just like borrowing a book from a library, families can check out a backpack filled with tools for learning about both Arches and Canyonlands national parks. Peruse the field guides, take a closer look at a sunflower with the hand lens magnifier, and give the activities in the binder a whirl. Be sure to make a journal entry of your family's discoveries. Backpacks can be returned to either Arches or Island in the Sky visitor centers. Use of the backpack is free with a credit-card imprint in case of loss or damage to the pack or enclosed items. ☎ *435/719–2299* ✉ *Free.*

WHAT'S NEARBY

NEARBY TOWNS

Moab is the major gateway to both Arches and Canyonlands national parks. Near the Colorado River in a beautiful valley between red rock cliffs, with the La Sal Mountains rising to 12,000 feet just 20 mi away, Moab is an interesting, eclectic place to visit, especially if you're looking for fine restaurants with good wine lists, abundant shopping, art galleries, and varied lodging. Also, here you'll find the area's greatest number of sports outfitters to help you enjoy the parks. For those who want civilization and culture with their outdoor itineraries, Moab is the place to be.

The next-closest town to Arches, about 47 mi to the northwest, is **Green River.** Unlike hip Moab, this sleepy little town is more traditional and off the tourists' radar screen. It's worth a visit for the **Crystal Geyser,** which erupts unpredictably for approximately 30 minutes every 14 to 16 hours. Also, each September the fragrance of fresh cantaloupe, watermelon, and honeydew fills the air, especially during Melon Days, a family-fun event celebrating the harvest on the third weekend of September.

VISITOR INFORMATION

Green River Information Center ✉ *885 E. Main St., Green River* ☎ *435/564–3427.* **Moab Information Center** ✉ *Center and Main Sts., Moab* ☎ *435/259–8825 or 800/635–6622* ⊕ *www.discovermoab.com.*

NEARBY ATTRACTIONS

Courthouse Wash. Although this rock-art panel fell victim to an unusual case of vandalism in 1980, when someone scoured the petroglyphs and pictographs that had been left by four cultures. You can still see ancient images if you take a short walk from the parking area on the left-hand side of the road, heading south. ✉ *U.S. 191, about 2 mi south of Arches National Park entrance.*

John Wesley Powell River History Museum. At this riverfront museum you can see what it was like to travel down the Green and Colorado rivers in the 1800s. A series of displays tracks the Powell Party's arduous, dangerous 1869 journey and visitors can watch the award-winning film *Journey into the Unknown* for a cinematic taste of the white-water adventure.

FESTIVALS AND EVENTS

WINTER

Western Stars Cowboy Poetry Gathering. A fast-growing tradition in Moab, Western Stars brings cowboy poets and singers to the heart of town in mid-February. A Dutch-oven cook-off, horsemanship demonstrations, traditional western dancing and crafts, and western art shows make Presidents' Day holiday weekend a great time to visit Moab and Arches National Park. ☎ 435/259–6272 ⊕ www.moabwesternstars.com.

SPRING

Moab Art Walk. Moab galleries, shops, and cafés chase the winter blues away by launching the first Art Walk of the season. Art Walks are held the second Saturday of the month from March through June and September through November. Stroll the streets to see and purchase original art by Moab's talent. ☎ 435/259–4446 ⊕ www.moabartwalk.com.

Moab Arts Festival. Every Memorial Day weekend, artists from across the West gather at Moab's Swanny City Park to show their wares, including pottery, photography, and paintings. The festival is small enough to be fun and prices are affordable. Live music, cultural entertainment, and lots of food keep everyone happy. ☎ 435/259–2742 ⊕ www.moabartsfestival.org.

SUMMER

Canyonlands PRCA Rodeo. Cowboys come to the Old Spanish Trails Arena (just south of Moab) for three days in early June to try their luck on thrashing bulls and broncs at this annual western tradition. ☎ 435/259–6226.

4th of July Celebration. Moab dishes out a real slice of Americana each Independence Day, with apple-pie baking contests, fireworks, a good ol' fashioned parade, a kiddie carnival (including a dunk tank for temporarily sinking town officials), watermelon-eating contests, the mayor's address, and local bands and dance groups. The free community festivities fill Swanny City Park and end with a traditional bang: fireworks. ☎ 435/259–7814.

FALL

Green River Melon Days. All the watermelon you can eat, an old-fashioned parade, and other small-town-America activities await you on the third Saturday of September. ☎ 435/564–3526.

Moab Music Festival. Listen to world-class music—classical, jazz, and traditional—among the red rocks, embark on a short "musical walk," or attend a special river concert 30 mi downstream on the Colorado River in Canyonlands National Park. Musicians from all over the globe perform, and it's one event truly worth driving great distances to attend. The festival starts the Thursday before Labor Day and runs two to three weeks. ☎ 435/259–7003 ⊕ www.moabmusicfest.org.

24 Hours of Moab Bike Race. This 24-hour race whips 1,500 competitors through the desert near Moab. Riders bike laps of 15 mi, covering a total combined distance of close to 68,000 mi. About 2,000 fans (mostly friends and family of the riders) camp and cheer the riders on. ☎ 304/259–5533 ⊕ www.grannygear.com.

The center also houses the River Runner's Hall of Fame, a tribute to those have followed in Powell's wake. An art gallery reserved for works thematically linked to river exploration is also on-site. ✉ *1765 E. Main St.* ☎ *435/564–3427* ⊕ *www.jwprhm.com* 🗌 *$4* ☉ *Apr.–Oct., daily 8–7; Nov.–Mar., Tues.–Sat. 9–5.*

For a small taste of history in the Moab area and a chance to test out an old player piano, stop by the **Museum of Moab.** Ancient and historic American Indians are remembered in exhibits of sandals, baskets, pottery, and other artifacts. Other displays chronicle the early Spanish expeditions into the area and the history of uranium discovery and exploration. ✉ *118 E. Center St., Moab* ☎ *435/259–7985* ⊕ *www. moabmuseum.org* 🗌 *$3* ☉ *Apr.–Oct., weekdays 10–6, Sat. noon–6; Nov.–Mar., weekdays 10–3, Sat. noon–5.*

Sego Canyon. About 39 mi from Moab, this is one of the most dramatic and mystifying rock-art sights in the area. On the canyon walls you can see large, ghostlike rock-art figures etched by American Indians approximately 4,000 years ago. There's also art left by the Ute Indians 400–700 years ago. This canyon is a little out of the way, but well worth the drive. ✉ *About 4 mi off I–70 exit 187, Thompson Springs.*

⇨ *Canyonlands National Park (chapter 11) for additional area listings.*

AREA ACTIVITIES

SPORTS AND THE OUTDOORS
BIRD-WATCHING
Scott M. Matheson Wetlands Preserve. The best place around for bird-watching, this desert oasis is home to hundreds of species of birds, including such treasures as the pied-billed grebe, the cinnamon teal, and the northern flicker. It's possible that you might even spot beaver and muskrat playing in the water. The preserve is home to several bat species such as the western pipistrel, the pallid bat, and the hoary bat. A boardwalk winds through the preserve to a viewing shelter. ✉ *Near the intersection of 500 West and Kane Creek Blvd.* ☎ *435/259–4629.*

GOLF
★ **Moab Golf Course** is undoubtedly one of the most beautiful in the world. The 18-hole, par-72 course has lush greens set against a red rock sandstone backdrop, a lovely visual combination that's been know to distract even the most focused golfer. ✉ *2705 S. East Bench Rd.* ☎ *435/259–6488* 🗌 *Greens fees $42 for 18 holes, including cart rental.*

RAFTING
Fisher Towers. On the Colorado River northeast of Arches and very near Moab, you can take one of America's most scenic—yet unintimidating—river-raft rides. This is the perfect place to take the family or to learn to kayak with the help of an outfitter. The river rolls by the red Fisher Towers as they rise into the sky in front of the La Sal Mountains. A day trip on this stretch of the river will take you about 14 mi. Outfitters offer full- or half-day adventures here. ✉ *17 mi upriver from Rte. 128 near Moab.*

Gray–Desolation Canyon. Desolation is not really a fair name for this beautiful, lush canyon along the Green River. It's a favorite destination of canoe paddlers, kayakers, and beginning rafters. There are lots of rapids on this stretch of the Green, but they are on the small side and deliver lots of laughs. Families with children of almost any age can share this adventure and even paddle on their own under the watchful eyes of a guide. This trip requires four or five days to complete. ⊠ *On the Green River.*

Westwater Canyon. In this narrow, winding canyon near the Utah–Colorado border, the Colorado River cuts through the oldest exposed geologic layer on earth. The result is craggy black granite jutting out of the water with red sandstone walls towering above. This section of the river is rocky and considered highly technical for rafters and kayakers, but it dishes out a great white-water experience in a short period of time. Most Moab outfitters offer this trip as a one-day getaway, but you may also linger in the canyon as long as three days to complete the journey. ⊠ *About 51 mi northeast of Moab on the Colorado River.*

OUTFITTERS
AND
EXPEDITIONS Longtime Moab outfitter **Sheri Griffith Expeditions** (⊠ *2231 S. U.S. 191, Moab* ☎ *435/259–8229 or 800/332–2439* ⊕ *www.griffithexp.com*) offers trips through the white water of Cataract, Westwater, and Desolation canyons, on the Colorado and Green rivers. Specialty expeditions include river trips for women, writers, and families. You might also enjoy one of their more luxurious expeditions, which make roughing it a little more comfortable. **Tag-A-Long Expeditions** (⊠ *452 N. Main St., Moab* ☎ *435/259–8946 or 800/453–3292* ⊕ *www.tagalong.com*) has been taking people into the white water of Cataract Canyon and Canyonlands longer than any other outfitter in Moab. It also runs four-wheel-drive expeditions into the backcountry of the park plus calm-water excursions on the Colorado and Green rivers. Trips run from a half day to six days.

ARTS AND ENTERTAINMENT

Moab Arts and Recreation Center. The hub of arts activities in Moab, the center hosts art exhibits featuring local artists every other month as well as concerts and exercise classes. ⊠ *111 E. 100 N, Moab* ☎ *435/259–6272.*

Canyonlands by Night. Operating from April to October, take a two-hour boat ride on the Colorado River after dark. While illuminating the canyon walls with 40,000 watts, the trip includes music and narration highlighting Moab's history, American Indian legends, and geologic formations along the river. You can combine the boat trip with a Dutch-oven dinner, too. ⊠ *U.S. 191, north of Colorado River bridge* ☎ *435/259–5261* ⊕ *www.canyonlandsbynight.com.*

SHOPPING

ART GALLERIES

The folks at **Lema's Kokopelli Gallery** (⊠ *70 N. Main St., Moab* ☎ *435/259–5055*) have built a reputation for fair prices on a giant selection of American Indian jewelry and art. Everything for sale here is authentic. Paintings, jewelry, sculpture, and American Indian pottery—much of which reflects the spirit of canyon country—can be found at **Overlook**

Gallery (✉ *83 E. Center St., Moab* ☎*435/259–3861*), an elegant little gallery just a short walk from Main Street. After you visit Arches and Canyonlands, stop at **Tom Till Gallery** (✉*61 N. Main St., Moab* ☎*435/259–9808*) to buy stunning original photographs of the parks by one of the nation's best-loved landscape photographers.

BOOKS

You can't beat the warm ambience or friendly service at the popular **Arches Book Company** (✉ *78 N. Main St., Moab* ☎*435/259–0782* ⊕ *www. archesbookcompany.com*). Every title you'd want, from the top best sellers to works by local authors, is here, along with your favorite coffee drink. Sit in the window, read a book, chat with locals, smell coffee beans (which they roast on-site) and watch people pass by as you sip an espresso. A decidedly "green" bookstore, **Back of Beyond Books** (✉ *83 N. Main St., Moab* ☎*435/259–5154 or 800/700–2859* ⊕ *www.backofbeyondbooks. com*) features an excellent selection of books on environmental studies, American Indian cultures, western water issues, and western history as well as a collection of rare antiquarian books of the Southwest.

WESTERN GOODS

A fun place to browse for a flavor of the Old West, **Western Image** (✉ *161 W. 100 N., Moab* ☎*435/259–3006*) has antiques, western art, cowboy hats, boots, belts, coins, badges, and other favorite but classy souvenirs.

SCENIC DRIVE

Colorado River Scenic Byway—Route 128. One of the most scenic drives in the country is Route 128, which intersects U.S. 191 3 mi south of Arches. The 44-mi highway runs along the Colorado River northeast to Interstate 70. The drive from Moab to Interstate 70 takes about an hour.

WHERE TO EAT AND STAY

ABOUT THE RESTAURANTS

Since most people come to Arches to play outside, casual is the modus operandi for dining. Whether you select an award-winning Continental restaurant in Moab or a tavern in Green River, you can dress comfortably in shorts or jeans. But don't let the relaxed attire fool you. There are some wonderful culinary surprises waiting for you, often with spectacular views as a bonus.

In the park itself, there are no dining facilities and no snack bars. Supermarkets, bakeries, and delis in downtown Moab will be happy to make you a sandwich to go. If you bring a packed lunch, there are several picnic areas from which to choose.

ABOUT THE HOTELS

Though there are no hotels or cabins in the park itself, in the surrounding area, every type of lodging is available, from economy chain motels to B&Bs and high-end, high-adventure resorts. It's important to know when popular events are held, however, as accommodations can, and do, fill up weeks ahead of time.

ABOUT THE CAMPGROUNDS

Campgrounds in and around Moab range from sprawling RV parks with every amenity you could dream of to quaint, shady retreats near a babbling brook. The Devils Garden Campground in the park is a wonderful spot to call home for a few days, though it is often full and does not provide an RV dump station. Another favorite is the Dead Horse State Park Campground, which is particularly popular with RV campers (⇨ *Canyonlands National Park*). Green River State Park is a shady glen positioned near the river and near a public golf course. River expeditions through Labyrinth and Stillwater canyons on the Green River begin here. The most centrally located campgrounds are in Moab and will generally provide services needed by RV travelers.

WHERE TO EAT

IN THE PARK

PICNIC AREAS **Balanced Rock.** The view is the best part of this picnic spot. There are no cooking facilities or water, but there are tables. If you sit just right you might find some shade under a small juniper; otherwise, this is an exposed site. Pit toilets are nearby. ⊠ *Opposite the Balanced Rock parking area, 9.2 mi from the park entrance on the main road.*

Devils Garden. There are grills, water, picnic tables, restrooms, and depending on the time of day, some shade from large junipers and rock walls. It's a good place for lunch before or after you go hiking. ⊠ *On the main road, 18 mi from the park entrance.*

OUTSIDE THE PARK

IN GREEN RIVER

¢–$ ✕ **Ben's Cafe.** At the local hot spot for homemade enchiladas you can
MEXICAN also get a good porterhouse steak. This unpretentious restaurant on Green River's main thoroughfare offers plenty of choices at reasonable prices. ⊠ *115 W. Main St., Green River* ☎ *435/564–3352* ⊕ *www.benscafe.com* ▭ *AE, D, DC, MC, V.*

$ ✕ **Ray's Tavern.** Ray's is something of a western legend and a favorite
AMERICAN hangout for river runners. Stop at this unassuming joint for great tales
★ about working on the river as well as the coldest beer and the best all-beef hamburger in two counties. ⊠ *25 S. Broadway, Green River* ☎ *435/564–3511* ▭ *AE, D, MC, V.*

IN MOAB

$$$–$$$$ ✕ **Buck's Grill House.** For a taste of the American West, try the buffalo
SOUTHWESTERN meat loaf or elk stew served at this popular dinner spot. The steaks are
Fodor'sChoice thick and tender, and the gravies will have you licking your fingers.
★ A selection of southwestern entrées, including duck tamales and rabbit *machaca*, round out the menu. Vegetarian diners, don't despair; there are some tasty choices for you, too. A surprisingly good wine list will complement your meal. The 21-plus crowd can mosey to the contemporary Vista Lounge, a cool contrast to the bustling main dining room, for dinner and drinks. Outdoor patio dining with the trickle of a waterfall will end your day perfectly. ⊠ *1393 N. U.S. 191, Moab* ☎ *435/259–5201* ⊕ *www.bucksgrillhouse.com* ▨ *$9–$38* ▭ *D, MC, V* ⊙ *Limited menu late Nov.–mid-Feb. No lunch.*

$$$–$$$$
AMERICAN
★

✕ **Center Café.** A block away from the hustle and bustle of the main thoroughfare, this "globally inspired" restaurant has a peaceful courtyard for outdoor dining. The mood inside is Spanish Mediterranean, made even more lovely by the fireplace. From grilled Black Angus beef tenderloin with bordelaise sauce to pan-seared lamb loin with roasted garlic flan, there's always something on the contemporary menu to make your taste buds go "aah." Be sure to ask for the impressive wine list. ✉ *60 N. 100 West St., Moab* ☎ *435/259–4295* ⊕ *www.centercafemoab.com* ▭ *D, MC, V* ⊙ *Closed Dec.–Jan. Open for tapas 4–6 PM. No lunch.*

$$–$$$
SOUTHWESTERN

✕ **Desert Bistro.** The 1896 ranch house, with sprigs of lavender decorating each table, has a seasonally changing menu with an emphasis on game. Try the Gorgonzola-encrusted fillet on the patio under the soft glow of strung white lights or enjoy quiet indoor conversation along with the ahi tuna appetizer and a bottle of *vino*. The cuisine's presentation is exemplary, the staff is warm and unpretentious and the historic setting coupled with the soft whoosh of a spring is both romantic and relaxing. If the petit dining room and patio are full, you might end up dining at one of the five tables in the wine cellar. ✉ *1266 N. Main St., Moab* ☎ *435/259–0756* ⊕ *www.desertbistro.com* ▭ *AE, D, MC, V* ⊙ *No lunch. No dinner Dec.–Feb.*

$–$$
AMERICAN
☕

✕ **Eddie McStiff's.** This casual restaurant and microbrewery serves homemade fish-and-chips, organic pizzas, burgers, and zesty Italian specialties to go with the 13 freshly brewed concoctions, such as raspberry and blueberry wheat beer, and a smooth cream ale. ✉ *57 S. Main St., Moab* ☎ *435/259–2337* ⊕ *www.eddiemcstiffs.com* ▭ *D, MC, V.*

¢–$
ECLECTIC

✕ **Eklecticafe.** This small place is easy to miss but worth searching out for one of the more creative, healthy menus in Moab. Breakfast and lunch items include a variety of burritos and wraps, scrambled tofu, salmon cakes, Indonesian satay kebabs, and many fresh, organic salads. On nice days you can take your meal outside to the large covered patio. In winter you'll want to stay inside by the wood-burning stove. ✉ *352 N. Main St., Moab* ☎ *435/259–6896* ▭ *D, MC, V* ⊙ *No dinner.*

$
MEXICAN

✕ **Fiesta Mexicana.** Authentic Mexican food and atmosphere abound in this warm restaurant with excellent service. Portions are large, so you won't go hungry, and you can have a cold *cerveza* (beer) or margarita with your entrée. Try the sizzling fajitas or create your own combo of chimichangas, tacos, and tamales and feel like you're south of the border. ✉ *202 S. Main St., Moab* ☎ *435/259–4366* ▭ *AE, D, MC, V.*

$–$$
AMERICAN

✕ **Jail House Café.** Only open for breakfast, the fare here should keep you going long into the afternoon. From eggs Benedict to waffles, the menu is designed to fill you up. Housed in what was once the county courthouse, the building actually held prisoners in the past. Plan your time carefully if you dine here; this is not fast food. ✉ *101 N. Main St., Moab* ☎ *435/259–3900* ▭ *AE, D, MC, V* ⊙ *No lunch or dinner. Closed Nov.–Feb.*

¢–$
MEXICAN

✕ **La Hacienda.** This family-run local favorite serves good south-of-the-border meals at an equally good price. The helpings are generous and the service is friendly. And yes, you can order a margarita. ✉ *574 N. Main St., Moab* ☎ *435/259–6319* ▭ *AE, MC, V.*

5

$-$$ ✕ **Moab Brewery.** You can always find someone to talk to about canyon
AMERICAN country adventure, since river runners, rock climbers, and locals all hang
  out here. There's a wide selection of menu choices, including fresh salads,
creative sandwiches, and hot soups. Try the gyros salad for a taste of
the Mediterranean, and cool off with house-made gelato. Last but not
least, this hot spot serves the best brew in town. ⊠ *686 S. Main, Moab*
435/259–6333 ⊕ *www.themoabbrewery.com* ═ *AE, D, MC, V.*

¢–$ ✕ **Moab Diner.** For breakfast, lunch, and dinner, this is the place where old-
AMERICAN time Moabites go. A mixture of good old-fashioned American food and
southwestern entrées gives you plenty to choose from. ⊠ *189 S. Main St.,*
Moab ☎ *435/259–4006* ⊕ *www.moabdiner.com* ═ *AE, D, MC, V.*

$-$$ ✕ **Pasta Jay's.** Mountain bikers, families, and couples pack this down-
ITALIAN town restaurant's patio from noon well into the evening. Perfect for the
  hungry adventurer, this bustling spot's friendly servers rapidly fill red-
checkered tablecloths with the likes of chicken Genovese (stuffed with
Italian sausage, roasted red peppers, provolone cheese and mushrooms
and baked in a tomato-basil sauce), pizza, and brew. A noisy motorcycle
passing by on Moab's main drag may cause you a moment's pause while
you're sipping a glass of Castle Creek wine, but it won't detract from
the energetic, bistro atmosphere. ⊠ *4 S. Main, Moab* ☎ *435/259–2900*
⊕ *www.pastajays.com* ═ *AE, MC, V.*

$$–$$$ ✕ **Sorrel River Grill.** The most scenic dining experience in the area is 17 mi
AMERICAN down the road from Moab at the Sorrel River Ranch. Both the casual dining room and the swankier upstairs seating have riverside outdoor dining,
which make the most of views over the Colorado, the La Sal Mountains,
and the red rock spires and towers surrounding the ranch. The seasonal
menu changes regularly for the freshest ingredients. Plenty of veggie entrées
round out the menu. ⊠ *Mile Marker 17.5, Rte. 128, Moab* ☎ *435/259–*
4642 ⊕ *www.sorrelriver.com* ═ *AE, D, MC, V* ⊘ *No lunch.*

$$–$$$ ✕ **Sunset Grill.** Housed in the cliff-side home of former uranium kingpin
AMERICAN Charlie Steen, this restaurant is a Moab landmark. The views into the
valley and of the Colorado River are magnificent, especially at sunset. The salmon is always reliable and the steaks are generously cut
and juicy. ⊠ *900 Hwy. 191., Moab* ☎ *435/259–7146* ═ *AE, D, MC, V*
⊘ *Closed Sun. No lunch.*

$-$$ ✕ **Zax.** Wood-fired pizza ovens are the focal point of this downtown
AMERICAN eatery and bar. Sit out on the patio to people watch or catch a game on
  one of the flat-screen TVs while dining at a spacious booth. For $13,
you can try the pizza-salad-soup buffet (a popular choice, so the pies
are constantly coming out of the oven), but don't overlook non-pizza
entrées such as mahimahi with mango salsa. The decor is contemporary southwestern and the staff is welcoming and attentive. Breakfast
is available Thursday through Monday from March through November. ⊠ *96 S. Main St., Moab* ☎ *435/259–6555* ⊕ *www.zaxmoab.com*
═ *AE, D, MC, V.*

WHERE TO STAY

IN THE PARK

CAMPING

$

★

Devils Garden Campground. This small campground is one of the most unusual—and gorgeous—in the national park system, and in the West, for that matter. Sites, which are tucked away into red rock outcroppings, are available on a first-come, first-served basis during the off-season, but March through October, campers are required to pre-register for a site (done at the visitor center between 7:30 and 8 AM, or at the campground entrance station after 8 AM). Also March through October, up to 28 of the campsites can be reserved in advance (at least four but no more than 240 days prior) by contacting National Recreation Reservation Service (NRRS) via phone or online. For the best views, pick a site at least halfway into the campground. **Pros:** incredible red rock surroundings; ample space between sites means privacy; pristine. **Cons:** requires early-bird ambition; some sites are exposed to the elements. ⊠ *18 mi from park entrance, off main road* ☎ *435/719–2299, 435/259–4351 group reservations, 877/444–6777 NRRS reservations* ⊕ *www.recreation.gov* ⚠ *54 tent/RV sites* ⚐ *Flush toilets, drinking water, fire grates, picnic tables* ☐ *No credit cards.*

OUTSIDE THE PARK

IN GREEN RIVER

$

Green River Comfort Inn. Right off Interstate 70, this reliable motel is convenient if you're only stopping for the night. There's a restaurant directly across the street. Rooms have a somewhat contemporary look, but mainly the decor is modern motel. **Pros:** convenient, clean and comfortable; close to Green River rafting action; kids under 18 stay for free. **Cons:** remote, sleepy town; close to I–70; not much in the way of dining or entertainment. ⊠ *1975 E. Main St., Green River* ☎ *435/564–3300* ⊕ *www.choicehotels.com* ⇆ *54 rooms, 3 suites* ⚐ *In-room: refrigerator, DVD (some), Wi-Fi. In-hotel: pool, gym, laundry facilities, Wi-Fi* ☐ *AE, D, DC, MC, V* ⊠ *CP.*

IN MOAB

$$–$$$

Adobe Abode. A lovely B&B near the nature preserve, this one-story inn surrounds you with solitude. When you're not out exploring, you can unwind in a picture-perfect common room with fireplace and Southwest decor. **Pros:** relaxing in the beautifully decorated common area; the entrée-of-the-day (sometimes ham and eggs or waffles) accompanying the Continental breakfast; peace and quiet. **Cons:** you can bicycle to town, but it's too far to walk; not the place for young children. ⊠ *778 W. Kane Creek Blvd., Moab* ☎ *435/260–2932 innkeeper's cell, 435/259–7716* ⊕ *www.adobeabodemoab.com* ⇆ *4 rooms, 2 suites* ⚐ *In-room: no phone, Wi-Fi. In-hotel: Wi-Fi, no kids under 16* ☐ *AE, D, MC, V* ⊠ *CP.*

$$–$$$

🐾

Best Western Canyonlands Inn. Remodeled in 2007, this comfortable, contemporary, impeccably clean hotel is ideally located in the center of Moab. It's within a few footsteps of many restaurants and shops, and within easy reach of the Mill Creek Parkway foot and bicycle trail. The staff is friendly and the rooms are quiet, despite the downtown location. Kids enjoy the playground, and both kids and grown-ups like the pool. **Pros:** downtown location; smiling and helpful staff; updated, sparkling rooms. **Cons:** no green space; for those seeking solitude, family-friendliness means the pool is bustling with happy children. ⊠ *16 S. Main St., Moab* ☎ *435/259–2300 or 800/649–5191* ⊕ *www.canyonlandsinn.com* ⌁ *46 rooms, 31 suites* ⌂ *In-room: kitchen (some), refrigerator, Internet (some), Wi-Fi. In-hotel: pool, gym, laundry facilities* ☰ *AE, D, DC, MC, V* ⍫ *BP.*

$$–$$$
Fodor's Choice
★

⊡ **Dream Keeper Inn.** Serenity is just a wish away at this B&B in a quiet Moab neighborhood, on large, shady grounds filled with flower and vegetable gardens. The rooms line a hallway in the ranch-style home, and each opens onto the pool, patio, and courtyard area, where you may want to have your morning coffee. Or, you may prefer to have breakfast in the sunny indoor dining area. Some rooms have jetted tubs; all have VCRs, and access to a large video collection. **Pros:** located on a quiet street; you can unwind in the shade near the pool; gourmet breakfast. **Cons:** you can't bring the kids along (which may be a pro for some). ⊠ *191 S. 200 East, Moab* ☎ *435/259–5998 or 888/230–3247* ⊕ *www. dreamkeeperinn.com* ⌁ *6 rooms* ⌂ *In-room: refrigerator, Wi-Fi. In-hotel: pool, Wi-Fi, no kids under 13* ☰ *AE, D, MC, V* ⍫ *BP.*

$

⊡ **Moab Springs Ranch.** About 1 mi from Arches and 1 mi from downtown Moab, this 18-acre property was first developed by William Granstaff (known not-so-politically-correctly in Moab as Negro Bill) in the late 1800s. The 1896 ranch house now houses the on-site restaurant, Desert Bistro (⇨ *Where to Eat),* and the meandering spring has given recent life to one-, two- and three-bedroom, contemporary, comfortable, spotless condos. Relax by the pool, splash in the stream, kick back on a hammock in the shade of sycamores, mulberry trees and cottonwoods, or fill water bottles directly from the clear spring. **Pros:** large green, shaded space filled with a natural spring and ponds; excellent on-site restaurant; new, comfortable condos. **Cons:** some Route 191 traffic noise might drift to your balcony or patio; too far to walk to downtown Moab. ⊠ *1266 N. Main St., Moab* ☎ *435/259–7891 or 888/259–5759* ⊕ *www. moabspringsranch.com* ⌁ *12 condo units* ⌂ *In-room: kitchen, refrigerator, DVD, Internet (some), Wi-Fi. In-hotel: restaurant, pool, laundry facilities, Wi-Fi* ☰ *AE, D, MC, V.*

$$$$
★

⊡ **Red Cliffs Adventure Lodge.** You can have it all at this gorgeous, classically western lodge. The Colorado River rolls by right outside your door, and canyon walls reach for the sky in all their red glory; you can gaze at it all from your private riverfront patio. Rooms are Western in flavor, with log furniture, lots of wood, and Saltillo tile. Added attractions include an on-site winery, a movie memorabilia museum, as well as guided rafting, biking, and horseback-riding adventures into the desert. The setting is fabulous, but note that you're 14 mi from town. **Pros:** ranch setting on the river; a smorgasbord of adventures; afternoon wine tasting. **Cons:** a ways from town. ⊠ *Rte. 128, mile marker 14, Moab* ☎ *435/259–2002 or 866/812–2002* ⊕ *www.redcliffslodge.com* ⌁ *79 rooms, 30 cabins, 1 suite* ⌂ *In-room: kitchen (some), refrigerators, Internet, Wi-Fi. In-hotel: restaurant, room service, bar, pool, tennis courts, gym, laundry facilities, Wi-Fi, some pets allowed* ☰ *AE, D, MC, V* ⍫ *CP.*

¢–$

⊡ **Red Stone Inn.** One of the best bargains near the parks, this motel offers small but adequate rooms in a location convenient to restaurants and shops. Knotty-pine walls and western furnishings give it a little more flair than most motels in this price range. **Pros:** walking distance to Moab restaurants and shops; the price is right. **Cons:** not a lot of green space nearby; no frills; petit rooms. ☒ *535 S. Main St., Moab* ☎ *435/259–3500 or 800/722–1972* ⊕ *www.moabredstone.com* ⇨ *52 rooms* ⌂ *In-room: refrigerator, DVD (some), Internet. In-hotel: pool, laundry facilities, some pets allowed* ⊟ *AE, D, MC, V.*

\$\$\$\$
Fodor'sChoice
★

🏨 **Sorrel River Ranch Resort & Spa.** This luxury ranch on the banks of the Colorado River 17 mi from Moab is the ultimate getaway. No matter which way you look in a landscape studded with towering red cliffs, buttes, and spires, the vista is spectacular. Rooms are furnished with hefty log beds, tables, and chairs, along with western art and rugs. Some of the bathtubs even have views of the river and sandstone cliffs. For an extra cost, you can choose to relax in the spa with aromatherapy and a pedicure, go river rafting or mountain biking, or take an ATV out for a spin. At the Sorrel River Grill (⇨ *Where to Eat*), the most scenic dining experience in the Moab area, the seasonal menu changes regularly to incorporate the freshest ingredients. **Pros:** swanky grounds and dining; comfortable, luxurious rooms; red rock setting away from town on the Colorado River. **Cons:** more than 17 mi from Moab; prices are befitting the luxury (i.e., steep). ☒ *Rte. 128, mile marker 17.5, 17 mi from Moab* ☎ *435/259–4642 or 877/359–2715* ⊕ *www.sorrelriver.com* ⇨ *23 rooms, 32 suites* ⌂ *In-room: refrigerator, DVD (some), Wi-Fi. In-hotel: restaurant, bar, room service, tennis court, pool, gym, spa, laundry service, Wi-Fi* ⊟ *AE, D, MC, V.*

CAMPING
\$\$–\$\$\$
☾

🏕 **Canyonlands Campground.** Although this camping park is in downtown Moab, you get the feeling you are in a shady retreat. Because it's downtown, all local attractions are convenient. **Pros:** in town; shade trees; all the camping amenities. **Cons:** sites are close together, so not much privacy; downtown, so it lacks the solitude of off-the-beaten-path campgrounds. ☒ *555 S. Main St., Moab* ☎ *435/259–6848 or 888/522–6848* ⊕ *www.canyonlandsrv.com* 🏕 *32 tent sites, 90 RV sites, 8 cabins* ⌂ *Flush toilets, full hookups, partial hookups (electric and water), dump station, drinking water, guest laundry, showers, grills, picnic tables, electricity, public telephone, general store, service station, play area, swimming (pool)* ⊟ *AE, D, MC, V.*

\$\$

🏕 **Slickrock Campground.** At one of Moab's older campgrounds you find lots of mature shade trees and all of the basic amenities—plus three hot tubs where adults have priority. About 3 mi from Arches National Park and next to Buck's Grill House, this can make a comfortable home base. Wi-Fi is available at the campground office but not at the individual sites. **Pros:** close to Arches and a top-notch restaurant; campfires allowed at these shady sites; clean and convenient. **Cons:** trees, but not much in the way of grass; you can almost reach out and touch your neighbor (i.e., sites are close); popular, and therefore busy, campground. ☒ *1301½ N. U.S. 191, Moab* ☎ *435/259–7660 or 800/448–8873* ⊕ *www.slickrockcampground.com* 🏕 *182 tent/RV sites (115 with hookups), 14 cabins* ⌂ *Flush toilets, full hookups, partial hookups (electric and water), dump station, drinking water, guest laundry, showers, grills, picnic tables, food service, electricity, public telephone, general store, swimming (pool), Wi-Fi* ⊟ *MC, V.*

$$–$$$ △ **Moab Valley RV Resort.** Near the Colorado River, this campground with
🕐   an expansive view seems to get bigger and better every year. Just 2 mi
★   from Arches National Park, it's convenient for sightseeing, river rafting,
and all types of area attractions and activities. On-site you can pitch some
horseshoes, perfect your putting, embark on a scavenger hunt, or soak in
the hot tub. Kids and parents alike will enjoy all the playgrounds, including a giant chess- and checkerboard. The place is spotlessly clean, with
everything from tent sites to cottages. **Pros:** plenty of family fun to be had;
close to Arches and relatively close to town; clean and welcoming. **Cons:**
tent sites are covered, but lack grass; big and fun also means busy; sites
are close to one another. ✉ *1773 N. U.S. 191, Moab* ☎ *435/259–4469*
⊕ *www.moabvalleyrv.com* △ *69 RV sites, 39 tent sites, 33 cabins* △ *Flush
toilets, full hookups, dump station, drinking water, guest laundry, showers, grills, picnic tables, electricity, public telephone, general store, play
area, swimming (pool), Wi-Fi* ▭ *AE, D, MC, V.*

$$$–$$$$ △ **Up the Creek Campground.** This neighborhood campground lies under
★   big cottonwoods on the banks of Mill Creek. Even though you are near
downtown, you'll feel like you're in the woods—the campground has
walk-in tent sites only. Dogs are allowed for an additional payment of
$5 per day. **Pros:** sleeping beside a creek; shade trees and grass; peace
and quiet of the walk-in campground setting. **Cons:** sorry, RVers: tents
only; no campfires; you have to schlep your gear from your car to the
site, but carts for hauling goods are provided. ✉ *210 E. 300 South,
Moab* ☎ *435/260–1888* ⊕ *www.moabupthecreek.com* △ *20 tent sites*
△ *Flush toilets, drinking water, showers, grills, picnic tables* ▭ *MC, V*
☾ *Mid-Mar.–Oct.*

Badlands National Park

WORD OF MOUTH

"I recently visited Badlands National Park as part of a two-week road trip. The bold colors of the mounds and sky, as well as the interesting cloud formations, really struck me. The clouds almost recreated the Badlands rock formations in the sky, and the weather allowed me to fully experience the dramatic landscape."

—photo by Andrew Mace, Fodors.com member

WELCOME TO BADLANDS

TOP REASONS TO GO

★ **Fossils:** From the mid-1800s, the fossil-rich Badlands area has welcomed paleontologists, research institutions, and fossil hunters who have discovered the fossil remnants of numerous species from ancient days.

★ **A world of wildlife:** Badlands National Park is home to a wide array of wildlife: antelope, deer, black-footed ferret, prairie dogs, rabbits, coyotes, foxes, badgers.

★ **Missiles:** The Minuteman Missile Silo, located at the entrance to the park, represents the only remaining intact components of a nuclear-missile field that consisted of 150 Minuteman II missiles and 15 launch control centers, and covered over 13,500 square mi of southwestern South Dakota.

★ **Stars aplenty:** Due to its remote location and vastly open country, Badlands National Park contains some of the clearest and cleanest air in the country, which makes it perfect for viewing the night sky.

1 North Unit. This is the most easily accessible of the three units and attracts the most visitors. It includes the Badlands Wilderness Area.

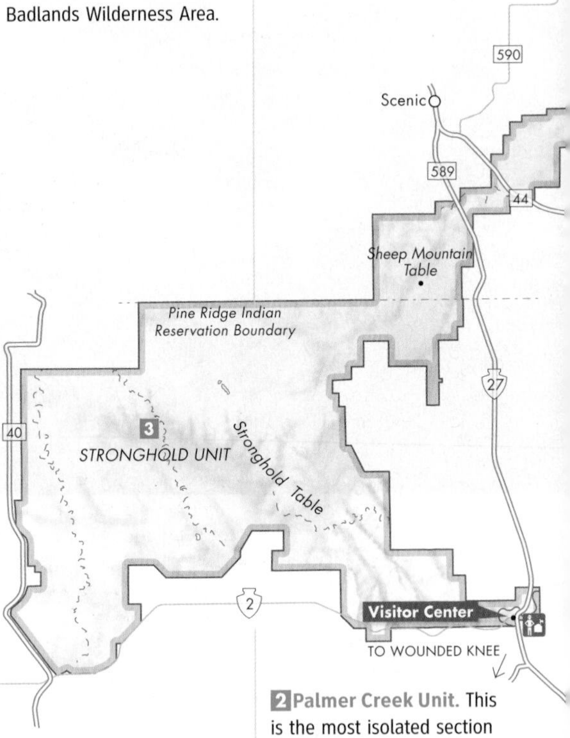

Scenic

590

589

44

Sheep Mountain Table

Pine Ridge Indian Reservation Boundary

27

40

3 STRONGHOLD UNIT

Stronghold Table

2

Visitor Center

TO WOUNDED KNEE

2 Palmer Creek Unit. This is the most isolated section of the park—no recognized roads pass through its borders. You must obtain permission from private landowners to pass through their property (contact the White River Visitor Center on how to do so). If you plan on exploring here, count on spending two days—one day to hike in and one day out.

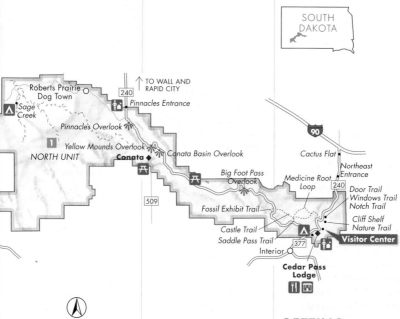

SOUTH DAKOTA

TO WALL AND RAPID CITY

Roberts Prairie Dog Town

Sage Creek

Pinnacles Entrance

Pinnacles Overlook

Yellow Mounds Overlook

1

NORTH UNIT

Conata ◆

Conata Basin Overlook

Cactus Flat

90

Big Foot Pass Overlook

Northeast Entrance

Medicine Root Loop

240

Door Trail

Windows Trail

Notch Trail

Fossil Exhibit Trail

509

Castle Trail

Saddle Pass Trail

Cliff Shelf Nature Trail

Visitor Center

377

Interior

Cedar Pass Lodge

6

0   4 mi
0   4 km

2

PALMER CREEK UNIT

TO WOUNDED KNEE

KEY
🏠 Ranger Station
⛺ Campground
🌲 Picnic Area
🍴 Restaurant
🖼 Lodge
🚶 Trailhead
🚻 Restrooms
➤ Scenic Viewpoint
⋯⋯ Walking/Hiking Trails

3 Stronghold Unit. This was used as a gunnery range for the United States Air Force and the South Dakota National Guard from 1942 until the late 1960s. Discarded remnants and unexploded ordnance make this area potentially dangerous, so mind your step here. If you do find fragments of this era, do not handle them. Report the location to a ranger.

GETTING ORIENTED

The park is divided into three units: the North Unit, and the southern Stronghold and Palmer units. The two southern units are within Pine Ridge Indian Reservation and are jointly managed by the National Park Service and the Oglala Sioux Tribe. Much of the southern park is accessible only on foot or horseback, or by a high-clearance four-wheel drive or ATV.

BADLANDS PLANNER

When to Go

Most visitors see the park between Memorial Day and Labor Day. The park's vast size and isolation prevent it from ever being too packed—**though it is usually crowded the first week of August,** when hundreds of thousands of motorcycle enthusiasts flock to the Black Hills for the annual Sturgis Motorcycle Rally. In summer, temperatures typically hover around 90°F—though it can get as hot as 116°F—and sudden mid-afternoon thunderstorms are not unusual. Storms put on a spectacular show of thunder and lightning, but it rarely rains for more than 10 or 15 minutes (the average annual rainfall is 15 inches). Autumn weather is generally sunny and warm. Snow usually appears by late October. Winter can be as low as -40°F. Early spring is often wet, cold, and unpredictable. By May the weather usually stabilizes, bringing pleasant 70°F days.

Ave. High/Low Temps

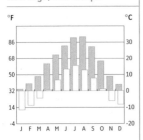

Flora and Fauna

The park's sharply defined cliffs, canyons, and mesas are near-deserts with little plant growth. Most of the park, however, is made up of mixed-grass prairies, where more than 460 species of hardy grasses and wildflowers flourish in the warmer months. Prairie coneflower, yellow plains prickly pear, pale-green yucca, buffalo grass, and sideoats grama are just a few of the plants on the badlands plateau. Trees and shrubs are rare and usually confined to dry creek beds. The most common trees are Rocky Mountain junipers and Plains cottonwoods.

It's common to see pronghorn antelope and mule deer dart across the flat plateaus; bison grazing on the buttes; prairie dogs and sharp-tailed grouse; and, soaring above, golden eagles, turkey vultures, and hawks. Also present are coyotes, swift foxes, jackrabbits, bats, gophers, porcupines, skunks, bobcats, horned lizards, bighorn sheep, and prairie rattlers. The latter are the only venomous reptiles in the park—watch for them near rocky outcroppings. Backcountry hikers might consider heavy boots and long pants reinforced with leather or canvas. Although rarely seen, weasels, mountain lions, and the endangered black-footed ferret roam the park.

Getting Here and Around

Badlands National Park is 70 mi east of Rapid City and 73 mi northeast of Wind Cave National Park in western South Dakota. It's accessed via exit 110 or 131 off Interstate 90, or Route 44 east to Route 377. Few roads, paved or otherwise, pass within the park. Badlands Loop Road (Route 240) is the most traveled and the only one that intersects I-90. It's well maintained and rarely crowded. Parts of Route 44 and Route 27 run at the fringes of the badlands, connecting the visitor centers and Rapid City. Unpaved roads should be traveled with care when wet. Sheep Mountain Table Road, the only public road into the Stronghold Unit, is impassable when wet, with deep ruts—sometimes only high-clearance vehicles can get through. Off-road driving is prohibited. There's free parking at visitor centers, overlooks, and trailheads.

By T. D. Griffith and Dustin D. Floyd

So stark and forbidding are the chiseled spires, ragged ridgelines, and deep ravines of South Dakota's badlands that Lieutenant Colonel George Custer once described them as "hell with the fires burned out." Although a bit more accessible than the depths of the underworld, the landscape is easily the strangest in the Great Plains. Ruthlessly ravaged over the ages by wind and rain, the 380 square mi of wild terrain continue to erode and evolve, sometimes visibly changing shape in a few days. Prairie creatures thrive on the untamed territory, and animal fossils are in abundance.

6

PARK ESSENTIALS

ACCESSIBILITY
Cedar Pass Lodge and the visitor centers are all fully wheelchair accessible. The Fossil Exhibit Trail and the Window Trail have reserved parking and are accessible by ramp, although they are quite steep in places. The Door, Cliff Shelf, and Prairie Wind trails are accessible by boardwalk. Cedar Pass Campground has two fully accessible sites, plus many other sites that are sculpted and easily negotiated by wheelchair users; its office and amphitheater also are accessible. The Bigfoot picnic area has reserved parking, ramps, and an accessible pit toilet. Other areas of the park can be difficult or impossible to navigate by those with limited mobility.

ADMISSION FEES AND PERMITS
The entrance fee is $7 per person or $15 per vehicle, and is good for seven days. A annual park pass is $30. A backcountry permit isn't required for hiking or camping in Badlands National Park, but it's a good idea to check in at park headquarters before setting out on a backcountry journey. Backpackers may set up camps anywhere except within a half mile of roads or trails. Open fires are prohibited.

ADMISSION HOURS
The park is open 24/7 year-round and is in the mountain time zone.

ATMS/BANKS
An ATM is located at Cedar Pass Lodge; other ATMs may be found in surrounding communities. The nearest full-service bank is in Wall.

CELL-PHONE RECEPTION
Usually near the interstate you can pick up a cell-phone signal, but within the majority of the park there is no service. You'll find pay phones at the Cedar Pass Lodge and Cedar Pass Campground.

PARK CONTACT INFORMATION
Badlands National Park ✆ *P.O. Box 6, Interior, SD 57750* ☎ *605/433–5361* ⊕ *www.nps.gov/badl.*

SCENIC DRIVES

For the average visitor, a casual drive is the essential means by which to see Badlands National Park. To do the scenery justice, drive slowly, and don't hesitate to get out and explore on foot when the occasion calls for it.

★ **Badlands Loop Road.** The simplest drive is on two-lane Badlands Loop Road (Route 240). The drive circles from exit 110 off Interstate 90 through the park and back to the interstate at exit 131. Start from either end and make your way around to the various overlooks along the way. Pinnacles and Yellow Mounds overlooks are outstanding places to examine the sandy pink- and brown-toned ridges and spires distinctive to the badlands. At a certain point the landscape flattens out slightly to the north, revealing spectacular views of mixed-grass prairies. The Cedar Pass area of the drive has some of the park's best trails.

WHAT TO SEE

HISTORIC SITES
Big Pig Dig. Until August 2008, paleontologists dug for fossils at this site named for a large fossil originally thought to be of a prehistoric pig (it actually turned out to be a small, hornless rhinoceros). Visitors will find interpretive signage detailing fossils discovered at the site. ⊠ *Conata Picnic Area, 17 mi northwest of the Ben Reifel Visitor Center.*

Stronghold Unit. With few paved roads and no campgrounds, the park's southwest section is difficult to access without a four-wheel-drive or high-clearance vehicle. However, if you're willing to trek, the unit's isolation provides a rare opportunity to explore badlands rock formations and prairies completely undisturbed. From 1942 to 1968 the U.S. Air Force and South Dakota National Guard used much of the Stronghold Unit as a gunnery range. Hundreds of fossils were destroyed by bomber pilots, who frequently targeted the large fossil remains of an elephant-size titanothere (an extinct relative of the rhinoceros), which gleamed bright white from the air. Beware of such remnants as old automobiles turned targets, unexploded bombs, shells, rockets, and other hazardous materials. If you see unexploded ordnance (UXO) while hiking in the Stronghold Unit, steer clear of it and find another route—however, note

BADLANDS IN ONE DAY

With a packed lunch and plenty of water, arrive at the park via the northeast entrance (off I–90 at exit 131) and follow Route 240 (Badlands Loop Road) southwest toward the **Ben Reifel Visitor Center.** You can pick up park maps and information here, and also pay the park entrance fee (if the booth at the entrance was closed).

Next, stop at the **Big Badlands Overlook,** just south of the northeast entrance, to get a good feel for the landscape. As you head toward the visitor center, hike any one of several trails you'll pass, or if you prefer guided walks, arrive at the visitor center in time to look at the exhibits and talk with rangers before heading down to the Fossil Exhibit Trail, where you can join the Fossil Talk at 10:30 AM (with repeats at 1:30 and 3:30 PM), usually available from early June to mid-August. Even if you miss the talk, hike this ¼-mi trail before your morning is over. The badlands are one of the richest fossil fields in the world, and along the trail are examples of six extinct creatures, now protected under clear plastic domes. After your walk, drive a couple of miles to the **Big Foot Pass Overlook,** up on the right. Here you can enjoy a packed lunch amid grassy prairies, with the rocky badland formations all around you.

After lunch, continue driving along Badlands Loop Road, stopping at the various overlooks for views and a hike or two. Near the Conata Picnic Area, you'll find the **Big Pig Dig,** a fossil site that was excavated by paleontologists through the summer of 2008. When you reach the junction with **Sage Creek Rim Road,** turn left and follow it along the northern border of the 100-square-mi **Badlands Wilderness Area,** which is home to hundreds of bison. Provided the road is dry, take a side trip 5 mi down Sage Creek Rim Road to **Roberts Prairie Dog Town,** inhabited by a huge colony of the chattering critters. Children will love to watch these small rodents, which bark warning calls and dive underground if you get too close to their colony. The animals built burrow networks that once covered the Great Plains, but since European settlers established ranches in the region during the late 19th century, prairie dogs have become a far rarer sight. The park is less developed the farther you travel on Sage Creek Rim Road, allowing you to admire the sheer isolation and untouched beauty of badlands country. Hold out for a glorious sunset over the shadows of the nearby Black Hills, and keep your eyes open for animals stirring about.

6

the location so you can report it to a ranger later. Within the Stronghold Unit, the **Stronghold Table,** a 3-mi-long plateau, can be reached only by crossing a narrow land bridge just wide enough to let a wagon pass. It was here, just before the Massacre at Wounded Knee in 1890, that some 600 Sioux gathered to perform one of the last known Ghost Dances, a ritual in which the Sioux wore white shirts that they believed would protect them from bullets. Permission from private landowners is required to gain access to the table; contact the White River Visitor Center for details. ✉ *North and west of White River Visitor Center; entrance off Hwy. 27.*

People in the Park

Much of the credit for setting aside South Dakota's badlands as public lands is owed to Peter Norbeck, a powerful politician who was also largely responsible for establishing nearby Custer State Park and obtaining federal funding for Mount Rushmore National Memorial. Convinced that the state's badlands formations were more distinctive than those in other parts of the American West, Norbeck began lobbying for a new national park almost immediately after he was elected a U.S. Senator in 1920. Political maneuvering tied up the proposal in Congress for nearly 10 years, and land issues delayed the measure for another decade. Finally, on March 4, 1929, the region was declared Badlands National Monument by President Calvin Coolidge. It was promoted to a national park in 1978.

SCENIC STOPS

★ **Badlands Wilderness Area.** Covering about 25% of the park, this 100-square-mi area is part of the United States' largest prairie wilderness. About two-thirds of the Sage Creek region is mixed-grass prairie, making it the ideal grazing grounds for bison, pronghorn, and many of the park's other native animals. The Hay Butte Overlook 2 mi northwest on Sage Creek Rim Road and the Pinnacles Overlook 1 mi south of the Pinnacles entrance are the best places to get an overview of the wilderness area. Feel free to park beside the road and hike your own route into the untamed, unmarked prairie—just remember that all water is unfit for drinking. ⊠ *25 mi northwest of Ben Reifel Visitor Center.*

Big Badlands Overlook. From this spot just south of the park's northeast entrance, 90% of the park's 1 million annual visitors get their first views of the White River Badlands. ⊠ *5 mi northeast of the Ben Reifel Visitor Center.*

⟳ **Roberts Prairie Dog Town.** Once a homestead, the site today contains one of the country's largest (if not the largest) colonies of black-tailed prairie dogs. ⊠ *5 mi west of Badlands Loop Rd. on Sage Creek Rim Rd.*

Yellow Mounds Overlook. Contrasting sharply with the whites, grays, and browns of the badlands pinnacles, the mounds viewed from here greet you with soft yet vivid yellows, reds, and purples. ⊠ *16 mi northwest of the Ben Reifel Visitor Center.*

VISITOR CENTERS

Ben Reifel Visitor Center. Open year-round, this is the park's main information hub. Stop here on your way in to pick up brochures and maps. A 22-minute video about Badlands geology and wildlife runs continually. The facility is named for a Sioux activist and the first Lakota to serve in Congress. Born on the nearby Rosebud Indian Reservation, Ben Reifel also served in the Army during World War II. ⊠ *On Badlands Loop Rd., near Hwy. 377 junction, 8 mi from northeast entrance* ☎ 605/433–5361 ⊙ *June 4–Aug. 19, daily 7 AM–8 PM; Aug. 20–Sept. 9, daily 8–6; Sept. 10–June 3, daily 9–4.*

White River Visitor Center. Open only three months out of the year, this small center serves almost exclusively serious hikers and campers venturing into the Stronghold or Palmer units. If you're heading into one of the southern units, stop here for maps and details about road and trail conditions. The center is located on the Pine Ridge Indian Reservation. While here, you can see fossils and Lakota artifacts, and learn about Sioux culture. ✉ *25 mi south of Hwy. 44 via Hwy. 27* ☎ *605/455–2878* ☺ *June–Aug., daily 10–4.*

SPORTS AND THE OUTDOORS

Pure, unspoiled, empty space is the greatest asset of Badlands National Park, and it can only be experienced to its highest degree if you're on foot. Spring and autumn are the best times of the year to do wilderness exploring, since the brutal extremes of summer and winter can—and do—kill. In fact, the two biggest enemies to hikers and bicyclists in the Badlands are heat and lightning. Before you venture out, make sure you have at least one gallon of water per person per day, and be prepared to take shelter from freak thunderstorms, which often strike in the late afternoon with little warning.

AIR TOURS

OUTFITTER AND EXPEDITIONS

★ Owned and operated for 25 years by Steve Bower, **Black Hills Balloons** (☎ *605/673–2520* ⊕ *www.blackhillsballoons.com* ✉ *$245–$500*), based in Custer, provides amazing bird's-eye views of some of the Black Hills' most picturesque locations. Reservations are essential.

BICYCLING

Bicycles are permitted only on designated roads, which may be paved or unpaved. They are prohibited from closed roads, trails, and the backcountry. Flat-resistant tires are recommended.

Sheep Mountain Table Road. This 7-mi dirt road in the Stronghold Unit is ideal for mountain biking, but should be biked only when dry. The terrain is level for the first 3 mi; then it climbs the table and levels out again. At the top you can take in great views of the area. ✉ *About 14 mi north of the White River Visitor Center.*

OUTFITTER Family-owned and -operated **Two Wheeler Dealer Cycle and Fitness** (☎ *605/343–0524* ⊕ *www.twowheelerdealer.com*), founded in 1972 and based in Rapid City, stocks more than 1,000 new bikes for sale or rent. Service is exceptional. Get trail and route information for Badlands National Park and the Black Hills at the counter.

BIRD-WATCHING

Especially around sunset, get set to watch the badlands come to life. More than 215 bird species have been recorded in the area, including herons, pelicans, cormorants, egrets, swans, geese, hawks, golden and bald eagles, falcons, vultures, cranes, doves, and cuckoos. Established roads and trails are the best places from which to watch for nesting species. The Cliff Shelf Nature Trail and the Castle Trail, which both traverse areas with surprisingly thick vegetation, are especially good locations. You may even catch sight of a rare burrowing owl at the Roberts Prairie Dog Town. Be sure to bring along a pair of binoculars.

6

HIKING

Fossil Exhibit Trail and Cliff Shelf Nature Trail are must-dos, but even these popular trails are primitive, so don't expect to see bathrooms or any hiking surfaces other than packed dirt and gravel. Because the weather here can be so variable, rangers suggest that you be prepared for anything. Wear sunglasses, a hat, and long pants, and have rain gear available. It's illegal to interfere with park resources, which includes everything from rocks and fossils to plants and artifacts. Stay at least 100 yards away from wildlife. Due to the dry climate, open fires are never allowed. Tell friends, relatives, and the park rangers if you're going to embark on a multiday expedition. If you have a cell phone with you, assume that it won't get a signal in the park. But most importantly of all, be sure to bring your own water. Sources of water in the park are few and far between, and none of them are drinkable. All water in the park is contaminated by minerals and sediment, and park authorities warn that it's untreatable. If you're backpacking into the wilderness, bring at least a gallon of water per person per day. For day hikes, rangers suggest you drink at least a quart per person per hour.

> **TIPS FOR MULTIDAY TRIPS**
>
> Before you begin a multiday visit to the badlands, stock up on enough drinking water and food; both resources are hard to come by in the park. This is especially true in the backcountry, where water is so laden with silt and minerals that it's impossible to purify. Also bring a compass, topographical map, and rain gear.

EASY

Fossil Exhibit Trail. The trail, in place since 1964, has fossils of early mammals displayed under glass along its ¼-mi length, which is now completely wheelchair accessible. Give yourself at least an hour to fully enjoy this popular hike. ⊠ *Trail begins 5 mi northwest of the Ben Reifel Visitor Center, off Hwy. 240.*

Fodor's Choice ★

Window Trail. This 200-yard round-trip trail ends at a natural hole, or window, in a rock wall. Looking though, you'll see more of the distinctive badlands pinnacles and spires. ⊠ *Trail begins 2 mi north of the Ben Reifel Visitor Center, off Hwy. 240.*

MODERATE

★ **Cliff Shelf Nature Trail.** This ½-mi loop winds through a wooded prairie oasis in the middle of dry, rocky ridges and climbs 200 feet to a peak above White River Valley for an incomparable view. Look for chipmunks, squirrels, and red-winged blackbirds in the wet wood, and eagles, hawks, and vultures at hilltop. Even casual hikers can complete this trail in far less than an hour, but if you want to observe the true diversity of wildlife present here, stay longer. ⊠ *Trail begins 1 mi east of the Ben Reifel Visitor Center, off Hwy. 240.*

Notch Trail. One of the park's more interesting hikes, this 1½-mi round-trip trail takes you over moderately difficult terrain and up a ladder. Winds at the notch can be fierce, but it's worth lingering for the view of the White River Valley and the Pine Ridge Indian Reservation. If you take a couple of breaks and enjoy the views, you'll probably want to plan on spending a little more than an hour on this hike. ⊠ *Trail begins 2 mi north of the Ben Reifel Visitor Center, off Hwy. 240.*

DIFFICULT

Saddle Pass Trail. This route, which connects with Castle Trail and Medicine Root Loop, is a steep, ¼-mi climb up and down the side of "The Wall," an impressive rock formation. Plan on spending about an hour on this climb. ⊠ *Trail begins 2 mi west of the Ben Reifel Visitor Center, off Hwy. 240.*

HORSEBACK RIDING

★ The park has one of the largest and most beautiful territories in the state in which to ride a horse. Riding is allowed in most of the park except for some marked trails, roads, and developed areas. The mixed-grass prairie of the Badlands Wilderness Area is especially popular with riders. However, note that the weather in the Badlands Wilderness Area can be very unpredictable. Only experienced riders or people accompanied by experienced riders should venture far from more developed areas.

There are several restrictions and regulations that you must be aware of if you plan to ride your own horse. Potable water for visitors and animals is a rarity. Riders must bring enough water for themselves and their stock. Only certified weed-free hay is approved in the park. Horses are not allowed to run free within the borders of the park. It's essential that all visitors with horses contact park officials for other restrictions that may apply.

OUTFITTER A local outfitter since 1968, **Gunsel Horse Adventures** (☎ 605/343–7608
★ ⊕ *www.gunselhorseadventures.com* ✉ *$250 per day*) arranges pack trips into the badlands, Black Hills National Forest, and Buffalo Gap National Grassland. The four-day trips are based in one central campsite and are all-inclusive; you bring your own sleeping bag. Also available are 7- and 10-day trips. Reservations are essential.

EDUCATIONAL OFFERINGS

RANGER PROGRAMS

Evening Program. Watch a 40-minute outdoor audiovisual presentation on the wildlife, natural history, paleontology, or another aspect of the badlands. The shows typically begin around 9 PM. Check with a ranger for exact times and topics. ⊠ *Cedar Pass Campground amphitheater* ⊗ *Mid-June–mid-Aug., daily usually around 9 PM.*

Fossil Talk. What were the badlands like many years ago? This tour of protected fossil exhibits will inspire and answer all your questions. ⊠ *Fossil Exhibit Trail, 5 mi west of the Ben Reifel Visitor Center* ⊗ *Mid-June–mid-Aug., daily at 10:30 AM, 1:30 PM, and 3:30 PM.*

Geology Walk. Learn the geologic story of the White River badlands in a 45-minute walk. The terrain can be rough in places, so be sure to wear hiking boots or sneakers. A hat is a good idea, too. ⊠ *Door and Window trails parking area, 2 mi east of the Ben Reifel Visitor Center* ⊗ *Mid-June–mid-Aug., daily at 8:30 AM.*

Junior Ranger Program. Children ages 7–12 may participate in this 45-minute adventure, typically a short hike, game, or other hands-on

BLACK HILLS AND BADLANDS TOURS

★ **Affordable Adventures Badlands Tour.** Take a seven-hour narrated tour through the park and surrounding badlands for $110 per person. Tours can easily be customized and are available year-round. 🔗 *P.O. Box 203, Box Elder 57719* . ☎ *605/342-7691 or 888/888-8249* ⊕ *www.affordableadventuresbh.com* 💲 *$110.*

Golden Circle Tours. This company gives a seven-hour, narrated van tour out of Custer to several venues, including Mount Rushmore, Crazy Horse Memorial, and Custer State Park. Other Black Hills tours are available. ⊠ *695 W. Mt. Rushmore Rd., Custer* ☎ *605/673-4349* ⊕ *www.goldencircletours.com* 💲 *$73 for main tour* ⊗ *Apr. 15–Oct. 15, weather permitting.*

Gray Line of the Black Hills. This outfit offers bus tours from Rapid City to Mount Rushmore, Black Hills National Forest, Custer State Park, and Crazy Horse Memorial, as well as other tours tied to special events such as the Mount Rushmore fireworks and the Custer State Park Buffalo Roundup. ⊠ *1600 E. St. Patrick St., Rapid City* ☎ *800/456-4461* ⊕ *www.blackhillsgrayline.com* 💲 *$60–$65* ⊗ *May–Oct.*

★ ⏾ **Mount Rushmore Tours.** Beginning at Fort Hayes on the *Dances with Wolves* film set and then moving to Mount Rushmore, Custer State Park, and Crazy Horse Memorial, this nine-hour trip around the Black Hills includes a cowboy show plus breakfast and dinner (guests are responsible for their own lunch at the State Game Lodge). ⊠ *2255 Fort Hayes Dr., Rapid City* ☎ *888/343-3113* ⊕ *www. rushmoretours.com* 💲 *$74* ⊗ *Mid-May–mid-Oct.*

activity focused on badlands wildlife, geology, or fossils. Parents are welcome. ⊠ *Cedar Pass Campground amphitheater* ☎ *605/433–5361* ⊗ *June–Aug., daily at 10:30* AM.

WHAT'S NEARBY

Badlands National Park is situated off Interstate 90 with two separate entrances. Badlands can be a one- or two-day stop for visitors who are traveling through the area or a place of frequent visits to locals. Located 50 mi east of the edge of the Black Hills (and Rapid City, the largest community on this side of the state), Badlands allows travelers a unique stop in a highly dense area of national parks, monuments, and memorials. Its close proximity to national treasures such as Mount Rushmore National Memorial, Wind Cave National Park, Jewel Cave National Monument, Devils Tower National Monument, and Custer State Park allow visitors to take in a wealth of sightseeing excursions in a relatively small area. The Black Hills provide a wonderful backdrop for the dry canyon and dusty buttes of the badlands.

FESTIVALS AND EVENTS

JANUARY–FEBRUARY

Black Hills Stock Show and Rodeo. Watch world-champion wild-horse races, bucking horses, timed sheepdog trials, draft-horse contests, and steer wrestling during this two-week-long professional rodeo at the Rushmore Plaza Civic Center in Rapid City. Don't miss the stockman's banquet and ball. ☎ 605/258–2863.

MARCH

Badlands Quilters Weekend Getaway. A three-day display of the region's finest hand- and machine-made quilts, plus quilting classes, demonstrations, and sales, are held in Wall's community center. ☎ 605/279–2945.

JUNE–AUGUST

Red Cloud Indian Art Show. American Indian artists' paintings and sculptures are the focus of this 11-week-long exhibition, beginning on the second Sunday in June, at the Red Cloud Indian School in Pine Ridge. ☎ 605/867–5491.

NEARBY TOWNS

6

Built against a steep ridge of badland rock, **Wall** was founded in 1907 as a railroad station, and is among the closest towns to Badlands National Park, 8 mi from the Pinnacles entrance to the North Unit. Wall is home to about 850 residents and the world-famous Wall Drug Store, best known for its fabled jackalopes and free ice water. **Pine Ridge,** about 35 mi south of the Stronghold Unit, is on the cusp of Pine Ridge Indian Reservation. The town was established in 1877 as an Indian agency for Chief Red Cloud and his band of followers. With 2,800 square mi, the reservation, home, and headquarters of the Oglala Sioux, is second in size only to Arizona's Navajo Reservation. **Rapid City,** in the eastern buttes of the Black Hills, is South Dakota's second-largest city and a good base from which to explore the treasures of the state's south-western corner, including the neighboring Black Hills National Forest, the badlands 70 mi to the east, and Mount Rushmore and Wind Cave National Park, 25 mi and 50 mi to the south respectively.

VISITOR INFORMATION

Oglala Sioux Tribe (Pine Ridge) ☝ *P.O. Box 570, Kyle, SD 57764* ☎ *605/455–2584.* **Rapid City Chamber of Commerce, and Convention and Visitors Bureau** ✉ *444 Mt. Rushmore Rd. N, Rapid City 57701* ☎ *605/343–1744 or 800/487–3223* ⊕ *www.rapidcitycvb.com.* **Wall–Badlands Area Chamber of Commerce** ✉ *501 Main St., Wall 57790* ☎ *605/279–2665 or 888/852–9255* ⊕ *www.wall-badlands.com.*

NEARBY ATTRACTIONS

For attractions in Rapid City and the Black Hills, ⇨ *Wind Cave National Park (chapter 36).*

Fodor'sChoice ★ **Mount Rushmore National Memorial.** One of the nation's most popular attractions, the giant likenesses of Washington, Jefferson, Lincoln, and Theodore Roosevelt lie just 65 mi west of Badlands. An excellent visitor center and viewing station makes the trip even more pleasurable. ⇨ *For more on Mount Rushmore, see Wind Cave National Park, chapter 36.* ✉ *Rte. 244, Keystone* ☎ *605/574–2523* 🌐 *www.nps.gov/moru* 🎫 *Parking $10* ⏲ *Monument daily 24 hrs; visitor facilities and museums hrs vary.*

FAMILY PICKS

- Badlands Loop Tour
- Fossil Exhibit Trail
- Mount Rushmore
- Robert's Prairie Dog Town
- Wall Drug

Fodor's Choice ★ **Wall Drug Store.** This South Dakota original got its start by offering free ice water to road-weary travelers. Today its four dining rooms seat 520 visitors. The walls are covered with art for sale. A life-size mechanical Cowboy Orchestra and Chuckwagon Quartet greet you in the store, and in the Wall Drug backyard you'll see an animated T. rex and replicas of Mount Rushmore and a native village. The attached Western Mall has 14 shops selling all kinds of souvenirs, from T-shirts to fudge. ✉ *510 Main St., Wall* ☎ *605/279–2175* 🌐 *www.walldrug.com* 🎫 *Free* ⏲ *Late May–early Sept., daily 6 AM–10 PM; early Sept.–late May, daily 6:30–6.*

Wounded Knee Historical Site. A solitary stone obelisk commemorates the site of the December 29, 1890, massacre at Wounded Knee, the last major conflict between the U.S. military and American Indians. Only a handful of visitors make pilgrimages to the remote site today, which is simple and largely unchanged from its 1890 appearance. Nonetheless, in a society that still largely forgets the last days of the Indian Wars—and mostly ignores this part of the country, which is among the most impoverished parts of the nation—a visit to this site has never been more important. ✉ *12 mi northwest of Pine Ridge, along U.S. 18* 🎫 *Free* ⏲ *24/7 year-round.*

★ **Wounded Knee: The Museum.** This modern facility interprets the history of the December 29, 1890, Wounded Knee Massacre through interactive exhibits with historical photos and documents. Although a tour of the museum is an excellent companion to a visit to the actual site of the massacre, many visitors choose to stop at this convenient location off Interstate 90 in lieu of a stop at the isolated battleground 80 mi to the south. ✉ *207 10th Ave., Wall* ☎ *605/279–2573* 🌐 *www.woundedkneemuseum.org* 🎫 *$4* ⏲ *Apr.–mid-Oct., daily 8:30 AM–5:30 PM.*

WHERE TO EAT AND STAY

ABOUT THE RESTAURANTS

Dining on the prairies of South Dakota has always been a casual and family-oriented experience, and in that sense, very little has changed in the past century. Even the fare, which consists largely of steak and potatoes, has stayed consistent (in fact, in some towns, "vegetarian" can be a dirty word). But for its lack of comparative sophistication, the grub in the restaurants surrounding Badlands National Park is typically very good. You'll probably never have a better steak—beef or buffalo—outside this area. You should also try cuisine influenced by American

Wounded Knee Massacre

In late December 1890 the men of the 7th Cavalry, armed with a federal mandate (and some light artillery), intercepted a group of 350 Lakota in southwest South Dakota with the intention of disarming them and marching them to Nebraska, where they would be forced onto scattered reservations. The disarming process was remarkably peaceful—that is, until soldiers approached a warrior named Black Coyote. According to several accounts, Black Coyote wouldn't relinquish his weapon without compensation, since he had bought the firearm himself. Somehow, a weapon was discharged, and at least one soldier ordered the troops to open fire. Fearful of an impending attack, the cavalry did so, even bringing their artillery to bear on the Lakota camp. Warriors scrambled to retrieve their seized rifles to re-arm themselves. By the time the smoke had cleared, about 150 Lakota and 25 U.S. soldiers lay dead. While most of the remaining Lakota managed to escape, the majority perished in the elements, the victims of a sudden blizzard. When a burial party returned to the site after the storm, they found the frozen and contorted bodies of nearly 300 Lakota, mostly women and children, which they placed in a common grave.

Lakota Chief Spotted Elk (later known as Big Foot)

In the following days, newspapers and government officials referred to the confrontation as a "battle," but it was none other than wholesale slaughter. Within a year, the army had awarded 23 Medals of Honor to members of the Seventh Cavalry for "valor" shown in the carnage (modern-day activists are seeking to have them rescinded). Even so, there was no cover-up of this affair. The American people were incensed, and from this point on, any government-led extermination of the Indian people ended. The blood in the snow at Wounded Knee melted in the spring of 1891, and as it thawed and ran across the prairie in a thousand rivulets, it carried with it a way of life for the American Indian.

Indian cooking. The most popular (and well-known) is the Indian taco, made from spiced meat and flat bread. In the park itself there's only one restaurant. The food is quite good, but don't hesitate to explore other options farther afield. You'll find the most choices in Wall.

ABOUT THE HOTELS

Badlands National Park is oft visited by families on a vacation to see the American West, but very few opt to stay overnight here, especially when there's a profusion of accommodations in the Black Hills, situated a mere 50 mi east. As a result, there are very few lodging options in and around the park, and if you're determined to bed down within park boundaries, you have only one choice: Cedar Pass Lodge. Though rustic, it's comfortable and inexpensive.

The rustic-but-comfy formula is repeated by the area's few motels, hotels, and inns. Most are chain hotels in Wall, grouped around the interstate. Whether you stay inside or outside the park, you shouldn't ever have to worry about making reservations very far in advance, except during the first full week of August, when the entire region is inundated with more than half a million motorcyclists for the annual Sturgis Motorcycle Rally. Rooms for miles around book up more than a year in advance.

ABOUT THE CAMPGROUNDS

Pitching a tent and sleeping under the stars is one of the greatest ways to fully experience the sheer isolation and unadulterated empty spaces of Badlands National Park. You'll find two relatively easy-access campgrounds within park boundaries, but only one has any sort of amenities. The second is little more than a flat patch of ground with some signs. Unless you desperately need a flush toilet to have an enjoyable camping experience, you're just as well off hiking into the wilderness and choosing your own campsite. The additional isolation will be well worth the extra effort. You can set up camp anywhere that's at least ½ mi from a road or trail, and is not visible from any road or trail.

The handful of campgrounds located outside the park typically have more of the accoutrements of civilization. These more developed sites are more likely to attract vacationing retirees and young families, while the primitive campgrounds (and wilderness areas) seem to draw younger outdoors enthusiasts. Pets are almost universally accepted, but remember to check with each individual campground. Fires may be allowed at private campgrounds outside the park, but they are never allowed within park boundaries, and the rule is rigorously enforced.

WHERE TO EAT

IN THE PARK

$–$$
AMERICAN
✕ **Cedar Pass Lodge Restaurant.** Cool off within dark, knotty-pine walls under an exposed-beam ceiling, and enjoy a hearty meal of steak, trout, or Indian tacos and fry bread. ⊠ *1 Cedar St. (Rte. 240), Interior* ☏ *605/433–5460* ⊕ *www.cedarpasslodge.com* ▭ *AE, D, MC, V* ☉ *Closed Nov.–Mar.*

PICNIC AREAS
The National Park Service provides several structured picnic areas, though you may picnic wherever your heart desires. The wind may blow hard enough to make picnicking a challenge, but the views are unrivaled.

Bigfoot Pass Overlook. There are only a handful of tables here and no water, but the incredible view makes it a lovely spot to have lunch. Restrooms are available. ⊠ *7 mi northwest of the Ben Reifel Visitor Center on Badlands Loop Rd.*

Conata Picnic Area. A dozen or so covered picnic tables are scattered over this area, which rests against a badlands wall ½ mi south of Badlands Loop Road. There's no potable water, but there are bathroom facilities and you can enjoy your lunch in peaceful isolation at the threshold of the Badlands Wilderness Area. The Conata Basin area is to the east, and Sage Creek area is to the west. ⊠ *15 mi northwest of the Ben Reifel Visitor Center on Conata Rd.*

OUTSIDE THE PARK

For restaurants in Rapid City and the Black Hills, ⇨ *Wind Cave National Park (chapter 36).*

$–$$
AMERICAN
✕ **Cactus Family Restaurant and Lounge.** Delicious hotcakes and pies await you at this full-menu restaurant in downtown Wall. In summer you'll find a roast-beef buffet large enough for any appetite. ⊠ *519 Main St., Wall* ☎ *605/279–2561* ▭ *D, MC, V.*

¢–$$
AMERICAN
✕ **Elkton House Restaurant.** For a terrific hot roast-beef sandwich served on white bread with gravy and mashed potatoes, make your way to this comfortable, family-friendly restaurant. The dining room is sunlit and the service is fast. ⊠ *203 South Blvd., Wall* ☎ *605/279–2152* ⊕ *www. blackhillsbadlands.com/elkton* ▭ *D, MC, V.*

¢–$
AMERICAN
★
✕ **Western Art Gallery Restaurant.** This large restaurant in the Wall Drug store displays more than 200 original oil paintings, all with a western theme. Try a hot beef sandwich or a buffalo burger. The old-fashioned soda fountain has milk shakes and homemade ice cream. ⊠ *510 Main St., Wall* ☎ *605/279–2175* ⊕ *www.walldrug.com* ▭ *AE, D, MC, V.*

6

WHERE TO STAY

IN THE PARK

$–$$$
★
⊡ **Cedar Pass Lodge.** Each small, stucco, white cabin has two twin beds and views of the badlands peaks. A gallery at the lodge displays the work of local artists, and the gift shop is well stocked with local crafts, including turquoise and beadwork. There are also hiking trails on the premises. **Pros:** best star-gazing in South Dakota. **Cons:** remote location; long drive to other restaurants. ⊠ *20681 Hwy. 240., Interior* ☎ *605/433–5460* ⊕ *www. cedarpasslodge.com* ⊅ *24 cabins* ⌂ *In-room: no phone, no TV. In-hotel: restaurant, some pets allowed* ▭ *AE, D, MC, V* ⊗ *Closed Oct.–Apr.*

CAMPING
$
★
⚠ **Cedar Pass Campground.** Although it has only tent sites, this is the most developed campground in the park, and it's near the Ben Reifel Visitor Center, Cedar Pass Lodge, and a half dozen hiking trails. Recently renovated to include paved interior roads, new dump station, and improved facilities. You can buy $2 bags of ice at the lodge. **Pros:** you may feel like you have the place to yourself. **Cons:** remote location; lack of shade trees; reservations not accepted. ⊠ *Hwy. 377, ¼ mi south of Badlands Loop Rd.* ☎ *605/433–5361* ⊕ *www.cedarpasslodge.com* ⚠ *96 campsites* ⌂ *Flush toilets, pit toilets, dump station, drinking water, public telephone, ranger station* ▭ *No credit cards* ⊗ *Closed mid-Oct.–mid-Apr.*

¢
(FREE)
⚠ **Sage Creek Primitive Campground.** The word to remember here is primitive. If you want to get away from it all, this lovely, isolated spot surrounded by nothing but fields and crickets is the right camp for you. There are no designated campsites, and the only facilities are pit toilets and horse hitches. **Pros:** isolated, middle of nowhere feel. **Cons:** as primitive as it gets; long way to potable water, shopping, or restaurants. ⊠ *Sage Creek Rim Rd., 25 mi west of Badlands Loop Rd.* ☎ *No phone* ⚠ *No designated sites* ⌂ *Pit toilets.*

OUTSIDE THE PARK

For lodging in Rapid City and the Black Hills, ⇨ Wind Cave National Park (chapter 36).

¢ 🖼 🏕 **Badlands Budget Host Motel.** Every room in this motel has views of the Buffalo Gap National Grasslands, 1 mi away. You can have breakfast and dinner on the premises or walk to a nearby restaurant. Badlands Budget also has 70 campsites ($–$$), some with full hookups. A game room and volleyball court are on site. **Pros:** clean and comfortable; close to the grasslands and the park. **Cons:** standard rooms with no frills. ✉ *Rte. 377, Interior* ☎ *605/433–5335 or 800/388–4643* 📞 *21 rooms* 🏕 *70 campsites* ⛄ *In-hotel: restaurant, pool, laundry facilities, some pets allowed. Campground: full hookups, guest laundry, showers, play area, fire pits, swimming (pool)* ▭ *D, MC, V* ⊘ *Closed Oct.–Apr.*

$–$$ 🖼 **Circle View Guest Ranch.** This B&B has spectacular views and is located ⚘ in the heart of the badlands. Rooms have been upgraded with queen and king beds, private baths, a/c, and free Wi-Fi throughout the guest ranch. In the morning a full ranch breakfast (generally a hearty meal of eggs, meat, potatoes, toast, juice, and coffee) is served. A fireplace in the common area warms up visitors on cool evenings. **Pros:** friendly people; beautiful views; great for groups. **Cons:** small and isolated. ✉ *20055 Hwy. 44 E, Scenic* ☎ *605/433–5582* ⊕ *www.circleviewranch.com* 📞 *8 rooms* ⛄ *In-room: kitchen, a/c, Wi-Fi* ▭ *D, MC, V.*

$–$$$ 🖼 **Coyote Blues Village B&B.** This European-style lodge on 30 Black Hills ★ acres (12 mi north of Hill City) displays an unusual mix of antique furnishings and contemporary art. Swiss, "no need for lunch" breakfasts include a variety of baked goods. Some rooms have a private deck with a hot tub. A creek runs through the property. **Pros:** probably the only touch of Europe in Black Hills; tucked away 1 mi from highway with no neighbors; exceptional food. **Cons:** not within walking distance of other restaurants. ✉ *23165 Horseman's Ranch Rd., Rapid City* ☎ *605/574–4477 or 888/253–4477* ⊕ *www.coyotebluesvillage.com* 📞 *10 rooms* ⛄ *In-room: refrigerator. In-hotel: gym* ▭ *AE, D, MC, V.*

CAMPING 🏕 **Badlands/White River KOA.** Four miles southeast of Interior, this award-
$$–$$$ winning campground's green, shady sites spread over 31 acres are pleas-
⚘ ant and cool after a day among the dry rocks of the national park. White River and a small creek border the property on two sides. Cabins and cottages are also available, and you can play miniature golf and rent bikes. The campsites have cable hookups at no extra charge. **Pros:** quiet rural setting; lots of shade; friendly and efficient. **Cons:** remote location; relatively large and busy. ✉ *20720 Hwy. 44, Interior* ☎ *605/433–5337* ⊕ *www.koa.com* ⛄ *Flush toilets, full hookups, partial hookups (electric and water), dump station, drinking water, showers, fire grates, picnic tables, food service, public telephone, general store, play area, swimming (pool), Wi-Fi* 🏕 *144 sites (44 with full hookups, 38 with partial hookups), 8 cabins* ▭ *D, MC, V* ⊘ *Closed Oct.–mid-Apr.*

Banff National Park

WORD OF MOUTH

"We stopped at Bow Summit and Peyto Lake. From the parking lot, it is a short uphill walk to the overlook. The evergreen trees on this walk were all covered with snow and just sparkled in the sun. It looked like a winter wonderland. The view of Peyto Lake with the mountains and blue sky was amazing."

—LindainOhio

WELCOME TO BANFF

TOP REASONS TO GO

★ **Scenery:** Visitors are often unprepared for the sheer scale of the Canadian Rockies. Scattered between the peaks are glaciers, forests, valleys, meadows, rivers, and the bluest lakes of the planet.

★ **Spectacular ski slopes:** Lake Louise Mountain Resort is Canada's largest single ski area, with skiing on four mountain faces, 4,200 skiable acres, and 113 named trails—and that's only one of the three ski resorts in Banff.

★ **Trails galore:** More than 1,600 km (1,000 mi) of defined hiking trails in the park lead to scenic lakes, alpine meadows, glaciers, forests, and deep canyons.

★ **Banff Upper Hot Springs:** Relax in naturally hot mineral springs as you watch snowflakes swirl around you, or gaze at the stars as you "take the waters" on a cool summer's evening.

★ **Icefields Parkway:** One of the most scenic drives on the continent, this 230-km (143-mi) roadway links Banff and Jasper.

TO JASPER AND JASPER NATIONAL PARK

1 Icefields Parkway. There are many sites to be seen along this spectacular 230-km (143-mi) stretch of road. The Crowfoot Glacier, Bow Pass, Mistaya Canyon, Saskatchewan Crossing, and the Columbia Icefield are the primary highlights in the Banff section.

2 Lake Louise, Moraine Lake, and the Bow Valley Parkway. Backed by snowcapped mountains, fantastically ice-blue, Lake Louise is one of the most photographed lakes in the world. Lake Louise, Morraine Lake and the Valley of the Ten Peaks, and stunning Johnston Canyon are highlights of this region.

3 Banff Townsite. The hub of the park, Banff Townsite is the place to go to find shops, restaurants, hotels, and other facilities. Highlights of the townsite: Banff Information Centre, Canada Place, Whyte Museum, Banff Centre, Upper Hot Springs Pool, Sulphur Mountain Gondola, Lake Minnewanka, Vermillion Lakes, and the Hoodoos.

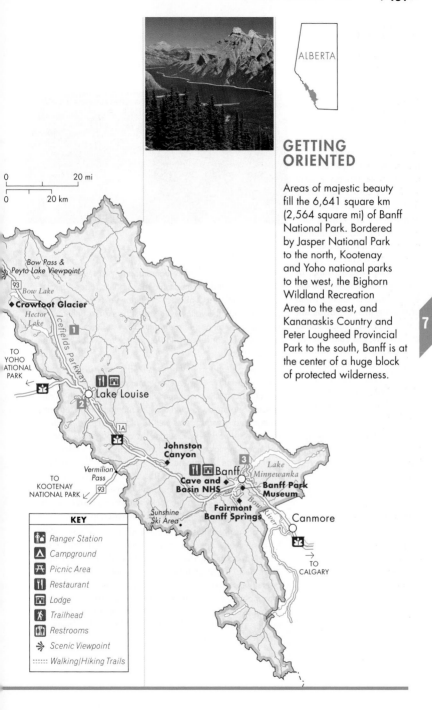

ALBERTA

GETTING ORIENTED

Areas of majestic beauty fill the 6,641 square km (2,564 square mi) of Banff National Park. Bordered by Jasper National Park to the north, Kootenay and Yoho national parks to the west, the Bighorn Wildland Recreation Area to the east, and Kananaskis Country and Peter Lougheed Provincial Park to the south, Banff is at the center of a huge block of protected wilderness.

7

0   20 mi
0   20 km

Bow Pass &
Peyto Lake Viewpoint
93
Bow Lake
◆ **Crowfoot Glacier**
Hector
Lake
1

TO
YOHO
NATIONAL
PARK

Lake Louise
2

1A

Johnston
Canyon

Vermilion
Pass
TO
KOOTENAY
NATIONAL PARK
93

3
Banff
Lake
Minnewanka
Cave and
Basin NHS
Banff Park
Museum

Sunshine
Ski Area
Fairmont
Banff Springs
Canmore

TO
CALGARY

KEY

👫	Ranger Station
⛺	Campground
�picnic	Picnic Area
🍴	Restaurant
🏨	Lodge
🚶	Trailhead
🚻	Restrooms
⚜	Scenic Viewpoint
⋯⋯	Walking/Hiking Trails

BANFF PLANNER

When to Go

Banff National Park is an all-season destination. Visit in summer to hike the mountain trails or go in winter to enjoy some of the world's best skiing. Millions of people visit the park every year with the vast majority traveling during July and August, the warmest and driest months in the park. **If you can visit in late spring (May to June) or early fall (September), you will be in shoulder season when prices are lower, crowds are fewer, and the temperatures are usually still comfortable.** The downside to an off-season visit is the fact that you miss the summer interpretive programs and the wildflowers that reach their peak from early July to mid-August.

Both of the park's information centers are open all year, with extended hours during the summer months.

Avg. High/Low Temps.

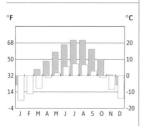

Flora and Fauna

Awesome forces of nature combined to thrust wildly folded sedimentary and metamorphic rock up into ragged peaks and high cliffs. Add glaciers and snowfields to the lofty peaks, carpet the valleys with forests, mix in a generous helping of small and large mammals, wildflowers, rivers, and crystal-clear lakes, and you've got the recipe for Banff National Park.

This diverse topography has resulted in three complex life zones in Banff: montane, subalpine, and alpine. Each zone has characteristic physical environments along with its own species of plants and animals. The montane zone features valleys and grasslands as well as alders, willows, birches, and cottonwoods. The Douglas firs and lodgepole pines that cover the lower slopes of the mountains are also in the montane zone. Subalpine forest extends from the montane to about 6,500 feet and is made up of mostly spruce and pine trees. The fragile alpine zone is found at the highest elevations in the park. The rocky terrain and cold howling winds mean far fewer plants and animals can survive there.

Most of the wildlife is found in the montane life zone where bighorn sheep, deer, elk, and caribou abound. Moose and mountain goats can also be seen, as well as the occasional black bear. Other animals in the park include grizzly bears, wolves, coyotes, and cougars, as well as smaller mammals such as squirrels, marmots, muskrats, porcupines, and beavers. Birds commonly spotted are grouse, larks, finches, ptarmigans, bald eagles, golden eagles, loons, and Canada geese.

Getting Here and Around

Banff National Park, in west-central Alberta, is located 128 km (80 mi) west of Calgary, 401 km (249 mi) southwest of Edmonton, and 850 km (528 mi) east of Vancouver. The closest international airports are in Calgary and Edmonton. Major airlines serve both airports.

A car allows the most flexible travel in the Canadian Rockies, and the easiest way to get from Calgary to Banff is by car on the Trans-Canada Highway 1. Use Icefields Parkway (Highway 93) to get from Jasper to Banff. International car rental agencies are available at Edmonton and Calgary airports and in Banff, Lake Louise, and Jasper.

Brewster Sightseeing Excursions (📞 800/760–6934 ⊕ www.explorerockies.com) provides bus transportation between Calgary International Airport and Banff.

For travel within the towns of Banff and Lake Louise, there is a public transit system as well as several local taxi companies to choose from. Public buses also run between Banff and Lake Louise, and in the winter there is a ski shuttle service that picks up at most area hotels and transports guests to the park's three ski resorts.

Park Publication

The Mountain Guide is distributed by parks staff upon entry to Banff National Park. It contains maps and good general park information such as points of interest, safety messages, programs and events, camping information and fees. If you want to use it for advance planning, it is also available on the Parks Canada Web site (⊕ www.pc.gc.ca/banff) under "Visitor Information."

Family Picks

Canada Place. At Canada Place you can see what it feels like to step into a real birch-bark canoe or participate in fun games and programs designed to teach you more about Canada. It's free and there are many hands-on activities.

Athabasca Glacier. This glacier is the most accessible one in the park, and a short walk leads you right to its toe. You can explore the free displays at the Icefield Centre and even take an Ice Explorer vehicle onto the ice. (Note: Do not venture onto the ice without a trained guide! It can be deadly.)

Canoe adventure. Rent a canoe at Lake Minnewanka, Moraine Lake, or Lake Louise and learn to paddle like early explorers once did.

Enjoy the view. You can't beat the views from the Banff Gondola during the steep eight-minute ride to the 7,500-foot summit of Sulphur Mountain. From the main deck you can hike the short distance to the summit of Sanson Peak and perhaps catch sight of grazing bighorn sheep.

Adrenaline rush. Try whitewater rafting in summer or dog-sledding and skiing in winter. The local ski hills have excellent children's programs.

By Debbie Olsen

Comparing mountains is a subjective and imprecise business. Yet few would deny that the Canadian Rockies are one of the most extravagantly beautiful ranges on Earth. The mountains and vast stretches of wilderness that make up the birthplace of Canada's first national park offer stunning scenery of glaciers, lakes, valleys, and snowcapped mountain peaks. Large mammals such as deer and elk can be observed in all seasons from the roadside.

PARK ESSENTIALS

ACCESSIBILITY

Both visitor information centers are fully accessible and many of the campgrounds are also wheelchair accessible. There are also several trails in the park that are wheelchair accessible and Banff Transit operates one fully accessible shuttle. To find out specifics on accessible campgrounds and trails, call the information center at ☎ *403/762–1550.*

ADMISSION FEES AND PERMITS

A park entrance pass is C$9.80 per person or C$19.60 maximum per vehicle per day. An annual pass will cost C$67.70 per adult or C$136.40 per family or group. Larger buses and vans pay a group commercial rate. If you're planning to stay a week or more, your best bet is an annual pass.

Permits are required for backcountry camping and some other activities in the park. Backcountry camping permits ($9.80 per day), fire permits ($8.80 per day), dumping station permits ($8.80 per day), and fishing permits ($9.80 per day) are available at the park visitor information center or at some campgrounds. In some cases a fire permit is included in your camping fees. Be sure to check with campground staff.

ADMISSION HOURS

The park is open 24/7 year-round. It's in the mountain time zone.

ATMS/BANKS

There are at least a dozen ATMs in Banff Townsite. The Bank of Montreal, Bow Valley Credit Union, and Canadian Imperial Bank of Commerce (CIBC) operate full-service branches in Banff.

CELL-PHONE RECEPTION

Cell-phone service in the park is sometimes unpredictable. Public telephones can be found at the information centers, at most hotels and bars, and at several key spots around the townsite of Banff and the village of Lake Louise.

PARK CONTACT INFORMATION

Banff National Park ✆ *P.O. Box 900, Banff, Alberta, Canada T1L 1K2* ☎ *403/762–1550* ⊕ *www.pc.gc.ca/banff.*

Note that all prices in this chapter are in Canadian dollars, unless stated otherwise.

BANFF IN ONE DAY

Start with a visit to the **Banff Information Centre** to pick up maps and information on the major sites. Buy lunch provisions and drive to beautiful **Lake Louise**. Walk the flat shoreline trail and venture upward along the **Lake Agnes Trail** to the Teahouse (or turn back once you get a lofty view of Lake Louise). On the drive back to Banff townsite, stop at Johnston Canyon and allow an hour for the easy round-trip hike to the dramatic waterfall. Have dinner at **Fairmont Banff Springs Hotel**. Afterward, explore the hotel's interior, then end the day with an evening dip in the **Banff Upper Hot Springs**.

SCENIC DRIVES

Fodor's Choice ★ **Icefields Parkway.** The Icefields Parkway stretches 230 km (138 mi) and connects Banff National Park with Jasper National Park. It is an absolute highlight of the Canadian Rockies (⇨ *Icefields Parkway box).*

Lake Minnewanka Loop. It's easy to spend the day along this 25-km (15-mi) loop. Traveling clockwise, you can explore Lower Bankhead and Upper Bankhead, an abandoned coal mine and mining community. Just 3 km (2 mi) farther you come to Lake Minnewanka, the largest lake in the park at 20 km (12 mi). Boat and fishing rentals are available at the lake. Farther along are more lakes and picnic areas.

Mount Noquay Drive. The highlight of this 6½-km (4-mi) route is the viewpoint near the top over the Banff Townsite. Bighorn sheep and mule deer are often sighted along the twisting road. Trailheads at the top lead to Stoney Squaw Summit and Cascade Amphitheatre.

Tunnel Mountain Drive. On the east side of Banff, Tunnel Mountain Drive makes a scenic 5-km (3-mi) loop. It's closed in winter, but just off the drive, the **hoodoos**—fingerlike, eroded rock formations—are accessible year-round (signs on Banff's main street direct you to the hoodoos).

Icefields Parkway

Powerfully rugged mountain scenery, glaciers, waterfalls and icefalls, and wildlife: the Icefields Parkway reveals all of these and more as it snakes its way between Lake Louise and Jasper.

There aren't any gas stations along the route, so be sure to check the gas gauge before setting out. Although you could drive this winding road in three to four hours, it's more likely to be a full-day trip when you add in stops. The road rises to near the tree line at several points, and the weather can be chilly and unsettled at these high elevations, even in midsummer, so it's a good idea to bring warm clothing along.

Elk, moose, deer, and bighorn sheep are fairly common along this route, and occasionally you can see bears and mountain goats. In summer, alpine wildflowers carpet Bow Pass and Sunwapta Pass.

The most dramatic scenery is in the north end of Banff National Park and the south end of Jasper National Park, where ice fields and glaciers become common on the high mountains flanking the route (ice fields are massive reservoirs of ice; glaciers are the slow-moving rivers of ice that flow from the ice fields). Scenic overlooks and signposted hiking trails abound along the route.

At 6,787 feet, **Bow Summit** (⊠ *40 km [25 mi] north of Lake Louise, 190 km [118 mi] south of Jasper*) is the highest drivable pass in the national parks of the Canadian Rockies. It is famous for its postcard viewpoint of Peyto Lake. To reach the summit viewpoint, park in the lot on the west side of the highway and take the trail from there that leads 1½ km (1 mi) through alpine forest to a scenic point above the timberline. On the south side of the pass is Bow Lake, source of the Bow River, which flows through Banff. You may wish to stop for lunch or supper at **Simpson's Num-Ti-Jah Lodge** (⊠ *40 km [25 mi] north of Lake Louise on Hwy. 93* ☎ *403/522–2167* ⊕ *www.num-ti-jah.com*) at Bow Lake. This rustic lodge with simple guest rooms specializes in excellent regional Canadian cuisine. Outside, walking paths circle the lake. Above Bow Lake hangs the Crowfoot Glacier, so named because of its resemblance to a three-toed crow's foot. At least that's how it looked when it was named at the beginning of the 20th century. In the Canadian Rockies, glaciers, including Crowfoot, have been receding. The lowest toe completely melted away 50 years ago, and now only the upper two toes remain. On the north side of Bow Pass is **Peyto Lake**; its star-tlingly intense aqua-blue color comes from the minerals in glacial runoff. Wildflowers blossom along the pass in summer, but note that it can be covered with snow as late as May and as early as September.

The short (2½ km [1½ mi]), steep **Parker Ridge Trail** is one of the easiest hikes in the national parks to bring you above the tree line. There's an excellent view of the Saskatch-ewan Glacier, where the river of the same name begins, though you've got to make it to the top of the ridge to get the view. Snowbanks can persist into early summer, but carpets of wildflowers cross the trail in late July and August. Stay on the path to keep erosion to a minimum. The trailhead is about 4 km (2½ mi) south of the boundary between Banff and Jasper parks.

Sunwapta Pass (⊠ *122 km [76 mi] north of Lake Louise, 108 km [67 mi] south of Jasper*) marks the border between Banff and Jasper national parks. Wildlife is most visible in spring and autumn after a snowfall, when herds of bighorn sheep come to the road to lick up the salt used to melt snow and ice. At 6,675 feet, Sunwapta is the second-highest drivable pass in the national parks. Be prepared for a series of hairpin turns as you switch-back up to the pass summit.

★ Fodor's Choice   The **Athabasca Glacier** (⊠ *127 km [79 mi] north of Lake Louise, 103 km [64 mi] south of Jasper*) is a 7-km (4½-mi) tongue of ice flowing from the immense Columbia Icefield almost to the highway. A century ago the ice flowed over the current location of the highway; signposts depict the gradual retreat of the ice since that time. Several other glaciers are visible from here; they all originate from the Columbia Icefield, a giant alpine lake of ice covering 325 square km (125 square mi), whose edge is visible from the highway. You can hike up to the toe of the glacier, but venturing further without a trained guide is extremely dangerous because of hidden crevasses. **Athabasca Glacier Ice Walks** (☎ *800/565-7547* ⊕ *www.icewalks. com*) offers three-, five-, and six-hour guided walks (C$36–C$45), which can be reserved at the Icefield Centre or through **Jasper Adventure Centre** (☎ *780/852-5595 or 800/565-7547* ⊕ *www.jasperadventurecentre.com*), in Jasper (⇨ *chapter 23*). You can also take a trip onto the Athabasca Glacier in **Brewster Tours' Ice Explorers**, which have been modified

to drive on ice (tickets are available at the Icefield Centre for C$29.86).

The **Icefield Centre** opposite Atha-basca Glacier houses interpretive exhibits, a gift shop, and two dining facilities (one cafeteria style, one buf-fet style). The summer midday rush between 11 and 3 can be intense. The **Glacier View Inn** is located opposite the Icefiels and has 32 hotel rooms, available from early May to mid-October. Book through **Brewster Sightseeing Excursions** (☎ *800/ 760-6934* ⊕ *www.explorerockies.com*) in Banff. ⊠ *Opposite Athabasca Gla-cier on Hwy. 93, 127 km (79 mi) north of Lake Louise, 103 km (64 mi) south of Jasper* ☎ *877/423-7433* 🎫 *Free* ☉ *Late May–mid-June and Sept.–early Oct., daily 10–5; mid-June–Aug., daily 10–7.*

As you continue north from the Ice-field Centre through Jasper National Park toward Jasper Townsite, you'll see some of the most spectacular scenery in the Canadian Rockies. One of the most stunning sites is the **Stut-field Glacier**, 95 km (57 mi) south of Jasper Townsite. The glacier stretches down 3,000 feet of cliff face, forming a set of double icefalls visible from a roadside viewpoint. Continuing along the parkway, you'll pass the access to spectacular **Sunwapta Falls**, 57 km (33 mi) south of the town of Jasper. You'll also want to stop at **Athabasca Falls**, 31 km (19 mi) south of Jasper Townsite. These powerful falls are created as the Athabasca River is compressed through a narrow gorge, producing a violent torrent of water. The falls are especially dramatic in early summer. Trails and overlooks provide good viewpoints.

7

Catching a view from Moraine Lake as the sunlight plays on the snow-drizzled mountains around it.

WHAT TO SEE

HISTORIC SITES

Banff Park Museum National Historic Site of Canada. This National Historic Site, made for the 1893 World Exhibition in Chicago, is western Canada's oldest natural-history museum. ⊠ *91 Banff Ave., north of the bridge* ☎ *403/762–1558* ⊕ *www.pc.gc.ca/banff* 💲 *C$3.90* ⊙ *Mid-May–Sept., daily 10–6; Oct.–mid-May, daily 1–5.*

★ **Banff Upper Hot Springs.** The sulfur pool of hot springwater can be soothing, invigorating, or both. The water is especially inviting on a dull, cold day. Lockers, bathing suits (circa 1920s or modern), and towels can be rented, and spa services are available. ⊠ *Mountain Ave., 3 km (2 mi) south of downtown (or a 20-min hike up a steep trail from the Fairmont Banff Springs parking area)* ☎ *403/762–1515 or 800/767–1611, 403/760–2500 for spa bookings* ⊕ *www.hotspring.ca* 💲 *C$7.30* ⊙ *Mid-May–mid-Sept., daily 9 AM–11 PM; mid-Sept.–mid-May, Sun.–Thurs. 10–10, Fri. and Sat. 10 AM–11 PM.*

Cave and Basin National Historic Site. This was given national park protection in 1885, becoming the birthplace of the Canadian Rockies park system. Two interpretive trails explain the area's geology and plant life, while hands-on interpretive displays offer information on the wildlife and history of the national park. You can take a guided tour of the cave daily mid-May through September and weekends throughout the rest of the year. A boardwalk leads to a marsh where the warm springwater supports tropical fish illegally dumped into the waters many years ago. ⊠ *Cave Ave., 2 km (1 mi) west of downtown* ☎ *403/762–1566* ⊕ *www.*

pc.gc.ca/banff ✉ *C$3.90* ☉ *Mid-May–Sept., daily 9–6; Oct.–mid-May, weekdays 11–4, weekends 9:30–5.*

★ **Fairmont Banff Springs.** This hotel, 2 km (1 mi) south of downtown Banff, is the town's architectural showpiece and a National Historic Site. Built in 1888, the hotel is easily recognized by its castle-like exterior. Heritage Hall, a small, free museum above the Grand Lobby, has rotating exhibits on the area's history and is open from 9 AM to 9 PM. Historical tours are offered Tuesday through Saturday at 3 PM and are free for hotel guests or C$15 for nonguests. ⊠ *405 Spray Ave.* ☎ *403/762–2211 or 800/441–1414* ⊕ *www.fairmont.com.*

★ **Fairmont Château Lake Louise.** The massive hotel, opened in 1890, overlooks blue-green Lake Louise and the Victoria Glacier. The hotel is also a departure point for several short, moderately strenuous, well-traveled hiking routes. The most popular hike (about 3 km [2 mi]) is to Lake Agnes. The tiny lake hangs on a mountain-surrounded shelf that opens to the east with a bird's-eye view of the Beehives and Mount Whitehorn. ⊠ *111 Lake Louise Dr.* ☎ *403/522–3511.*

SCENIC STOPS

⇨ *Icefields Parkway box for stops along the famous parkway.*

☾ **Banff Gondola.** Views during the steep eight-minute ride to and from the 7,500-foot summit are spectacular. From the upper gondola terminal you can hike the short distance to the summit of Sanson Peak and perhaps catch sight of grazing bighorn sheep, or visit the gift shop or the reasonably priced restaurant. The gondola is south from the center of Banff; you can catch a public Banff transit bus. ⊠ *Mountain Ave., 3 km (2 mi) south of downtown (lower terminal next to Upper Hot Springs), Banff* ☎ *403/762–5438 or 403/762–2523* ⊕ *www.banffgondola.com* ✉ *C$27.62 round-trip* ☉ *Late May–late Aug., daily 8:30 AM–9 PM; late Aug.–mid-Oct., daily 8:30–6:30; mid-Oct.–early Nov., daily 8:30–4:30; early Nov.–early May, daily 10–4.*

☾ **Lake Louise Sightseeing Gondola.** Ride this to an alpine plateau for a stunning view that includes more than a dozen glaciers. The deck of the Wildlife Interpretive Centre is a good place to enjoy an ice-cream cone, a drink, or a picnic lunch or you can buy a ticket that includes buffet breakfast or buffet lunch that is enjoyed at the lodge near the base of the gondola. Guided interpretive walks take place at 10:30, 12:30, and 2:30 daily and last about 45 minutes. ⊠ *Whitehorn Rd., off Hwy. 1 (Lake Louise exit)* ☎ *403/522–3555* ⊕ *www.lakelouisegondola.com* ✉ *C$25.95 ride only, C$28.60 ride with breakfast, $32.25 ride with lunch* ☉ *May 15–June 12, daily 9–4:30; June 13–Sept. 7, daily 9–5; Sept. 8–30, daily 9–4:30.*

★ **Moraine Lake.** This beauty, 11 km (7 mi) south of Lake Louise, is a photographic highlight of Banff National Park. Set in the Valley of the Ten Peaks, the lake reflects the snow-clad mountaintops that rise abruptly around it. The lake is a major stop for tour buses as well as a popular departure point for hikers and a place to canoe. Visit early or late in the day to avoid crowds. Moderate hiking trails lead from the lodge at Moraine Lake into some spectacular alpine country. Call ahead for special trail restrictions.

7

VISITOR CENTERS

Banff Information Centre. Park wardens and staff here have excellent information on camping, hiking, interpretive programs, and sightseeing. ✉ *224 Banff Ave., Banff* ☎ *403/762–1550* ⊕ *www.pc.gc.ca/banff* ⊗ *Jan.–mid-May, daily 9–5; mid-May–mid-June and Sept., daily 8–6; mid-June–Aug., daily 8–8.*

Banff Lake Louise Tourism. Located in the same building as the Banff Information Centre, this information desk can provide you with information on hotels, restaurants, and services in the towns of Banff and Lake Louise. ✉ *224 Banff Ave.* ☎ *403/762–8421* ⊕ *www.banfflakelouise.com* ⊗ *Jan.–mid-May, daily 9–5; mid-May–mid-June and Sept., daily 8–6; mid-June–Aug., daily 8–8.*

Lake Louise Visitor Centre. Stop here to get maps and information about area attractions and trails. The Banff Lake Louise Tourism desk can provide information on area accommodations and amenities, and you can purchase educational books and other materials from the Friends of Banff National Park. ✉ *Village of Lake Louise, next to Samson Mall* ☎ *403/522–3833* ⊕ *www.pc.gc.ca/banff* ⊗ *Mid-Sept.–Apr., daily 9–4; May–mid-June, daily 9–5; mid-June–mid-Sept., daily 9–8.*

SPORTS AND THE OUTDOORS

AIR TOURS

OUTFITTERS AND EXPEDITIONS
Helicopter sightseeing and heli-hiking in the Canadian Rockies are the specialty at **Alpine Helicopters** (✉ *91 Bow Valley Tr., Canmore* ☎ *403/678–4802* ⊕ *www.alpinehelicopter.com*). **CMH** (✉ *217 Bear St., Banff* ☎ *403/762–7100 or 800/661–0252* ⊕ *www.canadianmountainholidays.com*) can arrange multiday heli-hiking, heli-mountaineering, and heli-skiing with accommodation in remote mountain lodges.

Soar above the Columbia Icefields with **Icefield Helicopter Tours** (✎ *Site 7, RR #2, P.O. Box 7, Rocky Mountain House T4T 2A2* ☎ *888/844–3514 or 403/721–2100* ✄ *Tours $59–$589 per person* ⊕ *www.icefieldheli.com*), an outfitter that not only offers helicopter tours but has heli-yoga, heli-horseback riding, heli-hiking, and heli-fishing. Flights take off from the company's base in the Kootenay Plains area of Alberta, just north of Lake Louise.

BICYCLING

The biking season typically runs from May through October and the more than 189 km (118 mi) of mountain-bike trails include those suitable for beginners and advanced bikers. Bikers and hikers often share the trails in the park, with hikers having the right-of-way. Those who wish to enjoy free riding or down-hilling should go to nearby areas like Calgary's Canada Olympic Park, Fernie, or Golden. Those riders who like pavement can choose from a wide variety of scenic rides that run from a few hours to several days in length. Shorter rides include the Bow Lake trail, Vermillion Lakes Drive, and the loop around Tunnel Mountain.

For equipment shops, ⇨ Multisport Outfitters and Expeditions box.

BIRD-WATCHING

Birdlife is abundant in the montane and wetland habitats of the lower Bow Valley, and more than 260 species of birds have been recorded in the park. Come in the spring to observe the annual migration of waterfowl, including common species of ducks and Canada geese as well as occasional tundra swans, cinnamon teal, Northern shovelers, white-winged and surf scoters, and hooded and common mergansers. Bald eagles are also seen regularly. Come in mid-October if you want to observe the annual migration of golden eagles along the "super flyway" of the Canadian Rockies. Interpreters and guides are on hand to explain the phenomenon.

BOATING

Lake Minnewanka, near town, is the only place in Banff National Park that allows private motorboats. Aluminum fishing boats with 8-horsepower motors can be rented at the dock (call Lake Minnewanka Boat Tours (⇨ *below*).

Canoe rentals are available at Lake Louise, Moraine Lake, and in Banff where you launch along the Bow River and explore the waterways of the Bow Valley.

Rafting options range from scenic float trips to family-friendly white-water excursions on the Kananaskis River to the intense white water of the Kicking Horse River, with its Class IV rapids.

OUTFITTERS AND EXPEDITIONS

At **Banff Rafting Centre** (☎ *403/760–2007 or 866/330–7238* 🌐 *www.chinookrafting.com*) you can book half-day or full-day rafting adventures suitable for families as well as some for truly adventurous adults. Explore the waterways of Bow Valley with **Blue Canoe Rentals** ((☎ *403/760–5007 or 877/565–9372* 🌐 *www.banfftours.com*), paddling 40 Mile Creek, Vermillion Lakes, or the Bow River. Scenic floats and thrilling white-water rafting tours on the Bow and Kananaskis rivers are available with local experts at **Canadian Rockies Rafting** (☎ *403/678–6535 or 877/226–7625* 🌐 *www.rafting.ca*). Pickups in Banff and Canmore are included.

Paddle the tranquil waters of Lake Louise with the **Fairmont Château Lake Louise Canoe Experience** (☎ *403/522–3511 or 800/441–1414*). **Hydra River Guides** (☎ *403/762–4554 or 800/644–8888* 🌐 *www.raftbanff.com*) is where you want to go for thrills. The guides here take you through the Class IV rapids on the Kicking Horse River. A variety of boating trips, ranging from scenic raft floats on the Toby or Kootenay River to Class IV white-water rafting on the Kicking Horse, are available through **Kootenay River Runners** (☎ *250/347–9210 or 800/599–4399* 🌐 *www.raftingtherockies.com*). A unique Voyageur Canoe Experience is also an option. For white-water rafting on the Kicking Horse, guests meet at the boat launch about 90 minutes from Banff Townsite.

From mid-May to mid-October, **Minnewanka Lake Cruise** (☎ *403/762–3473 or 800/760–6934* 🌐 *www.explorerockies.com/minnewanka*) offers 1½-hour, C$41.91 tours on the lake. From June through September, paddle on beautiful Moraine Lake with a canoe rental from the **Moraine Lake Lodge** (☎ *403/522–3733 or 877/522–2777* 🌐 *www.morainelake.com*), at the end of Moraine Lake Road in Lake Louise. Canoes can be rented right from the dock area.

Banff-based **Rocky Mountain Raft Tours** (☎ *403/762–3632* ⊕ *www.banfframttours.com*) specializes in one- and two-hour float trips on the Bow River, starting at $42. **Wild Water Adventures Ltd.** (☎ *403/522–2212 or 888/647–6444* ⊕ *www.wildwater.com*), based 40 km (25 mi) north of Lake Louise, has trips ranging from gentle floats to intense whitewater experiences. Single-day and multiday trips are available.

FISHING

You can experience world-class trout fishing on the Bow River in Banff and enjoy fishing for trophy lake trout on Lake Minnewanka and several other mountain lakes. You will need a National Park fishing permit to fish within the park and must follow strict fishing regulations, including no use of live bait. Some waterways are permanently closed to anglers, while others are open only at certain times per year. Before heading out on your own, read the regulations or speak to the park staff.

OUTFITTERS AND EXPEDITIONS
Alpine Anglers (✉ *208 Bear St., Banff* ☎ *403/762–8223 or 877/740–8222* ⊕ *www.alpineanglers.com*) is a full-service fly shop with spin- and fly-rod rentals, float trips, and a fly-fishing guide service. Choose from full-day or multiday guided trout-fishing trips. A wide variety of fishing experiences from trolling for trophy lake trout to fly-fishing on the Bow River are available from the experienced guides at **Banff Fishing Unlimited** (⌂ *P.O. Box 8281, Canmore T1W 2V1* ☎ *403/678–2486 or 866/678–2486* ⊕ *www.banff-fishing.com*). In the winter, the outfitter also offers ice-fishing excursions. Learn how to fly-fish with a local guide by signing up with **Hawgwild Fly Fishing Guides** (⌂ *P.O. Box 2534, Banff T1L 1C3* ☎ *403/760–2446* ⊕ *www.flyfishingbanff.com*). Day-long and multiday fly-fishing trips can be arranged through **Tightline Adventures** (✉ *129 Banff Ave., Banff T1L 1E2* ☎ *403/762–4548* ⊕ *www.tightlineadventures.com*).

GOLF

Banff Springs Golf Course. The Stanley Thompson–designed championship course has breathtaking views in every direction. Its challenging 27 holes wind along the Bow River beneath snowcapped mountain peaks. ✉ *405 Spray Ave.* ☎ *403/762–6801 or 877/591–2525* ⊕ *www.fairmontgolf.com.*

HIKING

The trail system in Banff National Park allows you to access the heart of the Canadian Rockies. The scenery is spectacular and you can see wildlife such as birds, squirrels, deer, and sheep along many of the trails. Make noise as you travel the trails, so you don't surprise a bear or other large animal. Also, prepare for any and all weather conditions by dressing in layers and bringing at least ½ gallon of drinking water along per person on all full-day hikes. Get a trail map at the information center. Some of the more popular trails have bathrooms or outhouses at the trailhead. Dogs should be leashed at all times. *For guided hikes, ⇨ Multisport Outfitters and Expeditions box.*

EASY

Bow River HooDoos Trail. This 4.8-km (3-mi) trail feels as if it is a world away from the busy townsite. It begins with a view of a waterfall on Bow River and then leads through meadows and forests and past sheer

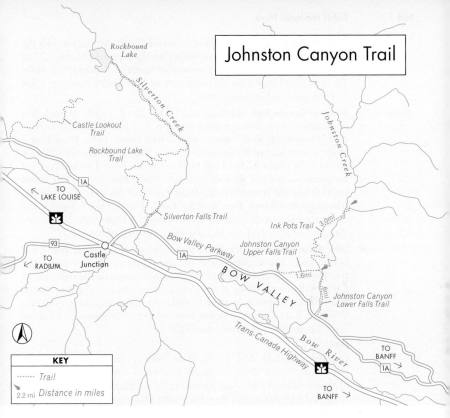

Rockbound
Lake

Silverton Creek

Castle Lookout
Trail

Rockbound Lake
Trail

Johnston Creek

TO
LAKE LOUISE

1A

Silverton Falls Trail

Ink Pots Trail — 3.0mi

Bow Valley Parkway

Johnston Canyon
Upper Falls Trail

93

Castle
Junction

1A

1.6mi

TO
RADIUM

B O W   V A L L E Y

.6mi

Johnston Canyon
Lower Falls Trail

Trans-Canada Highway

Bow River

TO
BANFF

1A

TO
BANFF

KEY

------ *Trail*

2.2 mi *Distance in miles*

cliffs, ending at the hoodoos in the east part of Banff Townsite. ⊠ *Trail-head at the Bow Falls Overlook on Tunnel Mountain Dr.*

Discovery Trail and Marsh Trail. On a hillside above the Cave and Basin Centennial Centre, this 0.8-km (½-mi) boardwalk takes you past the vent of the cave to a spring flowing out of the hillside. Interpretive signage explains the geology and history of the Cave and Basin. Follow the Marsh Trail to get a good view of the lush vegetation that is fed by the mineral water and to see the birdlife. Along the boardwalk are telescopes, benches, and interpretive signage as well as a bird blind on the marsh itself. Wheelchairs have limited access to the boardwalk. ⊠ *Trailhead at the parking lot of Cave and Basin National Historic Site.*

Fenland Trail. It will take about an hour round-trip to walk the 2-km (1-mi) trail that slowly changes from marsh to dense forest. Watch for beavers, muskrat, and waterfowl. The trail is popular with joggers and cyclists. ⊠ *Trailhead at Forty Mile Picnic Area.*

MODERATE

Boom Lake Trail. This 5-km (3.2-mi) hike climbs through a forest of pine, fir, and spruce. Surrounded by mountains and glaciers, the waters of the lake are crystal clear. The trail will take a half day round-trip. ⊠ *Trailhead off Hwy. 93 S, 7 km (4½-mi) west of Castle Junction.*

Castle Lookout Trail. Outstanding views of Castle Mountain and the mountains above the Bow River Valley are the highlight of this 3.7-km (2.3-mi) one-way trail that is somewhat steep. ☒ *Trailhead off Hwy. 1A at the parking lot on the north side of Bow Valley Parkway 5 km (3.1 mi) west of Castle Junction.*

Fodor's Choice
★
Johnston Canyon Trail. Rushing water has carved a path through this limestone canyon that is a must-see stop. The first 1.1 km (0.7 mi) is a paved walkway that leads to the 33-foot Lower Falls. From here a slightly more rugged 2.7-km (1¾-mi) trail leads to the almost-100-foot Upper Falls and a 5-km (3-mi) trail to the Ink Pots. The Ink Pots are six green pools filled with springwater. It will take four to five hours to complete the return trip. ☒ *Trails begin off Hwy. 1A* ✢ *From the Norquay Interchange drive west 5.5 km (3.4 mi) on the Trans-Canada Highway and take the Bow Valley Parkway (1A Highway). Drive along this road 18 km (11.1 mi) to Johnston Canyon parking lot.*

★ **Lake Agnes Teahouse Trail.** Winding north of Lake Louise, this 7-km (4½-mi) trail has stunning views of Lake Agnes and Mirror Lake. The trail passes through an old-growth forest and comes up the right side of a waterfall before ending at a teahouse where you can stop for dessert. It will take four hours or more to make the return trip along this trail. ✢ *Follow Lake Louise Shoreline Trail in front of the Fairmont Chateau Lake Louise up to the Teahouse Trail.*

DIFFICULT

Cory Pass Loop Trail. This 13-km (8-mi) hike is one of the park's most difficult and takes about six hours to do; it is only recommended for experienced hikers who are able to trace a difficult route. Hikers are rewarded with awesome views. The return route loops around Mt. Edith and descends the Edith Pass Trail. ☒ *Trailhead at Fireside picnic area, the eastern end of the Bow Valley Parkway.*

Sulphur Mountain Summit Trail. This well-maintained trail crisscrosses underneath the gondola on Sulphur Mountain and climbs from the parking lot to the summit. You may choose to hike up and take the gondola down, but you should check schedules first. A restaurant and cafeteria are located at the summit along with a viewing platform and interpretive signage. It will take four hours to hike the trail round-trip. ☒ *Trailhead at the corner of the Upper Hot Springs parking lot closest to the pool.*

HORSEBACK RIDING

Experiencing the Canadian Rockies on horseback takes you back to the era of Banff's early explorers. One-hour, half-day, full-day, and multiday guided trips within the park are offered by several outfitters. Make your reservations well in advance, especially during the peak summer months and for multiday journeys. Hourly rides start at $34 per person. Short-term boarding is available in Canmore and a few other communities outside Banff.

OUTFITTERS
AND
EXPEDITIONS
Experience the "Cowboy Way of Life" by moving cattle and doing chores on overnight mountain pack tours with **Brewster Adventures** (✉ *P.O. Box 964, Banff T1L 1A5* ☎ *403/762–5454 or 800/691–5085* ⊕ *www.brewsteradventures.com*), a Banff company that also has daily summer trail rides to the Plain of Six Glaciers, Lake Agnes Tea House, Paradise Valley,

and the Giant Steps. In the winter, sleigh rides are available at Brewsters' Lake Louise Stable, which is near the Fairmont Chateau Lake Louise.

⟳ **Holiday on Horseback** (✉ *132 Banff Ave., Banff* ☎ *403/762–4551 or 800/661–8352* ⊕ *www.horseback.com*) arranges hourly or daily rides, as well as lessons and multiday backcountry trips. The company operates out of three different locations in Banff (the main stable is located at the Fairmont Banff Springs). It also offers carriage rides in summer and sleigh rides in winter. Multiday all-inclusive horseback, stagecoach, and bring-your-own horse holidays can be had at the **Outpost at Warden Rock** (⌂ *P.O. Box 461, Banff T1L 1A6* ☎ *403/762–2767 or 877/762–2767* ⊕ *www.outpostatwardenrock.com*). The outpost is open mid-May to mid-October and is located 50 mi north of Banff Townsite.

Trail rides ranging from 10 minutes to 10 days can be arranged with **Timberline Tours** (⌂ *P.O. Box 14, Lake Louise T0L 1E0* ☎ *403/522– 3743 or 888/858–3388* ⊕ *www.timberlinetours.ca*).

SWIMMING

⟳ **Banff Centre.** Amenities here include a 25-meter swimming pool, a wading pool, an outdoor sundeck, climbing wall, fitness center, gymnasium, and squash center, as well as fitness classes. ✉ *St. Julien Rd. (on Tunnel Mountain), Banff* ☎ *403/762–6450* ⊕ *www.banffcentre.ca* 🖾 *C$4.50 public swim, C$10 day pass* ⊙ *Weekdays 6 AM–10 PM, weekends 7 AM–10 PM.*

WINTER SPORTS

Whether you're driving a dogsled across a frozen lake, ice climbing, snowshoeing, skiing at one of the world's top mountain ski resorts— or simply taking in the northern lights—there's no shortage of winter activities to choose from at Banff.

Skis and snowboards can be rented on the slopes or at many shops in town, concentrated along Bear Street and Banff Avenue.

CROSS-COUNTRY SKIING

Canmore Nordic Centre. The best place in the Rockies to learn how to cross-country ski is with a lesson at this center built for the 1988 Winter Olympic Games. IT has rental equipment, a day lodge, and miles of trails to enjoy. ✉ *#7 1988 Olympic Way, Canmore* ☎ *403/678–2400.*

DOWNHILL SKIING

⟳ **Lake Louise Ski Area.** The downhill terrain at is large and varied, with
★ a fairly even spread of novice, intermediate, and expert runs spread across three mountains and north-facing back bowls. The vertical drop is 3,257 feet, there are 105 runs, 11 lifts, and a terrain park. ✉ *1 Whitehorn Rd., off Lake Louise Dr., Lake Louise* ☎ *403/522–3555* ⊕ *www. skilouise.com.*

Ski Banff at Norquay. Locals like this five-lift, 28-run mountain, and so do Olympic and World Cup trainees. It has night skiing, too. The vertical drop is 1,650. ⌂ *P.O. Box 1520, Banff T1L 1B4* ☎ *403/762–4421* ⊕ *www.banffnorquay.com.*

Sunshine Village. Eight kilometers (5 mi) west of the town of Banff, the terrain here offers options for all levels of skiers. The vertical drop is 3,514 feet, and there are 103 trails and 12 lifts. ✉ *Off Hwy. 1, Banff* ☎ *403/762–6500 or 877/542–2633* ⊕ *www.skibanff.com.*

MULTISPORT OUTFITTERS AND EXPEDITIONS

Abominable Ski & Sportswear. Rent or buy ski and snowboarding equipment in winter and bikes and accessories in summer. ⊠ *229 Banff Ave., Banff* ☎ *403/762-2905.*

Bactrax Bike Rentals. This supplier has Banff's largest selection of rental skis and snowboards. It also rents bikes in the summer and arranges one- to four-hour guided interpretive bike tours on local Banff trails, which are suitable for any age or physical ability. ⊠ *225 Bear St., Banff* ☎ *403/762-8177* ⊕ *www.snowtips-bactrax.com.*

Banff Adventures Unlimited. Rent bikes here, or come here to sign up for almost any area activity. ⊠ *211 Bear St., Banff* ☎ *403/762-4554* ⊕ *www.banffadventures.com.*

Chute High Adventures. Mountain climbing, rock climbing, ice climbing, and guided hiking can be arranged through this outfitter. ✑ *P.O. Box 1876, Banff T1L1B7* ☎ *403/762-4068.*

Discover Banff Tours Ltd. Sign up here for guided sightseeing, wildlife safaris, nature walks, ice walks, and snowshoeing adventures. ⊠ *Sundance Mall, Main Level, 215 Banff Ave., Banff* ☎ *403/760-5007 or 877/565-9372* ⊕ *www.banfftours.com.*

Great Divide Nature Interpretation. Guided interpretive hikes and snowshoeing trips are the specialty here. ✑ *P.O. Box 343, Lake Louise T0L 1E0* ☎ *403/522-2735* ⊕ *www.greatdivide.ca.*

Mountain Edge. This gear shop sells clothing and equipment for wintertime fun—downhill skis, snowboards, and helmets. ⊠ *Lake Louise Ski Area, off Lake Louise Dr.* ☎ *403/522-3555.*

Mountain Magic Equipment. Canada's largest independent climbing outfitter has three floors of hiking, climbing, skiing, running, and biking gear and a 30-foot indoor climbing wall for testing equipment. ⊠ *224 Bear St.* ☎ *403/762-2591.*

The Ski Stop. This great spot rents bicycles as well as provides a bike shuttle and valet service and has guided soft-adventure tours and self-guided hard-adventure tours. There's also a demo-to-buy ski rental program that allows you to put your ski rental toward the purchase of your skis. Additionally, the shop has free equipment pickup and return for skis and snowboards. ⊠ *203 A Bear St., Banff* ☎ *403/760-1650* ⊕ *www.theskistop.com.*

White Mountain Adventures. Daily guided hikes, backpacking, and heli-hiking can be arranged through this outfitter. In winter, you can try snowshoeing, cross-country skiing, or a guided ice walk. ⊠ *#7 107 Boulder Crescent, Canmore* ☎ *403/678-4099 or 800/408-0005* ⊕ *www.whitemountainadventures.com.*

Yamnuska Inc. Canada's largest mountain-guide company has programs for groups and individuals. ⊠ *200, 50 Lincoln Park, Canmore* ☎ *403/678-4164* ⊕ *www.yamnuska.com.*

DID YOU KNOW?

A staggering 33 feet of powder fall on Banff's Sunshine Village each year, creating a winter sports paradise. Snowboarders and skiers can hit over 3,300 acres of terrain on three mountains.

■TIP➔ A good bargain is a $239.85, three-day pass that allows you to ski at Sunshine Village, Ski Banff at Norquay, and Lake Louise. It includes free shuttle service to the slopes. You can purchase the pass at the ski areas or at Banff Ski Hub store.

For equipment shops, ⇨ *Mulitport Outfitters and Expeditions box.*

EDUCATIONAL OFFERINGS

There is a wide range of park interpretive programs in Banff. At the Banff Information Centre and at Cave and Basin, there are slide shows and presentations throughout the year. In the summer months you can enjoy campground interpretive programs, guided hikes, bicycle tours, film showings, and adventure games at Banff Avenue square.

Friends of Banff National Park. This nonprofit group provides roving naturalist programs, guided hikes, and junior naturalist programs designed especially for children. The junior naturalist programs take place at Tunnel Mountain Campground, Johnston Canyon Campground, Two Jack Lakeside Campground, and Lake Louise Campground Theatre. ⊠ *224 Banff Ave., Banff* ☎ *403/762–8918* ⊠ *Free or nominal fee* ⊕ *www.friendsofbanff.com.*

☾ **Mountain World Heritage Interpretive Theatre.** Each summer Parks Canada's
★ troupe of professional actors put on entertaining and educational free performances for park guests. Performances take place at the Upper Hot Springs, around the townsite, and at the Johnston Canyon Mountain Theatre. ☎ *403/760–1328* ☾ *July and Aug.*

ARTS AND ENTERTAINMENT

ARTS VENUES

★ **Banff Centre.** Most of the cultural activity in the Canadian Rockies takes place in and around Banff, and the hub of that activity is at this center composed of 16 buildings across 43 acres. It presents a performing-arts grab bag throughout the year of pop and classical music, theater, and dance. The season peaks in summer with the monthlong **Banff Arts Festival** (☎ *403/762–6300*), with concerts, performances, films, and discussions. The **Walter Phillips Gallery** (☎ *403/762–6281* ⊠ *Free* ☾ *Tues., Wed., and Fri.–Sun. noon–5, Thurs. noon–9*) within the center showcases contemporary artwork by Canadian and international artists. ⊠ *St. Julien Rd., on Tunnel Mountain* ☎ *403/762–6100, 800/413–8368 in Alberta and British Columbia* ⊕ *www.banffcentre.ca.*

WHAT'S NEARBY

NEARBY TOWNS

About 25 km (15 mi) southeast of Banff Townsite, **Canmore** became a modest boomtown with the 1988 Olympics. It attracts a mix of tourists, residents who seek a mountain lifestyle, and Calgary residents who feel the hour-long commute is a fair trade-off for living in the mountains.

FESTIVALS AND EVENTS

JANUARY

Ice Magic ice-sculpting contest. On weekends, beginning the third Friday in January, ice carvers from around the world compete in this annual competition held at various locations in Lake Louise. This free exhibition remains on display until the first of March, weather permitting. ☎ *403/762-8421* ⊕ *www. banfflakelouise.com.*

Banff–Lake Louise Winter Festival. Winter sports are the highlight of the festival that also features outdoor events, nightly bar activities, and a town party. It begins on the third Friday in January and runs for 10 days. ☎ *403/762-8421* ⊕ *www. banfflakelouise.com.*

APRIL

Easter at Sunshine Village. Stop in for Easter-egg hunts, church service at the top of the strawberry chairlift, and visits by the Easter Bunny. ☎ *403/762-6508.*

JUNE–AUGUST

Banff Summer Arts Festival. Every summer the Banff Centre presents film screenings, visual-art displays, theater, opera, dance, and musical productions. ☎ *403/762-6300* ⊕ *www.banffcentre.ca/bsaf.*

JULY

Canada Day Celebration. Canada Day means free admission to the national park and it means big celebrations in Canmore and Banff including a parade, fireworks, and live music. ☎ *403/762-0285.*

NOVEMBER–DECEMBER

Christmas in the Rockies and Santa Claus Parade. Banff welcomes the Christmas season with a one-day event with photos with Santa in Central Park, treats, crafts, and an evening parade of lights. On Christmas Day, Santa skis at the three area ski resorts. ☎ *403/762-8421.*

Canmore makes a good base for exploring both Kananaskis Country and Banff National Park, without the crowds or cost of Banff.

Three provincial parks make up the 4,200-square-km (1,600-square-mi) recreational region known as **Kananaskis Country,** whose northern entrance is 26 km (16 mi) southeast of Canmore. The area includes grand mountain scenery, though perhaps not quite a match for that in the adjacent national parks. You can take part in the same activities you'd find in the national parks, and Kananaskis allows some activities that are prohibited within the national-park system, such as snowmobiling, motorized boating, off-road driving, and mountain biking. The main route through Kananaskis Country is Highway 40, also known as the Kananaskis Trail. It runs north–south through the front ranges of the Rockies. Only the northern 40 km (25 mi) of the road remain open from December 1 through June 15, in part because of the extreme conditions of Highwood Pass (at 7,280 feet, the highest drivable pass in Canada), and in part to protect winter wildlife habitats in Peter Lougheed Provincial Park and southward. Highway 40 continues south to join Highway 541, west of Longview. Access to East Kananaskis Country, a popular area for horseback trips, is on Highway 66, which heads west from the town of Priddis.

VISITOR INFORMATION

Banff Lake Louise Tourism ⊠ *224 Banff Ave., Banff* ✆ *P.O. Box 1298, Banff, Alberta, Canada T1L 1B3* ☎ *403/762–8421* ⊕ *www.banfflakelouise.com.* **Tourism Canmore** ⊠ *907 7th Ave., Canmore* ✆ *P.O. Box 8608, T1W 2V3* ☎ *403/678–1295 or 866/226–6673* ⊕ *www.tourismcanmore.com.*

AREA ACTIVITIES

SPORTS AND THE OUTDOORS

Many of the outfitters and operators who run tours in Banff National Park are based in Canmore, so if you're staying here, you can often join the tour from Canmore rather than having to drive to the park. Equipment for activities can be rented at most sports shops in Canmore.

GOLF

Kananaskis Country Golf Course (⊠ *Off Hwy. 40* ☎ *403/591–7272 or 877/591–2525* ⊕ *www.kananaskisgolf.com*), one of the premier golf courses in the Canadian Rockies, has two 18-hole, par-72 links. Eighteen-hole, par-72 **Silvertip Golf Course** (⊠ *1000 Silvertip Trail* ☎ *403/678–1600 or 877/877–5444* ⊕ *www.silvertipresort.com*) offers spectacular elevation changes and views of the valley and mountains from most holes.

SPELUNKING

OUTFITTERS AND EXPEDITIONS ☾ If you have ever wanted to don a headlamp and explore an undeveloped cave, you can have **Canmore Caverns Ltd.** (⊠ *1009 Larch Pl.* ☎ *403/678–8819 or 877/317–1178* ⊕ *www.canadianrockies.net/wildcavetours*) arrange a suitable caving experience. The outfitter supplies the equipment and you bring the enthusiasm. Children should be at least nine years of age to participate.

WATER SPORTS

OUTFITTERS AND EXPEDITIONS ☾ Unique guided kayak adventures using inflatable kayaks on white water are available through **Blast Adventures** (⊠ *120 B Rundle Dr., Canmore* ☎ *403/609–2009 or 888/802–5278* ⊕ *www.blastadventures.com*). Transportation from Banff or Canmore is included.

WINTER SPORTS

☾ ★ **Canmore Nordic Centre.** Built for the 1988 Olympic Nordic skiing events, Canmore Nordic Centre has 70 km (43 mi) of groomed cross-country trails in winter that become mountain-biking trails in summer. Some trails are lighted for night skiing, and a 1½-km (1-mi) paved trail is open in summer for roller skiing and rollerblading. This state-of-the-art facility is in the northwest corner of Kananaskis Country, south of Canmore. In late January, the annual **Canmore International Dogsled Race**—a two-day event—takes place here, attracting more than 100 international teams. ⊠ *1988 Olympic Way* ☎ *403/678–2400* ⌨ *Trails free Apr.–Oct., C$7.50 per day Nov.–Mar.* ☉ *Lodge daily 9–5:30; trails open 7* AM–11 PM, *some trails illuminated until 9* PM.

Nakiska. The site of the 1988 Olympic alpine events, Nakiska is 45 minutes southeast of Banff and has wide-trail intermediate skiing and a sophisticated snowmaking system. The vertical drop is 2,412 feet, and there are four lifts. ⊠ *Off Hwy. 40, Kananaskis Village* ☎ *403/591–7777.*

WHERE TO EAT AND STAY

ABOUT THE RESTAURANTS

Eating out is, for the most part, a casual affair with an emphasis on good fresh food served in large quantities. Trout, venison, elk, moose, and bison appear on the menus of even many modest establishments. Prices everywhere are slightly inflated.

ABOUT THE HOTELS

The lodgings in Banff compose an eclectic list that includes backcountry lodges without electricity or running water, campgrounds, hostels with shared bathroom facilities, standard roadside motels, quaint B&Bs, supremely luxurious hotels, and historic mountain resorts. Most accommodations do not provide meal plans, but some include breakfast.

With just a few exceptions, room rates are often highest from mid-June to late September and between Christmas and New Year's. In many cases, the best accommodation rates can be found during the months of October to mid-November and May to mid-June when rates can drop by as much as 50%. Lodgings in this chapter are listed with their peak-season rates. Check in advance for off-season rates.

If you want to save money, consider staying in nearby Canmore and in Kananaskis Country.

ABOUT THE CAMPGROUNDS

Parks Canada operates 13 campgrounds in Banff National Park (not including backcountry sites for backpackers and climbers). The camping season generally runs from mid-May through October, although the Tunnel Mountain and Lake Louise campgrounds remain open year-round. Hookups are available at most of the campgrounds and at four of the 31 Kananaskis Country campgrounds. Prices for a one-night stay range from C$16 to C$38. A fire permit is required to use a fire pit. In some cases the permit is purchased separately and in others it's included in the rates. Banff and Lake Louise participate in a reservation system that allows visitors to prebook campsites at Tunnel Mountain and Lake Louise campgrounds for a fee of C$11. The other campgrounds in the park operate on a first-come, first-served basis. To reserve a campsite, visit ⊕ *www.pccamping.ca* or call ☎ *905/566–4321 or 877/737–3783.* For backcountry camping in Banff or Lake Louise, call Lake Louise Backcountry Trails Office at ☎ *403/522–1264.* Numerous privately run campgrounds can be found outside park boundaries.

WHERE TO EAT

IN THE PARK

$$$$ ✕**Banffshire Club.** The Scottish influence in the region becomes immedi-
CONTINENTAL ately apparent when you enter the exclusive Banffshire Club, with its vaulted ceilings, oak paneling, tartan drapes, and reproduction Stuart-era furniture. Named for the Scottish town from which Banff gets its name, this intimate restaurant serves exceptional gourmet cuisine made from Canada's finest ingredients. Entrées include butter-poached Nova Scotia lobster, roast young partridge with truffles, and pecan-crusted

caribou. Staff members are all sommelier trained to help you choose from the extensive wine cellar. While some people may choose to dress for dinner, you don't have to here: the dress code is resort casual. ✉ *Fairmont Banff Springs, 405 Spray Ave., Banff* ☎ *403/762–6860* ⊕ *www.fairmont.com/banffsprings* ⚔ *Reservations essential* ▭ *AE, D, DC, MC, V* ☉ *Closed Sun. and Mon. No lunch.*

$$$ ✕ **The Bison.** Chef-owner Ryan Rivard combines fresh, local, organically
CANADIAN grown ingredients to create innovative cuisine he calls "Rocky Mountain comfort food." The restaurant has its own charcuterie that produces delicious smoked regional meats, and Rivard has experience and a flare for selecting cheeses to accompany them. There is an emphasis on slow cooking and making everything from scratch—even the ketchup and mustard for the bison burgers are made in-house. There's a lounge on the lower level where you can enjoy a glass of wine and a snack or a light meal without breaking the bank, or you can pop upstairs and enjoy a multicourse gourmet meal in the dining room or on the outdoor patio. The decor is modern and contemporary with hardwood floors and vaulted ceilings and an open kitchen. The Rocky Mountain charcuterie board, the grilled bison strip loin with roasted pear salad, or the AAA Alberta beef tenderloin with goat-cheese whipped potatoes are regional specialties on the dinner menu. ✉ *211 Bear St., Banff* ☎ *403/762–5550* ⊕ *www.thebison.ca* ▭ *AE, MC, V* ☉ *No lunch weekdays.*

$$$$ ✕ **Bow Valley Grill.** Serving breakfast, lunch, and dinner in a relaxed dining
CANADIAN room with magnificent views of the Fairholme Mountain Range and the Bow Valley, this is one of the most popular restaurants in the Fairmont Banff Springs hotel. You can choose between à la carte or buffet dining. There's a tantalizing selection of fresh market rotisserie-grilled meats, salads, and seafood, plus bread from an on-site bakery. The weekend brunches are legendary, with a wonderful selection of breakfast and dinner favorites including made-to-order omelets, prime rib, smoked salmon, salads, and a wide selection of tantalizing desserts. ✉ *Fairmont Banff Springs, 405 Spray Ave., Banff* ☎ *403/762–6860* ⊕ *www.fairmont.com* ⚔ *Reservations essential* ▭ *AE, D, DC, MC, V.*

$$$ ✕ **Coyotes Deli & Grill.** Fresh, healthy ingredients are used to create a
SOUTHWESTERN wide array of southwestern-style dishes for breakfast, lunch, and dinner. Breakfast favorites include scrambled eggs and salmon, stuffed French toast, and warm seven-grain cereal topped with fresh berries, pecans, and yogurt. For lunch or dinner you can't go wrong with the spicy black-bean burrito, the southwestern polenta with ratatouille, or the oven-baked salmon. There are a good number of vegetarian selections and the in-house deli can prepare picnic lunches to go. The small restaurant is decorated with log beams and warm Santa Fe colors. ✉ *206 Caribou St., Banff* ☎ *403/762–3963* ▭ *AE, D, MC, V.*

$$$$ ✕ **Eden.** Luxurious decor and magnificent mountain views form the
CONTINENTAL backdrop for a dinner of regionally influenced French cuisine. The Eden
Fodor's Choice has won numerous awards and is the only AAA/CAA five-diamond
★ restaurant in western Canada. Food is prepared à-la-minute from fresh ingredients and the menu is constantly changing. There are four fixed dining options, but the main courses constantly change; previous entrées have included pan-seared venison loin, red deer with preserved

Often found nibbling, elk like to eat such plants as beargrass, aspen leaves, sagebrush, and chokecherries.

cranberry and beets, and cinnamon-smoked short ribs. The prix-fixe menu is C$95 for three courses, C$110 for four courses, or C$125 for five courses. Wine pairings from an extensive wine collection can be added; if you don't indulge in wine, consider having the sommelier do a tea pairing with your meal. ⊠ *Rimrock Resort Hotel, 100 Mountain Ave., Banff* ☎ *403/762–1865* ⊕ *www.rimrockresort.com* ⌚ *Reservations essential* ═ *AE, D, DC, MC, V* ⊙ *No lunch.*

\$\$
CANADIAN
✕ **Elk & Oarsman.** This second-floor pub is popular with locals and serves quality pub fare such as elk burgers, Tuscan-sausage pizzas, fish-and-chips, and steaks. All pizzas are C$9 on Mondays and you can get a steak sandwich on Tuesdays for only $8. Ask for a table by the window so you can watch the action along Banff Avenue. Families are welcome daily until 10 PM. ⊠ *119 Banff Ave., Banff* ☎ *403/762–4616* ═ *AE, MC, V.*

\$\$
FRENCH
✕ **Le Beaujolais Café de Paris.** This café is a recent addition to one of Banff's well-known and widely acclaimed fine-dining restaurants. French bistro fare at reasonable prices—trout almondine (trout with almonds), *moules* and *frites* (mussels and fries) featuring PEI (Prince Edward Island) mussels, and elk meatloaf—is served in a casual dining atmosphere. Ask for a table next to the window so you can people-watch on Banff Avenue. ⊠ *Banff Ave. and Buffalo St., Banff* ☎ *403/762–2712* ═ *AE, MC, V.*

\$\$\$\$
CONTINENTAL
Fodor's Choice
★
✕ **Post Hotel.** The Post dining room is a destination all by itself—one of the true epicurean experiences in the Canadian Rockies. A low, exposed-beam ceiling and a stone, wood-burning hearth in the corner lend a warm, in-from-the-cold atmosphere; white tablecloths and fanned napkins provide an elegant touch. The combination of modern and classic dishes leads to daring regionally inspired fresh market cuisine. Look for innovative dishes prepared with fresh fish, game, or Alberta beef.

The Post is one of only four restaurants in Canada to receive the *Wine Spectator* Grand Award with a 2,200-label wine list and an incredible cellar that boasts more than 32,000 bottles of wine. For a unique dining experience with a group of six or more, ask to dine in the private cellar dining room. ⊠ *200 Pipestone Rd., Lake Louise* ☎ *403/522–3989 or 800/661–1586* ⚲ *Reservations essential* ▭ *AE, MC, V.*

$$$$ ✕ **The Sleeping Buffalo.** Located in the main lodge of the Buffalo Mountain
CANADIAN Lodge, this rustic, casual dining room serves breakfast, lunch, and dinner. Historic photos and native artifacts adorn the light green walls, and there are plenty of windows to let in natural light. Fresh indigenous berries, wild fruits, local meats, and regional vegetables are skillfully and artistically combined with fresh herbs grown in the lodge's large garden to create fine Rocky Mountain cuisine. The lodge has its own game farm, and smoked, cured, or roasted wild game is a specialty here. Try the pulled-elk sandwich for lunch or the grilled buffalo rib eye with potato and spinach gratin, tempura cornmeal onions, and sour cherry black pepper sauce for dinner. The wine list is extensive. ⊠ *700 Tunnel Mountain Rd., 1 mi west of Banff* ☎ *403/762–2400* ⊕ *www.crmr.com* ▭ *AE, DC, MC, V.*

$ ✕ **Trailhead Cafe.** Local work crews, mountain guides, and park wardens
CAFE come to this small café in the Samson Mall for a hot breakfast or lunch. There's a good selection of baked goods, made-to-order sandwiches, wraps, and salads, as well as hot and cold drinks. It's a good place to pick up a sandwich if you're driving north on the Icefields Parkway. ⊠ *Samson Mall, off Hwy. 1, Lake Louise* ☎ *403/522–2006* ▭ *MC, V.*

$$$$ ✕ **Walliser Stube.** For something that's fun and a little different, try this
SWISS Swiss wine bar with warm cherrywood and a large selection of fondues. Choose from bison, beef, tuna, or seafood in broth, or classic cheese fondues. Meat and seafood fondues are served with young vegetables, steamed potatoes, mushrooms, and a selection of sauces. Be sure to save room for dessert: a Swiss chocolate dessert fondue served with banana bread, fresh fruit, marshmallows, and whipped cream. There is also an excellent selection of fine wines kept in the back room, which is affectionately known as the wine library because the floor-to-ceiling shelves are lined with wine, not books. ⊠ *Fairmont Château Lake Louise, Lake Louise Dr., Lake Louise* ☎ *403/522–3511 Ext. 1817* ⊕ *www.fairmont. com/lakelouise* ▭ *AE, D, DC, MC, V* ◔ *No lunch.*

PICNIC AREAS **Bow Lake picnic area.** Situated on the shores of stunning Bow Lake, on the Icefields Parkway, this picnic area has a kitchen shelter, five tables, toilets, and fireboxes. ⊠ *Icefields Pkwy., at the edge of Bow Lake.*

Cascade picnic area. This spot has 60 tables, a kitchen shelter, fireplaces, and flush toilets. ⊠ *Off Lake Minnewanka Rd.*

Fireside picnic area. Located on the Bow Valley Parkway, this picnic area has picnic tables and toilets nearby. ⊠ *Off Bow Valley Pkwy.*

☾
★ **Lake Minnewanka picnic area.** This popular picnic area has three picnic shelters, 35 tables, flush toilets, two fire rings, and six fireplaces. Hike, rent a boat, or try your luck at fishing. ⊠ *10 km (6 mi) from Banff on the Minnewanka Loop.*

Moraine Lake picnic area. One of the most beautiful lakes in the Canadian Rockies is the setting for this picnic area located near Lake Louise.

There are two kitchen shelters, eight tables, and toilets at this site. ⊠ *Off Moraine Lake Rd., 5 km (3 mi) from the village of Lake Louise.*

OUTSIDE THE PARK

$$$
ECLECTIC

✕**The Trough Dining Co.** Fine dining without the attitude is the theme for this intimate restaurant with hardwood floors, a glass waterfall, and orange-terracotta walls. Selected by *Where* magazine as one of the top 10 new restaurants in Canada in 2007, the Trough has an ever-changing menu that features fresh locally-grown ingredients that are carefully prepared and creatively displayed. Slow cooking is the norm—the ribs are marinated for four days and the balsamic braised Alberta lamb shank is slow roasted for an entire day. There's a good selection of wines and a palate-cleansing sorbet is served between the appetizer and the main course. ⊠ *725 B 9 St., Canmore* ☎ *403/678–2820* ⊕ *www.thetrough.ca* ▭ *AE, MC, V* ⊗ *No lunch.*

WHERE TO STAY

IN THE PARK

$$$$

▦ **Banff Caribou Lodge & Spa.** Hand-hewn logs, slate flooring, and a massive fieldstone fireplace give the lobby of this hotel a mountain lodge ambience. Rooms have a western feel with basic pine furnishings; some have balconies and wood-burning fireplaces. There is a hot tub and steam room, and the Red Earth Spa is one of the largest spas in Banff with six treatment rooms offering a variety of services. The hotel adds extra value by offering free Internet, free local calling, inexpensive long-distance rates, complimentary bus transportation, and free heated underground parking. **Pros:** large lobby; value-added amenities like free Internet; excellent spa. **Cons:** average rooms; 10-minute walk to downtown. ⊠ *521 Banff Ave., Banff* ☎ *403/762–5887 or 800/563–8764 in North America* ⊕ *www.bestofbanff.com/banff-caribou-lodge* ⟿ *195 rooms, 6 suites* ⚘ *In-room: no a/c, Wi-Fi. In-hotel: restaurant, room service, gym, spa, laundry facilities, laundry service, parking (free), Wi-Fi* ▭ *AE, D, DC, MC, V.*

$$$$

▦ **Delta Banff Royal Canadian Lodge.** They take service so seriously at this intimate boutique-style lodge that every night—rain or shine (or snow)—they clean the windshields of their guests' cars. Rooms at the hotel are standard size but well appointed. Some rooms have fireplaces, and five rooms have access to a private garden terrace that is particularly nice during the summer months. The grotto-style indoor mineral pool is made to mimic a natural hot springs and is a highlight of the property. There is a good lounge and restaurant on-site. **Pros:** intimate property; 10-minute walk to downtown; mineral pool and steam room. **Cons:** fee for parking; gym is very small. ⊠ *459 Banff Ave.* ☎ *403/762–3307, 800/661–1379* ⊕ *www.charltonresorts.com* ⟿ *99 rooms* ⚘ *In-room: refrigerator, Wi-Fi. In-hotel: restaurant, room service, pool, gym, parking (paid), Wi-Fi* ▭ *AE, D, MC, V.*

$$$$
⟳

▦ **Douglas Fir Resort & Chalets.** The huge indoor water park and playground at this resort on Tunnel Mountain are a sure-fire hit with families. The water park has two waterslides, a swimming pool, a kiddie pool, two hot tubs, a sauna, and a steam room. Nearby is a fitness room, where you can work out while watching the kids play in the water park.

Outside are tennis courts, basketball courts, and a barbecue station. The array of room types ranges from bachelor suites for two people to one-bedroom loft condos with a separate kitchen and a living room that accommodate six comfortably. Or choose one of two A-frame chalets with multiple bedrooms. No matter the option, the units aren't fancy—just clean and comfortable, with basic wooden furnishings. All have well-equipped kitchens, and most have wood-burning fireplaces and balconies or patios. **Pros:** large indoor playground and water park; kitchen facilities. **Cons:** 10-minute drive to townsite; abundance of children at the resort. ⊠ *Tunnel Mountain Rd.* ☏ *403/762–5591, 800/661–9267 in North America* ⊕ *www.douglasfir.com* ⇱ *130 condo rooms, 3 specialty suites, 9 chalets* ⟅ *In-room: kitchen, Wi-Fi. In-hotel: tennis courts, pool, gym, laundry facilities, Internet terminal, Wi-Fi, parking (free) some pets allowed* ☐ *AE, MC, V.*

$$$$
Fodor's Choice
★
Fairmont Banff Springs. Affectionately known as "The Castle in the Rockies," this massive hotel built by the Canadian Pacific Railway in 1888 marked the beginning of Banff's tourism boom. The hotel retains its historic elegance—not to mention magnificent views of the Bow River and surrounding peaks—but it also includes modern amenities that make for a luxurious lodging experience. Pampering is a form of art at the world-class Willow Stream spa. Restaurants, bars, and lounges of varying formality and cuisine create a small culinary universe. In the summer, about 200 rooms per night are reserved for individual travelers on inclusive resort packages. If the hotel is the focus of your visit to Banff, these packages represent good value. Rates decrease substantially off-season. If you join the free Fairmont's President's Club prior to your visit, then during your stay you can enjoy complimentary access to the Internet and health club, a free shoe shine, and discounts at the spa. Riding stables are on the grounds. **Pros:** ultra-luxurious; many amenities; historical property. **Cons:** costly rooms and dining. ⊠ *405 Spray Ave.* ☏ *403/762–2211 or 800/441–1414* ⊕ *www.fairmont.com/banffsprings* ⇱ *770 rooms, 70 suites* ⟅ *In-room: Internet. In-hotel: 10 restaurants, room service, bars, golf course, tennis courts, pools, gym, spa, Wi-Fi, parking (paid), some pets allowed* ☐ *AE, D, DC, MC, V.*

$$$$
★
Fairmont Château Lake Louise. There's a good chance that no hotel anywhere has a more dramatic view out its back door. Terraces and lawns reach to the famous aquamarine lake, backed by the Victoria Glacier. Guest rooms have neocolonial furnishings, and some have terraces. The hotel began as a wooden chalet in 1890, but it was largely destroyed by 1924 fire. It was soon rebuilt into the present grand stone-facade structure. The nearly half-dozen dining choices range from family dining in the Brasserie to night-on-the-town elegance in the Fairview Dining Room (jacket required for dinner during the summer). If you join the free Fairmont's President's Club prior to your visit, then during your stay you can enjoy free use of the Internet and health club, a shoe shine, and discounts at the spa. Riding stables and canoe rentals are available on the property during the summer months. In the winter, you can enjoy a sleigh ride around the lake or rent ice skates and enjoy skating on Lake Louise. **Pros:** stunning setting; abundant amenities; luxurious accommodations. **Cons:** costly rooms and dining; farther away from the

townsite than some of the other lodging options. ✉ *Lake Louise Dr., Lake Louise* ☎ *403/522–3511 or 800/441–1414* ⊕ *www.fairmont.com/ lakelouise* ⇋ *433 rooms, 54 suites* ⚲ *In-room: no a/c (some), Internet. In-hotel: 5 restaurants, pool, gym, spa, laundry service, Wi-Fi, parking (paid), some pets allowed* ⊟ *AE, D, DC, MC, V.*

$$$$
★
Fox Hotel & Suites. One of the newest hotels in Banff, the Fox is close enough to the busy downtown core that you can walk to most of the shopping and nightlife and far enough away that you won't be bothered by the noise of it. Rooms are mostly suites with kitchenettes and separate living-room areas. Some rooms at the back of the property have views of the mountains. All rooms open to a central courtyard area, and there is a man-made replica hot springs in the basement with faux rock walls. Several freebies are part of the deal: Internet access, local calling (plus inexpensive long distance), bus transportation, and heated underground parking. **Pros:** kitchen facilities; value-added amenities like free Internet; good interior design. **Cons:** small fitness facility; parking is tight. ✉ *461 Banff Ave., Banff* ☎ *403/760–8500 or 800/563–8764* ⊕ *www. bestofbanff.com/fox-hotel-suites* ⇋ *116 rooms, 66 suites* ⚲ *In-room: no a/c (some), Wi-Fi. In-hotel: restaurant, room service, pool, gym, laundry facilities, laundry service, parking (free)* ⊟ *AE, D, DC, MC, V.*

¢
HI Banff Alpine Centre. This hostel is one of the best accommodation values in the park. You can purchase packages that include lift tickets in winter or adventure activities in the summer. There are plenty of dorm-style rooms (some with private baths), six private ensuites, and two cabins; guests at the hostel have access to a fridge, communal kitchen, TV room, library, and dining area. The hostel has an activities program, but the activities are designed for the young adults who tend to stay here and are generally not appropriate for children. This property is a long walk from the townsite; however, a free bus pass is included in the rates. **Pros:** economical; good for singles; free Wi-Fi. **Cons:** few private rooms; a long walk from townsite. ✉ *801 Hidden Ridge Way* ☎ *403/670–7580 or 866/762–4122* ⊕ *www.hihostels.ca* ⇋ *146 4- to 6-bedroom dorms with shared bath, 65 4- to 6- bedroom dorms with private bath, 6 private rooms, 2 cabins* ⚲ *In-room: no a/c, Wi-Fi. In-hotel: restaurant; laundry facilities, Internet terminal, Wi-Fi, parking (free)* ⊟ *MC, V.*

$$$$
★
Post Hotel. Part of the exclusive Relais & Châteaux hotel group, the Post is one of the best retreats in the Rocky Mountains. It has an understated elegance that has garnered international attention. The bright red roof and post-and-beam log construction make this hotel a landmark in Lake Louise. The gourmet restaurant features fresh market cuisine (using fresh, in-season ingredients) and is regularly rated as one of the best in the Canadian Rockies; the wine cellar is one of the best in Alberta. Rooms come in 15 configurations, from standard doubles to units with a sleeping loft, balcony, fireplace, and whirlpool tub. The deluxe suites each have a king-size bed and a large living room with a river-stone fireplace. If you like old-fashioned, in-the-mountains romance, try one of the three streamside log cabins. Furnishings are solid Canadian pine throughout. Room rates decrease by about 40% off-season. **Pros:** gourmet dining on site; luxurious. **Cons:** costly rooms and dining; rustic ambience. ✉ *200 Pipestone Rd., Lake Louise* ☎ *403/522–3989 or*

7

800/661–1586 ⊕ *www.posthotel.com* 🛏 *69 rooms, 26 suites, 3 cabins* ⌂ *In-room: no a/c, Wi-Fi. In-hotel: restaurant, pool, gym, spa, Wi-Fi, parking (free)* ⊟ *AE, MC, V.*

$$ 🏨 **Red Carpet Inn.** There's nothing fancy here—just clean, simple, comfortable motel rooms. All rooms have mini-fridges and there is a free Continental breakfast included in the room price. Other features like free local calling and free wireless Internet make this inn one of the best values in Banff. The suites offer options for large families or for couples who want a Jacuzzi and/or fireplace in their room at a reasonable price. There's an on-site hot tub, and guests also have access to the pool, sauna, and hot tub at the High Country Inn. Rooms at the back of the property are quieter and have the best views of the mountains. **Pros:** good value; free breakfast and Wi-Fi; 10-minute walk to townsite. **Cons:** small lobby; few amenities. ✉ *425 Banff Ave.* ☎ *403/762–4184, 800/563–4609 in North America* ⊕ *www.banffredcarpet.com* 🛏 *70 rooms* ⌂ *In-room: refrigerator, Wi-Fi. In-hotel: Wi-Fi, Internet terminal, parking (free)* ⊟ *AE, MC, V* ⏐◎⏐ *CP.*

$$$$ 🏨 **Rimrock Resort Hotel.** Luxury and natural splendor coexist in harmony at
★ this 11-story hotel perched on the steep slope of Sulphur Mountain. The Grand Lobby has a 25-foot ceiling, giant windows, a balcony facing the Rockies, and an oversize marble fireplace. There are two lounges and two restaurants on site, including Eden *(F ⇨ Where to Eat),* one of only seven AAA-rated five-diamond restaurants in all of Canada. Nearly all rooms have views of the Bow Valley or Spray Valley, though the views from the lower floors are compromised by trees. Off-season rates drop by 50%. You can catch a free Banff transit bus to Banff Townsite. There's also an excellent fitness facility on-site with squash and racquetball courts, a steam room, sauna, and hot tub. **Pros:** spectacular views; close to hot springs and a gondola; top-notch gourmet dining. **Cons:** farther from townsite than some other options; there is a fee to use the gym and take the fitness classes. ✉ *300 Mountain Ave.* ☎ *403/762–3356 or 888/746–7625* ⊕ *www.rimrockresort.com* 🛏 *346 rooms, 6 suites* ⌂ *In-room: Wi-Fi. In-hotel: 2 restaurants, pool, gym, spa, Wi-Fi, parking (paid)* ⊟ *AE, D, DC, MC, V.*

CAMPING ⛺ **Castle Mountain Campground.** This campground is located in a beau-
$$ tiful wooded area close to a small store, a gas bar, and a restaurant. **Pros:** lovely setting; flush toilets. **Cons:** no electricity; no showers. ✉ *34 km (21 mi) from Banff on Bow Valley Pkwy.* ☎ *403/762–1550* ⛺ *43 tent/RV sites* ⌂ *Flush toilets* ⚑ *Reservations not accepted* ⊟ *AE, MC, V* ⊙ *Open mid-May–early Sept.*

$$ ⛺ **Johnston Canyon Campground.** The scenery is spectacular and the wildlife abundant in and around this campground, which is across from Johnston Canyon. A small creek flows right by the camping area. Sites are first-come, first-served. **Pros:** pretty spot close to Johnston Canyon. **Cons:** no electricity; many tourists during the day. ✉ *25 km (15½ mi) from Banff on Bow Valley Pkwy.* ☎ *403/762–1550* ⛺ *132 tent/RV sites* ⌂ *Flush toilets, showers* ⊟ *AE, MC, V* ⊙ *Open early June–mid-Sept.*

$$ ⛺ **Lake Louise Campground.** This forested area next to the Bow River is open
☾ year-round, but in early spring and late fall tents and soft-sided trailers
★ are not permitted in order to protect both people and bears. A protective electrical fence with a Texas gate surrounds the campground. There are

plenty of hiking and biking trails nearby. **Pros:** many amenities; on-site interpretive programs. **Cons:** busy campground; decreased privacy. ⊠ *1 km (½ mi) from Lake Louise Village and 4 km (2½ mi) from the Lake* ☏ *877/737–3783* ⚠ *206 tent sites, 189 RV sites* ⚬ *Flush toilets, partial hookups (electric), dump station, showers, fire pits* ⊟ *AE, MC, V.*

$$–$$$ ⚠ **Tunnel Mountain Campground.** Situated close to the townsite, this campground has a great view of the valley, hoodoos, and the Banff Springs golf course. There are 321 full-service sites in the trailer court, 188 power-only sites in Village II, and 618 nonserviced sites in Village I. **Pros:** close to Banff Townsite; many amenities (electricity, shows, flush toilets); on-site interpretive programs. **Cons:** busy campground; decreased privacy. ⊠ *2½ km (1½ mi) from Banff Townsite on Tunnel Mountain* ☏ *877/737–3783* ⚠ *618 tent sites, 509 RV sites* ⚬ *Flush toilets, full hookups, showers, fire pits* ⊟ *AE, MC, V* ⊙ *Open mid-May–early Oct.*

$$ ⚠ **Two Jack Main Campground.** This secluded camp is situated in a beautiful wooded area with lots of wildlife. You can explore the ruins of the coal-mining town of Bankhead, located nearby. If you want showers, stay at Two Jack Lakeside Campground right across the road. **Pros:** secluded setting; flush toilets. **Cons:** no showers; farther away from town. ⊠ *12 km (7½ mi) from Banff on the Minnewanka Loop* ☏ *403/762–1550* ⚠ *380 tent/RV sites* ⚬ *Flush toilets* ⚘ *Reservations not accepted* ⊟ *AE, MC, V* ⊙ *Open mid-May–early Sept.*

OUTSIDE THE PARK

$$$ 🏨 **Delta Lodge at Kananaskis.** Now part of the Kananaskis Village built for the 1988 Olympics, this hotel started life as a Canadian Pacific luxury hotel. Rooms are large and lavish—many have fireplaces, hot tubs, and sitting areas. Rooms in the Signature Club building are a little larger and have extra amenities like free Internet service, separate concierge service, an honor bar, Continental breakfast, and afternoon hors d'oeuvres. The resort has a large pool, an indoor-outdoor hot tub, tennis courts, a eucalyptus-infused steam room, and a well-equipped fitness center. The Summit Spa offers treatments for both men and women, and there is an activities program for children during peak seasons. In the summer months you can rent bicycles in Kananaskis Village and enjoy miles of excellent trails or enjoy a round of golf at the nearby golf course. Free shuttle service to the adjacent Nakiska Ski Resort is available in the winter. Several on-site restaurants, skewed toward elegance, serve everything from pizza and burgers to haute cuisine. **Pros:** beautiful mountain setting; family-friendly resort; hiking, biking, golf, skiing nearby. **Cons:** isolated: 25- to 30-minute drive to Canmore and one-hour drive to Banff. ⊠ *Hwy. 40, 28 km (17 mi) south of Hwy. 1, Kananaskis Village* ☏ *403/591–7711 or 888/244–8666 in North America* ⊕ *www.deltahotels.com* ⟿ *412 rooms* ⚬ *In-room: Internet. In-hotel: 4 restaurants, bar, room service, pool, spa, gym, laundry facilities, Wi-Fi* ⊟ *AE, D, MC, V.*

$$$ 🏨 **Falcon Crest Lodge.** This place is ideal for families or couples who enjoy cooking some of their own meals. The luxurious condos, only 20 minutes outside Banff, have marvelous views of the Three Sisters, Ha-Ling, and Rundle Mountain, and they're stuffed with the comforts of home: fully-equipped kitchens with granite countertops, marble bathrooms, gas fireplaces, balconies with individual gas barbecues, and modern furnishings.

7

The two outdoor hot tubs have great views and there is a Vietnamese restaurant on-site. There are laundry facilities in the lodge, but if you reserve a one-bedroom unit or larger, you'll have a washer and dryer right inside your condo. **Pros:** feels like a home away from home; great views; free Wi-Fi. **Cons:** 20-minute drive to Banff; no pool; small gym. ✉ *190 Kananaskis Way, Canmore* ☎ *403/678–6150, 866/609–3222 in North America* ⊕ *www.falconcrestlodge.ca* ⮡ *46 1-bedroom condos, 8 2-bedroom condos, 18 studio suites* ⚐ *In-room: kitchen, DVD, Wi-Fi. In-hotel: restaurant, gym, laundry facilities, Internet terminal, Wi-Fi* ⊟ *AE, MC, V.*

CAMPING
$$–$$$$

⚠ **Sundance Lodges Campground.** If you have always wanted to see what it is like to sleep in a real teepee, this is the place to go. This family campground has teepee camping, tent and RV sites, and old-fashioned trapper's tents. Campsites are set in a wooded area near a small creek. It's a quiet, secluded campground designed for peace and tranquility. There are no electrical hookups, but there are outlets in the washroom. There is a small fee for pets. If you don't have camping gear, you can borrow some for a small fee. **Pros:** beautiful setting in a treed area 3-km (1.9 mi) outside of Kananaskis Village; ideal for families; reasonable prices. **Cons:** secluded; farther from restaurants and services. ⌁ *P.O. Box 190, Kananaskis Village T0L 2H0* ☎ *403/591–7122* ⊕ *www. sundancelodges.com* ⚠ *30 tent/RV sites, 12 teepees, 18 trapper's tents* ⚐ *Pit toilets, drinking water, guest laundry, showers, fire pits, public telephone, general store* ⊟ *MC, V.*

Big Bend National Park

WORD OF MOUTH

"Big Bend is spectacular. Besides the National Park itself, the ghost town Terlingua is really cute, and for spectacular scenery, you should drive on highway 170 west of Lajitas for a couple of miles. It is a very, very scenic road."

—Traveller1959

WELCOME TO BIG BEND

TOP REASONS TO GO

★ **Varied terrain:** Visit gilded desert, a fabled river, bird-filled woods, and mountain spirals all in the same day.

★ **Wonderful wildlife:** Catch sight of the park's extremely diverse number of animals, including approximately two dozen shy mountain lions and eight to twelve lumbering bears.

★ **Bird-watching:** Spy a pied-billed grebe or another member of the park's more than 400 bird species, including the Lucifer hummingbird and the unique-to-this-area *pato mexicano* (Mexican duck).

★ **Hot spots:** Dip into the natural hot springs (105°F) near Rio Grande Village.

★ **Mile-high mountains:** Lace up those hiking boots and climb the Chisos Mountains, reaching almost 8,000 feet skyward in some places and remaining cool even during the most scorching Southern summer.

1 **North Rosillos.** Dinosaur fossils have been found in this remote, northern portion of the park. Made up primarily of back roads, this is where nomadic warriors traveled into Mexico via the Comanche Trail.

2 **Chisos Basin.** This bowl-shaped canyon amid the Chisos Mountains is at the heart of Big Bend. It's the place to watch a sunset and begin a hike.

3 **Castolon.** Just east of Santa Elena Canyon, this historic district was once used by ranchers and the U.S. military, earning it a place on the National Register of Historic Places.

4 **Rio Grande Village.** Tall, shady cottonwoods highlight the park's eastern fringe along the Mexican border and Rio Grande. It's popular with RVers and bird-watchers.

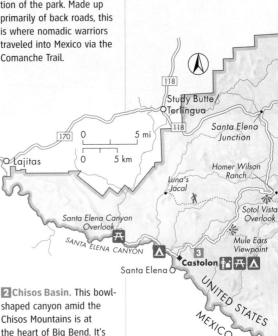

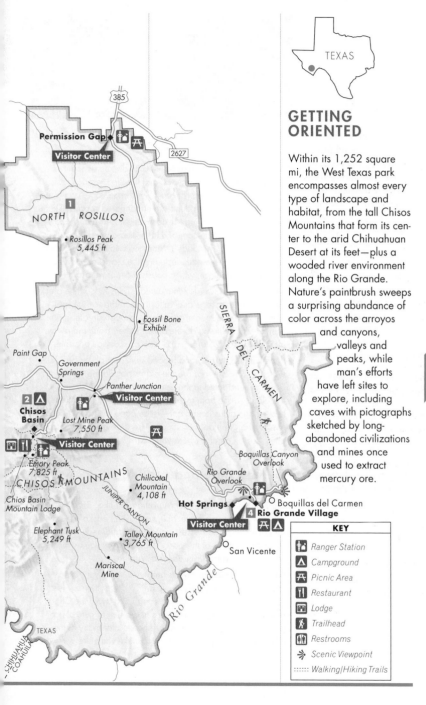

TEXAS

GETTING ORIENTED

Within its 1,252 square mi, the West Texas park encompasses almost every type of landscape and habitat, from the tall Chisos Mountains that form its center to the arid Chihuahuan Desert at its feet—plus a wooded river environment along the Rio Grande. Nature's paintbrush sweeps a surprising abundance of color across the arroyos and canyons, valleys and peaks, while man's efforts have left sites to explore, including caves with pictographs sketched by long-abandoned civilizations and mines once used to extract mercury ore.

385

Permission Gap

Visitor Center

2627

1

NORTH ROSILLOS

• Rosillos Peak
5,445 ft

• Fossil Bone Exhibit

SIERRA DEL CARMEN

Paint Gap

Government Springs

Panther Junction
Visitor Center

2 Chisos Basin

Lost Mine Peak
7,550 ft

Visitor Center

• Emory Peak
7,825 ft

CHISOS MOUNTAINS

Chisos Basin Mountain Lodge

JUNIPER CANYON

Chilicotal Mountain
4,108 ft

Boquillas Canyon Overlook

Rio Grande Overlook

Hot Springs

4 **Rio Grande Village**

Visitor Center

O Boquillas del Carmen

• Elephant Tusk
5,249 ft

Talley Mountain
3,765 ft

O San Vicente

Mariscal Mine

Rio Grande

TEXAS

CHIHUAHUA
COAHUILA

8

KEY	
🧍	Ranger Station
△	Campground
🛆	Picnic Area
🍴	Restaurant
🏨	Lodge
🚶	Trailhead
🚻	Restrooms
✳	Scenic Viewpoint
⋯⋯	Walking/Hiking Trails

BIG BEND PLANNER

When to Go

There is never a bad time to make a Big Bend foray—except during Thanksgiving, Christmas, and spring break. During these holidays, competition for rooms at the Chisos Mountains Lodge and campsites is fierce—with reservations for campsites and rooms needed up to a year in advance.

Depending on the season, Big Bend sizzles or drizzles, steams up collars or chills fingertips. Many shun the park in the summer, because temperatures skyrocket (up to 120°F), and the Rio Grande lowers.

In winter, temperatures rarely dip below 30°F. During those few times the mercury takes a dive, visitors might be rewarded with a rare snowfall.

The mountains routinely are 5 to 10 degrees cooler than the rest of the park, while the sweltering stretches of Rio Grande are 5 to 10 degrees warmer.

AVG. HIGH/LOW TEMPS

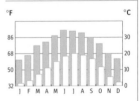

Flora and Fauna

Because Big Bend contains habitats as diverse as spent volcanoes, slick-sided canyons, and the Rio Grande, it follows that species here are extremely diverse, too. Among the park's most notable residents are endangered species like the agave- and cactus-eating Mexican long-nosed bat, shadow-dappled peregrine falcon, and fat-bellied horned lizard (Texans call them "horny toads"). More than 450 species of birds wing throughout the park, including the black-capped vireo and the turkey vulture, which boasts a 6-foot wingspan.

In the highlands two-dozen mountain lions lurk, while black bears loll in the crags and valleys. Your chances of spotting the reclusive creatures are rare, though greater in the early morning. If you do encounter either, don't run away. Instead, stand tall, shout, and look as scary as possible.

If the winged, furred, and legged denizens of Big Bend are watch-worthy, so, too, are the plants populating the region. Supremely adapted to the arroyos, valleys, and slopes, the plants range from the endangered Chisos Mountains hedgehog cactus (found only in the park) to the towering rasp of the giant dagger yucca. Also here are 60 types of cacti—so be careful where you tread.

Getting Here and Around

Big Bend is 39 mi south of Marathon, off U.S. 385; 81 mi south of Alpine, off Route 118; and 69 mi east of Presidio, off Route 170. The nearest airport is in Midland, three-and-a-half hours north of the park. The bus takes you as far as Marathon, and the train as far as Alpine.

Paved park roads have twists and turns, some very extreme in higher elevations; if you have an RV longer than 24 feet or a trailer longer than 20 feet, you should avoid the Chisos Basin Road into higher elevations in Big Bend's central portion. Four-wheel-drive vehicles are needed for many of the backcountry roads. At parking areas take valuables with you.

By Jennifer Edwards
Updated by Patrick Dearen

Cradled in the warm, southwestern elbow of Texas, the 801,163 acres of Big Bend National Park hang suspended above the deserts of northern Mexico. From the craggy, forested Chisos Mountains rising up to almost 8,000 feet to the flat and stark plains of the Chihuahuan Desert, Big Bend is one of the nation's most geographically diverse parks, with the kind of territory that inspired Hollywood's first western sets. Visitors can ride the rapids of the Rio Grande, trek through the classic, Old West landscape, and marvel at the moonscape that skirts Boquillas, Mexico.

8

PARK ESSENTIALS

ACCESSIBILITY
Visitor centers and some campsites at Rio Grande Village and Chisos Basin are wheelchair accessible. The Founder's Walk and Panther Path at Panther Junction; Window View Trail at Chisos Basin; and Rio Grande Village Nature Trail boardwalk are wheelchair-accessible trails. The Rio Grande and Chisos Basin amphitheaters also are accessible.

ADMISSION FEES AND PERMITS
It costs $20 to enter at the gate, and your pass is good for seven days. Camping fees in developed campgrounds are $14 per night, while backcountry camping is $10 for up to 14 days. Mandatory backcountry camping, boating, and fishing permits are available at visitor centers.

ADMISSION HOURS
Big Bend National Park never closes. Visitor centers may be closed Christmas Day. The park is in the central time zone.

ATMS/BANKS
The Rio Grande Village store and Chisos Basin Lodge have ATMs.

BIG BEND IN ONE DAY

You can drive the paved roads of the park in a day, but you miss the most striking parts if you don't get out and hike. Two not-to-miss trails are those through the rifts and boulders of **Santa Elena Canyon** and the rocky pinnacles of the **Chisos Mountain Basin**.

Access the Santa Elena trailhead from a turnaround at the end of **Ross Maxwell Scenic Drive** at the southwestern rim of the park. From there, take the **Santa Elena Canyon Trail** (1.7 mi round-trip). You'll need to wade Terlingua Creek, and then enter the canyon, home to gargantuan rocks, singular rock formations, and the Rio Grande sandwiched between sheer cliffs. Back at the trailhead take Ross Maxwell Scenic Drive 30 mi back north and turn east at Santa Elena Junction.

Drive to the **Chisos Mountains Basin Junction** and turn south on **Chisos Basin Road**. This scenic drive will take you to the heart of Big Bend, where you can amble leisurely along a less-than-half-mile hike along the **Window View Trail**. Settle in for a picnic lunch near the **Chisos Basin Visitor Center**.

Drive north back to the junction, turn east, and drive 23 mi to **Rio Grande Village**. Stroll through the tall, shady cottonwoods in the picnic area, home to many birds, including roadrunners. If you have the time, follow the signs to the natural hot spring and take a dip.

Before calling it a day, drive east to the **Boquillas Canyon** overlook and view the Mexican village of Boquillas on the south side of the Rio Grande.

CELL-PHONE RECEPTION
Cell phones do not often work in the park. Public telephones can be found at the visitor centers.

PARK CONTACT INFORMATION
Big Bend National Park ✉ *P.O. Box 129, Big Bend National Park 79834* ☎ *432/477–2251* ⊕ *www.nps.gov/bibe.*

SCENIC DRIVES

Chisos Basin Road. This road leads south from Chisos Basin Junction. By driving into higher elevations (the heart of Big Bend), you're likely to spot lions and bears as well as white-tailed deer amid juniper trees and pinyon pines. You'll also see lovely, red-barked Texas madrone along with some Chisos oaks and Douglas fir trees. Avoid this drive, however, if you are in an RV longer than 24 feet, because of sharp curves.

Fodor'sChoice ★ **Ross Maxwell Scenic Drive.** This route takes you 30 mi through pyramid-shaped volcanic mountains. If you don't mind a little grate in your gait from the gravel that blankets the road, you can make this drive a loop by starting out at the west park entrance and turning southwest onto Old Maverick Road (unpaved) for 12.8 mi to the Santa Elena Canyon overlook—where you can get a taste of the lowland desert. ■TIP→ If you're in an RV, don't even attempt Old Maverick Road. The road isn't paved and is rough going in some spots.

WHAT TO SEE

HISTORIC SITES

Castolon Historic District. Adobe buildings and wooden shacks serve as reminders of the farming and military community of Castolon. The Magdalena House has historical exhibits. ⊠ *At the end of the Ross Maxwell Scenic Dr., southwest portion of the park* ☎ *432/477–2225 ranger station.*

☼ **Hot Springs.** Hikers soak themselves in the 105°F waters alongside the Rio Grande and petroglyphs (rock art) coat the canyon walls nearby. The remains of a post office, motel, and bathhouse point to the old commercial establishment operating here in the early 1900s. ⊠ *15 mi southeast of Panther Junction, near Rio Grande Village.*

Mariscal Mine. Hardy, hard-working men and women once coaxed cinnabar, or mercury ore, from the Mariscal Mine, located at the north end of Mariscal Mountain. They left the mines and surrounding stone buildings behind for visitors to explore. If you stop here, take care not to touch the timeworn stones, as they may contain poisonous mercury residue. ⊠ *5 mi west of Rio Grande Village, on River Rd. E.*

SCENIC STOPS

★ **Chisos Basin.** Panoramic vistas, a restaurant with an up-close view of the mountains, and glimpses of the Colima warbler (which summers in Big Bend) await in the forested Chisos Basin. This central site also has hiking trails, a lodge, a campground, a grocery store, and a gift shop. ⊠ *Off Chisos Basin Rd., 7 mi southwest of Chisos Basin Junction and 9 mi southwest of Panther Junction.*

★ **Santa Elena Canyon.** The finale of a short hike (1.7 mi round-trip) is a spectacular view of the Rio Grande and cliffs that rise 1,500 feet to create a natural box. ⊠ *30 mi southwest of Santa Elena Junction via Ross Maxwell Scenic Dr.; 14 mi southwest of Rte. 118 via Old Maverick Rd.*

VISITOR CENTERS

Castolon Visitor Center. Here you'll find some of the most hands-on exhibits the park has to offer, with touchable fossils, plants, and implements used by the farmers and miners who settled here in the 1800s and early 1900s. ⊠ *In the Castolon Historic District, southwest side of the park, at the end of the Ross Maxwell Scenic Dr.* ☎ *432/477–2666* ☉ *Nov.–Apr., daily 10–5; closed for lunch.*

Fodor'sChoice ★ **Chisos Basin Visitor Center.** The center is one of the better equipped, as it offers an interactive computer exhibit and a bookstore, while an adjacent general store has camping supplies, picnic fare, and some produce. There are plenty of nods to the wild, with natural resource and geology exhibits and a larger-than-life representation of a mountain lion. ⊠ *Off Chisos Basin Rd., 7 mi southwest of Chisos Basin Junction and 9 mi southwest of Panther Junction* ☎ *432/477–2264* ☉ *Nov.–Mar., daily 8–3:30; Apr.–Oct., daily 9–4:30; closed for lunch.*

Panther Junction Visitor Center. The park's main visitor center includes a bookstore and exhibits on the park's mountain, river, and desert environments. Nearby, a gas station offers limited groceries such as chips, premade sandwiches, and picnic items. ⊠ *30 mi south of U.S. 385 junction leading to north park boundary* ☎ *432/477–1158* ☉ *Daily 8–6.*

8

West Texas fauna includes prairie dogs, jackrabbits, and roadrunners, while its flora includes yuccas.

Persimmon Gap Visitor Center. Complete with exhibits and a bookstore, this visitor center is the northern boundary gateway into miles of flat-lands that surround the more scenic heart of Big Bend. Dinosaur fossils have been found here; the **Fossil Bone Exhibit** is on the road between Persimmon Gap and Panther Junction. ⊠ *3 mi south of U.S. 385 junction* ☎ *432/477–2393* ☉ *Daily 9–4:30.*

Rio Grande Village Visitor Center. Opening days and hours are sporadic here, but if you do find this center open, then view videos of Big Bend's geological and natural features at its mini-theater. There are also exhibits dealing with the Rio Grande. ⊠ *22 mi southeast of Panther Junction* ☎ *432/477–2271* ☉ *Nov.–Apr., daily 8:30–4; closed for lunch.*

SPORTS AND THE OUTDOORS

Spectacular and varied scenery plus more than 300 mi of road spell adventure for hikers, bikers, horseback riders, or those simply in need of a ramble on foot or by Jeep. A web of dusty, unpaved roads lures experienced hikers deep into the backcountry, while paved roads make casual walks easier. Because the park has nearly half of the bird species in North America, birding ranks high. Boating is also popular, since some of the park's most striking features are accessible only via the Rio Grande.

BICYCLING

Mountain biking the backcountry roads can be so solitary that you're unlikely to encounter another human being. However, the solitude also means you should be extraordinarily prepared for the unexpected with ample supplies, especially water (summer heat is brutal, and you're unlikely to find shade except in forested areas of Chisos Basin). Biking is recommended only during the cooler months (October–April).

On paved roads, a regular road bike should suffice, but you'll have to bring your own—outfitters tend to only stock mountain bikes. Off-road cycling is not allowed in the park. For an easy ride on mostly level ground, try the 13-mi (one way) unpaved **Old Maverick Road** on the west side of the park off Route 118. For a challenge, take the unpaved **Old Ore Road** for 27 mi from the park's north area to near Rio Grande Village on the east side. *For bike rentals and expeditions, ⇨ Multisport Outfitters box.*

> **NOTABLE QUOTE**
>
> "I'd rather be broke down and lost in the wilds of Big Bend, any day, than wake up some morning in a penthouse suite high above the megalomania of Dallas or Houston."
>
> —Environmental writer Edward Abbey

BIRD-WATCHING

Situated on north–south migratory pathways, Big Bend is home to approximately 450 species of birds—more than any other national park. In fact, the birds that flit, waddle, soar, and swim in the park represent more than half the bird species found in North America, including the Colima warbler, found nowhere else in the United States. To glimpse darting hummingbirds, turkey vultures, golden eagles, and the famous Colima, look to the Chisos Mountains. To spy woodpeckers and scaled quail (distinctive for dangling crests), look to the desert scrub. And for cuckoos, cardinals, and screech owls, you must prowl along the river. Rangers lead birding talks *(⇨ Ranger Programs, under Educational Offerings).*

☾ Fodor's Choice ★ **Rio Grande Village.** Considered the best birding habitat in Big Bend, this river wetland has summer tanagers and vermilion flycatchers among many other species. The trail's a good one for kids, and a portion is wheelchair accessible. ⊠ *22 mi southeast of Panther Junction.*

OUTFITTERS AND EXPEDITIONS **Mark Smith Nature Tours.** The nine-day April trip, which includes the Texas Hill Country as well as Big Bend, runs $2,185. The trip either begins in El Paso and concludes in San Antonio or goes from San Antonio to El Paso. ⌂ *P.O. Box 3831, Portland, OR 97208* ☎ *800/821–0401 Willamette International Travel* ⊕ *www.marksmithnaturetours.com/destinations/bigbend.html.*

WINGS Birding Tours Worldwide. In the spring, this Arizona-based company offers a 10-day trip that encompasses Big Bend and the Davis Mountains. ⊠ *1643 N. Alvernon, Suite 109, Tucson, AZ 85712* ☎ *888/293–6443* ⊕ *www.wingsbirds.com/tours.*

BOATING AND RAFTING

Much is made of the park's hiking trails and the exquisite views they offer. Likewise, the watery pathway that is the Rio Grande should be mentioned for the spectacular views it affords. The 118 mi of the Rio Grande that border the park form its backbone, defining the vegetation, landforms, and animals found at the park's southern rim. By turns

8

shallow and deep, the river flows through stunning canyons and picks up speed over small and large rapids.

By turns soothing and exciting (Class II and III rapids develop here, particularly after the summer rains), the river can be traversed in several ways, from guided rafting tours to more strenuous kayak and canoe expeditions. In general, rafting trips spell smoother sailing for families, though thrills are inherent when soaring over the river's meringue-like tips and troughs. Always respect this river, however, for fatalities have occurred. ■TIP➜ Be sure to check the river levels before planning an outing—many times during the year the river's too low to get a decent rafting experience.

You can bring your own raft to the boat launch at the Rio Grande, but you must obtain a $10 river-use permit (which allows you to camp along the river) from a visitor center. Leave the Jet Skis at home; no motorized vehicles are allowed on the Rio Grande. For less fuss, go with a tour guide or outfitter on trips that range from a few hours to several days. Most outfitters are in the communities of Study Butte, Terlingua, and Lajitas, just west of the park boundary off Route 170. They rent rafts, canoes, kayaks, and inflatable kayaks (nicknamed "duckies") for when the river is low. Their guided trips last anywhere from a couple of hours to several days, and cost in the tens of dollars to thousands of dollars. Personalized river tours are available all year long, and since this is the Lone Star State, they might include gourmet rafting tours that end with beef Wellington and live country music. Though many of the rafting trips are relatively smooth, thus safe for younger boaters, be sure to tell the equipment-rental agent or guide if a party member weighs less that 100 pounds or more that 200, since special life jackets may be needed. ➪ *Multisport Outfitters box.*

FISHING

You can cast a line into the Rio Grande all year long for free, as long as you obtain a permit from one of the park's visitor centers. You cannot use jug lines, traps, or other nontraditional fishing methods.

HIKING

Each of the park's zones has its own appeal. The east side offers demanding mountain hikes, border canyons, limestone aplenty, and sandy washes with geographic spectacles. West-side trails go down into striking scenery in the Santa Elena Canyon and up into towering volcanic landforms. Descend into gorges and springs or ascend into the must-see scenic windows of Grapevine Hills. The heart of the park has abandoned mines, scrub vegetation around the Chisos, and deserts lying just below soaring Chisos Mountain aeries. ■TIP➜ Carry enough drinking water—a gallon per person daily (more when extremely hot).

While Big Bend certainly has "expedition level" trails to test the most veteran backpacker, many are very demanding and potentially dangerous (sometimes resulting in fatalities). So no "difficult" trails are noted below. Instead, the ones included here are representative of trails at Big Bend that most physically fit people can accomplish.

For group hiking expeditions, ➪ *Multisport Outfitters box.*

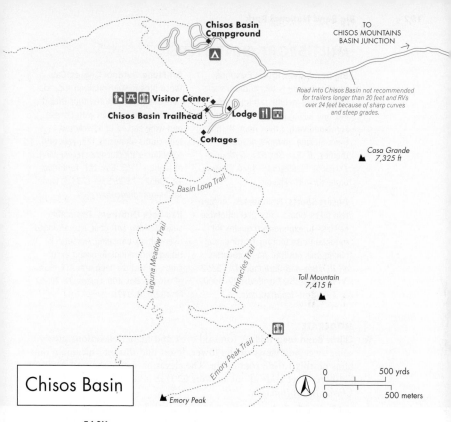

Chisos Basin

0 | 500 yrds
0 | 500 meters

EASY

☪ ★ **Chihuahuan Desert Nature Trail.** A windmill and spring form a desert oasis, a refreshing backdrop to a ½-mi, hot and flat nature trail; wild doves are abundant, the hike is pleasant, and kids will do just fine. While you're there, keep an eye out for the elf owl, one of the sought-after birds on the Big Bend's "Top 10" list. ⊠ *Trail accessed at Dugout Wells, 5 mi southeast of Panther Junction.*

☪ **Rio Grande Village Nature Trail.** This ¾-mi trail is short and easy yet packs a powerful wildlife punch. The village is considered one of the best spots in the park to see rare birds, and the variety of other wildlife isn't in short supply either. Keep a lookout for coyotes, javelinas (they look like wild pigs), and other mammals. Although this is a good trail for kids to lay their tootsies on, it isn't the most remote, so expect higher traffic. Nearby facilities are closed in the summer. Restrooms (open year-round) are nearby, and the trail can be done in less than an hour, even when lingering. The first ¼ mi is wheelchair accessible. ⊠ *Trail accessed 22 mi southeast of Panther Junction.*

☪ **Window View Nature Trail.** This 0.3-mi nature trail is wheelchair accessible and great for little ones. Take in the beautiful, craggy-sided Chisos with ease, as this self-guided trail is easily accomplished in less than an hour. ⊠ *Trail begins in the Chisos Basin.*

MULTISPORT OUTFITTERS

Big Bend River Tours. Exploring the Rio Grande is this outfitter's specialty. Tours include rafting, canoeing, and hiking and horseback trips combined with a river float. Rafting tours include gourmet or music themes. 🏠 *P.O. Box 317, Terlingua, TX 79852* 📞 *800/545–4240* ⊕ *www.bigbendrivertours.com.*

Desert Sports. From rentals—mountain bikes, boats, rafts, and inflatable kayaks—to experienced guides for mountain-bike touring, boating, and hiking, this outfitter has it covered. 🏠 *P.O. Box 448, Terlingua, TX 79852* 📞 *432/371–2727 or 888/989–6900* ⊕ *www.desertsportstx.com.*

Far Flung Outdoor Center. Call these pros for personalized trips via rafts and 4X4s. Tailored trips include gourmet rafting tours with cheese and wine served on checkered tablecloths alongside the river, and sometimes spectacular star-viewing at night. 🏠 *P.O. Box 377, Terlingua, TX 79852* 📞 *800/839–7238* ⊕ *www.farflungoutdoorcenter.com.*

Red Rock Outfitters. This outfitter sells clothing and gear, and arranges river-rafting, canoeing, horseback-riding, and mountain-biking excursions, as well as Jeep and ATV tours. 🏠 *HC 70, Box 400, Lajitas, TX 79852* 📞 *432/424–5170.*

MODERATE

★ **Chisos Basin Loop Trail.** A forested area and higher elevations give you some sweeping views of the lower desert and distant volcanic mountains on this 1.6-mi round-trip. The elevation where the trail begins is 5,400 feet. Set aside about an hour. ⊠ *Trail accessed 7 mi southwest of Chisos Basin Junction.*

Hot Springs Trail. An abandoned motel and a bathhouse foundation are among the sights along this 2-mi hike. The Rio Grande is heard at every turn, and trees shelter the walkway. Temperatures can soar to 120°F, so hike it during cooler months. ⊠ *Trail accessed 22 mi southeast of Panther Junction.*

The Lost Mine Trail. Set aside about two hours to leisurely explore the nature of the Chisos Mountains along this elevation-climbing trail. It starts at 5,700 feet, one of the highest elevations in the park, and climbs to an even higher vantage point. Though the air is thinner, all but the smallest kids should enjoy this trail because of the sweeping cliff view at the end of the first mile. The entire length of the trail is 4.8-mi round-trip. ⊠ *Trail begins at mile marker 5 on the Basin Rd.*

Fodor'sChoice **Santa Elena Canyon Trail.** A 1.7-mi round-trip crosses Terlingua Creek and
★ takes hikers to a view of steep cliffs jutting above the Rio Grande. Try to end up there near sunset, when the dying sun stains the cliffs a rich red-brown chestnut—its beauty can inspire poetry. It's a moderate-to-difficult trail, and worth every bead of sweat. ⊠ *Trail accessed 8 mi west of Castolon, accessible via Ross Maxwell Scenic Dr. or Old Maverick Rd.*

JEEP TOURS

Wheeled traffic is welcome in the park, up to a point. RVs, trucks, cars, and Jeeps are allowed in designated areas, though personal ATV use is prohibited. Jeep rental isn't available inside the park, but Jeep and ATV tours just outside the park are possible through outfitters. Jeep tours can cost as little as $49 for a two-hour tour, while ATV tours ring up at about $125 for the first person, with reduced rates for a second rider.

SWIMMING

Though it might be tempting to doff sweat-drenched T-shirts in favor of bathing suits, be careful where you take your dips. The Rio Grande has ample waters, but swimming isn't recommended due to dangerous currents and high pollution levels.

GOOD READS

■ *Naturalist's Big Bend,* by Roland H. Wauer and Carl M. Fleming, paints a picture of the park's diverse plants and animals.

■ *Big Bend, The Story Behind the Scenery,* by Carol E. Sperling and Mary L. Van Camp, is rife with colorful photos illustrating the park's history and geology.

■ For gleeful and awestruck thoughts on the Big Bend wilderness, check out *God's Country or Devil's Playground,* which collects the writing of nearly 60 authors.

EDUCATIONAL OFFERINGS

CLASSES AND SEMINARS

Big Bend Seminars. The Big Bend National History Association offers one- to two-day seminars covering subjects such as wildflowers, geology, and desert survival. Class size is limited, generally from five to 15, and the seminars are operated by the Far Flung Outdoor Center (⇨ *Multisport Outfitters box*). ⊠ *Held at locations throughout the park, P.O. Box 377, Terlingua 79852* ☎ *877/839–5337* ⊕ *www.farflungoutdoorcenter.com* ✎ *Fees vary.*

RANGER PROGRAMS

Birding Talks. Rangers lead two-hour birding tours; binoculars are needed. ⊠ *Chisos Basin Visitor Center* ☎ *432/477–2264* ⊙ *Nov.–Mar., daily 8–3:30; Apr.–Oct., daily 9–4:30; closed for lunch.*

Interpretive Activities. Ranger-guided activities include slide shows, talks, and walks on natural and cultural history. Check visitor centers and campground bulletin boards for event postings. ☎ *432/477–2251.*

Junior Ranger Program. This self-guided program for kids of all ages is taught via a $2 booklet of nature-based activities (available at visitor centers). Upon completion of the course, kids are given a Junior Ranger badge or patch, a certificate, and a bookmark. ☎ *432/477–2251.*

WHAT'S NEARBY

Just as many of Big Bend's zones are geographically isolated, the park itself is isolated among hundreds upon hundreds of miles of West Texas desert and scrub. The nearest metropolis is El Paso, 329 mi away, while

FESTIVALS AND EVENTS

FEBRUARY

Texas Cowboy Poetry Gathering.
Ranchers and cowboys congregate
at Sul Ross State University to regale
audiences with original poetry and
washtub-bass tributes to singers like
Bob Wills. ⊠ *Alpine* ☎ *432/837–*
2326 or 800/561–3712 ⊕ *www.*
cowboy-poetry.org.

SEPTEMBER

Big Bend Balloon Bash. Brightly
splashed hot-air balloons create
Kodak moments as they ascend
Alpine skies each Labor Day weekend. When the sun goes down, the
balloons light up, and the flames are
choreographed to music. ⊠ *Alpine*
79830 ☎ *432/837–7486.*

Marfa Lights Festival. A Labor Day
weekend celebration of nighttime,
multicolored mystery lights that dot
the Chinati Mountains. Visitors gather
to watch a parade, listen to live
music and frequent the food booths.

⊠ *Marfa Courthouse, Marfa 79843*
☎ *800/650–9696.*

NOVEMBER

Alpine Gallery Night Artwalk.
Each year, the peculiar mix of ranching and artist culture that inhabits
Alpine overflows the galleries and
seeps into the town's main drag, Holland Avenue. Musicians play at the
train depot, barbecue vendors crowd
the streets, and local artists display
their works in many downtown businesses. ⊠ *Alpine* ☎ *800/561–3712*
⊕ *www.alpinegallerynight.com.*
Terlingua International Chili
Championship. Each November, top
chili chefs spice up cooling weather
with four days of chili cooking, bragging, and gathering at Rancho CASI,
on the north side of Highway 170,
11 mi west of Study Butte. Some of
the prize-winning cooks dole out
samples. ⊠ *Terlingua* ☎ *210/887–*
8827 ⊕ *www.chili.org/terlingua.html*
or *www.krazyflats.com.*

the nearest sizable cities are Odessa and Midland, 222 and 242 mi,
respectively, to the northeast.

NEARBY TOWNS

Marathon, just 39 mi to the north, is one of the closest towns to Big Bend.
Once a shipping hub, the population-500 town still contains reminders
of its Old West railroad days. **Alpine,** a town of about 6,000, hunkers
down among the Davis Mountains 81 mi north of the park. The town
is known for its extensive college agriculture program at Sul Ross State
University. It also attracts celebrities like Will Smith and Jada Pinkett-
Smith, who have been spotted at its historic Holland Hotel. About 26
mi west of Alpine is **Marfa,** a population-2,000, middle-of-nowhere West
Texas city known for its spooky, unexplained "Marfa lights," attributed
to everything from atmospheric disturbances to imagination. Once the
headquarters of quicksilver mining (now defunct), **Terlingua** is just 7 mi
from the park's west entrance on Highway 118. Four mi to east of
Terlingua is **Study Butte,** which also has its roots in the old quicksilver
mining industry. The combined Terlingua-Study Butte population is
about 300. Follow Highway 170 west from Terlingua for 13 mi and
you come upon the flat-rock formations of tiny (pop. 75) **Lajitas.** Once

a U.S. Cavalry outpost, Lajitas, which means "little flat stones," has been converted to a resort area offering plenty of golf. The border town of **Presidio,** 69 mi from the park's west exit, is regarded as the gateway to northern Mexico. Across the border from Presidio is a spring-break favorite, **Ojinaga, Mexico,** famous for its partylike atmosphere. It's also a springboard to Copper Canyon, a striking series of canyons that runs down the west side of the Sierra Tarahumara.

Once a mining boomtown that fed off rich minerals and silver, **Boquillas, Mexico,** has shrunk to a small pool of families. It doesn't help matters that visitors are no longer able to just splash across the Rio Grande and into the city, which made money by selling hand-carved canes and the like. Instead, visitors are required to travel to this city via the legal checkpoints at Presidio or Del Rio. The best way to see the region is now from the belly of a raft.

From Presidio it's easy to cross the border. You can hail a cab, park and walk, or drive your vehicle across. Many people choose public transportation or walking, because in order to drive your car into Mexico, you may have to have a permit, Mexican auto insurance, and a tourist card. Bring your passport. For details, see the Department of State's Web site (⊕ *www.state.gov*).

VISITOR INFORMATION

Alpine Chamber of Commerce ⊠ *106 N. 3rd St., Alpine* ☏ *800/5613712 or 432/837–2326* ⊕ *www.alpinetexas.com.* **Big Bend Chamber of Commerce** ⊠ *No address* ☏ *No phone* ⊕ *www.bigbendchamberofcommerce.com.* **Del Rio Chamber of Commerce** ⊠ *1915 Veterans Blvd., Del Rio* ☏ *800/889–8149* ⊕ *www.drchamber.com.* **Marathon Chamber of Commerce** ⊠ *105 Hwy. 90 W, Marathon* ☏ *432/386–4516* ⊕ *www.marathontexas.net.* **Marfa Chamber of Commerce** ⊠ *207 N. Highland St., Marfa* ☏ *800/650–9696* ⊕ *www.marfacc. com.* **Presidio Chamber of Commerce** ⌖ *P.O. Box 2497, Presidio 79845* ☏ *432/229–3199* ⊕ *www.presidiotex.com.*

NEARBY ATTRACTIONS

Barton Warnock Environmental Education Center. A self-guided walking tour takes you through indoor and outdoor exhibits providing insight into cultural history and natural resources of the Big Bend area. It's a good way to become oriented to the Chihuahuan Desert before touring Big Bend. In the summer, the center offers Desert Garden Tours through a two-acre botanical expanse with representative Chihuahuan Desert flora. ⊠ *Off Rte. 170, 1 mi east of Lajitas* ☏ *432/424–3327* ⊕ *www.tpwd.state.tx.us/park/barton/ barton.htm* ⌦ *$3, Desert Garden Tours $14 per group* ☉ *Daily 8–4:30.*

Big Bend Ranch State Park. As a western buffer to Big Bend National Park, this rugged desert wilderness extends along the Rio Grande across more than 300,000 acres from southeast of Lajitas to Presidio. You can hike, backpack, raft, and even round up longhorn steers on the annual cattle drive put on by the park in April or October of each year. ⊠ *Entrance road at Fort Leaton, 4 mi southeast of Presidio off Rte. 170, Presidio* ☏ *432/229–3416* ⊕ *www.tpwd.state.tx.us/park/bigbend/bigbend.htm* ⌦ *$3* ☉ *Park 24 hrs; visitor centers daily 8–4:30.*

Fort Leaton State Historic Site. The 23-acre site in Presidio County contains a thick-walled adobe trading post that dates back to pioneer days. There are exhibits, a ½-mi trail, picnic sites, and a store. The park is day use only—no camping is available. ⊠ *4 mi south of Presidio on Hwy. 170, Presidio* ☎ *432/229–3613* ⊕ *www.tpwd. state.tx.us/spdest/findadest/parks/ fort_leaton* ☞ *$3* ☉ *Daily 8–4:30.*

McDonald Observatory Visitors Center. There's plenty to do here. Check out exhibits, examine sunspots and flares safely via film, or peer into the research telescopes. After nightfall, the observatory offers public observing activities at Star Parties. ⊠ *Hwy. 118 north through Alpine and Fort Davis, Fort Davis* ☎ *432/426–3640* ⊕ *www.mcdonaldobservatory.org* ☞ *Programs, $8; star parties, $10* ☉ *Observatory programs, 11 AM and 2 PM daily; star parties, after nightfall Tues., Fri., and Sat.*

Museum of the Big Bend. With 5,000 square feet of space, this history-lover's haven has exhibits representing the life and cultures of the region and sponsors an annual show on ranching handiwork (such as saddles, reins, and spurs) held in conjunction with the Cowboy Poetry Gathering each February. ⊠ *Sul Ross State University Campus, Alpine* ☎ *432/837–8730* ⊕ *www.sulross.edu/~museum* ☞ *Donations accepted* ☉ *Tues.–Sat. 9–5, Sun. 1–5.*

AREA ACTIVITIES

ARTS AND ENTERTAINMENT

While recreation and the outdoor adventures are alive inside the park, the arts are vibrant outside it. Activities include live poetry readings and Cinco de Mayo festivals that fill up streets and shut down towns.

The **Chinati Foundation** (🖃 *P.O. Box 1135, Marfa 79843* ☎ *432/729–4362* ⊕ *www.chinati.org*) changes its exhibits regularly and has a well-attended annual open house. People fly from all over the country to see the collection, and the foundation conducts tours of its huge contemporary-art holdings by appointment. Getting to the museum can be tricky, so call for directions or visit the Web site.

Ballroom Marfa (⊠ *108 E. San Antonio St., Marfa* ☎ *432/729–3600* ⊕ *www. ballroommarfa.org*) is part gallery, part performance art and live music venue. Young, hip, modern, and undeniably cool, the Ballroom welcomes visitors Thursday through Sunday from noon to 6; live music and arts performances take the stage on many Friday and Saturday evenings.

The West of the Pecos Rodeo, held each summer in Pecos (a small town 150 mi north of Big Bend), features dancing after the rodeo events have

BORDER CROSSING AT BIG BEND

Concerns about terrorism have led to strict border-crossing security at the Big Bend National Park boundary line. Villagers used to wait at the Rio Grande crossing with burros and pickup trucks to transport you into town just across the border. But no more. You'll also no longer see a rowboat operated by villagers from Santa Elena that once ferried visitors across the Rio Grande at the crossing point near Castolon in Big Bend National Park. Similarly, once upon a time, Big Bend visitors could splash across the Rio Grande and into the confines of Boquillas and Santa Elena, small Mexican towns that buttered their bread with the money they made selling Americans handicrafts. Now, if you want to visit one of the border towns, you must do so by entering official checkpoints in Texas. ⚠ If you try to re-enter the United States through the Big Bend park, you are subject to thousands in fines, one year's imprisonment, or both.

That said, it's easy to cross the border from Presidio, 69 mi from the park's west exit, and Del Rio, 220 mi east of Big Bend, as long as you know what documentation to bring. Once you're ready to cross, you'll be faced with a few options: hail a cab, park and walk, or drive your vehicle across. Many people choose public transportation or walking, because in order to drive your car into Mexico, you may have to have a permit, Mexican auto insurance, and a tourist card. To re-enter the United States, you'll need a passport, while children 16 and under will also need birth certificates. For more on this, visit the Department of State's Web site, ⊕ *www.state.gov.* ⚠ Do not take a rental car into Mexico without first checking with the rental car company—most U.S. rentals are not covered in Mexico, and you may be liable if anything happens to the car on the other side of the border. If you leave your car on the U.S. side, you can park it in a lot and just walk across the border, or take a cab. No matter what, bring a passport—it's required to cross back into the United States.

Once you get to Mexico, don't fret about language difficulties or money incompatibility. Border towns are very tourist friendly (sometimes overly so, as storekeepers get aggressive when trying to get visitors into their stores), and most there speak English. American money is also accepted, so it probably won't be necessary to get your greenbacks exchanged. Just don't carry too much money, as that will make you a target—just as in American cities. Most Mexican border towns are easy to get to and can be explored in as little as one or two days.

While you're there, be wary of the water, which carries germs to which most Americans have not developed immunity. Worse, the water supply has in the past been laced with high levels of dangerous chemicals. Dining should not be a concern if you stay on the tourist-frequented streets of Ojinaga, but exercise caution outside the tourist district. If food looks or smells spoiled, the vendor's hands don't look clean, or you see questionable sanitary practices, don't eat there.

8

MEXICO CUSTOMS

WHAT TO BRING TO MEXICO

■ **A passport.**

■ **Additional documentation.** Just in case, bring photo ID such as your driver's license or voter-registration card. Children 16 and under will need birth certificates to re-enter the United States.

■ **Your own water.** Although border towns are used to catering to U.S. tourists, their water supplies do not meet U.S. standards and have been shown to be laced with arsenic and other harmful compounds.

WHAT NOT TO BRING TO MEXICO

■ **Drugs.** Border patrol agents use drug-sniffing dogs on many cars leaving the park, and Mexican officials may search cars at customs.

■ **Ammo or guns.**

■ **Large amounts of cash.** It makes you a target.

■ **Flashy accessories.** Don't wear expensive jewelry or flaunt nice cameras.

ended for the night. Rodeo events take place throughout town, but the main event is conducted at Buck Jackson Rodeo Arena. ⊠ *Take Exit 42 off I-20, Pecos* ☎ *800/588-2855* ⊕ *www.pecosrodeo.com.*

WHERE TO EAT AND STAY

ABOUT THE RESTAURANTS

One word can sum up the fare available in the park: casual. You can wear jeans and sneakers to the one park restaurant, which has American-style fare. Outside the park, Alpine and Marfa in West Texas have the biggest selection.

ABOUT THE HOTELS

At the only hotel in the park, the Chisos Basin Mountain Lodge, visitors can select from a freestanding cabin or a hotel room, both within a pace or two of spectacular views—Chisos sunsets are not to be missed. It's fun to stay here because it's close to trails, and has a nice little gift shop and the park's only restaurant. Even if you don't stay here, go just to see the stunning view through the wall-sized dining room windows.

ABOUT THE CAMPGROUNDS

The park's copious campsites are separated, roughly, into two categories—frontcountry and backcountry. Each of its four frontcountry sites except Rio Grande Village RV Campground has toilet facilities at a minimum. You can reserve a spot at the other three locations from November 15 to April 15, and rangers recommend doing so as far in advance as possible. During the off-season, sites are given on a first-come, first-served basis. Make reservations by phone at ☎ 877/444-6777 or online at ⊕ *www.reserveusa.com.*

Far more numerous are the primitive backcountry sites, which have no amenities and are generally inaccessible via RV. Permits, available for $10 each from the visitor center, are needed to camp there. Primitive

Bluebonnets: the Pride of Texas

Ever since men first explored the prairies of Texas, the bluebonnet has been revered. American Indians wove folktales around this bright bluish-violet flower; early-day Spanish priests planted it thickly around their newly established missions; and the cotton boll and cactus competed fiercely with it for the state flower—the bluebonnet won the title in 1901.

Nearly half a dozen varieties of the bluebonnet, distinctive for flowers resembling pioneers' sunbonnets, exist throughout the state. From mid-January until late March, at least one of the famous flowers carpets the park: the Big Bend (also called Chisos)

bluebonnet has been described as the most majestic species, as its deep-blue flower spikes can shoot up to three feet in height. The Big Bend bluebonnets can be found beginning in late winter on the flats of the park as well as along the El Camino del Rio (Highway 170), which follows the legendary Rio Grande between Lajitas and Presidio, Texas.

For information on viewing the bluebonnets at their peak, March through May, call the Texas Department of Transportation Hotline ☎ 800/452–9292.

—Marge Peterson

campsites with spectacular views are accessed via the following back-country roads: River Road, Glenn Springs, Old Ore Road, Paint Gap, Old Maverick Road, Grapevine Hills, Pine Canyon, and Croton Springs. There are also some along these main roads: Nine Point Draw, Hannold Draw, and K-Bar.

8

WHERE TO EAT

IN THE PARK

¢–$$

AMERICAN

✕ **Chisos Mountains Lodge Restaurant.** Views of the imposing Chisos Mountains are a pleasant accompaniment to nicely prepared fare such as chicken-fried steak, hamburgers, Mexican food, and rainbow trout. The view is probably the best from any Texas restaurant and the salad bar isn't bad; there is a takeout hiker's lunch. ⊠ *7 mi southwest of Chisos Basin Junction and 9 mi southwest of Panther Junction* ☎ *432/477–2292* ▭ *AE, D, DC, MC, V.*

PICNIC AREAS

Castolon Area. There are two tables here next to the store parking lot.

Chisos Basin Area. There are about half a dozen tables scattered near the parking lot, as well as a few grills. The tables provide an awesome view of the Chisos Mountains. ⊠ *Off Chisos Basin Rd., 7 mi southwest of Chisos Basin Junction and 9 mi southwest of Panther Junction.*

Dugout Wells Area. There is a picnic table under the shady cottonwoods off the Dugout Wells Trail loop. There is also a vault toilet here (these type of facilities are more pleasant than pit toilets). However, as with all vault toilets in the park, there is no running water to wash your hands. We suggest bringing some hand wipes. ⊠ *6 mi southeast of Panther Junction.*

Persimmon Gap Area. Quiet and remote, this new picnic area has tables shaded by metal roofs called ramadas. There are no grills; there is a pit toilet. ⊠ *North Big Bend, 4 mi south of U.S. 385 junction.*

Rio Grande Village Area. Half a dozen picnic tables are scattered under cottonwoods south of the store. Half a mile away at Daniels Ranch there are two tables and a grill. Wood fires aren't allowed (charcoal and propane okay). ⊠ *2 mi southeast of Panther Junction.*

Santa Elena Canyon Area. Two tables sit in the shade next to the parking lot at the trailhead. There is a vault toilet. ⊠ *8 mi west of Castolon, accessible via Ross Maxwell scenic drive or Old Maverick Rd.*

OUTSIDE THE PARK

$–$$$
AMERICAN

✕ **Candelilla Cafe and Thirsty Goat Saloon.** Steaks, southwestern dishes, and Mexican-inspired fare are Candelilla's specialties. Glass walls give you unobstructed views of sunsets, and a quick stroll next door finds you a nightcap at the Thirsty Goat Saloon. ⊠ *Lajitas Resort, off Rte. 170, 25 mi west of park entrance, Lajita, 79852* ☎ *432/424–5000* ➌ *AE, D, DC, MC, V.*

$–$$$
CAFÉ

✕ **La Trattoria.** This impressive little café offers candlelight dinners and specializes in pasta dishes with authentic tomato basil sauce that lends a taste of Italy to the Chihuahuan Desert. If you prefer more traditional West Texas fare, there's Black Angus Rib-Eye. Walk-ins are welcome, but it's a good idea to reserve a table on weekends and during special events in the city. ⊠ *901 E. Holland Ave., Alpine* ☎ *432/837–2200* ➌ *AE, D, DC, MC, V.*

¢–$
PIZZA

✕ **Pizza Foundation.** This funky gas station turned hip pizza joint will appeal to most park visitors, and especially families, because of its casual atmosphere, good-smelling interior, and, most of all, the quality pizza the native Rhode Island owners turn out. Kids will dig the fun pizza names such as the Faux Caeser, as well as several varieties of limeade, including blueberry and melon. ⊠ *100 E. San Antonio St., Marfa* ☎ *432/729–3377* ➌ *AE, D, DC, MC, V.*

$–$$$
TEX-MEX

✕ **Reata.** This is a favorite eatery for many West Texans spending the day in Alpine. The restaurant feels both welcoming and upscale, with lots of wood, big tables, and an overall rustic feel. The menu features Tex-Mex touches such as tortilla soup and tenderloin tamales, while reflecting its Texas roots with dishes like calf fries and gravy. ⊠ *203 N. Fifth St., Alpine* ☎ *432/424–9232* ➌ *AE, D, DC, MC, V.*

WHERE TO STAY

IN THE PARK

$$
☾

▩ **Chisos Mountains Lodge.** Views of desert peaks and staying in the cooler, forested section of Big Bend's higher elevations complement comfortable rooms with refrigerators and microwaves. With ranger talks just next door at the visitor center, miles of hiking trails to suit all levels of fitness, and plenty of wildlife, this is a great place for kids. Remodeling of selected units was underway in 2009. Make advance reservations during the October-to-May busy season—up to a year's lead time is not out of the question for spring break and holidays. Guests can rent a TV/DVD player and movies. **Pros:** refrigerators; microwaves. **Cons:** no phones or TVs. ⊠ *7 mi southwest of Chisos Basin Junction and 9 mi southwest of Panther Junction, 79834* ☎ *432/477–2291* ⊕ *www. chisosmountainslodge.com* ⤳ *72 rooms* ⚴ *In-room: no phone, no TV. In-hotel: restaurant, some pets allowed* ▭ *AE, D, DC, MC, V.*

CAMPING   ⚿ **Chisos Basin Campground.** Scenic views and cool shade are the high-
$ lights here. Steep grades and twisting curves mean trailers longer than 20 feet and RVs longer than 24 feet are not recommended. **Pros:** has shelters; 360-degree views. **Cons:** Offers little privacy; often is full. ⊠ *7 mi southwest of Chisos Basin Junction* ☎ *432/477–2251* ⚴ *60 sites* ⚴ *Flush toilets, drinking water, grills, picnic tables, food service, public telephone, general store, ranger station* ▭ No credit cards.

$ ⚿ **Cottonwood Campground.** This Castolon-area campground is a popu-
lar bird-watching spot. The grounds are generator-free. **Pros:** has shady trees; less crowded than some other campgrounds in area. **Cons:** blazing seasonal heat; sometimes has pesky insects. ⊠ *Off Ross Maxwell Scenic Dr., 22 mi southwest of Santa Elena Junction* ☎ *432/477–2251* ⚴ *35 sites* ⚴ *Pit toilets, drinking water, grills, picnic tables, general store, ranger station* ▭ No credit cards.

$ ⚿ **Rio Grande Village Campground.** A shady oasis, this campground is a
☂   birding "hot spot." It's also a great site for kids and seniors, due to the
★   ease of accessing facilities. RV parking is available. **Pros:** river environ-
ment; convenient to store. **Cons:** blazing seasonal heat; often full in winter. ⊠ *22 mi southeast of Panther Junction* ☎ *432/477–2251* ⚴ *100 sites* ⚴ *Flush toilets, dump station, drinking water, guest laundry, show-ers, grills, picnic tables, public telephone, general store, service station, ranger station* ▭ No credit cards.

$$ ⚿ **Rio Grande Village RV Park.** Often full during holidays, this is one
☂   of the best sites for families because of the mini-theater and proxim-
ity to the hot spring, which is fun to soak in at night. Register at the Rio Grande Village Store (22 mi southeast of Panther Junction). Only 30-amp electrical connections are available. You must have a 3-inch sewer connection to stay here. **Pros:** river environment; convenient to store. **Cons:** no reservations permitted. ⊠ *22 mi southeast of Panther Junction* ☎ *432/477–2293* ⚴ *25 RV sites* ⚴ *Dump station, drinking water, guest laundry, grills, picnic tables, electricity, public telephone, general store, service station, ranger station* ▭ *AE, D, MC, V.*

OUTSIDE THE PARK

$–$$ ⌂ **Holland Hotel.** Once just a stop on the transcontinental railroad, the
Holland Hotel is now a historic landmark in downtown Alpine. Still hung with its original, vertical sign, the hotel is set on the town's main, bustling drag—just doors down from a quaint café and across from a coffee shop. Choose from a light-filled penthouse at the top of the motel, a 1,000-square-foot loft, or basic rooms on the second and third floor. **Pros:** an affordable retreat to the past; complimentary breakfast. **Cons:** nearby trains make a lot of noise (but management provides earplugs). ⊠ *209 W. Holland Ave., Alpine* ☎ *800/535–8040* ⊕ *www.hollandhotel. net* ⤳ *28 rooms* ⚴ *In-room: no phone (some), kitchen (some), Wi-Fi* ▭ *AE, D, MC, V* ⦿ *BP.*

8

$-$$ ☷ **Hotel Paisano.** Once the playground of Liz Taylor, Rock Hudson, and
Fodor'sChoice   James Dean, who stayed here while filming *Giant,* the Paisano has kept
★   its glamour with beautiful Mediterranean architecture and a fountain
in the center. It's located amid downtown Marfa's quirky buildings and
just down the street from the historic courthouse. **Pros:** exudes a wonderful "Hollywood golden age" nostalgia; in the center of town. **Cons:**
no elevator. ⊠ *207 N. Highland St., Marfa* ☎ *432/729–3669* ⊕ *www.
hotelpaisano.com* ⌂ *41 rooms* ⌂ *In-room: no phone (some), Wi-Fi.
In-hotel: pool, Wi-Fi* ⊟ *AE, D, MC, V.*

$$-$$$$ ☷ **Lajitas Resort.** This is the nicest place to eat, shop, and overnight
Fodor'sChoice   within 25 mi of the park. Various theme motels and lodging options are
★   available (under the same ownership) in this revived ghost town con-
verted into a classy, Old West–style resort community alongside the Rio
Grande. Conveniences within walking distance of Lajitas include a res-
taurant and lounge. Make reservations well in advance of holidays and
spring break. The resort is under new ownership, but some visitors have
noted that service can lag behind the reputation. **Pros:** resort is a town
unto itself; many luxury activities, including full spa and golf course.
Cons: quite expensive. ⊠ *Hwy. 170, 17 mi west of Hwy. 118* ⌂ *HC
70, Box 400, Lajitas 79852* ☎ *432/424–5000, 877/525–4827 reserva-
tions* ⊕ *www.lajitas.com* ⌂ *72 rooms, 16 suites, 2 cottages* ⌂ *In-room:
kitchen (some), refrigerator (some). In-hotel: 3 restaurants, bar, golf
course, pool, spa, bicycles, laundry service* ⊟ *AE, D, DC, MC, V.*

CAMPING   ⚠ **Big Bend Resort & Adventures.** Under new ownership, the motel units
$-$$ were undergoing impressive renovation in 2009. Shade trees and a scenic setting make the full-service RV park a nice roosting place within
3 mi of the west park entrance. It has a restaurant, gas station, gift shop,
and golf course. **Pros:** phones and TVs in all rooms; full-service RV
park. **Cons:** adjacent to horse stables. ⊠ *Hwy. 118, 3 mi west of west
park entrance, Terlingua* ☎ *800/848–2363* ⊕ *www.bigbendresorts.com*
⚠ *85 motel rooms, 125 RV sites, separate informal tent area* ⌂ *Flush
toilets, full hookups, drinking water, guest laundry, showers, grills,
picnic tables, food service, electricity, public telephone, general store,
service station* ⊟ *AE, D, DC, MC, V.*

Black Canyon of the Gunnison National Park

WORD OF MOUTH

"Stop and listen to the roar of the Gunnison River that runs through the canyon 2,000 to 2,700 feet below the rim. This park has good overlooks, roads, parking, restrooms, and picnic areas. There are also lots of hiking opportunities."

—Msheinberg

WELCOME TO BLACK CANYON

TOP REASONS TO GO

★ **Sheer of heights:** Play it safe, but edge as close to the canyon rim as you dare and peer over into an abyss that's more than 2,700 feet deep in some places.

★ **Rapids transit:** Experienced paddlers can tackle Class-V rapids and 50°F water with the occasional portage past untamable sections of the Gunnison River.

★ **Fine fishing:** Fish the rare Gold Medal Waters of the Gunnison. Of the 9,000 mi of trout streams in Colorado, only 168 mi have this "gold medal" distinction.

★ **Triple-park action:** Check out Curecanti National Recreation Area and Gunnison Gorge National Conservation Area, which bookend Black Canyon.

★ **Cliff-hangers:** Watch experts climb the Painted Wall—Colorado's tallest vertical wall at 2,250 feet—and other challenging rock faces.

1 East Portal. The only way you can get down to the river via automobile in Black Canyon is on the steep East Portal Road. There's a campground and picnic area here, as well as fishing and trail access.

KEY	
🚻	*Ranger Station*
⛺	*Campground*
🏕	*Picnic Area*
🥾	*Trailhead*
🚻	*Restrooms*
⚜	*Scenic Viewpoint*
------	*Walking/Hiking Trails*

2 North Rim. If you want to access this side of the canyon from the south, expect a drive of up to three hours as you wind around the canyon. The area's remoteness and difficult location mean the North Rim is never crowded; the road is partially unpaved and closes in the winter. There's also a small ranger station here.

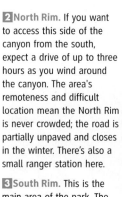

COLORADO

GETTING ORIENTED

3 South Rim. This is the main area of the park. The park's only visitor center is here, along with a campground and a few picnic areas. The South Rim Road closes at Gunnison Point in the winter, when skiers and snowshoers take over.

Black Canyon of the Gunnison is a park of extremes—great depths, narrow widths, tall cliffs, and steep descents. It is not a large park, but it offers incredible scenery and unforgettable experiences, whether you're hiking, fishing, or just taking it all in from the car. The adjacent parks and other open spaces offer even more opportunity for adventure.

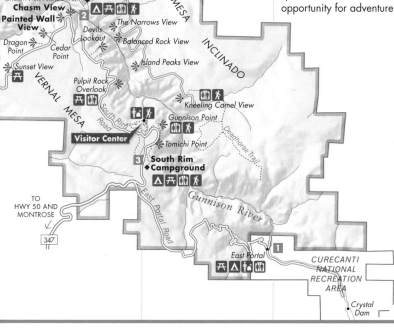

North Rim Road (closed in winter)

North Vista Trail

North Rim Campground

North Rim Ranger Station

Chasm View Nature Trail

Chasm View

Painted Wall View

The Narrows View

Devils Lookout

Balanced Rock View

MESA

Dragon Point

Cedar Point

Island Peaks View

INCLINADO

Sunset View

VERNAL MESA

Pulpit Rock Overlook

South Rim Road

Kneeling Camel View

Gunnison Point

Visitor Center

Tomichi Point

Deadhorse Trail

3 **South Rim Campground**

9

TO HWY 50 AND MONTROSE

347

East Portal Road

Gunnison River

East Portal

1

CURECANTI NATIONAL RECREATION AREA

Crystal Dam

BLACK CANYON OF THE GUNNISON PLANNER

When to Go

Summer is the busiest season, with July experiencing the greatest crowds. **A spring or fall visit gives you two advantages: fewer people and cooler temperatures**—in summer, especially in years with little rainfall, daytime temperatures can reach into the 90s. A winter visit to the park brings even more solitude, as all but one section of campsites are shut down and only about 2 mi of South Rim Road, the park's main road, are plowed.

November through February is when the snow hits, with 9 to 24 inches of it monthly on average. April and May, and September through November are the rainiest, with a monthly average of 1.7 to 2.2 inches of rain. June is generally the driest month, with only about 1 inch of rain on average.

Temperatures at the bottom of the canyon are about 8 degrees warmer than at the rim.

Flora and Fauna

You may spot peregrine falcons nesting in May and June, or other birds of prey such as red-tailed hawks, Cooper's hawks, and golden eagles circling overhead at any time of year. In summer, turkey vultures join the flying corps, and in winter, bald eagles. Mule deer, elk, and the very shy bobcat also call the park home. In spring and fall, you may see a porcupine among pinyon pines on the rims. Listen for the high-pitched chirp of the yellow-bellied marmot, which hangs out on sunny, rocky outcrops. Though rarely seen, mountain lions and black bears also live in the park.

Getting Here and Around

Located in southwest Colorado, Black Canyon of the Gunnison lies between the cities of Gunnison and Montrose. Both have small regional airports.

The park has three roads. South Rim Road, reached by Route 347, is the primary thoroughfare and winds along the canyon's South Rim. From about late November to early April, the road is not plowed past the visitor center at Gunnison Point. North Rim Road, reached by Route 92, is usually open from May through Thanksgiving; in winter, the road is unplowed. The serpentine East Portal Road descends abruptly to the Gunnison River on the park's south side. The road is usually open from the beginning of May through the end of November. Because of the grade, vehicles or vehicle-trailer combinations longer than 22 feet are not permitted. The park has no public transportation.

Avg. High/Low Temps

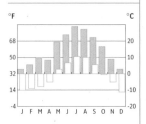

°F   °C

68   20

50   10

32   0

14   -10

-4   -20

J F M A M J J A S O N D

Updated
by Martha
Connors

The Black Canyon of the Gunnison River is one of Colorado's, and indeed the West's, most awe-inspiring places. A vivid testament to the powers of erosion, the canyon is roughly 2,000 feet deep. At its narrowest point, it spans 1,000 feet at the rim and only 40 feet at the bottom. The steep angles of the cliffs make it difficult for sunlight to fully break through during much of the day, and ever-present shadows blanket the canyon walls, leaving some places in almost perpetual darkness. No wonder it's called the "Black Canyon."

PARK ESSENTIALS

9

ACCESSIBILITY

South Rim Visitor Center is accessible to people with mobility impairments, as are most of the sites at South Rim Campground. Drive-to overlooks on the South Rim include Tomichi Point, the alternate gravel viewpoint at Pulpit Rock (the main one is not accessible), Chasm View (gravel), Sunset View, and High Point. Balanced Rock (gravel) is the only drive-to viewpoint on the North Rim. None of the park's hiking trails is accessible by car.

ADMISSION FEES AND PERMITS

Entrance fees are $15 per week per vehicle. Visitors entering on bicycle, motorcycle, or on foot pay $7 for a weekly pass. To access the inner canyon, whether for hiking, climbing, camping, or kayaking, you must pick up a backcountry permit (no fee) at South Rim Visitor Center, North Rim ranger station, or East Portal ranger station, in adjoining Curecanti National Recreation Area.

ADMISSION HOURS

The park is open 24/7 year-round. It's in the mountain time zone.

ATMS/BANKS

The park has no ATMs. The nearest ATMs are in Montrose.

BLACK CANYON IN ONE DAY

Pack a lunch and head to the canyon's South Rim, beginning with a stop at the **South Rim Visitor Center**. Before getting back into the car, take in your first view of Black Canyon from **Gunnison Point**, adjacent to the visitor center. Then set out on a driving tour of the 7-mi **South Rim Road**, allowing the rest of the morning to stop at the various viewpoints that overlook the canyon. Don't miss **Chasm View**

and **Painted Wall View**, and be sure to stretch your legs along the short (0.7-mi round-trip) **Cedar Point Nature Trail**. If your timing is good, you'll reach **High Point**, the end of the road, around lunchtime.

After lunch, head out on **Warner Point Nature Trail** for an hour hike (1½ mi round-trip). Then retrace your drive along South Rim Road back to the visitor center.

CELL-PHONE RECEPTION

Cell-phone reception in the park is unreliable and sporadic. There are public telephones at South Rim Visitor Center and South Rim Campground.

PARK CONTACT INFORMATION

Black Canyon of the Gunnison National Park ✉ *102 Elk Creek, Gunnison, CO* ☎ *970/641–2337* ⊕ *www.nps.gov/blca.*

SCENIC DRIVES

Two scenic rim roads offer deep and distant views into the canyon. Both also offer several lookout points and short trails along the rim. The trails that go into the canyon are steep and strenuous, not to mention relatively unmarked, and so are reserved for experienced (and very fit) hikers only. To get an up-close look at the bottom of the canyon, you'll have to drive down the East Portal Road.

East Portal Road. The only way to access the Gunnison River from the park by car is via this paved route, which drops approximately 2,000 feet down to the water in only 5 mi, giving it a steep, 16% grade. (Vehicles longer than 22 feet are not allowed on the road; if you're towing a trailer, you can unhitch it at a parking area near the entrance to South Rim campground.) The bottom of the road is actually in the adjacent Curecanti National Recreation Area. A tour of East Portal Road, with a brief stop at the bottom, takes about 45 minutes.

North Rim Road. Black Canyon's North Rim is much less frequented, but no less spectacular—the walls here are near vertical—than the South Rim. To reach the 15½-mi-long North Rim Road, take the signed turnoff from Route 92 about 3 mi south of Crawford. The road is paved for about the first 4 mi; the rest is gravel. After 11 mi, turn left at the intersection (the North Rim Campground and ranger station are to the right). There are six overlooks as the road snakes along the rim's edge. Kneeling Camel, 4½ mi out at road's end, provides the broadest view of the canyon. Set aside about two hours for a tour of the North Rim.

South Rim Road. This paved 7-mi stretch from Tomichi Point to High Point is the park's main road. The drive follows the canyon's level South Rim; 12 overlooks are accessible from the road, most via short gravel trails. Several short hikes along the rim also begin roadside. Allow between two and three hours round-trip.

WHAT TO SEE

SCENIC STOPS

★ **Chasm and Painted Wall Views.** At the heart-in-your-throat Chasm viewpoint, the canyon walls plummet 1,820 feet to the river, but are only 1,100 feet apart at the top. As you peer down into the depths, keep in mind that this section is where the Gunnison River descends at its steepest rate, dropping 240 feet within the span a mile. A few hundred yards farther, you'll find the best place to see Painted Wall, Colorado's tallest cliff. Pinkish swaths of pegmatite (a crystalline, granitelike rock) give the wall its colorful, marbled appearance. ⊠ *Approximately 3½ mi from the Visitor Center on South Rim Rd.*

Narrows View. Look upriver from this North Rim overlook and you'll be able to see into the canyon's narrowest section, just a slot really, with only 40 feet between the walls at the bottom. The canyon is also taller (1,725 feet) here than it is wide at the rim (1,150 feet). ⊠ *North Rim Rd., first overlook past the ranger station.*

★ **Warner Point.** This viewpoint delivers awesome views of the canyon's deepest point (2,722 feet), plus the nearby San Juan and West Elk mountain ranges. ⊠ *End of Warner Point Nature Trail, westernmost end of South Rim Rd.*

VISITOR CENTERS AND RANGER STATIONS

North Rim ranger station. This small facility on the park's North Rim is open in the summer. Rangers here that can provide information and assistance, as well as issue permits for backcountry use and rock climbing. ⊠ *North Rim Rd., 11 mi from Rte. 92 turnoff* ☎ 970/641–2337 ⊗ *Late May–Labor Day, daily 8–6.*

South Rim Visitor Center. The park's only visitor center offers interactive exhibits as well as two orientation videos—one details the geology and history of the canyon, the other includes the history of the Gunnison Water Diversion Tunnel and flora and fauna in the park. ⊠ *1½ mi from the entrance station on South Rim Rd.* ☎ 970/249–1914 Ext. 423 ⊗ *Late May–early Sept., daily 8–6; early Sept.–late May, daily 8:30–4.*

SPORTS AND THE OUTDOORS

Recreational activities in Black Canyon run the gamut from short and easy nature trails to world-class (and experts-only) rock climbing and kayaking. The cold waters of the Gunnison River are well known to trout anglers.

9

BIRD-WATCHING

The sheer cliffs of Black Canyon, though prohibitive to human habitation, provide a great habitat for birds. Naturally, cliff dwellers such as peregrine falcons and white-throated swifts revel in the dizzying heights, while at river level the American dipper is a common sight as it forages for food in the rushing waters. Canyon wrens, which nest in the cliffs, are more often heard than seen, but their hauntingly beautiful songs are unforgettable. Great horned owls and Steller's jays frequent the canyon rims. Best times for birding: spring and early summer.

BOATING AND KAYAKING

★ The Gunnison River is one of the premier kayak challenges in North America, with Class IV and Class V rapids, and difficult portages required around bigger drops. The spectacular 14-mi stretch of the river that passes through the park is so narrow in some sections that the rim seems to be closing up above your head. Once you're downstream from the rapids (and out of the park), the canyon opens up into what is called the Gunnison Gorge. The rapids ease considerably, and the trip becomes more of a quiet float on Class I to Class III water. Kayaking the river through the park requires a wilderness use permit (and lots of expertise), and rafting is not allowed. However, several outfitters offer guided raft and kayak trips in the Gunnison Gorge and other sections of the Gunnison River. *For kayaking and rafting outfitters, ⇨ Area Activities in the What's Nearby section.*

BOAT TOURS Running twice daily (except Tuesday) in the summer, at 10 AM and 12:30 PM, **Morrow Point Boat Tours** (⊠ *Pine Creek Boat Dock* ☎ *970/641–2337, ext. 205*) take up to 42 passengers on a 90-minute tour via pontoon boat. The cost is $16. Reservations are required.

FISHING

★ The three dams built upriver from the park in Curecanti National Recreation Area have created prime trout fishing in the waters below. In fact, the section of Gunnison River that goes through the park is designated Gold Medal Water, with abundant rainbow and brown trout. Certain restrictions apply: Only artificial flies and lures are permitted, and a Colorado fishing license is required for people aged 16 and older. Rainbow trout are catch-and-release only, and there are size and possession limits on brown trout (check at the visitor center). Most anglers access the river from the bottom of East Portal Road; an undeveloped trail goes along the riverbank for about ¾ mi.

GOOD READS

■ *The Gunnison Country*, by Duane Vandenbusche, is almost 500 pages of historical photographs and essays on the park.

■ *The Essential Guide to Black Canyon of the Gunnison National Park*, by John Jenkins, is one of the definitive guides to the park.

■ *A Kid's Guide to Exploring Black Canyon of the Gunnison*, by Renee Skelton, is perfect for the 6–12 set.

DID YOU KNOW?

While Hells Canyon, in Idaho and Oregon, is the continent's deepest canyon, at 7,913 feet, the 53-mi-long Black Canyon of the Gunnison impresses with its sheer cliffs, depth of up to 2,722 feet (at Warner Point), and powerful river running through it that at times drops 240 feet per mile. The canyon also has a narrow opening that at its tightest is only 40 feet across. It is about 8 degrees cooler at the bottom of the canyon than at the top.

HIKING

All trails can be hot in summer and most don't receive much shade, so bring water, a hat, and plenty of sunscreen. Dogs are permitted, on leash, on Rim Rock, Cedar Point Nature, and Chasm View Nature trails. Hiking into the inner canyon, while doable, is not for the faint of heart—or step. Six named routes lead down to the river, but they are not maintained or marked. In fact, the park staff won't even call them trails; they refer to them as "controlled slides." These super-steep, rocky routes vary in one-way distance from 1 to 2¾ mi, and the descent can be anywhere from 1,800 to 2,702 feet. Your reward, of course, is a rare look at the bottom of the canyon and the fast-flowing Gunnison. ■ TIP→ Don't attempt an inner-canyon hike without plenty of water (the park's recommendation is one gallon per person, per day). For descriptions of the routes, and the necessary permit to hike them, stop at the visitor center at the South Rim or North Rim ranger station. Dogs are not permitted in the inner canyon.

EASY

Cedar Point Nature Trail. This 0.7-mi round-trip interpretive trail leads out from South Rim Road to two overlooks. It's an easy stroll, and signs along the way detail the surrounding plants. ⊠ *Trailhead off South Rim Rd., 4.2 mi from South Rim Visitor Center.*

Deadhorse Trail. Despite its unpleasant name, Deadhorse Trail (about 5 mi round-trip) is actually an easy-to-moderate hike, starting on an old service road from the Kneeling Camel View on the North Rim Road. The trail's farthest point provides the park's easternmost viewpoint. From this overlook, the canyon is much more open, with pinnacles and spires rising along its sides. If you want to give yourself a bit of a scare, take the mile-long loop detour, about halfway through the hike. (The detour isn't marked; just look for the only other visible trail). At the two informal overlooks, you'll be perched—without guardrails—atop the highest cliff in this part of the canyon. Make sure to keep your children by your side at all times. ⊠ *Trailhead at the southernmost end of North Rim Rd.*

MODERATE

Chasm View Nature Trail. The park's shortest trail (0.3 mi round-trip) starts at North Rim Campground and offers an impressive 50-yard walk right along the canyon rim as well as an eye-popping view downstream of Painted Wall, 1,100 feet across on the South Rim. ⊠ *Trailhead at North Rim Campground, 11¼ mi from Rte. 92.*

North Vista Trail. The moderate round-trip hike to and from Exclamation Point is 3 mi; a more difficult foray to the top of 8,563-foot Green Mountain (a mesa, really), with about 800 feet of elevation gain, is 7 mi round-trip. You'll hike along the North Rim; keep an eye out for especially gnarled pinyon pines—the North Rim is the site of some of the oldest groves of pinyons in North America, between 400 and 700 years old. ⊠ *Trailhead at North Rim ranger station, off North Rim Rd., 11 mi from Rte. 92 turnoff.*

Fodor'sChoice
★
Warner Point Nature Trail. The 1½-mi round-trip hike starts from High Point. You'll enjoy fabulous vistas of the San Juan and West Elk Mountains and Uncompahgre Valley. Warner Point, at trail's end, has the

steepest drop-off from rim to river: a dizzying 2,722 feet. ⊠ *Trailhead: at the end of South Rim Rd.*

DIFFICULT

Oak Flat Trail. This 2-mi loop trail is the most demanding of the South Rim hikes, as it brings you about 300 feet below the canyon rim. In places, the trail is narrow and crosses some steep slopes, but you won't have to navigate any steep drop-offs. Oak Flat is the shadiest of all the South Rim trails; small groves of aspen and thick stands of Douglas fir along the loop offer some respite from the sun. ⊠ *Trailhead: just west of the South Rim Visitor Center.*

HORSEBACK RIDING

Although its name might indicate otherwise, Deadhorse Trail is actually the only trail in the park where horses are allowed. The trail is an easy-to-moderate 5-mi loop that begins east of North Rim Road. Horses are not allowed on the South Rim, and can be on the North Rim only on the Deadhorse Trail, in the North Rim Campground, or on the North Rim Road during transport in a trailer.

Black Canyon of the Gunnison has no facilities geared toward horses. If you bring your own horse, go to the end of North Rim Road and park your trailer at Kneeling Camel Overlook to access Deadhorse Trail. No permit is required.

OUTFITTERS AND EXPEDITIONS Run by the Montrose Recreation District, **Elk Ridge Trail Rides** (⊠ *10203 Bostwick Park Rd., Montrose* ☎ *970/240–6007* ⊕ *www.elkridgeranchinc. com* ⊙ *May–Sept., daily, weather permitting*) is the only outfitter allowed to guide rides in Black Canyon National Park. It offers a four-hour ride to the canyon rim along the Deadhorse Trail. Riders must be in good physical condition, at least 8 years old, and weigh no more than 230 pounds.

ROCK CLIMBING

Fodor's Choice ★ For advanced rock climbers, climbing the sheer cliffs of the Black Canyon is one of Colorado's premier big-wall challenges. Some routes can take several days to complete, with climbers sleeping on narrow ledges or "portaledges." Though there's no official guide to climbing in the park, reports from other climbers are kept on file at the South Rim Visitor Center. Nesting birds of prey may lead to wall closure at certain times of year.

Rock climbing in the park is for experts only, but if you want to get in some easier climbing, head for the Marmot Rocks bouldering area, about 100 feet south of South Rim Road between Painted Wall and Cedar Point overlooks (park at Painted Wall). Four boulder groupings offer a variety of routes rated from easy to very difficult; a pamphlet with a diagrammed map of the area is available at the South Rim Visitor Center.

OUTFITTERS AND EXPEDITIONS In the summer months, advanced climbers can take a full-day guided tour with **Crested Butte Mountain Guides** (⊠ *218 Maroon Ave.* ⊕ *P.O. Box 1718, Crested Butte 81224* ☎ *970/349–5430* ⊕ *www.crestedbutteguides. com*) for $300 (one person), $450 (two people), or $525 (three people). Come winter, the guides also lead day-long ice-climbing trips in the park for $270 for one to two people, $135 for each additional person. Intermediate to advanced climbers can take a one-, three-, or five-day

9

guided tour with **Skyward Mountaineering** (✉ *P.O. Box 323, Ridgway 81432* ☎ *970/209–2985* ⊕ *www.skywardmountaineering.com* ☉ *Mar.–Nov.*); per-day rates are $350 for one person, $450 for two, and $600 for three.

WINTER SPORTS

From late November to early April, South Rim Road is not plowed past the visitor center, offering park guests a unique opportunity to cross-country ski or snowshoe on the road. It's possible to ski or snowshoe on the unplowed North Rim Road, too, but it's about 4 mi from where the road closes, through sagebrush flats, to the canyon rim.

OUTFITTERS
AND
EXPEDITIONS

In winter, rangers offers **Guided Snowshoe Walks** (☎ *970/249–1914 Ext. 423*), usually once a day on weekends. Tours leave from the South Rim Visitor Center and go along the rim for about 2 mi, often on Rim Rock Trail. A limited supply of snowshoe gear is available for use at no charge. Call ahead to reserve equipment and a space on a tour.

EDUCATIONAL OFFERINGS

RANGER PROGRAMS

☸ **Junior Ranger Program.** Kids ages 5–12 can participate in this program with an activities booklet to fill in while exploring the park.

WHAT'S NEARBY

While not totally out of the way, Black Canyon of the Gunnison and its two neighboring recreation playgrounds—the Curecanti National Recreation Area and the Gunnison Gorge National Conservation Area—are far enough removed from civilization (i.e., big cities) to maintain a sense of getting-away-from-it-all isolation. It's a good 250 mi from Denver, and 240 mi from Colorado Springs, and touristy towns such as Durango and Telluride are 120 mi and 80 mi away, respectively. Colorado National Monument is about 85 mi distant.

NEARBY TOWNS

The primary gateway to Black Canyon is **Montrose**, 15 mi northeast of the park. The legendary Ute chief, Ouray, and his wife, Chipeta, lived near here in the mid-19th century. Today, Montrose straddles the important agricultural and mining regions along the Uncompahgre River, and its traditional downtown is a shopping hub. The closest town to Black Canyon's North Rim is **Crawford**, about 3 mi from the entrance to the North Rim Road, a small hillside enclave amid the sheep and cattle ranches of the North Fork Valley with a small downtown area. Northeast on Route 92 (20 mi) is **Paonia**, a unique and charming blend of the old and new West. Here, career environmentalists and hippie types who have escaped the mainstream mingle with longtime ranchers, miners, and fruit growers. Eleven miles northwest of Crawford on Route 92 is the small ranching and mining community of **Hotchkiss**. The trappings and sensibilities of the Old West are here, from cowboy bars and fields of livestock to the annual summertime rodeo.

VISITOR INFORMATION
Crawford Area Chamber of Commerce ⌂ *P.O. Box 22, Crawford, CO 81415* ☎ *970/921–4000* ⊕ *www.crawfordcountry.org.* Hotchkiss Chamber of Commerce ⌂ *P.O. Box 158, Hotchkiss, CO 81419* ☎ *970/872–3226* ⊕ *www.hotchkisschamber.com.* Montrose Visitors and Convention Bureau ✉ *1519 E. Main St., Montrose, CO 81401* ☎ *800/873-0244* ⊕ *visitmontrose.com.* Paonia Chamber of Commerce ⌂ *P.O. Box 366, Paonia, CO 81428* ☎ *970/527-3886* ⊕ *www.paoniachamber.com.*

TOP FAMILY PICKS

Cimarron Visitor Center. See a vintage, circa-1882 railroad trestle, which is listed on the National Register of Historic Places.

Main in Motion. Be entertained by street-corner performers and strolling musicians during this Thursday evening event every summer in downtown Montrose.

Morrow Point Boat Tour. Relax and check out a calmer stretch of the Gunnison on this 90-minute summertime-only tour.

NEARBY ATTRACTIONS

Crawford State Park. The focus of this 337-acre park is Crawford Reservoir, created in 1963 when a dam was built to increase the supply of irrigated water to the surrounding ranches and farms. Boating and waterskiing are permitted on the reservoir, as are swimming and fishing (the lake is stocked with rainbow trout). The park has a 1-mi wheelchair-accessible hiking trail along with the primitive ½-mi Indian Fire Nature Trail, which runs along the reservoir on the park's west side. ✉ *1 mi south of Crawford, at 40468 Hwy. 92* ☎ *970/921–5721* ⊕ *parks.state.co.us/Parks/crawford* ⌂ *$5* ☉ *Daily 8* AM*–4* PM.

★ **Curecanti National Recreation Area.** Curecanti, named in honor of a Ute Indian chief, encompasses 40 mi of striking eroded volcanic landscape along U.S. 50, between Gunnison and Montrose. Three reservoirs were created by dams constructed in the 1960s: Morrow Point, Crystal Dam, and Blue Mesa, Colorado's largest lake at almost 20-mi long. You can go boating (paid permit required for Blue Mesa), windsurfing, fishing, and swimming in all three. Camping, horseback riding, and hiking (pets are allowed on all trails but must be leashed) are also available. At the western entrance to the recreation area, about 15 mi from Black Canyon, the **Cimarron Visitor Center** displays vintage railroad cars, an 1882 trestle listed on the National Register of Historic Places, and a reconstruction of a railroad stockyard. ✉ *35 mi west of Gunnison in Cimarron* ☎ *970/249–4074* ☉ *Late May–Labor Day, daily 9–4* ⌂ *Free.*

The Elk Creek visitor center along U.S. 50 also has more information. ✉ *102 Elk Creek, Gunnison* ☎ *970/641–2337* ⊕ *www.nps.gov/cure* ⌂ *$15 entrance fee at East Portal entrance only* ☉ *Park, daily; visitor centers, hrs. vary.*

9

FESTIVALS AND EVENTS

JULY–AUGUST

Main in Motion. From 6–8 PM every Thursday in the summer, Main Street in Montrose is the place to be. Street performers and other artisans join Historic Downtown Montrose restaurants and shops to make for a pleasant evening stroll. ☎ *970/249–6295* ⊕ *www.maininmotion.com.*

JULY

Paonia Cherry Days. One of Colorado's longest-running annual events, this small-town fair around the 4th of July includes a parade, food, crafts, sidewalk sales, and a variety of entertainment celebrating local cherry crops (and the other fruits that have made Paonia famous). ☎ *970/527–3886.*

AREA ACTIVITIES

SPORTS AND THE OUTDOORS

BOATING

OUTFITTER You can put your boat into the Blue Mesa Reservoir or rent a slip for it at the **Lake Fork Marina** (✉ *16171 Hwy. 92, Gunnison* ☎ *877/258–6372 or 970/641–3048* ⊕ *www.bluemesares.com* ☉ *May–Sept.*) or at Elk Creek Marina, about 12 mi up the road. If you don't have a boat, you can rent one at either place.

FISHING

OUTFITTER **Recreation Resource Management** (✉ *24830 U.S. Hwy 50, Gunnison* ☎ *877/258–6372 or 970/641–0707* ⊕ *www.bluemesares.com* ☉ *May–Sept.*) operates out of Elk Creek Marina and operates guided fishing tours on the Blue Mesa Reservoir. Common catches include brown, brook, rainbow, and lake trout.

KAYAKING AND RAFTING

OUTFITTERS AND EXPEDITIONS Beginners can book a 1-day white-water rafting trip on the Gunnison River with **Dvorak Kayak and Rafting Expeditions** (✉ *17921 U.S. Hwy 285, Nathrop* ☎ *800/824–3795 or 719/539–6851* ⊕ *www.dvorakexpeditions. com* 🖅 *$263 per person for rafting trip, $263–$814 per person for kayaking trips* ☉ *May–Sept.*). This outfitter also offers 1- and 2-day kayaking trips for intermediate-level paddlers in the Gunnison Gorge, as well as instructional seminars in rafting and kayaking. **Wilderness Aware Rafting** (✉ *12600 U.S. Hwy. 24, Buena Vista* ☎ *800/462–7238 or 719/395–2112* ⊕ *www.inaraft.com* 🖅 *$250–$798 per person* ☉ *May–Sept.*) takes visitors on single- or multi-day rafting or fishing trips in the Gunnison Gorge National Conservation Area.

SHOPPING

FOOD Pack a picnic lunch for the Black Canyon from the **Montrose Farmer's Market** (✉ *S. Cascade St. between S. First and S. Second Sts., Montrose* ☎ *970/209–8463* ⊕ *www.montrosefarmersmarket.com* ☉ *May–mid-July and late Sept.–Oct., Sat. 8:30–1; mid-July–late Sept., Wed. 8:30–1*). The **Russell Stover Factory Outlet** (✉ *2185 Stover Ave., Montrose* ☎ *970/249–5372*), south of downtown Montrose off U.S. Hwy 550, sells fresh chocolates made right across the street.

Colorado National Monument

Sheer red-rock canyons filled with colorful cliffs and monoliths that sprout as high as 450 feet make the **Colorado National Monument** one of the great landscapes of the American West. President William Howard Taft declared this 32-square-mi tract of rugged, ragged terrain a national monument in 1911 after an eccentric named John Otto built trails where many thought would be impossible. Otto went on to become the monument's first custodian.

Cold Shivers Point is just one of the many dramatic overlooks along **Rim Rock Drive**, a 23-mi-long road that takes visitors past 19 signed overlooks and more than a dozen short and backcountry trails that range in length from ¼ mi to 8½ mi. An easy 30-minute stroll with sweeping canyon views, **Otto's Trail** greets hikers with breezes scented by sagebrush

and juniper, which stand out from the dull red rock and sand. The trail leads to stunning, sheer drop-offs. **Serpents Trail**, with more than 50 switchbacks, ascends several hundred feet and takes about two hours to complete.

Scheduled programs, such as guided walks and porch talks, are posted at the **Visitor Center**. Maps and trail information are also available. Rock climbing is popular at the monument, as are cross-country skiing, biking, and camping.

CONTACT INFORMATION

✉ *About 4 mi south of Fruita on Hwy. 340* ☎ *970/858–3617* ⊕ *www.nps.gov/colm* 💲 *$7 weekly pass per vehicle. $4 weekly pass for those entering on bicycle, motorcycle, or foot* ☉ *Monument, daily; visitor center, daily 8–6, late May–Sept. 30; daily 9–5, Sept. 30–late May.*

WHERE TO EAT AND STAY

9

ABOUT THE RESTAURANTS
The park itself has no eateries, but nearby towns have choices ranging from traditional American to an eclectic café and bakery.

ABOUT THE HOTELS
Black Canyon is devoid of hotels. Smaller hotels, some excellent B&Bs, and rustic lodges are nearby, as are a few of the larger chains.

ABOUT THE CAMPGROUNDS
There are two campgrounds in the national park. The smaller North Rim Campground is first-come, first served, and is closed in the winter. South Rim Campground is considerably larger, and has a loop that's open year-round. Reservations are accepted in South Rim Loops A and B. Power hookups only exist in Loop B, and vehicles more than 35 feet long are discouraged from either campground. At both of the park's drive-to campgrounds there's a limit of eight people per site, and camping is limited to 14 days. Water has to be trucked up to the campgrounds, so use it in moderation; it's shut off in mid- to late September. Generators are not allowed at South Rim and are highly discouraged on the North Rim. Nearby communities such as Montrose have RV parks with more amenities, and Crawford State Park has options that include a boat ramp.

WHERE TO EAT

IN THE PARK

PICNIC AREAS   There are a variety of picnic areas at Black Canyon of the Gunnison, all with pit toilets; all are closed when it snows.

East Portal. This picnic area, located at the bottom of the canyon, accommodates large groups. There are tables, fire grates, bathrooms, and a large shaded shelter. ⊠ *East Portal Rd. at the Gunnison River.*

High Point. When the sun is unforgiving, this overlook offers more shade than most of the other picnic areas. There are tables and bathrooms but no fire grates. ⊠ *West end of South Rim Rd.*

North and South Rim campgrounds. Feel free to use unoccupied camping sites for a picnic lunch. There are tables, fire grates, and bathrooms. ⊠ *North Rim: West end of North Rim Rd.; South Rim: About 1 mi east of South Rim Visitor Center on South Rim Rd.*

OUTSIDE THE PARK

$–$$ ✕ **Amelia's Hacienda Restaurante.** While there's no shortage of Mexican
MEXICAN   restaurants in this part of the country, Amelia's still stands out for its great food, atmosphere (in the dining room and on the patio), and speedy service. It's family friendly, but they also make a mean margarita and have a full bar stocked with Mexican beers and tequilas. ⊠ *44 S. Grand Ave., Montrose* ☎ *970/249–1881* ⊕ *www.ameliashacienda. com* ⊟ *AE, D, MC, V.*

$$ ✕ **Camp Robber.** This chic restaurant serves Montrose's most creative
SOUTHWESTERN   cuisine (when weather permits, you can sit in the patio). Try entrées such as basil-crusted salmon, spicy shrimp pasta, or the house specialty: pork medallions crusted in green chili pistachios. At lunch, salads, sandwiches (such as mesquite-grilled chicken cordon bleu), or blue-corn enchiladas fuel hungry hikers, and the Sunday brunch will leave you happily stuffed. ⊠ *1515 Ogden Rd., Montrose* ☎ *970/240–1590* ⊕ *www.camprobber.com* ⊟ *AE, D, MC, V* ⊙ *No dinner Sun.*

$$ ✕ **The Flying Fork Café & Bakery.** This charming café turns out tasty Italian
ECLECTIC   fare for lunch and dinner in a comfortable dining room—and, in the summer, a shady outdoor garden—plus an assortment of artisan breads and pastries sold in the small bakery at the front of the building (you can also order your meal to go from here). Local ingredients are used whenever possible to create dishes like farfalle covered in a sauce of smoked chicken, pear, and Gorgonzola, salads of organic filed greens, and braised Colorado lamb shank. The individual pizzas (made with whole-wheat flour and fresh basil and mozzarella) are especially good for smaller appetites. ⊠ *101 3rd St., Paonia* ☎ *970/527–3203* ⊕ *www. flyingforkcafe.com* ⊟ *AE, D, MC, V* ⊙ *Café, closed Mon.*

$ ✕ **Zack's Bar-B-Q.** On Saturday nights, the local ranching families flock
SOUTHERN   to Zack's for the tastiest barbecue around; choose from ham, beef, chicken, or ribs. Steak and catfish dinners are also available Friday through Sunday nights. A favorite is the chef salad, made with barbequed chicken straight off the grill. This informal eatery serves breakfast too. ⊠ *721 E. Bridge St., near the intersection of Hwys. 133 and 92, Hotchkiss* ☎ *970/872–3199* ⊟ *AE, MC, V* ⊙ *Closed Mon.*

WHERE TO STAY

IN THE PARK

CAMPING

$

Fodor's Choice

★

South Rim Campground. Stay on the canyon rim at this main campground right inside the park entrance. Loops A and C have tent sites only. The RV hookups are in Loop B, and those sites are priced higher than those in other parts of the campground. It's possible to camp here year-round (Loop A stays open all winter), but the loops are not plowed, so you'll have to hike in with your tent. **Pros:** easy access to the canyon; never crowded. **Cons:** extra-large vehicles (more than 35 feet long) aren't recommended; because park staff must bring in all water by truck, there's no water for dishes or bathing (just drinking fountains). ⊠ *South Rim Rd., 1 mi from the visitor center* ⚠ *65 tent sites, 23 RV sites* ⚐ *Pit toilets, partial hookups (electric) in Loop B, drinking water, fire grates, picnic tables, public telephone* ➡ *No credit cards* ⊙ *Loops B and C closed Nov.–Apr.*

$

North Rim Campground. This small campground, nestled amid pine trees, offers the basics along the quiet North Rim. **Pros:** amazing views; fragrant campsites among pinions and junipers. **Cons:** occasionally fills on summer weekends; close proximity to the rim makes it less than ideal for small children; no hookups. ⊠ *North Rim Rd., 11¼ mi from Rte. 92* ⚠ *13 tent/RV sites* ⚐ *Pit toilets, drinking water, fire grates, picnic tables, ranger station* ➡ *No credit cards* ⊙ *Closed Nov.–Apr.*

OUTSIDE THE PARK

$–$$

Best Western Red Arrow Motor Inn. This low-key establishment is one of the nicest lodgings in the area, mainly because of the large, pretty rooms filled with handsome dark-wood furnishings. Some rooms include soothing whirlpool tubs. **Pros:** spacious and comfortable rooms; good Continental breakfast; pets welcome. **Cons:** pets add an extra $10 per day. ⊠ *1702 E. Main St., Montrose* ☎ *970/249–9641 or 800/468–9323* ⊕ *www.bestwestern.com* ⌁ *57 rooms, 2 suites* ⚐ *In-room: refrigerator, Wi-Fi. In-hotel: pool, gym, laundry facilities, laundry service, pets allowed* ➡ *AE, D, DC, MC, V.*

¢–$

Black Canyon Motel. One of Montrose's better values, this motel has rooms that are large and clean, with a good selection of amenities. **Pros:** inexpensive; central location; hot tub. **Cons:** older facility that's showing its age; some rooms and common areas are a little gloomy. ⊠ *1605 E. Main St. (U.S. 50), Montrose* ☎ *970/249–3495 or 800/348–3495* ⊕ *www.blackcanyonmotel.com* ⌁ *46 rooms, 3 suites* ⚐ *In-room: refrigerator, Wi-Fi. In-hotel: Wi-Fi, pool, laundry facilities, pets allowed* ➡ *AE, D, DC, MC, V.*

¢–$

Country Lodge. This homey, family- (and pet-) friendly motel has knotty-pine walls, a garden courtyard with pool and hot tub, and two separate play areas for older and younger kids. A newer three-bedroom log cabin with full kitchen and washer-dryer is available for nightly rentals in summer. Guests have access to a hot tub. **Pros:** spotless, comfortable rooms with cabin-style furniture and handmade quilts; friendly and helpful staff; close to several restaurants. **Cons:** the rustic decor can feel a little overdone. ⊠ *1624 E. Main St. (U.S. 50), Montrose* ☎ *970/249–4567* ⊕ *www.countrylodgecolorado.com* ⌁ *22 rooms,*

9

1 cabin ⚿ *In-room: kitchen (some), refrigerator, Wi-Fi. In-hotel: pool, some pets allowed* ⊟ *AE, D, DC, MC, V.*

CAMPING

$$ ⚿ **Cedar Creek RV Park.** This close-to-town park in Montrose has a minia-ture golf course and a shop with RV supplies. You can pitch a tent along Cedar Creek, but there are no individual sites. On the grounds is also a two-room cabin you can rent for $35 a night (bedding is $5 extra). **Pros:** friendly, family-owned facility; close to restaurants and shopping. **Cons:** sites feel crowded, without much room for bigger RVs. ⊠ *126 Rose La., Montrose* 🕾 *970/249–3884 or 877/425–3884* ⊕ *www.cedarcreekrv.com* ⚿ *8 tent sites, 47 RV sites with full hookups, 16 RV sites with partial hookups* ⚿ *Flush toilets, full hookups, partial hookups (electric and water), dump station, drinking water, guest laundry, showers, fire pits, picnic tables, public telephone, play area, Wi-Fi* ⊟ *D, MC, V.*

$$ ⚿ **Montrose RV Resort.** Located just off Main Street, this clean, welcom-ing campground offers all the amenities, including a very nice pool and cable TV in the RV hookups. They're also pet friendly (bonus: a 12-acre field for your dog to romp in). **Pros:** friendly staff; absolutely immaculate facility; very nice pool (and hot tub) and laundry room. **Cons:** pricier than other camping options; tent campers don't have a lot of shade. ⊠ *200 N. Cedar Ave., Montrose* 🕾 *970/249–9177* ⊕ *www.montroservresort.com* ⚿ *50 tent sites, 71 RV sites with full hookups, 4 camping cabins, 2 cabins with kitchen and bath* ⚿ *Flush toilets, show-ers, guest laundry, swimming (pool), Wi-Fi* ⊟ *MC, V.*

$ ⚿ **East Portal.** Though technically in Curecanti National Recreation Area, this shady riverside campground is accessible only via the East Portal Road in the Black Canyon National Park. **Pros:** beautiful setting right next to the river; never crowded. **Cons:** no hookups; the access road is steep and twisting, meaning vehicles longer than 22 feet aren't permit-ted. ⊠ *Bottom of East Portal Rd., Gunnison* 🕾 *970/641–2337* ⊕ *www.nps.gov/cure* ⚿ *15 tent/RV sites* ⚿ *Pit toilets, drinking water, fire grates, picnic tables, ranger station* ⊟ *No credit cards* ⊙ *Early May–late Nov.*

Bryce Canyon National Park

WORD OF MOUTH

"The brilliant colors of the mysterious hoodoos at Bryce Canyon were more impressive than I remembered from a trip there as a child. I've been to many of the parks in the NPS system and Bryce is unquestionably at the top of my list."

—photo by Stephanie Ripley, Fodors.com member

WELCOME TO BRYCE CANYON

TOP REASONS TO GO

★ **Hoodoo heaven:** The brashly colored limestone spires—called hoodoos—are the main attraction of Bryce Canyon.

★ **Famous fresh air:** To say the air around Bryce Canyon is rarified is not an exaggeration. With some of the clearest skies anywhere, the park offers views that, on a clear day, extend 200 mi and into three states.

★ **Spectacular sunrises and sunsets:** The deep orange and crimson hues of the park's hoodoos are intensified by the light of the sun at either end of the day.

★ **Dramatically different zones:** From the highest point of the rim to canyon base the park spans 2,000 feet, so you can explore three unique climatic zones: spruce–fir forest, ponderosa pine forest, and pinyon pine–juniper forest.

★ **Gasp-worthy geology:** You won't believe the bold colors adorning the rock layers, columns, arches, pinnacles, knobs, and other indescribable million-year old sandstone shapes.

1 Bryce Amphitheater. Here is the park's densest collection of attractions, including the historic Bryce Canyon Lodge and the points Sunrise, Sunset, and Inspiration. Paria View looks far south into Grand Staircase–Escalante National Monument.

2 Under-the-Rim Trail. Though it more or less parallels most of the scenic drive and accesses many popular sites, from Bryce Point to the vicinity of Swamp Canyon, this trail is the best way to reach the Bryce Canyon backcountry. A handful of primitive campgrounds line the route.

3 Rainbow and Yovimpa Points. The end of the scenic road, but not of the scenery, here you can hike a trail to see some ancient bristlecone pines and look south into Grand Staircase–Escalante National Monument.

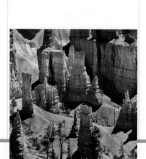

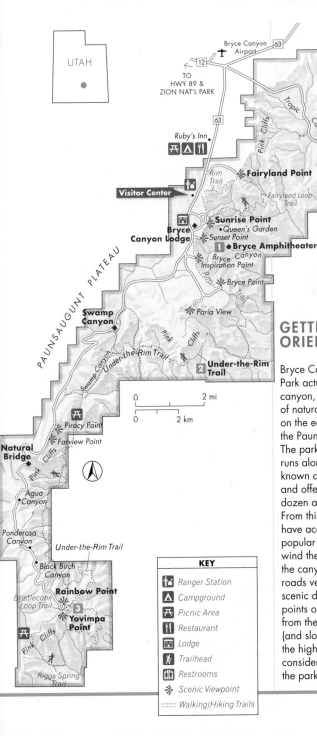

GETTING ORIENTED

Bryce Canyon National Park actually isn't a single canyon, but rather a series of natural amphitheaters on the eastern edge of the Paunsaugunt Plateau. The park's scenic drive runs along a formation known as the Pink Cliffs and offers more than a dozen amazing overlooks. From this road you'll also have access to the most popular hiking trails, which wind their way down into the canyons. A handful of roads veer to the east of the scenic drive to access other points of interest. As relief from the frequent heavy (and slow) traffic during the high season of summer, consider riding in one of the park's shuttle buses.

10

Map labels

UTAH

Bryce Canyon Airport — 63
12
TO HWY 89 & ZION NAT'L PARK
63
Tropic Canyon
Pink Cliffs
12 TO ESCALANTE

Ruby's Inn
Rim Trail
Fairyland Point
Visitor Center
Fairyland Loop Trail
Sunrise Point
Queen's Garden
Bryce Canyon Lodge
Sunset Point
Bryce Amphitheater
Inspiration Point
Bryce Canyon
Bryce Point
Rim Trail
PAUNSAUGUNT PLATEAU
Paria View
Swamp Canyon
Pink Cliffs
Under-the-Rim Trail
Swamp Canyon
Under-the-Rim Trail

0   2 mi
0   2 km

Piracy Point
Farview Point
Natural Bridge
Pink Cliffs
Agua Canyon
Ponderosa Canyon
Under-the-Rim Trail
Black Birch Canyon
Rainbow Point
Bristlecone Loop Trail
Yovimpa Point
Pink Cliffs
Riggs Spring Trail

KEY

🛉	Ranger Station
⛺	Campground
🌲	Picnic Area
🍴	Restaurant
🏨	Lodge
🚶	Trailhead
🚻	Restrooms
☀	Scenic Viewpoint
⋯⋯	Walking/Hiking Trails

BRYCE CANYON PLANNER

When to Go

Around Bryce Canyon National Park and the nearby Cedar Breaks National Monument area, elevations approach and surpass 9,000 feet, making for temperamental weather, intermittent and seasonal road closures due to snow, and downright cold nights well into June. The air is cooler on the rim of the canyon than it is at lower altitudes. **If you choose to see Bryce Canyon in July, August, or September, you'll be visiting with the rest of the world.** During these months, traffic on the main road can be crowded with cars following slow-moving RVs, so consider taking one of the park shuttle buses.

If it's solitude you're looking for, come to Bryce any time between October and March. The park is open all year long, so if you come during the cooler months you might just have a trail all to yourself.

AVG. HIGH/LOW TEMPS.

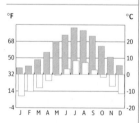

Flora and Fauna

Due to elevations approaching 9,000 feet, many of Bryce Canyon's 400 plant species are unlike those you'll see at less lofty places. Look at exposed slopes and you might catch a glimpse of the pygmy pinyon, or the gnarled, thousand-year-old bristlecone pine. At lower altitudes are the Douglas fir, ponderosa pine, and the quaking aspen, sitting in groves of twinkling leaves. No fewer than three kinds of sagebrush—big, black, and fringed—grow here, as well as the blue columbine.

Mule deer are common, and chipmunks will scamper along the trails with you. The Utah prairie dog is also a resident. Give them a wide berth; they may be cute, but they bite and their fleas can carry disease. Other animals include elk, black-tailed jackrabbits, and the desert cottontail. Below 7,000 feet, black bear have been seen in the trees, but infrequently. It's far more likely you'll see the soaring forms of golden and bald eagles, or perhaps a peregrine falcon diving into the amphitheaters at speeds approaching 200 MPH.

Getting Here and Around

The closest major cities to Bryce Canyon are Salt Lake City and Las Vegas, each about 270 mi away. The nearest commercial airport is 80 mi west in Cedar City, Utah. The park is reached via Route 63, just 3 mi south of the junction with Highway 12.

You can see the park's highlights by driving along the well-maintained road running the length of the main scenic area. Bryce has no restrictions on automobiles on the main road, but in the summer you may encounter heavy traffic and full parking lots. A shuttle bus system operates from mid-May through September. Use of it comes free with your park entrance fee. The shuttle departs from the staging area off Highway 12 about 3 mi north of the park entrance every 15 minutes. Stops include Best Western Ruby's Inn, the North Campground, the visitor center, and all major overlooks in the northern portion of the park. The shuttle can be helpful in planning a one-way hike.

Updated by
Swain Scheps

A land that captures the imagination and the heart, Bryce is a favorite among Utah's national parks. Although its splendor had been well known for decades, Bryce Canyon wasn't designated a national park until 1928. The park is named for Ebenezer Bryce, a pioneer cattleman and the first permanent settler in the area. His description of the landscape not being hospitable to cows has oft been repeated. Even more than his famous quote, however, Bryce Canyon is known for its fanciful "hoodoos," best viewed at sunrise or sunset, when the light plays off the red rock.

In geological terms, Bryce is actually an amphitheater, not a canyon. The hoodoos in the amphitheater took on their unusual shapes because the top layer of rock—"cap rock"—is harder than the layers below it. If erosion undercuts the soft rock beneath the cap too much, the hoodoo will tumble. Bryce continues to evolve today, but the hoodoos are a permanent feature; old ones may die, but new ones are constantly forming as the amphitheater rim recedes.

10

PARK ESSENTIALS

ACCESSIBILITY

Most park facilities were constructed between 1930 and 1960. Some have been upgraded for wheelchair accessibility, while others can be used with some assistance. The Sunset campground offers two sites with wheelchair access. Few of the trails, however, can be managed in a standard wheelchair due to the sandy, rocky, or uneven terrain. The section of the Rim Trail between Sunrise and Inspiration points is wheelchair accessible. The 1-mi bristlecone Loop Trail at Rainbow Point has a hard surface and could be used with assistance, but several grades do not meet standards. Accessible parking is marked at all overlooks and public facilities.

ADMISSION FEES

The entrance fee is $20 per vehicle for a seven-day pass and $10 for pedestrians or bicyclists. The entrance fee includes unlimited use of the park shuttle. An annual Bryce Canyon park pass, good for one year from the date of purchase, costs $30. If you leave your private vehicle outside the park—at the shuttle staging area or Ruby's Inn—the one-time entrance fee, including transportation on the shuttle, is $10.

A $5 backcountry permit, available from the visitor center, is required for camping in the park's interior, allowed only on Under-the-Rim Trail and Rigg's Spring Loop, both south of Bryce Point. Campfires are not permitted.

ADMISSION HOURS

The park is open 24/7, year-round. It's in the mountain time zone.

ATMS/BANKS

Ruby's Inn has an ATM. The nearest bank is in Panguitch.

AUTOMOBILE SERVICE STATIONS

Just outside the park you can fuel up, get your oil and tires changed, and have car repairs done.

CELL-PHONE RECEPTION

Cell-phone reception is hit-and-miss in the park. If you're getting reception, take advantage of it and make your calls; you may not have another chance. Bryce Canyon Lodge, Bryce Canyon Pines General Store, Ruby's Inn, Sunset Campground, and the visitor center all have public telephones.

EMERGENCIES

In an emergency, dial 911. To contact park police or if you need first aid, go to the visitor center or speak to a park ranger. (In the summer months only, there is also first aid at Bryce Canyon Lodge.) The nearest hospital is in Panguitch.

POST OFFICE

You can mail letters and buy stamps from Bryce Canyon Lodge. Ruby's Inn also has a full-service post office.

PARK CONTACT INFORMATION

Bryce Canyon National Park 🖂 *P.O. Box 170001, Bryce 84717* ☎ *435/834–5322 or 888/362–2642* ⊕ *www.nps.gov/brca.*

SCENIC DRIVE

Fodor'sChoice **Main Park Road.** Following miles of canyon rim, this thoroughfare gives
★ access to more than a dozen scenic overlooks between the park entrance and Rainbow Point. Allow two to three hours to travel the entire 36 mi round-trip. The road is open year-round, but may be closed temporarily after heavy snowfalls to allow for clearing. Major overlooks are rarely more than a few minutes' walk from the parking areas, and many let you see more than 100 mi on clear days. ■ TIP➔ The park shuttle is an easy way to get around but if you must drive all overlooks lie east of the road—to keep things simple (and left turns to a minimum), you can proceed to the southern end of the park and stop at the overlooks on your north-bound return. Trailers are not allowed beyond Sunset Campground. Day users may park trailers at the visitor center or other designated sites;

BRYCE CANYON IN ONE DAY

Begin your day at the **visitor center** to get an overview of the park and to purchase books and maps. Watch the video and peruse exhibits about the natural and cultural history of Bryce Canyon. Then, drive to the historic **Bryce Canyon Lodge.** From here, stroll along the relaxing **Rim Trail.** Afterward, drive the 18-mi **main park road,** stopping at the overlooks along the way. Allowing for traffic, and if you stop at all 13 overlooks, this drive will take you between two and three hours.

If you have the time and energy for a hike, the easiest route into the amphitheater is the **Queen's Garden Trail** at Sunrise Point. A short,

rolling hike along the **Bristlecone Loop Trail** at Rainbow Point rewards you with spectacular views and a cool walk through a forest of bristlecone pines. If you don't have time to drive the 18 mi to the end of the park, skip Bryce Canyon Lodge and drive 2 mi from the visitor center to **Inspiration Point** and the next 2 mi to **Bryce Point.**

End your day with sunset at Inspiration Point and dinner at Bryce Canyon Lodge (reserve ahead). As you leave the park, stop at **Ruby's Inn** for Native American jewelry, souvenirs for the kids, and snacks for the road.

check with park staff for parking options. RVs can drive throughout the park, but vehicles longer than 25 feet are not allowed at Paria View.

WHAT TO SEE

HISTORIC SITE

Bryce Canyon Lodge. The lodge's architect, Gilbert Stanley Underwood, was a national park specialist, having designed lodges at Zion and Grand Canyon before turning his T-square to Bryce in 1923. The results are worth a visit, even if you plan to sleep elsewhere; this National Historic Landmark has been faithfully restored, right down to the lobby's huge limestone fireplace and log and wrought-iron chandelier. The bark-covered hickory furniture isn't original, but renovators ordered them from the same company that created the originals. Inside the historic building are a restaurant and a gift shop, as well as plenty of information on park activities. Guests of the lodge stay in the numerous log cabins on the wooded grounds (⇨ *Where to Eat and Stay*). ⊠ *2 mi south of park entrance* ☎ *435/834–5361.*

SCENIC STOPS

Agua Canyon. When you stop at this overlook in the southern section of the park, pick out among the hoodoos the formation known as the Hunter, which actually has a few small hardy trees growing on its cap. The play of light and colorful contrasts are especially noticeable here. ⊠ *12 mi south of park entrance.*

★ **Fairyland Point.** Just north of the visitor center, this scenic overlook atop Boat Mesa is a great first stop after you enter the park. There are splendid views of Fairyland Amphitheater and its delicate, fanciful forms. The Sinking Ship and other formations stand before the grand backdrop

10

of the Aquarius Plateau and distant Navajo Mountain. Nearby is the Fairyland Loop trailhead; it's about a five-hour hike. ⊠ *1 mi off main park road, 1 mi north of visitor center.*

Inspiration Point. Not far at all (0.3 mi) east along the Rim Trail from Bryce Point is Inspiration Point, site of a wonderful vista on the main amphitheater and one of the best places in the park to see the sunset. ⊠ *5½ mi south of park entrance on Inspiration Point Rd.*

★ **Natural Bridge.** This 85-foot arch formation is an essential Bryce photo-op. The rusty buttress, formed over millions of years by wind, water, and chemical erosion, contrasts sharply against the pine forest that peeks through from below. ⊠ *11 mi south of park entrance.*

Rainbow and Yovimpa Points. Separated by less than a mile, Rainbow and Yovimpa points offer two fine panoramas facing opposite directions. Rainbow Point's best view is to the north overlooking the southern rim of the amphitheater and giving a glimpse of Grand Staircase–Escalante National Monument. Yovimpa Point's vista spreads out to the south. On a clear day you can see all the way to Arizona, 100 mi away. Yovimpa Point also has a shady and quiet picnic area with tables and restrooms. Hike between them on the Bristlecone Loop Trail or the more strenuous 8½-mi Riggs Spring Loop Trail. ⊠ *18 mi south of park entrance.*

★ **Sunrise Point.** Named for its stunning views at dawn, this overlook is a popular stop for the summer crowds that come to Bryce Canyon and is the starting point for the Queen's Garden Trail and the Fairyland Loop Trail. You have to descend the Queen's Garden Trail to get a regal glimpse of **Queen Victoria,** a hoodoo that appears to sport a crown and glorious full skirt. The trail is popular and marked clearly, but moderately strenuous with 300 feet of elevation change. ⊠ *2 mi south of park entrance near Bryce Canyon Lodge.*

Sunset Point. Watch the late-day sun paint its magic on the hoodoos here. You can only see **Thor's Hammer,** a delicate formation similar to a balanced rock when you hike 521 feet down into the amphitheater on the Navajo Loop Trail. ⊠ *2 mi south of park entrance near Bryce Canyon Lodge.*

VISITOR CENTER

Bryce Canyon Visitor Center. Sure, you're anxious to hit the hoodoos, but the informational movie *Shadows of Time* about Bryce Canyon's history and geology is a wonderful primer. You can't miss it—the spacious building looks like a cross between a barn and a fire station. There are also exhibits, books, maps, and back-country camping permits for sale. First aid, emergency, and lost-and-found services are offered here.

GOOD READS

■ *Bryce Canyon Auto and Hiking Guide,* by Tully Stoud, includes information on the geology and history of the area.

■ Supplement the free park map with *Bryce Canyon Hiking Guide,* which includes an amphitheater hiking map and aerial photo.

■ To prepare kids ages 5–10 for a trip to the park, consider ordering the 32-page *Kid's Guide to Bryce Canyon.*

10

If you want coffee, head to nearby Ruby's Inn. ✉ *1 mi south of park entrance* ☎ *435/834–5322* ⊕ *www.nps.gov/brca* ◷ *Oct.–June, daily 8–4:30; July–Sept., daily 8–8.*

SPORTS AND THE OUTDOORS

Most visitors explore Bryce Canyon by car, but the hiking trails are far more rewarding. At these elevations, you'll have to stop to catch your breath more often than you're used to. It gets warm in the summer but rarely uncomfortably hot, so hiking farther into the depths of the park is not difficult so long as you don't pick a hike that is beyond your abilities.

AIR TOURS

OUTFITTERS AND EXPEDITIONS

For a bird's-eye view of Bryce Canyon National Park, take a dramatic helicopter ride over the fantastic sandstone formations with **Bryce Canyon Airlines & Helicopters** (☎ *435/834–5341* ⊕ *www.rubysinn.com/bryce-canyon-airlines.html* 🖃 *$55–$225*). Flights depart from Ruby's Inn Heliport. Trips can last from 20 minutes to more than an hour. Bring a jacket.

BIRD-WATCHING

More than 170 bird species have been identified in Bryce. Violet green swallows and white-throated swifts are common, as are Steller's jays, American coots, rufous hummingbirds, and mountain bluebirds. Lucky bird-watchers will see golden eagles floating across the skies above the pink rocks of the amphitheater and experienced birders might spot an osprey nest high in the canyon wall. The best time in the park for avian variety is from May through July.

HIKING

To get up close and personal with the park's hoodoos, set aside a half day to hike into the amphitheater. There are no elevators, so remember that after you descend below the rim you'll have to get back up. The air gets warmer the lower you go, and the altitude will have you huffing and puffing unless you're a mountain native. The uneven terrain calls for sturdy hiking boots; no below-rim trails are paved. For trail maps, information, and ranger recommendations, stop at the visitor center. Bathrooms are located at most trailheads but not down in the amphitheater.

EASY

Bristlecone Loop Trail. This 1-mi trail with a modest 100 feet of elevation gain alternates between spruce and fir forest and wide-open vistas of the Paunsaugunt Plateau and beyond. You might see yellow-bellied marmots and blue grouse, critters not found at lower elevations in the park. The most challenging part of the hike is ungluing your eyes from the scenery long enough to read the signage at the many trail forks. Plan on 45 minutes to an hour. ✉ *Trailhead at Rainbow Point parking area, 18 mi south of park entrance.*

� **Queen's Garden Trail.** This hike is the easiest way down into the amphitheater. Three hundred feet of elevation change will lead you to a short tunnel, quirky hoodoos, and many like-minded hikers. Allow two hours total to hike the 1.5-mi trail plus the ½-mi rim-side path back to the parking area. ✉ *Trailhead at Sunrise Point, 2 mi south of park entrance.*

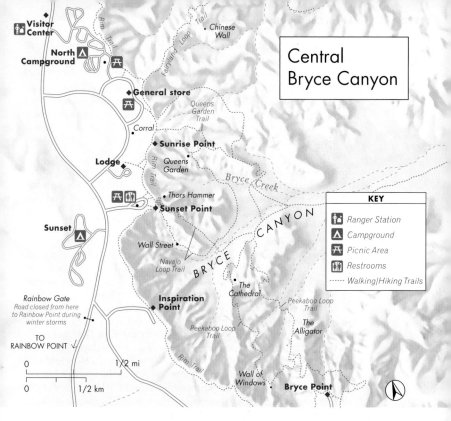

Central Bryce Canyon

KEY

🏢 Ranger Station
🏕 Campground
🎋 Picnic Area
🚻 Restrooms
⋯⋯ Walking|Hiking Trails

MODERATE

Navajo Loop Trail. A steep descent via a series of switchbacks leads to Wall Street, a claustrophobic hallway of rock only 20 feet wide in places with walls 100 feet high. Geology buffs will love the striations in the canyon walls. The northern end of the trail brings Thor's Hammer into view. Allow one to two hours on this 1½-mi trail with 500 feet of elevation change. ⊠ *Trailhead at Sunset Point, 2 mi south of park entrance.*

★ **Navajo/Queen's Garden Combination Loop.** By walking this extended 3-mi loop, you can see some of the best of Bryce; it takes two to three hours. The route passes fantastic formations and an open forest of pine and juniper on the amphitheater floor. Descend into the amphitheater from Sunset Point on the Navajo Trail and ascend via the less demanding Queen's Garden Trail; return to your starting point via the Rim Trail. ⊠ *Trailheads at Sunset and Sunrise points, 2 mi south of park entrance.*

DIFFICULT

Fairyland Loop Trail. Hike into whimsical Fairyland Canyon on this strenuous and uncrowded 8-mi trail, popular with cross-country skiers in winter. It winds around hoodoos, across trickles of water, and finally to a natural window in the rock at Tower Bridge, 1½ mi from Sunrise Point and 4 mi from Fairyland Point. The pink-and-white badlands and hoodoos surround you the whole way. Allow at least five hours for the round trip with

10

1,000 feet of elevation change. You can pick up the loop at Fairyland Point or Sunrise Point. ⊠ *Trailhead at Fairyland Point, 1 mi off main park road, 1 mi south of park entrance; Sunrise Point, 2 mi south of park entrance.*

★ **Peekaboo Loop.** The reward of this steep trail is the Wall of Windows and the Three Wise Men. ■TIP➔ Horses use this trail in spring, summer, and fall and have the right-of-way. Start at Bryce, Sunrise, or Sunset Point and allow four to five hours to hike the 5-mi trail or 7-mi loop. ⊠ *Trailheads at Bryce Point, 2 mi off main park road, 5½ mi south of park entrance; Sunrise and Sunset points, 2 mi south of park entrance.*

Trail to the Hat Shop. The sedimentary haberdashery sits 2 mi from the trailhead. Hard gray caps balance precariously atop narrow pedestals of softer, rust-colored rock. Allow three to four hours to travel this strenuous 4-mi round-trip trail. ⊠ *Trailhead at Bryce Point, 2 mi off main park road, 5½ mi south of park entrance.*

Under-the-Rim Trail. This is how serious backpackers immerse themselves in the landscape of Bryce. Starting at Bryce Point, the trail travels 22½ mi to Rainbow Point, passing through the Pink Cliffs, traversing Agua Canyon and Ponderosa Canyon, and taking you by several springs. Most of the hike is on the amphitheater floor, characterized by up-and-down terrain among stands of ponderosa pine; the elevation change totals about 1,500 feet. Four trailheads along the main park road allow you to connect to the Under-the-Rim Trail and cover its length as a series of day hikes. Allow at least two days to hike the route in its entirety, and there's plenty to see to make it a more leisurely three-day affair. Obtain a backcountry permit at the visitor center if you intend to stay in the amphitheater overnight. Also inquire about the current availability of water along the trail. ⊠ *Trailheads at Bryce Point, Swamp Canyon, Ponderosa Canyon, and Rainbow Point.*

HORSEBACK RIDING

Many of the park's hiking trails were first formed beneath the hooves of cattle wranglers. Today, hikers and riders share the trails and a number of outfitters can set you up with a gentle mount and lead you to the park's best sights. Not only can you cover more ground than you would walking, but equine traffic has the right-of-way at all times. Call ahead to the stables for reservations to find a trip that's right for you, from half an hour to overnight. The biggest outfitters have over 100 horses and mules to choose from, but those under the age of 7 or who weigh more than 220 pounds are prohibited.

OUTFITTERS
AND
EXPEDITIONS

Canyon Trail Rides (⊠ *Bryce Canyon Lodge* ☎ *435/679–8665* ⊕ *www.canyonrides.com*) descend to the floor of the Bryce Canyon amphitheater via horse or mule. Most who take this expedition have no riding experience, so don't hesitate to join in. A $50 two-hour ride ambles along the amphitheater floor to the Fairy Castle before returning to Sunrise Point. The $75 half-day expedition follows Peekaboo Trail, winds past the Fairy Castle and the Alligator, and passes the Wall of Windows before returning to Sunrise Point. Two rides a day of each type leave in the morning and early afternoon; there are no rides in winter. To reserve a trail ride, call or stop by their desk in the lodge. Retrace trails taken by outlaw Butch Cassidy in Red Canyon National Forest, Bryce Canyon,

Hikers in Bryce are rewarded with vistas highlighting the park's colorful landscape.

or Grand Staircase—Escalante National Monument on **Ruby's Red Canyon Horseback Rides** (☎ *866/782–0002* ⊕ *www.horserides.net*), which last from half an hour to a $125 all day ride that includes lunch.

WINTER SPORTS

Unlike Utah's other national parks, Bryce Canyon receives plenty of snow, making it a popular cross-country ski area. The park's 2½-mi Fairyland Ski Loop is marked but ungroomed, as is the 5-mi Paria Loop, which runs through ponderosa forests into long, open meadows.

The National Park Service lends out snowshoes free of charge at the visitor center; just leave your driver's license or a major credit card with a ranger. You can snowshoe on the rim trails, but the Park Service discourages their use below the rim.

OUTFITTERS AND EXPEDITIONS **Best Western Ruby's Inn** (⊠ *Rte. 63, 1 mi north of park entrance* ☎ *435/834–5341*) grooms a 31-mi private trail that connects to an ungroomed trail in the park. Rental equipment is available.

EDUCATIONAL OFFERINGS

RANGER PROGRAMS

The base of operations for all ranger activities is the visitor center, located 4½ mi south of the intersection of Highways 12 and 63. Admission is free, but meeting times and locations vary. Stop by the visitor center or call ☎ *435/834–5322* for more information.

Canyon Hike. Take an early morning walk among the hoodoos of Queen's Garden or Navajo Loop Trail. A ranger points out the formations and explains some of the amphitheater's features as you go. The hike is 2–3 mi long and takes two to three hours to complete.

Campfire and Auditorium Programs. Bryce Canyon's natural diversity comes alive in the park's two campgrounds or at Bryce Canyon Lodge. Lectures, slide programs, and audience participation introduce you to geology, astronomy, wildlife, history, and many other topics related to Bryce Canyon and the West. ☎ *435/834–5322.*

Geology Talk. Rangers relate the geologic story of Bryce Canyon in short sessions held at various times and locations around the park.

Junior Ranger Program. Running from Memorial Day to Labor Day; children ages six to 12 can sign up at the park visitor center. Activities vary depending on the park ranger, but a session might involve learning about geology and wildlife using arts and crafts and games. Schedules of events and topics are posted at the visitor center, Bryce Canyon Lodge, and on North and Sunset campgrounds bulletin boards.

Moonlight Hike. Three times a month, at or near full moon, rangers lead this two-hour hike. You must make reservations in person at the visitor center on the day of the hike.

Fodor's Choice ★ **Night Sky Program.** Up to 7,500 stars are visible on a clear night at Bryce Canyon—one of the best places in the country for sky watching. A combination of rangers and volunteers team up to give low-key astronomy lectures or multimedia presentations, followed by telescope viewing.

Rim Walk. Stroll along the gorgeous rim of Bryce Canyon with a park ranger on a 1-mi, 1½-hour outing.

WHAT'S NEARBY

Bryce Canyon is a bit off the beaten path, often a side trip for those who visit Zion National Park to the southwest and far from major roads or large cities (both Las Vegas and Salt Lake City are approximately 270 mi away). The park is just one of a number of beautiful or unique natural areas in southern Utah worth exploring. Towns close to the park pulse with western personality and are excellent bases for exploring beyond Bryce. The expansive and remote Grand Staircase—Escalante National Monument is about an hour to the northeast, and Red Canyon offers spectacular, bright red-rock formations and a paved bike path. Nearby State Parks are great side trips: Escalante Petrified Forest and Kodachrome Basin.

VISITOR INFORMATION

Garfield County Travel Council (Escalante, Panguitch) ⊠ 55 S. Main St., Panguitch ☎ 435/676–1160 or 800/444–6689 ⊕ www.brycecanyoncountry.com. **Iron County Travel Council (Cedar City)** ⊠ 581 N. Main, Ste. A, Cedar City ☎ 800/354–4849 or 435/586–5124 ⊕ www.scenicsouthernutah.com.

NEARBY TOWNS AND ATTRACTIONS

NEARBY TOWNS

Decent amenities, inexpensive lodging, and an excellent location 24 mi northwest of Bryce Canyon National Park on U.S. 89 make **Panguitch** a comfortable launching pad for recreation in the area. The town is noted for the distinctive brick architecture of its early homes and outbuildings, and for the original facades of some of its late-19th-century Main Street commercial structures. Northeast of Bryce 47 mi, **Escalante** has modern amenities and is a western gateway to the Grand Staircase–Escalante National Monument. If you're traveling through southwestern Utah on Interstate 15, **Cedar City** will be your exit to Bryce. The largest city you'll encounter in this part of Utah, it's 78 mi from Bryce Canyon. The campus of Southern Utah University is here, and their Shakespearean Festival draws fans of the Bard from all over the country.

NEARBY ATTRACTIONS

★ **Cedar Breaks National Monument.** From the rim of Cedar Breaks, a natural amphitheater similar to Bryce Canyon plunges 2,000 feet into the Markagunt Plateau. Short alpine hiking trails along the rim make this a wonderful summer stop. Although its roads may be closed in winter due to heavy snow, the monument stays open for cross-country skiing and snowmobiling. ⊠ *Rte. 14, 23 mi east of Cedar City, Brian Head* ☎ *435/586–0787* ⊕ *www.nps.gov/cebr* ☜ *$4 per person* ☉ *Visitor center open late May–mid-Oct., daily 8–6.*

Dixie National Forest. This expansive natural area divided into four noncontiguous swaths covers a total of two million acres. Adjacent to three national parks, two national monuments, and several state parks, this area has 26 developed campgrounds in a variety of backdrops: lakeside, mountainside, in the depths of pine and spruce forests. Recreational opportunities abound: hiking, camping, picnicking, horseback riding, and fishing. Call ahead to see if your preferred activity requires a permit or a fee. ⊠ *Dixie National Forest Headquarters, 1789 N. Wedgewood La., Cedar City* ☎ *435/865–3200, 800/280–2267 campground information* ⊕ *www.fs.fed.us/dxnf* ☜ *Free.*

☼ **Escalante Petrified Forest State Park.** This park 48 mi east of Bryce Canyon off Route 12 was created to protect a huge repository of fossilized wood and dinosaur bones. Learn all about petrified wood, which is easily spotted along two short interpretive trails. There's an attractive swimming beach at the park's Wide Hollow Reservoir, which is also good for boating, fishing, and birding. ⊠ *710 N. Reservoir Rd., Escalante* ☎ *435/826–4466* ⊕ *www.stateparks.utah.gov* ☜ *Day use $6, camping $16* ☉ *June–Aug., 7 AM–10 PM; Sept.–May, 8 AM–10 PM.*

Kodachrome Basin State Park. As soon as you see it, you'll understand why the park earned this colorful photographic name from the National Geographic Society. The sand pipes seen here cannot be found anywhere else in the world. Hike any of the trails to spot some of the 67 pipes in and around the park. The short Angels Palace Trail takes you quickly into the park's interior, up, over, and around some of the badlands. ⊠ *Cottonwood Canyon Rd., 7 mi southeast of Cannonville*

10

FESTIVALS AND EVENTS

FEBRUARY
Bryce Canyon Winter Festival.
This event at Ruby's Best Western Inn features cross-country ski races, snow-sculpting contests, and ski archery. ☎ 435/834–5341 or 866/866–6616 ⊕ www.rubysinn.com.

JUNE
Panguitch Valley Balloon Rally.
Watch two dozen or more colorful hot-air balloons rise into the air at Panguitch and float over canyon country. ☎ 866/590–4134 ⊕ www.panguitch.org.

Quilt Walk Festival. During the bitter winter of 1864, Panguitch residents were on the verge of starvation. A group of men from the settlement set out over the mountains to fetch provisions from the town of Parowan, 40 mi away. When they hit waist-deep snowdrifts they were forced to abandon their oxen. Legend says the men, frustrated and ready to turn back, laid a quilt on the snow and knelt to pray. Soon they realized the quilt had kept them from sinking into the snow. Spreading quilts before them as they walked, leapfrog style, the

men traveled to Parowan and back, returning with lifesaving provisions. This three-day event commemorates the event with quilting classes, a tour of Panguitch's pioneer homes, crafts shows, and a dinner-theater production in which the story is acted out. ☎ 435/676–1160 ⊕ www.quiltwalk.com.

JUNE–OCTOBER
Utah Shakespearean Festival. Join the hurly burly as Cedar City features several of the Bard's stage productions as well as a outdoor Greenshow before each play, with jugglers, puppet shows, and folks dressed in Elizabethan period costume. ☎ 435/586–7880 or 800/752–9849 ⊕ www.bard.org.

JULY
Panguitch Pioneer Day Celebration. At one of the biggest Pioneer Day celebrations in the state, Panguitch does it right with an invitational rodeo, parade, historical program, chuck-wagon breakfast and barbecue, children's races, and dancing. ☎ 435/676–1160 or 800/444–6689.

☎ 435/679–8562 ⊕ www.stateparks.utah.gov ✉ Day use $6, camping $16 ⊙ Daily 6 AM–10 PM.

AREA ACTIVITIES

SPORTS AND THE OUTDOORS

OUTFITTERS AND EXCURSIONS

Excursions of Escalante. Hikers, bikers, climbers, anglers, and photographers are all served by this company, where tours are custom-fit to your schedule and needs. The specialty is canyoneering: using basic climbing equipment to move through slot chutes or rappel down walls and other obstacles. No experience is required; all gear is provided, and tours last from four hours to eight days. ✉ 125 E. Main St., Escalante ☎ 800/839–7567 ⊕ www.excursionsofescalante.com ⊙ Mid-Apr.–mid-Nov. or by appointment.

Grand Staircase—Escalante

In September 1996, President Bill Clinton designated 1.7 million acres in south-central Utah as **Grand Staircase—Escalante National Monument,** the first monument to be administered by the Bureau of Land Management instead of the National Park Service. Its three distinct sections—the Grand Staircase, the Kaiparowits Plateau, and the Canyons of the Escalante—offer remote backcountry experiences hard to find elsewhere in the Lower 48. Waterfalls, Native American ruins, and petroglyphs, shoulder-width slot canyons, and improbable colors all characterize this wilderness. Highway 12 which straddles the northern border of the monument, is one of the most scenic stretches of road in the Southwest. The small towns of Escalante and Boulder offer access, information, outfitters, lodging, and dining.

Larger than most national parks, this formidable monument is popular with backpackers, hikers, canyoneers, and hard-core mountain-bike enthusiasts. You can explore the rocky landscape, including slot canyons and wilderness, via dirt roads with a four-wheel-drive vehicle; most roads depart from Highway 12. Views into the monument are most impressive from Highway 12 between Escalante and Boulder. Calf Creek Falls is an easy 6-mi round-trip hike from the trailhead at Calf Creek Recreation Area (on Route 12 north of Escalante). At the end of your walk, a large waterfall explodes over a cliff hundreds of feet above. It costs nothing to visit the park, but fees apply for camping and backcountry permits. ⊠ *318 N. 100 East, Kanab* ☎ *435/644-6400* ⊕ *www.ut.blm.gov/ monument* ⊠ *Free.*

BICYCLING

A good long-distance mountain-bike ride in the isolated Escalante region follows the 44-mi **Hell's Backbone Road** from Escalante to Boulder. The grade is steep, but the views of Box Death Hollow make it all worthwhile. The road leaves from the center of town and signage is good.

SCENIC DRIVES AND VISTAS

10

Fodor's Choice
★

Highway 12 Scenic Byway. Keep your camera handy and steering wheel steady along this route between Escalante and Loa, near Capitol Reef National Park. Though the highway starts at the intersection of U.S. 89, west of Bryce Canyon National Park, the stretch that begins in Escalante is one of the most spectacular. The road passes through Grand Staircase–Escalante National Monument and on to Capitol Reef along one of the most scenic stretches of highway in the United States. Be sure to stop at the scenic overlooks; almost every one will give you an eye-popping view. Don't get distracted, though; the paved road is twisting and steep, and at times climbs over a hogback with sheer drop-offs on both sides.

U.S. 89/Utah's Heritage Highway. Winding north from the Arizona border all the way to Spanish Fork Canyon an hour south of Salt Lake City, U.S. 89 is known as the Heritage Highway for its role in shaping Utah history. At its southern end, Kanab is known as "Little Hollywood," having provided the backdrop for many famous western movies and TV commercials. The town has since grown considerably to accommodate tourists who flock here to see where Ronald Reagan once slept and Clint Eastwood drew his guns. Other towns north along this famous road may not have the same notoriety in these parts, but they do provide a quiet, uncrowded, and inexpensive place to stay near Zion and Bryce Canyon National Parks. East of Kanab, U.S. 89 runs along the southern edge of the Grand Staircase–Escalante National Monument.

WHERE TO EAT AND STAY

ABOUT THE RESTAURANTS

Dining options in the park proper are limited to Bryce Canyon Lodge; the nearby Ruby's Inn complex is your best eating bet close by. The restaurants in nearby locales tend to be of the meat-and-potatoes variety. Utah's drinking laws can be confusing so ask your server what is available: beer is more common than wine and spirits.

ABOUT THE HOTELS

Lodging options in Bryce Canyon include both rustic and modern amenities, but all fill up fast in summer. Bryce Canyon Lodge is the only hotel inside the park. It's a charming facility, and you'll be close to everything. Panguitch has some particularly good options for budget and last-minute travelers.

ABOUT THE CAMPGROUNDS

Campgrounds in Bryce Canyon fill up fast, especially during the summer, and are family friendly. All are drive-in, except for the handful of backcountry sites that only backpackers and gung-ho day hikers ever see. Most are first-come, first-served during the high season, but call to inquire about those available for reservation. Most of the area's state parks have camping facilities, and Dixie National Forest contains many wonderful sites. Campgrounds may close seasonally because of lack of services (one loop of North Campground remains open year-round), and roads may occasionally close in winter while heavy snow is cleared.

WHERE TO EAT

IN THE PARK

$$ ✕ **Bryce Canyon Lodge.** Set among towering pines, this rustic old lodge is the only place to dine within the park. Many menu items change each year. Try anything with the tomatillo sauce, and stick with the simpler dishes. Be sure to make a reservation during peak season. ⊠ *About 2 mi south of the park entrance* ☎ *435/834–5361* ⊕ *www.brycecanyonlodge.com* ☖ *Reservations essential* ▭ *AE, D, DC, MC, V* ☽ *Closed Nov.–Mar.*

PICNIC AREAS **North Campground.** This area, a shady, alpine setting among ponderosa pine, has picnic tables and grills. ⊠ *About ¼ mi south of the visitor center.*

Yovimpa Point. At the southern end of the park, this shady, quiet spot looks out onto the 100-mi vistas from the rim. There are tables and restrooms. ⊠ *18 mi south of the park entrance.*

OUTSIDE THE PARK

$ ✕ **Bryce Canyon Restaurant.** Part of the Bryce Canyon Pines motel, this
AMERICAN eatery is known for homemade soups like tomato-broccoli and corn
chowder, and for fresh berry and cream pies. ⊠ *Hwy. 12, about 15 mi
west from Tropic* ☎ *800/892–7923* ⊕ *www.brycecanyonmotel.com*
═ *AE, D, DC, MC, V.*

$–$$ ✕ **Cowboy Blues.** Walk back into the Old West for basic but good American
AMERICAN food in this rustic restaurant adorned with ranching memorabilia. Steaks,
ribs, and Utah trout dominate the dinner menu, while lunch serves tried-
and-true sandwiches, salads, and burgers. A full liquor license, a rarity in
these parts, allows beer, wine, and cocktails to be served here. ⊠ *530 W.
Main St., Escalante* ☎ *435/826–4577* ═ *AE, D, MC, V.*

¢ ✕ **Esca-Latte Coffee Shop & Pizza Parlor.** Fuel up for your hike with the best
CAFÉ coffee in town. When you're spent after a day of exploration, there's
no better place to sit back and relax with friends. Try a turkey sub or
pizza with a cold draft microbrew, or do the salad bar. When dining
on the patio, watch hummingbirds fight the wind at the feeders. ⊠ *310
W. Main St., Escalante* ☎ *435/826–4266* ═ *D, MC, V.*

$ ✕ **Fosters Family Steakhouse.** With a stone fireplace and picture windows,
STEAK Fosters is a relatively quiet, modern steak house, and one of the most
pleasant restaurants in the area. The menu features prime rib, steaks,
and basic chicken and seafood dishes. Beer is the only alcohol served.
⊠ *1150 Highway 12 (2 mi west of the junction with Rte. 63), Panguitch*
☎ *435/834–5227* ═ *AE, D, MC, V* ☯ *Closed Mon.–Thurs. in Jan.*

$–$$ ✕ **Harold's Place.** About 15 mi west of Bryce Canyon, on Highway 12
AMERICAN at the entrance to Red Canyon stands this establishment designed to
resemble a log cabin. The large dinner menu includes a variety of steaks,
lamb, seafood, pastas, and salads. Try Harold's Favorite for breakfast:
eggs any way you like, potatoes, your choice of meat, and a bottomless
cup of coffee. ⊠ *3066 Rte. 12, 7 mi east from Panguitch* ☎ *435/676–
2350* ═ *MC, V* ☯ *Closed Nov.–Mar. No lunch.*

$$$ ✕ **Milt's Stage Stop.** Locals and an increasing number of tourists have
AMERICAN discovered the terrific food at this dinner spot in beautiful Cedar Can-
FodorśChoice yon, about 78 mi from Bryce Canyon and 5 mi east of Cedar City. It's
★ known for rib-eye steak, fajitas, and fresh seafood dishes. In winter,
deer feed in front of the restaurant as a fireplace blazes away inside.
A number of hunting trophies decorate the rustic building's interior,
and splendid views of the surrounding mountains delight patrons year-
round. ⊠ *3560 E. Highway 14, Cedar City* ☎ *435/586–9344* ═ *AE, D,
DC, MC, V* ☯ *No lunch.*

10

WHERE TO STAY

IN THE PARK

$$$ ⌂ **Bryce Canyon Lodge.** A few feet from the amphitheater's rim and trail-
FodorśChoice heads is this rugged stone-and-wood lodge. You have your choice of
★ suites on the lodge's second level, motel-style rooms in separate buildings (with balconies or porches), and cozy lodgepole-pine cabins, some
with cathedral ceilings and gas fireplaces. ■ TIP→ Reservations are hard
to come by, so call several months ahead. Horseback rides into the park's
interior can be arranged in the lobby. Reservations are essential for

dinner at the lodge restaurant. Recent renovations to the historic property paid careful attention to details, but remember the focus here is lodge, not luxury. **Pros:** fine western-style lodging; friendly and attentive staff; bright orange hoodoos only a short walk away. **Cons:** closed in the winter; few amenities; grounds are dark at night, so bring a flashlight to dinner! ⊠ *2 mi south of park entrance* ⌂ *P.O. Box 640079, Bryce, 84764* ☎ *435/834–5361 or 888/297–2757* ⊕ *www.brycecanyonlodge. com* ⟿ *70 rooms, 3 suites, 40 cabins* ⌂ *In-room: no a/c, no TV. In-hotel: restaurant* ▤ *AE, D, DC, MC, V* ⊙ *Closed Nov.–Mar.*

CAMPING

$ ⚠ **North Campground.** A cool, shady retreat in a forest of ponderosa pines, this is a great home base for your exploration of Bryce Canyon. You're near the general store, Bryce Canyon Lodge, trailheads, and the visitor center. Reservations are accepted for sites during part of the year, but usually it's first-come, first-served, and the campground usually fills by early afternoon in July, August, and September. **Pros:** a trail leads right to the visitor center; Loop D is close to the general store and outdoor theater. **Cons:** not quite as scenic as the Sunset Campground; some sites feel crowded and un-private. ⊠ *Main park road, ½ mi south of visitor center* ☎ *435/834–5322* ⚠ *56 tent sites, 47 RV sites* ⌂ *Flush toilets, dump station, drinking water, fire grates, picnic tables, public telephone, general store* ▤ *No credit cards.*

$ ⚠ **Sunset Campground.** This serene alpine campground is within walking distance of Bryce Canyon Lodge and many trailheads. All sites are filled on a first-come, first-served basis. The campground fills by early afternoon in July though September, so get your campsite before you sightsee. Reservations are required for the group site. **Pros:** shady tent sites; a great place to watch the sun go down. **Cons:** as one of the most accessible hiking areas of the park, it can be crowded; only one group site. ⊠ *Main park road, 2 mi south of visitor center* ☎ *435/834–5322* ⚠ *47 tent sites, 49 RV sites (no hookups)* ⌂ *Flush toilets, dump station, drinking water, fire grates, picnic tables, public telephone, general store* ▤ *No credit cards* ⊙ *May–Oct.*

OUTSIDE THE PARK

$–$$ ⊞ **Bard's Inn Bed and Breakfast.** Rooms in this restored turn-of-the-20th-century house 78 mi from Bryce Canyon are named after heroines in Shakespeare's plays. There are wonderful antiques throughout and handcrafted quilts grace the beds. Enjoy a full breakfast that includes fresh home-baked breads, such as nutmeg-blueberry muffins, plus fruit, juices, and oven-shirred eggs. **Pros:** immaculate rooms; good restaurant next door; close to festival grounds. **Cons:** Shakespeare is everywhere you look, and often the subject of conversation at breakfast; must book ahead for festival season (June–October). ⊠ *150 S. 100 West St., Cedar City* ☎ *435/586–6612* ⊕ *bards.qwestoffice.net/* ⟿ *11 rooms* ⌂ *In-room: no phone. In-hotel: no-smoking rooms* ▤ *AE, MC, V* ⦿ *BP.*

$$–$$$ ⊞ **Best Western Grand.** This four story 164-room chain hotel opened ★ its doors in the summer of 2009. If you're into creature comforts but can do without charm, this is your place. One of the hotels in the area (as opposed to motels, the Grand's room are accessed from inside), the property also offers a pool and patio areas. Rooms are relatively posh, with solid mattresses, pillows, and bedding, spacious bathrooms,

and modern appliances. **Pros:** one of the nicest hotels this side of Las Vegas; lots of indoor amenities. **Cons:** feels perfect for the business traveler, with predictability favored over personality; no pets allowed. ⊠ *30 N. 100 East, Bryce* ☎ *866/866–6636* ⊕ *www.brycecanyongrand. com* ↗ *164 rooms, 31 suites* ⚲ *In-room: refrigerator, Wi-Fi. In-hotel: Internet terminal, pool, laundry service, gym* ▭ *AE, D, DC, MC, V.*

\$\$ 🛏 **Best Western Ruby's Inn.** North of the park entrance this is "Grand
★ Central Station" for visitors to Bryce. Ruby's has anything the weary traveler might need, and a few things they don't. There's a beauty salon, a service station, and a liquor store here. Ruby's has expanded with the popularity of the park, adding wings of rooms that now vary in size and attractiveness. All of the guest rooms are consistently comfortable, however. Centered between the gift shop and restaurant, the lobby of rough-hewn log beams and poles sets a southwestern mood. **Pros:** has it all—general store, post office, campground, restaurants, gas and more; a good place to mingle with other park visitors and swap stories and advice on hiking the park. **Cons:** expansion has caused it to lose some of its charm; this is no sleepy vacation spot—the lobby scan get very busy. ⊠ *26 S. Main St., Bryce* ☎ *435/834–5341 or 866/866–6616* ⊕ *www. rubysinn.com* ↗ *383 rooms, 2 suites* ⚲ *In-room: Wi-Fi. In-hotel: 2 restaurants, pools, laundry facilities* ▭ *AE, D, DC, MC, V.*

\$\$ 🛏 **Escalante's Grand Staircase Bed & Breakfast Inn.** Rooms are separate
★ from the main house giving this property some motel privacy along with B-and-B amenities. Skylights, tile floors, log furniture, and murals reproducing area petroglyphs add decoration. You can relax on the outdoor porches or in the library, or make use of the rental bikes to explore the adjacent national monument. **Pros:** spacious rooms; cute back porch for horizon gazing. **Cons:** bring your own computer cable for Internet access—seriously. ⊠ *280 W. Main St., Escalante* ☎ *435/826–4890 or 866/826–4890* ⊕ *www.escalantebnb.com* ↗ *8 rooms* ⚲ *In-room: Internet. In-hotel: bicycles, Internet terminal, Wi-Fi, no kids under 10* ▭ *D, MC, V* ⱺ| *BP.*

¢ 🛏 **Escalante Outfitters.** Stay here if you want a one-stop place to plan and gear up for your outdoor adventure or if you're on a budget and don't care about amenities. The seven log bunkhouse cabins share a single bathhouse. Tent sites are available too. **Pros:** the café food is a pleasant surprise; large outdoor store on-site. **Cons:** right on the highway; communal showers mean you may have to wait in line. ⊠ *310 W. Main St., Escalante* ☎ *435/826–4266* ⊕ *www.escalanteoutfitters. com* ↗ *7 double-occupancy cabins* ⚲ *In-room: no a/c, no TV. In-hotel: restaurant* ▭ *D, MC, V.*

¢–\$ 🛏 **Marianna Inn.** Choose from one-, two-, three-, and four-bed cabin-
🌙 style rooms at this family-friendly one-story motel; those with whirlpool baths are \$25 extra. You can barbecue your own supper on one of the grills and eat your meal on the covered patio. Relax afterward on a hammock or in the summer-only outdoor spa. **Pros:** lovely cedar deck and patio; cooling ceiling fans. **Cons:** pastel paint colors may not appeal to all; tiny rooms. ⊠ *699 N. Main St., Panguitch* ☎ *435/676–8844* ⊕ *www.mariannainn.com* ↗ *34 rooms* ⚲ *In-hotel: some pets allowed* ▭ *AE, D, DC, MC, V.*

10

CAMPING

$$–$$$

Fodor's Choice

★

⚠ **Best Western Ruby's Inn Campground and RV Park.** North of the entrance to Bryce Canyon National Park, this campground sits amid pine and fir trees a few steps from the main Ruby's complex. Sites are shaded and you can also rent a cabin or a tepee. **Pros:** practically on top of the park entrance; whatever you need, Ruby will provide; RV pull-throughs can handle the largest vehicles. **Cons:** because of all that Ruby's has to offer, peace, serenity, and solitude are in short supply. ⊠ *20 S. Main St., Bryce* ☎ *866/866–6616 or 435/834–5314* ⊕ *www.brycecanyoncampgrounds. com* ⚠ *200 tent/RV sites; 5 cabins, 8 tepees* ♿ *Flush toilets, full hookups, dump station, drinking water, guest laundry, showers, grills, picnic tables, electricity, public telephone, general store, swimming (pool)* ⊟ *AE, D, DC, MC, V* ⊗ *Apr.–Oct.*

$$

☾

⚠ **Bryce Valley KOA.** On the quiet side of Bryce, this campground has the lowest (and warmest) elevation of any camping spot near Bryce Canyon. Everything you need for a quiet night of sleep and comfort is right here, near the slot canyons of the Paria River, and the scenery is spectacular. There's a cooking pavilion for group get-togethers. **Pros:** gorgeous setting; heated pool great for cool evenings early and late in the season; close to Kodachrome Basin State Park. **Cons:** some RV sites are narrow; some public water sites are hard to reach. ⊠ *Hwy. 12 at the Kodachrome Basin turnoff, Cannonville* ☎ *435/679–8988 or 888/562–4710* ⊕ *www. koa.com* ⚠ *65 RV sites, 20 tent sites, 5 cabins* ♿ *Flush toilets, full hookups, dump station, drinking water, guest laundry, showers, fire grates, grills, picnic tables, electricity, Wi-Fi, public telephone, general store, play area, swimming (pool)* ⊟ *AE, D, MC, V* ⊗ *Mar.–Nov.*

Canyonlands National Park

WORD OF MOUTH

"If you are going to make the drive to Dead Horse Point, then make time for Mesa Arch and Green River Overlook! WHAT A VIEW! And, if time allows, Grand View Point."

—utahtea

WELCOME TO CANYONLANDS

TOP REASONS TO GO

★ **Solitude:** Take time for reflection in this rarely crowded park.

★ **Radical rapids:** Experience some white-water adventure in Cataract Canyon on the Colorado River.

★ **American Indian artifacts:** View rock art and Ancestral Puebloan dwellings in the park.

★ **Last Holdout for wilderness:** Walk, raft, or drive through some of this country's wildest, most untouched country.

★ **Bighorn sheep:** Snap a photo of these intriguing creatures grazing along the roadway.

★ **The night skies:** Far away from city lights, Canyonlands is ideal for stargazing.

1 Island in the Sky. From any of the overlooks here you can see for miles and look down thousands of feet to canyon floors. Chocolate-brown canyons are capped by white rock, and deep-red monuments rise nearby.

2 Needles. Pink, orange, and red rock is layered with white rock and stands in spires and pinnacles around grassy meadows. Extravagantly red mesas and buttes interrupt the horizon, as in a picture postcard of the Old West.

3 The Maze. Only the most-adventurous visitors walk in the footsteps of Butch Cassidy in this area, for it is accessible only by four-wheel-drive vehicles.

4 Rivers. The park's waterways are as untamed and undammed as when John Wesley Powell explored them in the mid-1800s.

5 Horseshoe Canyon. This unit, part of the Maze, is just northwest of the Glen Canyon Recreation Area. The famous rock art panel "Great Gallery" is the reward at the end of a long hike.

GETTING ORIENTED

Canyonlands National Park, in southeastern Utah, is divided into three distinct land districts and the river district, so it can be a little daunting to visit. Unless you have several days, you will need to choose between the Island in the Sky or the Needles districts.

KEY	
🏚	Ranger Station
◭	Campground
🏕	Picnic Area
🍴	Restaurant
🏨	Lodge
🚶	Trailhead
🚻	Restrooms
⟿	Scenic Viewpoint
⋯⋯	Walking/Hiking Trails

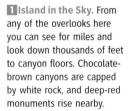

11

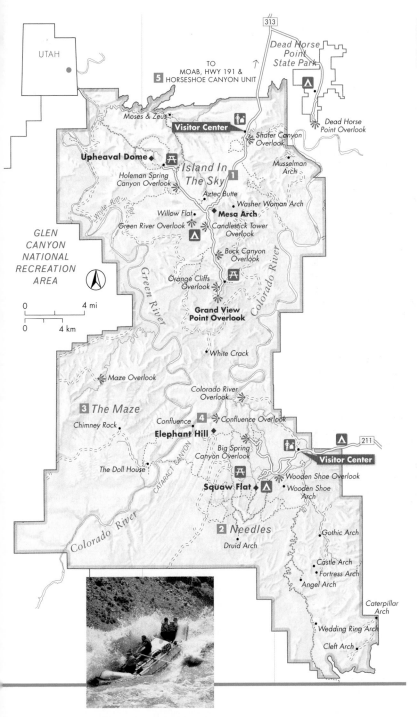

UTAH

Dead Horse
Point
State Park

TO
MOAB, HWY 191 &
HORSESHOE CANYON UNIT
5

Moses & Zeus

Visitor Center

Shafer Canyon
Overlook

Dead Horse
Point Overlook

Upheaval Dome ◆

*Island In
The Sky* **1**

Musselman
Arch

Holeman Spring
Canyon Overlook

Aztec Butte

• Washer Woman Arch

Willow Flat •

Mesa Arch

Green River Overlook •

Candlestick Tower
Overlook

*GLEN
CANYON
NATIONAL
RECREATION
AREA*

Green River

Buck Canyon
Overlook

0   4 mi

0   4 km

Orange Cliffs
Overlook

Colorado River

**Grand View
Point Overlook**

• White Crack

Maze Overlook •

Colorado River
Overlook

3 *The Maze*

Confluence **4** ⚡ Confluence Overlook

Chimney Rock •

Elephant Hill ◆

Big Spring
Canyon Overlook

211

Visitor Center

CATARACT CANYON

The Doll House •

Wooden Shoe Overlook

Squaw Flat ◆

• Wooden Shoe
Arch

Colorado River

2 *Needles*

Druid Arch •

Gothic Arch •

Castle Arch •
• Fortress Arch
Angel Arch •

Caterpillar
Arch

• Wedding Ring Arch

Cleft Arch •

CANYONLANDS PLANNER

When to Go

The busiest times of year for the park are spring and fall. Canyonlands is seldom crowded, but in the spring, backpackers and four-wheelers populate the trails and roads. During Easter week, some of the four-wheel-drive trails in the park are used for Jeep Safari, an annual event drawing thousands of visitors to town.

The crowds thin out by July as the thermostat approaches 100°F and beyond for about four weeks. It's a great time to get out on the Colorado or Green River winding through the park. October can be rainy, but the region only receives 8 inches of rain annually.

The well-kept secret is that winter is the best time in the park. Crowds are gone, roads are good, and snowcapped mountains stand in the background.

AVG. HIGH/LOW TEMPS.

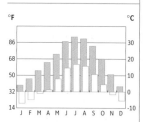

Flora and Fauna

Your chances of seeing wildlife are fairly good in Canyonlands because there are fewer people and less traffic to scare the animals away. Cool mornings and evenings are the best time to spot them, especially during the summer when the heat keeps them in cool, shady areas. Mule deer are nearly always seen along the roadway as you enter the Needles District, and you'll no doubt see jackrabbits and small rodents darting across the roadway. Approximately 250 bighorns populate the park in the Island in the Sky District, and the Maze shelters about 100 more. If you happen upon one of these regal animals, do not approach it even if it is alone, as bighorn sheep are skittish by nature and easily stressed. Also, report your sighting to a ranger.

Getting Here and Around

Off U.S. 191, Canyonlands' Island in the Sky is 21 mi from Arches National Park and 32 mi from Moab on Route 313 west of U.S. 191; the Needles District is reached via Route 211, west of U.S. 191. The nearest airport is Canyonlands Field, also know as Grand County Airport (☎ 435/259–4849), 18 mi north of Moab. Flights are limited. The nearest train "station" is a solitary Amtrak stop in Green River, about 50 mi northwest of Moab. For train inquiries, call Amtrak (☎ 800/872–7245).

Before starting a journey to any of Canyonlands' three districts, make sure your gas tank is topped off, as there are no services inside the large park. Island in the Sky is 32 mi from Moab, Needles District is 80 mi from Moab, and the Maze is more than 100 mi from Moab. The Island in the Sky road from the district entrance to Grand View Point is 12 mi, with one 5-mi spur to Upheaval Dome. The Needles scenic drive is 10 mi with two spurs about 3 mi each. Roads in the Maze, suitable only for rugged, high-clearance, four-wheel-drive vehicles, wind for hundreds of miles through the canyons. Within the parks, safety and courtesy mandate that you always park only in designated pullouts or parking areas.

Updated by
Jane Gendron

While Arches looks like Mars, Canyonlands resembles the moon. Mushroomlike rock formations rise randomly out of the ground, twisting into all manner of shapes: pinnacles, spires, buttes, and mesas. It's a desert landscape, but it's not devoid of water or color. The Green and Colorado rivers traverse the canyons, where the rich browns, verdant greens, and fresh yellows of the pinyon-juniper forests complement the deep reds, baby pinks, bright oranges, and milky whites of the rocks. The park's dirt roads appeal to mountain bikers, and the rising rapids of Cataract Canyon challenge rafters.

PARK ESSENTIALS

ACCESSIBILITY

There are currently no trails in Canyonlands that are accessible to people in wheelchairs, but Grand View Point and Buck Canyon Overlook at Island in the Sky are wheelchair accessible. The visitor centers at the Island in the Sky and Needles districts are also accessible, and the park's pit toilets are accessible with some assistance.

ADMISSION FEES AND PERMITS

Admission is $10 per vehicle and $5 per person on foot, motorcycle, or bicycle, good for seven days. Your Canyonlands pass is good for all the park's districts. There's no entrance fee to the Maze District of Canyonlands. A $25 local park pass grants you admission to both Arches and Canyonlands as well as Natural Bridges and Hovenweep national monuments for one year.

You need a permit for overnight backpacking, four-wheel-drive camping, mountain-bike camping, four-wheel-drive day use in Horse and Lavender canyons (Needles District), and river trips. Reservations need to be made two weeks (or more) in advance. The backcountry reservations office can be reached at ☎ 435/259–4351.

ADMISSION HOURS

Canyonlands National Park is open 24 hours a day, seven days a week, year-round. It is in the mountain time zone.

ATMS/BANKS

The park has no ATM. The nearest ATMs and banks are in Moab.

CELL-PHONE RECEPTION

Cell-phone reception may be available in some parts of the park, but not reliably so. Public telephones are at the park's visitor centers.

PARK CONTACT INFORMATION

Canyonlands National Park ⊠ 2282 W. Resource Blvd., Moab ☎ 435/719–2313 ⊕ www.nps.gov/cany.

SCENIC DRIVES

Island in the Sky Park Road. This 12-mi long road connects to a 5-mi side road to the Upheaval Dome area. You can enjoy many of the park's vistas by stopping at the overlooks—get out of your car for the best views. Once you get to the park, allow about two hours to explore.

Needles District Park Road. You'll feel certain that you've driven into a picture postcard as you roll along the park road in the Needles District. Red mesas and buttes rise against the horizon, blue mountain ranges interrupt the rangelands, and the colorful red and white needles stand like soldiers on the far side of grassy meadows. The drive, about 10 mi one way, takes about half an hour.

WHAT TO SEE

HISTORIC SITES

IN ISLAND IN THE SKY

Shafer Trail. This road was probably first established by ancient American Indians, but in the early 1900s ranchers used it to drive cattle into the canyon. Originally narrow and rugged, it was upgraded during the uranium boom, when miners hauled ore by truck from the canyon floor. You can see the road's winding route down canyon walls from Shafer Canyon Overlook. Today, Shafer Trail is used by daring four-wheelers and energetic mountain bikers. It descends 1,400 feet to the White Rim. ⊠ *Off main road, less than 1 mi from park entrance, Island in the Sky.*

IN NEEDLES

☾ **Cowboy Line Camp.** The remnants here include furniture and camp gear.
★ The artifacts are found on the **Cave Springs Trail,** which is short but requires some ladder climbing and sloping slickrock navigating. ⊠ *Off Cave Springs Rd., 2.3 mi from park entrance, Needles.*

SCENIC STOPS

IN ISLAND IN THE SKY

★ **Grand View Point.** At the end of the main road of Island in the Sky, don't miss this 360-degree view that extends all the way to the San Juan Mountains in Colorado on a clear day. ⊠ *Off main road, 12 mi from park entrance, Island in the Sky.*

CANYONLANDS IN ONE DAY

Your day begins with a choice: Island in the Sky or Needles. If you want expansive vistas looking across southeast Utah's canyons, head for the Island, where you stand atop a giant mesa. If you want to drive and walk among the Canyonland's needles and buttes, Needles is your destination. If you have a second or third day in the area, consider contacting an outfitter to take you on a 4X4 adventure. ■TIP➔ Before venturing into the park, top off your gas tank, pack a picnic lunch, and stock up on plenty of water.

A DAY IN ISLAND IN THE SKY

Make your first stop along the main park road at **Shafer Canyon Overlook**. A short walk takes you out on a finger of land with views of the canyon over both sides. From here you can see Shafer Trail hugging the wall below.

Drive next to **Mesa Arch**. Grab your camera and water bottle for the short hike out to the arch perched on the cliff's edge. After your hike, continue on the main park road to **Grand View Point**. Stroll along the edge of the rim, and see how many landmarks you can spot in

the distance. Have your lunch at the Grand View Point picnic area. Afterward, turn back toward the visitor center but take a left on Upheaval Dome Road. Stop at Island in the Sky Campground so you can see the Green River from the nearby overlook.

Lastly, head to the Upheaval Dome parking lot to stretch your legs with a hike up to the first **Upheaval Dome** viewpoint. If you still have energy, time, and a little sense of adventure, continue to the second overlook.

A DAY IN NEEDLES

If you can stay overnight as well, then begin today by setting up camp at one of the Needles' wonderful campgrounds. Then hit the **Joint Trail**, or any of the trails that begin from Squaw Flat campground, and spend the day hiking in the backcountry of the park. (Or, if you really want to cram a lot in, begin the morning with a brief but terrific little hike to **Cave Springs** before tackling a lengthier trail.) Sleep under more stars than you've seen in a long time.

★ **Mesa Arch.** Even though it can be crowded, you simply can't visit Island in the Sky without taking the quick ½-mi walk to Mesa Arch. The arch is above a cliff that drops 800 feet to the canyon bottom. Views through Washerwoman Arch and surrounding buttes, spires, and canyons make this a favorite photo opportunity. ⊠ *Off main road, 6 mi from park entrance, Island in the Sky.*

Upheaval Dome. This colorful, mysterious crater is one of the many wonders of Island in the Sky. Some geologists believe it to be an eroded salt dome, but others have theorized that it is an eroded meteorite-impact dome. To see it, you'll have to walk a short distance to the overlook. ⊠ *Off Upheaval Dome Rd., 11 mi from park entrance, Island in the Sky.*

IN NEEDLES

Pothole Point Trail. This is an especially good stop after a rainstorm, which fills the potholes with water. Stop to study the communities of tiny creatures, including fairy shrimp, that thrive in the slickrock hollows. Along the way, discover dramatic views of the Needles and Six Shooter Peak, too. The easy 0.6-mi round-trip walk takes about 45 minutes. There's no shade, so wear a hat. ⊠ *Off main road, about 9 mi from park entrance, Needles.*

VISITOR CENTERS

Hans Flat Ranger Station. This remote spot is nothing more than a stopping point for permits, books, and maps before you strike out into the Maze District of Canyonlands. To get here, you must drive 46 mi on a dirt road that is sometimes impassable to two-wheel-drive vehicles. There's a pit toilet, but no water, food, or services of any kind. ⊠ *46 mi east of Rte. 24; 21 mi south and east of the Y-junction and Horseshoe Canyon kiosk on the dirt road, Maze* ☎ *435/259–2652* ☉ *Daily 8–4:30.*

Island in the Sky Visitor Center. Stop and watch the orientation film and then browse the bookstore for information about the Canyonlands region. Exhibits help explain animal adaptations as well as some of the history of the park. ⊠ *Past park entrance off the main park road, Island in the Sky* ☎ *435/259–4712* ☉ *Daily 9–4:30 with expanded hrs Mar.–Oct.*

Needles District Visitor Center. This gorgeous building that blends into the landscape is worth seeing, even if you don't need the books, trail maps, or other information available inside. ⊠ *Less than 1 mi from park entrance off the main park road, Needles* ☎ *435/259–4711* ☉ *Daily 9–4:30 with expanded hrs Mar.–Oct.*

> ### MEET ME AT SUNSET
>
> Sunset is one of the picture-perfect times in Canyonlands, as the slanting sun shines over the vast network of canyons that stretch out below Island in the Sky. A moonlight drive to Grand View Point can also give you lasting memories as the moon drenches the white sandstone in the light. Likewise, late afternoon color in the spires and towers at the Needles District is a humbling, awe-inspiring scene.

SPORTS AND THE OUTDOORS

Canyonlands is one of the world's best destinations for adrenaline junkies. You can rock climb, mountain bike treacherous terrain, tackle world-class white-water rapids, and make your 4X4 crawl over steep cliffs along precipitous drops. Compared to other national parks, Canyonlands allows you to enjoy an amazing amount of solitude while having the adventure of a lifetime.

BICYCLING

White Rim Road. Mountain bikers all over the world like to brag that they've ridden this 112-mi road around Island in the Sky. The trail's fame is well-deserved: it traverses steep roads, broken rock, and ledges as well as long stretches that wind through the canyons and look down onto others. There's always a chance you'll see bighorn sheep here, too. Permits are not required for day use, but if you're biking White Rim without an outfitter you'll need careful planning and backcountry reservations (make them as far in advance as possible through the reservation office, ☎ 435/259–4351). Information about permits can be found at ⊕ *www.nps.gov/cany*. There's no water on this route. White Rim Road starts at the end of Shafer Trail. ✛ *Off the main park road about 1 mi from the entrance, then about 11 mi on Shafer Trail; or off Potash Rd. (Rte. 279) at the Jug Handle Arch turnoff about 18 mi from U.S. 191, then about 5 mi on Shafer Trail; Island in the Sky.*

⇨ *Four-Wheeling, for more routes.*

OUTFITTERS AND EXPEDITIONS

Nichols Expeditions. These professional outfitters take about a dozen multiday bike trips a year into the backcountry of Canyonlands National Park. Departure dates and routes are predetermined, so contact them for a schedule. ⊠ *497 N. Main St., Moab* ☎ *435/259–3999 or 800/648–8488* ⊕ *www.nicholsexpeditions.com.*

Magpie Cycling Adventures. Owners and seasoned bikers, Mike Holme and Maggie Wilson lead groups (or the lone rider) on daylong and multiday bike trips exploring the White Rim, Needles, and the Maze, as well as Moab and beyond. Whichever outfitter you go with, your guide will meet you in Moab at a bike shop. ✑ *P.O. Box 1496, Moab 84532* ☎ *435/259–4464 or 800/546–4245* ⊕ *www.magpieadventures.com.*

BIRD-WATCHING

Without getting on the Colorado River, you can see a variety of wrens, including the rock wren, canyon wren, and Bewick's wren. Blue-gray gnatcatchers are fairly common in the summer, along with the solitary vireo and black-throated gray warbler and Virginia's warbler. You'll have the most fun spotting the American kestrel or peregrine falcon or prairie falcon and watching golden and bald eagles soar overhead. The common raven is everywhere you look, as are the juniper titmouse, mountain chickadee, and a variety of jays. Once on the Colorado River, you'll stand a chance of glimpsing the elusive white-faced ibis, and you'll almost certainly see a great blue heron swooping along the water or standing regally on a sandbar.

BOATING AND RAFTING

Seeing Canyonlands National Park from the river is a great and rare pleasure. Long stretches of calm water on the Green River are perfect for lazy canoe trips. In Labyrinth Canyon, north of the park boundary, and in Stillwater Canyon, in the Island in the Sky District, the river is quiet and calm and there's plenty of shoreside camping. The Island in the Sky leg of the Colorado River, from Moab to its confluence with the Green River and downstream a few more miles to Spanish Bottom, is ideal for both canoeing and for rides with an outfitter in a large, stable jet boat. If you want to take a self-guided flat-water float trip in the park you must obtain a $20 permit, which you have to request by mail or fax. Make your upstream travel arrangements with a shuttle company before you request a permit. For permits, contact the reservation office at park headquarters (☎ 435/259–4351).

Below Spanish Bottom, about 64 mi downstream from Moab, 49 mi from the Potash Road ramp, and 4 mi south of the confluence, the Colorado churns into the first rapids of legendary Cataract Canyon. Home of some of the best white water in the United States, this piece of river between the Maze and the Needles districts rivals the Grand Canyon stretch of the Colorado River for adventure. During spring melt-off these rapids can rise to staggering heights and deliver heart-stopping excitement. The canyon cuts through the very heart of Canyonlands, where you can see this amazing wilderness area in its most pristine form. The water calms down a bit in summer but still offers enough thrills for most people. Outfitters will take you for the ride of your life in this wild canyon, where the river drops more steeply than anywhere else on the Colorado River (in ¾ mi, the river drops 39 feet). You can join an expedition lasting anywhere from one to six days, or you can purchase a $30 permit for a self-guided trip from park headquarters.

Oars (⊠ *2540 S. Hwy. 191., Moab* ☎ *435/259–5865 or 800/342–5938* ⊕ *www.oarsutah.com*) can take you for several days of rafting on the Colorado and Green rivers and four-wheeling in the parks. For those not into white water they also offer the occasional calm-water ride on the Colorado.

For additional outfitters, ⇨ Arches National Park (chapter 5).

FOUR-WHEELING

Nearly 200 mi of challenging backcountry roads lead to campsites, trail-heads, and natural and cultural features in Canyonlands. All of the roads require high-clearance, four-wheel-drive vehicles, and many are inappropriate for inexperienced drivers. Especially before you tackle the Maze, be sure that your four-wheel-drive skills are well honed and that you are capable of making basic road and vehicle repairs. Carry at least one full-size spare tire, extra gas, extra water, a shovel, a high-lift jack, and—October through April—chains for all four tires. Double-check to see that your vehicle is in top-notch condition, for you definitely don't want to break down in the interior of the park: towing expenses can exceed $1,000. For overnight four-wheeling trips you must purchase a $30 permit, which you can reserve in advance by contacting the Backcountry Reservations Office (☎ *435/259–4351*). Cyclists share all roads, so be aware and cautious of their presence. Vehicular traffic traveling uphill has the right-of-way. It's best to check at the visitor center for current road conditions before taking off into the backcountry. You must carry a washable, reusable toilet with you in the Maze District and carry out all waste.

For guided 4X4 trips, ⇨ Outfitters and Expeditions, in Arches National Park (chapter 5).

ISLAND IN THE SKY

★ **White Rim Road.** Winding around and below the Island in the Sky mesa top, the dramatic 112-mi White Rim Road offers a once-in-a-lifetime driving experience. As you tackle Murphy's Hogback, Hardscrabble Hill, and more formidable obstacles, you will get some fantastic views of the park. A trip around the loop takes two to three days and you must make reservations almost a year in advance for an overnight campsite—unless you manage to snap up a no-show or cancellation. For reservation information, call the Backcountry Reservation Office (☎ *435/259–4351*). White Rim Road starts at the end of Shafer Trail. ⊹ *Off the main park road about 1 mi from the entrance, then about 11 mi on Shafer Trail; or off*

Potash Rd. (Rte. 279) at the Jug Handle Arch turnoff about 18 mi from U.S. 191, then about 5 mi on Shafer Trail; Island in the Sky.

NEEDLES

★ **Elephant Hill.** The Needles route is so difficult—steep grades, loose rock, and stair-step drops—that many people get out and walk. In fact you can walk it faster than you can drive it. From Elephant Hill Trailhead to Devil's Kitchen it's 3½ mi; from the trailhead to the Confluence Overlook, it's a 14½-mi round-trip and requires at least eight hours. ⊠ *Off the main park road, 7 mi from park entrance, Needles.*

THE MAZE

Flint Trail. This remote, rugged road is the most used road in the Maze District, but don't let that fool you into thinking it's smooth sailing. It's very technical with 2 mi of switchbacks that drop down the side of a cliff face. You reach Flint Trail from the Hans Flat Ranger Station, which is 46 mi from the closest paved road (Route 24 off I–70). From Hans Flat to the end of the road at the Doll House it's 41 mi, a drive that takes five to seven hours one way. From Hans Flat to the Maze Overlook it's 34 mi. The Maze is not generally a destination for a day trip, so you'll have to purchase an overnight backcountry permit for $30. ⊠ *Hans Flat Ranger Station (46 mi east of Rte. 24, Maze).*

HIKING

Canyonlands National Park is a good place to saturate yourself in the intoxicating colors, smells, and textures of the desert. Many of the trails are long, rolling routes over slickrock and sand in landscapes dotted with juniper, pinyon, and sagebrush. Interconnecting trails in the Needles District provide excellent opportunities for weeklong backpacking excursions. The Maze trails are primarily accessed via four-wheel-drive vehicle. In the separate Horseshoe Canyon area, Horseshoe Canyon Trail takes a considerable amount of effort to reach, as it is more than 100 mi from Moab, 32 mi of which are a bumpy, and often sandy, dirt road.

ISLAND IN THE SKY

EASY   **Aztec Butte Trail.** Chances are good you'll enjoy this hike in solitude. It begins level, then climbs up a steep slope of slickrock. The highlight of the 2-mi round-trip hike is the chance to see Ancestral Puebloan granaries. ⊠ *Trailhead on Upheaval Dome Rd., about 6 mi from park entrance, Island in the Sky.*

Grand View Point Trail. If you're looking for a level walk with some of the grandest views in the world, stop at Grand View Point and wander the 2-mi round-trip trail along the cliff edge. Most people just stop at the overlook and drive on, so the trail is not as crowded as you might think. On a clear day you can see up to 100 mi to the Maze and Needles districts of the park, the confluence of the Green and Colorado rivers, and each of Utah's major laccolithic mountain ranges: the Henrys, Abajos, and La Sals. ⊠ *Trailhead on the main park road, 12 mi from park entrance, Island in the Sky.*

Fodor's Choice   **Mesa Arch Trail.** By far the most popular trail in the park, this ½-mi loop
★   acquaints you with desert plants and terrain. The highlight of the hike is a natural arch window perched over a 800-foot drop below. It gives a

DID YOU KNOW?

The more than 100-mile White Rim Road, which cuts through Island in the Sky near the Green River, is popular with those in Jeeps and those on mountain bikes. In fact, campgrounds close to the road are sometimes booked up to a year in advance, especially in the spring and fall. A permit from the park is required for overnight trips; you can register at the Island in the Sky Visitor Center. The Green River separates the Maze district from Island in the Sky.

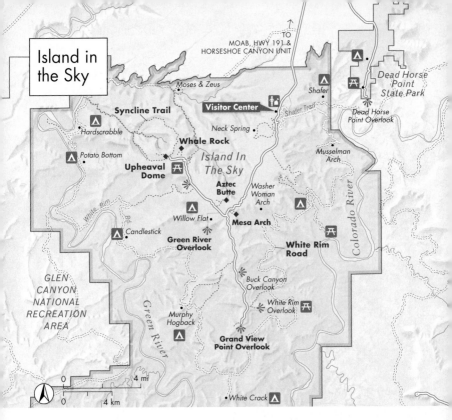

rare downward glimpse of a vast canyon, rather than the usual vantage point of peering skyward through arches. ⊠ *Trailhead 6 mi from the Island in the Sky Visitor Center.*

Whale Rock Trail. If you've been hankering to walk across some of that pavement-smooth stuff they call slickrock, the hike to Whale Rock will make your feet happy. This 1-mi round-trip adventure, complete with handrails to help you make the tough 100-foot climb, takes you to the very top of the whale's back. Once you get there, you are rewarded with great views of Upheaval Dome and Trail Canyon. ⊠ *Trailhead on Upheaval Dome Rd., 11 mi from park entrance, Island in the Sky.*

DIFFICULT **Syncline Loop Trail.** If you're up for a full, strenuous day of hiking, try this 8-mi trail that circles Upheaval Dome. You get limited views of the dome itself as you actually make a complete loop around the outside of the crater. Stretches of the trail are rocky, rugged, and steep. ⊠ *Trailhead on Upheaval Dome Rd., 11 mi from park entrance, Island in the Sky.*

★ **Upheaval Dome Trail.** It's worth the steep hike to see this formation, which is either an eroded salt dome or a meteorite crash site. You reach the main overlook after just ½ mi, but you can double your pleasure by going on to a second overlook for a better view. The trail becomes steep and rough after the first overlook. Round-trip to the second overlook is 2 mi. ⊠ *Trailhead on Upheaval Dome Rd., 11 mi from park entrance, Island in the Sky.*

THE MAZE

DIFFICULT ★ **Horseshoe Canyon Trail.** You arrive at this detached unit of Canyonlands National Park via a washboard-like, two-wheel-drive dirt road. Park at the lip of the canyon and hike 6½ mi round-trip to the Great Gallery, considered by some to be the most significant rock-art panel in North America. Ghostly life-size figures in the Barrier Canyon style populate the amazing panel. The hike is moderately strenuous, with a 750-foot descent. Allow at least six hours for the trip and take a gallon of water per person. There's no camping allowed in the canyon, although you can camp on top near the parking lot. ⊠ *Trailhead 32 mi east of Rte. 24 (on a mostly dirt road, which can be impassable when rainy), Maze.*

NEEDLES

EASY **Slickrock Trail.** If you're on this trail in summer, make sure you're wearing a hat, because you won't find any shade along the 2.4-mi round-trip trek across slickrock. This is one of the few front-country sites where you might see bighorn sheep. ⊠ *Trailhead on the main park road, about 10 mi from park entrance, Needles.*

MODERATE ↻ ★ **Cave Spring Trail.** One of the best, most diverse trails in the park takes you past a historic cowboy camp, prehistoric American Indian pictographs, and great views along the way. About half of the trail is in shade, as it meanders under overhangs. Slanted, bumpy slickrock make this hike more difficult than others, and two ladders make the 0.6-mi round-trip walk even more of an adventure. Allow about 45 minutes. ⊠ *Trailhead off the main park road on Cave Springs Rd., 2.3 mi from park entrance, Needles.*

DIFFICULT **Chesler Park Loop.** Chesler Park is a grassy meadow dotted with spires and enclosed by a circular wall of colorful "needles." One of Canyonlands' more popular trails leads through the area to the famous Joint Trail. The trail is 6 mi round-trip to the viewpoint. The entire loop is 11 mi. ⊠ *Accessed via the Elephant Hill Trailhead, off the main park road, about 7 mi from park entrance, Needles.*

★ **Joint Trail.** Part of the Chesler Park Loop, this well-loved trail follows a series of deep, narrow fractures in the rock. A shady spot in summer, it will give you good views of the Needles formations for which the district is named. The loop travels briefly along a four-wheel-drive road and is 11 mi round-trip; allow at least five hours to complete the hike. ⊠ *Accessed by the Elephant Hill Trailhead, off the main park road, 7 mi from park entrance, Needles.*

ROCK CLIMBING

Fodor's Choice ★ Canyonlands and many of the surrounding areas draw climbers from all over the world. Permits are not required, but because of the sensitive archaeological nature of the park, it's imperative that you stop at the visitor center to pick up regulations pertaining to the park's cultural resources. Popular climbing routes include Moses and Zeus towers in Taylor Canyon, and Monster Tower and Washerwoman Tower on the White Rim Road. Like most routes in Canyonlands, these climbs are for experienced climbers only. Just outside the Needles disctrict, in Indian Creek, is one of the country's best traditional climbing areas.

For climbing outfitters, ⇨ Outfitters and Expeditions box, in Arches National Park (chapter 5).

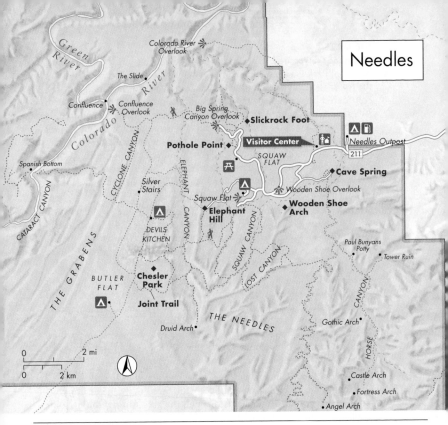

EDUCATIONAL OFFERINGS

RANGER PROGRAMS

For more information on current schedules and locations of park programs, contact the visitor centers (☎ 435/259–4712 Island in the Sky, 435/259–4711 Needles) or check the bulletin boards throughout the park. Note that programs change periodically and may sometimes be cancelled because of limited staffing.

Grand View Point Overlook Talk. By attending this ranger-led session you can learn something about the geology that created Utah's Canyonlands. ✉ Grand View Point, 12 mi from park entrance off the main park road, Island in the Sky ☜ $10 per vehicle ⊙ Apr.–Oct., daily; check at park visitor centers for times and locations.

Junior Ranger Program. Kids ages 6 to 12 can pick up a Junior Ranger booklet at the visitor centers. It's full of activities, word games, drawings, and educational material about the park and the wildlife. To earn the Junior Ranger badge, they must complete several activities in the booklet, attend a ranger program, watch the park film or gather a bag of litter. For ranger program veterans, ages 8 and up, ask about the "extra credit" Red Rock Ranger Program. ☎ 435/259–4712 Island in the Sky, 435/259–4711 Needles ☜ Free.

EDUCATIONAL RESOURCES

Red Rock Explorer Pack. Just like borrowing a book from a library, families can check out a backpack filled with tools for learning about both Canyonlands and Arches national parks. Peruse the field guides, take a closer look at a juniper tree with the hand lens magnifier and give the activities in the binder a whirl. Be sure to make a journal entry of your family's discoveries. Backpacks can be returned to either Arches or Island in the Sky visitor center. Use of the backpack is free with a credit card imprint in case of loss or damage to the pack or enclosed items. ☎ *435/719–2299* 🖅 *Free.*

WHAT'S NEARBY

NEARBY TOWNS

Moab is the major gateway to both Arches and Canyonlands national parks, with the most outfitters, shops, and lodging options of the area. *For more on Moab, see* ⇨ *Arches National Park (chapter 5).* A handful of communities, which are much smaller and with fewer amenities, are scattered around the Needles and Island in the Sky districts along U.S. 191.

Roughly 55 mi south of Moab is **Monticello.** Convenient to the Needles District, it lies at an elevation of 7,000 feet, making it a cool summer refuge from the desert heat. In winter, it gets downright cold and sees deep snow; the Abajo Mountains, whose highest point is 11,360 feet, rise to the west of town. Monticello motels serve the steady stream of tourists who venture south of Moab, but the town offers few dining or shopping opportunities. **Blanding,** 21 mi south of Monticello, prides itself on old-fashioned conservative values. By popular vote there's a ban on the sale of liquor, beer, and wine, so the town has no state liquor store and its restaurants do not serve alcoholic beverages. Blanding is a good resting point if you're traveling south from Canyonlands to Natural Bridges Natural Monument, Grand Gulch, Lake Powell, or the Navajo Nation. About 25 mi south of Blanding, tiny **Bluff** is doing its best to stay that way. It's a great place to stop if you aren't looking for many amenities but value beautiful scenery, silence, and starry nights. Bluff is the most common starting point for trips on the San Juan River, which serves as the northern boundary for the Navajo Reservation; it's also a wonderful place to overnight if you're planning a visit to Hovenweep National Monument, about 30 mi away.

VISITOR INFORMATION

Blanding Visitor Center ✉ *12 N. Grayson Pkwy., Blanding* ☎ *435/678–3662.* **Monticello Welcome Center** ✉ *216 S. Main St., Monticello* ☎ *435/587–3401* ⊕ *www.monticelloutah.org.* **San Juan County Community Development and Visitor Services (Bluff, Blanding, and Monticello)** ✉ *117 S. Main St., Monticello* ☎ *435/587–3235 or 800/574–4386* ⊕ *www.utahscanyoncountry.com.*

NEARBY ATTRACTIONS

For additional area listings, ⇨ *Arches National Park (chapter 5).*

Dead Horse Point State Park. One of the finest state parks in Utah overlooks a sweeping oxbow of the Colorado River, some 2,000 feet below, as well as the upside-down landscapes of Canyonlands National Park. Dead Horse Point itself is a small peninsula connected to the main mesa by a narrow neck of land. As the story goes, cowboys used to drive wild mustangs onto the point and pen them there with a brush fence. Some were accidentally forgotten and left to perish. There's a modern visitor center and museum as well as a 21-site campground with drinking water and an overlook. Be sure to walk the 4-mi rim trail loop and drive to the park's eponymous point. ⊠ *34 mi west from Moab at the end of Rte. 313* ☎ *435/259–2614, 800/322–3770 for campground reservations* ⊕ *www.stateparks.utah.gov* ✉ *$10 per vehicle* ⊗ *Visitor center daily 8–5, park daily 6* AM–*10* PM.

★ **Edge of the Cedars State Park Museum.** Tucked away on a backstreet in Blanding is one of the nation's foremost museums dedicated to the ancestral Puebloan Indians. The museum displays a variety of pots, baskets, spear points, and rare artifacts, even a pair of sandals said to date back 1,500 years. Behind the museum, you can visit an Anasazi ruin. ⊠ *660 W. 400 North St., Blanding* ☎ *435/678–2238* ⊕ *www.stateparks. utah.gov* ✉ *$20 per vehicle or $5 per person* ⊗ *May–Sept., Mon.–Sat., 9–5; Oct.–Apr., Tues.–Sat. 9–5.*

Natural Bridges National Monument. When visitor Elliot McClure came to Natural Bridges National Monument in 1931, his car slowly disintegrated. First his headlights fell off. Next, his doors dropped off. Finally, his bumpers worked loose, and the radiator broke away. Today a drive to the three stone bridges is far less hazardous. All roads are paved and a scenic 9-mi route takes you to stops that overlook Sipapu, Owachomo, and Kachina bridges. Natural Bridges was designated the first International Dark Sky park and has a 13-site primitive campground for optimum stargazing. The national monument is a drive of about 100 mi southwest from the Needles District of Canyonlands National Park. ⊠ *Rte. 275 off Rte. 95* ☎ *435/692–1234* ⊕ *www.nps.gov/nabr* ✉ *$6 per vehicle, $3 per bike or motorcycle* ⊗ *Daily 8:30* AM–*6:30* PM.

★ **Newspaper Rock Recreation Site.** One of the West's most famous rock-art sites, this large panel contains American Indian etchings that accumulated on the rock over the course of 2,000 years. Apparently, early pioneers and explorers to the region named the site Newspaper Rock because they believed the rock, crowded with drawings, constituted a written language with which early people communicated. Archaeologists now agree the petroglyphs do not represent language. This is one of many "newspaper rocks" throughout the Southwest. ⊠ *Rte. 211, about 15 mi west of U.S. 191.*

Wilson Arch. Between Arches and the Needles District of Canyonlands, this giant roadside arch makes a great photo stop. In Moab, you can still find historical photos of an airplane flying through this arch. No one has tried the stunt lately, probably because it's now illegal. ⊠ *26 mi south of Moab on U.S. 191.*

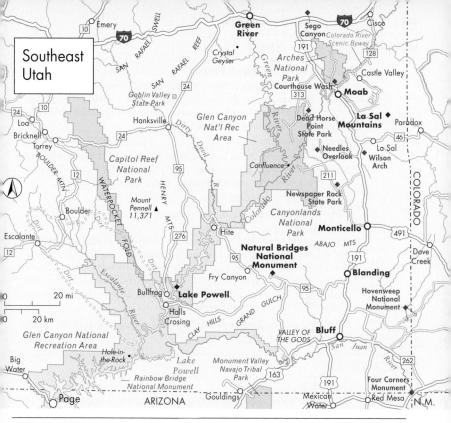

Southeast Utah

SHOPPING

Thin Bear Indian Arts. This tiny little trading post has operated in the same location for 35 years. Authentic jewelry, rugs, baskets and pottery are for sale at this friendly spot. ⊠ *1944 S. Main St., Blanding* ☎ *435/678–2940.*

SCENIC DRIVES AND VISTAS

Colorado Riverway Scenic Byway–Route 279. If you're interested in American Indian rock art, this scenic drive along the Colorado River is a perfect place to spend a couple of hours. If you start late in the afternoon, the cliffs will be glowing orange as the sun sets. Along the first part of the route you'll see signs reading INDIAN WRITINGS. Park in designated areas to view the petroglyphs on the cliff. At the 18-mi marker you'll see Jug Handle Arch on the cliff side of the road. A few miles later the road turns to four-wheel-drive only into the Island in the Sky District. Allow about two hours round-trip for the drive.

WHERE TO EAT AND STAY

ABOUT THE RESTAURANTS

There are no dining facilities in the park itself. Needles Outpost, just outside the entrance to the Needles District, has a small grocery store for picnicking necessities. Restaurants in Monticello and Blanding offer simple meals, and most do not serve alcohol.

ABOUT THE HOTELS

There is no lodging inside Canyonlands. The towns of Monticello and Blanding offer basic motels, both family-owned and national chains. Bluff also has motels and B&Bs and offers a quiet place to stay.

ABOUT THE CAMPGROUNDS

Canyonlands campgrounds are some of the most beautiful in the National Park System. At the Needles District, campers will enjoy fairly private campsites tucked against red rock walls and dotted with pinyon and juniper trees. At Island in the Sky, starry nights and spectacular vistas make the small campground an intimate treasure. Hookups are not available in either of the park's campgrounds; however, the sites are long enough to accommodate units up to 28 feet long. There are no RV dump stations in the park.

For dining and lodging in Moab, ⇨ *Where to Eat and Stay, in Arches National Park (chapter 5).*

WHERE TO EAT

IN THE PARK

PICNIC AREAS **Grand View Point.** Stopping here for a picnic lunch might be one of your more memorable vacation events. It's a pleasant spot in which to recharge your energy and stretch your legs. There are picnic tables, grills, restrooms, and shade. ⊠ *12 mi from park entrance on the main road, Island in the Sky.*

Needles District Picnic Area. The most convenient picnic spot in the Needles District is a sunny location right near the roadway. There are picnic tables, but no grills, restrooms, water, or other amenities. ⊠ *About 5 mi from the park visitor center, Needles.*

OUTSIDE THE PARK

$–$$$ ✕ **Homestead Steak House.** The folks here specialize in authentic Navajo
AMERICAN   fry bread and Navajo tacos. The popular—and big!—sheepherder's sandwich, is made with the fry bread and comes with your choice of beef, turkey, or ham and all the trimmings. No alcohol is served. ⊠ *121 E. Center St., Blanding* ☎ *435/678–3456* ▭ *AE, D, MC, V.*

WHERE TO STAY

IN THE PARK

CAMPING   △ **Squaw Flat Campground.** Squaw Flat is one of the best campgrounds in
$ the National Park System. The sites are spread out in two different areas,
★   giving each site almost unparalleled privacy. Each site has a rock wall at its back, and shade trees. The sites are filled on a first-come, first-served

basis. **Pros:** close to great day hikes like Chesler Park; private; each site has some much-needed shade. **Cons:** fills up in spring and fall, so have a back-up plan; no hookups for RVs; toasty in summer. ⌧ *About 5 mi from park entrance off the main road, Needles* ☏ *435/259–7164* ⌂ *26 tent/RV sites* ⌂ *Flush toilets, drinking water, fire pits, picnic tables* ▭ *No credit cards.*

¢ ⌂ **Willow Flat Campground.** From this little campground on a mesa top, you can walk to spectacular views of the Green River. Most sites have a bit of shade from juniper trees. To get to Willow Flat you travel through some tight and tricky turns, so RVs, in particular, need to take it slow. It is filled on a first-come, first-served basis only. Arrive early and set up camp in time to take a short walk to Green River Overlook for sunset. **Pros:** walk to Green River Overlook and close to Mesa Arch; pristine; relatively remote; usually peaceful. **Cons:** not much shade; remote; no water. ⌧ *About 9 mi from park entrance off the main park road, Island in the Sky* ☏ *435/259–4712* ⌂ *12 tent/RV sites* ⌂ *Pit toilets, fire pits, picnic tables* ▭ *No credit cards.*

OUTSIDE THE PARK

$ ⊡ **Days Inn.** One of the largest properties in Monticello, this is also one of the nicest, with a heated indoor pool and a hot tub that's just what the doctor ordered for soaking adventure-weary bodies. **Pros:** management takes good care of the reliable chain rooms; splashing about in the pool; close to Needles District. **Cons:** sits near the highway, so might be noisy (ask for a room on the back side); not much action in Monticello (but town is just a mile away); three smoking rooms (a pro if you're a smoker; avoidable if you're not). ⌧ *533 N. Main St.* ☏ *435/587–2458* ⊕ *www.daysinn.com* ⇆ *43 rooms* ⌂ *In-room: refrigerator (some), Wi-Fi. In-hotel: pool* ▭ *AE, D, MC, V* ⊙ *CP.*

$–$$ ⊡ **Desert Rose Inn and Cabins.** Bluff's largest motel is truly a rose in the
Fodor's Choice desert. It's an attractive log-cabin-style structure with a front porch
  ★   that gives it a nostalgic touch, and all rooms are spacious and clean with uncommonly large bathrooms. The cabins have small refrigerators and microwaves. **Pros:** beautiful motel with comfortable rooms; clean; friendly staff. **Cons:** has no particular historic charm; Bluff's not too happening (but close to Hovenweep, San Juan River trips, and other natural wonders); not a culinary hub. ⌧ *701 W. Main St. (U.S. 191)* ☏ *435/672–2303 or 888/475–7673* ⊕ *www.desertroseinn.com* ⇆ *30 rooms, 6 cabins* ⌂ *In-room: refrigerator (some), Wi-Fi. In-hotel: laundry facilities* ▭ *AE, D, MC, V.*

¢–$ ⊡ **Recapture Lodge.** Known for its friendliness, this older but popular and regionally famous inn has knowledgeable owners ready to give guests detailed tips for exploring the surrounding canyon country. They even present nightly slide shows about local geology, art, and history. The plain motel rooms offered at good prices book up fast, so call ahead for reservations. Horses can spend the night in the on-site corral. A playground is on site. **Pros:** quiet lodge set on shady grounds; welcoming owners; Jim (one of the owners) is a wildlife biologist willing to share his knowledge. **Cons:** older property; small rooms and basic amenities; Bluff (pop. 350) is about as small town as it gets (which could be a pro). ⌧ *220 E. Main St. (U.S. 191)* ☏ *435/672–2281* ⊕ *www.*

recapturelodge.com ⤳ *26 rooms, 2 houses* ♿ *In-room: kitchen (some) refrigerator (some), Wi-Fi. In-hotel: pool, laundry facilities, some pets allowed* ⊟ *AE, D, MC, V.*

CAMPING **Bureau of Land Management Campgrounds.** There are 350 sites at 22 dif-
$ ferent BLM campgrounds near Arches and Canyonlands national parks. Most of these are in the Moab area near Arches and Canyonlands' Island in the Sky District, along the Route 128 Colorado River corridor, on Kane Creek Road, and on Sand Flats Road. *For additional BLM campgrounds,* ⇨ *Where to Stay, in Arches National Park (chapter 5).* All sites are primitive, though Wind Whistle and Hatch Point do have water. Campsites go on a first-come, first-served basis. They are all open year-round. ☎ *435/259–2100* ⊕ *www.blm.gov/utah/moab* ⊟ *No credit cards.*

$ ⚠ **Dead Horse Point State Park Campground.** A favorite of almost everyone
★ who has ever camped here, either in RVs or tents, this mesa-top site fills up at about the same pace as the national park campgrounds. It is impressively set near the edge of a 2,000-foot cliff above the Colorado River. If you want to pay for your stay with a credit card you must do so during business hours (8–5 daily); otherwise you must pay in cash in the after-hours drop box. Four of the campsites are first-come, first-served. **Pros:** a couple of miles from the dramatic Dead Horse Point; shaded picnic area and grill at each site; clean and relatively private. **Cons:** gigantic drop-offs (keep an eye on little ones on rim trails and outlooks); no wood fires. ✉ *Dead Horse Point State Park, Rte. 313, 18 mi off U.S. 191 (right outside the entrance to Canyonlands National Park)* ☎ *435/259–2614, 800/322–3770 reservations* ⊕ *www.stateparks.utah. gov* ⚠ *21 tent/RV sites and 1 group site* ♿ *Flush toilets, dump station, drinking water, picnic tables, electricity, ranger station* ⊟ *AE, MC, V.*

Capitol Reef
National Park

WORD OF MOUTH

"I'd suggest spending your time in Capitol Reef—we did a good part of the Cohab Canyon hike and it was spectacular! Hickman Bridge is nice but pretty short; a nice morning stroll. We did the hike to Surprise Canyon (off of the Burr Trail) a few years back and it was nice but not as scenic as trails in Cap Reef."

—sharondi

WELCOME TO CAPITOL REEF

TOP REASONS TO GO

★ **The Waterpocket Fold:** See an excellent example of a monocline—a fold in the earth's crust with one very steep side in an area that is otherwise horizontal. This one's almost 100 mi long.

★ **No crowds:** Experience the best of southern Utah weather, rock formations, and wide-open spaces without the crowds of nearby parks such as Zion and Bryce Canyon.

★ **Fresh fruit:** Pick apples, pears, apricots, and peaches in season at the pioneer-planted orchards at historic Fruita. These trees still produce plenty of fruit.

★ **Rock art:** View ancient pictographs and petroglyphs left by the Fremont people, who lived in this area from AD 700 to 1300.

★ **Pioneer artifacts:** Buy faithfully reproduced tools and utensils like those used by Mormon pioneers, at the Gifford Farmhouse.

1 Fruita. This historic pioneer village is at the heart of what most people see of Capitol Reef. The one and only park visitor center nearby is the place to get maps, and travel and weather information. The scenic drive through Capitol Gorge provides a view of the Golden Throne.

2 Cathedral Valley. The views are stunning and the silence deafening in the park's remote northern section. High-clearance vehicles are required, as is a crossing of the Fremont River. Driving in this valley is next to impossible when the Cathedral Valley Road is wet, so ask at the visitor center about current weather and road conditions.

3 Muley Twist Canyon. At the southern reaches of the park, this canyon is accessed via Notom-Bullfrog Road from the north, and Burr Trail Road from the west and southeast. High-clearance vehicles are required for much of it.

GETTING ORIENTED

At the heart of this 378-square-mi park is the massive natural feature known as the Waterpocket Fold, which runs roughly northwest to southeast along the park's spine. Capitol Reef itself is named for a formation along the fold near the Fremont River. A historic pioneer settlement, the green oasis of Fruita is easily accessed by car, and a 9-mi scenic drive provides a good overview of the canyons and rock formations that populate the park. Colors here range from deep, rich reds to sage greens to crumbling gray sediments. The absence of large towns nearby ensures that night skies are brilliant starscapes.

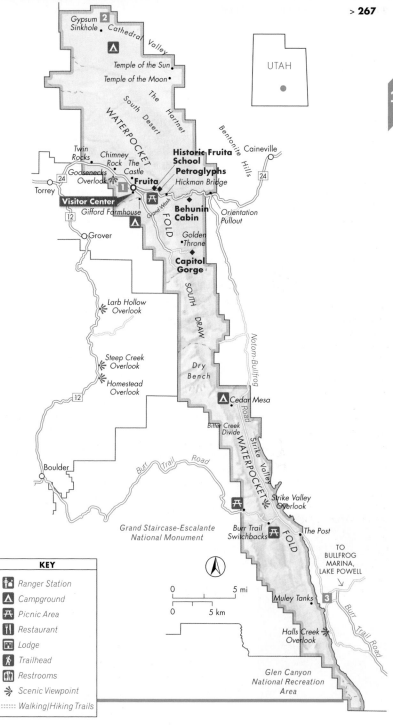

UTAH

12

Gypsum Sinkhole

Cathedral Valley

Temple of the Sun
Temple of the Moon

The Hartnet

South Desert

WATERPOCKET

Bentonite Hills

Caineville

Twin Rocks
Chimney Rock
The Castle

Historic Fruita School
Petroglyphs

Goosenecks Overlook

Torrey

24

Fruita
Hickman Bridge

Grand Wash

Visitor Center

Gifford Farmhouse

Behunin Cabin

Orientation Pullout

24

12

Grover

FOLD

Golden Throne

Capitol Gorge

Larb Hollow Overlook

SOUTH DRAW

Steep Creek Overlook

Notom-Bullfrog

Dry Bench

Homestead Overlook

12

Cedar Mesa

Bitter Creek Divide

Boulder

WATERPOCKET

Strike Valley

Strike Valley Overlook

Burr Trail Road

Burr Trail Switchbacks

FOLD

The Post

Grand Staircase-Escalante
National Monument

TO BULLFROG MARINA, LAKE POWELL

3

Muley Tanks

Burr Trail Road

Halls Creek Overlook

Glen Canyon
National Recreation
Area

	KEY
🏚	Ranger Station
△	Campground
🖼	Picnic Area
🍴	Restaurant
🏠	Lodge
🚶	Trailhead
🚻	Restrooms
✷	Scenic Viewpoint
⋯⋯	Walking/Hiking Trails

0   5 mi

0   5 km

CAPITOL REEF PLANNER

When to Go

Spring and early summer are most bustling. Folks clear out in the midsummer heat, and then return for the apple harvest and crisp temperatures of autumn. Still, the park is seldom crowded—though the campground fills quickly except in winter. Annual rainfall is scant, but when it does rain, flash floods can wipe out park roads. Snowfall is usually light. Sudden, short-lived snowstorms—and thunderstorms—are not uncommon in the spring.

AVG. HIGH/LOW TEMPS.

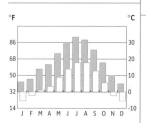

°F

86	
68	
50	
32	
14	

J F M A M J J A S O N D

°C

	30
	20
	10
	0
	-10

Flora and Fauna

The golden rock and rainbow cliffs are at their finest at sunset, when it seems as if they are lighted from within. That's also when mule deer wander through the orchards near the campground. The deer are quite tame, but do not feed them; their digestive systems are harmed by people food. Many of the park's animals move about only at night to escape the heat of the day, but pinyon jays and black-billed magpies flit around the park all day. The best place to see wildlife is near the Fremont River, where animals are drawn to drink. Ducks and small mammals such as the yellow-bellied marmot live nearby. Desert bighorn sheep also live in Capitol Reef, but they are elusive. Your best chance of spotting the sheep is during a long hike deep within the park. If you should encounter a sheep, do not approach it, as they've been known to charge human beings.

Getting Here and Around

Though far from big cities, Capitol Reef country can be reached by a variety of approaches. The main high-speed arteries through the region are Interstates 70 and 15, but any route will require travel of some secondary roads such as U.S. 50, U.S. 89, Highway 24, or Route 72. All are well-maintained, safe roads that bisect rich agricultural communities steeped in Mormon history (such as the nearby towns of Bicknell and Loa). Interstate 15 is the fastest way through central Utah, but U.S. 89 and the local roads that feed onto it will give you a more direct path into Utah's past and present-day character. Highway 24 runs across the middle of Capitol Reef National Park, so even those traveling between points west and east of the park with no intention of touring the park get a scenic treat on their way. Once inside the park, there is no shuttle service like at nearby Zion and Bryce Canyon national parks.

12

By John
Blodgett

Your senses will be delighted by a visit to Capitol Reef National Park. Here, you are saturated in colors that are more dramatic than anywhere else in the West. The dominant Moenkopi rock formation is a rich, red-chocolate hue. Deep blue-green juniper and pinyon stand out against it. Other sandstone layers are gold, ivory, and lavender. Sunset brings out the colors in an explosion of copper, platinum, and orange, then dusk turns the cliffs purple and blue. The texture of rock deposited in ancient inland seas and worn by subsequent erosion is pure art.

The park preserves the Waterpocket Fold, a giant wrinkle in the earth that extends a hundred miles between Thousand Lake Mountain and Lake Powell. When you climb high onto the rocks or into the mountains, you can see this remarkable geologic wonder and the jumble of colorful cliffs, massive domes, soaring spires, and twisting canyons that surround it. It's no wonder American Indians called this part of the country the "land of sleeping rainbow."

But your eyes will not be alone in their joy. The fragrance of pine and sage rises from the earth, and canyon wrens sing to you as you sit by the water. Flowing across the heart of Capitol Reef is the Fremont River, a narrow little creek that can turn into a swollen, raging torrent during desert flash floods. The river sustains cottonwoods, wildlife, and verdant valleys rich with fruit. During the harvest, your sensory experience is complete when you bite into a perfect ripe peach or apple from the park's orchards. Your soul, too, will be gratified here. You can walk the trails in relative solitude and enjoy the beauty without confronting crowds on the roads or paths. All around you are signs of those who came before: ancient American Indians of the Fremont culture, Mormon pioneers who settled the land, and other courageous explorers who traveled the canyons. It is a rare thrill to feel the past overtake the present.

PARK ESSENTIALS

ACCESSIBILITY

Capitol Reef doesn't have many trails that are accessible to people in wheelchairs. The visitor center, museum, slide show, and restrooms are all accessible, as is the campground amphitheater where evening programs are held. The Fruita Campground Loop C restroom is accessible, as is the boardwalk to the petroglyph panel on Highway 24, 1.2 mi east of the visitor center.

ADMISSION FEES AND PERMITS

There is no fee to enter the park, but it's $5 per vehicle (or $3 per pedestrian) to travel on Scenic Drive beyond Fruita Campground; this fee is good for one week. Backcountry camping permits are free; pick them up at the visitor center.

ADMISSION HOURS

The park is open 24/7 year-round. It is in the mountain time zone.

ATMS/BANKS

The nearest ATM is at the travel plaza at the junction of Highways 24 and 12 in Torrey. There are banks in Loa and Escalante.

CELL-PHONE RECEPTION

Cell-phone reception is best near the visitor center and campground areas. Pay phones are at the visitor center and at Fruita Campground.

PARK CONTACT INFORMATION

Capitol Reef National Park ⊠ HC 70, P.O. Box 15, Torrey, UT ☎ 435/425–3791 ⊕ www.nps.gov/care.

SCENIC DRIVE

Capitol Reef Scenic Drive. This paved road starts at the visitor center and winds its way through the Fruita Historic District and colorful sandstone cliffs into Capitol Gorge; a side road, Grand Wash Road, provides access into the canyon. At Capitol Gorge, the route becomes unpaved, and road conditions may vary because of weather and amount of use. Check with the visitor center before entering Capitol Gorge. Capitol Reef Scenic Drive, called simply Scenic Drive by locals, is 9 mi long, with about the last quarter of it unpaved.

For the **Cathedral Valley Scenic Backway** *drive,* ⇨ *Four-Wheeling, in Sports and the Outdoors.*

WHAT TO SEE

HISTORIC SITES

Behunin Cabin. Elijah Cutlar Behunin used blocks of sandstone to build this cabin in 1882. Floods in the lowlands made life too difficult, and he moved before the turn of that century. The house is empty, but you can peep through a window. ⊠ *Hwy. 24, 6.2 mi east of visitor center.*

Fruita Historic District. In 1880 Nels Johnson became the first homesteader in the Fremont River Valley, building his home near the confluence of Sulphur Creek and the Fremont River. Other Mormon settlers followed

CAPITOL REEF IN ONE DAY

Pack a picnic lunch, snacks, and cold drinks to take with you, because there are no restaurants in the park. As you enter the park, look to your left for Chimney Rock; in a landscape of spires, cliffs, and knobs, this deep-red landmark is unmistakable. Start your journey at the **visitor center**, where you can study a three-dimensional map of the area, watch the short slide show, and browse the many books and maps related to the park. Then head for the park's scenic drive, stopping at the **Fruita Historic District** to see some of the sites associated with the park's Mormon history. Stop at the **Gifford Farmhouse** for a tour and a visit to the gift shop.

As you continue on with your tour, check out the **Fremont Indian Petroglyphs,** and if you feel like some exertion, take a hike on the Hickman Bridge Trail. From the trail (or if you skip the hike, from Highway 24 about 2 mi east of the visitor center), you'll see **Capitol Dome.** Along this stretch of Highway 24 stop to see the old one-room **Fruita Schoolhouse,** the **petroglyphs,** and the **Behunin Cabin.** Next you'll have to backtrack a few miles on Highway 24 to find the **Goosenecks Trail.** At the same parking lot you'll find the trailhead for **Sunset Point Trail**; take this short hike in time to watch the setting sun hit the colorful cliffs.

12

and established small farms and orchards near the confluence, creating the village of Junction. The orchards thrived, and in 1902 the settlement's name was changed to Fruita. The orchards are preserved and protected as a Rural Historic Landscape.

An old **blacksmith shop** (⊠ *Scenic Dr., less than 1 mi south of visitor center*) exhibits tools, farm machinery, and harnesses dating from the late 1800s, along with Fruita's first tractor.

Pioneer Register. Travelers passing through Capitol Gorge in the 19th and early 20th centuries etched the canyon wall with their names and the date they passed. Directly across the canyon from the Pioneer Register and about 50 feet up are signatures etched into the canyon wall by an early United States Geologic Survey crew. It's illegal to write or scratch on the canyon walls today. You can reach the register via an easy 1-mi hike from the end of the road. ⊠ *Off Scenic Dr., 9 mi south of visitor center.*

SCENIC STOPS

Capitol Dome. One of the rock formations that gave the park its name, this giant, golden dome is visible in the vicinity of the Hickman Bridge trailhead. ⊠ *Hwy. 24, about 2 mi east of visitor center.*

Capitol Gorge. At the entrance to this gorge Scenic Drive becomes unpaved. The narrow, twisting road on the floor of the gorge was a route for pioneer wagons traversing this part of Utah starting in the 1860s. After every flash flood, pioneers would laboriously clear the route so wagons could continue to go through. The gorge became the main automobile route in the area until 1962, when Highway 24 was built. The short drive to the end of the road leads to some interesting hiking trails to the water-holding "tanks" eroded into the sandstone. ⊠ *Scenic Dr., 9 mi south of visitor center.*

Chimney Rock. Even in a landscape of spires, cliffs, and knobs, this deep-red landform is unmistakable. ☒ *Hwy. 24, about 3 mi west of the visitor center.*

☾ **Fremont Indian Petroglyphs.** Nearly 1,000 years ago the Capitol Reef area was occupied by the Fremont Indians, whose culture was tied closely to the ancestral Puebloan culture. Fremont rock art can be identified by the large trapezoidal figures often depicted wearing headdresses and ear baubles. ☒ *Hwy. 24, 1.2 mi east of visitor center.*

The Waterpocket Fold. A giant wrinkle in the earth that extends almost 100 mi between Thousand Lake Mountain and Lake Powell, the Waterpocket Fold is not to be missed. You can glimpse the fold by driving south on Scenic Drive—after it branches off Highway 24—past the Fruita Historic District, but for complete immersion enter the park via the 66-mi Burr Trail from the town of Boulder. Travel through the southernmost reaches of the park requires a substantial amount of driving on unpaved roads. It's accessible to most vehicles during dry weather; check at the visitor center for road conditions and recommendations.

GEOLOGY BEHIND THE PARK'S NAME

When water wears away layers of sandstone, basins can appear in the rock. These are called waterpockets. The 100-mi-long Waterpocket Fold—a massive rift in the Earth's crust, where geothermal pressure pushed one side 7,000 feet higher than the other (today it's settled to 2,600 feet)—is full of these waterpockets. Early explorers with seafaring backgrounds called the fold a reef, since it was a barrier to travel. Some of the rocks, due to erosion, also have domelike formations resembling capitol rotundas.

VISITOR CENTER

Capitol Reef Visitor Center. Watch a film, talk with rangers, or peruse the many books, maps, and materials offered for sale in the bookstore. Towering over the center is the Castle, one of the park's most prominent rock formations. ☒ *Hwy. 24, 11 mi east of Torrey* ☏ *435/425–3791* ☽ *Late May–Sept., daily 8–6; Oct. and mid-Apr.–late May, daily 8–5; Nov.–mid-Apr., daily 8–4:30.*

SPORTS AND THE OUTDOORS

The main outdoor activity at Capitol Reef is hiking. There are trails for all levels. Remember: whenever you venture into the desert—that is, wherever you go in Capitol Reef—take, and drink, plenty of water.

BICYCLING

Bicycles are allowed only on established roads in the park. Since Highway 24 is a state highway and receives a substantial amount of through traffic, it's not the best place to pedal. Scenic Drive is better, but the road is narrow, and you have to contend with drivers dazed by the beautiful surroundings. Four-wheel-drive roads are certainly less traveled, but they are often sandy, rocky, and steep. You cannot ride your bicycle in washes or on hiking trails.

GOOD READS

- *Capitol Reef: Canyon Country Eden*, by Rose Houk, is an award-winning collection of photographs and lyrical essays on the park.

- *Dwellers of the Rainbow, Fremont Culture in Capitol Reef National Park*, by Rose Houk, offers a brief background of the Fremont culture in Capitol Reef.

- *Explore Capitol Reef Trails*, by Marjorie Miller and John Foster, is a comprehensive hiking guide.

- *Geology of Capitol Reef National Park*, by Michael Collier, teaches the basic geology of the park.

- *Red Rock Eden*, by George Davidson, tells the story of historic Fruita, its settlements, and orchards.

Hondoo Rivers & Trails (⇨ *Multisport Outfitters and Expeditions box)* organizes rides in the park.

Cathedral Valley Scenic Backway. In the remote northern end of the park you can enjoy solitude and a true backcountry ride on this trail. You'll be riding on surfaces that include dirt, sand, bentonite clay, and rock, and you will also ford the Fremont River; you should be prepared to encounter steep hills and switchbacks, wash crossings, and stretches of deep sand. Summer is not a good time to try this ride, as water is very difficult to find and temperatures may exceed 100°F. The entire route is about 58 mi long; during a multiday trip you can camp at the primitive campground with five sites, about midway through the loop. ⊠ *Off Hwy. 24 at Caineville, or at River Ford Rd., 5 mi west of Caineville on Hwy. 24.*

South Draw Road. This is a very strenuous ride that traverses dirt, sand, and rocky surfaces, and crosses several creeks that may be muddy. It's not recommended in winter or spring because of deep snow at higher elevations. If you like fast downhill rides, though, this trip is for you—it will make you feel like you have wings. The route starts at an elevation of 8,500 feet on Boulder Mountain and ends 15 mi later at 5,500 feet in the Pleasant Creek parking area at the end of Scenic Drive. ⊠ *At the junction of Bowns Reservoir Rd. and Hwy. 12, 13 mi south of Torrey.*

FOUR-WHEELING

You can explore Capitol Reef in a 4X4 on a number of exciting backcountry routes. Road conditions can vary greatly depending on recent weather patterns. Spring and summer rains can leave the roads muddy, washed out, and impassable even to four-wheel-drive vehicles. Always check at the park visitor center for current conditions before you set out, and take water, supplies, and a cell phone with you.

Hondoo Rivers & Trails (⇨ *Multisport Outfitters and Expeditions box)* has guided four-wheeling trips in the park.

Cathedral Valley Scenic Backway. The north end of Capitol Reef, along this backcountry road, is filled with towering monoliths, panoramic vistas, and a stark desert landscape. The area is remote and the road through it unpaved, so do not enter without a high-clearance vehicle, some planning, and a cell phone (although reception is spotty). The drive through the valley is a 58-mi loop that you can begin at River Ford

MULTISPORT OUTFITTERS AND EXPEDITIONS

Hondoo Rivers & Trails. With a reputation for high-quality, educational trips into the backcountry of Capitol Reef National Park, these folks pride themselves on delivering a unique, private experience. From April to October, the company offers adventures on horseback, on foot, or via four-wheel-drive vehicle in Capitol Reef and the mountains and deserts surrounding it. Trips are designed to explore the geologic landforms in the area, seek out wildflowers in season, and to encounter free-roaming mustangs, bison, and bighorn sheep when possible. Single- or multiday trips can be arranged. ⊠ *90 E. Main St., Torrey* ☎ *435/425–3519 or 800/332–2696* ⊕ *www.hondoo.com.*

Road off Highway 24. From there, the loop travels northwest, giving you access to Glass Mountain, South Desert, and Gypsum Sinkhole. Turning southeast at the sinkhole, the loop takes you past the side road that accesses the Temples of the Moon and Sun, then becomes Caineville Wash Road before ending at Highway 24, 7 mi east of your starting point. Caineville Wash Road has two water crossings. Including stops, allow a half day for this drive. ■TIP→ If your time is limited, you may want to tour only the Caineville Wash Road, which takes about two hours. At the visitor center you can check for road conditions and pick up a self-guided auto tour brochure for $2. ⊠ *River Ford Rd., 11.7 mi east of visitor center on Hwy. 24.*

HIKING

Many park trails in Capitol Reef include steep climbs, but there are a few easy-to-moderate hikes. A short drive from the visitor center takes you to a dozen trails, and a park ranger can advise you on combining trails or locating additional routes.

Guided hikes can be arranged with Hondoo Rivers & Trails (⇨ *Multisport Outfitters and Expeditions box).*

EASY

Goosenecks Trail. This nice little walk gives you a good introduction to the land surrounding Capitol Reef. Enjoy the dizzying views from the overlook. It's only 0.3 mi round-trip. ⊠ *Trailhead at Hwy. 24, about 3 mi west of the visitor center.*

Grand Wash Trail. At the end of unpaved Grand Wash Road you can continue on foot through the canyon to its end at the Fremont River. You're bound to love the trip. This flat hike takes you through a wide wash between canyon walls. It's an excellent place to study the geology up close. The round-trip hike is 4½ mi; allow two to three hours for your walk. Check at the ranger station for flash-flood warnings before entering the wash. ⊠ *Trailhead at Hwy. 24, east of Hickman Bridge parking lot, or at end of Grand Wash Rd., off Scenic Dr. about 5 mi from visitor center.*

Sunset Point Trail. The trail starts from the same parking lot as the Goosenecks Trail. Benches along this easy, 0.7-mi round-trip invite you to sit and meditate surrounded by the colorful desert. At the trail's end, you will be rewarded with broad vistas into the park; it's even better at sunset. ⊠ *Trailhead at Hwy. 24, about 3 mi west of visitor center.*

MODERATE

★ **Capitol Gorge Trail and the Tanks.** Starting at the Pioneer Register, about a mile from the Capitol Gorge parking lot, is a trail that climbs to the Tanks, two holes in the sandstone, formed by erosion, that hold water after it rains. After a scramble up about 0.2 mi of steep trail with cliff drop-offs, you can look down into the Tanks and can also see a natural bridge below the lower tank. Including the walk to the Pioneer Register, allow an hour or two for this interesting little hike. ⊠ *Trailhead at end of Scenic Dr., 9 mi south of visitor center.*

☺ **Cohab Canyon Trail.** Children particularly love this trail for the geological features and native creatures, such as rock wrens and Western pipistrelles (canyon bats), that you see along the way. One end of the trail is directly across from the Fruita Campground on Scenic Drive, and the other is across from the Hickman Bridge parking lot. The first ¼ mi from Fruita is pretty strenuous, but then the walk becomes easy except for turnoffs to the overlooks, which are strenuous but short. Along the way you'll find miniature arches, skinny side canyons, and honeycombed patterns on canyon walls where the wrens make nests. The trail is 3.2 mi round-trip to the Hickman Bridge parking lot. The Overlook Trail adds 2 mi to the journey. Allow one to two hours to overlooks and back; allow two to three hours to Hickman Bridge parking lot and back. ⊠ *About 1 mi south of visitor center on Scenic Dr., or about 2 mi east of visitor center on Hwy. 24.*

Fremont River Trail. What starts as a quiet little stroll beside the river turns into an adventure. The first ½ mi of the trail is wheelchair accessible as you wander past the orchards next to the Fremont River. After you pass through a narrow gate, the trail changes personality and you're in for a steep climb on an exposed ledge with drop-offs. The views at the top of the 770-foot ascent are worth it as you look down into the Fruita Historic District. The trail is 2½ mi round-trip; allow two hours. ⊠ *Near amphitheater off Loop C of Fruita Campground, about 1 mi from visitor center.*

Golden Throne Trail. As you hike to the base of the Golden Throne, you may be fortunate enough to see one of the park's elusive desert bighorn sheep. You're more likely, however, to spot their small, split-hoof tracks in the sand. The trail itself is 2 mi of gradual elevation gain with some steps and drop-offs. The Golden Throne is hidden until you near the end of the trail, then suddenly you find yourself looking at a huge sandstone monolith. If you hike near sundown the throne burns gold, salmon, and platinum. The round-trip hike is 4 mi and you should allow two to three hours. ⊠ *At end of Capitol Gorge Rd., at Capitol Gorge trailhead, 9 mi south of visitor center.*

Hickman Bridge Trail. This trail is a perfect introduction to the park. It leads to a natural bridge of Kayenta sandstone, which has a 135-foot opening carved by intermittent flash floods. Early on, the route climbs a set of steps along the Fremont River, and as the trail tops out onto a bench, you'll find a slight depression in the earth. This is what remains of an ancient Fremont pit house, a kind of home that was dug into the ground

Temple of the Sun, a monolith in Capitol Reef's Cathedral Valley, is a favorite with photographers.

and covered with brush. The trail splits, leading along the right-hand branch to a strenuous uphill climb to the Rim Overlook and Navajo Knobs. Stay to your left to see the bridge, and you'll encounter a moderate up-and-down trail. As you continue up the wash on your way to the bridge, you'll notice a Fremont granary on the right side of the small canyon. Allow about 1½ hours to walk the 2-mi round-trip. The walk to the bridge is one of the most popular trails in the park, so expect lots of company along the way. ⊠ *Hwy. 24, 2 mi east of visitor center.*

DIFFICULT

Chimney Rock Trail. You're almost sure to see ravens drifting on thermal winds around the deep red Mummy Cliff that rings the base of this trail. This loop trail begins with a steep climb to a rim above Chimney Rock. The trail is 3½ mi round-trip, with a 600-foot elevation change. Allow three to four hours. ⊠ *Hwy. 24, about 3 mi west of visitor center.*

EDUCATIONAL OFFERINGS

RANGER PROGRAMS

From late May to early September, ranger programs are offered at no charge. You can obtain current information about ranger talks and other park events at the visitor center or campground bulletin boards.

Evening Program. Learn about Capitol Reef's geology, American Indian cultures, wildlife, and more at a free lecture, slide show, or other ranger-led activities. A schedule of programs is offered from May to September nightly, a half hour after sunset. A schedule of topics and times is posted

FESTIVALS AND EVENTS

JULY

Bicknell International Film Festival. *Don't* get out your best black beret to attend this event—it's a spoof on serious film festivals. It begins with the world's fastest parade, a 55-MPH procession from Torrey to Bicknell. Past themes have included "UFO Flicks," "Japanese Monster Movies," and "Viva! Elvis." ☎ *No phone* ⊕ *www.thebiff.org*

AUGUST

Wayne County Fair. The great American county fair tradition is at its finest in Loa. Horse shows, turkey shoots, and the Tilt-A-Whirl are all standards, as is a rodeo and a parade. Look at handmade quilts and other crafts, see agricultural exhibits, play games, and eat plenty of good food while you spend a day at the fair. ☎ *435/836–2614*.

at the visitor center. ⊠ *Amphitheater, Loop C, Fruita Campground, about 1 mi from visitor center on Scenic Dr.* ☎ *435/425–3791.*

Junior Ranger Program. Each child who participates in this self-guided program completes a combination of activities in the Junior Ranger booklet, attends a ranger program, interviews a park ranger, and/or picks up litter. ⊠ *At the visitor center* ☎ *435/425–3791* 🎫 *Free.*

Ranger Talks. Each day at the visitor center rangers give brief talks on park geology. Times change, so check at the center for a current schedule. ⊠ *At the visitor center* ☎ *435/425–3791* 🎫 *Free* ☽ *May–Sept., daily.*

WHAT'S NEARBY

NEARBY TOWNS

Probably the best home base for exploring the park, the pretty town of **Torrey,** just outside the park, has lots of personality. Giant old cottonwood trees make it a shady, cool place to stay, and the townspeople are friendly and accommodating. A little farther west on Highway 24, tiny **Teasdale** is a charming settlement cradled in a cove of the Aquarius Plateau. The homes, many of which are well-preserved older structures, look out onto brilliantly colored cliffs and green fields. **Bicknell** lies another few miles west of Capitol Reef. Not much happens here, making it a wonderfully quiet place to rest your head. The Wayne County seat of **Loa,** 10 mi west of Torrey, was settled by pioneers in the 1870s. If you head south from Torrey instead of west, you can take a spectacular 32-mi drive along Highway 12 to **Boulder,** a town so remote that its mail was carried on horseback until 1940. Nearby is Anasazi State Park. In the opposite direction, 51 mi east, **Hanksville** is more a crossroads than anything else.

VISITOR INFORMATION

Capitol Reef Country Travel Council (Bicknell, Hanksville, Loa, Teasdale, Torrey) 🗊 *P.O. Box 7, Teasdale 84773* ☎ *800/858–7951* ⊕ *www.capitolreef.org.* **Garfield County Travel Council (Boulder)** ⊠ *55 S. Main St., Panguitch 84759* ☎ *800/444–6689* ⊕ *www.brycecanyoncountry.com.*

NEARBY ATTRACTIONS

Anasazi State Park. *Anasazi* is a Navajo word interpreted to mean "ancient enemies." What the Anasazi called themselves we will never know, but their descendants, the Hopi people, prefer the term ancestral Puebloan. This state park is dedicated to the study of that mysterious culture, with a largely unexcavated dwelling site, an interactive museum, and a reproduction of a pueblo. ⊠ *460 N. Hwy. 12, Boulder* ☎ *435/335–7308* ⊕ *www.stateparks.utah.gov* ☜ *$4 per person* ☉ *Late May–early Sept., daily 8–6; early Sept.–late May, daily 9–5.*

♲ **Goblin Valley State Park.** All of the landscape in this part of the country is strange and surreal, but Goblin Valley takes the cake as the weirdest of all. It's full of hundreds of gnomelike rock formations colored in a dramatic orange hue. Short, easy trails wind through the goblins, which delight children. ⊠ *Hwy. 24, 12 mi north of Hanksville* ☎ *435/564–3633* ⊕ *www.stateparks.utah.gov* ☜ *$7 per vehicle* ☉ *Daily 8 AM–sunset.*

San Rafael Swell. About 80 mi long and 30 mi wide, this massive fold and uplift in the Earth's crust rises 2,100 feet above the desert. The Swell, as it is known locally, is northeast of Capitol Reef, between Interstate 70 and Highway 24. You can take photos from several viewpoints. ⊠ *BLM San Rafael Resource Area, 125 S. 600 W, Price* ☎ *435/636–3600* ⊕ *www.blm.gov/ut/st/en/fo/price.html.*

AREA ACTIVITIES

SPORTS AND THE OUTDOORS

FISHING

Fishlake National Forest. Sitting at an elevation of 8,800 feet is Fish Lake, which lies in the heart of its namesake, 1.4-million-acre forest. The area has several campgrounds and wonderful lodges. The lake is stocked annually with lake and rainbow trout, mackinaw, and splake. A large population of brown trout is native to the lake. The Fremont River Ranger District office can provide all the information you need on camping, fishing, and hiking in the forest. ⊠ *Fremont River Ranger District office, 138 S. Main St., Loa* ☎ *435/836–2811* ⊕ *www.fs.fed.us/r4/fishlake.*

OUTFITTERS AND EXPEDITIONS **Alpine Adventures** (⊠ *310 W. Main St., Torrey* ☎ *435/425–3660* ⊕ *www.alpineadventuresutah.com*) has a stellar reputation for personalized attention during fly-fishing trips into the high backcountry around Capitol Reef, as well as trophy hunting and horseback tours.

ARTS AND ENTERTAINMENT

ART GALLERIES

Gallery 24. This pleasing space sells contemporary fine art from Utah-based artists that includes sculpture, handcrafted furniture, folk art, photography, and ceramics. ⊠ *135 E. Main St., Torrey* ☎ *435/425–2124.*

PERFORMING ARTS

Robbers' Roost. Open from March through October, the Roost, whose name comes from Butch Cassidy's hideout region, is an excellent place to stop to browse, talk about trails, or find out what's going on around town. It's part coffee bar, part bookstore, and part performance space, all contained in the late Utah writer Ward Roylance's practically pyramid-shaped house. ⊠ *185 W. Main St./Hwy. 24, Torrey* ☎ *435/425–3265.*

SHOPPING

Unique and unexpected, the nifty **Flute Shop** (⊠ *2650 S. Hwy. 12, 4 mi south of junction of Hwys. 12 and 24* ☎ *435/425–3144*) is open year-round and sells American Indian–style flutes and gifts.

12

SCENIC DRIVES

★ **Burr Trail Scenic Backway.** Branching east off Highway 12 in Boulder, Burr Trail travels through the Circle Cliffs area of Grand Staircase–Escalante National Monument into Capitol Reef. The views are of backcountry canyons and gulches. The road is paved between Boulder and the eastern boundary of Capitol Reef. It leads into a hair-raising set of switchbacks—not suitable for RVs or trailers—that ascends 800 feet in ½ mi. Before attempting to drive this route, check with the Capitol Reef Visitor Center for road conditions. From Boulder to its intersection with Notom-Bullfrog Road the route is 36 mi long.

Fodor's Choice
★ **Utah Scenic Byway 12.** Named as one of only 20 All-American Roads in the United States by the National Scenic Byways Program, Highway 12 is not to be missed. The 32-mi stretch between Torrey and Boulder winds through alpine forests and passes vistas of some of America's most remote and wild landscape. It is not for the faint of heart or those afraid of narrow, winding mountain roads.

Utah Scenic Byway 24. For 62 mi between Loa and Hanksville, you'll cut right through Capitol Reef National Park. Colorful rock formations in all their hues of red, cream, pink, gold, and deep purple extend from one end of the route to the other. The closer you get to the park the more colorful the landscape becomes. The vibrant rock finally gives way to lush green hills and the mountains west of Loa.

WHERE TO EAT AND STAY

ABOUT THE RESTAURANTS

There is not even a snack bar within Capitol Reef, but dining options exist close by in Torrey, where you can find everything from one of Utah's best restaurants serving high-end southwestern cuisine to basic hamburger joints offering up consistently good food.

ABOUT THE HOTELS

There are no lodging options within Capitol Reef, but you'll have no problem finding clean and comfortable accommodations no matter what your budget in nearby Torrey and not far beyond in Bicknell and Loa. Drive farther into the region's towns, and you are more likely to find locally owned low- to moderate-price motels and a few nice bed-and-breakfasts. Reservations are recommended in summer.

DID YOU KNOW?

The 3.5-mile, round-trip trek up to Chimney Rock has some steep switchbacks, but the journey yields panoramic views. The trailhead is 3 mi from the park visitor center, near the entrance. It is forbidden to rock climb on it.

12

ABOUT THE CAMPGROUNDS

Campgrounds in Capitol Reef fill up fast between Memorial Day and Labor Day, though that goes mainly for the super-convenient Fruita Campground and not the more remote backcountry sites. Most of the area's state parks have camping facilities, and the region's two national forests offer many wonderful sites.

WHERE TO EAT

IN THE PARK

PICNIC AREA **Gifford Farmhouse.** In a grassy meadow with the Fremont River flowing by, this is an idyllic, shady spot in the Fruita Historic District for a sack lunch. Picnic tables, drinking water, grills and a convenient restroom make it perfect. ⊠ *1 mi south of visitor center on Scenic Dr.*

OUTSIDE THE PARK

$$$

SOUTHWESTERN

Fodor's Choice

★

✕ **Cafe Diablo.** This popular ever-expanding Torrey restaurant keeps getting better, and indeed is one of the state's best. Saltillo-tile floors and matte-plaster white walls are a perfect setting for the southwestern art that lines the walls in this intimate restaurant. Innovative southwestern entrées include fire-roasted pork tenderloin and usually some variation of tamales. The rattlesnake cakes, made with free-range desert rattler and served with ancho-rosemary aioli, are delicious and a steadfast menu item. ⊠ *599 W. Main St./Hwy. 24, Torrey* ☎ *435/425–3070* ⊕ *www. cafediablo.net* ⊟ *AE, D, MC, V* ⊗ *Closed mid-Oct.–Apr. No lunch.*

$–$$

AMERICAN

✕ **Capitol Reef Café.** For standard fare that will please everyone in the family, visit this unpretentious restaurant. Favorites include the 10-vegetable salad and the flaky smoked or grilled fillet of rainbow trout, and the breakfasts are both delicious and hearty. A handful of vegetarian offerings—including mushroom lasagna—make for a refreshing break from beef and beans. A surprisingly expansive beer and wine list makes for an out-of-town dining experience. ⊠ *360 W. Main St./Hwy. 24, Torrey* ☎ *435/425–3271* ⊕ *www. capitolreefinn.com* ⊟ *AE, D, MC, V* ⊗ *Closed Nov.–Mar.*

$$–$$$

ECLETIC

★

✕ **Hell's Backbone Grill.** One of the best restaurants in Southern Utah, this remote spot is worth the drive from any distance. The menu is inspired by American Indian, western range, southwestern, and Mormon pioneer recipes. The owners, who are also the chefs, use only fresh, organic foods that have a historical connection to the area. Because they insist on fresh foods, the menu changes weekly. ⊠ *20 N. Hwy. 12, Boulder* ☎ *435/335–7464* ⊕ *www.hellsbackbonegrill.com* ⊟ *AE, D, MC, V* ⊗ *Closed Nov.–Mar.*

¢

FAST FOOD

✕ **Stan's Burger Shack.** This is the traditional pit stop between Lake Powell and Capitol Reef, featuring great burgers, fries, and shakes—and the only homemade onion rings you'll find for miles and miles. ⊠ *140 S. Hwy. 95, Hanksville* ☎ *435/542–3330* ⊟ *D, MC, V.*

WHERE TO STAY

IN THE PARK

CAMPING   ⚠ **Cathedral Valley Campground.** You'll
¢   find this primitive campground,
(FREE)   about 30 mi from Highway 24, in the
park's remote northern district. The
only way here is via a high-clearance
road that should not be attempted
when wet. **Pros:** away-from-it-all
wonderful; stunning views. Sites are
first come, first served. **Cons:** difficult to access; bare bones. ⊠ *Hartnet
Junction, on Caineville Wash Rd.* ☎ *435/425–3791* ⚠ *6 tent sites* ⌂ *Pit
toilets, grills, picnic tables.*

¢   ⚠ **Cedar Mesa Campground.** Wonderful views of the Waterpocket Fold
(FREE)   and Henry Mountains surround this primitive campground in the park's
southern district. The road to the campground does not require a high-
clearance vehicle, but it's not paved and you should not attempt to drive
it if the road is wet. Sites are first-come, first-served. **Pros:** too small to
get crowded; quiet. **Cons:** somewhat difficult to access; far from any
amenities. ⊠ *Notom-Bullfrog Rd., 22 mi south of Hwy. 24* ☎ *435/425–
3791* ⚠ *5 tent sites* ⌂ *Pit toilets, grills, picnic tables.*

$ ⚠ **Fruita Campground.** Near the orchards and the Fremont River, this
☼   shady campground is a great place to call home for a few days. The
Fodor's Choice   sites nearest the river or the orchards are the very best. Loop C is most
★   appropriate for RVs, although the campground has no hookups. Sites
are first-come, first-served, and in summer the campground fills up
early in the day. **Pros:** central park location; cool and shady. **Cons:** fills
quickly; 10-minute drive from Torrey. ⊠ *Scenic Dr., about 1 mi south of
the visitor center* ☎ *435/425–3791* ⚠ *71 tent/RV sites* ⌂ *Flush toilets,
drinking water, grills, picnic tables* ▭ *No credit cards.*

OUTSIDE THE PARK

¢   ⚏ **Aquarius Motel & Restaurant.** Large, comfortable rooms and recreational
facilities such as an indoor pool and basketball and volleyball courts
make this an attractive place for families. The restaurant next door
serves decent comfort food. **Pros:** not too far from Torrey and Capitol
Reef. **Cons:** Bicknell might be too tiny and quiet for some; can fill quickly
on summer weekends. ⊠ *240 W. Main St., Bicknell* ☎ *435/425–3835 or
800/833–5379* ⊕ *www.aquariusinn.com* ⇲ *27 rooms* ⌂ *In-room: DVD,
Wi-Fi. In-hotel: pool, Wi-Fi, some pets allowed* ▭ *AE, D, DC, MC, V.*

$-$$ ⚏ **Boulder Mountain Lodge.** If you're traveling between Capitol Reef and
★   Bryce Canyon national parks, don't miss this wonderful lodge along
scenic Highway 12. A 5-acre pond on the pastoral grounds is a sanctuary for ducks and other waterfowl; horses graze in a meadow opposite.
Large rooms with balconies or patios offer gorgeous views of the wetlands. The main lodge contains a great room with fireplace, and there's
a fine art gallery and remarkably good restaurant on the premises.
Pros: a perfect spot for peace and solitude; the service and care given
to guests is impeccable. **Cons:** some might find the middle-of-nowhere
location too remote. ⊠ *Hwy. 12 at Burr Trail, Boulder* ☎ *435/335–7460*

or *800/556–3446* ⊕ *www.boulder-utah.com* ⇆ *20 rooms* ⌂ *In-room: Wi-Fi. In-hotel: Wi-Fi, some pets allowed* ⊟ *D, MC, V.*

$–$$
(CABINS)
$$$–$$$$
(HOTELS)

Fish Lake Lodge. This large, lakeside lodge built in 1932 exudes rustic charm and character and has great views. It houses the resort's restaurant, gift shop, game room, and even a dance hall. Guests stay in cabins that sleep 2 to 18 people. The larger houses are excellent for family reunions. Some of the lodgings are quite rustic. The larger cabins are the newest, but all focus on function rather than cute amenities. The lodge, general store, and restaurant are closed from early September to late May; cabins are available year-round. An RV park also has 24 sites for $20 a night, May–October. **Pros:** great place for families and groups to congregate. **Cons:** some cabins are a little close together— so not the best for solitude. ⊠ *HC80, Rte. 25, Loa* ☎ *435/638–1000* ⊕ *www.fishlake.com* ⇆ *45 cabins* ⌂ *In-room: no a/c, kitchen, no TV (some). In-hotel: restaurant* ⊟ *D, MC, V.*

$$$–$$$$
Fodor's Choice
★

Lodge at Red River Ranch. You'll swear you've walked into one of the great lodges of western legend when you walk through the doors at Red River Ranch. The great room is decorated with wagon-wheel chandeliers, American Indian rugs, leather furniture, and original Frederick Remington sculptures. Guest rooms are meticulously and individually decorated with fine antiques and art; each has a fireplace and each have a patio or balcony overlooking the grounds. **Pros:** furnishings and artifacts so distinctive they could grace the pages of a design magazine. **Cons:** rooms are on the small side; in summer you may wish for air-conditioning. ⊠ *2900 W. Hwy. 24, Teasdale* ☎ *435/425–3322 or 800/205–6343* ⊕ *www.redriverranch.com* ⇆ *15 rooms* ⌂ *In-room: a/c, no TV. In-hotel: restaurant* ⊟ *DC, MC, V.*

$–$$
★

Muley Twist Inn. This gorgeous B and B sits on 30 acres of land, with expansive views of the colorful landscape that surrounds it. A wraparound porch, contemporary furnishings, and classical music drifting through the air add to a stay here. **Pros:** dramatic setting against a beautiful rock cliff; a place you can slow down and unwind. **Cons:** might be too far away from it all for some. ⊠ *125 S. 250 W, Teasdale* ☎ *435/425–3640 or 800/530–1038* ⊕ *www.muleytwistinn.com* ⇆ *5 rooms* ⌂ *In-room: no TV, Wi-Fi. In-hotel: laundry service, Wi-Fi* ⊟ *AE, MC, V* ⊙ *Closed Nov.–Mar.*

¢

Rim Rock Inn. Situated on a bluff with outstanding views into the desert, this motel was the first one built to accommodate visitors to Capitol Reef. Under energetic management it has been completely renovated, so rooms are clean and ample—and a good bargain, to boot. The on-site restaurant is a local favorite. **Pros:** stunning views in every direction. **Cons:** predictable motel-style rooms; no shade on property. ⊠ *2523 E. Hwy. 24, Torrey* ☎ *435/428–3398* ⊕ *www.therimrock.net* ⇆ *19 rooms* ⌂ *In-hotel: restaurant* ⊟ *AE, MC, V* ⊙ *Closed Dec.–Feb.*

$

The Snuggle Inn. On the second floor of a row of shops on Main Street, this hostelry has the feel of an old-time hotel. The rooms are spacious, with modern decorations and touches like Internet access. Each room has a pillow-top queen bed. For families, there's a sofa bed in one room. The suite has two separate bedrooms, a living room, and a full kitchen. **Pros:** character, character, character! **Cons:** located in a small farming community with few restaurants. ⊠ *55 S. Main St., Loa* ☎ *435/836–2898 or 877/505–1936* ⊕ *www.thesnuggleinn.com* ↗ *5 rooms, 1 suite* ⚭ *In-room: kitchen (some), refrigerator, Wi-Fi. In-hotel: Wi-Fi* ⊟ *AE, D, DC, MC, V.*

¢ 🖼 **Sunglow Motel and Restaurant.** This well-maintained and inexpensive motel is right in the heart of Bicknell. Rooms are basic but clean, recently upgraded and inexpensive. Try the buttermilk and oatmeal pie at the restaurant next door—and don't knock the sounds of Pickle Pie and Pinto Bean Pie, for they are legendary, and rightfully so. **Pros:** friendly owner who makes amazing pies! **Cons:** few amenities, either at this motel or in this small town. ⊠ *91 E. Main St., Bicknell* ☎ *435/425–3821* ⊕ *www.sunglowpies.com* ↗ *15 rooms* ⚭ *In-room: Wi-Fi. In-hotel: restaurant, Wi-Fi* ⊟ *AE, D, MC, V.*

CAMPING $ ⚠ **Fish Lake Campgrounds.** There are four Forest Service campgrounds in the Fish Lake area, about 7–15 mi northwest on Route 25 or Route 72. All are comfortable and well maintained. The two best are **Doctor Creek** and **Mackinaw.** Doctor Creek is a short drive from Fish Lake in a grove of aspen and pine. Mackinaw sits on a hill overlooking Fish Lake, giving campers a good view of the surrounding basin. The showers here are a rarity in Forest Service campgrounds. **Pros:** beautiful surroundings; lots of space. **Cons:** not all sites available for online reservation; gets cold quickly at higher elevations. ⊠ *Fremont River Ranger District Office, 138 S. Main St., Loa* ☎ *435/836–2811, 877/444–6777 reservations* ⊕ *www.reserveamerica.com* ⚠ *60 tent sites at Mackinaw, 30 tent sites at Doctor Creek* ⚭ *Pit toilets, dump station (Doctor Creek only), drinking water, showers (Mackinaw only)* ⊟ *AE, D, MC, V (for online or phone reservations only)* ☾ *Closed Nov.–Apr.*

$–$$ ⚠ **Thousand Lakes RV Park and Campground.** This is one of the area's most popular RV parks. There's lots of grass and shade, and the level 22-acre site provides good views of the surrounding red cliffs. The cabins come either bare-bones or with bath, microwave, refrigerator, and TV. There's free wireless Internet access. **Pros:** family friendly; convenient. **Cons:** if you seek peace and quiet, look elsewhere. ⊠ *1050 W. Rte 24, Torrey* ☎ *435/425–3500 or 800/355–8995* ⊕ *www.thousandlakesrvpark.com* ⚠ *46 RV sites with full hookups, 16 RV sites with partial hookups, 16 tent sites, 8 cabins* ⚭ *Flush toilets, full hookups, partial hookups (electric and water), dump station, drinking water, guest laundry, showers, fire pits, grills, picnic tables, electricity, public telephone, general store, play area, swimming (pool)* ⊟ *D, MC, V* ☾ *Closed Nov.–Mar.*

Carlsbad Caverns National Park

WORD OF MOUTH

"Nothing can prepare you for the size and scope of the caverns. As you descend into the cave, you keep thinking that you must be near the bottom, but then you realize you're nowhere near. There are giant rooms the size of cathedrals that you keep passing through. It feels like another planet, otherwordly."

—bkluvsNola

WELCOME TO CARLSBAD CAVERNS

TOP REASONS TO GO

★ **400,000 hungry bats:** Every night and every day, bats wing to and from the caverns in a swirling, visible tornado.

★ **Take a guided tour through the underworld:** Plummet 75 stories underground and step into enormous caves hung with stalactites and bristling with stalagmites.

★ **Living Desert Zoo and Gardens:** More preserve than zoo, this 1,500-acre park houses scores of rare species, including endangered Mexican wolves and Bolson tortoises, and now boasts a new black bear exhibit.

★ **Birding at Rattlesnake Springs:** Nine-tenths of the park's 330 bird species, including roadrunners, golden eagles, and acrobatic cave swallows, visit this green desert oasis.

★ **Pecos River:** The Pecos River, a Southwest landmark, flows through the nearby town of Carlsbad. The river is always soothing, but gets festive for holiday floaters when riverside homeowners lavishly decorate their homes.

1 Bat Flight. Cowboy Jim White discovered the caverns after noticing that a swirling smokestack of bats appeared there each morning and evening. White is long gone, but the 300,000-member bat colony is still here, snatching up 3 tons of bugs a night. Watch them leave at dusk from the amphitheater located near the park visitor center.

2 Carlsbad Caverns Big Room Tour. Travel 75 stories below the surface to visit the Big Room, where you can traipse beneath a 255-foot-tall ceiling and take in immense and eerie cave formations. Situated directly beneath the park visitor center, the room can be accessed via quick-moving elevator or the natural cave entrance.

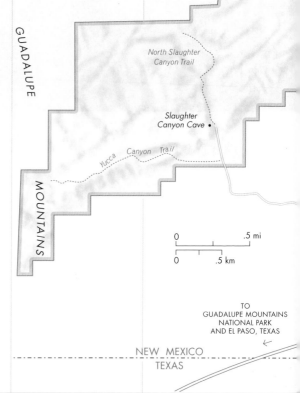

GUADALUPE

MOUNTAINS

North Slaughter Canyon Trail

Slaughter Canyon Cave •

Yucca Canyon Trail

0   .5 mi
0   .5 km

TO
GUADALUPE MOUNTAINS
NATIONAL PARK
AND EL PASO, TEXAS
←

NEW MEXICO
TEXAS

3 **Living Desert Zoo and Gardens.** Endangered river cooters, Bolson tortoises, and Mexican wolves all roam in the Living Desert Zoo and Gardens. You can also skip alongside roadrunners and slim wild turkeys in the park's aviary, or visit a small group of cougars. The Living Desert is located within the town of Carlsbad, New Mexico, 23 mi to the north of the park.

4 **The Pecos River.** Running through the town of Carlsbad, the Pecos River is a landmark of the Southwest. It skims through town and makes for excellent boating, waterskiing, and fishing. In the winter, residents gussy up dozens of riverside homes for the holiday season.

NEW MEXICO

13

GETTING ORIENTED

To get at the essence of Carlsbad Caverns National Park, you have to delve below the surface—literally. Most of the park's key sights are underground in a massive network of caves (there are 113 in all, although not all are open to visitors; a variety of tours leave from the visitor center). The park also has a handful of trails above ground, where you can experience the Chihuahua Desert and some magnificent geological formations.

5 **Rattlesnake Springs.** Despite 30,000-plus acres in which to roam, nine-tenths of the park's 330-plus species of birds show up at Rattlesnake Springs at one time or another—probably because it's one of the very few water sources in this area.

KEY	
	Ranger Station
▲	Campground
⊼	Picnic Area
🍴	Restaurant
▦	Lodge
🚶	Trailhead
🚻	Restrooms
⇬	Scenic Viewpoint
::::::	Walking/Hiking Trails

CARLSBAD CAVERNS PLANNER

When to Go

While the desert above may alternately bake or freeze, the caverns remain in the mid-50s. If you're coming to see the Mexican free-tailed bat, come between spring and late fall.

Getting Here and Around

Carlsbad Caverns is 27 mi southwest of Carlsbad, New Mexico, and 35 mi north of Guadalupe Mountains National Park via U.S. 62/180. The nearest full-service airport is in El Paso, 154 mi away. The 9½-mi Walnut Canyon Desert Drive loop is one-way. It's a curvy, gravel road and is not recommended for motor homes or trailers. Be alert for wildlife crossing roadways, especially in the early morning and at night.

AVG. HIGH/LOW TEMPS.

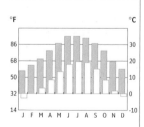

Flora and Fauna

Without a doubt, the park's most prominent and popular residents are Mexican free-tailed bats. These bats have bodies that barely span a woman's hand, yet sport wings that would cover a workingman's boot. Female bats give birth to a single pup each year, which usually weighs more than a quarter of what an adult bat does. Their tiny noses and big ears enable them to search for the many tons of bugs they consume over their lifetime. Numbering nearly a third of a million, these tiny creatures are the park's mascot.

Famous fanged flyers aside, there is much more wildlife to recommend in the park. One of New Mexico's best birding areas is at Rattlesnake Springs. Summer and fall migrations give you the best chance of spotting the most varieties of the more than 330 species of birds. Lucky visitors may spot a golden eagle, a rare visitor, or get the thrill of glimpsing a brilliant, gray-and-crimson vermilion flycatcher.

Snakes generally appear in summer. ■TIP→ If you're out walking, be wary of different rattlesnake species, such as banded-rock and diamondbacks. If you see one, don't panic. Rangers say they are more scared of us than we are of them. Just don't make any sudden moves, and slowly walk away or back around the vipers.

This area is also remarkable because of its location in the Chihuahua Desert, which sprouts unique plant life. There are thick stands of raspy-leaved yuccas, as well as the agave (mescal) plants that were once a food source for early Apache tribes. The leaves of this leggy plant are still roasted in sand pits by Apache elders during traditional celebrations.

In spring, thick stands of yucca plants unfold yellow flowers on their tall stalks. Blossoming cacti and desert wildflowers are one of the natural wonders of Walnut Canyon. You'll see bright red blossoms adorning ocotillo plants, and sunny yellow blooms sprouting from prickly pear cactus.

13

By Jennifer
Edwards

On the surface, Carlsbad Caverns National Park is deceptively normal—but all bets are off once visitors set foot in the elevator, which plunges 75 stories underground. The country beneath the surface is part silky darkness, part subterranean hallucination. The snaky, illuminated walkway seems less like a trail and more like a foray across the River Styx and into the underworld. Within more than 14 football fields of subterranean space are hundreds of formations that alternately resemble cakes, soda straws, ocean waves, and the large, leering face of a mountain troll.

PARK ESSENTIALS

ACCESSIBILITY

Though the park covers a huge expanse above ground (and there are paved roads traversing the grounds), most of the parts you'll want to see are below the surface. Routes through the caverns are paved and well maintained, and portions of the paved Big Room trails in Carlsbad Caverns are accessible to wheelchairs. A map defining appropriate routes is available at the visitor center information desk. Strollers are not permitted on trails (use a baby pack instead). Individuals who may have difficulty walking should access the Big Room via elevator.

ADMISSION FEES AND PERMITS

No fee is charged for parking or to enter the above-ground portion of the park. It costs $6 to descend into Carlsbad Caverns either by elevator or through the Natural Entrance. Costs for special tours range from $7 to $20 plus general admission.

Those planning overnight hikes must obtain a free backcountry permit, and all hikers are advised to stop at the visitor center information desk for current information about trails. Trails are poorly defined, but can be followed with a topographic map. Dogs are not allowed in the park, but a kennel is available at the park visitor center.

ADMISSION HOURS

The park is open year-round, except Christmas Day. From Memorial Day weekend through Labor Day, tours are conducted from 8:30 to 5; the last entry into the cave via the Natural Entrance is at 3:30, and the last entry into the cave via the elevator is at 5. After Labor Day until Memorial Day weekend, tours are conducted from 8:30 to 3:30; the last entry into the cave via the Natural Entrance is at 2, and the last entry into the cave via the elevator is 3:30. Carlsbad Caverns is in the mountain time zone.

ATMS/BANKS

There are no ATMs in the park; the nearest ones are in White's City or Carlsbad.

CELL-PHONE RECEPTION

Cell phones only work about 10% of the time in the park. Public telephones are at the visitor center.

PART CONTACT INFORMATION

Carlsbad Caverns National Park ✉ *3225 National Parks Hwy., Carlsbad, NM* ☎ *575/785–2232, 800/967–2283 reservations for special cave tours, 800/388–2733 cancellations* ⊕ *www.nps.gov/cave.*

SCENIC DRIVE

Walnut Canyon Desert Drive. This scenic drive begins ½ mi from the visitor center. It travels 9½ mi along the top of a ridge to the edge of Rattlesnake Canyon and sinks back down through upper Walnut Canyon to the main entrance road. The backcountry scenery on this one-way gravel loop is stunning; go late in the afternoon or early in the morning to enjoy the full spectrum of changing light and dancing colors. Along the way, you'll be able to see Big Hill Seep's trickling water, the tall, flowing ridges of the Guadalupe Mountain range, and maybe even some robust mule deer.

WHAT TO SEE

SCENIC STOPS

ℭ   **The Big Room.** With a floor space equal to about 14 football fields, this

Fodor's Choice   underground focal point of Carlsbad Caverns clues visitors in to just

★   how large the caverns really are. Its caverns are close enough to the trail to cause voices to echo, but the chamber itself is so vast voices don't echo far; the White House could fit in just one corner of the Big Room, and wouldn't come close to grazing the 255-foot ceiling. The 1-mi loop walk on a mostly level, paved trail is self-guided. An audio guide is also available from park rangers for a few dollars. Kids under 15 are admitted free of charge. ✉ *At the visitor center* 🎫 *$6* ☉ *Late May–early Sept., daily 8–5 (last entry into the Natural Entrance is at 3:30; last entry into the elevator is at 5); early Sept.–late May, daily 8:30–3:30 (last entry into the Natural Entrance at 2; last entry into the elevator at 3:30).*

CARLSBAD CAVERNS IN ONE DAY

In a single day, visitors can easily view both the eerie, exotic caverns and the volcano of bats that erupts from the caverns each morning and evening. Unless you're attending the annual Bat Breakfast, when visitors have the morning meal with rangers and then view the early morning bat return, go ahead and sleep past sunrise and then stroll into the caves.

For the full experience, begin by taking the **Natural Entrance Route Tour,** which allows visitors to trek into the cave from surface level. This tour winds past the Boneyard, with its intricate ossifications, and a 200,000-ton boulder called the Iceberg. After 1¼ mi, or about an hour, the route links up with the **Big Room Route.** If you're not in good health or are traveling with young children, you might want to skip the Natural Entrance and start with the Big Room Route, which begins at the foot of the elevator. This underground walk extends 1¼ mi on level, paved ground, and takes about 1½ hours to complete. If you have made reservations in advance or happen upon some openings, you also can take the additional **King's Palace** guided tour for 1 mi and an additional 1½ hours. At 83 stories deep, the Palace is the lowest rung the public can visit. By this time, you will have spent four hours in the cave. Take the elevator back up to the top. If you're not yet tuckered out, consider a short hike along the sunny, self-guided ½-mi **Desert Nature Walk** by the visitor center.

To picnic by the birds, bees, and water of **Rattlesnake Springs,** take U.S. 62/180 south from White's City 5½ mi, and turn back west onto Route 418. You'll find old-growth shade trees, grass, picnic tables, and water. Many varieties of birds flit from tree to tree. Return to the Carlsbad Caverns entrance road and take the 9½-mi Walnut Canyon Desert Drive loop. Leave yourself enough time to return to the **visitor center** for the evening bat flight.

Natural Entrance. A self-guided, paved trail leads from the natural cave entrance. The route is winding and sometimes slick from water seepage above ground. A steep descent of about 750 feet takes you about a mile through the main corridor and past features such as the Bat Cave and the Boneyard. (Despite its eerie name, the formations here don't look much like femurs and fibulas; they're more like spongy bone insides.) Iceberg Rock is a 200,000-ton boulder that dropped from the cave ceiling some millennia ago. After about a mile, you'll link up underground with the 1-mi Big Room trail and return to the surface via elevator. ⊠ *At the visitor center* 🖾 *$6* ☉ *Late May–early Sept., daily 8:30–3:30; early Sept.–late May, daily 9–2.*

Rattlesnake Springs. Enormous cottonwood trees shade the picnic and recreation area at this cool oasis near Black River. The rare desert wetland harbors butterflies, mammals, and reptiles, as well as 90% of the park's 330 bird species. Don't let its name scare you; there may be rattlesnakes here, but not more than at any other similar site in the Southwest. Overnight camping and parking are not allowed. ⊠ *Hwy. 418* ⊹ *Take U.S. 62/180 5½ mi south of White's City and turn west onto Hwy. 418 for 2½ mi.*

VISITOR CENTER

Carlsbad Caverns National Park Visitor Center. A 75-seat theater offers an engrossing film about the different types of caves, as well as an orientation video that explains cave etiquette. Some of the rules include staying on paths so you don't get lost, keeping objects and trash in your pockets and not on the ground, and not touching the formations. Besides laying down the ground rules, visitor center exhibits offer a primer on bats, geology, wildlife, and the early tribes and nomads that once lived in and passed through the Carlsbad Caverns area. Friendly rangers staff an information desk, where tickets and maps are sold. Two gift shops also are on the premises. ✉ *7 mi west of park entrance at White's City, off U.S. 62/180* ☎ *575/785–2232* ⊙ *Late May–late Aug., daily 8–7; early Sept.–late May, daily 8–5.*

SPORTS AND THE OUTDOORS

BIRD-WATCHING

From warty-headed turkey vultures to svelte golden eagles, about 330 species of birds have been identified in Carlsbad Caverns National Park. Ask for a checklist at the visitor center and then start looking for greater roadrunners, red-winged blackbirds, white-throated swifts, northern flickers, and pygmy nuthatches.

Ⓒ

Fodor's Choice

★

Rattlesnake Springs. Offering one of the best bird habitats in New Mexico, this is a natural wetland with old-growth cottonwoods. Because southern New Mexico is in the northernmost region of the Chihuahua Desert, you're likely to see birds that can't be found anywhere else in the United States outside extreme southern Texas and Arizona. If you see a flash of crimson, you might have spotted a vermilion flycatcher. Wild turkeys also flap around this oasis. ✉ *Hwy. 418, 2½ mi west of U.S. 62/180, 5½ mi south of White's City.*

HIKING

Deep, dark, and mysterious, the Carlsbad Caverns are such a park focal point that the 30,000-plus acres of wilderness above them have gone largely undeveloped. This is great news for people who pull on their hiking boots when they're looking for solitude. What you find are rudimentary trails that crisscross the dry, textured terrain and lead up to elevations of 6,000 feet or more. These routes often take a half-day or more to travel; at least one, Guadalupe Ridge Trail, is long enough that it calls for an overnight stay. Walkers who just want a little dusty taste of desert flowers and wildlife should try the Desert Nature Walk.

Finding the older, less well-maintained trails can be difficult. Pick up a topographical map at the visitor center bookstore, and be sure to pack a lot of water. There's none out in the desert, and you'll need at least a gallon

per person per day. The high elevation coupled with a potent sunshine
punch can deliver a nasty sunburn,
so be sure to pack SPF 30 (or higher)
sunblock and a hat, even in winter.
You can't bring a pet or a gun, but
you do have to bring a backcountry
permit if you're camping. They're
free at the visitor center.

13

EASY

Desert Nature Walk. While waiting for the night bat-flight program, try
taking the ½-mi self-guided hike. The tagged and identified flowers and
plants make this a good place to get acquainted with much of the local
desert flora. The paved trail is wheelchair accessible and an easy jaunt
for even the littlest ones. The payoff is great for everyone, too: a big,
vivid view of the desert basin. ⊠ *Trail begins off the cavern entrance
trail, 200 yards east of the visitor center.*

Rattlesnake Canyon Overlook Trail. A ¼-mi stroll off Walnut Canyon Desert Drive offers a nice overlook of the greenery of Rattlesnake Canyon.
⊠ *Trail begins at mile marker 9 on Walnut Canyon Desert Dr.*

MODERATE

Juniper Ridge Trail. Climb up in elevation as you head north on this nearly
3-mi trail, which leads to the northern edge of the park and then turns
toward Crooked Canyon. While not the most notable trail, it's challenging enough to keep things interesting. Allow yourself half a day,
and be sure to bring lots of water, especially when the temperature is
high. ⊠ *Trailhead at mile marker 8.8 of Desert Loop Dr.*

Old Guano Road Trail. Meandering a little more than 3½ mi one way on
mostly flat terrain, the trail dips sharply toward White's City campground, where the trail ends. Give yourself about half a day to complete the walk. Depending on the temperature, this walk can be taxing.
Drink lots of water. ⊠ *Trailhead at the Bat Flight Amphitheater, near
the Natural Cave entrance and visitor center.*

Rattlesnake Canyon Trail. Rock cairns loom over this trail, which descends
from 4,570 to 3,900 feet as it winds into the canyon. Allow half a day
to trek down into the canyon and make the somewhat strenuous climb
out; the total trip is about 6 mi. ⊠ *Trail begins at mile marker 9 on
Walnut Canyon Desert Dr.*

Fodor's Choice **Yucca Canyon Trail.** Sweeping views of the Guadalupe Mountains and
★ El Capitan give allure to this trail. Drive past Rattlesnake Springs and
stop at the park boundary before reaching the Slaughter Canyon Cave
parking lot. Turn west along the boundary fence line to the trailhead.
The 6-mi round-trip begins at the mouth of Yucca Canyon, and climbs
up to the top of the escarpment. Here you find the panoramic view.
Most people turn around at this point; the hearty can continue along
a poorly maintained route that follows the top of the ridge. The first
part of the hike takes half a day. If you continue on, the hike takes a
full day. ⊠ *Trail begins at Slaughter Canyon Cave parking lot, Hwy.
418, 10 mi west of U.S. 62/180.*

DIFFICULT

Guadalupe Ridge Trail. This long, winding ramble follows an old road all the way to the west edge of the park. Because of its length (about 12 mi), an overnight stay in the backcountry is suggested. The hike may be long, but for serious hikers the up-close-and-personal views into Rattlesnake and Slaughter canyons are more than worth it—not to mention the serenity of being miles and miles away from civilization. ⊠ *Trailhead 4.8 mi down Desert Loop Dr.*

North Slaughter Canyon Trail. Beginning at the Slaughter Canyon Cave parking lot, the trail traverses a heavily vegetated canyon bottom into a remote part of the park. As you begin hiking, look off to the east (to your right) to see the dun-colored ridges and wrinkles of the Elephant Back formation, the first of many dramatic limestone formations visible from the trail. The route travels 5½ mi one way, the last 3 mi steeply climbing onto a limestone ridge escarpment. Allow a full day for the round-trip. ⊠ *Trail begins at Slaughter Canyon Cave parking lot, Hwy. 418, 10 mi west of U.S. 62/180.*

SPELUNKING

Carlsbad Caverns is famous for the beauty and breadth of its inky depths, as well as for the accessibility of some of its largest caves. All cave tours are ranger led, so safety is rarely an issue in the caves, no matter how remote. There are no other tour guides in the area, nor is there an equipment retailer other than the Wal-Mart located in Carlsbad, 23 mi away. Depending on the difficulty of your cave selection (Spider Cave is the hardest to navigate), you'll need at most knee pads, flashlight batteries, sturdy pants, hiking boots with ankle support, and some water.

Hall of the White Giant. Plan to squirm through some tight passages for long distances to access a very remote chamber, where you'll see towering, glistening white formations that explain the name of this feature. This strenuous, ranger-led tour lasts about four hours. Steep drop-offs might elate you—or make you queasy. Wear sturdy hiking shoes and bring four AA batteries with you. Visitors must be at least 12 years old. ⊠ *At the visitor center* ☎ *800/967–2283* ⌦ *$20* ⌂ *Reservations essential* ⊗ *Tour Sat. at 1.*

King's Palace. Throughout King's Palace, you'll see leggy "soda straws" large enough for a giant to sip and multi-tiered curtains of stone—sometimes by the light of just a few flashlights. The mile-long walk is on a paved trail, but there's one very steep hill. This ranger-guided tour lasts about 1½ hours and gives you the chance to experience a blackout, when all lights are extinguished. While advance reservations are highly recommended, this is the one tour you might be able to sign up for on the spot. Children younger than 4 aren't allowed on this tour. ⊠ *At the visitor center* ☎ *800/967–2283* ⌦ *$8* ⊗ *Tours late May–early Sept., daily 10, 11, 2, and 3; early Sept.–late May, daily 10 and 2.*

Lower Cave. Fifty-foot vertical ladders and a dirt path will take you into undeveloped portions of Carlsbad Caverns. It takes about half a day to negotiate this moderately strenuous side trip led by a knowledgeable ranger. Children younger than 12 are not allowed on this tour. ⊠ *At the*

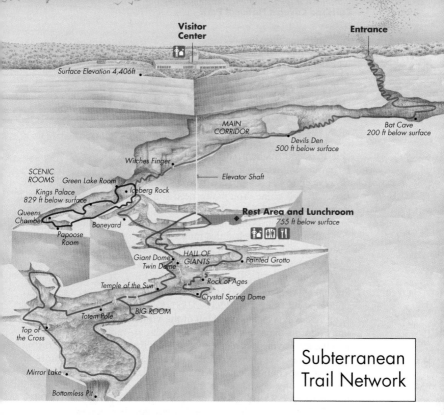

Visitor Center

Entrance

Surface Elevation 4,406ft

MAIN
CORRIDOR

Bat Cave
200 ft below surface

Devils Den
500 ft below surface

Witches Finger

SCENIC
ROOMS   Green Lake Room

Elevator Shaft

Kings Palace
829 ft below surface

Iceberg Rock

Queens
Chamber

Rest Area and Lunchroom
755 ft below surface

Papoose
Room

Boneyard

Giant Dome   HALL OF
Twin Dome   GIANTS

Painted Grotto

Temple of the Sun

Rock of Ages

Crystal Spring Dome

Totem Pole   BIG ROOM

Top of
the Cross

Mirror Lake

Bottomless Pit

Subterranean
Trail Network

visitor center ☎ 800/967–2283 🎟 *$20* ⌲ *Reservations essential* ⊙ *Tour weekdays at 1.*

★ **Slaughter Canyon Cave.** Discovered in the 1930s by a local goatherd, this cave is one of the most popular secondary sites in the park, about 23 mi southwest of the main Carlsbad Caverns and visitor center. Both the hike to the cave mouth and the tour will take about half a day, but it's worth it to view the deep cavern darkness as it's punctuated only by flashlights and, sometimes, headlamps. From the Slaughter Canyon parking area, give yourself 45 minutes to make the steep ½-mi climb up a trail leading to the mouth of the cave. Arrange to be there a quarter of an hour earlier than the appointed time. You'll find that the cave consists primarily of a single corridor, 1,140 feet long, with numerous side passages.

You can take some worthwhile pictures of this cave. Wear hiking shoes with ankle support, and carry plenty of water. You're also expected to bring your own two-D-cell flashlight. Children younger than 6 are not permitted. It's a great adventure if you're in shape and love caving. ⊠ *End of Hwy. 418, 10 mi west of U.S. 62/180* ☎ *800/967–2283* 🎟 *$15* ⌲ *Reservations essential* ⊙ *Tours Memorial Day–Labor Day, daily at 10 and 1; post–Labor Day–Dec., weekends at 10; Jan.–Memorial Day, weekends at 10 and 1.*

Spider Cave. Visitors may not expect to have an adventure in a cavern system as developed and well stocked as Carlsbad Caverns, but serious cavers and energetic types have the chance to clamber up tight tunnels, stoop under overhangs, and climb up steep, rocky pitches. This backcountry cave is listed as "wild," a clue that you might need a similar nature to attempt a visit. Plan to wear your warm, but least-favorite clothes, as they'll probably get streaked with grime. You'll also need soft knee pads, 4 AA batteries, leather gloves, and water. The gloves and pads are to protect you on long, craggy clambers and the batteries are for your flashlight. It will take you half a day to complete this ranger-led tour noted for its adventure. Visitors must be at least 12 years old and absolutely not claustrophobic. ✉ *Meet at visitor center* ☎ *800/967–2283* 💲 *$20* ⛏ *Reservations essential* ⊙ *Tour Sun. at 1.*

> **FLYING BLIND**
>
> Bats use a type of sonar system called echolocation to orient themselves and locate their insect dinners at night. About 15 species of bats live in Carlsbad Caverns, although the Mexican free-tailed is the most predominant.

EXPEDITIONS   Spelunkers who wish to explore both developed and wild caves can go on **Ranger-led Tours** (☎ 800/967–2283). Reservations for the six different tours, which include the **Hall of the White Giant** and **Spider Cave,** known for its tight twists and grimy climbs, are required at least a day in advance. Payment is by credit card over the phone or online (or by mailing in a check, if you're making reservations 21 days or more in advance; but confirm first that space is available). Those who want to go it alone outside the more established caverns can get permits and information about 10 backcountry caves from the **Cave Resources Office** (☎ 575/785–2232). Heed rangers' advice for these remote, undeveloped, nearly unexplored caves.

EDUCATIONAL OFFERINGS

RANGER PROGRAMS

Fodor'sChoice   **Evening Bat Flight Program.** In the amphitheater at the Natural Cave
★   Entrance (off a short trail from main parking lot) a ranger discusses the park's batty residents before the creatures begin their sundown exodus. The bats aren't on any predictable schedule, so times are a little iffy. ✉ *Natural Cave Entrance, at the visitor center* 💲 *Free* ⊙ *Mid-May–mid-Oct., nightly at sundown.*

WHAT'S NEARBY

NEARBY TOWNS

On the Pecos River, with 2¾ mi of beaches and picturesque riverside pathways, **Carlsbad, New Mexico,** seems suspended between the past and the present. It's part university town, part Old West, with a robust Mexican kick. The Territorial town square, a block from the river, encircles a Pueblo-style country courthouse designed by New Mexican architect

FESTIVALS AND EVENTS

DECEMBER

Christmas on the Pecos. Stellar Christmas displays decorate Carlsbad mansions along a 3-mi-plus stretch of the Pecos River. Boat tours ($17.50 Friday and Saturday, $12.50 Sunday–Thursday) run from Thanksgiving night through New Year's Eve except Christmas Eve. ☎ 575/887–6516, 575/628–0952 after Oct. 1.

MAY

Mescal Roast and Mountain Spirit Dances. This May celebration commemorates the connection that indigenous Mescalero Apaches have long had with the Guadalupe Mountains, where mescal plants were gathered for food. Descendants of the original Mescaleros perform a blessing in their native language, and everyone gets to taste the fruit from the mescal-baking pits. Fruit and candy is available as well. ☎ 575/887–5516.

AUGUST

Bat Flight Breakfast. On the second Thursday in August, early risers gather at the cave's entrance to eat breakfast and watch tens of thousands of bats come home ($7 for adults, $3 for kids). ☎ 575/887–6516.

13

John Gaw Meem. Seven miles east of the caverns is **White's City,** grown from a tiny outpost to a small outpost. This privately owned town is the nearest place to Carlsbad Caverns and contains dining and lodging options, plus the essentials.

VISITOR INFORMATION

Carlsbad Chamber of Commerce ✉ 302 S. Canal St., Carlsbad, NM ☎ 575/887–6516 ⊕ www.carlsbadchamber.com. White's City Inc. ✉ 17 Carlsbad Caverns Hwy., White's City, NM ☎ 800/228–3767 or 800/228–3767.

NEARBY ATTRACTIONS

Brantley Lake State Park. In addition to 42,000-acre Brantley Lake, this park 12 mi north of Carlsbad offers primitive camping areas, nature trails, a visitor center, more than 51 fully equipped campsites, and fine fishing for largemouth bass, bluegill, crappie, and walleye pike (though authorities recommend practicing catch-and-release due to the high levels of contaminants in fish caught here). You can boat here, too. ✉ County Rd. 30 (Capitan Reef Rd.), 5 mi off U.S. 285 ☎ 575/457–2384 ⊕ www.emnrd.state.nm.us/PRD/ParksPages/Brantley.htm ☜ $5 per vehicle ⊗ Daily, dawn to dusk.

Carlsbad Museum and Arts Center. Pueblo pottery, American Indian artifacts, and early cowboy and ranch memorabilia are here, along with exhibitions of contemporary art. The real treasure, though, is the McAdoo Collection, with works by painters of the Taos Society of Artists. ✉ 418 W. Fox St., Carlsbad ☎ 575/887–0276 ☜ Free ⊗ Mon.–Sat. 10–5.

Ⓒ ★ **Living Desert Zoo and Gardens State Park.** The park contains impressive plants and animals native to the Chihuahua Desert. The Desert Arboretum has hundreds of exotic cacti and succulents, and the Living Desert Zoo—more a reserve than a traditional zoo—is home to mountain lions, deer, elk, wolves, bison, and endangered Mexican wolves, which are more petite than their snarly kin. Nocturnal exhibits and dioramas let you in on the area's nighttime wildlife, too. Though there are shaded rest areas, restrooms, and water fountains, in hot weather it's best to visit during the early morning or early evening, when it's cooler. ✉ *1504 Miehls Dr., off U.S. 285* ☎ *575/887–5516* 🎫 *Tour $5* ☉ *Late May–early Sept., daily 8–5; early Sept.–late May, daily 8–5; last admission 1½ hrs before closing.*

WHERE TO EAT AND STAY

ABOUT THE RESTAURANTS

Choice isn't an issue inside Carlsbad Caverns National Park because there are just three dining options—the surface-level café, the underground restaurant, and the bring-it-in-yourself option. Luckily, everything is reasonably priced (especially for national park eateries).

ABOUT THE HOTELS

The only overnight option within the arid, rugged park is to make your own campsite in the backcountry, at least half a mile from any trail.

Outside the park, however, options expand. White's City, which is less than 10 mi to the east of the park, contains two motels. Both are near the boardwalk that connects shopping and entertainment options. In Carlsbad there are even more choices, but many of them aren't as appealing as they once were. The hotels here are aging and not particularly well maintained, so don't expect a mint on your pillow. Still, most are clean, if less than opulent.

ABOUT THE CAMPGROUNDS

Backcountry camping is by permit only (obtained for free at the visitor center). No campfires allowed in the park, and all camping is hike-to. Commercial sites can be found in White's City and Carlsbad.

WHERE TO EAT

IN THE PARK

$ ✕ **Carlsbad Caverns Restaurant.** This comfy, diner-style restaurant has AMERICAN the essentials—hamburgers, sandwiches, and hot roast beef. ✉ *Visitor center, 7 mi west of U.S. 62/180 at the end of the main park road* ☎ *575/785–2281* ▭ *AE, D, MC, V* ☉ *Closes at 6:30* PM *Memorial Day weekend–Labor Day, at 5* PM *after Labor Day.*

$ ✕ **Underground Lunchroom.** Grab a treat, soft drink, or club sandwich FAST FOOD for a quick break. Service is quick, even when there's a crowd. ✉ *Visitor center, 7 mi west of U.S. 62/180 at the end of the main park road* ☎ *575/785–2281* ▭ *AE, D, MC, V* ☉ *No dinner. Closes at 5* PM *Memorial Day weekend–Labor Day, at 3:30* PM *after Labor Day.*

PICNIC AREAS **Rattlesnake Springs.** Of the couple of places to picnic in the park, this is the best by far. There are about a dozen picnic tables and grills here, and drinking water and chemical toilets are available. ✉ *Hwy. 418, 2½ mi west of U.S. 62/180.*

Mexican free-tailed bats swarm out of the caves each evening to hunt for food; they return just before dawn.

OUTSIDE THE PARK

$
CHINESE
★

✕ **Bamboo Garden Restaurant.** This popular restaurant—one of few Asian options in southeast New Mexico—was recently remodeled. It looks lovely now, and residents like the buffet. ⊠ *1511 N. Canal St., Carlsbad* ☎ *575/887–5145* ▭ *MC, V* ☻ *Closed Mon.*

$$
AMERICAN

✕ **J.J.'s Steakhouse.** Formerly the Velvet Garter, J.J's serves steaks, chicken, shrimp, and Mexican food in an Old West atmosphere, and the salad bar is popular. You won't find gourmet meals here, but it's a convenient place for a decent meal if you don't want to drive an additional 20 mi north to Carlsbad. There's also a full-service bar. ⊠ *26 Carlsbad Caverns Hwy., White's City* ☎ *800/228–3767* ▭ *AE, D, MC, V.*

$
MEXICAN
★

✕ **Lucy's Mexicali Restaurant & Entertainment Club.** "The best margaritas and hottest chile in the world" is the motto of this family-owned Mexican food oasis. All the New Mexican staples are prepared here, plus some not-so-standard items such as chicken fajita burritos and enchiladas served the New Mexico way—that is, flat with an egg on top. Try the Tucson-style chimichangas and brisket *carnitas* (beef brisket or chicken sautéed with chilies and seasonings). Low-fat and fat-free Mexican dishes and 12 microbrewery beers are served—or try Lucy's original Mexicali beer with a slice of orange. There's live entertainment on weekends. ⊠ *701 S. Canal St., Carlsbad* ☎ *575/887–7714* ▭ *AE, D, DC, MC, V.*

$
BARBECUE

✕ **Red Chimney.** If you hanker for sweet-and-tangy barbecue, this homey, log-cabin-style spot is the place for you. Sauce from an old family recipe is slathered on chicken, pork, beef, turkey, and ham here; fried catfish and other home-style dishes are also served. If wall-mounted animal heads make you squeamish, though, you might want to dine elsewhere. ⊠ *817 N. Canal St., Carlsbad* ☎ *575/885–8744* ▭ *MC, V* ☻ *Closed weekends.*

WHERE TO STAY

IN THE PARK

CAMPING Backcountry camping is the only lodging option in the park (⇨ *About the Campgrounds*).

OUTSIDE THE PARK

$$
★

☷ **Best Western Stevens Inn.** Up until the Holiday Inn was finished in 2008, this family-owned hotel was known regionally as the best-maintained hotel in town. To be honest, it needs updating but it's still a nice place to stay. Etched glass and carved wooden doors add a touch of elegance, and prints of western landscapes decorate the spacious rooms while prime rib and steaks are served in the evening at the motel's Flume Room Restaurant and Coffee Shop, which opens at 5:30 AM daily. **Pros:** established and comfortable; lots of discounts offered; airport shuttle. **Cons:** aging property. ⊠ *1829 S. Canal St., Carlsbad* ☎ *575/887–2851 or 800/730–2851* ⤴ *222 rooms* ⧖ *In-room: kitchen (some), refrigerator (some), Wi-Fi. In-hotel: restaurant, bar, pool, laundry facilities, some pets allowed* ⊟ *AE, D, DC, MC, V* ⌾⏐ *BP.*

$$
Fodor's Choice
★

☷ **Holiday Inn Express.** The area isn't renowned for its luxurious accommodations, so residents and travelers were happy when this hotel came on the scene in 2008. With its indoor pool and nicely updated fitness center, the hotel quickly became a favorite. **Pros:** everything still has that new and sparkling-clean feel; full, hot breakfast. **Cons:** a little farther away from the park than other hotels. ⊠ *2210 W. Pierce, Carlsbad* ☎ *575/234–1252* ⤴ *80 rooms, 24 suites* ⧖ *In-room: Wi-Fi. In-hotel: pool, gym, public Internet* ⊟ *AE, D, DC, MC, V* ⌾⏐ *BP.*

CAMPING
$$–$$$

⚠ **Carlsbad RV Park & Campground.** This full-service campground inside the city limits has level gravel sites and an indoor swimming pool. Camping cabins with heating and air-conditioning are available, as are phone hookups and a meeting room. Reservations are recommended in summer. A professional RV service center where repairs can be made is next door. **Pros:** full-service campground, free Wi-Fi. **Cons:** sites are close together. ⊠ *4301 National Parks Hwy., Carlsbad* ☎ *575/885–6333* ⊕ *www.carlsbadrvpark.com* ⚠ *96 RV sites, 41 tent sites* ⧖ *Flush toilets, full hookups, partial hookups, dump station, drinking water, guest laundry, showers, grills, picnic tables, electricity, public telephone, general store, play area, swimming (pool)* ⊟ *MC, V.*

Channel Islands National Park

WORD OF MOUTH

"The Channel Islands are a national park, so you can go to the Web site for great photos of the islands. You book a campsite through the national park reservations system and you can reserve a boat trip over to the islands from Ventura . . . No, there are not flush toilets. To stay there, you backpack."

—sandals

WELCOME TO CHANNEL ISLANDS

TOP REASONS TO GO

★ **Rare flora and fauna:** The Channel Islands are home to 145 species of terrestrial plants and animals found nowhere else on Earth.

★ **Time travel:** With no cars, phones, or services, these undeveloped islands provide a glimpse of what California was like hundreds of years ago, away from hectic modern life.

★ **Underwater adventures:** The incredibly healthy channel waters rank among the top 10 diving destinations on the planet— but you can also visit the kelp forest virtually via an underwater video program.

★ **Marvelous marine mammals:** More than 30 species of seals, sea lions, whales, and other marine mammals ply the park's waters at various times of year.

★ **Sea-cave kayaking:** Paddle around otherwise inaccessible portions of the park's 175 mi of gorgeous coastline— including one of the world's largest sea caves.

1 Anacapa. Tiny Anacapa is a 5-mi stretch of three islets, with towering cliffs, caves, natural bridges, and rich kelp forests.

2 San Miguel. Isolated, windswept San Miguel, the park's westernmost island, has an ancient caliche forest and hundreds of archaeological sites chronicling the Chumash Indian's 11,000-year history on the island. More than 30,000 pinnipeds (seals and sea lions) hang out on the island's beaches during certain times of year.

3 Santa Barbara. Nearly 6 mi of scenic trails crisscross this tiny island, known for its excellent wildlife viewing and native plants. It's a favorite destination for diving, snorkeling, and kayaking.

Santa Ynez Peak 4,298 ft

Harris Point
Point Bennett
Cuyler Harbor
Cabrillo Monument
Lester Ranch site
West Point
Carrington Point
Vail & Vickers Ranch
Bechers Bay
2
Tyler Bight
Sandy Point
San Miguel Passage
San Miguel Island
5
Torrey Pines
East Point
Soledad Peak 1,574 ft
Johnsons Lee
Santa Rosa Island
South Point
Santa Cruz Channel

PACIFIC OCEAN

4 Santa Cruz. The park's largest island offers some of the best hikes and kayaking opportunities, one of the world's largest and deepest sea caves, and more species of flora and fauna than any other park island.

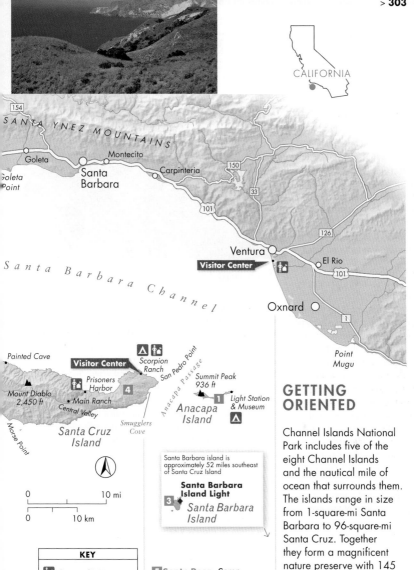

CALIFORNIA

14

Santa Ynez Mountains

Goleta
Goleta Point
Montecito
Santa Barbara
Carpinteria
Ventura
Visitor Center
El Rio
Oxnard

Santa Barbara Channel

Point Mugu

Painted Cave
Visitor Center
Scorpion Ranch
Prisoners Harbor
San Pedro Point
Summit Peak 936 ft
Light Station & Museum
Mount Diablo 2,450 ft
Main Ranch
Central Valley
Smugglers Cove
Anacapa Passage
Anacapa Island
Santa Cruz Island
Morse Point

0 _____ 10 mi
0 _____ 10 km

Santa Barbara island is approximately 52 miles southeast of Santa Cruz Island

Santa Barbara Island Light
3
Santa Barbara Island

KEY	
🛉	Ranger Station
⛺	Campground
⟁	Picnic Area
🍴	Restaurant
🏠	Lodge
🏃	Trailhead
🚻	Restrooms
⟿	Scenic Viewpoint
⋯⋯	Walking/Hiking Trails

5 Santa Rosa. Campers love to stay on Santa Rosa, with its myriad hiking opportunities, stunning white-sand beaches, and rare grove of Torrey pines. It's also the only island accessible by plane.

GETTING ORIENTED

Channel Islands National Park includes five of the eight Channel Islands and the nautical mile of ocean that surrounds them. The islands range in size from 1-square-mi Santa Barbara to 96-square-mi Santa Cruz. Together they form a magnificent nature preserve with 145 endemic or unique species of plants and animals. Half the park lies underwater, and the 5 mi of surrounding channel waters are teeming with life, including dolphins, whales, seals, sea lions, and seabirds.

CHANNEL ISLANDS PLANNER

When to Go

Channel Islands National Park records about 620,000 visitors each year, but many never venture beyond the visitor center. The busiest times are holidays and summer weekends. If you're going then, make your transportation and accommodation arrangements far in advance.

The warm, dry summer months are the best time to go camping. Humpback and blue whales arrive to feed from late June through early fall. The rains usually come from December through March—but this is also the best time to spot gray whales and to get discounts at area hotels. In the late spring, thousands of migratory birds descend on the islands to hatch their young, and wildflowers carpet the slopes. The water temperature is nearly always cool, so bring a wet suit if you plan to spend much time in the ocean, even in the summer. Fog, high winds, and rough seas can happen any time of the year.

Flora and Fauna

The Channel Islands are home to species found nowhere else on Earth: mammals such as the island fox and the island deer mouse, birds like the island scrub jay, and plants such as the Santa Barbara Island live forever, on the endangered species list. Thousands of western gulls hatch each summer on Anacapa, then fly off to the mainland where they spend about four years learning all their bad habits. Then they return to the island to roost and have chicks of their own. It all adds up to a living laboratory not unlike the one naturalist Charles Darwin discovered off the coast of South America 200 years ago, which is why the Channel Islands are often called the North American Galapagos.

Good Reads

You can find a handful of books about this little-known gem in the Channel Islands Visitor Center in Ventura. A few good ones are:

- *Channel Islands National Park,* by Susan Lamb

- *Channel Islands National Park,* by Tim Hauf.

- *Island of the Blue Dolphins,* by Scott O'Dell (great for kids).

AVG. HIGH/LOW TEMPS.

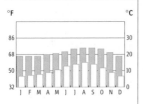

Getting Here and Around

The visitor center for Channel Islands National Park is on California's mainland, in the town of Ventura, off U.S. 101. From the harbors at Ventura, Santa Barbara, and Oxnard you can board a boat to one of the islands. You also can catch a flight to some of the islands from the Camarillo Airport, near Oxnard, and the Santa Barbara Airport.

If you have your own boat, you can land at any of the islands, but each island has certain closed and restricted areas, so boaters should contact the park ranger on each island for instructions. Private vehicles are not permitted on the islands. Pets are also not allowed in the park.

Several private companies provide transportation by boat or plane to and from the mainland to one of more of the Channel Islands (⇨ *Island Operators, at right*).

To reach the Ventura harbor, exit U.S. 101 in Ventura at Seaward Boulevard or Victoria Avenue and follow the signs to Ventura Harbor/Spinnaker Drive. In Santa Barbara, exit U.S. 101 at Castillo Street and head south to Cabrillo Boulevard, then turn right for the harbor entrance. To access Channel Islands Harbor in Oxnard, exit U.S. 101 at Victoria Avenue and head south approximately 7 mi to Channel Islands Boulevard. Amtrak makes stops in Santa Barbara, Ventura, and Oxnard; from the Amtrak station, just take a taxi or waterfront shuttle bus to the harbor.

Transit Times to the Islands

ISLAND	DISTANCE AND TIME BY BOAT	COST (per hiker/camper)
Anacapa Island	12 mi/1 hr from Oxnard	$48/$58
San Miguel Island	58 mi/3½–4 hrs from Ventura	$75/$108
Santa Barbara Island	55 mi/2½–3 hrs from Ventura	$60/$90
Santa Cruz Island	20 mi/1–1½ hrs from Ventura	$48/$64
Santa Rosa Island	46 mi/2½–3 hrs from Ventura	$65/$90

Island Operators

Island Packers and Truth Aquatics go from the mainland to all of the islands. Channel Islands Aviation flies solely to Santa Rosa Island.

Channel Islands Aviation (✉ 305 Durley Ave., Camarillo ☎ 805/987–1301 ⊕ www.flycia.com ⌨ $160 per person, $250 per person if camping) provides day excursions, surf fishing, and camper transportation year-round, flying from Camarillo Airport, about 10 mi east of Oxnard, to an airstrip on Santa Rosa. The operator will also pick up groups of six or more at Santa Barbara Airport, but no camper transportation is available from Santa Barbara.

Sailing on two high-speed catamarans from Ventura or Oxnard, **Island Packers** (✉ 3600 S. Harbor Blvd., Oxnard ☎ 805/642–1393 ✉ 1691 Spinnaker Dr., Ventura ☎ 805/642–1393 ⊕ www.islandpackers.com ⌨ $32–$65) goes to Santa Cruz Island daily most of the year, weather permitting. The boats also go to Anacapa several days a week, and to the other islands three or four times a month, most frequently May through October. **Truth Aquatics** (✉ 301 W. Cabrillo Blvd., Santa Barbara ☎ 805/962–1127 ⊕ www.truthaquatics.com ⌨ $120 for scuba day trips, average of $170 per day for all-inclusive trips) departs from Santa Barbara for scuba trips and multiday excursions (where travelers sleep aboard ship) to the islands.

14

By Cheryl Crabtree

On crystal-clear days the craggy peaks of Channel Islands are easy to see from the mainland, jutting from the Pacific in such sharp detail it seems you could reach out and touch them. The islands really aren't that far away—a high-speed boat will whisk you to the closest ones in less than an hour—yet very few people ever visit them. Those fearless, adventurous types who do will experience one of the most splendid land-and-sea wilderness areas on the planet.

PARK ESSENTIALS

ACCESSIBILITY

The Channel Islands Visitor Center is fully accessible. The islands themselves have few facilities and are not easy to navigate by individuals in wheelchairs or those with limited mobility. Limited wheelchair access is available on Santa Rosa Island via air transportation.

ADMISSION FEES AND PERMITS

There is no fee to enter Channel Islands National Park, but unless you have your own boat, you will pay $32 or more per person for a ride with a boat operator. The cost of taking a boat to the park varies depending on which operator you choose. Also, there is a $15 per day fee for staying in one of the islands' campgrounds.

If you take your own boat, landing permits are not required to visit Channel Islands because there are no public moorings; if you anchor in a nearby cove, at least one person should remain aboard the boat at all times. Boaters who want to land on the Nature Conservancy preserve on Santa Cruz Island should call ☎ 805/898–1642 for permit information or visit ⊕ *www.nature.org/cruzpermit*; allow 10 business days to process your permit application. To hike on San Miguel, call ☎ 805/658–5711 to be matched up to a ranger, which must accompany you there. Anglers must have a state fishing license; for details, call the California Department of Fish and Game at ☎ 916/653–7664. Thirteen Marine Protected

Areas (MPAs) with special resource protection regulations surround the islands, so read the guidelines before you depart.

ADMISSION HOURS

The islands are open every day of the year. Channel Islands Visitor Center in Ventura is closed on Thanksgiving and Christmas. Channel Islands National Park is located in the Pacific time zone.

ATMS/BANKS

There are no ATMs on the islands. ATMs can be found in Santa Barbara, Oxnard, Ventura, and the Camarillo Airport. Santa Barbara and Port Hueneme have banks.

CELL-PHONE RECEPTION

In general, cell-phone reception is spotty. The rangers rely on satellite phones. Public telephones are available on the mainland near the Channel Islands Visitor Center but not on the islands.

PARK CONTACT INFORMATION

Channel Islands Visitor Center ⊠ *1901 Spinnaker Dr., Ventura, CA* ☎ *805/658–5730* ⊕ *www.nps.gov/chis.*

CHANNEL ISLANDS IN ONE DAY

If you have a few hours or a day to visit the Channel Islands, start with viewing the exhibits at the **Channel Islands Visitor Center** in Ventura. Then cruise over to **East Anacapa** for sweeping views of Santa Cruz Island and the mainland—provided it's not too foggy—and hiking, the primary activity here. Wander through western gull rookeries or peer down from steep cliffs and watch the antics of sea lions and seals. Alternatively, zip out to Scorpion Landing or Prisoner's Harbor on **Santa Cruz Island** on a high-speed catamaran run by Island Packers for more extended hiking, snorkeling, or kayaking.

14

WHAT TO SEE

THE ISLANDS

★ **ANACAPA ISLAND**

Although most people think of it as an island, **Anacapa Island** is actually comprised of three narrow islets. The tips of these volcanic formations nearly touch but are inaccessible from one another except by boat. All three islets have towering cliffs, isolated sea caves, and natural bridges; Arch Rock, on East Anacapa, is one of the best-known symbols of Channel Islands National Park. Wildlife viewing is the reason most people come to East Anacapa—particularly in summer when seagull chicks are newly hatched and sea lions and seals lounge on the beaches. Trips to Middle Anacapa Island require a ranger escort.

The compact **museum** on East Anacapa tells the history of the island and houses, among other things, the original lead-crystal Fresnel lens from the island's lighthouse (circa 1937).

Depending on the season and the number of desirable species lurking about there, a limited number of boats travel to **Frenchy's Cove** at West Anacapa, where there are pristine tide pools where you might see anemones, limpets, barnacles, mussel beds, and colorful marine algae. The rest of West Anacapa is closed to protect nesting brown pelicans.

Ⓑ Watch the **Channel Islands Live Dive Program** (✉ *Landing Cove, Anacapa Island* 🎟 *Free* ☉ *Summer, Tues.–Thurs. at 2*), in which divers armed with video cameras explore the undersea world of the kelp forest off Anacapa Island; images are transmitted to monitors located on the dock at Landing Cove and in the mainland visitor center. You see bright red sea stars, spiny sea urchins, and brilliant orange Garibaldis. You can even ask the divers questions via interactive lines.

SAN MIGUEL ISLAND

The westernmost of the Channel Islands, **San Miguel Island** is frequently battered by storms sweeping across the North Pacific. The 15-square-mi island's wild, windswept landscape is lush with vegetation. Point Bennett, at the western tip, offers one of the world's most spectacular wildlife displays when more than 30,000 pinnipeds hit its beach. Explorer Juan Rodríguez Cabrillo was the first European to visit this island; he claimed it for Spain in 1542. Legend holds that Cabrillo died on one of the Channel Islands—no one knows where he's buried, but there's a memorial to him on a bluff above Cuyler Harbor.

SANTA BARBARA ISLAND

At about 1 square mi, **Santa Barbara Island** is the smallest of the Channel Islands and nearly 35 mi south of the others. Triangular in shape, Santa Barbara's steep cliffs—which offer a perfect nesting spot for the Xantus's murrelet, a rare seabird—are topped by twin peaks. In spring, you can enjoy a brilliant display of yellow coreopsis. Learn about the wildlife on and around the islands at the island's small **museum.** ✉ *Santa Barbara Island* ☎ *No phone* ☉ *Daily 10–5.*

SANTA CRUZ ISLAND

Five miles west of Anacapa, 96-square-mi **Santa Cruz Island** is the largest of the Channel Islands. The National Park Service manages the easternmost 24% of the island; the rest is owned by the Nature Conservancy, which requires a permit to land. When your boat drops you off on the 70 mi of craggy coastline, you see two rugged mountain ranges with peaks soaring to 2,500 feet and deep canyons traversed by streams. This landscape is the habitat of a remarkable variety of flora and fauna—more than 600 types of plants, 140 kinds of land birds, 11 mammal species, five varieties of reptiles, and three amphibian species live here. Bird-watchers may want to look for the endemic island scrub jay, which is found nowhere else in the world.

★ The largest and deepest sea cave in the world, **Painted Cave,** lies along the northwest coast of Santa Cruz. Named for the colorful lichen and algae that cover its walls, Painted Cave is nearly ¼ mi long and 100 feet wide. In spring a waterfall cascades over the entrance. Kayakers may encounter seals or sea lions cruising alongside their boats inside the cave. The Channel Islands hold some of the richest archeological resources in North America; all artifacts are protected within the park. Remnants of a dozen Chumash villages can be seen on the island. The largest of these villages, at the eastern end of the island, occupied the area now called **Scorpion Ranch.** The Chumash mined extensive chert deposits on the island for tools to produce shell-bead money, which they traded with people on the mainland. You can learn about Chumash history and view artifacts, tools, and exhibits on native plant and wildlife at the interpretive visitor center near the landing dock. Visitors can also explore remnants of the early-1900s ranching era in the restored historic adobe and outbuildings.

SANTA ROSA ISLAND

Set between Santa Cruz and San Miguel, **Santa Rosa Island** is the second largest of the Channel Islands and has a relatively low profile, broken by a central mountain range rising to 1,589 feet. The coastal areas range from broad sandy beaches to sheer cliffs. The island is home to about 500 species of plants, including the rare Torrey pine. Three unusual mammals—the endemic island fox, spotted skunk, and deer mouse—are among those that make their home here. They hardly compare to the mammoths that once roamed the island; a nearly complete skeleton of a 6-foot-tall pygmy mammoth was unearthed here in 1994.

The island was once home to the **Vail & Vickers Ranch,** where sheep and cattle were raised from 1901 to 1998. You can catch a glimpse of what the operation was like when you walk from the landing dock to the campground; the route passes by the historic ranch buildings, barns, equipment, and the wooden pier where cattle were brought onto the island. (Note that these buildings are not accessible to the public.)

VISITOR CENTERS

Channel Islands National Park Robert J. Lagomarsino Visitor Center. The park's main visitor center has a museum, a bookstore, a three-story observation tower with telescopes, and exhibits about the islands. There's also a marine life exhibit where you can see sea stars clinging to rocks, anemones waving their colorful, spiny tentacles, and a brilliant orange garibaldi darting around. The center also has full-size reproductions of a male northern elephant seal and the pygmy mammoth skeleton unearthed on Santa Rosa Island in 1994. Rangers lead various free public programs describing park resources on weekends and holidays at 11 and 3; they can also give you a detailed map and trip-planning packet if you're interested in visiting the actual islands. ⊠ *1901 Spinnaker Dr., Ventura* ☎ *805/658–5730* ⊕ *www.nps.gov/chis* ☉ *Daily 8:30–5.*

Outdoors Santa Barbara Visitor Center. The small office in the Santa Barbara Harbor provides maps and other information about Channel Islands National Park and Channel Islands National Marine Sanctuary; the Santa Barbara Maritime Museum is housed in the same building. Call ahead to verify hours. ⊠ *113 Harbor Way, Santa Barbara* ☎ *805/884–1475* ⊕ *www.outdoorsb.noaa.gov* ☉ *Daily 11–5.*

SPORTS AND THE OUTDOORS

DIVING

Some of the best snorkeling and diving in the world can be found in the cool waters surrounding the Channel Islands. In the relatively warm water around Anacapa and eastern Santa Cruz, photographers can get great shots of rarely seen giant black bass swimming among the kelp forests. Here you also find a reef covered with red brittle starfish. If you're an experienced diver, you might swim among five species of seals

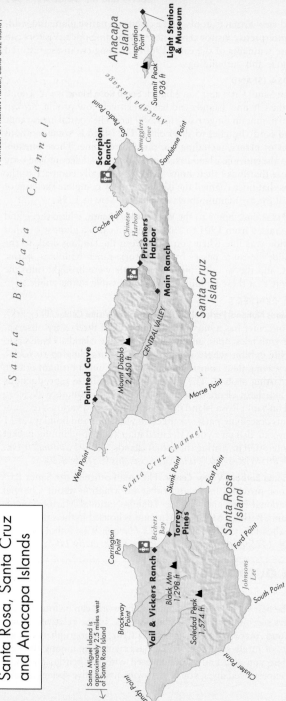

Santa Rosa, Santa Cruz and Anacapa Islands

Ventura is approximately 28 miles
Northeast of Prisoners Harbor, Santa Cruz Island

Santa Barbara Island is
approximately 52 miles southeast
of Santa Cruz Island

Santa Barbara Channel

Painted Cave

West Point

Mount Diablo
2,450 ft

CENTRAL VALLEY

Morse Point

Coche Point

Chinese Harbor

Prisoners Harbor

Main Ranch

Santa Cruz Island

San Pedro Point

Smugglers Cove

Sandstone Point

Scorpion Ranch

Anacapa Passage

Anacapa Island

Inspiration
Point

Summit Peak
936 ft

**Light Station
& Museum**

PACIFIC OCEAN

Santa Miguel Island is
approximately 2.5 miles west
of Santa Rosa Island

Sandy Point

Brockway
Point

Carrington
Point

*Bechers
Bay*

Vail & Vickers Ranch

Black Mtn
1,298 ft

Soledad Peak
1,574 ft

**Torrey
Pines**

Santa Cruz Channel

Skunk Point

East Point

Santa Rosa Island

Ford Point

*Johnsons
Lee*

South Point

Cluster Point

0   5 mi
0   5 km

and sea lions, or try your hand at spearing rockfish or halibut near San Miguel and Santa Rosa. The best time to scuba dive is in the summer and fall, when the water is often clear up to a 100-foot depth.

Ventura Harbor–based **Peace Dive Boat** (⊠ *1691 Spinnaker Dr., Dock G, Ventura* ☎ *805/650–3483* ⊕ *www.peaceboat.com* ✉ *Day trips start at $105*) runs single and multiday diving adventures near all the Channel Islands. Travelers sleep aboard ship. The **Spectre Dive Boat** (⊠ *1575 Spinnaker Dr., Suite 105B-75, Ventura* ☎ *866/225–3483 or 805/486–1166* ⊕ *www.calboatdiving.com* ✉ *$85–$115*) runs single-day diving trips to Anacapa, Santa Cruz, Santa Rosa, and San Miguel. Fees include three or four dives, air, and food. Trips to the Channel Islands lasting a day or more can be arranged through Santa Barbara–based operator **Truth Aquatics** (⊠ *301 W. Cabrillo Blvd., Santa Barbara* ☎ *805/962–1127* ⊕ *www.truthaquatics.com* ✉ *$109–$835*). You live aboard the boats on multiday trips; all meals are provided.

14

HIKING

The terrain on most of the islands ranges from flat to moderately hilly. There are no services (and no public phones; cell-phone reception is dicey) on the islands—you need to bring all your own food, water (except on Santa Cruz and Santa Rosa, where there are water faucets at campgrounds), and supplies.

Truth Aquatics (⊠ *301 W. Cabrillo Blvd., Santa Barbara* ☎ *805/962–1127* ⊕ *www.truthaquatics.com* ✉ *$340–$835*) serves all the park's islands for multiday overnight trips that include naturalist-led hikes (you sleep and eat on board the 65-foot twin-engine single-hull vessels).

EASY

Cuyler Harbor Beach Trail. This easy walk takes you along a 2-mi-long white sand beach on San Miguel. The eastern section is occasionally cut off by high tides. ⊠ *Trailhead at San Miguel Campground, San Miguel Island.*

Historic Ranch Trail. This easy ½-mi walk on Santa Cruz Island takes you to a historic ranch where you can visit an interpretive center in an 1800s adobe and see remnants of a cattle ranch. ⊠ *Trailhead at Scorpion Beach, Santa Cruz Island.*

♺ **Inspiration Point Trail.** This 1½-mi hike along flat terrain takes in most of
★ East Anacapa; there are great views from Inspiration Point and Cathedral Cove. ⊠ *Trailhead at Landing Cove, Anacapa Island.*

Water Canyon Trail. Starting at Santa Rosa Campground, this 2-mi walk along a white-sand beach includes some exceptional beachcombing. Frequent strong winds can turn this easy hike into a fairly strenuous excursion, so be prepared. If you extend your walk into Water Canyon, you can follow animal paths to a lush canyon full of native vegetation. ⊠ *Trailhead at Santa Rosa Campground, Santa Rosa Island.*

MODERATE

♺ **Cavern Point Trail.** This moderate 2-mi hike takes you to the bluffs northwest of Scorpion harbor on Santa Cruz, where there are magnificent coastal views and see pods of migrating gray whales from December through March. ⊠ *Trailhead at Santa Cruz Campground, Santa Barbara Island.*

Elephant Seal Cove Trail. This moderate to strenuous walk takes you across Santa Barbara to a point where you can view magnificent elephant seals from steep cliffs. ⊠ *Trailhead at Landing Cove, Santa Barbara Island.*

Fodor'sChoice ★ **Prisoners Harbor/Pelican Cove Trail.** Taking in quite a bit of Santa Cruz, this moderate to strenuous 3-mi trail to Pelican Cove is one of the best hikes in the park. You must be accompanied by an Island Packers naturalist (⇨ *Island Operators in chapter planner)*, or secure a permit (call ☎ *805/898–1642* or visit ⊕ *www.nature.org/cruzpermit*; allow 10 business days to process your application), as the hike takes you through Nature Conservancy property. ⊠ *Trailhead at Prisoners Harbor, Santa Cruz Island.*

DIFFICULT

Lester Ranch Trail. This short but strenuous 2-mi hike leads up a spectacular canyon filled with waterfalls and lush native plants. At the end of a steep climb to the top of a peak, views of the historic Lester Ranch and the Cabrillo Monument await. (If you plan to hike beyond the Lester Ranch, you'll need a hiking permit; call ☎ *805/658–5730*.) ⊠ *Trailhead at San Miguel Campground, San Miguel Island.*

Point Bennett Trail. Rangers conduct 15-mi hikes across San Miguel to Point Bennett, where more than 30,000 pinnipeds (three different species) can be seen. ⊠ *Trailhead at San Miguel Campground, San Miguel Island.*

KAYAKING

The most remote parts of the Channel Islands are accessible only by a sea kayak. Some of the best kayaking in the park can be found on Anacapa, Santa Barbara, and the eastern tip of Santa Cruz. Anacapa has plenty of sea caves, tidal pools, and even natural bridges you can paddle beneath. Santa Cruz has plenty of secluded beaches to explore, as well as seabird nesting sites and seal and sea lion rookeries. One of the world's largest colonies of Xantus's murrelets resides here, and brown pelicans, cormorants, and storm petrels nest in Santa Barbara's steep cliffs.

It's too far to kayak from the mainland out to the islands, but outfitters have tours that take you to the islands. Tours are offered year-round, but high seas may cause trip cancellations between December and March. ⚠ Channel waters can be unpredictable and challenging. Don't venture out alone unless you are an experienced kayaker; guided trips are highly recommended. All kayakers should carry proper safety gear and equipment and be prepared for sudden strong winds and weather changes.

The operators listed below hold permits from the National Park Service to conduct kayak tours; if you choose a different company, verify that it holds the proper permits.

OUTFIT-
TERS AND
EXPEDITIONS
Highly regarded **Aquasports** (☎ *800/773–2309 or 805/968–7231* ⊕ *www. islandkayaking.com* ✉ *$175–$395*), based in Goleta, offers guided one-, two-, and three-day trips to Scorpion Landing on Santa Cruz and one-day trips to Santa Barbara Island for beginner to expert kayakers. Cross-channel passage, instruction, equipment, and guides are included. ■ TIP→ This is a very popular trip—book early! You can take a one-day trip

Like much of California's central coast, Santa Cruz looks as rugged and undeveloped as it did centuries ago.

to one of the five islands, or overnight multiday excursions to several islands with **Paddle Sports** (☎ 888/254–2094, 805/899–4925 Ext. 303 ⊕ www.kayaksb.com ✉ $195–$700), with shops in Santa Barbara and Carpinteria. All trips include equipment, instruction, and transportation across the channel. Full-service outfitter **Santa Barbara Adventure Company** (☎ 805/898–0671 or 888/773–3239 ⊕ www.sbadventureco.com ✉ $165–$235 day trips) conducts guided kayaking single- and multiday excursions to the Channel Islands. Trips include transportation, equipment, guides, and paddling lessons.

WHALE-WATCHING

About a third of the world's cetacean species (27 to be exact) can be seen in the Santa Barbara Channel. In July and August, humpback and blue whales feed off the north shore of Santa Rosa. From late December through March, up to 10,000 gray whales pass through the Santa Barbara Channel on their way from Alaska to Mexico and back again, and on a whale-watching trip this during timeframe, you should see one or more of them. Other types of whales, but fewer in number, swim the channel June through August.

EXPEDITION ☾ ★ Depending on the season, you can take a three-hour tour or an all-day tour from either Ventura or Channel Islands harbors with **Island Packers** (✉ 1691 Spinnaker Dr., Ventura ☎ 805/642–1393 ⊕ www.islandpackers.com ✉ $32–$64). From January through March you're almost guaranteed to see gray whales in the channel.

EDUCATIONAL OFFERINGS

RANGER PROGRAMS

Ranger programs are held at the Channel Islands National Park Visitor Center in Ventura.

Interpreting the Language of the Park. Presentations by different rangers focus on the park's rich history; topics include everything from tidal pools and marine life to shipwrecks and the area's cultural history. ⊠ *Channel Islands National Park Visitor Center, 1901 Spinnaker Rd., Ventura* ☎ *805/658–5730* ⌨ *Free* ☉ *Weekends and holidays at 3* PM.

Tidepool Talk. Explore the area's marine habitat without getting your feet wet. Rangers at the Channel Islands Visitor Center demonstrate how animals and plants adapt to the harsh conditions found in tidal pools of the Channel Islands. ⊠ *Channel Islands National Park Visitor Center, 1901 Spinnaker Rd., Ventura* ☎ *805/658–5730* ⌨ *Free* ☉ *Weekends and holidays at 11* AM.

WHAT'S NEARBY

NEARBY TOWNS

With a population of more than 100,000, **Ventura** is the main gateway to Channel Islands National Park. It's a classic California beach town filled with interesting restaurants, a wide range of accommodations, and miles of clean, white beaches. South of Ventura is **Oxnard,** a community of 162,000 boasting a busy harbor and uncrowded beaches. Known for its Spanish ambience, **Santa Barbara** has a beautiful waterfront set against a backdrop of towering mountains—plus glistening palm-lined beaches, whitewashed adobe structures with red-tile roofs, and plenty of genteel charm.

VISITOR INFORMATION

Oxnard Convention & Visitors Bureau ⊠ *1000 Town Center Dr. #130., Oxnard* ☎ *805/385–7545 or 800/269–6273* ⊕ *www.visitoxnard.com.* **Santa Barbara Conference & Visitors Bureau and Film Commission** ⊠ *1601 Anacapa St., Santa Barbara* ☎ *805/966–9222 or 800/676–1266* ⊕ *www.santabarbaraca. com.* **Ventura Visitors & Convention Bureau** ⊠ *101 S. California St., Ventura* ☎ *805/648–2075 or 800/483–6214* ⊕ *www.ventura-usa.com.*

NEARBY ATTRACTIONS

Mission San Buenaventura. The ninth of the 21 California missions, Mission San Buenaventura was established in 1872 but burned to the ground in the 1790s. It was rebuilt and rededicated in 1809. A self-guided tour takes you through a small museum, a quiet courtyard, and a chapel with 250-year-old paintings. ⊠ *211 E. Main St., Ventura* ☎ *805/643–4318* ⊕ *www.sanbuenaventuramission.org* ⌨ *$2* ☉ *Weekdays 10–5, Sat. 9–5, Sun. 10–4.*

Fodor'sChoice ★   **Mission Santa Barbara.** Widely referred to as the "Queen of Missions," this is one of the most beautiful and frequently photographed buildings in coastal California. ⊠ *2201 Laguna St., Santa Barbara* ☎ *805/682–4149 or 805/682–4713* ⊕ *www.santabarbaramission.org* ▣ *$5* ☉ *Daily 9–4:30.*

☾ **Santa Barbara Museum of Natural History.** The gigantic skeleton of a blue whale greets you at the entrance of this complex, where major draws include a planetarium, space-related activities and exhibits, a gem and mineral display, and dioramas illustrating Chumash Indian history and culture; many exhibits have interactive components. ⊠ *2559 Puesta del Sol Rd., Santa Barbara* ☎ *805/682–4711* ⊕ *www.sbnature.org* ▣ *$10* ☉ *Daily 10–5.*

Stearns Wharf. Built in 1872, historic Stearns Wharf is Santa Barbara's most visited landmark. Expansive views of the mountains, cityscape, and harbor unfold from every vantage point on the three-block-long pier, which has shops and restaurants. ⊠ *Cabrillo Blvd. at the foot of State St., Santa Barbara* ☎ *805/897–2683 or 805/564–5531.*

14

Ventura Oceanfront. The city of San Buenaventura (*aka* Ventura) edges 4 mi of gorgeous coastline, stretching from the county fairgrounds at the northern border through San Buenaventura State Beach down to Ventura Harbor in the south. The main attraction here is the San Buenaventura City Pier, a historic landmark built in 1872 and restored in 1993. Stroll to the end of the pier and sit on a bench to take in the spectacular ocean, mountain, and island views. Surfers rip the waves just north of the pier, and sunbathers relax on white-sand beaches on either side. The 1-mi-long promenade and the Omer Rains Bike Trail north of the pier attract scores of joggers, surrey cyclers, and bikers throughout the year. ⊠ *Hub at end of California St. at ocean's edge, Ventura* ☎ *805/648–2075 or 800/333–2989* ⊕ *www.ventura-usa.com* ▣ *Free (except parking areas at state beaches).*

WHERE TO EAT AND STAY

ABOUT THE RESTAURANTS

Out on the islands, you won't have any trouble deciding where to dine—there are no restaurants, no snack bars, and in some cases, no potable water. Pack a fancy picnic or a simple sandwich—and don't forget it in your car or hotel room unless you want to starve. For a quick meal before or after your island trip, each of the harbors has a number of decent eateries nearby.

Back on the mainland, though, it's a dining gold mine. Santa Barbara has a longstanding reputation for culinary excellence, and a "foodie" renaissance in recent years has transformed Ventura into a dining destination—with dozens of new restaurants touting nouvelle cuisine made with organic produce and meats. Fresh seafood is a standout, whether it's prepared simply in wharf-side hangouts or incorporated into sophisticated bistro menus. Dining attire is generally casual, though slightly dressy casual wear is the custom at pricier restaurants.

ABOUT THE HOTELS

It's easy to choose where to stay in the park—your only option is sleeping in your tent in a no-frills campground. If you hanker for more creature comforts, you can splurge on a bunk and meals on a park concessionaire dive boat.

There's a huge range of lodging options on the mainland, from seaside camping to posh international resorts. The most affordable options are in Oxnard, Ventura, and Carpinteria, a small seaside community between Santa Barbara and Ventura. Despite rates that range from pricey to downright shocking, Santa Barbara's numerous hotels and bed-and-breakfasts attract thousands of patrons year-round. Wherever you stay, be sure to make reservations for the summer and holiday weekends (especially Memorial Day, Labor Day, and Thanksgiving) well ahead of time; it's not unusual for coastal accommodations to fill completely during these busy times. Also be aware that some hotels double their rates during festivals and other events.

ABOUT THE CAMPGROUNDS

Camping is the best way to experience the natural beauty and isolation of Channel Islands National Park. Unrestricted by tour schedules, you have plenty of time to explore mountain trails, snorkel in the kelp forests, or kayak into sea caves. Campsites are primitive, with no water (except on Santa Rosa and Santa Cruz) or electricity. Campfires are not allowed on the islands, though you may use enclosed camp stoves. Use the bear boxes for storing your food. You must carry all your gear and pack out all trash. Campers must arrange transportation to the islands before reserving a campsite (and yes, park personnel do check). You can get specifics on each campground and reserve a campsite ($15 per night) by contacting the **National Park Service Reservation System** (☎ *877/444–6777* ⊕ *www.recreation.gov*) up to six months in advance.

WHERE TO EAT

IN THE PARK

Picnic Areas. Picnic tables are available on all the islands except San Miguel. You can also picnic on some of the beaches of Santa Cruz, Santa Rosa, and San Miguel; be aware that high winds are always a possibility on Santa Rosa and San Miguel.

OUTSIDE THE PARK

OXNARD

$–$$

MEXICAN

✕ **Cabo Seafood Grill and Cantina.** A crowd of locals in the know gathers at this lively restaurant and bar close to downtown Oxnard for south of the border seafood specialties served with fresh handmade tortillas. The rainbow-hued dining rooms and patio are casual and cheery. If you're not a seafood fan, try the carne asada (marinated strips of beef) or one of the large combination plates. ⊠ *1041 S. Oxnard Blvd., Oxnard* ☎ *805/487–6933* ▱ *AE, D, DC, MC, V.*

$$$

AMERICAN

✕ **The Whale's Tail.** This popular seafood house in Channel Islands Harbor includes a casual upstairs shellfish bar with indoor/outdoor seating and a more formal main dining room downstairs; practically all the tables let in waterfront views. Fresh fish is delivered to the restaurant's dock daily. ⊠ *3950 Bluefin Circle, Oxnard* ☎ *805/985–2511* ⌕ *Reservations essential* ▱ *AE, MC, V.*

SANTA BARBARA

$$
SEAFOOD
✕ **Brophy Bros.** The outdoor tables at this casual harborside restaurant in Santa Barbara have perfect views of the marina and mountains. The staff serves enormous, exceptionally fresh fish dishes—don't miss the seafood salad and chowder. They'll give you a pager if there's a long wait so you can stroll along the waterfront until your table is ready. This place is hugely popular—be aware that it can be crowded and loud, especially on weekend evenings. ⊠ *119 Harbor Way, Santa Barbara* ☎ *805/966–4418* ▭ *AE, MC, V.*

$
MEXICAN
★
✕ **La Super-Rica Taqueria.** Praised by Julia Child, this food stand with a patio on the east side of Santa Barbara serves some of the spiciest and most authentic Mexican dishes between Los Angeles and San Francisco. Fans drive for miles to fill up on the soft tacos served with yummy spicy or mild sauces and legendary beans. Three specials are offered each day. Portions are on the small side, so order several dishes and share. ⊠ *622 N. Milpas, at Alphonse St., Santa Barbara* ☎ *805/963–4940* ▭ *No credit cards.* ⊘ *Closed Wed.*

VENTURA

$
SEAFOOD
✕ **Andria's Seafood.** The specialties at this casual, family-oriented restaurant in Ventura Harbor Village are fresh fish-and-chips and homemade clam chowder. After placing your order at the counter, you can sit outside on the patio and enjoy the view of the harbor and marina. ⊠ *1449 Spinnaker Dr., Suite A, Ventura* ☎ *805/654–0546* ▭ *MC, V.*

$$$
AMERICAN
✕ **Brooks.** Innovative chef Andy Brooks and his wife, Jayme—whose grandfather co-owned the famous Chi Chi supper club in Palm Springs in the 1960s—serve some of Ventura's finest meals in a slick, contemporary downtown dining room. The fare centers around seasonal, mostly local, organic ingredients and features nightly three- and five-course tasting menus, which might include *limoncello* steamed mussels, cornmeal fried oysters, or prime rib with smoked cheddar grits. Ask for the romaine salad dressed in the legendary Chi Chi creamy garlic dressing. Live music and drinks attract a loyal following after 9 PM on weekends. ⊠ *545 E. Thompson Blvd., Ventura* ☎ *805/652–7070* ▭ *AE, D, MC, V* ⊘ *Closed Mon. No lunch Sat.–Wed.*

$$
SEAFOOD
✕ **Brophy Bros.** The Ventura outpost of the wildly popular Santa Barbara restaurant serves the same fresh-seafood-oriented meals in a spacious second-story setting overlooking the harbor. Feast on everything from fish-and-chips and crab cakes to chowder and delectable fish—often straight from the boats moored below. ⊠ *1559 Spinnaker Dr., in Ventura Harbor Village, Ventura* ☎ *805/639–0865* ⌂ *Reservations not accepted* ▭ *AE, MC, V.*

WHERE TO STAY

IN THE PARK

CAMPING
$
△ **Del Norte Campground.** This remote campground on Santa Cruz, the newest on the islands, offers backpackers sweeping ocean views from its 1,500-foot perch. It's accessed via a 3½-mi hike through a series of canyons and ridges. Bear boxes are on-site. **Pros:** serene; away from busy main campground; fantastic views. **Cons:** tiny; long hike to access

site; very rustic. ✉ *Scorpion Beach landing* ☎ *877/444–6777* ⊕ *www. recreation.gov* 🏕 *4 tent sites* ♿ *Pit toilets, picnic tables* ▭ *D, MC, V.*

$ 🏕 **East Anacapa Campground.** You need to walk ½ mi and ascend more than 150 steps to reach this open, treeless camping area above Cathedral Cove. Bear boxes are on-site. **Pros:** some of the best views in the park; near lighthouse; easy access from mainland. **Cons:** small; 150 steps to campground; nesting gulls can be noisy. ✉ *East Anacapa landing* ☎ *877/444–6777* ⊕ *www.recreation.gov* 🏕 *7 tent sites* ♿ *Pit toilets, picnic tables, ranger station* ▭ *D, MC, V.*

$ 🏕 **San Miguel Campground.** Accessed by a steep 1½-mi hike across the beach and through a lush canyon, this campground is on the site of the Lester Ranch; the Cabrillo Monument is nearby. Be aware that strong winds and thick fog are common here. Bear boxes are on-site. **Pros:** fantastic backpacking experience; ranger-escorted hikes to largest pinniped rookery in the world. **Cons:** can be windy; sites are primitive; infrequent transportation options. ✉ *Cuyler Harbor landing* ☎ *877/444–6777* ⊕ *www.recreation.gov* 🏕 *9 tent sites* ♿ *Pit toilets, picnic tables, ranger station, swimming (ocean)* ▭ *D, MC, V.*

$ 🏕 **Santa Barbara Campground.** This seldom-visited campground perched on a cliff above Landing Cove is reached via a challenging ½-mi uphill climb. Three-day trips are permitted. **Pros:** far from civilization; gorgeous vistas; snorkel with seals and sea lions. Bear boxes are on-site. **Cons:** tiny island with few trails; sometimes closed for pelican nesting. ✉ *Landing Cove* ☎ *877/444–6777* ⊕ *www.recreation.gov* 🏕 *10 tent sites* ♿ *Pit toilets, picnic tables, ranger station, swimming (ocean)* ▭ *D, MC, V.*

$ 🏕 **Santa Cruz Scorpion Campground.** In a grove of eucalyptus trees, ★ this campground is near the historic buildings of Scorpion Ranch. It's accessed via an easy, ½-mi, flat trail from Scorpion Beach landing. **Pros:** sheltered site in canyon; running water; easy access to many hiking trails. **Cons:** one of busiest campgrounds; wild animals sometimes raid food. Bear boxes are on-site. ✉ *Scorpion Beach landing* ☎ *877/444–6777* ⊕ *www.recreation.gov* 🏕 *40 tent sites* ♿ *Pit toilets, drinking water, picnic tables, swimming (ocean)* ▭ *D, MC, V.*

$ 🏕 **Santa Rosa Campground.** Backcountry beach camping for kayakers is available on this island; it's a 1½-mi flat walk to the campground. There's a spectacular view of Santa Cruz Island across the water. There's easy access to fantastic hiking trails, swimming in the nearby ocean, and bathrooms are nice. Bear boxes are on site. **Pros:** near gorgeous white-sand beach; running water. **Cons:** can be windy; must carry equipment a long distance. ✉ *Bechers Bay landing* ☎ *877/444–6777* ⊕ *www. recreation.gov* 🏕 *15 tent sites* ♿ *Pit toilets, drinking water, showers (cold), picnic tables, swimming (ocean)* ▭ *D, MC, V.*

OUTSIDE THE PARK
OXNARD

$$–$$$ 🏨 **Embassy Suites Mandalay Beach Resort.** Tropical gardens, small waterfalls, and sprawling pool areas surround this Spanish-Mediterranean complex, set on eight acres of white-sand beach north of Channel Islands Harbor. The two- and three-room suites all have marble baths, and rates include complimentary cooked-to-order breakfasts. Capistrano's restaurant serves California cuisine in a garden courtyard and Polynesian-inspired dining

rooms (don't miss the Sunday brunch). **Pros:** on the beach, just a mile to island transportation boats; family friendly. **Cons:** 4 mi from island transportation from Ventura Harbor; no Wi-Fi in rooms; no full kitchens. ⊠ *2101 Mandalay Beach Rd., Oxnard* ☎ *805/984–2500 or 800/362–2779* ⊕ *www.embassymandalay.com* ⤵ *248 suites* ⟐ *In-room: refrigerator (some), Internet. In-hotel: restaurant, room service, bar, tennis court, pool, gym, beachfront, water sports, bicycles, laundry facilities, laundry service, Internet terminal, Wi-Fi* ⊟ *AE, D, DC, MC, V* ⦿ *BP.*

SANTA BARBARA

$$$ 🏨 **Franciscan Inn.** Part of this Spanish-Mediterranean motel, a block from the harbor and West Beach, dates back to the 1920s. The friendly staff and range of cheery, spacious country-themed rooms—from singles to mini- and family suites—make this a good choice for families. **Pros:** walking distance from waterfront and harbor; family-friendly; great value. **Cons:** busy lobby; pool can be crowded. ⊠ *109 Bath St., Santa Barbara* ☎ *805/963–8845* ⊕ *www.franciscaninn.com* ⤵ *48 rooms, 5 suites* ⟐ *In-room: kitchen (some), refrigerator (some). In-hotel: pool, laundry facilities* ⊟ *AE, DC, MC, V* ⦿ *CP.*

$$$$ 🏨 **San Ysidro Ranch.** John and Jackie Kennedy spent their honeymoon
★ at this romantic hideaway, and Oprah sends her out-of-town guests here. Guest cottages are scattered among groves of orange trees and flower beds; all have down comforters and fireplaces, and many have private outdoor spas—one even has its own pool. Hiking trails crisscross 500 acres of open space surrounding the property, and the resort's Stonehouse Restaurant and Plow & Angel Bistro are Santa Barbara institutions. Note that there is a two-night minimum stay on weekends (three nights for holiday weekends). **Pros:** ultimate privacy; surrounded by nature; pet-friendly. **Cons:** very expensive; too remote for some. ⊠ *900 San Ysidro La., Montecito* ☎ *805/565–1700 or 800/368–6788* ⊕ *www.sanysidroranch.com* ⤵ *23 rooms, 4 suites, 14 cottages* ⟐ *In-room: refrigerator, DVD, Internet, Wi-Fi. In-hotel: 2 restaurants, room service, bar, pool, gym, some pets allowed* ⊟ *AE, MC, V.*

VENTURA

$$ 🏨 **Four Points by Sheraton Ventura Harbor.** The spacious, contemporary rooms here are still gleaming from a total renovation that was completed in 2009. An on-site restaurant and a slew of amenities make this 17-acre property (which includes sister hotel Holiday Inn Express) a popular and practical choice for Channel Island visitors. The hotel sits on the edge of the harbor, just a few minutes drive from the national park visitor center and concessionaire boat launches. All of the nautical-themed rooms have flat-screen TVs; most have private patios or balconies. (For the best views, request a second-floor marina-facing balcony room.) **Pros:** close to island transportation; mostly quiet; short drive or bus ride to historic downtown Ventura. **Cons:** not in the heart of downtown; noisy seagulls sometimes congregate nearby. ⊠ *1050 Schooner Dr., Ventura* ☎ *805/658–1212* ⊕ *www.fourpoints.com/ventura* ⤵ *102 rooms, 4 suites* ⟐ *In-room: refrigerator, Wi-Fi. In-hotel: restaurant, room service, bar, pool, gym, laundry service, Internet terminal, Wi-Fi, some pets allowed* ⊟ *AE, D, DC, MC, V* ⦿ *BP.*

14

$$–$$$ ⊡ **Ventura Beach Marriott.** Spacious, contemporary rooms and a peaceful location just steps from San Buenaventura State Beach—plus easy access to historic downtown Ventura's arts and culture district—make this Marriott a popular choice for travelers who want to explore Ventura before and after an island excursion. It's a joy to hang out in the public areas: the marble-tiled lobby doubles as an art gallery, with rotating exhibits of works produced by local photography students, and waterfalls, lush gardens, and a koi pond with turtles contribute to the tropical theme indoors and out. Ask for a room with a private balcony. **Pros:** walk to beach and biking/jogging trails; a block from historic pier; great value for location. **Cons:** close to highway; near busy intersection. ⊠ *2055 E. Harbor Blvd., Ventura* ☎ *805/643–6000 or 800/228–9290* ⊕ *www.marriottventurabeach.com* ⤺ *272 rooms, 12 suites* ♿ *In-room: Internet. In-hotel: restaurant, room service, bar, pool, gym, bicycles, laundry facilities, laundry service, Internet terminal, Wi-Fi, parking (fee), some pets allowed, laundry service, Internet terminal, Wi-Fi, some pets allowed* ▭ *AE, D, DC, MC, V* ⎜◉⎜ *BP.*

Crater Lake National Park

WORD OF MOUTH

"After arriving the evening before amidst fog and snow, we awoke to the incredible blue lake and fresh snow."
— photo by William A. McConnell, Fodors.com member

WELCOME TO CRATER LAKE

TOP REASONS TO GO

★ **The lake:** Cruise inside the caldera basin and gaze into the extraordinary sapphire blue water of the country's deepest lake.

★ **Native land:** Enjoy the rare luxury of interacting with totally unspoiled terrain.

★ **The night sky:** Billions of stars glisten in the pitch-black darkness of an unpolluted sky.

★ **Splendid hikes:** Accessible trails spool off the main roads and wind past colorful bursts of wildflowers and cascading waterfalls.

★ **Camping at its best:** Pitch a tent or pull up a motor home at Mazama Campground, a beautifully situated, guest-friendly, and well-maintained campground.

1 Crater Lake. The focal point of the park, this non-recreational, scenic destination is known for its deep blue hue.

2 Wizard Island. Visitors can take boat rides to this protruding landmass rising from the western section of Crater Lake; it's a great place for a hike or a picnic.

3 Mazama Village. This is your best bet for stocking up on snacks, beverages, and fuel in the park; it's about 5 mi from Rim Drive.

4 Cleetwood Cove Trail. The only safe, designated trail to hike down the caldera and reach the lake's edge is on the rim's north side off Rim Drive.

GETTING ORIENTED

Crater Lake National Park covers 183,224 acres. Located in southern Oregon less than 100 mi from the California border, it's surrounded by several Cascade Range forests, including the Winema and Rogue River national forests. Of the nearby towns, Medford is closest at 59 mi southwest of the park; Ashland, to the southwest, and Klamath Falls, to the south, are each approximately 90 mi from the lake, with Roseburg the farthest away at 119 mi northwest of the park.

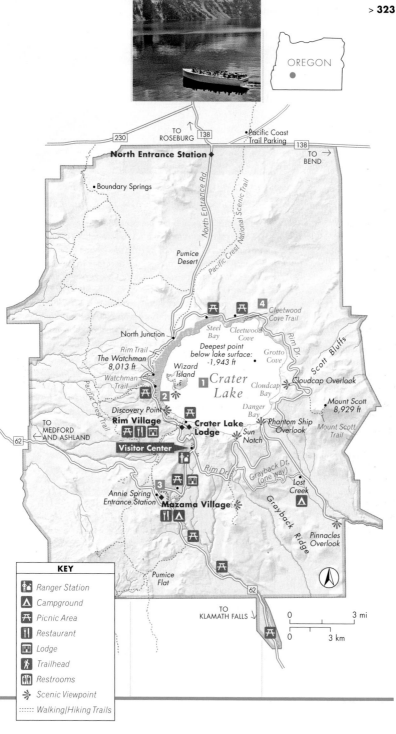

OREGON

TO
ROSEBURG
230
138
•Pacific Coast
Trail Parking
138
TO →
BEND

North Entrance Station ◆

•Boundary Springs

North Entrance Rd.

Pacific Crest National Scenic Trail

Pumice
Desert

Steel
Bay
Cleetwood
Cove
4 Cleetwood
Cove Trail

North Junction

Rim Trail
The Watchman
8,013 ft
Wizard
Island
1
Crater
Lake

Deepest point
below lake surface:
-1,943 ft

Grotto
Cove

Rim Dr.

Scott Bluffs

Watchman
Trail

2

Cloudcap
Bay

Cloudcap Overlook

Mount Scott
8,929 ft

Discovery Point

Rim Village

TO
MEDFORD
AND ASHLAND
62

Crater Lake
Lodge

Danger
Bay

Phantom Ship
Overlook

Mount Scott
Trail

Sun
Notch

Visitor Center

Pacific Crest Trail

3

Rim Dr.

Grayback Dr.
(one way)

Lost
Creek

Annie Spring
Entrance Station

Mazama Village

Grayback
Ridge

Pinnacles
Overlook

Pumice
Flat

62

TO
KLAMATH FALLS

0   3 mi

0   3 km

KEY

🧍 *Ranger Station*
△ *Campground*
🏕 *Picnic Area*
🍴 *Restaurant*
🏛 *Lodge*
🚶 *Trailhead*
🚻 *Restrooms*
➻ *Scenic Viewpoint*
⋯⋯ *Walking/Hiking Trails*

CRATER LAKE PLANNER

When to Go

The park's high season is July and August. September and early October tend to draw smaller crowds. From October through June, the entire park virtually closes due to heavy snowfall. The road is kept open just to the rim in winter, except during severe weather.

Getting Here and Around

Most of the park is only accessible in late June–early July through mid-October. The rest of the year, snow blocks all park roadways and entrances except Highway 62 and the access road to Rim Village from Mazama Village. Rim Drive is typically closed because of heavy snowfall from mid-October to mid-July, and you could encounter icy conditions any month of the year, particularly in early morning.

AVG. HIGH/LOW TEMPS.

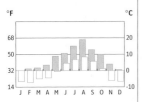

Flora and Fauna

Two primary types of fish swim beneath the surface of Crater Lake: kokanee salmon and rainbow trout. It's estimated that hundreds of thousands of kokanee inhabit the lake, but since boating and recreational access is so limited they elude many would-be sportsman. Kokanees average about 8 inches in length, but they can grow to nearly 18 inches. Rainbow trout are larger than the kokanee but are less abundant in Crater Lake. Trout—including bull, Eastern brook, rainbow, and German brown—swim in the park's many streams and rivers; they usually remain elusive because these waterways flow near inaccessibly steep canyons.

Remote canyons shelter the park's elk and deer populations, which can sometimes be seen at dusk and dawn feeding at forest's edge. Black bears and pine martens—cousins of the short-tailed weasel—also call Crater Lake home. Birds such as hairy woodpeckers, California gulls, red-tailed hawks, and great horned owls are more commonly seen in summer in forests below the lake.

Good Reads

■ *Crater Lake National Park: A Global Treasure,* by former park rangers Ann and Myron Sutton, celebrates the park's first 100 years with stunning photography, charts, and drawings.

■ Ron Warfield's *A Guide to Crater Lake National Park and The Mountain That Used to Be* gives a useful and lushly illustrated overview of Crater Lake's history and physical features.

■ The National Park Service uses Stephen Harris's *Fire Mountains of the West* in its ranger training; the detailed handbook covers Cascade Range geology.

■ *Wildflowers of the Olympics and Cascades,* by Charles Stewart, is an easy-to-use guide to the area's flora and fauna.

By Christine Vovakes

The pure, crystalline blue of Crater Lake astounds visitors at first sight. More than 5 mi wide and ringed by cliffs almost 2,000 feet high, the lake was created approximately 7,700 years ago, following Mt. Mazama's fiery explosion. Days after the eruption, the mountain collapsed on an underground chamber emptied of lava. Rain and snowmelt filled the caldera, creating a sapphire-blue lake so clear that sunlight penetrates to a depth of 400 feet (the lake's depth is 1,943 feet). Today it's both the clearest and deepest lake in the United States—and the seventh deepest in the world.

15

PARK ESSENTIALS

ACCESSIBILITY

All the overlooks along Rim Drive are accessible to those with impaired mobility, as are Crater Lake Lodge, the facilities at Rim Village, and Steel Information Center. A half-dozen accessible campsites are available at Mazama Campground.

ADMISSION FEES AND PERMITS

Admission to the park is $10 per vehicle, good for seven days. Backcountry campers and hikers must obtain a free wilderness permit at Rim Visitor Center or Steel Information Center for all overnight trips.

ADMISSION HOURS

Crater Lake National Park is open 24 hours a day year-round; however, snow closes most park roadways October through June. Lodging and dining facilities usually are open from late May to mid-October. The park is located in the Pacific Time Zone.

ATMS/BANKS

There's an ATM at the Mazama Camper Store near the park's Annie Spring entrance station. Look for banks in nearby towns.

CRATER LAKE IN ONE DAY

Begin at **Steel Information Center**, where interpretive displays and a short video introduce you to the story of the lake's formation and its unique characteristics. Then begin your circumnavigation of the crater's rim by heading northeast on **Rim Drive**, allowing an hour to stop at overlooks—check out the Phantom Ship rock formation in the lake—before you reach **Cleetwood Cove Trail** trailhead, the only safe and legal access to the lake. Hike down the trail to reach the dock, and hop aboard one of the **tour boats** for an almost-two-hour tour around the lake. If you have time, add on a trip to **Wizard Island** for a picnic lunch.

Back on Rim Drive, continue around the lake, stopping at the **Watchman Trail** for a short but steep hike to this peak above the rim, which affords not only a splendid view of the lake, but a broad vista of the surrounding southern Cascades. Wind up your visit at **Crater Lake Lodge**—allow time to wander the lobby of the 1915 structure perched on the rim. Dinner at the lodge restaurant, overlooking the lake and the Cascade sunset, caps the day.

CELL-PHONE RECEPTION
Cell phone reception in the park is unreliable. You'll find public telephones at Steel Information Center, Rim Village, Crater Lake Lodge, and the Mazama Village complex.

PARK CONTACT INFORMATION
Crater Lake National Park ⌂ *P.O. Box 7, Crater Lake, OR 97604* ☎ *541/594–3000* ⊕ *www.nps.gov/crla.*

SCENIC DRIVE

★ **Rim Drive.** The 33-mi loop around the lake is the main scenic route, affording views of the lake and its cliffs from every conceivable angle. The drive alone takes up to two hours; frequent stops at overlooks and short hikes can easily stretch this to a half day. Be aware that Rim Drive is typically closed due to heavy snowfall from mid-October to mid-June, and icy conditions can be encountered any month of the year, particularly in early morning. ⊠ *Rim Dr. leads from Annie Spring entrance station to Rim Village, where the drive circles around the rim; it's about 7 mi from the entrance station to Rim Village. To get to Rim Dr. from the park's north entrance, access the north entrance road via either Rte. 230 or Hwy. 138, and follow it for about 10 mi.*

WHAT TO SEE

For most visitors, the star attractions of Crater Lake are the lake itself and the breathtakingly situated Crater Lake Lodge. Other park highlights include the natural, unspoiled beauty of the forest and the geological marvels that you can access along the 33-mi Rim Drive.

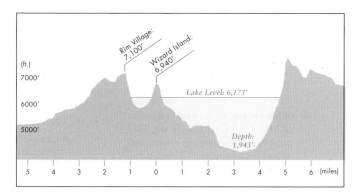

HISTORIC SITE

Fodor's Choice ★ **Crater Lake Lodge.** First built in 1915, this classic log-and-stone structure still boasts the original lodgepole-pine pillars, beams, and stone fireplaces. The lobby, fondly referred to as the Great Hall, serves as a warm, welcoming gathering place where you can play games, socialize with a cocktail, or gaze out of the many windows to view spectacular sunrises and sunsets by a crackling fire. ⊠ *Rim Village, just east of Rim Visitor Center.*

SCENIC STOPS

Cloudcap Overlook. The highest road-access overlook on the Crater Lake rim, Cloudcap has a westward view across the lake to Wizard Island and an eastward view of Mt. Scott, the volcanic cone that is the park's highest point, just 2 mi away. ⊠ *2 mi off Rim Dr., 13 mi northeast of Steel Information Center.*

Discovery Point. This overlook marks the spot at which prospectors first spied the lake in 1853. Wizard Island is just northeast, close to shore. ⊠ *Rim Dr., 1½ mi north of Rim Village.*

Mazama Village. In summer a campground, motor inn, amphitheater, gas station, post office, and small store are open here. ⊠ *Mazama Village Rd., off Hwy. 62, near Annie Spring entrance station* ☎ 541/594–2255 or 888/774–2728 ⊕ *www.nps.gov/crla* ☉ *June–Sept., daily 8–6.*

Phantom Ship Overlook. From this point you can get a close look at Phantom Ship, a rock formation that resembles a schooner with furled masts, and looks ghostly in fog. ⊠ *Rim Dr., 7 mi northeast of Steel Information Center.*

Pinnacles Overlook. Ascending from the banks of Sand and Wheeler creeks, unearthly spires of eroded ash resemble the peaks of fairy-tale castles. Once upon a time, the road continued east to a former entrance. A path now replaces the old road and follows the rim of Sand Creek (affording more views of pinnacles) to where the entrance arch still stands. ⊠ *5 mi northeast of Steel Information Center, then 2 mi east on Pinnacles Spur Rd.*

Sun Notch. It's a moderate ¼-mi hike through wildflowers and dry meadow to this overlook, which has views of Crater Lake and Phantom Ship. Mind the cliff edges. ⊠ *Rim Dr., 4.4 mi east of Steel Information Center, east side of the lake.*

★ **Wizard Island.** To get here you've got to hike down Cleetwood Cove Trail (and back up upon your return) and board the tour boat (⇨ *Educational Offerings*) for a 1¾-hour ride. Bring a picnic. If you're in top shape take the very strenuous 2-mi hike to Wizard Summit that leads to a path around the 90-foot deep crater at the top. A more moderate hike is the 1.8-mi trek on a rocky trail along the shore of the island. ⊠ *Via Cleetwood Cove Trail to the Wizard Island dock* ☎ *541/594–2255 or 888/774–2728* ⊕ *www.craterlakelodges.com* ⊗ *Late June–mid-Sept., daily.*

VISITOR CENTERS

Rim Visitor Center. In summer you can obtain park information here, take a ranger-led tour, or stop into the nearby Sinnott Memorial, with a small museum and a 900-foot view down to the lake's surface. In winter, snowshoe walks are offered on weekends and holidays. The Rim Village Gift Store and cafeteria are the only services open in winter. ⊠ *Rim Dr. on the south side of the lake, 7 mi north of Annie Spring entrance station* ☎ *541/594–3090* ⊕ *www.nps.gov/crla* ⊗ *Late May–mid-Sept., daily 9:30–5.*

Steel Information Center. The information center is part of the park's headquarters; you'll find restrooms and a first-aid station here. There's also a small post office and a shop that sells books, maps, and postcards. In the auditorium, an ongoing 18-minute film, *The Mirror of Heaven,* describes Crater Lake's formation. ⊠ *Rim Dr., 4 mi north of Annie Spring entrance station* ☎ *541/594–3100* ⊕ *www.nps.gov/crla* ⊗ *Mid-Apr.–early Nov., daily 9–5; early Nov.–mid-Apr., daily 10–4.*

SPORTS AND THE OUTDOORS

FISHING

Fishing is allowed in the lake, but you may find the experience frustrating—in such a massive body of water, the problem is finding the fish. Try your luck near the Cleetwood Cove boat dock, or take poles on the boat tour and fish off Wizard Island. Rainbow trout and kokanee salmon lurk in Crater Lake's aquamarine depths, and some grow to enormous sizes. You don't need a state fishing license, but to protect the lake's pristine waters use only artificial bait as opposed to live worms. Private boats are prohibited on the lake.

HIKING
EASY

Castle Crest Wildflower Trail. The 1.4-mi, creek-side loop in the upper part of Munson Valley is one of the park's flatter and less demanding hikes. Wildflowers burst into full bloom here in July. ⊠ *Across the street from Steel Information Center parking lot, Rim Dr.*

Godfrey Glen Trail. This 1-mi loop trail is an easy stroll through an old-growth forest with canyon views. Its dirt path is accessible to wheelchairs with assistance. ⊠ *2.4 mi south of Steel Information Center.*

15

MODERATE

Annie Creek Canyon Trail. This somewhat strenuous 1.7-mi hike loops through a deep stream-cut canyon, providing views of the narrow cleft scarred by volcanic activity. This is a good spot to look for flowers and deer. ⊠ *Mazama Campground, Mazama Village Rd., near Annie Spring entrance station.*

Boundary Springs Trail. If you feel like sleuthing, take this moderate 5-mi round-trip hike to the headwaters of the Rogue River. The trail isn't always well marked, so a detailed trail guide is necessary. You'll see streams, forests, and wildflowers along the way before discovering Boundary Springs pouring out of the side of a low ridge. ⊠ *Pullout on Hwy. 230, near milepost 19, about 5 mi west of the junction with Hwy. 138.*

The Watchman Trail. This is the best short hike in the park. Though it's less than a mile each way, the trail climbs more than 400 feet—not counting the steps up to the actual lookout, which has great views of Wizard Island and the lake. ⊠ *Watchman Overlook, 3.8 mi northwest of Rim Village on Rim Dr., west side of the lake.*

DIFFICULT

Cleetwood Cove Trail. This strenuous 2.2-mi round-trip hike descends 700 feet down nearly vertical cliffs along the lake to the boat dock. ⊠ *Cleetwood Cove trailhead, Rim Dr., 11 mi north of Rim Village, north side of the lake.*

Fodor's Choice ★ **Mt. Scott Trail.** This 5-mi round-trip trail takes you to the park's highest point—the top of Mt. Scott, the oldest volcanic cone of Mt. Mazama, at 8,929 feet. It will take the average hiker 90 minutes to make the steep uphill trek—and nearly 60 minutes to get down. The trail starts at an elevation of about 7,450 feet, so the climb is not extreme but does get steep in spots. Views of the lake and the broad Klamath Basin are spectacular. ⊠ *14 mi east of Steel Information Center on Rim Dr., east side of the lake, across from the road to Cloudcap Overlook.*

Pacific Crest Trail. You can hike a portion of the Pacific Crest Trail, which extends from Mexico to Canada and winds through the park for 33 mi. For this prime backcountry experience, catch the trail off Highway 138 about a mile east of the north entrance road, where it heads toward the west rim of the lake and circles it for about 6 mi, then descends down Dutton Creek to the Mazama Village area. An online brochure offers further details. ⊠ *Pacific Crest Trail parking lot, north access road off Hwy. 138, 2 mi east of the Hwy. 138–north entrance road junction* ⊕ *www.nps. gov/crla/brochures/pct.htm.*

FAMILY PICKS

Boat Tour. Climb aboard for a closeup view of Crater Lake.

Annie Creek Restaurant. Chow down on a picnic feast at this eatery's outdoor seating area.

Crater Lake Lodge. Tour this historic inn.

EDUCATIONAL OFFERINGS

RANGER PROGRAMS

Boat Tours. The most extensively used guided tours in Crater Lake are on the water, aboard launches that carry 49 passengers on a one-hour, 45-minute tour accompanied by a ranger. The boats circle the lake; two of the seven daily boats stop at Wizard Island, where you can get off and re-board a minimum of three hours later, or six hours later if you catch the morning boat. The first tour leaves the dock at 10 AM; the last departs at 3 PM. To get to the dock you must hike down Cleetwood Cove Trail, a strenuous 1.1-mi walk that drops 700 feet; only those in excellent physical shape should attempt the hike. Bring adequate water with you. Purchase boat tour tickets at the top of the trail. Restrooms are available at the top and bottom of the trail. ⊠ *Cleetwood Cove Trail, off Rim Dr., 10 mi north of Rim Village on the north side of the lake* 🕾 *541/594–2255 or 888/774–2728* ⊕ *www.craterlakelodges.com* 🖾 *$26; $36 with island drop-off* ☺ *Late June–mid-Sept., daily.*

Junior Ranger Program. Junior Ranger booklets and badges are available at Steel Information Center and Rim Visitor Center. 🕾 *541/594–3090.*

WHAT'S NEARBY

NEARBY TOWNS

Three small cities serve as gateways to Crater Lake—each a 2- to 2½-hour drive to the park. Klamath Lake, the largest freshwater lake in Oregon, is anchored at its south end by the city of **Klamath Falls,** population 21,000. Boasting 300 days of sunshine per year, Klamath Falls is home to acres of parks and marinas from which to enjoy water sports and bird-watching. **Roseburg's** location at the west edge of the southern Cascades led to its status as a timber-industry center—still the heart of the town's economy—but its site along the Umpqua River has drawn fishermen here for years. **Ashland,** one of the premier destinations in the Northwest, is a charming small city set in the foothills of the Siskiyou Mountains. The foundation of the city's appeal is its famed Oregon Shakespeare Festival and its dozens of fine small inns, shops, and restaurants.

VISITOR INFORMATION
Ashland Chamber of Commerce
⊠ *110 E. Main St., Ashland* ☎ *541/482–3486* ⊕ *www.ashlandchamber.com.*
Discover Klamath Visitor and Convention Bureau ⊠ *125 W. Main St., Klamath Falls* ☎ *541/882–1501 or 800/445–6728* ⊕ *www.discoverklamath.com.* **Klamath County Chamber of Commerce** ⊠ *203 Riverside Dr., Klamath Falls* ☎ *541/884–5193* ⊕ *www.klamath.org.* **Roseburg Visitors & Convention Bureau** ⊠ *410 S.E. Spruce St., Roseburg* ☎ *541/672–9731 or 800/444–9584* ⊕ *www.visitroseburg.com.*

FESTIVAL

More than 375,000 Bard-loving buffs descend on Ashland (90 mi from Crater Lake) for the annual **Oregon Shakespeare Festival**. Plays run from February to November in three theaters; peak season is July, August, and September. ☎ *541/482–4331.*

NEARBY ATTRACTIONS

15

Fodor's Choice ★ **Klamath Basin National Wildlife Refuge Complex.** As many as 1,000 bald eagles make Klamath Basin their rest stop, amounting to the largest wintering concentration of these birds in the contiguous United States. Located along the Pacific Flyway bird migration route, the vast acres of freshwater wetlands in the refuge complex serve as a stopover for nearly 1 million waterfowl in the fall. Any time of year is bird-watching season; more than 400 species of birds have been spotted in the Klamath Basin, 24 mi south of Klamath Falls on the California–Oregon border. For a leisurely ramble by car take the tour routes in the Lower Klamath and Tule Lake Refuges. ⊠ *4009 Hill Rd., 20 mi south of Klamath Falls via U.S. 97 or Rte. 39, Tulelake, CA* ☎ *530/667–2231* ⊕ *www.fws.gov/klamathbasinrefuges/* ⊠ *Free* ☉ *Weekdays 8–4:30, weekends 9–4.*

Fodor's Choice ★ **Oregon Caves National Monument.** Marble caves, large calcite formations, and huge underground rooms shape this rare adventure in geology. Above ground, the surrounding valley holds an old-growth forest with some of the state's largest trees. Guided cave tours take place on the hour in late spring and fall, and every half-hour in July and August. The 90-minute 0.6-mi tour is moderately strenuous with low passageways, twisting turns and more than 500 stairs; children must be at least 42 inches tall to go on the tour. The monument closes in winter. ⊠ *19000 Caves Hwy. (Rte. 46), 20 mi south of Hwy. 199, Cave Junction* ☎ *541/592–2100 Ext. 262* ⊕ *www.nps.gov/orca* ⊠ *$8.50* ☉ *Late Mar.–late May and mid-Oct.–late Nov., daily 10–4; late May–late June and early Sept.–mid-Oct., daily 9–5; late June–early Sept., daily 9–6.*

WHERE TO EAT AND STAY

ABOUT THE RESTAURANTS

There are a few casual eateries and convenience stores within the park. For fantastic upscale dining on the caldera's rim, head to the Crater Lake Lodge.

ABOUT THE HOTELS

Crater Lake's summer season is relatively brief, and the park's main lodge is generally booked with guest reservations a year in advance. If you don't snag one, check availability as your trip approaches—cancellations are always possible. Outside the park are options in Prospect, Klamath Falls, Roseburg, Medford, or Ashland.

ABOUT THE CAMPGROUNDS

Both tent campers and RV enthusiasts will enjoy the heavily wooded and well-equipped setting of Mazama Campground. Drinking water, showers, and laundry facilities help ensure that you don't have to rough it too much. Lost Creek Campground is much smaller, with minimal amenities and a more "rustic" Crater Lake experience.

WHERE TO EAT

IN THE PARK

$–$$
ITALIAN

✕**Annie Creek Restaurant.** It's family-style buffet dining here; pizza and pasta, along with ham and roast beef, are the main features. The outdoor seating area is surrounded by towering pine trees. ✉ *Mazama Village Rd., near Annie Spring entrance station* ☎ *541/594–2255 Ext. 4533* ▭ *AE, D, MC, V* ⊘ *Closed mid-Sept.–mid-June.*

$$$–$$$$
AMERICAN
Fodor'sChoice
★

✕**Dining Room at Crater Lake Lodge.** Virtually the only place where you can dine well once you're in the park, the lodge's culinary emphasis is on fresh, regional Northwest cuisine. The dining room is magnificent, with a large stone fireplace and views of Crater Lake's clear blue waters. Breakfast and lunch are enjoyable here, but the evening menu is the main attraction, with tempting delights such as thyme-seared wild Alaskan salmon, citrus duck filet mignon with a mushroom merlot sauce, and grilled venison. An extensive wine list tops off the gourmet experience. ✉ *Crater Lake Lodge, Rim Village, east of Rim Visitor Center* ☎ *541/594–2255* ⬦ *Reservations essential* ▭ *AE, D, MC, V* ⊘ *Closed late Sept.–mid-May.*

PICNIC AREAS

Rim Drive. About a half-dozen picnic-area turnouts encircle the lake; all have good views, but they can get very windy. Most have pit toilets, and a few have fire grills, but none have running water. ✉ *Rim Dr.*

Rim Village. This is the only park picnic area with running water. The tables are set behind the visitor center, and most have a view of the lake below. There are flush toilets inside the visitor center. ✉ *Rim Dr. on the south side of the lake, 7 mi north of Annie Spring entrance station.*

Wizard Island. The park's best picnic venue is on Wizard Island; pack a picnic lunch and book yourself on one of the early morning boat tour departures, reserving space on an afternoon return. There are no formal picnic areas and just pit toilets, but there are plenty of sunny, protected spots where you can have a quiet meal and appreciate the astounding scene that surrounds you. The island is accessible by boat tour only (⇨ *Educational Offerings*).

OUTSIDE THE PARK

$$$–$$$$
FRENCH

✕**Chateaulin.** One of southern Oregon's most romantic restaurants occupies an ivy-covered storefront a block from the Oregon Shakespeare Festival Center. Chef Steven Breckenridge dispenses French food, local wine, and impeccable service with equal facility. During outdoor theater season (from April to November), late night dining is offered to satisfy post-play hunger. Try the pan-roasted rack of lamb or the Black Angus filet mignon, or check offerings on the three-course, prix-fixe menu. ⊠ *50 E. Main St., Ashland* 🕾 *541/482–2264* ▱ *AE, D, MC, V* ⊗ *No lunch Sun.–Tues.*

$–$$

ECLECTIC

✕ **Morning Glory Restaurant.** Stepping inside this sunny converted bungalow with its Matisse-blue walls, creamy yellow ceiling, and fresh flowers on the table jostles your senses awake even before you've had a whiff of caffeine. Chef-owner Patricia Groth uses organic ingredients whenever possible. You can try dishes like Tandoori tofu scramble or chorizo eggs with tortillas along with inventive renditions of American classics—one bite of the scrumptious cranberry walnut French toast with lemon butter and you'll know why it's so popular. ⊠ *1149 Siskiyou Blvd., Ashland* 🕾 *541/488–8636* ⊕ *www.morninggloryrestaurant.com* ⌂ *Reservations not accepted* ▱ *MC, V* ⊗ *No dinner.*

WHERE TO STAY

15

IN THE PARK

$$

🏠 **The Cabins at Mazama Village.** In a wooded area 7 mi south of the lake, this complex is made up of several A-frame buildings. Most of the modest rooms have two queen beds and a private bath. These rooms fill up fast, so book early. A convenience store and gas station are nearby in the village. **Pros:** clean and well-kept facility. **Cons:** lots of traffic into adjacent campground. ⊠ *Mazama Village, near Annie Spring entrance station* 🕾 *541/594–2255 or 888/774–2728* ⊕ *www.craterlakelodges. com* ⇌ *40 rooms* ⌂ *In-room: no a/c, no phone, no TV. In-hotel: laundry facilities* ▱ *AE, D, MC, V* ⊗ *Closed mid-Oct.–late May.*

$$$–$$$$

🏠 **Crater Lake Lodge.** The period feel of this 1915 lodge on the caldera's rim is reflected in its lodgepole-pine columns, gleaming wood floors, and stone fireplaces in the common areas. With magnificent lake views—and the all-too-brief tourist season at Crater Lake—rooms at this popular spot are often booked a year in advance. Plan ahead, as this is the only "in-park" place to stay by the lake. **Pros:** ideal location for watching sunrise and sunset reflected on the lake. **Cons:** very difficult to reserve rooms. ⊠ *Rim Village, east of Rim Visitor Center, 1 Lodge Loop Rd., Crater Lake* 🕾 *541/594–2255 or 888/774–2728* ⊕ *www. craterlakelodges.com* ⇌ *71 rooms* ⌂ *In-room: no phone, no TV. In-hotel: restaurant* ▱ *AE, D, MC, V* ⊗ *Closed mid-Oct.–late May.*

CAMPING

$

△ **Lost Creek Campground.** The small, remote sites here are usually available on a daily basis. In July and August arrive early to secure a spot. Lost Creek is for tent campers only; RVs must stay at Mazama. **Pros:** close to the fossil spires of Pinnacles Overlook. **Cons:** open only for a brief period each summer; no reservations. ⊠ *3 mi south of Rim Rd. on Pinnacles Spur Rd. at Grayback Dr.* 🕾 *541/594–3100* △ *16 tent sites* ⌂ *Flush toilets, drinking water, fire grates* ⊗ *Closed mid-Sept.–mid-July.*

$$

△ **Mazama Campground.** Crater Lake National Park's major visitor accommodation, aside from the famed lodge on the rim, is set well below the lake caldera in the pine and fir forest of the Cascades. Not far from the main access road (Highway 62), it offers convenience more than outdoor serenity—although adjacent hiking trails lead away from the roadside bustle. About half the spaces are pull-throughs, some with electricity; no hookups are available. The best tent spots are on some of the outer loops above Annie Creek Canyon. **Pros:** close to the Annie Spring and Pacific Crest trails. **Cons:** because it's popular, it's a noisy, crowded place during the busiest summer weeks. ⊠ *Mazama Village, near Annie Spring entrance station* ☎ *541/594–2255 or 888/774–2728* ⊕ *www.craterlakelodges.com* ♨ *212 tent/RV sites* ⚐ *Flush toilets, dump station, drinking water, guest laundry, showers, fire grates, public telephone* ⊟ *AE, D, MC, V* ⊙ *Mid-June–early Oct.*

OUTSIDE THE PARK

$–$$ ⚏ **Prospect Historic Hotel Bed and Breakfast.** Noted individuals such as ★ Theodore Roosevelt, Zane Grey, Jack London, and William Jennings Bryan have stayed here (in rooms that now bear their names). Located 39 mi southwest of the park entrance on Highway 62, the main house has quaint, country-style guest accommodations. The elegant Dinner House restaurant serves hearty pasta, chicken, and the signature prime rib special to hotel guests and the public from May through October. Behind the main house are clean, well-equipped motel units. **Pros:** three waterfalls within walking distance; large property with beautiful grounds; on-site owners. **Cons:** Prospect is a very small town. ⊠ *391 Mill Creek Dr., Prospect* ☎ *541/560–3664 or 800/944–6490* ⊕ *www. prospecthotel.com* ☞ *10 main house rooms, 14 motel rooms* ⚐ *In-room: refrigerator (some), Wi-Fi. In-hotel: Wi-Fi, some pets allowed* ⊟ *D, DC, MC, V.*

$$$–$$$$ ⚏ **Running Y Ranch Resort.** Golfers rave about the Arnold Palmer– designed course here, which wends its way through a juniper-and-ponderosa–shaded canyon overlooking Upper Klamath Lake. Hiking, biking, horseback riding, sailing, fishing, and wildlife watching are some of the prime activities. Rooms in the main lodge are spacious and modern; the two- to three-bedroom town houses have a plethora of amenities, such as built-in entertainment centers and outdoor hot tubs. **Pros:** a playground and miniature golf course make this a good place for kids. **Cons:** may be a bit too far off the beaten path for some. ⊠ *5500 Running Y Rd., 8 mi north of Klamath Falls, Klamath Falls* ☎ *541/850–5500 or 800/851–6013* ⊕ *www.runningy.com* ☞ *82 rooms, 43 houses* ⚐ *In-room: refrigerator (some), Wi-Fi. In-hotel: restaurant, bar, golf course, tennis courts, pool, gym, spa, laundry service, Wi-Fi, some pets allowed* ⊟ *AE, D, DC, MC, V* ⧉ *CP.*

Death Valley National Park

WORD OF MOUTH

"DV is worth more than one day trip. The drive down into it is fantastic. We usually drive north on 95 to Beatty and then go west over the hump and down into the valley, stopping at Rhyolite if we're with someone who hasn't been to a ghost town."

—emalloy

WELCOME TO DEATH VALLEY

TOP REASONS TO GO

★ **Weird science:** Death Valley's Racetrack is home to a moving boulder, an unexplained phenomenon that has scientists baffled.

★ **Lowest spot on the continent:** Stand on the lowest spot on the continent at Badwater, 282 feet below sea level.

★ **Wildflower explosion:** During the spring, this desert landscape is ablaze with greenery and colorful flowers, especially between Badwater and Ashford Mill.

★ **Ghost towns:** Death Valley is renowned for its Wild West heritage and is home to dozens of crumbling settlements including Ballarat, Cerro Gordo, Chloride City, Greenwater, Harrisburg, Keeler, Leadfield, Panamint City, Rhyolite, and Skidoo.

★ **Natural wonders:** From canyons to sand dunes to salt flats and dry lake beds, Death Valley serves up plenty of geological treasures.

1 Central Death Valley. Furnace Creek sits in the heart of Death Valley—if you only have a short time in the park, this is where you'll want to start. You can visit gorgeous Golden Canyon, Zabriskie Point, the Salt Creek Interpretive Trail, and Artist's Drive, among other popular points of interest.

2 Northern Death Valley. This region is uphill from Furnace Creek, which means marginally cooler temperatures. Be sure to stop by Rhyolite Ghost Town on Highway 374 before entering the park and exploring Moorish Scotty's Castle, colorful Titus Canyon, crumbling Keane Wonder Mine, and jaw-dropping Ubehebe Crater.

3 Southern Death Valley. This is a desolate area, but there are plenty of sights that help convey Death Valley's rich history. Don't miss the Dublin Gulch Caves, or the famous Amargosa Opera House, where aging ballerina Marta Becket still wows the crowds.

4 Western Death Valley. Panamint Springs Resort is a nice place to grab a meal and get your bearings before moving on to quaint Darwin Falls, smooth rolling sand dunes, beehive-shaped Wildrose Charcoal Kilns, and historic Stovepipe Wells Village. On the way in, stop at Cerro Gordo Ghost Town, where you can view restored buildings dating back to 1867.

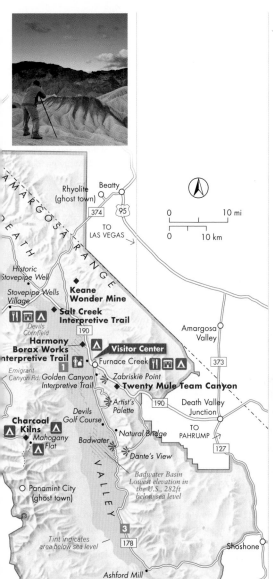

CALIFORNIA

GETTING ORIENTED

Death Valley National Park covers 5,310 square mi, ranges from 6 to 60 mi wide, and measures 140 mi north to south. Within the park, the Panamint Range parallels Death Valley to the west, the Amargosa Range to the east. Nearly all of the park lies in southeastern California, with a small eastern portion crossing over into Nevada.

16

KEY	
👥	Ranger Station
△	Campground
🛆	Picnic Area
🍴	Restaurant
🏠	Lodge
🚶	Trailhead
🚻	Restrooms
⇘	Scenic Viewpoint
⋯⋯	Walking/Hiking Trails
===	4-Wheel Drive Dirt Road
===	2-Wheel Drive Dirt Road

DEATH VALLEY PLANNER

When to Go

Most of the park's one million annual visitors still come between late fall and early spring, taking advantage of moderate temperatures and the lack of rainfall. During these cooler months you will need to book a room in advance, but don't worry: the park never feels crowded. If you visit during summer, believe everything you've ever heard about desert heat—it can be brutal, with temperatures often topping 120°F. The dry air wicks moisture from the body without causing a sweat, so drink plenty of water. Bring sunglasses, a hat, and sufficient clothing to block the sun's rays and the wind. Flash floods are common; sections of roadway can be flooded or washed away. The wettest month is February, when the park receives an average of 0.3 inch of rain.

AVG. HIGH/LOW TEMPS.

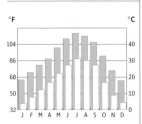

Flora and Fauna

There's a general misconception that Death Valley National Park consists of mile upon endless mile of flat desert sands, scattered cacti, and an occasional cow skull. Many people don't realize that across the valley floor from Badwater—the lowest point in the Western Hemisphere—Telescope Peak towers at 11,049 feet above sea level. The extreme topography of Death Valley is a lesson in geology. Two hundred million years ago seas covered the area, depositing layers of sediment and fossils. Between 3.5 million and 5 million years ago faults in the Earth's crust and volcanic activity pushed and folded the ground, causing mountain ranges to rise and the valley floor to drop. The valley was then filled periodically by lakes, which eroded the surrounding rocks into fantastic formations and deposited the salts that now cover the floor of the basin.

Most animal life in Death Valley (51 mammal, 36 reptile, 307 bird, and three amphibian species) is found near the limited sources of water. The bighorn sheep spend most of their time in the secluded upper reaches of the park's rugged canyons and ridges. Coyotes can often be seen lazing in the shade next to the golf course and have been known to run onto the fairways to steal a golf ball. The only native fish in the park is the pupfish, which grows to slightly longer than 1 inch. In winter, when the water is cold, the fish lie dormant in the bottom mud, becoming active again in spring. Because they are wary of large moving shapes, you must stand quietly over a pool at Salt Creek to see them.

Botanists say there are more than 1,000 species of plants here (21 exist nowhere else in the world), though many annual plants lie dormant as seeds for all but a few months in spring, when rains trigger a bloom. The rest congregate around limited sources of water. Most of the low-elevation vegetation grows around the oases at Furnace Creek and Scotty's Castle, where oleanders, palms, and salt cedar grow. At higher elevations you will find pinyon, juniper, and bristlecone pine.

Getting Here and Around

It can take more than three hours to cross from one side of the park to another, so it's important to choose an entrance point that makes sense for what you want to see. If you're driving from Los Angeles, enter through the western portion along Highway 395; enter from the north at Beatty, Nevada, or via the central entrance at Death Valley Junction if you're coming from Las Vegas. Travelers from Orange County, San Diego, and the Inland Empire should access the park via I–15 North at Baker.

Distances can be deceiving within the park: what seems close can be very far away. Much of the park can be toured on regularly scheduled bus tours, but these often don't allow time for hikes to sites not seen from the road, such as Salt Creek, Golden Canyon, and Natural Bridge. The best option is to drive to a number of the sites, get out of the car, and walk.

When driving in Death Valley, reliable maps are a must, as signage is often limited or, in a few places, nonexistent. Other important accessories include a compass, a mobile phone (though these don't always work in remote areas), and extra food and water (3 gallons per person per day is recommended, plus additional radiator water). If you're able to take a four-wheel-drive vehicle, bring it: many of Death Valley's most spectacular canyons are otherwise inaccessible. Be aware of possible winter closures or driving restrictions due to snow.

The **California State Department of Transportation Hotline** (☎ 916/445–7623 or 800/427–7623 ⊕ www.dot. ca.gov) has updates on Death Valley road conditions. The **California Highway Patrol** (☎ 760/256–1727 near Barstow, 760/872–5900 near Bishop ⊕ cad.chp.ca.gov) offers the latest traffic incident information.

Maps and Info

The Death Valley Natural History Association sells a variety of books on the area and publishes a pamphlet outlining a self-guided tour of Golden Canyon, which costs 50¢ and is available from the association or the bookstore at the visitor center. The association also sells a waterproof, tear-proof topographical map of the entire park for $11.95. Additional topo maps covering select areas are $6 each and available at the visitor center or from the **Death Valley Natural History Association** (☎ 760/786–2146 or 800/478–8564 ⊕ www.dvnha.org).

Festivals and Events

MAR. **Diaz Lake Trout Derby.** The first Saturday of the month, you can take a shot at the "big one." Admission is free. ☎ 760/876–4444.

APR. **Shoshone Desert Art Show.** Admission is free for this annual arts-and-crafts show and sale weekend. ☎ 760/852–4254 or 775/727–5460.

MAY **Bishop Mule Days.** Entertainment includes top country-music stars, steer roping, barbecues, country dances, and the longest-running nonmotorized parade in the U.S. Admission is free. ☎ 760/872–4263 ⊕ www.muledays.org.

OCT. **Lone Pine Film Festival.** Every Columbus Day weekend, this town pays tribute to its Hollywood history with three days of tours, films, lectures, and Old West celebrity guests. ☎ 760/876–9103 ⊕ www.lonepinefilmfestival.org.

NOV. **Death Valley 49er Encampment Days.** Originally a centennial celebration held in 1949 to honor the area's first European visitors, this event draws thousands of people from around the world. The weeklong celebration includes art shows, organized seminars, walks, and dances. ⊕ www.deathvalley49ers.org.

Shoshone Old West Days. Just outside of Death Valley National Park, this annual festival celebrates Wild West heritage. ☎ 760/852–4524.

16

Updated by
Reed Parsell

The desert is no Disneyland. With its scorching summer heat and vast, sparsely populated tracts of land, it's not often at the top of the list when most people plan their California vacations. But the natural riches of Death Valley—the largest national park outside Alaska—are overwhelming: rolling waves of sand dunes, black cinder cones thrusting up hundreds of feet from a blistered desert floor, riotous sheets of wildflowers, bizarrely shaped Joshua trees basking in the orange glow of a sunset, tiny pupfish that enthrall youngsters, and a silence that is both dramatic and startling.

PARK ESSENTIALS

ACCESSIBILITY

All of Death Valley's visitor centers, contact stations, and museums are accessible to all visitors. The campgrounds at Furnace Creek, Sunset, and Stovepipe Wells have wheelchair-accessible sites. The grounds at Scotty's Castle are accessible to the mobility impaired and the guided tour of the main house has provisions for a wheelchair lift to the upper floors. Highway 190, Badwater Road, Scotty's Castle Road, and paved roads to Dante's View and Wildrose provide access to the major scenic viewpoints and historic points of interest.

ADMISSION FEES AND PERMITS

The entrance fee is $20 per vehicle and $10 for those entering on foot, bus, bike, or motorcycle. The payment, valid for seven consecutive days, is collected at the park's entrance stations and at the visitor center at Furnace Creek. (If you enter the park on Highway 190, there is no entrance station; remember to stop by the visitor center to pay the fee.) Annual park passes, valid only at Death Valley, are $40.

DEATH VALLEY IN ONE DAY

If you begin the day in Furnace Creek, you can see many different sights without doing much driving. Bring plenty of water with you, and some food, too. Get up early and drive the 20 mi on Badwater Road to **Badwater**, which looks out on the lowest point in the Western Hemisphere and is a dramatic place to watch the sunrise. Returning north, stop at **Natural Bridge**, a medium-size conglomerate rock formation that has been hollowed at its base to form a span across the canyon, and then at the **Devil's Golf Course**, so named because of the large pinnacles of salt present here. Detour to the right onto **Artist's Drive**, a 9-mi one-way, northbound route that passes **Artist's Palette**.

The reds, yellows, oranges, and greens come from minerals in the rocks and the earth. Four miles north of Artist's Drive you will come to the **Golden Canyon Interpretive Trail**, a 2-mi round-trip that winds through a canyon with colorful rock walls. Just before Furnace Creek, take Highway 190 3 mi east to **Zabriskie Point**, overlooking dramatic, furrowed red-brown hills and the **Twenty Mule Team Canyon**. Return to Furnace Creek, where you can have lunch and visit the museum at the Furnace Creek Visitor Center. Heading north from Furnace Creek, pull off the highway and take a look at the **Harmony Borax Works**.

16

A permit is not required for groups of 14 or fewer, but if you're planning an overnight visit to the backcountry, complete a registration form at the Furnace Creek Visitor Center. Backcountry camping is allowed in areas that are at least 2 mi from maintained campgrounds and the main paved or unpaved roads, and ¼ mi from water sources. Most abandoned mining areas are restricted to day use.

ADMISSION HOURS
Most facilities within the park remain open year-round, daily 8–6.

ATMS/BANKS
There is an ATM at the Furnace Creek Ranch Registration Office.

CELL-PHONE RECEPTION
Results vary, but in general you should be able to get fairly good cell-phone reception on the valley floor. In the surrounding mountains, however, don't count on it.

PARK CONTACT INFORMATION
Death Valley National Park P.O. Box 579, Death Valley 92328 ☎ 760/786–2331 ⊕ www.nps.gov/deva.

SCENIC DRIVE

★ **Artist's Drive.** This 9-mi, one-way route skirts the foothills of the Black Mountains and provides intimate views of the changing landscape. Once inside the palette, the huge expanses of the valley are replaced by the small-scale natural beauty of pigments created by volcanic deposits. It's a quiet, lonely drive, and shouldn't be rushed. Reach Artist's Palette by heading north off Badwater Road.

WHAT TO SEE

HISTORIC SITES

Charcoal Kilns. Ten well-preserved stone kilns, each 25 feet high and 30 feet wide, stand as if on parade. The kilns, built by Chinese laborers for a mining company in 1877, were used to burn wood from pinyon pines to turn it into charcoal. The charcoal was then transported over the mountains into Death Valley, where it was used to extract lead and silver from the ore mined there. If you hike nearby Wildrose Peak, you will be rewarded with terrific views of the kilns. ⊠ *Wildrose Canyon Rd., 37 mi south of Stovepipe Wells.*

Harmony Borax Works. Death Valley's mule teams hauled borax from here to the railroad town of Mojave, 165 mi away. The teams plied the route until 1889, when the railroad finally arrived in Zabriskie. Constructed in 1883, one of the oldest buildings in Death Valley houses the Borax Museum, 2 mi south of the borax works. Originally a miners' bunkhouse, the building once stood in Twenty Mule Team Canyon. Now it displays mining machinery and historical exhibits. The adjacent structure is the original mule-team barn. ⊠ *Harmony Borax Works Rd., west of Hwy. 190, 2 mi north of Furnace Creek* ☉ *Daily 10–5.*

Fodor's Choice ★ **Keane Wonder Mine.** The tram towers and cables from the old mill used to process gold from Keane Wonder Mine are still here, leading up to the crumbling mine, which is a steep 1-mi hike up the mountain. A nearby path leads north to Keane Wonder Spring. ⊠ *Access road off Beatty Cutoff Rd., 17½ mi north of Furnace Creek.*

☾ ★ **Scotty's Castle.** This Moorish-style mansion, begun in 1924 and never completed, takes its name from Walter Scott, better known as Death Valley Scotty. An ex-cowboy, prospector, and performer in Buffalo Bill's Wild West Show, Scotty always told people the castle was his, financed by gold from a secret mine. In reality, there was no mine, and the house belonged to a Chicago millionaire named Albert Johnson, whom Scott had finagled into investing in the fictitious mine. Despite the con, Johnson and Scott became great friends. The house functioned for a while as a hotel and still contains works of art, imported carpets, handmade European furniture, and a tremendous pipe organ. Costumed rangers, to varying degrees of enthusiasm, re-create life at the castle circa 1939. Check out the Underground Mysteries Tour, which takes you through a ¼-mile tunnel in the castle basement. ⊠ *Scotty's Castle Rd. (Hwy. 267), 53 mi north of Furnace Creek Interpretive Trail* ☏ *760/786–2392* ⊕ *www.nps.gov/deva* 🖃 *$11* ☉ *Daily 8:30–5, tours daily 9–5.*

SCENIC STOPS

★ **Artist's Palette.** So called for the contrasting colors of its volcanic deposits, this is one of signature sights of Death Valley. Artist's Drive, the approach to the area, is one way heading north off Badwater Road, so if you're visiting Badwater, come here on the way back. The drive winds through foothills of sedimentary and volcanic rocks. About 4 mi into the drive, a short side road veers right to a parking lot that's a few hundred feet before the "palette," whose natural colors include shades of green, gold, and pink. ⊠ *11 mi south of Furnace Creek, off Badwater Rd.*

★ **Badwater.** At 282 feet below sea level, Badwater is the lowest spot on land in the Western Hemisphere—and also one of the hottest. Stairs and wheelchair ramps descend from the parking lot to a wooden platform that overlooks a sodium chloride pool, a small but remarkably persistent reminder that the valley floor used to contain a lake. You can continue past the platform on a broad, white path that peters out after a half-mile or so. Badwater is one of the most popular and easily accessible sites within the park. From this lowest point, be sure to look across to Telescope Peak, which towers more than 2 mi above the valley floor. ⊠ *Badwater Rd., 19 mi south of Furnace Creek.*

Fodor'sChoice **Dante's View.** This lookout is more than 5,000 feet up in the Black
★ Mountains. In the dry desert air you can see across most of 110-mi-wide Death Valley. The view is astounding. Take a 10-minute, mildly strenuous walk from the parking lot toward a series of rocky overlooks, where with binoculars you can spot some of Death Valley's signature sites. A few interpretive signs point out the highlights below in the valley and across, in the Sierra. Getting here from Furnace Creek takes an hour—time well invested. ⊠ *Dante's View Rd., off Hwy. 190, 35 mi from Badwater, 20 mi south of Twenty Mule Team Canyon.*

Darwin Falls. Named for Dr. Darwin French, who explored this desert wilderness in 1860, the 80-foot Darwin Falls are a unique sight in the arid, unforgiving desert. This rocky landscape, accented with trees and moss, pours down into a cool plunge pool. (Swimming is not permitted.) ⊠ *Hwy. 190, 1 mi west of Panamint Springs. Exit south on the signed dirt road and travel 2½ mi to the parking area.*

Devil's Golf Course. Thousands of miniature salt pinnacles carved into surreal shapes by the desert wind dot this wildly varied landscape. The salt was pushed up to the earth's surface by pressure created as underground salt- and water-bearing gravel crystallized. Get out of your vehicle and take a closer look; you'll see perfectly round holes descending into the ground. ⊠ *Badwater Rd., 13 mi south of Furnace Creek. Turn right onto dirt road and drive 1 mi.*

Golden Canyon. Just South of Furnace Creek, these glimmering mountains are perhaps best known for their role in the original *Star Wars*. The canyon is also a fine hiking spot, with gorgeous views of the Panamint Mountains, ancient dry lake beds, and alluvial fans. If you fork out a quarter for the small trail guide, be forewarned that several of the numbered signs it refers to are missing. ⊠ *From the Furnace Creek Visitor Center, drive 2 mi south on Hwy. 190, then 2 mi south on Hwy. 178 to the parking area. The lot has a kiosk with trail guides.*

★ **Racetrack.** Getting here involves a 27-mi journey over a rough and almost nonexistent dirt road, but the trip is well worth the reward. Where else in the world do rocks move on their own? This phenomenon has baffled scientists for years. No one has actually seen the rocks in motion, but theory has it that when it rains, the hard-packed lake bed becomes slippery enough that gusty winds push the rocks along—sometimes for several hundred yards. When the mud dries, a telltale trail remains. The trek to the Racetrack can be made in a passenger vehicle, but high clearance is suggested. ⊠ *27 mi west of Ubehebe Crater via dirt road.*

16

"I loved how soft the dunes in Death Valley National Park looked from a distance in the early morning light. I ventured out far from the road to capture the serene isolation, and found these unexpected print trails.

Sand Dunes at Mesquite Flat. These dunes, made up of minute pieces of quartz and other rock, are ever-changing products of the wind-rippled hills, with curving crests and a sun-bleached hue. The dunes are the most photographed destination in the park, and you can see them at their best at sunrise and sunset. Keep your eyes open for animal tracks—you may even spot a coyote or fox. Bring plenty of water, and note where you parked your car: it's easy to become disoriented in this ocean of sand. If you lose your bearings, climb to the top of a dune and scan the horizon for the parking lot. ⊠ *19 mi north of Hwy. 190, northeast of Stovepipe Wells Village.*

Stovepipe Wells Village. This tiny 1926 town, the first resort in Death Valley, takes its name from the stovepipe that an early prospector left to indicate where he found water. The area contains a motel, restaurant, grocery store, campgrounds, and landing strip, though first-time park visitors are better off staying in Furnace Creek, which is more central. Off Highway 190, on a 3-mi gravel road immediately southwest, are the multicolor walls of **Mosaic Canyon.** ⊠ *Hwy. 190, 2 mi from Sand Dunes, 77 mi east of Lone Pine.*

★ **Titus Canyon.** Titus Canyon is a popular 28-mi drive from Beatty south along Scotty's Castle Road. Along the way you'll pass Leadville Ghost Town, petroglyphs at Klare Spring, and spectacular limestone and dolomite narrows at the end of the canyon. Toward the end, a two-section of gravel road will lead you into the mouth of the canyon. ⊠ *Access road off Scotty's Castle Rd., 33 mi northwest of Furnace Creek.*

Twenty Mule Team Canyon. This canyon was named for the 20-mule teams that, between 1883 and 1889, carried 10-ton loads of borax through the burning desert. At places along the loop road off Highway 190 the soft

One from a person along the ridge, and several straight animal prints. The group of tourists in the distance really give us an idea of the enormous vastness of the landscape." —photo by Evan Spiler, Fodors.com member

rock walls reach high on both sides, making it seem like you're on an amusement-park ride. Remains of prospectors' tunnels are visible here, along with some brilliant rock formations. ⊠ *20 Mule Team Rd., off Hwy. 190, 4 mi south of Furnace Creek, 20 mi west of Death Valley Junction.*

Ubehebe Crater. At 500 feet deep and ½ mi across, this crater resulted from underground steam and gas explosions about 3,000 years ago. Volcanic ash spreads out over most of the area, and the cinders lie as deep as 150 feet, near the crater's rim. Trek down to the crater's floor or walk around it on a fairly level path. Either way, you need about an hour and will be treated to fantastic views. ⊠ *N. Death Valley Hwy., 8 mi northwest of Scotty's Castle.*

★ **Zabriskie Point.** Although only about 710 feet in elevation, this is one of Death Valley National Park's most scenic spots, overlooking a striking panorama of wrinkled, multicolor hills. It's a great place to watch the sunrise, but it can be bustling any time of day. Pair it with a drive out to magnificent Dante's View. ⊠ *Hwy. 190, 5 mi south of Furnace Creek.*

VISITOR CENTERS

Furnace Creek Visitor Center and Museum. The exhibits and artifacts here provide a broad overview of how Death Valley formed; you can pick up maps at the bookstore run by the Death Valley Natural History Association. This is also the place to sign up for ranger-led walks (available November through April) or check out a live presentation about the valley's cultural and natural history. The center offers 12-minute slide shows about the park every 30 minutes. Your children are likely to receive plenty of individual attention from the enthusiastic rangers.

✉ *Hwy. 190, 30 mi northwest of Death Valley Junction* ☎ *760/786–3200* ⊕ *www.nps.gov/deva* ☉ *Daily 8–6.*

Scotty's Castle Visitor Center and Museum. If you visit Death Valley, you'll likely make a stop here at the main ticket center for Scotty's Castle living-history tours. Here you'll also find a nice display of exhibits, books, self-guided tour pamphlets, and displays about the castle's creators, Death Valley Scotty and Albert M. Johnson. Fuel up with gasoline, sandwiches, or souvenirs before heading back out to the park. ✉ *Rte. 267, 53 mi northwest of Furnace Creek and 45 mi northwest of Stovepipe Wells Village* ☎ *760/786–2392* ⊕ *www.nps.gov/deva* ☉ *Daily 7:30–5.*

SPORTS AND THE OUTDOORS

BICYCLING

There are no bike rentals in the park, but mountain biking is permitted on any of the back roads open to the public. A free flier with suggested bike routes is at the Furnace Creek Visitor Center. Bicycle Trail, a 4-mi round-trip trek from the visitor center to Mustard Canyon, is a good place to start, as is Desolation Canyon, an easy 2-mi round-trip trail 4 mi south of Badwater Road. For a better workout, try the moderate 6-mi round-trip journey to Keane Wonder Mine, which begins 17 mi north of the Beatty cutoff road, or the 10-mi round-trip journey to Big Four Mine, starting 9½ mi south of Badwater Road.

OUTFITTER AND EXPEDITIONS Mountain bike into the heart of Death Valley during a six-day adventure through the national park with **Spirit of the Mojave Mountain Biking Tour** (*Escape Adventures* ☎ *800/596–2953 or 702/838–6966* ⊕ *www.escapeadventures.com*). The 110-mi journey includes accommodations (both camping and inns). Tours are $995 per person; bikes, tents, sleeping bags, helmets, and other gear may be rented for an additional price. Tours are available February–April and October only.

BIRD-WATCHING

Approximately 350 bird species have been identified in Death Valley. The best place to see the park's birds is along the Salt Creek Interpretive Trail, where you can spot ravens, common snipes, killdeer, spotted sandpipers, and great blue herons. Along the fairways at Furnace Creek Golf Club, you can see kingfishers, peregrine falcons, hawks, Canada geese, yellow warblers, and the occasional golden eagle—just remember to stay off the greens. Scotty's Castle attracts wintering birds from around the globe who are attracted to its running water, shady trees, and shrubs. Other good spots to find birds are at Saratoga Springs, Mesquite Springs, Travertine Springs, and Grimshaw Lake near Tecopa. You can download a complete park bird checklist, divided by season, at ⊕ *www.nps.gov/deva/naturescience/birds.htm*. Rangers at Furnace Creek Visitor Center often lead birding walks through Salt Creek between November and March.

FOUR-WHEELING

Maps and SUV guidebooks for four-wheel-drive and other backcountry roads (including the popular Cottonwood/Marble canyons, Racetrack, Eureka Dunes, Saratoga Springs, Warm Springs Canyon) are offered at the Furnace Creek Visitor Center. Remember: never travel alone and be sure to pack plenty of water and snacks. Driving off established roads is strictly prohibited in the park.

Butte Valley. This 21-mi road in the southwest part of the park climbs from 200 feet below sea level to an elevation of 4,000 feet. The geological formations along the drive reveal the development of Death Valley. ⊠ *Trailhead on Warm Spring Canyon Rd., 50 mi south of Furnace Creek Visitor Center.*

Hunter Mountain. From Teakettle Junction to the park boundary, this 20-mi road climbs from 4,100 feet to 7,200 feet, winding through a pinyon-and-juniper forest. This route may be closed or muddy in winter and spring. ⊠ *Trailhead 28 mi southwest of Scotty's Castle.*

Warm Springs Canyon. This route takes you past Warm Springs talc mine and through Butte Valley, over Mengel Pass and toward **Geologists Cabin,** a charming and cheery little cabin where you can spend the night (if nobody else beats you to it!). The cabin, which sits under a cottonwood tree, has a fireplace, table and chairs, and a sink. Farther up the road, the cabins at Mengel's Home and Russell Camp are also open for public use. Keep the historic cabins clean and restock any items that you use. ⊠ *Warm Springs Canyon Rd., off Hwy. 190/Badwater Rd.*

16

OUTFITTER AND EXPEDITION
The 10-hour **Death Valley SUV Tour** (*Death Valley Tours* ☎ 800/719–3768 ⊕ *www.deathvalleytours.net*) departs from Las Vegas and takes you on a fully narrated whirl through Death Valley in a four-wheel-drive Jeep. Tours ($205 per person) depart Monday and Wednesday at 7 AM and include free pickup from designated hotels. Bottled water and snacks are provided, and camera rentals, tripods, and film are available for an additional fee.

GOLF

Furnace Creek Golf Club. Play 9 or 18 holes at the lowest golf course in the world (214 feet below sea level). Its improbably green fairways are lined with date palms and tamarisk trees, and its level of difficulty is rated surprisingly high. The club rents clubs and carts, and greens fees are reduced for Furnace Creek Ranch or Furnace Creek Inn guests. In winter, reservations are essential. ⊠ *Hwy. 190, Furnace Creek* ☎ *760/786–2301* ⊕ *www.furnacecreekresort.com* ⬚ *$30–$55* ☉ *Tee times 6 AM–3:30 PM; pro shop 6 AM–5 PM.*

HIKING

Plan to hike before or after midday in the spring, summer, or fall, unless you're in the mood for a masochistic baking. Carry plenty of water, wear protective clothing, and keep an eye out for tarantulas, black widows, scorpions, snakes, and other potentially dangerous creatures. Some of the best trails are unmarked; if the opportunity arises, ask for directions.

OUTFITTERS AND EXPEDITIONS
Available during the spring months, **Death Valley National Park and Red Rock Canyon Hiking Tour** (*Death Valley Tours* ☎ 800/719–3768 ⊕ *www.deathvalleytours.net*) is a six-day adventure that begins in Las Vegas. All transportation, permits, park fees, food, beverages, first aid, and camping gear is included. Tours are $1,230 per person.

Join an experienced guide and spend six days exploring Death Valley's most popular sights with **Death Valley National Park and Red Rock**

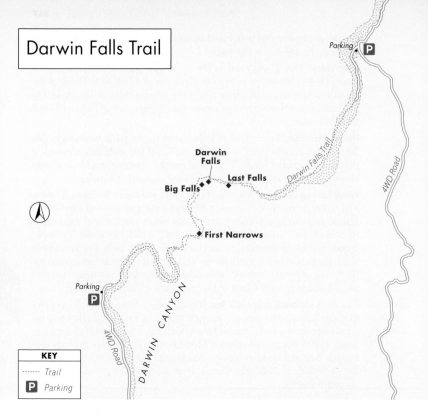

Darwin Falls Trail

Darwin Falls

Big Falls ♦ **Last Falls** ♦

♦ **First Narrows**

Darwin Falls Trail

4WD Road

Parking 🅿

Parking 🅿

DARWIN CANYON

4WD Road

KEY

------ *Trail*

🅿 *Parking*

Hiker (*Escape Adventures* ☎ 800/596–2953 or 702/838–6966 🌐 *www. escapeadventures.com*). The tour ($995), offered October and February–April, also spends two days in Red Rock Canyon National Conservation Area. For an additional fee, you can rent hiking shoes, tents, sleeping bags, trekking poles, water bottles, and more. The price includes a night in the Furnace Creek Inn.

EASY

☾ **Darwin Falls.** This lovely 2-mi round-trip hike rewards you with a refreshing waterfall surrounded by thick vegetation and a rocky gorge.

Fodor's Choice No swimming or bathing is allowed, but it's a beautiful place for a pic-

★ nic. Adventurous hikers can scramble higher toward more rewarding views of the falls. ✉ *Access the 2-mi graded dirt road and parking area off Hwy. 190, 1 mi west of Panamint Springs Resort.*

Natural Bridge Canyon. A 2-mi access road with potholes that could swallow basketballs leads to a parking lot. From there, set off to see interesting geological features in addition to the bridge, which is ¼-mi away. The one-way trail continues for a few hundred meters, but scenic returns diminish quickly and eventually you're confronted with climbing boulders. ✉ *Access road off Badwater Rd., 15 mi south of Furnace Creek.*

☺ **Salt Creek Interpretive Trail.** This trail, a ½-mi boardwalk circuit, loops through a spring-fed wash. The nearby hills are brown and gray, but the floor of the wash is alive with aquatic plants such as pickerelweed and salt grass. The stream and ponds here are among the few places in the park to see the rare pupfish, the only native fish species in Death Valley. Animals such as bobcats, fox, coyotes, and snakes visit the spring, and you may also see ravens, common snipes, killdeer, and great blue herons. ⊠ *Off Hwy. 190, 14 mi north of Furnace Creek.*

MODERATE

Fall Canyon. This is a 3½-mi one-way hike from the Titus canyon parking area. First, walk ½ mi north along the base of the mountains to a large wash, then go 2½ mi up the canyon to a 35-foot dry fall. You can continue by climbing around to the falls on the south side. ⊠ *Access road off Scotty's Castle Rd., 33 mi northwest of Furnace Creek.*

☺ **Mosaic Canyon.** A gradual uphill trail (4 mi round-trip) winds through the smoothly polished walls of this narrow canyon. There are dry falls to climb at the upper end. ⊠ *Access road off Hwy. 190, ½ mi west of Stovepipe Wells Village.*

DIFFICULT

Fodor's Choice
★

Keane Wonder Mine. Allow two hours for the 2-mi round-trip trail that follows an out-of-service aerial tramway to this mine. The way is steep, but the views of the valley are spectacular. Do not enter the tunnels or hike beyond the top of the tramway—it's dangerous. The trailhead is 2 mi down an unpaved and bumpy access road. ⊠ *Access road off Beatty Cutoff Rd., 17½ mi north of Furnace Creek.*

Telescope Peak Trail. The 14-mi round-trip begins at Mahogany Flat Campground, which is accessible by a very rough dirt road. The steep and at some points treacherous trail winds through pinyon, juniper, and bristlecone pines, with excellent views of Death Valley and Panamint Valley. Ice axes and crampons may be necessary in winter—check at the Furnace Creek Visitor Center. It takes a minimum of eight hours to hike to the top of the 11,049-foot peak and then return. Getting to the peak is a strenuous endeavor; take plenty of water and only attempt it in fall unless you're an experienced hiker. ⊠ *Off Wildrose Rd., south of Charcoal Kilns.*

HORSEBACK AND CARRIAGE RIDES

OUTFITTERS
AND
EXPEDITIONS

Set off on a one- or two-hour guided horseback or carriage ride ($10–$60) from **Furnace Creek Stables** (⊠ *Hwy. 190, Furnace Creek* ☎ *760/786-2345 Ext. 339* ⊕ *www.furnacecreekstables.net*). The rides traverse trails with views of the surrounding mountains, where multicolor volcanic rock and

---

MOTORCYCLE TOURS

Sign up for a guided **Death Valley Dualsport Tour** (*Adventure Motorcycle [AdMo] Tours* ☎ *760/249-1105* ⊕ *www.admotours.com*). The four-day tour ($1,530) through Death Valley on a rented Suzuki DR-Z400S (or your own) bike covers about 400 mi of terrain. The tours, which run October–May, include bike rental, gasoline, snacks, hotel accommodations for three nights, and a professional guide. To join, you'll need a motorcycle driver's license, health insurance, and protective gear.

16

"I'd always wanted to photograph this remote location, and on my drive into Death Valley I was rewarded at Zabriskie Point with this amazing view." —photo by Rodney Ee, Fodors.com member

alluvial fans form a background for date palms and other vegetation. Evening carriage rides take passengers around the golf course and Furnace Creek Ranch. Cocktail rides, with champagne, margaritas, and hot spiced wine, are available. The stables are open October–May only.

EDUCATIONAL OFFERINGS

GUIDED TOURS

Death Valley & Scotty's Castle Adventure Tour. This 11-hour luxury motor-coach tour of the park passes through its most famous landmarks. Tours include lunch and hotel pickup from designated Las Vegas–area hotels. ☎ 800/719–3768 *Death Valley Tours, 800/566–5868 or 702/233–1627 Look Tours* ✉ *$205* ⊙ *Tues., Fri., and Sun. at 7* AM.

Furnace Creek Visitor Center tours. This center has the most tour options, including a weekly 2-mi Harmony Borax Walk and guided hikes to Keane Wonder Mine, Mosaic Canyon, and Golden Canyon. Less strenuous options include wildflower walks, birding walks, geology walks, and a Furnace Creek Inn historical tour. The Furnace Creek Visitor Center is where you hop aboard a distinctive, pink four-wheel-drive vehicle with **Pink Jeep Tours Las Vegas** (☎ 702/895–6777 ⊕ *www.pinkjeep.com*), to visit places—the Charcola Kilns, the Racetrack, and Titus Canyon among them—that your own vehicle might not be able to handle. Pink Jeep tours last two to six hours and cost $59 to $159. The visitor center also offers orientation programs every half hour, daily from 8 to 6. ✉ *Furnace Creek Visitor Center, Rte. 190, 30 mi northwest of Death Valley Junction* ☎ *760/786–2331.*

RANGER PROGRAMS

☽ **Junior Ranger Program.** Children can join this program at any of the three visitor centers, where they can pick up a workbook and complete up to 15 projects (based on their age) to earn souvenir badge.

ARTS AND ENTERTAINMENT

Marta Becket's Amargosa Opera House. An artist and dancer from New York, Becket first visited the former railway town of Amargosa while on tour in 1964. Three years later she returned to town and bought a boarded-up theater that sat amid a group of rundown mock–Spanish colonial buildings. To compensate for the sparse audiences in the early days, Becket painted a Renaissance-era Spanish crowd on the walls and ceiling, turning the theater into a trompe l'oeil masterpiece. Now in her late 70s, Becket performs her blend of ballet, mime, and 19th-century melodrama to sellout crowds. After the show you can meet her in the adjacent gallery, where she sells her paintings and autographs her books. There are no performances mid-May through September. Reservations are required. ⊠ *Rte. 127, Death Valley Junction* ☎ *760/852–4441* ⊕ *www.amargosa-opera-house.com* ⌑ *$15* ☽ *Oct.–May (through Mother's Day weekend).*

16

WHAT'S NEARBY

NEARBY TOWNS

Founded at the turn of the 20th century, **Beatty** sits 16 mi east of the California-Nevada border on Death Valley's northern side. Named for a single pine tree found at the bottom of the canyon of the same name, **Lone Pine,** on the park's west side, is where you'll find Mt. Whitney, the highest peak in the continental United States, at 14,496 feet. The nearby Alabama Hills have been used in many movies and TV scenes, including segments in *The Lone Ranger.* Down south, unincorporated **Shoshone,** a very small town at the edge of Death Valley, started out as a mining town. The area, dotted with tamarisk trees and date palms, is home to a natural warm-springs pool fed by an underwater river.

VISITOR INFORMATION

Contacts Beatty Chamber of Commerce ⊠ *119 E. Main St., Beatty, NV* ☎ *775/553–2424* ⊕ *www.governet.net/nv/as/bea.* **Death Valley Chamber of Commerce** ⊠ *118 S. Rte. 127, Shoshone* ☎ *760/852–4524* ⊕ *www.deathvalleychamber.org.* **Lone Pine Chamber of Commerce** ⊠ *126 S. Main St., Lone Pine* ☎ *760/876–4444 or 877/253–8981* ⊕ *www.lonepinechamber.org.* **Shoshone Development** ⌂ *P.O. Box 67, Shoshone, 92384* ☎ *760/852–4224.*

NEARBY ATTRACTIONS

☽
★ **Ancient Bristlecone Pine Forest.** Here you can see some of the oldest living trees on earth, some of which date back more than 40 centuries. At the Schulman Grove Visitor Center (☎ *760/873–2500* ⊕ *www.fs.fed.us/r5/inyo/about*), open 8–4:30 weekdays, late May–October, you can learn

about the bristlecone and take a walk to the 4,700-year-old Methuselah tree. ⊠ *North from Independence on Hwy. 395, turn onto Hwy. 168 and follow signs for 31 mi* 🖼 *$3.*

Ballarat Ghost Town. This crusty, dusty town saw its heyday between 1897 and 1917. It's watched over by two lonely but lovable caretakers, George Novak and his son, Rocky, who run a working store-museum where you can grab a cold soda and hear a story or two before venturing out to explore the crumbling landscape. Ballarat's more infamous draw is **Barker Ranch,** accessible with four-wheel drive, where convicted murderer Charles Manson and his "family" were captured after the 1969 Sharon Tate murder spree. ⊠ *From Hwy. 395, exit SR-178 and travel 45 mi to the historic marker; Ballarat is 3½ mi from the pavement* 🕾 *No phone.*

Cerro Gordo Ghost Town. Discovered by Mexican miner Pablo Flores in 1865, Cerro Gordo was California's biggest producer of silver and lead, raking in almost $13 million before it shut down in 1959. Today, the privately owned ghost town offers overnight accommodations in the **Belshaw House** for $150 per night (up to five people), billing itself the only bed-and-cook-your-own-breakfast ghost town in the world. Visit during the summer months, as its 8,300-foot elevation proves impassable during the winter. Four-wheel-drive is recommended for the steep road into the ghost town. Admission includes a tour if arranged in advance. Guests are forbidden to take artifacts from the area or explore nearby mines. ⊠ *From Hwy. 395 at Lone Pine, take Hwy. 136 for 13 mi to Keeler, then travel 7½ miles up Cerro Gordo Rd. From Panamint Springs, travel 31 mi west on Hwy. 190 until it merges with Hwy. 136; travel 5 more mi to Cerro Gordo Rd.* 🕾 *760/876–5030* ⊕ *www.cerrogordo.us* 🖼 *$5.*

Manzanar National Historic Site. A reminder of an ugly episode in U.S. history, the former Manzanar War Relocation Center is where some 10,000 Japanese-Americans were confined behind barbed-wire fences between 1942 and 1945. Today not much remains of Manzanar but a guard post, the auditorium, and some concrete foundations. But you can drive the one-way dirt road past the ruins to a small cemetery, where a monument stands. Signs mark where the barracks, a hospital, school, and fire station once stood. An outstanding 8,000-square-foot interpretive center has exhibits and a 15-minute film. ⊠ *Hwy. 395, 11 mi north of Lone Pine* 🕾 *760/878–2932* ⊕ *www.nps.gov/manz* 🖼 *Free* ☉ *Daily 9–4:30.*

FodorsChoice
★
Petroglyph Canyons. The only way to see these amazing spectacles is on a guided tour conducted by the **Maturango Museum** (⊠ *100 E. Las Flores Ave., Ridgecrest* 🕾 *760/375–6900* ⊕ *www.maturango.org com*). Tours ($35) depart from the museum February–June, and September or October–early December; call for tour times. Children under 10 are not allowed on the tour. The two canyons, commonly called Big Petroglyph and Little Petroglyph, are in the Coso Mountain range on the million-acre U.S. Naval Weapons Center at China Lake. Each of the canyons holds a superlative concentration of ancient rock art, the largest of its kind in the Northern Hemisphere. Thousands of well-preserved images of animals and humans are scratched or pecked into dark basaltic rocks. The military requires everyone to produce a valid driver's license, social security

number, passport, and vehicle registration before the trip (nondrivers must provide a birth certificate).

ℭ **Randsburg.** The Rand Mining District first boomed when gold was discovered in the Rand Mountains in 1895. Along with neighboring settlements, it grew further due to the success of the Yellow Aster Mine, which yielded $3 million worth of gold before 1900. Rich tungsten ore, used in World War I to make steel alloy, was discovered in 1907, and silver was found in 1919. Randsburg is one of the few gold-rush communities not to have become a ghost town; the tiny city jail is among the original buildings still standing in this town with a population under 100. In nearby Johannesburg, 1 mi south of Randsburg, spirits are said to dwell in the stunning Old West cemetery in the hills above town. ⊠ *Hwy. 395, near the junction with Rte. 14.*

Fodor'sChoice ★

<aside>
FAMILY PICKS

Salt Creek. Look for pupfish here.

Sand Dunes. Ride a piece of cardboard down the dunes.

Caves of Dublin Gulch. Come here for some fun exploring in Shoshone.

Horseback Tour. Furnace Creek Ranch offers tours via horse.

Ghost towns. Venture through a real-live at Cerro Gordo or Rhyolite.
</aside>

16

ℭ **Rhyolite.** Though it's not within the boundary of Death Valley National
★ Park, this Nevada ghost town, named for the silica volcanic rock nearby, is still a big draw. Around 1904, Rhyolite's Montgomery Shoshone Mine caused a financial boom, and fancy buildings sprung up all over town. Today you can still explore many of the crumbling edifices. The Bottle House, built by miner Tom Kelly out of almost 50,000 Adolphus Busch beer bottles, is a must-see. ⊠ *Hwy. 374, 35 mi north of Furnace Creek Visitor Center and 5 mi west of Beatty, NV* ☎ *No phone.*

Shoshone Museum. The museum chronicles the local history of Death Valley and houses a unique collection of period items, and minerals and rocks from the area. The building also houses the Death Valley Chamber of Commerce and functions as the visitor center for the southeastern entrance to Death Valley. ⊠ *Rte. 127, Shoshone* ☎ *760/852–4414* ☜ *Free* ☉ *Daily 8–4.*

WHERE TO EAT AND STAY

ABOUT THE RESTAURANTS

Inside the park, if you're looking for a special evening out in Death Valley, head to the Furnace Creek Dining Room, where you'll be spoiled with fine wines and gourmet fare such as rattlesnake empanadas or a juicy New York steak. It's also a great spot to start the day with a hearty gourmet breakfast. Most other spots within the park are mom-and-pop type places with basic American fare. Outside the park, dining choices are much the same, with little cafés and homey diners serving up coffee shop–style burgers, chicken, and steaks.

ABOUT THE HOTELS

It's difficult to find lodging anywhere in Death Valley that doesn't have breathtaking views of the park and surrounding mountains. Most accommodations, aside from Furnace Creek Inn, are homey and rustic. Rooms fill up quickly during the fall and spring seasons, and reservations are required about three months in advance for the prime weekends.

Outside the park, head to Beatty or Amargosa Valley in Nevada for a bit of nightlife and casino action. The western side of Death Valley, along the eastern Sierras, is a gorgeous setting, though it's quite a distance from Furnace Creek. Here, you can stay in the historic Dow Villa Motel, where John Wayne spent many a night, or head farther south to the ghost towns of Randsburg or Cerro Gordo for a true Wild West experience.

ABOUT THE CAMPGROUNDS

Backcountry camping is allowed in areas that are at least 2 mi from maintained campgrounds and the main paved or unpaved roads, and ¼ mi from water sources. You will need a high-clearance or a 4X4 vehicle to reach these locations. For your own safety, fill out a voluntary backcountry registration form so the rangers will know where to find you.

You may build fires in the fire grates that are available at all campgrounds except Sunset and Emigrant. Fires may be restricted during summer at Thorndike, Mahogany Flat, and Wildrose (check with rangers about current conditions). Wood gathering is prohibited at all campgrounds. A limited supply of firewood is available at general stores in Furnace Creek and Stovepipe Wells, but since prices are high and supplies limited, you're better off bringing your own if you intend to camp. Camping is prohibited in the historic Inyo, Los Burro, and Ubehebe Crater areas as well as day-use spots including Aguerberry Point Road, Cottonwood Canyon Road, Racetrack Road, Skidoo Road, Titus Canyon Road, Wildrose Road, and West Side Road.

WHERE TO EAT

IN THE PARK

¢–$
AMERICAN

✕ **19th Hole.** Next to the clubhouse of the world's lowest golf course, this open-air spot serves hamburgers, hot dogs, chicken, and sandwiches. There is drive-through service for golfers in carts. ⊠ *Furnace Creek Golf Club, Hwy. 190, Furnace Creek* ☎ *760/786–2345* ⊟ *AE, D, DC, MC, V* ⊗ *Closed June–Sept. No dinner.*

$–$$
CAFÉ
🕘

✕ **Forty-Niner Cafe.** This casual coffee shop serves typical American fare for breakfast, lunch, and dinner. It's done up in a rustic mining style with whitewashed pine walls, vintage map-covered tables, and prospector-branded chairs. Past menus and old photographs decorate the walls. ⊠ *Furnace Creek Ranch, Hwy. 190, Furnace Creek* ☎ *760/786–2345* ⊕ *www.furnacecreekresort.com* ⊟ *AE, D, DC, MC, V.*

$$$–$$$$
AMERICAN
Fodor'sChoice
★

✕ **Furnace Creek Inn Dining Room.** Fireplaces, beamed ceilings, and spectacular views provide a visual feast to match the inn's ambitious menu. Dishes may include such desert-theme items as rattlesnake empanadas and crispy cactus, and simpler fare such as salmon, free-range chicken, and lamb chops. For vegetarians, there's squash lasagna and polenta.

An evening dress code (no jeans, T-shirts, or shorts) is enforced. Lunch is served October–May only, but you can always have afternoon tea, an inn tradition since 1927. Breakfast and Sunday brunch are also served. ✉ *Furnace Creek Inn Resort, Hwy. 190, Furnace Creek* ☎ *760/786–2345* ⊕ *www.furnacecreekresort.com* ⚞ *Reservations essential* ▭ *AE, D, DC, MC, V* ⊘ *No lunch June–Sept.*

$–$$ ✕ **Panamint Springs Resort Restaurant.** This is a great place for steak and a
AMERICAN beer, or pasta and a salad. In summer, evening meals are served outdoors on the porch, which has spectacular views of Panamint Valley. Breakfast and lunch are also served. ✉ *Hwy. 190, 31 mi west of Stovepipe Wells* ☎ *775/482–7680* ⚞ *Reservations essential* ▭ *AE, D, MC, V.*

$$$–$$$$ ✕ **Wrangler Buffet and Steakhouse.** This casual, family-style restaurant has
STEAK a buffet for breakfast and lunch, and steak-house favorites for dinner.
☾ It's slightly more formal than the other restaurant at the Furnace Creek Resort, the Forty-Niner Cafe. ✉ *Furnace Creek Ranch, Hwy. 190, Furnace Creek* ☎ *760/786–2345* ⊕ *www.furnacecreekresort.com* ▭ *AE, D, DC, MC, V* ⊘ *No buffet lunch for 3 wks after Thanksgiving.*

OUTSIDE THE PARK

$–$$ ✕ **Café C'est Si Bon.** This funky little café and Internet lounge serves a
FRENCH variety of delectable treats like homemade croissants slathered with
★ homemade fruit preserves, Thai iced tea, and wafer-thin crêepes stuffed with Gorgonzola, Armenian feta, and smooth Brie cheeses. ✉ *Rte. 127, Shoshone* ☎ *760/852–4307* ▭ *MC, V* ⊘ *Closed Tues.*

$ ✕ **Miner's Union Restaurant and General Store.** Built as Randsburg's Drug
AMERICAN Store in 1896, this popular biker and family spot is one of the area's
☾ few surviving ghost-town buildings with original furnishings intact,
★ such as tin ceiling, light fixtures, and a 1906 marble-and-stained-glass soda fountain. You can still enjoy a phosphate soda from that same fountain, cool down with a draft beer, or lunch on the signature Yellow Aster ham and cheese sandwich and blueberry milkshake. ✉ *35 Butte Ave., Randsburg* ☎ *760/374–2180* ▭ *AE, D, MC, V.*

¢–$ ✕ **Mt. Whitney Restaurant.** A boisterous family-friendly restaurant with a
AMERICAN game room and 50-inch television, this place serves the best burgers in town—but in addition to the usual beef variety, you can choose from ostrich, venison, and buffalo burgers. ✉ *227 S. Main St., Lone Pine* ☎ *760/876–5751* ▭ *D, MC, V* ⊘ *Closed Sun. No lunch.*

WHERE TO STAY

IN THE PARK

During the busy season (November–March) you should make reservations for lodgings within the park at least one month in advance.

$$$$ ⊡ **Furnace Creek Inn.** This is Death Valley's most luxurious accommoda-
Fodor's Choice tions, going so far as to have valet parking. Built in 1927, this adobe-
★ brick-and-stone lodge is nestled in one of the park's greenest oases. A warm mineral stream gurgles across the property, and its 85°F waters feed into a swimming pool. The rooms are decorated in earth tones, with tasteful furnishings. The top-notch Furnace Creek Inn Dining Room ($$$) serves desert-theme dishes such as rattlesnake empanadas and crispy cactus, as well as less exotic fare such as cumin-lime shrimp,

16

lamb, and New York strip steak. Afternoon tea has been a tradition since 1927. **Pros:** refined; comfortable; great views. **Cons:** a far cry from roughing it; expensive. ✉ *Furnace Creek Village, near intersection of Hwy. 190 and Badwater Rd.* ✆ *P.O. Box 187, Death Valley 92328* ☎ *760/786–2345* ⊕ *www.furnacecreekresort.com* ⇆ *66 rooms* ⬧ *In-room: Internet. In-hotel: restaurant, room service, bar, tennis courts, pool* ▬ *AE, D, DC, MC, V* ⊗ *Closed mid-May–mid-Oct.*

$$–$$$ ☷ **Furnace Creek Ranch.** Originally crew headquarters for the Pacific Coast Borax Company, the four buildings here have motel-style rooms that are good for families. The best ones overlook the green lawns of the resort and the surrounding mountains. The property is adjacent to a golf course with its own team of pros, and also has a general store and a campground. The pool here is very popular, but you'll likely have the tennis courts to yourself. The family-style Wrangler Steak House and Forty-Niner Cafe serve American fare in simple surroundings. **Pros:** good family atmosphere; central location. **Cons:** rooms can get hot despite air-conditioning; parking near your room can be problematic. ✉ *Hwy. 190, Furnace Creek* ✆ *P.O. Box 1, Death Valley 92328* ☎ *760/786–2345 or 800/528–6367* ⊕ *www.furnacecreekresort. com* ⇆ *224 rooms* ⬧ *In-room: Internet. In-hotel: restaurant, room service, bar, tennis courts, pool* ▬ *AE, D, DC, MC, V.*

$ ☷ **Panamint Springs Resort.** Ten miles inside the west entrance of the park, this low-key resort overlooks the sand dunes and peculiar geological formations of the Panamint Valley. It's a modest mom-and-pop-style operation with a wraparound porch and rustic furnishings. One room has a king-size bed, and two of the rooms accommodate up to six people. A pay phone, a gas pump, and a grocery store are on the premises. The resort uses satellite telephones to link to the outside world, so it is sometimes difficult to reach the property via phone. **Pros:** slow-paced; friendly; there's a glorious amount of peace and quiet after sundown. **Cons:** far from the park's main attractions. ✉ *Hwy. 190, 28 mi west of Stovepipe Wells* ✆ *P.O. Box 395, Ridgecrest, 93556* ☎ *775/482–7680* ⊕ *www.deathvalley.com/ psr* ⇆ *14 rooms, 1 cabin* ⬧ *In-room: no a/c (some), no phone, no TV. In-hotel: restaurant, bar, some pets allowed* ▬ *AE, D, MC, V.*

$–$$ ☷ **Stovepipe Wells Village.** If you prefer quiet nights and an unfettered view of the night sky and nearby sand dunes, this property is for you. No telephones break the silence here, and only the deluxe rooms have televisions and some refrigerators. Rooms are simple yet comfortable and provide wide-open desert vistas. The Toll Road Restaurant serves American breakfast, lunch, and dinner favorites, from omelets and sandwiches to burgers and steaks. RV campsites with full hookups ($23) are available on a first-come, first-served basis. **Pros:** intimate, relaxed; no big-time partying; authentic desert community ambience. **Cons:** isolated; a bit dated; can feel a bit dodgy after dark. ✉ *Hwy. 190, Stovepipe Wells* ✆ *P.O. Box 559, Death Valley 92328* ☎ *760/786–2387* ⊕ *www.stovepipewells.com* ⇆ *83 rooms* ⬧ *In-room: no phone (some), refrigerator (some). In-hotel: restaurant, bar, pool, some pets allowed* ▬ *AE, D, MC, V.*

CAMPING ⚠ **Furnace Creek.** This campground, 196 feet below sea level, has some

$$ shaded tent sites. Pay showers, a laundry, and a swimming pool are at nearby Furnace Creek Ranch. Reservations are accepted for stays between mid-October and mid-April; at other times sites are available on a first-come, first-served basis. Two group campsites that can accommodate 40 people each. **Pros:** inexpensive; central to park's main attractions; many tent-only sites have trees for limited shade. **Cons:** the campground often is full or parts of it are closed; tent-only sites are hard and pebbly; RV spots have no shade. ⊠ *Hwy. 190, Furnace Creek* ☎ *301/722–1257, 800/365–2267 reservations* ⤵ *136 tent/RV sites* ♿ *Flush toilets, dump station, drinking water, fire grates, picnic tables, public telephone, ranger station* ▭ *AE, DC, MC, V (credit cards accepted for reservations only).*

¢   △ **Mahogany Flat.** If you have a four-wheel-drive vehicle and want to scale
(FREE)   Telescope Peak, the park's highest mountain, you might want to sleep
★   at one of the few shaded spots in Death Valley, at a cool 8,133 feet. It's the most scenic campground, set among pinyon pines and junipers, with a view of the valley. Reservations are not accepted. **Pros:** great scenery; cool; free. **Cons:** remote; no frills or water; road has been in awful shape for years. ⊠ *Off Wildrose Rd., south of Charcoal Kilns* ☎ *No phone* ⤵ *13 tent sites* ♿ *Pit toilets, fire grates, picnic tables* ⊗ *Mar.–Nov.*

$–$$ △ **Panamint Springs Resort.** Part of a complex that includes a motel and cabin, this campground is surrounded by cottonwoods. The daily fee includes use of the showers and restrooms. **Pros:** at an elevation of 1,000 feet, it's cooler than the valley floor; has water and electricity. **Cons:** road to it has many potholes; some reports of rude hosts. ⊠ *Hwy. 190, 28 mi west of Stovepipe Wells* ☎ *775/482–7680* ⤵ *11 RV sites, 26 tent sites, 30 water-only RV sites* ♿ *Flush toilets, full hookups, partial hookups (water), dump station, drinking water, showers, fire grates, picnic tables, public telephone, general store, service station (gas only)* ▭ *AE, D, MC, V.*

$–$$ △ **Stovepipe Wells Village.** This is the second-largest campground in the park. This area is little more than a giant parking lot, but pay showers and laundry facilities are available at the adjacent motel. It's first-come, first-served. **Pros:** creature comforts are nearby, including a saloon; near the sand dunes; lots of socializing possibilities. **Cons:** nothing special as a camping experience, as there's no shade or frills inside the campground. ⊠ *Hwy. 190, Stovepipe Wells* ☎ *760/786–2387* ⤵ *190 tent sites, 14 RV sites* ♿ *Flush toilets, full hookups, dump station, drinking water, public telephone, general store, swimming (pool)* ▭ *No credit cards* ⊗ *Mid-Oct.–mid-Apr.*

$ △ **Sunset Campground.** This first-come, first-served campground is a gravel-and-asphalt RV city. Hookups are not available, but you can walk across the street to the showers, laundry facilities, and swimming pool at Furnace Creek Ranch. Many of Sunset's denizens are senior citizens who migrate to Death Valley each winter to play golf and tennis or just to enjoy the mild, dry climate. No fires are allowed here. **Pros:** good for large rigs; wonderful views; centrally located. **Cons:** can be noisy with RV generators running; dumpsters strangely dominate the immediate surroundings. ⊠ *Sunset Campground Rd., 1 mi north of Furnace Creek* ☎ *760/786–2331* ⤵ *750 tent/RV sites* ♿ *Flush toilets, dump station, drinking water, public telephone, ranger station, play area* ▭ *No credit cards* ⊗ *Mid-Oct.–mid-Apr.*

16

$
★

⚠ **Texas Spring.** This campsite south of the Furnace Creek Visitor Center has good facilities and is a few dollars cheaper than Furnace Creek. No generators are allowed. In spring, not all sites may be available for RV use. **Pros:** spectacular views as it's slightly above the valley floor; centrally located; quiet. **Cons:** not open year-round. ⊠ *Off Badwater Rd., south of the Furnace Creek Visitor Center* ☎ *800/365–2267* ⤴ *92 tent/RV sites* ⚑ *Flush toilets, dump station, drinking water, fire grates, picnic tables* ⚑ *Reservations not accepted* ▭ *No credit cards* ☽ *Mid-Oct.–mid-Apr.*

¢

(FREE)

⚠ **Wildrose.** Since it's on a paved road at a lower elevation (4,100 feet) than nearby Mahogany Flat, Wildrose is less likely to be closed because of snow in winter. The view here is not as spectacular as that from the campground at Mahogany Flat, but it does overlook the northern end of the valley. It's first-come, first-served. **Pros:** availability is rarely an issue; has refreshing higher-altitude breezes. **Cons:** remote; nothing fancy. ⊠ *Wildrose Canyon Rd., 37 mi south of Stovepipe Wells* ☎ *No phone* ⤴ *30 tent/RV sites* ⚑ *Pit toilets, drinking water (Apr.–Nov. only), fire grates, picnic tables* ⚑ *Reservations not accepted.*

OUTSIDE THE PARK

$–$$

▭ **Dow Villa Motel and Hotel.** John Wayne slept here, and you can, too. Built in 1923 to cater to the film industry, Dow Villa is in the center of Lone Pine. Some rooms have views of the mountains; both buildings are within walking distance of just about everything in town. There are in-room coffeemakers and whirlpool tubs, though some of the guest rooms share bathrooms. Pets are allowed only in smoking rooms. Many units have an Old West feel, and are decorated with antique furniture and pictures of John Wayne or Mt. Whitney. **Pros:** authentic eastern Sierra feel; clean rooms; great mountain views. **Cons:** somewhat dated décor; Lone Pine is not all that thrilling. ⊠ *310 S. Main St., Lone Pine* ☎ *760/876–5521 or 800/824–9317* ⊕ *www.dowvillamotel.com* ⤴ *91 rooms* ⚑ *In-room: refrigerator, Internet (some), Wi-Fi (some). In-hotel: pool* ▭ *AE, D, DC, MC, V.*

Glacier and Waterton Lakes National Parks

WORD OF MOUTH

"And then it was time for the sunrise . . . The sun hit that pyramidal mountain that stands alone, directly across the lake from the lodge, and set it afire. First pink, then gold, hovering above the still-dark lake—the stuff of famous photographs."

—Enzian

WELCOME TO GLACIER AND WATERTON

TOP REASONS TO GO

★ **Witness the Divide:** The rugged mountains that weave their way through Glacier and Waterton along the Continental Divide seem to have glaciers in every hollow melting into tiny streams, raging rivers, and icy-cold mountain lakes.

★ **Just hike it:** There are hundreds of miles of trails that cater to hikers of all levels—from all-day hikes to short strolls. It's little wonder the readers of *Backpacker Magazine* rated Glacier the number-one backcountry hiking park in America.

★ **Go to the sun:** Crossing the Continental Divide at the 6,646-foot-high Logan Pass, Glacier's Going-to-the-Sun Road is a spectacular drive.

★ **View the wildlife:** This is one of the few places in North America where all native carnivores, including grizzlies and wolves, still survive. Bighorn sheep, mule deer, coyotes, grizzly bears, and black bears can often be seen from roadways.

1 West Glacier. Known to the Kootenai people as "sacred dancing lake," Lake McDonald is the largest glacial water basin lake in Glacier National Park.

2 Logan Pass. At 6,646 feet, this is the highest point on the Going-to-the-Sun Road. From mid-June to mid-October, a 1½-mi board-walk leads to an overlook that crosses an area filled with lush meadows and wildflowers.

3 East Glacier. St. Mary Lake and Many Glacier are the major highlights of the eastern side of Glacier. Services and amenities are located at both sites.

4 Backcountry. This is some of the most incredible terrain in North America and provides the right combination of beautiful scenery and isolation. Although Waterton is a much smaller park, its backcountry trails connect with hiking trails in both Glacier and British Columbia's Akamina-Kishinena Provincial Park.

5 Waterton Lakes. The Canadian national park is the meeting of two worlds: the flatlands of the prairie and the abrupt upthrust of the mountains.

GETTING ORIENTED

In the rocky northwest corner of Montana, Glacier National Park encompasses 1.2 million acres (1,563 square mi) of untrammeled wilds. Within the park, there are 37 named glaciers (which are ever-so-slowly diminishing), 200 lakes, and 1,000 mi of streams. Neighboring Waterton Lakes National Park, across the border in Alberta, Canada, covers another 130,000 acres. In 1932, the parks were unified to form the Waterton-Glacier International Peace Park—the first international peace park in the world—in recognition of the two nations' friendship and dedication to peace.

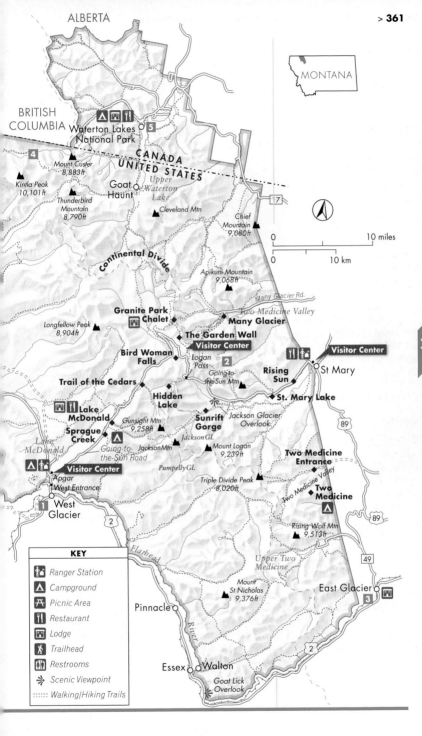

ALBERTA

BRITISH
COLUMBIA

MONTANA

Waterton Lakes
National Park

5

4

Mount Custer
8,883 ft

Kintla Peak
10,101 ft

Thunderbird
Mountain
8,790 ft

Goat
Haunt

Upper
Waterton
Lake

CANADA
UNITED STATES

Cleveland Mtn

Chief
Mountain
9,080 ft

17

Continental Divide

Apikuni Mountain
9,068 ft

Many Glacier Rd.

Two Medicine Valley

Granite Park
Chalet

Longfellow Peak
8,904 ft

The Garden Wall

Visitor Center

Bird Woman
Falls

Logan
Pass

Many Glacier

2

Going to
the Sun Mtn

Visitor Center

St Mary

Rising
Sun

Trail of the Cedars

Hidden
Lake

St. Mary Lake

Lake
McDonald

Gunsight Mtn
9,258 ft

Sunrift
Gorge

Jackson Glacier
Overlook

Sprague
Creek

Jackson Gl.

Lower
McDonald

Going-to-
the-Sun Road

Jackson Mtn

Mount Logan
9,239 ft

Two Medicine
Entrance

Pumpelly Gl.

Visitor Center

Triple Divide Peak
8,020 ft

Two Medicine Valley

Two
Medicine

Apgar
West Entrance

West
Glacier

1

2

Rising Wolf Mtn
9,513 ft

89

89

49

Flathead

Upper Two
Medicine

KEY

Ranger Station

Campground

Picnic Area

Restaurant

Lodge

Trailhead

Restrooms

Scenic Viewpoint

Walking/Hiking Trails

Mount
St Nicholas
9,376 ft

Pinnacle

East Glacier

3

River

Essex

Walton

Goat Lick
Overlook

2

0 —— 10 miles

0 —— 10 km

GLACIER AND WATERTON LAKES PLANNER

When to Go

Of the 2 million annual visitors to Glacier and 400,000 to Waterton, most drive come between July 1 and September 15, when the streams are flowing and wildlife is roaming. Snow removal on the alpine portion of Going-to-the-Sun Road is usually completed by mid-June; the opening of Logan Pass at the road's summit marks the summer opening of Glacier. Canada's Victoria Day in late May marks the beginning of the season in Waterton. Spring and fall are quieter. By October, snow forces the closing of most park roads.

Flora and Fauna

In summer, a profusion of new flowers, grasses, and budding trees covers the landscape high and low. Spring attracts countless birds, from golden eagles riding thermals north to Canada and Alaska, to rare harlequin ducks dipping in creeks. Snow-white mountain goats, with their wispy white beards and curious stares, are seen in alpine areas, and sure-footed bighorn sheep graze the high meadows in the short summers. The largest population of grizzly bears in the lower 48 states live in the wild in and around the park. Feeding the animals is illegal.

Visiting Glacier in winter makes for easy tracking of many large animals like moose, elk, deer, mountain lions, wolf, lynx, and their smaller neighbors—the snowshoe hare, pine marten, beaver, and muskrat.

In park lakes, sportfishing species include burbot (ling), northern pike, whitefish, grayling, cutthroat, rainbow, lake (Mackinaw), kokanee salmon, and brook trout.

AVG. HIGH/LOW TEMPS

Glacier

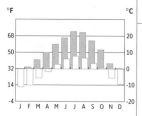

Waterton Lakes

Tours

Glacier Park Inc. schedules driver-narrated van tours that cover most of the park accessible by road. The tour of Going-to-the-Sun Road is a favorite, with plenty of photo opportunities at roadside pull-outs. Some of the tours are conducted in "jammers," vintage 1936 red buses with roll-back tops. Short trips and full-day trips are available. Reservations are essential. 🏠 *P.O. Box 2025, Columbia Falls, MT 59912* ☎ *406/892–2525 or 403/236–3400* 🌐 *www.glacierparkinc.com* 💳 *$45–$90* ☺ *June–Sept.*

Getting Here and Around

On the east, U.S. 89 accesses Many Glacier and St. Mary, Route 49 reaches Two Medicine. On the west, U.S. 2 goes to West Glacier. Take the Chief Mountain Highway to access Waterton Lakes during the summer or Highway 89 to Alberta Highway 2 through Cardston and then west to the park via Highway 5 any time of the year. The nearest airports to Glacier are in Great Falls and Kalispell, Montana. The nearest airport to Waterton Lakes is in Calgary.

The roads in both parks are either paved or gravel and become deteriorated from freezing and thawing. Drive slowly and anticipate that rocks and wildlife may be around the corner. Road reconstruction is part of the park experience as there are only a few warm months in which road crews can complete projects. Scenic pull-outs are frequent; watch for other vehicles pulling in or out, and watch for children in parking areas. Most development and services center around St. Mary Lake on the east and Lake McDonald on the west.

Glacier Park Inc. (☏ 406/226–5666 ⊕ www.glacierpark-inc.com) operates a shuttle along the Going-to-the-Sun Road July 1 to Labor Day. Buses make stops at major trailheads, campgrounds, and other developed areas between Lake McDonald Lodge and Rising Sun Motor Inn.

Border Crossings

A passport is required of everyone crossing the Canadian/U.S. border. Kids traveling with only one parent need a notarized letter from the other parent giving permission to enter Canada or the United States. If you are traveling with pets, you need proof of up-to-date immunizations to cross the border in either direction. Citizens from most countries (Canada, Mexico, and Bermuda are exceptions) entering the United States from Canada must pay $6 (cash only) at the border for a required I–94 or I–94W Arrival-Departure Record form, to be returned to border officials when leaving the U.S. Contact United States Customs (☏ 406/335–2611 ⊕ www.cbp.gov) or the Canada Border Services Agency (☏ 403/344–3767 ⊕ www.cbsa-asfc.gc.ca) for more information.

Safety Tips

Never approach a bear or any other park animal, no matter how cute, cuddly, and harmless it appears. If you encounter a bear, don't run. Back away slowly and assume a nonthreatening posture. If a brown or grizzly bear charges, drop into the fetal position, protect your head and neck, and do not move. It's the opposite if you encounter a black bear or mountain lion: act aggressively, throw rocks or sticks, and try to look large by holding up a pack or branches. If attacked, fight back, aiming for the nose.

To minimize the risk of contact with bears and mountain lions, hike only during the day, hike in groups, and make lots of noise by singing, talking loudly, and clapping hands, especially near blind corners and streams.

Check for ticks after walking through shrubs and high grasses. They are a problem especially in the spring.

Prepare for winter storms with survival kits that include snow tires or chains, a shovel and window scraper, flares or a reflector, a blanket or sleeping bag, a first-aid kit, sand, gravel or traction mats, a flashlight with extra batteries, matches, a lighter and candles, paper, nonperishable foods, drinking water, and a tow chain or rope.

17

By Debbie Olsen   The massive peaks of the Continental Divide in Northwest Montana are the backbone of Glacier National Park and its sister park in Canada, Waterton Lakes, which together make up the International Peace Park. From their slopes, melting snow and alpine glaciers yield the headwaters of rivers that flow west to the Pacific Ocean, north to the Arctic Ocean, and southeast to the Atlantic Ocean via the Gulf of Mexico. Coniferous forests, thickly vegetated stream bottoms, and green-carpeted meadows provide homes and sustenance for all kinds of wildlife.

PARK ESSENTIALS

ACCESSIBILITY
All visitor centers are wheelchair accessible, and most of the campgrounds and picnic areas are paved, with extended-length picnic tables and accessible restrooms. Three of Glacier's nature trails are wheelchair accessible: the Trail of the Cedars, Running Eagle Falls, and the Oberlin Bend Trail, just west of Logan Pass. In Waterton, the Linnet Lake Trail, Waterton Townsite Trail, Cameron Lake day-use area, and the International Peace Park Pavilion are wheelchair accessible.

ADMISSION FEES AND PERMITS
Entrance fees for Glacier are $25 per vehicle, or $12 for one person on foot or bike, good for seven days; it's $35 for a one-year pass. A day pass to Waterton Lakes costs C$7.80, and an annual pass costs C$39. *Passes to Glacier and Waterton must be paid separately.*

At Glacier the required backcountry permit is $5 per person per day from the Apgar Backcountry Permit Center after mid-April for the upcoming summer. Advance reservations cost $20. Mail a request and a check after mid-April to Backcountry Reservations, Glacier National Park Headquarters, P.O. Box 395, West Glacier, MT 59936.

Waterton requires backcountry camping permits for use of its 13 backcountry camp spots, with reservations available up to 90 days in advance. Buy the permit for C$9.80 per adult per night—reserve for an additional C$11—at the visitor reception center (☎ 403/858–5133).

ADMISSION HOURS

The parks are open year-round, but most roads and facilities close October through May. The parks are in the mountain time zone.

ATMS/BANKS

You'll find cash machines at Lake McDonald, Many Glacier, St. Mary Lodge, and Glacier Park lodges and in Waterton's Tamarack Village Square. Waterton has a full-service bank in the Waterton Townsite. The closest full-service bank in the Glacier area can be found in Columbia Falls, where there are several.

CELL-PHONE RECEPTION

Cell phones do not generally work in the mountains. Find pay phones at Avalanche Campground, Glacier Highland Motel and Store, Apgar, St. Mary Visitor Center, Two Medicine Campstore, and all lodges except Granite Park Chalet and Sperry Chalet.

RELIGIOUS SERVICES

In the summer, you can attend either Christian Ministry or Catholic services at Glacier, and Anglican, United, Catholic, or Mormon services in Waterton.

PARK CONTACT INFORMATION

Glacier National Park 🖃 *P.O. Box 128, West Glacier, MT 59936* ☎ *406/888–7800* ⊕ *www.nps.gov/glac.* **Waterton Lakes National Park** 🖃 *P.O. Box 200, Waterton Park, AlbertaCanada T0K 2M0* ☎ *403/859–2224 or 800/748–7275* ⊕ *www.pc.gc.ca/waterton.*

17

GLACIER NATIONAL PARK

SCENIC DRIVES

Fodor's Choice
★

Going-to-the-Sun Road. This magnificent, 50-mi highway—the only American roadway designated both a National Historic Landmark and a National Civil Engineering Landmark—crosses the crest of the Continental Divide at Logan Pass and traverses the towering Garden Wall. Open from mid-June to mid-September, this is one of the most stunning drives in Glacier National Park. A multiyear Sun Road rehabilitation project will result in some driving delays due to reconstruction.

Many Glacier Road. This 12-mi drive enters Glacier on the northeast side of the park, west of Babb, and travels along Sherburne Lake for almost 5 mi, penetrating a glacially carved valley surrounded by mountains. It passes through meadows and a scrubby forest of lodgepole pines, aspen, and cottonwood. The farther you travel up the valley, the more clearly you'll be able to see Grinnell and Salamander glaciers. The road passes Many Glacier Hotel and ends at the Swift Current Campground. It's usually closed from October to May.

GLACIER IN ONE DAY

It's hard to beat the **Going-to-the-Sun Road** for a one-day trip in Glacier National Park. This itinerary takes you from west to east—if you're starting from St. Mary, take the tour backwards. First, however, call the Glacier Park Boat Company (☎ 406/257–2426) to make a reservation for the **St. Mary Lake or Lake McDonald boat tour**, depending on where you end up. Then, drive up Going-to-the-Sun Road to **Avalanche Creek Campground**, and take a 30-minute stroll along the fragrant **Trail of the Cedars**. Afterward, continue driving up—you can see views of waterfalls and wildlife to the left and an awe-inspiring, precipitous drop to the right. At the summit, **Logan Pass**, your arduous climb is rewarded with a gorgeous view of immense peaks, sometimes complemented by a herd of mountain goats. Stop in at the **Logan Pass Visitor Center**, then take the 1½-mi **Hidden Lake Nature Trail** up to prime wildlife-viewing spots. Picnic at the overlook above Hidden Lake. In the afternoon, continue driving east over the mountains. Stop at the **Jackson Glacier Overlook** to view one of the park's largest glaciers. Continue down; eventually the forest thins, the vistas grow broader, and a gradual transition to the high plains begins. When you reach **Rising Sun Campground**, take the one-hour St. Mary Lake boat tour to St. Mary Falls. If you'd rather hike, the 1.2-mi **Sun Point Nature Trail** also leads to the falls. (Take the boat tour if you're driving from east to west.) The Going-to-the-Sun Road is generally closed from mid-September to mid-June.

WHAT TO SEE

HISTORIC SITES

☾ **Apgar.** On the southwest end of Lake McDonald, this tiny hamlet has a few stores, an ice-cream shop, motels, ranger buildings, a campground, and an historic schoolhouse. From November to mid-May, no services remain open, except the weekend-only visitor center. Across the street from the Apgar visitor center, **Apgar Discovery Cabin** is filled with animal posters, kids' activities, and maps. ⊠ *2 mi north of west entrance* ☎ *406/888–7939* ☾ *Cabin: mid-June–Labor Day, daily 1:30–3.*

SCENIC STOPS

⇨ *Going-to-the-Sun Road close-up for stops along that famous route.*

Goat Lick Overlook. Mountain goats frequent this natural salt lick on a cliff above the Middle Fork of the Flathead River. ⊠ *2½ mi east of Walton Ranger Station on U.S. 2.*

Grinnell and Salamander Glaciers. These glaciers formed as one ice mass, but in 1926 they broke apart and have been shrinking ever since. The best viewpoint is reached by the 5½-mi Grinnell Glacier Trail from Many Glacier. ⊠ *Trailhead for Grinnell Glacier Trail at the far northwestern end of Lake Josephine. Catch a boat to this trailhead or hike there via the trail behind the Many Glacier Hotel.*

Lake McDonald. This beautiful 10-mi-long lake is accessible year-round on Going-to-the-Sun Road. Take a boat ride to the middle for a view of the surrounding glacier-clad mountains. You can go fishing and horseback riding at either end, and in winter, snowshoe or cross-country ski. ⊠ *2 mi north of west entrance.*

Running Eagle Falls (Trick Falls). Cascading near Two Medicine, these are actually two different waterfalls from two different sources. In spring, when the water level is high, the upper falls join the lower falls for a 40-foot drop into Two Medicine River; in summer, the upper falls dry up, revealing the lower 20-foot falls that start midway down the precipice. ⊠ *2 mi east of Two Medicine entrance.*

Two Medicine Valley. Rugged, often windy, and always beautiful, the valley is a remote 9-mi drive from Route 49 and is surrounded by some of the park's most stark, rocky peaks. On and around the valley's lake you can rent a canoe, take a narrated boat tour, camp, and hike. Be aware that bears frequent the area. The road is closed from late October through late May. ⊠ *Two Medicine entrance, 9 mi east of Hwy. 49* ☎ *406/888–7800, 406/257–2426 boat tours.*

VISITOR CENTERS

Apgar Visitor Center. This is a great first stop if you're entering the park from the west. Here you can get all kinds of information, including maps, permits, books, and the *Junior Ranger* newspaper. You can plan your route on a large relief map to get a glimpse of where you're going. In winter, the rangers offer free snowshoe walks. Snowshoes can be rented for $2 at the visitor center. ⊠ *2 mi north of West Glacier in Apgar Village* ☎ *406/888–7800* ☉ *Mid-May–Oct., daily 8–8; Nov.–mid-May, weekends 9–4.*

Logan Pass Visitor Center. Built of stone, this center stands sturdy against the severe weather that forces it to close in winter. Books, maps, and more are stocked inside. Rangers staff the center and give 10-minute talks on the alpine environment. ⊠ *34 mi east of West Glacier, 18 mi west of St. Mary* ☎ *406/888–7800* ☉ *Mid-June–mid-Sept., daily 9–7.*

St. Mary Visitor Center. The park's largest visitor complex, it has a huge relief map of the park's peaks and valleys and provides a 15-minute video that orients visitors. Rangers host evening presentations during the peak summer months. Traditional Blackfeet dancing and drumming performances are offered throughout the summer. Check with the center for exact dates and times. The center has books and maps for sale, backcountry camping permits, and large viewing windows facing the 10-mi-long St. Mary Lake. ⊠ *Going-to-the-Sun Rd., off U.S. 89* ☎ *406/732–7750* ☉ *Mid-May–mid-Oct., daily 8–4:30 with extended hours during the peak summer months.*

SPORTS AND THE OUTDOORS

BICYCLING

Cyclists in Glacier must stay on roads or bike routes and are not permitted on hiking trails or in the backcountry. The one-lane, unpaved Inside North Fork Road from Apgar to Polebridge is well suited to mountain bikers. Two Medicine Road is an intermediate paved route, with a mild

17

Going-to-the-Sun Road

Going-to-the-Sun Road, arguably the most beautiful drive in the country, connects Lake McDonald on the west side of Glacier with St. Mary Lake on the east. Turnoffs provide views of the high country and glacier-carved valleys. The sights below are listed in order from west to east.

The Garden Wall. An abrupt and jagged wall of rock juts above the road and is visible for about 10 mi as it follows Logan Creek from just past Avalanche Creek Campground to Logan Pass. ⊠ *24–34 mi northeast of West Glacier.*

★ **Logan Pass.** At 6,660 feet, this is the highest point in the park accessible by motor vehicle. It presents unparalleled views of both sides of the Continental Divide and is frequented by mountain goats, bighorn sheep, and grizzly bears. It is extremely crowded in July and August. ⊠ *34 mi east of West Glacier, 18 mi west of St. Mary.*

Hidden Lake Overlook. Take a walk from Logan Pass up to see the crystalline Hidden Lake, which often still has ice clinging to it in early July. It's a 1½-mi hike on an uphill grade, partially on a boardwalk that protects the abundant wildflowers. ⊠ *Trailhead behind Logan Pass Visitor's Centre.*

Jackson Glacier Overlook. On the east side of the Continental Divide, you come into view of Jackson Glacier looming in a rocky pass across the upper St. Mary River valley. If it isn't covered with snow, you'll see sharp peaks of ice. The glacier is shrinking and may disappear in another 100 years. ⊠ *5 mi east of Logan Pass.*

St. Mary Lake. When the breezes calm, the lake mirrors the snowcapped granite peaks that line the St. Mary Valley. The Sun Point Nature Trail follows the lake's shore 1 mi each way. You can buy an interpretive brochure for 50¢ at the trailhead on the north side of the lake, then drop it off at the box at the trail's end to be recycled. ⊠ *1 mi west of St. Mary.*

■ TIP→ **The drive is susceptible to frequent delays in summer. To avoid traffic jams and parking problems, take the road early in the morning or late in the evening (when the lighting is ideal for photography and wildlife is most likely to appear).**

Vehicle size is restricted to under 21 feet long, 10 feet high, and 8 feet wide, including mirrors, between Avalanche Creek Campground and Sun Point. This roadway is open only from mid-June to mid-September, due to heavy snowfalls.

If you don't want to drive the Going-to-the-Sun Road, consider making the ride in a "jammer," an antique red bus operated by **Glacier Park Inc.** (☎ *406/892–2525* ⊕ *www.glacierpark-inc.com*). The drivers double as guides and they can roll back the tops of the vehicles to give you improved views. Reservations are required.

The scenic, 50-mile Going to the Sun road takes about two hours to drive, depending on how often you stop.

grade at the beginning, becoming steeper as you approach Two Medicine Campground. Much of the western half of Going-to-the-Sun Road is closed to bikes from 11 to 4. Other restrictions apply during peak traffic periods and road construction. You can find thrilling off-road trails just outside the park near Whitefish. There are no bike rental shops inside the park, but there is one in the nearby town of Whitefish.

OUTFITTER AND EXPEDITIONS Guided cycling tours inside the park with plenty of stops to identify plants, animals, and habitats can be arranged with **Glacier Adventure Guides** (⌂ *P.O. Box 4833, Whitefish 59937* ☎ *406/891–2173 or 877/735–9514* ⊕ *www.glacierparkskitours.com*). Rental bikes are included with the tours (but the company doesn't rent bikes otherwise). **Glacier Cyclery** (✉ *326 E. 2nd St., Whitefish* ☎ *403/862–6446* ⊕ *www.glaciercyclery. com*) has daily and weekly bike rentals on touring, road, and mountain bikes for all ages and skill levels. It also sells bikes and does repairs.

BOATING AND RAFTING

Glacier has many stunning lakes and rivers, and boating is a popular park activity. Glacier Park Boat Company offers guided tours of Lake McDonald, St. Mary Lake, and Two Medicine Lake, as well as Swiftcurrent Lake and Lake Josephine at Many Glacier from June to mid-September. You can rent small boats at Lake McDonald, Apgar, Two Medicine, and Many Glacier through the Glacier Park Boat Company. Watercraft such as Sea-Doos or Jet Skis are not allowed in the park.

Many rafting companies provide adventures along the border of the park on the Middle and North Forks of the Flathead River. The Middle Fork has some excellent white water, while the North Fork has both slow-moving and fast-moving sections. If you bring your own raft or kayak, stop at the Hungry Horse Ranger Station in the Flathead National Forest near West Glacier to obtain a permit.

OUTFITTERS
AND
EXPEDITIONS
★

Glacier Park Boat Company (☎ 406/257–2426 ⊕ *www.glacierparkboats. com* 🖃 *Tours $11.25–$22, rentals $18–$24 per hour* ☉ *May–Sept.*) gives tours on five lakes. A **Lake McDonald cruise** takes you from the dock at Lake McDonald Lodge to the middle of the lake for an unparalleled view of the Continental Divide's Garden Wall. **Many Glacier tours** on Swiftcurrent Lake and Lake Josephine depart from Many Glacier Lodge and provide views of the Continental Divide. **Two Medicine Lake cruises** leave from the dock near the ranger station and lead to several trails. **St. Mary Lake cruises** leave from the launch near Rising Sun Campground and head to Red Eagle Mountain and other spots. The tours last 45–90 minutes. You can rent kayaks, canoes, rowboats ($18 per hour), and small motorboats ($24 per hour) at Lake McDonald, Apgar, Two Medicine, and Many Glacier.

For rafting outfitters and expeditions, ⇨ *Multisport Outfitters.*

FISHING

Within Glacier there's an almost unlimited range of fishing possibilities, with a catch-and-release policy encouraged. You can fish in most waters of the park, but the best fishing is generally in the least accessible spots. A fishing license is not required inside the park boundary, but you must stop by a park office to pick up a copy of the regulations. The fishing season runs from the third Saturday in May to November 30. There are several companies that offer guided fishing trips in the area.

■ TIP➔ Fishing on both the North Fork and the Middle Fork of the Flathead River requires a Montana conservation license ($10) plus a Montana fishing license ($15 for two consecutive days or $60 for a season). They are available at most convenience stores, sports shops, and from the Montana Department of Fish, Wildlife, and Parks (☎ 406/752–5501 ⊕ www.fwp.mt.gov).

⇨ *Multisport Outfitters for additional fishing outfitters and expeditions.*

HIKING

With 730 mi of marked trails, Glacier is a hiker's paradise. Trail maps are available at all visitor centers and entrance stations. Before hiking, ask about trail closures due to bear or mountain lion activity. Never hike alone. For backcountry hiking, pick up a permit from park headquarters or the Apgar Backcountry Permit Center near Glacier's west entrance (☎ 406/888–7939).

EASY

Avalanche Lake Trail. From Avalanche Creek Campground, take this 3-mi trail leading to mountain-ringed Avalanche Lake. The walk is relatively easy (it ascends 500 feet), making this one of the most accessible backcountry lakes in the park. Crowds fill the parking area and trail during July and August, and on sunny weekends in May and June. ✉ *Trailhead across from Avalanche Creek Campground, 15 mi north of Apgar on Going-to-the-Sun Rd.*

🜁 **Baring Falls.** For a nice family hike, try the 1.3-mi path from the Sun Point parking area. It leads to a spruce and Douglas fir wood; cross a log bridge over Baring Creek and you arrive at the base of gushing Baring

MULTISPORT OUTFITTERS

Glacier Guides and Montana Raft Company. Take a raft trip through the stomach-churning white water of the Middle Fork of the Flathead and combine it with a hike, horseback ride, or a barbecue. The company also offers guided hikes and fly-fishing trips. ⊠ *11970 U.S. 2 E, 1 mi west of West Glacier* ☎ *406/387-5555 or 800/521-7238* ⊕ *www.glacierguides.com* ⌦ *$48–$87* ⊗ *May–Oct.*

Glacier Raft Company and Outdoor Center. In addition to running fishing trips, family float rides, and high-adrenaline white-water adventure rafting (including multiday excursions), this outfitter will set you up with camping, backpacking, and fishing gear. There's a full-service fly-fishing shop and outdoor store. You can stay in one of nine log cabins that sleep six to 14 people. ⊠ *11957 U.S. 2 E, West Glacier* ☎ *406/888-5454 or 800/235-6781* ⊕ *www.*

glacierraftco.com ⌦ *$48–$87* ⊗ *Year-round; rafting mid-May–Sept.*

Great Northern Whitewater. Sign up for daily white-water, kayaking, and fishing trips. This outfitter also rents Swiss-style chalets with views of Glacier's peaks. ⊠ *12127 Hwy. 2 E, 1 mi south of West Glacier* ☎ *406/387-5340 or 800/735-7897* ⊕ *www.gnwhitewater.com* ⌦ *$48–$82* ⊗ *May–Oct.*

Wild River Adventures. Brave the whitewater in an inflatable kayak or a traditional raft or enjoy a scenic float with these guys, who will paddle you over the Middle Fork of the Flathead, and peddle you tall tales all the while. They also provide trail rides, and scenic fishing trips on rivers around Glacier Park. ⊠ *11900 U.S. 2 E, 1 mi west of West Glacier* ☎ *406/387-9453 or 800/700-7056* ⊕ *www.riverwild.com* ⌦ *$48–$115* ⊗ *Mid-May–Sept.*

17

Falls. ⊠ *Trailhead 11 mi east of Logan Pass on Going-to-the-Sun Rd. at the Sun Point parking area.*

★ **Hidden Lake Nature Trail.** This uphill, 1½-mi trail runs from Logan Pass southwest to Hidden Lake Overlook, from which you get a beautiful view of the lake and McDonald Valley. In spring, ribbons of water pour off the rocks surrounding the lake. ⊠ *Trailhead directly behind Logan Pass Visitor Center.*

☾ **Trail of the Cedars.** This wheelchair-accessible, ½-mi boardwalk loop
★ through an ancient cedar and hemlock forest is a favorite of families with small children and people with disabilities. Interpretive signs describe the habitat and natural history of the rain forest. ⊠ *Trailhead across from Avalanche Creek Campground, 15 mi north of Apgar on Going-to-the-Sun Rd.*

MODERATE

Fodor'sChoice **Highline Trail.** From the Logan Pass parking lot, hike north along the
★ Garden Wall and just below the craggy Continental Divide. Wildflowers dominate the 7.6 mi to Granite Park Chalet, a National Historic Landmark, where hikers with reservations can overnight. Return to Logan Pass along the same trail or hike down 4½ mi (a 2,500-foot descent) on the Loop Trail. ⊠ *Trailhead at the Logan Pass Visitor Center.*

Iceberg Lake Trail. This moderately strenuous 9-mi round-trip hike passes the gushing Ptarmigan Falls, then climbs to its namesake, where icebergs bob in the chilly mountain loch. Mountain goats hang out on sheer cliffs above, bighorn sheep graze in the high mountain meadows, and grizzly bears dig for glacier lily bulbs, grubs, and other delicacies. Rangers lead hikes here almost daily in summer, leaving at 8:30 AM. ✉ *Trailhead at the Swiftcurrent Inn parking lot off Many Glacier Rd.*

> ### GLACIERS AWAY?
>
> Call it global warming or call it a natural progression, but the glaciers at Glacier National Park are feeling the heat. By 2050, or earlier, it is estimated that all of the glaciers in the park will have melted. Currently there are 50 glaciers in the park (at one time there were 200).

DIFFICULT

★ **Grinnell Glacier Trail.** The strenuous 5½-mi hike to Grinnell Glacier, the park's largest and most accessible glacier, is marked by several spectacular viewpoints. You start at Swiftcurrent Lake's picnic area, climb a moraine to Lake Josephine, then climb to the Grinnell Glacier overlook. Halfway up, turn around to see the prairie land to the northeast. You can shortcut the trail by 2 mi each way by taking two scenic boat rides across Swiftcurrent Lake and Lake Josephine. From July to mid-September, a ranger-led hike departs from the Many Glacier Hotel boat dock most mornings at 8:30. ✉ *Trail begins at Lake Josephine boat dock.*

Sun Point Nature Trail. This short, 1.3-mi well-groomed trail allows you to walk along the cliffs and shores of picturesque St. Mary Lake. There is a stunning waterfall at the end of the hike. You may choose to hike one-way and take a boat transfer back. ✉ *Trailhead is 11 mi east of Logan Pass on Going-to-the-Sun Rd. at the Sun Point parking area.*

Two Medicine Valley Trails. One of the least-developed parts of Glacier, the lovely southeast corner of the park is a good place for a quiet day hike, although you should look out for signs of bears. The trailhead to Upper Two Medicine Lake and Cobalt Lake begins west of the boat dock and camp supply store where you can make arrangements for a boat pick-up or drop-off across the lake. ✉ *Trailhead is west of the boat dock and camp supply store at Two Medicine Campground, 9 mi west of Rte. 49.*

HORSEBACK RIDING

Horses are permitted on many trails within the parks; check for seasonal exceptions. Horseback riding is prohibited on paved roads. You can pick up a brochure about suggested routes and outfitters from any visitor center or entrance station. The Sperry Chalet Trail to the view of Sperry Glacier above Lake McDonald is a tough 7-mi climb.

OUTFITTERS
AND
EXPEDITIONS
At **Glacier Gateway Outfitters** (☎ *406/226–4408, 406/338–5560* ⌨ *$25– $175* ☺ *May–Sept.*), in East Glacier, a Blackfoot cowboy guides riders through the park's Two Medicine area. Rides, which are one hour or one day, begin at Glacier Park Lodge and climb through aspen groves to high-country views of Dancing Lady and Bison mountains. Riders must be 8 and older, and reservations are essential. **Swan Mountain Outfitters** (☎ *877/888–5557 central reservations, 406/888–5010 Apgar Corral,*

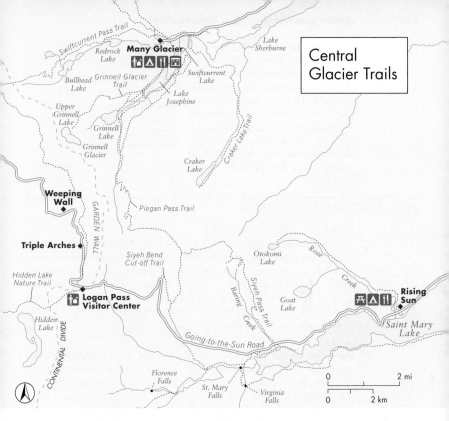

406/888–5121 Lake McDonald Corral, 406/732–4203 Many Glacier Corral ⊕ *www.swanmountainoutfitters.com/glacier* ✉ *$40 for 1 hr, $58 for 2 hrs, $105 for ½ day, $150 for full day* ⏱ *Late May–mid-Sept.*) begins its rides at Apgar, Lake McDonald, and Many Glacier, and is the only outfitter that offers horseback riding inside the park. Trips for beginning to advanced riders cover both flat and mountainous territory. Riders must be 7 or older and weigh less than 250 pounds. Reservations are essential.

SKIING AND SNOWSHOEING

Cross-country skiing and snowshoeing are increasingly popular in the park. Glacier distributes a free pamphlet entitled *Ski Trails of Glacier National Park*, with 16 noted trails. You can start at Lake McDonald Lodge and ski cross-country up Going-to-the-Sun Road. The 2½-mi Apgar Natural Trail is popular with snowshoers. No restaurants or stores are open in winter in Glacier.

OUTFITTERS AND EXPEDITIONS **Glacier Park Ski Tours** (⬁ *P.O. Box 4833, Whitefish 59937* ☎ *406/891–2173 or 877/735–9514* ⊕ *www.glacierparkskitours.com* ✉ *$30–$150* ⏱ *Mid-Nov.–May*) leads one-day or multiday guided ski or snowshoe trips on the park's scenic winter trails. On overnight trips, you stay in snow huts or tents. Just outside the southern edge of the park, the **Izaak Walton Inn** (⬁ *290 Izaak Walton Inn Rd. [off U.S. 2], Essex 59916* ☎ *406/888–5700* ⊕ *www.izaakwaltoninn.com* ▭ *MC, V* ✉ *$85–$200 full day [includes* *lunch]* ⊘ *Mid-Nov.–May*) has more than 20 mi of groomed cross-country ski trails on the property and offers guided ski and snowshoe tours inside the park. The hotel is one of the few places in the area that is both open during the winter months and accessible by Amtrak train—a nice perk, because then you don't have to worry about driving on icy mountain roads.

> ### NOTABLE QUOTATION
>
> "Get off the tracks at Belton Station (now West Glacier), and in a few minutes you will find yourself in the midst of what you are sure to say is the best care-killing scenery on the continent."
>
> —John Muir

EDUCATIONAL OFFERINGS

CLASSES AND SEMINARS

ⓒ **Glacier Institute.** Based near West Glacier at the Field Camp and on the remote western boundary at the Big Creek Outdoor Education Center, this learning institute offers more than 75 field courses for kids and adults. Year-round, experts in wildlife biology, native plants, and river ecology lead treks into Glacier's backcountry on daylong and multiday programs. ✉ *P.O. Box 7457, Kalispell 59901* ☎ *406/755–1211* ⊕ *www.glacierinstitute.org.*

KIDS' CAMPS

ⓒ **Adventure Camps.** Youngsters ages six to eight can partake of one-day naturalist courses, while kids 11–13 can take weeklong hiking and rafting trips. Some camps involve backcountry camping while others are based out of the Big Creek or Glacier Park field camps. Subjects range from ecology and birding to wildflowers, predators and prey, and backcountry medicine. ✉ *137 Main St., Kalispell* ☎ *406/755–1211* ⊕ *www.glacierinstitute.org* ☑ *$20–$300* ⊘ *June–Aug.*

RANGER PROGRAMS

These programs are free to visitors. Most run daily, July through Labor Day. For information on ranger programs, call ☎ *406/888–7800.*

ⓒ **Children's Programs.** Kids learn about bears, wolves, geology, and more via hands-on activities, such as role-playing skits and short hikes. Check the Apgar Education Cabin located near the Apgar Visitor Center for schedules and locations.

Evening Campfire Programs. Rangers lead discussions on the park's wildlife, geology, and history. The programs occur at park campgrounds, beginning at 8 or 9 PM. Topics and dates are posted at campgrounds, lodges, and the St. Mary Visitor Center.

ⓒ **Junior Ranger Program.** Year-round, children ages 6–12 can become a Junior Ranger by completing activities in the *Junior Ranger* newspaper available at the park Visitor Centers.

Naturalist Activities. Evening slide programs, guided hikes, and boat tours are among the ranger-led activities held at various sites in the park. A complete schedule of programs is listed in *Glacier Explorer,* a national park service publication distributed at the visitor centers.

The Crown of the Continent

The history of Glacier National Park started long before Congress named the spectacular wilderness a national park. American Indians, including the Blackfeet, Kootenai, and Salish, regularly traversed the area's valleys for centuries before white immigrants arrived. For the most part, these migratory people crossed the Rocky Mountains in search of sustenance in the form of roots, grasses, berries, and game. Many tribes felt that the mountains, with their unusual glacier-carved horns, cirques, and arêtes, were spiritually charged. Later, white people would be similarly inspired by Glacier's beauty and would nickname the area atop the Continental Divide the "Crown of the Continent."

White trappers arrived in the area as early as the 1780s. Then, in 1805, Lewis and Clark passed south of what is now Glacier National Park. Attracted by the expedition's reports of abundant beaver, many more trappers, primarily British, French, and Spanish, migrated to the region. For most of the early to mid-1800s, human activity in the area was limited to lone trappers and migrating Indians.

On their journey west, Lewis and Clark sought but did not find the elusive pass over the Rockies, now known as Marias Pass on the southern edge of the park. Whether their scouts were unaware of the relatively low elevation—5,200 feet—of the pass, or whether they feared the Blackfeet that controlled the region, is unknown. The pass went undiscovered until 1889, when surveyors for the Great Northern Railway found it in the dead of winter. By 1891 the Great Northern Railway's tracks had crossed Marias Pass, and by 1895 the railroad had completed its westward expansion.

As homesteaders, miners, and trappers poured into the Glacier area in the late 1800s, the American Indian population seriously declined. The Blackfeet were devastated by smallpox epidemics—a disease previously unknown in North America—from the mid-1800s until the early 1900s. The disease, and a reduced food supply due the overhunting of buffalo, stripped the Blackfeet of their power and, eventually, their land. In 1895, the tribe sold the area now within the park to the U.S. government, which opened it to miners. Returns on the mines were never very substantial, and most were abandoned by 1905.

Between the late 1880s and 1900, *Forest and Stream* magazine editor George Grinnel made several trips to the mountains of northwestern Montana. He was awed by the beauty of the area and urged the U.S. government to give it park status, thus protecting it from mining interests and homesteaders. At the same time, the Great Northern Railway company was spreading the word about the area's recreational opportunities. The company built seven backcountry chalets to house guests, and promised tourists from the East a back-to-nature experience with daylong hikes and horseback rides between the chalets. Visitors arrived by train at West Glacier, took a stagecoach to Lake McDonald, a boat to the lakeside Snyder Hotel, and began their nature adventures from there. Between Grinnel's political influence and the Great Northern's financial interests, Congress found reason enough to establish Glacier National Park; the bill was signed by president William Howard Taft in 1910.

17

TOURS

★ **Sun Tours.** Tour the park and learn the Blackfeet perspective with these native guides who concentrate on how Glacier's features are relevant to the Blackfeet Nation, past and present. In summer, tours depart daily from East Glacier at 29 Glacier Avenue at 8 AM and the St. Mary Visitor Center at 9:15 AM in air-conditioned coaches. ⊠ *29 Glacier Ave., East Glacier* ☎ *406/226–9220 or 800/786–9220* ⊕ *www.glacierinfo.com* ✉ *$35–$55* ☉ *June–Sept., daily at 8 AM (East Glacier) and 9:15 AM (St. Mary).*

WATERTON LAKES NATIONAL PARK

SCENIC DRIVES

Akamina Parkway. Take this winding 16-km (10-mi) road up to Cameron Lake. A relatively flat, paved, 1.6-km (1-mi) trail hugs the western shore and makes a nice walk. Bring your binoculars, because it's common to see grizzly bears on the lower slopes of the mountains at the far end of the lake.

Red Rock Parkway. The 15-km (9-mi) route takes you from the prairie up the Blakiston Valley to Red Rock Canyon, where water has cut through the earth, exposing red sedimentary rock.

WHAT TO SEE

HISTORIC SITES

First Oil Well in Western Canada. Alberta is known worldwide for its oil and gas production and the first oil well in western Canada was established in 1902 in what is now the park. Stop at this National Historic Site to explore the wellheads, drilling equipment, and remains of the Oil City boomtown. ⊠ *Watch for sign 7.7 km (4.8 mi) up the Akamina Pkwy.* ☎ *No phone.*

★ **Prince of Wales Hotel.** Named for the prince who later became King Edward VIII, this lovely hotel was constructed between 1926 and 1927 and was designated a National Historic Site in 1995. The lobby window affords a pretty view, and afternoon tea is a treat here. ⊠ *Off Hwy. 5* ☎ *406/756–2444 or 403/859–2231 mid-May–late Sept.* ⊕ *www.glacierparkinc.com* ☉ *Mid-May–late Sept.*

SCENIC STOPS

★ **Cameron Lake.** The jewel of Waterton, Cameron Lake sits in a land of glacially carved cirques (steep-walled basins). In summer, hundreds of varieties of alpine wildflowers fill the area, including 22 kinds of wild orchids. Canoes and pedal boats can be rented here. ⊠ *Akamina Pkwy., 13 km (8 mi) southwest of Waterton Park Townsite.*

Goat Haunt Ranger Station. Reached only by foot trail or tour boat from Waterton Townsite, this spot on the U.S. end of Waterton Lake is the stomping ground for mountain goats, moose, grizzlies, and black bears. The ranger posted at this remote station gives thrice-daily 10-minute overviews of Waterton Valley history. ⊠ *South end of Waterton Lake*

17

☎ *406/888–7800 or 403/859–2362* ⊕ *www.watertoncruise.com* 📧 *Tour boat $22 one-way* ⊗ *Mid-May–Oct.*

★ **Waterton Townsite.** This is a decidedly low-key community in roughly the geographical center of the park. In summer it swells with tourists, and local restaurants and shops open to serve them. In winter only a few motels are open, and services are limited.

VISITOR CENTER

Waterton Information Centre. Stop here on the eastern edge of Waterton Townsite to pick up brochures, maps, and books. Park interpreters are on hand to answer questions and give directions. ✉ *On Waterton Rd. before you reach the townsite* ☎ *403/859–5133 or 403/859–2224* ⊗ *Mid-May–mid-June, daily 8–6; mid-June–early Sept., daily 8–8; early Sept.–Oct. 8, daily 9–6.*

SPORTS AND THE OUTDOORS

The park contains numerous short hikes for day-trippers and some longer treks for backpackers. Upper and Middle Waterton and Cameron lakes provide peaceful havens for boaters. A tour boat cruises across Upper Waterton Lake, crossing the U.S.–Canada border, and the winds that rake across that lake create an exciting ride for windsurfers—bring a wet suit, though; the water remains numbingly cold throughout summer.

BICYCLING

Bikes are allowed on some trails, such as the 3-km (2-mi) Townsite Loop Trail. A ride on mildly sloping Red Rock Canyon Road isn't too difficult. Cameron Lake Road is an intermediate route.

OUTFITTER **Pat's Waterton.** Choose from surrey bikes, mountain bikes, or motorized scooters. Pat's also rents tennis rackets, strollers, and binoculars. ✉ *Corner of Mt. View Rd., Waterton Townsite* ☎ *403/859–2266.*

BOATING

Nonmotorized boats can be rented at Cameron Lake in summer; private craft can be used on Upper and Middle Waterton lakes.

OUTFITTERS AND EXPEDITIONS **Waterton Inter-Nation Shoreline Cruise Co.** This company's two-hour round-trip boat tour along Upper Waterton Lake from Waterton Townsite to Goat Haunt Ranger Station is one of the most popular activities in Waterton. (*Note that because Goat Haunt is in the United States, you must clear customs if you want to stay at Goat Haunt and hike into Glacier from there.*) The narrated tour passes scenic bays, sheer cliffs, and snow-clad peaks. ✉ *Waterton Townsite Marina, on the northwest corner of Waterton Lake near the Bayshore Inn* ☎ *403/859–2362* ⊕ *www.watertoncruise. com* 📧 *C$34* ⊗ *May–early Oct., cruises several times daily.*

HIKING

There are 225 km (191 mi) of trails in Waterton Lakes that range in difficulty from short strolls to strenuous treks. Some trails connect with the trail systems of Glacier and British Columbia's Akamina-Kishenina Provincial Park. The wildflowers in June are particularly stunning along most trails.

WATERTON IN ONE DAY

Begin your day with a stop at the **Waterton Information Centre** to pick up free maps and information about interpretive programs and schedules.

Behind the reception center is the **Bear's Hump Trailhead,** where you can enjoy a relatively easy 1.4-km (0.9-mi) hike to a beautiful scenic overlook. After the hike, drive up the hill to the historic **Prince of Wales Hotel** to enjoy the view.

Next, visit **Waterton Townsite** for an early lunch. Afterward, walk the easy 3-km (2-mi) **Townsite Loop Trail,** stopping to view **Cameron Falls** and explore the trail behind the falls.

End the day with a scenic, two-hour **Waterton Inter-Nation Shoreline Cruise** across the border to **Goat Haunt Ranger Station** and back.

EASY

🕑 ★ **Bear's Hump Trail.** This 2.7-km (1.7-mi) trail climbs up the mountainside to an overlook with a great view of Upper Waterton Lake and the town site. ⊠ *Trailhead directly behind the Waterton Information Centre bldg.*

🕑 **Cameron Lake Shore Trail.** This relatively flat paved 1½-km (1-mi) trail is a peaceful place for a walk. Look for grizzlies on the lower slopes of the mountains at the far end of the lake. ⊠ *Trailhead at the lakeshore in front of the parking lot, 13 km (8 mi) southwest of Waterton Townsite.*

Crandell Lake Trail. This easy 2½-km (1½ mi) trail follows an old wagon road to lead to Oil City. ⊠ *Trail begins about halfway up the Akamina Pkwy.*

MODERATE

Bertha Lake Trail. This 13-km (8-mi) trail leads from the Waterton Townsite through a Douglas fir forest to a beautiful overlook of Upper Waterton Lake, then on to Lower Bertha Falls. If you continue on, a steeper climb will take you past Upper Bertha Falls to Bertha Lake. The wildflowers are particularly stunning along this trail in June. ⊠ *Trailhead on south end of Waterton Townsite; head toward the lake and you will find a parking lot on the west side of the road.*

DIFFICULT

Fodor's Choice ★ **Crypt Lake Trail.** This awe-inspiring, strenuous, 9-km (5½-mi) trail is proclaimed by some to be one of the most stunning hikes in the Canadian Rockies. Conquering the trail involves a boat taxi across Waterton Lake, a climb of 2,300 feet, a crawl through a tunnel that measures almost 100 feet, and a climb along a sheer rock face. The reward is a 600-foot-tall cascading waterfall and the turquoise waters of Crypt Lake. ⊠ *Trailhead at Crypt Landing accessed by ferry from Waterton Townsite.*

HORSEBACK RIDING

Rolling hills, grasslands, and rugged mountains make riding in Waterton Lakes a real pleasure. Scenery, wildlife, and wildflowers are easily viewed from the saddle and many of the park trails allow horses.

17

OUTFITTERS AND EXPEDITIONS With **Alpine Stables** (⊠ *P.O. Box 53, Waterton Lakes National Park* ☎ *403/859–2462 May–Sept., 403/653–2449 Oct.–Apr.* ⊕ *www.alpinestables.com* ⊙ *May–Sept.*) you can arrange hour-long trail rides and all-day guided excursions within the park as well as multiday pack trips through the foothills of the Rockies.

SWIMMING

⟳ **Waterton Lakes.** These lakes are chilly year-round, but they are still a great place to cool off after a long hot day of hiking. Most visitors wade, but a few join the "polar bear club" and get completely submersed. ⊠ *Along the shoreline in Waterton Townsite.*

Waterton Health Club. This club, at the Waterton Lakes Lodge Resort, has an 18-meter (56-foot) saltwater pool, a hot tub, a sauna, and a gym. A one-week membership to the facility cost C$18 (or C$52 for a family). ⊠ *101 Clematis Ave.Waterton Townsite.*

> **HIKER'S SHUTTLE**
>
> **Tamarack Outdoor Outfitters.** This is the headquarters for hiker shuttle services that run throughout Waterton to most of the major trailheads; they can also arrange certified hiking guides for groups. You can reserve shuttles two months in advance. ⊠ *Tamarack Village Sq., Waterton Lakes National Park* ☎ *403/859–2378* ⊕ *www.watertonvisitorservices.com* ⊙ *May–Sept.*

EDUCATIONAL OFFERINGS

Evening interpretive programs are offered from late June until Labor Day, at the Falls Theatre, near Cameron Falls and the townsite campground. These one-hour sessions begin at 8 PM. A guided International Peace Park hike is held every Wednesday and Saturday in July and August. The 14-km (9-mi) hike begins at the Bertha trailhead, and is led by Canadian and American park interpreters. You take lunch at the International Border, before continuing on to Goat Haunt in Glacier National Park, Montana, and returning to Waterton via boat. A fee is charged for the return boat trip. You must pre-register for this hike at the Waterton Information Centre.

WHAT'S NEARBY

You can easily spend a week exploring Waterton and Glacier, but you may wish to take in some nearby sights as well. The Canadian town of Cardston is about 30 minutes east of Waterton Lakes National Park and is the site of the Remington Carriage Museum, containing North America's largest collection of horse-drawn vehicles. About 90 minutes northeast you can visit Head-Smashed-In Buffalo Jump, a UNESCO World Heritage Site, outside the town of Fort Macleod. You can also camp overnight in a traditional Blackfoot tepee at this site. Outside Glacier National Park are the gateway towns of East Glacier, West Glacier, and Columbia Falls, where you can find tour operators, accommodations, restaurants, and stores. Not far from Glacier Park are the towns of Essex, Kalispell, Whitefish, Browning, and Bigfork. Here you will

FAMILY PICKS

Hidden Lake Nature Trail. This uphill, 1½-mi, self-guided trail runs from Logan Pass southwest to Hidden Lake Overlook, from which you get a beautiful view of the lake and McDonald Valley. In spring, ribbons of water pour off the rocks surrounding the lake. A boardwalk protects the abundant wildflowers and spongy tundra on the way.

Lake McDonald. Rent a canoe and enjoy paddling around the lake. If you work up a sweat, you can go for a swim in the lake afterwards.

Climb Bear's Hump. This 2.7-km (1.7-mi) trail takes you from the Waterton Information Centre up the mountainside to an overlook with a great view of Upper Waterton Lake and the townsite.

A surrey and a swim. Rent a surrey bike at Pat's Waterton store and enjoy peddling around the townsite. A surrey bike has a flat seat and a canopy and can hold up to three people, so it is great for families. Cool off afterwards with a swim in icy cold Waterton Lake.

find some excellent golf courses, world-class cross-country and downhill skiing, summer and winter festivals, diverse recreational opportunities, accommodations, and restaurants.

NEARBY TOWNS

17

Early tourists to Glacier National Park first stopped in **East Glacier,** where the Great Northern Railway had established a station. Although most people coming from the east now enter by car through St. Mary, East Glacier, population about 400, attracts visitors with its quiet, secluded surroundings and lovely Glacier Park Lodge. **Browning,** 35 mi to the east of Glacier, is the center of the Blackfeet Nation, whose name is thought to have been derived from the color of their painted or dyed black moccasins; there are about 13,000 enrolled tribal members. The green waters of the Flathead River's Middle Fork and several top-notch outfitters make **West Glacier** an ideal base for river sports. The small town of **Columbia Falls,** only 15 mi west of Glacier National Park, has restaurants, services and accommodations.

The best base for the park is **Whitefish,** 25 mi west of Glacier and with a population of 6,000. The town has a well-developed nightlife scene, good restaurants, galleries, and shops. The village of **Essex** borders the southern tip of the park and is the site of the main rail and bus terminals for visitors coming to the park. About 45 minutes from Glacier's west entrance on Flathead Lake's pristine northeast shore, **Bigfork** twinkles with decorative lights that adorn its shops, galleries, and restaurants. Just 28 mi east of Waterton, **Cardston** is home to the Alberta Temple, built by the Mormon pioneers who established the town. The Remington Carriage Museum contains North America's largest collection of horse-drawn vehicles.

VISITOR INFORMATION

Glacier-Waterton Visitors Association (⌂ *P.O. Box 96, West Glacier, MT 59936* ☎ *406/387-4053* ⊕ *www.glacierwaterton.com*). **Waterton Chamber of Commerce and Visitors Association** (⌂ *P.O. Box 50, Waterton Lakes National Park, Alberta, T0K 2M0* ☎ *403/859-2224*). **Bigfork Area Chamber of Commerce** (✉ *8155 Hwy. 35, Bigfork, MT 59911* ☎ *406/837-5888* ⊕ *www.bigfork. org*). **East Glacier Chamber of Commerce** (⌂ *P.O. Box 260, East Glacier, MT 59434* ☎ *406/226-4403*). **Town of Cardston** (⌂ *P.O. Box 280, Cardston, Alberta T0K 0K0* ☎ *403/653-3366 or 888/434-3366* ⊕ *www.town.cardston.ab.ca*). **Whitefish Chamber of Commerce** (✉ *520 E. 2nd St., Whitefish, MT 59937* ☎ *403/862-3501 or 877/862-3548* ⊕ *www.whitefishchamber.org*).

NEARBY ATTRACTIONS

☾ **Big Sky Waterpark.** During summer, the most popular place between the hardworking lumber town of Columbia Falls and Glacier National Park is the Big Sky Waterpark. Besides the 10 waterslides and a golf course, there are arcade games, bumper cars, a carousel, barbecue grills, a picnic area, and food service. ✉ *7211 U.S. 2 E, junction of U.S. 2 and Hwy. 206, Columbia Falls, MT* ☎ *406/892-5025 or 406/892-2139* ⊕ *www. bigskywp.com* ⌑ *$24* ☯ *Memorial Day–Labor Day, daily 10–8.*

★ **Museum of the Plains Indian.** The stunning collection of artifacts from the Blackfeet at this museum includes clothing, saddlebags, and artwork. ✉ *U.S. 2 at U.S. 89, Browning, MT* ☎ *406/338-2230* ⌑ *$4, June–Sept., free Oct.– May* ☯ *June–Sept., daily 9–4:45; Oct.–May, weekdays 10–4:30.*

AREA ACTIVITIES

SPORTS AND THE OUTDOORS

DOGSLEDDING

☾ The dogs are raring to run late November to mid-April at **Dog Sled Adventures** (✉ *U.S. 93, 20 mi north of Whitefish, 2 mi north of Olney,* ⌂ *P.O. Box 34, Olney, MT 59927* ☎ *406/881-2275* ⊕ *www. dogsledadventuresmt.com*). Your friendly musher will gear the ride to the passengers, from kids to senior citizens; bundled up in a sled, you'll be whisked through Stillwater State Forest on a 1½-hour ride over a 12-mi trail. Reservations are necessary.

SKIING AND SNOW-BOARDING

☾ **Big Mountain Ski and Summer Resort.** Just 8 mi from Whitefish, this has been one of Montana's top ski areas since the 1930s and it remains comfortably small. Big Mountain is popular among train travelers from the Pacific Northwest and the upper Midwest. A daily lift ticket is $61. In the summer there are bike trails, an alpine slide, and a zip line. The mountain's stats include a 2,500-foot vertical drop; 3,000 skiable acres; terrain that is 25% beginner, 50% intermediate, and 25% advanced; two high-speed quad chairs, one quad chair, four triple chairs, one double chair, and three surface lifts. ⌂ *P.O. Box 1400, Whitefish, MT 59937* ☎ *406/862-1900 or 800/858-4152 information, 406/862- 2909 ski and snowboard school, 406/862-7669 or 800/847-4868 snow report* ⊕ *www.skiwhitefish.com* ⌑ *Lift ticket $61, lesson $65* ☯ *Thanksgiving–early Apr. and mid-June–mid-Sept., daily 9–4:30.*

ARTS AND ENTERTAINMENT

When the West was young, weekend nights were reserved for community barn dances. It was an opportunity to get together with friends, enjoy live music, and kick up your heels. You can relive those times at **The Great Canadian Barn Dance** and dinner almost every weekend during the summer months on a Hillspring farm, about 30 minutes east of Waterton Lakes National Park. It's a good idea to reserve your tickets to the dinner and dance in advance. ✉ *60 mi. southwest from Lethbridge. Take Hwy. 2 south, turn west on Hwy. 505 to Wynder Rd., then turn North and travel 1.5 mi to the barn.* ✆ *P.O. Box 163, Hillspring, Alberta T0K 1E0* ☎ *403/626–3407 or 866/626–3407* ⊕ *www. greatcanadianbarndance.com* ⊠ *Dinner and dance $40* ⊙ *June–Sept., Fri.–Sat., dinner at 5:30 PM, dance at 7:30 PM.*

WHERE TO EAT AND STAY

ABOUT THE RESTAURANTS

Steak houses featuring certified Angus beef are typical of the region; in recent years, resort communities have diversified their menus to include bison meat, fresh fish, and savory vegetarian options. Small cafés offer hearty, inexpensive meals, and you can pick up on local history through conversation with the local denizens. Trout, venison, elk, moose, and bison appear on the menus inside the park. Attire everywhere is decidedly casual.

ABOUT THE HOTELS

Lodgings in the parks tend to be fairly rustic and simple, though there are a few grand lodges and some modern accommodations. There are a few modern hotels that offer facilities such as swimming pools, hot tubs, boat rentals, guided excursions, or fine dining. Although there is a limited supply of rooms within both parks, the prices are relatively reasonable. It's best to reserve well in advance, especially for July and August.

ABOUT THE CAMPGROUNDS

There are 10 major campgrounds in Glacier National Park and excellent backcountry sites for backpackers. Reservations for Fish Creek and St. Mary Campgrounds are available through the National Park Reservation Service (☎ *877/444–6777 or 518/885–3639* ⊕ *www.recreation. gov*). Reservations may be made up to five months in advance. Parks Canada operates four campgrounds in Waterton Lakes that range from fully serviced to unserviced sites. There are also some backcountry campsites. Visitors can prebook campsites for a fee of C$11. To do so, visit ⊕ *www.pc.gc.ca* or call ☎ *905/426–4648 or 877/737–3783.*

Outside the park campgrounds vary from no-services, remote state or federal campsites to upscale commercial operations. During July and August it's best to reserve a site. Ask locally about bears and always store food inside a bear box or a closed hard-side vehicle (not a tent).

17

FESTIVALS AND EVENTS

JANUARY

Ski Fest. This worldwide cross-country ski celebration introduces newcomers to kick-and-glide skiing. Equipment demonstrations and family activities are scheduled at the Izaak Walton Inn in Essex, MT. ☎ *406/888–5700* ⊕ *www.izaakwaltoninn.com.*

FEBRUARY

Whitefish Winter Carnival. For more than 40 years, Whitefish, MT, has been the scene of outstanding winter fun, including a grand parade, and a torchlight parade on skis. ☎ *406/862–3501 or 877/862–3548.*

JUNE

Waterton Wildflower Festival. Wildflower walks, horseback rides, hikes, watercolor workshops, photography classes, and family events help visitors and locals celebrate the annual blooming of Waterton's wildflowers. ☎ *403/859–2009 or 800/215–2395* ⊕ *www.watertonwildflowers.com.*

Summer Concert Series. Running each Thursday from mid-June to late August, the series is held in the Don Lawrence Amphitheater at Marantette Park in Columbia Falls. Types of music vary, but the Don Lawrence Big Band has a performance every year. ☎ *406/892–2072.*

JULY

Canada Day. In honor of Canada's birthday, all guests get into the national parks free of charge. Waterton also has special activities for families such as treasure hunts and street-theater performances. ☎ *403/859–5133.*

NW Montana Antique Threshing Bee. Steam threshing machines, steam plows, antique tractors, and engines flex muscles in the Parade of Power, organized by the Northwest Montana Antique Power Association in Columbia Falls. Participants challenge friends and neighbors to tractor barrel races and shingle-making events, while children of all ages enjoy miniature steam-train rides, music, food, and entertainment. ☎ *406/837–4795 or 406/892–2072.*

SEPTEMBER

Waterton Wildlife Weekend. Wildlife viewing is at its best in Waterton during the fall. This weekend features wildlife events including viewing on foot, on horseback and by boat. There are also photography, drawing, and sketching courses. ☎ *800/215–2395 or 403/859–2663.*

WHERE TO EAT

IN THE PARKS
GLACIER

$$ ✕ **Eddie's Café, Gifts & Grocery.** Whether you stop in for burgers and fries or
AMERICAN enjoy a salad with a trout dinner, the food is simple and good at Eddie's. Try
🕙 the huckleberry cobbler or pop next door to the ice cream shop and enjoy some huckleberry ice cream for dessert. Eddie's serves breakfast, lunch, and dinner and they can even pack up a picnic lunch to go. ⌂ *P.O. Box 69, Apgar Village 59936* ☎ *406/888–5361* ⊛ *Reservations not accepted* ▭ *D, DC, MC, V* ⊕ *www.eddiescafegifts.com* ☉ *Closed mid Sept.–late May.*

$$–$$$ ✕ **Lake McDonald Lodge Restaurants.** In Russell's Fireside Dining Room,
AMERICAN take in a great view while choosing between standards such as pasta,
★ steak, wild game, and salmon. There are also some delicious salads and

other local favorites on the menu. Don't miss the apple bread pudding with caramel-cinnamon sauce for dessert. The restaurant has an excellent breakfast buffet, a children's menu, and box lunches are available on request. Across the parking lot is a cheaper alternative, **Jammer Joe's Grill & Pizzeria** (¢–$),which serves burgers and pasta for lunch and dinner. ⊠ *10 mi north of Apgar on Going-to-the-Sun Rd.* ☎*406/888–5431 or 406/892–2525* ▭ *AE, D, MC, V* ☙ *Closed early Oct.–early June.*

$$
AMERICAN

✕ **Ptarmigan Dining Room.** Sophisticated cuisine is served in the dining room of early-20th-century, chaletlike Many Glacier Hotel. As the sun sets over Swiftcurrent Lake just outside the massive windows, French-American cuisine is served amid Swiss-style decor. Signature dishes include the wild game sausage sampler, buffalo Stroganoff, and Rocky Mountain trout. Each night there's a chef's special such as fresh fish or pork prime rib with a huckleberry demi-glace. For a true Montana creation, have a huckleberry daiquiri. ⊠ *Many Glacier Rd.* ☎*406/732–4411* ▭ *AE, D, MC, V* ☙ *Closed late Sept.–early June.*

PICNIC AREAS

There are picnic spots at most campgrounds and visitor centers. Each has tables, grills, and drinking water in summer.

★

Sun Point. On the north side of St. Mary Lake, this is one of the most beautiful places in the park for a picnic. ⊠ *Sun Point Trailhead.*

WATERTON LAKES

$$$
CANADIAN

✕ **Prince of Wales Dining Room.** Enjoy upmarket cuisine before a dazzling view of Waterton Lake in the dining room of this century-old chalet high on a hill. Choose from a fine selection of wines to accompany your meal. Every afternoon the lodge's main culinary event unfolds: a British high tea served in the lobby includes finger sandwiches, scones and other pastries, and chocolate-dipped fruits and is enjoyed with live piano music. ⊠ *Off Hwy. 5 in the Prince of Wales Hotel outside Waterton Townsite* ☎*403/859–2231* ▭ *AE, D, MC, V* ☙ *Closed Oct.–May.*

OUTSIDE THE PARKS

$$$
AMERICAN
★

✕ **Belton Chalet Grill Dining Room.** This is a lovely dining room with original wainscoting and leaded-glass windows, but if the weather is nice you should ask for a table on the deck where you can see the sunset behind the mountains or watch the trains roll by. Menu specialties include buffalo meatloaf, chili-rubbed wild Alaska salmon, and the bacon-wrapped bourbon and brown-sugar-cured beef fillet. The restaurant remains open most of the year (weekends only in the winter months). ⊠ *Rte. 49, next to railroad station, East Glacier* ☎*406/226–5600* ⌥ *Reservations recommended* ▭ *AE, D, MC, V* ☙ *Closed early Oct.–early Dec. and late Mar.–late May. Closed Mon.–Thurs. early Dec.–late Mar. (brunch only on Sun. Dec.–Mar.) No lunch.*

$
MEXICAN
★

✕ **Serrano's.** After a day on the dusty trail, fresh Mexican food is quite a treat whether dining inside or on the back patio. Try a taco salad, a beef burrito, or a chicken enchilada with one of the restaurant's famous margaritas. Don't be surprised if there's a lineup during July, August, and early September—the restaurant is a favorite with locals and visitors alike and doesn't take reservations. ⊠ *29 Dawson Ave., East Glacier* ☎*406/226–9392* ⊕ *www.serranosmexican.com* ⌥ *Reservations not accepted* ▭ *AE, D, DC, MC, V* ☙ *Closed Oct.–Apr.*

17

Jammer Joe

Harkening back to the early days of automobile touring in the parks, each summer a fleet of red "jammers"—vintage buses—weaves through Glacier and Waterton Lakes national parks. Drivers began jamming gears on the coaches in 1936, but today only guides licensed with Glacier Park Inc. (☎ 406/892–2525 ⊕ www.glacierparkinc.com) operate them. Park visitors ride them for special tours, as well as to traverse the park and go up the incredible Going-to-the-Sun Road.

One of the most popular drivers is Joe Kendall, known as "Jammer Joe" to passengers. "I love doing it. It's absolutely the best job," he says. "What I enjoy the most is the fact that we have the most pristine, beautiful, scenic area in the mountains … to show that to our visitors is a lot of fun."

His lively narration and colorful descriptions of Glacier have endeared him to many park visitors. In fact, he has so won the hearts of fans over his 10 years of service that the park has named a pizza parlor (near Lake McDonald Lodge) after him. "I think it's great," Kendall says. "It's as close to what you might call famous as I'll ever be."

Kendall's interest in Glacier began in 1949, when he joined the park's summer staff, which was all college-aged kids at the time, in 1949. He worked as a dishwasher that summer and then came back the following summer to be a busboy.

In those years, he says, you had to be a pre-law or pre-med student in order to have the coveted job of driving the jammers. He was training to be a farmer, so he never thought he'd have a chance to drive one of the famous red buses.

But in the 1990s the park's concessionaire, Glacier Park Inc., started hiring seniors, and Kendall, who turned 81 in late February, got his chance. "It's every bit as good as we thought it was in the early days," he says.

Besides driving the jammer, he has just been happy to be back in Glacier. "You know how the mountains are," he says. "There's something just spectacular about them. It had that effect on me in those earlier years, and I've just never gotten over it."

Kendall's wife of 57 years, Geri, also works for Glacier Park Inc., as tour director for the dozen or so six-day Great Lodges of Glacier Tours each summer. During the off-season, the couple lives in Illinois.

—Debbie Harmsen

WHERE TO STAY

INSIDE THE PARKS
GLACIER

$$$ ⌂ **Granite Park Chalet.** Early tourists used to ride horses through the park 7 to 9 mi each day and stay at a different chalet each night. The Granite Park is one of two chalets still standing (the other one is the Sperry Chalet). You can reach it only via hiking trails. You must bring sleeping bags and your own food and water, and you need a reservation. A rustic kitchen, limited refrigeration, and pit toilets are near the chalet. You can park at Logan Pass Visitor Center and hike 7.6 mi or at the Loop Trailhead and hike uphill 4 mi. **Pros:** beautiful scenery; secluded. **Cons:** difficult to access; rustic; far from services. ⊠ *7.6 mi south of Logan Pass on Going-to-the-Sun Rd.* ☎ *888/345–2649* ⊕ *www.graniteparkchalet. com* ⊃ *12 rooms* ⌂ *In-room: no a/c, no TV In-hotel: kitchen, refrigerator* ⊟ *AE, D, MC, V* ⊘ *Closed mid-Sept.–late June.*

$$$ ⌂ **Lake McDonald Lodge.** One of the great historic lodges of the West
Fodor's Choice   anchors this complex on the shore of lovely Lake McDonald. On the
★   Going-to-the-Sun Road not far from Apgar and West Glacier, this lodge is an ideal base for exploring the western side of the park. Scenic cruises of the park's largest lake depart from the boat docks right behind the lodge or you can rent private boats by the hour or by the day. Take a room in the lodge itself, where public spaces are filled with massive timbers, stone fireplaces, and animal trophies. Rooms are located on the second and third floors of the lodge and there is no elevator. Cabins sleep up to four and don't have kitchens; there are also motel-style rooms separate from the lodge. All rooms are no-smoking and there are four wheelchair accessible. **Pros:** lovely lakeside setting; historic property; close to Apgar, West Glacier, and Going-to-the-Sun Road. **Cons:** rustic; no TV; small bathrooms. ⊠ *Going-to-the-Sun Rd.* ⊕ *P.O. Box 2025, Columbia Falls 59912* ☎ *406/892–2525 or 406/888–5431* ⊕ *www.glacierparkinc.com* ⊃ *32 lodge rooms, 38 cabins, 30 motor-inn rooms* ⌂ *In-room: no a/c, no TV. In-hotel: restaurant, bar* ⊟ *AE, D, MC, V.*

$$$ ⌂ **Many Glacier Hotel.** The most isolated of the grand hotels—it's on Swift-
★   current Lake on the northeast side of the park—this is also one of the most scenic, especially if you nab one of the lake-view balcony rooms. There's a large fireplace in the lobby where guests gather on chilly mornings. Rooms are small and sparsely decorated, but the location and the view can't be beat. There are several wonderful hikes to enjoy in this area including ranger-guided hikes to Grinnell Glacier and Iceberg Lake. You can combine the hikes with a scenic boat tour to substantially decrease the hiking distance. Wildlife is often seen in this part of the park and bear sightings are common in August when the huckleberries ripen. All rooms at the hotel are no-smoking. **Pros:** stunning views from lodge; secluded; good hiking trails nearby. **Cons:** rustic rooms; no TV; no Internet. ⊠ *Many Glacier Rd., 12 mi west of Babb* ⊕ *P.O. Box 2025, Columbia Falls 59912* ☎ *406/892–2525 or 406/732–4411* ⊕ *www.glacierparkinc.com* ⊃ *206 rooms, 6 family rooms, 2 suites* ⌂ *In-room: no a/c, no TV. In-hotel: restaurant, bar* ⊟ *AE, D, MC, V.*

$$$$ ⌂ **Sperry Chalet.** This elegant backcountry lodge, built in 1913 by the Great Northern Railway, is accessible only by a steep, 6.7-mi trail with

17

a 3,300-foot vertical rise. Either hike in or arrive on horseback. Guest rooms have no electricity, heat, or running water, but who cares when the view includes Glacier's Gunsite Mountain, Mt. Edwards, Lake McDonald, and mountain goats in wildflowers. Informal meals, such as turkey with the trimmings, are simple yet filling. Note that the reservations office is closed in September and October. **Pros:** spectacular views; lovely secluded mountain setting; meals included. **Cons:** difficult to access; far from services; no electricity or running water. ⊠ *On the west side of Gunsite Mountain. Trail to chalet begins at Lake Macdonald Lodge on the Going-to-the-Sun Rd.* ⌂ *P.O. Box 188, West Glacier 59936* ☎ *406/387–5654 or 888/345–2649* ⊕ *www.sperrychalet.com* ⤵ *17 rooms* ⅂ *In-room: no a/c, no phone, no TV. In-hotel: restaurant* ▭ *AE, MC, V* ⊘ *Closed mid-Sept.–early July* ¶⃝ *FAP.*

$$ ⊡ **Village Inn.** On Lake McDonald, this motel could use some updating, but it is very popular and offers a great view. All of the plain but serviceable rooms, some with kitchenettes, face the lake. A restaurant, bar, and coffee shop are nearby. **Pros:** great views; nice location in Apgar Village. **Cons:** rustic motel; smaller property; few amenities. ⊠ *Apgar Village* ⌂ *P.O. Box 2025, Columbia Falls 59912* ☎ *406/756–2444* ⊕ *www.villageinnatapgar. com* ⤵ *36 rooms* ⅂ *In-room: no a/c, kitchen (some)* ▭ *AE, D, MC, V.*

CAMPING   ⚠ **Apgar Campground.** This popular and large campground on the southern
$$ shore of Lake McDonald has many activities and services. From here you can hike; boat, fish, or swim and sign up for trail rides. About 25 sites are suitable for RVs. **Pros:** close to many activities and services; scenic spot; many campground amenities. **Cons:** large campground; less secluded. ⊠ *Apgar Rd.* ☎ *406/888–7800* ⚠ *169 tent sites, 25 RV sites* ⅂ *Flush toilets, pit toilets, dump station, drinking water, bear boxes, fire grates, picnic tables, food service, public telephone, general store, ranger station, swimming (lake)* ▭ *AE, D, MC, V* ⊘ *Closed mid-Oct.–early May.*

$$ ⚠ **Avalanche Creek Campground.** This peaceful campground is shaded by huge red cedars and bordered by Avalanche Creek. Trail of the Cedars begins here, and it's along Going-to-the-Sun Road. Some campsites and the washroom facilities are wheelchair accessible. There are 50 sites for RVs up to 26 feet. **Pros:** nice setting near a creek; wheelchair accessible. **Cons:** 10-minute drive to most services. ⊠ *15.7 mi. from the West entrance on the Going-to-the-Sun Rd.* ☎ *406/888–7800* ⚠ *37 tent sites, 50 RV sites,* ⅂ *Flush toilets, drinking water, fire grates, picnic tables, public telephone* ▭ *AE, D, MC, V* ⊘ *Closed early Sept.–early June.*

$$ ⚠ **Kintla Lake Campground.** Beautiful and remote, this is a trout fisherman's favorite. Trails lead into the backcountry. The dirt access road is rough, so RVs are not recommended. **Pros:** beautiful setting; remote; good fishing nearby. **Cons:** difficult to access; not good for trailers or RVs. ⊠ *14 mi north of Polebridge Ranger Station on Inside North Fork Rd.* ⚠ *13 tent sites* ⅂ *Pit toilets, dump station, bear boxes, fire grates, picnic tables* ⚠ *Reservations not accepted* ▭ *No credit cards* ⊘ *Closed mid-Sept.–mid-May.*

$$ ⚠ **Many Glacier Campground.** One of the most beautiful spots in the park is
★ also a favorite for bears. Several hiking trails take off from here, and often ranger-led hikes climb to Grinnell Glacier. Always check posted notices for areas closed because of bears. **Pros:** beautiful scenery; nice hiking trails in the area; ranger-led hikes nearby. **Cons:** beware of bears. ⊠ *Next to the*

Swiftcurrent Motor Inn on Many Glacier Rd. ☎ *406/888–7800* ⚐ *97 tent sites, 13 RV sites* ♿ *Flush toilets, pit toilets, drinking water, showers, bear boxes, fire grates, picnic tables, food service, public telephone, ranger station, swimming (lake)* ▭ *AE, D, MC, V* ☉ *Closed Oct.–Apr.*

$$$ ⚐ **St. Mary Campground.** This large, grassy spot alongside the lake and stream has mountain views and cool breezes. It always seems to be the campground that fills first. **Pros:** beautiful scenery; flush toilets and showers. **Cons:** large, busy campground. ✉ *0.9 mi from the St. Mary entrance to the Going-to-the-Sun Rd.* ☎ *406/888–7800* ⚐ *123 tent sites, 25 RV sites* ♿ *Flush toilets, pit toilets, drinking water, showers, bear boxes, fire grates, picnic tables, food service, public telephone, swimming (lake)* ▭ *AE, D, MC, V* ☉ *Closed Oct.–Apr.*

$$ ⚐ **Sprague Creek Campground.** This sometimes noisy roadside campground for tents, RVs, and truck campers (no towed units) offers spectacular views of the lake and sunsets, fishing from shore, and great rock skipping on the beach. Restaurants, gift shops, and a grocery store are 1 mi north on Going-to-the-Sun Road. Sites are first-come, first-served. **Pros:** small campground; spectacular views; 1 mi from stores and services. **Cons:** can be noisy; no trailers allowed. ✉ *Going-to-the-Sun Rd., 1 mi south of Lake McDonald Lodge* ☎ *406/888–7800* ⚐ *25 tent/RV sites* ♿ *Flush toilets, drinking water, bear boxes, fire grates, picnic tables* ♿ *Reservations not accepted* ▭ *No credit cards* ☉ *Closed mid-Sept.–mid-May.*

$$ ⚐ **Two Medicine Campground.** Because of its distance from the Going-to-the-Sun Road, this is often the last campground to fill during the height of summer. A general store, snack bar, and boat rentals are available. **Pros:** lots of onsite amenities; flush toilets and showers; pretty setting. **Cons:** farther away from popular areas along the Going-to-the-Sun Rd. ✉ *14 mi from East Glacier at the end of Two Medicine Rd.* ☎ *406/888–7800* ⚐ *86 tent sites, 13 RV sites* ♿ *Flush toilets, pit toilets, drinking water, showers, bear boxes, fire grates, picnic tables, food service, public telephone, general store, swimming (lake)* ▭ *AE, D, MC, V* ☉ *Closed Oct.–Apr.*

WATERTON

$$$$ ☷ **Prince of Wales Hotel.** Perched between two lakes, with a high mountain backdrop, this hotel has the best view in town. A high steeple crowns the building, which is fantastically ornamented with eaves, balconies, and turrets. The two-story windows in the lobby have stunning views of the valley and the townsite. Even if you don't choose to stay in the hotel, you should stop by and visit the well-stocked gift shop or enjoy afternoon tea, which is served in the lobby daily. Expect creaks and rattles at night—the old hotel, built in the 1920s, is exposed to rough winds. Rates decrease by about 25% off-season. **Pros:** spectacular view; historic property; bellmen wear kilts. **Cons:** rustic rooms; no TV; no a/c. ✉ *Off Hwy. 5; access road is opposite the Waterton Information Center* ✉ *P.O. Box 33, Waterton Park T0K 2M0* ☎ *406/756–2444, 403/859–2231 mid-May–late Sept.* ⊕ *www.glacierparkinc.com* ⌾ *86 rooms* ♿ *In-room: no a/c, no TV. In-hotel: restaurant* ▭ *AE, MC, V* ☉ *Closed late Sept.–mid-May.*

$$$$ ☷ **Waterton Glacier Suites.** Located in the heart of the townsite, this property is walking distance to restaurants, shopping, and the boat dock

on beautiful Waterton Lake. It is one of the newer accommodations in the park and is particularly nice for couples. Rooms come in several different configurations and have microwaves, mini-refrigerators, and fireplaces. All rooms here are no-smoking. **Pros:** modern convenient suites; good for couples; open year-round. **Cons:** no view; pull-out sofas uncomfortable. ✉ *107 Wildflower Ave.* ✆ *P.O. Box 51, Waterton Park T0K 2M0* ☎ *403/859–2211 or 866/621–3330* ⊕ *www.watertonsuites. com* ⤳ *26 rooms* ♿ *In-room: safe, refrigerator, DVD, Wi-Fi. In-hotel: laundry facilities, laundry service, Wi-Fi* ☰ *AE, MC, V.*

CAMPING   ⚠ **Waterton Townsite Campground.** Though the campground is busy,
$$ noisy, and windy, sites here are grassy and flat with access to kitchen shelters and have views down the lake into the U.S. part of the peace park. The town's restaurants and shops are within walking distance. **Pros:** right in town; walking distance to restaurants and other amenities; flush toilets and showers. **Cons:** busy campground; windy. ✉ *Waterton and Vimy Aves.* ☎ *905/426–4648 or 877/737–3783* ⊕ *www.pc.gc.ca/ waterton* ⚠ *143 tent sites, 95 RV sites* ♿ *Flush toilets, full hookups, dump station, drinking water, guest laundry, showers, fire grates, picnic tables, public telephone* ☰ *AE, MC, V* ⊙ *Closed early Oct.–late Apr.*

OUTSIDE THE PARKS

$$$ ▦ **Belton Chalet.** This carefully restored 1910 railroad hotel, the original winter headquarters for the park, has a great location just outside the West Glacier entrance. Rooms are cozy and bright, with original woodwork around the windows and period furnishings. Some rooms open up to a private deck area with lovely views. The Lewis and Clark Cottages, which remain open in winter, are snug up against the evergreen forest behind the lodge. If train noise bothers you, ask for a room at the back of the hotel. **Pros:** excellent restaurant on site; wraparound decks with lovely views; historic property. **Cons:** train noise; rustic; no a/c or TV. ✉ *12575 U.S. 2 E, West Glacier, MT 59936* ☎ *406/888–5000 or 888/235–8665* ⊕ *www.beltonchalet.com* ⤳ *25 rooms, 2 cottages* ♿ *In-room: no a/c, no phone, no TV. In-hotel: restaurant, bar, spa, bicycles* ☰ *MC, V* ⏐◯⏐ *BP.*

$$ ▦ **Glacier Park Lodge.** Just outside the east side of the park, across from
★ the Amtrak station, you'll find this beautiful hotel built in 1913. The full-service lodge is supported by 500- to 800-year-old fir and 3-foot-thick cedar logs. Rooms are sparsely decorated, but there are historic framed posters on the walls in the halls. Cottages and a house are also available on the grounds next to the golf course. If you golf on the spectacular course, watch out for moose. Entertainers delight guests with storytelling and singing in the great hall. **Pros:** on-site golf course; scenic location; lots of activities. **Cons:** small bathrooms; no elevator; no a/c. ✉ *Off U.S. 2, East Glacier* ✆ *P.O. Box 2025, Columbia Falls, MT 59912* ☎ *406/892–2525 or 406/226–9311* ⊕ *www.glacierparkinc. com* ⤳ *161 rooms* ♿ *In-room: no a/c, no TV. In-hotel: restaurant, bar, golf course, pool, spa* ☰ *AE, D, MC, V.*

$$ ▦ **Good Medicine Lodge.** Built of cedar timbers and decorated in a west-
★ ern style, this comfortable lodge-style bed-and-breakfast is warm and inviting. A hearty breakfast is served at individual tables in the dining room in the mornings and hors d'oeuvres are served by the fireplace

17

in the afternoon. All rooms have private baths and most have balconies with mountain views. There is a lovely garden and deck with a gas fire pit and a hot tub for guests to enjoy. The lodge is very close to Whitefish Mountain Resort. There is a ski room with boot and glove dryers and the snow bus to the ski resort stops right outside. **Pros:** good breakfast included; many amenities, including free Wi-Fi; one wheelchair-accessible room. **Cons:** no TV in most rooms; small property. ⊠ *537 Wisconsin Ave., Whitefish, MT 59937* ☏ *406/862–5489 or 800/860–5488* ⊕ *www.goodmedicinelodge.com* ↝ *6 rooms, 3 suites* ⚬ *In-room: no TV, Wi-Fi. In-hotel: Wi-Fi; laundry facilities, Internet terminal* ⊟ *AE, D, MC, V* ¶◎¶ *BP.*

$$ ⬚ **Izaak Walton Inn.** This historic lodge sits on the southern edge of Glacier and under the shadow of the Great Bear Wilderness. Originally built to house railway workers, the inn has retained its historic ties and is decorated with railroad memorabilia. The on-site restaurant is designed to look like an old-fashioned railway dining car and serves excellent Montana-style dishes such as steaks, elk burgers, pan-seared Montana trout, and huckleberry cobbler. You can ride Amtrak to the back door and stay either in quaint lodge rooms, in refurbished train cabooses, or in newly constructed family cabins. Lodge rooms have knotty-pine paneling and simple furnishings; caboose cottages (three-night minimum for $723) sleep up to four people and have kitchenettes. In winter you can ski or snowshoe from the door. **Pros:** good location in the middle between East and West Glacier; open year-round. **Cons:** train noise can be a problem; no phones or TVs in rooms; no cell-phone access. ⊠ *290 Izaak Walton Inn Rd., off U.S. 2, Essex, MT 59916* ☏ *406/888–5700* ⊕ *www.izaakwaltoninn.com* ↝ *33 rooms, 4 caboose cottages, 6 family cabins* ⚬ *In-room: no a/c, no phone, kitchen (some), no TV. In-hotel: restaurant, bar, bicycles* ⊟ *MC, V.*

CAMPING   ⚠ **Sundance RV Park and Campground.** This older campground, 6 mi
$$ south of West Glacier, was built with families in mind. It's close to a water park, and offers free Wi-Fi. Bicyclists and hikers drop in for $4 showers. You can also rent a tepee or a cabin here. **Pros:** close to water park; flush toilets and showers; free Internet. **Cons:** outside the park. ⊠ *10545 U.S. 2 E, Coram, MT* ☏ *406/387–5016* ⚠ *31 RV sites, 2 cabins, 1 teepee* ⚬ *Flush toilets, partial hookups (electric and water), dump station, drinking water, guest laundry, showers, fire grates, picnic tables, play area* ⊟ *MC, V* ⊗ *Closed Oct. 15–May 15.*

Grand Canyon National Park

WORD OF MOUTH

"What I remember most . . . is how clear the night sky was. It seemed as though you could see every star in the Milky Way! Seeing the night sky is worth every penny you spend at the Grand Canyon!"

—crazyhorse42

WELCOME TO THE GRAND CANYON

TOP REASONS TO GO

★ **Its status:** This is one of those places where you really want to say, "Been there, done that!"

★ **Awesome vistas:** Painted desert, sandstone canyon walls, pine and fir forests, mesas, plateaus, volcanic features, the Colorado River, streams, and waterfalls make for some jaw-dropping moments.

★ **Year-round adventure:** Outdoor junkies can bike, boat, camp, fish, hike, ride mules, whitewater raft, watch birds and wildlife, cross-country ski, and snowshoe.

★ **Continuing education:** Adults and kids can get schooled, thanks to free park-sponsored nature walks and interpretive programs.

★ **Sky-high and river-low experiences:** Experience the canyon via plane, train, and automobile, as well as helicopter, boat, bike, mule, or on foot.

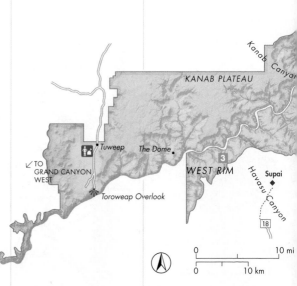

1 South Rim. The South Rim is where the action is: Grand Canyon Village's lodging, camping, eateries, stores, and museums, plus plenty of trailheads into the canyon. Visitor services and facilities are open and available every day of the year, including holidays. Three free shuttle routes cover 30-some stops, and visitors who'd rather relax than rough it can treat themselves to comfy hotel rooms and elegant restaurant meals (lodging and camping reservations are essential).

2 North Rim. Of the nearly 5 million people who visit the park annually, 90% enter at the South Rim, but many believe the North Rim is even more gorgeous—and worth the extra effort. Accessible only from mid-May to mid-October (or the first good snowfall), the North Rim has legitimate bragging rights: at more than 8,000 feet above sea level (and 1,000 feet higher than the South Rim), it offers precious solitude and seven developed viewpoints. Rather than staring into the canyon's depths, you get a true sense of its expanse.

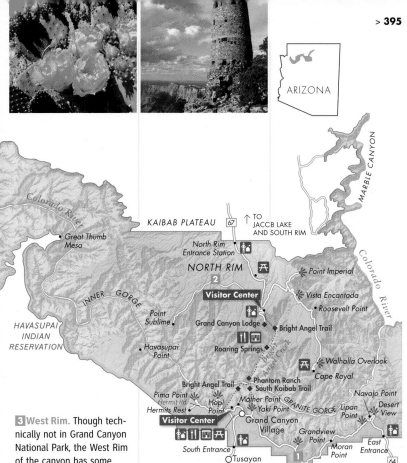

ARIZONA

MARBLE CANYON

Colorado River

KAIBAB PLATEAU   67   ↑ TO
JACCB LAKE
AND SOUTH RIM

• Great Thumb
Mesa

North Rim
Entrance Station

NORTH RIM

Colorado River

2

• Point Imperial

Visitor Center

INNER GORGE

Point
Sublime

Grand Canyon Lodge

• Vista Encantada
• Roosevelt Point

HAVASUPAI
INDIAN
RESERVATION

• Bright Angel Trail

• Havasupai
Point

Roaring Springs

Walhalla Overlook

Cape Royal

Bright Angel Trail

Phantom Ranch
South Kaibab Trail

GRANITE GORGE

Navajo Point

Pima Point
Hermit Rd.
Hermits Rest •

Hopi
Point

Mather Point

Lipan
Point

Desert
View

3 **West Rim.** Though technically not in Grand Canyon
National Park, the West Rim
of the canyon has some
spectacular scenery. The
Skywalk, part of the Hualapai Tribe's efforts to expand
its tourism offerings on the
West Rim, is a U-shaped
glass bridge suspended
above the Colorado River—
not for the faint of heart.

Visitor Center

Grand Canyon
Village

Grandview
Point

Moran
Point

East
Entrance

South Entrance

Tusayan

Grand Canyon
Airport

64

SOUTH RIM

TO CAMERON
AND NORTH RIM

64

180   ↓ TO FLAGSTAFF,
WILLIAMS

18

GETTING
ORIENTED

Grand Canyon National
Park is a superstar—
biologically, historically,
and recreationally. One of
the world's best examples
of arid-land erosion, the
canyon provides a record
of three of the four eras of
geological time. In addi-
tion to its diverse fossil

record, the park is home to
several major ecosystems,
five of the world's seven
life zones, three of North
America's four desert
types, and all kinds of rare,
endemic, and protected
plant and animal species.

KEY	
🏚	Ranger Station
⚠	Campground
🌲	Picnic Area
🍴	Restaurant
🏠	Lodge
🥾	Trailhead
🚻	Restrooms
✷	Scenic Viewpoint
⫶⫶⫶	Walking/Hiking Trails

GRAND CANYON PLANNER

When to Go

There's no bad time to visit the canyon, though the busiest times of year are summer and spring break. Visiting during these peak seasons, as well as holidays, requires patience and a tolerance for crowds. Note that weather changes on a whim in this exposed high-desert region. The North Rim is closed in the winter.

AVG. HIGH/LOW TEMPS.

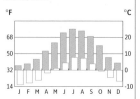

South Rim

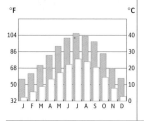

North Rim

Inner Canyon

Flora and Fauna

Eighty-nine mammalian species inhabit the Grand Canyon, as well as 355 species of birds and 56 kinds of reptiles and amphibians. The rare Kaibab squirrel is found only on the North Rim—you can recognize them by their all-white tails and the long tufts of white hair on their ears. The pink Grand Canyon rattlesnake lives at lower elevations within the canyon. Hawks and ravens are visible year-round. The endangered California condor has been reintroduced to the canyon. Park rangers give daily talks on the magnificent birds, whose wingspan measures 9 feet. In spring, summer, and fall, mule deer, recognizable by their large antlers, are abundant at the South Rim. Don't be fooled by gentle appearances; these guys can be aggressive. It's illegal to feed them.

The best times to see wildlife are early in the morning and late in the afternoon. Look for out-of-place shapes and motions, keeping in mind that animals occupy all layers in a natural habitat and not just at your eye level.

More than 1,700 species of plants color the park. The South Rim's Coconino Plateau is fairly flat, at an elevation of about 7,000 feet, and covered with stands of pinyon and ponderosa pines, junipers, and Gambel oak trees. On the Kaibab Plateau on the North Rim, Douglas fir, spruce, quaking aspen, and more ponderosas prevail. In spring you're likely to see asters, sunflowers, and lupine in bloom at both rims.

Getting Here

Nearly 5 million visitors come to the Grand Canyon each year. They can access the canyon via two main points: the South Rim and the North Rim. A third option, though not within the national park, are the tribal lands of the Hualapai and the Havasupai on the West Rim of the canyon.

The best route into the park from the east or south is from Flagstaff. Take U.S. 180 northwest to the park's southern entrance and Grand Canyon Village. To go on to the North Rim, go north from Flagstaff on Highway 89 to Bitter Springs, then take Highway 89A to the junction of Highway 67 and travel south on the highway for about 40 mi. From the west on Interstate 40, the most direct route to the South Rim is on U.S. 180 and Highway 64. The more remote North Rim is off-limits during winter. From mid-October (or the first heavy snowfall) through mid-May, there are no services, and Hwy. 67 south of Jacob Lake is closed.

The West Rim is a five-hour drive from the South Rim. From Kingman, Arizona, drive north 42 mi on Stockton Hill Road. Turn right (north) on to Pierce Ferry Road and follow for 7 mi. Turn right (east) on to Diamond Bar Road and follow for 21 mi to Grand Canyon West entrance.

■TIP→ When driving off major highways in low-lying areas, watch for rain clouds. Flash floods from sudden summer rains can be deadly. To check on road conditions, call the Arizona Department of Transportation's recorded hotline (☎ 888/411–7623).

Getting Around

The park is most crowded near the east and south entrances and in Grand Canyon Village, as well as on the 23-mi Desert View Drive. After you enter the park's South Rim you can drive on the roads that are open to traffic (Hermits Rest is only open to shuttles from March through November), or you can try to avoid the congestion by parking your car in the village parking lot and taking advantage of the free shuttles. By car, traveling between the South Rim and the North Rim requires a 215-mi drive via Highways 64, 89, and 67. By foot, it's a steep and strenuous trek of at least 21 mi on arduous hiking trails down the canyon to Phantom Ranch and then up the other side via the North and South Kaibab trails. At the West Rim, visitors aren't allowed to travel in their own vehicles to the viewpoints once they reach the rim; they must purchase a tour package from Destination Grand Canyon West.

Nearby Airports

Several carriers fly to the **Grand Canyon National Parks Airport** (☎ 928/638–2446) from Las Vegas, including **Grand Canyon Express** (☎ 800/940–2550 ⊕ www.airvegas.com), **Scenic Airlines** (☎ 800/634–6801 ⊕ www.scenic.com), and **Vision Holidays** (☎ 702/261–3850 or 800/256–8767 ⊕ www.visionholidays.com). You also can make connections into the Grand Canyon from **Phoenix Sky Harbor International Airport (PHX)** (☎ 602/273–3300 ⊕ www.phoenix.gov/skyharborairport). The nearest airport to the North Rim is 164 mi away in Utah, **St. George Municipal Airport** (☎ 435/634–5822 ⊕ www.sgcity.org/airport).

18

Planning Ahead

Grand Canyon National Park is one of the most popular parks in the country, so if you're planning to sleep at a lodge in the park, it's essential that you make your reservation for your in-park stay early—reservations can be made up to 13 months in advance. Reservations for mule rides also fill up quickly, so book at least six months in advance, and one year ahead for the busy season.

■TIP→ Before you head to the park, get the complimentary Trip Planner from the Grand Canyon National Park Web site (⊕ www.nps.gov/grca).

Updated by
Carrie Frasure

When it comes to the Grand Canyon, there are statistics, and there are sensations. While the former are impressive—the canyon measures in at an average width of 10 mi, length of 277 mi, and depth of a mile—they don't truly prepare you for that first impression. Seeing the canyon for the first time is an astounding experience—one that's hard to wrap your head around. In fact, it's more than an experience, it's an emotion, one that is only just beginning to be captured with the superlative "Grand."

PARK ESSENTIALS

ACESSIBILITY

Rim Trail and all the viewpoints along the South Rim are accessible to wheelchairs. For detailed information, see *The Grand Canyon Accessibility Guide,* available free at Canyon View Information Plaza, Yavapai Information Station, Tusayan Museum, Desert View Information Center, and all entrance stations. There are free wheelchairs for use inside the park; inquire at one of the information centers. Temporary handicapped parking permits are available at Canyon View Information Plaza, Yavapai Observation Center, and all entrance stations.

ADMISSION FEES AND PERMITS

A fee of $25 per vehicle (or $12 per person for pedestrians and cyclists) is collected at the east entrance near Cameron, the south entrance near Tusayan for the South Rim, and the main entrance at the North Rim. The fee covers up to one week's access and is good for both rims. The annual Grand Canyon Pass is $50.

Unless they have a reservation to stay at Phantom Ranch, hikers descending into the canyon for an overnight stay need a backcountry permit; request one in person, or by mail at ✏ *P.O. Box 129, Grand Canyon 86023.* Cost is $10 for the permit, plus $5 per person per night. Permits are limited, so make your reservation as far in advance as possible—they're taken up to four months ahead of arrival. A limited number of last-minute permits are available for the corridor campgrounds (Indian Garden, Bright Angel, and Cottonwood) on a daily basis.

ADMISSION HOURS

The South Rim is open 24/7, year-round. The North Rim is open mid-May through mid-October, depending on the weather. Highway 67 from Jacob Lake is closed due to snowfall from around mid-October to mid-May. The entrance gates are open 24 hours, but are generally staffed from about 7 AM to 7 PM. If you arrive when there's no one at the gate, you may enter legally without paying.

ATMS/BANKS

There is a full-service bank and ATM at the South Rim Chase Bank office in Market Plaza near the general store and an ATM at Maswik Lodge. Near the North Rim, there's an ATM at Jacob Lake Inn.

CELL-PHONE RECEPTION

Cell-phone reception is not possible in many areas of the park. There are telephones at all visitor centers and lodgings.

PARK CONTACT INFORMATION

Grand Canyon National Park ⌂ *P.O. Box 129, Grand Canyon 86023* ☎ *928/638–7888* ⊕ *www.nps.gov/grca.*

GRAND CANYON SOUTH RIM

SCENIC DRIVES

18

Hermit Road. The Santa Fe Company built Hermit Road, formerly known as West Rim Drive, in 1912 as a scenic tour route. Nine overlooks dot this 7-mi stretch, each worth a visit. The road is filled with hairpin turns, so make sure you adhere to posted speed limits. The historic roadway reopened after an extensive rehabilitation in 2008. As part of the project, a 3-mi Greenway Trail now offers easy access to cyclists looking to enjoy the original 1913 Hermit Rim Road. From March through November, the improved Hermit Road is closed to private auto traffic because of congestion; during this period, a free shuttle bus will carry you to all the overlooks. Riding the bus round-trip without getting off at any of the viewpoints takes 75 minutes; the return trip stops only at Mohave and Hopi points.

WHAT TO SEE

HISTORIC SITES

Tusayan Ruin and Museum. Completed in 1932, the museum offers a quick orientation to the lifestyles of the native tribes associated with the Grand Canyon and the Colorado Plateau. Adjacent, an excavation of an 800-year-old dwelling gives a glimpse at the lives of some of the area's earliest residents. ⊠ *About 20 mi east of Grand Canyon Village on Desert View Dr.* ☎ *928/638–7968* ⓦ *Free* ⊗ *Daily 9–5.*

THE SOUTH RIM IN ONE DAY

Start early, pack a picnic lunch, and take the shuttle to **Canyon View Information Plaza** just north of the south entrance, to pick up information and see your first incredible view at **Mather Point**. Continue east along **Desert View Drive** for about 2 mi to **Yaki Point**, your first stop. Next, hop back on the shuttle to head 7 mi east to **Grandview Point**, for a good view of the Krishna Shrine and Vishnu Temple buttes. Go 4 mi east and catch the view at **Moran Point**, then 3 mi to the **Tusayan Ruin and Museum**, where a small display is devoted to the history of the ancestral Puebloans. Continue another mile east to **Lipan**

Point to view the Colorado River. The final stop along the shuttle route is **Desert View and Watchtower**, where you can use telescopes for even better views.

On the return shuttle, hop off at any of the picnic areas for lunch. Once back at Grand Canyon Village, walk the paved **Rim Trail** to **Maricopa Point**. Stop at the historic **El Tovar Hotel** for dinner (be sure to make reservations well in advance). If you have time, take the shuttle on **Hermit Road** to **Hermits Rest**, 7 mi away. It's a good place to watch the sunset.

SCENIC STOPS

The Abyss. At an elevation of 6,720 feet, the Abyss is one of the most awesome stops on Hermit Road, revealing a sheer drop of 3,000 feet to the Tonto Platform, a wide terrace of Tapeats sandstone layers about two-thirds of the way down the canyon. From the Abyss you'll also see several isolated sandstone columns, the largest of which is called the Monument. ⊠ *5 mi west of Hermit Road Junction on Hermit Rd.*

★ **Desert View and Watchtower.** From the top of the 70-foot stone-and-mortar watchtower, even the muted hues of the distant Painted Desert to the east and the Vermilion Cliffs rising from a high plateau near the Utah border are visible. In the chasm below, angling to the north toward Marble Canyon, an imposing stretch of the Colorado River reveals itself. Up several flights of stairs, the Watchtower houses a glass-enclosed observatory with powerful telescopes. ⊠ *About 23 mi east of Grand Canyon Village on Desert View Dr.* ☎ *928/638–2736* ☉ *Daily 8–8, hrs vary in winter.*

Grandview Point. At an elevation of 7,496 feet, the view from here is one of the finest in the canyon. To the northeast is a group of dominant buttes, including Krishna Shrine, Vishnu Temple, Rama Shrine, and Shiva Temple. A short stretch of the Colorado River is also visible. Directly below the point, and accessible by the steep and rugged Grandview Trail, is Horseshoe Mesa, where you can see remnants of Last Chance Copper Mine. ⊠ *About 12 mi east of Grand Canyon Village on Desert View Dr.*

Hermits Rest. This westernmost viewpoint and Hermit Trail, which descends from it, were named for "hermit" Louis Boucher, a 19th-century French-Canadian prospector who had a number of mining claims and a roughly built home down in the canyon. Views from here

Tips for Avoiding Canyon Crowds

"I find that in contemplating the natural world, my pleasure is greater if there are not too many others contemplating it with me, at the same time."—Edward Abbey

TAKE ANOTHER ROUTE

Avoid road rage by choosing a different route to the South Rim, foregoing the traditional routes, Highway 64 and U.S. 180 from Flagstaff. Take Highway 89 north from Flagstaff instead, passing near Sunset Crater and Wupatki national monuments. When you reach the Cameron Trading Post at the junction with Highway 64, take a break—or stay overnight. This is a good place to shop for high-quality Navajo rugs, jewelry, and other authentic handicrafts. You also can sample Navajo tacos. Highway 64 to the west takes you directly to the park's east entrance; the scenery along the Little Colorado River Gorge en route is eye-popping. It's 23 mi from the Grand Canyon east entrance to the visitor center at Canyon View Information Plaza.

BYPASS THE SOUTH RIM

Although at the narrowest divide, the North Rim is just 10 mi across from the South Rim, the trip to get from one rim to the other by car is a five-hour drive of 215 mi. At first it might not sound like the trip would be worth it, but the payoff is huge. Along the way, you will travel through some of the prettiest parts of the state and be granted even more stunning views than those on the more easily accessible South Rim. Those who visit the North Rim often insist it offers the canyon's most beautiful views and best hiking.

To get to the North Rim from Flagstaff, take Highway 89 north past Cameron, turning left onto Highway 89A at Bitter Springs. En route you'll pass the area known as Vermilion Cliffs. At Jacob Lake, take Highway 67 directly to the Grand Canyon North Rim. The road to the North Rim closes from around mid-October through mid-May due to heavy snow, but in summer and early fall, it's a wonderful way to beat the crowds at the South Rim.

RIDE THE RAILS

There is no need to deal with all of the other drivers racing to the South Rim. Forget the hassle of the twisting rim roads, jaywalking pedestrians, and jammed parking lots, and sit back and relax in the comfy train cars of the **Grand Canyon Railway.** Live music and storytelling enliven the trip as you journey past the landscape through prairie, ranch, and national park land to the log-cabin train station in Grand Canyon Village. You won't see the Grand Canyon from the train, but you can walk or catch the shuttle at the restored, historic Grand Canyon Railway Station. The vintage train departs from the Williams Depot each morning, and makes the 65-mi journey in 2¼ hours. You can do the round-trip in a single day; however, you may choose to stay overnight at the South Rim and return to Williams the following afternoon. ⊠ *Williams Depot, 233 N. Grand Canyon Blvd., at Fray Marcos Blvd., Williams* ☎ *800/843–8724 railway reservations and information* ⊕ *www.thetrain.com* ⊴ *$70–$190 round-trip* ⊙ *Departs from Williams daily between 9:30 and 10:30* AM, *depending on the season, and from the South Rim between 3:30 and 4:30* PM.

18

SHUTTLE SERVICE

There are three shuttle routes. **The Hermits Rest Route** operates March through November, between Grand Canyon Village and Hermits Rest. **The Village Route** operates year-round in the village area; it provides the easiest access to the Canyon View Information Center. The **Kaibab Trail Route** goes from Canyon View Information Center to Yaki Point, including a stop at the South Kaibab Trailhead. Running from one hour before sunrise until one hour after sunset, shuttles arrive every 15 to 30 minutes. The roughly 30 stops are clearly marked throughout the park.

From mid-May to mid-October, you can get from the South Rim to the North Rim and vice versa via the **Transcanyon Shuttle** (☎ *928/638–2820* ⊕ *www.trans-canyonshuttle. com*). It leaves Bright Angel Lodge at 1:30 PM and arrives at the North Rim's Grand Canyon Lodge about 6:30 PM. The return trip leaves the North Rim each morning at 7 AM, arriving at the South Rim at about noon. One-way fare is $80, round-trip $150. A 50% deposit is required two weeks in advance. Reservations are required.

include Hermit Rapids and the towering cliffs of the Supai and Redwall formations. The stone building at Hermits Rest sells curios and refreshments. ⊠ *About 8 mi west of Hermit Road Junction on Hermit Rd.*

★ **Hopi Point.** From this elevation of 7,071 feet, you can see a large section of the Colorado River; although it appears as a thin line, the river is nearly 350 feet wide below this overlook. The overlook extends farther into the canyon than any other point on Hermit Road. The unobstructed views make this a popular place to watch the sunset. ⊠ *About 4 mi west of Hermit Road Junction on Hermit Rd.*

Lipan Point. Here, at the canyon's widest point, you can get an astonishing visual profile of the gorge's geologic history, with a view of every eroded layer of the canyon. The spacious panorama stretches to the Vermilion Cliffs on the northeastern horizon and features a multitude of imaginatively named spires, buttes, and temples—intriguing rock formations named after their resemblance to ancient pyramids. You can also see Unkar Delta, where a creek joins the Colorado to form powerful rapids and a broad beach. Ancestral Puebloan farmers worked the Unkar Delta for hundreds of years, growing corn, beans, and melons. ⊠ *About 25 mi east of Grand Canyon Village on Desert View Dr.*

★ **Mather Point.** You'll likely get your first glimpse of the canyon from this viewpoint, one of the most impressive and accessible (and most crowded) on the South Rim. Named for the National Park Service's first director, Stephen Mather, this spot yields extraordinary views of the Grand Canyon, including deep into the Inner Gorge and numerous buttes: Wotan's Throne, Brahma Temple, and Zoroaster Temple, among others. The Grand Canyon Lodge, on the North Rim, is almost directly north from Mather Point and only 10 mi away—yet you have to drive 215 mi to get from one spot to the other. ⊠ *Near Canyon View Information Plaza.*

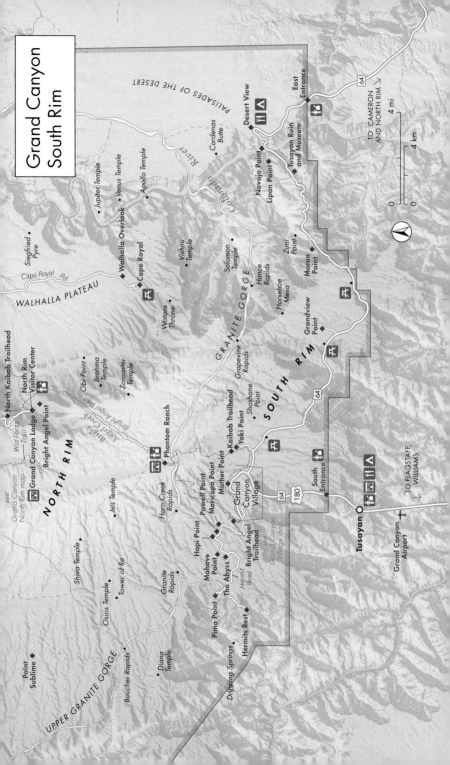

Moran Point. This point was named for American landscape artist Thomas Moran, who was especially fond of the play of light and shadows from this location. He first visited the canyon with John Wesley Powell in 1873. "Thomas Moran's name, more than any other, with the possible exception of Major Powell's, is to be associated with the Grand Canyon," wrote noted canyon photographer Ellsworth Kolb. It's fitting that Moran Point is a favorite spot of photographers and painters. ⊠ *About 17 mi east of Grand Canyon Village on Desert View Dr.*

Trailview Overlook. Look down on a dramatic view of the Bright Angel and Plateau Point trails as they zigzag down the canyon. In the deep gorge to the north flows Bright Angel Creek, one of the region's few permanent tributary streams of the Colorado River. Toward the south is an unobstructed view of the distant San Francisco Peaks, as well as Bill Williams Mountain (on the horizon) and Red Butte (about 15 mi south of the canyon rim). ⊠ *About 2 mi west of Hermit Road Junction on Hermit Rd.*

> ### ILLUMINATING VIEWS
>
> The best time of day to see the canyon is before 10 AM and after 2 PM, when the angle of the sun brings out the colors of the rock, and clouds and shadows add dimension.
>
> Colors deepen dramatically among the contrasting layers of the canyon walls just before and during sunrise and sunset. Hopi Point is the top spot on the South Rim to watch the sun set; Yaki and Pima points also offer vivid views. For a grand sunrise, try Mather or Yaki points. Arrive at least 30 minutes early for sunrise views and as much as 90 minutes for sunset views.

Yaki Point. Stop here for an exceptional view of Wotan's Throne, a flattop butte named by François Matthes, a U.S. Geological Survey scientist who developed the first topographical map of the Grand Canyon. The overlook juts out over the canyon, providing unobstructed views of inner canyon rock formations, South Rim cliffs, and Clear Creek Canyon. This point marks the beginning of the South Kaibab Trail and is one of the best places on the South Rim to watch the sunset. ⊠ *2 mi east of Grand Canyon Village on Desert View Dr.*

Fodor'sChoice ★ **Yavapai Point.** The word *yavapai* means "sun people" in Paiute, a group of nomadic American Indians associated with the Grand Canyon. Appropriately, this is one of the best locations on the South Rim to watch the sunset. Dominated by the Yavapai Observation Station, this point offers panoramic views of the mighty gorge through a wall of windows. Exhibits showcased here include videos of the canyon floor and the Colorado River, a scaled diorama of the canyon with national park boundaries, fossils and rock fragments used to re-create the complex layers of the canyon walls, and a display on the natural forces used to carve the chasm. Rangers dig even deeper into Grand Canyon geology with the free ranger program Geo-Glimpse, offered twice daily. A guided afternoon nature walk completes the offerings. Check ahead for special event and walk schedules. ⊠ *Adjacent to Grand Canyon Village* ☼ *Daily 8–8; hrs vary in winter.*

VISITOR CENTERS

Canyon View Information Plaza. The park's main orientation center near Mather Point provides pamphlets and resources to help plan your sightseeing. Park rangers are on hand to answer questions and aid in planning canyon excursions. A bookstore is stocked with books covering all topics on the Grand Canyon, and a daily schedule of ranger-led hikes and evening lectures is posted on a bulletin board inside. The information center can be reached by a short walk from Mather Point, by a short ride on the shuttle bus Village Route, or by a leisurely 1-mi walk on the Greenway Trail—a paved pathway that meanders through the forest. ⊠ *East side of Grand Canyon Village* ☎ *928/638–7888* ☉ *Daily 8–5; outdoor exhibits may be viewed anytime.*

Desert View Information Center. Near the Watchtower, at Desert View Point, the Grand Canyon Association offers a nice selection of books, park pamphlets, and educational materials. ⊠ *East entrance* ☎ *800/858– 2808 or 928/638–7893* ☉ *Daily 9–5; hrs vary in winter.*

Verkamp's Visitor Center. After 102 years of selling memorabilia and knickknacks on the South Rim, Verkamp's Curios closed in 2008 only to reopen a couple of months later as the park's newest visitor center. The building now serves as a bookstore, ranger station, and museum with exhibits on the pioneer history of the region. ⊠ *Desert View Dr., across from El Tovar Hotel, Grand Canyon Village* ☎ *928/638–7146* ☉ *Daily 8–5.*

Yavapai Observation Station. Shop in the bookstore, catch the park shuttle bus, or pick up information for the Rim Trail here. ⊠ *1 mi east of Market Plaza, Grand Canyon* ☎ *928/638–7890* ☉ *Daily 8–8; hrs vary in winter.*

SPORTS AND THE OUTDOORS

AIR TOURS

★ Flights by plane and helicopter over the canyon are offered by a number of companies, departing for the Grand Canyon Airport at the south end of Tusayan. You'll have more visibility from a helicopter but they are louder and more expensive than the fixed-wing planes. Prices and lengths of tours vary, but you can expect to pay about $109–$120 per adult for short plane trips and approximately $145–$235 for brief helicopter tours.

TOUR OPERATORS **Air Grand Canyon** (⊠ *Grand Canyon Airport, Grand Canyon* ☎ *928/638– 2686 or 800/247–4726* ⊕ *www.airgrandcanyon.com*) offers 40- to 50-minute fixed-wing air tours over the North Rim, the Kaibab Plateau, and the Dragon Corridor, one of the cross canyons. Tours start at 9 AM and run every hour on the hour. **Grand Canyon Airlines** (⊠ *Grand Canyon Airport* ☎ *928/638–2359 or 866/235–9422* ⊕ *www.grandcanyonairlines.com*) flies a fixed-wing on a 50-minute tour of the eastern edge of the Grand Canyon, the North Rim, and the Kaibab Plateau. All-day combination tours combine flightseeing with jeep tours and float trips on the Colorado River. Get an up-close view of Grand Canyon geology and the Colorado River on 30- and 50-minute tours with **Grand Canyon Helicopters** (⊠ *Grand Canyon Airport* ☎ *928/638–2764 or 800/541– 4537* ⊕ *www.grandcanyonhelicoptersaz.com/gch*). **Maverick Helicopters** (⊠ *Grand Canyon Airport* ☎ *928/638–2622 or 800/962–3869* ⊕ *www.*

maverickhelicopters.com) offers 25- and 45-minute tours of the eastern Grand Canyon, the North Rim, and the Dragon Corridor. A landing tour option sets you down in the canyon for a short snack below the rim. **Papillon Grand Canyon Helicopters** (⊠ *Grand Canyon Airport* ☎ *928/638–2419 or 800/528–2418* ⊕ *www.papillon.com*) offers both fixed-wing and helicopter tours of the canyon and combination tours with off-road Jeep tours and smooth-water rafting trips.

HIKING

Although permits are not required for day hikes, you must have a backcountry permit for longer trips (⇨ *Admission Fees and Permits, at the start of chapter*). Some of the more popular trails are listed in this chapter; more detailed information and maps can be obtained from the Backcountry Information Center. Also, rangers can help design a trip to suit your abilities.

Remember that the canyon has significant elevation changes and, in summer, extreme temperature ranges, which can pose problems for people who aren't in good shape or who have heart or respiratory problems. ■ TIP→ Carry plenty of water and energy foods. The majority of each year's 400 search-and-rescue incidents result from hikers underestimating the size of the canyon, hiking beyond their abilities, or not packing sufficient food and water.

⚠ Under no circumstances should you attempt a day hike from the rim to the river and back. Remember that when it's 80°F on the South Rim, it's 110°F on the canyon floor. Allow two to four days if you want to hike rim to rim (it's easier to descend from the North Rim, as it is more than 1,000 feet higher than the South Rim). Hiking steep trails from rim to rim is a strenuous trek of at least 21 mi and should be attempted only by experienced canyon hikers.

EASY

Fodor's Choice ★

Rim Trail. The South Rim's most popular walking path is the 9-mi (one way) Rim Trail, which runs along the edge of the canyon from Mather Point (the first overlook on Desert View Drive) to Hermits Rest. This walk, which is paved to Maricopa Point, visits several of the South Rim's historic landmarks. Allow anywhere from 15 minutes to a full day, depending on how much of the trail you want to explore. If you want to cover all it, the Rim Trail is an ideal day hike, as it varies only a few hundred feet in elevation from Mather Point (7,120 feet) to the trailhead at Hermits Rest (6,640 feet). ⚠ On the Rim Trail, water is only available in the Grand Canyon Village area and at Hermits Rest. ⊠ *Trailheads: from the major viewpoints along Hermit Road, which are serviced by shuttle buses during the busy summer months.*

■ NEED A BREAK?

If you've been driving too long and want some exercise, along with great views of the canyon, it's an easy 1¼-mi-long hike from the Information Plaza to El Tovar Hotel. The Greenway Trail runs through a quiet wooded area for about ½ mi, and then along the rim for another ¾ mi.

Grand Canyon Park Insider: Chuck Wahler

When Chuck Wahler tells people to "take a hike," he means it in the most helpful, encouraging sense. An 19-year employee at Grand Canyon National Park, Wahler knows the lay of the land, and he encourages folks to get a feel for it on foot. A hike "either along the rim or into the canyon" ranks among his top "must-do" suggestions for park visitors.

As Chief of the Operations Branch for the park's Division of Interpretation and Resource Education, Wahler manages front-line operations for the division. "The staff that works with me operates the park visitor centers and museums, and presents interpretive programs to our visitors," he explains.

Those programs include the popular Junior Ranger activities, which also make Wahler's must-do list: "If there are children in your group, have them participate."

Variety is the spice of park life, as far as Wahler is concerned, and the range of activities is his favorite thing about his workplace. "It is a constantly changing place," he says, "different from minute to minute, day to day, and season to season." That diversity inspires another suggestion: "Views of the canyon from along Hermit Road are very different from those along Desert View Drive," explains Wahler. "If you have the time, plan to experience both areas of the park."

Navigating the 1,904-square-mi park is a sizeable task, but it's made easier by the free shuttle system. The buses stop at 30-some points of interest, and Wahler advocates hopping aboard whenever possible. "You'll spend more of your time exploring the park and less time looking for a place to park."

For another insider tip, he touts the park's aptly named newspaper, which is distributed at the entrance station. "*The Guide* provides visitors with all the basic information they need to plan their visit to the park. Taking a few minutes to read the newspaper will help make a visit more enjoyable."

Wahler also urges travelers to consider coming during "the off-season" (late fall through early spring). "The weather can delightful, and the park is often less crowded than in the summer."

No matter the season, Wahler's final must-do is a simple one: "Find a quiet place along the rim, and just sit and enjoy the canyon."

—Jill Koch

18

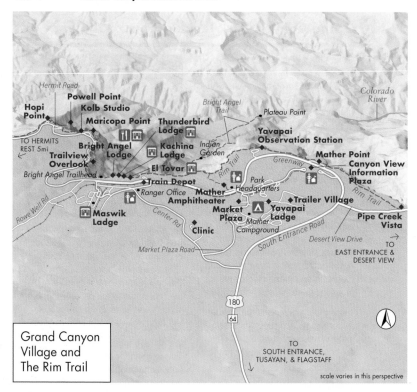

Grand Canyon
Village and
The Rim Trail

MODERATE

★ **Bright Angel Trail.** Well-maintained, this is one of the most scenic hiking paths from the South Rim to the bottom of the canyon (9.6 mi each way). Rest houses are equipped with water at the 1½- and 3-mi points from May through September and at Indian Garden (4 mi) year-round. Water is also available at Bright Angel Campground, 9¼ mi below the trailhead. Plateau Point, about 1½ mi below Indian Garden, is as far as you should attempt to go on a day hike; plan on spending six to nine hours. Bright Angel Trail is the easiest of all the footpaths into the canyon, but because the climb out from the bottom is an ascent of 5,510 feet, the trip should be attempted only by those in good physical condition and should be avoided in midsummer due to extreme heat. The top of the trail, a tight set of switchbacks called Jacob's Ladder, can be icy in winter. Originally a bighorn sheep path and later used by the Havasupai, the trail was widened late in the 19th century for prospectors. It is used by those taking mule rides as well as those on foot. ■**TIP→** Hikers going downhill should yield to those going uphill. Also note that mule trains have the right-of-way—and sometimes leave unpleasant surprises in your path. ⊠ *Trailhead: near Bright Angel Lodge.*

DIFFICULT

★ **South Kaibab Trail.** Because the route is so steep—descending from the trailhead at 7,260 feet down to 2,480 feet at the Colorado River—and has no water, many hikers return via the less-demanding Bright Angel Trail; allow four to six hours. During this 6.4-mi trek to the Colorado River, you're likely to encounter mule trains and riders. At the river, the trail crosses a suspension bridge and runs on to Phantom Ranch. Along the trail there is no water and very little shade. There are no campgrounds, though there are portable toilets at Cedar Ridge (6,320 feet), 1½ mi from the trailhead. Toilets and an emergency phone are also available at the Tipoff, 4.6 mi down the trail (3 mi past Cedar Ridge). The trail corkscrews down through some spectacular geology. Look for (but don't remove) fossils in the limestone when taking water breaks. ■TIP→ Even though an immense network of trails winds through the Grand Canyon, the popular corridor trails (Bright Angel and South Kaibab) are recommended for hikers new to the region. ⊠ *Trailhead: at Yaki Point on Desert View Drive, 4 mi east of Grand Canyon Village.*

MULE RIDES

★ Mule rides provide an intimate glimpse into the canyon for those who have the time, but not the stamina to see the canyon on foot. ■TIP→ Reservations are essential and are accepted up to 13 months in advance.

These trips have been conducted since the early 1900s. A comforting fact as you ride the narrow trail: no one's ever been killed while riding a mule that fell off a cliff. (Nevertheless, the treks are not for the faint of heart or people in questionable health.)

OUTFITTERS **Grand Canyon National Park Lodges Mule Rides** (☎*303/297–2757 or 888/297–2757 ⊕ www.grandcanyonlodges.com ⊙ May–Sept.*) delve into the canyon from the South Rim. Riders must be at least 55 inches tall, weigh less than 200 pounds, and understand English. Children under 15 must be accompanied by an adult. Riders must be in fairly good physical condition, and pregnant women are advised not to take these trips. The all-day ride to Plateau Point costs $154 (box lunch included). An overnight with a stay at Phantom Ranch at the bottom of the canyon is $420 ($743 for two riders). Two nights at Phantom Ranch, an option available from November through March, will set you back $593 ($991 for two). Meals are included. Reservations, especially during the busy summer months, are a must, but you can check at the Bright Angel Transportation Desk to be placed on the waiting list.

EDUCATIONAL OFFERINGS

Grand Canyon Field Institute. Instructors lead guided educational tours, hikes around the canyon, and weekend programs at the South Rim. With more than 100 classes a year, tour topics include everything from archaeology and backcountry medicine to photography and natural history. Contact GCFI for a schedule and price list; reserving ahead is essential. Discounted classes are available for members. Dues for an individual membership is $35 a year. ⟟ *P.O. Box 399, Grand Canyon 86023 ☎928/638–2485 or 866/471–4435 ⊕ www.grandcanyon.org/fieldinstitute ⟳ $105–$695.*

18

Interpretive Ranger Programs. The National Park Service sponsors all sorts of orientation activities, such as daily guided hikes and talks. The focus may be on any aspect of the canyon—from geology and flora and fauna to history and early inhabitants. For schedules on the South Rim, go to Canyon View Information Plaza, pick up a free copy of *The Guide*, or check online. ☎ 928/638–7888 ⊕ *www.nps.gov/grca* ☑ *Free.*

☼ **Junior Ranger Program.** The Junior Ranger Program provides a free, fun way to look at the cultural and natural history of this sublime destination. These hands-on educational programs for children ages 4 to 14 include guided adventure hikes, ranger-led "discovery" programs, and book readings. ☎ 928/638–7888 ⊕ *www.nps.gov/grca* ☑ *Free.*

Xanterra Motorcoach Tours. Narrated by knowledgeable guides, tours include the Hermits Rest Tour, which travels along the old wagon road built by the Santa Fe Railway; the Desert View Tour, which glimpses the Colorado River's rapids and stops at Lipan Point; Sunrise and Sunset Tours; and Combination Tours. Children 16 and younger are free when accompanied by a paying adult. ⊕ *6312 S. Fiddlers Green Circle, Suite 600, N. Greenwood Village, CO 80111* ☎ *303/297–2757 or 888/297–2757* ⊕ *www.grandcanyonlodges.com* ☑ *$18–$50.*

GRAND CANYON NORTH RIM

The North Rim stands 1,000 feet higher than the South Rim and has a more alpine climate, with twice as much annual precipitation. Here, in the deep forests of the Kaibab Plateau, the crowds are thinner, the facilities fewer, and the views even more spectacular. Due to snow, the North Rim is off-limits in the winter. The park buildings are closed mid-October through mid-May. The road closes when the snow makes it impassable—usually by the end of November.

Lodgings are available but limited; the North Rim only offers one historic lodge and restaurant and a single campground. Dining options have opened up a little with the addition of the Grand Cookout, offered nightly with live entertainment under the stars. Your best bet may be to pack your camping gear and hiking boots and take several days to explore the lush Kaibab Forest. The canyon's highest, most dramatic rim views also can be enjoyed on two wheels (via primitive dirt access roads) and on four legs (courtesy of a trusty mule).

SCENIC DRIVE

★ **Highway 67.** Open mid-May to mid-October (and often until Thanksgiving), the two-lane paved road running from Jacob Lake to Bright Angel Point climbs 1,400 feet in elevation as it passes through the Kaibab National Forest. Also called the "North Rim Parkway," this scenic route crosses the limestone-capped Kaibab Plateau—passing broad meadows, sun-dappled forests, and small lakes and springs—before abruptly falling away at the abyss of the Grand Canyon. Wildlife abounds in the thick ponderosa pine forests and lush mountain meadows. It's common to see deer, turkeys, and coyotes as you drive through this remote region. Point Imperial and Cape Royal can be reached by spurs off this scenic drive.

WHAT TO SEE

HISTORIC SITES

Grand Canyon Lodge. Built in 1928 by the Union Pacific Railroad, the massive stone structure is listed on the National Register of Historic Places. Its huge sunroom has hardwood floors, high-beam ceilings, and a marvelous view of the canyon through plate-glass windows. On warm days, visitors sit in the sun and drink in the surrounding beauty on an outdoor viewing deck, where National Park Service employees deliver free lectures on geology and history. ⊠ *Off Hwy. 67, near Bright Angel Point, North Rim.*

SCENIC STOPS

★ **Bright Angel Point.** The trail leading to Bright Angel Point, one of the most awe-inspiring overlooks on either rim, starts on the grounds of the Grand Canyon Lodge and runs along the crest of a point of rocks that juts into the canyon for several hundred yards. The walk is only ½ mi round-trip, but it's an exciting trek accented by sheer drops on each side of the trail. In a few spots where the route is extremely narrow, metal railings ensure visitors' safety. The temptation to clamber out to precarious perches to have your picture taken could get you killed—every year several people die from falls at the Grand Canyon. ⊠ *North Rim Dr.*

Cape Royal. A popular sunset destination, Cape Royal showcases the canyon's jagged landscape; you'll also get a glimpse of the Colorado River, framed by a natural stone arch called Angels Window. In autumn, the aspens turn a beautiful gold, adding even more color to an already magnificent scene of the forested surroundings. At Angels Window Overlook, **Cliff Springs Trail** starts its 1-mi route (round-trip) through a forested ravine. The trail terminates at Cliff Springs, where the forest opens to another impressive view of the canyon walls. ⊠ *Cape Royal Scenic Dr., 23 mi southeast of Grand Canyon Lodge.*

△ Practice basic safety precautions to reduce the risks of summer-storm-related dangers. The safest place to be during a thunderstorm is in a building or in a vehicle with the windows closed.

Point Imperial. At 8,803 feet, Point Imperial has the highest vista point at either rim; it offers magnificent views of both the canyon and the distant country: the Vermilion Cliffs to the north, the 10,000-foot Navajo Mountain to the northeast in Utah, the Painted Desert to the east, and the Little Colorado River Canyon to the southeast. ⊠ *2.7 mi left off Cape Royal Scenic Dr. on Point Imperial Rd., 11 mi northeast of Grand Canyon Lodge.*

Fodor'sChoice **Point Sublime.** Talk about solitude. Here you can camp within feet of the
★ canyon's edge. Sunrises and sunsets are spectacular. The winding road, through gorgeous high country, is only 17 mi, but it will take you at least two hours, one way. The road is intended only for vehicles with high-road clearance (pickups and four-wheel-drive vehicles). It is also necessary to be properly equipped for wilderness road travel. Check with a park ranger or at the information desk at Grand Canyon Lodge before taking this journey. You may camp here only with a permit from the Backcountry Office. ⊠ *North Rim Dr., Grand Canyon; about 20 mi west of North Rim Visitor Center.*

18

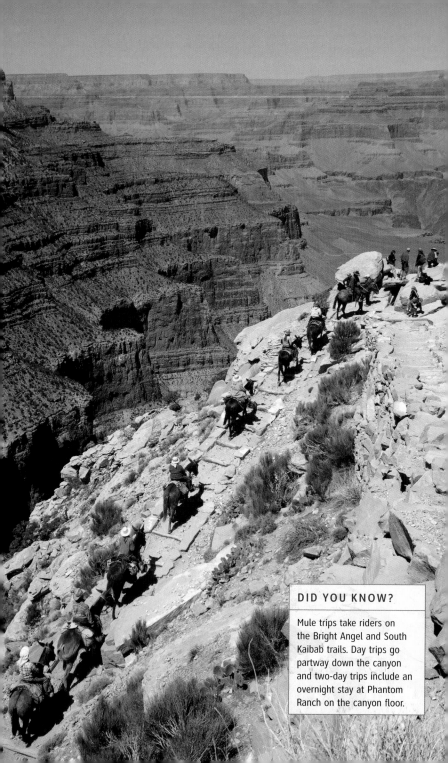

DID YOU KNOW?

Mule trips take riders on the Bright Angel and South Kaibab trails. Day trips go partway down the canyon and two-day trips include an overnight stay at Phantom Ranch on the canyon floor.

THE NORTH RIM IN ONE DAY

For your day at the North Rim, we suggest a hike and a drive. The most popular trails on the North Rim are **Transept Trail**, which starts near the Grand Canyon Lodge and has little elevation change, making it good for children; and **Cliff Springs Trail**, which starts near Cape Royal and leads to good views of the canyon.

For your drive, travel up the two-lane Cape Royal Road through the Kaibab National Forest to **Point Imperial**— at 8,803 feet, it's the highest vista

on either rim and has views of the Vermilion Cliffs, the Painted Desert, Navajo Mountain, and more. If you have more time, you can take a **mule ride** into the canyon. The trails for the mules are a bit easier on this side of the canyon. Riders must be at least age 7. Or listen to a **ranger-led talk**. Schedules are posted at the Grand Canyon Lodge near the North Rim Visitor Center.

Roosevelt Point. Named after the president who gave the Grand Canyon its national park status in 1919, this is the best place to see the confluence of the Little Colorado River and the Grand Canyon. The cliffs south of the junction are known as the Palisades of the Desert. A short woodland loop trail leads to this eastern viewpoint. ⊠ *Cape Royal Rd., 18 mi southeast of Grand Canyon Lodge.*

VISITOR CENTER

North Rim Visitor Center. View exhibits, peruse the bookstore, and pick up useful maps and brochures. Interpretive programs are often scheduled in the summer. If you're craving coffee, it's a short walk from here to the Roughrider Saloon at the Grand Canyon Lodge. ⊠ *Near the parking lot on Bright Angel Peninsula* ☎ *928/638–7864* ⏱ *Mid-May–mid-Oct., daily 8–6.*

18

SPORTS AND THE OUTDOORS

HIKING

EASY

Cape Final Trail. This 2-mi hike follows an old Jeep trail through a ponderosa pine forest to the canyon overlook at Cape Final with panoramic views of the northern canyon, the Palisades of the Desert, and the impressive spectacle of Juno Temple. ⊠ *Trailhead: parking lot 5 mi south of Roosevelt Point on Cape Royal Rd.*

Cape Royal Trail. Informative signs on natural history add to this popular 0.6-mi, round-trip, paved path to Cape Royal; allow 30 minutes round-trip. At an elevation of 7,685 feet on the southern edge of the Walhalla Plateau, the popular Cape Royal viewpoint offers expansive vistas of Wotans Throne, Vishnu Temple, Freya Castle, Horseshoe Mesa, and the Colorado River. The trail also offers several nice views of Angels Window. ⊠ *Trailhead: at the Cape Royal parking area.*

★ **Cliff Springs Trail.** An easy 1-mi (round-trip), one-hour walk near Cape Royal, Cliff Springs Trail leads through a forested ravine to an excellent

Grand Canyon
North Rim

0 ____ 5 mi
0 ____ 5 km

SOUTH CANYON

MARBLE CANYON

Tatahatso Point

Point Hansbrough

PAINTED DESERT

NAVAJO INDIAN RESERVATION

Colorado River

445

KAIBAB PLATEAU

TO JACOB LAKE, MARBLE CANYON AND SOUTH RIM

67

North Rim Entrance Station

TO POINT SUBLIME

Point Imperial

Bourke Point

Nankoweap Rapids

Nankoweap Mesa

Kwagunt Butte

NORTH RIM

Point Imperial Road

Ken Patrick Trail

Wildforss Trail

North Rim Visitor Center

Grand Canyon Lodge

Bright Angel Point

Cottonwood Campground

Bright Angel Creek

North Kaibab Trail

Shiva Temple

Osiris Temple

Isis Temple

Obi Point

Brahma Temple

Zoroaster Temple

WALHALLA PLATEAU

Cape Royal Road

Vista Encantada

Tritle Peak

Roosevelt Point

Atoko Point

Siegfried Pyre

Chuar Butte

Temple Butte

Jupiter Temple

Venus Temple

Apollo Temple

Cape Final Trail

Walhalla Ruins

Cape Royal

Cliff Springs Trail

Wotans Throne

Cape Royal Trail

Vishnu Temple

PALISADES OF THE DESERT

Cardenas Butte

Granite Rapids

Horn Creek Rapids

Phantom Ranch

Bright Angel Trail

SOUTH RIM

South Kaibab Trail

GRANITE GORGE

Solomon Temple

Hopi Point

The Abyss

Mather Point

Hermit Road

Yaki Point

64

Grand Canyon Village

Grapevine Rapids

Hance Rapids

Desert View

Navajo Point

Lipan Point

TO FLAGSTAFF, WILLIAMS

view of the canyon. Narrow and precarious in spots, it passes ancient dwellings, winds beneath a limestone overhang, and ends at Cliff Springs. ⊠ *Trailhead: across from Angels Window Overlook.*

☘ **Transept Trail.** This 3-mi (round-trip), 1½-hour trail begins at 8,255 feet. Well-maintained and -marked, it has little elevation change, sticking

near the rim before reaching a dramatic view of a large stream through Bright Angel Canyon. The route leads to a side canyon called Transept Canyon, which geologist Clarence Dutton named in 1882, declaring it "far grander than Yosemite." Check the posted schedule to find a ranger talk along this trail; it's also a great place to view fall foliage. ⊠ *Trailhead: near the Grand Canyon Lodge's east patio.*

MODERATE

Uncle Jim Trail. This 5-mi, three-hour loop trail starts at 8,300 feet and winds south through the forest, past Roaring Springs Canyon and Bright Angel Canyon. The highlight of this rim hike is Uncle Jim Point, which, at 8,244 feet, overlooks the upper sections of the North Kaibab Trail. ⊠ *Trailhead: at the North Kaibab Trail parking lot.*

★ **Widforss Trail.** Round-trip, Widforss Trail is 9.8 mi, with an elevation change of 200 feet. The trailhead is at 8,080 feet. Allow six hours for the hike, which passes through shady forests of pine, spruce, fir, and aspen on its way to Widforss Point, at 7,900 feet. Here you'll have good views of five temples: Zoroaster, Brahma, and Deva to the southeast and Buddha and Manu to the southwest. You are likely to see wildflowers in summer, and this is a good trail for viewing fall foliage. It's named in honor of artist Gunnar M. Widforss, renowned for his paintings of national park landscapes. ⊠ *Trailhead: across from the North Kaibab Trail parking lot.*

18

DIFFICULT

North Kaibab Trail. At 8,241 feet, this trail is open only from May through October. It is recommended for experienced hikers only, who should allow four days for the full hike. The long, steep path drops 5,840 feet over a distance of 14.5 mi to Phantom Ranch and the Colorado River, so the National Park Service suggests that day hikers not go farther than Roaring Springs (5,020 feet) before turning to hike back up out of the canyon. After about 7 mi, Cottonwood Campground (4,080 feet) has drinking water in summer, restrooms, shade trees, and a ranger. ■ TIP→ For a fee, a shuttle takes hikers to the North Kaibab Trailhead twice daily from Grand Canyon Lodge. ⊠ *Trailhead: about 2 mi north of the Grand Canyon Lodge.*

MULE RIDES

OUTFITTER **Canyon Trail Rides** (☎ 435/679–8665 ⊕ *www.canyonrides.com*) leads mule
☘ rides on the easier trails of the North Rim. A one-hour ride (minimum age 7) runs $40. Half-day trips on the rim or into the canyon (minimum age 10) cost $75; full-day trips (minimum age 12) go for $165. Full-day trips into the canyon follow the North Kaibab Trail to Roaring Springs

where you'll have time to explore and eat a sack lunch. Weight limits vary from 200 to 220 pounds. Available daily from May 15 to October 15, these excursions are popular, so make reservations in advance.

EDUCATIONAL OFFERINGS

☺ **Junior Ranger Program.** Children ages 9 to 14 can take part in these hands-on educational programs and earn a Junior Ranger certificate and badge. ☎ *928/638–7967* ⊕ *www.nps.gov/grca* ✉ *Free.*

Interpretive Ranger Programs. Daily guided hikes and talks may focus on any aspect of the canyon—from geology and flora and fauna to history and the canyon's early inhabitants. For schedules, go to the Grand Canyon Lodge or pick up a free copy of *The Guide* to the North Rim. ☎ *928/638–7967* ⊕ *www.nps.gov/grca* ✉ *Free.*

GRAND CANYON WEST RIM

The West Rim, a five-hour drive away from the South Rim, is not part of the national park but belongs to the Pai Indians—the Hualapai and Havasupai. These natives have lived along the Colorado River and the vast Colorado Plateau for more than 1,000 years.

WHAT TO SEE

Visitors aren't allowed to travel in their own vehicles to the viewpoints once they reach the West Rim, but must purchase a tour package from **Destination Grand Canyon West.** The Hualapai Tribe offers the basic **Hualapai Legacy tour package** ($29.95 per person plus tax), which includes a Hualapai visitation permit and shuttle transportation. A free shuttle will take you to Eagle Point, where the Indian Village walking tour visits authentic dwellings; Hualapai Ranch, site of Western performances, cookouts, and horseback and wagon rides; and Guano Point, where the "High Point Hike" offers panoramic views of the Colorado River. For an extra cost you can add a helicopter trip into the canyon, a boat trip on the Colorado, an off-road Hummer adventure, a horseback or wagon ride to the canyon rim, or a walk on the Skywalk. Local Hualapai guides add a American Indian perspective to a canyon trip that you won't find on North Rim and South Rim tours.

The **Skywalk** is a cantilevered glass bridge suspended nearly 4,000 feet above the Colorado River and extending 70 feet from the edge of the Grand Canyon that opened in 2007. Approximately 10 feet wide, the bridge's deck, made of tempered glass several inches thick, has 5-foot glass railings on each side making an unobstructed open-air platform. Visitors must store all personal effects, including cameras, cell phones, and video cameras, in lockers before entering the Skywalk. A professional photographer takes personal photographs on the walkway, which can be purchased from the gift shop. At this writing, a three-level, 6,000-square-foot visitor center is under construction at the site. Slated to be completed in 2009, it will include a museum, movie theater, VIP lounge, gift shop, and multiple restaurants. A short walk takes visitors to the Indian Village, where educational displays uncover the culture of five different American Indian tribes (Havasupai, Plains, Hopi,

Hualapai, and Navajo). Intertribal, powwow-style dance performances entertain visitors at the nearby amphitheater. ✉ *Grand Canyon West* ☎ *702/878–9378 or 877/716–9378* ⊕ *www.destinationgrandcanyon.com* ✉ *Hualapai Legacy tour $29.95, impact fee $8, Skywalk $29.95* ⊙ *Daily.*

WHAT'S NEARBY

The northwest section of Arizona is geographically fascinating. In addition to the Grand Canyon, it's home to national forests, national monuments, and national recreation areas. Towns, however, are small and scattered. Many of them cater to visiting adventurers, and American Indian reservations dot the map.

NEARBY TOWNS

Towns near the canyon's South Rim include the tiny town of Tusayan, just 1 mi south of the entrance station, and Williams, the "Gateway to the Grand Canyon," 58 mi south. **Tusayan** has the basic amenities and an airport that serves as a starting point for airplane and helicopter tours of the canyon. The cozy mountain town of **Williams,** founded in 1882 when the railroad passed through, was once a rough-and-tumble joint, replete with saloons and bordellos. Today it reflects a much milder side of the Wild West, with 3,000 residents and 1,512 motel rooms. Wander along main street—part of historic Route 66, but locally named, like the town, after trapper Bill Williams—and indulge in Route 66 nostalgia inside antiques shops or souvenir and T-shirt stores.

The communities closest to the North Rim include Fredonia, 76 mi north; Marble Canyon, 80 mi northeast; Lees Ferry, 85 mi east; and Jacob Lake, 45 mi north. **Fredonia,** a small community of about 1,200, approximately an hour's drive north of the Grand Canyon, is often referred to as the gateway to the North Rim; it's also relatively close to Zion and Bryce Canyon national parks. **Marble Canyon** marks the geographical beginning of the Grand Canyon at its northeastern tip. It's a good stopping point if you are driving Highway 89 to the North Rim. En route from the South Rim to the North Rim is **Lees Ferry,** where most of the area's river rafts start their journey. The tiny town of **Jacob Lake,** nestled high in pine country at an elevation of 7,925 feet, was named after Mormon explorer Jacob Hamblin, also known as the "Buckskin Missionary." It has a hotel, café, campground, and lush mountain countryside.

18

Continued on page 426

EXPLORING THE
COLORADO RIVER

By Carrie Frasure

High in Colorado's Rocky Mountains, the Colorado River begins as a catch-all for the snowmelt off the mountains west of the Continental Divide. By the time it reaches the Grand Canyon, the Colorado has been joined by multiple tributaries to become a raging river, red with silt as it sculpts spectacular landscapes. A network of dams can only partially tame this mighty river.

Snaking its way through five states, the Colorado River is an essential water source to the arid Southwest. Its natural course runs 1,450 mi from its origin in Colorado's La Poudre Pass Lake in Rocky Mountain National Park to its final destination in the Gulf of California, also called the Sea of Cortez. In northern Arizona, the Colorado River has been a powerful force in shaping the Grand Canyon, where it flows 4,000 to 6,000 feet below the rim. Beyond the canyon, the red river takes a lazy turn at the Arizona–Nevada border, where Hoover Dam creates the reservoir at Lake Mead. The Colorado continues at a relaxed pace along the Arizona–California border, providing energy and irrigation in Arizona, California, and Nevada before draining into northwestern Mexico.

A RIVER RUNS THROUGH IT

Stretching along 277 mi of the Colorado River is one of the seven natural wonders of the world, the Grand Canyon. The river here ranges in width from 4 to 18 mi, while the canyon walls around it soar up to a mile high. The canyon's geologic history and majesty are revealed in exposed tiers of rock cut deep in the Colorado Plateau. What caused this incredible marvel of nature? No one knows for sure. Erosion by water coupled with driving wind are most likely the major culprits: under the sculpting power of wind and water, the shale layers eroded into slopes and the harder sandstone and limestone layers created terraced cliffs. Other forces that may have helped shape the canyon include ice, volcanic activity, continental drift, and earthquakes.

WHO LIVES HERE
Native tribes have lived in the canyon for thousands of years and continue to do so, looking to the river for subsistence. The plateau-dwelling Hualapai ("people of the tall pines") live on a million acres along 108 mi of the Colorado River in the West Rim. The Havasupai ("people of the blue green water") live deep within the walls of the 12-mi-long Havasu Canyon—a major side canyon connected to the Grand Canyon.

ENVIRONMENTAL CONCERNS
When the Grand Canyon achieved national park status in 1919, only 44,173 people made the grueling overland trip to see it—quite a contrast from today's nearly 5 million annual visitors. The tremendous increase in visitation has greatly impacted the fragile ecosystems, as has Lake Powell's Glen Canyon Dam, which was constructed in the 1950s and '60s. The dam has changed the composition of the Colorado River, replacing warm water rich in sediments (nature's way of nourishing the riverbed and banks) with mostly cool, much clearer water. This has introduced non-native plants and animals that threaten the extinction of several native species.

Above and right, views of Colorado River in the Grand Canyon from Toroweap.

DID YOU KNOW?

The North Rim's isolated Toroweap overlook (also called Tuweep) is perched 3,000 feet above the canyon floor: a height equal to stacking the Sears Tower and Empire State Building on top of each other.

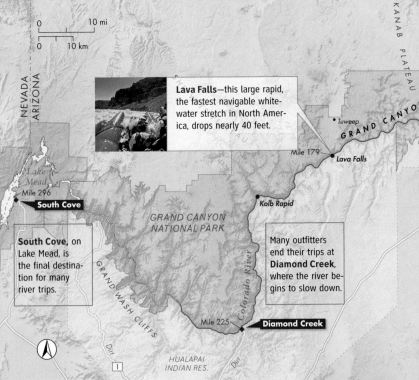

RIVER RAFTING THROUGH THE GRAND CANYON

Viewing the Colorado River from a canyon overlook is one thing, but looking up at the canyon from the middle of the river is quite another experience. If you're ready to tackle the churning white water of the Colorado River as it rumbles and hisses its way through the Grand Canyon, take a look at this map of what you might encounter along the way.

0   10 mi
0   10 km

NEVADA
ARIZONA

KANAB PLATEAU

GRAND CANYON

Lava Falls—this large rapid, the fastest navigable white-water stretch in North America, drops nearly 40 feet.

Tuweep

Mile 179   Lava Falls

Lake Mead
Mile 296
South Cove

Kolb Rapid

GRAND CANYON NATIONAL PARK

South Cove, on Lake Mead, is the final destination for many river trips.

Colorado River

Many outfitters end their trips at **Diamond Creek**, where the river begins to slow down.

GRAND WASH CLIFFS

Mile 225   **Diamond Creek**

Dirt

1

HUALAPAI INDIAN RES.

Dirt

COLORADO RIVER TRIPS

Time and Length	Entry and Exit points	Cost/person
1 day	Glen Canyon Dam to Lees Ferry	$75-$400
3-4 days	Lees Ferry to Phantom Ranch	*$650-$1,200
6 days, 89 mi	Phantom Ranch to Diamond Creek	$1,800-$2,100
9-10 days, 136 mi	Lees Ferry to Diamond Creek	$2,300-$3,000
14-16 days, 225 mi	Lees Ferry to South Cove	$3,250-$3,900

*Trips either begin or end at Phantom Ranch/Bright Angel Beach at the bottom of the Grand Canyon, at river mile 87

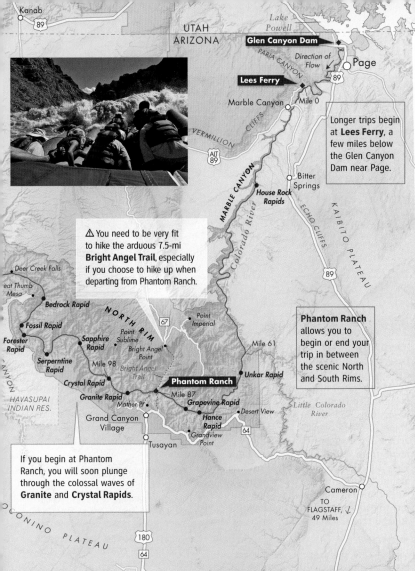

Kanab

89

UTAH
ARIZONA

Lake
Powell

Glen Canyon Dam

Direction
of Flow

Page

89

Lees Ferry

Mile 0

Marble Canyon

Longer trips begin
at **Lees Ferry**, a
few miles below
the Glen Canyon
Dam near Page.

VERMILLION CLIFFS

PARIA CANYON

Bitter
Springs

89

KAIBITO PLATEAU

ECHO CLIFFS

House Rock
Rapids

MARBLE CANYON

Colorado River

Deer Creek Falls

eat Thumb
Mesa

⚠ You need to be very fit
to hike the arduous 7.5-mi
Bright Angel Trail, especially
if you choose to hike up when
departing from Phantom Ranch.

Bedrock Rapid

NORTH RIM

67

Point
Imperial

Phantom Ranch
allows you to
begin or end your
trip in between
the scenic North
and South Rims.

Fossil Rapid

**Sapphire
Rapid**

Point
Sublime

Bright Angel
Point

Mile 61

**Forester
Rapid**

**Serpentine
Rapid**

Mile 98

Bright Angel
Trail

Crystal Rapid

Phantom Ranch

Unkar Rapid

CANYON

HAVASUPAI
INDIAN RES.

Granite Rapid

Mile 87

Mather Pt

Grapevine Rapid

Little Colorado
River

Desert View

Grand Canyon
Village

**Hance
Rapid**

18

If you begin at Phantom
Ranch, you will soon plunge
through the colossal waves of
Granite and **Crystal Rapids**.

Tusayan

Grandview
Point

64

Cameron

TO
FLAGSTAFF, ↓
49 Miles

COCONINO PLATEAU

180

64

NOT JUST RAPIDS

Don't think that your experience will be
non-stop white-water adrenaline. Most of
the Colorado River features long, relaxing
stretches of water, where you rift amid
grandiose rock formations. You might even
spot a mountain goat or two. Multiday trips
include camping on the shore.

PLANNING YOUR RIVER RAFTING TRIP

PADDLE, MOTOR, OR HYBRID?

Base the type of trip you choose on the amount of effort you want to put in. Motor rafts, which are the roomiest of the choices, cover the most miles in less time and are the most comfortable. All-paddle trips are the most active and require the most involvement from guests. They're good for physically fit individuals who thrive on action. Hybrid trips are the most popular because they offer both the opportunity to paddle and to relax and have the guide do the tough rowing.

THE GEAR

Life jackets, beverages, tents, sheets, tarps, sleeping bags, dry bags, first aid, and food are provided—but you'll still need to plan ahead by packing clothing, hats, sunscreen, toiletries, and other sundries. Commercial outfitters allow each river runner two waterproof bags to store items during the day—just keep in mind that one of these will be filled up with the provided sleeping bag and tarp. ■TIP→ Bring a rain suit: summer thunderstorms are frequent and chilly.

WHEN TO GO

Lots of people book trips for summer's peak period: June through August. If you're flexible, take advantage of the Arizona weather and go from May to early June or in September. ■TIP→ Seats fill up quickly; make reservations for multiday trips a year or two in advance.

TOUR OPERATORS

Arizona Raft Adventures ⌂ 4050 E. Huntington Rd., Flagstaff 86004 ☎ 928/526-8200 or 800/786-7238 ⊕ www.azraft.com

Canyoneers ⌂ P.O. Box 2997, Flagstaff 86003 ☎ 928/526-0924 or 800/525-0924 ⊕ www.canyoneers.com

Grand Canyon Expeditions ⌂ P.O. Box O, Kanab, UT 84741 ☎ 435/644-2691 or 800/544-2691 ⊕ www.gcex.com

Hualapai River Runners ⌂ 887 Rte. 66, Peach Springs 86434 ☎ 928/769-2219 or 888/255-9550 ⊕ www.destinationgrandcanyon.com

⇨ See "Rafting" in the Sports and the Outdoors section of Area Activities in the What's Nearby section of this chapter for more information.

Above, Getting wet—and loving it—on a hybrid raft.

DID YOU KNOW?

As you're hanging on for dear life, consider this: Civil War veteran John Wesley Powell chartered these treacherous rapids in 1869—not only were conditions more dangerous then, but he had only one arm.

VISITOR INFORMATION
Kaibab National Forest, North District ✉ *430 S. Main St., Fredonia 86022*
☎ *928/643–7395* ⊕ *www.fs.fed.us/r3/kai.* **Kaibab National Forest, Tusayan**
Ranger District ✉ *Hwy. 64, Grand Canyon 86023* ☎ *928/638–2443* ⊕ *www.*
fs.fed.us/r3/kai. **Kaibab National Forest, Williams Ranger District** ✉ *742 S.*
Clover Rd., Williams 86046 ☎ *928/635–5600* ⊕ *www.fs.fed.us/r3/kai.* **Kaibab**
Plateau Visitor Center ✉ *Hwy. 89A/AZ 67, Jacob Lake 86022* ☎ *928/643–7298*
⊕ *www.fs.fed.us/r3/kai.* **Williams Visitor Center** ✉ *200 W. Railroad Ave., at*
Grand Canyon Blvd., Williams ☎ *928/635–1418 or 800/863–0546* ⊕ *www.*
williamschamber.com ☾ *Sept.–May, daily 8–5; June–Aug., daily 8–6:30.*

NEARBY ATTRACTIONS

National Geographic Visitor Center Grand Canyon. Here you can schedule and purchase tickets for air tours and daily Colorado River trips, buy a national park pass, and access the park by special entry lanes. However, the biggest draw at the visitor center is the six-story IMAX screen that features the 34-minute movie *Grand Canyon: Discovery & Adventure*—you can learn about the geologic and natural history of the canyon, soar above stunning rock formations, and ride the rapids through the rocky gorge. ✉ *Hwy. 64/U.S. 180, 2 mi south of the Grand Canyon's south entrance, Tusayan* ☎ *928/638–2203 or 928/638–2468* ⊕ *www.explorethecanyon.com* 🎟 *$12.81* ☾ *Mar.–Oct., daily 8:30–8:30; Nov.–Feb., daily 10:30–6:30.*

★ **Vermilion Cliffs.** West from the town of Marble Canyon are these spectacular cliffs, more than 3,000 feet high in many places. Keep an eye out for condors; the giant endangered birds were reintroduced into the area in 1996. Reports suggest that the birds, once in captivity, are surviving well in the wilderness.

AREA ACTIVITIES

SPORTS AND THE OUTDOORS
FISHING

The stretch of ice-cold, crystal-clear water at Lees Ferry off the North Rim provides arguably the best trout fishing in the Southwest. Many rafters and anglers stay the night in a campground near the river or in nearby Marble Canyon before hitting the river at dawn. At a number of lakes surrounding Williams, fish for trout, crappie, catfish, and smallmouth bass. Anglers ages 14 and older are required to obtain a fishing license from the **Arizona Game and Fish Department** (⌂ *3500 S. Lake Mary Rd., Flagstaff 86001* ☎ *928/774–5045* ⊕ *www.gf.state.az.us*).

OUTFITTERS
AND
EXPEDITIONS

Marble Canyon Outfitters (☎ *928/355–2225 or 800/726–1789* ⊕ *www.leesferryflyfishing.com*), at Marble Canyon Lodge, sells Arizona fishing licenses and offers guided fishing trips. **Lees Ferry Anglers** (☎ *928/355–2261, 800/962–9755 outside Arizona* ⊕ *www.leesferry.com*), at Milepost 547 on North Highway 89A, sells state fishing licenses and has guides and gear.

WHERE TO EAT AND STAY

ABOUT THE RESTAURANTS

Inside the park, you can find everything from cafeteria food to casual café fare to elegant evening specials. There's even a coffeehouse with organic joe. Reservations are accepted (and recommended) only at El Tovar Dining Room; they can be made up to six months in advance in conjuction with El Tovar room reservations, up to 30 days in advance without. The dress code is casual across the board, but El Tovar is your best option if you're looking to dress up a bit and thumb through an extensive wine list. On the North Rim there is one restaurant, a cafeteria, and the Grand Cookout experience. Drinking water and restrooms are not available at most picnic spots. Options outside the park, in Tusayan and Williams to the south and Jacob Lake to the north, range from fast food to nice sit-down restaurants. Near the park, even the priciest places allow casual dress. On the Hualapai Reservation on the West Rim, dining is limited.

ABOUT THE HOTELS

The park's accommodations include three "historic rustic" facilities and four motel-style lodges. Of the 922 rooms, cabins, and suites, only 203, all at the Grand Canyon Lodge, are at the North Rim. Outside El Tovar Hotel, the canyon's architectural crown jewel, frills are hard to find. Rooms are basic but comfortable, and most guests would agree that the best in-room amenity is a view of the canyon. Though rates vary widely, most rooms fall in the $125 to $175 range.

■TIP→ Reservations are a must, especially during the busy summer season. If you want to get your first choice (especially Bright Angel Lodge or El Tovar), make reservations as far in advance as possible; they're taken up to 13 months ahead. You might find a last-minute cancellation, but you shouldn't count on it. Although lodging at the South Rim will keep you close to the action, the frenetic activity and crowded facilities are off-putting to some. With short notice, the best time to find a room on the South Rim is during winter. And though the North Rim is less crowded than the South Rim, lodging (remember that rooms are limited) is available only from mid-May through mid-October.

Grand Canyon National Park Lodges (☎ *303/297–2757 or 888/297–2757* ⊕ *www.grandcanyonlodges.com*) runs the park lodging on the South Rim.

Outside the park, Tusayan's hotels offer a convenient location but no bargains, while Williams can provide price breaks on food and lodging, as well as a respite from the crowds. Extra amenities (e.g., swimming pools and Internet access) are also more abundant. Lodging options are even more limited on the West Rim.

ABOUT THE CAMPGROUNDS

Inside the park, camping is permitted only in designated campsites. Some campgrounds charge nightly camping fees in addition to entrance fees, and some accept reservations up to five months in advance through ⊕ *www.recreation.gov*. Others are first-come, first-served. The South Rim has three campgrounds, one with RV hookups. The North Rim's single in-park campground does not offer hookups. All four campgrounds are near the rims and easily accessible. In-park camping in a spot other than a developed rim campground requires a permit from the Backcountry Information Center, which also serves as your reservation. Permits can be requested by mail or fax; applying well in advance is recommended. Call ☎ 928/638–7875 between 1 and 5 weekdays for information. Numerous backcountry campsites dot the canyon—be prepared for a considerable hike. The three established backcountry campgrounds require a trek of 4.6 to 16.6 mi. Outside the park, two campgrounds, one with hookups, are within 7 mi of the South Rim, and two are within about 45 mi of the North Rim. Developed and undeveloped campsites are available, first-come, first-served, in the Kaibab National Forest. There is no camping on the West Rim, but you can pitch a tent on the beach near the Colorado River at the primitive campground on Diamond Creek Road.

WHERE TO EAT

IN THE PARK
SOUTH RIM

$$$ ✕ **Arizona Room.** The canyon views from this casual southwestern-style
STEAK steak house are the best of any restaurant at the South Rim. The menu includes such delicacies as chili-crusted pan-seared wild salmon, chipotle barbecue baby back ribs, roasted-vegetable-and-black-bean enchiladas, and blackened prime rib. For dessert, try the cheesecake with prickly-pear syrup paired with one of the house-specialty coffee drinks. Seating is first-come, first served, so arrive early to avoid the crowds. ⊠ *Bright Angel Lodge, Desert View Dr., Grand Canyon Village* ☎ *928/638–2631* ⊕ *www.grandcanyonlodges.com* ⌖ *Reservations not accepted* ⊟ *AE, D, DC, MC, V* ⊙ *Closed Jan.–mid-Feb. No lunch Nov.–Feb.*

$$ ✕ **Bright Angel Restaurant.** No-surprises dishes will fill your belly at break-
SOUTHWESTERN fast, lunch, or dinner. Entrées include such basics as salads, steaks, pasta, fajitas, and fish. Or you can step it up a notch and order some of the same selections straight from the Arizona Room menu including prime rib, baby back ribs, and wild salmon. For dessert try the warm apple grunt (sliced apples with granola and ice cream). Be prepared to wait for a table: the dining room bustles all day long. The plain decor is broken up with large-pane windows and original artwork. Don't wait until the last minute to use the restroom: you have to leave the restaurant, walk through the lobby, and down a flight of stairs to get there—where you'll most likely need to wait in line with all of the other canyon visitors. ⊠ *Bright Angel Lodge, Desert View Dr., Grand Canyon Village* ☎ *928/638–2631* ⊕ *www.grandcanyonlodges.com* ⌖ *Reservations not accepted* ⊟ *AE, D, DC, MC, V.*

¢ ✕ **Canyon Café.** Fast-food favorites here include pastries, burgers, and
CAFE pizza. Open for breakfast, lunch, and dinner, the cafeteria also serves specials, chicken potpie, fried catfish, and fried chicken. There isn't a fancy bar here, but you can order beer and wine with your meal. Resembling an old-fashioned diner, this cafeteria seats 345 guests at a time and has easy-to-read signs that point the way to your favorite foods. ⊠ *Yavapai Lodge, Desert View Dr., Grand Canyon Village*

☎ 928/638–2631 ⊕ www.grandcanyonlodges.com ⌕ Reservations not accepted ☰ AE, D, DC, MC, V ⊙ Closed mid-Dec.–Feb.

$$$ ✕ **El Tovar Dining Room.** No doubt about it—this is the best restaurant for
SOUTHWESTERN miles. Modeled after a European hunting lodge, this rustic 19th-century
Fodor's Choice dining room built of hand-hewn logs is worth a visit. Breakfast, lunch,
★ and dinner are served beneath the beamed ceiling. The cuisine is modern
southwestern with an exotic flair. Start with the buffalo carpaccio on
roasted poblano crostini or the mozzarella roulades with prosciutto and
basil pesto. The dinner menu includes such dishes as citrus-marmalade-
glazed duck with roasted-poblano-and-black-bean rice, grilled New
York strip steak with buttermilk-cornmeal onion rings, and a salmon
tostada topped with organic greens and tequila vinaigrette. The dining
room also offers an extensive wine list. ■TIP→ Dinner reservations can
be made up to six months in advance with room reservations and 30 days in
advance for all other visitors. *⊠ El Tovar Hotel, Desert View Dr., Grand
Canyon Village ☎ 303/297–2757 or 888/297–2757 (reservations only),
928/638–2631 Ext. 6432 ⊕ www.grandcanyonlodges.com ⌕ Reserva-
tions essential ☰ AE, D, DC, MC, V.*

¢ ✕ **Maswik Cafeteria.** You can get a burger, hot sandwich, pasta, or Mexi-
CAFE can fare at this food court. This casual eatery is ¼ mi from the rim. Lines
will be long during high season lunch and dinner, but everything moves
fairly quickly. *⊠ Maswik Lodge, Desert View Dr., Grand Canyon Vil-
lage ☎ 928/638–2631 ⊕ www.grandcanyonlodges.com ⌕ Reservations
not accepted ☰ AE, D, DC, MC, V.*

PICNIC AREAS **Buggeln.** Come here for some secluded, shady spots. *⊠ 15 mi east of
Grand Canyon Village, off Desert View Dr.*

Grandview Point. As the name implies, this spot has grand views. *⊠ 12 mi
east of Grand Canyon Village, off Desert View Dr.*

NORTH RIM

¢ ✕ **Deli in the Pines.** Dining choices are very limited on the North Rim, but
AMERICAN this is your best bet for a meal on a budget. The selection includes pizza,
salads, deli sandwiches, hot dogs, homemade breakfast pastries, and
soft-serve ice cream. Best of all, there is an outdoor seating area for din-
ing alfresco. It's open for breakfast, lunch, and dinner. *⊠ Grand Canyon
Lodge, Bright Angel Point ☎ 928/638–2611 Ext. 766 ⌕ Reservations
not accepted ☰ AE, D, DC, MC, V ⊙ Closed mid-Oct.–mid-May.*

$$$ ✕ **Grand Canyon Lodge Dining Room.** The historic lodge has a huge, high-
AMERICAN ceilinged dining room with spectacular views and very good food; you
★ might find pork medallions, roast chicken, and salmon steaks on the
dinner menu. Food here takes a flavorful turn with southwestern spices
and organic selections. It's also open for breakfast and lunch. A full-
service bar and an impressive wine list add to the relaxed atmosphere
of the only full-service, sit-down restaurant on the North Rim. *⊠ Grand
Canyon Lodge, Bright Angel Point ☎ 928/638–2611 Ext. 760 ☰ AE,
D, DC, MC, V ⊙ Closed mid-Oct.–mid-May.*

$$$$ ✕ **Grand Cookout.** Dine under the stars and enjoy live entertainment at
AMERICAN this chuck-wagon-style dining experience—the newest addition to the
⊙ North Rim's limited dining options. Fill up on western favorites including barbecue beef brisket, roasted chicken, baked beans, and cowboy
biscuits. The food is basic and tasty, but the real draw is the nightly

18

performance of western music and tall tales. Transportation from the Grand Canyon Lodge to the cookout is included in the price. Be sure to call before 4 PM for dinner reservations. Advance reservations are taken up to seven days in advance at the Grand Canyon Lodge registration desk. ⊠ *Grand Canyon Lodge* ☎ *928/638–2611* ⌔ *Reservations essential* ⊟ *AE, D, DC, MC, V* ☾ *Closed mid-Oct.–mid-May.*

PICNIC AREAS   **Cape Royal.** Due to its panoramic views, this is the most popular designated picnic area on the North Rim. ⊠ *23 mi south of the North Rim Visitor Center.*

Point Imperial. Enjoy shade and some privacy here. ⊠ *11 mi northeast of the North Rim Visitor Center.*

OUTSIDE THE PARK

TUSAYAN

$ ✕ **Café Tusayan.** This cozy café might not look like much, but it serves up STEAK some of the most filling and wholesome food in Tusayan. You won't find fancy entrées with special French sauces. What you will find is a large menu of omelets, salads, burgers, salmon, pasta, and steaks. Breakfast is served all day long and the homemade pies are worth a stop all on their own. ⊠ *Hwy. 64/U.S. 180* ☎ *928/638–2151* ⊟ *MC, V.*

$$ ✕ **Canyon Star Restaurant and Saloon.** Relax in the rustic dining room AMERICAN at the Grand Hotel for breakfast, lunch, or dinner. The dinner menu ☾ includes steak, grilled chicken, barbecue ribs, enchiladas, and salmon. Most nights there's entertainment: live music, karaoke, or American Indian dance performances—all great for families. There's even a kids' menu. In the summer, be sure to reserve a table. ⊠ *Hwy. 64/U.S. 180* ☎ *928/638–3333* ⊟ *AE, DC, MC, V.*

$$ ✕ **The Coronado Room.** When pizza and burgers just won't do, the restau-CONTINENTAL rant at the Best Western Grand Canyon Squire Inn is the best upscale choice in Tusayan. The menu has everything from escargot to elk steak. Even though the Coronado Room takes pride in its fine-dining atmosphere, dress is casual and comfortable. Reservations are a good idea, particularly in the busy season. ⊠ *Hwy. 64/U.S. 180* ☎ *928/638–2681* ⊟ *AE, D, DC, MC, V* ☾ *No lunch.*

WILLIAMS

$ ✕ **Cruisers Café 66.** Talk about nostalgia. Imagine your favorite '50s-style, AMERICAN high-school hangout—with cocktail service. Good burgers, salads, and ☾ malts are family-priced, but a choice steak is available, too, for $25. Fodor's Choice The Grand Canyon Brewery, accessed by a side entrance, adds to the ★ casual fun—just saddle up to a hand-carved log barstool and order one of five microbrews on tap. A large mural of the town's heyday along the "Mother Road" and historic cars out front make this a Route 66 favorite. Kids enjoy the relaxed atmosphere and jukebox tunes. ⊠ *233 W. Rte. 66* ☎ *928/635–2445* ⊟ *AE, D, MC, V.*

WHERE TO STAY

IN THE PARK
SOUTH RIM

$–$$ **Bright Angel Lodge.** Famed architect Mary Jane Colter designed this 1935 log-and-stone structure, which sits within a few yards of the canyon rim and blends superbly with the canyon walls. It offers a similar location to El Tovar for about half the price. Accommodations are in motel-style rooms or cabins. Lodge rooms don't have TVs, and some rooms do not have private bathrooms. Scattered among the pines are 50 cabins, which do have TVs and private baths; some have fireplaces. Expect historic charm but not luxury. The Bright Angel Dining Room serves family-style meals all day and desserts are large enough to share. The Arizona Room serves dinner only. Adding to the experience are an ice-cream parlor, gift shop, and small history museum. **Pros:** some rooms have canyon views; all rooms are steps away from the rim; Internet kiosks and transportation desk for the mule ride check-in are in the lobby. **Cons:** the popular lobby is always packed; parking here is problematic; stairs throughout the building and lack of elevators make accessibility an issue. ⊠ *Desert View Dr., Grand Canyon Village* ☎ *888/297–2757 reservations only, 928/638–2631* ⊕ *www.grandcanyonlodges.com* ⌁ *37 rooms, 6 with shared toilet and shower, 13 with shared shower; 50 cabins* ⚬ *In-room: no a/c (some), safe (some), refrigerator (some), no TV (some). In-hotel: 2 restaurants, bar* ⊟ *AE, D, DC, MC, V.*

$$$ **El Tovar Hotel.** A registered National Historic Landmark, the "architectural crown jewel of the Grand Canyon" was built in 1905 of Oregon pine logs and native stone. The hotel's proximity to all of the canyon's facilities, its European hunting-lodge atmosphere, and its renowned dining room make it the best place to stay on the South Rim. It's usually booked well in advance (up to 13 months ahead), though it's easier to get a room during winter months. Three suites (El Tovar, Fred Harvey, and Mary Jane Colter) and several rooms have canyon views (these are booked early), but you can enjoy the view anytime from the cocktail-lounge back porch. **Pros:** historic lodging just steps from the South Rim; fabulous lounge with outdoor seating and canyon views; best in-park dining on-site. **Cons:** books up quickly, no Internet access. ⊠ *Desert View Dr., Grand Canyon Village* ☎ *888/297–2757 reservations only, 928/638–2631* ⊕ *www.grandcanyonlodges.com* ⌁ *66 rooms, 12 suites* ⚬ *In-room: refrigerator. In-hotel: restaurant, room service, bar* ⊟ *AE, D, DC, MC, V.*

Fodor's Choice
★

$$$ **Kachina Lodge.** On the rim halfway between El Tovar and Bright Angel Lodge, this motel-style lodge has many rooms with partial canyon views ($10 extra). Although lacking the historical charm of the neighboring lodges, these rooms are a good bet for families and are within easy walking distance of dining facilities at El Tovar and Bright Angel Lodge. There are also several rooms for people with physical disabilities. There's no air-conditioning, but evaporative coolers keep the heat at bay. Check in at El Tovar Hotel to the east. **Pros:** partial canyon views in half the rooms; family-friendly; accessible rooms. **Cons:** no Internet access; check-in takes place at El Tovar Hotel; limited parking. ⊠ *Desert View Dr., Grand Canyon Village* ☎ *888/297–2757 reserva-*

18

tions only, 928/638–2631 ⊕ www.grandcanyonlodges.com ⤳ 49 rooms ♻ *In-room: safe, refrigerator* ☰ *AE, D, DC, MC, V.*

$ ⊞**Maswik Lodge.** The lodge, named for a Hopi kachina who is said to
♻ guard the canyon, is ¼ mi from the rim. Accommodations, nestled in the
ponderosa pine forest, range from rustic cabins to more modern rooms.
The cabins are the cheapest option but are available only spring through
fall. Some rooms have air-conditioning, and the rest have ceiling fans.
Teenagers like the lounge, where they can shoot pool, throw darts, or
watch the big-screen TV. There is also an Internet room. Kids under
16 stay free. **Pros:** larger rooms here than in historic lodgings; good for
families; Internet access; affordable dining options. **Cons:** plain rooms
lack historic charm; tucked away from the rim in the forest. ⊠ *Grand
Canyon Village* ☎ *888/297–2757 reservations only, 928/638–2631*
⊕ *www.grandcanyonlodges.com* ⤳ *250 rooms, 28 cabins* ♻ *In-room:
no a/c (some), safe (some), refrigerator (some). In-hotel: restaurant, bar,
Internet terminal* ☰ *AE, D, DC, MC, V.*

¢ ⊞**Phantom Ranch.** In a grove of cottonwood trees on the canyon floor,
Phantom Ranch is accessible only to hikers and mule trekkers. The
wood-and-stone buildings originally made up a hunting camp built
in 1922. There are 40 dormitory beds and 14 beds in cabins, all with
shared baths. Seven additional cabins are reserved for mule riders, who
buy their trips as a package. The mess-hall-style restaurant, one of the
most remote eating establishments in the United States, serves family-
style meals, with breakfast, dinner, and box lunches available. Reservations, taken up to 13 months in advance, are a must for services
and lodging. **Pros:** only inner-canyon lodging option; fabulous canyon views; remote access limits crowds. **Cons:** accessible only by foot
or mule; few amenities. ⊠ *On canyon floor, at intersection of Bright
Angel and Kaibab trails* ☎ *303/297–2757 or 888/297–2757* ⊕ *www.
grandcanyonlodges.com* ⤳ *4 dormitories and 2 cabins for hikers, 7 cabins with outside showers for mule riders* ♻ *In-room: no a/c, no phone,
no TV. In-hotel: restaurant* ☰ *AE, D, DC, MC, V.*

$$$ ⊞**Thunderbird Lodge.** This motel with comfortable, no-nonsense rooms
is next to Bright Angel Lodge in Grand Canyon Village. For $10 more,
you can get a room with a partial view of the canyon. Rooms have either
two queen beds or one king. Check in at Bright Angel Lodge, the next
hotel to the west. Some rooms do not have air-conditioning, but instead
have evaporative coolers. **Pros:** partial canyon views in some rooms;
family-friendly; accessible rooms. **Cons:** no Internet access; check-in
takes place at Bright Angel Lodge; limited parking. ⊠ *Desert View Dr.,
Grand Canyon Village* ☎ *888/297–2757 reservations only, 928/638–
2631* ⊕ *www.grandcanyonlodges.com* ⤳ *55 rooms* ♻ *In-room: safe,
refrigerator* ☰ *AE, D, DC, MC, V.*

$$–$$$ ⊞**Yavapai Lodge.** The largest motel-style lodge in the park is tucked in a
pinyon and juniper forest at the eastern end of Grand Canyon Village,
near the RV park. The basic rooms are near a park general store, ½ mi
from the visitor center, and ¼ mi from the rim. The cafeteria, open for
breakfast, lunch, and dinner, serves standard park-service food. An Inter-
net room is available to guests. **Pros:** transportation-activities desk on-
site in the lobby; near Market Plaza in Grand Canyon Village; forested

grounds. **Cons:** no Internet access in rooms; farthest in-park lodging from the rim. ⊠ *Grand Canyon Village* ☎ *888/297–2757 reservations only, 928/638–2961* ⊕ *www.grand-canyonlodges.com* ⤴ *358 rooms* ⌂ *In-room: no a/c (some), refrigerator (some). In-hotel: restaurant, Internet terminal* ⊟ *AE, D, DC, MC, V* ⊘ *Closed Jan. and Feb.*

> DUFFEL SERVICE:
> LIGHTEN YOUR LOAD
>
> Hikers staying at either Phantom Ranch or Bright Angel camp-ground can also take advantage of the ranch's duffel service: bags or packs weighing 30 pounds or less can be transported to the ranch by mule for a fee of $62.43 each way. Reservations are a must.

CAMPING
¢ ⚠ **Bright Angel Campground.** This campground is near Phantom Ranch on the South and North Kaibab trails, at the bottom of the canyon. There are toilet facilities and running water, but no showers. If you plan to eat at the Phantom Ranch Canteen, book your meals ahead of time. Reservations for all services, taken up to four months in advance, are a must. A backcountry permit, which serves as your reservation, is required to stay here. ⊠ *Intersection of South and North Kaibab trails, Grand Canyon* ⚏ *Backcountry Office, Box 129, Grand Canyon 86023* ☎ *928/638–7875* ⚠ *30 tent sites, 2 group sites* ⌂ *Flush toilets, drinking water, picnic tables* ⚒ *Backcountry permit required.*

$ ⚠ **Desert View Campground.** Popular for spectacular views of the canyon from the nearby Watchtower, this campground fills up fast in summer. Fifty RV (without hookups) and tent sites are available on a first-come, first-served basis (reservations are not accepted). ⊠ *Desert View Dr., 23 mi east of Grand Canyon Village off Hwy. 64* ⚏ *Backcountry Office, Box 129, Grand Canyon 86023* ☎ *928/638–7875* ⌂ *Flush toilets, drinking water, grills, picnic tables* ⚠ *50 tent/RV sites* ⊘ *Closed mid-Oct.–mid-May.*

$$ ⚠ **Mather Campground.** Mather has RV and tent sites but no hookups.
★ No reservations are accepted from December to March, but the rest of the year, especially during the busy spring and summer seasons, they are a good idea, and can be made up to five months in advance. Ask at the campground entrance for same-day availability. ⊠ *Off Village Loop Dr., Grand Canyon Village* ☎ *877/444–6777* ⊕ *www.recreation.gov* ⚠ *308 tent/RV sites* ⌂ *Flush toilets, dump station, drinking water, guest laundry, showers, fire grates, picnic tables, public telephone.*

$$ ⚠ **Trailer Village.** This campground in Grand Canyon Village has RV-only sites with full hookups and bathroom facilities ½ mi away. The $28 fee is good for two people, with an extra $2 fee for each additional person over age 16. The facility is very busy during spring and summer, so make reservations ahead of time (not accepted December through March). The dump station is closed in winter. ⊠ *Off Village Loop Dr., Grand Canyon Village* ☎ *303/297–2757 or 888/297–2757 (reservations only)* ⊕ *www. grandcanyonlodges.com* ⚠ *79 RV sites* ⌂ *Flush toilets, full hookups, dump station, drinking water, guest laundry, showers, fire grates.*

NORTH RIM

$$$ ⌂ **Grand Canyon Lodge.** This historic property, constructed mainly in the
Fodor'sChoice 1920s and '30s, is the premier lodging facility in the North Rim area.
★ The main building has locally quarried limestone walls and timbered ceilings. Lodging options include small, rustic cabins; larger cabins

18

(some with a canyon view and some with two bedrooms); and slightly more modern motel rooms. The two-bedroom Pioneer cabins got a face-lift in 2008 and now sleep up to six people. The hand-carved Aspen lodge furniture adds to the rustic atmosphere. However, the best of the bunch are the Rim View Western, especially log cabins 301 and 306, which have private porches perched on the lip of the canyon. Other cabins with fabulous canyon views include 305, 309, and 310. Because of their premier location, these cabins are snapped up fast and need to be reserved a year in advance. You can access the Internet at the general store. **Pros:** steps away from gorgeous North Rim views; close to several easy hiking trails. **Cons:** as the only in-park North Rim lodging option, it fills up fast; few amenities. ⊠ *Grand Canyon National Park, Hwy. 67* ☎ *877/386–4383, 928/638–2611 May–Oct., 928/645–6865 Nov.–Apr.* ⊕ *www.grandcanyonforever.com* 🛏 *40 rooms, 178 cabins* ⚐ *In-room: no a/c, refrigerator (some), no TV. In-hotel: 3 restaurants, bar, bicycles, laundry facilities (at the North Rim Campground)* ▤ *AE, D, MC, V* ☉ *Closed mid-Oct.–mid-May.*

CAMPING
$$
🏕 **North Rim Campground.** The only designated campground at the North Rim of Grand Canyon National Park sits 3 mi north of the rim, and has 83 RV and tent sites (no hookups). You can reserve a site up to five months in advance and reservations are essential to secure a spot. Leashed pets are allowed at the campground. ⊠ *Hwy. 67, North Rim* ☎ *877/444–6777* ⊕ *www.recreation.gov* 🏕 *83 tent/RV sites* ⚐ *Flush toilets, dump station, drinking water, guest laundry, showers, fire grates, picnic tables, general store* ☉ *Closed mid-Oct.–mid-May.*

OUTSIDE THE PARK
FREDONIA AND MARBLE CANYON

$
🏨 **Jacob Lake Inn.** The bustling lodge at Jacob Lake Inn is a popular stop for those heading to the North Rim. This 5-acre complex in Kaibab National Forest has basic cabins and standard motel rooms overlooking the highways. Avoid the older facilities by asking for one of the new rooms. They aren't as nostalgic and private as the cabins, but they do offer fresher surroundings. **Pros:** grocery store, coffee shop, and restaurant on the premises; quiet rooms. **Cons:** small bathroom in cabins; worn furnishings. ⊠ *Hwy. 67/Hwy. 89A, Fredonia* ☎ *928/643–7232* ⊕ *www.jacoblake.com* 🛏 *32 rooms, 26 cabins* ⚐ *In-room: no a/c (some), no phone (some), no TV (some), Internet (some), Wi-Fi (some). In-hotel: restaurant, some pets allowed* ▤ *AE, D, MC, V.*

$
★
🏨 **Marble Canyon Lodge.** Play the 1920s piano or sit on the porch swing of the native-rock lodge and look out on Vermilion Cliffs and the desert. Zane Grey and Gary Cooper are among well-known past guests. Types of accommodations available are rooms in the original building, standard motel rooms in the newer building, and two-bedroom apartments. **Pros:** convenience store and trading post; great fishing on the Colorado River. **Cons:** no-frills rustic lodging; more than 70 mi to the Grand Canyon North Rim. ⊠ *¼ mi west of Navajo Bridge on Hwy. 89A, Marble Canyon 86036* ☎ *928/355–2225 or 800/726–1789* 🛏 *46 rooms, 8 apartments* ⚐ *In-room: no a/c (some), no phone, Wi-Fi. In-hotel: restaurant, bar, laundry facilities, some pets allowed* ▤ *AE, D, MC, V.*

TUSAYAN

$$$ [] **Best Western Grand Canyon Squire Inn.** About 1 mi south of the park's
☾ south entrance, this motel lacks the historic charm of the older lodges
★ at the canyon rim, but has more amenities, including a small cowboy
museum in the lobby and an upscale gift shop. Children enjoy the
bowling alley, arcade, and outdoor swimming pool. Updated rooms
with flat-screen TVs are spacious and furnished in southwestern style.
Those in the rear have a view of the woods. Kiosks in the lobby provide
Internet access to registered guests. **Pros:** a cool pool in the summer and
a steamy sauna for cold winter nights; children's activities at the Fam-
ily Fun Center; high-speed Internet. **Cons:** hall noise can be an issue
with all of the in-hotel activities. ✉ *100 Hwy. 64* ☎ *928/638–2681 or
800/622–6966* ⊕ *www.grandcanyonsquire.com* ⇴ *250 rooms, 4 suites*
⚬ *In-room: refrigerator (some), Wi-Fi. In-hotel: restaurant, bar, pool,
gym, laundry facilities, Wi-Fi* ▭ *AE, D, DC, MC, V.*

$$$ [] **The Grand Hotel.** At the south end of Tusayan, this popular hotel has
★ bright, clean rooms decorated in Southwestern colors. The lobby has
a stone-and-timber design, cozy seating areas, and Wi-Fi access. Live
American Indian dancing and cowboy singers lead the entertainment
in the Canyon Star Wild West Saloon during evenings in the peak season. At the bar, you can sit on a saddle that was once used for canyon
mule trips. **Pros:** coffee stand for a quick morning pick-me-up; gift
shop stocked with outdoor gear and regional books. **Cons:** no in-room
Internet access; restaurant and lounge hours are not reliable; facilities
often closed during off-season. ✉ *Hwy. 64/U.S. 180* ☎ *928/638–3333
or 888/634–7263* ⊕ *www.grandcanyongrandhotel.com* ⇴ *120 rooms,
12 suites* ⚬ *In-hotel: restaurant, bar, pool, gym, laundry facilities, Wi-Fi*
▭ *AE, D, DC, MC, V.*

WILLIAMS

$$$ [] **Grand Canyon Railway Hotel and Resort.** This hotel was designed to
★ resemble the train depot's original Fray Marcos lodge. Neoclassical
Greek columns flank the grand entrance, which leads to a lobby with
maple-wood balustrades, an enormous flagstone fireplace, and oil paint-
ings of the Grand Canyon by local artist Kenneth McKenna. Original
bronzes by Frederic Remington also adorn the lobby. The pleasant
southwestern-style accommodations have large bathrooms. Adjacent
to the lobby is Spenser's, a pub with an ornate 19th-century hand-
carved bar. Riding the train to the canyon in railcars that date from
the 1920s can be a relaxing alternative to the long drive. **Pros:** Grand
Canyon Railway package options; pet resort; game room and outdoor
playground for family fun. **Cons:** noisy location; high traffic volume;
limited food options. ✉ *235 N. Grand Canyon Blvd.* ☎ *928/635–4010
or 800/843–8724* ⊕ *www.thetrain.com* ⇴ *288 rooms, 10 suites* ⚬ *In-
room: refrigerator (some), Internet. In-hotel: restaurant, bar, pool, gym,
laundry facilities, Wi-Fi* ▭ *AE, D, MC, V.*

$$$ [] **Sheridan House Inn.** Nestled among 2 acres of pine trees near Route
★ 66, this B&B has decks looking to the tall ponderosa pines and a flag-
stone patio with a hot tub. Average-size bedrooms all have king beds
and marble bathrooms. Hearty breakfasts—scrambled eggs, fruit plates,
bacon, sausage, potatoes, eggs Benedict, and buttermilk pancakes—will

18

ready you for the hour-long drive to the canyon. K.C. and Mary Seidner are gracious hosts who will gladly help guests plan itineraries. **Pros:** quiet location; game room has puzzles and board games; the entertainment room has a pool table and piano. **Cons:** a long drive to the canyon and a short drive from downtown Williams; parking is at the bottom of the hill. ⊠ *460 E. Sheridan Ave.* ☎ *928/635–9441 or 888/635–9345* ⊕ *www.grandcanyonbbinn.com* ⇌ *6 rooms, 2 suites* ⚹ *In-room: no a/c, DVD (some), Wi-Fi* ⊟ *AE, D, MC, V* ⍩ *BP.*

CAMPING ⚠ **Grand Canyon Camper Village and RV Park.** More a city than a village,
$$–$$$ this popular RV park and campground has tent sites and full-hookup RV sites. Fourteen sites have 50 amp hookups; the rest are 20 and 30 amp. Reservations are a good idea during the busy spring and summer seasons. ⊠ *Off Hwy. 64/U.S. 180, Tusayan* ☎ *928/638–2887* ⚑ *50 tent sites, 200 RV sites* ⚹ *Flush toilets, full hookups, dump station, drinking water, showers, picnic tables, general store, play area.*

Grand Teton National Park

WORD OF MOUTH

"The scenery in Grand Teton is breathtaking! I literally gasped as we drove up Hwy. 89 in Jackson, came around the curve and we got our first glimpse of the Teton Range!"

—luv2globetrot

WELCOME TO GRAND TETON

TOP REASONS TO GO

★ **Heavenward hikes:** Trek where grizzled frontiersmen roamed. Jackson Hole got its name from mountain man David Jackson; now there are dozens of trails for you to explore.

★ **Wildlife big and small:** Keep an eye out for little fellows like short-tailed weasels and beaver, as well as bison, elk, wolves, and both black and grizzly bears.

★ **Waves to make:** Float the Snake River or take a canoe onto Jackson Lake or Jenny Lake.

★ **Homesteader history:** Visit the 1890s barns and ranch buildings of Mormon Row or Menor's Ferry.

★ **Rare bird-watching:** Raise the binoculars—or just your head—to see more than 300 species of birds, including trumpeter swans, bald eagles, and osprey.

★ **Trout trophies:** Grab your rod and slither over to the Snake River, where cutthroat trout are an angler's delight.

1 Antelope Flats. Buffalo and antelope frequently roam across this sagebrush-covered area of the park northeast of Moose, and it is also where homesteader barns along Mormon Row dot the landscape. It's a popular place for wildflower viewing and bicycle rides.

2 Jenny Lake. In this developed area, you can go to the visitor center, purchase supplies, or talk to a ranger—plus ride a boat across the lake, hike around it, have a picnic, or camp nearby.

3 Moose. Just north of Craig Thomas Discovery and Visitor Center, this historical area is home to the Chapel of the Transfiguration, and was once the stomping grounds of early settlers at Menor's Ferry.

4 Oxbow Bend. At this famously scenic spot the Snake River, its inhabitants, and the Tetons all converge, especially in early morning or near dusk. You're likely to see moose feeding in willows, elk grazing in aspen stands, and birds such as bald eagles, osprey, sandhill cranes, ducks, and American white pelicans.

GETTING ORIENTED

Grand Teton's immense peaks jut dramatically up from the Jackson Hole valley floor. Without any foothills to soften the blow, the sight of these glacier-scoured crags is truly striking. Several alpine lakes reflect the mountains, and the winding Snake River cuts south along the eastern side of the park. The northern portion of the park is outstanding wildlife-watching territory—you can see everything from rare birds to lumbering moose to the big predators (mountain lions and black and grizzly bears). Two main roads run through the 310,000-acre park; Highway 26/89/191 curves along the eastern or outer side and Teton Park Road (also called the inner park road, which is closed during winter) runs closer to the mountain range.

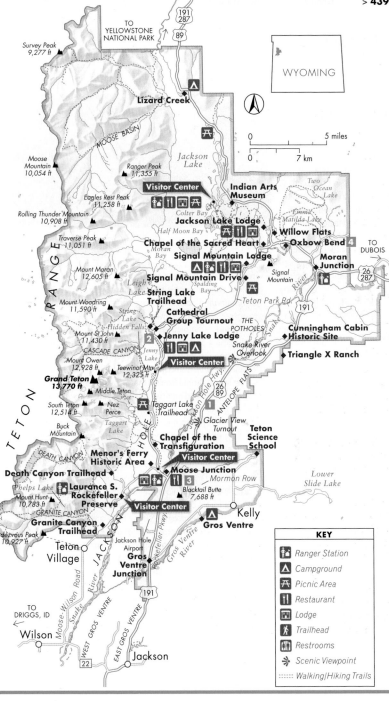

TO
YELLOWSTONE
NATIONAL PARK

191
287
89

Survey Peak
9,277 ft

WYOMING

Lizard Creek

MOOSE BASIN

Moose
Mountain
10,054 ft

Jackson
Lake

Ranger Peak
11,355 ft

Two
Ocean
Lake

0   5 miles
0   7 km

Eagles Rest Peak
11,258 ft

Visitor Center

**Indian Arts
Museum**

Emma
Matilda Lake

Rolling Thunder Mountain
10,908 ft

Colter Bay

Jackson Lake Lodge

TO
DUBOIS

Traverse Peak
11,051 ft

Half Moon Bay

Willow Flats

Chapel of the Sacred Heart

Oxbow Bend 4

R
A
N
G
E

Moran
Bay

Signal Mountain Lodge

**Moran
Junction**

26
287

Mount Moran
12,605 ft

Signal Mountain Drive

Signal
Mountain

Leigh
Lake

Spalding
Bay

**String Lake
Trailhead**

Teton Park Rd

191

Mount Woodring
11,590 ft

**Cathedral
Group Tournout**

THE
POTHOLES

**Cunningham Cabin
Historic Site**

String
Lake

Hidden Falls

2

Jenny Lake Lodge

Snake River
Overlook

Triangle X Ranch

Mount St John
11,430 ft

CASCADE CANYON

Jenny
Lake

Visitor Center

Mount Owen
12,928 ft

Teewinot Mtn
12,325 ft

T
E
T
O
N

**Grand Teton
13,770 ft**

Middle Teton

26
89

1

ANTELOPE FLATS

South Teton
12,514 ft

Nez
Perce

**Taggart Lake
Trailhead**

**Glacier View
Turnout**

19

Buck
Mountain

Taggart
Lake

**Teton
Science
School**

J
A
C
K
S
O
N

DEATH CANYON

**Chapel of the
Transfiguration**

Lower
Slide Lake

**Menor's Ferry
Historic Area**

Visitor Center

Death Canyon Trailhead

Phelps Lake

Moose Junction

3

Mount Hunt
10,783 ft

**Laurance S.
Rockefeller
Preserve**

Mormon Row

Blacktail Butte
7,688 ft

GRANITE CANYON

Visitor Center

**Granite Canyon
Trailhead**

Rendezvous Peak
10,927 ft

Kelly

Gros Ventre

**Teton
Village**

Jackson Hole
Airport

H
O
L
E

**Gros
Ventre
Junction**

Gros Ventre River

191

TO
DRIGGS, ID

Moose–Wilson Road

Snake River

Rockefeller Pkwy

WEST GROS VENTRE

Wilson

22

EAST GROS VENTRE

Jackson

KEY	
🚹🚺	*Ranger Station*
⛺	*Campground*
⛾	*Picnic Area*
🍴	*Restaurant*
▦	*Lodge*
🚶	*Trailhead*
🚻	*Restrooms*
✳	*Scenic Viewpoint*
⋯⋯	*Walking/Hiking Trails*

GRAND TETON PLANNER

When to Go

In July and August all the roads, trails, and visitor centers are open, and the Snake River's float season is in full swing. **To have access to most services without the crowds, plan a trip between May and June or in September.** Lower rates and smaller crowds can be found in spring and fall, but some services and roads are limited. Grand Teton Lodge Company, the park's major outfitter, winds down its activities in September, and most of Teton Park Road closes from late October through early May.

Towns outside the park rev up in winter. Teton Village and Jackson both buzz with the energy of Snow King Resort and Jackson Hole Mountain Resort, the former conveniently in town, the latter an international skiing hot spot deep in the valley. (Prices rise for the peak winter season.) Because of the many skiers, U.S. Highway 26/191/89 stays open all winter.

AVG. HIGH/LOW TEMPS.

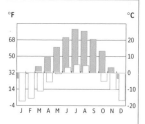

Flora and Fauna

Grand Teton's short growing season and arid climate create a complex ecosystem and hardy plant species. The dominant elements are big sagebrush, which gives a gray-green cast to the valley, lodgepole pine trees, quaking aspen, and ground-covering wildflowers such as bluish-purple alpine forget-me-nots. In spring and early summer you will see the vibrant yellow arrowleaf balsamroot and the delicate blue camas, a plant prized by American Indians for its nutritional value. The growing season in Jackson Hole is short, but gives rise to spectacular though short-lived displays of wildflowers. The best time to see these natural displays are mid-June to early July, although the changing of the aspen and cottonwood leaves in early fall can be equally spectacular.

On almost any trip to Grand Teton, you will see bison, antelope, and moose. More rarely you will see a black or grizzly bear or a mountain lion or wolf. Watch for elk along the forest edge, and, in the summer, on Teton Park Road. Oxbow Bend and Willow Flats are good places to look for moose, beaver, and otter any time of year. Pronghorn antelope and bison appear in summer along Jackson Hole Highway and Antelope Flats Road. If animals are crossing the road, they have the right-of-way.

The park's smaller animals—yellow-bellied marmots and golden-mantled ground squirrel, as well as a variety of birds and waterfowl—are commonly seen along park trails and waterways. Seek out the water sources—the Snake River, the alpine lakes, and marshy areas—to see birds such as bald eagles, ospreys, ducks, and trumpeter swans. Your best chance to see wildlife is at dawn or dusk.

Getting Here and Around

The best way to see Grand Teton National Park is by car. Unlike Yellowstone's Grand Loop, Grand Teton's road system doesn't allow for easy tour-bus access to the major sights. Only a car will get you close to Jenny Lake, into the remote east Jackson Hole hills, and to the top of Signal Mountain. You can stop at many points along the roads within the park for a hike or a view. Be extremely cautious in winter when whiteouts and ice are not uncommon. There are adequate road signs throughout the park, but a good road map is handy to have in the vehicle.

Jackson Hole Highway (U.S. 89/191) runs the entire length of the park, from Jackson to Yellowstone National Park's south entrance. (This highway is also called Route 26 south of Moran Junction and U.S. 287 north of Moran Junction.) This road is open all year from Jackson to Moran Junction and north to Flagg Ranch, 2 mi south of Yellowstone. Depending on traffic, the southern (Moose) entrance to Grand Teton is about 15 minutes from downtown Jackson via Jackson Hole Highway. Coming from the opposite direction on the same road, the northern boundary of the park is about 15 minutes south of Yellowstone National Park. Also open year-round, U.S. 26/287 runs east from Dubois over Togwotee Pass to the Moran entrance station, a drive of about one hour.

Two back-road entrances to Grand Teton require high-clearance vehicles. Both are closed by snow from November through mid-May and are heavily rutted through June. Moose-Wilson Road (Route 390) starts at Route 22 in Wilson (west of Jackson) and travels 12 mi north past Teton Village, then turns into an unpaved road for 3 mi leading to the Moose entrance. It's closed to large trucks, trailers, and RVs. Even rougher is 60-mi Grassy Lake Road, which heads east from Route 32 in Ashton, Idaho, through Targhee National Forest. It connects with U.S. 89/287 in the John D. Rockefeller Jr. Memorial Parkway, sandwiched between Grand Teton and Yellowstone.

Festivals and Events

YEAR-ROUND Grand Teton **Music Festival** presents monthly concerts featuring solo performers as well as duos and groups at Walk Festival Hall in Teton Village. Tickets range from $25–$50, but there are many free events throughout the year. ☎ *307/733–1128* ⊕ *www.gtmf.org.*

MARCH The **Pole-Pedal-Paddle** is a mini-marathon, ski-cycle-canoe relay race held every year in March or April, starting at Jackson Hole Ski Resort and finishing down the Snake River. ☎ *307/733–6433* ⊕ *www.polepedalpaddle.com.*

MAY Jackson's **Old West Days** includes a rodeo, American Indian dancers, a western swing-dance contest, Mountain Man Rendezvous, and cowboy poetry readings. ☎ *307/733–3316.*

MAY–SEPTEMBER Gunslingers stage **The Shootout** in the summer at 6:15 PM daily (except Sunday) on the southeast corner of the Jackson Town Square. Don't worry, the bullets aren't real. ☎ *307/733–3316.*

19

Updated by
Brian Kevin

Your jaw will probably drop the first time you see the Teton Range jabbing up from the Jackson Hole valley floor. With no foothills to get in the way, you'll have a close-up, unimpeded view of magnificent, jagged, snowcapped peaks. This massif is long on natural beauty. Before your eyes, mountain glaciers creep imperceptibly down 12,605-foot Mt. Moran. Large and small lakes gleam along the range's base. Many of the West's iconic animals (elk, bears, bald eagles) call this park home.

PARK ESSENTIALS

ACCESSIBILITY
The frontcountry portions of Grand Teton are largely accessible to people using wheelchairs. There's designated parking at most sites, and some interpretive trails are easily accessible. There are accessible restrooms at visitor centers. For the *Accessibility* brochure, a guide to accessible trails and facilities, stop by any visitor center.

ADMISSION FEES AND PERMITS
Park entrance fees are $25 per car, truck, or RV; $20 per motorcycle; and $12 per person on foot or bicycle, good for seven days in both Grand Teton and Yellowstone parks. Annual park passes are $40. A winter day-use fee is $5.

Backcountry permits, which must be retrieved in person at the Craig Thomas Visitor Center, Colter Bay Visitor Center, or Jenny Lake Ranger Station, are $25 to reserve in advance or free to pick up one day before your hike. Permits are required for all overnight stays outside designated campgrounds. Seven-day boat permits, available year-round at Craig Thomas Discovery and Visitor Center and in summer at Colter Bay and Signal Mountain ranger stations, cost $20 for motorized craft and $10 for nonmotorized craft and are good for seven days. Annual permits are $40 for motorized craft and $20 for nonmotorized craft.

ADMISSION HOURS

The park is open 24/7 year-round. It's in the mountain time zone.

ATMS/BANKS

In the park, ATMs are at Colter Bay Grocery and General Store, Dornan's, Jackson Lake Lodge, and Signal Mountain Lodge. You can also find ATMs at Flagg Ranch Resort, which is north of the park before the southern entrance to Yellowstone. The nearest full-service banks are in Jackson and Dubois.

CELL-PHONE RECEPTION

Cell phones work in most developed areas and occasionally on trails. Public phones are at Moose, Dornan's, south Jenny Lake, Signal Mountain Lodge, Moran Entrance Station, Jackson Lake Lodge, Colter Bay Village, Leeks Marina, and Flagg Ranch.

RELIGIOUS SERVICES

Late spring through early autumn, Christian services are held on weekends at the park's two chapels (⇨ *Scenic Stops under What to See*).

PARK CONTACT INFORMATION

Grand Teton National Park ✍ *P.O. Box 170, Moose, WY 83012* ☎ *307/739–3300* ⊕ *www.nps.gov/grte.*

SCENIC DRIVES

🕑 **Antelope Flats Road.** Off U.S. 191/89/26, about 2 mi north of Moose Junction, this narrow road wanders eastward over rolling plains, rising buttes, and sagebrush flats. The road intersects Mormon Row, where you can turn off to see abandoned homesteaders' barns and houses from the turn of the 20th century. Less than 2 mi past Mormon Row is a four-way intersection where you can turn right to loop around past the town of Kelly and Gros Ventre campground and rejoin U.S. 191/26/89 at Gros Ventre Junction. Keep an eye out for pronghorn, bison, moose, and mountain bikers.

Fodor'sChoice ★ **Jenny Lake Scenic Drive.** This 4-mi, one-way loop provides the park's best roadside close-ups of the Tetons as it winds south through groves of lodgepole-pine and open meadows. Roughly 1.5 mi off Teton Park Road, the Cathedral Group Turnout faces 13,770-foot Grand Teton (the range's highest peak), flanked by 12,928-foot Mt. Owen and 12,325-foot Mt. Teewinot. ✉ *Jenny Lake.*

🕑 Fodor'sChoice ★ **Signal Mountain Road.** This exciting drive climbs Signal Mountain's 1,040-foot prominence along a 4-mi stretch of switchbacks. As you travel through forest you can catch glimpses of Jackson Lake and Mt. Moran. At the top of the winding road you can park and follow the well-marked dirt path to be treated to one of the best panoramic views in the park. From 7,720 feet above sea level your gaze can sweep over all of Jackson Hole and the 40-mi Teton Range. The views are particularly dramatic at sunset. The road is not appropriate for long trailers and is closed in winter. ✉ *Off Teton Park Rd., south of Jackson Lake Junction and near Chapel of the Sacred Heart.*

19

GRAND TETON IN ONE DAY

Begin the day by packing a picnic lunch or picking one up at a Jackson eatery. Arrive at **Craig Thomas Discovery and Visitor Center** in time for a 9 AM, two-hour, guided Snake River float trip (make reservations in advance with one of the dozen or so outfitters that offer the trip). When you're back on dry ground, drive north on Teton Park Road, stopping at scenic turnouts—don't miss Teton Glacier—until you reach Jenny Lake Road, which is one-way headed south.

After a brief stop at **Cathedral Group Turnout**, park at the Jenny Lake ranger station and take the 20-minute boat ride to **Cascade Canyon** trailhead for a short hike. Return to your car by mid-afternoon, drive back to Teton Park Road, and head north to Signal Mountain Road

to catch a top-of-the-park view of the Tetons. In late afternoon descend the mountain and continue north on Teton Park Road.

At Jackson Lake Junction, you can go east to **Oxbow Bend** or north to **Willow Flats**, both excellent spots for wildlife viewing before you head to **Jackson Lake Lodge** for dinner and an evening watching the sun set over the Tetons. Or if you'd like to get back on the water, drive to **Colter Bay Marina**, where you can board a 1½-hour sunset cruise across Jackson Lake to Waterfalls Canyon. You can reverse this route if you're heading south from Yellowstone: start the day with a 7:30 AM breakfast cruise from Colter Bay and end it with a sunset float down the Snake River.

WHAT TO SEE

HISTORIC AND CULTURAL SITES

☙ **Indian Arts Museum.** This collection's standout exhibits include Plains Indian weapons and clothing. You will see Crow blanket strips with elegant beadwork, sashes from both the Shawnee and Hopi tribes, as well as weapons, games, toys, flutes, drums, and a large collection of moccasins from many tribes. From June through early September, watch crafts demonstrations, take guided museum tours, and listen to a 45-minute program on American Indian culture. ⌧ *Colter Bay Visitor Center, 2 mi off U.S. 89/191/287, 5 mi north of Jackson Lake Junction* ☏ *307/739–3594* ⌸ *Free* ☯ *June–early Sept., daily 8–7; early Sept.–mid-Oct., daily 8–5.*

★ **Menor's Ferry Historic Area.** Down a path from the Chapel of the Transfiguration, the ferry on display here is not the original, but it's an accurate re-creation of the double-pontoon craft built by Bill Menor in 1894. It demonstrates how people crossed the Snake River before bridges were built. In the cluster of turn-of-the-20th-century buildings there are historical displays, including a collection of photos taken in the area; one building has been turned into a small general store. Pick up a pamphlet for a self-guided tour, and check out the nearby general supplies store, where candy and pop are sold in the summer. The ferry typically runs after spring runoff, between June and August, and only when a park ranger is available to operate it. ⊠ *½ mi off Teton Park Rd., 1 mi north of Moose Junction* ⊙ *Daily dawn–dusk.*

Mormon Row Historic Area. Settled by homesteaders between 1896 and 1907, this area received its name because many of them were members of the Church of Jesus Christ of Latter-day Saints, otherwise known as the Mormons. The remaining barns, homes, and outbuildings are representative of early homesteading in the West. You can wander among the buildings, hike the row, and take photographs. ⊠ *Just off Antelope Flats Rd., 2 mi north of Moose Junction* ⊙ *Daily.*

SCENIC STOPS

Chapel of the Sacred Heart. This small log chapel sits in the pine forest with a view of Jackson Lake. It's open only for services, but you can enjoy the view anytime. ⊠ *½ mi north of Signal Mountain Lodge, off Teton Park Rd.* ☎ *307/733–2516* ⊙ *Services June–Sept., Sat. at 5:30* PM *and Sun. at 5* PM.

Fodor's Choice ★ **Chapel of the Transfiguration.** This tiny chapel built in 1925 on land donated by Maud Noble is still a functioning Episcopal church. Couples come here to exchange vows with the Tetons as a backdrop, and tourists come to take photos of the small church with its awe-inspiring view. ⊠ *½ mi off Teton Park Rd., 1.1 mi north of Moose Junction, 2 mi north of Moose* ⊹ *Turn off Teton Park Rd. onto Chapel of the Transfiguration Rd.* ☎ *307/733–2603* ⊙ *Late May–late Sept., Sun., Eucharist at 8* AM, *service at 10* AM.

Fodor's Choice ★ **Jackson Lake.** The biggest of Grand Teton's glacier-carved lakes, this body of water in the northern reaches of the park was enlarged by construction of the Jackson Lake Dam in 1906. You can fish, sail, and windsurf here. Three marinas (Colter Bay, Leeks, and Signal Mountain) provide access for boaters, and several picnic areas, campgrounds, and lodges overlook the lake. ⊠ *U.S. 89/191/287 from Lizard Creek to Jackson Lake Junction, and Teton Park Rd. from Jackson Lake Junction to Signal Mountain Lodge, Oxbow Bend.*

★ **Jenny Lake.** Named for the wife of mountain man Beaver Dick Leigh, this alpine lake south of Jackson Lake draws paddle-sports enthusiasts to its pristine waters and hikers to its tree-shaded trails. ⊠ *Off Teton Park Rd. midway between Moose and Jackson Lake.*

Fodor's Choice ★ **Oxbow Bend.** This peaceful and much-admired spot overlooks a quiet backwater left by the Snake River when it cut a new southern channel. White pelicans stop here on their spring migration (many stay on through summer), sandhill cranes and trumpeter swans visit frequently, and great blue herons nest amid the cottonwoods along the river. Use binoculars to search for bald eagles, ospreys, moose, beaver, and otter. The Oxbow is known for the reflection of Mt. Moran that marks its calm waters in early morning. ⊠ *U.S. 89/191/287, 2.5 mi east of Jackson Lake Junction.*

★ **Willow Flats.** You will almost always see moose grazing in the marshy area here, in parts because of its good growth of willow trees, where moose both eat and hide. This is also a good place to see birds and waterfowl. ⊠ *U.S. 89/191/287, 1 mi north of Jackson Lake Junction, Oxbow Bend.*

19

VISITOR CENTERS

If you plan to do any hiking or exploring on your own, it is important to stop at a visitor center to get up-to-date information about weather conditions. Rangers also will know if any trails are temporarily closed due to wildlife activity. Before beginning any backcountry explorations, you must obtain permits, which you can get at visitor centers.

Colter Bay Visitor Center. The auditorium here hosts several free daily programs about American Indian culture and natural history. Also, at 11 and 3 daily, a 30-minute Teton Highlights ranger lecture provides tips on park activities. ⊠ *Colter Bay, ½ mi west of Colter Bay Junction on Hwy. 89/191/287, Oxbow Bend* ☎ *307/739–3594* ☉ *June–early Sept., daily 8–7; early Sept.–mid-Oct., daily 8–5.*

Craig Thomas Discovery and Visitor Center. Completed in August 2007, this center has interactive and interpretive exhibits dedicated to themes of preservation, mountaineering, and local wildlife. There's also a 3-D map of the park and streaming video along a footpath showing the area's intricate natural features. ⊠ *½ mi west of Moose Junction, Moose* ☎ *307/739–3399* ☉ *Early June–early Sept., daily 8–7; early Sept.–early June, daily 8–5.*

Jenny Lake Visitor Center. Geology exhibits, including a relief model of the Teton Range, are on display here. ⊠ *S. Jenny Lake Junction, 8 mi north of Moose Junction on Teton Park Rd., Jenny Lake* ☎ *307/739–3392* ☉ *June–early Sept., daily 8–7; early Sept.–late Sept., daily 8–5.*

★ **Laurance S. Rockefeller Preserve Interpretive Center.** The park's newest and eco-friendliest visitor center opened its doors 2008, a modern, wood-and-steel structure that feels more like an art gallery than an interpretive facility. The elegant, LEED-certified building is more than just eye candy—you can experience the sounds of the park in a cylindrical audio chamber, and laminated maps in the reading room are great for trip planning. ⊠ *East side of Moose-Wilson Rd., about 4 mi south of Moose and 3 mi north of Granite Canyon Entrance Station* ☎ *307/739–3654* ☉ *Late May–early Sept., daily 8–6; early-Sept.–late Sept., daily 8–5.*

SPORTS AND THE OUTDOORS

BICYCLING

Teton Park Road and Jackson Hole Highway are generally flat with long, gradual inclines, and have well-marked shoulders. Cyclists should be very careful when sharing the road with vehicles, especially RVs and trailers. The first phase of a paved bike path along Teton Park Road was completed in 2008 and runs between Moose and the visitor center at Jenny Lake. A bike lane allows for northbound bike traffic along the one-way Jenny Lake Loop Road, a one-hour ride. The River Road, 4 mi north of Moose, is an easy four-hour mountain-bike ride along a ridge above the Snake River on a gravel road. Bicycles are not allowed on trails or in the backcountry.

In Jackson, ride the Snow King trails system that begins at Snow King resort. The Cache Creek to Game Creek loop is a 25-mi ride on dirt roads and trails. The two trails systems also link together. In addition,

GOOD READS

■ *Teewinot: Climbing and Contemplating the Teton Range,* by Jack Turner. A trained philosopher turned climbing guide, Turner reflects on mountain ecology and mountain culture in essays both poetic and precise.

■ *A Naturalist's Guide to Grand Teton and Yellowstone National Parks,* by Frank Craighead. An accessible homage to greater Yellowstone, Craighead's text reveals natural patterns

and concordances in the Tetons, week to week and season to season.

■ *Windows into the Earth: The Geologic Story of Yellowstone and Grand Teton National Parks,* by Robert B. Smith and Lee J. Siegel. The graphic-heavy text is handily the best book on the market for non-specialists hoping to grasp Teton and Yellowstone geology.

the surrounding Bridger-Teton National Forest has abundant mountain-biking trails and roads.

OUTFITTERS AND EXPEDITIONS Jackson's hub for cycling culture, **Fitzgerald's Bicycles** (⊠ *245 W. Hansen St., Jackson* ☎ *307/734–6886*) offers mountain- and road-bike rentals, sales, accessories, and repairs.

BIRD-WATCHING

With over 300 species of birds in the park, the Tetons make for excellent bird-watching country. Here you might spot both the calliope hummingbird (the smallest North American hummingbird) and the trumpeter swan (the world's largest waterfowl). The two riparian habitats described below draw lots of attention, but there are many other bird-busy areas as well. Birds of prey circle around Antelope Flats Road, for instance—the surrounding fields are good hunting turf for red-tailed hawks and prairie falcons. At Taggart Lake you'll see woodpeckers, bluebirds, and hummingbirds. Look for songbirds, such as pine and evening grosbeaks and Cassin's finches, in surrounding open pine and aspen forests.

Oxbow Bend. Some seriously impressive birds tend to congregate at this quiet spot (⇨ *Scenic Stops)*. In spring, white pelicans stop by during their northerly migration; in summer, bald eagles, great blue herons, and osprey nest nearby. Year-round, you'll have a good chance of seeing trumpeter swans. Nearby Willow Flats has similar bird life, plus sandhill cranes. ⊠ *U.S. 89/191/287, 2 mi east of Jackson Lake Junction.*

Phelps Lake. The moderate 1.8-mi round-trip Phelps Lake Overlook Trail takes you from the Death Canyon trailhead up conifer- and aspen-lined glacial moraine to a view that's accessible only by trail. Expect abundant bird life: Western tanagers, northern flickers, and ruby-crowned kinglets thrive in the bordering woods, and hummingbirds feed on scarlet gilia beneath the overlook. Don't neglect the newly opened Phelps Lake Trail, which circles the lake and is accessible from either Death Canyon or the Rockefeller Preserve. ⊠ *Moose-Wilson Rd., about 3 mi off Teton Park Rd.*

19

BOATING AND WATER SPORTS

Water sports in Grand Teton are diverse. You can float the Snake River, which runs high and fast early in the season (May and June) and more slowly during the latter part of the summer. Canoes and kayaks dominate the smaller lakes and share the water with motorboats on the impressively large Jackson Lake. Motorboats are allowed on Jenny, Jackson, and Phelps lakes. On Jenny Lake, there's an engine limit of 10 horsepower. You can launch your boat at Colter Bay, Leek's Marina, Signal Mountain, and Spalding Bay.

If you're floating the Snake River on your own, you are required to purchase a permit ($20 per raft for the entire season, or $10 per raft for seven days). Permits are available year-round at Craig Thomas Discovery and Visitor Center and at Colter Bay, Signal Mountain, and Buffalo (near the Moran entrance) ranger stations in summer. Before you set out, check with park rangers for current conditions.

You may prefer to take one of the many guided float trips through calm-water sections of the Snake; outfitters pick you up at the float-trip parking area near Craig Thomas Discovery and Visitor Center for a 10- to 20-minute drive to upriver launch sites. Ponchos and life preservers are provided. Early-morning and evening floats are your best bets for wildlife viewing, but be sure to carry a jacket or sweater. Float season runs mid-April to December.

MARINAS

Colter Bay Marina. All types of services are available to boaters, including free parking for boat trailers and vehicles, free mooring, boat rentals, guided fishing trips, and fuel. ⊠ *On Jackson Lake* ☎ *307/543–3100, 307/543–2811, or 800/628–9988.*

Leek's Marina. Both day and short-term parking for boat trailers and vehicles are available for up to three nights maximum. There are no boat rentals, but you can get fuel, and there's free short-term docking plus a pizza restaurant. This marina is operated by park concessionaire Signal Mountain Lodge. ⊠ *U.S. 89/191/287, 6 mi north of Jackson Lake Junction* ☎ *307/543–2831* ⊙ *Mid-May–late Sept.*

Signal Mountain Lodge Marina. The marina rents pontoon boats, deck cruisers, motorboats, kayaks, and canoes by the hour or for full-day cruising; rates range from $12 an hour for a kayak to $62 an hour for a pontoon boat. ⊠ *Teton Park Rd., 3 mi south of Jackson Lake Junction* ☎ *307/543–2831* ⊙ *Mid-May–late Sept.*

OUTFITTERS AND EXPEDITIONS Travel the peaceful parts of the Snake River looking for wildlife as knowledgeable guides on **Barker-Ewing Float Trips** (☎ *307/733–1800 or 800/365–1800* ⊕ *www.barkerewing.com* ☎ *$55* ⊙ *May–Sept.*) talk about area history, plants, and animals. Rent motorboats, kayaks, and canoes at **Colter Bay Marina** from **Grand Teton Lodge Company** (☎ *307/543–3100, 307/543–2811, or 800/628–9988* ⊕ *www.gtlc.com* ☎ *Motorboats $30/hr, canoes $14/hr, kayaks $13–$15/hr* ⊙ *Late May–late Sept.*). On **Grand Teton Lodge Company Snake River Float Trips** (☎ *307/543–3100 or 800/628–9988* ⊕ *www.gtlc.com* ☎ *Scenic float $53, lunch float $64, steak-fry float $70* ⊙ *June–Aug.*) choose from a scenic float trip with or without lunch, or an evening trip with a steak-fry dinner. Make reservations at the activities desk at Colter Bay Village or Jackson Lake Lodge. **Mad River Boat Trips** (☎ *307/733–6203 or 800/458–7238* ⊕ *www.mad-river.com* 🖃 *$59–$92* ☽ *Mid-May–Sept.*) leads a variety of white-water and scenic float trips, some combined with breakfast, lunch, or dinner. Obtain some instruction in the fine art of paddling with **Snake River Kayak and Canoe** (☎ *307/733–9999 or 800/529–2501* ⊕ *www.snakeriverkayak.com* 🖃 *Raft trips $45–$125, 1-day clinics $200–$300, multiday instruction $275–$1,400* ☽ *Apr.–Oct.*), then test yourself on the river. **Triangle X Float Trips** (☎ *307/733–5500 or 888/860–0005* ⊕ *www.trianglex.com* 🖃 *$60–$75* ☽ *Mid-May–late Sept.*) offers subdued river trips in Grand Teton National Park, including a sunset supper float.

CLIMBING

The Teton Range has some of the nation's most diverse general mountaineering. Excellent rock, snow, and ice routes abound for climbers of all experience levels. Unless you're already a pro, it's recommended that you take a course from one of the area's climbing schools before tackling the tough terrain.

OUTFITTERS AND EXPEDITIONS **Exum Mountain Guides** (☎ *307/733–2297* ⊕ *www.exumguides.com* 🖃 *1-day climbs $295–$395, climbing schools $135–$165*) leads a variety of climbing experiences, including one-day mountain climbs and backcountry adventures on skis and snowboards. **Jackson Hole Mountain Guides** (☎ *307/733–4979 or 800/239–7642* ⊕ *www.jhmg.com* 🖃 *1-day guided climbs $250–$400, climbing classes $140–$375*) instructs beginning to advanced climbers.

FISHING

Rainbow, brook, lake, and native cutthroat trout inhabit the park's waters. The Snake's 75 mi of river and tributary are world-renowned for their fishing. To fish in Grand Teton National Park, you need a Wyoming fishing license. A day permit for nonresidents is $10, and an annual permit is $65 plus a $10 conservation stamp; for state residents a license costs $15 per season plus $10 for a conservation stamp. Children under age 14 can fish free with an adult who has a license.

Buy a fishing license at Colter Bay Marina, Moose Village Store, Signal Mountain Lodge, and at area sporting-goods stores, where you also can get solid information on good fishing spots and the best flies or lures to use. Or obtain a license from the **Wyoming Game and Fish Department** (✉ *420 N. Cache St., Jackson* ☎ *307/733–2321* ⊕ *gf.state.wy.us*).

OUTFITTERS AND EXPEDITIONS The park's major concessionaire, **Grand Teton Lodge Company** (✉ *Colter Bay Marina or Jackson Lake Lodge* ☎ *307/543–3100 or 800/628–9988* ⊕ *www.gtlc.com* 🖃 *$150–$450 and up* ☽ *June–Sept.*) operates guided fishing trips on Jackson Lake that include boat and tackle, and guided fly-fishing trips on the Snake River. Make reservations at the activities desks at Colter Bay Village or Jackson Lake Lodge, where trips originate. Hourly and half-day Jackson Lake fishing trips with a guide leave from the marina at **Signal Mountain Lodge** (✉ *Teton Park Rd., 3 mi south of Jackson Lake Junction* ☎ *307/543–2831* ⊕ *www. signalmountainlodge.com* 🖃 *$80/hr* ☽ *Mid-May–late Sept.*). Equipment and tackle are included in the price.

19

HIKING

Most of Grand Teton's trails are unpaved, with just a few short paved sections in the vicinity of developed areas. You can get trail maps and information about hiking conditions from rangers at the park visitor centers at Moose, Jenny Lake, or Colter Bay, where you will also find bathrooms or outhouses; there are no facilities along the trails themselves. Of the more than 250 mi of maintained trails, the most popular are those around Jenny Lake, the Leigh and String lakes area, and Taggart Lake Trail, with views of Avalanche Canyon.

Front country or backcountry, you may see moose and bears, but keep your distance. Pets are not permitted on trails or in the backcountry, but you can take them on paved front-country trails so long as they are on a leash no more than 6 feet long. Always sign in at trailheads, let someone know where you are going and when you expect to return, and carry plenty of water, snacks and a cell phone.

EASY

🕭 **Cascade Canyon Trail.** Take the 20-minute boat ride from the Jenny Lake dock to the start of a gentle, ½-mi climb to 200-foot Hidden Falls, the park's most popular and crowded trail destination. With the boat ride, plan on a couple of hours to experience this trail. Listen here for the distinctive bleating of the rabbitlike pikas among the glacial boulders and pines. The trail continues ½ mi to Inspiration Point over a rocky path that is moderately steep. There are two points on the climb that afford good views of Jenny Lake and the surrounding area, but keep climbing; after passing a rock wall you'll finally reach the true Inspiration Point, with the best views. To avoid crowds, try to make your way to Inspiration Point in early morning or late afternoon. To reach the Cascade Canyon trailhead, go to the Jenny Lake Visitor Center to catch a ride across Jenny Lake with **Jenny Lake Boating** (☎ 307/734–9227 ☒ $5–$7 ☉ *June–early Sept.*). ☒ *Access trailhead from Jenny Lake Visitor Center, Jenny Lake, 2 mi off Teton Park Rd., 8 mi north of Moose Junction.*

Colter Bay Nature Trail Loop. This very easy, 1¾-mi round-trip excursion treats you to views of Jackson Lake and the Tetons. As you follow the level trail from Colter Bay Visitor Center and along the forest's edge, you may see moose and bald eagles. Allow yourself two hours to complete the walk. ☒ *Trailhead at Colter Bay Visitor Center, 2 mi off U.S. 89/191/287, 5 mi north of Jackson Lake Junction.*

Lunchtree Hill Trail. One of the park's easiest trails begins at Jackson Lake Lodge and leads ½ mi to the top of a hill above Willow Flats. The area's willow thickets, beaver ponds, and wet, grassy meadows make it a birder's paradise. Look for sandhill cranes, hummingbirds, and the many types of songbirds described in the free bird guide available at visitor centers. You might also see moose. The round-trip walk takes no more than half an hour. ☒ *Trailhead at Jackson Lake Lodge, U.S. 89/191/287, ½ mi north of Jackson Lake Junction.*

MODERATE

🕭 **Jenny Lake Trail.** You can walk to Hidden Falls from Jenny Lake ranger
★ station by following the mostly level trail around the south shore of the lake to Cascade Canyon Trail. Jenny Lake Trail continues around the

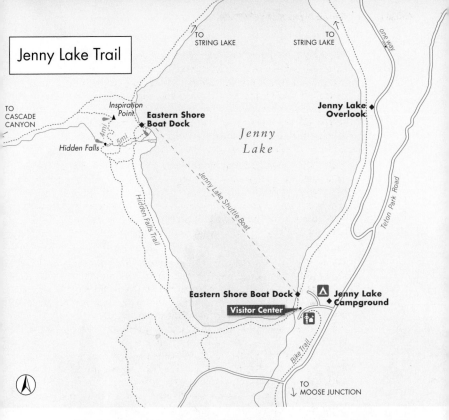

Jenny Lake Trail

TO STRING LAKE

TO STRING LAKE

one way

TO CASCADE CANYON

Inspiration Point

Eastern Shore Boat Dock

Jenny Lake Overlook

Jenny Lake

.4mi

.9mi

Hidden Falls

Hidden Falls Trail

Jenny Lake Shuttle Boat

Teton Park Road

Eastern Shore Boat Dock

Jenny Lake Campground

Visitor Center

Bike Trail

TO MOOSE JUNCTION

lake for 6½ mi. It's an easy trail—classed here as moderate because of its length—that will take you two to three hours. You'll walk through a lodgepole-pine forest, have expansive views of the lake and the land to the east, and hug the shoulder of the massive Teton range itself. Along the way you are likely to see elk, pikas, golden mantle ground squirrels, a variety of ducks and water birds, plus you may hear elk bugling, birdsong, and the chatter of squirrels. ⊠ *Trailhead at Jenny Lake Visitor Center, S. Jenny Lake Junction, ½ mi off Teton Park Rd., 8 mi north of Moose Junction.*

Leigh Lake Trail. The flat trail follows String Lake's northeastern shore to Leigh Lake's south shore, covering 2 mi in a round-trip of about an hour. You can extend your hike into a moderate 7½-mi, four-hour round-trip by following the forested east shore of Leigh Lake to Bearpaw Lake. Along the way you'll have views of Mt. Moran across the lake, and you may be lucky enough to spot a moose. ⊠ *Leigh Lake Trailhead, northwest corner of String Lake Picnic Area, ½ mi west of Jenny Lake Rd., 2 mi off Teton Park Rd., 12 mi north of Moose Junction.*

String Lake Trail. This moderate 3½-mi, three-hour loop around String Lake lies in the shadows of 11,144-foot Rockchuck Peak and 11,430-foot Mt. Saint John. This is also a good place to see moose, hear songbirds, and view wildflowers. This trail is a bit more difficult than other

DID YOU KNOW?

The Grand Tetons have been called many things—"the three pinnacles," "pilot knobs," and "the hoary brothers" among them. But the name that struck was given by French fur trappers, who referred to the mountains as *les Trois Teton* (the Three Beasts).

mid-length trails in the park, which means it is also less crowded. ⊠ *String Lake Trailhead, ¼ mi west of Jenny Lake Rd., 2 mi off Teton Park Rd., 12 mi north of Moose Junction.*

DIFFICULT

Death Canyon Trail. This 7.6-mi trail is a strenuous hike with lots of hills to traverse, ending with a climb up into Death Canyon. Plan to spend most of the day on this steep trail. ⊠ *Death Canyon Trailhead, off Moose-Wilson Rd., 4 mi south of Moose Junction.*

HORSEBACK RIDING

You can arrange a guided horseback tour at Colter Bay Village and Jackson Lake Lodge corrals or with a number of private outfitters. Most offer rides of an hour or two up to all-day excursions. If you want to spend even more time riding in Grand Teton and the surrounding mountains, consider a stay at a dude ranch. Shorter rides are almost all appropriate for novice riders, while more experienced cowboys and cowgirls will enjoy the longer journeys where the terrain gets steeper and you may wind through deep forests. For any ride be sure to wear long pants and boots (cowboy boots or hiking boots). Because you may ride through trees, a long-sleeve shirt is also a good idea and a hat is always appropriate, but it should have a stampede string to make sure it stays on your head if the wind comes up.

OUTFITTERS AND EXPEDITIONS One- and two-hour rides leave **Colter Bay Village Corral** (⊠ *2 mi off U.S. 89/191/287, 5 mi north of Jackson Lake Junction* ☎ *307/543–3100 or 800/628–9988* ⊕ *www.gtlc.com* ⊠ *1-hr rides $36, 2-hr rides $54* ☉ *June–Aug.*) for a variety of destinations, while half-day trips—for advanced riders only—go to Hermitage Point. One-hour trail rides at **Jackson Lake Lodge Corral** (⊠ *U.S. 89/191/287, ½ mi north of Jackson Lake Junction* ☎ *307/543–3100 or 800/628–9988* ⊕ *www.gtlc.com* ⊠ *1-hr rides $36, 2-hr rides $54* ☉ *June–Aug.*) give an overview of the Jackson Lake Lodge area; two-hour rides go to Emma Matilda Lake, Oxbow Bend, and Christian Pond. Experienced riders can take a half-day ride to Two Ocean Lake.

WINTER SPORTS

Grand Teton has some of North America's finest and most varied cross-country skiing. (And don't forget the nearby Jackson Hole Mountain Resort; ⇨ *What's Nearby*.) Ski the gentle 3-mi Swan Lake–Heron Pond Loop near Colter Bay Visitor Center, the mostly level 10-mi Jenny Lake Trail, or the moderate 4-mi Taggart Lake–Beaver Creek Loop and 5-mi Phelps Lake Overlook Trail. Advanced skiers should head for the Teton Crest Trail. In winter, overnight backcountry travelers must register or make a reservation at the Craig Thomas Discovery and Visitor Center. The Jackson Hole Mountain Resort aerial tram from Teton Village deposits riders at the mountains' crest of the range, from where they can access backcountry on both sides of the range.

Snowmobiling is permitted on Jackson Lake. Since snowmobiles must be towed into the park, sledders pay only the regular park entrance fees. Snowmobilers wishing to proceed north from Flagg Ranch into Yellowstone National Park must be with a commercial tour guide. The speed limit for snowmobiles on Jackson Lake is 45 MPH. The Flagg

Ranch Information Station closed beginning with the 2007–08 winter season, and consequently ski and snowshoe trails went unmarked (in fact, any references in brochures or maps to signed or maintained trails should be disregarded until further notice). For a ranger-guided snowshoe walk, call the Craig Thomas Visitor Center (⇨ *Visitor Centers*).

OUTFITTERS AND EXPEDITIONS

Jack Dennis Outdoor Shop (✉ *50 E. Broadway Ave., Jackson* ☎ *307/733–3270 Jackson, 307/733–6838 Teton Village* ⊕ *www.jackdennis.com* ✉ *Ski rental $27–$49, snowboard and boot rental $27–$36*) stocks skis and snowboards for sale and rent,

and outdoor gear for any season. In Teton Village you can buy or rent skis or snowboards at **Pepi Stiegler Sports** (✉ *Teton Village* ☎ *307/733–4505* ⊕ *www.jackdennis.com/pepis* ✉ *Ski or snowboard rental $27–$49* ⊙ *Nov.–Apr.*), conveniently located at the base of the Jackson Hole ski mountain. Rent a snowmobile at **Togwotee Mountain Lodge** (✉ *U.S. 26/287, Moran* ☎ *307/543–2847 or 866/278–4245* ⊕ *www.togwoteelodge.com* ✉ *Snowmobile rentals $149–$210 per day* ⊙ *Nov.–Apr.*) and then ride it on an extensive trail network along the Continental Divide.

EDUCATIONAL OFFERINGS

CLASSES AND SEMINARS

Teton Science School. Adults and families can join one of the school's single- or multiday wildlife expeditions in Grand Teton, Yellowstone, and surrounding forests to see and learn about wolves, bears, mountain sheep, and other animals. Junior high and high school students can take multiweek field ecology courses while living at the school, backpacking and camping out. Weekdays, kids in grades one through six can join Young Naturalists programs that don't involve sleepovers. ✉ *700 Coyote Canyon Rd., Jackson* ☎ *307/733–1313* ⊕ *www.tetonscience.org* ✉ *Wildlife expeditions $69–$1,995, youth programs $200–$3,600*

PROGRAMS AND TOURS

Grand Teton Lodge Company Bus Tours. Half-day tours depart from Jackson Lake Lodge and include visits to scenic viewpoints, visitor centers, and other park sites. Interpretive guides provide information about the park geology, history, wildlife and ecosystems. Buy tickets in advance at Colter Bay or Jackson Lake Lodge activities desks. Tours include Grand Teton, Yellowstone or a combination of the two parks. ✉ *Jackson Lake Lodge* ☎ *307/543–2811 or 800/628–9988* ⊕ *www.gtlc.com* ✉ *$36–$66* ⊙ *Mid-May–early Oct., Mon.–Sat.*

Gray Line Bus Tours. Full-day bus tours provide an overview of Grand Teton National Park. They depart from Jackson and you will learn about the park's geology, history, birds, plants, and wildlife. ✉ *1580*

19

W. Martin La., Jackson ☎ *307/733–4325 or 800/443–6133* ⊕ *www. graylinejh.com* ⬛ *$100 plus $12 park entrance fee* ⊙ *Memorial Day–Sept., Mon., Wed., and Sat.*

Jackson Lake Cruises. Grand Teton Lodge Company runs 1½-hour Jackson Lake scenic cruises from Colter Bay Marina throughout the day as well as breakfast cruises, and sunset steak-fry cruises. Interpretive guides explain how forest fires and glaciers have shaped the Grand Teton landscape. ⊠ *2 mi off U.S. 89/191/287, 5 mi north of Jackson Lake Junction* ☎ *307/543–3100, 307/543–2811, or 800/628–9988* ⊕ *www.gtlc.com* ⬛ *Scenic cruise $24, breakfast cruise $36, steak-fry cruise $57* ⊙ *Late May–mid-Sept.*

RANGER PROGRAMS

Campfire Programs. Park rangers lead free nightly slide shows from June through September at the Colter Bay, Gros Ventre, and Signal Mountain amphitheaters. For schedules of topics check the park newspaper, *Teewinot,* or at visitor centers. ⊠ *Colter Bay Amphitheater, 2 mi off U.S. 89/191/287, 5 mi north of Jackson Lake Junction* ⊠ *Gros Ventre Amphitheater, 4 mi off U.S. 26/89/191 and 2½ mi west of Kelly on Gros Ventre River Rd., 6 mi south of Moose Junction* ⊠ *Signal Mountain Amphitheate, Teton Park Rd., 4 mi south of Jackson Lake Junction* ☎ *307/739–3399 or 307/739–3594* ⊙ *June and July, nightly at 9:30; Aug. and Sept., nightly at 9.*

Jackson Lake Lodge Ranger Talks. Visit the Wapiti Room to hear a slide-illustrated ranger presentation on topics such as area plants and animals, geology, and natural history. Also, you can chat with the ranger on the back deck of the lodge 6:30 PM–8 PM daily, early June through early September. ⊠ *U.S. 89/191/287, ½ mi north of Jackson Lake Junction* ☎ *307/739–3300* ⊙ *Late June–mid-Aug., nightly at 8:30.*

⟳ **Ranger Walks.** Rangers lead free walks throughout the park in summer, from a one-hour lakeside stroll at Colter Bay to a three-hour hike from Jenny Lake. The talks focus on a variety of subjects from wildlife to birds and flower species to geology. Call for itineraries, times, and reservations. ☎ *307/739–3300* ⊙ *Early June–early Sept.*

⟳ **Junior Rangers Program.** Children ages 8–12 learn about the natural world of the park as they take an easy 2-mi hike with a ranger. Kids should wear old clothes and bring water, rain gear, and insect repellent. The hike, which takes place at Moose, Jenny Lake, or Colter Bay, is 1½ hours long and is limited to 12 children. ⊠ *Moose: meet at fireplace in Craig Thomas Discovery and Visitor Center; Jenny Lake: meet at the flagpole in front of the visitor center; Colter Bay: meet at the visitor center* ☎ *307/739–3399 or 307/739–3594* ⊙ *Mid-June–mid-Aug., daily 1:30.*

⟳ **Nature Explorer's Backpack Program.** Rangers lend a nature journal and a backpack full of activities to children ages 6 through 12 before sending them out along the trails at the Rockefeller Preserve. ⊠ *Laurance S. Rockefeller Preserve Interpretive Center, on east side of Moose-Wilson Rd., about 4 mi south of Moose and 3 mi north of Granite Canyon Entrance Station* ☎ *307/739–3654* ⊙ *June–early Sept., backpacks available daily 8–6.*

WHAT'S NEARBY

NEARBY TOWNS

The major gateway to Grand Teton National Park is **Jackson**—but don't confuse this with Jackson Hole. Jackson Hole is the mountain-ringed valley that houses Jackson and much of Grand Teton National Park. The town of Jackson, located south of the park, is a small community (roughly 7,000 residents) that gets flooded with more than 3 million visitors annually. Expensive homes and fashionable shops have sprung up all over, but Jackson manages to maintain at least part of its true western character. With its raised wooden sidewalks and old-fashioned storefronts, the town center still looks a bit like a western movie set. There's a lot to do here, both downtown and in the surrounding countryside.

If it's skiing you're after, **Snow King Resort** is the oldest resort in the valley, and its 7,808-foot mountain overlooks the town of Jackson and the National Elk Refuge. It's at the end of Snow King Avenue. **Teton Village,** on the southwestern side of the park, is a cluster of businesses centered around the facilities of the Jackson Hole Mountain Resort—a ski and snowboard area with an aerial tram, gondola, and various other lifts. There are plenty of places to eat, stay, and shop here.

On the "back side of the Tetons," as eastern Idaho is known, is **Driggs,** the western gateway to Yellowstone and Grand Teton. Easygoing and rural, Driggs resembles the Jackson of a few decades ago. To reach the park from here you have to cross a major mountain pass that is sometimes closed in winter by avalanches. **Dubois,** about 85 mi east of Jackson, is the least known of the gateway communities to Grand Teton and Yellowstone, but this town of 1,000 has all the services of the bigger towns. You can still get a room for the night here during the peak summer travel period without making a reservation weeks or months in advance (though it's a good idea to call a week or so before you intend to arrive).

About an hour to the south is **Pinedale,** another small Wyoming town with lodging, restaurants, and attractions. Energy development has made the area a hopping place these days, so be sure to plan ahead if you want to stay in town.

VISITOR INFORMATION

Stop at the **Jackson Hole and Greater Yellowstone Visitor Center** (⊠ *532 N. Cache St., Jackson* ☎*307/733–3316* ⊕ *www.fs.fed.us/jhgyvc* ⊙ *Late May–Sept., daily 8–7; Oct.–late May, daily 9–5*) to get information about area attractions and events and to see wildlife displays that include bronze elk sculptures outside and a stuffed herd of elk in the lobby. The center is jointly operated by several organizations and governmental agencies—State of Wyoming, Jackson Hole Chamber of Commerce, U.S. Forest Service, U.S. Fish and Wildlife Service, U.S. Department of the Interior, and Wyoming Game and Fish Department—so you can get information related to all public lands in the region.

19

Dubois Chamber of Commerce ⬠ *P.O. Box 632Y, Dubois, WY 82513* ☎ *307/455–2556* ⊕ *www.duboiswyoming.org.* **Eastern Idaho Visitor Information Center** ✉ *630 W. Broadway, Idaho Falls, ID 83405* ☎ *208/523–1010 or 866/365–6943.* **Jackson Chamber of Commerce** ⬠ *P.O. Box 550, Jackson, WY 83001* ☎ *307/733–3316* ⊕ *www.jacksonholechamber.com.* **Jackson Lake/ Colter Bay Visitor Center** ✉ *2 mi off U.S. 89/191/287, 6 mi north of Jackson Lake Junction, Moran, WY 83013* ☎ *307/739–3594.* **Sublette County Chamber of Commerce** ✉ *32 E. Pine St., Pinedale, WY 82941* ☎ *307/367–2242* ⊕ *www. pinedalechamber.com.* **Teton Valley Chamber of Commerce** ✉ *29 N. Main St., Driggs, ID 83452* ☎ *208/354–2500* ⊕ *www.tetonvalleychamber.com.*

NEARBY ATTRACTIONS

DUBOIS

ⓒ ★ **National Bighorn Sheep Interpretive Center.** The local variety is known as the Rocky Mountain bighorn, but you can learn about all kinds of bighorn sheep here. Among the exhibits of mounted specimens here are the Super Slam diorama, with one of each type of wild sheep in the world, and two bighorn rams fighting during the rut. Hands-on exhibits illustrate a bighorn's body language, characteristics, and habitat. Wildlife-viewing tours ($25; reserve ahead) are conducted in winter to Whiskey Mountain to see the wild sheep in their natural habitat. ✉ *907 W. Ramshorn Ave., Dubois* ☎ *307/455–3429 or 888/209–2795* ⊕ *www.bighorn.org* 🎫 *$2.50* ⊙ *Memorial Day–Labor Day, daily 9–7; early Sept.–late May, Mon.–Sat. 9–5; wildlife-viewing tours mid-Nov.–Mar.*

JACKSON

Bridger-Teton National Forest. This 3.4-million-acre forest has something for everyone: history, hiking, camping, and wildlife. It encompasses the Teton Wilderness east of Grand Teton National Park and south of Yellowstone National Park, the Gros Ventre Wilderness southeast of Jackson, and the Bridger Wilderness farther south and east. No motor vehicles are allowed in the wilderness, but there are many scenic drives, natural springs (including Granite Hot Springs, ⇨ *see box*) where you can swim or soak throughout the year (in winter access is on snowmobiles or dogsleds), and cultural sights like abandoned lumber camps in the national forest between the wildernesses. The peaks reach higher than 13,000 feet, and the area is liberally sprinkled with more than a thousand high-mountain lakes, where fishing is generally excellent. ✉ *340 N. Cache St., Jackson* ☎ *307/739–5500* ✉ *29 E. Fremont Lake Rd.* ☎ *307/367–4326* ⊕ *www.fs.fed.us/r4/btnf* 🎫 *Free, some picnic sites $5.*

ⓒ **Jackson Hole Museum.** See exhibits about area homesteaders and find out how Dead Man's Bar got its name. You can also learn about Jackson's all-female town government, not to mention a lady sheriff who claimed to have killed three men before hanging up her spurs. Among the exhibits are American Indian, ranching, and cowboy artifacts. ✉ *Glenwood St. and Deloney Ave., Jackson* ☎ *307/733–2414* ⊕ *www.jacksonholehistory. org* 🎫 *$3* ⊙ *Memorial Day–Sept., Mon.–Sat. 9:30–6, Sun. 10–5.*

ⓒ **National Elk Refuge.** Wildlife abounds on this 25,000-acre refuge year-round at the foot of "Sleeping Indian" mountain. But from around late November through March, the real highlight is the more than 7,000 elk,

Fodor's Choice ★

Granite Hot Springs

Soothing thermal baths in pristine outback country awaits in the heart of the Bridger-Teton National Forest, just a short drive south of Jackson. Concerted local and federal efforts have preserved the wild lands in this hunter and fisherman's paradise where ranches dot the Teton Valley floor. The Snake River turns west and the contours sheer into steep vertical faces. By Hoback Junction there's white-water excitement. The drive south along U.S. 191 provides good views of the river's bends and turns and the life-jacketed rafters and kayakers who float through the Hoback canyon. At Hoback Junction, about 11 mi south of Jackson, head east (toward Pinedale) on U.S. Highway 189/191 and follow the Hoback River east through its beautiful canyon.

A tributary canyon 10 mi east of the junction is followed by a well-maintained and -marked gravel road to Granite Hot Springs, in the Bridger-Teton National Forest. Drive 9 mi off U.S. 189/191 (northeast) on Granite Creek Road to reach the hot springs. People also come for the shady, creek-side campground and moderate hikes up Granite Canyon to passes with panoramic views. You'll want to drive with some caution, as there are elevated turns, the possibility of a felled tree, and wandering livestock that can own the road ahead on blind curves. In winter there's a popular snowmobile and dogsled trail from the highway. The 93°F to 112°F thermal bath at the end of the road is pure physical therapy, but it's closed from November through mid-December. Admission is $6 per person.

---

many with enormous antler racks, that winter here. There are also buffalo and limited hunts, depending on population size, to cull the herds. The Refuge Road entrance lies about 1 mi from the Town Square just past St. John's hospital on East Broadway. Elk can also be observed from various pullouts along U.S. 191 or up close by slowly driving your car on the refuge's winding unpaved roads. In winter you can take a horse-drawn sleigh ride for the chance to see the elk stand or eat calmly as sleighs loaded with families and supplied with alfalfa pellets move in their midst. Among the other animals that make their home here are buffalo, coyote, mountain sheep, trumpeter swan, and other waterfowl, though in the summer, the range is light on big game. Arrange for sleigh rides through the Jackson Hole and Greater Yellowstone Visitor Center (☏ *307/733–3316*); wear warm clothing, including hats, gloves, boots, long johns, and coats. ⊠ *Northeast of Jackson along Refuge Rd.* ⌖ *Jackson Hole and Greater Yellowstone Visitor Center, 532 N. Cache Dr., Jackson* ☏ *307/733–5771 refuge, 307/733–3316 visitor center* ⊕ *www. fws.gov/nationalelkrefuge* ☐ *Free. Sleigh rides $18* ⊙ *Daily, dawn to dusk. Sleigh rides mid-Dec.–Mar.*

★ **National Museum of Wildlife Art.** An impressive collection of wildlife art—most of it devoted to North American species—is displayed in the 14 galleries displaying the work of artists Karl Bodmer, Albert Bierstadt, Charles Russell, John Clymer, Robert Bateman, Carl Rungius, and others. A deck here affords views across the National Elk Refuge,

19

where, particularly in winter, you can see wildlife in a natural habitat. ⌧ *2820 Rungius Rd., 3 mi north of Jackson* ☎ *307/733–5771* ⊕ *www. wildlifeart.org* ⌦ *$10* ☉ *Mid-May–mid-Oct., daily 9–5; mid-Oct.–mid-May, Mon.–Sat. 9–5, Sun. 1–5.*

PINEDALE

☽ **Museum of the Mountain Man.** Preserving the history of the area's trapper ★ heritage, this museum displays of 19th-century guns, traps, clothing, and beaver pelts. There's also an interpretive exhibit devoted to the pioneer and ranch history of Sublette County as well as an overview of the western fur trade. In summer the museum hosts living-history demonstrations, children's events, a reenactment of the early 19th-century Green River Rendezvous, and lectures. ⌧ *700 E. Hennick Rd., Pinedale* ☎ *307/367–4101 or 877/686–6266* ⊕ *www.museumofthemountainman. com* ⌦ *$5* ☉ *May–Sept., daily 9–5; Oct., daily 9–4.*

AREA ACTIVITIES

SPORTS AND THE OUTDOORS

GOLF

Jackson Hole Golf and Tennis Club (⌧ *5000 Spring Gulch Rd.* ⌧ ✛ *9 mi north of Jackson on U.S. 189 then 2 mi west at Gros Ventre Junction to Spring Gulch Rd.* ☎ *307/733–3111, 307/543–2811, or 800/628–9988* ⊕ *www.jhgtc.com* ⌦ *$60–$175* ☉ *May–mid-Oct.*), an 18-hole course redesigned by Robert Trent Jones, has views of the Teton Range and an eco-friendly, LEED-certified clubhouse. It has been ranked as Wyoming's top course by *Golf Magazine*. Designed by Arnold Palmer and Ed Seay, **Teton Pines Resort and Country Tennis Club** (⌧ *3450 N. Clubhouse Dr., Wilson* ☎ *307/733–1005 or 800/238–2223* ⊕ *www.tetonpines.com* ⌦ *$65–$160* ☉ *Early June–mid-Oct.*) is a relatively flat 18-hole course near Teton Village affords views of the Tetons and abundant wildlife. It's certified as an Audubon course.

WINTER SPORTS

Skiers and snowboarders love **Jackson Hole Mountain Resort** (⌧ *P.O. Box 290, Teton Village* ☎ *307/733–2292 or 800/333–7766* ⊕ *www. jacksonhole.com*), one of the great skiing experiences in America. There are literally thousands of routes up and down the mountain, and not all of them are hellishly steep, despite Jackson's reputation.

ARTS AND ENTERTAINMENT

ART GALLERIES

Jackson's hot spot for contemporary work, **JH Muse Gallery** (⌧ *62 S. Glenwood St., Jackson* ☎ *307/733–0555* ⊕ *www.jhmusegallery.com*), leaves wildlife and landscape art behind in favor of hip and often playful painting, sculpture, and jewelry. It's a bit of SoHo nestled in the Rockies. **Trailside Galleries** (⌧ *130 E. Broadway, Jackson* ☎ *307/733–3186* ⊕ *www.trailsidegalleries.com*) has traditional western art, including paintings by the biggest names—Charles M. Russell, John Clymer, and Howard Terpening—along with today's most talented western painters, such as Z. S. Laing, Nancy Glazier, Bill Anton, and Tim Cox.

Fodor's Choice ★ Abi Garaman has been capturing images of Jackson Hole and Grand Teton National Park on film for more than 50 years. Many of his wide selection of images of wildlife, mountains, barns, and more are displayed at **Under the Willow Photo Gallery** (✉ 50 S. Cache St., Jackson ☎ 307/733–6633 ⊕ www.underthewillow.com).

SHOPPING

The Cowboy Shop (✉ 129 W. Pine St., Pinedale ☎ 307/367–4300) sells western and cowboy clothing for all ages, including hats, boots and leather goods. It also has a decent selection of books. Well stocked with the best in outdoor equipment for winter and summer, **Jack Dennis Sports** (✉ 50 E. Broadway Ave., Jackson ☎ 307/733–3270) is Jackson's premier sports shop, and in fact is known internationally as a fishing and sporting headquarters. You can get everything from a canoe or backpack to skis and kayaks, plus clothing and other supplies. Fishing equipment can be rented as well.

FAMILY PICKS

Float the Snake. Climb aboard a big rubber raft and hang on for a float trip on the Snake River (not suitable for very young children).

Mount a horse. Rent a horse for a couple of hours, take a guided tour, or stay at a guest ranch where you can ride every day.

Ride a stagecoach. Experience the Old West with a stagecoach ride around the Town Square in Jackson.

WHERE TO EAT AND STAY

ABOUT THE RESTAURANTS

Though the park itself has some excellent restaurants, don't miss dining in Jackson, where restaurants combine game, fowl, and fish with the enticing spices and sauces of European cuisine and the lean ingredients, vegetarian entrées, and meat cuts that reflect the desires of health-consciousness diners. Steaks are usually cut from grass-fed Wyoming beef, but you'll also find buffalo and elk on the menu; poultry and pasta are offered by most restaurants, and you'll find fresh salads and fish (trout, tilapia, and salmon are most common). Just about everywhere, you can order a burger or a bowl of homemade soup. Casual is the word for most dining both within and outside the park. An exception is Jenny Lake Lodge, where jackets and ties are recommended for dinner. Breakfast is big: steak and eggs, pancakes, biscuits and gravy; lunches are lighter, often taken in a sack to enjoy on the trail.

ABOUT THE HOTELS

The choice of lodging properties within the park is as diverse as the landscape itself. Here you'll find simple campgrounds, cabins, and basic motel rooms. You can also settle into a homey bed-and-breakfast, or a luxurious suite in a full-service resort. Between June and August, room rates go up and are harder to get without advanced reservations. Nonetheless, if you're looking to stay in a national park that's tailored to individual pursuits, this is it. Although this park is becoming more popular and crowded each year, it still resembles the haven its found-

19

ers envisioned in 1929 and again in 1950, a place where man can contemplate and interact with nature.

ABOUT THE CAMPGROUNDS

You'll find a variety of campgrounds, from small areas where only tents are allowed, to full RV parks with all services. If you don't have a tent, but want to bring your sleeping bags, you can take advantage of the tent cabins at Colter Bay, where you have a hard floor, cots, and canvas walls for shelter. Standard campsites include a place to pitch your tent or park your trailer/camper, a fire pit for cooking, and a picnic table. All developed campgrounds have toilets and water; plan to bring your own firewood. Check in at National Park Service campsites as early as possible—sites are assigned on a first-come, first-served basis.

You can camp in the park's backcountry year-round, provided you have the requisite permit and are able to gain access to your site. Between June 1 and September 15, backcountry campers in the park are limited to one stay of up to 10 days. Campfires are prohibited in the backcountry except at designated lakeshore campsites. You can reserve a backcountry campsite between January 1 and May 15 for a $25 nonrefundable fee (Social Security numbers must be included on all checks) using the online reservation system, by fax, or in writing to **GTNP-Backcountry Permits** (⌂ *P.O. Box 170, Moose, WY 83012* ☏ *307/739–3438* ⊕ *www.nps. gov/grte*). You can also take a chance that the site you want will be open when you arrive in the park, in which case you pay no fee at all, but a trip to Craig Thomas Visitor and Discovery Center or Jenny Lake Ranger Station is still required for a permit and mandatory bear-proof canister. Campfires are prohibited in the backcountry except at designated lakeshore campsites. Jackson Hole Mountain Resort tram provides access to the park's backcountry, which can also be reached on foot.

■ TIP➔ Because bears and lions live in the park, campers should store food in bear containers and never in the tent.

WHERE TO EAT

IN THE PARK

$$–$$$
BARBECUE
☺
★
✕ **Dornan's Chuck Wagon.** Hearty portions of beef, beans, potatoes, short ribs, stew, and lemonade or hot coffee are the dinner standbys at Dornan's. Locals know this spot for the barbecue cooked over wood fires. At breakfast, count on old-fashioned staples such as sourdough pancakes or biscuits and gravy. You can eat your chuck-wagon meal inside one of the restaurant's teepees if it happens to be raining or windy; otherwise, sit at outdoor picnic tables with views of the Snake River and the Tetons. The quick service and inexpensive prices make this a good choice for families. Weekly "Hootenanny" open-mic nights attract family tourists as well as rowdy young Jacksonians. A pizza parlor (⇨ *Doran's Restaurant*) serves lunch year-round. ⊠ *10 Moose Rd., off Teton Park Rd. at Moose Junction* ☏ *307/733–2415* ⊕ *www.dornans. com* ▤ *AE, D, MC, V* ☉ *Closed early Sept.–mid-June.*

$$
PIZZA
✕ **Dornan's Restaurant.** Tasty pizzas and pastas are the main standbys at Dornan's, located at Moose on a longtime family inholding, but you'll also find generous margaritas, a surprisingly diverse wine list, and occasional

live music. Place your order at the front counter, and your food is brought out to you—either at a picnic table facing the Tetons, inside one of the huge teepees (ideal in rainy weather, or for those traveling with kids), or upstairs on the roof with stunning mountain views, the perfect hangout to unwind with a margarita after a strenuous day's hike. The extremely popular eatery serves both steak and pasta and has an extensive salad bar. There's also a long inside bar with stellar views and friendly barkeeps. Check Dornan's schedule for live music and be sure to explore the wine shop next door: it's one of the most varied and well stocked in the valley. It's where local resident and movie star Harrison Ford has been seen buying his *vino*. ⌧ *10 Moose Rd., off Teton Park Rd. at Moose Junction* ☎ *307/733–2415* ⊕ *www.dornans.com* ▭ *AE, D, MC, V.*

$$–$$$$
AMERICAN
Fodor'sChoice
★
✕ **Jackson Lake Lodge Mural Room.** The ultimate park dining experience is found in this large room that gets its name from a 700-square-foot mural painted by western artist Carl Roters. The mural details an 1837 Wyoming mountain man rendezvous and covers two walls of the dining room. Select from a menu that includes trout, elk, beef, and chicken. The plantain-crusted trout is a great choice, or try the bison prime rib. The tables face tall windows affording a panoramic view of Willow Flats and Jackson Lake to the northern Tetons. ⌧ *U.S. 89/191/287, ½ mi north of Jackson Lake Junction* ☎ *307/543–3463 or 800/628– 9988* ⊕ *www.gtlc.com* ▭ *AE, MC, V* ☾ *Closed mid-Oct.–late May.*

$–$$$
AMERICAN–
CASUAL
✕ **Jackson Lake Lodge Pioneer Grill.** With an old-fashioned soda fountain, friendly service, and seats along a winding counter, this eatery recalls a 1950s-era luncheonette. Tuck into burgers, sundaes, and other classic American fare here. ⌧ *U.S. 89/191/287, ½ mi north of Jackson Lake Junction* ☎ *307/543–2811* ⊕ *www.gtlc.com* ▭ *AE, MC, V* ☾ *Closed early Oct.–late May.*

$$$$
AMERICAN
★
✕ **Jenny Lake Lodge Dining Room.** Elegant yet rustic, this is Grand Teton National Park's finest dining establishment, with easily the most ambitious menu in any national park. The menu is ever changing and offers ambitious items like tempura squash blossoms and pinot-glazed veal checks; the wine list is extensive. Dinner is prix-fixe, and though lunch is à la carte, the inventive soups and *panini* are no less decadent. Jackets are encouraged for men at dinner. ⌧ *Jenny Lake Rd., 2 mi off Teton Park Rd., 12 mi north of Moose Junction* ☎ *307/733–4647 or 800/628– 9988* ⊕ *www.gtlc.com* ⌕ *Reservations essential* ▭ *AE, MC, V* ☾ *Closed early Oct.–late May.*

¢–$
MEXICAN
✕ **John Colter Cafe Court.** At this Colter Bay Village spot you can buy tacos and burritos, plus a few American faves like burgers and hot dogs. The southwestern theme extends to the cafeteria's décor. ⌧ *5 mi north of Jackson Lake Lodge* ☎ *307/543–2811* ⊕ *www.gtlc.com* ▭ *AE, MC, V* ☾ *Closed early Sept.–early June.*

$$$–$$$$
AMERICAN
✕ **The Peaks.** Part of Signal Mountain Lodge, this casual room has exposed ceiling beams and big square windows overlooking southern Jackson Lake and the Tetons. The emphasis here is on fish: Rocky Mountain trout is marinated, lightly floured, and grilled, or simply grilled and topped with lemon-parsley butter. ⌧ *Teton Park Rd., 4 mi south of Jackson Lake Junction* ☎ *307/543–2831* ⊕ *www.signalmountainlodge. com* ▭ *AE, D, MC, V* ☾ *Closed mid-Oct.–mid-May.*

19

$–$$$ ✕ **Ranch House at Colter Bay Village.** New in 2009, the Ranch House delivers quick service and inexpensive prices, making it a good choice for families or travelers on a budget. Dinner entrees skew Western: thick steaks, barbecued ribs, chicken with chile sauce. The kitchen will also prep your day's catch if you deliver it by 4 PM. ⊠ *2 mi off U.S. 89/191/287, 5 mi north of Jackson Lake Junction, Colter Bay* ☎ *307/543–2811* ⊕ *www.gtlc.com* ⊟ *AE, MC, V* ⊘ *Closed late Sept.–late May.*

AMERICAN

PICNIC AREAS   The park has 11 designated picnic areas, each with tables and grills, and most with pit toilets and water pumps or faucets. In addition to those listed here you can find picnic areas at Colter Bay Village Campground, Cottonwood Creek, the east shore of Jackson Lake, and South Jenny Lake and String Lake trailhead.

Chapel of the Sacred Heart. From this intimate lakeside picnic area you can look across southern Jackson Lake to Mt. Moran. ⊠ *¼ mi east of Signal Mountain Lodge, off Teton Park Rd.*

Colter Bay Visitor Center. This big picnic area, spectacularly located right on the beach at Jackson Lake, gets crowded in July and August. It's conveniently close to flush toilets and stores. ⊠ *2 mi off U.S. 89/191/287, 5 mi north of Jackson Lake Junction.*

Hidden Falls. Adjacent to the Jenny Lake shuttle boat dock is this shaded, pine-scented picnic site. An easy ½-mi hike takes you to the falls. Take the shuttle boat across Jenny Lake to reach the Cascade Canyon trailhead. ⊠ *At the Cascade Canyon trailhead.*

OUTSIDE THE PARK

$$–$$$ ✕ **Bar J Chuckwagon.** This may be the best value in Jackson Hole. You get a full ranch-style meal plus a complete western show. Served on a tin plate, the food is barbecued roast beef, chicken, or rib-eye steak with potatoes, beans, biscuits, applesauce, spice cake, and ranch coffee or lemonade. The talented Bar J Wranglers sing, play instruments, share cowboy stories and poetry, and even yodel. The dinner and show take place inside, so don't let the weather keep you away. The doors open at 5:30, so you can explore the Bar J's western village—including a saloon and several shops—before the dinner bell rings at 7:30. Reservations are strongly suggested. ⊠ *Off Moose-Wilson Rd., 1 mi north of Hwy. 22, Wilson* ☎ *307/733–3370* ⊕ *www.barjchuckwagon.com* ⊟ *D, MC, V* ⊘ *Closed Oct.–Memorial Day.*

BARBECUE
Fodor's Choice
★

$$ ✕ **Billy's Giant Hamburgers and Cadillac Grille.** True to its name, Billy's serves big—really big—burgers and waffle fries that are really, really good, albeit greasy. There are also hot dogs and several deli-style sandwiches that you can munch on, around a 1950s-style lunch counter with clear views of the Town Square. The portions are generally huge. Service is quick and unpretentious. Billy's shares space with the more refined but equally fun Cadillac Grille, where you can enjoy a casual atmosphere of a few booths and tables or grab a stool (if you can find one) around its usually jam-packed circular bar. ⊠ *55 N. Cache Dr., Jackson* ☎ *307/733–3279* ⊕ *www.cadillac-grille.com* ⊟ *AE, MC, V.*

AMERICAN
★

¢–$$ ✕ **The Bunnery.** Lunch is served year-round and dinner is served in summer at the Bunnery, but it's the breakfasts of omelets and home-baked pastries that are irresistible; the coffee is also very good. All of the breads are made on the premises, most from OSM flour (oats,

AMERICAN
★

sunflower, millet). It's elbow to elbow inside, so you may have to wait to be seated on busy mornings, but any inconvenience is well worth it. There's also a decent vegetarian selection here. Try a giant almond stick, sticky bun, or a piece of Very Berry Pie made from raspberries, strawberries, and blueberries. In summer there's outdoor seating. On-street parking can be hard to find here. ⊠ *Hole-in-the-Wall Mall, 130 N. Cache St., Jackson* ☎ *307/734–0075* ⊕ *www.bunnery.com* ⊟ *AE, D, MC, V* ☉ *No dinner Sept.–May.*

$$$$

AMERICAN

Fodor's Choice

★

✕ **Couloir.** The gondola at Teton Village provides access to this stylish dining room at 9,095 feet, where diners can look out over Jackson Hole while lingering over signature cocktails and a smart, contemporary prix-fixe dinner menu. Entrée options might include house-smoked bison cuts or fork-ready Kurobuta pork, along with clever sides like chickpea pancakes and fried-green "Wyomatoes," a favorite local tomato variety. Fake cowhide upholstery, exposed ductwork, and a towering back-bar give the room a fun, modern feel. Foodies buzzed when Couloir opened in 2007, and the clamor hasn't died down much since. Days and hours can change with the seasons, so call for reservations. ⊠ *Atop the gondola at Teton Village* ☎ *307/739–2675* ⊲ *Reservations essential* ⊟ *AE, D, MC, V* ☉ *Closed Mon. and Tues. Closed late Sept.–late Nov. and Apr.–mid-June. No lunch.*

¢–$$

AMERICAN

✕ **Jedediah's House of Sourdough.** Friendly, noisy, and elbow knocking, this restaurant a block east of Town Square—which also has a branch at the airport—makes breakfast and lunch for those with big appetites. There are plenty of excellent "sourjacks" (sourdough flapjacks) and biscuits and gravy. Burgers are mountain-man size. The menu at the airport location tends to be more expensive than in the restaurant downtown, but it's open later. ⊠ *135 E. Broadway Ave., Jackson* ☎ *307/733–5671* ⊠ *1250 Airport Rd., Jackson* ☎ *307/733–6063* ⊟ *AE, D, MC, V* ☉ *No dinner.*

$–$$$

AMERICAN

✕ **Mangy Moose.** Folks pour in off the ski slopes for a lot of food and talk at this two-level restaurant with a bar and an outdoor deck. There's a high noise level but decent food consisting of Alaska halibut, buffalo meat loaf, and fish and pasta dishes. The place is adorned with antiques, including a full-size stuffed moose and sleigh suspended from the ceiling. The attached bar is a popular nightspot, with live music and frequent concerts by top bands. ⊠ *3295 Village Dr., Teton Village* ☎ *307/733–4913* ⊕ *www.mangymoose.net* ⊟ *AE, MC, V.*

$$–$$$$

ITALIAN

★

✕ **Nani's Genuine Pasta House.** The ever-changing menu at this cozy restaurant—a longtime favorite with locals—may include braised veal shanks with saffron risotto, quail marinated with honey and balsamic vinegar, or other regional Italian cooking. Whether Nani's is "authentic" or Americanized Italian is open to debate. The knowledgeable staff will help you through the rotating menu, which focuses on a different region each month. The place is almost hidden behind a motel and is designed to attract gourmets who will really appreciate the cuisine. The wine list features a wide range of sparkling wines, regional Italian and non-Italian wines, and wines by the glass. Vegan choices are offered. ⊠ *242 N. Glenwood St., Jackson* ☎ *307/733–3888* ⊕ *www.nanis.com* ⊟ *AE, MC, V.*

19

$$–$$$$

AMERICAN

★

✕ **Snake River Grill.** One of Jackson's best dining options, this sophisticated dining room offers creatively prepared free-range veal chops, grilled venison buffalo strip steak, elk chops, and grilled Idaho redrainbow trout on a menu that changes seasonally. The extensive wine list seems to pick up another award every year or so. ⊠ *84 E. Broadway Ave., Jackson* ☎ *307/733–0557* ⊕ *www.snakerivergrill.com* ▭ *AE, DC, MC, V* ☾ *Closed Apr. and Nov. No lunch.*

$–$$

THAI

Fodor'sChoice

★

✕ **Teton Thai.** For the best Thai this side of San Francisco—and maybe the entire inner-mountain west—this family-owned local favorite tops the list of everyone in Jackson. Just one block off Town Square—across from the Teton Theatre and next to Gaslight Alley—it's always packed. In winter there's takeout or counter seating right in the kitchen, but in summer you can sit on the patio outside, where the atmosphere can become boisterous with big crowds and nightly DJs. Service can sometimes be slow, but the *tom kha gai* (coconut milk, lemongrass, and chicken soup) or tofu curry dishes are always worth the wait. A Teton Village location is in the works. ⊠ *135 N. Cache Dr., Jackson* ☎ *307/733–0022* ⊠ *32 W. Birch St., Victor* ☎ *208/787–8424* ⊕ *www.tetonthai.com* ▭ *No credit cards at Jackson location; MC, V accepted in Victor* ☾ *Closed Nov. No lunch weekends. Jackson location closed Sun.*

WHERE TO STAY

IN THE PARK

$$

🏠 **Colter Bay Village.** Near Jackson Lake, this complex of western-style cabins—some with one room, others with two or more rooms—are within walking distance of the lake. The property has splendid views and an excellent marina and beach for the windsurfing crowd (you'll need a wet suit because of the cold). There are also camping options: a 112-space RV park as well as tent cabins (⇨ *Camping, below*), which share communal baths. **Pros:** prices are good for what you get; many nearby facilities. **Cons:** little sense of privacy; not all cabins have bathrooms. ⊠ *2 mi off U.S. 89/191/287, 10 mi north of Jackson Lake Junction, Colter Bay* ☎ *307/543–3100 or 800/628–9988* ⊕ *www.gtlc.com* ⌁ *166 cabins (9 with shared baths), 66 tent cabins* ☊ *In-room: no a/c, no phone, no TV. In-hotel: 2 restaurants, bar, laundry facilities, some pets allowed, Wi-Fi* ▭ *AE, MC, V* ☾ *Closed late Sept.–late May (shorter season for tent cabins).*

$$$–$$$$

🏠 **Dornan's Spur Ranch Cabins.** Part of Dornan's all-in-one shopping–dining–recreation development at Moose, these one- and two-bedroom cabins have great views of the Tetons and the Snake River. Each cabin has a full kitchen, with electric stove, toaster, pots, pans, dishes, coffeemaker, and utensils as well as a generously sized living-dining room and a furnished porch with a Weber grill in summer. However, there's only one microwave on-site, so you'll want to request it early. **Pros:** cabins are simple but clean; full kitchens allow you to make your own meals to save money. **Cons:** proximity of cabins means not much privacy; cabins have little atmosphere and no fireplaces. ⊠ *10 Moose Rd., off Teton Park Rd. at Moose Junction, Moose* ☎ *307/733–2522* ⊕ *www.dornans. com* ⌁ *8 1-bedroom cabins, 4 2-bedroom cabins* ☊ *In-room: no a/c, kitchen, no TV. In-hotel: 2 restaurants, bar* ▭ *AE, D, MC, V.*

$$$$ ⌂ **Jackson Lake Lodge.** This large, full-service resort stands on a bluff with spectacular views across Jackson Lake to the Tetons. (And we do mean full service: there's everything from live music in the bar to in-house religious services.) The upper lobby has 60-foot picture windows and a collection of American Indian artifacts and western art. Many guest rooms have spectacular lake and mountain views, while others have little or no view, so ask when you book. A top-down renovation in late 2008 freshened up rooms with refurbished oak furniture, new upholstery, and some cool photos from the lodge's early days. **Pros:** central location for visiting both Grand Teton and Yellowstone; heated outdoor pool; on-site medical clinic. **Cons:** rooms without views are pricey for what you get; the hotel hosts a lot of large meetings. ⊠ *U.S. 89/191/287, ½ mi north of Jackson Lake Junction* ☎ *307/543–3100 or 800/628–9988* ⊕ *www.gtlc.com* ⌁ *385 rooms* ⌂ *In-room: no a/c, refrigerator (some), no TV. In-hotel: 2 restaurants, bar, pool, some pets allowed, Wi-Fi* ▭ *AE, MC, V* ☉ *Closed early Oct.–mid-May.*

$$$$ ⌂ **Jenny Lake Lodge.** This lodge (the most expensive in any U.S. national park) has been serving tourists, sportspeople, and travelers since the 1920s. Nestled off the scenic one-way Jenny Lake Loop Road, bordering a wildflower meadow, its guest cabins are well spaced in lodgepole-pine groves. Cabin interiors, with sturdy pine beds and handmade quilts and electric blankets, live up to the elegant rustic theme, and cabin suites have fireplaces. Bathroom renovations in 2008 added new stonework and rain-dome showerheads. Breakfast, bicycle use, horseback riding, and dinner are always included the price. Room telephones are provided only on request. **Pros:** maximum comfort in a pristine setting; perhaps the best hotel in the national park system. **Cons:** very expensive; not suitable for families with kids under 17; pretty formal for a national-park property. ⊠ *Jenny Lake Rd., 2 mi off Teton Park Rd., 12 mi north of Moose Junction* ☎ *307/733–4647 or 800/628–9988* ⊕ *www.gtlc.com* ⌁ *37 cabins* ⌂ *In-room: no a/c, no TV. In-hotel: restaurant, bicycles, Wi-Fi* ▭ *AE, MC, V* ☉ *Closed early Oct.–late May* ⦶ *MAP.*

$–$$$ ⌂ **Moulton Ranch Cabins.** Along Mormon Row, these cabins stand a few
Fodor'sChoice dozen yards south of the famous Moulton Barn, which you see on bro-
★ chures, jigsaw puzzles, and photographs of the park. The land was once part of the T. A. Moulton homestead, and the cabins are still owned by the Moulton family. The quiet property has views of the Teton and the Gros Ventre ranges, and the owners can regale you with stories about early homesteaders. There's a dance hall in the barn, making this an ideal place for family and small group reunions. Smoking is not permitted on the premises. There's no Sunday check-in. **Pros:** quiet and secluded; as picturesque as any lodging in the park. **Cons:** fairly basic accommodations; little nightlife nearby. ⊠ *Off Antelope Flats Rd., off U.S. 26/89/191, 2 mi north of Moose Junction* ☎ *307/733–3749 or 208/529–2354* ⊕ *www.moultonranchcabins.com* ⌁ *5 cabins* ⌂ *In-room: no a/c, kitchen (some), no TV* ▭ *MC, V* ☉ *Closed Oct.–May.*

$$–$$$ ⌂ **Signal Mountain Lodge.** These relaxed, pine-shaded cabins sit on Jackson Lake's southern shoreline. The main building has a cozy lounge and a grand pine deck overlooking the lake. Some cabins are equipped with sleek kitchens and pine tables. The smaller log cabins are in shaded areas,

19

and eight of them have a fireplace. Rooms 151–178 have lake views, and there are a handful of suite and bungalow options as well. **Pros:** restaurants and bar are popular hot spots; on-site gas station; general store sells ice. **Cons:** rooms are pretty motel-basic; fireplaces are gas. ⊠ *Teton Park Rd., 3 mi south of Jackson Lake Junction* ☏ *307/543–2831* ⊕ *www. signalmountainlodge.com* ↰ *47 rooms, 32 cabins* ⌂ *In-room: no a/c, kitchen (some), refrigerator (some), no TV. In-hotel: 2 restaurants, bar, Wi-Fi* ⊟ *AE, D, MC, V* ⊙ *Closed mid-Oct.–mid-May.*

CAMPING

$$

★

🔺 **Colter Bay Campground.** Busy, noisy, and filled by noon, this campground has both tent and trailer or RV sites—and one great advantage: it's centrally located. Try to get a site as far from the nearby cabin road as possible. This campground also has hot showers at the nearby Colter Bay launderette. The maximum stay is 14 days. Reservations are not accepted. **Pros:** most amenities of any campground in the park; lake access; flush toilets. **Cons:** very crowded in peak season; fills up early. ⊠ *2 mi off U.S. 89/191/287, 5 mi north of Jackson Lake Junction, Colter Bay* ☏ *307/543–3100 or 800/628–9988* ⊕ *www.gtlc.com* 🔺 *350 tent/RV sites* ⌂ *Flush toilets, dump station, drinking water, guest laundry, showers, bear boxes, fire grates, picnic tables* ⊟ *AE, MC, V* ⊙ *Late May–late Sept.*

$$$–$$$$

🔺 **Colter Bay Tent Village and RV Park.** Adjacent to the Colter Bay campground, this slightly more developed area is the only RV park in Grand Teton Park. You'll find showers nearby, too. **Pros:** water, sewer, and electric hookups available; five-minute walk to Jackson Lake. **Cons:** no open fires in RV park; no bedding provided in tent village. ⊠ *2 mi off U.S. 89/191/287, 5 mi north of Jackson Lake Junction, Colter Bay* ☏ *307/543–3100 or 800/628–9988* ⊕ *www.gtlc.com* 🔺 *66 tent cabins, 112 RV sites* ⌂ *Flush toilets, full hookups, drinking water, guest laundry, showers, bear boxes, fire grates, picnic tables* ⊟ *AE, MC, V* ⊙ *June–Sept.*

$$

🔺 **Gros Ventre.** The park's biggest campground is set in an open, grassy area on the bank of the Gros Ventre River, away from the mountains and 2 mi southwest of Kelly, WY. Try to get a site close to the river. The campground usually doesn't fill until nightfall, if at all. There's a maximum stay of 14 days. Reservations are not accepted. **Pros:** low traffic on Gros Ventre Rd.; many wooded sites; often doesn't fill. **Cons:** crowded in peak season; no showers; nearest general store in Kelly. ⊠ *4½ mi off U.S. 26/89/191, 2½ mi west of Kelly on Gros Ventre Rd., 6 mi south of Moose Junction* ☏ *307/543–3100 or 800/628–9988* 🔺 *350 tent/RV sites, 5 group sites* ⌂ *Flush toilets, dump station, drinking water, bear boxes, fire grates, picnic tables* ⊟ *AE, MC, V* ⊙ *May–mid-Oct.*

¢–$$

★

🔺 **Jenny Lake.** Wooded sites and Teton views make this the most desirable campground in the park, and it fills early. The small, quiet facility allows tents only, and there's a maximum of one vehicle (no longer than 14 feet) per campsite. Reservations are not accepted. **Pros:** no loud RVs; stunning views; central location. **Cons:** no showers. ⊠ *Jenny Lake, ½ mi off Teton Park Rd., 8 mi north of Moose Junction, Jenny Lake* ☏ *307/543–3100 or 800/628–9988* 🔺 *49 tent sites (10 walk-in)* ⌂ *Flush toilets, drinking water, bear boxes, fire grates, picnic tables* ⊟ *No credit cards* ⊙ *Mid-May–late Sept.*

¢–$$

🔺 **Lizard Creek.** Views of Jackson Lake, wooded sites, and the relative isolation of this campground make it a relaxing choice. No vehicles over

30 feet are allowed, and there's a 14-day limit. Reservations are not accepted. **Pros:** no crowds; well-spaced sites. **Cons:** no staffed amenities; low lake levels sometimes lead to mudflat views. ☒ *U.S. 89/191/287, 13 mi north of Jackson Lake Junction* ☎ *307/543–2831 or 800/672–6012* ⚠ *61 tent/RV sites* � *Flush toilets, drinking water, bear boxes, fire grates, picnic tables* ▭ *No credit cards* ☉ *Early June–late Aug.*

$$ ⚠ **Signal Mountain.** This campground in a hilly setting on Jackson Lake has boat access to the lake. Many campsites offer spectacular views of the Tetons across the lake. No vehicles or trailers over 30 feet are allowed, and there's a maximum stay of 14 days. Reservations are not accepted. **Pros:** nightly ranger programs at the amphitheater; walking distance to Signal Mountain Lodge amenities. **Cons:** high noise level in peak season; many sites close to road. ☒ *Teton Park Rd., 3 mi south of Jackson Lake Junction* ☎ *307/543–2831 or 800/672–6012* ⚠ *81 tent/RV sites* ⚑ *Flush toilets, dump station, drinking water, fire grates, picnic tables* ▭ *AE, D, MC, V* ☉ *Early May–mid-Oct.*

OUTSIDE THE PARK

$$-$$$$ ⊞ **Alpenhof Lodge.** This small Austrian-style hotel is in the heart of Jackson Hole Mountain Resort, next to the tram. Hand-carved Bavarian furniture fills the rooms. All the deluxe rooms have balconies, and some have fireplaces and bathtub jets. Standard rooms are smaller and don't have balconies. Entrées such as wild game loaf, Wiener schnitzel, and fondue are served in the dining room, and a relatively quiet bistro/nightclub offers casual dining. **Pros:** quaint, Old World feel; cozy surroundings; spa treatments available. **Cons:** some rooms are more small than cozy, especially for the price. ☒ *Teton Village, adjacent to aerial tram* ☎ *307/733–3242 or 800/732–3244* ⊕ *www.alpenhoflodge.com* ⌕ *42 rooms* ⚑ *In-room: a/c, refrigerator (some), Wi-Fi. In-hotel: 2 restaurants, bar, pool, spa, laundry facilities, some pets allowed* ▭ *AE, D, DC, MC, V* ☉ *Closed mid-Oct–Dec. 1 and early Apr.–May 1* ⁑*BP.*

$$$$ ⊞ **Amangani.** This exclusive resort built of sandstone and redwood melds
★ into the landscape of Gros Ventre Butte, affording beautiful views of Spring Creek Valley from its cliff-top location. The warm hospitality is Western, but the setting is that of Eastern (as in Asian) simplicity, with tall ceilings, clean lines, and rooms with platform beds, large soaking tubs, and plenty of space. The amenities here are the best in Jackson Hole and include horseback riding, tennis, and nearby cross-country skiing and sleigh rides in winter. **Pros:** extremely luxurious; impeccable service; excellent views of the Tetons. **Cons:** very expensive; too detached from the mundane world below (even by Jackson standards); decor seems a bit too exotic for western Wyoming. ☒ *1535 N.E. Butte Rd., Jackson* ☎ *307/734–7333 or 877/734–7333* ⊕ *www.amangani.com* ⌕ *40 suites* ⚑ *In-room: safe, refrigerator, DVD, Wi-Fi. In-hotel: restaurant, room service, bar, tennis courts, pool, spa, laundry service* ▭ *AE, D, DC, MC, V.*

$$-$$$ ⊞ **Antler Inn.** As real estate agents say, location, location, location, and perhaps no motel in Jackson has a better location than the Antler, one block south of Town Square. Some rooms have fireplaces, two have Jacuzzis, but otherwise they're standard motel rooms (indeed, the neon sign advertises it as the Antler Motel). In winter there's a complimentary ski shuttle. **Pros:** restaurants nearby; family-run operation with

19

owner on premises; good prices in the off-season. **Cons:** frequently booked in summer; can get rowdy during "Hill Climb," a snowmobile festival in March at nearby Snow King. ✉ *43 W. Pearl St., Jackson* ☎ *307/733–2535 or 800/483–8667* ⊕ *www.townsquareinns.com/ antler-inn* ↵ *110 rooms* ♿ *In-room: Wi-Fi. In-hotel: some pets allowed* ▭ *AE, D, DC, MC, V.*

$$$$ ▦ **Hotel Terra.** Other properties talk the eco-talk, but Hotel Terra takes green hospitality to the next level. From café seat backs made of recycled seat belts to custom-made, non-chemical mattresses, and from bottle-free water stations to the building's abundance of natural light, there's a true conservation mindset at the heart of this hotel. It's also luxe to the core, with a hip, urban feel and all the amenities the price tag suggests. Il Villaggio Osteria ($$$–$$$$), the on-site restaurant, is a sexy space with a top-notch wine list. **Pros:** greenest hotel ever; expert staff; organic spa. **Cons:** not for budget-conscious; located in a crowded corner of Teton Village. ✉ *Teton Village, just west of Mangy Moose* ☎ *307/379–4000 or 800/631–6281* ⊕ *www.hotelterrajacksonhole.com* ↵ *132 rooms* ♿ *In-room: kitchen (some), refrigerator, Wi-Fi. In-hotel: 2 restaurants, room service, bar, pool, spa* ▭ *AE, D, MC, V.*

$$$$ ▦ **Parkway Inn.** From the moment you enter its ground floor "salon,"
★ a vintage ambience soothes the soul in period furniture and black-and-white photographs, showing the rise of east Jackson. Each room has a distinctive look—with oak or wicker furniture—and each is filled with antiques from the 19th century onward. The overall effect is homey and delightful, especially if you plan to stay a few days or longer. Continental breakfast is served in an antique-filled lounge. This quiet property is just three blocks from the Town Square. **Pros:** walking distance to many restaurants; quiet; boutique atmosphere. **Cons:** not a full-service hotel; no on-the-premises restaurant. ✉ *125 N. Jackson St., Jackson Hole* ☎ *307/733–3143 or 800/247–8390* ⊕ *www.parkwayinn.com* ↵ *33 rooms, 12 suites* ♿ *In-hotel: pool, gym, Internet terminal, Wi-Fi* ▭ *AE, D, MC, V* ◑ *CP.*

$$$–$$$$ ▦ **R Lazy S Ranch.** Jackson Hole, with the spectacle of the Tetons in
☺ the background, is true dude-ranch country, and the R Lazy S is one of the largest dude ranches in the area. Horseback riding and instruction are the main attraction, with a secondary emphasis on fishing in private waters on the ranch. Kids activities counselors keep youngsters busy through late August—after that it's adults-only. Guests stay in log-cabin guest cottages and gather for meals in the large main lodge. **Pros:** authentic dude ranch experience, very popular with older kids and preteens, absolutely beautiful setting. **Cons:** few modern trappings, not for the high-maintenance traveler. ✉ *1 mi north of Teton Village on the outskirts of Grand Teton National Park, Grand Teton* ☎ *307/733–2655* ⊕ *www.rlazys.com* ↵ *14 cabins* ♿ *In-room: no a/c, no TV. In-hotel: Wi-Fi, no kids under 7* ▭ No *credit cards* ☉ *Closed Oct.–mid-June* ◑ *FAP* ✄ *1-week minimum.*

$$$$ ▦ **Teton Tree House.** On a steep hillside and surrounded by trees, this is a real retreat. Ninety-five steps lead to this cozy lodgepole-pine B and B tucked away in the forest. Decks abound, rooms are full of wood furniture and warm southwestern colors, and an inviting common area has a two-story old-fashioned adobe fireplace. **Pros:** scenic locale; good breakfast; knowledgeable hosts. **Cons:** not open in winter; must drive to town; small climb up to the B and B. ☒ *6175 Heck of a Hill Rd., Wilson* ☎ *307/733–3233* ⮑ *6 rooms* ⏷ *In-room: no a/c, no TV, Wi-Fi. In-hotel: no kids under 5* ▤ *D, MC, V* ⦿❘ *BP* ☉ *Closed Oct.–Apr.*

$$$$ ⊡ **Trapper Inn & Suites.** This motel is within walking distance of Town Square and has some of the best-appointed rooms in Jackson for people with disabilities. It's also undergone a major renovation geared toward turning it into an executive-stay hotel. Downstairs, you'll find an open reception desk with friendly and helpful staff, free coffee, plenty of tall windows, ample sitting space, free Wi-Fi, a stone fireplace, and vintage trapper gear big enough to snare a grizzly. **Pros:** walking distance to town; small pool and Jacuzzi. **Cons:** limited views; must drive to mountains. ☒ *285 N. Cache St., Jackson* ☎ *307/733–2648 or 888/771–2648* ⊕ *www.trapperinn.com* ⮑ *89 rooms, 53 suites* ⏷ *In-room: kitchen (some), refrigerator, Wi-Fi. In-hotel: pool, laundry facilities, Internet terminal* ▤ *AE, MC, V* ⦿❘ *BP.*

$$$$ ⊡ **The Wildflower Inn.** This log country inn built in 1989 is cozy, clean, comfortable, and serves gourmet breakfasts. Just down the road from Jackson Hole Mountain Resort and Teton Village, the inn is surrounded by three acres of aspen and pine trees frequented by moose, deer, and other native wildlife. Each room has a private deck and bathroom, handcrafted log bed piled high with comforters, and its own alpine theme. There's also a plant-filled solarium, hot tub, and a sunlit dining room. **Pros:** excellent views; frequent wildlife sightings just outside; plenty of loaner gear available. **Cons:** books far in advance; 12 mi from Jackson itself. ☒ *3725 Moose-Wilson Rd., Jackson* ☎ *307/733–4710* ⊕ *www.jacksonholewildflower.com* ⮑ *5 rooms* ⏷ *In-room: refrigerator (some), Wi-Fi. In-hotel: bicycles* ▤ *MC, V* ⦿❘ *BP.*

$$$$ ⊡ **The Wort Hotel.** This brick Victorian hotel near the Town Square, built in
Fodor's Choice   1941, seems to have been around as long as the Tetons, but it feels fresh
★   inside (there's even property-wide Wi-Fi). A fireplace warms the lobby, and a sitting area is just up the stairs. Locally made western-style furnishings include lodgepole-pine beds and pine dressers; carpets, drapes, and bed coverings are warm, muted blues and mauves. You can sip a drink in the Silver Dollar Bar & Grill ($$$)—aptly named for the 2,032 silver dollars embedded on top of the bar—or amble through swinging doors into the restaurant for a fine meal. **Pros:** charming old building with lots of history; convenient location in town; some good-value packages offered. **Cons:** limited views; must drive to parks and mountains. ☒ *50 N. Glenwood St., Jackson* ☎ *307/733–2190 or 800/322–2727* ⊕ *www.worthotel. com* ⮑ *59 rooms, 5 suites* ⏷ *In-room: refrigerator (some), Wi-Fi. In-hotel: restaurant, room service, bar, gym* ▤ *AE, D, MC, V* ⦿❘ *BP.*

19

CAMPING   ⛰ **Curtis Canyon.** Numerous trees surround this simple campground
$ northeast of Jackson Hole. Part of Bridger-Teton National Forest, the campground is near a popular mountain-biking area and sits at an elevation of 6,600 feet. Reservations are not accepted. Be sure to keep your camp clean and free of food and other bear attractants. Trailers longer than 30 feet are not allowed; there's a 10-day stay limit. **Pros:** ideal for budget-conscious campers; isolated and quiet. **Cons:** no

staffed amenities; rough road for cars without four-wheel drive; not suitable for large RVs. ⊠ *Bridger-Teton National Forest, Jackson from Elk Refuge Headquarters in Jackson, take Flat Creek Rd. northeast 7 mi* ☎ *307/739–5400 or 307/543–2386* ⊕ *www.fs.fed.us/r4/btnf* ⚠ *11 tent/RV sites* ⚐ *Pit toilets, drinking water, fire pits, picnic tables* ⊟ *No credit cards* ☉ *June–Sept.*

$ ⚠ **Granite Creek.** Part of Bridger-Teton National Forest, this wooded, 52-site campground is a sprawling place convenient to hiking and mountain-biking trails. An added bonus is the thermally heated pool of Granite Hot Springs ($6/person). The elevation is 7,100 feet and there are wheelchair-accessible sites. Sites are first-come, first served. **Pros:** hot springs just up the road; rarely fills up; abundant wildlife. **Cons:** no staffed amenities; rough road for cars without four-wheel drive; not suitable for large RVs. ⊠ *Bridger-Teton National Forest, Granite Creek Rd. off U.S. 189/191, 35 mi southeast of Jackson* ☎ *307/739–5400 or 307/543–2386* ⊕ *www.fs.fed.us/btnf* ⚠ *52 tent/RV sites* ⚐ *Flush toilets, pit toilets, drinking water, fire pits, picnic tables* ⊟ *No credit cards* ☉ *Late May–Sept.*

Great Basin
National Park

WORD OF MOUTH

"An interesting cave is Lehman Caves in Great Basin National Park (Nevada). Not too many visitors there. . . . I love that park. It's vertical! You can camp at a variety of elevations."

—elnap29

WELCOME TO GREAT BASIN

TOP REASONS TO GO

★ **Ancient tree spottings:** The bristlecone pines in Great Basin are thousands of years old.

★ **Being away from it all:** Among the least visited of America's national parks, Great Basin doesn't know the meaning of the word "crowds."

★ **Wallet stays in the pocket:** There is no fee required to enter the park.

★ **Gather your pine nuts while you may:** Come in the fall and go a little nutty, as you can gather up to three gunnysacks of pinyon pine nuts, found in abundance throughout the park and tasting oh so yummy— they're great on salads.

1 Lehman Caves. Highlighted by the limestone cavern, this area is in some ways the heart of Great Basin. It includes a popular visitor center and two of the main campgrounds (both accessible for RVers). Nearby is the start of the Wheeler Peak Scenic Drive.

2 Wheeler Peak. Rarely is a crown jewel truly so—but just look at this 13,063-footer when it's capped with snow. Hikers can climb the mountain via day-use-only trails, which also lead to three small alpine lakes, a glacier, and some ancient bristlecone pines.

3 Granite Basin. This is the less-crowded part of an already sparsely visited park. Trails follow a handful of creeks around Pyramid Peak, and six primitive campgrounds line Snake Creek. A bristlecone pine grove is nearby, though far off any beaten path.

4 Arch Canyon. A high-clearance vehicle is nice to have, and stout boots are mandatory to get to Lexington Arch, which is unusual in that it is formed of limestone, not sandstone as most arches are. This is a day-use-only area.

GETTING ORIENTED

One of the smallest and least crowded national parks in the country (77,180 acres), Great Basin National Park, in eastern Nevada, occupies only a minute fraction of the almost 200,000 square mi of the Great Basin desert—yet it exemplifies the landscape and ecology of the region. This high desert (4,500–6,200 feet in elevation), the largest desert in the United States, is bordered by the Sierra Nevada Range, the Rocky Mountains, the Columbia Plateau, and the Mojave and Sonoran deserts. It covers 75% of the state of Nevada and extends into California, Utah, and Idaho.

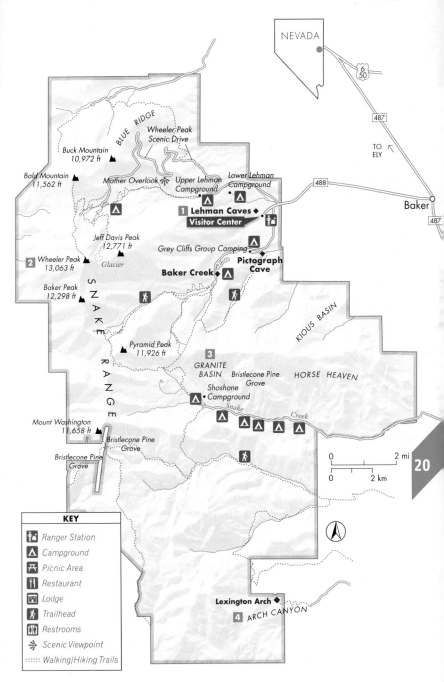

NEVADA

TO
ELY

Baker

Buck Mountain
10,972 ft

BLUE RIDGE

Wheeler Peak
Scenic Drive

Bald Mountain
11,562 ft

Mather Overlook

Upper Lehman
Campground

Lower Lehman
Campground

1 **Lehman Caves**
Visitor Center

Jeff Davis Peak
12,771 ft

Grey Cliffs Group Camping

2 Wheeler Peak
13,063 ft

Glacier

Pictograph
Cave

Baker Peak
12,298 ft

Baker Creek

SNAKE RANGE

KIOUS BASIN

Pyramid Peak
11,926 ft

3

GRANITE
BASIN

Bristlecone Pine
Grove

HORSE HEAVEN

Shoshone
Campground

Snake   Creek

Mount Washington
11,658 ft

Bristlecone Pine
Grove

Bristlecone Pine
Grove

20

0   2 mi

0   2 km

KEY

🚻	Ranger Station
▲	Campground
🌳	Picnic Area
🍴	Restaurant
🏨	Lodge
🥾	Trailhead
🚻	Restrooms
✳	Scenic Viewpoint
∷∷∷	Walking/Hiking Trails

Lexington Arch

4 ARCH CANYON

GREAT BASIN PLANNER

When to Go

As one of the least visited national parks in the country, attracting fewer than 100,000 people each year, **Great Basin National Park is never crowded.** Few visitors ensure that most any time is a fine time to visit this park, though of course much of that number will pass through the entry gates during the warmer months. In summer the high desert weather here is typically mild, so you'll be comfortable in shorts and T-shirts during the day—though temperatures drop at night, so bring light jackets and pants.

A winter visit can be sublime in its solitude, but the hardy visitor must be prepared for the elements, especially if the back-country is a destination. With temperatures hovering in the low teens, heavy coats, jeans, and sweaters are recommended. Some roads might be impassable in inclement weather; check ahead with a park ranger.

AVG. HIGH/LOW TEMPS.

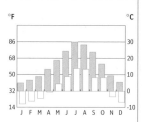

Flora and Fauna

Despite the cold, dry conditions in Great Basin, 411 plant species thrive; 13 are considered sensitive species. The region gets less than 10 inches of rain a year, so plants have developed some ingenious methods of dealing with the desert's harshness. For instance, many flowering plants will only grow and produce seeds in a year when there is enough water. Spruces, pines, and junipers have set down roots here and the bristlecone pine has been doing so for thousands of years.

The park's plants provide a variety of habitats for animals and for more than 230 bird species. In the sagebrush are jackrabbits, ground squirrels, chipmunks, and pronghorns. Mule deer and striped skunks abound in the pygmy forest of pinyon pine and juniper trees. Shrews, ringtail cats, and weasels make their homes around the springs and streams. Mountain lions, bobcats, and sheep live on the rugged slopes and in valleys. The park is also home to coyotes, kit fox, and badgers. Treat the Great Basin rattlesnake with respect. Bites are uncommon and rarely fatal, but if you're bitten, remain calm and contact a ranger immediately.

Getting Here and Around

The entrance to Great Basin is on Route 488, 5 mi west of its junction with Route 487. From Ely, take U.S. 6/50 to Route 487. From Salt Lake City or Cedar City, UT, take I–15 South to 6/50 West; from Las Vegas, drive north on I–15 and then north on Route 93 to access U.S. 6/50. The nearest airports are in Cedar City (120 mi), Salt Lake City (240 mi), and Las Vegas (287 mi).

In the park, Baker Creek Road and portions of Wheeler Peak Scenic Drive, above Upper Lehman Creek, are closed from November to June. The road to the visitor center and the roads to the developed campgrounds are paved, but the going is tough in winter and two-wheel-drive cars don't do well. RVs and trailers aren't allowed above Lower Lehman Creek. With an 8% grade, the road to Wheeler Peak is steep and curvy, but not dangerous if you take it slow. Motorcyclists should watch for gravel on the road's surface.

By John
Blodgett

Here, just off the Loneliest Road in America, small mountain ranges parade across farmland on the north, and a huge desert stretches south to central Utah. There are a few rivers, but in this arid land their waters evaporate in the dry air or fade into the soil quickly, adding to the sense of isolation that many visitors seek in this off-the-beaten-path park. Surface water in the Great Basin has no outlet to the sea, so it pools in more than 200 small basins throughout the steep mountain ranges. Along with these alpine lakes, the dramatic mountains shelter lush meadows, limestone caves, and ancient bristlecone pines. Within the park is the southernmost permanent glacier on the continent.

PARK ESSENTIALS

20

ACCESSIBILITY

Designated handicap parking spaces are available at both visitor centers. The center itself is all on one level, fully accessible to those with impaired mobility. The park slide show is captioned. At the front desk you can borrow wheelchairs to use in the center and in the first room of Lehman Caves. A cut curb provides access to a table and fire grate at the picnic area near the visitor center, which also has accessible restrooms. Baker Creek Campground, Upper Lehman Creek Campground, and Wheeler Peak Campground are accessible, though the restroom access ramp at Upper Lehman Creek Campground is steep.

ADMISSION FEES AND PERMITS

Admission to the park is free, but if you want to tour Lehman Caves there's a fee ($4–$10, depending on age and tour length). To fish in Great Basin National Park, those 12 and older need a Nevada state fishing license (contact the Nevada Department of Wildlife:

GREAT BASIN IN ONE DAY

Start your visit with a tour of the fascinating limestone caverns of **Lehman Caves**, the park's most famous attraction. If you have time before or after the tour, hike the short and family friendly **Mountain View Nature Trail**, near the Lehman Caves Visitor Center, to get your first taste of the area's pinyon-juniper forests. Stop for lunch at the Lehman Caves Cafe or have a picnic near the visitor center.

In the afternoon, take a leisurely drive up to **Wheeler Peak**, the park's tallest mountain at just over 13,000 feet. You can stop about halfway along your drive to hike the short **Osceola Ditch Trail**, a remnant of the park's gold-mining day, or, alternatively, just enjoy the fantastic views from the two overlooks. If you're feeling energetic when you reach Wheeler Peak, hike some of the trails there.

⊕ *www.ndow.org*). The resident license costs $13 for kids 12–15 and $29 for those 16 and older; the one-day nonresident license is $9, plus $3 for each additional day at time of purchase. Backcountry hikers do not need permits, but for your own safety you should fill out a form at the visitor center before setting out.

ADMISSION HOURS
The park is open 24/7 year-round, and it's in the Pacific time zone.

ATMS/BANKS
There are no ATMs in the park. The nearest ATM is in Baker, and the nearest banks are in Ely.

CELL-PHONE RECEPTION
The only public phone in the park is at the visitor center. There is no reliable cell-phone reception.

PARK CONTACT INFORMATION
Great Basin National Park ✉ *Rte. 488, Baker, NV* ☎ *775/234–7331* ⊕ *www. nps.gov/grba.*

SCENIC DRIVES

Baker Creek Road. Though less popular than the Wheeler Peak Scenic Drive, this well-maintained gravel road affords gorgeous views of Wheeler Peak, the Baker Creek Drainage, and Snake Valley. The road is closed in the winter, and there are no pull-outs or scenic overlooks.

Wheeler Peak Scenic Drive. Less than a mile from the visitor center off Route 488, turn onto this paved road that winds its way up to elevations of 10,000 feet. The road takes you through pygmy forest in lower elevations; as you climb, the air cools. Along the way, two overlooks offer awe-inspiring views of the Snake Range mountains, and a short hiking trail leads to views of an old mining site. Turn off at Mather Overlook, elevation 9,000 feet, for the best photo ops. Allow 1½ hours for the 24-mi round-trip, not including hikes.

Lehman Caves: it's amazing what a little water and air can do to a room.

WHAT TO SEE

HISTORIC SITES

★ **Lehman Caves.** In 1885, rancher and miner Absalom Lehman discovered the underground wonder that's now named after him. Although the name suggests that there's more than one cave here, Lehman is a single limestone and marble cavern ¼ mi long. Inside, stalactites, stalagmites, helictites, flowstone, popcorn, and other bizarre mineral formations cover almost every surface. Lehman Caves is one of the best places to see rare shield formations, created when calcite-rich water is forced from tiny cracks in a cave wall, ceiling, or floor. Year-round the cave maintains a constant, damp temperature of 50°F, so wear a light jacket and nonskid shoes when you take the tour. Guided tours conducted by the park service run 60–90 minutes; the full 90-minute tour route is just over ½ mi round-trip. Children under age 5 are not allowed on the 90-minute tours; those under 16 must be accompanied by an adult. Tours run four times a day. Next to the cave visitor center, peek into **Rhodes Cabin**, where black-and-white photographs of the park's earlier days line the walls. ✉ *Lehman Caves Visitor Center* ☎ *775/234–7331* 🎫 *$4–$10* 🕐 *Daily 8–4:30.*

VISITOR CENTERS

Great Basin Visitor Center. Here you can see exhibits on the flora, fauna, and geology of the park, or ask a ranger to suggest a favorite hike. Books, videos, and souvenirs are for sale; a coffee shop is attached. ✉ *Rte. 487, just north of Baker* ☎ *775/234–7331* 🕐 *Oct.–mid-May, daily 8–4:30; mid-May–Sept., daily 8–5:30.*

Lehman Caves Visitor Center. Regularly scheduled tours, for durations of 60 and 90 minutes, depart from here. Exhibits highlight the gnarled and ancient bristlecone pine and other park flora, plus cave formations. Buy gifts for friends and family back home at the bookstore. ⊠ *Rte. 488, ½ mi inside park boundary* ☎ *775/234–7331* 🖃 *$8–$10* ⊗ *Daily 8–4:30.*

SPORTS AND THE OUTDOORS

Great Basin National Park is a great place for experienced outdoor enthusiasts. There are no outfitters to guide you, and there are no nearby shops that rent or sell sporting equipment, so bring everything you might need and be prepared to go it alone. Permits are not required to go off the beaten path, but such adventurers are encouraged to register with a ranger just in case. The effort is worth it, for the backcountry is wide open and not at all crowded no matter the time of year (just keep an eye on the weather). As is the case in all national parks, bicycling is restricted to existing roads, but as the park sees fewer visitors than other national parks, road cyclists will find few cars to trouble them.

BIRD-WATCHING

Great Basin National Park might not be crowded with people, but it sports an impressive list of bird species that have been sighted—238, according to the National Park Service checklist. Some species, such as the common raven and American robin, can be seen at most locations. Others, such as the red-naped sapsucker, are more commonly seen near Lehman Creek.

CROSS-COUNTRY SKIING

Lehman Creek Trail is the most popular cross-country skiing trail in the park. It's marked with orange flags, making it easy to find. You may need snowshoes to reach the skiable upper section.

HIKING

You'll witness beautiful views by driving along the Wheeler Peak Scenic Drive and other park roads, but hiking allows an in-depth experience that just can't be matched. Trails at Great Basin run the gamut from relaxing ¼-mi trails to multiday backpacking specials, so everyone can find a path that matches personal ability, fitness level, and desired destination, be it mountain peak, flowered meadow, or evergreen forest. When you pick up a trail map at the visitor center, ask about weather and trail conditions (many are unpaved, and some are maintained less than others) and bring appropriate clothing when you set out from any trailhead. No matter the trail length, always carry water, and remember that the trails are at high elevations, so pace yourself accordingly. Do not enter abandoned mineshafts or tunnels, for they are unstable and potentially dangerous. Those who head out for the backcountry need not obtain a permit, but are encouraged to register at either of the two visitor centers. Though Great Basin is a high desert, winters can be harsh, so always inquire about the weather ahead of time at the visitor center.

EASY

☾ **Mountain View Nature Trail.** Just past the Rhodes Cabin on the right side of the visitor center, this short and easy trail (0.3 mi) through pinyon pine and juniper trees is marked with signs describing the plants. The path passes the original entrance to Lehman Caves and loops back to the visitor center. It's a great way to spend a half hour or so while you wait for your cave tour to start. ⊠ *Trailhead at Lehman Caves Visitor Center.*

Osceola Ditch Trail. In 1890, at a cost of $108,223, the Osceola Gravel Mining Company constructed an 18-mi-long trench. The ditch was part of an attempt to glean gold from the South Snake Range, but water shortages and the company's failure to find much gold forced the mining operation to shut down in 1905. You can reach portions of the eastern section of the ditch on foot via the Osceola Ditch Trail, which passes through pine and fir trees. Allow 30 minutes for this easy 0.3-mi round-trip hike. ⊠ *Access from Wheeler Peak Scenic Dr.*

GOOD READS

■ *Hiking Great Basin National Park,* by Bruce Grubbs, will get your Great Basin trip off on the right foot.

■ *Trails to Explore in Great Basin National Park,* by Rose Houk, is all about hiking in the park.

■ *Geology of the Great Basin,* by Bill Fiero, or *Basin and Range,* by John McPhee, presents a geological tour of the Great Basin.

MODERATE

Fodor's Choice ★ **Bristlecone Pine Trail.** Though the park has several bristlecone pine groves, the only way to see the ancient trees up close is to hike this trail. From the parking area to the grove, it's a moderate 1.4-mi hike that takes about an hour each way. Rangers offer guided hikes daily in season; inquire at the visitor center.

Bristlecone Pine Trail leads to two other trails. To the right, as you head past the grove, is the **Alpine Lakes Loop Trail,** a moderate 2.7-mi trek that loops past stellar Stella and Teresa lakes and returns you to Bristlecone Pine Trail in about two hours. Bring your camera. Turn left off Bristlecone Pine Trail past the grove to connect with **Glacier Trail.** The trail skirts the southernmost permanent ice field on the continent and ends with a view of a small alpine glacier, the only one in Nevada. From there it's less than 5 mi back to the parking lot. Allow 2½ hours for the moderate hike. ⊠ *Access from Summit Trail parking area, Wheeler Peak Scenic Dr., 12 mi from Lehman Caves Visitor Center.*

20

DIFFICULT

Baker Lake Trail. This full-day 12-mi hike can easily be made into a two-day backpacking trip. You'll gain a total of 2,620 feet in elevation on the way to Baker Lake, a jewel-like alpine lake with a backdrop of mountainous cliffs. ⊠ *Access from Baker Creek Rd., going south from just east of the Lehman Caves Visitor Center.*

Wheeler Peak Summit Trail. Begin this full-day, 8.6-mi hike early in the day so as to minimize exposure to the storms that sometimes strike the mountain in the afternoon. Most of the route follows a ridge up the mountain to the summit. Elevation gain is 2,900 feet, so hikers should have good stamina. ⊠ *Wheeler Peak Scenic Dr., Summit Trail parking area.*

EDUCATIONAL OFFERINGS

Campfire programs. On summer evenings the park offers these programs at two of its campgrounds, Upper Lehman Creek and Wheeler Peak. The 40- to 60-minute programs cover a range of subjects related to the Great Basin's cultural and natural history, and resources. Dress warmly and bring a flashlight. Program times vary, so call for information. ⊠ *Wheeler Peak Scenic Dr., 4 mi (Upper Lehman Creek) and 12 mi (Wheeler Peak) from the Lehman Caves Visitor Center* ☎ *775/234–7331* 🈵 *Free* ☉ *Mid-June–Labor Day; check Lehman Caves Visitor Center for schedule.*

☾ **Junior Ranger Program.** Youngsters who complete the program will be sworn in as Junior Rangers and receive a Great Basin Bristlecone patch. ☎ *775/234–7331* ⊕ *www.nps.gov/grba.*

WHAT'S NEARBY

NEARBY TOWNS

An hour's drive west of the park, at the intersection of three U.S. highways, **Ely** (population 4,008) is the biggest town in the area. It grew up in the second wave of the early Nevada mining boom, right at the optimistic turn of the 20th century. For 70 years copper kept the town in business, but when it ran out in the early 1980s Ely declined fast. Then, in 1986, the National Park Service designated Great Basin National Park 68 mi to the east and the town got a boost. Ely has since been rebuilt and revitalized and is now home to a railroad museum, the county seat, and a great old hotel-casino (Hotel Nevada), as well as the basic tourist amenities. If you want to get closer to the park you can stay in tiny **Baker** (population roughly 50), which sits at the main park entrance. Really just a cluster of small businesses a few miles south of U.S. 6/50 on Route 487, the hamlet is 5 mi from the visitor center.

VISITOR INFORMATION

Bristlecone Convention Center ⊠ *150 6th St., Ely* ☎ *800/496–9350.* **Great Basin Business and Tourism Council** ⊠ *10 Main St., Baker* ☎ *No phone* ⊕ *www.greatbasinpark.com.* **White Pine Chamber of Commerce** ⊠ *636 Aultman St., Ely* ☎ *775/289–8877* ⊕ *www.whitepinechamber.com.*

NEARBY ATTRACTIONS

Cave Lake State Park. High in the pine and juniper forest of the big Schell Creek Range that borders Ely on the east, this is an idyllic spot. You can spend a day fishing for rainbow and brown trout in the reservoir and a night sleeping under the stars. Arrive early; it gets crowded. Access may be restricted in winter. ⊠ *15 mi southeast of Ely via U.S. 50/6/93* ☎ *775/728–4460* ⊕ *www.parks.nv.gov/cl.htm* 🈵 *$4* ☉ *Daily, 24 hrs.*

Nevada Northern Railway Museum. During the mining boom the Nevada Northern Railroad connected East Ely, Ruth, and McGill to the transcontinental rail line in the northeast corner of Nevada. The whole operation is now a museum. You can tour the depot, offices, warehouses, yard, roundhouses, and repair shops, and catch a ride on one of the trains in the summer. ⊠ *1100 Ave. A, Ely* ☎ *866/407–8326* ⊕ *www. nevadanorthernrailway.net* ⊠ *$4* ☉ *Wed.–Sat. 8–5, Sun. 8–3.*

Ward Charcoal Ovens State Historic Park. In the desert south of Ely is this row of ovens. The ovens turned pinyon, juniper, and mountain mahogany into charcoal, which was used for refining local silver and copper ore. It's worth the drive from Ely to take in this well-preserved piece of Nevada mining history. ⊠ *7 mi south of Ely on U.S. 50/6/93, and 11 mi southwest on Cave Valley Rd.* ☎ *775/728– 4460* ⊕ *www.parks.nv.gov/ww.htm* ⊠ *$4* ☉ *Daily, 24 hrs.*

SCENIC DRIVE

U.S. 93 Scenic Byway. The 68 mi between the park and Ely make a beautiful drive with diverse views of Nevada's paradoxical geography: desert vegetation and lush mountains. You'll catch an occasional glimpse of a snake, perhaps a rattler, slithering on the road's shoulder, or a lizard sunning on a rock. Watch for deer. A straight drive to Ely takes a little more than an hour; if you have the time to take a dirt-road adventure, don't miss the Ward Charcoal Ovens or a peek at Cave Lake.

WHERE TO EAT AND STAY

20

ABOUT THE RESTAURANTS

Dining in the park itself is limited to the basic lunch fare at the Lehman Caves Cafe and Gift Shop. Nearby Baker has a handful of dining and grocery options.

ABOUT THE HOTELS

There is no lodging in the park, so unless you're willing and able to snag one of the park's first-come, first-served campsites, or expect to camp in the backcountry, plan on lodging in nearby Baker or in Ely.

ABOUT THE CAMPGROUNDS

Great Basin has four developed campgrounds, all easily accessible by car, but only the Lower Lehman Creek Campground is open year-round. One campground, Grey Cliffs, is specifically for groups, and is open Memorial Day through Labor Day, or until snow closes it; contact the park for details on staying there.

Primitive campsites around Snake and Strawberry creeks are open year-round and are free; however, snow and rain can make access to the sites difficult. Permits for backcountry camping are not required, though such park users are encouraged to fill out a registration form and become familiar with backcountry weather conditions at the visitor center.

None of the campgrounds in the park accept credit cards, and none have RV hookups (but RVers can stay at Whispering Elms in nearby Baker), and reservations are not accepted. Water is only provided at the developed campgrounds in summer; if you're camping in winter, bring your own. Camping parties are limited to eight people and two vehicles per site. Though not allowed on any park trails, pets can be led on a leash in the campgrounds—just be sure that the leash is no more than six feet in length. For the safety of your pet as well as that of park wildlife, stay clear of any wild animals that might cross your path.

> **FESTIVALS AND EVENTS**
>
> **MAY–SEPTEMBER**
> **Silver State Classic Challenge.** The country's largest (and longest-held) open-road race for amateur fast-car enthusiasts shows off street-legal muscle cars that zoom up to 200 MPH. The event occurs south of Ely on Route 318, from Lund to Hiko. ☎ *702/631–6166.*
>
> **AUGUST**
> **White Pine County Fair.** Livestock, flower, and vegetable judging, plus a hay contest, carnival rides, a midway, food booths, dancing, and a buckaroo breakfast make this fair, held at the County Fairgrounds in Ely, the real thing. ☎ *775/289–8877.*

WHERE TO EAT

IN THE PARK

¢   ✕ **Lehman Caves Cafe and Gift Shop.** The menu here includes light break-
AMERICAN   fast, soup-and-sandwich lunches, hot drinks, soft drinks, and home-
☺   baked desserts. They hand-make large ice-cream sandwiches. ⊠ *Next to the visitor center* ☎ *775/234–7221* ▭ *AE, D, MC, V* ☯ *Closed Nov.– Mar. No dinner.*

PICNIC AREAS   **Lehman Caves Visitor Center Picnic Area.** This full-service picnic site, with tables, fire grills, water, and restrooms (the latter two available during the summer), is a short walk from the visitor center. Summer hours are often extended beyond the standard 8 AM–4:30 PM. ⊠ *Just north of Lehman Caves Visitor Center.*

Pole Canyon Trailhead Picnic Area. Inaccessible in the winter when Baker Creek Road is closed, this area at the mouth of a canyon has a handful of picnic tables and fire grills but no water. It does have a restroom. Access is via an unimproved road. ⊠ *East of entrance to Grey Cliffs Group Camping site, at the mouth of Pole Canyon.*

Upper Lehman Creek Campground. There are a handful of sites here where you can sit down for a bite and a breather. A group picnic site requires a reservation at least two weeks in advance, but areas near the host site and amphitheater are first-come, first-served. Water is available. ⊠ *4 mi from the Lehman Caves Visitor Center on Wheeler Peak Scenic Dr.*

OUTSIDE THE PARK

¢–$ ✕ **The Border Inn.** This part of Nevada is ranch country, so it's no surprise
AMERICAN that meat and potatoes dominate the menu at the Border Inn. You'll find
hearty fare like hamburgers, chicken-fried steak, pork chops, and, of
course, steaks. Breakfast is also served. ⊠ *U.S. 6/50, 13 mi east of Great
Basin National Park, Baker* ☎ *775/234–7300* ▭ *D, MC, V.*

¢–$$ ✕ **T and D's Country Store, Restaurant, and Lounge.** The bright and cheer-
AMERICAN ful restaurant in this large white-brick building occupies a sunroom,
where windows line the walls. Salads, hot and cold sandwiches, ribs,
and chicken are the core of the menu; you can order pizza and Ital-
ian and Mexican food as well. ⊠ *1 Main St., Baker* ☎ *775/234–7264*
▭ *D, MC, V.*

WHERE TO STAY

IN THE PARK

CAMPING ⛺ **Baker Creek Campground.** The turnoff is just past the park entrance,
$ on the left as you approach the Lehman Caves Visitor Center. **Pros:**
wheelchair access to two sites; central location. **Cons:** fills quickly in
summer; no reservations. ⊠ *2½ mi south of Rte. 488, 3 mi from the
visitor center* ☎ *No phone* ⛺ *34 sites* ☐ *Pit toilets, drinking water, fire
grates, picnic tables* ▭ *No credit cards* ☼ *May–Sept., depending on
weather conditions.*

$ ⛺ **Lower Lehman Creek Campground.** Other than Great Basin's primitive
sites, this is the only campground in the park that is open year-round.
It's the first turnoff past the Lehman Caves Visitor Center. **Pros:** open
all year; nearby the popular Lehman Caves. **Cons:** water only available
during summer; no wheelchair access; no reservations. ⊠ *2½ mi from the
visitor center on Wheeler Peak Scenic Dr.* ☎ *No phone* ⛺ *11 sites* ☐ *Pit
toilets, drinking water, fire grates, picnic tables* ▭ *No credit cards.*

$ ⛺ **Upper Lehman Creek Campground.** The entrance is about a mile past the
Lower Lehman Creek turnoff. **Pros:** wheelchair access to one site. **Cons:**
fills quickly during summer; no reservations. ⊠ *4 mi from the visitor
center on Wheeler Peak Scenic Dr.* ☎ *No phone* ⛺ *22 sites* ☐ *Pit toilets,
drinking water, fire grates, picnic tables* ▭ *No credit cards* ☼ *May–Sept.,
depending on weather conditions.*

$ ⛺ **Wheeler Peak Campground.** This scenic, cool campground is at the
Fodor's Choice end of Wheeler Peak Scenic Drive, at an elevation of 10,000 feet. RVs
★ cannot camp here because they cannot negotiate the twisting road past
Upper Lehman Creek. In fact, nothing over 24-feet long is allowed
beyond this point. The campground is closed for most of the year
because of snow. **Pros:** stunning views; close to trailhead. **Cons:** single
vehicles and trailers more than 24 feet long not allowed; limited sea-
son; no reservations. ⊠ *12 mi from the Lehman Caves Visitor Center
on Wheeler Peak Scenic Dr.* ☎ *No phone* ⛺ *37 tent sites* ☐ *Pit toilets,
drinking water, fire grates, picnic tables* ▭ *No credit cards* ☼ *June–Sept.,
depending on weather conditions.*

20

OUTSIDE THE PARK

¢ ⚏ **The Border Inn.** Located on the Utah-Nevada border, this motel has air-conditioned rooms with twin, double, and queen beds. The only gas station in the area is right here. **Pros:** 24-hour gas and grocery services; self-contained. **Cons:** far from area attractions; no Internet. ⊠ *U.S. 6/50, 13 mi east of Great Basin National Park, Baker* ☎ *775/234–7300* ⤵ *29 rooms* ⚐ *In-room: kitchen (some). In-hotel: restaurant* ⊟ *AE, D, MC, V.*

¢–$$ ⚏ **Hotel Nevada.** One of the oldest hotel buildings in the state, this land-
Fodor's Choice mark in the middle of town is nonetheless in excellent shape. Built in
★ 1908, it's a big square brick building in downtown Ely. The luxury rooms are especially nice, most named after the celebrities who have allegedly stayed within—Gary Cooper, Mickey Rooney, and others. The hotel has a casino and leathered bikers obstruct the entrance. **Pros:** coolest lodging facility in town; caters to motorcyclists; restaurant has incredible double-burgers. **Cons:** tobacco smoke permeates the entire property. ⊠ *501 Ault-man St., Ely* ☎ *775/289–6665 or 888/406–3055* ⊕ *www.hotelnevada.com* ⤵ *67 rooms* ⚐ *In-room: Wi-Fi. In-hotel: restaurant, room service, bars, Wi-Fi, some pets allowed* ⊟ *AE, D, DC, MC, V.*

¢–$ ⚏ **Silver Jack Inn.** This tiny-town motel surrounds a cozy lawn with trees
★ and a patio—a nice place to relax in the early evening. The motel also rents out three off-site efficiency units. Rooms are simple, quiet, and, most important, close to the entrance of Great Basin National Park. The Inn's funky Lectrolux Gallery Café and Movie House serves up fresh pastries, coffee, and a surprisingly varied selection of wine, beer, and spirits—not to mention breakfast, lunch, and dinner according to season. Movies are shown every Wednesday and Saturday evening. **Pros:** funky artistic decor; eclectic menu. **Cons:** Baker is too laid back for some. ⊠ *10 Main St., Baker* ☎ *775/234–7323* ⊕ *www.silverjackinn.com* ⤵ *10 rooms* ⚐ *In-room: no phone. In-hotel: some pets allowed* ⊟ *MC, V.*

CAMPING ⚠ **Whispering Elms Campground.** The largest camping facility close to
$–$$ but not inside the park is also the nearest to offer hookups for RVs. It is open year-round. **Pros:** tent sites include use of shower; laundry facilities. **Cons:** no reservations; staying in Baker is not for the easily bored. ⊠ *Rte. 487, behind Great Basin Lodge, Baker* ☎ *775/234–9900* ⚠ *45 sites* ⚐ *Flush toilets, full hookups, dump station, guest laundry, showers, picnic tables, play area* ⊟ *MC, V.*

Great Sand Dunes National Park

WORD OF MOUTH

"Great Sand Dunes is one of my favorite places to go, but the sand can get hot in summer. I haven't camped there but stayed in town at a B&B. I'd love to camp inside the park."

—colokid

WELCOME TO GREAT SAND DUNES

TOP REASONS TO GO

★ **Dune climbing:** Trek through the 30 square mi of main dunes in this landlocked dune field.

★ **Unrivaled diversity:** You can see eight completely different life zones in this park, ranging from salty wetlands and lush forests to parched sand sheet and frozen alpine peaks, all in a single day.

★ **Bounty of bison:** Take a ride around the west end of the park, where more than 2,000 bison roam in the grasslands and wetlands.

★ **Aspens in autumn:** Take a hike—or, if you've got a high-clearance four-wheel-drive vehicle and good driving skills, take the rough road—up to Medano Pass during fall foliage season when the aspens turn gold.

★ **Vigorous hikes:** Pack a picnic lunch and climb up to High Dune, followed by the more strenuous stretch over to Star Dune. Or tackle the dramatic Music Pass Trail, which takes you to the tree line and covers 3½ mi (and 2,000 feet in elevation change) each way.

1 Sand dunes. The 30-square-mi field of sand has no designated trails. The highest dune in the park—and, in fact, in North America—is 750-foot-high Star Dune.

2 Sangre de Cristo Mountains. Named the "Blood of Christ" Mountains by Spanish explorers because of their ruddy color—especially at sunrise and sunset—the range contains 10 of Colorado's 54 fourteeners (mountains higher than 14,000 feet). Six that are more than 13,000 feet tall are within the preserve itself.

3 Forest. Ponderosa pines populate the forested areas around the Sangre de Cristo Mountains in the preserve and park's eastern boundaries.

4 Grasslands. Wildlife, such as elk and bison, feed on the park's grassy areas, primarily found in the park's southern area and the Great Sand Dunes National Preserve.

5 Wetlands. Popular with a variety of birds and amphibians, these seasonal wetlands form in the area around Medano Creek, where cottonwood and willow trees also thrive.

SAN LUIS VALLEY

SAND SHEET

SABKHA

← TO MOSCA

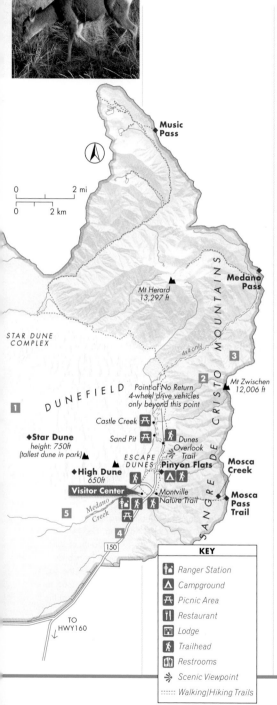

COLORADO

GETTING ORIENTED

The Great Sand Dunes Park and Preserve encompasses 150,000 acres (about 234 square mi) of land and mountains surrounding the dunes. Looking at the dunes from the west, your eye sweeps over the grassland and sand sheet, a vast expanse of smaller dunes and flatter sections of sand and knee-high brush. The Sangre de Cristo Mountains rear up in the east behind the dunes, forming a dramatic backdrop and creating a stunning juxtaposition of color and form. Depending on the time of year, you'll hear a quiet gurgle or a real rush from Medano Creek, which flows along the eastern edge of the dunes (*medano* is Spanish for "sand dune," and it's pronounced *meh*-dah-noh). Hiking trails thread these mountains—the "preserve" area—where you can walk quietly through aspens and evergreens.

GREAT SAND DUNES PLANNER

When to Go

About 300,000 visitors come to the park each year, most on summer weekends; they tend to congregate around the main parking area and Medano Creek. To avoid the crowds, hike away from the main area up to the High Dune. Or come in the winter, when the park is a place for contemplation and repose—as well as skiing and sledding.

Fall and spring are the prettiest times to visit, with the surrounding mountains still capped with snow in May, and leaves on the aspen trees turning gold in September and early October. In summer, the surface temperature of the sand can climb to 140°F in the afternoon, so climbing the dunes is best in the morning or late afternoon. Since you're at a high altitude—about 8,200 feet at the visitor center—the air temperatures in the park itself remain in the 70s most of the summer.

AVG. HIGH/LOW TEMPS.

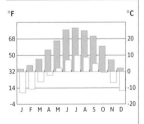

Flora and Fauna

The salty wetlands are dotted with sedges, rushes, and other plants that are tolerant of changes in water salinity and levels, while the sand sheet and grasslands have prickly pear, rabbit brush, and yucca. The dune field looks barren from afar, but up close you see various grasses have rooted in swales among the dunes. Juniper pinyon, and ponderosa pine trees grow on the lower portions of the mountain, hardy spruce and fir trees survive in the subalpine forest zone, and lichens and tiny flowers cling to the rock at the top.

Birds inhabit the wetlands; short-horned lizards, elk, and pronghorns live in the sand sheet and grassland; and Great Sand Dunes tiger beetles and Ord's kangaroo rats breed in the dune field. In the forests and on the mountainsides, raptors fly overhead, while mule deer and Rocky Mountain bighorn sheep graze.

■TIP➔ Be cautious around wild animals and never approach them. (If you're taking pictures, this is a good time to use a telephoto lens.) Campers should check with rangers about precautions to avoid bear problems.

Getting Here and Around

Great Sand Dunes National Park and Preserve is about 240 mi from both Denver and Albuquerque, and roughly 180 mi from Colorado Springs and Santa Fe. The fastest route from the north is Interstate 25 south to U.S. 160, heading west to just past Blanca, to Highway 150 north, which goes right to the park's main entrance. For a more scenic route, take U.S. 285 over Kenosha, Red Hill, and Poncha Passes, turn onto Highway 17 just south of Villa Grove, then take County Lane 6 to the park (watch for signs just south of Hooper). When traveling from the south, go north on I–25 to Santa Fe, then north on U.S. 285 to Alamosa, then U.S. 160 east to Highway 150. From the west, Highway 17 and County Lane 6 take you to the park. The park entrance station is about 3 mi from the park boundary, and it's about a mile from there to the visitor center; the main parking lot is about a mile farther.

Updated by Martha Connors

Created by winds that sweep the San Luis Valley floor, the enormous sand dunes that form the heart of Great Sand Dunes National Park and Preserve are an improbable, unforgettable sight. The dunes, as curvaceous as Rubens' nudes, stretch for more than 30 square mi. Because they're made of sand, the dunes' very existence seem tenuous, as if they might blow away before your eyes, yet they're solid enough to withstand thousands of years of Mother Nature—and the modern stress of hikers and saucer-riding thrill-seekers.

PARK ESSENTIALS

ACCESSIBILITY
The park has two wheelchairs with balloon tires (for the sand) that can be borrowed; someone must push them. You can reserve one by calling the visitor center. There is one accessible campsite.

ADMISSION FEES AND PERMITS
Entrance fees are $3 per adult above age 16 and are valid for one week from date of purchase. Children are admitted free at all times. Pick up camping permits ($14 per night per site at Pinyon Flats Campground) and backpacking permits (free) at the visitor center.

ADMISSION HOURS
The park is open 24/7. It is in the mountain time zone.

ATMS/BANKS
The park has no ATM. The nearest bank is 35 mi away in Alamosa.

CELL-PHONE RECEPTION
Cell-phone reception in the park is sporadic. Public telephones are at the visitor center, dunes parking lot, and at the Pinyon Flats campground—you need a calling card (these aren't coin-operated phones).

GREAT SAND DUNES IN ONE DAY

Arrive early in the day during the summertime so you can hike up to **High Dune** and get a view of the entire dune field. Round-trip, the walk itself should take about 1½ to 2 hours (plus time to jump off or slide down the dunes). In the afternoon, hop into the car and head to Zapata Falls, hike on the short-and-shady Montville Nature Trail, or head for the longer Mosca Pass Trail, which follows a small creek through cool aspens and evergreens to one of the lower mountain passes.

In the spring and early summer or fall, when the temperatures are cooler, first walk up to the High Dune to enjoy the view. If you're game to hike farther, head to **Star Dune** for a picnic lunch. Hike down the eastern ridge to Medano Creek, then head to the western end of the park to explore the sand sheet, grasslands, and wetlands. If you're here on a morning when there's a hayride (or four-wheel-drive) tour to see the bison, take it and then head off on your hikes.

PARK CONTACT INFORMATION
Great Sand Dunes National Park and Preserve ✉ *11999 Hwy. 150, Mosca* ☎ *719/378–6399* ⊕ *www.nps.gov/grsa.*

SCENIC DRIVE

★ **Medano Pass Primitive Road.** This 22-mi road connects Great Sand Dunes with the Wet Mountain Valley and Highway 69 on the east side of the Sangre de Cristo Mountains via a climb to Medano Pass (about 10,000 feet above sea level). It also provides access to campsites in the national preserve. It is a four-wheel-drive-only road that is best driven by someone who already has good driving skills on rough, unpaved roads. (Your four-wheel-drive vehicle must have high clearance and be engineered to go over rough roads, and you may need to drop your tires' air pressure.) The road has sections of deep, loose sand, and it crosses Medano Creek nine times. Before you go, stop at the visitor center for a map and ask about current road conditions. Drive time pavement to pavement is 2½ to 3 hours.

WHAT TO SEE

★ **Dune Field.** The more than 30 square mi of big dunes in the heart of the park is the main attraction, although the surrounding sand sheet does have some smaller dunes. You can start putting your feet in the sand three mi past the main park entrance.

High Dune. This isn't the park's highest dune, but it's high enough in the dune field to provide a view of all the dunes from its summit. It's on the first ridge of dunes you see from the main parking area.

VISITOR CENTER
Great Sand Dunes Visitor Center. View exhibits, browse in the bookstore, and watch a 20-minute film with an overview of the dunes. Rangers are on hand to answer questions. Facilities include restrooms and a vending

machine stocked with soft drinks spring, summer, and fall, but no food. (The Great Sand Dunes Oasis, just outside the park boundary, has a café that is open May through late-September.) ⊠ *Near the park entrance* ☎ *719/378–6399* ⊙ *Late May–early Sept., daily 9–6; early Sept.–late May, hrs vary (call ahead).*

SPORTS AND THE OUTDOORS

BIRD-WATCHING

The San Luis Valley is famous for its migratory birds, many of which make a stop in the park. Great Sand Dunes also has many permanent feathered residents. In the wetlands, you might see American white pelicans and the American avocet. On the forested sections of the mountains there are goshawks, northern harriers, gray jays, and Steller's jays. And in the alpine tundra there are golden eagles, hawks, horned larks, and white-tailed ptarmigan.

FISHING

Fly fishermen can angle for Rio Grande cutthroat trout in the upper reaches of Medano Creek, which is accessible by four-wheel-drive vehicle. It's catch and release only, and a Colorado license is required (☎ *800/244–5613*). There's also fishing in Upper and Lower Sand Creek Lakes, but it's a very long hike (3 or 4 mi from the Music Pass Trailhead, located on the far side of the park in the San Isabel National Forest).

HIKING

Visitors can walk just about anywhere on the sand dunes in the heart of the park. The best view of all the dunes is from the top of High Dune. There are no formal trails because the sand keeps shifting, but you don't really need them: There's no way you'd get lost out here.

■ TIP➔ Before taking any of the trails in the preserve, rangers recommend stopping at the visitor center and picking up the handout that lists the trails, including their degree of difficulty. The dunes can get very hot in the summer, reaching up to 140°F in the afternoon. If you're hiking, carry plenty of water; if you're going into the backcountry to camp overnight, carry even more water and a water filtration system. A free permit is needed to backpack in the park. Also, watch for weather changes. If there's a thunderstorm and lightning, get off the dunes or trail immediately, and seek shelter. Before hiking, leave word with someone indicating where you're to hike and when you expect to be back. Tell that contact to call 911 if you don't show up when expected.

EASY

Hike to High Dune. Get a panoramic view of all the surrounding dunes. Since there's no formal path, the smartest approach is to zigzag up the dune ridgelines. High Dune is 650 feet high, and to get there and back takes about 1½ to 2 hours. It's 1.2 mi each way, but it can feel like a lot longer if there's been no rain for awhile and the sand is soft. If you add on the walk to Star Dune, which is a few more miles, plan on another two hours and a strenuous workout up and down the dunes to get there. ⊠ *Start from main dune field.*

American Indians used to peel ponderosa pines in order to eat the inner bark (which is rich in calcium) and use the pine gum for medicinal purposes. You can view many of these "culturally modified" trees at Great Sand Dunes.

MODERATE

Fodor'sChoice ★ **Mosca Pass Trail.** This moderately easy trail follows the route laid out centuries ago by Native Americans, which became the Mosca Pass toll road used in the late 1800s and early 1900s. This is a good afternoon hike, because the trail rises through the trees and subalpine meadows, often following Mosca Creek. It is 3½ miles one way, with a 1,480-foot gain in elevation. Hiking time is two to three hours each way. ⊠ *The lower end of the trail begins at the Montville Trailhead, just north of the visitor center.*

DIFFICULT

Music Pass Trail. This steep trail offers superb views of the glacially carved Upper Sand Creek Basin, ringed by many 13,000-foot peaks and the Wet Mountain Valley to the east. At the top of the pass you are about 11,000 feet above sea level and surrounded by yet higher mountain peaks. It's 3½ mi and a 2,000-foot elevation gain one way from the lower parking lot on the east side of the preserve, off Forest Service Road 119, and 1 mi from the upper parking lot (only reachable in a four-wheel-drive vehicle). Depending on how fit you are and how often you stop, it could take six hours round-trip. ⊠ *Trail begins on eastern side of park, reached via Hwy. 69, 4½ mi south of Westcliffe.* ⊹ *Turn off Hwy. 69 to the west at the sign for Music Pass and South Colony Lakes Trails. At the "T" junction, turn left onto South Colony Rd. At the end of the ranch fence on the right you'll see another sign for Music Pass.*

EDUCATIONAL OFFERINGS

PROGRAMS AND TOURS

☺ **Bison Tour.** The Nature Conservancy, an international nonprofit conservation organization, owns a 103,000-acre ranch that includes a herd of roughly 2,000 bison in the 50,000-acre Medano Ranch section, in the southwest corner of the park. The conservancy offers a two-hour tour focused on the "Wild West" section of the park, where bison—along with coyotes, elk, deer, pronghorns, porcupines, and birds such as great horned owls and red-tailed hawks, roam in the grasslands and wetlands. Depending on the season, the tour will be led as a hayride or a four-wheel-drive vehicle drive. ⊠ *Tours begin at the Nature Conservancy's Zapata Ranch Headquarters, 5303 Hwy. 150, Mosca* ☎ *888/592–7282 or 719/378–2356* ⊕ *www.zranch.org* ⊠ *$50.*

RANGER PROGRAMS

Interpretive Programs. Terrace talks and nature walks designed to help visitors learn more about the park are scheduled most days from late May through September. (Contact the park in advance about any programs from October through April.) ⊠ *Programs begin at the visitor center* ☎ *719/378–6399* ⊠ *Free.*

🪶 **Junior Ranger Programs.** During summer months, children ages 3 through 12 can join age-appropriate activities to learn about plants, animals, and the park's ecology, and they can become Junior Rangers by working successfully through an activity booklet. Ask for schedules and activity booklets at the visitor center. Youngsters can learn about the park prior to their trip via an interactive online program for kids at ⊕ *www.nps.gov/grsa/forkids/beaujuniorranger.htm.* Sign up at the visitor center. ☎ *719/378–6399* 📧 *Free.*

WHAT'S NEARBY

The vast open expanse one sees from the dunes is the San Luis Valley. Covering 8,000 square mi (and with an average altitude of 7,500 feet), the San Luis Valley is the world's largest alpine valley, sprawling on a broad, flat, dry plain between the San Juan mountains to the west and the Sangre de Cristo range to the east. The area is one of the state's major agricultural producers.

NEARBY TOWNS

Alamosa, the San Luis Valley's major city, is 35 mi southwest of Great Sand Dunes via U.S. 160 and Highway 150. It's a casual, central base for exploring the park and the surrounding region. The rest of the area is dotted with tiny towns, including **Mosca, Blanca,** Antonito, and **Fort Garland,** to the south of the park, and **Monte Vista, Del Norte,** and Hooper to the west. They are all within an hour or so drive from the park.

VISITOR INFORMATION
Alamosa Convention & Visitors Bureau ✉ *601 State Ave., Alamosa* ☎ *800/258–7597 or 719/589–3681* ⊕ *www.alamosa.org.* **Antonito Chamber of Commerce & Visitor Center** ✉ *307 Main St., Antonito* ☎ *719/376–2277* ⊕ *www.antonito.org.* **Del Norte Chamber of Commerce** ✉ *505 Grade Ave., Del Norte* ☎ *888/616–4638 or 719/657–2845* ⊕ *www.delnortechamber.org.* **Monte Vista Chamber of Commerce** ✉ *947 1st Ave., Monte Vista* ☎ *719/852–2731* ⊕ *www.monte-vista.org.*

NEARBY ATTRACTIONS

San Luis Valley National Wildlife Refuges. Less than an hour southwest of the park are two sanctuaries for songbirds, water birds, and raptors (they're also home to many other types of birds, along with mule deer, beavers, and coyotes). The smaller of the two is the **Alamosa National Wildlife Refuge** (✉ *9383 El Rancho La., Alamosa* ☎ *719/589–4021* ⊕ *www.fws.gov/alamosa* 📧 *Free* ☉ *Daily sunrise–sunset*), comprising

Near water in the park's grasslands area is where you might see elk, mule deer, and lizards.

nearly 12,000 acres of natural and man-made wetlands bordering the Rio Grande. You can take a 2-mi hike along the river or a 3½-mi drive along the bluff overlook on the park's eastern side. Just west of the Alamosa refuge is its sister sanctuary, the **Monte Vista National Wildlife Refuge** (✉ *6120 Hwy. 15, Monte Vista* ☎ *719/589–4021* ⊕ *www.fws. gov/alamosa* ✉ *Free* ☉ *Daily sunrise–sunset*), a 15,000-acre park that's a stopping point for up to 20,000 migrating cranes. It hosts an annual Crane Festival, held one weekend in mid-March in the nearby town of Monte Vista. You can see the sanctuary via a 4-mi driving tour.

☼ **Zapata Falls Recreation Area.** If it's a hot day, take a drive to the falls section of the Zapata Falls Recreation Area, about 7 mi south of Great Sand Dunes National Park (and about 10 mi north of Alamosa). From the trailhead, it's a ½-mi hike to the 40-foot waterfall and a mildly steep trail, which can include wading in a stream and walking through a narrow gorge to view the falls (depending on water levels). Air temperatures in the gorge are always cool and inviting, and the falls are beautiful, but be careful of the current (and slippery rocks) here. a picnic area and restrooms are at the entrance. The trailhead is 3½ mi off Highway 150, between mile markers 10 and 11. ✉ *San Luis Public Lands Center, 1803 W. Hwy. 160, Monte Vista* ☎ *719/852–5941* ✉ *free* ☉ *Daily.*

AREA ACTIVITIES

SPORTS AND THE OUTDOORS

FISHING

There are many reservoirs and lakes in the area where you can fish for trout, pike, and perch, including the Rio Grande, the Conejos River, and the Sanchez, Smith, and Platoro reservoirs. A Colorado fishing license is required. ⊠ *Colorado Division of Wildlife, SE Region Service Center, 4255 Sinton Rd., Colorado Springs* ☎ *719/227–5200* ⊕ *wildlife.state. co.us/fishing.*

EDUCATIONAL OFFERINGS

Colorado Field Institute. This nonprofit teams up with the experts at the park and other area organizations, such as the Rio Grande National Forest, San Luis Valley National Wildlife Refuges Complex, and the Nature Conservancy's Medano/Zapata Ranch to conduct in-depth outdoor educational programs on the natural and cultural resources of the area. ⌂ *P.O. Box 1753, Alamosa 81101* ☎ *719/378–6384* ⊕ *www.coloradofieldinstitute.org* ✉ *Free* ⊙ *Times and locations vary; call ahead.*

EVENT

21

☾ **Alamosa Round-Up Rodeo.** The last weekend in June marks the annual rodeo competition in Alamosa, a genuine Wild West event including barrel racers, bulls, broncos, and bareback riding. ⌂ *Alamosa Fairgrounds, P.O. Box 239, Alamosa 81101* ☎ *719/589–9444* ⊕ *www. alamosaroundup.com* ✉ *$12* ⊙ *Times vary; call ahead for details.*

SCENIC DRIVES AND RIDES

Manassa, San Luis, and Fort Garland Loop. To get a real feel for this area, take an easy driving loop from Alamosa through much of the San Luis Valley (the whole trip is about 95 mi). Head east on U.S 160 to Fort Garland, south on Highway 159 to San Luis, west on Highways 159 and 142 to Manassa, then north on U.S. 285 back to Alamosa. More than half of the route is part the Los Caminos Antiguos Drive, one of Colorado's Scenic Byways.

☾ **Scenic Train Rides.** Two train companies in this region take passengers through stunning scenery. Take a day trip on the **Cumbres & Toltec Scenic Railroad** (☎ *888/286–2737* ⊕ *www.cumbrestoltec.com* ✉ *$74–$120, $148–$153 for a seat in the adults-only parlor car* ⊙ *May–Oct.*), an 1880s-era steam locomotive that chugs through portions of Colorado's and northern New Mexico's rugged mountains that you can't reach via roads. It's the country's longest and highest narrow-gauge railroad. The company offers two round-trip train routes—either Antonito to Osier or Chama, NM. to Osier—plus several bus-and-train combinations and one-way trips. Cumbres & Toltec offers themed rides, including a special Christmastime train ride called "The Cinder Bear." A second option is **Rio Grande Scenic Railroad** (☎ *877/726–7245* ⊕ *www. riograndescenicrailroad.com* ✉ *$12–$87* ⊙ *May–Oct.*), which carries passengers on excursions between Alamosa and La Veta or Monte Vista; also offered is a side trip from La Veta, via motorcoach, to the Great Sand Dunes. Or you can catch a Rio Grande train to Antonito, where you'll connect with the Combres & Toltec train on its way to Osier or Chama. The Rio Grande offers a round-trip "Winter Wonderland Express" train from Alamosa to La Veta from November to May and other themed trips throughout the year.

WHERE TO EAT AND STAY

ABOUT THE RESTAURANTS

There are no dining establishments in the park. In the visitor center and at the campground there are vending machines with drinks that are stocked mid-spring through mid-fall. There is one picnic area in the park.

ABOUT THE HOTELS

There are no hotels, motels, or lodges in the park. The nearest lodge is right outside the park entrance, and there are many hotels in Alamosa and other surrounding towns.

ABOUT THE CAMPGROUNDS

Great Sand Dunes has one campground that is open year-round. During weekends in the summer, it can fill up with RVs and tents by mid-afternoon. Black bears live in the preserve, so when camping there, keep your food, trash, and toiletries in the trunk of your car (or use bear-proof containers). There is one campground and RV park near the entrance to Great Sand Dunes, and several others in the area.

WHERE TO EAT

IN THE PARK

PICNIC AREA **Mosca Creek.** The park's only picnic area is shaded by cottonwood trees. It has a dozen places where visitors can park a car or small RV near a picnic table and a grill. ⊠ *South of the dunes parking lot.*

OUTSIDE THE PARK

¢–$ ✕ **East West Grill.** Noodles and teriyaki top the menu at this casual,
ASIAN   almost fast-food-style place with dine-in or carry-out options. The salads and bento boxes are great. ⊠ *408 4th St., Alamosa* ☎ *719/589–4600* ⊕ *www.east-westgrill.com* ▭ *D, MC, V.*

$ ✕ **The Oasis Cafe.** The no-frills restaurant in the Great Sand Dunes Oasis
AMERICAN   (which includes a grocery store and gas station as well as motel rooms and campsites), just outside the park entrance, is open for breakfast, lunch, and dinner. The Navajo taco (served on fry bread) and beef or chicken burritos are among the most popular items, although the menu ranges from grilled-cheese sandwiches to steaks. ⊠ *5400 Hwy. 150, Mosca* ☎ *719/378–2222* ⊕ *www.greatdunes.com* ▭ *AE, D, MC, V* ☾ *May–late-Sept.*

$$ ✕ **True Grits.** At this steak house, the cuts of beef are predictably good,
STEAK   but that's not the real draw. As the name implies, the restaurant is a shrine to John Wayne. His portraits hang everywhere: the Duke in action, the Duke in repose, the Duke lost in thought. ⊠ *100 Santa Fe Ave., Alamosa* ☎ *719/589–9954* ▭ *AE, D, MC, V.*

WHERE TO STAY

IN THE PARK

CAMPING

$ **Pinyon Flats Campground.** Set in a pine forest about a mile past the visitor center, this campground has a trail leading to the dunes. Sites are available on a first-come, first-served basis, although groups of 10 or more might be able to reserve in advance. (Register at the kiosk.) RVs are allowed, but there are no hookups. The campground can fill up on summer weekends, and tends to have lots of families when school is out. Quiet hours start at 10 PM. **Pros:** only campground in park; close to main dunes. **Cons:** can get crowded, especially on summer weekends; best for smaller RVs. ⊠ *On the main park road, near the visitor center* ☎ *719/378–6399* ⚠ *88 tent/ RV sites* ⚐ *Flush toilets, fire grates, picnic tables* ⊟ *D, MC, V.*

OUTSIDE THE PARK

$–$$ **Best Western Alamosa Inn.** This sprawling, well-maintained complex is your best bet for budget lodgings. Rooms are spacious and offer the standard amenities. All rooms are nonsmoking. **Pros:** reliable basic accommodations; easy to find. **Cons:** noisy street; nothing but fast food nearby. ⊠ *2005 Main St., Alamosa* ☎ *719/589–2567* ⊕ *www. bestwestern.com/alamosainn* ⟿ *53 rooms, 1 suite* ⚐ *In-room: refrigerator. In-hotel: pool, some pets allowed* ⊟ *AE, D, DC, MC, V.*

$–$$ **Conejos Canyon River Ranch.** Located within the Rio Grande National Forest on the Conejos River, this peaceful, family-friendly retreat is about 42 mi southwest of Alamosa. One of the draws is the great fishing in the area: The ranch has its own privately stocked section of river (and separate kids' fishing pond), plus access to many more streams and tributaries. Staff can set you up with fishing guides and lessons. The main lodge is more than 100 years old, and the cabins and guest rooms are outfitted with ranch-style decor, including lodgepole pine furnishings. There's an outdoor barbecue and campfire area, stocked with firewood. Breakfast is complimentary for lodge guests. **Pros:** gorgeous riverfront setting; access to national forest; plenty of activities for adults and kids; on-site gift shop. **Cons:** no amenities nearby; more than an hour from the Great Sand Dunes. ⊠ *25390 Hwy. 17, Antonito* ☎ *719/376–2464* ⊕ *www.conejosranch.com* ⟿ *8 rooms, 8 cabins* ⚐ *In-room: no a/c, kitchen (some), no TV. In-hotel: restaurant* ⊟ *D, MC, V* ⊙ *Limited rooms and cabins available Dec.–Apr.* ⊩ *BP.*

$ **Ft. Garland Motor Inn.** This cheerful, squeaky-clean motel is just a few miles south of the Great Sand Dunes, in the tiny town of Ft. Garland, and makes a great base from which to visit the park and other San Luis Valley attractions. **Pros:** spotless, comfortable rooms; 20 minutes from park. **Cons:** no pool or other recreational amenities in hotel; no great eating options nearby. ⊠ *411 Hwy. 160, Ft. Garland* ☎ *800/379–2993 or 719/379–2993* ⊕ *www.garlandmotorinn.com* ⟿ *15 rooms* ⚐ *In-room: safe, kitchen (some), Wi-Fi. In-hotel: Wi-Fi* ⊟ *AE, D, MC, V.*

$$ **Inn of the Rio Grande.** Alamosa's largest hotel is a dog-friendly property, with comfortable rooms and suites. It's a full-service hotel, with a unique (and enormous) indoor water park that kids will love. Breakfast in the hotel's restaurant is included. **Pros:** great for families with children and/or pets; close to restaurants and other amenities in town; sauna and hot tub.

Cons: water park and gym area can get crowded; big property with the feel of a convention center. ✉ *333 Santa Fe Dr., Alamosa* ☎ *800/669/1658 or 719/589–5833* ⊕ *www.innoftherio.com* ⤳ *120 rooms, 5 suites* ♿ *In-room: a/c, refrigerator (some), Wi-Fi. In-hotel: restaurant, bar, pool, gym, Wi-Fi, some pets allowed* ▭ *AE, D, MC, V* ⦿| *BP.*

$$$$ ⬚ **Zapata Ranch.** The Zapata Ranch is part of a 103,000-acre working cattle and bison ranch owned by the Nature Conservancy. Its guest operations are focused mainly on all-inclusive, week-long stays, during which guests learn about bison, land conservation and renewable ranching practices, and participate in ranch activities (including branding cattle and mending fences), but it also offers rooms on a per-night basis. An overnight stay includes all meals and use of the ranch's hot tub and hiking trails. **Pros:** beautiful setting among mature cottonwoods; historic lodge buildings; terrific restaurant with indoor and outdoor seating. **Cons:** much pricier than other area accommodations; limited capacity (the ranch rents only those rooms that aren't reserved for guest ranch visitors). ✉ *5305 State Hwy. 150, Mosca* ☎ *888/592–7282 or 719/378–2356* ⊕ *www.zranch.org* ⤳ *15 rooms* ♿ *In-room: no a/c, no phone, no TV. In-hotel: restaurant, Wi-Fi* ▭ *AE, D, MC, V* ⦿| *AI.*

CAMPING ⛺ **Great Sand Dunes Oasis.** Just outside the park, the Great Sand Dunes
$$ Oasis has a campground with both tent and RV sites and a few spartan
☾ cabins; they also have two motel rooms, each with two queen-sized beds and maid service. Ice-cream socials are sometimes held on summer evenings. On the premises are a restaurant, general store, and gas station. Pets are allowed. **Pros:** as close to the park as you can get (and the closest campground with hookups); friendly and helpful staff. **Cons:** not much shade for campers; facilities could use some updating. ✉ *5400 Hwy. 150, Mosca* ☎ *719/378–2222* ⊕ *www.greatdunes.com* ⛺ *130 tent sites, 20 RV sites, 4 cabins, 2 motel rooms* ▭ *AE, D, MC, V* ♿ *Flush toilets, full hook-ups, guest laundry, showers, fire pits, food service, picnic tables, general store, service station (gas only), play area* ⊙ *Closed Sept.–Mar.*

$ ⛺ **San Luis State Park.** About 15 minutes from Great Sand Dunes on County Lane 6 North, this state park has a modern campground with access to the parks' pristine lake and about 9 mi of easy (and kid-friendly) hiking trails. **Pros:** close to lake (and boating and fishing); clean, modern bathhouse; nice wide sites with great views of the lake and mountains. **Cons:** access to campgrounds is over a bumpy (unpaved) road; proximity to wetlands means plenty of biting bugs. ⌖ *P.O. Box 150, Mosca 81146* ☎ *719/738–2020 or 719/738–2376* ⊕ *www.parks. state.co.us* ⛺ *51 tent/RV sites* ♿ *Flush toilets, guest laundry, showers, fire pits, picnic tables, electricity* ▭ *D, MC, V Closed Sept.–May.*

Guadalupe Mountains National Park

WORD OF MOUTH

"Compared to other national parks, Guadalupe is fairly empty. That's worked out great for us, as we hoped we'd have the mountain all to ourselves. There were some people on the mountain, but not many."

—bkluvsNola

WELCOME TO
GUADALUPE MOUNTAINS

TOP REASONS TO GO

★ **Tower over Texas:** The park is home to 8,749-foot Guadalupe Peak, the highest point in the state.

★ **Fall for fiery foliage:** Though surrounded by arid desert and rocky soil, the park has miles of beautiful foliage in McKittrick Canyon. In late October you can watch it burst into flaming colors.

★ **Hike unhindered:** The main activity at the park is hiking its rugged, remote, and often challenging trails: 80 mi worth will keep you captivated and spry—and far away from civilization.

★ **Eat with elk, loll with lions:** Despite the surrounding arid region, a variety of wildlife—including shaggy brown elk, sneaky mountain lions, and shy black bears—traipses the mountains, woods, and desert here.

1 **Guadalupe Peak.** This crude, rocky pinnacle tops 8,700 feet and towers over the rest of the park's peaks. Those who brave the seven-hour-plus round-trip to the summit are rewarded with breathtaking views of New Mexico and southwestern Texas.

2 **McKittrick Canyon.** In late October and early November, the lush green foliage along McKittrick Canyon's trout-filled desert stream bursts into russet, amber, and gold hues. An easy, wheelchair-accessible ramble takes visitors through this geological wonder.

3 **El Capitan.** Not to be confused with equally impressive El Capitan in Yosemite National Park, this 8,000-foot cliff dominates the view at the southern end of the Guadalupe Range. It has visitors talking and hikers walking: a 6- to 11-mi-plus trail winds around the base of this massive limestone formation.

4 **Manzanita Spring.** The area around this idyllic stream and picnic spot has a little bit of everything: a spring feeds lush grasses and trees, giving life to hundreds of wildflowers. Birds hang out here to enjoy the tasty seeds and insects that the water, shade, and vegetation provide. Plus, it's only a 0.2-mi, paved ramble from here to the Frijole Ranch Museum.

5 **Frijole Ranch Museum.** This easily accessible historic ranch site houses the stone ruins of the oldest structure in the park. The recently restored ranch-house museum injects a bit of man-made history into the natural surroundings. Five nearby springs are just a refreshing stroll away.

NEW MEXICO
TEXAS

Cutoff Mountai
6,933

Butterfield Route

TEXAS

22

137

Dog Canyon
△ 🏕 🚻

Pratt Cabin

BROKEOFF MOUNTAINS

CUTOFF RIDGE

2 🚻
McKittrick Canyon

▲ *Lost Peak 7,830 ft*

◆ **Grotto**
🏕

GUADALUPE MOUNTAINS

FRIJOLE RIDGE

62 180

Bush Mountain 8,631 ft ▲

Bartlett Peak 8,508 ft ▲

Shumard Peak 8,615 ft ▲

5

▲ *Hunter Peak 8,368 ft*

Frijole Ranch Museum

1

Guadalupe Peak (highest point in Texas) 8,749 ft ◆

4

Pine Springs ◆
△ 🏕 🚻

Stay Station Ruins

Visitor Center

Williams Ranch ◆

El Capitan 8,085 ft ▲ **3**

Williams Ranch Rd.

62 180

0 _____ 2 mi

0 _____ 2 km

🧭

Quail Mountain 4,962 ft ▲

GETTING ORIENTED

The park is off U.S. 62/180, 110 mi east of El Paso, Texas; 40 mi southwest of Carlsbad Caverns National Park; and 55 mi southwest of Carlsbad, New Mexico. White's City, New Mexico, is 35 mi northeast of the park on U.S. 62/180.

KEY	
🚻	*Ranger Station*
△	*Campground*
🏕	*Picnic Area*
🍴	*Restaurant*
🏨	*Lodge*
🚶	*Trailhead*
🚻	*Restrooms*
⚹	*Scenic Viewpoint*
∷∷∷∷	*Walking/Hiking Trails*

GUADALUPE MOUNTAINS PLANNER

When to Go

Trails here are rarely crowded, except in fall, when foliage changes colors in McKittrick Canyon, and during Spring Break in March. Still, this is a very remote area, and you probably won't find too much congestion at any time. Hikers are more apt to explore backcountry trails in spring and fall, when it's cooler but not too cold. Snow, not uncommon in the winter months, can linger in the higher elevations.

Getting Here and Around

Since about half of the Guadalupe Mountains is a designated wilderness, few roadways penetrate the park. Most sites are accessible off U.S. 62/180. Dog Canyon Campground on the north end of the park can be reached via Route 137.

AVG. HIGH/LOW TEMPS.

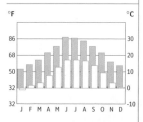

Flora and Fauna

Despite the constant wind and the arid conditions, more than a thousand species of plants populate the mountains, chasms, and salt dunes that make up the park's different geologic zones. Some grow many feet in a single night; others bloom so infrequently they're called "century plants." In fall, McKittrick Canyon's oaks, bigtooth maples, and velvet ashes go Technicolor above the little stream that traverses it. Barren-looking cacti burst into yellow, red, and purple bloom in spring, and wildflowers can carpet the park for thousands of acres after unusually heavy rains.

More than 86,000 acres of mountains, chasms, canyons, woods, and deserts house an incredible diversity of wildlife, including hallmark southwestern species like roadrunners and long-limbed jackrabbits, which run so fast they appear to float on their enormous, black-tipped ears. Other furry residents include coyotes, black bears, and badgers. You may also spot elk and winged creatures: nearly 300 different bird species, 90 types of butterflies, and 16 species of bats.

Plenty of reptiles and insects make their homes here, too: coachwhip snakes, diamondback rattlers, and lovelorn tarantulas (the only time you might spy them is in the fall, when they search for mates), to name a few. Texas's famous horned lizards—affectionately called "horny toads"—can also be seen waddling across the soil in search of ants and other insects. Rangers caution parents not to let little ones run too far ahead on the trails.

■ TIP➔ Rattlesnakes are common here. They're not aggressive, but give a wide berth to any you spot.

By Jennifer Edwards

Guadalupe Mountains National Park is a study in extremes: it has mountaintop forests but also rocky canyons; arid deserts and yet a stream that winds through verdant woods. The park is home to the Texas madrone tree, found commonly only here and in Big Bend National Park. Guadalupe Mountains National Park also has the distinction of hosting the loftiest spot in Texas: 8,749-foot Guadalupe Peak. The mountain dominates the view from every approach, but it's just one member of a rugged range carved by wind, water, and time.

PARK ESSENTIALS

ACCESSIBILITY
The wheelchair-accessible Headquarters Visitor Center has a wheelchair available for use. The ¾-mi round-trip Pinery Trail from the visitor center to Butterfield Stage Ruins is wheelchair accessible, as is McKittrick Contact Station.

ADMISSION HOURS
The park is open 24/7, year-round. It is in the mountain time zone.

ADMISSION FEES AND PERMITS
An admission fee of $8 is collected at the visitor center. For overnight backpacking trips, you must get a free permit from either Headquarters Visitor Center or Dog Canyon Ranger Station.

ATMS/BANKS
There are no ATMs in the park. The nearest ones are in White's City or Carlsbad.

GUADALUPE MOUNTAINS IN ONE DAY

Start your tour at **Headquarters Visitor Center,** where an exhibit and slide show introduce the park's wildlife and geology. Nearby is the ¾-mi round-trip, wheelchair-accessible **Pinery Trail,** which rambles to the Pinery Bitterfield Stage Station ruins. As you take in the sights, do not to touch the ruins' fragile walls; the site is quite vulnerable. Next, head to the **Frijole Ranch Museum,** built in 1876.

Once you're done gawking at the old structures, turn onto the paved trailhead behind the ranch house for the 0.2-mi stroll to the calming waters of **Manzanita Spring,** one of five springs that gurgle within a couple of miles of the museum. Park staff call such areas riparian zones. These oases supply the fragile wildlife here, and can sometimes look like Pre-Raphaelite paintings, with mirrored-surface ponds and delicate flowers and greenery.

Afterward, pay a visit to the famed **McKittrick Canyon.** Regardless of the season, the dense foliage and basin stream are worth the hike—though it's best to visit it in late October and early November when the trees burst into color. There isn't a direct route, but you can get here quickly by driving northeast from the visitor center on U.S. 62/180. Follow it to the gate at the western turnoff, which is locked at sunset. Head northwest through the gate (ignoring the service road) in your car, and you'll arrive at the canyon.

Take your time walking the **McKittrick Canyon Trail** that leads to Pratt Lodge, or the strenuous but rewarding 8.4-mi **Permian Reef Trail,** which takes you up thousands of feet, past monumental geological formations. Or traverse the easy, short (less than 1 mi) **McKittrick Canyon Nature Loop.**

CELL-PHONE RECEPTION
Cell phones with far-reaching service can pick up signals at key points along trails. Alternatively, public phones are located at Dog Canyon Ranger Station, Headquarters Visitor Center, McKittrick Contact Station, and Pine Springs Campground.

PARK CONTACT INFORMATION
Headquarters Visitor Center ⊠ *U.S. 62/180, 55 mi southwest of Carlsbad, 110 mi northeast of El Paso* ⌂ *HC 60, Box 400, Salt Flat, TX 79847* ☎ *915/828–3251* ⊕ *www.nps.gov/gumo.*

SCENIC DRIVE

Williams Ranch Road. Take in panoramic views and view limestone cliffs up close on this 7¼-mi, one-way drive over what was once the Bitterfield Overland Mail Stage Line. The closest highway, U.S. 180, parallels the old trail. The route is rough —you need a high-clearance, four-wheel-drive vehicle—but enjoyable. The road leads to an old ranch house, where James "Dolph" Williams worked with his partner, an Indian named Geronimo (no relation to the historical figure). ■ TIP➔ **The drive is locked, so pick up a gate key at the visitor center.** ✛ *Drive west on U.S. 62/180 for 8¼ mi until you see a brown metal gate on the north side* *with a National Park Service sign. Continue through two locked gates (lock them behind you)* ⊙ *Daily, dawn to dusk.*

WHAT TO SEE

HISTORIC SITES

⊙ **Frijole Ranch Museum.** Displays and photographs depict ranch life and early park history inside this old ranch-house museum. Hiking trails, which are easy to travel and great for kids, are adjacent to the shady, tree-lined grounds; Some of them lead to the **Manzanita Spring.** ⊠ *Access road 1 mi northeast of Headquarters Visitors Center* ☎ *915/828–3251* ⊑ *Free* ⊙ *Call for hrs.*

★ **Pinery Bitterfield Stage Station Ruins.** In the mid-1800s passengers en route from St. Louis or San Francisco on the old Bitterfield Overland Mail stagecoach route would stop here for rest and refreshment. You can drive here or take a paved ¾-mi round-trip trail from the visitors center. ⊠ *½ mi east of Headquarters Visitors Center.*

SCENIC STOP

Fodor'sChoice **McKittrick Canyon.** A desert creek flows through this canyon, which is
★ lined with walnut, maple, and other trees that explode into brilliant colors each fall. Call the visitor center to find out the progress of the colorful fall foliage; the spectacular changing of the leaves can often take until November, depending on the weather. You're likely to spot mule deer heading for the water here. ⊠ *4 mi off U.S. 62/180, about 7 mi northeast of Headquarters Visitor Center* ⊙ *Highway gate open Nov.–Apr., daily 8–4:30; May–Sept., daily 8–6.*

VISITOR CENTERS

Headquarters Visitor Center. You can pick up maps, brochures, and other information about the park at the main park visitor center. Exhibits and a slide show here give you a quick introduction to the park, half of which is a wilderness area. Some nicely crafted exhibits depict typical wildlife and plant scenes. ⊠ *U.S. 62/180, 55 mi southwest of Carlsbad, 110 mi east of El Paso* ☎ *915/828–3251* ⊙ *June–Aug., daily 8–6; Sept.–May, daily 8–4:30.*

McKittrick Contact Station. Poster-size illustrations in a shaded, outdoor patio area tell the geological story of the Guadalupe Mountains, believed to have been carved from an ancient sea. You can also hear the recorded memoirs of oilman Wallace Pratt, who donated his ranch and surrounding area to the federal government for preservation. ⊠ *4 mi off U.S. 62/180, 7 mi northeast of Headquarters Visitor Center* ☎ *915/828–3251 (Headquarters Visitor Center)* ⊙ *June–Aug., daily 8–6; Sept.–May, daily 8–4:30.*

SPORTS AND THE OUTDOORS

BIRD-WATCHING

More than 300 species of birds have been spotted in the park, including the ladder-backed woodpecker, Scott's oriole, Say's phoebe, and white-throated swift. Many non-native birds—such as fleeting hummingbirds and larger but less graceful turkey vultures—stop at Guadalupe during spring and fall migrations. **Manzanita Springs,** located near the Frijole

Ranch Museum, is an excellent bird-ing spot. As with hiking, there aren't any local guides, but rangers at the Dog Canyon and Pine Springs ranger stations can help you spot some native species. Books on birding are available at the Pine Springs Ranger Station; visitors might find the Nat-ural History Association's birding checklist for Guadalupe Mountains National Park especially helpful. It will be easy to spot the larger birds of prey circling overhead, such as keen-beaked golden eagles and swift, red-tailed hawks. Be on the lookout for owls in the **Bowl** area, and watch for swift-footed roadrunners in the desert areas (they're quick, but not as speedy as their cartoon counterpart).

> **NOTABLE QUOTE**
>
> "May your trails be crooked, wind-ing, lonesome, dangerous, leading to the most amazing view. May your mountains rise into and above the clouds."
>
> —Edward Abbey, environmental writer and activist

HIKING

No matter which trail you select, be sure to pack wisely—the park doesn't sell anything. This includes the recommended gallon of water per day per person, as well as sunscreen and hats. (Bring $5, too—that's the additional cost to use the trails, payable at the visitor centers.) The area has a triple-whammy as far as sun ailments are concerned: it's very open, very sunny, and has a high altitude (which makes sunburns more likely). Slather up. And be sure to leave Fido at home—few of the park's trails allow pets.

HIKING RESOURCES The staff at the **Dog Canyon Ranger Station** (☎ 505/981–2418) can help you plan your hike. The bookstore at the **Pine Springs Ranger Station** also sells hiking guides. These and other guides can also be found at ⊕ *www.ccgma.org.*

EASY

☺ **Indian Meadows Nature Trail.** This trail in Dog Canyon is a very easy, mostly level 0.5-mi hike that crosses an arroyo into meadowlands. It's a good way to spend about 45 minutes savoring the countryside. ⊠ *Trail-head access is directly across from the Dog Canyon Ranger Station.*

☺ **McKittrick Nature Loop.** Signs along the way explain the geological and Fodor'sChoice biological history of the area. The trail is wheelchair-accessible and ★ great for little ones. Plus, you can see the canyon's signature foliage in the late fall. ⊠ *Trail accessed via the McKittrick Canyon Trailhead at the northeast corner of the park.*

MODERATE

Bush Mountain. A 4.5-mi round-trip rewards you with a panoramic view of West Dog Canyon. Set aside about half a day for it. ⊠ *Trail accessed at Rte. 137, 60 mi southwest of U.S. 285.*

Devil's Hall Trail. Wind through through Chihuahua Desert habitat thick with spiked agave plants, prickly pear cacti, and giant boulders, and Devil's Hall, a narrow canyon about 10 feet wide and 100 feet deep. If you travel at a leisurely pace, this 4-mi trail will take about a day. ⊠ *Trail accessed via the Pine Springs Trailhead, in the RV section of Pine Springs Campground.*

The sun sets over the desert landscape of West Texas at Guadalupe Mountains National Park.

★ **El Capitan/Salt Basin Overlook Trails.** These trails form a popular loop through the low desert. El Capitan skirts the base of El Capitan peak for about 3.5 mi, leading to a junction with Salt Basin Overlook. The 4.5-mi Salt Basin Overlook trail begins at the Pine Springs Trailhead and has views of the stark, white salt flat below and loops back onto the El Capitan Trail. Though moderate, the 11.3-mi round-trip is not recommended during the intense heat of summer, since there is absolutely no shade. ⊠ *Trail accessed behind Headquarters Visitors Center at Pine Springs Campground.*

Frijole/Foothills Trail. Branching off the Frijole Ranch Trail, this hike leads to Pine Springs Campground behind Headquarters Visitors Center. The 5.5-mi round-trip route through desert vistas takes about five hours. ⊠ *Trail begins at the Frijole Ranch History Museum.*

Trail to Grotto Picnic Area. The 6.75-mi round-trip trek to this picnic area affords views of a flowing stream and surface rock that resembles formations in an underground cave with jagged overhangs. Plan on about five hours at a leisurely pace. ⊠ *Starts at the McKittrick Contact Station.*

Pratt Lodge Trail. View stream and canyon woodland areas along a 4½-mi round-trip excursion that leads to the vacant Pratt Lodge. Plan on at least two hours if you walk at a fast pace, but give yourself another hour or two if you want to take your time. ⊠ *Trail accessed 4 mi off U.S. 62/180, about 7 mi northeast of Headquarters Visitors Center.*

☾ **Smith Spring Trail.** Departing from the Frijole Ranch Trailhead, the trail takes you through a shady oasis where you're likely to spot mule deer alongside a spring and a small waterfall. Allow 1½ hours to complete the 2.2-mi round-trip walk. This is a good hike for older kids, whose legs won't tire as easily. ⊠ *Trailhead off access road 1 mi northeast of Headquarters Visitors Center.*

DIFFICULT

★ **The Bowl.** Cutting through forests of pine and Douglas fir, this is considered one of the most gorgeous trails in the park. The strenuous 9-mi round-trip—which can take up to 10 hours, depending on your pace—is where rangers go when they want to enjoy themselves. ■TIP➔ Don't forget to drink (and bring) lots of water! ⊠ *Trail accessed from the Pine Springs Trailhead ✛ From Pine Springs Campground, follow the Frijole/Foothills Trail, and Bear Canyon Trail to the top; then turn left onto the Bowl Trail.*

> **PARK PUBLICATIONS**
>
> ■ The Guadalupe Mountains' natural features and history are the subjects of the illustrated *The Guadalupes,* by Dan Murphy, a booklet published by the Carlsbad Caverns Guadalupe Mountains Association.
>
> ■ Other booklets include *Trails of the Guadalupes,* by Don Kurtz and William D. Goran, and *Hiking Carlsbad Caverns and Guadalupe Mountains National Parks,* by Bill Schneider. These and other publications are available at the visitor center.

Guadalupe Peak Trail. The 8.5-mi strenuous workout over a steep grade offers some great views of exposed cliff faces. The hike can take up to eight hours to complete. ⊠ *Trail accessed via the Pine Springs Trail, in the RV section of Pine Springs Campground.*

Lost Peak. The somewhat strenuous trek from Dog Canyon into a coniferous forest is 6.5-mi round-trip and will take about six hours to complete at a fairly slow pace. ⊠ *Access via the Dog Canyon Trailhead. From there, follow the Tejas Trail into the canyon and to a junction with McKittrick Ridge Trail.*

Permian Reef Geology Trail. If you're in shape and have a serious geological bent, you may want to hike this approximately 8.5-mi round-trip climb. It heads through open, expansive desert country to a forested ridge with Douglas fir and ponderosa pines. Panoramic views of McKittrick Canyon and the surrounding mountain ranges allow you to see many rock layers. Set aside at least eight hours for this trek. ⊠ *Trail accessed via the McKittrick Canyon Trailhead at the northeast corner of the park.*

MOUNTAIN BIKING

If you've got a mountain bike or a high-clearance, four-wheel-drive vehicle, cruise to the **Williams Ranch Trail.** Skittering down it will only take about an hour one way (for vehicles) and will lead you to the Williams Ranch House, which sits alone at the base of a 3,000-foot cliff. ■TIP➔ Before you set out, check out the gate key at the Headquarters Visitor Center. Then head west on Highway 62/180. Drive 8¼ mi to the brown metal gate with NATIONAL PARK signs; be sure to lock the gate behind you once you're through. Proceed for another ¾ mi to another gate; lock this one as well once you're through it. Follow the worn dirt road, which runs past arid scenery and cacti that bloom in the spring months, to the ranch house—and enjoy a great view of El Capitan. Leave before sundown and return the key to the visitor center.

22

EDUCATIONAL OFFERINGS

RANGER PROGRAM

☺ **Junior Ranger Program.** The park offers a self-guided Junior Pro-
★ gram: kids choose activities from a workbook—including taking nature
hikes and answering questions based on park exhibits—and earn a patch
and certificate once they've completed three. If they complete six, they earn
an additional patch. ✉ *Headquarters Visitors Center* ☎ *915/828–3251
Ext. 118* ⬚ *Free* ☉ *June–Aug., daily 8–6; Sept.–May, daily 8–4:30.*

WHAT'S NEARBY

Tiny **White's City, New Mexico,** 35 mi to the northeast off U.S. 62/180, is
more a crossroads than a town. The town of **Carlsbad, New Mexico,** 55 mi
northeast of the park, has more amenities. *For more information about
both cities,* ➪ *Carlsbad Caverns National Park (chapter 13).*

WHERE TO EAT AND STAY

ABOUT THE RESTAURANTS

Dining in the park is a do-it-yourself affair. Ranger stations don't serve
meals or sell picnic items, though nearby White's City offers some
basics—sodas, snacks, and the like.

ABOUT THE HOTELS

There are no hotels within the park. Your best options are in White's
City or Carlsbad.

ABOUT THE CAMPGROUNDS

The park has two developed campgrounds that charge fees, and a number of designated primitive, backcountry sites where you can camp for
free—visitors haul their supplies for miles to stretch out on the unsoiled
land of these backcountry sites. In the backcountry, no restrooms are
provided; visitors may dig their own privies, but toilet paper and other
paper waste should be packed out. Wood and charcoal fires are prohibited throughout the park, but you can use your camp stove at both
the developed and backcountry sites. For backcountry sites, check with
the park's main visitor center (☎ *915/828–3251*).

WHERE TO EAT

IN THE PARK

The park has no snack bars or restaurants, but several picnic areas are
available. Wood and charcoal fires are not allowed anywhere in the
park. If you want to cook a hot meal, bring a camp stove.

PICNIC AREAS **Dog Canyon Campground.** Thirteen campsites have picnic tables, which
you can use during the day for free. This is a lovely shaded area where
you're very likely to see mule deer. Drinking water and restrooms are
available at the site. This area is about a 2½-hour hike from the Headquarters Visitors Center (you also can drive here). ✉ *Off Rte. 137, 65
mi southwest of Carlsbad.*

Frijole Ranch Museum. This area is much cooler than nearby Pine Springs Campground. Two picnic tables are set up under tall trees; restrooms are available at the ranch house. ⊠ *Access road 1 mi northeast of Headquarters Visitors Center.*

Pine Springs Campground. Shade varies depending on the time of day, so it can be hard to find a cool spot. There are restrooms and drinking water here. ⊠ *Behind Headquarters Visitors Center.*

OUTSIDE THE PARK

For dining options near the park, ⇨ *Where to Eat in Carlsbad Caverns National Park (chapter 13).*

WHERE TO STAY

IN THE PARK

CAMPING

⛺ **Dog Canyon Campground.** This campground is remote and a little tricky to find, but well worth the effort. Located on the north side of Guadalupe National Park, it can be accessed by turning west on County Road 408 off U.S. 62/180, about 9 mi south of Carlsbad. Drive 23 mi on this county road; then turn south on Highway 137. Travel 43 mi through Lincoln National Forest until the road dead-ends just at the park boundary, at the New Mexico–Texas state line. The very well maintained camping area is located in a coniferous forest, with hiking trails nearby. **Pros:** cooler than some of the other backcountry sites. **Cons:** no open fires allowed. ⊠ *Just within the park's northern entrance* ☎ *505/981–2418* ⛺ *9 tent sites, 4 RV sites* ⟁ *Flush toilets, drinking water, picnic tables, public telephone, ranger station* ▭ *AE, D, MC, V.*

⛺ **Pine Springs Campground.** You'll be snuggled amid pinyon and juniper trees at the base of a tall mountain peak at this site behind the Guadalupe Mountains National Park Visitor Center. Wood and charcoal fires are prohibited, although camp stoves are allowed. Shade here can be a bit sparse in the intense summer heat. Advance reservations are accepted for group sites only. **Pros:** easily accessible; lots of sites for both tents and RVs. **Cons:** may be more crowded than other campground during popular times. ⊠ *Behind the visitor center at the park's east entrance, off U.S. 62/180* ☎ *915/828–3251* ⛺ *20 tent sites, 18 RV sites, 1 wheelchair-accessible site, 2 group sites* ⟁ *Flush toilets, drinking water, picnic tables, public telephone, ranger station* ▭ *AE, D, MC, V.*

OUTSIDE THE PARK

For lodging options near the park, ⇨ *Where to Stay in Carlsbad Caverns National Park (chapter 13).*

Jasper National Park

WORD OF MOUTH

"Drove to Maligne Lake the second day . . . saw TONS of mountain goats, bighorn sheep, some elk, deer, a couple of bears— including one little cub munching obliviously by the side of the road, with dozens of people climbing out of their cars to get closer."
                                                                —SarahJake68

WELCOME TO JASPER

TOP REASONS TO GO

★ **Larger than life:** Almost as large as the entire state of Connecticut, Jasper is the largest of the Canadian Rocky Mountain national parks, and one of the world's largest protected mountain ecosystems.

★ **Spectacular scenery:** Jasper's scenery is rugged and mountainous. Within its boundaries are crystal-clear mountain lakes, thundering waterfalls, jagged mountain peaks, and ancient glaciers.

★ **Wonderful wildlife:** The Canadian Rockies provide a diverse habitat for 277 bird species and 69 species of mammals, including deer, elk, moose, sheep, goats, and bears.

★ **Columbia Icefield:** The largest ice field south of Alaska, the Columbia Icefield is also the hydrographic apex of North America, with water flowing to three different oceans from one point.

1 Yellowhead Corridor. Trans-Canada Highway 16 (Yellowhead Highway) travels through the foothills and main ranges of the Canadian Rockies. Highlights are views of the Jasper Lake sand dunes (Km 27), Disaster Point Animal Lick (Km 39.5), Pocahontas Townsite (Km 39.5), the Coal Mine Interpretive Trail (Km 39.5), and Miette Hot Springs (Km 43).

2 Jasper Townsite. Shops, restaurants, nightclubs, and the main park information center are here. Just outside town are Lac Beauvert, Lake Annette, and Lake Edith, plus Old Fort Point, and Whistlers Tramway.

3 Maligne Valley. Highlights of this region include the Athabasca Valley Lookout (Km 5.8), Maligne Canyon (Km 7), Medicine Lake (Km 20.7), and Maligne Lake (Km 45), where the paved road ends.

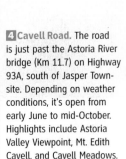

4 Cavell Road. The road is just past the Astoria River bridge (Km 11.7) on Highway 93A, south of Jasper Townsite. Depending on weather conditions, it's open from early June to mid-October. Highlights include Astoria Valley Viewpoint, Mt. Edith Cavell, and Cavell Meadows.

5 Icefield Parkway. Highway 93 spans 210 km (130 mi) between Jasper Townsite and Lake Louise and is one of the world's most spectacular drives. Highlights include Athabasca Falls (Km 31), Sunwapta Falls (Km 55), Columbia Icefield (Km 103), Sunwapta Pass (Km 108), and the Weeping Wall (Km 125).

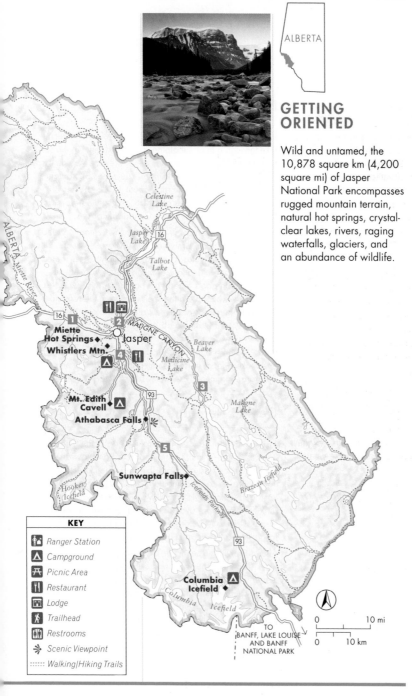

ALBERTA

GETTING ORIENTED

23

Wild and untamed, the 10,878 square km (4,200 square mi) of Jasper National Park encompasses rugged mountain terrain, natural hot springs, crystal-clear lakes, rivers, raging waterfalls, glaciers, and an abundance of wildlife.

Celestine Lake

Jasper Lake

Talbot Lake

ALBERTA
Miette River

16

1

2 MALIGNE CANYON

Miette Hot Springs ◆

Jasper

Whistlers Mtn. ◆

4

Beaver Lake

Medicine Lake

3

93

Mt. Edith Cavell ◆

Maligne Lake

Athabasca Falls ◆

5

Sunwapta Falls ◆

Hooker Icefield

Icefields Parkway

Brazeau Icefield

93

Columbia Icefield ◆

Columbia Icefield

TO
BANFF, LAKE LOUISE
AND BANFF
NATIONAL PARK

0   10 mi

0   10 km

KEY

👫 *Ranger Station*
⛺ *Campground*
🛆 *Picnic Area*
🍴 *Restaurant*
🖼 *Lodge*
🚶 *Trailhead*
🚻 *Restrooms*
🔆 *Scenic Viewpoint*
⋯⋯ *Walking/Hiking Trails*

JASPER PLANNER

When to Go

An old saying in the Canadian Rockies states: "If you don't like the weather, just wait a minute." The weather in Jasper National Park is unpredictable and ever changing, so you need to prepare for all weather conditions, especially when hiking. The summer months can be hot enough for swimming in Lake Edith one day and icy cold the next. Temperatures in winter are usually well below freezing, but occasionally warm Chinook winds blow in and begin to melt the snow.

July and August are the peak travel months for visitors— and the best time for hiking and viewing wildflowers. If you are traveling then, book accommodations well in advance and expect to pay a bit more.

Temporary road closures may occur due to adverse weather conditions.

AVG. HIGH/LOW TEMPS.

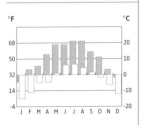

Flora and Fauna

In Jasper it is possible to stand in a field of wildflowers, hike through a thick subalpine forest, and revel in the solitude of the fragile alpine zone all in one day. A wide array of plants occupies the parks' three life zones of montane, alpine, and subalpine. In fact, about 1,300 species of plants and 20,000 types of insects and spiders are part of the complex web of life in the Canadian Rockies.

Jasper's vast wilderness is one of the few remaining places with a full range of carnivores, such as grizzly bears, black bears, wolves, coyotes, cougars, and wolverines. There are also large populations of elk, deer, bighorn sheep, and mountain goats among the park's nearly 53 species of mammals—which are often seen right from the roadsides. Each year hundreds of animals are killed along Jasper's highways, so it is vital to observe all speed limits and especially to slow down in special animal-sighting speed-zone areas. When hiking, keep your distance from wild animals and make a lot of noise as a means of avoiding contact with large mammals, especially bears.

Getting Here and Around

Jasper National Park is in central Alberta in the Canadian Rockies. It is 178 km (111 mi) north of Banff Townsite and 50 km (31 mi) east of Jasper Townsite. The closest international airports are in Edmonton, 362 km (225 mi) to the east, and Calgary, 480 km (298 mi) to the southeast. Car rental agencies are available at both airports, as well as in Jasper. Driving is the easiest way to get from Edmonton to Jasper (on Yellowhead Highway 16).

Alternatively, train service is available three times per week (Monday, Thursday, and Saturday) from Edmonton to Jasper with **VIA Rail Canada** (☎ 888/842–7245 ⊕ www. viarail.ca). **Brewster Sightseeing Excurions** (☎ 800/760–6934 ⊕ www.explorerockies.com) provides transportation between Calgary International Airport and Jasper.

23

By Debbie
Olsen

Jagged mountain peaks, shimmering glaciers, and crystal-clear lakes are just part of the incredible scenery that make up the largest and wildest of Canada's Rocky Mountain parks. Situated along the eastern slopes of the Rockies in west-central Alberta, Jasper National Park encompasses 10,878 square km (4,200 square mi) of land and is home to an astonishing variety of wildlife.

PARK ESSENTIALS

ACCESSIBILITY
Miette Hot Springs has wheelchair-accessible restrooms and changing rooms and a ramp descending into the pool with a railing. Several trails, scenic viewpoints, and day-use areas are paved. Whistlers Campground has two paved sites, each with adapted picnic tables and fireboxes. Ask for a key at the kiosk for wheelchair-accessible showers. Other camp-grounds have various facilities for disabled access.

ADMISSION FEES AND PERMITS
A park entrance pass is C$9.80 per person or C$19.60 maximum per vehicle per day. Larger buses and vans pay a group rate. An annual pass costs $67.70 per adult or $136.40 per family or group.

Permits, obtained from the park's information center (☎ 780/852–6177) are required for backcountry camping (C$9.80 per day), camp-fires (C$8.80 per day), using dumping stations (C$8.80 per day), and fishing (C$9.80 per day).

ADMISSION HOURS
The park is open 24/7, year-round. It is in the mountain time zone.

ATMS/CURRENCY EXCHANGE
There are four banks with ATM and currency exchange service and plenty of private ATMs in Jasper Townsite. Whistlers Inn also has a currency exchange service and an ATM.

JASPER IN ONE DAY

Make a stop at the **Jasper Information Centre** to get maps of the park and information about any special activities before driving up to **Mt. Edith Cavell.** The 1 km (½-mi) trail from the parking lot leads to the base of an imposing cliff where you can see the stunning Angel Glacier. If you are feeling energetic, take the steep 3-km (2-mi) trail that climbs up the valley to **Cavell Meadows,** which are carpeted with wildflowers from mid-July to mid-August. Return to Jasper Townsite for lunch.

In the afternoon, take the 45-minute drive southeast of the townsite to beautiful **Maligne Lake,** the second-largest glacier-fed lake in the world. Explore the lake and make a stop at **Spirit Island** on a 1½-hour guided boat tour with **Maligne Lake Scenic Cruises.** Return to the townsite for supper and end your day by participating in a free ranger-led evening interpretive program at **Whistlers Outdoor Theatre,** south of Jasper Townsite at Whistlers Campground.

CELL-PHONE RECEPTION

Cell phones generally only work in and around the town of Jasper. Look in Jasper Townsite, at the information center, outside the Robinsons AG Foods Store, by the Shell gas station, next to Super A Foods, and inside hotels. Also at the Icefields Centre, along some roadways, and at major sites such as Athabasca Falls, Sunwapta Falls, and Mt. Christie picnic area.

RELIGIOUS SERVICES

There are seven chapels offering services in Jasper Townsite. Denominations represented are Anglican, Baptist, Catholic, Lutheran, Pentecostal, Presbyterian, and United.

PARK CONTACT INFORMATION

Jasper National Park *P.O. Box 10, Jasper, AB T0E 1E0* 780/852–6176 *www.pc.gc.ca/jasper.*

Note that all prices in this chapter are in Canadian dollars, unless stated otherwise.

SCENIC DRIVES

Scenic drives skirt the base of glaciers, stunning lakes, and exceptional wildlife-viewing areas. The 230-km (143-mi) **Icefields Parkway** that connects Jasper with Banff provides access to the largest ice field south of Alaska and takes you to the very edge of the treeless alpine tundra. *For more details on the parkway,* ⇨ *Banff National Park, chapter 7.*

Within Jasper, **Maligne Lake Road** and **Pyramid Lake Road** are good scenic drives, south and north of the townsite, respectively.

WHAT TO SEE

HISTORIC SITES

There are five National Historic Sites within the boundaries of Jasper National Park: Jasper Information Centre, Athabasca Pass, Yellowhead Pass, Jasper House, and Henry House.

SCENIC STOPS

At **Athabasca Falls,** the Athabasca River is compressed through a narrow gorge, producing a violent torrent of water. Trails and overlooks provide good viewpoints. ✉ *Icefields Pkwy. and Hwy. 93A, 31 km (19 mi) south of Jasper.*

23

Disaster Point Animal Lick, less than 5 km (3 mi) before Highway 16 from Jasper reaches the turn for Miette Hot Springs, is the most easily accessible spot in the park for encountering bighorn sheep; it's a rare summer moment when the sheep haven't descended from the adjacent steep slopes to lick up the mineral-rich mud, wandering back and forth across the road. You're likely to see numerous cars stopped by the side of the road. ✉ *Hwy. 16, 53 km (33 mi) northeast of Jasper.*

The **Jasper Tramway** whisks you 3,191 vertical feet up the steep flank of Whistlers Mountain to an impressive overlook of the townsite and the surrounding mountains. The seven-minute ride takes you to the upper station, above the tree line (be sure to bring warm clothes). A 30- to 45-minute hike from here takes you to the summit, which is 8,085 feet above sea level. Several unmarked trails lead through the alpine meadows beyond. ✉ *Whistlers Mountain Rd., 3 km (2 mi) south of Jasper off Hwy. 93* ☎ *780/852–3093* ⊕ *www.jaspertramway.com* 💳 *C$20 round-trip* ⊙ *Apr., May, and Oct., daily 9:30–4:30; June–early Sept., daily 8:30 AM–10 PM; rest of Sept., daily 9:30–6:30.*

The Maligne River cuts a 165-foot-deep gorge through limestone bedrock at **Maligne Canyon.** An interpretive trail winds its way along the river, switching from side to side over six bridges as the canyon progressively deepens. The 4-km (2½-mi) trail along the canyon can be crowded, especially near the trailhead. Just off the path, at the Maligne Canyon teahouse, are a restaurant and a good Native American crafts store. If you visit in winter, a Maligne Canyon ice walk offers spectacular scenery from the bottom of the frozen canyon. ✉ *Maligne Lake Rd., 11 km (7 mi) south of Jasper.*

The remarkably blue, 22-km-long (14-mi-long) **Maligne Lake** is one of the largest glacier-fed lakes in the world. The first outsider known to visit the lake was Henry MacLeod, a surveyor looking for a possible route for the Canadian Pacific Railway, in 1875. You can explore the lake in a rented canoe or on a 1½-hour **scenic cruise** with **Maligne Tours** (*627 Patricia St., Jasper* ☎ *780/852–3370 or 780/852–4803* ⊕ *www.malignelake.com* 💳 *C$55* ⊙ *Every hr on the hr: June and Sept.–early Oct., daily 10–4; July and Aug., daily 10–5*). A couple of day hikes (approximately four hours round-trip), with some steep sections, lead to alpine meadows that have panoramic views of the lake and the surrounding mountain ranges. You can also take horseback-riding and fishing trips, and there's an excellent cafeteria. ✉ *Maligne Lake Rd., 44 km (27 mi) southeast of Jasper* ⊕ *www.malignelake.com.*

The naturally heated mineral waters of **Miette Hot Springs** originate from three springs and are cooled to 104°F to allow bathing in the two hot pools. There's also an adjacent cold pool—especially liked by the younger crowd—which is definitely on the cool side, at about 59°F. A short walk leads to the remnants of the original hot-springs facility, where several springs still pour hot sulfurous water into the adjacent creek. Day passes and bathing suit, locker, and towel rentals are available. ✉ *Miette Hot Springs Rd., off Hwy. 16, 58 km (36 mi) northeast of Jasper* ☎ *780/866–3939* ⊕ *www.parkscanada.gc.ca/hotsprings* 🎫 *C$6.05* ⊙ *Mid-May–late June and early Sept.–early Oct., daily 10:30–9; late June–early Sept., daily 8:30 AM–10:30 PM.*

↻   **Mt. Edith Cavell,** the highest mountain in the vicinity of Jasper, towers at
Fodor'sChoice   11,033 feet and shows its permanently snow-clad north face to the town.
★   It's named after a World War I British nurse who stayed in Belgium to treat wounded Allied soldiers after Brussels fell to the Germans; she was executed for helping prisoners of war escape. The mountain is arguably the most spectacular site in the park reachable by car. From Highway 93A, a narrow, winding 14½-km (9-mi) road (often closed until the beginning of June) leads to a parking lot at the base of the mountain. Trailers are not permitted on this road, but they can be left at a separate parking lot near the junction with 93A. Several scenic lookouts along the route offer access to trails leading up the **Tonquin Valley,** one of the premier hiking area. ✉ *Off Hwy. 93A, 27 km (17 mi) south of Jasper.*

VISITOR CENTER

Jasper Information Centre. A registered National Historic Site, this information center is in Jasper Townsite and is worth a stop even if you don't need advice. Completed in 1914, this building was designed by Edmonton architect A.M. Calderon and is constructed of cobblestone and timber and is one of the finest examples of rustic architecture in Canada's national parks. You can pick up maps, informative brochures, and other materials to help you explore the parks and its trails. A small gift shop and restroom facilities are also inside the building. Parks Canada also operates an information desk at the Icefields Centre, 103 km (64 mi) south of Jasper Townsite. ✉ *500 Connaught Dr.* ☎ *780/852–6176, 780/852–6177 trail office* ⊕ *www.pc.gc.ca/jasper* ⊙ *Apr.–June 14 and Oct., daily 9–5; June 15–Sept. 4, daily 8:30–7; Sept. 5–30, daily 9–6; Nov.–Mar., daily 9–4.*

SPORTS AND THE OUTDOORS

In the northern half of the park, backpacking and horse-packing trips offer wilderness seclusion, while the park's southern half rewards trekkers with dramatic glacial scenery. Day hikes are popular around Mt. Edith Cavell, Miette Hot Springs, and Maligne Lake; Pyramid Lake and the Fairmont Jasper Park Lodge are destinations for horseback riding.

AIR TOURS

OUTFITTERS   Contact **High Country Helicopter Tours Ltd.** (☎ *877/777–4354 or 780/852–*
AND   *0125* ⊕ *www.hcheli.com* ✉ *Tours $118–$834 per person*) to enjoy a
EXPEDITIONS   helicopter tour of the park, or to arrange heli-hiking or snowshoeing. Flights take off from Jasper Hinton Airport, just outside the park. **Icefield Helicopter Tours** (☎ *888/844–3514 or 403/721–2100* ⊕ *www.*

icefieldheli.com ⤳ *Tours $59–$589 per person)* offers helicopter tours of the Columbia Icefields. They also have heli-yoga, heli-horseback riding, heli-hiking, heli-fishing, and other helicopter tours outside the park. Flights take off from their Icefield heli-base.

BICYCLING

There are hundreds of miles of mountain bike trails and scenic road-ways to enjoy in the park. Riders are expected to stick to designated trails. *For bike rentals and expeditions,* ⇨ *Multisport Outfitters box.*

BIRD-WATCHING

An astonishing 277 species of birds make their home in the Canadian Rockies. The golden eagle migration, which occurs in the spring and fall, is the biggest birding event in the park. In late September and early October, you may be able to see more than 200 eagles in one day at the east end of the park (Pocahontas area). At other times of year, the best place to observe birds is at **Cottonwood Slough** along Pyramid Lake Road. This spot is a good place to find Barrow's goldeneye, warblers, snipes, soras and hummingbirds, and red-necked grebe.

BOATING AND RAFTING

Boating in rowboats and canoes is allowed on most of the ponds and lakes in the park. Boats with electric motors without on-board generators are allowed on most road-accessible lakes, but the use of gas-powered motors is restricted. It's always wise to ask park staff about restrictions before launching your boat.

The rafting season runs from May through September and children as young as six years of age can participate on some of the float trips. The Athabasca River has Class II white-water rapids; the Sunwapta and Fraser rivers have Class III rapids.

OUTFITTERS AND EXPEDITIONS **Jasper Raft Tours** (☎ 780/852–3613 ⊕ *www.jasperrafttours.com*) runs half-day float trips on the Athabasca. **Jasper Whitewater Rafting Ltd.** (☎ 780/852–7238 or 800/557–7238 ⊕ *www.whitewaterraftingjasper.com*) runs a variety of rafting adventures on the Athabasca and Sunwapta rivers. **Maligne Tours** (✉ *Maligne Lake* ☎ 780/852–3370 or 866/625–4463 ⊕ *www.mra.ab.ca*) rents boats on beautiful Maligne Lake, and offers rafting on the Athabasca, Sunwapta, and Fraser rivers. **Raven Adventures Ltd.** (☎ 780/852–4292 or 866/496–7238 ⊕ *www.ravenadventure.com*) offers mild to wild raft trips on the Athabasca or Sunwapta rivers and multiday trips on the Smokey River. **Rocky Mountain River Guides** (☎ 780/852–3777 ⊕ *www.rmriverguides.com*) conducts a variety of rafting trips for different levels of rafters. **Whitewater Rafting (Jasper) Ltd.** (☎ 780/852–7238 or 800/557–7238) offers half-day trips on the Athabasca and Sunwapta rivers.

For additional boating outfitters, ⇨ *Multisport Outfitters box.*

FISHING

OUTFITTERS AND EXPEDITIONS **Currie's Guiding** (✉ *406 Patricia St.* ☎ 780/852–5650 ⊕ *www.curries-guidingjasper.com*) offers half-day and full-day guided fishing trips. Prices begin at around C$189. Stop in at **On-Line Sport & Tackle** (✉ *600 Patricia St.* ☎ 780/852–3630) to arrange a guided fishing trip or a fly fishing lesson. Half-day trips start at C$169.

GOLF

The **Fairmont Jasper Park Lodge** (⊠ *Off Hwy. 16* ☎ *780/852–6090* ⊕ *www.fairmont.com/jasper/recreation*) has a championship 18-hole, par-71 course that was voted the best golf resort in Canada by *Score Magazine* in 2005.

HIKING

Long before Jasper was established as a national park, a vast network of trails provided an essential passageway for wildlife, First Nations people, explorers, and fur traders. More than 1,200 km (746 mi) of hiking trails in Jasper provide an opportunity to truly experience wilderness, and hardcore backpackers will find multiday loops of more than 160 km (100 mi).

A few of these trails are restricted to pedestrians, but hikers, mountain bikers, and equestrian users may share most of them. There are several paved trails that are suitable for wheelchairs, while others are rugged backcountry trails designed for backpacking trips. Bathrooms are found along the most used day-use trails. You may see elk, bighorn sheep, moose, and mountain goats along the way. It is never a good idea to surprise a large animal such as an elk or bear, so make plenty of noise as you go along, avoid hiking alone, and stick to designated trails. The trails at Mt. Edith Cavell and Maligne Canyon should not be missed.

EASY

Lake Annette Loop. This short loop trail with interpretive signage is paved and mostly level and was designed especially for wheelchair use. Toilets are at two locations, and there is a shelter halfway around the 2.4-km (1½-mi) loop that will take an hour to complete. ⊠ *Trailhead on the right side of the Lake Annette picnic area western parking lot* ⊹ *Take Hwy. 16 east of Jasper Townsite for 1.9 km (1.2 mi) and turn right onto the Maligne Rd. Angle right onto Lodge Rd., then turn left at the sign for Lake Annette. Keep right at major intersections to reach the Lake Annette picnic area parking lot.*

Maligne Canyon. This 2.1-km (1.3-mi), one-way trail 8 km (5 mi) east ★ of Jasper Townsite leads to views of Jasper's famous limestone gorge and will take one to two hours to complete. Six bridges stretch across the canyon and a winding trail gains about 328 feet in elevation. Signage lines the trail that leads to a waterfall at the head of the canyon. ⊠ *Trailhead at Fifth Bridge, 8 km (5 mi) east of Jasper via Highway 16 and the Maligne Rd.*

★ **Old Fort Point Loop.** Shaped by glaciers, Old Fort Point is a bedrock knob that provides an excellent view of Jasper. It will take one to two hours to complete the 3½-km (2.2-mi) loop trail. There is a wide, easy path that begins behind the trail information kiosk and leads to a section of trail that is very steep. It's common to see Rocky Mountain Bighorn Sheep, the provincial mammal of Alberta, from this trail. The trail passes the oldest rock in Jasper National Park, but the real highlight is the view from the top. ⊠ *Trailhead 1.6 km (1 mi) from Jasper Townsite* ⊹ *From Jasper Townsite or from Hwy. 16, follow Hwy. 93A to the Old Fort Point/Lac Beauvert access road. Turn left, cross the Athabasca River on the old iron bridge, then park in the lot on the right.*

⟲ **Path of the Glacier Loop.** This short 1.6-km (1-mi) trail only takes about an hour and is a must-do. The start of the trail is paved and runs across a rocky landscape that was once covered in glacial ice. Eventually you come to Cavell Pond, which is fed by Cavell Glacier. Small icebergs often float in the water. Across the valley, you will have a good view of the Angel Glacier resting her wings between Mt. Edith Cavell and Sorrow Peak. Follow the trail back along Cavell Creek to the parking lot. ⊠ *Trail begins at parking lot at the end of Cavell Rd.* ✛ *Travel south of Jasper Townsite on the Icefields Pkwy. (Hwy. 93), go 7 km (4.3 mi) past the park gate and turn right on Hwy. 93A. Follow 93A for 5.5 km (3.4 mi) and turn right on Cavell Rd. and drive 15 km (9.3 mi) to the end.*

⟲ **Valley of the Five Lakes.** It will take two to three hours to complete the 4.2 km (2.3 mi) of this family-friendly hike just 9 km (5½ mi) south of Jasper Townsite. Five small lakes are the highlight of the trip, which takes you through a lodgepole pine forest, across the Wabasso Creek wetlands, and through a flowery meadow. Watch for birds, beavers, and other wildlife along the way. Note: You can turn this into a moderate hike by continuing another 10 km (6.2 mi) to Old Fort Point. ⊠ *Trailhead 9 km (5.6 mi) south of Jasper townsite on Hwy. 93.*

MODERATE

Cavell Meadows Loop. This moderately steep 8-km (5-mi) trail will take four to six hours. The upper section is still covered in snow and is not recommended in early summer, but from mid-July to mid-August you can enjoy the carpet of wildflowers. There's also an excellent view of the Angel Glacier. ⊠ *Trail begins at parking lot at the end of Cavell Rd.* ✛ *Travel south of Jasper Townsite on the Icefields Pkwy. (Hwy. 93), past the park gate; at 7 km (4.3 mi) then turn right on Hwy. 93A. Follow 93A for 5.5 km (3.4 mi) and turn right on Cavell Rd. and drive 15 km (9.3 mi) to the end.*

DIFFICULT

★ **Wilcox Pass.** Excellent views of the Athabasca Glacier are the highlight of this strenuous 8-km (5-mi) hike near the Icefield Centre. This pass was originally used by explorers and First Nations people and is fairly steep. Keep an eye out for wildflowers and bighorn sheep. Be sure to dress in warm layers, because this pass can be snowy until late July. ⊠ *Trailhead at parking area on left-hand side of the Wilcox Creek Campground entrance road, 3.1 km (1.9 mi) south of the Icefield Centre.*

WILDERNESS HIKING Jasper's backcountry is some of the wildest and most pristine of any mountain park in the world. For information on overnight camping quotas on the Skyline and Tonquin Valley trails or on any of the hundreds of hiking and mountain-biking trails in the area, contact the park information center. The **Skyline Trail** meanders for 44 km (27 mi) past some of the park's best scenery, at or above the tree line. **Tonquin Valley,** near Mt. Edith Cavell, is one of Canada's classic backpacking areas. Its high mountain lakes, bounded by a series of steep rocky peaks known as the Ramparts, attract many hikers in high summer.

HORSEBACK RIDING

Several outfitters offer one-hour, half-day, full-day, and multiday guided trips within the park. Participants must be at least age six to participate in a riding trip, but pony rides are available for younger children. It's wise to make your reservations well in advance, especially during the peak summer months and for multiday journeys. Horses can be boarded at the commercial holding facilities available through the Cottonwood Corral Association at Pyramid Riding Stables.

OUTFITTERS AND EXPEDITIONS

Pyramid Riding Stables (✉ *Pyramid Resort, Pyramid Lake Rd.* ☎ *780/852–3562*) offers rides and full-day excursions in the hills overlooking Jasper; there are also pony and carriage rides. **Skyline Trail Rides** (✉ *Fairmont Jasper Park Lodge, off Hwy. 16* ☎ *780/852–4215, 780/852–3301 Ext. 6189, or 888/852–7787* ⊕ *www.skylinetrail.com*) has lessons and one-hour to half-day rides. Multiday trips into the backcountry are also available. **Tonquin Valley Pack Trips** (☎ *780/852–3909* ⊕ *www.tonquinvalley.com*) has an all-inclusive three- or five-day pack trip into the Tonquin Valley staying at a lake-front backcountry lodge.

SWIMMING

Lakes Annette and Edith (✉ *Near Fairmont Jasper Park Lodge, off Hwy. 16*) have sandy beaches and water that reaches the low 70s°F during warm spells. As the name implies, **Horseshoe Lake** (✉ *Approximately 25 km [15½ mi] south of Jasper Townsite on Hwy. 93*) is shaped like a horseshoe and is surrounded by cliffs. Although the water can be cold, locals like to swim and jump from the rocks and cliffs into the lake.

Jasper Aquatic Center has a 180-foot indoor waterslide, a kids' pool, and a 25-meter regular pool. A steam room and a hot tub are also on-site, and towel and suit rentals are available. ✉ *401 Pyramid Lake Rd.* ☎ *780/852–3663* 🎟 *C$6.50* ⊙ *Public swimming daily 2–9.*

WINTER SPORTS

With more than 300-km (186 mi) of trails, Jasper is one of the largest cross-country ski areas in Canada. There is a wide choice of groomed and natural trails for skiing and snowshoeing, and equipment and local guides can be arranged through local ski shops. Current cross-country ski information is available at the park visitor center. **Pyramid and Patricia lakes** (✉ *Pyramid Lake Rd.*) have excellent groomed cross-country trails. **Marmot Basin** (✉ *Off Hwy. 93A* ☎ *780/852–3816* ⊕ *www.skimarmot.com*), near Jasper, has a wide mix of downhill skiing terrain (75 runs, 9 lifts, and a terrain park with all the toys), and the slopes are a little less crowded than those around Banff, especially on weekdays. This area has three day lodges, two of which are at mid-mountain; the vertical drop is 2,944 feet. For the 2009–2010 ski season, Marmot installed the longest high-speed quad chair in the Alberta Canadian Rockies.

EDUCATIONAL OFFERINGS

INTERPRETIVE PROGRAMS

Friends of Jasper National Park. This group of enthusiastic volunteers runs a number of excellent programs during the summer months for both children and adults. The offerings include a junior naturalist program for children, birding tours, hiking tours, and historical walks. The Friends also loan out hiking kits with binoculars, maps, first-aid materials, and other useful items. Kits can be picked up at the Friends store in the information center. All programs and kits are free, but the

MULTISPORT OUTFITTERS AND EXPEDITIONS

The Boat House (✉ *Fairmont Jasper Park Lodge, off Hwy. 16* ☎ *780/852–5708*) rents adult and children's mountain bikes, as well as paddleboats and canoes. Gravity Gear (✉ *618A Patricia St.* ☎ *780/852–3155 or 888/852–3155* ⊕ *www.gravitygearjasper.com*) can arrange for ice climbing, backcountry skiing, and mountaineering trips led by certified guides. Jasper Adventure Centre (✉ *618 Connaught Dr.* ☎ *780/852–5595 or 800/565–7547* ⊕ *www.jasperadventurecentre.com*) can arrange a variety of tours and adventures inside Jasper and Banff including guided hiking adventures, icewalks on the Athabasca Glacier, tours of the Icefield Parkway, and train excursions.

Jasper Source for Sports (✉ *406 Patricia St.* ☎ *780/852–3654* ⊕ *www.jaspersports.com*) rents bikes, fishing and camping equipment, and ski and snowboard equipment. Pyramid Lake Boat Rentals (✉ *Pyramid Lake Resort* ☎ *780/852–4900 or 800/717–1277*) rents canoes, kayaks, electric boats, and paddleboats. They also sell fishing licenses and have rod and reel rentals.

Tonquin Valley Backcountry Lodge (☎ *780/852–3909* ⊕ *www. tonquinvalley.com*) arranges hiking, skiing, and horseback trips into the Tonquin Valley, with guests staying at a similar backcountry lodge. Reservations for backcountry huts can be made through the Alpine Club of Canada (☎ *403/678–3200* ⊕ *www. alpineclubofcanada.ca*). Totem Ski Shop (✉ *408 Connaught Dr.* ☎ *780/852–3078 or 800/363–3078*) sells summer and winter sports equipment and clothing.

organization appreciates donations. ✉ *Jasper Information Centre, 500 Connaught Dr.* ☎ *780/852–4767* ⊕ *www.friendsofjasper.com*.

🕑 **Mountain World Heritage Interpretive Theatre.** Parks Canada's troupe of
★ professional actors put on entertaining performances designed to educate park guests about the Canadian Rocky Mountain Parks. Shows run on select dates in Jasper. ☎ *403/760–1328* ☉ *July and Aug.*

🕑 **Whistlers Outdoor Theatre.** Interpretive programs are offered daily through
★ the summer months at the Whistlers Campground theater. Programs are appropriate for both children and adults, and a schedule of seminars and activities is available at the information center. ✉ *Whistlers Campground* 🎟 *Free* ☉ *Late June–early Sept.*

TOURS

🕑 **Jasper Adventure Centre.** Guided tours, birding trips, ice walks, and snowshoeing tours are all available here. Rates start at C$65 per person, with most tours lasting three hours. The center also handles bookings for other adventure companies (canoeing, rafting, and other sports). ✉ *604 Connaught Dr.* ☎ *780/852–5595* ⊕ *www.jasperadventurecentre.com*.

Overlander Trekking and Tours. Overlander offers everything from day treks to overnight backpacking trips and heli-hiking excursions. The outfitter's Maligne Canyon Icewalk is a very popular tour during the winter months. Rates start at C$55 per person. ✉ *414 Connaught Dr.* ☎ *780/852–0167* ⊕ *www.overlandertrekking.com*.

FESTIVALS AND EVENTS

JANUARY

Jasper in January. Fun events for the entire family during Jasper's biggest winter celebration include an ice-sculpting contest, wine tasting, great live music, a chili cook-off, Taste of the Town, outdoor contests, and more. Accommodation deals and reduced ski-lift ticket prices are available. ☎ *780/852–3858* ⊕ *jasperinjanuary.com.*

JULY

Canada Day. July 1, Canada's birthday, is celebrated with a parade, a full day of activities, and fireworks at dusk. ☎ *780/852–6176.*

Parks Day. Celebrating national parks, this annual event takes place in mid-July. There are activities for the whole family, a fair on the Information center lawn in the middle of town and free guided hikes to some of Jasper National Park's most interesting spots. ☎ *780/852–6176.*

NOVEMBER–DECEMBER

Jasper Welcomes Winter. Jasper's annual winter kick-off festival marks winter's arrival. Special activities for the entire family include the Santa Claus Parade, the Christmas Craft Fair, and shopping festivities. Special hotel rates are available. ☎ *780/852–3858.*

Walks and Talks Jasper. Birding trips, nature walks, guided hiking, cross-country ski tours, and ice-field tours are some of this company's offerings. Rates start at C$55 per person, with most tours lasting about three hours. ⊠ *626 Connaught Dr.* ☎ *780/852–4994* ⊕ *www.walksntalks.com.*

WHAT'S NEARBY

Jasper National Park is 287 km (178 mi) north of Banff National Park, 400 km (249 mi) northwest of the city of **Calgary**, 360 km (224 mi) west of the city of **Edmonton**, and 55 km (34 mi) west of the town of **Hinton** and the Jasper/Hinton Airport. Most visitors arrive through either Calgary or Edmonton, where the major highway and the two major international airports are located.

VISITOR INFORMATION

Jasper Tourism and Commerce ⌖ *P.O. Box 98, Jasper, AB T0E 1E0* ☎ *780/852–3858* ⊕ *www.jaspercanadianrockies.com.*

WHERE TO EAT AND STAY

ABOUT THE RESTAURANTS

Jasper's casual restaurants offer a wide variety of cuisines, including Greek, Italian, Japanese, French, and North American. Regional specialties include Alberta beef, lamb, pheasant, venison, elk, bison, trout, and BC (British Columbia) salmon. For the best views in town, try the cafeteria-style Treeline Restaurant at the top of the Jasper Tramway, 7,500 feet above sea level. Just know that people go to Treeline for the view, not the food.

ABOUT THE HOTELS

Accommodations in this area include luxury resorts, fine hotels, reasonably priced motels, rustic cabins, and backcountry lodges. Reserve your accommodations in advance if you are traveling during the peak summer season.

ABOUT THE CAMPGROUNDS

Parks Canada operates 10 campgrounds in Jasper National Park that have a total of 1,772 available sites during the peak season. There is winter camping only at Wapiti campground. Hookup sites are available at Whistlers and Wapiti campgrounds only, so reserve a site in advance if you are traveling during the peak summer season. Reservations (☎ 877/737–3783 ⊕ www.pccamping.ca) can be made only at Pocahontas, Whistlers, Wapiti, and Wabasso campgrounds and there is a C$10.80 reservation fee. Other campgrounds work on a first-come, first-served basis and campers line up for sites early in the morning. You can pay using a credit card, but at remote campsites, you may wish to pay cash so that you don't have to wait for the mobile truck to come around to take your credit card payment. If your campsite has a fire pit, you will need to purchase a fire permit for C$8.80 before using it.

If you arrive at the park without a reservation and cannot obtain a serviced (with hookup) site, you may choose to take an unserviced site for the first night; campground staff can advise you on how to go about getting a hookup site for the rest of your stay. Another option is to travel to nearby Hinton, outside the park, where there are a number of serviced campsites and several good campgrounds. For general campground information, call ☎ 780/852–6176.

WHERE TO EAT

$$$
CONTINENTAL
Fodor'sChoice
★

✕**Andy's Bistro.** If you want a quick meal, this is not the place to go. This intimate bistro in downtown Jasper is known for its fresh market ingredients and its slow-food dining experience. Chef and owner Andy Allenbach is Swiss born and trained and is one of only 700 certified Chefs de Cuisine in Canada. His dishes have a European flare and regional influence, and include in-season organic fruits and vegetables, wild game, and fresh herbs. From November to April enjoy a three-course table d'hôte for $33. ⊠ 606 Patricia St., Jasper ☎ 780/852–4559 ⊕ www.andysbistro.com ⚐ Reservations essential ▭ AE, MC, V.

¢
CAFE

✕**Bear's Paw Bakery.** This cozy little downtown bakery is a great stop for breakfast or lunch. The staff here makes yummy muffins and fresh cinnamon buns, and serves a variety of coffees and teas. There are a few tables for dining inside. You can also stop by to pick up freshly made sandwiches, trail cookies (made with trail mix), pastries, or artisan breads to put together your own picnic lunch. ⊠ 4 Cedar Ave. (near Connaught Dr.), Jasper ☎ 780/852–3233 ⊕ www.bearspawbakery.com ⚐ Reservations not accepted ▭ AE, MC, V.

$$$$
CANADIAN

✕**Becker's Gourmet Restaurant.** Many visitors to Jasper miss Becker's because of its out-of-town location, but it's a favorite with locals. Spectacular panoramic views of the Athabasca River and Mt. Kerkeslin from a glass-enclosed dining room are a suitable accompaniment to the fine food. Fresh and local cuisine is the specialty here—wild game, pesto-crusted rack of Alberta lamb, BC Salmon, or an excellent Alberta beefsteak are always good bets. After dinner you can stroll along the upper bank of the Athabasca River. There's a breakfast buffet from 8 to 11. ⊠ *Beside Becker's Chalets, Hwy. 93, 5 km (3 mi) south of Jasper* ☎ *780/852–3535* ⊕ *www.beckerschalets.com* ⊟ *AE, MC, V* ⊙ *Closed mid–Oct.–mid-May. No lunch.*

$$$ ✕ **Evil Dave's.** A modern and funky atmosphere and creative menus make
CANADIAN this downtown restaurant a good bet. Although the original owner Dave is no longer running the place, the current chef is the only female Red Seal chef in Jasper. Enjoy such fun specialties as Malicious Salmon (blackened salmon with sweet curry yogurt), Nefarious Chicken (parmesan crusted with salsa), and The Glad Cow (vegetarian lasagna). The lollipop shrimp make delicious appetizers. There's also a creative kids' menu for guests under 18. ⊠ *622 Patricia St., Jasper* ☎ *780/852–3323* ⊟ *AE, DC, MC, V* ⊙ *No lunch.*

$$$ ✕ **La Fiesta.** Mexican dishes such as tacos *pollo* (chicken tacos) with
MEXICAN chili-corn marmalade, spicy beef enchiladas, and classic burritos share
★ the menu with tapas dishes such as steamed mussels, artichoke dip, and calamari. Paella is a specialty here. Try the paella Valencia made with mussels, prawns, pork, chicken, and tomato-saffron rice. For dessert the orange-tequila crème brûlée or the churros are good choices. There is free delivery on a specialized Mexican take-out menu. ⊠ *Fairmont Jasper Park Lodge, off Hwy. 16, 7 km (4½ mi) northeast of Jasper* ☎ *780/852–0404* ⊟ *MC, V* ⊙ *No lunch Oct.–May.*

$$$$ ✕ **Moose's Nook Northern Grill.** The cuisine is contemporary Canadian
CANADIAN and the atmosphere is rustic and casual at this restaurant located in the upscale Fairmont Jasper Park Lodge. Live music plays every night during the summer, and fresh local ingredients from the Rockies and Alberta prairies are on the menu. Wild game, prime rib of Alberta beef, AAA Alberta beef tenderloin wrapped in boar bacon, and fresh fish are some of the highlights. For an intimate dining experience, ask for a fireplace table. Children younger than 5 eat free and children under the age of 12 enjoy a special menu or eat from the regular menu for 50% off. There's no breakfast here. ⊠ *Fairmont Jasper Park Lodge, off Hwy. 16, 7 km (4½ mi) northeast of Jasper* ☎ *780/852–3301 or 800/441–1414* ⊕ *www.fairmont.com/jasper* ⊟ *AE, D, DC, MC, V* ⊙ *No lunch.*

$$$ ✕ **Oka Sushi.** Only about a dozen people can fit into this tiny restaurant
JAPANESE with tiled walls in white and burgundy and a central sushi bar. There is just one chef and one server, and patrons sit either at tables along the perimeter or at the small bar, watching the sushi as it's prepared. Mr. Oka, the owner and chef, is famous for using the freshest ingredients and creating a variety of tantalizing sushi combinations. *Nigiri* sushi and rolled sushi are both available and come in a range of combinations. Try the Jasper Roll, which is made with crabmeat and shrimp, and is served with a spicy sauce. Sapporo beer and sake provide a nice complement to the meal. Reservations are only possible for the 6 or 6:30 seating and should be made well in advance. If you don't have a reservation, try going later. ⊠ *Fairmont Jasper Park Lodge, off Hwy. 16, 7 km (4½ mi) northeast of Jasper* ☎ *780/852–1114* ⊟ *AE, MC, V* ⊙ *No lunch.*

23

PICNIC AREAS **Airport picnic area.** This large area has a shelter and is ideal for family reunions, because it can be reserved in advance. ⊠ *Off Hwy. 16 E, 15 km (9 mi) from Jasper Townsite.*

Athabasca Falls picnic area. Dine beside the stunning Athabasca Falls. ⊠ *Off Icefields Pkwy., 30 km (19 mi) from Jasper Townsite.*

Lake Annette. Beside Lake Annette, this picnic area has shelters and tables and is a favorite with families who come to the lake to swim. ⊠ *Near the junction of Maligne Lake Rd. and Hwy. 16.*

Sixth Bridge. This picnic area is right beside the Maligne River just before it flows into the Athabasca River. There are no shelters, but it is a preferred picnic areas with locals because of the scenic location. ⊠ *Off Maligne Lake Rd., 2.2 km (1.3 mi) from the Hwy. 16 junction.*

WHERE TO STAY

IN THE PARK

$$$–$$$$ **Becker's Chalets.** On the Icefields Parkway, 5 km (3 mi) south of the town of Jasper, this quaint, family-run log cabin resort is set in a picturesque forest glade along the shores of the Athabasca River. Cabins range from one-bedroom cottages to four-room chalets and have fireplaces and kitchenettes. There are also some inexpensive, motel-style rooms. Its restaurant is one of the best in Jasper. The cabins next to the river have lovely views. There's a playground outside. **Pros:** nice, secluded setting; cute log cabins; excellent restaurant. **Cons:** 5-km (3-mi) drive into townsite; trains pass right behind the property. ⊠ *On the Icefields Parkway, 5 km (3 mi) south of the town of Jasper* ⌂ *P.O. Box 579, Jasper T0E 1E0* ☎ *780/852–3779* ⊕ *www.beckerschalets.com* ➴ *118 rooms* ⌂ *In-room: no a/c, no phone, kitchen (some), refrigerator. In-hotel: restaurant, laundry facilities parking (free)* ▤ *AE, MC, V* ⊗ *Closed mid-Oct.–May.*

$$$$ **Fairmont Jasper Park Lodge.** With abundant on-site recreational amenities, this lakeside resort, 7 km (4½ mi) northeast of Jasper, is a destination in itself, whether or not you stay overnight. Accommodations vary from cedar chalets and log cabins to specialty cabins with up to eight bedrooms. Rooms include down duvets, and all have either a porch, patio, or balcony. Guests love the year-round outdoor swimming pool, heated to 86°F in winter. Canoe rentals, golf, and horseback riding are available in the summer and skate rentals, cross-country ski trails, tobogganing, and sleigh rides are offered in the winter. The golf course was voted the best golf resort in Canada by readers of *Score Magazine* in 2005, and nearby Marmot Basin has world-class skiing. **Pros:** abundant amenities; beautiful setting; top-notch dining. **Cons:** 10-minute drive to townsite; on-site dining can be pricey. ⊠ *At the end of Old Lodge Rd., off Old Fort Point Road, 1½ km (1 mi) from the Highway 93A junction, 4 km (2.5 mi) east of Jasper Townsite* ⌂ *P.O. Box 40, Jasper T0E 1E0* ☎ *780/852–3301 or 800/441–1414* ⊕ *www.fairmont.com/ jasper* ➴ *446 rooms, 100 suites* ⌂ *In-room: no a/c, Internet. In-hotel: 9 restaurants, room service, bar, golf course, tennis courts, pool, gym, bicycles, Wi-Fi* ▤ *AE, D, DC, MC, V.*

Fodor's Choice ★

$$$ **Patricia Lake Bungalows.** Lakefront solitude is the highlight of these ★ comfortable basic lodgings. Though the motel rooms are the least expensive of the accommodations, the cabins—at a 20% premium over

the motel units—are the most popular. Ten luxury cabins also are available. Rates decrease by up to 50% off-season. **Pros:** good value; quiet lakefront location; well-kept property and grounds. **Cons:** five-minute drive from townsite. ✉ *Off Pyramid Lake Rd.* 🖃 *P.O. Box 657, Jasper T0E 1E0* ☎ *780/852–3560* ⊕ *www.patricialakebungalows.com* 🛏 *10 rooms, 16 suites, 22 cabins* ⚤ *In-room: some a/c, no phone. In-hotel: bicycles, laundry facilities, water sports, Internet terminal* 🖃 *MC, V* ☺ *Closed mid-Oct.–Apr.*

$$$ ⛺ **Pine Bungalows.** On the banks of the Athabasca River, this property is ideal for families because it has 72 rustic cabins with outdoor barbecues, picnic tables, and tubs with showers. Many cabins have fireplaces and most have kitchens; there are laundry facilities on-site. Wildlife sightings are common on the property. **Pros:** natural setting; 10-minute walk to townsite. **Cons:** no TV; no Internet. ✉ *2 Cottonwood Creek Rd., approximately 2 km (1 mi) east of Jasper Townsite, Jasper* ☎ *780/852–3491* ⊕ *www.pinebungalows.com* 🛏 *72 cabins* ⚤ *In-room: no a/c, no phone, kitchen, no TV. In-hotel: laundry facilities* 🖃 *AE, MC, V* ☺ *Closed mid-Oct.–Apr.*

CAMPING ⛺ **Columbia Icefield Campground.** This rustic campground is near a creek

$ and has great views of the Columbia Icefield. Warm camping gear is recommended. The site is not appropriate for RVs and reservations are not accepted. **Pros:** close to the Icefield; secluded, picturesque setting. **Cons:** primitive; few services. ✉ *106 km (66 mi) south of Jasper on Hwy. 93* ☎ *780/852–6176* ⛺ *33 tent sites* ⚤ *Drinking water* 🖃 *AE, MC, V* ☺ *Closed early Oct.–mid-May.*

$ ⛺ **Jonas Creek Campground.** This small, primitive campground is in a quiet spot along a creek off the Icefields Parkway. Sites are first-come, first-served. **Pros:** quiet campground; secluded locale. **Cons:** primitive—very few amenities. ✉ *75 km (47 mi) south of Jasper Townsite* ☎ *780/852–6176* ⛺ *25 tent/RV sites* ⚤ *Picnic tables, public telephone* 🖃 *AE, MC, V* ☺ *Closed early Sept.–mid-May.*

$ ⛺ **Mt. Kerkeslin Campground.** This is a very basic campground with few facilities. Tent camping is available, and there are fire pits for cooking. **Pros:** quiet campground; secluded locale. Sites are first-come, first-served. **Cons:** primitive—very few amenities. ✉ *35 km (22 mi) south of Jasper Townsite on Hwy. 93* ☎ *780/852–6176* ⛺ *45 tent/RV sites* ⚤ *Fire pits* 🖃 *AE, MC, V* ☺ *Closed early Sept.–early June.*

$$ ⛺ **Wabasso Campground.** Families flock to this campground because of its playground and many amenities. **Pros:** lots of amenities; on-site playground. **Cons:** no showers. ✉ *16 km (10 mi) south of Jasper Townsite on Hwy. 93A* ☎ *877/737–3783* ⛺ *228 tent/RV sites* ⚤ *Flush toilets, dump station, drinking water, public telephone, play area* 🖃 *AE, MC, V* ☺ *Closed early Sept.–late June.*

$$ ⛺ **Wapiti Campground.** Close to Jasper, this campground is near a number of good hiking trails. There are 53 unserviced sites that are open during the winter season. **Pros:** lots of amenities including showers; half the size of Whistlers campground; good hiking trails nearby. **Cons:** no on-site interpretive programs. ✉ *5 km (3 mi) south of Jasper Townsite on Hwy. 93* ☎ *877/737–3782* ⛺ *322 tent/RV sites, 40 partial hookup (electric)*

23

RV sites ♿ Flush toilets, dump station, drinking water, showers, some hookups, electricity, public telephones ▭ AE, MC, V.

$$–$$$ ⛺ **Whistlers Campground.** This campground is the largest and has the ☾ most amenities. It's the number-one choice for families because of the on-site interpretive programs at Whistlers Theatre. **Pros:** on-site interpretive programs; large campground with many amenities. **Cons:** most popular campground in the park, so it tends to be more crowded than others. ✉ *3 km (2 mi) south of Jasper Townsite on Hwy. 93* ☏ *877/737–3783* ⛺ *604 unserviced tent/RV sites, 100 partial hookup RV sites (electric), 77 fully serviced RV sites sites ♿ Flush toilets, dump station, drinking water, showers, electricity, public telephone ▭ AE, MC, V* ☾ *Closed early Oct.–mid-May.*

OUTSIDE THE PARK

CAMPING ⛺ **Hinton/Jasper KOA Campground.** This campground is 15 minutes from
$$–$$$ the east entrance of Jasper National Park and about five minutes from the town of Hinton. It's situated in a meadow bordered by three creeks and has many amenities, including 81 fully serviced sites, rustic camping cabins, a shared camper kitchen, and wheelchair-accessible showers and restrooms. Horseback riding, hayrides, and hiking trails are nearby. **Pros:** lots of amenities; accessible showers; pretty locale. **Cons:** far from Jasper Townsite; no on-site interpretive programs. ✉ *Hwy. 16, 4 km (2½ mi) west of Hinton* ☏ *780/865–5061 or 888/562–4714* ⊕ *www.koa.com* ⛺ *106 tent/RV sites ♿ Flush toilets, showers, fire pits, picnic tables, play area ▭ MC, V.*

Joshua Tree National Park

WORD OF MOUTH

"I can only comment on Joshua Tree, it's a stunning pace to unwind for awhile. I keep going back when in S. California. I've seen great sunrises and desert flowers (spring). Nice hiking. I really enjoyed the drive out from San Diego. We always stop in Palm Springs for supplies and wine and make a nice dinner."

—blondiegal

WELCOME TO JOSHUA TREE

TOP REASONS TO GO

★ **Rock climbing:** Joshua Tree is a world-class site with challenges for climbers of just about every skill level.

★ **Peace and quiet:** Savor the solitude of one of the last great wildernesses in America.

★ **Stargazing:** You'll be mesmerized by the Milky Way flowing across the dark night sky. For spectacular natural fireworks, visit in mid-August during the Perseid meteor shower and watch shooting stars streak overhead.

★ **Wildflowers:** In spring, the hillsides explode in a patchwork of yellow, blue, pink, and white.

★ **Sunsets:** Twilight is a special time here, especially during the winter, when the setting sun casts a golden glow on the mountains.

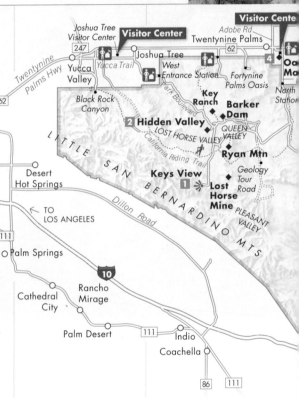

1 Keys View. This is the most dramatic overlook in the park—on clear days you can see Signal Mountain in Mexico.

2 Hidden Valley. Crawl between the big rocks and you'll understand why this boulder-strewn area was once a cattle rustlers' hideout.

3 Cholla Cactus Garden. Come here in the late afternoon, when the spiky stalks of the bigelow (jumping) cholla cactus are backlit against an intense blue sky.

4 Oasis of Mara. Walk the nature trail around this desert oasis, which the first settlers, the Serrano, dubbed "the place of little springs and much grass."

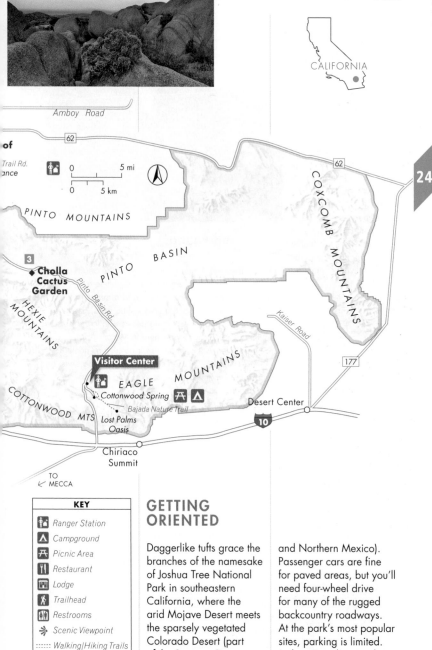

CALIFORNIA

24

Amboy Road

62

of

Trail Rd.
ance

0   5 mi

0   5 km

PINTO   MOUNTAINS

62

COXCOMB   MOUNTAINS

3
◆ **Cholla Cactus Garden**

PINTO   BASIN

Pinto Basin Rd.

HEXIE MOUNTAINS

Kaiser Road

177

Visitor Center

EAGLE   MOUNTAINS

Cottonwood Spring
Bajada Nature Trail

COTTONWOOD MTS

Lost Palms Oasis

Desert Center

10

Chiriaco Summit

TO
MECCA

KEY

👫	Ranger Station
⛺	Campground
🪑	Picnic Area
🍴	Restaurant
🏨	Lodge
🥾	Trailhead
🚻	Restrooms
⤳	Scenic Viewpoint
⋯⋯⋯	Walking/Hiking Trails

GETTING ORIENTED

Daggerlike tufts grace the branches of the namesake of Joshua Tree National Park in southeastern California, where the arid Mojave Desert meets the sparsely vegetated Colorado Desert (part of the Sonoran Desert, which lies within California and Northern Mexico). Passenger cars are fine for paved areas, but you'll need four-wheel drive for many of the rugged backcountry roadways. At the park's most popular sites, parking is limited. Joshua Tree does not have public transportation.

JOSHUA TREE PLANNER

When to Go

October through May, when the desert is cooler, is when most of visitors arrive. Daytime temperatures range from the mid-70s in December and January to mid-90s in October and May. Lows can dip to near freezing in mid-winter, and you may even encounter snow at the higher elevations. Summers can be torrid, with daytime temperatures reaching 110°F.

Festivals and Events

FEB. Riverside County Fair & National Date Festival. Head to Indio for camel and ostrich races. ☎ 800/811–3247.

MAY Pony Express Ride and Barbecue. This reenactment of the historic mail delivery service runs from Yucca Valley to Pioneertown. ☎ 760/365–6323.

OCT. Pioneer Days. Outhouse races, beard contests, and arm-wrestling mark this annual celebration in Twentynine Palms. ☎ 760/367–3445.

AVG. HIGH/LOW TEMPS.

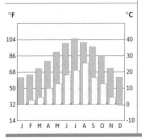

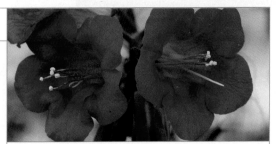

Flora and Fauna

Joshua Tree will shatter your notions of the desert as a vast wasteland. Life flourishes in this land of little rain, as flora and fauna have adapted to heat and drought. In most areas you'll be walking among native Joshua trees, ocotillos, and yuccas. One of the best spring desert wildflower displays in Southern California blooms here in March, April, and May. You'll see plenty of animals—reptiles such as nocturnal sidewinders, birds like golden eagles or burrowing owls, and occasionally mammals like coyotes and bobcats.

Getting Here and Around

An isolated island of pristine wilderness—a rarity these days—Joshua Tree National Park is within a short drive of 11 million Southern California residents. Most visitors, in fact, make the two-hour drive from the Los Angeles area to enjoy a weekend of solitude in 792,726 acres of untouched desert. The urban sprawl of Palm Springs (home to the nearest airport) is 45 mi away, but gateway towns Joshua Tree, Yucca Valley, and Twentynine Palms are just north of the park. If you're staying in the Palm Springs area, you can enjoy the highlights of the park in one day, including a stop for a picnic at a scenic spot.

■ TIP→ If you'd prefer not to drive, most Palm Springs area hotels can arrange a half or full day tour that hits the highlights of Joshua Tree National Park. But you'll need to spend two or three days camping here to truly experience the quiet beauty of the desert.

24

By Bobbi Zane

Ruggedly beautiful desert scenery attracts nearly 2 million visitors each year to Joshua Tree National Park, one of the last great wildernesses in the continental United States. Its mountains support mounds of enormous boulders and jagged rock; natural cactus gardens and lush oases shaded by tall fan palms mark the meeting place of the Mojave (high) and Sonora (low) deserts. Extensive stands of Joshua trees gave the park its name; the plants (members of the Yucca family of shrubs) reminded early white settlers of the biblical Joshua, with their thick, stubby branches representing the prophet raising his arms toward heaven.

PARK ESSENTIALS

ACCESSIBILITY
Black Rock Canyon and Jumbo Rocks campgrounds each have one accessible campsite. Nature trails at Oasis of Mara, Bajada, Keys View, and Cap Rock are accessible. Some trails at roadside viewpoints can be negotiated by those with limited mobility.

ADMISSION FEES AND PERMITS
Park admission is $15 per car, $5 per person on foot. The Joshua Tree Pass, good for one year, is $30. Free permits—available at all visitor centers—are required for rock climbing.

ADMISSION HOURS
The park is open every day, around the clock. The park is in the Pacific time zone.

ATMS/BANKS
There are no ATMs in the park. ATMs and banks can be found in Yucca Valley and Joshua Tree.

CELL-PHONE RECEPTION

Cell phones don't work in most areas of the park. Pay phones are at Oasis Visitor Center and Black Rock Canyon Campground; there are no telephones in the interior of the park.

PARK CONTACT INFORMATION

Joshua Tree National Park ⊠ *74485 National Park Dr., Twentynine Palms, CA* ☎ *760/367–5500* ⊕ *www.nps.gov/jotr.*

SCENIC DRIVES

Geology Tour Road. Some of the park's most fascinating landscapes can be observed from this 18-mi dirt road. Parts of the journey are rough, so make sure you have a 4X4. Sights to see include a 100-year-old stone dam called Squaw Tank, defunct mines, and a large plain with an abundance of Joshua trees. There are 16 stops along the way, so give yourself about two hours to make the round-trip. ⊠ *South of Park Blvd., west of Jumbo Rocks.*

★ **Park Boulevard.** Traversing the most scenic portions of Joshua Tree, this well-paved road connects the north and west entrances in the park's high desert section. Along with some sweeping desert views, you'll see jumbles of splendid boulder formations, stands of Joshua trees, and Hidden Valley and Barker Dam, remnants of the area's wild and woolly past. From the Oasis Visitor Center, drive south. After about 5 mi, the road forks; turn right and head west toward Jumbo Rocks (clearly marked with a road sign).

WHAT TO SEE

You can experience Joshua Tree National Park on several levels. Even on a short excursion along Park Boulevard between the Joshua Tree entrance station and Oasis of Mara, you'll see some of the best desert scenery in North America—including a staggering abundance of flora visible along a dozen self-guided nature trails. You'll also see remnants of homesteads from a century ago, now mostly abandoned and wind-worn. If rock climbing is your passion, this is the place for you; boulder-strewn mountaintops and slopes beckon. But in the end, Joshua Tree National Park is a pristine wilderness where you can enjoy a solitary stroll along an animal trail and commune with nature. The sites listed below include most of the highlights, each appealing in its own way. Be sure to take some time to explore on your own and enjoy the peace and quiet.

HISTORIC SITES

Hidden Valley. This legendary cattle-rustlers hideout is set among big boulders, which kids love to scramble over and around. ⊠ *Park Blvd., 14 mi south of West Entrance.*

★ **Keys Ranch.** This 150-acre ranch that once belonged to William and Frances Keys illustrates one of the area's most successful attempts at homesteading. The couple raised five children under extreme desert conditions. Most of the original buildings, including the house, school, store, and workshop, have been restored to the way it was when William died in 1969. The only way to see the ranch is on one of the 60-minute, ranger-led walking tours, offered weekdays October–May (⇨ *Educational Offerings*); tour reservations are essential. ✉ *2 mi north of Barker Dam Rd.* ☎ 760/367–5555 ✑ *$5* ⊙ *Oct.–May, tours weekdays at 10 and 1.*

Lost Horse Mine. This historic mine, which produced 10,000 ounces of gold and 16,000 ounces of silver between 1894 and 1931, illustrates gold prospecting and mining activities. The 10-stamp mill is considered one of the best preserved of its type in the park system. The site is accessed via a fairly strenuous 2-mi hike. ✉ *Keys View Rd., about 15 mi south of West Entrance.*

SCENIC STOPS

Cholla Cactus Garden. This stand of bigelow cholla (sometimes called jumping cholla, since its hooked spines seem to jump at you) is best seen and photographed in late afternoon, when the backlit spiky stalks stand out against a colorful sky. ✉ *Pinto Basin Rd., 20 mi north of Cottonwood Visitor Center.*

Cottonwood Spring. Home to the native Cahuilla people for centuries, this spring provided water for travelers and early prospectors. The area, which supports a large stand of fan palms, is a stop for migrating birds and a winter water source for bighorn sheep. A number of gold mills were located here, and the area still has some remains, including an *arrastra* (gold-mining tool) and concrete pillars. You can access the site via a 1-mi paved trail that begins at sites 13A and 13B of the Cottonwood Campground. ✉ *Cottonwood Visitor Center.*

Fortynine Palms Oasis. A short drive off Highway 62, this site is a bit of a preview of what the park's interior has to offer: stands of fan palms, interesting petroglyphs, and evidence of fires built by early American Indians. Since animals frequent this area, you may spot a coyote, bobcat, or roadrunner. ✉ *End of Canyon Rd., 4 mi west of Twentynine Palms.*

★ **Keys View.** At 5,185 feet, this point affords a sweeping view of the Santa Rosa Mountains and Coachella Valley, the mountains of the San Bernardino National Forest, the Salton Sea, San Andreas Fault, and—on a rare clear day—Signal Mountain in Mexico. Sunrise and sunset are magical times, when the light throws rocks and trees into high relief before bathing the hills in brilliant shades of red, orange, and gold. ✉ *Keys View Rd., 21 mi south of west entrance.*

Lost Palms Oasis. More than 100 fan palms comprise the largest group of the exotic plants in the park. A spring bubbles from between the rocks, but disappears into the sandy, boulder-strewn canyon. As you hike along the 4-mi trail, you might spot bighorn sheep. ⊠ *Cottonwood Visitor Center*.

Ocotillo Patch. Stop here for a roadside exhibit on the dramatic display made by the red-tipped succulent after even the shortest rain shower. ⊠ *Pinto Basin Rd., about 3 mi east of Cholla Cactus Gardens*.

> **LOOK, DON'T TOUCH—REALLY**
>
> Some cactus needles, like those on the cholla, can become embedded in your skin with just the slightest touch. If you do get zapped, use tweezers to gently pull it out.

VISITOR CENTERS

Cottonwood Visitor Center. Exhibits in this small center, staffed by rangers and volunteers, illustrate the region's natural history. ⊠ *Pinto Basin Rd.* ☏ *No phone* ⊕ *www.nps.gov/jotr* ⊙ *Daily 8–4*.

Joshua Tree Visitor Center. This visitor center, opened in summer 2006, holds exhibits illustrating park geology, cultural and historic sites, and hiking and rock-climbing activities. There's also a small bookstore. ⊠ *6554 Park Blvd.Joshua Tree* ☏ *760/367–5500* ⊕ *www.nps.gov/jotr* ⊙ *Daily 8–5*.

Oasis Visitor Center. Exhibits here illustrate how Joshua Tree was formed, reveal the differences between the two types of desert within the park, and demonstrate how plants and animals eke out an existence in this arid climate. Take the .5-mi nature walk through the nearby Oasis of Mara, which is alive with cottonwood trees, palm trees, and mesquite shrubs. ⊠ *74485 National Park Dr., Twentynine Palms* ☏ *760/367–5500* ⊕ *www.nps.gov/jotr* ⊙ *Daily 8–4:30*.

SPORTS AND THE OUTDOORS

BICYCLING

Mountain biking is a great way to see Joshua Tree. Bikers are restricted to roads that are used by motorized vehicles, including the main park roads and a few four-wheel-drive trails. Most scenic stops, picnic areas, and trailheads have bike racks.

Black Eagle Mountain Road. This dead-end, 9-mi road peppered with defunct mines runs along the edge of a former lake bed, then crosses a number of dry washes before navigating several of Eagle Mountain's canyons. ⊠ *Trailhead off Pinto Basin Rd., 6½ mi north of Cottonwood Visitor Center*.

Covington Flats. This 4-mi trail leads you past impressive Joshua trees as well as pinyon pines, junipers, and areas of lush desert vegetation. It's tough going toward the end, but once you reach 5,516-foot Eureka Peak, you have great views of Palm Springs, the Morongo Basin, and the surrounding mountains. ⊠ *Trailhead at Covington Flats picnic area, La Contenta Rd., 10 mi south of Rte. 62*.

Pinkham Canyon and Thermal Canyon Roads. This challenging unpaved 20-mi route loops through the Cottonwood Mountains; it begins at

DID YOU KNOW?

Found only in Arizona, California, Nevada, and Utah, the Joshua Tree (*Yucca brevifolia*) is actually a member of the lily family, and as such, it doesn't have tree rings to indicate its age. American Indians used the yucca's hearty foliage like leather, forming it into everyday items like baskets and shoes. Later, early settlers used its core and limbs for building fences to contain their livestock.

the Cottonwood Visitor Center. The trail follows Smoke Tree Wash through Pinkham Canyon, rounds Thermal Canyon, and loops back to the beginning. Rough in places, the road travels through soft sand and rocky flood plains. ⊠ *Trailhead at Cottonwood Visitor Center.*

Queen Valley. This 13.4-mi network of mostly level roads winds through one of the park's most impressive groves of Joshua trees. Bike racks at the Barker Dam and Hidden Valley trailheads allow you to park your ride and go hiking. ⊠ *Trailhead at Hidden Valley Campground.*

BIRD-WATCHING

Joshua Tree, located on the inland portion of the Pacific Flyway, hosts about 250 species of birds, and the park is a popular seasonal location for birdwatching. During the fall migration, which runs from mid-September through mid-October, there are several reliable sighting areas. At Barker Dam you might spot white-throated swifts, several types of swallows, or red-tailed hawks. Lucy's warbler, lesser goldfinches, and Anna's hummingbirds cruise around Cottonwood Spring, a serene palm-shaded setting where you'll likely see the largest concentrations of birds in the park. At Black Rock Canyon and Covington Flats, you're likely to see La Conte's thrashers, ruby-crowned kinglets, and warbling vireos. Rufus hummingbirds, Pacific slope flycatchers, and various warblers are frequent visitors to Indian Cove. Lists of birds found in the park, as well as information on recent sightings, are available at visitor centers.

HIKING

There are more than 191 mi of hiking trails in Joshua Tree, ranging from quarter-of-a-mile nature trails to 35-mi treks. Some connect with each other, so you can design your own desert maze. Remember that drinking water is hard to come by—you won't find water in the park except at the entrances. Bring along at least a gallon per person for all but the shortest hikes, more if the weather is hot. Before striking out on a hike or apparent nature trail, check out the signage. Roadside signage identifies hiking- and rock-climbing routes.

EASY

Bajada All Access. Learn all about what plants do to survive in the desert on this easy, wheelchair-accessible ¼-mi loop. ⊠ *Trailhead south of Cottonwood Visitor Center, ½ mi from park entrance.*

Cap Rock. This ½-mi wheelchair-accessible loop—named after a boulder that sits atop a huge rock formation like a cap—winds through fascinating rock formations and has signs that explain the geology of the Mojave Desert. ⊠ *Trailhead at junction of Park Blvd. and Keys View Rd.*

High View Nature Trail. This 1.3-mi loop climbs nearly to the top of 4,500-foot Summit Peak. The views of nearby Mt. San Gorgonio (snow-capped in winter) make the moderately steep journey worth the effort. ⊠ *Trailhead ½ mi west of Black Rock Canyon Campground.*

Indian Cove Trail. Look for lizards and roadrunners along this ½-mi loop that follows a desert wash. This easy trail has signs with interesting facts about these and other animals of the Mojave Desert. ⊠ *Trailhead at west end of Indian Cove Campground.*

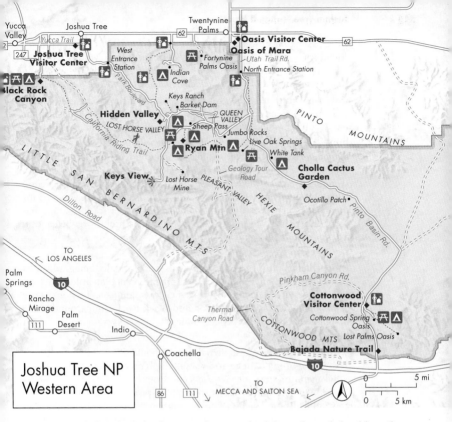

Skull Rock Trail. The ¼-mi loop guides hikers through boulder piles, desert washes, and a rocky alley. It's named for what is perhaps the park's most famous rock formation, which resembles a human head. ⊠ *Trailhead at Jumbo Rocks Campground.*

MODERATE

California Riding and Hiking Trail. This well-traveled route stretches for 35 mi between the Black Rock Canyon Entrance and the North Entrance. You can access the trail for a short or long hike at several points. ⊠ *Trailheads at Upper Covington Flats, Ryan Campground, Twin Tanks, south of north park entrance, and Black Rock Canyon.*

Fodor's Choice
★

Ryan Mountain Trail. The payoff for hiking to the top of 5,461-foot Ryan Mountain is one of the best panoramic views of Joshua Tree. From here you can see Mt. San Jacinto, Mt. San Gorgonio, Lost Horse Valley, and the Pinto Basin. You'll need two to three hours to complete the 3-mi round-trip. ⊠ *Trailhead at Ryan Mountain parking area, 16 mi southeast of park's west entrance or Sheep Pass, 16 mi southwest of Oasis Visitor Center.*

DIFFICULT

Boy Scout Trail. The moderately strenuous 8-mi trail, suitable for back-packers, extends from Indian Cove to Park Boulevard. It runs through the westernmost edge of the Wonderland of Rocks (where you're likely to see climbers on the outcroppings), passing through a forest of Joshua trees, past granite towers, and around willow-lined pools. Completing the round-trip journey requires camping along the way, so you may want to hike only part of the trail or have a car waiting at the other end. ⊠ *Trailhead between Quail Springs Picnic Area and Indian Cove Campground.*

Lost Palms Oasis Trail. Allow four to six hours for the moderately strenuous, 7½-mi round-trip, which leads to the most impressive oasis in the park. You'll find more than 100 fan palms and an abundance of wildflowers here. ⊠ *Trailhead at Cottonwood Spring Oasis.*

★ **Mastodon Peak Trail.** Some boulder scrambling is required on this 3-mi hike up 3,371-foot Mastodon Peak, but the journey rewards you with stunning views of the Salton Sea. The trail passes through a region where gold was mined from 1919 to 1932, so be on the lookout for open mines. The peak draws its name from a large rock formation that early miners believed looked like the head of a prehistoric behemoth. ⊠ *Trailhead at Cottonwood Spring Oasis.*

HORSEBACK RIDING

More than 200 mi of equestrian trails are gradually being added as part of a backcountry and wilderness management plan at Joshua Tree, and visitors are welcome to bring their own animals. Trail maps are available at visitor centers. Ryan and Black Rock campgrounds have designated areas for horses and mules.

ROCK CLIMBING

Fodor's Choice ★ With an abundance of weathered igneous boulder outcroppings, Joshua Tree is one of the nation's top winter climbing destinations and offers a full menu of climbing experiences—from bouldering for beginners in the Wonderland of Rocks to multiple-pitch climbs at Echo Rock and Saddle Rock. The best-known climb in the park is Hidden Valley's Sports Challenge Rock. A map inside the *Joshua Tree Guide* shows locations of selected wilderness and nonwilderness climbs.

OUTFIT-
TERS AND
EXPEDITIONS
Joshua Tree Rock Climbing School offers several programs, from one-day introductory classes to multiday programs for experienced climbers. The school provides all needed equipment. Beginning classes are limited to six people age 13 or older. ⌂ *Box 3034, Joshua Tree, CA 92252* ☎ *760/366–4745 or 800/890–4745* ⊕ *www.joshuatreerockclimbing. com* ✉ *$125 for beginner class.*

Vertical Adventures Rock Climbing School trains about 1,000 climbers each year in Joshua Tree National Park. Classes meet at a designated location in the park, and all equipment is provided. ☎ *800/514–8785* ⊕ *www.vertical-adventures.com* ✉ *$125 per person for one-day class* ☉ *Sept.–June.*

EDUCATIONAL OFFERINGS

LECTURES AND FIELD TRIPS

The Desert Institute of Joshua Tree National Park Association. This organization offers a full schedule of educational lectures on topics like the birds of Joshua Tree National Park, wildflower wanderings, the desert night sky, and basket weaving. University credit is available for some lectures. Classes meet at various locations; many include field trips within the

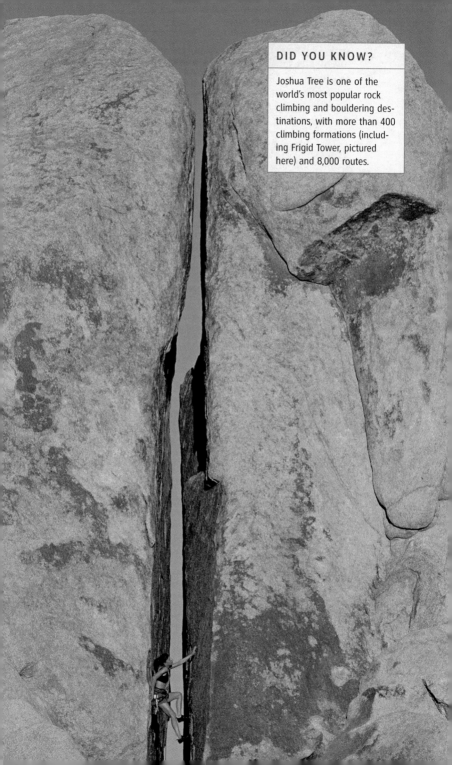

park. Call for current schedule and prices. ⊠ *74485 National Park Dr., Twentynine Palms* ☎ *760/367–5525* ⊕ *www.joshuatree.org.*

Star Parties. See the full night sky in its natural, unpolluted state during informal monthly star parties and telescope viewing presented by members of the Andromeda Astronomical Society at sunset on Saturday nights close to the new moon. Check for dates at visitor centers. ⊠ *Hidden Valley Picnic Area.*

RANGER PROGRAMS
Rangers offer a full schedule of hour-long programs to help you explore the park fall through spring; the schedule is limited in the hot summer months. Refer to the guide available at visitor centers for specific schedule, as times and destinations vary.

Keys Ranch Tour. A guide takes you through the former home of a struggling homesteading family. The 90-minute tour begins at the Barker Dam parking area. Rangers tell about the Tickets are $5 per person, and tours often sell out, and you can book by phone (☎ *760/367–5555*), at the Joshua Tree or Oasis visitor centers (prior to the day of the tour), or, if space is still available, at the ranch gate on the day of the tour. ⊠ *Hidden Valley Picnic Area.*

Evening Programs. Rangers present hour-long Saturday evening lectures at Black Rock Canyon Nature Center, Cottonwood Amphitheater, Indian Cove Amphitheater, and Jumbo Rocks Campground. Topics range from natural history to local lore. The schedule is posted at the visitor centers. ▨ *Free* ☉ *Oct.–Apr., Sat. at 7; May, Sat. at 8.*

ORGANIZED TOURS
TOUR
OPERATORS
Based in Palm Desert, **Big Wheel Tours** (☎ *760/779–1837* ⊕ *www.bwbtours. com* ✉ *$99 per person*) offers van excursions through the park. **Desert Adventures** (☎ *760/340–2345* ⊕ *www.red-jeep.com*) offers off-road jeep tours. **Desert Safari Guides** (☎ *760/325–4453 or 888/324–4453* ⊕ *www. palmspringshiking.com*) has short tours of Joshua Tree from Palm Springs. **Elite Land Tours** (☎ *760/318–1200* ⊕ *www.elitelandtours.com*) explores Joshua Tree via luxury Hummers.

WHAT'S NEARBY

NEARBY TOWNS

Palm Springs, about a 45-minute drive from the North Entrance Station at Joshua Tree, serves as the home base for most park visitors. This city of 43,000 has 95 golf courses, 600 tennis courts, and 30,000 swimming pools. A hideout for Hollywood stars since the 1920s, Palm Springs offers a glittering array of shops, restaurants, and hotels. Stroll down Palm Canyon Drive and you're sure to run into a celebrity or two. About 9 mi north of Palm Springs and closer to the park is **Desert Hot Springs,** which has more than 1,000 natural hot mineral pools and 40 health spas ranging from low-key to luxurious. **Yucca Valley** is the largest and fastest growing of the communities straddling the park's northern border. The town boasts a handful of motels, supermarkets, and a Wal-Mart. Tiny **Joshua Tree,** the closest community to the park's West Entrance, is where the serious rock climbers make their headquarters. **Twentynine Palms,** known as "two-nine" by locals, is sandwiched between the Marine Corps Air Ground Task Force Center to the north and Joshua Tree National Park to the south. Here you'll find a smattering of coffeehouses, antiques shops, and cafés.

VISITOR INFORMATION

California Welcome Center Yucca Valley ✉ *56711 Twentynine Palms Hwy.* ☎ *760/365–5464* ⊕ *www.visitcwc.com.* **Joshua Tree Chamber of Commerce** ✉ *6470 Veterans Way, Joshua Tree* ☎ *760/366–3723* ⊕ *www. joshuatreechamber.org.* **Palm Springs Bureau of Tourism** ✉ *777 N. Palm Canyon Dr., Palm Springs* ☎ *760/778–8415 or 800/348–7746* ⊕ *www.palm-springs. org.* **Twentynine Palms Chamber of Commerce** ✉ *73660 Civic Center, Suite C and D, Twentynine Palms* ☎ *760/367–3445* ⊕ *www.29chamber.com.* **Yucca Valley Chamber of Commerce** ✉ *56711 Twentynine Palms Hwy., Yucca Valley* ☎ *760/365–6323* ⊕ *www.yuccavalley.org.*

24

NEARBY ATTRACTIONS

Big Morongo Canyon Preserve. A serene oasis located about 11 mi north of Interstate 10, this serene preserve attracts birds and other animals to a riparian woodland filled with cottonwoods and willows. A shaded meadow is a nice place for a picnic. Pets are not permitted. ✉ *East Dr., Morongo Valley* ☎ *760/363–7190* ⊕ *www.bigmorongo.org* 🎟 *Free* ☉ *Daily 7:30–sunset.*

☾ **Hi-Desert Nature Museum.** Check out this small zoo containing creatures that make their homes in Joshua Tree, including scorpions, snakes, ground squirrels, and chuckwallas (a type of lizard). There's also a collection of rocks, minerals, and fossils from the Paleozoic era, an American Indian collection, and an interactive exhibit room for children. ✉ *57116 Twentynine Palms Hwy., Yucca Valley* ☎ *760/369–7212* ⊕ *www.yucca-valley.org* 🎟 *Free* ☉ *Tues.–Sun. 10–5.*

Oasis of Murals. This collection of 17 murals painted on the sides of buildings depicts the history of Twentynine Palms and the daily lives of its citizens. If you drive around town, you can't miss them.

Pioneertown. A hangout built by movie stars Roy Rogers, Gene Autry, and Russ Hayden in the 1940s, this 1880s-style Old West movie set is complete with hitching posts, a saloon, and an OK Corral. Although filming still takes place here, you can stroll the wooden sidewalks past false-fronted stores, clapboard houses and a historic bowling alley. Pappy & Harriett's old-time saloon and eatery is a popular venue for local and touring bands and singers. Gunfighters face off Old-West style in the dusty Mane Street on weekend afternoons. ✉ *4 mi north of Yucca Valley on Pioneertown Rd.* ☎ *No phone* ⊕ *www.pioneertown.com.*

Learn about the park's flora and fauna by attending the ranger programs.

WHERE TO EAT AND STAY

ABOUT THE RESTAURANTS

Dining options in the gateway towns around Joshua Tree National Park are extremely limited—you'll mostly find fast-food outlets and a few casual cafés in Yucca Valley and Twentynine Palms. The exception is the restaurant at 29 Palms Inn, which has an interesting California cuisine menu that features lots of veggies. Still, you'll have to travel to the Palm Springs desert resort area for a fine-dining experience.

ABOUT THE HOTELS

Lodging choices in the Joshua Tree National Park area are limited to a few motels, chain hotels, and a luxury bed-and-breakfast establishment in the gateway towns. In general, most offer few amenities and are modestly priced. Book ahead for the spring wildflower season—reservations may be difficult to obtain then.

For more extensive range of lodging options, you'll need to head to Palm Springs and the surrounding desert resort communities.

ABOUT THE CAMPGROUNDS

Camping is the best way to experience the stark, exquisite beauty of Joshua Tree. You'll also have a rare opportunity to sleep outside in a semi-wilderness setting. The campgrounds, set at elevations from 3,000 to 4,500 feet, have only primitive facilities; few have drinking water. Black Rock and Indian Cove campgrounds, located on the northern edge of the park (but not on a road that transits the park) accept reservations up to six months in advance (☎ 877/444–6777 ⊕ *www. recreation.gov*). Campsites elsewhere are on a first-come, first-served basis. Camping fees are $10 to $15 per site per night. You can pay for camping with your credit card (AE, MC, V) at a visitor center; otherwise it's cash or personal check only at the self-registration stations at the campgrounds.

During the busy fall and spring weekends, plan to arrive early in the day to ensure a site, or if you have an organized group, reserve one of the group sites in advance. Temperatures can drop at night during any part of the year—bring a sweater or light jacket. If you plan to camp in late winter or early spring, be prepared for the gusty Santa Ana winds that may sweep through the park. Backcountry camping is permitted in certain wilderness areas of Joshua Tree. You must sign in at a backcountry register board if you plan to stay overnight. For more information, stop at the visitor centers or ranger stations.

> **FAMILY PICKS**
>
> **Mane Street.** Walk in the footsteps of "real" spaghetti-western movie cowboys along this street in Pioneertown.
>
> **Theatre 29.** See a family-oriented live show at this place in Twentynine Palms.
>
> **Knotts Soak City.** Get in the swim of things at this Palm Springs attraction with 13 waterslides and a huge wave pool.

24

WHERE TO EAT

IN THE PARK

PICNIC AREAS **Black Rock Canyon.** Set among Joshua trees, pinyon pines, and junipers, this popular picnic area has barbecue grills and drinking water. It's one of the few with flush toilets. ⊠ *End of Joshua Lane at the Black Rock Canyon Campground.*

Covington Flats. This is a great place to get away from crowds. There's just one table, and it's surrounded by flat open desert dotted here and there by Joshua trees. ⊠ *La Contenta Rd., 10 mi from Rte. 62.*

Hidden Valley. Set among huge rock formations, with picnic tables shaded by dense trees, this is one of the most pleasant places in the park to stop for lunch. ⊠ *Park Blvd., 14 mi south of the west entrance.*

OUTSIDE THE PARK

$ ✕ **Edchada's.** Rock climbers who spend their days in Joshua Tree swear MEXICAN by the margaritas at this Mexican restaurant. Specialties include prodigious portions of fajitas, carnitas, seafood enchiladas, and fish tacos. ⊠ *73502 Twentynine Palms Hwy., Twentynine Palms* ☎ *760/367–2131* ▭ *AE, D, MC, V.*

$$$ ✕ **Pappy & Harriet's Pioneertown Palace.** Smack in the middle of a west-AMERICAN ern-movie-set town is this western-movie-set saloon, where you can have dinner, dance to live country music, or just relax with a drink at the bar. The food ranges from Tex-Mex to Santa Maria barbecue to steak and burgers—no surprises but plenty of fun. It may be in the middle of nowhere, but you'll need reservations for dinner on weekends. ⊠ *53688 Pioneertown Rd., Pioneertown* ☎ *760/365–5956* ⊕ *www. pappyandharriets.com* ▭ *AE, D, MC, V* ⊗ *Closed Tues. and Wed.*

$ ✕ **Park Rock Café.** If you're on your way to the national park on Highway CAFE 62, stop in the town of Joshua Tree to grab a hearty breakfast bagel sandwich and order a box lunch to take with you. The café creates some interesting sandwiches, including chicken Caesar and a healthy concoction with avocado and nuts on squaw bread (a dense, multi-grain bread made with molasses). The lentil barley soup is a favorite. Outside dining is pleasant here. ✉ *6554 Park Blvd., Joshua Tree* ☎ *760/366–8200* ▤ *MC, V* ☻ *Closed Mon.*

WHERE TO STAY

IN THE PARK

CAMPING

⌃ △ **Belle Campground.** This small campground is popular with families, as there are a number of boulders kids can scramble over and around. Campsites here are small and not recommended for recreational vehicles. Reservations are not accepted. **Pros:** secluded. **Cons:** small sites; no water. ✉ *9 mi south of Oasis of Mara* ☎ *760/367–5500* ⊕ *www.nps.gov/jotr/* △ *18 tent/RV sites* ⚲ *Pit toilets, fire pits, picnic tables* ▤ *No credit cards.*

$ △ **Black Rock Canyon Campground.** Set among juniper bushes, cholla cacti, and other desert shrubs, Black Rock Canyon is one of the prettiest campgrounds in Joshua Tree. South of Yucca Valley, it's the closest campground to most of the desert communities. Located on the California Riding and Hiking Trail, it has facilities for horses and mules. **Pros:** reservations available; good choice for RVs; ranger talks. **Cons:** fills up early; outside the main park. ✉ *Joshua La., south of Hwy. 62 and Hwy. 247* ☎ *760/367–5500, 877/444–6777 for reservations* ⊕ *www.recreation.gov* △ *100 tent/RV sites* ⚲ *Flush toilets, dump station, drinking water, fire pits, picnic tables, ranger station* ▤ *AE, D, MC, V.*

$ △ **Cottonwood Campground.** In spring this campground, the southern-most one in the park (and therefore often the last to fill up), is surrounded by some of the desert's finest wildflowers. Reservations are not accepted. **Pros:** great desert views; near oasis; good hiking. **Cons:** long drive to major park attractions. ✉ *Pinto Basin Rd., 32 mi south of North Entrance Station* ☎ *760/367–5500* ⊕ *www.nps.gov/jotr* △ *62 tent/RV sites, 3 group sites* ⚲ *Flush toilets, dump station, fire pits, picnic tables, ranger station* ▤ *AE, D, MC, V.*

$ △ **Hidden Valley Campground.** This campground is a favorite with rock climbers, who make their way up valley formations that have names like the Blob, Old Woman, and Chimney Rock. RVs are permitted. Reservations are not accepted. **Pros:** nicely spaced sites. **Cons:** no water; no RV hookups. ✉ *Off Park Blvd., 20 mi southwest of Oasis of Mara* ☎ *760/367–5500* ⊕ *www.nps.gov/jotr/* △ *39 tent/RV sites* ⚲ *Pit toilets, fire pits, picnic tables* ▤ *No credit cards.*

$ △ **Indian Cove Campground.** This is a very sought-after spot for rock climbers, primarily because it lies among the 50 square mi of rugged terrain at the Wonderland of Rocks. Popular climbs near the campground include Pixie Rock, Feudal Wall, and Corral Wall. Call ahead to reserve one of the 13 group sites. Reservations are essential to nab any site September through May. **Pros:** near hiking trails; popular with climbers. **Cons:** no water; no road to park interior. ✉ *Indian Cove Rd., south of Hwy. 62* ☎ *760/367–5500, 877/444–6777 for reservations*

⊕ *www.nps.gov/jotr/* ⌂ *101 tent/ RV sites, 13 group sites* ⌂ *Pit toilets, fire pits, picnic tables* ⊟ *AE, D, MC, V.*

$ ⌂ **Jumbo Rocks.** Each campsite at this well-regarded campground tucked among giant boulders has a bit of privacy. It's a good home base for visiting many of Joshua Tree's attractions, including Geology Tour Road. Sites are first-come, first-served. **Pros:** good stargazing. **Cons:** crowded in spring; some small sites. ⊠ *Park Blvd., 11 mi from Oasis of Mara* ☎ *760/367–5500* ⊕ *www.nps.gov/jotr/* ⌂ *125 tent/RV sites* ⌂ *Pit toilets, fire pits, picnic tables* ⊟ *No credit cards.*

$ ⌂ **White Tank.** This small, quiet campground is popular with families because a nearby trail leads to a natural arch. Campsites are small and not recommended for RVs or trailers. Reservations are not accepted. **Pros:** access to trails. **Cons:** no water. ⊠ *Pinto Basin Rd., 11 mi south of Oasis of Mara* ☎ *760/367–5500* ⊕ *www.nps.gov/jotr* ⌂ *15 tent sites* ⌂ *Pit toilets, fire pits, picnic tables* ⊟ *No credit cards.*

OUTSIDE THE PARK

$$$ 📺 **29 Palms Inn.** The funky 29 Palms, on the Oasis of Mara, is the lodging option closest to the Oasis entrance to Joshua Tree National Park. The collection of adobe and wood-frame cottages scattered over 70 acres of palm-shaded grounds includes a number of units suitable for families. Innkeeper Jane Smith's warm, personal service more than makes up for the cottages' rustic qualities. The contemporary fare at the inn's restaurant ($$–$$$) is more sophisticated than its Old West appearance might suggest. Art classes can be arranged through the inn. **Pros:** comfortable camping in the desert. **Cons:** limited amenities. ⊠ *73– 950 Inn Ave., Twentynine Palms* ☎ *760/367–3505* ⊕ *www.29palmsinn. com* ⋈ *15 rooms, 5 suites* ⌂ *In-room: no a/c, no phone. In-hotel: restaurant, pool, some pets allowed* ⊟ *AE, D, MC, V* ⊺⊙⫯ *CP.*

$$ 📺 **Best Western Yucca Valley Hotel & Suites.** This new hotel, opened in 2008, is a welcome addition to the slim pickings near Joshua Tree National Park. Rooms are spacious, nicely appointed, and decorated in soft desert colors. There are two sections: one is exclusively extended-stay while the other is for short-term guests. Continental breakfast, served in the parlor, is included in the price. **Pros:** convenient to Joshua Tree National Park; pleasant lounge. **Cons:** location on busy highway; limited services. ⊠ *56525 Twentynine Palms Hwy., Yucca Valley* ☎ *760/365–3555* ⊕ *www.bestwestern.com* ⋈ *95 rooms* ⌂ *In-room: safe, kitchens (some), refrigerators, Wi-Fi. In-hotel: pool, gym, laundry facilities, Internet terminal, Wi-Fi* ⊟ *AE, D, DC, MC, V* ⊺⊙⫯ *CP.*

$–$$$ 📺 **Casa Cody.** An excellent headquarters for families, the Casa Cody has spacious simply furnished studios and one- and two-bedroom suites that have kitchens. The homey rooms are situated in four buildings surrounding courtyards lushly landscaped with bougainvillea and citrus. Continental breakfast is included in the rates. **Pros:** kids stay free; large rooms. **Cons:** about an hour's drive from the park; lots of families. ⊠ *175 S. Cahuilla Rd., Palm Springs* ☎ *760/320–9346* ⊕ *www. casacodypalmsprings.com* ⋈ *16 rooms, 7 suites, 2 cottages* ⌂ *In-room: kitchen (some), refrigerator, Wi-Fi. In-hotel: pool, some pets allowed* ⊟ *AE, D, MC, V* ⊺⊙⫯ *CP.*

24

$$$$ 　🔲 **Movie Colony Hotel.** This intimate hotel, designed in 1935 by Albert
★ 　　 Frey, evokes mid-century minimalist ambience. Its sparkling, white,
two-story buildings, with balconies and porthole windows, evoke the
image of a luxury yacht. Rooms are elegantly appointed with soft desert
colors accented by bright reds and yellows; many features, including
tiny showers, are authentic to the period. A cool vibe prevails in late
afternoon, as sophisticated young guests share experiences during the
wine hour and again over morning coffee and a sumptuous Continental breakfast served in the flower-decked courtyard. **Pros:** architectural
icon; "Dean Martinis" at happy hour; cruiser bikes. **Cons:** close quarters; off the beaten path; staff is not available 24 hours. ⊠ *726 N. Indian
Canyon Dr., Palm Springs* ☎ *760/320–6340 or 888/953–5700* ⊕ *www.
moviecolonyhotel.com* ⤶ *13 rooms, 3 suites* ⚠ *In-room: refrigerator,
DVD, Internet, Wi-Fi (some). In-hotel: bar, pools, bicycles, Internet terminal Wi-Fi, parking (free), no kids under 21* ⊟ *AE, MC, V* ⦿ *CP.*

$$–$$$ 　🔲 **Roughley Manor.** Cost was no object for the wealthy pioneer who
★ 　　 erected this stone mansion, now a B and B. A 50-foot-long planked
maple floor is the pride of the great room, the carpentry on the walls
throughout is intricate, and huge stone fireplaces warm the house on
the rare cold night. Original fixtures still gleam in the bathrooms, and
bedrooms hold pencil and canopy beds and some fireplaces. Many
have private patios. The innkeepers serve afternoon tea and evening
dessert. An acre of gardens shaded by Washingtonian palms surrounds
the house. **Pros:** resident barn owl; palm-shaded pool; rose gardens.
Cons: somewhat formal. ⊠ *74–744 Joe Davis Rd., Twentynine Palms*
☎ *760/367–3238* ⊕ *www.roughleymanor.com* ⤶ *10 rooms, 3 suites*
⚠ *In-room: kitchen, Wi-Fi. In-hotel: pool, some pets allowed* ⊟ *AE,
D, MC, V* ⦿ *BP.*

$ 　🔲 **Pioneertown Lodge and Stables.** Built in 1946 as a bunkhouse for west-
ern film stars shooting in Pioneertown, this motel sticks to its roots.
Each room—from the Cowboy Room to the Twilight Zone Room—
has a theme that matches its name. For example, the Flower Room is
all about buds and blooms. Hiking trails outside the motel lead into
the desert. Bring your horse—there are corrals for visiting animals.
Pros: cowboy ambience; hitching posts for your horse. **Cons:** limited
room amenities; located in the middle of nowhere. ⊠ *5040 Curtis Rd.,
Pioneertown* ☎ *760/365–4879* ⊕ *www.pioneertownmotel.com* ⤶ *18
rooms* ⚠ *In-room: no a/c (some), no phone, kitchen (some), refrigerator
(some), no TV (some). In-hotel: some pets allowed* ⊟ *MC, V.*

CAMPING 　🏕 **Twentynine Palms RV Resort.** This well-equipped RV park caters to
$$$ 　　 snowbirds in winter who stay two or three months at a time to enjoy
warm weather, an active social life, and an array of amenities. **Pros:**
accommodates large rigs. **Cons:** no cable TV. ⊠ *4949 Desert Knoll Ave,
Twentynine Palms* ☎ *760/367–3320* ⊕ *www.29palmsgolfresort.com*
🏕 *197 RV sites, 26 cottages* ⚠ *Full hookups, guest laundry, swimming
(pool), Wi-Fi* ⊟ *MC, V.*

Lassen Volcanic National Park

WORD OF MOUTH

"We were in Lassen on June 29th and there was still a very thick layer of snow throughout the park. Many of the picnic areas and trails were closed due to the snow. It was lovely to drive, through . . . Burney Falls is a lovely area as are the roads along the Russian River and the little town of Paradise."

—BJinHolland

WELCOME TO LASSEN

TOP REASONS TO GO

★ **Hike a volcano:** The 2½-mi trek up Lassen Peak rewards you with a spectacular view of far northern California.

★ **Spot a rare bloom:** The Lassen Smelowskia, a small white-to-pinkish flower, grows only in Lassen Volcanic National Park, mainly on Lassen Peak.

★ **View volcano varieties:** All four types of volcanoes found in the world—shield, plug dome, cinder cone, and composite—are represented in Lassen Volcanic National Park.

★ **Listen to the earth:** The park's thumping mudpots and venting fumaroles roil, gurgle, and belch a raucous symphony from beneath the earth's crust.

★ **Escape the crowds:** Lassen, in sparsely populated far northern California, is one of the least-visited national parks.

1 Southwest. Geothermal activity is greatest in the southwest area; you'll see evidence on hikes to Bump-ass Hell and Devil's Kitchen. Walkways beside the former Sulphur Works on Lassen Park Road, just past the Kohm Yah-mah-nee Visitor Center, provide easy access to smelly, belching fumaroles.

2 Middle. Marsh meadows and stunning falls highlight the Kings Creek area in the park's southern midsection. Farther north, Summit Lake—in the midst of a red fir forest at an elevation of about 6,700 feet—has two camp-grounds and a trail leading to several smaller lakes.

3 **Northwest.** Lassen Park Road winds past the barren rubble of Devastated Area, providing stunning views of Lassen Peak and passing Chaos Jumbles before reaching lush, wooded Manzanita Lake.

4 **Eastern.** Among the delights found in the least-accessible and least-visited part of the park are Cinder Cone and Ash Butte, lava beds, and meadows, plus beautiful Snag and Juniper Lakes and the many creeks that flow out of them.

CALIFORNIA

GETTING ORIENTED

From gurgling mudpots and hissing steam vents, to tranquil lakes and lily-covered ponds, to jagged mountain peaks bordered by flowering meadows, Lassen Volcanic National Park's varied landscapes are certain to soothe, awe, and intrigue. Whether you want to climb to the top of a dormant volcano or simply loll at the water's edge as birdsong drifts down from tall pines, you'll find unexpected pleasures in this park formed by molten lava.

25

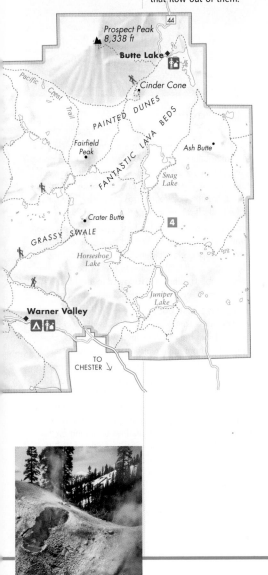

KEY	
🧍	Ranger Station
⛺	Campground
⛩	Picnic Area
🍴	Restaurant
🖼	Lodge
🚶	Trailhead
🚻	Restrooms
⇗	Scenic Viewpoint
∷∷∷	Walking/Hiking Trails

LASSEN PLANNER

When to Go

The park is open year-round, though most roads are closed from late October to mid-June due to snow.

Getting Here and Around

From the north, take the Highway 44 exit off Interstate 5 and travel east about 48 mi to Highway 89. Turn right and drive 1 mi to the northwest entrance station. From the south, take the second Red Bluff exit off I–5, head east, and turn left onto Highway 36. Drive approximately 45 mi, and turn left onto Highway 89. From there it's about 8 mi to the southwest entrance ranger station. The 30-mi main park road, Lassen Park Road/Highway 89, starts at the southwest entrance, loops around three sides of Lassen Peak, and exits the park on the northwest side.

AVG. HIGH/LOW TEMPS.

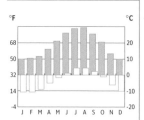

Flora and Fauna

Because of its varying elevations, Lassen has several different ecological habitats. Below 6,500 feet you can find ponderosa pine, Jeffrey pine, sugar pine, white fir, and several species of manzanita, gooseberry, and ceanothus. Wildflowers—wild iris, spotted coralroot, pyrola, violets, and lupine—surround the hiking trails in spring and early summer.

The Manzanita Lake area has the best bird-watching opportunities, with pygmy and great horned owls, white-headed and downy woodpeckers, golden-crowned kinglets, and Steller's jays. The area is also home to rubber boas, garter snakes, brush rabbits, Sierra Nevada red foxes, black-tailed deer, coyotes, and the occasional mountain lion.

At elevations of 6,500–8,000 feet are red fir forests populated by many of the same wildlife as the lower regions, with the addition of black-backed three-toed woodpeckers, blue grouse, snowshoe hare, pine martens, and the hermit thrush.

Above 8,000 feet the environment is harsher, with bare patches of land between subalpine forests. You'll find whitebark pine, groves of mountain hemlock, and the occasional wolverine. Bird-watchers should look for gray-crowned rosy finches, rock wrens, pikas, golden eagles, falcons, and hawks. California tortoiseshell butterflies are found on the highest peaks. If you can visit in winter, you'll see one of the park's most magnificent seasonal sights: massive snowdrifts up to 30 and 40 feet high.

Updated
by Christine
Vovakes

A dormant plug dome, Lassen Peak is the focus of Lassen Volcanic National Park. The peak began erupting in May 1914, sending pumice, rock, and snow thundering down the mountain, and gas and hot ash billowing into the atmosphere. Lassen's most spectacular outburst was in 1915 when it blew a cloud of ash almost 6 mi high. The resulting mudflow destroyed vegetation for miles in some directions; the evidence is still visible today, especially in Devastated Area. The volcano finally came to rest in 1921.

25

PARK ESSENTIALS

ACCESSIBILITY
Park headquarters and the Loomis Museum are both fully accessible to those with limited mobility. The Devastated Area interpretive trail is accessible, as are most ranger programs.

ADMISSION FEES AND PERMITS
The $10 fee per car covers seven days. Those entering by bus, bicycle, horse, motorcycle, or on foot pay $5. There's also a $25 annual park pass that also covers Whiskeytown NRA. For backcountry camping, pick up a free wilderness permit at the Loomis Museum or north and south entrance ranger stations, or download one at ⊕ *www.nps.gov/lavo*.

ADMISSION HOURS
The park is open 24/7, year-round. It is in the Pacific time zone.

CELL-PHONE RECEPTION
Cell phones don't work in many parts of the park. There are telephones at the Manzanita Camper Store and the Loomis Plaza.

PARK CONTACT INFORMATION
Lassen Volcanic National Park Headquarters ⊠ *38050 Rte. 36 E, P.O. Box 100, Mineral, CA 96063* ☎ *530/595–4444* ⊕ *www.nps.gov/lavo*.

LASSEN VOLCANIC IN ONE DAY

Start your day early at the park's northwest entrance, accessible via Route 44 from Redding. Make a stop at the **Loomis Museum**, where you can view exhibits before taking the easy, 1-mi round-trip **Lily Pond Nature Trail**. Back at the museum, drive down to **Manzanita Lake**; take a mid-morning break and pick up supplies for a picnic lunch at the **Camper Store** before taking the main road toward **Lassen Peak**. As you circle the peak on its northern flank, you come upon

Devastated Area, testimony to the damage done by the 1915 eruptions. Continue to **Summit Lake**, where you can picnic and swim, or to **Kings Creek**, an area of lush meadows and where you can hike to **Kings Creek Falls**. Allow at least two hours to make the 3-mi hike, which ends in a 700-foot descent to the falls. If time permits, continue to the **Sulphur Works** to stroll sidewalks that skirt sulphur-emitting steam vents.

SCENIC DRIVES

Fodor'sChoice
★

Lassen Scenic Byway. This 185-mi scenic drive begins in Chester and loops through the forests, volcanic peaks, geothermal springs, and lava fields of Lassen National Forest and Lassen National Park, providing for an all-day excursion into dramatic wilderness. The road is partially inaccessible in winter (call Caltrans for details on road closures). From Chester, take Route 36 west to Route 89 north through the park (subject to closures due to snow), then Route 44 east to Route 36 west. ☎ *800/427–7623 for Caltrans.*

WHAT TO SEE

The four types of volcanoes in the world—cinder cone, composite, plug dome, and shield—are all represented in the park. These, along with fumaroles, mudpots, lakes, and bubbling hot springs create a fascinating, but dangerous, landscape. ⚠ Stay on the trails and railed boardwalks to avoid falling into boiling water or through thin-crusted areas.

HISTORIC SITE

Loomis Museum. Here you can view artifacts from the park's 1914–15 eruptions, including dramatic original photographs taken by Benjamin Loomis, who documented the event and was instrumental in the park's establishment. The museum also has a bookstore, films about the park's history, and excellent exhibits on the area's American Indian heritage. ⊠ *Lassen Park Rd. at Manzanita Lake* ☎ *530/595–4444 Ext. 5180* ⌨ *Free* ☉ *Memorial Day–late Oct., daily 9–5.*

SCENIC STOPS

Boiling Springs Lake. A worthwhile, if occasionally muddy, 1.8-mi hike from the Drakesbad Guest Ranch, Boiling Springs Lake is surrounded by steep cliffs topped with trees. Constant bubbles release sulfuric steam into the air. ⊠ *At the end of Warner Valley Rd.*

★   **Bumpass Hell.** This site's quirky name came about when a man with the last name of Bumpass was severely burned after falling into the boiling springs. A scenic but strenuous 3-mi round-trip hike (⇨ *Hiking*) brings you up close to hot springs, hissing steam vents, and roiling mudpots. ⊠ *Lassen Park Rd., 6 mi north of the southwest entrance ranger station.*

Chaos Jumbles. More than 350 years ago, an avalanche from the Chaos Crags lava domes scattered hundreds of thousands of rocks—many of them 2–3 feet in diameter—over a couple of square miles. ⊠ *Lassen Park Rd., 2 mi north of the northwest entrance ranger station.*

Devastated Area. Lassen Peak's 1915 eruptions cleared the area of all vegetation, though there are a few signs of life after all these years. An easy interpretive trail loop, less than ½-mi total, is paved and wheelchair accessible. ⊠ *Lassen Park Rd., 2½ mi north of Summit Lake.*

Devil's Kitchen. One of the park's three main geothermal areas, this is a great place to view mudpots, steam vents, and boiling waters, as well as wildlife. It's much less frequented than Bumpass Hell, so you can expect more solitude during your moderately difficult 4.2-mi round-trip hike. You need to drive on a partially paved road to reach the trailhead. ⊠ *Off Warner Valley Rd., at Drakesbad Guest Ranch.*

Fodor's Choice   **Lassen Peak.** When this now-dormant plug dome volcano erupted in
★   1915, it spewed a huge mushroom cloud with debris almost 6 mi into the air. A fabulous panoramic view makes the strenuous 2½-mi hike to the 10,457-foot summit worth the effort. ⊠ *Lassen Park Rd., 7 mi from the southwest entrance ranger station.*

Manzanita Lake. Lassen Peak is reflected in the waters of Manzanita Lake, which has good catch-and-release trout fishing, as well as a pleasant trail from which to view the area's abundant wildlife. ⊠ *Lassen Park Rd. at northwest entrance ranger station.*

☼   **Sulphur Works Thermal Area.** Proof of Lassen Peak's volatility becomes evident shortly after you enter the park at the southwest entrance. Sidewalks skirt boiling springs and sulphur-emitting steam vents. This area is usually the last site to close because of snow. ⊠ *Lassen Park Rd., 1 mi from the southwest entrance ranger station.*

Summit Lake. The midpoint between the northern and southern entrances, Summit Lake is a good place to take a midday swim. A trail leads around the lakeshore, and several other trails diverge toward a cluster of smaller lakes in the more remote eastern section of the park. ⊠ *Lassen Park Rd., 17½ mi from southwest entrance ranger station.*

VISITOR CENTER

Kohm Yah-mah-nee Visitor Center. Pick up maps, trail and road guides, and inquire about children's activities and ranger-led programs here. Completed in 2008, this center at the park's southwest entrance shows a park film in digital surround-sound and has interactive exhibits that will wow the kids. There are restrooms and first aid facilities; drinks, food, souvenirs and books are available at Lassen Café and Gifts, which is inside the center. ⊠ *Rte. 89, north of Mineral* ☎ *530/595–4444* ☼ *Late May–late Oct., daily 9–6; late Oct.–late May, daily 9–5*

SPORTS AND THE OUTDOORS

Lassen is a rugged adventurer's paradise, but be prepared for sudden changes in the weather: in summer, hot temperatures can make high-altitude hikers woozy, and fierce thunderstorms drench the mountains; in winter, blizzard conditions can develop quickly.

> **A GOOD READ**
>
> *Lassen Volcanic National Park & Vicinity,* by Jeffrey P. Schaffer, is one of the most comprehensive books about the park.

BICYCLING

Biking is allowed on park roads, but not park trails. Cyclists under 18 must wear a helmet. Skateboarding and rollerblading are prohibited.

A one-day rental at **Bikes, Etc.** (✉ *2400 Athens Ave., Redding* ☎ *530/246–2453* ⊙ *Mon.–Sat. 9:30–6*) is $20. Rent mountain bikes at **Bodfish Bicycles & Quiet Mountain Sports** (✉ *149 Main, Chester* ☎ *530/258–2338* ⊙ *Tues.–Sat. 10–5*) for $10 an hour, with a two-hour minimum, or pay $30 a day. Bike rentals at **Redding Sports, Ltd.** (✉ *950 Hilltop Dr., Redding* ☎ *530/221–7333* ⊙ *Mon.–Sat. 9–7, Sun. 10–6*) run $30–$40 per day.

25

FISHING

The best place to fish is in Manzanita Lake—but it's catch and release only in the park. Butte, Snag, and Horseshoe lakes are also popular fishing destinations within the park. Anglers will need a California freshwater fishing license; you can pick up an application at most sporting-goods stores or download it from the California Department of Fish and Game's Web site (⊕ *www.dfg.ca.gov*). Ask about fishing conditions at bait-and-tackle shops.

OUTFITTERS Stop by **Ayoobs Hardware** (✉ *201 Main St., Chester* ☎ *530/258–2611* ⊙ *Mon.–Sat. 7:30–5, Sun. 8–1*) for tackle, bait, and local yore. **The Fishin' Hole** (✉ *3844 Shasta Dam Blvd., Shasta Lake City* ☎ *530/275–4123* ⊙ *Daily 6–6*), a few miles from Shasta Lake, sells bait, tackle, and fishing licenses. Ask about fishing conditions. Famous among fly fishers, **The Fly Shop** (✉ *4140 Churn Creek Rd., Redding* ☎ *530/222–3555* ⊙ *Daily 7:30–6)* carries tackle and equipment and offers guide service. Buy fishing and camping gear at **The Sports Nut** (✉ *208 Main St., Chester* ☎ *530/258–3327* ⊙ *May–Dec., Mon.–Sat. 8–5 and Sun. 8–2*).

HIKING

Of the 150 mi of hiking trails within the park, 17 mi are part of the Pacific Crest Trail. Trails vary greatly, some winding through coniferous forest, and others across alpine tundra or along waterways.

EASY

Lily Pond Nature Trail. This 1-mi jaunt loops past a small lake and through a wooded area, ending at a pond that is filled with yellow water lilies in summer. Marked with interpretive signs, this easy trail is a good choice for families with kids. ✉ *Trailhead across the road from Loomis Museum, Lassen Park Rd., near the northwest entrance ranger station.*

MODERATE

Fodor's Choice ★ **Bumpass Hell Trail.** Boiling springs, steam vents, and mudpots highlight this 3.2-mi round-trip hike. Expect the loop to take about three hours. During the first mile of the hike there's a gradual climb of 500 feet before a steep 250-foot descent to the basin. Stay on trails and boardwalks near the thermal areas: what appears to be firm ground may be only a thin crust over scalding mud. ⊠ *Trailhead at end of paved parking area off Lassen Park Rd., 6 mi from the southwest entrance ranger station.*

Crumbaugh Lake Hike. A 3-mi round-trip hike through meadows and forests to Cold Boiling and Crumbaugh lakes, this excursion is an excellent way to view spring wildflowers. ⊠ *Trailhead off access road 0.1 mi from Kings Creek picnic area, Lassen Park Rd., 13 mi north of the southwest entrance ranger station.*

★ **Kings Creek Falls Hike.** Nature photographers love this 3-mi round-trip hike through forests dotted with wildflowers. A steep 700-foot descent leads to the spectacular falls. It can be slippery in spots, so watch your step. ⊠ *Trailhead on southeast side of Lassen Park Rd., 12 mi from the southwest entrance ranger station.*

Mill Creek Falls. This 2½-hour (4.6-mi) hike through forests and wildflowers takes you to where East Sulphur and Bumpass creeks merge to create the park's highest waterfall. ⊠ *Trailhead on the east side of the parking lot for the Southwest Walk-In Campground, near the southwest entrance ranger station.*

DIFFICULT

Cinder Cone Trail. Though a little out of the way, this is one of Lassen's most fascinating trails. It's for more experienced hikers, since the 4-mi round-trip hike to the cone summit includes a steep 800-foot climb over ground that's slippery in parts with loose cinders. Pick up the trail brochure at Loomis Museum or Kohm Yah-mah-nee Visitor Center. ⊠ *Trailhead at the west end of Butte Lake Campground, on Rte. 44, 35 mi northwest of Susanville.*

Fodor's Choice ★ **Lassen Peak Hike.** This trail winds 2½ mi to the mountaintop. It's a tough climb—2,000 feet uphill on a steady, steep grade—but the reward is a spectacular view. At the peak you can see into the rim and view the entire park (and much of the California's far north). Bring sunscreen, water, and a jacket since it's often windy and much cooler at the summit. ⊠ *Trailhead past a paved parking area off Lassen Park Rd., 7 mi north of the southwest entrance ranger station.*

HORSEBACK RIDING

Drakesbad Guest Ranch (⊠ *End of Warner Valley Rd.* ☎ *530/529–1512 Ext. 120* 💲 *$24–$185* ⊙ *Mid-June–mid-Oct.*), an in-park property, offers guided rides to nonguests who make reservations in advance. Take a 45-minute trip to Boiling Springs or a two-hour lope to Devil's Kitchen. There's also a five-lake loop for advanced riders.

SNOWSHOEING

You can try snowshoeing anywhere in the park. The gentlest places are in the northern district, while more challenging terrain is in the south.

■ TIP→ Beware of hidden cavities in the snow. Park officials warn that heated sulphur emissions, especially in the Sulphur Works Area, can melt out dangerous snow caverns, which may be camouflaged by thin layers of fresh snow that skiiers and snowshoers can easily fall through.

At **Bodfish Bicycles & Quiet Mountain Sports** (⌂ *149 Main, Chester* ☎ *530/258–2338* ☉ *Tues.–Sat. 10–5*), snowshoes, skis, boots, and poles are $18 per day. At **Lassen Mineral Lodge** (⌂ *Rte. 36, Mineral* ☎ *530/595–4422*) snowshoes are $12 a day; skis and poles are $16. At **Redding Sports, Ltd.** (⌂ *950 Hilltop Dr., Redding* ☎ *530/221–7333* ☉ *Mon.–Sat. 9–7, Sun. 10–6*) snowshoes are $15 per pair per day; skis, boots, and poles are $20 per day.

EXPEDITIONS   On weekends from early January through early April, park rangers lead 1- to 2-mi **Snowshoe Walks** (⌂ *Lassen Park Rd. near the southwest entrance ranger station* ☎ *530/595–4444* 🕮 *Free* ☉ *Early Jan.–early Apr., weekends at 1:30*) that explore the park's geology and winter ecology. The hikes require moderate exertion at an elevation of 7,000 feet; children younger than 8 are not allowed. You can rent the shoes for $1 per person. Walks are first-come, first-served; meet outside the Kohm Yah-mah-nee Visitor Center.

25

EDUCATIONAL OFFERINGS

If you're wondering why fumaroles fume, how lava tubes are formed, or which critter left those tracks beside the creek, check out the array of ranger-led programs. Most groups meet outside Loomis Museum or near Manzanita Lake. To learn what's available, see park bulletin boards.

RANGER PROGRAMS

Bear Necessities. Learn about black bears in this under-an-hour ranger-led talk. ⌂ *Outside Loomis Museum, the north entrance to the park* ☎ *530/595–4444* ☉ *Late June–mid-Aug., Wed. at 2*

Blown from a Volcano. Explore the park's history through its rocks. ⌂ *Meet outside Loomis Museum* ☎ *530/595–4444* ☉ *Wed. at 10* AM.

Early Birds. Take a morning stroll and learn about the birds of Manzanita Lake. ⌂ *Meet outside the Manzanita Lake Camp Store* ☎ *530/595–4444* ☉ *Sat. at 8* AM.

★   **Kids Program.** Junior rangers, for ages seven through 12, meet for two
☉   hours three times a week with rangers. Junior Firefighters gather on Thursday mornings to learn about the role wildfires have in shaping our national parks. Youngsters unable to attend the sessions can earn badges by completing certain requirements. Kids under 7 can join the Chipmunk Club and get a sticker after filling out a nature sheet. ⌂ *Outside the Loomis Museum and Manzanita Lake Amphitheater* ☎ *530/595–4444*.

Starry Nights. Rangers discuss myths and contemporary theories about galaxies, stars, and planets, beneath the night sky in a 45-minute program. ⌂ *Devastated Area parking lot, Lassen Park Rd., 2½ mi north of Summit Lake* ☎ *530/595–4444* ☉ *Wed. at 9* PM.

WHAT'S NEARBY

NEARBY TOWNS

The tiny logging town of **Chester,** 17 mi from the park on Route 36, serves as the commercial center for the entire Lake Almanor area. It's one of the best kicking-off points for the park, but the accommodations and services are limited. **Susanville,** 35 mi east of Chester, is a high-desert town named after a pioneer's daughter. **Red Bluff** maintains a mix of Old West toughness and late 1800s gentility: restored Victorians line the streets west of Main Street, while the downtown looks like a stage set for a western. This small town is a good place to stock up before heading into the park; it's 50 mi from Lassen's south entrance via Route 36. With a population of 90,000, **Redding** is the largest city in the far northern portion of California; it's the area's main commercial center. Redding is 32 mi north of Red Bluff via Interstate 5 and 50 mi west of the park's north entrance via Route 44. Both Red Bluff and Redding offer the most accommodations and services in the area; each is an hour's drive from the park.

VISITOR INFORMATION

Chester & Lake Almanor Chamber of Commerce ⊠ *529 Main St., Chester* ☎ *800/350–4838 or 530/258–2426* ⊕ *www.chester-lakealmanor.com.* **Lassen County Chamber of Commerce** ⊠ *75 N. Weatherlow, Susanville* ☎ *530/257–4323* ⊕ *www.lassencountychamber.org.* **Red Bluff Chamber of Commerce** ⊠ *100 Main St., Box 850, Red Bluff* ☎ *530/527–6220* ⊕ *www.redbluffchamberofcommerce.com.* **Redding Convention and Visitors Bureau** ⊠ *777 Auditorium Dr., Redding* ☎ *800/874–7562 or 530/225–4100* ⊕ *www.visitredding.org.*

NEARBY ATTRACTIONS

Fodor'sChoice ★ **Lake Shasta Caverns.** Get an eyeful of geological formations on a one-hour tour that begins with a catamaran ride across Lake Shasta. ⊠ *Shasta Caverns Rd., 2 mi off I–5 exit 695, 17 mi north of Redding* ☎ *530/238–2341 or 800/795–2283* ⊕ *www.lakeshastacaverns.com* ☎ *$22* ۞ *June–Aug., tours on the half hour, daily 9–4; Apr., May, and Sept., tours on the hour, daily 9–3; Oct.–Mar., tours at 10, noon, and 2.*

۞ Fodor'sChoice ★ **Turtle Bay Exploration Park.** Here you find walking trails, an arboretum and botanical gardens, and lots of interactive exhibits for kids, including a gold-panning area and the seasonal butterfly exhibit. The main draw is the stunning **Sundial Bridge,** which links the Sacramento River Trail and the park's arboretum and gardens. Access to the bridge and arboretum is free, but there's a fee for the museum and gardens. ⊠ *840 Sundial Bridge Dr., Redding* ☎ *530/243–8850* ⊕ *www.turtlebay.org* ☎ *$13; $4 for arboretum and botanical gardens only* ۞ *Apr.–Oct., daily 9–5; Nov.–Mar., Wed.–Mon. 9–5.*

AREA ACTIVITIES

Whether you want to camp in national forests, wade in creeks, watch dragonflies dip over meadows thick with wildflowers, or star-gaze while listening to a chorus of crickets, the great outdoors is the draw here.

When you're ready to merge with civilization, the towns near Lassen Volcanic offer shopping, movies, dining, and the ever-popular activity, people-watching.

SPORTS AND THE OUTDOORS

BOATING AND FISHING ★ Twenty-one types of fish, including rainbow trout and salmon, inhabit Lake Shasta. The lake area also has one of the state's largest nesting populations of bald eagles. Rent boats, Jet Skis, and windsurfing boards at marinas and resorts along the 370-mi shoreline. The Sacrament River and its numerous creeks and tributaries also attract fishing enthusiasts from across the country.

WHERE TO EAT AND STAY

ABOUT THE RESTAURANTS

The best dining in the park might be the fresh catch any anglers in your group snag. Otherwise, you'll find simple fare at Lassen Café and Gifts and at the Manzanita Lake Camper Store. Those hiking or camping near Drakesbad Guest Ranch can call ahead and reserve a place at their table (☎ *530/529–1512 or 866/999–0914*). Enjoy a variety of dining choices, ranging from grilled steaks to ethnic specialties, in Red Bluff, Redding, and Chester.

ABOUT THE HOTELS

Drakesbad Guest Ranch is the only lodging available inside Lassen. It's rustic—no electricity, just old-fashioned kerosene lamps—and expensive, but reservations are often fully booked a year or more in advance. In towns surrounding the park there's everything from elegant B and Bs to chain hotels to simple, inexpensive rooms.

ABOUT THE CAMPGROUNDS

Sites at Lassen's eight campgrounds have wide appeal, from large groups singing around the campfire to solitary hikers seeking a quiet place under the stars. You can drive a vehicle to all campgrounds except the Southwest Walk-In; no trailers or RVs are allowed at Juniper Lake and Warner Valley campgrounds. Campfires are restricted to fire rings. Lassen has black bears, so be sure to secure your food and garbage properly by using the bear boxes provided at the park's campsites. To reserve campsites call ☎ 877/444–6777 or go to ⊕ *www.recreation.gov*. To hear recorded camping information, call ☎ *530/335–7029*.

WHERE TO EAT

IN THE PARK

¢ ✕ **Lassen Café & Gifts.** Purchase soft drinks, coffee, hot cocoa, wine, and CAFÉ beer, plus sandwiches, hot dogs, and chili. ⊠ *Lassen Park Rd., inside Kohm Yah-mah-nee Visitor Center* ☎ *530/595–4444 or 530/529–1512* ▭ *AE, D, MC, V* ☺ *Closed weekdays mid-Oct.–late May.*

¢ ✕ **Manzanita Lake Camper Store.** Pick up simple prepared food items and CAFÉ refreshments here. ⊠ *Lassen Park Rd., near Manzanita Lake* ☎ *530/335–7557 or 530/529–1512* ▭ *AE, D, MC, V* ☺ *Closed mid-Oct.–late May.*

25

PICNIC AREAS **Kings Creek.** Picnic tables are beside a creek in a shady area. There are no amenities except vault toilets. ⊠ *Off Lassen Park Rd., 11½-mi north of the southwest entrance ranger station.*

Lake Helen. This site, with picnic tables and vault toilets, has views of several peaks, including Lassen Peak. ⊠ *Lassen Park Rd., 6 mi north of southwest entrance ranger station near the Bumpass Hell trailhead.*

Manzanita Lake. In addition to the Camper Store, there are picnic tables and potable water here and restrooms nearby. ⊠ *Lassen Park Rd., near the northwest entrance ranger station.*

OUTSIDE THE PARK

$–$$
SEAFOOD   ✕ **Buz's Crab.** This casual restaurant in central Redding shares space with a bustling seafood market where locals snap up ocean-fresh Dungeness crab in season. The fish-and-chips and seafood combos are popular, but crab is what keeps the customers coming back. ⊠ *2159 East St., Redding* ☎ 530/243–2120 ⊟ D, MC, V.

$–$$
AMERICAN   ✕ **Feedbag Grill.** Locals gather at this friendly diner from early morning till late evening. For breakfast try the "Trail Boss"—three eggs, a hefty side of sausage, and hash browns; for dinner dig into the barbecued pork ribs for dinner; and anytime of day order a slice of the house-made pie. ⊠ *259 S. Main St., Red Bluff* ☎ 530/528–8777 ⚓ *Reservations not accepted* ⊟ MC, V ☾ *No dinner Sun.*

$$–$$$
STEAK   ✕ **Green Barn Steakhouse.** You're likely to find cowboys sporting Stetsons and spurs feasting on sizzling porterhouse, baby back ribs, and filet mignon at Red Bluff's premier steak house. For lighter fare, there's garlicky scampi or fettuccine primavera, along with fresh fish specials. For dessert, don't miss the bread pudding with rum sauce. The lounge is usually hopping, especially when there's an event at the nearby rodeo grounds. ⊠ *5 Chestnut Ave., Red Bluff* ☎ 530/527–3161 ⚓ *Reservations not accepted* ⊟ AE, D, MC, V ☾ *Closed Sun.*

$–$$
MEXICAN   ✕ **Maria and Walker's Mexican Restaurant.** A festive atmosphere prevails at this family-friendly restaurant and lounge, which serves traditional south-of-the-border fare. Lunch specials and children's plates are available. It's one of the few restaurants in the area with a full bar, the perfect place to enjoy a margarita at the end of a long day of hiking. ⊠ *159 Main St., Chester* ☎ 530/258–2262 ⚓ *Reservations are not accepted* ⊟ D, MC, V ☾ *Closed Sun.*

WHERE TO STAY

IN THE PARK

$$$$
🏨 **Drakesbad Guest Ranch.** Near Lassen's southern border, this ranch is accessible only by a partially paved road leading out of Chester. From propane furnaces to the kerosene lamps in lieu of electricity, everything about this more-than-100-year-old property is rustic. Meals, casual during the day and rather elegant in the evening, are included in the room rate. The waiting list for room reservations can be up to two years long. **Pros:** a true back-to-nature experience; great for family adventures. **Cons:** difficult to get a reservation during peak season. ⊠ *Chester–Warner Valley Rd., north from Rte. 36. Booking office: 2150 N. Main St., Suite 5, Red Bluff 96080* ☎ 530/529–1512 *or*

866/999–0914 ⊕ *www.drakesbad.com* ⤺ *19 rooms* ⚇ *In-hotel: pool.* ▭ *AE, D, MC, V* ⊗ *Closed early Oct.–early June* ⫶⊙⫶*FAP.*

CAMPING ⚠ **Juniper Lake.** On the east shore of the park's largest lake, campsites
$ are close to the water in a wooded area. To reach the campgrounds, you
have to take a rough dirt road that leads 13 mi north of Chester and
enters at the park's southeast corner. No trailers or RVs are allowed,
and there is no potable water. **Pros:** off-the-grid campers love this campground. **Cons:** may be too rustic for inexperienced campers; only group
sites can be reserved. ⊠ *Chester Juniper Lake Rd, approximately 13 mi
north of Rte. 36* ☎ *877/444–6777* ⊕ *www.nps.gov/lavo/planyourvisit/
campground-reservations.htm* ⚠ *18 tent sites* ⚇ *Pit toilets, bear boxes,
fire pits, picnic tables, swimming (lake)* ⊗ *Closed mid Sept.–June.*

$$ ⚠ **Manzanita Lake Campground.** The largest of Lassen campgrounds
Fodor'sChoice accommodates RVs up to 35 feet. Many ranger programs begin here,
★ and a trail nearby leads to a crater that now holds Crags Lake. Summer
reservations for group sites can be made up to 12 months in advance.
There is no running water from late September until snow closes the
grounds. **Pros:** next to Loomis Museum; showers available at Manza-
nita Camp Store. **Cons:** one of the park's busiest campgrounds; no RV
hookups. ⊠ *Off Lassen Park Rd., 2 mi east of junction of Rtes. 44 and
89* ☎ *530/595–4444* ⊕ *www.nps.gov/lavo/planyourvisit/campground-
reservations.htm* ⚠ *148 tent/RV sites, 31 tent sites* ⚇ *Flush toilets,
dump station, drinking water, showers, fire pits, picnic tables* ▭ *D,
MC, V* ⊗ *Closed late Oct.–Mid-May, depending on snowfall.*

$$ ⚠ **Summit Lake North.** This completely forested campground has easy
access to backcountry trails. You'll likely observe deer grazing. RVs up
to 30 feet long can park here. **Pros:** good fishing spot; easy trail with
beautiful views of Lassen Peak. **Cons:** can be noisy and crowded in peak
season. ⊠ *Lassen Park Rd., 12 mi south of Manzanita Lake and 17½ mi
north of southwest entrance* ☎ *877/444–6777* ⊕ *www.nps.gov/lavo/
planyourvisit/campground-reservations.htm* ⚠ *46 tent/RV sites* ⚇ *Flush
toilets, drinking water, bear boxes, fire pits, picnic tables, swimming
(lake)* ⊗ *Closed mid Sept.–early June.*

$ ⚠ **Southwest Walk-In.** This relatively small campground lies within a red fir
forest and has views of Brokeoff Peak. From September to June no drinking water is available. RVs can park overnight in the southwest entrance
parking area for $10; register at the campground. Vehicles must stay in
the parking area, a ¼-mi walk from the campsites. **Pros:** easy access for
year-round camping; close to Kohm Yah-mah-nee Visitor Center. **Cons:** no
reservable sites. ⊠ *Near southwest entrance* ⚠ *21 tent sites* ⚇ *Flush toilets,
pit toilets, drinking water (summer), bear boxes, fire grates, picnic tables.*

$ ⚠ **Summit Lake South.** Less crowded than its neighbor to the north, this
campground has wet meadows where wildflowers grow in the spring.
RVs up to 30 feet long can park here. **Pros:** great spot for canoes and
kayaks. **Cons:** can be crowded in July and August. ⊠ *Lassen Park
Rd., 12 mi south of Manzanita Lake and 17½ mi north of southwest entrance* ☎ *877/444–6777* ⊕ *www.nps.gov/lavo/planyourvisit/
campground-reservations.htm* ⚠ *48 tent/RV sites* ⚇ *Pit toilets, drinking water, bear boxes, fire pits, picnic tables, swimming (lake)* ⊗ *Closed
late Oct.–early June.*

25

OUTSIDE THE PARK

$–$$ 🛏 **Best Western Rose Quartz Inn.** Down the road from Lake Almanor and close to Lassen Volcanic National Park, this small town inn with its modern "wired" rooms lets you venture into the wilderness and stay in touch with cyberspace. A large lustrous piece of polished rose quartz anchors the cozy lobby. **Pros:** near Lassen Park; modern conveniences in a rural setting; small pets allowed. **Cons:** standard motel rooms are on the pricey side. ⊠ *306 Main St., Chester* ☎ *530/258–2002 or 888/571–4885* ⊕ *www.bestwesterncalifornia.com/chester-hotels* ⤵ *50 rooms* ⟐ *In-room: Internet. In-hotel: gym, Wi-Fi, some pets allowed* ⊟ *AE, D, MC, V* ⟐⟐ *CP.*

$–$$$ 🛏 **Bidwell House.** Chairs and swings on the front porch of this 1901 ranch
Fodor'sChoice house are inviting, and there are puzzles and games aplenty in the sun-
★ room. Some guest rooms have wood-burning stoves, claw-foot or Jacuzzi tubs, hardwood floors, and antiques. A separate cottage with kitchen sleeps six. The blueberry-walnut pancakes are the stars of the inn's gourmet three-course breakfast. **Pros:** unique decor in each room; standout breakfast. **Cons:** not ideal for kids. ⊠ *1 Main St., Chester* ☎ *530/258–3338* ⊕ *www.bidwellhouse.com* ⤵ *14 rooms, 2 with shared bath* ⟐ *In-room: no a/c, no phone, Wi-Fi. In-hotel: Wi-Fi* ⊟ *MC, V* ⟐⟐ *BP.*

$ 🛏 **High Country Inn.** Rooms are spacious in this two-story, colonial-style motel on the east edge of town. A complimentary Continental breakfast is provided; more extensive dining is available next door at the Sage Hen. **Pros:** great mountain views; heated pool. **Cons:** must drive to town's historic center. ⊠ *3015 Riverside Dr., Susanville* ☎ *530/257–3450 or 866/454–4566* ⊕ *www.high-country-inn.com* ⤵ *66 rooms* ⟐ *In-room: refrigerator, Wi-Fi. In-hotel: pool, gym, Wi-Fi* ⊟ *AE, D, MC, V* ⟐⟐ *CP.*

Mesa Verde National Park

WORD OF MOUTH

"Wetherill Mesa, which has some amazing cliff dwellings, is not open until Memorial Day. It isn't that hot here at that time; in fact, it is quite nice. Two nights in Mesa Verde is sufficient; it will give you plenty of time to see all of the dwellings, do some hikes, and drive the loop."

—DebitNM

WELCOME TO MESA VERDE

TOP REASONS TO GO

★ **Cliff dwellings:** Built atop the pinyon-covered mesa tops and hidden in the park's valleys is a wondrous collection of 600 ancient dwellings, some carved directly into the sandstone cliff faces.

★ **Ancient artifacts:** Mesa Verde is a time capsule for the Ancestral Puebloan culture that flourished here 700 years ago; more than 4,000 archaeological sites and three million Puebloan objects have been unearthed at Mesa Verde.

★ **Geological marvels:** View the unique geology that drew the Ancestral Puebloan people to the area: protected desert canyons, massive alcoves in the cliff walls, thick bands of sandstone, continuous seep springs, and soils that could be used for both agriculture and architecture.

★ **Bright nights:** Mesa Verde's dearth of pollution makes for cloudless nights that provide a spectacular vision of the heavens punctuated by shooting stars, passing satellites, and—if the conditions are right— eerie lightning flashes from distant thunderheads.

1 **Morefield Campground.** Near the park entrance, this large campground includes a village area with a gas station and grocery store. The park's best-known sites are farther in, but some of the best hiking trails are close by.

2 **Far View Visitor Center.** Almost an hour's drive (but just 18 mi) from Mesa Verde's entrance, Far View is the park's center of gravity, with a visitor center, restaurants, and the park's only overnight lodge. You can buy tickets for the popular ranger-led tours here.

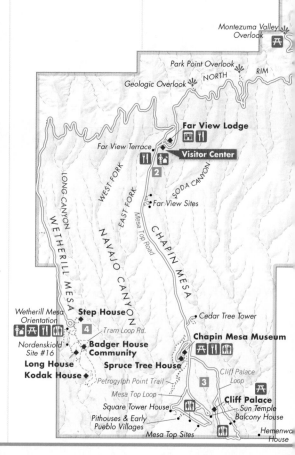

← TO CORTEZ

Montezuma Valley Overlook

Park Point Overlook

Geologic Overlook

NORTH RIM

Far View Lodge

Far View Terrace

Visitor Center

2

Far View Sites

LONG CANYON

WEST FORK

EAST FORK

Mesa Top Road

SODA CANYON

CHAPIN MESA

WETHERILL MESA

NAVAJO CANYON

Wetherill Mesa Orientation

4

Tram Loop Rd.

Step House

Cedar Tree Tower

Nordenskiold Site #16

Badger House Community

Chapin Mesa Museum

Long House

Spruce Tree House

Kodak House

Petrogylph Point Trail

Cliff Palace Loop

3

Mesa Top Loop

Square Tower House

Cliff Palace

Sun Temple

Balcony House

Pithouses & Early Pueblo Villages

Mesa Top Sites

Hemenwa House

3 Chapin Mesa. Home to the park's most famous cliff dwellings and archeological sites, Chapin Mesa includes the 150-room Cliff House dwelling.

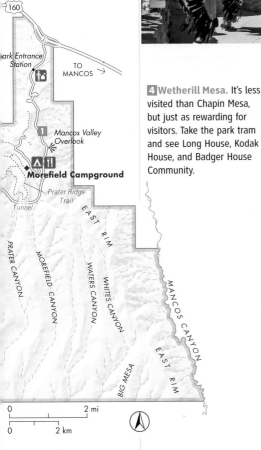

4 Wetherill Mesa. It's less visited than Chapin Mesa, but just as rewarding for visitors. Take the park tram and see Long House, Kodak House, and Badger House Community.

COLORADO

GETTING ORIENTED

Perhaps no other area offers as much evidence into the Ancestral Pueblo's existence as Mesa Verde National Park. Several thousand archaeological sites have been found, and research is ongoing to discover more. The carved-out homes and assorted artifacts displayed at the park's Chapin Mesa Archeological Museum belonged to ancestors of today's Hopi, Zuni, and Pueblo tribes, among others. Due to the sensitive nature of these remnants, hiking in the park is restricted to designated trails, and certain cliff dwellings may only be accessed under accompaniment of a ranger during the peak summer season.

26

KEY
🧍 *Ranger Station*
⛺ *Campground*
🌲 *Picnic Area*
🍴 *Restaurant*
🏨 *Lodge*
🚶 *Trailhead*
🚻 *Restrooms*
⚜ *Scenic Viewpoint*
⋯⋯ *Walking/Hiking Trails*

MESA VERDE PLANNER

When to Go

The best times to visit the park are late May, early June, and most of September, when the weather is fine but the summer crowds have thinned. **Mid-June through August are Mesa Verde's most crowded months.** In July and August, lines at the museum and visitor center may last half an hour. Afternoon thunder showers are common in July and August.

The mesa gets as much as 100 inches of snow in winter. Snow may fall as late as May and as early as October, but there's rarely enough to hamper travel. In winter, the Wetherill Mesa Road and Far View Lodge are closed, but the sight of the sandstone dwellings sheltered from the snow in their cliff coves is spectacular.

AVG. HIGH/LOW TEMPS.

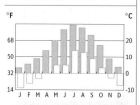

Flora and Fauna

Many areas of the park have extensive fire damage. In fact, wildfires here have been so destructive they are given names, just like hurricanes. The Bircher Fire in 2000 consumed 20,000 acres of brush and forest. It will take several centuries for the woodland to look as verdant as the area atop Chapin Mesa. But in the meantime, you'll have a chance to glimpse nature's powerful rejuvenating processes in action; the landscape is already filling in with vegetation specially adapted to thrive in a post-fire environment.

During warmer months you'll see brightly colored blossoms, like the yellow perky Sue, sage, yucca, and mountain mahogany. Sand-loving blue lupines are seen along the roadways in the higher elevations, and bright-red Indian paintbrushes are scattered throughout the rocky cliffs.

Drive slowly along the park's roads; mule deer are everywhere. You may spot wild horses grazing, and black bear encounters are not unheard of on the hiking trails. About 200 species of birds, including red-tailed hawks, golden eagles, and noisy ravens live here. Keep your eyes and ears open for the poisonous—but shy—prairie rattle snake. Animals are most active in the early morning and at dusk.

Getting Here and Around

The park has just one entrance, off U.S. 160, between Cortez and Durango in what's known as the Four Corners area. Durango, Colorado—35 mi east of the park entrance—has an airport.

Most of the scenic drives at Mesa Verde involve steep grades and hairpin turns, particularly on Wetherill Mesa. Vehicles over 8,000 pounds or 25 feet are prohibited on this road. Towed vehicles are prohibited past Morefield Campground. Check the condition of your vehicle's brakes before driving the road to Wetherill Mesa. For the latest road information, tune to 1610 AM, or call ☎ 970/529–4461. Off-road vehicles are prohibited in the park.

At less-visited Wetherill Mesa, you must leave you car behind and hike or ride the tram to Long House, Kodak House, and Badger House Community.

26

Updated by
Swain Scheps

Unlike most national parks of the west, Mesa Verde earned its status from its rich cultural history rather than its geological treasures. President Theodore Roosevelt established it in 1906 as the first national park to "preserve the works of man." The Ancestral Puebloan people, who lived in the region from roughly 600 to 1300, left behind more than 4,000 archaeological sites spread out over 80 square mi. Their ancient dwellings, set high into the sandstone cliffs, are the heart of the park.

Mesa Verde ("Green Table" in Spanish) is much more than an archaeologist's dreamland, however. It's one of those windswept places where man's footprints and nature's paintbrush—some would say chisel—meet. Rising dramatically from the San Juan Basin, the jutting cliffs are cut by a series of complex canyons and covered with green, from pines in the higher elevations down to sage and other mountain brush on the desert floor. From the tops of the smaller mesas, you can look across to the cliff dwellings in the opposite rock faces. Dwarfed by the towering cliffs, the sand-color dwellings look almost like a natural occurrence in the midst of the desert's harsh beauty.

PARK ESSENTIALS

ACCESSIBILITY

Accessibility to most of the archeological sites is limited within Mesa Verde as they require climbing ladders, squeezing through tunnels, and working your way up and down steep paths. Service dogs cannot be taken into Balcony House, Cliff Palace, or Long House because of ladders in those sites. None of these sites is accessible to those with mobility impairments. If you have heart or respiratory ailments, you may have trouble breathing in the thin air at 7,000 to 8,000 feet. Wheelchairs with wide-rim wheels are recommended on trails, some of which do not meet legal grade requirements. Mesa Top Loop Road provides the most comprehensive and accessible view of all the archaeological sites.

ADMISSION FEES AND PERMITS
Admission is $15 per vehicle for a seven-day permit. An annual pass is $30. Ranger-led tours of Cliff Palace, Long House, and Balcony House are $3 per person. Backcountry hiking and fishing are not permitted at Mesa Verde.

ADMISSION HOURS
The facilities open each day at 8 AM and close at sunset from Memorial Day through Labor Day. The rest of the year, the facilities close at 5. Wetherill Mesa, all the major cliff dwellings, and Morefield ranger station are open only from Memorial Day through Labor Day. Far View Visitor Center, Far View Lodge, and Morefield Campground are open mid-April through mid-October.

ATM/BANKS
There are no ATMs in the park. The nearest bank is in Mancos, just 5 mi east of the park.

CELL-PHONE RECEPTION
Cellular reception in the park varies in quality depending on your location. Morefield Village and the north part of the park get better reception than the south. Public telephones can be found at Morefield Campground and Morefield Village, Far View Visitor Center, Far View Lodge, Far View Terrace, Spruce Tree Terrace, park headquarters (5 mi from the Far View Visitor Center), and the Wetherill Mesa snack bar. Far View Lodge has free Wi-Fi in the lobby.

SHOPS AND GROCERS
Morefield Campground has a nicely stocked grocery store that is open 7 AM to 9 PM, mid-May to early October. The gift shops at Far View and on Mesa Top Loop Road have a small collection of essentials.

PARK CONTACT INFORMATION
Mesa Verde National Park ✉ *P.O. Box 8, Mesa Verde, CO 81330* ☎ *970/529–4465* ⊕ *www.nps.gov/meve.*

SCENIC DRIVES

Mesa Top Road. This 12-mi drive skirts the scenic rim of Chapin Mesa, and splits into two loops—**Mesa Top Loop** and **Cliff Palace Loop**—that reach many of Mesa Verde's most important archaeological sites. Two of the parks' most impressive viewpoints are also on this road: Navajo Canyon Overlook and Sun Point Overlook, from which you can see Cliff Palace, Sunset House, and other dwellings. ⊘ *Daily 8* AM–*sunset.*

Park Entrance Road. The main park road leads you from the entrance off U.S. 160 to the Far View complex 18 mi away. You can stop at a couple of pretty overlooks along the way as a break from the switchbacks, but hold out for **Park Point**, which, at the mesa's highest elevation (8,572 feet), affords unobstructed 360-degree views.

MESA VERDE IN ONE DAY

For a full experience, take at least one ranger-led tour of a major cliff dwelling site, as well as a few self-guided walks. Arrive early; it's about a 45-minute drive from the park entrance to your first stop, the **Far View Visitor Center**, where you can purchase tickets for Cliff Palace and Balcony House tours on Chapin Mesa. If it's going to be a hot day, you might want to take an early morning or late-afternoon tour. Drive to the **Chapin Mesa Museum** to watch a 25-minute film introducing you to the area and its history. Just behind the museum, hike the ½-mi-long **Spruce Tree House trail**, which leads to the best preserved cliff dwelling in the park. Then drive to Balcony House for a ranger-led tour.

Have lunch at the Spruce Tree House cafeteria or the Cliff Palace picnic area. Afterward take the ranger-led tour of **Cliff Palace**. Use the rest of the day to explore the overlooks and trails off the two 6-mi loops of **Mesa Top Loop Road**. Take **Petroglyph Point Trail** to see a great example of Ancestral Puebloan rock carvings. A leisurely walk along the Mesa Top's **Soda Canyon Overlook Trail** gives you a beautiful bird's-eye view of the canyon below.

On the drive back to the entrance stop and see the view from **Park Point**.

26

WHAT TO SEE

HISTORIC SITES

Badger House Community. A self-guided walk takes you through a group of subterranean dwellings, called pit houses, and aboveground storage rooms. The community dates back to 650, the Basket Maker Period, and covers seven acres of land. Most of the pit houses and kivas—religious or ceremonial rooms—were connected by an intricate system of tunnels, some up to 41 feet long. Allow about an hour to see all the sites. ⊠ *Wetherill Mesa Rd., 12 mi from the Far View Visitor Center* ⊑ *Free* ☉ *June–Aug., daily 8–4:30.*

⊙ **Balcony House.** The stonework of this 40-room cliff dwelling, which
★ housed about 40 or 50 people, is impressive, but you're likely to be even more awed by the skill it took to reach this place. Perched in a sandstone cove 600 feet above the floor of Soda Canyon, Balcony House seems almost suspended in space. Even with the aid of modern steps and a partially paved trail, today's visitors must climb two wooden ladders (the first one 32 feet high) to enter. Surrounding the house is a courtyard with a parapet wall and the intact balcony for which the house is named. A favorite with kids, the dwelling is accessible only on a ranger-led tour. Youngsters love climbing the ladders, crawling through the tunnels, and clambering around its nooks and crannies. Purchase your ticket at the Far View Visitor Center. ⊠ *Cliff Palace Loop Rd., 8½ mi southeast of the Far View Visitor Center* ⊑ *$3* ☉ *Late-May–mid-Oct., daily 9–5.*

Fodor's Choice
★

Cliff Palace. This was the first major Mesa Verde dwelling seen by cowboys Charlie Mason and Richard Wetherill in 1888. It is also the largest, containing about 150 rooms and 23 kivas on three levels. Getting there involves a steep downhill hike and four ladders. Purchase tickets at the Far View Visitor Center for the one-hour, ranger-led tour through this dwelling. From June to August, special Sunset Tour ranger-led evenings (⇨ *Ranger-Led Tours, in Educational Offerings*) offers a more in-depth look. ⊠ *Cliff Palace Loop Rd., 7 mi south of the Far View Visitor Center* 🖾 *Basic tour $3, Sunset Tour $10* ⊙ *Mid-May–mid-Oct., daily 9–5.*

> **GOOD READS**
>
> ■ *Mesa Verde National Park: The First 100 Years,* by Rose Houk, Faith Marcovecchio, and Duane A. Smith, captures the park as it celebrated its centennial.
>
> ■ *Fire on the Mesa,* by Tracey Chavis, discusses the wildfires that have been scarring Mesa Verde.
>
> ■ *Mesa Verde: Ancient Architecture,* by Jesse Walter Fewkes, tells the stories behind the park's dwellings.

Far View Sites Complex. This is believed to have been one of the most densely populated areas in Mesa Verde, comprising as many as 50 villages in a ½-square-mi area at the top of Chapin Mesa. Most of the sites here were built between 900 and 1300. Begin the self-guided tour at the interpretive panels in the parking lot, then proceed down a ½-mi, level trail. The ranger-led Far View Sites Walk takes place daily at 4. ⊠ *Park entrance road, 1½ mi south of the Far View Visitor Center* 🖾 *Free* ⊙ *Mid-May–mid-Oct., daily 8–6:30.*

Long House. Excavated in 1959 through 1961, this Wetherill Mesa cliff dwelling is the second largest in Mesa Verde. It is believed that about 150 people lived in Long House, so named because of the size of its cliff alcove. The spring at the back of the cave is still active today. The ranger-led tour begins a short distance from the parking lot and takes about 45 minutes. ⊠ *Wetherill Mesa Rd., 12 mi from the Far View Visitor Center* 🖾 *Tours $3* ⊙ *June–Aug., daily 10–4.*

☼
★

Spruce Tree House. This 114-room complex is the best-preserved site in the park, and the rooms and ceremonial chambers are more accessible to visitors. Here you can actually enter a kiva, via a short ladder, just as the original inhabitants did. It's a great place for kids to explore. Combined with its location in the heart of the most popular sites in the park, Spruce Tree House can resemble a playground during busy periods. Tours are self-guided, but a park ranger is on site to answer questions. The trail leading to Spruce Tree House starts behind the museum and leads you 170 feet down into the canyon. You may find yourself breathing hard by the time you make it back up to the parking lot. ⊠ *Park entrance road, 5 mi south of the Far View Visitor Center* 🖾 *Free* ⊙ *Mar.–Nov., daily 9–5.*

Triple Village Pueblo Sites. Three dwellings built atop each other from 750 to 1150 at first look like a mass of jumbled walls, but an interpretive panel helps identify the dwellings. The 325-foot trail from the walking area is paved and wheelchair accessible. ⊠ *Mesa Top Loop Rd., 8 mi south of the Far View Visitor Center* 🖾 *Free* ⊙ *Daily.*

SCENIC STOPS

Cedar Tree Tower. A self-guided tour takes you to, but not through, a tower and kiva built between 1100 and 1300 and connected by a tunnel. The tower-and-kiva combinations in the park are thought to have been either religious structures or signal towers. ⊠ *Park entrance road, 4 mi south of the Far View Visitor Center.*

Kodak House Overlook. Get an impressive view into Kodak House and its several small kivas from here. The house, closed to the public, was named for a Swedish researcher who absentmindedly left his Kodak camera behind here in 1891. ⊠ *Wetherill Mesa Rd., 12 mi from the Far View Visitor Center* ⊙ *June–Aug.*

Soda Canyon Overlook. Get your best view of Balcony House here and read interpretive panels about the dwelling and canyon geology. ⊠ *Mesa Top Loop Rd., 9 mi south of the Far View Visitor Center.*

VISITOR CENTERS

There are two visitor centers at Mesa Verde, though one is called a museum (but in fact, it serves as the official visitor center when the other closes for the season in the middle of October).

★ **Chapin Mesa Archeological Museum.** This is an excellent first stop for park visitors for an introduction to Ancestral Puebloan culture as well as the area's development into a national park. Exhibits showcase original textiles and other artifacts and a theater plays a well-done movie every 30 minutes. Rangers are available to answer your questions and there's also a sign-in sheet for hiking trails. The museum sits at the south end of the park entrance rode and overlooks Spruce Tree House, nearby you'll find park headquarters, a research library, a gift shop, cafeteria, and bathrooms. ⊠ *Park entrance road, 5 mi south of the Far View Visitor Center* ☎ 970/529–4465 ☒ *Free* ⊙ *Apr.–mid-Oct., daily 8–6:30; mid-Oct.–Mar., daily 8–5.*

★ **Far View Visitor Center.** You can't miss the cylindrical brick building on the east side of the road in the Far View complex, but you actually must park across the street and walk through the tunnel under the road to get to the center. ■ TIP→ Stop here first and buy tickets for the Cliff Palace, Balcony House, and Long House ranger-led tours here. Pick out a less-crowded tour if you want; computer screens show the number of available spaces left for each time. This center also acts as a mini-gift shop, viewing platform, and museum. An extensive selection of books, maps, and videos on the history of the park are available and rangers are on hand to answer questions and explain the history of the Ancestral Puebloans. ⊠ *15 mi south of the park entrance on main park road* ☎ 970/529–5036 ⊙ *Mid-Apr.–mid-Oct., daily 8–5.*

SPORTS AND THE OUTDOORS

Outdoor activities are restricted due to the fragile nature of the archeological treasures here. Hiking is the best option, especially as a way to view some of the Ancestral Puebloan dwellings.

BIRD-WATCHING

Turkey vultures soar between April and October, large flocks of ravens hang around all summer, and ducks and waterfowl fly through Mesa Verde from mid-September through mid-October. Among the park's other large birds are red-tailed hawks, great horned owls, and a few golden eagles. The Steller's jay (the male looks like a blue jay with a dark hat on) frequently pierces the pinyon-juniper forest with its cries, and hummingbirds dart from flower to flower. Any visit to cliff dwellings late in the day will include frolicking white-throated swifts who make their home in rock crevices overhead.

HIKING

A handful of trails lead beyond Mesa Verde's most visited sites and offer more solitude than the crowded cliff dwellings. The best canyon vistas can be reached if you're willing to huff and puff your way through elevation changes and switchbacks. Bring more water than you think you'll need, wear sunscreen, and bring rain gear—cloudbursts can come seemingly out of nowhere. Certain trails are seasonal only, so check with a ranger before heading out. No backcountry hiking is permitted in Mesa Verde due to the fragile nature of the ancient dwellings and artifacts.

26

EASY

Farming Terrace Trail. This 30-minute, 0.5-mi loop beginning and ending on the spur road to Cedar Tree Tower meanders through a series of check dams the Ancestral Puebloans built in order to create farming terraces. ⊠ *Trailhead: Park entrance road, 4 mi south of the Far View Visitor Center.*

Soda Canyon Overlook Trail. One of the easiest and most rewarding strolls in the park, this little trail travels 1.5-mi round-trip through the forest on almost completely level ground. The overlook is an excellent point from which to photograph the cliff dwellings. The trailhead is about ¼ mi past the Balcony House parking area. ⊠ *Trailhead: Cliff Palace Loop Rd., 8½ mi southeast of the Far View Visitor Center.*

MODERATE

Fodor's Choice
★ **Petroglyph Point Trail.** Scramble along the narrow side of the canyon wall from Spruce Tree House to reach the largest and best-known petroglyphs in Mesa Verde. Older literature occasionally refers to the destination of this 2.8-mi loop hike as "Pictograph Point" but pictographs are painted onto the rock, petroglyphs are carved into it. If you pose for a photo just right, you can just manage to block out the gigantic DON'T TOUCH sign next to the rock art. The trail's 50¢ self-guide brochure—available at any ranger station—points out three dozen points of interest along the two-hour trail. ⊠ *Trailhead: Park entrance road, 5 mi south of the Far View Visitor Center* ⊙ *Mar.–Nov., daily 9–5.*

Spruce Canyon Trail. Petroglyph Point Trail takes you along the side of the canyon, this trail ventures down into the canyon. It's only 2 mi long, but you can go down about 600 feet in elevation. Remember to save your strength; what goes down must come up again. ⊠ *Trailhead: Park entrance road, 5 mi south of the Far View Visitor Center* ⊙ *Mar.–Nov., daily 9–5.*

FESTIVALS AND EVENTS

JUNE

Mountain Ute Bear Dance. This traditional dance, held on the Tawaoc Ute reservation south of Cortez in June, celebrates spring and the legacy of the bear who taught the Ute people its secrets. ☎ *970/565–3751* ⊕ *www.utemountainute.com.*

JULY

Durango Fiesta Days. A parade, rodeo, barbecue, street dance, and pie auction come to the La Plata County Fair Grounds in Durango on the last weekend of the month. ☎ *970/247–8835* ⊕ *www. durangofiestadays.com.*

OCTOBER

Durango Cowboy Poetry Gathering. A parade and dance accompany art exhibitions, poetry readings, and storytelling to celebrate the traditions of the American West the first weekend in October. ☎ *970/749–2995 or 800/525–8855* ⊕ *www. durangocowboygathering.org.*

DIFFICULT

Prater Ridge Trail. This 7.8-mi round-trip loop, which starts and finishes at Morefield Campground, is the longest hike you can take inside the park and affords fine views of Morefield Canyon to the south and the San Juan Mountains to the north. ⊠ *Trailhead: Morefield Campground, 4 mi from the park entrance.*

STARGAZING

Since there are no large cities in the Four Corners area, there is very little artificial light to detract from the stars in the night sky. Far View Lodge and Morefield Campground are great for sky-watching.

EDUCATIONAL OFFERINGS

BUS TOURS

ARAMARK Tours. If you want a well-rounded visit to the park's most popular sites, consider a group tour. The park concessionaire provides all-day and half-day guided tours of the Mesa Top Loop Road sites departing in air-conditioned busses from either Morefield Campground or Far View Lodge. Tour guides trade off with park rangers in educating you on history, geology, and excavation process in Mesa Verde. ☎ *970/564–4300 or 800/449–2288* ⊕ *www.visitmesaverde.com* ⊠ *$39–$65* ☉ *Mid-Apr.– mid-Oct., daily, tours depart at 8* AM *and 1* PM.

RANGER PROGRAMS

☾ **Evening Ranger Campfire Program.** A park ranger presents a different 45-minute program or slide presentation each night of the week. ⊠ *Morefield Campground Amphitheater, 4 mi south of the park entrance* ☎ *970/529–4465* ⊠ *Free* ☉ *June–Aug., daily 9* PM–*9:45* PM.

☾ **Junior Ranger Program.** Children ages four through 12 can earn a certificate and badge for successfully completing a two-page questionnaire about the park. ⊠ *Far View Visitor Center or Chapin Mesa Museum* ☎ *970/529–4465.*

The Cliff Palace at Mesa Verde National Park is lit up for Christmas.

★ **Ranger-Led Tours.** Balcony House, Cliff Palace, and Long House can only be explored on a ranger-led tour; each lasts about an hour. Buy tickets for these at Far View Visitor Center the day of the tour, or at the Morefield Campground Ranger Station the evening before the tour, 5 PM–8:30 PM. These are active tours; each requires climbing ladders without handrails and squeezing through tight spaces. If you have any concerns, you should ask the ranger ahead of time if the tour is right for you. During the summer, you can take a Sunset Tour of Cliff Palace, where a park ranger takes on the identity of an important figure in the park's history (such as archeologist Dr. J. Walter Fewkes, who led the restoration of many of the cliff dwellings in the 1920s). Anyone interested in a deeper knowledge of the site will love it, but kids may find it boring. Bring water, sunscreen, and bug spray. ☎ 970/529–4465 ⊠ Tour $3, Sunset Tour $10 ⊙ Mid-Apr.–mid-Oct.

Cliff Palace/Sun Temple Talks. Interpretive talks on park-related subjects are held twice daily at Cliff Palace Overlook near the Sun Temple parking area. ⊠ Cliff Palace Overlook, Mesa Top Loop Rd. ☎ 970/529–4465 ⊠ Free ⊙ June–Aug., daily at 10 and 4.

WHAT'S NEARBY

NEARBY TOWNS

A onetime market center for sheep and cattle ranchers 30 mi from the park, **Cortez** is now the largest gateway town to Mesa Verde and a base for tourists visiting the Four Corners region of Colorado. You can still see a rodeo and cattle drive here at least once a year. **Dolores**, steeped in a rich railroad history, is set on the Dolores River, 20 mi north of Mesa Verde. Neighboring both the San Juan National Forest and McPhee Reservoir, the second-largest lake in the state, Dolores is a favorite of outdoor enthusiasts. East of Mesa Verde by 36 mi, **Durango,** the region's main hub, comes complete with chain restaurants and hotels, shopping, and outdoor equipment rental. Durango became a town in 1881 when the Denver and Rio Grande Railroad pushed its tracks across the neighboring San Juan Mountains.

VISITOR INFORMATION

Mesa Verde National Park ⌂ *P.O. Box 8, Mesa Verde 81330–0008* ☎ *970/ 529–4465* ⊕ *www.nps.gov/meve.* **Dolores Chamber of Commerce** ✉ *201 Railroad Ave., Dolores 81323* ☎ *970/882–4018 or 800/807–4712* ⊕ *www. doloreschamber.com.* **Durango Area Tourism Office** ✉ *111 S. Camino del Rio, Durango 81302* ☎ *970/247–0312 or 800/525–8855* ⊕ *www.durango.org.* **Mesa Verde Visitor Information Bureau** ✉ *928 E. Main St., Cortez 81321* ☎ *970/565–8227 or 800/253–1616* ⊕ *www.swcolo.org.*

NEARBY ATTRACTIONS

★ **Anasazi Heritage Center.** More than three million American Indian artifacts, including pottery, ornaments, and tools, were excavated from sites all over the Four Corners region and are preserved and exhibited in this state-of-the-art museum. (The term "Anasazi" is slowly being replaced by "Ancestral Puebloans" for reasons of cultural and linguistic pride.) A hands-on tour gives you the chance to grind corn, weave on a loom, and wander through a full-scale replica of an Ancestral Puebloan pithouse dwelling. ✉ *27501 Rte. 184, Dolores* ☎ *970/882–5600* ⊕ *www. co.blm.gov/ahc* ⊠ *Mar.–Oct. $3, Nov.–Feb. free* ☉ *Mar.–Oct., daily 9–5, Nov.–Feb., daily 10–4.*

Crow Canyon Archaeological Center. Think of it as an archaeology summer camp. This nonprofit research institution offers a hands-on educational experience covering all aspects of American Indian archaeology: in the classroom, laboratory, and in the field. A one-day archaeology program explains the excavation process and the Ancestral Puebloan culture through a hands-on laboratory tour and a visit to a current excavation site. The campus has overnight accommodations and a cafeteria for the weeklong experiences, aimed at families, students, and teachers. ✉ *23390 Rd. K, Cortez* ☎ *970/565–8975 or 800/422–8975* ⊕ *www. crowcanyon.org* ⊠ *Daylong program $50, weeklong programs $1,150 and up* ☉ *Mar.–Oct.*

AREA ACTIVITIES

SPORTS AND THE OUTDOORS

FISHING

McPhee Reservoir, the second-largest lake in Colorado, is both out of the way and relatively young (constructed in 1985) and as such offers great boating, waterskiing, and fishing—minus the crowds. The lake stays fully stocked with fish, including trout, bass, bluegills, crappies, and kokanee salmon. ✉ *Hwy. 184, Dolores* ☎ *970/882–7296.*

CLOSE UP

Marketing the Four Corners Monument

There's no view to speak of at Four Corners Monument, but it's a popular photo-op nonetheless. Set on Navajo land, about one usually-dusty mile off U.S. 60, the monument is the only place in the nation where the borders of four states meet. The first permanent marker, a simple "look-what's-here," was erected at the intersection of Colorado, Utah, New Mexico, and Arizona in 1912. As long as there have been cameras, people have gone out of their way just to stand in such a way as to be in four states at once.

The monument was refurbished in 1992, and a larger marker, consisting of a bronze disk embedded in granite, was put in place. Though bigger and more ornate than the first marker, it still seems far too unassuming to have attracted the bazaar that surrounds it. In response to a ready market of tourists and trinket hounds, the main drive is rimmed with plywood booths hawking Ute, Navajo, Apache, and other American Indian artwork, crafts, artifacts, and rugs. You can also buy fry bread and corn on the cob. It's all genuine, but the opportunistic nature of the site—it costs $3 per vehicle just to enter—detracts from what began as the simple fascination of standing at the very point where four southwestern states meet.

No major cities are nearby. Cortez, Colorado, is 40 mi away on U.S. 60; tiny Teec Nos Pos, Arizona, is 6 mi away; Shiprock, New Mexico, is about 25 mi to the east; and Bluff, Utah, is 50 mi distant.

The Navajo Nation Parks and Recreation Department administers the Four Corners Monument, along with numerous natural sites and thousands of square miles of pristine wilderness. The site is open 7 AM–8 PM May through mid-August and 8–5 mid-August through April. For more information, call ☎ 928/871–6647.

26

OUTFITTERS   Stop at the **McPhee Marina & Restaurant** (✉ 25021 Hwy. 184, 8 mi north of Dolores ☎ 970/882–2257), to buy your fishing license, bait, and tackle, and get the latest report on what's biting. Boat rentals are also available.

RAFTING

Beginning in the San Juan Mountains of southwestern Colorado, the Dolores River runs north for more than 150 mi before joining the Colorado River near Moab, Utah. This is one of those rivers that tends to flow madly in spring and diminish considerably by midsummer, and for that reason rafting trips are usually run between April and June.

OUTFITTERS   **Durango Rivertrippers** runs two- and four-hour trips down the Animas River, as well as one-, three-, and six-day wilderness expeditions on the Dolores River. ✉ 720 Main Ave., Durango ☎ 970/259–0289 or 800/292–2885 ⊕ www.durangorivertrippers.com.

ARTS AND ENTERTAINMENT

★ The **Cortez Cultural Center** has exhibits on regional artists and Ancestral Puebloan culture, as well as events and fairs. Summer evening programs include dances, sand painting, rug weaving, pottery-making demonstrations, theater, and storytelling. The adjacent park contains an authentic tepee. ✉ 25 N. Market St., Cortez ☎ 970/565–1151

⊕ *www.cortezculturalcenter.org* ✉ *Free* ⊙ *June–Aug., weekdays 10–9, Sat. 1–9; May and Sept., Mon.–Sat. 10–6; Oct.–Apr., weekdays 10–5.*

ART GALLERIES

Toh-Atin Gallery is one of the best galleries in Colorado, specializing in Navajo rugs and weavings. There's also a wide range of paintings, pottery, and prints. ✉ *145 W. 9th St., Durango* ☎ *970/247–8277 or 800/525– 0384* ⊕ *www.toh-atin.com* ⊙ *Mon.–Sat. 9–6, Sun. 10–5.*

NIGHTLIFE Legend has it the **Diamond Belle Saloon** inside the old Strater Hotel inspired some of Louis L'Amour's greatest creations of fiction. The décor and staff looked like they were plucked from the year 1880 and you can get lunch and dinner with your sarsaparilla. ✉ *699 Main Ave., Durango* ☎ *970/247–4431* ⊕ *www.strater.com.*

SHOPPING

Notah Dineh Trading Company and Museum specializes in rugs, hand-carved kachina dolls, cradleboards, baskets, beadwork, and silver jewelry. Stop in at the museum (entry is free) to see relics of the Old West as well as a noteworthy rug in the Two Grey Hills pattern. ✉ *345 W. Main St., Cortez* ☎ *970/565–9607 or 800/444–2024* ⊕ *www.notahdineh.com.*

SCENIC DRIVES AND VISTAS

TRAIN RIDE

⟳ **Durango & Silverton Narrow Gauge Railroad.** In service since 1882, this train Fodor's Choice still makes its daily 3½-hour, 45-mi runs between Silverton and Durango ★ in season. The nine-hour round-trip journey includes a stopover; it's an entertaining way to relive the halcyon days of steam-powered travel. Passengers travel in restored 1882 parlor cars or in the open-air gondolas as the locomotive chugs along the Animas River Valley and, at times, clings precariously to the hillside. There are age restrictions for the first-class seats. ✉ *479 Main Ave., Durango* ☎ *970/247–2733 or 877/872–4607* ⊕ *www. durangotrain.com* ✉ *$79–$159* ⚖ *Reservations essential* ⊙ *Early May– late Oct., with four departures daily June–Aug. and one daily at other times. A shorter excursion to Cascade Canyon is available in winter.*

WHERE TO EAT AND STAY

ABOUT THE RESTAURANTS

Dining options in Mesa Verde are limited inside the park, but comparatively plentiful and varied if you're staying in a nearby town. In surrounding communities, southwestern restaurants and steak houses are favored.

ABOUT THE HOTELS

All 150 rooms of the park's Far View Lodge, open April through October, have private balconies and fill up quickly—so reservations are recommended, especially if you plan to visit on a weekend in the summer. Options in the surrounding area range from chain hotels to bed-and-breakfast inns. Durango in particular has a number of hotels in fine old buildings reminiscent of the Old West.

ABOUT THE CAMPGROUNDS

Morefield Campground is the only option within the park and is an excellent one. Reservations are accepted; it's open April through October. Nearby, Mancos has a campground with full amenities, while the San Juan National Forest offers backcountry camping.

WHERE TO EAT

IN THE PARK

¢–$ ✕ **Far View Terrace.** This full-service cafeteria offers great views, plentiful choices, and reasonable prices. A coffee counter provides the requisite caffeine for the day's activities, and they'll cook your omelet and pancakes to order as you watch. Dinner options might include a Navajo taco piled high with all the fixings. Don't miss the creamy malts and homemade fudge. ⊠ *Mesa Top Loop Rd., across from the Far View Visitor Center* ☎ *970/529–4444* ⊟ *D, MC, V* ☉ *Closed late Oct.–early Apr.*

¢ ✕ **Knife's Edge Cafe.** An all-you-can-eat pancake breakfast is served every morning from 7:30 to 10, and at night there's an all-you-can-eat barbecue dinner from 5 to 8. ⊠ *4 mi south of the park entrance* ☎ *970/565–2133* ⊟ *AE, D, MC, V* ☉ *Closed Sept.–May. No lunch.*

$$–$$$ ✕ **Metate Room.** The rugged high-desert terrain contrasts with this relaxing
★ space just off the lobby of the Far View Lodge. Tables in this southwestern-style dining room are candlelit and cloth covered, but the atmosphere remains casual. A wall of windows affords wonderful Mesa Verde vistas. Entrées include American staples like steak and seafood, or you can try one of the dishes centered on regional game such as elk, bison, quail, venison, and rabbit. Every table gets mesa bread and black bean hummus for starters. There's a solid array of wines and cocktails with kitschy names, like the "mesa-tini." ⊠ *Far View Lodge, across from the Far View Visitor Center, 15 mi southwest of park entrance* ☎ *970/529–4421* ⊟ *AE, D, DC, MC, V* ☉ *Closed late Oct.–early Apr. No lunch.*

¢–$ ✕ **Spruce Tree Terrace.** A limited selection of hot food and sandwiches is all you'll find at this cafeteria, but the patio is pleasant, and it's conveniently across the street from the museum. The Terrace is also the only food concession open year-round for lunch. ⊠ *Park entrance road, 5 mi south of the Far View Visitor Center* ☎ *970/529–4521* ⊟ *AE, D, DC, MC, V* ☉ *No dinner Dec.–Feb.*

PICNIC AREAS **Park Headquarters Loop Picnic Area.** This is the nicest and largest picnic
☺ area in the park. It has 40 tables under shade trees and a great view into Spruce Canyon, as well as flush toilets and running water. ⊠ *6 mi south of the Far View Visitor Center.*

Wetherill Mesa Picnic Area. Ten tables placed under lush shade trees, along with drinking water and restrooms, make this a pleasant spot for lunch. ⊠ *12 mi southwest of the Far View Visitor Center.*

OUTSIDE THE PARK

¢–$ ✕ **Brickhouse Cafe & Coffee Bar.** This popular little place may look like
CAFÉ a bed-and-breakfast, but they take their coffee and tea seriously. In a restored Victorian house with wonderful yard landscaping, Brickhouse serves breakfast and lunch food all day. Don't miss the malted buttermilk

26

waffle, pigs in a blanket, or big burgers. ✉ *1849 Main Ave., Durango* ☎ *970/247–3760* ⊕ *www.brickhousecafe.com* ▭ *AE, D, MC.*

$–$$
GERMAN

✕ **German Stone Oven Restaurant & Bakery.** Favorites include Wiener schnitzel, sauerbraten, pork chops, and imported beer; there are also vegetarian dishes. Antiques and collectibles fill the dining room or you could eat on the patio. ✉ *811 Railroad Ave., Dolores* ☎ *970/882–7033* ▭ *MC, V* ☾ *Closed Tues., Wed., and Jan.–Apr.*

$$
AMERICAN
★

✕ **Millwood Junction.** This rambling restaurant, made of wood from seven local barns, has everything you'd want for a fun night out: good drinks, good food, and, on summer weekends, top-notch entertainment. Try the pasta, chicken, or steak specials; most meals come with a large salad bar. An excellent all you can eat Friday-night seafood buffet for $13.95 draws folks from four states. ✉ *U.S. 160 at Main St., Mancos* ☎ *970/533–7338* ⊕ *www.millwoodjunction.com* ▭ *MC, V* ☾ *No lunch weekends.*

¢–$
CAFÉ

✕ **Olde Tymer's Café.** Locals flock to this former drugstore for the hamburgers, and to bask in the feel of days gone by. Known as the OTC, they serve soups, salads, and sandwiches. The tin ceiling, artifacts, and photos give it the appearance of a 1920s dance hall, and when the weather's nice, take your chow to the patio. ✉ *1000 Main Ave., Durango* ☎ *970/259–2990* ⊕ *www.otcdgo.com* ▭ *AE, MC, V.*

$$–$$$$
STEAKHOUSE

✕ **Ore House.** Durango is a meat-and-potatoes kind of town, and this is Durango's idea of a steak house. The aroma of beef smacks you in the face as you walk past, but there are chicken and seafood dishes available too. This local favorite serves enormous slabs of aged Angus that are hand-cut daily. If you're watching your cholesterol, steer clear. ✉ *147 E. College Dr., Durango* ☎ *970/247–5707* ⊕ *www.orehouserestaurant.com* ▭ *D, MC, V.*

WHERE TO STAY

IN THE PARK

$
★

⊡ **Far View Lodge.** Talk about a view—all rooms have a private balcony, from which you can admire the neighboring states of Arizona, Utah, and New Mexico up to 100 mi in the distance. The spartan-meets-southwestern rooms don't have a lot of space to spare but the only other in-park lodging option is camping. Upgrade to a kiva room for a little more space and a few more amenities (including air-conditioning). The staff is friendly and you can take in nightly talks by guest speakers on various park topics in the lobby. The hotel also offers enthusiastic guided tours of the park. The Metate Room (⇨ *Where to Eat*), the lodge's main dining room, is acclaimed for its fine steaks and excellent southwestern fare. Above it is a cocktail lounge that offers late night appetizers. **Pros:** close to the key sites; views are spectacular; nights are quiet and mystical; no television! **Cons:** no television?; simple rooms and amenities; walls are thin and less than soundproof. ✉ *Across from the Far View Visitor Center, 15 mi southwest of park entrance* ⊡ *P.O. Box 277, Mancos 81328* ☎ *970/564–4300 or 800/449–2288* ⊕ *www.visitmesaverde.com* ⇆ *150 rooms* ⚏ *In-room: no a/c (some), refrigerator (some). In-hotel: restaurant, bar, laundry facilities, Wi-Fi, some pets allowed* ▭ *AE, D, DC, MC, V* ☾ *Closed Nov.–Mar.*

CAMPING
$$
Fodor's Choice
★

⚠ **Morefield Campground.** With more than 400 shaded campsites, access to trailheads, and plenty of amenities, the only campground in the park is an appealing mini-city for campers. It's a 40-minute drive to reach the park's most popular sites. Reservations are accepted only for tent and group sites. **Pros:** the village has a gas station and store; inside park boundaries. **Cons:** still far from key sites at the north end of the park. ⊠ *4 mi south of park entrance, P.O. Box 8, Mesa Verde* ☎ *970/564–4300 or 800/449–2288* ⊕ *www.visitmesaverde.com* ↴ *365 tent/RV sites, 15 RV sites* ♿ *Flush toilets, partial hookups (some), dump station, drinking water, guest laundry, showers, fire grates, grills, picnic tables, food service, electricity, public telephone, general store, ranger station, service station* ▭ *AE, D, DC, MC, V* ☽ *Late-Apr.–mid-Oct.*

OUTSIDE THE PARK

$

🏨 **Anasazi Motor Inn.** This is definitely the nicest hotel in downtown Cortez, mostly because its air-conditioned rooms are spacious, carpeted, and pleasantly decorated with furniture in southwestern colors. Outside, you'll find horseshoes and volleyball pits. The lounge features live music on the weekends. **Pros:** Cortez is closer than Durango at only 10 mi from the park entrance; pool is heated in the cooler months. **Cons:** less than charming from the outside. ⊠ *640 S. Broadway, Cortez* ☎ *970/565–3773 or 800/972–6232* ⊕ *www.anasazimotorinn.com* ↴ *87 rooms* ♿ *In-room: Wi-Fi. In-hotel: restaurant, bar, pool, some pets allowed* ▭ *AE, D, DC, MC, V.*

$$–$$$
★

🏨 **Jarvis Suite Hotel.** This former theater in the center of downtown Durango became an all-suites hotel in 1984, about a century after its curtain first went up. It's loaded with western relics. **Pros:** condo-style lodging with full kitchens and fold-out sofas. **Cons:** neighbors may be noisy. ⊠ *125 W. 10th St., Durango* ☎ *970/259–6190 or 800/824–1024* ↴ *21 suites* ♿ *In-room: kitchen, Wi-Fi. In-hotel: laundry facilities* ▭ *AE, D, DC, MC, V.*

$$–$$$$
★

🏨 **Rochester Hotel.** The rooms in this small, 19th-century hotel are decorated in an Old West style and named after some of the many Hollywood films that were made in Durango. Movie posters, mismatched furniture, and wagon-wheel chandeliers make for a chic but funky interior. A full gourmet breakfast includes plenty of coffee and several varieties of tempting mini-muffins and scones. The 10-room Leland House is a sister property across the street that offers more of a bed-and-breakfast experience. **Pros:** central location; airy and spacious rooms; comfortable beds; well appointed bathrooms. **Cons:** it's a 100-year-old house, so expect the walls to be thin and the floorboards to groan underfoot. ⊠ *726 E. 2nd Ave., Durango* ☎ *970/385–1920 or 800/664–1920* ⊕ *www.rochesterhotel.com* ↴ *13 rooms, 1 suite* ♿ *In-room: kitchen (some), refrigerator, Wi-Fi. In-hotel: some pets allowed* ▭ *AE, D, DC, MC, V* ⍨ *BP.*

$$$–$$$$
Fodor's Choice
★

🏨 **Strater Hotel.** This Victorian beauty opened in 1887 and is the flagship hotel of old town Durango complete with crystal chandeliers, beveled windows, original oak beams, flocked wallpaper, and plush velour curtains. The individually decorated rooms are swooningly exquisite: after all, the hotel owns the country's largest collection of Victorian walnut antiques and has its own wood-carving shop to create exact period reproductions. Your room might have entertained Butch Cassidy (the real one, not Paul Newman), Louis L'Amour (he worked on the Sacketts

26

series here), and Francis Ford Coppola. Other former guests include John F. Kennedy and Marilyn Monroe (no, not at the same time). **Pros:** in the heart of Durango; a living piece of history beautifully restored. **Cons:** rooms in the post-Victorian annex are not quite as charming; the provided white noise machine is necessary at night if your room is near the stairs; thin mattresses. ✉ *699 Main Ave., Durango* 🕾 *970/247–4431 or 800/247–4431* ⊕ *www.strater.com* 📞 *93 rooms* 🔥 *In-room: Wi-Fi. In-hotel: restaurant, bar* ▤ *AE, D, DC, MC, V.*

CAMPING
$$–$$$
☺
★

⚠ **A & A Mesa Verde RV Park and Campground.** This 30-acre lot, directly across the highway from the national park, has many creature comforts you'd find in a hotel. There are kitchen facilities, a rec room with games, miniature golf course, sports field, a pool and hot tub, and a kennel. You can even stay in a log cabin. **Pros:** a stone's throw from the park entrance; the swimming pool is a welcome sight on a summer afternoon. **Cons:** "family friendly" can be good news or bad news depending on your perspective; a nearby donkey corral means you'll need good earplugs if you want to sleep late; choose your site wisely. ✉ *34979 U.S. Highway 160, Mancos* 🕾 *970/565–3517 or 800/972–6620* ⊕ *www.mesaverdecamping.com* 📞 *28 tent sites, 45 RV sites; 4 cabins* 🔥 *Flush toilets, full hookups, dump station, drinking water, guest laundry, showers, fire grates, grills, picnic tables, electricity, public telephone, general store, play area, swimming (pool), Wi-Fi* ▤ *D, MC, V* ☾ *Closed Oct.–May.*

$

⚠ **McPhee Campground.** The largest and best-equipped campground in the San Juan National Forest, McPhee is surrounded by paved roads and has several wheelchair-accessible sites. The campground overlooks McPhee Reservoir, the second biggest lake in Colorado, and a popular destination for boating and fishing. Reach it by taking Route 184 south 7 mi from Dolores to County Road 25, then turn north to onto Forest Road 271. **Pros:** centrally located in the four corners region; the only campsite with showers in the San Juan Forest; full hookups for RV's and facilities for large gatherings. **Cons:** perched on a mesa that can get stuffy in warm weather; no actual lakefront campsites in spite of the reservoir's proximity. ✉ *Forest Rd. 271, Durango* 🕾 *877/444–6777 or 970/247–4874* ⊕ *www.fs.fed.us/r2/sanjuan* 📞 *60 tent sites, 16 RV sites* 🔥 *Flush toilets, partial hookups (electric and water), dump station, drinking water, showers, fire pits, grills, picnic tables, electricity, public telephone* ☾ *Closed Oct.–Apr.*

Mount Rainier National Park

WORD OF MOUTH

"I took this photo at Paradise on Mt. Rainier. It is the nearest thing to Switzerland this side of the Atlantic!"
—photo by chinana, Fodors.com member

WELCOME TO MOUNT RAINIER

TOP REASONS TO GO

★ **The mountain:** Some say Mt. Rainier is the most magical mountain in America. At 14,411 feet, it is a popular peak for climbing, with more than 10,000 attempts per year—half of which are successful.

★ **The glaciers:** About 35 square mi of glaciers and snowfields encircle Mt. Rainier, including Carbon Glacier and Emmons Glacier, the largest glaciers by volume and area, respectively, in the continental United States.

★ **The wildflowers:** More than 100 species of wildflowers bloom in the high meadows of the national park; the display dazzles from midsummer until the snow flies.

★ **Fabulous hiking:** More than 240 mi of maintained trails provide access to old-growth forest, river valleys, lakes, subalpine meadows, and rugged ridges.

★ **Unencumbered wilderness:** Under the provisions of the 1964 Wilderness Act and the National Wilderness Preservation System, 97% of the park is preserved as wilderness.

1 Longmire. Inside the Nisqually Gate explore Longmire historic district's museum and visitor center, ruins of the park's first hotel, or the nature loop. Nearby, delicate footbridges span the thundering Christine and Narada falls.

2 Paradise. The park's most popular destination is famous for wildflowers in summer and skiing in winter. Skyline Trail is one of many hiking routes that crisscross the base of the mountain; the larger of the two park lodges is also here.

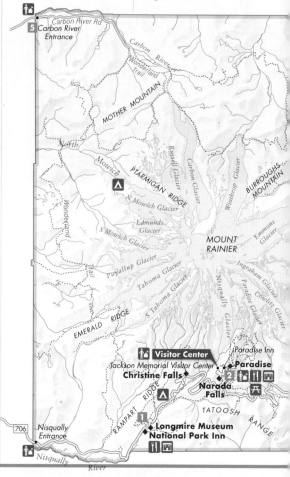

3 **Ohanapecosh.** Closest to the southeast entrance and the town of Packwood, the old-growth trees of the Grove of Patriarchs are a must-see. Another short trail around nearby Tipsoo Lake has great views.

4 **Sunrise and White River.** This side of the park is easy to visit in summer if you enter from the east side, but it's a long drive from the southwest entrance. Sunrise is the highest stretch of road in the park and a great place to take in the alpenglow—reddish light on the peak of the mountain near sunrise and sunset. Mt. Rainier's premier mountain-biking area, White River, is also the gateway to more than a dozen hiking trails.

5 **Carbon River and Mowich Lake.** Before entering the isolated northwest corner of the park, visit the Wilderness Information Center in downtown Wilkeson. Near the Carbon River Entrance Station is a swath of temperate forest, but to really get away from it all, follow the windy gravel roads to remote Mowich Lake.

WASHINGTON

GETTING ORIENTED

The jagged white crown of Mount Rainier is the showpiece of the Cascades and the focal point of this 337-square-mi national park. The most popular destination in the park, Paradise, is in the park's southern region, and Ohanapecosh, the Grove of Patriarchs, and Tipsoo Lake are in the southeastern corner. Mount Rainier National Park's eastern and northern areas are dominated by wilderness. The snowy folds of the Cascade mountain range stretch out from this Washington park; Seattle is roughly 50 mi north and the volcanic ruins of Mt. St. Helens 100 mi south.

27

KEY	
👫	Ranger Station
△	Campground
🛆	Picnic Area
🍴	Restaurant
🏠	Lodge
🚶	Trailhead
🚻	Restrooms
⟿	Scenic Viewpoint
⋯⋯	Walking/Hiking Trails

Sunrise
Visitor Center

White River
Entrance

White River

Crystal Mountain Ski Area

Pacific Crest Trail

410

Tipsoo Lake

123

Grove of the Patriarchs

Stevens Canyon Entrance

0   2 mi
0   2 km

Ohanapecosh
Visitor Center **3**

123

MOUNT RAINIER PLANNER

When to Go

Rainier is the Puget Sound's weather vane: if you can see it, the weather is going to be fine. Visitors are most likely to see the summit in July, August, and September. **Crowds are heaviest in summer,** too, meaning the parking lots at Paradise and Sunrise often fill before noon, campsites are reserved months in advance, and other lodgings are reserved as much as a year ahead.

True to its name, Paradise is often sunny during periods when the lowlands are under a cloud layer. The rest of the year, Rainier's summit gathers lenticular clouds whenever a Pacific storm approaches; once the peak vanishes from view it's time to haul out rain gear. The rare periods of clear winter weather bring residents up to Paradise for cross-country skiing.

AVG. HIGH/LOW TEMPS.

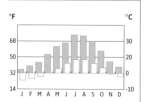

Flora and Fauna

Wildflower season in the meadows at and above timberline is mid-July through August. Large mammals like deer, elk, black bears, and cougars tend to occupy the less accessible wilderness areas of the park and thus elude the average visitor; smaller animals, such as squirrels and marmots are easier to spot. The best times to see wildlife are at dawn and dusk at the forest's edge. Fawns are born to the park's does in May, and the bugling of bull elk on the high ridges can be heard in late September and October, especially on the park's eastern side.

Getting Here and Around

The Nisqually entrance is on Highway 706, 14 mi east of Route 7; the Ohanapecosh entrance is on Route 123, 5 mi north of U.S. 12; and the White River entrance is on Route 410, 3 mi north of the Chinook and Cayuse passes. These highways become mountain roads as they reach Rainier, winding up and down many steep slopes, so cautious driving is essential: use a lower gear, especially on downhill sections, and take care not to overheat brakes by constant use. These roads are subject to storms any time of year and are repaired in the summer from winter damage and washouts. Expect to encounter roadwork delays.

The side roads going into the park's western slope are all narrower, unpaved, and subject to frequent flooding and washouts. All are closed by snow in winter except Highway 706 to Paradise and Carbon River Road, though the latter tends to flood near the park boundary. (Route 410 is open to the Crystal Mountain access road entrance.)

Park roads have a maximum speed of 35 MPH in most places, and you have to watch for pedestrians, cyclists, and wildlife. Parking can be very difficult to find during the peak summer season, especially at Paradise, Sunrise, the Grove of Patriarchs, and at the trailheads between Longmire and Paradise; it's best to arrive early in the day if you plan to visit these sites. All off-road-vehicle use—4X4 vehicles, ATVs, motorcycles, snowmobiles—is prohibited in Mount Rainier National Park.

Updated by
Holly S. Smith

Like a mysterious, white-clad woman, often veiled in clouds even when the surrounding forests and fields are bathed in sunlight, Mt. Rainier is the centerpiece of its namesake park. The impressive volcanic peak stands at an elevation of 14,411 feet, making it the fifth-highest peak in the lower 48 states. More than 2 million visitors a year enjoy spectacular views of the mountain and return home with a lifelong memory of its image.

27

The mountain holds the largest glacial system in the contiguous United States, with more than two-dozen major glaciers. On the lower slopes you find silent forests made up of cathedral-like groves of Douglas fir, western hemlock, and western red cedar, some more than 1,000 years old. Water and lush greenery are everywhere in the park, and dozens of thundering waterfalls, accessible from the road or by a short hike, fill the air with mist.

PARK ESSENTIALS

ACCESSIBILITY
The only trail in the park that is fully accessible to those with impaired mobility is Kautz Creek Trail, a ½-mi boardwalk that leads to a splendid view of the mountain. Parts of the Trail of the Shadows at Longmire and the Grove of the Patriarchs at Ohanapecosh are also accessible. Campgrounds at Cougar Rock, Ohanapecosh, and Sunshine Point have several accessible sites. All main visitor centers, as well as National Park Inn at Longmire, are accessible.

ADMISSION FEES AND PERMITS
The entrance fee of $15 per vehicle and $5 for those on foot, motorcycle, or bicycle, is good for seven days. Annual passes are $30. Climbing permits are $30 per person per climb or glacier trek. Wilderness camping permits must be obtained for all backcountry trips, and advance reservations are highly recommended.

ADMISSION HOURS

Mt. Rainier National Park is open 24/7 year-round, but with limited access in winter. Gates at Nisqually (Longmire) are staffed year-round during the day; facilities at Paradise and Ohanapecosh are open daily from late May to mid-October; and Sunrise is open daily July to early October. During off-hours you can buy passes at the gates from machines that accept credit and debit cards. Winter access to the park is limited to the Nisqually entrance, and the Jackson Memorial Visitor Center at Paradise is open on weekends and holidays in winter.

ATMS/BANKS

There are no ATMs in the park. ATMs are available at stores, gas stations, and bank branches in Ashford, Packwood, and Eatonville.

CELL-PHONE RECEPTION

Cell-phone reception is unreliable throughout much of the park, although access is clear at Paradise, Sunrise, and Crystal Mountain. Public telephones are at all park visitor centers, at the National Park Inn at Longmire, and at Paradise Inn at Paradise.

PARK CONTACT INFORMATION

Mount Rainier National Park ⊠ *Tahoma Woods, Star Rte., Ashford, WA* ☎ *360/569–2211* ⊕ *www.nps.gov/mora.*

SCENIC DRIVES

★ **Chinook Pass Road.** Route 410 (the highway to Yakima) follows the eastern edge of the park to Chinook Pass, where it climbs the steep, 5,432-foot pass via a series of switchbacks. At its top, take in broad views of Rainier and the east slope of the Cascades.

★ **Mowich Lake Road.** In the northwest corner of the park, this 24-mi mountain road begins in Wilkeson and heads up the Rainier foothills to Mowich Lake, traversing beautiful mountain meadows along the way. Mowich Lake is a pleasant spot for a picnic.

Paradise Road. This 9-mi stretch of Highway 706 winds its way up the mountain's southwest flank from Longmire to Paradise, taking you from lowland forest to the ever-expanding vistas of the mountain above. Visit on a weekday if possible, especially in peak summer months, when the road is packed with cars. The route is open year-round.

Sunrise Road. This popular (read: crowded) scenic road carves its way 11 mi up Sunrise Ridge from the White River Valley on the northeast side of the park. As you top the ridge there are sweeping views of the surrounding lowlands. The road is open late June to October.

WHAT TO SEE

HISTORIC SITES

National Park Inn. Even if you don't plan to stay overnight, you can stop by year-round to observe the architecture of this 1917 inn, which is on the National Register of Historic Places. While you're here, relax in front of the fireplace in the lounge, stop at the gift shop, or dine at

MOUNT RAINIER IN ONE DAY

The best way to get a complete overview of Mount Rainier in a day is to enter via Nisqually and begin your tour by browsing in **Longmire Museum.** When you're done, get to know the environment in and around Longmire Meadow and the overgrown ruins of Longmire Springs Hotel on the ½-mi **Trail of the Shadows** nature loop.

From Longmire, Highway 706 East climbs northeast into the mountains toward Paradise. Take a moment to explore gorgeous **Christine Falls,** just north of the road 1½ mi past Cougar Rock Campground, and **Narada Falls,** 3 mi farther on; both are spanned by graceful stone footbridges. Fantastic mountain views, alpine meadows crosshatched with

nature trails, a welcoming lodge and restaurant, and the excellent **Jackson Memorial Visitor Center** combine to make lofty Paradise the primary goal of most park visitors. One outstanding (but challenging) way to explore the high country is to hike the 5-mi round-trip **Skyline Trail** to Panorama Point, which rewards you with stunning 360-degree views.

Continue eastward on Highway 706 East for 21 mi and leave your car to explore the incomparable, thousand-year-old **Grove of the Patriarchs.** Afterward, turn your car north toward White River and **Sunrise Visitor Center,** where you can watch the alpenglow fade from Mt. Rainier's domed summit.

27

the restaurant. ⊠ *Longmire Visitor Complex, Hwy. 706, 10 mi east of Nisqually entrance, Longmire* ☎ *360/569–2411.*

SCENIC STOPS

Christine Falls. These two-tiered falls were named in honor of Christine Louise Van Trump, who climbed to the 10,000-foot level on Mt. Rainier in 1889 at the age of 9, despite having a crippling nervous-system disorder. ⊠ *Next to Hwy. 706, about 2½ mi east of Cougar Rock Campground.*

Fodor'sChoice
★ **Grove of the Patriarchs.** Protected from the periodic fires that swept through the surrounding areas, this small island of 1,000-year-old trees is one of Mount Rainier National Park's most memorable features. A 1½-mi loop trail heads through the old-growth forest of Douglas fir, cedar, and hemlock. ⊠ *Rte. 123, west of the Stevens Canyon entrance.*

★ **Narada Falls.** A steep but short trail leads to the viewing area for these spectacular 168-foot falls, which expand to a width of 75 feet during peak flow times. In winter the frozen falls are popular with ice climbers. ⊠ *Along Hwy. 706, 1 mi west of the turnoff for Paradise, 6 mi east of Cougar Rock Campground.*

☾ **Tipsoo Lake.** The short, pleasant trail that circles the lake here—ideal for families—provides breathtaking views. Enjoy the subalpine wildflower meadows during the summer months; in early fall there is an abundant supply of huckleberries. ⊠ *Off Cayuse Pass east on Hwy. 410.*

VISITOR CENTERS

Jackson Memorial Visitor Center. High on the mountain's southern flank, this center houses exhibits on geology, mountaineering, glaciology, and alpine ecology. Multimedia programs are staged in the theater; there's also a snack bar and gift shop. This is the park's most popular visitor destination, and it can be quite crowded in summer. ⊠ *Hwy. 706 E, 19 mi. east of the Nisqually park entrance* ☎ *360/569–6036* ⊙ *May–mid-Oct., daily 10–6; Nov.–Apr., weekends and holidays 10–5.*

> ## FLOOD DAMAGE
>
> Harsh winter weather and heavy spring rains cause road damage and closings every year. Those with the most snow and storm debris usually include Carbon River Road, Stevens Canyon Road, Westside Road to Dry Creek, and Highway 706 from Longmire to Paradise. ■TIP→ Before your trip, confirm site and road openings with one of the park's visitor centers.

★ **Longmire Museum and Visitor Center.** Glass cases inside this museum preserve plants and animals from the park—including a stuffed cougar—and historical photographs and geographical displays provide a worthwhile overview of the park's history. The adjacent visitor center has some perfunctory exhibits on the surrounding forest and its inhabitants, as well as pamphlets and information about park activities. ⊠ *Hwy. 706, 17 mi east of Ashford* ☎ *360/569–2211 Ext. 3314* 🔁 *Free* ⊙ *July–mid-Oct., daily 9–5; mid-Oct.–June, daily 9–4:30.*

Ohanapecosh Visitor Center. Learn about the region's dense old-growth forests through interpretive displays and videos at this visitor center, near the Grove of the Patriarchs. ⊠ *Rte. 123, 11 mi north of Packwood* ☎ *360/569–6046* ⊙ *Late May–Oct., daily 9–6.*

Sunrise Visitor Center. Exhibits at this center explain the region's sparser alpine and subalpine ecology. A network of nearby loop trails leads you through alpine meadows and forest to overlooks that have broad views of the Cascades and Rainier. ⊠ *Sunrise Rd., 15 mi from the White River park entrance* ☎ *360/663–2425* ⊙ *Early July–early Sept, daily 9–6.*

SPORTS AND THE OUTDOORS

BIRD-WATCHING

★ Be alert for kestrels, red-tailed hawks, and, occasionally, golden eagles on snags in the lowland forests. Also present at Rainier, but rarely seen, are great horned owls, spotted owls, and screech owls. Iridescent rufous hummingbirds flit from blossom to blossom in the drowsy summer lowlands, and sprightly water ouzels flutter in the many forest creeks. Raucous Steller's jays and gray jays scold passersby from trees, often darting boldly down to steal morsels from unguarded picnic tables. At higher elevations, look for the pure white plumage of the white-tailed ptarmigan as it hunts for seeds and insects in winter. Waxwings, vireos, nuthatches, sapsuckers, warblers, flycatchers, larks, thrushes, siskins, tanagers, and finches are common throughout the park.

HIKING

★ Although the mountain can seem remarkably benign on calm summer days, hiking Rainier is not a city-park stroll. Dozens of hikers and trekkers annually lose their way and must be rescued—and lives are lost on the mountain each year. Weather that approaches cyclonic levels can appear quite suddenly, any month of the year. With the possible exception of the short loop hikes listed below, all visitors venturing far from vehicle access points should carry day packs with warm clothing, food, and other emergency supplies.

⇨ *Multisport Outfitters box for hiking outfitters and expeditions.*

EASY

Nisqually Vista Trail. Equally popular in summer and winter, this trail is a 1¼-mi round-trip through subalpine meadows to an overlook point for Nisqually Glacier. The gradually sloping path is a favorite venue for cross-country skiers in winter; in summer, listen for the shrill alarm calls of the area's marmots. ⊠ *Trailhead at Jackson Memorial Visitor Center, Rte. 123, 1 mi north of Ohanapecosh, at the high point of Hwy. 706.*

Sourdough Ridge Trail. The mile-long loop of this self-guided trail takes you through the delicate subalpine meadows near the Sunrise Visitor Center. A gradual climb to the ridgetop yields magnificent views of Mt. Rainier and the more distant volcanic cones of Mts. Baker, Adams, Glacier, and Hood. ⊠ *Access trail at Sunrise Visitor Center, Sunrise Rd., 15 mi from the White River park entrance.*

Trail of the Shadows. This ½-mi walk is notable for its glimpses of meadowland ecology, its colorful soda springs (don't drink the water), James Longmire's old homestead cabin, and the foundation of the old Longmire Springs Hotel, which was destroyed by fire around 1900. ⊠ *Trailhead at Hwy. 706, 10 mi east of Nisqually entrance.*

MODERATE

Fodor's Choice **Skyline Trail.** This 5-mi loop, one of the highest trails in the park, beck-
★ ons day-trippers with a vista of alpine ridges and, in summer, meadows filled with brilliant flowers and birds. At 6,800 feet, Panorama Point, the spine of the Cascade Range, spreads away to the east, and Nisqually Glacier tumbles downslope. ⊠ *Jackson Memorial Visitor Center, Rte. 123, 1 mi north of Ohanapecosh at the high point of Hwy. 706.*

Van Trump Park Trail. You gain an exhilarating 2,200 feet on this route while hiking through a vast expanse of meadow with views of the southern Puget Sound. The 5-mi track provides good footing, and the average hiker can make it up in three to four hours. ⊠ *Hwy. 706 at Christine Falls, 4.4 mi east of Longmire.*

DIFFICULT

Fodor's Choice **Wonderland Trail.** All other Mt. Rainier hikes pale in comparison to this
★ stunning 93-mi trek, which completely encircles the mountain. The trail passes through all the major life zones of the park, from the old-growth forests of the lowlands to the alpine meadows and goat-haunted glaciers of the highlands—pick up a mountain-goat sighting card from a ranger station or visitor center if you want to help in the park's effort to learn more about these elusive animals. Wonderland is a rugged trail; elevation gains and losses totaling 3,500 feet are common in a day's hike,

27

Mount Rainier, Looking North

MOUNT RAINIER

Columbia Crest
14,411 ft

Liberty Cap
14,122 ft

Point Success
14,153 ft

Gibraltar Rock
12,660 ft

St. Andrews Rock
10,992 ft

SUNSET AMPHITHEATER

SUCCESS CLEAVER

Wilson Glacier

Nisqually Glacier

Kautz Glacier

WAPOWETY CLEAVER

Success Glaciers

Tahoma Glacier

PUYALLUP CLEAVER

Tahoma Glacier

GLACIER ISLAND

SOUTH TAHOMA DIVIDE

Pyramid Glaciers

Van Trump Glaciers

Van Trump Park

VAN TRUMP PARK

Mildred Point

PYRAMID PARK

Pyramid Peak
6,937 ft

Tokaloo Rock
7,684 ft

Iron Mountain
6,283 ft

EMERALD RIDGE

Disappointment Cleaver

Little Tahoma Peak
11,138 ft

Ingraham Glacier

CATHEDRAL ROCKS

Anvil Rock
9,584 ft

Paradise Glaciers

McClure Rock
7,385 ft

Snowfield

Muir Snowfield

Camp Muir
10,188 ft

Panorama Point
6,800 ft

Skyline Trail

Alta Vista

Paradise

Henry M. Jackson
Memorial Visitor Center

Unicorn Peak
6,917 ft

Louise Lake

The Castle

Reflection Lakes

Pinnacle Peak
6,562 ft

Plummer Peak
6,370 ft

Lane Peak
6,012 ft

Wahpenayo Peak
6,231 ft

Chutla Peak

CUSHMAN CREST

TATOOSH RANGE

Eagle Peak
5,958 ft

Cougar Rock

Pyramid Creek

Rampart Ridge Trail

RAMPART RIDGE

THE RAMPARTS

Longmire

KEY

— Paved Roads
--- Hiking Trails
···· Climbing Routes

which averages 8 mi. Most hikers start out from Longmire or Sunrise and take 10–14 days to cover the 93-mi route. Snow lingers on the high passes well into June (sometimes July); count on rain any time of the year. Campsites are wilderness areas with pit toilets and water that must be purified before drinking. Only hardy, well-equipped, and experienced wilderness trekkers should attempt this trip, but those who do will be amply rewarded. Wilderness permits are required, and reservations are strongly recommended. △ **Parts of the Wonderland Trail can be severely damaged due to floods. Check with a visitor center for the trail's current status.** For a summer-day hike, it's easiest to explore from Longmire, where a broad, easy section of track climbs through open, wildflower-filled slopes toward a vast panorama of ice-covered ridges. ⊠ *Longmire Visitor Center, Hwy. 706, 17 mi east of Ashford; Sunrise Visitor Center, Sunrise Rd., 15 mi west of the White River park entrance.*

MOUNTAIN CLIMBING

★ Climbing Mt. Rainier is not for amateurs; each year, climbers die on the mountain, and many climbers become lost and must be rescued. Near-catastrophic weather can appear quite suddenly, any month of the year. If you're experienced in technical, high-elevation snow, rock, and ice-field adventuring, Mt. Rainier can be a memorable adventure. Climbers can fill out a climbing card at the Paradise, White River, or Carbon River ranger stations and lead their own groups of two or more. Climbers must register with a ranger before leaving and check out upon return. A $30 annual climbing fee applies to anyone venturing above 10,000 feet or onto one of Rainier's glaciers. During peak season it is recommended that you make a climbing reservation ($20 per group) in advance; reservations are taken by fax beginning in April on a first-come, first-served basis (find the reservation form at ⊕ *www.nps.gov/mora/planyourvisit/climbing.htm*).

For climbing outfitters, ⇨ Multisport Outfitters box.

SKIING AND SNOWSHOEING

Mt. Rainier is a major Nordic ski center for cross-country and telemark skiing. Although trails are not groomed, those around Paradise are extremely popular. If you want to ski with fewer people, try the trails in and around the Ohanapecosh–Stevens Canyon area, which are just as beautiful and, because of their more easterly exposure, slightly less subject to the rains that can douse the Longmire side, even in the dead of winter. You should never ski on the plowed main roads, especially in the Paradise area—the snowplow operator can't see you. No rentals are available on the eastern side of the park.

★ Deep snows make Mt. Rainier a snowshoeing pleasure. The Paradise area, with its network of trails, is the best choice. The park's east side roads, Routes 123 and 410, are unplowed and provide other good snowshoeing venues, although you must share the main parts of the road with snowmobilers.

Paradise Ski Area. You can cross-country ski or, in the Snowplay Area north of the upper parking lot at Paradise, sled using inner tubes and soft platters from December to April. Check with rangers for any restrictions. In summer, many trails around this side of the mountain are accessible from Paradise. During winter, the easy, 3½-mile Nordic ski route begins

MULTISPORT OUTFITTER

Rainier Mountaineering Inc.
Reserve a private hiking guide through this highly regarded outfitter, or take part in its one-day mountaineering classes (mid-May through late September), where participants are evaluated on their fitness for the climb and must be able to withstand a 16-mi round-trip hike with a 9,000-foot gain in elevation. The company also arranges private cross-country skiing and snowshoeing guides. ✉ 30027 Hwy. 706 E, Ashford ☎ 888/892-5462 or 360/569-2227

⊕ www.rmiguides.com ✉ $805 for three-day summit climb package

Whittaker Mountaineering. You can rent hiking and climbing gear, skis, snowshoes, snowboards and other outdoor equipment through at this all-purpose Rainier Base Camp outfitter, which also arranges for private cross-country skiing and hiking guides. (✉ 30027 Hwy. 706 E, Ashford ☎ 800/238-5756 or 360/569-2142 ⊕ www. whittakermountaineering.com).

at the Paradise parking lot, and follows Paradise Valley/Stevens Canyon Road to Reflection Lakes. Equipment rentals are available at Whittaker Mountaineering in Ashford, or at the National Park Inn's General Store in Longmire. ✉ *Accessible from Nisqually entrance at park's southwest corner and (summer only) from Stevens Canyon entrance at park's southeast corner* ☎ *360/569-2211* ⊕ *www.nps.gov/mora* ☉ *May–mid-Oct., daily, sunrise–sunset; mid-Oct.–Apr., weekends sunrise–sunset.*

OUTFIT-
TERS AND
EXPEDITIONS

Adjacent to the National Park Inn, **Rainier Ski Touring Center** (✉ *Hwy. 706, 10 mi east of Nisqually entrance, Longmire* ☎ *360/569-2411, 360/569-2271 weekdays*) rents cross-country ski equipment and provides lessons from mid-December through Easter, depending on snow conditions. Park rangers lead **Snowshoe Walks** (✉ *1 mi north of Ohanapecosh on Rte. 123, at the high point of Hwy. 706* ☎ *360/569-2211 Ext. 2328* ✉ *Free* ☉ *Late Dec.–Apr., weekends and holidays*) that start at Jackson Memorial Visitor Center at Paradise and cover 1¼ mi in about two hours. Check park publications for exact dates.

For additional outfitters, ⇨ *Multisport Outfitters box.*

EDUCATIONAL OFFERINGS

RANGER PROGRAMS

☾ **Junior Ranger Program.** Youngsters can pick up the activity booklet to fill out as they explore the park. ☎ *360/569-2211 Ext. 3314* ✉ *Free.*

Ranger programs. Park ranger-led activities include **guided snowshoe walks** in the winter (most suitable for those older than 8) as well as **evening programs** at White River Campground on Thursday, Friday, and Saturday nights in July and August. Talks around the campfire may cover subjects such as park history, its flora and fauna, or interesting facts on climbing Mt. Rainier. ☎ *360/569-2211* ✉ *Free.*

TALKS

Summer Speaker Series. The Mount Rainier Institute hosts a lectures series on summer weekend evenings by speakers with various backgrounds and expertise. Past topics have included "National Parks during the Great Depression and World War II," "Mount Saint Helens and the Cascade Volcanoes," and "Fifty Years of Climate, Culture, and Landscape Change." ⊠ *Paradise Inn or Ohanapecosh Campground* ☎ *360/569–2211* ✆ *Free* ☉ *July–early Sept.*

TOURS

Fodor's Choice
★ **Gray Line Bus Tours.** Join a one-day or longer sightseeing tour from Seattle to Mount Rainier and Olympic national parks, Mt. St. Helens, the North Cascades, and the Washington Wine Country (Yakima Valley). ⊠ *4500 Marginal Way SW, Seattle* ☎ *206/624–5077 or 800/426–7532* ⊕ *www.graylineofseattle.com.*

WHAT'S NEARBY

NEARBY TOWNS

Ashford sits astride an ancient trail across the Cascades used by the Yakama Indians to trade with the coastal tribes of western Washington. The town began as a logging railway terminal; today, it's the main gateway to Mount Rainier—and the only year-round access point to the park—with lodges, restaurants, grocery stores, and gift shops. Surrounded by Cascade peaks, **Packwood** is a pretty mountain village on U.S. 12, below White Pass. Between Mt. Rainier and Mt. St. Helens, it's a perfect jumping-off point for exploring local wilderness areas.

VISITOR INFORMATION
Destination Packwood Association ☎ *360/494–2223 or 800/963–7898* ⊕ *www.destinationpackwood.com.*

NEARBY ATTRACTIONS

★ **Coldwater Ridge Visitor Center.** Exhibits at this multimillion-dollar facility document the great blast of Mt. St. Helens and its effects on the surrounding 150,000 acres, which were devastated but are in the process of a remarkable recovery. A ¼-mi trail leads from the visitor center to Coldwater Lake, which has a recreation area. ⊠ *Rte. 504, 43 mi east of I–5* ☎ *360/274–2131* ✆ *Free* ☉ *May–Oct., daily 10–6.*

★ **Goat Rocks Wilderness.** The crags in Gifford Pinchot National Forest, south of Mt. Rainier, are aptly named: you often see mountain goats here, especially when you hike into the backcountry; Goat Lake is a particularly good spot for viewing the elusive creatures. See the goats without backpacking by taking Forest Road 2140 south from U.S. 12 near Packwood to Stonewall Ridge. Ask for exact directions in Packwood, or ask a national forest ranger. The goats will be on Stonewall Ridge looming up ahead of you. ⊠ *Gifford Pinchot National Forest, 10600 N.E. 51st St. Circle, Vancouver* ✛ *Wilderness entrance points along U.S. 12, 2–10 mi east of White Pass* ☎ *360/891–5000* ⊕ *www.fs.fed.us/*

DID YOU KNOW?

Named after British admiral Peter Rainier in the late 18th century, Mount Rainier had an earlier name. Tahoma (also Takhoma), its American Indian name, means "the mountain that was God." Various unsuccessful attempts have been made to restore the aboriginal name to the peak. Of course, to most Puget Sound residents, Rainier is simply "the mountain."

gpnf/recreation/wilderness 🖳 *Free*
🕙 *Call for weather conditions.*

Johnston Ridge Observatory. With the
most spectacular views of the crater
and lava dome of Mt. St. Helens,
this observatory also has exhibits
that interpret the geology of the
mountain and explain how scientists
monitor an active volcano. ⊠ *Rte.
504, 53 mi east of I–5, Mount St.
Helens* 🕾 *360/274–2140* 🖳 *Free*
🕙 *May–Oct., daily 10–6.*

🕙 **Mount Rainier Scenic Railroad.** Begin-
★ ning at Elbe, 11 mi west of Ashford,
the train takes you southeast through
lush forests and across scenic bridges,

covering 14 mi of incomparable beauty. Seasonal theme trips, such as the
Great Pumpkin Express and the Snowball Express, are also available. At
this writing, departures are from Mineral, about 10 minutes from Elbe,
due to damage at the Nisqually Bridge in 2006; tickets and souvenirs can
still be purchased at the original Elbe depot on Route 7. ⊠ *349 Mineral
Creek Rd., Mineral* 🕾 *360/569–2588 or 888/783–2611* ⊕ *www.mrsr.com*
🖳 *$20* 🕙 *Memorial Day–Sept. Thurs. and Fri. at 2, weekends at 10:30
and 2; Dec., weekends, call for hrs.*

Mount St. Helens Visitor Center. This facility, one of three visitor centers
along Route 504 on the west side of the mountain, has exhibits docu-
menting the eruption, plus a walk-through volcano. ⊠ *Rte. 504, 5 mi
east of I–5, Silver Lake* 🕾 *360/274–2100* ⊕ *www.mounsthelens.com or
www.parks.wa.gov/mountsthelens.asp* 🖳 *$3* 🕙 *Late Oct.–Mar., daily
9–4; Apr.–late Oct., daily 9–5.*

★ **Northwest Trek Wildlife Park.** One of the pioneers in modern zoo operation, this park consists of large, natural enclosures where native animals
such as elk, caribou, moose, and deer roam free. Five miles of nature
trails meander near the enclosures, and the hands-on Cheney Discovery
Center provides an up-close wildlife experience. Hop on a tram for a
narrated tour of the park; another tour lets you accompany keepers
while they feed the wildlife. ⊠ *Rte. 161, about 35 mi west of Mount
Rainier National Park, Eatonville* 🕾 *360/832–6122* ⊕ *www.nwtrek.org*
🖳 *$15.50* 🕙 *Late June–early Sept., daily 9:30–6; rest of Sept., weekdays
9:30–4, weekends 9:30–5; Oct., weekdays 9:30–3, weekends 9:30–4;
Nov.–Feb., weekends 9:30–3; Mar., weekdays 9:30–3, weekends 9:30–
4; Apr., weekdays 9:30–4, weekends 9:30–5.*

WHERE TO EAT AND STAY

ABOUT THE RESTAURANTS

There are a limited number of restaurants inside the park, and a few worth checking out lie beyond its borders. Mount Rainier's picnic areas are justly famous, especially in summer, when wildflowers fill the meadows—resist the urge to feed the yellow pine chipmunks darting about.

ABOUT THE HOTELS

The Mount Rainier area is remarkably bereft of quality lodging. Rainier's two national park lodges, at Longmire and Paradise, are attractive and well maintained. They exude considerable history and charm, especially Paradise Inn, but unless you've made summer reservations a year in advance, getting a room can be a challenge. Dozens of motels and cabin complexes are near the park entrances, but the vast majority are overpriced and no-frills. With just a few exceptions, you're better off camping.

ABOUT THE CAMPGROUNDS

Five drive-in campgrounds are in the park—Cougar Rock, Ipsut Creek, Ohanapecosh, Sunshine Point, and White River—with almost 700 sites for tents and RVs. None have hot water or RV hookups; showers are available at Jackson Memorial Visitor Center. For backcountry camping, you must obtain a free wilderness permit at one of the visitor centers. Primitive sites are spaced at 7- to 8-mi intervals along the Wonderland Trail. A copy of *Wilderness Trip Planner: A Hiker's Guide to the Wilderness of Mount Rainier National Park,* available from any of the park's visitor centers or through the superintendent's office, is an invaluable guide if you're planning backcountry stays. Reservations for specific wilderness campsites are available from May 1 to September 30 for $20; for details, call the Wilderness Information Center at ☎ *360/569–4453.*

27

WHERE TO EAT

IN THE PARK

¢ ✕ **Jackson Memorial Visitor Center.** Traditional grill fare such as hot dogs,
AMERICAN hamburgers, and soft drinks are served daily from May through early
🕃 October and on weekends and holidays during the rest of the year.
⊠ *Rte. 123, 1 mi north of Ohanapecosh at the high point of Hwy. 706*
☎ *360/569–2211* ⊕ *www.mtrainierguestservices.com* ⊟ *No credit cards*
☉ *Closed weekdays early Oct.–Apr.*

$$–$$$ ✕ **National Park Inn.** Photos of Mt. Rainier taken by some of the North-
ECLECTIC west's top photographers adorn the walls of this inn's large dining room,
★ a bonus on the many days the mountain refuses to show itself. Meals, served family-style, are simple but tasty: maple hazelnut chicken, tenderloin tip stir-fry, and grilled red snapper with black bean sauce and corn relish. For breakfast, don't miss the home-baked cinnamon rolls with cream-cheese frosting. ⊠ *Hwy. 706, Longmire* ☎ *360/569–2411* ⊕ *www.mtrainierguestservices.com* ⚠ *Reservations not accepted* ⊟ *MC, V.*

$$–$$$ ✕ **Paradise Inn.** Where else can you get a decent Sunday brunch in a his-
CONTINENTAL toric heavy-timbered lodge halfway up a mountain? Tall, many-paned
★ windows provide terrific views of Rainier, and the warm glow of native wood permeates the large dining room. The lunch menu is simple and

healthy—grilled salmon, salads, and the like. For dinner, there's nothing like a hearty plate of the inn's signature bourbon buffalo meat loaf. ⊠ *Hwy. 706, Paradise* ☎ *360/569–2413* ⊕ *www.mtrainierguestservices. com* ⌣ *Reservations not accepted* ⊟ *MC, V* ⊘ *Closed Oct.–late May.*

AMERICAN   ¢ ✕ **Sunshine Lodge Food Service.** A cafeteria and grill here serve inexpensive hamburgers, chili, hot dogs, and snacks from early July to early
⊙ September. ⊠ *Sunrise Rd., 15 mi from the White River park entrance*
☎ *360/663–2425* ⊕ *www.mtrainierguestservices.com* ⊟ *No credit cards*
⊘ *Closed early Sept.–early July.*

PICNIC AREAS   Park picnic areas are open July through September only.

Paradise Picnic Area. This site has great views on clear days. After picnicking at Paradise, you can take an easy hike to one of the many waterfalls in the area—Sluiskin, Myrtle, or Narada, to name a few. ⊠ *Hwy. 706, 11 mi east of Longmire.*

Sunrise Picnic Area. Set in an alpine meadow that's filled with wildflowers in July and August, this picnic area provides expansive views of the mountain and surrounding ranges in good weather. ⊠ *Sunrise Rd., 11 mi west of the White River entrance.*

Sunshine Point Picnic Area. A small group of picnic tables at the Sunshine Point Campground sits in an open meadow along the burbling Nisqually River. ⊠ *Hwy. 706, 1 mi east of the Nisqually entrance.*

OUTSIDE THE PARK

$$–$$$ ✕ **Alexander's Country Inn & Restaurant.** Without a doubt, this classic,
AMERICAN   woodsy Northwest country inn built in 1912 serves the best food in
★   the area. Ceiling fans and wooden booths lining the walls make it look
like a country kitchen. Try the steak or trout—freshly caught from
the pond on the grounds. The homemade bread is fantastic, and the
blackberry pie is a must for dessert. Dine inside or outside on a patio
overlooking the trout pond and a waterfall. Box lunches for adventurers
are available upon request. ⊠ *37515 Hwy. 706, Ashford* ☎ *360/569–
2323 or 800/654–7615* ⊕ *www.alexanderscountryinn.com* ⊟ *D, MC,
V* ⊘ *Nov.–Apr., no lunch Fri. or weekends.*

¢   ✕ **Scaleburgers.** Once a 1939 logging-truck weigh station, the building
AMERICAN   is now a popular restaurant serving homemade hamburgers, fries, milk
⊙   shakes. Eat outside on tables overlooking the hills and scenic railroad.
The restaurant is 11 mi west of Ashford. ⊠ *54109 Mountain Hwy. E,
Elbe* ☎ *360/569–2247* ⊟ *No credit cards.*

WHERE TO STAY

IN THE PARK

$$ 🏨 **National Park Inn.** A large stone fireplace sits prominently in the com-
★   mon room of this country inn, the only one of the park's two inns
that's open year-round. Rustic details such as wrought-iron lamps and
antique bentwood headboards adorn the rooms. Simple American fare
is served in the restaurant (⇨ *Where to Eat).* The inn is operated as a
B&B from October through April. **Pros:** classic national park ambi-
ence; only lodging inside park open in winter and spring. **Cons:** jam-
packed in summer; must book far in advance; some rooms have shared
bath. ⊠ *Longmire Visitor Complex, Hwy. 706, 10 mi east of Nisqually*

entrance, Longmire ☎*360/569–2275* ⊕ *www.mtrainierguestservices. com* ↳ *25 rooms, 18 with bath* ♿ *In-room: no a/c, no phone. In-hotel: restaurant*⊟*MC, V*❘◯❘ *BP.*

$$–$$$ 🖼 **Paradise Inn.** With its hand-carved Alaskan cedar logs, burnished
Fodor's Choice parquet floors, stone fireplaces, Indian rugs, and glorious mountain
★ views, this 1917 inn is a classic example of a national park lodge. German architect Hans Fraehnke designed the decorative woodwork. In addition to the full-service dining room *(▷ Where to Eat)*, there's a small snack bar and a snug lounge. **Pros:** central to trails; pristine vistas; nature-inspired details. **Cons:** noisy in high season. ⊠ *Hwy. 706, Paradise* ☍ *c/o Mount Rainier Guest Services, P.O. Box 108, Star Rte., Ashford 98304* ☎*360/569–2275* ⊕ *www.mtrainierguestservices.com* ↳ *121 rooms* ♿ *In-room: no phone, no TV. In-hotel: restaurant, bar* ⊟*MC, V* ◷ *Closed Nov.–mid-May.*

CAMPING ⛺ **Cougar Rock Campground.** A secluded, heavily wooded campground
$ with an amphitheater, Cougar Rock is one of the first to fill up. You
★ can reserve group sites for $3 per person, per night, with a minimum of 12 people per group. Reservations are accepted for summer only. **Pros:** ranger programs; isolated feeling. **Cons:** often crowded. ⊠ *2½ mi north of Longmire* ☎*301/722–1257 or 800/365–2267* ⛺ *173 tent/RV sites* ♿ *Flush toilets, dump station, drinking water, fire grates, ranger station* ⊟*AE, D, MC, V* ◷ *Closed mid-Oct.–Apr.*

¢ ⛺ **Mowich Lake Campground.** This is Rainier's only lakeside campground.
(FREE) At 4,959 feet, it's also peaceful and secluded. Note that the campground is accessible only by 5 mi of convoluted gravel roads, which are subject to weather damage and potential closure at any time. Reservations are not accepted. **Pros:** Mowich Lake setting; isolated. **Cons:** long drive on unpaved roads. ⊠ *Mowich Lake Rd., 6 mi east of the park boundary* ☎*360/568–2211* ⛺ *30 tent/RV sites* ♿ *Pit toilets, running water (non-potable), fire grates, picnic tables, ranger station* ◷ *Closed Nov.–mid July.*

$ ⛺ **Ohanapecosh Campground.** This lush, green campground in the park's
★ southeast corner has a visitor center, amphitheater, and self-guided trail. It's one of the first campgrounds to open. Reservations are accepted for summer only. **Pros:** great for families; open in early summer. **Cons:** popularity means busy facilities. ⊠ *Ohanapecosh Visitor Center, Hwy. 123, 1½ mi north of park boundary* ☎*301/722–1257 or 800/365–2267* ⛺ *188 tent/RV sites* ♿ *Flush toilets, dump station, drinking water, fire grates, ranger station* ⊟*AE, D, MC, V* ◷ *Closed late-Oct.–Apr.*

$ ⛺ **Sunshine Point Campground.** This pleasant, partly wooded campground is near the Nisqually River and the most popular entrance to the park. Sites are first-come, first-served. **Pros:** fewer campers than other spots. **Cons:** subject to spring floods; few amenities. ⊠ *5 mi past the Nisqually entrance* ☎*360/569–2211* ⛺ *18 tent/RV sites* ♿ *Pit toilets, drinking water, fire grates* ⊟*AE, D, MC, V.*

$ ⛺ **White River Campground.** At an elevation of 4,400 feet, White River is one of the park's highest and least-wooded campgrounds. Here you can enjoy campfire programs, self-guided trails, and partial views of Mt. Rainier's summit. Sites are first-come, first-served. **Pros:** breathtaking scenery. **Cons:** more exposure to the elements. ⊠ *5 mi west of White River entrance* ☎*360/569–2211* ↳ *112 sites* ♿ *Flush toilets, dump*

27

station, drinking water, fire grates, ranger station ⊟ *AE, D, MC, V* ⌑ *Reservations not accepted* ⊘ *Closed mid-Sept.–early June.*

OUTSIDE THE PARK

$$ 🏨 **Alexander's Country Inn.** Serving guests since 1912, Alexander's offers
★ premier lodging just a mile from Mt. Rainier. Antiques and fine linens
lend the main building romance; there are also two adjacent guest-
houses. Rates include a hearty breakfast and evening wine. The cozy
restaurant (⇨ *Where to Eat*; closed to off-site guests weekdays in win-
ter) is the best place in town for lunch or dinner. Stroll out back to view
verdant gardens, or take a dip in a hot tub set over the trout pond. **Pros:**
luxury extras; on-site day spa. **Cons:** lots of breakables means it's not
great for children. ⊠ *37515 Hwy. 706 E, 4 mi east of Ashford, Ashford*
☎ *360/569–2323 or 800/654–7615* ⊕ *www.alexanderscountryinn.com*
🛏 *12 rooms, 2 3-bedroom houses* ⌂ *In-room: DVD. In-hotel: restau-
rant, spa* ⊟ *MC, V* ⦿| *BP.*

¢–$$ 🏨 **Inn of Packwood.** Cascade mountain peaks tower above this inn,
centrally located in the village of Packwood. Pine paneling and fur-
niture lend the rooms rustic charm, and you can swim in an indoor
pool beneath skylights or have a picnic beneath a weeping willow.
Pros: convenient location for exploring; between Mount Rainier and
Mount St. Helens. **Cons:** not much privacy. ⊠ *13032 U.S. 12, Packwood,* ☎ *877/496–9666 or 360/494–5500* ⊕ *www.innofpackwood.com*
🛏 *33 rooms* ⌂ *In-room: kitchen (some), refrigerator (some). In-hotel:
pool* ⊟ *AE, MC, V* ⦿| *CP.*

$–$$$ 🏨 **Wellspring.** In the woodlands outside Ashford, the untraditional
★ accommodations here include tastefully designed log cabins, tent cab-
ins, a tree house, and a room in a greenhouse. The Tatoosh lodge, with
space for 14, has a huge stone fireplace. Each space is individually
decorated: for example, a queen-size feather bed is suspended by ropes
beneath a skylight in the Nest Room. This forest-inspired collection
of units, the only property of its kind in the area, is the creation of a
massage therapist; a variety of spalike amenities are available. **Pros:**
unique lodging option; some rooms good for groups or kids; relaxing
spa influence. **Cons:** limited amenities. ⊠ *54922 Kernehan Rd., Ashford*
☎ *360/569–2514* 🛏 *1 lodge, 6 cabins, 3 tent cabins, 1 tree house, 1 cot-
tage* ⌂ *In-room: no a/c, no phone, kitchen (some), refrigerator (some),
no TV (some). In-hotel: spa* ⊟ *MC, V* ⦿| *EP, CP.*

North Cascades National Park

WORD OF MOUTH

"We were very glad we decided to go to North Cascades, it is such an amazingly beautiful place. We stopped at Cascadian and had the raspberry ice cream on the way in and a pint of blueberries on the way out of the park. Both were delicious, thanks for the tip!"

—regalada

WELCOME TO NORTH CASCADES

TOP REASONS TO GO

★ **Pure wilderness:** Nearly 400 mi of mountain and meadow trails immerse hikers in pristine natural panoramas, with sure sightings of bald eagles, deer, elk, and other wildlife.

★ **Majestic glaciers:** The North Cascades are home to 318 moving ice masses, more than half of the glaciers in the United States.

★ **Splendid flora:** A bright palette of flowers blankets the hillsides in midsummer, while October's colors paint the landscape in vibrant autumn hues.

★ **Thrilling boat rides:** Lake Chelan, Lake Ross, and the Stehekin River are the starting points for kayaking, white-water rafting, and ferry trips.

★ **19th-century history:** Delve into the state's farming, lumber, and logging pasts in clapboard towns and homesteads around the park.

1 North Unit. The park's creek-cut northern wilderness, centered on snowy Mount Challenger, stretches north from Highway 20 over the Picket Range toward the Canadian border. It's an endless landscape of pine-topped peaks and ridges.

2 South Unit. Hike the South Unit's lake-filled mountain foothills in summer to take in vistas of blue skies and flower-filled meadows. Waterfalls and wildlife are abundant here.

3 Ross Lake National Recreation Area. Drawing a thick line from British Columbia all the way down to the North cascades Scenic Highway, placid Ross Lake is edged with pretty bays that draw swimmers and boaters.

4 Lake Chelan National Recreation Area. Ferries steam between small waterfront towns along this pristine waterway, while kayakers and hikers follow quiet trails along its edges. This is one of the Northwest's most popular summer escapes, with nature-bound activities, and rustic accommodations.

WASHINGTON

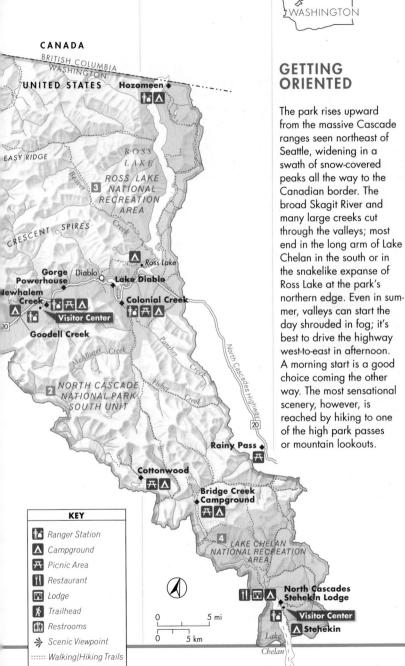

GETTING ORIENTED

The park rises upward from the massive Cascade ranges seen northeast of Seattle, widening in a swath of snow-covered peaks all the way to the Canadian border. The broad Skagit River and many large creeks cut through the valleys; most end in the long arm of Lake Chelan in the south or in the snakelike expanse of Ross Lake at the park's northern edge. Even in summer, valleys can start the day shrouded in fog; it's best to drive the highway west-to-east in afternoon. A morning start is a good choice coming the other way. The most sensational scenery, however, is reached by hiking to one of the high park passes or mountain lookouts.

28

KEY

| Ranger Station |
| Campground |
| Picnic Area |
| Restaurant |
| Lodge |
| Trailhead |
| Restrooms |
| Scenic Viewpoint |
| Walking/Hiking Trails |

0   5 mi
0   5 km

NORTH CASCADES PLANNER

When to Go

The spectacular, craggy peaks of the North Cascades—often likened to the Alps—are breathtaking in any season. **Summer is peak season,** especially along the alpine stretches of Route 20; weekends and holidays can be crowded. Summer is short and glorious in the high country, extending from snowmelt (late May to July, depending on the elevation and the amount of snow) to early September.

The North Cascades Highway is a popular autumn drive in September and October, when the changing leaves put on a colorful show. The lowland forest areas, such as the complex around Newhalem, can be visited almost any time of year. These can be wonderfully quiet in early spring or late autumn on mild, rainy days. Snow closes the North Cascades Highway from November through mid-April.

AVG. HIGH/LOW TEMPS.

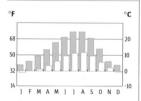

Flora and Fauna

Bald eagles are present year-round along the Skagit River and the various lakes—although in December, hundreds flock to the Skagit to feed on a rare winter salmon run; they remain through January. Black bears are often seen in spring and early summer along the roadsides in the high country, feeding on new green growth. Deer and elk can often be seen in early morning and late evening, grazing and browsing at the forest's edge. Other mountain residents include beaver, marmots, pika, otters, skunks, opossums, and smaller mammals, as well as a variety of forest and field birds.

Getting Here and Around

Highway 20, the North Cascades Highway, splits the park's north and south sections. The gravel Cascade River Road, which runs southeast from Marblemount, peels off Highway 20; Sibley Creek/Hidden Lake Road (USFS 1540) turns off Cascade River Road to the Cascade Pass trailhead. Thornton Creek Road is another rough four-wheel-drive track. For the Ross Lake area in the north, the unpaved Hozomeen Road (Silver–Skagit Road) provides access between Hope, British Columbia; Silver Lake; and Skagit Valley provincial parks. From Stehekin, the Stehekin Valley Road continues to High Bridge, Car Wash Falls, Bridge Creek, and Cottonwood campgrounds—although seasonal floods may cause washouts. Note that a day trip isn't nearly enough to make a thorough exploration of the park: roads are narrow and closed from October to June, many sights are off the beaten path, and the scenery is so spectacular that, once you're in it, you won't want to hurry through anyway.

By Holly S. Smith

Countless snow-clad mountain spires dwarf narrow glacial valleys in this 505,000-acre expanse of the North Cascades, which actually encompasses three diverse natural areas. North Cascades National Park is the core of the region, flanked by Lake Chelan National Recreation Area to the south and Ross Lake National Recreation Area to the north; all are part of the Stephen T. Mather Wilderness Area. This is an utterly spectacular gathering of snowy peaks, glacial meadows, plunging canyons, and cold, deep-blue lakes. Traditionally the lands of several American Indian tribes, it's fitting that it's still completely wild—and wildlife filled.

28

PARK ESSENTIALS

ACCESSIBILITY
All visitor centers along North Cascades Highway are accessible by wheelchair. Accessible hikes include Sterling Munro, Skagit River Loop, and Rock Shelter, three short trails into lowland old-growth forest, all at mile 120 along Route 20 near Newhalem; and the Happy Creek Forest Trail at mile 134.

ADMISSION FEES AND PERMITS
A Northwest Forest Pass, required for use of various park and forest facilities and trails, is $5 per vehicle for one calendar day or $30 for one year. A free wilderness permit is required for all overnight stays in the backcountry; these are available in person only. Dock permits for boat-in campgrounds are also $5 per day. Passes and permits are sold at visitor centers and ranger stations around the park area.

ADMISSION HOURS

The park never closes, but access is limited by snow in winter. Route 20 (North Cascades Highway), the major access to the park, is partially closed from mid-November to mid-April.

ATMS/BANKS

There are no ATMs in the park. Marblemount, Winthrop, and Chelan have banks with 24-hour ATMs.

CELL-PHONE RECEPTION

Cell-phone reception in the park is not reliable. Public telephones are found at the North Cascades Visitor Center and Skagit Information Center in Newhalem; and at the Golden West Visitor Center and North Cascades Stehekin Lodge in Stehekin.

PARK CONTACT INFORMATION

North Cascades National Park ⊠ *810 Rte. 20, Sedro-Woolley, WA* ☎ *360/856–5700 or 360/854–7200* ⊕ *www.nps.gov/noca.*

SCENIC DRIVES

★ **North Cascades Highway.** Also known as Highway 20, this classic scenic route first winds through the green pastures and woods of the upper Skagit Valley, the mountains looming in the distance. Beyond Concrete, a former cement-manufacturing town, the highway climbs into the mountains, passes the Ross and Diablo dams, and traverses Ross Lake National Recreation Area. Here several pullouts offer great views of the lake and the surrounding snowcapped peaks. From June to September, the meadows are covered with wildflowers, and from late September through October, the mountain slopes flame with fall foliage. The pinnacle point of this stretch is 5,477-foot-high Washington Pass: look east, to where the road descends quickly into a series of hairpin curves between Early Winters Creek and the Methow Valley. Remember, this section of the highway is closed from roughly November to April, depending on snowfall. From the Methow Valley, Highway 153 takes the scenic route along the Methow River's apple, nectarine, and peach orchards to Pateros, on the Columbia River; from here, you can continue east to Grand Coulee or south to Lake Chelan.

WHAT TO SEE

HISTORIC SITES

Buckner Homestead. Founded in 1912, this restored pioneer farm includes an apple orchard, farmhouse, barn, and many ranch buildings. One-hour ranger-guided tours of the property are offered weekends from July 4 through mid-September at 2:15; otherwise, you can pick up a self-guided tour booklet from the drop box. ⊠ *Stehekin Valley Rd., 3½ mi from Stehekin Landing, Stehekin* ☎ *360/854–7365 Ext. 340 option 14* ☉ *June–Sept., daily 9–5.*

Diablo Dam. Increased security has closed public access to Ross Powerhouse, the Incline Railway, and Diablo Dam (except on tours). From the tour center in Diablo, **Skagit Tours** (☎ *206/684–3030* ☜ *$25* ☉ *Tours July–Aug., Fri.–Sun. at 12:30; June and Sept., weekends at 12:30*) operates

NORTH CASCADES IN ONE DAY

The **North Cascades Highway,** with its breathtaking mountain and meadow scenery, is one of the most memorable drives in the United States. Although many travelers first head northeast from Seattle into the park and make this their grand finale, if you start out from Winthrop, at the south end of the route, traffic is lighter and there's less morning fog. Either way, the main highlight is **Washington Pass,** the road's highest point, where an overlook affords a sensational panorama of snow-covered peaks.

Rainy Pass, where the road heading north drops into the west slope valleys, is another good vantage point. Old-growth forest begins to appear, and after about an hour you reach **Gorge Creek Falls overlook** with its 242-foot cascade. Continue west to Newhalem and stop for lunch, then take a half-hour stroll along the **Trail of the Cedars.** Later, stop at the **North Cascades Visitor Center** and take another short hike. It's an hour drive down the Skagit Valley to Sedro-Woolley, where bald eagles are often seen along the river in winter.

a 2½-hour tour that takes you across Diablo Dam by motor coach and then on a boat cruise of Diablo Lake. Purchase snacks at the Skagit General Store or pack a picnic lunch for the trip. ⊠ *Diablo.*

SCENIC STOPS

Gorge Powerhouse/Ladder Creek Falls and Rock Gardens. A powerhouse is a powerhouse, but the rock gardens overlooking Ladder Creek Falls, 7 mi west of Diablo, are beautiful and inspiring. ⊠ *Rte. 20, 2 mi east of North Cascades Visitor Center, Newhalem* ☎ *206/684–3030* 🗫 *Free* ◷ *May–Sept., daily, dawn to dusk*

Fodor's Choice **Stehekin.** One of the most beautiful and secluded valleys in the Pacific ★ Northwest, Stehekin was homesteaded by hardy souls in the late 19th century. It's actually not a town, but rather a small community set at the northwest end of Lake Chelan, and it's accessible only by boat, floatplane, or trail. Year-round residents—who have intermittent outside communications, boat-delivered supplies, and just two-dozen cars between them—enjoy a wilderness lifestyle. Even during the peak summer season only around 200 visitors make the trek here.

VISITOR CENTERS

Chelan Ranger Station. The base for the Chelan National Recreation Area and Wenatchee National Forest has an information desk and a shop selling regional maps and books. ⊠ *Edge of Lake Chelan, Chelan* ☎ *509/682–2549* ◷ *Weekdays 7:45–4:30.*

Glacier Public Service Center. This office doubles as a headquarters for the Mt. Baker–Snoqualmie National Forest; it has maps, a book and souvenir shop, and a permits desk. The center is also right on the way to some of the park's main trailheads. ⊠ *Mt. Baker Hwy., east of Glacier* ☎ *360/599–2714* ◷ *Mar.–mid-Oct., daily 8–4:30; mid-Oct.–Mar., Sat.–Sun. 9–3.*

Golden West Visitor Center. Rangers here offer guidance on hiking, camping, and other activities, as well as audiovisual and children's programs and bike tours. There's also an arts and crafts gallery. Maps and concise displays explain the layered ecology of the valley, which encompasses in its length virtually every ecosystem in the Northwest. Note that access is by floatplane, ferry, or trail only. ⊠ *Stehekin Valley Rd., ¼ mi north of Stehekin Landing, Stehekin* 🕿 *360/854–7365 Ext. 14* ⊗ *Mid-Mar.– mid-Oct., daily 8:30–5.*

North Cascades National Park Headquarters Information Station. This is the park's major administrative center, and the place to pick up passes, permits, and information about current conditions. ⊠ *810 Rte. 20, Sedro-Woolley* 🕿 *360/856–5700 Ext. 515* ⊗ *Memorial Day–Oct., daily 8–4:30; Nov.–Memorial Day, weekdays 8–4:30.*

North Cascades Visitor Center. The main visitor facility for the park complex has extensive displays on surrounding landscape. Learn about the history and value of old-growth trees, the many creatures that depend on the rain forest ecology, and the effects of human activity on the ecosystem. Park rangers frequently conduct programs; check bulletin boards for schedules. ⊠ *Milepost 20, N. Cascades Hwy., Newhalem* 🕿 *206/386–4495 Ext. 11* ⊗ *May–June, daily 9–6; July–Aug., daily 9–7; Sept.–Oct., daily 9–6.*

Wilderness Information Center. The main stop to secure backcountry and climbing permits for North Cascades National Park and the Lake Chelan and Ross Lake recreational areas, this office has maps, a bookshop, and nature exhibits. If you arrive after hours, there's a self-register permit stop outside. ⊠ *Ranger Station Rd., off milepost 105.9, N. Cascades Hwy., Marblemount* 🕿 *360/873–4500 Ext. 39* ⊗ *May–June, Sun.–Thurs. 8–4:30, Fri. and Sat. 7 AM–6 PM; July–Aug., Sun.–Thurs. 7 AM–6 PM, Fri. and Sat. 7 AM–8 PM.*

SPORTS AND THE OUTDOORS

BICYCLING

Mountain bikes are permitted on all highways, unpaved back roads, and a few designated tracks around the park; however, you can't take a bike on any footpaths. Ranger stations have details on the best places to ride in each season, as well as notes on spots that are closed due to weather, mud, or other environmental factors. It's $15 round-trip to bring a bike on the Lake Chelan ferry.

OUTFITTER   You can rent mountain bikes at a self-serve rack in front of the Courtney Log Office in Stehekin for $4 per hour, $20 a day through **Discovery Bikes** (🕿 *509/682–3014* ⊕ *www.stehekindiscoverybikes.com*); helmets are provided.

BOATING

The boundaries of North Cascades National Park touch two long and sinewy expanses: Lake Chelan in the far south, and Ross Lake, which runs toward the Canadian border. Boat ramps, some with speed- and sailboat, paddleboat, kayak, and canoe rentals, are situated all around Lake Chelan, and passenger ferries cross between towns and campgrounds. Hozomeen, accessible via a 39-mi dirt road from Canada, is the boating base for Ross Lake; the site has a large boat ramp, and a boat taxi makes drops at campgrounds all around the shoreline. Diablo

Lake, in the center of the park, also has a ramp at Colonial Creek. Gorge Lake has a public ramp near the town of Diablo.

EXPEDITIONS   Diablo Lake excursions with **Skagit Tours** (☎ 206/684–3030 ⊕ *www. cityofseattle.net/light/tours/skagit* ☑ *$25* ◷ *Tours June, weekends at 12:30; July–Aug., Fri.–Sun. at 12:30; Sept., weekends at 12:30*) include transportation from Seattle.

HIKING

⚠ Black bears are often sighted along trails in the summer; DO NOT approach them! Back away carefully, and report sightings to the Golden West Visitor Center. Cougars, which are shy of humans and well aware of their presence, are rarely sighted in this region. Still, keep kids close and don't let them run ahead too far or lag behind on a trail. If you do spot a cougar, pick up children, have the whole group stand close together, and make yourself look as large as possible.

EASY

☺ **Happy Creek Forest Walk.** Old-growth forests are the focus of this kid-friendly boardwalk route, which loops just 0.3 mi through the trees right off the North Cascades Highway. Interpretive signs provide details about flora along the way. ☒ *Trailhead at milepost 135, Hwy. 20.*

Rainy Pass. An easy and accessible 1-mi paved trail leads to Rainy Lake, a waterfall, and glacier-view platform. ☒ *Trailhead off Hwy. 20, 38 mi east of visitor center at Newhalem.*

★ **Skagit River Loop.** Take this flat and easy, 1.8-mi, wheelchair-accessible trail down through stands of huge, old-growth firs and cedars toward the Skagit River. ☒ *Trailhead near North Cascades Visitor Center.*

Sterling Munro Trail. Starting from the North Cascades Headquarters and Information Station, this popular introductory stroll follows a board-walk path to a lookout above the forested Picket Range peaks. ☒ *Trailhead at 810 Hwy. 20.*

★ **Trail of the Cedars.** Only 0.5 mi long, this trail winds its way through one of the finest surviving stands of old-growth western red cedar in Washington. Some of the trees on the path are more than 1,000 years old. ☒ *Trailhead near North Cascades Visitor Center.*

MODERATE

Fodor's Choice **Cascade Pass.** The draws of this extremely popular 3.7-mi, four-hour trail
★ are stunning panoramas from the great mountain divide. Dozens of peaks line the horizon as you make your way up the fairly flat, hairpin-turn track, the scene fronted by a blanket of alpine wildflowers from July to mid-August. Arrive before noon if you want a parking spot at the trailhead. ☒ *Trailhead at end of Cascade River Rd., 14 mi from Marblemount.*

Diablo Lake Trail. Explore nearly 4 mi of waterside terrain on this moderate route, which is accessed from the Sourdough Creek parking lot. An excellent alternative for parties with small hikers is to take the Seattle City Light Ferry one way. ☒ *Trailhead at milepost 135, Hwy. 20.*

DIFFICULT

Thornton Lakes Trail. A 5-mi climb into an alpine basin with two pretty lakes, this steep and strenuous hike takes about five to six hours round-trip. ☒ *Trailhead off Hwy. 20, 3 mi west of Newhalem.*

28

HORSEBACK RIDING

Many hiking trails and backwoods paths are also popular horseback-riding routes, particularly around the park's southern fringes.

OUTFITTERS
AND
EXPEDITIONS

Cascade Corrals (⊕ *www.cascadecorrals.com* ✉ *$40–$50* ⊙ *June–mid-Sept., daily at 8:30 and 2:15*), a subsidiary of Stehekin Outfitters, organizes 2½-hour horseback trips to Coon Lake. English- and western-style riding lessons are also available. Reservations are taken at the Courtney Log Office at Stehekin Landing.

KAYAKING

The park's tangles of waterways offer access to remote areas inaccessible by road or trail; here are some of the most pristine and secluded mountain scenes on the continent. Bring your own kayak and you can launch from any boat ramp or beach; otherwise, companies in several nearby towns and Seattle suburbs offer kayak and canoe rentals, portage, and tours. The upper basin of Lake Chelan (at the park's southern end) and Ross Lake (at the top edge of the park) are two well-known kayaking expanses, but there are dozens of smaller lakes and creeks between. The Stehekin River also provides many kayaking possibilities.

OUTFITTERS
AND
EXPEDITIONS

Based in the mountain-sports center of Mazama, **Outward Bound U.S.A.** (☎ 866/467–7651 ⊕ *www.outwardbound.com*) stages canoe expeditions on Ross Lake. **Ross Lake Resort** (☎ 206/386–4437) rents kayaks and offers portage service for exploring Ross Lake; a water-taxi service is also available. Book a two-hour trip along the lake's upper estuary and western shoreline with **Stehekin Adventure Company** (⌂ *P.O. Box 36, Stehekin 98852* ☎ 509/682–4677 *or 800/536–0745* ⊕ *www.stehekinoutfitters.com* ✉ *Tour $35* ⊙ *Tours June–Sept., daily at 10. Rentals June–Sept., daily 10–4*), or just hire a kayak and set out on your own.

RAFTING

June through August is the park's white-water season, and rafting trips run through the lower section of the Stehekin River. Along the way take in views of cottonwood and pine forests, glimpses of Yawning Glacier on Magic Mountain, and placid vistas of Lake Chelan.

OUTFITTERS
AND
EXPEDITIONS

Downstream River Runners (✉ *3924 SW 106th St., Seattle* ☎ 206/906–9548 ⊕ *www.riverpeople.com*) covers rafting throughout the Northwest. June through October, **North Cascades River Expeditions** (☎ 360/435–0796 ⊕ *www.riverexpeditions.com*) focuses on regional rivers. White-water tours are available on the Skykomish and other area rivers April through September with **Orion River Expeditions** (☎ 509/548–1401 *or 800/553–7466* ⊕ *www.orionexp.com*). Guided trips on the class III Stehekin River leave from **Stehekin Valley Ranch** (☎ 509/682–4677 *or 800/536–0745* ⊕ *www.stehekinvalleyranch.com* ✉ *$50* ⊙ *June–Sept.*). Exciting half- and full-day rafting excursions with **Wildwater River Tours** (☎ 253/939–3337 *or 800/522–9453* ⊕ *www.wildwater-river.com*) include transportation and a picnic.

WINTER SPORTS

Mt. Baker, just off the park's far northwest corner, is one of the Northwest's premier skiing, snowboarding, and snowshoeing regions—the area set a U.S. record for most snow in a single season during the winter of 1998–99 (1,140 inches). The Mt. Baker Highway (Route 542) cuts through the slopes toward several major ski sites; main access is 17 mi east of the town of Glacier, and the season runs roughly from November to April. Salmon Ridge, 46 mi east of Bellingham at exit 255, has groomed trails and parking.

Stehekin is another base for winter sports. The Stehekin Valley alone has 20 mi of trails; some of the most popular are around Buckner Orchard, Coon Lake, and the Courtney Ranch (Cascade Corrals).

Mt. Baker. Off the park's northwest corner, this is the closest winter-sports area, with facilities for downhill and Nordic skiing, snowboarding, and other recreational ventures. The main base is the town of Glacier, 17 mi west of the slopes. Equipment, lodgings, restaurants, and tourist services are on-site. ✉ *Mt. Baker Hwy. 542, 62 mi east of Bellingham* ☎ *360/734–6771, 360/671–0211 for snow reports* ⊕ *www.mtbaker.us* ✉ *All-day lift ticket weekends and holidays $44, weekdays $36* ☉ *Nov.–Apr.*

EDUCATIONAL OFFERINGS

GUIDED TOURS

North Cascades Institute (NCI). Come here for information on park hiking, wildlife watching, horseback riding, climbing, boat rentals, and fishing, as well as classroom education and hands-on nature experiences. Guided tours staged from the center include mountain climbs, pack-train excursions, and float trips on the Skagit and Stehekin rivers. Choices range from forest ecology and backpacking trips to explorations of the Cascades hot springs. There's even a research library, a dock on Lake Diablo, an amphitheater, and overnight lodging. ✉ *810 Rte. 20, Sedro-Woolley, along Rte. 20, near Diablo Dam* ☎ *360/856–5700 Ext. 209* ⊕ *www.ncascades.org.*

RANGER PROGRAMS

In the summer, rangers conduct programs at the visitor centers, where you also can find exhibits and other park information. At the North Cascades Visitor Center (in Newhalem) you can learn about rain forest ecology, while at the Golden West Visitor Center (in Stehekin) there's an arts and crafts gallery as well as audiovisual and children's programs. Check center bulletin boards for schedules. ☎ *206/386–4495 Ext. 1, North Cascade Visitor Center; 360/854–7365 Ext. 14, Golden West Visitor Center* ☉ *Hrs vary.*

WHAT'S NEARBY

NEARBY TOWNS

Heading into North Cascades National Park from Seattle on Interstate 5 to Highway 2, **Sedro-Woolley** (pronounced "*see*-droh *wool*-lee") is the first main town you encounter. A former logging and steel-mill base settled by North Carolina pioneers, the settlement still has a 19th-century ambience throughout its rustic downtown area. Surrounded by farmlands, it's a pretty spot to stop and has basic visitor services like hotels, gas stations, and groceries. It's also home to the North Cascades National Park Headquarters. From here, it's about 40 mi to the park's

28

western edges. Along the way, you still have a chance to stop for supplies in **Concrete,** about 20 mi from the park along Highway 2.

Marblemount is 10 mi farther east, about 12 mi west of the North Cascades Visitor Center. It's another atmospheric former timber settlement nestled into the mountain foothills, and its growing collection of motels, cafés, and tour outfitters draw outdoor enthusiasts each summer. The park's base town, though, is **Newhalem,** tucked right along the highway between the north and south regions. This is the place to explore the visitor center and its surrounding trails, view exhibits, and pick up maps, permits, and tour information.

Still traveling east on Highway 20, it's about 5 mi from Newhalem to **Diablo,** where the local lake, dam, and overlook are all good reasons to stop. Keep going until the road turns south along the park's eastern side: this is the famed North Cascades Scenic Highway. From top to bottom, including Rainy Pass and the curve through the chilly Washington Pass overlook, this section is about 20 mi.

Winthrop, a relaxed, riverside rodeo town complete with clapboard cafés and five-and-dime charm, is about a 6-mi drive east of Washington Pass. This is also an outdoor-recreation base, offering activities that range from cross-country skiing to hiking, mountain biking, and white-water rafting. Less than 10 mi southeast of Winthrop, the tiny town of **Twisp** is settled into the farmlands and orchards, its streets lined with a few small lodgings and eateries.

The resort town of **Chelan,** nestled around its serene namesake lake, lies about 40 mi due south of Winthrop along Highway 153. It's a serene summer getaway for boating and swimming, as well as an access point for small villages and campgrounds along the shoreline. **Stehekin,** at the lake's northern end, is a favorite tourist stop for its peaceful isolation; without road connections, your options for getting here are by boat, floatplane, or trail. A ferry runs between Chelan and Stehekin.

VISITOR INFORMATION
Lake Chelan Chamber of Commerce ✉ *102 E. Johnson, Chelan* ☎ *509/682–3503 or 800/424–3526* ⊕ *www.lakechelan.com.* **North Cascades Visitor Information Center** ✉ *59831 Rte. 20, Marblemount* ☎ *360/873–4150* ⊕ *www.marblemount.com.* **Sedro-Woolley Chamber of Commerce** ✉ *714-B Metcalf St., Sedro-Woolley* ☎ *360/855–1841 or 888/225–8365* ⊕ *www.sedro-woolley.com.* **Twisp Visitor Information Center and Chamber of Commerce** ✉ *201 S. Methow Valley Hwy., Twisp* ☎ *509/997–2926* ⊕ *www.twispinfo.com.* **Winthrop Chamber of Commerce** ✉ *202 Hwy. 20, Winthrop* ☎ *509/996–2125 or 888/463–8469* ⊕ *www.winthropwashington.com.*

NEARBY ATTRACTIONS

★   **Lake Chelan.** This sinewy, 55-mi-long fjord—Washington's deepest lake—works its way southeast between the towns of Chelan, at its south end, and Stehekin, at the far northwest edge. The scenery is unparalleled, the flat blue water encircled by plunging gorges, with a vista of snow-slathered mountains beyond. No roads access the lake except for Chelan, so a floatplane or boat is needed to see the whole thing. Resorts dot the warmer eastern shores. ✉ *Alt. 97, Chelan* ☎ *360/856–5700 Ext. 340 option 14* 🌐 *www.nps.gov/lach.*

Lake Whatcom Railway. The steam-powered train makes short jaunts through the woods 11 mi north of Sedro-Woolley. Excursions run all summer and during special events, such as the December Christmas train rides with Santa. During peak weekends, tours depart around 9:30, noon, and 2:30, and children pay half-price. Note that the schedule changes seasonally. ✉ *Hwy. 9, Wickersham* ☎ *360/595–2218* 🎫 *$14* ⏲ *Call for hrs.*

FAMILY PICKS

Learn about nature. Join a guided walk, evening program, or or ranger-led children's event—and be sure to stop at the Northwest Cascades Institute.

Get out on the water. Take a Lake Chelan ferry, make a kayak exploration of river areas, or run the white water on the Stehekin River.

Travel back in time. Head to Winthrop for pioneer-style family fun.

Stehekin Boat Co. Working boats for this company haul supplies, mail, cars, and construction materials across Lake Chelan to Stehekin, but travelers are welcome aboard as well. The *Lady of the Lake II* makes journeys from May to October, departing Chelan at 8:30 and returning at 6. Tickets are $39 round-trip, half price for those ages two to 11. The *Lady Express,* a speedy catamaran, runs between Stehekin, Holden Village, the national park, and Lake Chelan from June to October, departing daily at 8:30 and returning at 2:45; tickets are $59 roundtrip. The vessels also can drop off and pick up at lakeshore trailheads. ✉ *1418 Woodin Ave., Chelan* ☎ *509/682–4584 or 888/682–4584* 🌐 *www.ladyofthelake.com* 🎫 *$39–$59* ⏲ *June–Sept., daily; check Web site for schedule.*

28

WHERE TO EAT AND STAY

ABOUT THE RESTAURANTS

There are no formal restaurants in North Cascades National Park, just a lakeside café at the North Cascades Environmental Learning Center. The only other place to eat out is in Stehekin, at the Stehekin Valley Ranch dining room or the Stehekin Pastry Company; both serve simple, hearty, country-style meals and sweets. Towns within a few hours of the park on either side all have a few small eateries, and some lodgings have small dining rooms. Don't expect fancy decor or gourmet frills—just friendly service and generally delicious homemade stews, roasts, grilled fare, soups, salads, and baked goods.

ABOUT THE HOTELS

Accommodations in North Cascades National Park are rustic, cozy, and comfortable. Options range from plush Stehekin lodges and homey cabin rentals to spartan Learning Center bunks and campgrounds. Expect to pay roughly $50 to $200 per night, depending on the rental size and the season. Book at least three months in advance, or even a year for popular accommodations in summer. Outside the park are numerous resorts, motels, bed-and-breakfasts, and even overnight boat rentals in Chelan, Concrete, Glacier, Marblemount, Sedro-Woolley, Twisp, and Winthrop.

ABOUT THE CAMPGROUNDS

Tent campers can choose between forest sites, riverside spots, lake grounds, or meadow spreads encircled by mountains. Here camping is as easy or challenging as you want to make it; some campgrounds are a short walk from ranger stations, while others are miles from the highway. Note that many campsites, particularly those around Stehekin, are completely remote and without road access anywhere, so you have to walk, boat, ride a horse, or take a floatplane to reach them. Most don't accept reservations, and spots fill up quickly May through September. If there's no ranger on-site, you can often sign in yourself—and always check in at a ranger station before you set out overnight. Note that some areas are occasionally closed due to flooding, forest fires, or other factors. Outside the park, each town has several managed camping spots, which can be at formal campgrounds or in the side yard of a motel.

WHERE TO EAT

IN THE PARK

¢–$ ✕ **Stehekin Pastry Company.** As you enter this lawn-framed timber chalet,
CAFE you're immersed in the tantalizing aromas of a European bakery. Glassed-in display cases are filled with trays of homemade baked goods, and the pungent espresso is eye-opening. Sit down at a window-side table and dig into an over-filled sandwich or rich bowl of soup—and don't forget dessert: we're guessing you'll never taste a better slice of pie, made with fruit fresh-picked from local orchards. Although it's outside of town, the shop is conveniently en route to Rainbow Falls and adjacent to the Norwegian Fjord Horses stables, which also makes it a popular summertime ice-cream stop for sightseers. ⊠ *Stehekin Valley Rd., about 2 mi from Stehekin Landing, on the way to Rainbow Falls, Stehekin* ☎ *509/682–4677* ▭ *No credit cards* ⊘ *Closed mid-Oct.–mid-May.*

$–$$ ✕ **Stehekin Valley Ranch.** Meals in the rustic log ranch house, served at
AMERICAN long, polished log tables, include buffet dinners of steak, ribs, hamburgers, salad, beans, and dessert. Note that breakfast is served 7 to 9, lunch is noon to 1, and dinner is 5:30 to 7; show up later, and the kitchen's closed. Transportation from Stehekin Landing is included for day visitors. ⊠ *Stehekin Valley Rd., 9 mi north of Stehekin Landing, Stehekin* ☎ *509/682–4677 or 800/536–0745* ▭ *No credit cards* ⊘ *Closed Oct.–mid-June.*

PICNIC AREAS Developed picnic areas at Rainy Pass (Route 20, 38 mi east of the park visitor center) and Washington Pass (Route 20, 42 mi east of the visitor center) each have a half-dozen picnic tables, drinking water, and pit toilets. The vistas of surrounding peaks are sensational at these two overlooks. More picnic facilities are located near the visitor center in Newhalem and at Colonial Creek Campground 10 mi east of the visitor center on Highway 20.

OUTSIDE THE PARK

$–$$$ ✕ **Buffalo Run Restaurant.** Buffalo, venison, elk, and ostrich are the spe-
AMERICAN cialties at this little place next to the Marblemount post office. Vegetarians need not worry, though—there are a few non-meat options. The atmosphere is completely casual, with buffalo heads and Old

West memorabilia lining the dining room walls. Outside, the patio adds warm-weather seating and garden views; it's a good spot to kick back with a glass of wine. The adjacent inn, run by the same management, is an inexpensive overnight option. ✉ *60084 Hwy. 20, Marblemount* ☎ *360/873–2461* ⊕ *www.buffaloruninn.com* ▭ *AE, D, MC, V* ⊗ *Closed Wed. and Nov.–Dec.*

$$$–$$$$ ✕ **Dining Room at Sun Mountain Lodge.** Cozy tables are surrounded by
SEAFOOD a woodsy decor in this spacious restaurant, where you can enjoy the mountain scenery while you dine. Farm-fresh produce, Washington beef, and locally caught seafood highlight the excellent menu, which includes such delicacies as rich forest-mushroom strudel; melt-in-your-mouth pork chops with caramelized apples and onions; and parchment-wrapped halibut cheeks served with saffron, orange, and basmati pilaf. Desserts range from seven-course cheese tastings to dark rum chocolate cake. The 5,000-bottle wine cellar is one of the best in the region. ✉ *Sun Mountain Lodge, Patterson Lake Rd., Winthrop* ☎ *509/996–2211* ⊕ *www.sunmountainlodge.com/dining* ▭ *AE, DC, MC, V.*

$–$$$ ✕ **Heenan's Burnt Finger Bar-B-Q & Steak House.** You can't get more authen-
SOUTHERN tic than a barbecue joint that serves slow-smoked sauce-slathered ribs and chicken right out of an old Conestoga wagon. Sidled up to the Methow River, the corral-style restaurant provides sweeping views of the water, the valley, and the farmlands beyond. Creamy coleslaw, crisp corn on the cob, and an assortment of salads and chilies round out the menu. Diners can relax inside the cozy dining rooms or outside by the grill, where evenings bring campfires and guitar-strumming cowboys. ✉ *7160 Hwy. 20 S, Winthrop* ☎ *509/996–8221* ▭ *MC, V* ⊗ *Closed Wed. and Oct.–Memorial Day weekend.*

¢ ✕ **Ship 'n' Shore Drive/Boat In.** The casual "dining room" here consists
AMERICAN of dockside picnic tables where hamburgers, hot dogs, and nachos are served. On hot days, kids line up for ice cream. ✉ *1230 W. Woodin Ave., Chelan* ☎ *509/682–5125* ⊗ *Closed Labor Day–mid-June.*

$–$$ ✕ **Twisp River Pub.** Buffalo wings, nachos, and an array of homemade soups
AMERICAN are tasty partners for the brewery's crisp house beers and regional wines. Choose from burgers, fish-and-chips, and meaty sandwiches at lunch; dinners include steak, salmon, coconut curry, and pad thai. Brunch is served Sunday. There's live music every weekend and jazz in the beer garden each Wednesday evening in summer. The shop sells quality T-shirts, beer glasses, and coffee mugs, as well as pub gift cards. Free Wi-Fi throughout the building is a bonus. ✉ *201 Hwy. 20, Twisp* ☎ *509/997–6822 or 888/220–3360* ⊕ *www.methowbrewing.com* ▭ *AE, D, DC, MC, V* ⊗ *Closed Mon. and Tues.*

28

WHERE TO STAY

IN THE PARK

$$$–$$$$ ⊞ **Silver Bay Inn.** Perched on a private little slip of land at the head of Lake Chelan, Silver Bay enjoys water and mountain views. Spacious timber cabins for two each have a loft, full kitchen, and wraparound cedar deck; the Riverview Room also has a kitchen and a deck over the Stehekin. The luxury two-bedroom Lakeview House is a Northwest-style escape with a sunroom, two baths, and many artistic touches.

Guests share a huge lawn, a waterside hot tub, and nightly bonfire cheer. Hiking, swimming, and relaxing are the top activities; you can also set out on a free bike or canoe. **Pros:** hot tub vistas; free canoe and bike use. **Cons:** summertime mosquitoes. ⊠ *Silver Bay Rd., P.O. Box 85, Stehekin* ☎ *509/699–2023 or 800/555–7781* ⊕ *www.silverbayinn. com* ↶ *1 room, 2 cabins, 1 house* ⚄ *In-room: no a/c, no phone, kitchen, no TV. In-hotel: bicycles, no kids under 12* ▭ *AE, MC, V.*

\$\$–\$\$\$ ▥ **Stehekin Landing Resort.** Large log cabins welcome you with crackling fires and Lake Chelan views. Standard rooms are in the Alpine House, which has a shared lounge and a lakeside deck; larger rooms in the Swiss Mont building each have a private deck overlooking the water. Kitchen units are also available, and the fully equipped Lake House comes with a fireplace, hot tub, and laundry. American fare is served in the restaurant, which is open all day in high season (lunch only October through April). For deep discounts, check out the lodge's seasonal packages, which combine accommodations, round-trip boat fare across Lake Chelan, a bus tour, parking, and sports equipment (like snowshoes). **Pros:** right on the water; on-site masseuse; tent-to-tent hiking excursions. **Cons:** pricey restaurant menu. ⊠ *About 5 mi south of Stehekin Landing on Lake Chelan* ☎ *509/682–4494* ⊕ *www.stehekinlanding. com* ↶ *27 rooms, 1 house* ⚄ *In-room: no a/c, no phone, kitchen (some), no TV. In-hotel: restaurant, Wi-Fi* ▭ *MC, V.*

\$–\$\$\$ ▥ **Stehekin Valley Ranch.** Nestled along pretty meadows at the edge of pine forest, this classic ranch is a center for hikers and horseback riders. Barnlike ranch cabins have cedar paneling, tile floors, and a private bath; canvas-roof tent cabins have bunk beds, kerosene lamps, and shared facilities; and two kitchen cabins have modern equipment. Enormous breakfasts and meaty dinner buffets are turned out family-style at picnic tables in the rustic wood restaurant (\$–\$\$). Rates for ranch and tent cabins include accommodations, linens, meals, and transport from Stehekin Landing. Credit cards are accepted only by phone. **Pros:** many activities; free vehicle use with kitchen cabins. **Cons:** no bathrooms in tent cabins. ⊠ *Stehekin Valley Rd., 9 mi north of Stehekin Landing, Stehekin* ☎ *509/682–4677 or 800/536–0745* ⊕ *www.stehekinvalleyranch.com* ↶ *34 cabins* ⚄ *In-room: no a/c, no phone, kitchen (some), no TV. In-hotel: restaurant, bicycles* ▭ *MC, V* ☺ *Closed Oct.–mid-June* ⦿⦿ *FAP.*

CAMPING △ **Lake Chelan National Recreation Area.** Many backcountry camping
¢ areas are accessible via park shuttles or boat. All require a free back-
(FREE) country permit; 12 boat-in sites also require a \$5 per day dock fee. Everything you bring must be hung on bear wires, so rethink those big coolers. **Purple Point,** the most popular campground due to its quick access to Stehekin Landing, has seven tent sites, bear boxes, and nearby road access. Reservations are not accepted, but group requests must be made in writing. **Pros:** beautiful location; easy water access. **Cons:** crowded in July and August. ⊠ *Stehekin Landing, NPS, P.O. Box 7, Stehekin, WA* ☎ *360/856–5700 Ext. 360 option 14* △ *7 tent sites* ⚄ *Pit toilets, drinking water, bear boxes* ▭ *No credit cards.*

\$ △ **Ross Lake National Recreation Area.** The National Park Service maintains three upper Skagit Valley campgrounds near Newhalem. All sites are on a first-come, first-served basis. All have fire grates and picnic tables. Colonial

Creek and Newhalem Creek have RV sites as well as tent sites, flush toilets, and drinking water, but are only open mid-May through mid-October. Goodell Creek is open year-round, with 21 tent sites and and drinking water (summer only) but only pit toilets. **Pros:** set amid forest. **Cons:** two are seasonal only. ☎ *360/856–5700 Ext. 515* ▭ *No credit cards.*

OUTSIDE THE PARK

$$$$ ▦ **Campbell's Resort.** A century old, this sprawling, stunningly renovated resort sits on landscaped grounds alongside Lake Chelan. Every room has a balcony with mountain and beach views; some have a kitchen or fireplace. Two-bedroom cabins with a kitchen and porch are on the east side of the property, near the marina. The elegant Veranda Bistro ($–$$), with a European feel and lake views, serves simple, rustic fare with an extensive menu of fine, reasonably priced local wines. The parklike, family-friendly setting includes pristine beaches, picnic areas, barbecues, and lots of room to romp. **Pros:** plenty of summer programs to keep kids busy; on-site day spa; great base for winter sports. **Cons:** tour buses, weddings, and conferences bring noisy crowds. ✉ *104 W. Woodin Ave., Chelan* ☎ *509/682–2561 or 800/553–8225* ⊕ *www.campbellsresort.com* ⤵ *172 rooms, 2 cottages* ⚬ *In-room: kitchen (some), refrigerator, Internet, Wi-Fi (some). In-hotel: restaurant, bar, pools, gym, spa, children's programs (ages 4–15)* ▭ *AE, MC, V.*

$–$$ ▦ **Methow Valley Inn.** Guest rooms in this lovely 1912 home are appointed with antiques and quilt-covered iron beds. A large stone fireplace fronts the Great Room; there's also a cozy library and light-filled sunroom. Fresh flowers and organic fruits come from the surrounding gardens, and seasonal events are hosted in the adjacent courtyard. **Pros:** gorgeous gardens in summer; lovely holiday decorations in winter; family-style friendliness. **Cons:** there isn't much to do in Twisp. ✉ *234 2nd Ave., Twisp* ☎ *509/997–2253* ⊕ *www.methowvalleyinn.com* ⤵ *7 rooms, 4 with private bath* ⚬ *In-room: no a/c, no phone, no TV. In-hotel: no kids under 12* ▭ *MC, V.*

$–$$ ▦ **Skagit River Resort.** The Clark Family runs this rambling resort at the western entrance to the North Cascades. Many of the clapboard cabins with kitchens have a gas or log fireplace; you also can stay in one of the charming second-floor bed-and-breakfast rooms, RVs with kitchens, or campsites along the Skagit River. You can book adventure tours, rent DVD and VCR players, enjoy the spacious picnic grounds, listen to live summer concerts, and try "bunny-hole golf" on a course dug by local rabbits. The Eatery—a quaint, country-style restaurant and museum fronted by a huge sawmill mural—serves homemade cinnamon rolls and chicken-fried steak. Savory pies are made by Tootsie Clark, whose grandmother arrived here in 1888 by Indian canoe and later named Marblemount. **Pros:** convenient location; great food; online coupons add discounts. **Cons:** a lot of rabbit droppings. ✉ *58468 Clark Cabin Rd. (milepost 103.5 on North Cascades Hwy.), Rockport* ☎ *360/873–2250 or 800/273–2606* ⊕ *www.northcascades.com* ⤵ *32 cabins, 4 B&B rooms with shared bath, 5 trailers, 30 RV sites, 15 tent sites* ⚬ *In-room: kitchen (some). In-hotel: restaurant, bicycles, laundry facilities* ▭ *MC, V.*

$$ ▦ **South Bay Bed and Breakfast.** Standing above Lake Whatcom, 20 mi north of Sedro-Woolley and 20 mi southeast of Bellingham, this

Craftsman-style house is surrounded by five acres of creek-laced cedar forests and beaches. Each elegant room comes with a fireplace, hot tub, and water views. More fireplaces are in the living room and sunroom, and hammocks and wicker chairs decorate the wraparound porch. **Pros:** unique rooms have historic flair; on-site solarium; trails just outside. **Cons:** breakfast can be elbow-to-elbow. ⊠ *4095 S. Bay Dr., Sedro-Woolley* ☎ *360/595–2086 or 877/595–2086* ⊕ *www.southbaybb.com* ↰ *6 rooms* ⚐ *In-room: no a/c, no phone, no TV. In-hotel: bicycles* ⊟ *MC, V* ⊚| *BP.*

$$$$ ⌂ **Sun Mountain Lodge.** A hilltop location gives guests panoramic views
★ of the Cascade Mountains and Methow Valley; some rooms face Mt. Gardner or Mt. Robinson. Accommodations mirror the lodge-style elegance of the main building; many have a fireplace, kitchen facilities, CD player, and a private deck. Luxury cabins are off-site, 1½ mi below on the Patterson lakefront. There are 100 mi of hiking, horseback-riding, and skiing trails nearby; afterward, you can indulge your sore muscles at the spa. The Dining Room (⇨ *Where to Eat*), with snowy mountain views from every table, serves Northwest fare and has a private wine cellar. **Pros:** year-round outdoor activities; award-winning wine cellar; kids stay free. **Cons:** roundabout eastern drive route is only access point from Seattle in winter. ⊠ *Patterson Lake Rd., Winthrop* ☎ *509/996–2211 or 800/572–0493* ⊕ *www.sunmountainlodge.com* ↰ *98 rooms, 17 cabins* ⚐ *In-room: kitchen (some), refrigerator (some), no TV, Wi-Fi (some). In-hotel: restaurant, room service, bar, tennis court, pools, spa, bicycles, Wi-Fi (hotel only), children's programs (ages 4–10)* ⊟ *AE, DC, MC, V.*

Olympic National Park

WORD OF MOUTH

"We had a wonderful time in Olympic National Park a few years ago. The beaches were so georgous! It was one of our most memorable trips! We LOVED the Kalaloch area . . . We wanted to stay in Kalaloch but they were booked. We actually ended up staying at the Lake Quinault Lodge. It was nice."

—txbluesky

WELCOME TO OLYMPIC

TOP REASONS TO GO

★ **Exotic rain forest:** A rain forest in the Pacific Northwest? Indeed, Olympic National Park is one of a few places in the world with this unique temperate landscape.

★ **Beachcombing:** Miles of spectacular, rugged coastline dotted with tidal pools, sea stacks, and driftwood hem the edges of the Olympic Peninsula.

★ **Nature's hot tubs:** Take a relaxing dip in the wooded heart of the park at the Sol Duc hot springs, a series of geothermal mineral pools.

★ **Lofty vistas:** The Olympics have plenty of peaks you can climb—or just drive up to Hurricane Ridge for endless views over the ranges.

★ **A sense of history:** The first evidence of humans on the Olympic Peninsula dates back 12,000 years. Today, eight tribes still have traditional ties to lands in Olympic National Park, and there are ample opportunities for exploring Native American history in and around the region.

1 Coastal Olympic.
Here the Pacific smashes endlessly into the rugged coastline, carving out some of the park's most memorable scenes in the massive, rocky sea stacks and islets just offshore. Back from the water are beaches and tide pools full of starfish, crabs, and anemones.

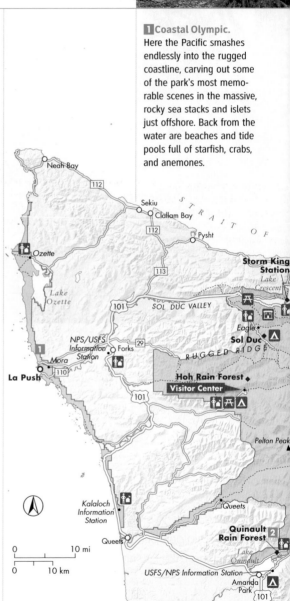

2 **The Rain Forest.** Centered on the Hoh, Queets, and Quinault river valleys, this is the region's most unique landscape. Fog-shrouded Douglas firs and Sitka spruces, some at more than 300 feet tall, huddle in this moist, pine-carpeted area, shading fern- and moss-draped cedars, maples, and alders.

3 **The Mountains.** Craggy gray peaks and snow-covered summits dominate the skyline. Low-level foliage and wildflower meadows make for excellent hiking in the plateaus. Even on the sunniest days, temperatures are brisk. Some roads are closed in winter months.

4 **Alpine Meadows.** In midsummer, the swath of colors is like a Monet canvas spread over the landscape, and wildlife teems among the honeyed flowers. Trails are never prettier, and views are crisp and vast.

WASHINGTON

GETTING ORIENTED

The Olympic peninsula's elegant snowcapped and forested landscape is edged on all sides by water: to the north, the Strait of Juan de Fuca separates the United States from Canada, a network of Puget Sound bays laces the east, the Chehalis River meanders along the southern end, and the massive gray Pacific Ocean guards the west side.

29

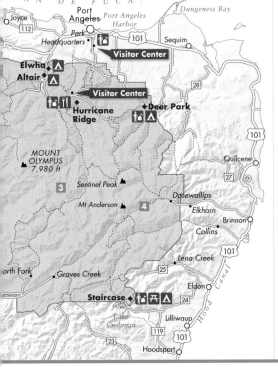

KEY	
👫	Ranger Station
⛕	Campground
⛗	Picnic Area
🍴	Restaurant
🏠	Lodge
🚶	Trailhead
👫	Restrooms
⇗	Scenic Viewpoint
⋯	Walking/Hiking Trails

OLYMPIC PLANNER

When to Go

Summer, with its long stretches of sun-filled days, is prime touring time for Olympic National Park. **June through September are the peak months;** Hurricane Ridge, the Hoh Rain Forest, Lake Crescent, and Ruby Beach are bustling by 10 AM.

Late spring and early autumn are also good bets for clear weather; any time between April and October, and you'll have a good chance of fair skies. Between Thanksgiving and Easter, it's a toss-up as to which days will turn out fair; prepare for heavy clouds, rain showers, and chilly temperatures, then hope for the best.

Winter is a great time to visit if you enjoy isolation. Locals are usually the only hardy souls during this time, except for weekend skiers heading to the snowfields around Hurricane Ridge. Many visitor facilities have limited hours or are closed from October to April.

AVG. HIGH/LOW TEMPS.

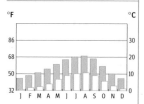

Flora and Fauna

Along the high mountain slopes hardy cedar, fir, and hemlock trees stand tough on the rugged land; the lower montane forests are filled with thickets of silver firs; and valleys stream with Douglas firs and western hemlock. The park's famous temperate rain forests are on the peninsula's western side, marked by broad western red cedars, towering red spruces, and ferns festooned with strands of mosses and patchwork lichens. This lower landscape is also home to some of the Northwest's largest trees: massive cedar and Sitka spruce near Lake Quinault can measure more than 700 inches around, and Douglas firs near the Queets and Hoh rivers are nearly as wide.

These landscapes are home to a variety of wildlife, including many large mammals and 15 creatures found nowhere else in the world. Hikers often come across Roosevelt's elk, black-tailed deer, mountain goats, beavers, raccoons, skunks, opossums, and foxes; Douglas squirrels and flying squirrels populate the heights of the forest. Less common are black bears (most prevalent from May through August); wolves, bobcats, and cougar are rarely seen. Birdlife includes bald eagles, red-tailed hawks, osprey, and great horned owls. Rivers and lakes are filled with freshwater fish, while beaches hold crabs, starfish, anemones, and other shelled creatures. Get out in a boat on the Pacific to spot seals, sea lions, and sea otters—and perhaps a pod of porpoises, orcas, or gray whales.

Beware of jellyfish around the shores—beached jellyfish can still sting. In the woods, check for ticks after every hike and after each shower. Biting nasties include black flies, horseflies, sand fleas, and the ever-present mosquitoes. Yellowjacket nests populate tree hollows along many trails; signs throughout the Hoh Rain Forest warn hikers to move quickly through these sections. If one or two chase you, remain calm and keep walking; these are just "guards" making sure you're keeping away from the hive. Poison oak is common, so familiarize yourself with its appearance. Bug repellent, sunscreen, and long pants and sleeves will go a long way toward making your experience more comfortable.

Getting Here and Around

U.S. 101 essentially encircles the main section of Olympic National Park, and a number of roads lead from the highway into the park's mountains and toward its beaches. You can reach U.S. 101 via Interstate 5 at Olympia, via Route 12 at Aberdeen, or via Route 104 from the Washington State ferry terminals at Bainbridge or Kingston. The ferries are the most direct route to the Olympic area from Seattle; contact **Washington State Ferries** (☎ 800/843–3779 or 206/464–6400 www.wsdot.wa.gov/ferries) for information. You can enter the park at a number of points, though access roads do not penetrate far, since the park is 95% wilderness. The best way to get around and to see many of the park's key sites is on foot.

Grays Harbor Transit (☎ 360/532–2770 or 800/562–9730 ⊕ www.ghtransit.com) runs daily buses from Aberdeen, Hoquiam, and Forks to Amanda Park, on the west end of Lake Quinault. **West Jefferson Transit** (☎ 800/436–3950 ⊕ www.jeffersontransit.com) runs a Forks–Amanda Park route Monday through Saturday.

Good Reads

■ Robert L. Wood's *Olympic Mountain Trail Guide* is a great resource for both day hikers and those planning longer excursions.

■ Stephen Whitney's *A Field Guide to the Cascades and Olympics* is an excellent trailside reference, covering more than 500 plant and animal species found in the park.

■ The park's newspaper, the *Olympic Bugler,* is a seasonal guide for activities and opportunities in the park. You can pick it up at the visitor centers. A handy online catalog of books, maps, and passes for northwest parks is available from **Discover Your Northwest** (⊕ www.discovernw.org).

Festivals and Events

MAY Irrigation Festival. Highlights of this Sequim festival include an antique-car show, logging demonstrations, arts and crafts, dancing, and a parade. ☎ 360/683–6197 ⊕ www.irrigationfestival.com.

JUNE–AUG. Centrum Summer Arts Festival. Fort Worden State Park, a 19th-century army base near Port Townsend, stages a summer-long line-up of concerts and workshops. ☎ 360/385–3102 ⊕ www.centrum.org.

JUNE–SEPT. Olympic Music Festival. A variety of classical concerts are performed in a renovated barn; picnic on the farm while you listen. ☎ 206/527–8839 ⊕ www. olympicmusicfestival.org.

JULY Fourth of July. A salmon bake, a parade, a demolition derby, and arts and crafts exhibits mark Forks' celebration. ☎ 360/374–5412 or 800/443–6757.

Lavender Festival. Mid-month, a street fair and farm tours celebrate Sequim's many fragrant lavender fields. ☎ 360/681–3035 or 877/681–3035 ⊕ www.lavenderfestival.com.

SEPT. Wooden Boat Festival. Hundreds of antique boats sail into Port Townsend. ☎ 360/385–3628 ⊕ www. woodenboat.org.

29

Updated by
Holly S. Smith

A spellbinding setting is tucked into the country's far-northwestern corner, within the heart-shaped Olympic Peninsula. Edged on all sides by water, the forested landscape is remote and pristine, and works its way around the sharpened ridges of the snow-capped Olympic Mountains. Big lakes cut pockets of blue in the rugged blanket of pine forests, and hot springs gurgle up from the foothills. Along the coast the sights are even more enchanting: wave-sculpted boulders, tidal pools teeming with sea life, and tree-topped sea stacks.

PARK ESSENTIALS

ACCESSIBILITY
There are wheelchair-accessible facilities—including trails, campgrounds, and visitor centers—throughout the park; contact visitor centers for more information.

ADMISSION FEES AND PERMITS
Seven-day vehicle admission fee is $10, plus $5 for each individual; an annual family pass is $30. Parking at Ozette, the trailhead for one of the park's most popular hikes, is $1 per day.

An overnight wilderness permit, available at visitor centers and ranger stations, is $5 (covers registration of your party for up to 14 days), plus $2 per person per night. A frequent-hiker pass, which covers all wilderness use fees, is $30 per year. Fishing in freshwater streams and lakes within Olympic National Park does not require a Washington State fishing license; however, anglers must acquire a salmon-steelhead punch card when fishing for those species. Ocean fishing and harvesting shellfish and seaweed require licenses, which are available at sporting goods and outdoor supply stores.

ADMISSION HOURS

Six park entrances are open 24/7; gate kiosk hours (for buying passes) vary widely according to season and location, but most kiosks are staffed during daylight hours. Olympic National Park is located in the Pacific time zone.

ATMS/BANKS

If you'll need cash for kayak rentals, groceries, or souvenirs during your visit, bring enough with you, because there are no ATMs in Olympic National Park. Some gas stations near the park in Port Angeles and Forks have ATMs, and major banks and grocery chains with ATMs are found in these towns and in Sequim.

CELL-PHONE RECEPTION

Note that there is no cell phone reception in wilderness areas. There are public telephones at the Olympic National Park Visitor Center, Hoh River Rain Forest Visitor Center, and the lodging properties within the park—Lake Crescent, Kalaloch, and Sol Duc Hot Springs. Fairholm General Store also has a phone.

PARK CONTACT INFORMATION

Olympic National Park ⊠ *600 E. Park Ave., Port Angeles, WA* ☎ *360/565–3130* ⊕ *www.nps.gov/olym.*

SCENIC DRIVE

★ **Port Angeles Visitor Center to Hurricane Ridge.** The premier scenic drive in Olympic National Park is a steep ribbon of curves, which climbs from thickly forested foothills and subalpine meadows into the upper stretches of pine-swathed peaks. At the top, the visitor center at Hurricane Ridge has some truly spectacular views over the heart of the peninsula and across the Strait of Juan de Fuca. (Backpackers note wryly that you have to hike a long way in other parts of the park to get the kinds of views you can drive to here.) Hurricane Ridge also has an uncommonly fine display of wildflowers in spring and summer.

29

WHAT TO SEE

Most of the park's attractions are found either off Highway 101 or down trails that require hikes of 15 minutes or longer. The west coast beaches are linked to the highway by downhill tracks; the number of cars parked alongside the road at the start of the paths indicate how crowded the beach will be.

HISTORIC SITES

La Push. At the mouth of Quileute River, La Push is the tribal center of the Quileute Indians. In fact, the town's name is a variation on the French *la bouche*, which means "the mouth." Offshore rock spires known as sea stacks dot the coast here, and you may catch a glimpse of bald eagles nesting in the nearby cliffs. ⊠ *Rte. 110, 14 mi west of Forks.*

★ **Lake Ozette.** The third-largest glacial impoundment in Washington anchors the coastal strip of Olympic National Park at its north end. The small town of Ozette, home to a coastal tribe, is the trailhead for two of the

OLYMPIC IN ONE DAY

Start at the **Lake Quinault Lodge**, in the park's southwest corner. From here, drive a half hour into the Quinault Valley via **South Shore Road**. Tackle the forested **Graves Creek Trail**, then head up **North Shore Road** to the Quinault Rain Forest Interpretive Trail. Next, head back to Highway 101 and drive to **Ruby Beach**, where a shoreline walk presents a breathtaking scene of sea stacks and sparkling, pink-hued sands.

Forks, and its **Timber Museum**, are your next stop; have lunch here, then drive 20 minutes to the beach at **La Push**. Next, head to **Lake Crescent**, around the corner to the northeast, where you can rent a boat, take a swim, or enjoy a picnic next to the sparkling teal waters. Drive through **Port Angeles to Hurricane Ridge**; count on an hour's drive from bottom to top if there aren't too many visitors. At the ridge, explore the visitor center or hike the 3-mi loop to **Hurricane Hill**, where you can see over the entire park north to Vancouver Island and south past Mt. Olympus.

park's better one-day hikes. Both 3-mi trails lead over boardwalks through swampy wetland and coastal old-growth forest to the ocean shore and uncrowded beaches. ⊠ *At the end of Hoko-Ozette Rd., 26 mi southwest of Hwy. 112 near Sekiu* ☎ *360/963–2725 Ozette Ranger Station.*

SCENIC STOPS

Fodor'sChoice   **Hoh River Rain Forest.** South of Forks, an 18-mi spur road links Highway
★   101 with this unique temperate rain forest, where spruce and hemlock trees soar to heights of more than 200 feet. Alders and big-leaf maples are so densely covered with mosses they look more like shaggy prehistoric animals than trees, and elk browse in shaded glens. Be prepared for precipitation: the region receives 140 inches or more each year. The visitor center is open daily July through September from 9 to 6, and Friday through Tuesday from 9 to 4 in other months. ⊠ *From Hwy. 101, at about 20 mi north of Kalaloch, turn onto Upper Hoh Rd. 18 mi east to Hoh Rain Forest Visitor Center* ☎ *360/374–6925.*

Fodor'sChoice   **Hurricane Ridge.** The panoramic view from this 5,200-foot-high ridge
★   encompasses the Olympic range, the Strait of Juan de Fuca, and Vancouver Island. Guided tours are given in summer along the many paved and unpaved trails, where wildflowers and wildlife such as deer and marmots flourish. ⊠ *Hurricane Ridge Rd., 17 mi south of Port Angeles* ☎ *360/565–3130 visitor center* ☉ *Visitor center daily 10–5.*

Kalaloch. With a lodge, a huge campground, miles of coastline, and easy access from the highway, this is another popular spot. Keen-eyed beachcombers may spot sea otters just offshore; they were reintroduced here in 1970. ⊠ *Hwy. 101, 32 mi northwest of Lake Quinault* ☎ *360/962–2283 Kalaloch ranger station.*

Lake Crescent. Visitors see Lake Crescent as Highway 101 winds along its southern shore, giving way to gorgeous views of teal waters rippling in a basin formed by Tuscan-like hills. In the evening, low bands of clouds caught between the surrounding mountains often linger over its

DID YOU KNOW?

Encompassing more than 70 miles of beachfront, Olympic is one of the few national parks of the West with an ocean beach (Redwood, Channel Islands, and some of the Alaskan parks are the others). This rare trait means the park is home to many marine animals, including sea otters, whales, sea lions, and seals.

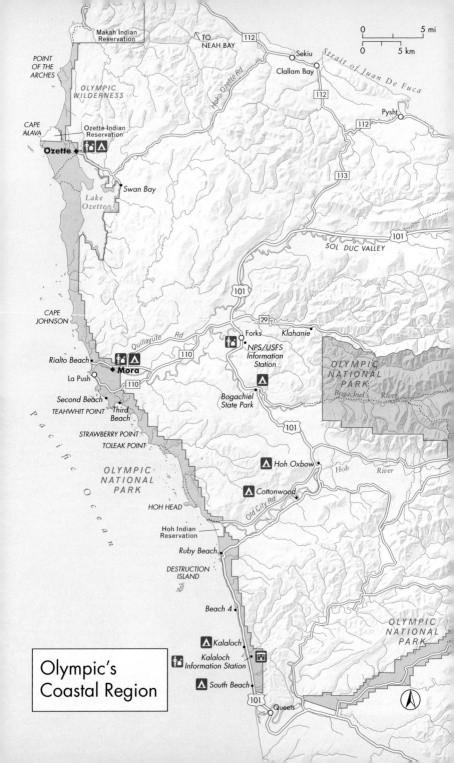

Olympic's Coastal Region

reflective surface. ⊠ *Hwy. 101, 16 mi west of Port Angeles and 28 mi east of Forks* ☎ *360/928–3380 Storm King ranger station.*

★ **Lake Quinault.** This glimmering lake, 4½ mi long and 300 feet deep, is the first landmark you'll reach when driving the west-side loop of U.S. 101. The rain forest is thickest here, with moss-draped maples and alders, and towering spruce, fir, and hemlock. Enchanted Valley, high up near the Quinault River's source, is a deeply glaciated valley that's closer to the Hood Canal than to the Pacific Ocean. A scenic loop drive circles the lake and travels around a section of the Quinault River. ⊠ *Hwy. 101, 38 mi north of Hoquiam* ☎ *360/288–2444 for Quinault River ranger station* ☉ *Ranger station May–Sept., daily 8–5.*

Second and Third Beaches. During low tide, the pools here brim with life, and you can walk out to some sea stacks. Gray whales play offshore during their annual spring migration, and most of the year the waves are great for surfing and kayaking (bring a wet suit). ⊠ *Hwy. 101, 32 mi north of Lake Quinault* ☎ *360/374–5460.*

Sol Duc. Sol Duc Valley is one of those magical places where all the Northwest's virtues seem at hand: lush lowland forests, sparkling river scenes, salmon runs, and serene hiking trails. Here, the popular Sol Duc Hot Springs area includes three attractive sulfuric pools ranging in temperature from 98°F to 104°F. ⊠ *Sol Duc Rd. south of U.S. 101, 1 mi past the west end of Lake Crescent* ☎ *360/374–6925 Hoh Rain Forest Visitor Center.*

Staircase. Unlike the forests of the park's south and west sides, Douglas fir is the dominant tree on the east slope of the Olympic Mountains. Fire has played an important role in creating the majestic forest here, as the Staircase Ranger Station explains in interpretive exhibits. ⊠ *At end of Rte. 119, 15 mi from U.S. 101 at Hoodsport* ☎ *360/877–5569 Staircase Ranger Station.*

VISITOR CENTERS

Forks Parks and Forest Information Center. The office has park maps and brochures; they also provide permits and rent bear-proof containers. ⊠ *Hwy. 101, Forks* ☎ *No phone* ⊕ *www.forks-web.com* ☉ *June–Aug., daily 9–4; Sept.–May, Fri.–Sun. 9–4.*

Hoh Rain Forest Visitor Center. Pick up park maps and pamphlets, permits, and activities lists in this busy, woodsy chalet; there's also a shop and exhibits on natural history. Several short interpretive trails and longer wilderness treks start from here. ⊠ *Upper Hoh Rd., Forks* ☎ *360/374–6925* ⊕ *www.nps.gov/olym* ☉ *Sept.–June daily 9–6, July and Aug., Fri.–Tues. 9–4.*

Hurricane Ridge Visitor Center. The upper level of this visitor center has exhibits, a gift shop, and a café; the lower level has open seating and nice views. Guided walks and programs start in late June, and you can also get details on the surrounding Winter Use Area ski and sledding slopes. ⊠ *Hurricane Ridge Rd., Port Angeles* ☎ *360/565–3131* ⊕ *www.nps.gov/olym* ☉ *Memorial Day–Labor Day, daily 9–7; late-Dec.–Apr., Fri.–Sun. 10–4.*

Olympic National Park Visitor Center. This modern, well-organized facility, staffed by park rangers, provides everything: maps, trail brochures, campground advice, listings of wildlife sightings, educational programs and exhibits, information on road and trail closures, and weather

29

forecasts. ⊠ *3002 Mount Angeles Rd., Port Angeles* ☎ *360/565–3130* ⊕ *www.nps.gov/olym* ☉ *May–Sept., daily 9–4; Oct.–Apr., daily 10–4.*

South Shore Quinault Ranger Station. This office at the Lake Quinault Lodge has maps, campground information, and program listings. ⊠ *S. Shore Lake Quinault Rd., Lake Quinault* ☎ *360/288–2444* ⊕ *www.nps.gov/ olym* ☉ *Memorial Day–Labor Day, weekdays 8–4:30, weekends 9–4.*

Wilderness Information Center (WIC). Located behind Olympic National Park Visitor Center, this facility provides all the information you'll need for a trip in the park, including trail conditions, safety tips, and weather bulletins. The office also issues camping permits, takes campground reservations, and rents bear-proof food canisters for $3. ⊠ *3002 Mount Angeles Rd., Port Angeles* ☎ *360/565–3100* ⊕ *www.nps.gov/olym* ☉ *Late June– Labor Day, Sun.–Thurs. 7:30–6, Fri. and Sat. 7:30–7.*

SPORTS AND THE OUTDOORS

BEACHCOMBING

★ The wild, shell-strewn Pacific coast teems with tide pools and clawed creatures. Crabs, sand dollars, anemones, starfish, and all sorts of shellfish are exposed at low tide, when flat beaches can stretch out for hundreds of yards. The most easily accessible sand-strolling spots are Rialto, Ruby, First, and Second beaches, near Mora and La Push, and Kalaloch Beach and Fourth Beach in the Kalaloch stretch.

The Wilderness Act and the park's code of ethics instruct visitors to leave all nonliving materials where they are for others to enjoy.

BICYCLING

The rough gravel car tracks to some of the park's remote sites were meant for four-wheel-drive vehicles, but can double as mountain-bike routes. The Quinault Valley, Queets River, Hoh River, and Sol Duc River roads have bike paths through old-growth forest. Graves Creek Road, in the southwest, is a mountain-bike path; Lake Crescent's north side is also edged by the bike-friendly Spruce Railroad Trail. More bike tracks run through the adjacent Olympic National Forest. Note that Highway 101 has heavy traffic and isn't recommended for cycling, although the western side has broad roads with beautiful scenery and can be biked off-season. Bikes are not permitted on foot trails.

OUTFITTERS AND EXPEDITIONS **Bicycle Adventures** (☎ *360/786–0989 or 800/443–6060* ⊕ *www.bicycleadventures.com*), an Olympia bike tour outfit, stages trips in and around the park area, including up Hurricane Ridge. **Mike's Bikes** (⊠ *150 W. Sequim Bay Rd., Sequim* ☎ *360/681–3868* ⊕ *www.mikes-bikes.net*), a bike, gear, and repair shop, is a great resource for advice on routes around the Olympic Peninsula. **Peak 6** (⊠ *4883 Upper Hoh Rd., Forks* ☎ *360/374–5254*), an adventure store on the way to the Hoh Rain Forest Visitor Center, rents mountain bikes. **Sound Bike & Kayak** (⊠ *120 E. Front St., Port Angeles* ☎ *360/457–1240* ⊕ *www.soundbikeskayaks.com*) rents and sells biking equipment.

CLIMBING

At 7,980 feet, Mt. Olympus is the highest peak in the park and the most popular climb in the region. To attempt the summit, participants must register at the Glacier Meadows Ranger Station. Mt. Constance, the third-highest Olympic peak at 7,743 feet, has a well-traversed climbing route that requires technical experience; reservations are recommended for the Lake Constance stop, which is limited to 20 campers. Mt. Deception is another possibility, though tricky snows have caused fatalities and injuries in the last decade. Climbing season runs from late June through September. Note that crevasse skills and self-rescue experience are highly recommended. Climbers must register with park officials and purchase wilderness permits before setting out. The best resource for climbing advice is the Wilderness Information Center in Port Angeles.

OUTFITTERS AND EXPEDITIONS

Alpine Ascents (⌧ *121 Mercer St., Seattle* ☎ *206/378–1927* ⊕ *www.alpineascents.com*) leads tours of the Olympic ranges. **Mountain Madness** (⌧ *4218 S.W. Alaska St., Ste. 206, Seattle* ☎ *206/937–8389 or 800/328–5925* ⊕ *www.mountainmadness.com*) offers adventure trips to summits around the Olympic Peninsula. **Olympic Mountaineering** (⌧ *140 W. Front St., Port Angeles* ☎ *360/452–0240* ⊕ *www.olymtn.com*) sells mountaineering gear and organizes climbs and hikes in the park.

FISHING

Bodies of water throughout the park offer numerous fishing possibilities. Lake Crescent is home to cutthroat and rainbow trout, as well as petite kokanee salmon; Lake Cushman, Lake Quinault, and Ozette Lake have trout, salmon, and steelhead; and Lake Mills has three trout varieties. As for rivers, the Bogachiel and Queets have steelhead salmon in season. The glacier-fed Hoh River is home to chinook salmon April to November, and coho salmon from August through November; the Sol Duc River offers all five species of salmon, plus cutthroat and steelhead trout. Rainbow trout are also found in the Dosewallips, Elwha, and Skykomish rivers. Other places to go after salmon and trout include the Duckabush, Quillayute, Quinault, and Salmon rivers. A Washington state punch card is required during salmon-spawning months; fishing regulations vary throughout the park. Licenses are available from sporting goods and outdoor supply stores.

OUTFITTERS AND EXPEDITIONS

Bob's Piscatorial Pursuits (☎ *866/347–4232* ⊕ *www.piscatorialpursuits.com*), based in Forks, offers year-round fishing trips around Olympic. **Blue Sky Outfitters** (⌧ *9674 50th Ave. SW, Seattle* ☎ *8206/938–4030 or 800/228–7238* ⊕ *www.blueskyoutfitters.com*), in Seattle, organizes custom-tailored fishing trips. White-water rafting trips are another specialty. **Kalaloch Lodge** (⌧ *157151 U.S. 101, Forks* ☎ *360/962–2271 or 866/525–2562* ⊕ *www.visitkalaloch.com*) organizes guided fishing expeditions around the Olympic Peninsula.

HIKING

Know your tides, or you might be trapped by high water. Tide tables are available at all visitor centers and ranger stations. Remember that a wilderness permit is required for all overnight backcountry visits.

29

Peak 6 (✉ *4883 Upper Hoh Rd., Forks* ☎ *360/374–5254*) runs guided hiking and camping trips. **Timberline Adventures** (☎ *800/417–2453* ⊕ *www.timbertours.com*) does weeklong excursions around the Olympic Peninsula.

EASY

☾ **Hoh Valley Trail.** Leaving from the Hoh Visitor Center, this rain forest jaunt takes you into the Hoh Valley, wending its way alongside the river, through moss-draped maple and alder trees, and past open meadows where elk roam in winter. ✉ *Hoh Visitor Center, 18 mi east of U.S. 101.*

Fodor's Choice
★

☾ **Hurricane Ridge Trail.** A 0.25-mi alpine loop, most of it wheelchair-accessible, leads through wildflower meadows overlooking numerous vistas of the interior Olympic peaks to the south and a panorama of the Strait of Juan de Fuca to the north. ✉ *Hurricane Ridge Rd., 17 mi south of Port Angeles.*

MODERATE

Boulder Creek Trail. The 5-mi round-trip walk up Boulder Creek leads to a half-dozen hot spring pools of varying temperatures; some are clothing-optional. ✉ *End of the Elwha River Rd., 4 mi south of Altair Campground.*

☾ **Cape Alva Trail.** Beginning at Ozette, this 3-mi trail leads from the forest
★ to wave-tossed headlands. ✉ *End of the Hoko-Ozette Rd., 26 mi south of Hwy. 112, west of Sekiu.*

Graves Creek Trail. This 6-mi-long moderately strenuous trail climbs from lowland rain forest to alpine territory at Sundown Pass. Due to spring floods, a fjord halfway up is often impassable in May and June. ✉ *End of S. Quinault Valley Rd., 23 mi east of U.S. 101.*

☾ **Sol Duc Trail.** The 1.5-mi gravel path off Sol Duc Road winds through thick
Fodor's Choice Douglas fir forests toward the thundering, three-chute Sol Duc Falls.
★ Just 0.1 mi from the road, below a wooden platform over the Sol Duc River, you'll come across the 70-foot Salmon Cascades. In late summer and autumn, thousands of salmon negotiate 50 mi or more of treacherous waters to reach the cascades and the tamer pools near Sol Duc Hot Springs. The popular 6-mi **Lovers Lane Loop Trail** links the Sol Duc falls with the hot springs. You can continue up from the falls 5 mi on the **Appleton Pass Trail,** at 3,100 feet. From there you can hike on to the 8.5-mi mark, where views at the High Divide are from 5,050 feet. ✉ *Sol Duc Rd., 11 mi south of U.S. 101.*

DIFFICULT

High Divide Trail. A 9-mi hike in the park's high country defines this trail, which includes some strenuous climbing on its last 4 mi before topping out at a small alpine lake. A return loop along High Divide wends its way an extra mile through alpine territory, with sensational views of Olympic peaks. This trail is only for dedicated, properly equipped hikers who are in good shape. ✉ *End of Sol Duc River Rd., 13 mi south of U.S. 101.*

KAYAKING AND CANOEING

Lake Crescent, a serene expanse of teal-colored waters surrounded by deep-green pine forests, is one of the park's best boating areas. Note that the west end is for swimming only; no speedboats are allowed here.

Lake Quinault has boating access from a gravel ramp on the north shore. From U.S. 101, take a right on North Shore Road, another right

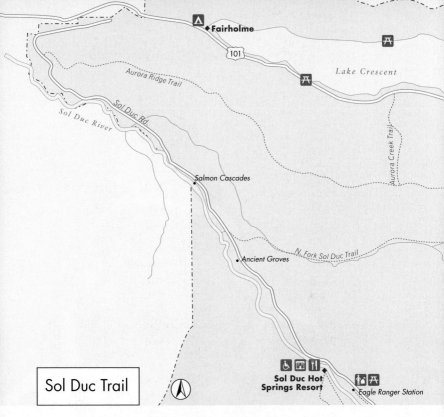

Fairholme

101

Aurora Ridge Trail

Sol Duc Rd.

Sol Duc River

Lake Crescent

Aurora Creek Trail

Salmon Cascades

N. Fork Sol Duc Trail

Ancient Groves

Sol Duc Hot
Springs Resort

Eagle Ranger Station

Sol Duc Trail

on Hemlock Way, and a left on Lakeview Drive. There are plank ramps at Falls Creek and Willoughby campgrounds on South Shore Drive, 0.1 mi and 0.2 mi past the Quinault Ranger Station, respectively.

Lake Ozette, with just one access road, is a good place for overnight trips. Only experienced canoe and kayak handlers should travel far from the put-in, since fierce storms occasionally strike—even in summer.

OUTFITTERS AND EXPEDITIONS **Fairholm General Store** (⊠ *U.S. 101, Fairholm* ☎ *360/928–3020* ⊕ *www.fairholmstore.com*) rents rowboats and canoes on Lake Crescent for $10 to $45. It's at the lake's west end, 27 mi west of Port Angeles. **Lake Crescent Lodge** (⊠ *416 Lake Crescent Rd.* ☎ *360/928–3211* ⊕ *www.lakecrescentlodge.com*) rents rowboats for $8.50 per hour and $35 per day. **Log Cabin Resort** (⊠ *Piedmont Rd., off U.S. 101* ☎ *360/928–3325* ⊕ *www.logcabinresort.net*), 17 mi west of Port Angeles, has boat rentals for $10 to $30. The dock provides easy access to Lake Crescent's northeast section. **Rain Forest Paddlers** (⊠ *4882 Upper Hoh Rd., Forks* ☎ *360/ 374–5254 or 866/457–8398* ⊕ *www.rainforestpaddlers.com*) takes kayakers down the Lizard Rock and Oxbow sections of the Hoh River.

RAFTING

Olympic has excellent rafting rivers, with Class II to Class V rapids. The Elwha River is a popular place to paddle, with some exciting turns. The Hoh is better for those who like a smooth, easy float.

DID YOU KNOW?

Olympic National Park is home to 13 species of amphibians (frogs, toads, and salamanders), including the Pacific Tree Frog. The park is a rare refuge for these animals, whose world populations have been declining due to air and water pollution (amphibians live in both environments, making them doubly susceptible).

OUTFITTERS
AND
EXPEDITIONS
Olympic Raft and Kayak (☎ *360/452–5268 or 888/452–1443 ⊕ www. raftandkayak.com*), based in Port Angeles, is the only rafting outfit allowed to venture into Olympic National Park.

WINTER SPORTS

Hurricane Ridge is the central spot for winter sports. Miles of downhill and Nordic ski tracks are open late December through March, and a ski lift, towropes, and ski school are open 10 to 4 weekends and holidays. Tubing areas for adults and children are open Friday through Sunday across from Hurricane Ridge Lodge.

OUTFITTERS
AND
EXPEDITIONS
Hurricane Ridge Visitor Center (✉ *Hurricane Ridge Rd., Port Angeles* ☎ *360/565–3131 information, 360/565–3136 tour reservations ⊕ www. nps.gov/olym*) rents ski equipment December through March; prices are $15 to $35. Free 90-minute snowshoe tours also depart from here every weekend from late December through March. Group bookings are at 10:30, with informal group tours at 2; sign-ups are at 1:30 and are first-come, first-served. A $5 per person donation is requested to cover trail and equipment maintenance. **Lost Mountain Lodge** (✉ *303 Sunny View Dr., Sequim* ☎ *360/683–2431 or 888/683–2431 ⊕ www.lostmountainlodge. com*), in Sequim, offers weekend Olympic Mountains snowshoe packages; gear rental and an in-room, fireside fondue are included.

EDUCATIONAL OFFERINGS

CLASSES AND SEMINARS

Olympic Park Institute. This first-class educational facility offers talks and excursions focusing on park ecology and history. Trips range from two-hour canoe trips ($20) to five-day camping, kayaking, and climbing excursions ($200 to $400 per person; family discounts are offered). ✉ *111 Barnes Point Rd., Port Angeles* ☎ *360/928–3720 or 800/775–3720 ⊕ www.yni.org/opi* ⊘ *Weekdays 8:30–4:30.*

29

WHAT'S NEARBY

NEARBY TOWNS

Although most Olympic Peninsula towns have evolved from their exclusive reliance on timber, **Forks,** outside the national park's northwest tip, remains one of the region's logging capitals. Washington state's wettest town (100 inches or more of rain a year), it's a small, friendly place with just 3,500 residents and a modicum of visitor facilities. **Port Angeles,** a city of 19,000, now focuses on its status as the main gateway to Olympic National Park and Victoria, BC. Set below the Strait of Juan de Fuca and looking north to Vancouver Island, it's an enviably scenic settlement filled with attractive, Craftsman-style homes. The Pacific Northwest has its very own "Banana Belt" in the waterfront community of **Sequim,** 15 mi east of Port Angeles along Highway 101. The town of 6,000 is located in the rain shadow of the Olympics and receives only 16 inches of rain per year (compared to the 40 inches that drench the Hoh Rain Forest just 40 mi away).

VISITOR INFORMATION

Contacts Forks Chamber of Commerce Visitor Center ✉ *1411 S. Forks Ave. (U.S. 101), Forks* ☎ *800/443–6757* ⊕ *www.forkswa.com.* **Port Angeles Chamber of Commerce Visitor Center** ✉ *121 E. Railroad Ave., Port Angeles* ☎ *360/452–2363* ⊕ *www.cityofpa.com.* **Sequim-Dungeness Valley Chamber of Commerce** ⌂ *P.O. Box 907, Sequim 98382* ☎ *360/693–6197 or 800/737–8462* ⊕ *www.cityofsequim.com.*

NEARBY ATTRACTIONS

Fodor'sChoice ★ **Dungeness Spit.** Curving 5½ mi into the Strait of Juan de Fuca, the longest natural sand spit in the United States is a wild, beautiful section of shoreline. More than 30,000 migratory waterfowl stop here each spring and fall, but you'll see plenty of birdlife any time of year. The entire spit is part of the **Dungeness National Wildlife Refuge.** At the end of the Dungeness Spit is the towering white **Dungeness Lighthouse** (☎ *360/683–9166* ⊕ *www.newdungenesslighthouse.com*); tours are available, though access is limited to those who can hike or kayak out 5 mi to the end of the spit. An adjacent, 64-site camping area, on the bluff above the Strait of Juan de Fuca, is open February through September. ✉ *Kitchen Rd., 3 mi north from U.S. 101, 4 mi west of Sequim* ☎ *360/457–8451 wildlife refuge, 360/683–5847 campground* ⌑ *$3 per family* ⊘ *Wildlife refuge daily sunrise–sunset.*

Timber Museum. The museum highlights Forks' logging history since the 1870s; a garden and fire tower are also on the grounds. ✉ *1421 S. Forks Ave., Forks* ☎ *360/374–9663* ⊘ *Open May–Oct., Tues.–Sat. 10–4.*

WHERE TO EAT AND STAY

ABOUT THE RESTAURANTS

The major resorts are your best bets for eating out in the park. Each has a main restaurant, café, and/or kiosk, as well as casually upscale dinner service, with regional seafood, meat, and produce complemented by a range of microbrews and good Washington and international wines. Reservations are either recommended or required.

Outside the park, Port Angeles is the place to go for a truly spectacular meal; several restaurants are internationally renowned by diners and chefs alike, and most are run by famous former chefs. Dozens of small, easygoing eateries offering hearty American-style fare line the main thoroughfares in Forks and Sequim.

ABOUT THE HOTELS

Major park resorts run from good to terrific, with generally comfortable rooms, excellent facilities, and easy access to trails, beaches, and activity centers. Midsize accommodations, like Sol Duc Hot Springs Resort, are often shockingly rustic—but remember, you're here for the park, not for the rooms.

The towns around the park have motels, hotels, and resorts for every budget. For high-priced stays with lots of perks, base yourself in Port Angeles. Sequim has many attractive, friendly B and Bs, plus lots of inexpensive chain hotels and motels. Forks is basically a motel town, with a few guesthouses around its fringes.

ABOUT THE CAMPGROUNDS

Note that only a few places take reservations; if you can't book in advance, you'll have to arrive early to get a place. Each site usually has a picnic table and grill or fire pit, and most campgrounds have water, toilets, and garbage containers; for hookups, showers, and laundry facilities, you'll have to head into the towns. Firewood is available from camp concessions, but if there's no store you can collect dead wood within 1 mi of your campsite. Dogs are allowed in campgrounds, but not on trails or in the backcountry. Trailers should be 21 feet long or less (15 feet or less at Queets Campground). There's a camping limit of two weeks.

If you have a backcountry pass, you can camp virtually anywhere throughout the park's forests and shores. Overnight wilderness permits are $5—plus $2 per person per night—and are available at visitor centers and ranger stations. Note that when you camp in the backcountry, you must choose a site at least ½ mi inside the park boundary.

WHERE TO EAT

IN THE PARK

$$–$$$
AMERICAN
★
✕ **Kalaloch Lodge.** A tranquil country setting and ocean views create the perfect backdrop for savoring local dinner specialties like cedar-planked salmon, fresh shellfish, wild mushrooms, and well-aged beef. Note that seating is every half hour after 5, and reservations are recommended. Hearty breakfasts and sandwich-style lunches are more casual. ✉ 157151 Hwy. 101, Kalaloch ☎ 866/525–2562 ▤ AE, MC, V.

$$–$$$
AMERICAN
★
✕ **Lake Crescent Lodge.** Part of the original 1916 lodge, the fir-paneled dining room overlooks the lake; you also won't find a better spot for a view of the sunset. Entrées include crab cakes, grilled salmon, halibut fish-and-chips, classic American steaks, and elk ribs. A good Northwest wine list complements the menu. Note that meals are only offered during set hours, but appetizers are served in the lounge—or out on the Sun Porch—from 2 to 10. ✉ 416 Lake Crescent Rd., Port Angeles ☎ 360/928–3211 ⚘ Reservations essential ▤ AE, D, DC, MC, V ☺ Closed mid-Oct.–May.

$$–$$$
AMERICAN
✕ **The Springs Restaurant.** The main Sol Duc Hot Springs Resort restaurant is a rustic, fir-and-cedar paneled dining room surrounded by trees. Big breakfasts are turned out daily 7:30 to 10; dinner is served daily between 5:30 and 9 (lunch and snacks are available 11 to 4 at the Poolside Deli or Espresso Hut). Evening choices include Northwest seafood and game highlighted by fresh-picked fruits and vegetables. ✉ 12076 Sol Duc Rd., at U.S. 101, Port Angeles ☎ 360/327–3583 ▤ AE, D, MC, V ☺ Closed mid-Oct.–mid-May.

PICNIC AREAS
All Olympic National Park campgrounds have adjacent picnic areas with tables, some shelters, and restrooms, but no cooking facilities. The same is true for major visitor centers, such as Hoh Rain Forest. Drinking water is available at ranger stations, interpretive centers, and inside campgrounds.

East Beach Picnic Area. Set on a grassy meadow overlooking Lake Crescent, this popular swimming spot has six picnic tables and vault toilets. ⊠ *At the far east end of Lake Crescent, off Hwy. 101, 17 mi west of Port Angeles.*

La Poel Picnic Area. Tall firs lean over a tiny gravel beach at this small picnic area, which has five picnic tables and a splendid view of Pyramid Mountain across Lake Crescent. ⊠ *Off Hwy. 101, 22 mi west of Port Angeles.*

Rialto Beach Picnic Area. Relatively secluded at the end of the road from Forks, this is one of the premier day-use areas in the park's Pacific coast segment. This site has 12 picnic tables, fire grills, and vault toilets. ⊠ *Rte. 110, 14 mi west of Forks.*

OUTSIDE THE PARK

$$$–$$$$ ✕ **C'est Si Bon.** Far more Euro-savvy than is typical on the Olympic
FRENCH   Peninsula, this first-rate restaurant stands out for its decor as well as
Fodor's Choice   for its food. The fanciful dining room is done up in bold red hues, with
★   crisp white linens, huge oil paintings, and glittering chandeliers; the spacious solarium takes an equally formal approach. The changing menu highlights homemade onion soup, Cornish hen, Dungeness crab soufflé, and filet mignon. The wine list is superb, with French, Australian, and Northwest choices to pair with everything. ⊠ *23 Cedar Park Rd., Port Angeles* ☎ *360/452–8888* ⊕ *www.cestsibon-frenchcuisine.com* ⌒ *Reservations essential* ⊟ *AE, DC, MC, V* ☉ *Closed Mon. No lunch.*

$–$$ ✕ **Deckside Grill.** With tremendous views of John Wayne Marina and
AMERICAN   Sequim Bay, this family restaurant is a fun place to watch the ships
★   placidly sail by. The casual menu includes coconut prawns, pasta, grilled chicken, and sandwiches. The kitchen also serves up excellent steak and lamb. ⊠ *2577 W. Sequim Bay Rd., Sequim* ☎ *360/683–7510* ⊟ *AE, D, MC, V* ☉ *Closed Mon. and Tues.*

$$–$$$ ✕ **Three Crabs.** An institution since 1958, this large crab shack on the
SEAFOOD   beach, 5 mi north of Sequim, specializes in Dungeness's famed crusta-
★   cean. Although the clawed creatures are served many ways here, these crabs are so fresh that it's best to simply have them with lemon and butter. ⊠ *11 Three Crabs Rd., Sequim* ☎ *360/683–4264* ⊕ *www.the3crabs.com* ⊟ *MC, V* ☉ *Closed Mon. and Tues.*

WHERE TO STAY

IN THE PARK

$$$–$$$$ 🏠 **Kalaloch Lodge.** A two-story cedar building overlooking the Pacific, Kalaloch has cozy rooms with sea views. The surrounding log cabins have a fireplace or woodstove, knotty-pine furnishings, earth-tone fabrics, and kitchenettes; the main lodge houses rustic oceanview rooms and suites; and wood-paneled motel-style quarters are in the Seacrest Building. Guests have pool privileges at the Lake Quinault Resort; towels are provided. The restaurant's ($$–$$$) menu changes seasonally, but usually includes local oysters, crab, and salmon. **Pros:** ranger tours; clam digging; supreme storm watching in winter. **Cons:** some units are two blocks from main lodge; cabins can smell like pets. ⊠ *157151 U.S. 101* ⌂ *HC 80, P.O. Box 1100, Forks 98331* ☎ *360/962–2271 or 866/525–2562* ⊕ *www.visitkalaloch.com* ⌁ *10 lodge rooms, 6 motel*

rooms, 3 motel suites, 44 cabins ⬡ In-room: no phone, kitchen, no TV. In-hotel: restaurant, bar, some pets allowed ⊟ AE, D, MC, V.

$$–$$$ ⊡ **Lake Crescent Lodge.** Deep in the forest at the foot of Mt. Storm King, this comfortable 1916 lodge has a wraparound veranda and picture windows that frame the lake's sapphire waters. Rooms in the rustic Roosevelt Cottage have polished wood floors, stone fireplaces, and lake views, while Tavern Cottage quarters resemble modern motel rooms. The historic lodge has second-floor rooms with shared baths. The lodge's fir-paneled dining room ($$–$$$) overlooks the lake, and the adjacent lounge is often crowded with campers. Seafood dishes like grilled salmon or steamed Quilcene oysters highlight the restaurant menu; reservations are required. **Pros:** gorgeous setting; free wireless access in the wilderness. **Cons:** no laundry; Roosevelt Cottages must be booked a year in advance. ⊠ *416 Lake Crescent Rd., Port Angeles* ☎ *360/928–3211* ⊕ *www.lakecrescentlodge.com* ⥅ *30 motel rooms, 17 cabins, 5 lodge rooms with shared bath* ⬡ *In-room: no phone, no TV. In-hotel: 2 restaurants* ⊟ *AE, DC, MC, V* ⊗ *Closed Nov.–Apr.*

$$$–$$$$ ⊡ **Lake Quinault Lodge.** On a lovely glacial lake in Olympic National Forest, this beautiful early-20th-century lodge complex is within walking distance of the lakeshore and hiking trails in the spectacular old-growth forest. A towering brick fireplace is the centerpiece of the great room, where antique wicker furnishings sit beneath ceiling beams painted with Native American designs. In the rooms, modern gadgets are traded in for old-fashioned comforts, such as claw-foot tubs, fireplaces, and walking sticks. The lively bar is a good place to unwind after a day outdoors, and the restaurant ($$$–$$$$) serves upscale seafood entrées like baked salmon with capers and onions. **Pros:** hosts summer campfires with s'mores; family-friendly ambience. **Cons:** kayaks and canoes rent out quickly in the summer. ⊠ *South Shore Rd., P.O. Box 7, Quinault* ☎ *360/288–2900 or 800/562–6672* ⊕ *www.visitlakequinault.com* ⥅ *92 rooms* ⬡ *In-room: no phone, no TV (some). In-hotel: restaurant, bar, pool, some pets allowed* ⊟ *AE, D, MC, V.*

$–$$ ⊡ **Log Cabin Resort.** This rustic hotel has an idyllic setting at the northeast end of Lake Crescent. Settle into one of the A-frame chalet units, standard cabins, small camping cabins, motel units, or RV sites, which include full hookups. Some rooms have full kitchens. Twelve of the units are on the lake. You can rent paddleboats or kayaks to use by the day. **Pros:** bikes and boats available on-site; weekly ranger talks. **Cons:** cabins are very rustic. ⊠ *3183 E. Beach Rd., Port Angeles* ☎ *360/928–3325* ⊕ *www.logcabinresort.net* ⥅ *4 lodge rooms, 24 cabins, 40 RV sites* ⬡ *In-room: no a/c, no phone, no TV. In-hotel: restaurant, laundry facilities, Wi-Fi* ⊟ *D, MC, V* ⊗ *Closed Nov.–Mar.*

$$–$$$ ⊡ **Sol Duc Hot Springs Resort.** Deep in the brooding forest along the Sol Duc River, this remote 1910 resort is surrounded by 5,000-foot-tall mountains. The main draw is the pool area, which surrounds a gathering of soothing mineral baths, and has a freshwater swimming pool. Some forest cabins have kitchens, but all are spartan; however, after a day's hike, a dip, and dinner at the Springs Restaurant ($$–$$$), you'll hardly notice. The attractive fir-and-cedar-paneled dining room serves unpretentious meals all day, drawing on top Northwest seafood and produce.

29

Pros: nearby trails; peaceful setting. **Cons:** steep pool rates. ⊠ *12076 Sol Duc Rd.* ⌂ *P.O. Box 2168, Port Angeles 98362* ☎ *360/327–3583 or 866/476–5382* ⊕ *www.visitsolduc.com* ⤵ *32 rooms, 6 cabins* ⌂ *In-room: no a/c (some), no phone (some), kitchen (some), no TV (some). In-hotel: restaurant, bar, pool* ⊟ *AE, DC, MC, V* ⊘ *Closed mid-Oct.–mid-Apr.*

CAMPING

$ ⚲ **Altair Campground.** This small campground sits amid an old-growth forest by the river in the rather narrow Elwha River Valley. The 3-mi West Elwha Trail leads downstream from the campground. **Pros:** river views; immediate hiking options. **Cons:** noisy on summer weekends. ⊠ *Elwha River Rd., 8 mi south of U.S. 101, Olympic National Park* ☎ *No phone* ⚲ *30 tent/RV sites* ⌂ *Flush toilets, drinking water, fire grates* ⊘ *Closed Nov.–Mar.*

$ ⚲ **Deer Park Campground.** At 5,400 feet, this is the park's only drive-to alpine campground. The part-gravel access road is steep and winding; RVs are prohibited. **Pros:** shaded sites; easy access by road. **Cons:** motor noises. ⊠ *Deer Park (Blue Mountain) Rd., 21 mi south of U.S. 101, Olympic National Park* ☎ *No phone* ⚲ *14 tent sites* ⌂ *Pit toilets, drinking water, fire grates* ⊘ *Closed Oct.–Apr.*

$ ⚲ **Elwha Campground.** The larger of the Elwha Valley's two campgrounds, this is one of Olympic's year-round facilities. Two campsite loops lie in an old-growth forest. **Pros:** spur-of-the-moment camping opportunity because it's not usually full; amphitheater nearby. **Cons:** no water in winter. ⊠ *Elwha River Rd., 7 mi south of U.S. 101, Olympic National Park* ☎ *No phone* ⚲ *40 tent/RV sites* ⌂ *Pit toilets, drinking water (summer only), fire grates, public telephone, ranger station* ⊟ *MC, V.*

$ ⚲ **Fairholme Campground.** One of just three lakeside campgrounds in the
★ park, Fairholm is near the Lake Crescent Resort. There is an on-site boat launch. **Pros:** gorgeous setting; well placed for lakeside explorations. **Cons:** very popular. ⊠ *U.S. 101, 28 mi west of Port Angeles, on the west end of Lake Crescent, Olympic National Park* ☎ *No phone* ⚲ *88 tent/RV sites* ⌂ *Flush toilets, dump station, drinking water, fire grates, public telephone, swimming (lake)* ⊘ *Closed Nov.–Mar.*

$ ⚲ **Heart O' the Hills Campground.** At the foot of Hurricane Ridge in a grove of tall firs, this popular year-round campground offers a regular slate of summer programs. **Pros:** lots of activities; closest campground to the ridge. **Cons:** only accessible on foot during off-season. ⊠ *Hurricane Ridge Rd., 4 mi south of the main park visitor center in Port Angeles, Olympic National Park* ☎ *No phone* ⚲ *105 tent/RV sites (tent-only in winter)* ⌂ *Flush toilets, drinking water, fire grates, public telephone, ranger station.*

$ ⚲ **Hoh Campground.** Crowds flock to this rain-forest site, near the Hoh Visitor Center under a canopy of moss-draped maples and towering spruce trees. **Pros:** kid-friendly day hikes; animal sightings. **Cons:** bears are sometimes spotted, especially during salmon season. ⊠ *Hoh River Rd., 17 mi east of U.S. 101, Olympic National Park* ☎ *No phone* ⚲ *88 tent/RV sites* ⌂ *Flush toilets, dump station, drinking water, fire grates, public telephone, ranger station* ⊟ *MC, V.*

$–$$ ⚲ **Kalaloch Campground.** Kalaloch is the biggest and most popular Olympic campground, and it's open all year. Its vantage of the Pacific is unmatched on the park's coastal stretch—although the campsites themselves are set back in the spruce fringe. **Pros:** bluff-top views, beach access. **Cons:** no reservations taken mid-September–mid-June. ⊠ *U.S. 101, ½ mi north of the Kalaloch Information Station, Olympic National Park* ☎ *360/962–2271 group bookings* △ *175 tent/RV sites* ⛲ *Flush toilets, dump station, drinking water, fire grates, public telephone, ranger station* ▭ *MC, V.*

$$ △ **Lake Quinault Rain Forest Resort Village Campground.** Stretching along the south shore of Lake Quinault, this RV campground has many recreation facilities, including beaches, canoes, ball fields, and horseshoe pits. Cabins, suites, and apartments are also available. **Pros:** close to Salmon House restaurant; on-site grocery. **Cons:** very busy in summer. ⊠ *3½ mi east of U.S. 101, South Shore Rd., Lake Quinault* ☎ *360/288–2535 or 800/255–6936* ⊕ *www.rainforestresort.com* △ *31 RV sites* ⛲ *Flush toilets, full hookups, drinking water, showers, grills, picnic tables, electricity, public telephone, general store* ▭ *AE, D, MC, V* ⊗ *Closed Nov.–Mar.*

$ △ **Mora Campground.** Along the Quillayute estuary, this campground
★ doubles as a popular staging point for hikes northward along the coast's wilderness stretch. **Pros:** some sites have river views; quick drive to Rialto Beach. **Cons:** throngs of hikers in summer. ⊠ *Rte. 110, 13 mi west of Forks, Olympic National Park* ☎ *No phone* △ *94 tent/RV sites (1 walk-in)* ⛲ *Flush toilets, dump station, drinking water, fire grates, public telephone, ranger station.*

$ △ **North Fork Campground.** The park's smallest campground is for self-sufficient travelers who want to enjoy the rain forest in peace. It's deep, wet woods here; RVs are not advised. **Pros:** good place to find solitude. **Cons:** damp setting; primitive. ⊠ *N. Quinault Valley Rd., 19 mi east of U.S. 101, Olympic National Park* ☎ *No phone* △ *7 tent sites* ⛲ *Pit toilets, fire grates, ranger station* ⊗ *Closed Oct.–Apr.*

$ △ **Ozette Campground.** Hikers heading to Cape Alava, a scenic promontory that is the westernmost point in the lower 48 states, use this lakeshore campground as a jumping-off point. There's a boat launch and a small beach. **Pros:** water activities; stunning panoramas. **Cons:** often closes in winter. ⊠ *Hoko-Ozette Rd., 26 mi south of Hwy. 112, Olympic National Park* ☎ *No phone* △ *15 tent/RV sites* ⛲ *Pit toilets, fire grates, ranger station* ▭ *MC, V* ⊗ *Call ahead in winter.*

$ △ **Sol Duc Campground.** Sol Duc resembles virtually all Olympic campgrounds save one distinguishing feature—the famed hot springs are a short walk away. **Pros:** easy access to pools; waterfalls close by, too. **Cons:** no water in winter. ⊠ *Sol Duc Rd., 11 mi south of U.S. 101, Olympic National Park* ☎ *360/327–3534* △ *82 tent/RV sites* ⛲ *Flush toilets, dump station, drinking water (spring–fall), fire grates, public telephone, ranger station, swimming (hot springs)* ⊗ *Closed Nov.–Apr.*

$ △ **Staircase Campground.** In deep woods away from the river, this campground is a popular jumping-off point for hikes into the Skokomish River Valley and the Olympic high country. **Pros:** some sites are next to the river; running water in summer. **Cons:** Staircase Road is closed to vehicles in winter. ⊠ *Rte. 119, 16 mi northwest of U.S. 101, Olympic National Park* ☎ *No phone* △ *56 tent/RV sites (tent-only in winter)* ⛲ *Flush toilets, drinking water, fire grates, public telephone, ranger station.*

29

OUTSIDE THE PARK

$$$–$$$$ ⊞ **Colette's Bed & Breakfast.** A contemporary mansion curving around 10
Fodor's Choice   acres of gorgeous waterfront property, this B and B offers more space,
★   service, and luxury than any other property in the area. Leather sofas
and chairs and a river-rock fireplace make the front room a lovely spot
to watch the water through expansive 20-foot windows. The suites,
which have such names as Iris, Azalea, and Cedar, also overlook the
water and have fireplaces, balconies, CD and DVD players, and two-
person hot tubs. A specially made outdoor fireplace means you can
enjoy the deck even in winter. Multicourse breakfasts include espresso-
based drinks and fresh fruit. **Pros:** water views to Victoria, BC; discreet
personal service. **Cons:** does not cater to families. ⊠ *339 Finn Hall Rd.,
10 mi east of town, Port Angeles* ☎ *360/457–9197 or 888/457–9777*
⊕ *www.colettes.com* ⇆ *5 suites* ⚭ *In-room: refrigerator. In-hotel: res-
taurant, no kids under 18* ⊟ *MC, V* ⊚ *BP.*

$$$–$$$$ ⊞ **Quality Inn Uptown.** South of town, at the green edge of the Olympic
Mountain foothills, this inn offers a stunning panorama of mountain
and harbor scenes. Perks include free wireless Internet and nightly
cookies. **Pros:** central location; great views. **Cons:** always busy. ⊠ *101
E. 2nd St., Port Angeles* ☎ *360/457–9434 or 800/858–3812* ⊕ *www.
qualityinnportangeles.com* ⇆ *51 rooms* ⚭ *In-room: kitchen (some),
refrigerator, Wi-Fi. In-hotel: Wi-Fi* ⊟ *AE, D, DC, MC, V* ⊚ *BP.*

Petrified Forest
National Park

WORD OF MOUTH

"If you are close by, a couple of hours is worth doing. I have seen
petrified trees at a couple of other spots, and this place is KING
of the Petrified Trees. Lots of them."

—spirobulldog

WELCOME TO PETRIFIED FOREST

TOP REASONS TO GO

★ **Terrific timber:** Be mesmerized by the clusters of petrified (fossilized) wood. The trees look like they're made of colorful stone.

★ **Route 66 kicks:** Put the top down on the Chevrolet. A section of the fabled road is preserved in the park, the only section of the highway protected in a national park.

★ **Triassic treasures:** Find an oasis of water in the desert, or at least evidence that it once existed. Clam fossils in the park indicate that waterways once prevailed where sand, stone, and trees now define the land.

★ **Corps creations:** Say thanks to FDR. The Painted Desert Inn, a National Historic Landmark, was modernized by the Civilian Conservation Corps (CCC) during the throes of the Great Depression. The recently renovated building is now a museum and bookstore.

1 Painted Desert. The main area of the park, in the northern section, is where park headquarters, the Painted Desert Inn, and Route 66 are located. It's also the best place for hiking. A permit is required for overnight camping in the wilderness area, but day users need not obtain one. The 28-mi park road begins here, off Interstate 40.

2 Blue Mesa. In the heart of the Painted Desert, this 1-mi loop trail begins off a loop road accessed from the park road. Petrified trees lie among hills of bluish bentonite clay.

3 Rainbow Forest Museum. Get a trail guide here for the short Giant Logs Trail located behind the museum, and keep an eye out for Old Faithful, a log almost 10 feet wide. The southern terminus for the park road is here.

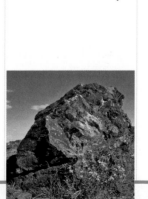

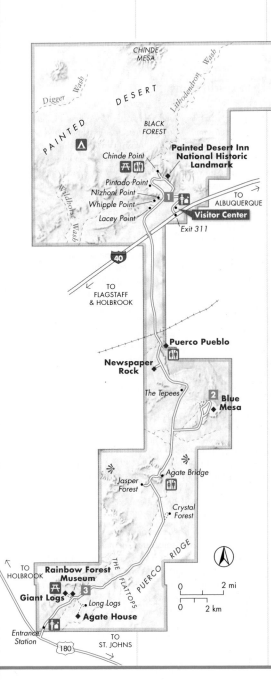

ARIZONA

GETTING ORIENTED

There are few places where the span of geologic and human history is as wide or apparent as it is at Petrified Forest National Park. Fossilized trees and countless other fossils date back to the Triassic Period, while a stretch of the famed Route 66 of more modern lore is protected within park boundaries. Ancestors of the Hopi, Zuni, and Navajo left petroglyphs, pottery, and even structures built of petrified wood. Nine park sites are on the National Register of Historic Places; the Painted Desert Inn is one of only 3% of such sites that are further listed as National Historic Landmarks.

30

KEY	
👫	Ranger Station
🔺	Campground
🌲	Picnic Area
🍴	Restaurant
🏨	Lodge
🚶	Trailhead
🚻	Restrooms
✳	Scenic Viewpoint
⋯⋯	Walking/Hiking Trails

PETRIFIED FOREST PLANNER

When to Go

The park is rarely crowded. **The best time to visit is in the autumn,** when nights are chilly but daytime temperatures hover near 70°F. Half of all yearly rain falls between June and August, so it's a good time to spot blooming wildflowers. In winter there are cold winds and occasional snow.

Festivals and Events

For details, call the park at ☎ 928/524–6228.

MAY National Wildflower Week. Activities include wildflower walks and an interactive wildflower display.

DEC. Petrified Forest Park Anniversary. A national monument since 1906 and a national park since 1962, Petrified Forest throws a party for its birthday, with homemade cider, cookies, and cultural demonstrations.

AVG. HIGH/LOW TEMPS.

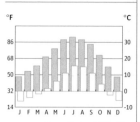

Flora and Fauna

Engelmann asters and sunflowers are among the blooms in the park each summer. Juniper trees, cottonwoods, and willows grow along Puerco River Wash, providing shelter for all manner of wildlife. You might spot mule deer, coyotes, prairie dogs, and foxes, although other inhabitants, like porcupines and bobcats, tend to hide. Bird-watchers should keep an eye out for mockingbirds, red-tailed and Swainson's hawks, roadrunners, swallows, and hummingbirds. Look for all three kinds of lizards—collared, side-blotched, and southern prairie—in rocks.

Beware of rattlesnakes. They are common but can generally be avoided if you use sense: Watch where you step, and don't step anywhere you can't see. If you do come across a rattler, give it plenty of space, and let it go its way before you continue yours. Other reptiles—and there are plenty—are just as common but not as worrisome. The gopher snake looks similar to a rattlesnake, but is nonpoisonous. The collared lizard, with its yellow head, can be seen scurrying out of your way just about everywhere in bursts measured at up to 15 MPH. They are not poisonous, but will bite in the rare instance of being caught.

Getting Here and Around

The nearest major airports are in Phoenix, AZ (259 mi away via U.S. 17 and U.S. 40), and Albuquerque, NM (204 mi distant via U.S. 40). Holbrook, the nearest large town, is roughly 20 mi from either of the park's two entrances on U.S. 40. By train you can take Amtrak to Flagstaff and Winslow (☎ 928/774–8679).

Parking is free, and there's ample space at all trailheads, as well as at the visitor center and the museum. The main park road extends 28 mi from the Painted Desert Visitor Center (north entrance) to the Rainbow Forest Museum (south entrance). For park road conditions, call ☎ 928/524–6228. For area road conditions, call the state of Arizona's road conditions line, ☎ 511, from any phone.

by Cara
LaBrie

Petrified logs scattered about a vast pink-hued lunarlike land-scape resemble a fairy-tale forest turned to stone at Petri-fied Forest National Park. The park's 218,533 acres, which include portions of the Painted Desert, are covered with petri-fied tree trunks whose wood cells were fossilized over centuries by brightly hued mineral deposits—silica, iron oxide, carbon, manganese, aluminum, copper, and lithium. The park holds plenty of other fossils; remnants of humans and their artifacts have been recovered at more than 500 sites in the park.

PARK ESSENTIALS

ACCESSIBILITY

The visitor center, museum, and overlooks on the scenic drive are wheel-chair accessible. All trails are paved, and all are accessible except Blue Mesa, which is very steep. For more information, call the park switch-board at ☎ 928/524–6228.

ADMISSION FEES AND PERMITS

Entrance fees are $10 per car for seven consecutive days or $5 per person on foot, bicycle, motorcycle, or bus. Permits are required for back-country hiking and camping, and are free (limit of 15 days) at Painted Desert Visitor Center or the Rainbow Forest Museum before 4 PM.

ADMISSION HOURS

The park is open daily 7 AM–7 PM late May through early September and daily 8 AM–5 PM from early September through late May. The park is in the mountain time zone.

PARK CONTACT INFORMATION

Petrified Forest National Park ✉ 1 Park Rd., Petrified Forest, AZ ☎ 928/524–6228 ⊕ www.nps.gov/pefo.

30

Different minerals in different concentrations create the rich colors in petrified wood.

SCENIC DRIVE

Painted Desert Scenic Drive. A 28-mi scenic drive takes you through the park from one entrance to the other. If you begin from the north, the first 5 mi of the drive takes you along the edge of a high mesa, with spectacular views of Painted Desert. Beyond lies the desolate Painted Desert Wilderness Area. After the 5 mi point, the road crosses Interstate 40, then swings south toward the Puerco River across a landscape covered with sagebrush, saltbrush, sunflowers, and Apache plume. Past the river, the road climbs onto a narrow mesa leading to Newspaper Rock, a panel of Pueblo Indian rock art. Then the road bends southeast, enters a barren stretch, and passes teepee-shaped buttes in the distance. Next you come to Blue Mesa, roughly the park's midpoint and a good place to stop for views of petrified logs. The next stop on the drive is Agate Bridge, really a 100-foot log over a wide wash. The remaining overlooks are Jasper Forest and Crystal Forest, where you can get a further glimpse of the accumulated petrified wood. On your way out of the park, stop at the Rainbow Forest Museum for a rest and to shop for a memento. ⊠ *Begins at Painted Desert Visitor Center.*

WHAT TO SEE

Though named for its famous fossilized trees, Petrified Forest has something to see for history buffs of all stripes, from a segment of Route 66 to ancient dwellings to even more ancient fossils. And the good thing is that most of Petrified Forest's treasures can easily be viewed without a great amount of athletic conditioning. Much can be seen by driving

PETRIFIED FOREST IN ONE DAY

A nonstop drive through the park (28 mi) takes only 45 minutes, but you can spend most of a day exploring if you stop along the way. From almost any vantage point you can see the multicolored rocks and hills that were home to prehistoric humans and ancient dinosaurs.

Entering the park from the north, stop at **Painted Desert Visitor Center** and see a 20-minute introductory film. **Painted Desert Inn visitor center**, 2 mi south of the north entrance, provides further orientation in the form of guided ranger tours. Drive south 8 mi to reach **Puerco Pueblo**, a 100-room pueblo built before 1400. Continuing south, you'll find Puebloan petroglyphs at **Newspaper Rock** and, just beyond, **the Teepees**, cone-shaped rock

formations covered with manganese and other minerals.

Blue Mesa is roughly the midpoint of the drive, and the start of a 1-mi, moderately steep loop hike that leads you around badland hills made of bentonite clay. Drive on for 5 mi until you come to **Jasper Forest**, just past **Agate Bridge**, with views of the landscape strewn with petrified logs. **Crystal Forest**, 18 mi south of the north entrance, is named for the smoky quartz, amethyst, and citrine along the 0.8-mi loop trail. **Rainbow Forest Museum**, at the park's south entrance, has restrooms, a bookstore, and exhibits. Just behind Rainbow Forest Museum is **Giant Logs**, a 0.4-mi loop that takes you to Old Faithful, the largest log in the park, estimated to weigh 44 tons

along the main road, from which historic sites are readily accessible. By combining a drive along the park road with a short hike here and there and a visit to one of the park's landmarks, you can see most of the sights in as little as half a day.

HISTORIC SITES

Agate House. This eight-room pueblo is thought to have been built entirely of petrified wood 700 years ago. Researchers believe it might have been used as a temporary dwelling by seasonal farmers or traders from one of the area tribes. ⊠ *Rainbow Forest Museum parking area.*

Newspaper Rock. See huge boulders covered with petroglyphs believed to have been carved by the Pueblo Indians more than 500 years ago. ⊠ *6 mi south of Painted Desert Visitor Center on the main park road.*

Painted Desert Inn National Historic Site. You'll find cultural-history exhibits, as well as the murals of Fred Kabotie, a popular 1940s artist whose work was commissioned by Mary Jane Colter. American Indian crafts are displayed in this museum and mini visitor center. Check the schedule for daily events. ⊠ *2 mi north of Painted Desert Visitor Center on the main park road* 🕿 *928/524–6228* ⊕ *www.nps.gov/pefo* 🎟 *Free* ☉ *Late May–early Sept., daily 7–7; early Sept.–late May, daily 8–5.*

Puerco Pueblo. This is a 100-room pueblo, built before 1400 and said to have housed Ancestral Puebloan people. Many visitors come to see petroglyphs, as well as a solar calendar. ⊠ *10 mi south of the Painted Desert Visitor Center on the main park road.*

30

SCENIC STOPS

★ **Agate Bridge.** Here you'll see a 100-foot log spanning a 40-foot-wide wash. ⊠ *19 mi south of Painted Desert Visitor Center on the main park road.*

Crystal Forest. The fragments of petrified wood strewn here once held clear quartz and amethyst crystals. ⊠ *20 mi south of Painted Desert Visitor Center on the main park road.*

★ **Giant Logs.** A short walk leads you past the park's largest log, known as Old Faithful. It's considered the largest because of its diameter (9 feet, 9 inches), as well as how tall it once was. ⊠ *28 mi south of Painted Desert Visitor Center on the main park road.*

Jasper Forest. More of an overlook than a forest, this spot has a large concentration of petrified trees in jasper or red. ⊠ *17 mi south of Painted Desert Visitor Center on the main park road.*

The Teepees. Witness the effects of time on these cone-shaped rock formations colored by iron, manganese, and other minerals. ⊠ *8 mi south of Painted Desert Visitor Center on the main park road.*

VISITOR CENTERS

Painted Desert Inn National Historic Site. This visitor center isn't as large as the other two, but here you can get information as well as view cultural history exhibits. ⊠ *2 mi north of Painted Desert Visitor Center on the main park road* ☎ *928/524–6228* ☉ *Late May–early Sept., daily 7–7; early Sept.–late May, daily 8–5.*

Painted Desert Visitor Center. This is the place to go for general park information and an informative 20-minute film on the park. Proceeds from books purchased here will fund continued research and interpretive activities for the park. ⊠ *North entrance, off I–40, 27 mi east of Holbrook* ☎ *928/524–6228* ☉ *Visitor center late May– early Sept., daily 7–7; early Sept.–late May, daily 8–5. Post office weekdays 11–1.*

Rainbow Forest Museum and Visitor Center. The museum houses artifacts of early reptiles, dinosaurs, and petrified wood. Be sure to see Gurtie, a skeleton of a phytosaur, a crocodile-like carnivore. ⊠ *South entrance, off U.S. 180, 18 mi southeast of Holbrook* ☎ *928/524–6228* ☉ *Labor Day–Memorial Day, daily 8–5; Labor Day–Memorial Day, daily 7–7.*

SPORTS AND THE OUTDOORS

As with visits to all national parks, you don't get the full experience unless you take time to smell the roses—or in this case, get close enough to see the multihued lines streaking a petrified log. However, because the park goes to great pains to maintain the integrity of the fossil- and artifact-strewn landscape, sports and outdoor options in the park are limited. Off-highway activity is restricted to on-trail hiking and horseback riding.

HIKING

All trails begin off the main road, with restrooms at or near the trailheads. Most maintained trails are relatively short, paved, clearly marked, and, with a few exceptions, easy to moderate in difficulty. Hikers with greater stamina can make their own trails in the wilderness area, located just north of the Painted Desert Visitor Center. Watch your step for rattlesnakes, which are common in the park—if left alone and given a wide berth, they are passed easily enough.

EASY

Crystal Forest Trail. The easy 0.8-mi loop leads you past petrified wood that once held quartz crystals and amethyst chips. ⊠ *Trailhead: 20 mi south of the Painted Desert Visitor Center.*

Giant Logs Trail. At 0.4 mi, Giant Logs is the park's shortest trail. The loop leads you to Old Faithful, the park's largest petrified log—9 feet, 9 inches at its base, weighing an estimated 44 tons. ⊠ *Trailhead: directly behind Rainbow Forest Museum, 28 mi south of Painted Desert Visitor Center.*

Long Logs Trail. Although barren, the easy 0.6-mi loop passes the largest concentration of wood in the park. ⊠ *Trailhead: 26 mi south of Painted Desert Visitor Center.*

♻ **Puerco Pueblo Trail.** A relatively flat and interesting 0.3-mi trail takes you past remains of a home of the Ancestral Puebloan people, built before 1400. The trail is paved and wheelchair accessible. ⊠ *Trailhead: 10 mi south of Painted Desert Visitor Center.*

MODERATE

Fodor's Choice ★ **Agate House.** A fairly flat 1-mi trip takes you to an eight-room pueblo sitting high on a knoll (⇨ *Historic Sites, in What to See*). ⊠ *Trailhead: 26 mi south of Painted Desert Visitor Center.*

Blue Mesa. Although it's only 1 mi long and it's significantly steeper than the rest, this trail at the park's midway point is one of the most popular. ⊠ *Trailhead: 14 mi south of Painted Desert Visitor Center.*

Painted Desert Rim. The 1-mi trail is at its best in early morning or late afternoon, when the sun accentuates the brilliant red, blue, purple, and other hues of the desert and petrified forest landscape. ⊠ *Trail runs between Tawa Point and Kachina Point, 1 mi north of Painted Desert Visitor Center; drive to either point from Visitor Center.*

DIFFICULT

Kachina Point. This is the trailhead for wilderness hiking. A 1-mi trail leads to the Wilderness Area, but from there you're on your own. With no developed trails, hiking here is cross-country style, but expect to see strange formations, beautifully colored landscape, and maybe, just maybe, a pronghorn antelope. ⊠ *Trailhead: on the northwest side of the Painted Desert Inn Museum.*

EDUCATIONAL OFFERINGS

RANGER PROGRAMS

Ranger Walks and Talks. Park rangers lead regular programs along the Great Logs Trail, inside the Painted Desert Inn Museum, and to the Puerco Pueblo. You can view which ranger programs are currently being offered at the visitor centers or online at ⊕ *www.nps.gov/pefo.*

Special tours. Ask at either park visitor center for the availability of special ranger-led tours, such as the after-hours lantern tour of the Painted Desert Inn Museum.

30

CLOSE UP

Petroglyphs: The Writing on the Wall

Like some other historic sites in eastern Arizona, Petrified Forest National Park is a great place to view petroglyphs and pictographs—designs pecked or scratched into the stone are called petroglyphs; those that are painted on the surface are pictographs. Few pictographs remain because of the deleterious effects of weathering, but the more durable petroglyphs number in the thousands.

WHERE TO FIND IT

The rock art of early American Indians is carved or painted on basalt boulders, on canyon walls, and on the underside of overhangs throughout the area. No one knows the exact meaning of these signs, and interpretations vary; they have been seen as elements in shamanistic or hunting rituals, as clan signs, maps, or even indications of visits by extraterrestrials.

Damaged by vandalism, many rock-art sites are not open to the public. Two good petroglyphs to check out are Newspaper Rock, an overlook near mile marker 12, and the Puerco Pueblo Trail near mile marker 11. Other sites in Arizona include Hieroglyphic Point in Salt River Canyon, Five-Mile Canyon in Snowflake, and Lyman Lake State Park.

DETERMINING ITS AGE

It's just as difficult to date a "glyph" as it is to understand it. Archaeologists try to determine a general time frame by judging the style, the date of the ruins and pottery in the vicinity, the amount of patination (formation of minerals) on the design, or the superimposition of newer images on top of older ones. Most of eastern Arizona's rock art is estimated to be at least 1,000 years old, and many of the glyphs were created even earlier.

VARIETY OF IMAGES

Some glyphs depict animals like bighorn sheep, deer, bear, and mountain lions; others are geometric patterns. The most unusual are the anthropomorphs, strange humanlike figures with elaborate headdresses. Concentric circles are a common design. A few of these circles served as solstice signs, indicating the summer and winter solstice and other important dates. At a certain time in the year, when the angle of the sun is just right, a shaft of light shines through a crack in a nearby rock, illuminating the center of the circle. Archaeologists believe that these solar calendars helped determine the time for ceremonies and planting.

Many solstice signs are in remote regions, but you can visit the Petrified Forest National Park around June 20 to see a concentric circle illuminated during the summer solstice. The glyph, reached by paved trail just a few hundred yards from the parking area, is visible year-round, but a finger of light shines directly in the center during the week of the solstice. The phenomenon occurs at 9 AM, a reasonable hour for looking at the calendar.

■TIP➔ Do not touch petroglyphs or pictographs—the oils from your hands can cause damage to the image.

—Janet Webb Farnsworth

The stones tell a story with ancient sketchings on Newspaper Rock.

🐾 **Junior Ranger.** Children 12 and younger can learn more about the park's extensive human, animal, and geologic history as they train to become a Junior Ranger.

WHAT'S NEARBY

Located in eastern Arizona just off Interstate 40, Petrified Forest National Park is set in an area of grasslands, overlooked by mountains in the distance. At nearly an hour from American Indian Nations, nearly two hours from Flagstaff and three hours from the Grand Canyon, the park is relatively remote and separated from many comforts of travel. Just a half-hour away, Holbrook, the nearest town, is the best place to grab a quick bite to eat or a brief rest.

NEARBY ATTRACTIONS

★ **Canyon de Chelly National Monument.** Home to Ancestral Puebloans from AD 350 to 1300, the nearly 84,000-acre Canyon de Chelly (pronounced d'*shay*) is one of the most spectacular natural wonders in the Southwest. On a smaller scale, it rivals the Grand Canyon for beauty. Its main gorges—the 26-mi-long Canyon de Chelly (Canyon in the Rock) and the adjoining 35-mi Canyon del Muerto (Canyon of the Dead)—comprise sheer, heavily eroded sandstone walls that rise to 1,100 feet above streams, hogans, tilled fields, and sheep-grazing lands. Ancient pictographs and petroglyphs decorate some of the cliffs, and within the canyon complex there are more than 7,000 archaeological sites. ✉ *Indian Hwy. 7, 3 mi* *east of U.S. 191, Chinle* ☎ *928/674–5500 visitor center* ⊕ *www.nps.gov/cach* ✉ *Free* ⊙ *Daily 8–5.*

★ **Homolovi Ruins State Park.** *Homolovi* is a Hopi word meaning "place of the little hills." The pueblo sites here are thought to have been occupied between AD 1200 and 1425, and include 40 ceremonial kivas and two pueblos containing more than 1,000 rooms each. Weekdays in June and July you can see archaeologists working the site. Rangers conduct guided tours. The Homolovi Visitor Center has a small museum with Hopi pottery and Ancestral Puebloan artifacts; it also hosts workshops on native art, ethnobotany, and traditional foods. ✉ *AZ 87, 5 mi northeast of Winslow, 53 mi east of Flagstaff, 33 mi west of Holbrook; exit 257 off I–40.* ⌂ *HCR 63, Box 5, Winslow 86047* ☎ *928/289–4106* ⊕ *www.azstateparks.com* ✉ *$5* ⊙ *Visitor center daily 8–5.*

> ## LOOK AND TOUCH, BUT DON'T TAKE!
>
> One of the most commonly asked questions about the Petrified Forest is, "Can I touch the wood?" Fortunately, yes! Park rangers encourage visitors to use their sense that's often ignored at museums and historical sites: touch. Feel comfortable to touch anything, pick it up, inspect it … just make sure you put it back exactly where you found it. Some of the park's visitor centers also have "touching tables" where you can more comfortably interact with objects. Feel free to ask questions and feel your way through the experience.

Rock Art Ranch. The Ancestral Puebloan petroglyphs of this working cattle ranch in Chevelon Canyon, are startlingly vivid after more than 1,000 years. Ranch owner Brantly Baird will guide you along the 0.25-mi trail, explaining western and archaeological history. It's mostly easy walking, except for the climb in and out of Chevelon Canyon, where there are handrails. Baird houses his American Indian artifacts and pioneer farming implements in his own private museum. It's out of the way and on a dirt road, but you'll see some of the best rock art in northern Arizona. Reservations are required. ✉ *Off AZ 87, 13 mi southeast of Winslow* ⌂ *P.O. Box 224, Joseph City 85032* ☎ *928/386–5047* ✉ *Fee varies* ⊙ *May–Oct., by appointment only.*

SHOPPING

McGee's Indian Art Gallery (✉ *2114 E. Navajo Blvd.* ☎ *928/524–1977 or 800/524–9183* ⊕ *www.hopiart.com*) is the area's premier source of high-quality American Indian jewelry, rugs, Hopi baskets, and kachina dolls. The owners have longstanding relationships with reservation artisans and a knowledgeable staff that adroitly assists first-time buyers and seasoned collectors.

WHERE TO EAT AND STAY

ABOUT THE RESTAURANTS

Dining in the park is limited to a cafeteria in the Painted Desert Visitor Center and snacks in the Rainbow Forest Museum. In and around the Navajo and Hopi reservations, be sure to sample Indian tacos, an authentic treat made with scrumptious fry bread, beans, and chilies. If you're searching for burgers-and-fries fare, Holbrook is your best bet.

ABOUT THE HOTELS

There is no lodging within Petrified Forest. Outside the park, lodging choices include modern resorts, rustic cabins, and small bed-and-breakfasts. Note that air-conditioning is not a standard amenity in the mountains, where the nights are cool enough for a blanket even in summer. Closer to the Navajo and Hopi reservations many establishments are run by American Indians, tribal enterprises intent on offering first-class service and hospitality. Nearby Holbrook offers most national chain hotels and comfortable accommodations.

ABOUT THE CAMPGROUNDS

There are no campgrounds in the park. Backpack, minimal-impact camping is allowed in a designated zone north of Lithodendron Wash in the Wilderness Area; a free permit must be obtained (pick up at the visitor center or museum), and group size is limited to eight. RVs are not allowed. There are no fire pits or designated sites, nor is any shade available. Note that if it rains, that pretty Painted Desert formation turns to sticky clay.

WHERE TO EAT

IN THE PARK

¢–$ ✕ **Painted Desert Visitor Center Cafeteria.** Serving standard cafeteria fare,
AMERICAN this is the only place in the park where you can get a full meal. ✉ *North entrance* ☎ *928/524–6228* ▭ *MC, V.*

PICNIC AREAS **Chinde Point Picnic Area.** Near the north entrance, this small spot has tables and restrooms. ✉ *2 mi north of Painted Desert Visitor Center.*

Rainbow Forest Museum Picnic Area. Near the south entrance, this small site has tables and restrooms. ✉ *Off I–40, 27 mi east of Holbrook.*

OUTSIDE THE PARK

$$ ✕ **Mesa Italiana Restaurant.** While getting your kicks on Route 66, stop by
ITALIAN to enjoy a hearty meal at one of Holbrook's most popular restaurants, where the chef prepares authentic-tasting traditional Italian dishes. Locals recommend the fresh pasta, including the spaghetti with Italian mushrooms. Don't forget the spumoni for dessert. For a more low-key environment, check out its adjoining grill that serves up burgers and steak. ✉ *2318 E. Navajo Blvd., Holbrook* ☎ *928/524–6696* ▭ *AE, D, MC, V* ☺ *No lunch.*

WHERE TO STAY

IN THE PARK

CAMPING ⚠ **Wilderness Area.** Backcountry camping is allowed year-round in a
¢ designated zone with a free permit and park admission fee. **Pros:** ideal
(FREE) for serious campers who want to sleep in a completely rustic environment with no comforts of home. **Cons:** no access to your cars at night; no water; probably not kid-friendly; not recommended for beginner campers. ✉ *North of Lithodendron Wash* ☎ *928/524–6228.*

30

OUTSIDE THE PARK

$ 🏨 **Holbrook Days Inn.** This clean, simple hotel has free Continental breakfast and local phone calls; it's a pleasant, convenient choice for a good price. Rooms have coffeemakers, hair dryers, and cable TV. **Pros:** heated indoor pool and hot tub; close to local restaurants. **Cons:** lacks the historic charm of most of its lodging neighbors. ⊠ *2601 Navajo Blvd.* 🕾 *928/524–6949* ⊕ *www.daysinn.com* ⟿ *52 rooms, 3 suites* ♿ *In-room: refrigerator (some), Wi-Fi. In-hotel: pool, laundry facilities* ▤ *AE, D, MC, V* ⦶⦶ *CP.*

$$–$$$ 🏨 **La Posada Winslow.** One of the great railroad hotels, La Posada (Resting Place) exudes the charm of an 18th-century Spanish hacienda. Architect Mary Colter, famous for her work at the Grand Canyon, designed and decorated the 68,000-square-foot hotel. Spanish and American Indian furniture, antiques, and art permeate her designs. The lobby is a gallery for paintings by Tina Mion, one of the owners. Individually decorated rooms are restored to 1930s style, and the lush gardens are a swath of green in the red-rock Colorado Plateau. Ongoing renovations will open La Posada's East Wing for the first time in 2010, and add 14 rooms to the property. If you can't stay for the night, take a self-guided tour of the hotel ($3 donation). **Pros:** historic charm; unique architecture. **Cons:** dated rooms; ongoing renovations. ⊠ *303 E. 2nd St., Winslow* 🕾 *928/289–4366* ⊕ *www.laposada.org* ⟿ *37 rooms* ♿ *In-room: no phone. In-hotel: restaurant, bar* ▤ *AE, D, MC, V.*

¢–$ 🏨 **Wigwam Motel.** One of the iconic images of Route 66 and listed on the National Register of Historic Places, the Wigwam consists of 15 bright-white concrete teepees where you can sleep inexpensively in a quirky environment. As you might expect, wigwams are phoneless, but—here's to Mother Progress—these have cable TV. A small lobby museum exhibits Mexican, American Indian, and military relics collected by the owner's family. The 180-pound, polished, petrified-wood sphere is one of the largest in the Southwest. All of the classic cars parked by the teepees also belong to the owners. **Pros:** impeccably kitschy; one of the signature spots along Route 66. **Cons:** very sparse accommodations. ⊠ *711 W. Hopi Dr.* 🕾 *928/524–3048* ⊕ *www.galerie-kokopelli.com/wigwam* ⟿ *15 rooms* ♿ *In-room: no phone* ▤ *MC, V.*

CAMPING ⛺ **Fool Hollow Lake Recreational Area.** In addition to camping, this year-
¢ round park is popular for boating, fishing, and wildlife-viewing. Set
(FREE) amid a piney 800 acres, a lake is stocked with rainbow trout, walleye, and bass. Camping here is free with recreational area admission fee ($6). **Pros:** year-round camping; beautiful setting in a ponderosa pine forest, modern conveniences such as restrooms. **Cons:** can be cold in winter months; far from Petrified Forest (two hours at least). ⊠ *1500 N. Fool Hollow Lake Rd., 2 mi north of U.S. 60 off AZ 260* 🕾 *928/537–3680* ⛺ *31 tent sites, 92 RV sites* ♿ *Showers, grills, picnic tables, play area.*

Redwood
National Park

WORD OF MOUTH

"September is a great time for the redwoods and the coast. The 'best' weather of the year starts after labor day. At that time of the year, if the sky is clear, the groves are spectacular about an hour before sunset."

—GP

WELCOME TO REDWOOD

TOP REASONS TO GO

★ **Giant trees:** These mature coastal redwoods are the tallest trees in the world.

★ **Hiking to the sea:** The park's trails wind between majestic redwood groves, and many connect to the Coastal Trail running along the western edge of the park.

★ **Rare wildlife:** Mighty Roosevelt elk favor the park's flat prairie and open lands; seldom-seen black bears roam the backcountry; trout and salmon leap through streams, and Pacific gray whales swim along the coast during their biannual migrations.

★ **Stepping back in time:** Hike Fern Canyon Trail, which weaves through a prehistoric scene of lush vegetation and giant ferns.

★ **Cheeps, not beeps:** Amid the majestic redwoods you're out of range for cell-phone service—and in range for the soothing sounds of warblers and burbling creeks.

1 Del Norte Coast Redwoods State Park. The rugged terrain of this far northwest corner of California combines stretches of treacherous surf, steep cliffs, and forested ridges. On a clear day it's postcard-perfect; with fog, it's mysteriously mesmerizing.

2 Jedediah Smith Redwoods State Park. Gargantuan old growth redwoods dominate the scenery here. The Smith River cuts through canyons and splits across boulders, carrying salmon to the inland creeks where they spawn.

3 Prairie Creek Redwoods State Park. The forests here give way to spacious, grassy plains where abundant wildlife thrives. Roosevelt elk are a common sight in the meadows and down to Gold Bluffs Beach.

4 Orick Area. The highlight of the southern portion of Redwood National Park is the Tall Trees Grove. It's difficult to reach and requires a special pass, but it's worth the hassle—this section has the tallest coast redwood trees, with a new record holder discovered in 2006.

31

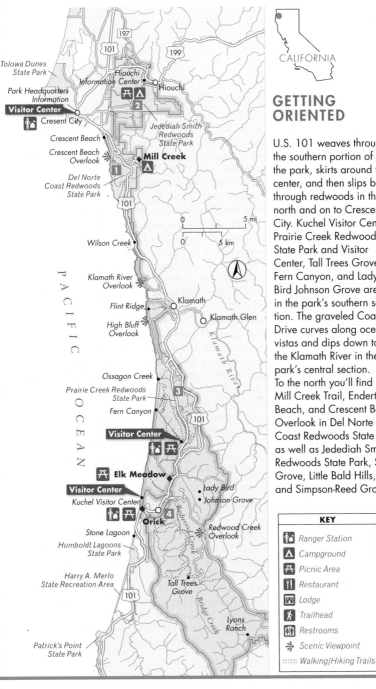

CALIFORNIA

GETTING ORIENTED

U.S. 101 weaves through the southern portion of the park, skirts around the center, and then slips back through redwoods in the north and on to Crescent City. Kuchel Visitor Center, Prairie Creek Redwoods State Park and Visitor Center, Tall Trees Grove, Fern Canyon, and Lady Bird Johnson Grove are all in the park's southern section. The graveled Coastal Drive curves along ocean vistas and dips down to the Klamath River in the park's central section. To the north you'll find Mill Creek Trail, Enderts Beach, and Crescent Beach Overlook in Del Norte Coast Redwoods State Park as well as Jedediah Smith Redwoods State Park, Stout Grove, Little Bald Hills, and Simpson-Reed Grove.

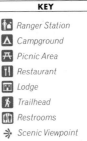

KEY	
👫	Ranger Station
◭	Campground
🛆	Picnic Area
🍴	Restaurant
🏨	Lodge
🥾	Trailhead
🚻	Restrooms
☀	Scenic Viewpoint
⋯⋯	Walking/Hiking Trails

REDWOOD PLANNER

When to Go

Campers and hikers flock to the park from mid-June to early September. Crowds disappear in winter, but you'll have to contend with frequent rains and nasty potholes on side roads. Temperatures fluctuate widely throughout the park: the foggy coastal lowland is much cooler than the higher-altitude interior.

The average annual rainfall here is 90 to 100 inches, and during dry summer months thick fog rolling in from the Pacific veils the forests, giving redwoods a large portion of their moisture intake.

AVG. HIGH/LOW TEMPS.

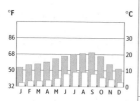

Flora and Fauna

Coast redwoods, the world's tallest trees (a new record holder, topping out at 379 feet, was found within the park in 2006) grow in the moist, temperate climate of California's North Coast. These ancient giants thrive in an environment that exists in only a few hundred coastal miles along the Pacific Ocean. They commonly live 600 years—though some have been around for 2,000 years.

A healthy redwood forest is diverse and includes Douglas firs, western hemlocks, tan oaks, and madrone trees. The complex soils of the forest floor support a verdant profusion of ferns, mosses, and fungi, along with numerous shrubs and berry bushes. In spring, California rhododendron bloom throughout the forest, providing a dazzling purple and pink contrast to the dense greenery.

Redwood National Park holds 45% of all California's old-growth redwood forests. Of the original 3,125 square mi (2 million acres) in the Redwoods Historic Range, only 4% remain following the logging that began in 1850; 1% is privately owned and managed, and 3% is on public land.

In the park's backcountry, you might spot mountain lions, black bears, black-tailed deer, river otters, beavers, and minks. Roosevelt elk roam the flatlands, and the rivers and streams teem with salmon and trout. Gray whales, seals, and sea lions cavort near the coastline. And thanks to the area's location along the Pacific Flyway, an amazing 402 species of birds have been sighted here.

Getting Here and Around

U.S. 101 runs north–south along the park, and Highway 199 cuts east–west through its northern portion. Access routes off 101 include Bald Hills Road, Davison Road, Newton B. Drury Scenic Parkway, Coastal Drive, Requa Road, and Enderts Beach Road. From 199 take South Fork Road to Howland Hill Road. Many of the park's roads aren't paved, and winter rains can turn them into obstacle courses; sometimes they're closed completely. RVs and trailers aren't permitted on some routes.

By Christine Vovakes

Soaring to more than 300 feet, the coastal redwoods that give this park its name are miracles of efficiency—some have survived hundreds of years (a few live for more than 2,000 years). These massive trees glean nutrients from the rich alluvial flats at their feet and from the moisture and nitrogen trapped in their uneven canopy. Their huge, thick-barked trunks can hold thousands of gallons of water, reservoirs that have helped them withstand centuries of firestorms.

PARK ESSENTIALS

ACCESSIBILITY
Park maps indicate which camping, picnic, and other areas are wheelchair accessible. Such spots include the visitor centers, Crescent Beach, Crescent Beach Overlook, Lagoon Creek, Klamath Overlook, High Bluff Overlook, Big Tree Wayside, and Lost Man Creek picnic areas.

ADMISSION FEES AND PERMITS
Admission to Redwood National Park is free. There's a $8 day-use fee to enter one or all of Redwood's state parks; for camping at these state parks it's an additional $35. To visit Tall Trees Grove, you must get a free permit at the Kuchel Information Center in Orick. Permits also are needed to camp in Redwood Creek backcountry.

ADMISSION HOURS
The park is open year-round, 24 hours a day.

ATMS/BANKS
There are no ATMs in Redwood. The nearest ATM and bank is in Crescent City.

CELL-PHONE RECEPTION
It's difficult to pick up a signal in the parks, especially in the camping and hiking areas. If you need a public telephone, go to the Prairie Creek or Jedediah Smith visitor center.

PARK CONTACT INFORMATION
Redwood National Park ⊠ 1111 2nd St., Crescent City, CA ☎ 707/465–7306
⊕ www.nps.gov/redw.

SCENIC DRIVES

★ **Coastal Drive.** This 8-mi, partially paved road is closed to trailers and RVs and takes about one hour to drive one way. The slow pace alongside stands of redwoods offers close-up views of the Klamath River and expansive panoramas of the Pacific. From here you'll find access to the Flint Ridge section of the Coastal Trail.

Howland Hill Road/Stout Grove. Take your time as you drive this 10 mi route along Mill Creek, which winds through old-growth redwoods and past the Smith River. Trailers and RVs are prohibited on this route.

Newton B. Drury Scenic Parkway/Big Tree Wayside. This 10-mi track, open to all non-commercial vehicles, threads through Prairie Creek Redwoods State Park and old-growth redwoods. Just north of the Prairie Creek Visitor Center you can make the 0.8-mi walk to Big Tree Wayside and observe Roosevelt elk in the prairie.

WHAT TO SEE

SCENIC STOPS

Crescent Beach Overlook. The scenery here includes ocean views and, in the distance, Crescent City and its working harbor; in balmy weather this is a great place for a picnic. From the overlook you can spot migrating gray whales November through December and March through April. ⊠ 2 mi south of Crescent City off Enderts Beach Rd.

★ **Fern Canyon.** Enter another world and be surrounded by 30-foot canyon walls covered with sword, maidenhair, and five-finger ferns. Allow an hour to explore the ¼-mi long vertical garden along a 0.7-mi loop. From the north end of Gold Bluffs Beach it's an easy walk, although you'll have to wade across a small stream several times (in addition to driving across streams on the way to the parking area). But the lush surroundings are otherworldly, and worth a visit when creeks aren't running too high. Be aware that RVs longer than 24 feet and all trailers are not allowed here. ⊠ 10 mi northwest of Prairie Creek Visitor Center, via Davison Rd. off U.S. 101.

Lady Bird Johnson Grove. This section of the park was dedicated by, and named for, the former first lady. A 1-mi, wheelchair-accessible nature loop follows an old logging road through a mature redwood forest. Allow 45 minutes to complete the trail. ⊠ 5 mi east of Kuchel Visitor Center, along U.S. 101 and Bald Hills Rd.

Redwoods State Parks. The three state parks have miles of trails that lead to magnificent redwood groves and overlooks with views of sea lion colonies and migrating whales. Birds inhabit bluffs, lagoons, and offshore rocks. All three parks are open year-round and have ranger programs for children, as well as ranger-led talks. Admission is $8 per day.

REDWOOD IN ONE DAY

31

Head south on U.S. 101. About a mile south of Klamath, detour onto the 8-mi-long, partially paved **Coastal Drive** (trailers and RVs not allowed), which loops north before reaching the ocean. Along the way, you'll pass the old **Douglas Memorial Bridge**, destroyed in the 1964 flood. Coastal Drive turns south above Flint Ridge. In less than a mile you'll reach the **World War II Radar Station**, which looks like a farmhouse, its disguise in the 1940s. Continue south to the intersection with Alder Camp Road, stopping at the **High Bluff Overlook**.

From the Coastal Drive turn left to reconnect with U.S. 101, or turn right onto **Newton B. Drury Scenic Parkway**, a 10-mi drive through an old-growth redwood forest with access to numerous trailheads. (This road is open to all noncommercial vehicles). Along the way, stop at **Prairie Creek Visitor Center**, housed in a small redwood lodge crafted in 1933. Enjoy a picnic lunch and an engaging tactile walk in a grove behind the lodge on the Revelation Trail, which was designed for people with diminished sight. Head north less than a mile and drive out unpaved **Cal-Barrel Road** (trailers and RVs not allowed), which leads east from the parkway through redwood forests. Return to the parkway, continue south about 2 mi to reconnect with U.S. 101, and turn west on **Davison Road**. It's partially unpaved; RVs longer than 24 feet and all trailers are prohibited. In about 30 minutes you'll reach **Gold Bluffs Beach**. Turn right and drive north, crossing a narrow creek a number of times, to the terminus at **Fern Canyon**.

Return to U.S. 101, and drive south to the turnoff for the **Kuchel Information Center**. Pick up free permits to visit the **Tall Trees Grove**, and then head north on U.S. 101 to the turnoff for **Bald Hills Road**, a steep route that doesn't allow trailers or RVs (park them at the trailhead or the information center). If you visit the grove, allow about four hours roundtrip from the information center. You could also bypass the turnoff to the grove and continue south on Bald Hills Road to 3,097-foot **Schoolhouse Peak**. For a simpler jaunt, turn onto Bald Hills Road and follow it for 2 mi to the **Lady Bird Johnson Grove Nature Loop Trail**. Take the footbridge to the easy 1-mi loop, which follows an old logging road through a mature redwood forest.

Seven miles southeast of Crescent City via U.S. 101, **Del Norte Coast Redwoods State Park** contains 15 memorial redwood groves. The growth extends down steep slopes almost to the shore. ⊠ *Crescent City Information Center, 1111 2nd St., off U.S. 101, Crescent City* ☎ *707/465–7306* ⊕ *www.parks.ca.gov* ☉ *Mid-May–mid-Oct., daily 9–6; mid-Oct.–mid-May, daily 9–4.*

Home to the Stout Memorial Grove, **Jedediah Smith Redwoods State Park** is named after a trapper who, in 1826, became the first white man to explore northern California's interior. You'll find 20 mi of hiking and nature trails here. The park is 2 mi west of Hiouchi and 9 mi east of Crescent City off Highway 199. ⊠ *Jedediah Smith Visitor Center, Hwy. 199, Hiouchi* ☎ *707/465–2144* ⊕ *www.parks.ca.gov* ☉ *Late May–late Sept., daily 9–5; late Sept.–May, Fri.–Sun. 10–6* ⊠ *Hiouchi*

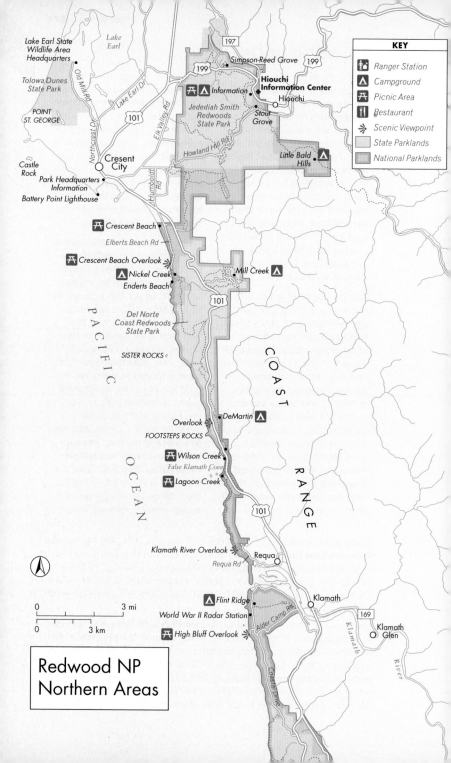

KEY

🛉	Ranger Station
🏕	Campground
🍴	Picnic Area
🍽	Restaurant
✳	Scenic Viewpoint
	State Parklands
	National Parklands

Lake Earl State
Wildlife Area
Headquarters

Lake
Earl

Tolowa Dunes
State Park

Simpson-Reed Grove

Hiouchi
Information Center

POINT
ST. GEORGE

199

Information

Hiouchi

Jedediah Smith
Redwoods
State Park

Stout
Grove

Castle
Rock

Cresent
City

Howland Hill Rd

Little Bald
Hills

Elk Valley Rd

Lake Earl Dr

Old Mill Rd

Northcrest Dr

Park Headquarters
Information
Battery Point Lighthouse

Crescent Beach

Elberts Beach Rd

Crescent Beach Overlook

Nickel Creek

Enderts Beach

Mill Creek

Humboldt Rd

P A C I F I C

Del Norte
Coast Redwoods
State Park

SISTER ROCKS

101

C O A S T

Overlook

DeMartin

FOOTSTEPS ROCKS

Wilson Creek

False Klamath Cove

Lagoon Creek

O C E A N

R A N G E

101

Klamath River Overlook

Requa

Requa Rd

Flint Ridge

World War II Radar Station

Alder Camp Rd

Klamath

High Bluff Overlook

169

Klamath
Glen

Klamath River

0   3 mi

0   3 km

Redwood NP
Northern Areas

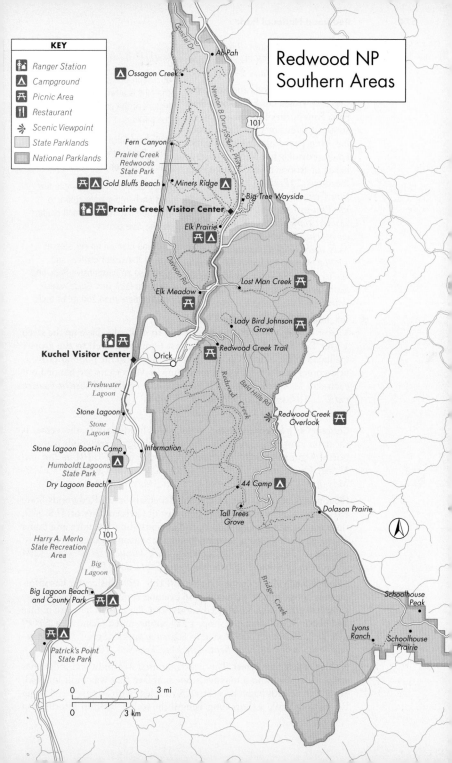

Redwood NP
Southern Areas

KEY

🚹	Ranger Station
🔺	Campground
⛩	Picnic Area
🍴	Restaurant
✦	Scenic Viewpoint
	State Parklands
	National Parklands

Coastal Dr.

Ah-Pah

Ossagon Creek

Newton B Drury Scenic Pkwy

101

Fern Canyon

Prairie Creek
Redwoods
State Park

Gold Bluffs Beach • Miners Ridge

Big Tree Wayside

Prairie Creek Visitor Center

Elk Prairie

Davison Rd.

Lost Man Creek

Elk Meadow

Lady Bird Johnson
Grove

Kuchel Visitor Center

Orick

Redwood Creek Trail

Freshwater
Lagoon

Redwood Creek

Bald Hills Rd.

Stone Lagoon

Redwood Creek
Overlook

Stone
Lagoon

Stone Lagoon Boat-in Camp

Information

**Humboldt Lagoons
State Park**

Dry Lagoon Beach

44 Camp

Tall Trees
Grove

Dolason Prairie

Harry A. Merlo
State Recreation
Area

101

Big
Lagoon

Bridge Creek

Big Lagoon Beach
and County Park

Schoolhouse
Peak

Lyons
Ranch

Schoolhouse
Prairie

Patrick's Point
State Park

0   3 mi

0   3 km

Information Center, Hwy. 199, Hiouchi ☎707/458–3294 ⊙ Late-May–mid-Sept., daily 9–6.

Spectacular redwoods and lush ferns make up **Prairie Creek Redwoods State Park,** 5 mi north of Orick and 50 mi south of Crescent City. Extra space has been paved alongside the park-lands, providing fine places to observe herds of Roosevelt elk in adjoining meadows. ⊠ *Prairie Creek Information Center, Newton B. Drury Scenic Pkwy., Orick ☎707/465–7354 ⊕ www.parks.ca.gov ⊙ Late May–early Sept., daily 9–6; early Sept.–late May, daily 9–5 ⊠ Thomas H. Kuchel Visitor Center, U.S. 101, Orick ☎707/465–7765 ⊙ Late May–early Sept., daily 9–6; early Sept.–late May, daily 9–5.*

★ **Tall Trees Grove.** From the Kuchel Visitor Center, you can get a free permit to make the drive up the steep 17-mi Tall Trees Access Road (the last 6 mi are gravel) to the grove's trailhead (trailers and RVs not allowed). Access to the popular grove is first-come, first-served, and a maximum of 50 permits are handed out each day. ⊠ *Access road is 10 mi drive east of Kuchel Visitor Center, via U.S. 101 and Bald Hills Rd.*

VISITOR CENTERS

Crescent City Information Center. As the park's headquarters, this center is the main information stop if you're approaching the redwoods from the north. A gift shop and picnic area are here. ⊠ *Off U.S. 101 at 2nd and K Sts., Crescent City ☎707/465–7306 ⊕ www.nps.gov/redw ⊙ Mid-May–mid-Oct., daily 9–6; mid-Oct.–mid-May, daily 9–4.*

Hiouchi Information Center. Located in Jedediah Smith Redwoods State Park, 2 mi west of Hiouchi and 9 mi east of Crescent City off U.S. 199, this center has a bookstore, film, and exhibits about the flora and fauna in the park. It's also a starting point for seasonal ranger programs. ⊠ *Hiouchi Information Center, Hwy. 199, Hiouchi ☎707/458–3294 ⊕ www.nps.gov/redw ⊙ Late May–mid-Sept., daily 9–6.*

Jedediah Smith Visitor Center. Located off U.S. 199, this center has information about ranger-led walks and evening campfire programs in the summer in Jedediah Smith Redwoods State Park. Also here are nature and history exhibits, a gift shop, a pay phone, and a picnic area. ⊠ *Off U.S. 199, Hiouchi ☎707/465–2144 ⊕ www.parks.ca.gov ⊙ Late May–late Sept., daily 9–5; late Sept.–late May, Fri.–Sun. 10–6.*

Prairie Creek Visitor Center. This center, housed in a redwood lodge, has wildlife displays and a massive stone fireplace that was built in 1933. Several trailheads begin here. Stretch your legs with an easy stroll along Revelation Trail, a short loop behind the lodge. Pick up information about summer programs in Prairie Creek Redwoods State Park. There's a pay phone, nature museum, gift shop, picnic area, and exhibits on flora and fauna. ✉ *Off southern end of Newton B. Drury Scenic Pkwy., Orick* ☎ *707/465–7354* ⊕ *www.parks.ca.gov* ☉ *Late May–early Sept., daily 9–6; early Sept.–late May, daily 9–5.*

Thomas H. Kuchel Visitor Center. Here you can get brochures, advice, and a free permit to drive up the access road to Tall Trees Grove. Whale-watchers will find the deck of the visitor center an excellent observation point, and bird-watchers will enjoy the nearby Freshwater Lagoon, a popular layover for migrating waterfowl. ✉ *Off U.S. 101, Orick* ☎ *707/465–7765* ⊕ *www.nps.gov/redw* ☉ *Late May–early Sept., daily 9–6; early Sept.–late May, daily 9–5.*

SPORTS AND THE OUTDOORS

BICYCLING

Besides the roadways, you can bike on several trails. Your best bets include the 11-mi Lost Man Creek Trail that begins 3 mi north of Orick; the 12-mi round-trip Coastal Trail (Last Chance Section) which starts at the south end of Enderts Beach Road and becomes steep and narrow as it travels through dense slopes of foggy redwood forests; and the 19-mi, single-track Ossagon Trail Loop, where you're likely to see elk as you cruise through redwoods before ending up ocean side for the last leg of the trail.

BIRD-WATCHING

Many rare and striking winged specimens inhabit the area, including chestnut-backed chickadees, brown pelicans, great blue herons, pileated woodpeckers, northern spotted owls, and marbled murrelets.

FISHING

Both deep-sea and freshwater fishing are popular here. Anglers often stake out sections of the Klamath and Smith rivers in their search for salmon and trout. (A single fishing license covers both ocean and river fishing.) Less serious anglers go crabbing and clamming on the coast, but check the tides carefully: rip currents and sneaker waves are deadly.

OUTFITTER AND EXPEDITIONS **Coast True Value** (✉ *900 Northcrest Dr., Crescent City* ☎ *707/464–3535*) is a good place to get fishing licenses (valid for both river and ocean fishing; $41.20 annual fee or $20.75 two-day fee for California residents; two-day and 10-day licenses for $20.75 and $41.20 can also be purchased by nonresidents). The store sells fishing gear, bait, and tackle.

HIKING

MODERATE

★ **Coastal Trail.** Although this easy-to-difficult trail runs along most of the park's length, smaller sections—of varying degrees of difficulty—are accessible via frequent, well-marked trailheads. The moderate to difficult DeMartin section leads past 5 mi of old growth redwoods and through prairie. If you're up for a real workout, you'll be well rewarded with the brutally difficult but stunning Flint Ridge section, a 4.5-mi stretch of steep grades and numerous switchbacks that leads past redwoods and Marshall Pond. The moderate 4-mi-long Hidden Beach section connects the Lagoon Creek picnic area with Klamath Overlook and provides coastal views and whale-watching opportunities. ⊠ *Flint Ridge trailhead: Douglas Bridge parking area, north end of Coastal Dr.*

DIFFICULT

West Ridge–Friendship Ridge–James Irvine Loop. For a moderately strenuous trek, try this 12.5-mi loop. The difficult West Ridge segment passes redwoods looming above a carpet of ferns. The difficult Friendship Ridge portion slopes down toward the coast through forests of spruce and hemlock. The moderate James Irvine Trail portion winds along a small creek and amid dense stands of redwoods. ⊠ *Trailhead at Prairie Creek Redwoods State Park information center, off Newton B. Drury Scenic Pkwy.*

KAYAKING

With many miles of often-shallow rivers and streams in the area, kayaking is a popular pastime in the park.

OUTFITTER AND EXPEDITIONS
You can rent hard-shell kayaks at **Adventure's Edge** (⊠ *650 10th St., Arcata* ☎ *707/822–4673* ☉ *Mon.–Sat. 9–6, Sun. 10–5*) for $35 a day. In business since 1970, this Arcata outfitter also rents camping equipment and tents.

WHALE-WATCHING

Good vantage points for whale-watching include Crescent Beach Overlook, the Kuchel Visitor Center in Orick, points along the Coastal Drive, and the Klamath River Overlook. Late November through January are the best months to see their southward migrations; February through April they return and generally pass closer to shore.

EDUCATIONAL OFFERINGS

RANGER PROGRAMS

Ranger-led programs explore the mysteries of both redwoods and the sea all summer long. Special events, such as bike rides, bat walks, and a December candlelight walk through an old-growth forest, take place in fall and winter. Check with visitor centers for offerings and times.

Field Seminars. State park rangers and other experts conduct one-day and overnight seminars with an emphasis on natural history. Subjects may include: photography, wildflowers, tide pools, Roosevelt elk, and stargazing. The programs often sell out in advance. ☎ *707/465–7325* ▭ *$30–$70.*

Junior Ranger Program. The state parks run these one-hour programs during the summer season. Rangers instruct children ages 7 through 12 on bird identification, outdoor survival skills, and more. ☎ *707/465–7765* ▭ *Free.*

Ranger Talks. From Memorial Day through Labor Day, state park rangers regularly lead discussions on the redwoods, tide pools, geology, and American Indian culture. Pick up a schedule at one of the visitor centers. ☎ *707/465–7765* ▭ *Free.*

WHAT'S NEARBY

NEARBY TOWNS

Crescent City, north of the park, is Del Norte County's largest town (pop. 7,500) and home to the Redwood National and State Park headquarters. Though it curves around a beautiful stretch of ocean and radiates small-town charm, rain and bone-chilling fog often prevail. The very small town of **Klamath** is outside park boundaries though very near to the middle section of the parks. It has a couple of lodging options but not much dining wise. Roughly 50 mi south of Crescent City, **Trinidad**'s cove harbor attracts fishermen and photographers, while campers head to nearby Patrick's Point State Park. Farther south, **Arcata** began life in 1850 as a base camp for miners and lumberjacks. Today this town of 17,000 residents is also home to the 7,800 students of Humboldt State University. Activity centers around Arcata Plaza, which is surrounded by restored buildings. Pick up the "Victorian Walking Tour" map at the chamber of commerce. Nearby **Eureka,** a city of 25,400 residents and filled with strip malls, was named after a gold miner's hearty exclamation. Its Old Town has a new waterfront boardwalk, a few good restaurants and shops, and the chamber of commerce has a free driving map to Victorian homes.

VISITOR INFORMATION

Arcata Chamber of Commerce ✉ *1635 Heindon Rd., Arcata* ☎ *707/822–3619* ⊕ *www.arcatachamber.com.* **Crescent City/Del Norte County Chamber of Commerce** ✉ *1001 Front St., Crescent City* ☎ *707/464–3174 or 800/343–8300* ⊕ *www.northerncalifornia.net.* **Eureka/Humboldt County Convention and Visitors Bureau** ✉ *1034 2nd St., Eureka* ☎ *707/443–5097 or 800/346–3482* ⊕ *www.redwoods.info.* **Klamath Chamber of Commerce** ✐ *P.O. Box 476, Klamath 95548* ☎ *800/200–2335.* **Trinidad Chamber of Commerce** ✐ *P.O. Box 356, Trinidad 95570* ☎ *707/677–1610* ⊕ *www.trinidadcalif.com.*

NEARBY ATTRACTIONS

Battery Point Lighthouse. At low tide, you can walk from the pier across the ocean floor to this working lighthouse, which was built in 1856. It houses a museum with nautical artifacts and photographs of shipwrecks, and even a resident ghost. Call ahead for guided group tours. ✉ *A St., Crescent City* ☎ *707/464–3089* 🎟 *$3* ⏱ *Apr.–Sept., daily 10–4; Oct.–Mar., weekends at low tide*

★ **California Western Railroad Skunk Train.** Following the same coastal route between Fort Bragg and Willits since 1885, the Skunk Train winds along the Noyo River, crosses some 30 bridges and passes through two tunnels in this scenic trip into the redwoods. The gas-powered locomotive replaced the steam engine on this train in 1925. Locals say, "You can smell 'em before you can see 'em." Hence, the nickname. You can take a four-hour or half-day trip. ✉ *100 W. Laurel St., Fort Bragg* ☎ *707/964–6371 or 866/457–5865* ⊕ *www.skunktrain.com* 🎟 *$35–$47* ⏱ *Mar.–Nov.*

Northcoast Marine Mammal Center. This nonprofit organization rescues and rehabilitates stranded, sick, or injured seals, sea lions, dolphins, and porpoises. This is not a museum per se, but you can see the rescued creatures through a fence enclosing individual pools, and learn via placards and information kiosks about marine mammals and coastal ecosystems. ⊠ *424 Howe Dr., Crescent City* ☎ *707/465–6265* ⊕ *www.northcoastmmc.org* ⊠ *Free* ☉ *Gift shop daily 10–4.*

NEED A BREAK?

A few doors down from the bay, combination diner–gift shop **Trinidad Bay Eatery and Gallery** (⊠ *Trinity and Parker Sts., Trinidad* ☎ *707/677-3777* ⊟ *AE, D, MC, V*) is famous for homemade blackberry cobbler.

WHERE TO EAT AND STAY

ABOUT THE RESTAURANTS

If you're an angler, fresh catch of the day is your best bet, since there are no dining facilities in the park itself. The seasonal Steelhead Lodge in Klamath Glen serves huge barbecued portions of steak, ribs, chicken, and fish. To sample ethnic cuisine, pub fare, and seafood delights, head to the towns north or south of the park. Crescent City and Eureka offer the broadest selections.

ABOUT THE HOTELS

There's only one lodging option—a hostel—within park boundaries. Orick and Klamath, the two towns on U.S. 101 near the park, have basic motels, plus the rustic Requa Inn, a two-story B and B on Requa Road beside the Klamath River. In towns north and south of the park you'll find numerous options, from elegant Victorians to seaside inns to no-frills rooms. Reservations at all lodgings should be made in advance for summer visits.

ABOUT THE CAMPGROUNDS

Within a 30-minute drive of Redwood National and State parks there are nearly 60 public and private camping facilities. None of the four primitive areas in Redwood—DeMartin, Flint Ridge, Little Bald Hills, and Nickel Creek—is a drive-in site. Although you don't need a permit at these four hike-in sites, stop at a ranger station to inquire about availability. You will need to get a permit from a ranger station for camping along Redwood Creek in the backcountry. Bring your own water, since drinking water isn't available in any of these sites.

If you'd rather drive than hike in, Redwood has four developed campgrounds—Elk Prairie, Gold Bluffs Beach, Jedediah Smith, and Mill Creek—that are within the state park boundaries. None has RV hookups, and some length restrictions apply. Fees are $35 in state park campgrounds. For details and reservations, call ☎ *800/444–7275* or check ⊕ *www.reserveamerica.com.*

WHERE TO EAT

IN THE PARK

PICNIC AREAS **Crescent Beach.** This beach has a grassy picnic area with tables, fire pits, and restrooms. There's an overlook south of the beach. ⊠ *2 mi south of Crescent City Visitor Center, on Enderts Beach Rd.*

Elk Prairie. In addition to many elk, this spot has a campground, a nature trail, and a ranger station. ⊠ *On Newton B. Drury Scenic Pkwy. in Prairie Creek Redwoods State Park.*

High Bluff Overlook. This picnic area's sunsets and whale-watching are unequaled. A 0.5-mi trail leads from here to the beach. ⊠ *On Coastal Dr., off U.S. 101, via Alder Camp Rd.*

OUTSIDE THE PARK

CRESCENT CITY

¢–$ ✕**Good Harvest Cafe.** Not only does the Good Harvest have a funky
AMERICAN atmosphere, but it serves the best breakfasts in town (along with superb
★ espresso). A lunch menu of salads, hamburgers, sandwiches, and veg-etarian specialties is served after 11 AM. There's also a second location, on U.S. 101 South, that stays open for dinner. ⊠ *700 Northcrest Dr., Crescent City* ☎ *707/465–6028* ▭ *D, MC, V* ☉ *No dinner.*

EUREKA

$–$$$ ✕**Cafe Waterfront.** This airy local landmark serves a solid basic menu
SEAFOOD of burgers and steaks, but the real standouts are the daily seafood specials—snapper, shrimp, crab and other treats fresh from the bay across the street. The building, listed on the National Register of Historic Places, was a saloon and brothel until the 1950s. Named after former ladies of the house, Sophie's Suite and Rachel's Room, two Victorian-style B&B rooms ($$$–$$$$), are available upstairs. ⊠ *102 F St., Eureka* ☎ *707/443–9190* ▭ *D, MC, V.*

KLAMATH

$$–$$$$ ✕**Steelhead Lodge.** Come hungry to this rustic lodge where huge por-
AMERICAN tions of beef, ribs, chicken, and fish are barbecued over a roaring hard-wood fire outside the restaurant's back door. Stop at the lounge with its curved wooden bar, artistic floor tiles that create a riverbed mosaic, and anglers perched on stools casting yarns. ⊠ *330 Terwer Riffle Rd., Klamath* ☎ *707/482–8145* ▭ *MC, V* ☉ *Closed mid-Oct.–Jan. and week-days Feb.–mid-June.*

WHERE TO STAY

IN THE PARK

¢ ▦ **Hostels International–Redwood.** Travelers of all ages are welcome at this vintage 1908 Edwardian-style hostel. Perks include an enthusiastic staff and a location across the highway from the ocean. There are three dorm rooms and three private rooms; linens are included. A wood-burning stove warms the common room, and kitchen and laundry facilities are available. Get clear directions or you might miss the turn off U.S. 101 onto Wilson Creek Road. **Pros:** stunning ocean views from dining area; big communal kitchen. **Cons:** even the private rooms share a bath; difficult to find. ⊠ *14480 U.S. 101* ☎ *707/482–8265 or 800/295–1905*

⊕ *www.norcalhostels.org/redwoods* 🛏 *28 beds in 3 dorm rooms, all with shared bath* ⚒ *In-hotel: parking (free), laundry facilities* ☰ *AE, D, MC, V* ☺ *Closed weekdays Nov.–Feb.*

CAMPING

¢

(FREE)

⚠ **DeMartin Campground.** This primitive hike-in area occupies a grassy prairie with a panoramic ocean view. **Pros:** great views. **Cons:** you must bring your own drinking water. ✉ *3 mi from Coastal Trail along U.S. 101* ☎ *707/465–7306* ⚠ *10 tent sites* ⚒ *Pit toilets, bear boxes, fire pits, picnic tables.*

$$

⚠ **Elk Prairie Campground.** Adjacent to a prairie and old-growth redwoods, this campground is popular with Roosevelt elk. To park here, RVs can be no longer than 27 feet, trailers no longer than 24 feet. **Pros:** easy access. **Cons:** can be crowded July–August. ✉ *On Newton B. Drury Scenic Pkwy. in Prairie Creek Redwoods State Park* ☎ *800/444–7275* ⚠ *75 tent/RV sites* ⚒ *Flush toilets, dump station, drinking water, showers, bear boxes, fire pits, picnic tables, public telephone, ranger station* ☰ *AE, D, MC, V.*

¢

(FREE)

⚠ **Flint Ridge Campground.** In old-growth forest with excellent wildlife-viewing opportunities, this primitive site is accessible from two trailheads along Coastal Drive: from the west, it's a 0.5-mi hike; from the east, it's 4.5 mi. **Pros:** easy access from Coastal Drive. **Cons:** must bring your own drinking water. ✉ *On Coastal Trail south of Klamath River estuary* ☎ *707/465–7306* ⚠ *10 tent sites* ⚒ *Pit toilets, bear boxes, fire pits, picnic tables.*

$

Fodor'sChoice

★

⚠ **Gold Bluffs Beach Campground.** You can camp in tents or RVs right on the beach at this Prairie Creek Redwoods State Park campground near Fern Canyon. Keep your eyes open for Roosevelt elk. Note that RVs must be less than 24 feet long and 8 feet wide, and trailers aren't allowed on the access road. You pay the fee at the campground. **Pros:** gorgeous setting. **Cons:** no reservations. ✉ *At end of Davison Rd., 5 mi north of Redwood Information Center off U.S. 101* ☎ *707/465–7354* ⚠ *26 tent/RV sites* ⚒ *Flush toilets, drinking water, showers, fire pits, picnic tables* ☰ *No credit cards.*

$$

⚠ **Jedediah Smith Campground.** This is one of the few places to camp—in tents or RVs—within groves of old-growth redwood forest. The length limit on RVs is 36 feet; for trailers it's 31 feet. **Pros:** family friendly; only campground with swimming. **Cons:** can get crowded. ✉ *8 mi northeast of Crescent City on U.S. 199* ☎ *800/444–7275* ⚠ *86 tent/RV sites* ⚒ *Flush toilets, dump station, drinking water, bear boxes, fire pits, picnic tables, public telephone, play area, ranger station, swimming (river)* ☰ *AE, D, MC, V.*

¢

(FREE)

⚠ **Little Bald Hills Campground.** You can hike, bike, or ride on horseback 4.5 mi through old-growth forest and prairies lined with fir and pine to this primitive area and its ridgetop vistas. There's a corral and horse troughs. **Pros:** good for horse lovers seeking an Old West ride. **Cons:** must bring your own drinking water. ✉ *East end of Howland Hill Rd.* ☎ *707/465–7306* ⚠ *5 tent sites* ⚒ *Pit toilets, running water (non-potable), bear boxes, fire pits, picnic tables.*

$$

⚠ **Mill Creek Campground.** Mill Creek is the largest of the state park campgrounds. **Pros:** good family campground. **Cons:** open only in summer. ✉ *West of U.S. 101, 7 mi southeast of Crescent City* ☎ *800/444–7275* ⚠ *145 tent/RV sites* ⚒ *Flush toilets, dump station, drinking water,*

Redwood trees, and the moss that often coats them, grow best in damp, shady environments.

showers, bear boxes, fire pits, picnic tables ▤ *AE, D, MC, V* ☺ *Closed Day after Labor Day–April.*

¢ 🏕 **Nickel Creek Campground.** An easy hike gets you to this primitive site, (FREE) which is near tide pools and has great ocean views. **Pros:** lush coastal environment. **Cons:** must bring drinking water or purify stream water. ✉ *On Coastal Trail ½ mi from end of Enderts Beach Rd.* ☎ *707/465–7306* 🏕 *5 tent sites* ♿ *Pit toilets, bear boxes, fire pits, picnic tables.*

OUTSIDE THE PARK

CRESCENT CITY

¢ 🏨 **Curly Redwood Lodge.** A single redwood tree produced the 57,000 board feet of lumber used to build this lodge in 1957. Furnishings make the most of that tree, with paneling, platform beds, and built-in dressers. It's a good value for the price. **Pros:** large rooms; several restaurants within walking distance. **Cons:** road noise can be bothersome. ✉ *701 Redwood Hwy. S, Crescent City* ☎ *707/464–2137* ⊕ *www.curlyredwoodlodge.com* ➷ *36 rooms, 3 suites* ♿ *In-room: no a/c, Wi-Fi. In-hotel: Wi-Fi* ▤ *AE, MC, V.*

EUREKA

$$–$$$$ 🏨 **Abigail's Elegant Victorian Mansion.** This meticulously restored Eastlake mansion in a residential neighborhood lives up to its name. Each room is completely decked out in period furnishings, down to the carved-wood beds, fringed lamp shades, and pull-chain commodes. You can also arrange for a guided tour of local Victoriana in an antique automobile. **Pros:** a delightful, knowledgeable innkeeper; history lodging buffs will love this place. **Cons:** may be overwhelming for tourists not interested in history. ✉ *1406 C St., Eureka* ☎ *707/444–3144*

⊕ *www.eureka-california.com* ⇆ *4 rooms, 2 with shared bath* ⟐ *In-hotel: laundry service* ▤ *MC, V.*

$$–$$$$ 🏨 **Cornelius Daly Inn.** Set in the heart of Eureka's historic area, this three-
★ story B&B was built in 1905 as the home of department store magnate
Cornelius Daly. Period touches include Victorian gardens, ornate flo-
ral wallpaper, a ballroom, and many antiques. Innkeepers Donna and
Bob Gafford serve complimentary refreshments in the afternoon. Five
rooms have wood-burning fireplaces; two rooms share a bath. **Pros:** a
beautifully furnished Victorian maintained by gracious hosts; outstand-
ing breakfast. **Cons:** not within easy walking distance to restaurants.
✉ *1125 H St., Eureka* ☎ *707/445–3638 or 800/321–9656* ⊕ *www.
dalyinn.com* ⇆ *3 rooms, 2 suites* ⟐ *In-room: no a/c, no phone, Wi-Fi.
In-hotel: laundry facilities, Wi-Fi* ▤ *AE, D, MC, V* ⏍ *BP.*

KLAMATH

$–$$$ 🏨 **Historic Requa Inn.** Neither TVs nor phones disrupt the serenity of
Fodor's Choice this 12-room B&B that overlooks the Klamath River a mile east of
★ where it meets the ocean. Set near the park's central section, the inn is
within easy reach of numerous trails and scenic drives. A scrumptious
breakfast is included. **Pros:** this is the park's most serene lodging choice
for non-campers; great central location. **Cons:** few dining options in
area. ✉ *451 Requa Rd., Klamath* ☎ *707/482–1425 or 866/800–8777*
⊕ *www.requainn.com* ⇆ *12 rooms* ⟐ *In-room: no a/c, no phone, Wi-Fi.
In-hotel: Wi-Fi* ▤ *AE, D, MC, V* ⏍ *Closed mid-Dec.–Jan.* ⏍ *BP.*

¢–$$ 🏨 **Ravenwood Motel.** Attentive on-site owners have converted this once
dowdy roadside motel into a class act. The 10 rooms and five suites—
four with full kitchens—are beautifully decorated with different themes.
Gazebos and fire pits set amid lovely landscaping offer a relaxing respite
at day's end. The exceptionally clean rooms are value priced: doubles
here are $65 in high season. **Pros:** great central location. **Cons:** non-suite
rooms are a bit small. ✉ *151 Klamath Blvd., Klamath* ☎ *707/482–5911
or 866/520–9875* ⊕ *ravenwoodmotel.com* ⇆ *10 rooms, 5 suites* ⟐ *In-
room: kitchen (some), Wi-Fi. In-hotel: Wi-Fi* ▤ *AE, D, MC, V* ⏍ *CP.*

TRINIDAD

$–$$$ 🏨 **Trinidad Inn.** These quiet cottage rooms nestled in the redwoods are
2 mi north of Trinidad Bay's harbor, restaurants, and shops. Individually
decorated, most rooms have full kitchens. It's an ideal home base from
which to explore the park's southern section. **Pros:** idyllic setting with
walking path through adjacent redwood grove; good place for kids; some
rooms have a VCR. **Cons:** older facility. ✉ *1170 Patrick's Point Dr., Trinidad* ☎ *707/677–3349* ⊕ *www.trinidadinn.com* ⇆ *10 rooms* ⟐ *In-room:
kitchen (some), Wi-Fi. In-hotel: Wi-Fi* ▤ *AE, D, MC, V* ⏍ *CP.*

Rocky Mountain National Park

WORD OF MOUTH

"If you're in RMNP for 9 days, I'd spend one day driving over Trail Ridge Road to Grand Lake. It would make a very nice, scenic day trip. Grand Lake is beautiful and there are lots of nice restaurants in the little town. Our kids used to like to play miniature golf there, too, which is also in town. And Trail Ridge Road is spectacular."

—MaureenB

WELCOME TO ROCKY MOUNTAIN

TOP REASONS TO GO

★ **Gorgeous scenery:** Peer out over dozens of lakes, gaze up at majestic mountain peaks, and look around at pine-scented woods that are perfect for whiling away an afternoon.

★ **Over 355 mi of trails:** Hike to your heart's content on mostly moderate trails crisscrossing the park.

★ **Continental Divide:** Straddle this great divide, which cuts through the western part of the park, separating water's flow to either the Pacific or Atlantic Ocean.

★ **Awesome ascents:** Trek to the summit of Longs Peak or go rock climbing on Lumpy Ridge. In winter, you can even ice climb.

★ **Wildlife viewing:** Spot elk and bighorn sheep; there are more than 2,000 and 800 of them, respectively.

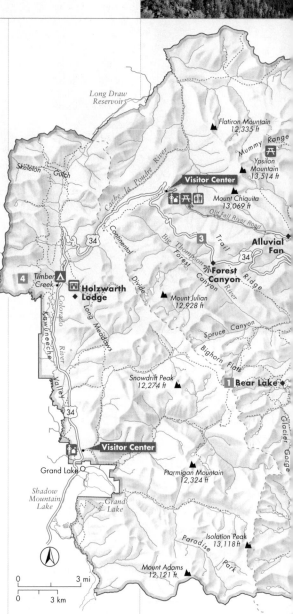

Long Draw Reservoirs

Skeleton Gulch

Cache la Poudre River

Flatiron Mountain 12,335 ft

Mummy Range

Ypsilon Mountain 13,514 ft

Visitor Center

Mount Chiquita 13,069 ft

Old Fall River Road

Continental

34

Big Thompson River

Forest Canyon

Trail Ridge

3

Alluvial Fan

34

4 Timber Creek

Divide

Forest Canyon

Holzwarth Lodge

Mount Julian 12,928 ft

Colorado River

Long Meadows

Spruce Canyon

Kawuneeche

Bighorn Flats

Snowdrift Peak 12,274 ft

1 **Bear Lake**

Valley

34

Visitor Center

Grand Lake

Ptarmigan Mountain 12,324 ft

Glacier Gorge

Shadow Mountain Lake

Grand Lake

Isolation Peak 13,118 ft

Paradise Park

Mount Adams 12,121 ft

0   3 mi

0   3 km

1 **Bear Lake.** One of the most photographed places in the park, Bear Lake is the hub for many trailheads. It gets crowded in summer.

2 **Longs Peak.** The highest peak in the park and the toughest to climb, this Fourteener pops up in many park vistas. If you want to reach the summit on a day-long trek, it's recommended you begin at 3 AM.

3 **Trail Ridge Road.** The alpine tundra of the park is the highlight here as the road climbs beyond the timberline.

4 **Timber Creek.** The park's western area is much less crowded, though it has its share of amenities and attractions, including a campground, historic sites, and a visitor center.

COLORADO

32

GETTING ORIENTED

Rocky Mountain National Park's 416-square-mi wilderness of meadows, mountains, and mirror-like lakes lie just 65 mi from Denver. The park is nine times smaller than Yellowstone, yet it receives almost as many visitors—3 million a year.

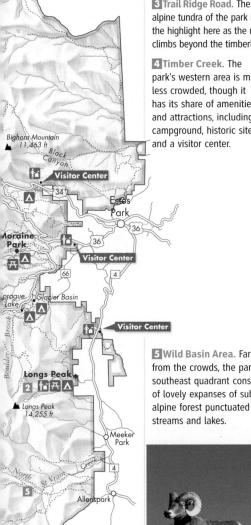

Bighorn Mountain
11,463 ft
Black Canyon

Visitor Center
34
Estes Park
36

Moraine Park
36
Visitor Center
66
4

Sprague Lake
Glacier Basin

Boulder Brook

Visitor Center

Longs Peak
2

Longs Peak
14,255 ft

Meeker Park

North St. Vrain Creek
4

5
Allenspark

5 **Wild Basin Area.** Far from the crowds, the park's southeast quadrant consists of lovely expanses of sub-alpine forest punctuated by streams and lakes.

KEY	
🏠	*Ranger Station*
▲	*Campground*
🌳	*Picnic Area*
🍴	*Restaurant*
🏨	*Lodge*
🚶	*Trailhead*
🚻	*Restrooms*
⚡	*Scenic Viewpoint*
⋯⋯	*Walking/Hiking Trails*

ROCKY MOUNTAIN PLANNER

When to Go

More than two-thirds of the park's annual 3 million visitors come in summer and fall. **For thinner high-season crowds, come in early June or September.** But there is a good reason to put up with summer crowds: only from Memorial Day to mid-October can you make the unforgettable drive over Trail Ridge Road (weather-permitting).

Spring is capricious—75°F one day and a blizzard the next (March sees the most snow). June can range from hot to cool and rainy. July typically ushers in high summer. Up on Trail Ridge Road, it can be 15°–20° cooler. Spring and summer are the best times for wildlife viewing and fishing. In early fall, the trees blaze with brilliant foliage. Winter, when backcountry snow can be 4 feet deep and the wind brutal, is the time for skiing, snowshoeing, and ice fishing.

AVG. HIGH/LOW TEMPS

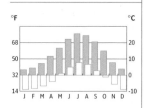

Flora and Fauna

Volcanic uplifts and the savage clawing of receding glaciers have brought about Rocky Mountain's majestic landscape. You'll find three distinct ecosystems here—verdant mountain valleys towering with proud ponderosa pines and Douglas firs; higher and colder subalpine mountains with wind-whipped trees (krummholz) that grow at right angles; and harsh, unforgiving alpine tundra with dollhouse-size versions of familiar plants and wildflowers. The high, wind-whipped ecosystem of alpine tundra is seldom found outside the Arctic, yet it makes up one-third of the park's terrain. Few plants can survive at the tundra's elevation, but many beautiful wildflowers—including alpine forget-me-nots—bloom briefly in late June or early July.

The park has so much wildlife that you can often enjoy prime viewing from the seat of your car. Fall, when many animals begin moving down from higher elevations, is an excellent time to spot the park's animal residents. This is also when you'll hear the male elk bugle mating calls (popular "listening" spots are Horseshoe Park, Moraine Park, and Upper Beaver Meadows).

May through mid-October is the best time to see the bighorn sheep that congregate in the Horseshoe Park–Sheep Lakes area, just past the Fall River entrance. If you want to glimpse a moose, try Kawuneeche Valley, on the park's western side. Other animals in the park include mule deer, squirrels, chipmunks, pikas, beavers, and marmot. Common birds are broad-tailed and rufous hummingbirds, peregrine falcons, woodpeckers, mountain bluebirds, and Clark's nutcracker, as well as the white-tailed ptarmigan, spotted year-round on the alpine tundra.

Mountain lions, black bears, and bobcats also inhabit the park but are rarely spotted by visitors. Altogether, the park is home to 63 species of mammals and 280 bird species.

Getting Here and Around

Estes Park and Grand Lake are the Rocky Mountain's gateway communities; from these you can enter the park via U.S. 34 or 36. The closest commercial airport is **Denver International Airport** (DEN). Its **Ground Transportation Information Center** (☎ 800/247–2336 or 303/342–4059) assists visitors with car rentals, door-to-door shuttles, and limousine services. From the airport, the eastern entrance of the park is 80 mi (about two hours). **Estes Park Shuttle** (☎ 970/586–5151; reservations essential) serves Estes Park and Rocky Mountain from Denver, the airport, and Boulder. Greyhound Lines serve Denver, Boulder, and Fort Collins, and Amtrak's California Zephyr stops in downtown Denver, Winter Park/Fraser, and Granby.

U.S. 36 runs from Denver through Boulder, Lyons, and Estes Park to the park; the portion between Boulder and Estes Park is heavily traveled—especially on summer weekends. Colorado Routes 119, 72, and 7 have much less traffic. If you're driving directly to Rocky Mountain from the airport, the E–470 tollway connects Peña Boulevard to Interstate 25.

The Colorado Department of Transportation (for road conditions, call ☎ 303/639–1111) plows roads efficiently, but winter snowstorms can slow traffic and create wet or icy conditions.

The main thoroughfare in the park is Trail Ridge Road; in winter, it's plowed up to Many Parks Curve on the east side and the Colorado River trailhead on the west side. Gravel-surfaced, extremely curvy Old Fall River Road is open from July to September. Pulled trailers and vehicles longer than 25 feet are prohibited.

Two free park shuttle-bus routes operate along the park's popular Bear Lake Road from mid-June to mid-October. Unless you arrive early enough to get one of the few parking spaces beyond the park-and-ride, you must take the shuttle. One bus line runs every 30 minutes between 7:30 AM and 7:30 PM from near the Fern Lake Trailhead to the Moraine Park Museum and on to Glacier Basin Campground. The other runs every 15 minutes between 7 AM and 7 PM from the campground to the Bear Lake Trailhead. There's also a hiker shuttle bus running from the Estes Park Visitor Center to the park during the peak summer season (call ☎ 970/586–1206 for times); it passes most lodging and shopping areas, and many visitors like to use it as a free sightseeing tour bus. You must have a park pass if you transfer to the buses that enter the national park.

Festivals and Events

32

MID-MAY Jazz Fest. Pack a picnic and bring the kids for a weekend afternoon of free jazz performances and an art walk at the outdoor amphitheater downtown. ⊠ Estes Park ☎ 800/443–7837 ⊕ www.estesnet.com/events/.

JUNE The Wool Market. Watch shearing, spinning, and herding contests, and view animal shows where angora goats, sheep, llamas, and alpacas are judged for their wool. ⊠ Estes Park ☎ 800/443–7837.

JULY Rooftop Rodeo. A tradition for more than 80 years, this six-day event features a parade and nightly rodeos. Admission runs $10–$15. ⊠ Fairgrounds, Estes Park ☎ 800/443–7837 ⊕ www.estesnet.com/events/.

SEPT. ★ Longs Peak Scottish/Irish Highland Festival. A traditional tattoo kicks off this four-day fair of athletic competitions, Celtic music, dancing, a parade, and seminars on topics such as heraldry and Scotch whisky. ⊠ Fairgrounds, Estes Park ☎ 970/586–6308 or 800/903–7837 ⊕ www.scotfest.com.

NOV.–APR. The **Estes Park Music Festival** stages concerts at 2 PM on Sunday afternoons from November through April at the Stanley Hotel (333 E. Wonderview Ave.). ⊠ 333 E. Wonderview Ave., Estes Park ☎ 970/586–9519 or 800/443–7837 ⊕ www.estesparkmusicfestival.org.

Updated
by Barbara
Colligan

Anyone who delights in alpine lakes, mountain peaks, and an abundance of wildlife—not to mention dizzying heights—should consider Rocky Mountain National Park. Here, a single hour's drive leads from a 7,800-foot elevation at park headquarters to the 12,183-foot apex of the twisting and turning Trail Ridge Road. More than 355 mi of hiking trails take you to the park's many treasures: meadows flushed with wildflowers, cool dense forests of lodgepole pine and Engelmann spruce, and the noticeable presence of wildlife, including elk and bighorn sheep.

PARK ESSENTIALS

ACCESSIBILITY

All visitor centers are fully accessible to mobility-impaired people. The Sprague Lake, Bear Lake, Coyote Valley, and Lily Lake trails are hard-packed gravel, ½0.5- to 1-mi, accessible loops. A backcountry camp-site at Sprague Lake accommodates up to 12 campers, including six in wheelchairs. Bear Lake shuttles are whee lchair accessible.

ADMISSION FEES AND PERMITS

Entrance fees are $20 for a weekly pass, or $10 if you enter on bicycle, motorcycle, or foot. An annual pass costs $40.

From May through October, the backcountry camping cost is $20 per party (it's free the rest of the year, but you still need a permit). Pick up the permit at the backcountry office, east of Beaver Meadows Visitor Center, or at Kawuneeche Visitor Center. Phone reservations for back-country campsites can be made between March 1 and May 15 and after October 1 by calling the backcountry office at ☎ 970/586–1242.

ADMISSION HOURS

The park is open 24/7, year-round; some roads close in winter. It is in the mountain time zone.

ROCKY MOUNTAIN IN ONE DAY

Begin your adventure with a hearty breakfast at the **Bighorn Restaurant** in Estes Park. While you're enjoying your short stack with apple-cinnamon-raisin topping, you can put in an order for a packed lunch.

Drive west on U.S. 34 into the park, and stop at the **Fall River Visitor Center** to watch the orientation film and pick up a park map. Also inquire about road conditions on Trail Ridge Road, which you should plan to drive either in the morning or afternoon, depending on the weather. If possible, save the drive for the afternoon, and use the morning to get out on the trails before any afternoon lightning threatens your safety.

For a beautiful and invigorating hike, follow the route that takes you from the trailhead at **Bear Lake** to **Nymph Lake** (an easy 0.5-mi hike), then onto **Dream Lake** (an additional 0.6 mi with a steeper ascent), and finally to **Emerald Lake** (an additional 0.7 mi of moderate to challenging terrain). You can stop at several places along the way. The trek down is much easier, and quicker, than the climb up. ■TIP→ If you prefer a shorter, simpler, yet still scenic walk, consider the **Bear Lake Nature Trail,** a 0.6-mi loop that is partially wheelchair and stroller accessible.

You'll need the better part of your afternoon to drive the scenic **Trail Ridge Road.** If you're heading to Grand Lake and destinations west, take Trail Ridge Road west, over the Continental Divide; otherwise, after you reach the top, take it back east and end your day with a ranger-led talk or evening campfire program.

ATMS/BANKS

There are no ATMs within the park. The nearest ATMs and banks are in Estes Park.

CELL-PHONE RECEPTION

Cell phones work in much of the park. Pay phones may be found at the Beaver Meadows, Kawuneeche, and Fall River visitor centers.

PARK CONTACT INFORMATION

Rocky Mountain National Park ⊠ *1000 U.S. 36, Estes Park, CO* ☎ *970/586–1206* ⊕ *www.nps.gov/romo.*

SCENIC DRIVES

Bear Lake Road. This 9-mi drive offers superlative views of Longs Peak (14,255-foot summit) and the glaciers surrounding Bear Lake, winding past shimmering waterfalls perpetually shrouded with rainbows. ⊠ *Runs from the Beaver Meadow Entrance Station to Bear Lake.*

Old Fall River Road. A one-way 11-mi loop up to the Alpine Visitor Center and back down along Trail Ridge Road is a scenic alternative to driving Trail Ridge Road twice. Start at West Horseshoe Park, which has the park's largest concentrations of sheep and elk, and head up the paved and gravel Old Fall River Road, passing Chasm Falls. Early visitors to the park traveled Old Fall River Road before Trail Ridge Road was built. ☉ *July–Sept.*

Fodor's Choice ★ **Trail Ridge Road.** This is the park's star attraction and the world's highest continuous paved highway, topping out at 12,183 feet. The 48-mi road connects the park's gateways of Estes Park and Grand Lake. The views around each bend—of moraines and glaciers, and craggy hills framing emerald meadows carpeted with columbine and Indian paintbrush— are truly awesome. As it passes through three ecosystems—montane, subalpine, and arctic tundra—the road climbs 4,300 feet in elevation. As you drive the road, take your time at the numerous turnouts to gaze over verdant valleys, brushed with yellowing aspen in fall, that slope between the glacier-etched granite peaks. **Many Parks Curve** affords views of the crest of the Continental Divide and of the **Alluvial Fan,** a huge gash a vicious flood created after an earthen dam broke in 1982. ■ TIP➔ Pick up a copy of the *Trail Ridge Road Guide,* available at visitor centers, for an overview of what you will be seeing as you drive the road. In normal traffic, it's a two-hour drive across the park, but it's best to give yourself three to four hours to allow for leisurely breaks at the overlooks. Note that the middle part of the road closes down again by mid-October, though you can still drive up about 10 mi from the west and 8 mi from the east. ⊠ *Trail Ridge Rd. (U.S. 34)* ⊗ *June–mid-Oct.*

WHAT TO SEE

HISTORIC SITES

Rocky Mountain has more than 100 sites of historic significance. In order to be nominated for the National Register of Historic Places, a park building must tie in strongly to the park's history in terms of architecture, archaeology, engineering, or culture. Most buildings at Rocky Mountain are done in the rustic style, a design preferred by the National Park Service's first director, Stephen Mather. The rustic style is a way to incorporate nature within man-made structures.

Holzwarth Historic Site. A scenic 0.5-mi interpretive trail leads you over the Colorado River to the original "dude ranch" that the Holzwarth family ran between the 1920s and 1950s. Allow about an hour to explore the buildings and chat with a ranger. It's a great place for families to learn about homesteading. ⊠ *Trail Ridge Rd., About 13 mi west of the Alpine Visitor Center* 🚍 *Free* ⊗ *Daily 10:30–4:30.*

Lulu City. A few remnants of cabins and mining equipment are all that's left of this onetime silver mining town, established in 1880. Reach it by hiking the 3.6-mi Colorado River Trail. Look for wagon ruts from the old Stewart Toll Road and the ruins of cabins in Shipler Park. The Colorado River is a mere stream at this point, flowing south from its headwaters at nearby La Poudre Pass. ⊠ *Off Trail Ridge Rd., 10½ mi north of Grand Lake.*

Moraine Park Museum. Lectures, slide shows, and displays explain the park's geology, botany, and history. ⊠ *Bear Lake Rd., off U.S. 36* 🚍 *Free* ⊗ *May–Sept., daily 9–5.*

SCENIC STOPS

Alluvial Fan. On July 15, 1982, the 79-year-old dam at Lawn Lake burst, and water roared into Estes Park, killing three people and causing major flooding. The flood created the alluvial fan, a pile of glacial and streambed debris up to 44 feet deep on the north side of Horseshoe Park. A 0.5-mi trail allows you to explore it up close. You also can view it from the Rainbow Curve lookout on Trail Ridge Road. ⊠ *Fall River Rd., 3 mi from the Fall River entrance station.*

★ **Bear Lake.** Thanks to its picturesque location, easy accessibility, and the good hiking trails nearby, this small alpine lake below Flattop Mountain and Hallett Peak is one of the most popular destinations in the park. Free park shuttle buses can take you here. ⊠ *Bear Lake Rd., 10 mi southwest of Beaver Meadows Visitor Center, off Highway 36.*

Forest Canyon Overlook. Beyond the classic U-shaped glacial valley lies a high-alpine circle of ice-blue pools (the Gorge Lakes) framed by ragged peaks. ⊠ *Trail Ridge Rd., 14 mi east of Alpine Visitor Center, on Highway 34.*

VISITOR CENTERS

Alpine Visitor Center. At the top of Trail Ridge Road, this visitor center is open only when that road is navigable. There's a snack bar inside. ⊠ *Trail Ridge Rd., at Fall River Pass 22 mi from the Beaver Meadows entrance, on Highway 34* ☎ *970/586–1206* ⊙ *June–mid-Oct., daily 9–5.*

★ **Beaver Meadows Visitor Center.** Housing park headquarters, this visitor center was designed by students of the Frank Lloyd Wright School of Architecture at Taliesen West using the park's popular rustic style, which integrates buildings into their natural surroundings. Completed in 1966, it was named a National Historic Landmark in 2001. The surrounding utility buildings are also on the National Register and are noteworthy examples of the rustic-style buildings that the Civilian Conservation Corps constructed during the Depression. The visitor center has a terrific orientation film and a large relief map of the park. ⊠ *U.S. 36, before the Beaver Meadows entrance* ☎ *970/586–1206* ⊙ *Mid-June–Labor Day, Mon.– Wed. 8–8 and Thurs.–Sat. 8–9; early Sept.–mid-June, daily 8–4:30.*

Fall River Visitor Center. The Discovery Room, which houses everything from old ranger outfits to elk antlers, coyote pelts, and bighorn sheep skulls for hands-on exploration, is a favorite with kids (and adults) at this northeast center. ⊠ *U.S. 34 at the Fall River entrance station* ☎ *970/586–1206* ⊙ *Mid-June–Labor Day, daily 9–5; winter hrs vary.*

Kawuneeche Visitor Center. The park's only west-side source of visitor information has exhibits on the plant and animal life of the area, as well as a large three-dimensional map of the park and an orientation film. ⊠ *U.S. 34, before the Grand Lake entrance station* ☎ *970/586–1206* ⊙ *Mid-June–mid-Aug., daily 8–6; mid-Aug.–mid-June, daily 8–4:30.*

ROCKY MOUNTAIN WILDLIFE

If you see a group of cars pulled over at a seemingly random section of road, with passengers staring intently at something in the distance, it's a good bet that an animal is within sight. May through mid-October is the best time to see the bighorn sheep that congregate in the Horseshoe Park–Sheep Lakes area, just past the Fall River entrance. Elk can be seen year-round in the park and the surrounding area. Kawuneeche Valley, on the park's western side, is the most likely location to glimpse a moose. At night, listen for the eerie vocalizing of coyotes.

Fall, when many animals begin moving down from the higher elevations, is an excellent time to spot wildlife. This is also when you'll hear the male elk bugle mating calls to their female counterparts, which draws large crowds to popular "listening" spots in the early evening: Horseshoe Park, Moraine Park, and Upper Beaver Meadows—in the early evening.

Spring and summer are the best times for bird-watching. Go early in the morning, before the crowds arrive. Lumpy Ridge is the nesting ground of raptors such as golden eagles, red-tailed hawks, and peregrine. You can see migratory songbirds from South America in their summer breeding grounds near the Endovalley Picnic Area. The alpine tundra is habitat for white-tailed ptarmigan. The alluvial fan, along the Roaring River, is an excellent place for viewing broad-tailed hummingbirds, hairy woodpeckers, robins, ouzels, and the occasional raptor.

Keep a telephoto lens handy for those close-ups of animals. Approaching, chasing, or feeding any wildlife in the park not only is forbidden, but unduly stresses the animals and diminishes the enjoyment of others watching the wildlife.

SPORTS AND THE OUTDOORS

BIRD-WATCHING

Spring and summer, early in the morning, are the best times for bird-watching in the park. **Lumpy Ridge** is a nesting ground for raptors such as golden eagles, red-tailed hawks, and peregrine falcons. Migratory songbirds from South America have summer breeding grounds near the **Endovalley Picnic Area.** The **alpine tundra** is habitat for white-tailed ptarmigan. The **alluvial fan** is the place for viewing broad-tailed hummingbirds, hairy woodpeckers, ouzels, and the occasional raptor.

FISHING

Rocky Mountain is a wonderful place to fish, especially for trout—German brown, brook, rainbow, cutthroat, and greenback cutthroat—but check at a visitor center about regulations and information on specific closures, catch-and-release areas, and limits on size and possession. No fishing is allowed at Bear Lake. Rangers recommend the more-remote backcountry lakes, since they are less crowded. To fish in the park, anyone 16 and older must have a valid Colorado fishing license, which you can obtain at local sporting-goods stores. See ⊕ *www.wildlife.state. co.us/fishing* for details.

DID YOU KNOW?

A pine beetle epidemic that is affecting forests nation-wide has caused some of the Rocky Mountain National Park's trees to turn a reddish color and eventually die. The mitigation efforts of the park service are to remove hazard trees and protect "high value" trees near campgrounds, pic-nic areas, and visitor centers.

Estes Angler (⊠ *338 W. Riverside Dr., Estes Park* ☎ *970/586–2110 or 800/586–2110* ⊕ *www.estesangler.com*) arranges four-, six-, and eight-hour fly-fishing trips—including on horseback—into the park's quieter regions. **Scot's Sporting Goods** (⊠ *2325 Spruce Ave.* ⊠ *870 Moraine Ave., Estes Park* ☎ *970/586–2877* ⊕ *www.scotssportinggoods.com* ☜ *$80– $190* ⊙ *May–Sept., daily 8–8*) rents and sells gear, and provides four-, six-, and eight-hour fishing instruction trips daily from May through September. Clinics, geared toward first-timers, focus on casting, reading the water, identifying insects for flies, and properly presenting natural and artificial flies to the fish. Half-day excursions into the park are available for three or more people. **Kirk's Fly Shop** (⊠ *230 E. Elkhorn Ave., Estes Park* ☎ *970/577–0790* ⊕ *www.kirksflyshop.com*) has various guided fly-fishing trips, as well as backpacking, horseback riding, showshoeing, and llama trips. The store also carries fishing and backpacking gear.

HIKING

Fodor's Choice
★ Rocky Mountain National Park contains more than 355 mi of hiking trails, so you could theoretically wander the park for weeks. Most visitors explore just a small portion of these trails, so some of the park's most accessible and scenic paths can resemble a backcountry highway on busy summer days. The high-alpine terrain around Bear Lake is the park's most popular hiking area, and it's well worth exploring. However, for a truly remote experience, hike one of the trails in the far northern end of the park or in the Wild Basin area to the south. Keep in mind that trails at higher elevations may have some snow on them even in July. And because of afternoon thunderstorms on most summer afternoons, an early morning start is highly recommended; the last place you want to be when a storm approaches is on a peak or anywhere above the tree line. All trails are round-trip unless stated otherwise.

EASY

★ **Bear Lake.** The virtually flat nature trail around Bear Lake is an easy, 1-mi walk that's wheelchair accessible. Sharing the route with you will likely be plenty of other hikers as well as songbirds and chipmunks. ⊠ *Trailhead at Bear Lake, Bear Lake Rd.*

☾ **Copeland Falls.** The 0.6-mi hike to these Wild Basin Area falls is a good option for families, as the terrain is relatively flat (only a 15-foot elevation gain). ⊠ *Trailhead at Wild Basin.*

Cub Lake. This 4.6-mi, three-hour hike takes you through meadows and stands of aspen trees and up 540 feet in elevation to a lake with water lilies. ⊠ *Trailhead at Cub Lake. Take Bear Lake Road to Moraine Park Campground, turn right, then left at road to trailhead.*

East Inlet Trail. You can get to **Adams Falls** in about 15 minutes on this 0.3-mi route with an 80-foot climb in elevation. The trail to the falls will likely be packed with visitors, so if you have time, continue east on the trail past the falls to enjoy more solitude, see wildlife, and catch views of Mount Craig from near the East Meadow campground. Note, however, that beyond the falls the elevation climbs between 1,500 and 1,900 feet, making it a challenging hike. ⊠ *Trailhead at East Inlet, end of W. Portal Road; W. Portal Road spurs off Trail Ridge Road by entrance to Grand Lake Village. Stay left at junction with Grand Ave.*

Glacier Gorge Trail. The 5-mi hike to **Mills Lake** can be crowded, but the reward is one the park's prettiest lakes, set against the breathtaking backdrop of Longs Peak, Pagoda Mountain, and the Keyboard of the Winds. There's a modest elevation gain of 700 feet. About 1 mi in, you pass **Alberta Falls**, a popular destination in and of itself. The hike travels along Glacier Creek, under the shade of a subalpine forest. Give yourself at least four hours for hiking and lingering time. ⊠ *Trailhead at off Bear Lake Road, 9 mi south of the Beaver Meadows entrance station.*

★ **Sprague Lake.** With virtually no elevation gain, this 1-mi, pine-lined path is wheelchair accessible and provides views of Hallet Peak and Flattop Mountain. ⊠ *Trailhead at Sprague Lake, Bear Lake Rd.*

HIKERS SHUTTLE

The many trails in the Bear Lake area of the park are so popular that parking areas at the trailheads usually cannot accommodate all of the hikers' cars. Shuttle buses connect a large park-and-ride facility at the Glacier Basin Campground with the Cub Lake, Fern Lake, Glacier Gorge Junction, Sprague Lake, and Bear Lake trailheads. Buses run daily between mid-June and mid-September. The Bear Lake shuttle runs approximately every 15 minutes between 7 AM and 7 PM; the Moraine Park shuttle runs approximately every 30 minutes between 7:30 AM and 7:30 PM.

MODERATE

Fodor's Choice **Bear Lake to Emerald Lake.** This scenic, caloric-burning hike begins at Bear
★ Lake and takes you first on a moderately level, 0.5-mi journey to **Nymph Lake.** From here, the trail gets steeper, with a 425-foot elevation gain, as it winds around for 0.6 mi to **Dream Lake.** The last stretch is the most arduous part of the hike, an almost all-uphill 0.7-mi trek to lovely **Emerald Lake**, where you can perch on a boulder and enjoy the view. Round-trip, the hike is 3.6 mi, with an elevation gain of 605 feet. Allow two hours or more, depending on stops. ⊠ *Trailhead at Bear Lake, off Bear Lake Rd.*

Colorado River Trail. This walk to the ghost town of Lulu City on the west side of the park is excellent for looking for the bighorn sheep, elk, and moose that reside in the area. Part of the former stagecoach route that went from Granby to Walden, the 7.4-mi trail parallels the infant Colorado River to the meadow where Lulu City once stood. Elevation gain is 350 feet. ⊠ *Trailhead at Colorado River, off Trail Ridge Rd.*

Fern Lake Trail. Heading to Odessa Lake from the north involves a steep hike, but usually you'll encounter fewer fellow hikers than if you begin at Bear Lake. Along the way, you'll come to the Arch Rocks; The Pool, an eroded formation in the Big Thompson River; two waterfalls; and Fern Lake (4 mi from your starting point). Odessa Lake itself lies at the foot of Tourmaline Gorge, below the craggy summits of Gabletop Mountain, Little Matterhorn, Knobtop Mountain, and Notchtop Mountain. For a full day of spectacular scenery, continue past Odessa to Bear Lake (8½ mi total), where you can pick up the shuttle back to the Fern Lake Trailhead. Total elevation gain is 1,375 feet. ⊠ *Trailhead off Bear Lake Road, about 1½ mi south of the Beaver Meadows entrance station.*

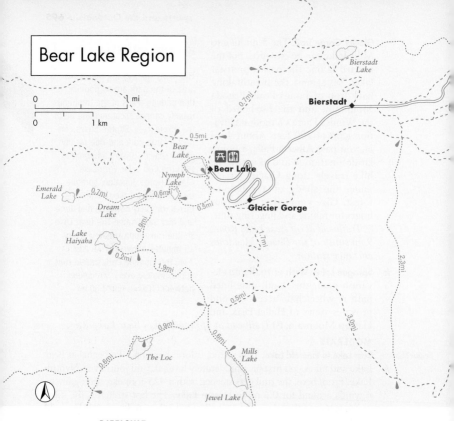

DIFFICULT

Chasm Lake Trail. Nestled in the shadow of Longs Peak and Mount Meeker, Chasm Lake offers one of Colorado's most impressive backdrops, so en route to it, expect to encounter plenty of other hikers. The 4.2-mi Chasm Lake trail, reached via the Longs Peak Trail, has a 2,360-foot elevation gain. Just before the lake, you'll need to climb a small rock ledge, which can be a bit of a challenge for the less surefooted; follow the cairns for the most straightforward route. Once atop the ledge, you'll catch your first memorable view of the lake. ⊠ *Trailhead at Rte. 7, 9 mi south of Estes Park.*

★ **Longs Peak Trail.** Climbing this 14,255-foot mountain (one of 54 "fourteeners" in Colorado) is an ambitious goal for many people—but only those who are very fit and acclimated to the altitude should attempt it. The 16-mi round-trip hike up Longs requires a predawn start (3 AM is ideal) so that you're off the summit before the typical summer afternoon thunderstorm hits. Also, the last 2 mi or so of the trail are very exposed—you have to traverse narrow ledges with vertigo-inducing drop-offs. That said, summiting Longs can be one of the most rewarding hikes you'll ever attempt. The Keyhole route is the traditional means of ascent, and the number of people going up it on a summer day can be astounding given the rigors of the hike. Though just as scenic, the

CLOSE UP

Longs Peak: The Northernmost Fourteener

At 14,255 feet above sea level, **Longs Peak** has long fascinated explorers to the region. Isabella L. Bird wrote of it, "It is one of the noblest of mountains, but in one's imagination it grows to be much more than a mountain. It becomes invested with a personality."

It was named after Major Stephen H. Long, who led an expedition in 1820 up the Platte River to the base of the Rockies. Long never ascended the mountain—in fact, he didn't even get within 40 mi of it—but a few decades later, in 1868, the one-armed Civil War veteran John Wesley Powell climbed to its summit.

In the park's southeast quadrant, Longs Peak is northernmost of the 54 mountains in Colorado that reach above the 14,000-foot mark, and one of more than 114 named mountains in the park higher than 10,000 feet. You can see its distinctive flat-top, rectangular summit from many spots on the park's east side and Trail Ridge Road.

If you want to make the ambitious climb to Longs summit—it's only recommended for those who are strong climbers and well acclimated to the altitude—begin by 3 AM so you're down from the summit when the typical afternoon thunderstorm hits.

32

Loft route, between Longs and Mount Meeker from Chasm Lake, is not clearly marked and is therefore difficult to navigate. ⊠ *Trailhead: off Rte. 7, 9 mi south of Estes Park.*

HORSEBACK RIDING

Horses and riders can access 260 mi of trails in Rocky Mountain.

OUTFITTERS AND EXPEDITIONS

National Park Gateway Stables and Cowpoke Corner Corrals. Guided trips into the national park range from two-hour rides to Little Horseshoe Park to full-day rides along the Roaring River to Lawn or Ypsilon Lake. ⊠ *46000 Fall River Rd., Estes Park* ☎ *970/586–5269 or 970/586–5890* ⊕ *www.nationalparkgatewaystables.com* ☜ *$45–$125* ▤ *D, MC, V* ☉ *Mid May–early Oct.*

Sombrero Ranches, Inc. Sombrero offers guided rides into the wilderness and national park, including scenic and relaxing early-morning breakfast rides and pack trips. The Boulder-based company also arranges private camping trips. Guided horseback riding trips last two to five hours. ⊠ *Grand Lake Stables, 304 W. Portal Rd., Grand Lake* ☎ *970/627–3514* ⊕ *www.sombrero.com* ☜ *$30–$80* ☉ *Mid-May–mid-Sept.* ⊠ *Glacier Creek Stables, Off Bear Lake Rd., near Sprague Lake* ☎ *970/586–3244* ⊠ *Moraine Park Stables, Off Bear Lake Rd.* ☎ *970/586–2327.*

ROCK CLIMBING

Expert rock climbers as well as novices can try hundreds of classic climbs here. The burgeoning sport of ice climbing also thrives in the park. The Diamond, Lumpy Ridge, and Petit Grepons are the places for rock climbing, while well-known ice-climbing spots include Hidden Falls, Loch Vale, and Emerald and Black lakes.

OUTFITTER ★

Colorado Mountain School is the oldest continuously operating U.S. guide service and an invaluable resource. You can take introductory half-day and one- to seven-day courses on climbing and rappelling technique, or sign up for guided introductory trips, full-day climbs, and longer expeditions. Make reservations as far as six weeks in advance for summer climbs. The school also runs a 16-bed hostel. ⊠ *341 Moraine Ave., Estes Park* ☎ *800/836–4008 Ext. 3* ⊕ *www.totalclimbing.com* ✉ *$75–$395.*

WINTER SPORTS

Each winter, the popularity of snowshoeing in the park increases. It's a wonderful way to experience Rocky Mountain's majestic winter side, when the jagged peaks are softened with a blanket of snow and the summer hordes are nonexistent. You can snowshoe any of the summer hiking trails that are accessible by road; many of them also become well-traveled cross-country ski trails.

Backcountry skiing within the park ranges from gentle cross-country outings to full-on telemarking down steep chutes and glaciers. Come spring, when avalanche danger decreases, the park has some classic ski descents for those on telemark or alpine touring equipment. Ask a ranger about conditions and gear up as if you were spending the night. If you plan on venturing off trail, take a shovel, probe pole, and avalanche transceiver. Two trails to try are Tonahutu Creek Trail (near Kawuneeche Visitor Center) and the Colorado River Trail to Lulu City (start at the Timber Creek Campground).

Only on the west side of the park are you permitted to snowmobile, but you must register at Kawuneeche Visitor Center before traveling up the unplowed section of Trail Ridge Road up to Milner Pass. Check the park newspaper, *High Country Headlines,* for ranger-guided tours.

OUTFITTERS AND EXPEDITIONS

Estes Park Mountain Shop. Rent snowshoes and skis here, as well as fishing, hiking, and climbing equipment. The store gives half- and full-day guided fly-fishing trips into the park year-round for all levels as well as four- and eight-hour climbing trips to areas near Rocky Mountain National Park. ⊠ *2050 Big Thompson Ave., Estes Park* ☎ *970/586–6548 or 866/303–6548* ⊕ *www.estesparkmountainshop.com.*

Never Summer Mountain Sports (⊠ *919 Grand Ave., Grand Lake* ☎ *970/627–3642*) rents cross-country skis, boots, and poles, and sells hiking and some climbing gear.

EDUCATIONAL OFFERINGS

ART PROGRAM

Artist-in-Residence. Professional writers, sculptors, composers, and visual and performing artists can stay in a rustic cabin for two weeks in summer while working on their art. During their stay, they must do two park presentations, and donate a piece of original work to Rocky Mountain that relates to their stay. Applications must be received by December for requests for the following summer. ☎ *970/586–1206.*

CLASSES AND SEMINARS

★ **Rocky Mountain Field Seminars.** The Rocky Mountain Nature Association sponsors some 100 hands-on seminars for adults and children on such topics as natural history, geology, bird-watching, wildflower identification, wildlife biology, photography, and sketching. Children's

FODOR'S FIRST PERSON

Barbara Colligan
Colorado Resident

32

In September and October, there are traffic jams in the park as people drive up to listen to the elk bugling. It's a lot of fun. The rangers and park volunteers keep track of where the elk are and direct visitors to the mating spots. The bugling is high-pitched, and if it's light enough, you can see the elk put his head in the air. He really puts his whole head and shoulders into it, and his throat puffs out. It's fascinating to listen to. It echoes across the forest.

The call is to let the other bulls know "These are my females. You other males stay away." They sometimes have clashes. I've seen a big elk chase a smaller one off. The females are grouped around the bulls. Once I saw a female start to move away and the bull pushed her back into line.

Having binoculars really makes a difference, too. With those I could see the elk even when it got dark.

classes run three hours, and adult classes last one to five days. All are taught by expert instructors. College students often receive academic credit, and teachers can receive recertification credit. ⊠ *1895 Fall River Rd., Estes Park* ☎ *970/586–3262* ⊕ *www.rmna.org* ⊠ *$20–$75 per day* ⊙ *Jan.–Oct.*

RANGER PROGRAMS

☺ **Junior Ranger Program.** Pick up a Junior Ranger activity book (in English or Spanish) at any visitor center. Program content has been developed for children ages 12 and under; the material focuses on environmental education, identifying birds and wildlife, and outdoor safety skills. Once a child has completed all of the activities, a ranger will look over the book and award a Junior Ranger badge. ☎ *970/586–1206* ⊠ *Free.*

☺ **Ranger-Led Programs.** With more than 150 programs each summer, there ★ are many opportunities to join in on free hikes, talks, and activities conducted by those who know the park best. Topics may include the wildlife, geology, vegetation, or park history. At night, storytelling, slide shows, and talks may be part of the evening campfire program, held in summer at park campgrounds and at Beaver Meadows Visitor Center. There are also evening hikes and stargazing sessions. On Friday, stories, songs, and marshmallow roasts take place at Holzwarth Historic Site. In winter, rangers lead snowshoeing and cross-country ski tours. Special programs for kids include "Ranger for a Day," "Skins and Skulls," and "Tales for Tots" (for preschool-age kids with an accompanying adult). Look for the extensive program schedule in the park's newspaper. ☎ *970/586–1206* ⊠ *Free.*

WHAT'S NEARBY

NEARBY TOWNS

Estes Park, 5 mi east of Rocky Mountain, is the park's most popular gateway. The town sits at an altitude of more than 7,500 feet, with 14,255-feet Longs Peak and a chorus of surrounding mountains as its stunning backdrop. Many of the small hotels lining the roads are mom-and-pop outfits that have been passed down through several generations. Estes Park's quieter cousin, **Grand Lake,** 1½ mi outside the park's west entrance, gets busy in summer, but overall has a low-key, Western graciousness. In winter, it's *the* snowmobiling capital and ice-fishing destination for Coloradans. At the park's southwestern entrance are Arapaho National/Roosevelt Forest, Arapaho National Recreational Area, and the small town of **Granby,** the place to go for big-game hunting, mountain biking, and skiing at nearby SolVista resort, Winter Park, and Mary Jane.

VISITOR INFORMATION

Estes Park Convention and Visitors Bureau ⊠ *500 Big Thompson Ave., Estes Park* ☎ *800/443–7837* ⊕ *www.estesparkcvb.com.* **Grand Lake Area Chamber of Commerce** ⊠ *14700 U.S. 34, Grand Lake* ☎ *800/531–1019* ⊕ *www. grandlakechamber.com.* **Greater Granby Area Chamber of Commerce** ⊠ *81 W. Jasper, P.O. Box 35, Granby* ☎ *970/887–2311 or 800/325–1661* ⊕ *www. granbychamber.com.*

NEARBY ATTRACTIONS

The Stanley Hotel. Genius entrepreneur F. O. Stanley, inventor of the Stanley Steamer automobile and several photographic processes, constructed this regal hotel on a promontory overlooking Estes Park in 1907 (it opened in 1909), after his doctors said he would soon die of tuberculosis. Stanley went on to live another 30-odd years, an extension that he attributed to the area's fresh air. The hotel soon became one of the most glamorous resorts in the Rockies, a reputation it holds to this day. The hotel was the inspiration for Stephen King's *The Shining,* part of which he wrote while staying here. ⊠ *333 East Wonderview Ave., Estes Park* ☎ *970/586–3371 or 800/976–1377* ⊕ *www.stanleyhotel.com* ☉ *Year-round.*

AREA ACTIVITIES

SPORTS AND THE OUTDOORS

FISHING

Anglers in the Grand Lake and Granby area enjoy plentiful trout, mackinaw, and kokanee salmon. Ice fishers will not want to miss the big contest held the first weekend in January on Lake Granby, where winners collect $20,000 in cash and prizes. Anyone older than 16 needs a Colorado fishing license, which you can obtain at local sporting-goods stores. See ⊕ *www.wildlife.state.co.us/fishing* for more information.

The Big Thompson River, east of Estes Park along U.S. 34, has a good stock of rainbow and brown trout. Anyone older than 16 needs a Colorado fishing license, which you can obtain at local sporting-goods stores (see ⊕ *www.wildlife.state.co.us/fishing* for more information).

OUTFITTERS AND EXPEDITIONS **Rocky Mountain Adventures** (☎ *970/586–6191 or 800/858–6808*) offers guided fly- and float-fishing trips on the Cache la Poudre River. **Trail Ridge Marina** (✉ *Shadow Mountain Lake, 4 mi south of Grand Lake on U.S. 34* ☎ *970/627–3586*) rents pontoons, runabouts, and fishing boats by the hour.

32

WINTER SPORTS

★ Many consider Grand Lake to be Colorado's snowmobiling capital, with more than 300 mi of trails (150 mi groomed), many winding through virgin forest. If you're visiting during the winter holidays, make reservations about three weeks ahead.

OUTFITTERS AND EXPEDITIONS **Grand Adventures LLC** (✉ *304 W. Portal Rd., Grand Lake* ☎ *970/627–3098 or 800/726–9247* ⊕ *www.grandadventures.com*) arranges unguided snowmobile rentals. **Never Summer Mountain Products** (✉ *919 Grand Ave., Grand Lake* ☎ *970/627–3642*) rents cross-country skis and snowshoes. **On The Trail** (✉ *1447 County Rd. 491, Grand Lake* ☎ *970/627–0171 or 888/627–2429* ⊕ *www.onthetrailrentals.com*) rents snowmobiles.

ARTS AND ENTERTAINMENT

ARTS

The **Rocky Ridge Music Center** (✉ *465 Longs Peak Rd., 9 mi south of Estes Park off CO Hwy. 7* ☎ *970/586–4031* ⊕ *www.rockyridge.org*) holds classical concerts June through August.

NIGHTLIFE

The **Lariat Saloon** (✉ *1121 Grand Ave., Grand Lake* ☎ *970/627–9965*) is the Grand Lake local hotspot with live rock music almost every night. Look for the talking buffalo. **The Tavern** (✉ *Mary's Lake Lodge, 2625 Mary's Lake Rd., Estes Park* ☎ *970/586–5958*) has live entertainment nightly in summer and five nights a week in winter.

SCENIC DRIVES

Peak-to-Peak Highway. Winding from Central City through Nederland to Estes Park, this is not the quickest way to get to the eastern gateway to Rocky Mountain National Park, but it's certainly the most scenic. It passes through the old mining towns of Ward and Allenspark and enjoy spectacular mountain vistas and, in fall, golden stands of aspen. Mount Meeker and Longs Peak rise magnificently behind every bend in the road, and the descent into Estes Park provides grand vistas of snow-covered alpine peaks and green valleys. ✉ *From Central City through Nederland to Estes Park* ✢ *From Nederland drive north on Hwy. 72. Turn left at intersection with Hwy. 7 and continue to Estes Park.*

WHERE TO EAT AND STAY

ABOUT THE RESTAURANTS

Restaurants in north central Colorado run the gamut from simple diners with tasty, homey basics to elegant establishments with extensive wine lists. Some restaurants take reservations, but many—particularly mid-range spots—seat on a first-come, first-served basis. In the park itself, there are no real dining establishments, though you can get snacks and light fare at the top of the Trail Ridge Road. The park also has a handful of scenic picnic areas, all with tables and pit or flush toilets.

ABOUT THE HOTELS

Bed-and-breakfasts and small inns in north central Colorado vary from old-fashioned fluffy cottages to sleek, modern buildings with understated lodge themes. If you want some pampering, there are guest ranches and spas. In Estes Park, Grand Lake, and nearby towns, the elevation keeps the climate cool, and you'll have a tough time finding air-conditioned lodging. For a historic spot, try the Stanley Hotel in Estes Park—with its stately structure, it would fit right in on Mackinac Island in Michigan. The park has no hotels or lodges.

ABOUT THE CAMPGROUNDS

Five top-notch campgrounds in the park meet the needs of campers, whether you're staying in a tent, trailer, or RV (only two campgrounds accept reservations; the others fill up on a first-come, first-served basis). Backcountry camping requires advance reservations or a day-of-trip permit; contact **Backcountry Permits, Rocky Mountain National Park** (⊠ *Beaver Meadows Visitor Center, U.S. 36 southwest of Estes Park* ☎ *970/586–1242* ☉ *May–Sept., daily 7–7; Oct.–Apr., daily 8–4:30*) before starting out.

WHERE TO EAT

IN THE PARK

¢ ✕ **Trail Ridge Store Snack Bar.** Pick up snacks and sandwiches, burgers,
AMERICAN and soups at the Alpine Visitor Center. ⊠ *Trail Ridge Rd.* ☎ *970/586–3097* ⊟ *AE, D, MC, V* ☉ *Closed mid-Oct.–May.*

PICNIC AREAS **Endovalley.** With 32 tables and 30 fire grates, this is the largest picnic area in the park. The views here are of aspen groves, Fall River Pass, and a beautiful lake. ⊠ *U.S. 34, at the beginning of Old Fall River Rd.*
Hollowell Park. In a meadow near Mill Creek, this lovely spot for a picnic has nine tables. The Mill Creek Basin trailhead is nearby. There are no running water and no fire grates. ⊠ *Off Bear Lake Rd., between the Moraine Park Museum and Glacier Basin campground.*

☉ **Sprague Lake.** With 23 tables, there's plenty of room for the whole gang at this dining alfresco spot. The wheelchair-accessible picnic area has restrooms, too. ⊠ *0.6 mi from the intersection of Bear Lake Road and U.S. 36.*

OUTSIDE THE PARK

ESTES PARK

$–$$ ✕ **Bighorn Restaurant.** An Estes Park staple since 1972, this family-run
AMERICAN outfit is where the locals go for breakfast. Opening as early as 6 AM, you
★ can get a double-cheese omelet, huevos rancheros, or grits before heading into the park. Owners Laura and Sid Brown are happy to pack up a lunch for you—just place your order with breakfast, and your sandwich, chips, homemade cookie, and drink will be ready to go when you leave. This homey spot also serves lunch and dinner. ⊠ *401 W. Elkhorn Ave., Estes Park* ☎ *970/586–2792* ⊟ *D, MC, V.*

32

$$$
STEAK
✗ **Hunter's Chophouse.** The locals head here for the savory and spicy barbecue: steaks, venison, buffalo, chicken, and seafood. If you're not hungry enough for a 20-ounce porterhouse steak, Hunter's has gourmet burgers like the avocado bacon burger and a list of sandwiches that spans a traditional French dip and salmon pancetta on focaccia. There's a good kids' menu, too, with fish-and-chips, a junior sirloin, and a mini chophouse burger. It fills quickly in the evening. ⊠ *1690 Big Thompson Ave.* ☎ *970/586–6962* ⚑ *Reservations essential* ▭ *MC, V.*

$$
ITALIAN
✗ **Mama Rose's.** After an active day in the park, head here for a $13 four-course meal, including all the salad, soup, bread, and spaghetti you can eat, with a good portion of spumoni to top it off. The lasagne and tricolor baked pasta are popular entrées, as are veal- or chicken parmigiana and fettuccine Alfredo. There's also a kids' menu. ⊠ *338 E. Elkhorn Ave., Estes Park* ☎ *970/586–3330* ⚑ *Reservations essential* ▭ *AE, D, DC, MC, V* ⊗ *Closed Jan–mid Feb. No lunch.*

$$
ECLECTIC
★
✗ **The Other Side.** View ducks from your table and listen to easy jazz at this delightful, rustic, high-ceilinged restaurant on Estes Park's west side. Specialties include trout, crab cakes, Alfredo chicken breast, and cowboy steak (a 16-ounce ribeye). Entrées come with soup or salad, and bread—you won't leave hungry. ⊠ *900 Moraine Ave., Estes Park* ☎ *970/586–2171* ⊕ *www.theothersideofestes.com* ▭ *AE, D, MC, V.*

$
PIZZA
✗ **Poppy's Pizza & Grill.** The spinach, artichoke, and feta pie with sun-dried tomato sauce at this family-friendly pizzeria is excellent. Try a pizza with Rocky Mountain smoked trout, capers, and cream cheese, or create your own specialty from the five sauces and more than 40 toppings on the menu. A portion of the profits go to local charities. ⊠ *342 E. Elkhorn Ave., Estes Park* ☎ *970/586–8282* ▭ *AE, D, DC, MC, V* ⊗ *Closed Jan.*

$$
ITALIAN
☾
★
✗ **Sweet Basilico Café.** This family-owned and family-friendly restaurant is the locals' favorite for basic Italian classics like lasagna, manicotti, and eggplant parmesan as well as the great service. The calamari *fritti* is crisp and spicy, sandwiches made with homemade focaccia are delicious, and the minestrone satisfies wonderfully. All meals, including home-style entrées like the savory and spicy chicken *scarpelli*, are prepared fresh. Enjoy dinner alfresco on the large covered patio or in the well-lighted, brick-wall dining room accented with photos of Italian scenery. Don't forget the spumoni cheesecake with mascarpone frosting for dessert. ⊠ *430 Prospect Village Dr.* ☎ *970/586–3899* ⚑ *Reservations essential* ▭ *AE, D, MC, V.*

GRANBY

$–$$
ECLECTIC
✗ **Longbranch Restaurant.** This smoke-free, Western-style coffee shop has a warm fireplace, rustic wood interior, and wagon-wheel chandeliers. It serves delicious German food: bratwurst, goulash, schnitzel, and sauerbraten. The traditional German desserts are authentic; the strudel gets particularly high marks. The bar serves many domestic and foreign beers, as well as a few microbrews. ⊠ *185 E. Agate Ave., U.S. 40 Granby* ☎ *970/887–2209* ▭ *D, MC, V* ⊗ *Closed Sun.*

GRAND LAKE

$ ✕**The Bear's Den.** The menu at this rustic, log restaurant includes Rocky
ECLECTIC Mountain oysters, New York strip steak, and seafood. But the standouts
here are the nightly specials—especially the fried chicken and chicken-
fried steak, cooked in cast-iron skillets for homemade flavor. ⊠ *612
Grand Ave., Grand Lake* ☎ *970/627–3385* ▭ *D, MC, V.*

$$ ✕**Sagebrush BBQ & Grill.** Barbecue ribs, chicken, and catfish draw local and
SOUTHERN out-of-town attention to this homey café. Comforting sides such as baked
beans, corn bread, cole slaw, and potatoes top off the large plates; meals
can be sized for smaller appetites. They also serve breakfast. ⊠ *1101
Grand Ave., Grand Lake* ☎ *970/627–1404* ▭ *AE, D, DC, MC, V.*

WHERE TO STAY

IN THE PARK

CAMPING ⚠**Aspenglen Campground.** This quiet, east-side spot near the north
$$ entrance is set in open pine woodland along Fall River. It doesn't have
the views of Moraine Park or Glacier Basin, but it is small and peace-
ful. There are a few excellent walk-in sites for those who want to pitch
a tent away from the crowds but still close to the car. All sites accommodate RVs, tents, trailers, or campers. Firewood and ice are for sale.
Reservations are not accepted. **Pros:** good paved road; very peaceful;
sites with trees; close to town but still very private. **Con:** no great mountain views. ⊠ *Drive past Fall River Visitor Center on U.S. 34 and turn
left at the campground road.* ☎ *No phone* ⚠ *54 tent/RV sites* ⚐ *Flush
toilets, drinking water, fire grates, public telephone* ⚐ *Reservations not
accepted* ▭ *AE, D, MC, V* ☉ *Closed mid-Sept.–late May.*

$$ ⚠**Glacier Basin Campground.** Rest near the banks of Glacier Creek and take
in views of the Continental Divide. There's easy access to a network of
many popular trails, and rangers come here for campfire programs. All
sites accommodate RVs, tents, trailers, or campers. Firewood and ice are
for sale. Reservations are essential. **Pros:** ranger-led campfire programs;
near many hiking trails. **Con:** trees have suffered damage from mountain
pine beetle, but new growth is evident. ⊠ *Drive 5 mi south from U.S.
36 along Bear Lake Rd.* ☎ *877/444–6777* ⚠ *150 tent/RV sites* ⚐ *Flush
toilets, dump station, drinking water, fire grates, public telephone* ⚐ *Res-
ervations essential* ▭ *AE, D, MC, V* ☉ *Closed mid-Sept.–late May.*

$$ ⚠**Longs Peak Campground.** Hikers going up Longs Peak can stay at
this year-round campground. Sites, which are first-come, first-served,
are limited to eight people; ice and firewood are sold in summer. **Pro:**
good camp site for Longs Peak hikers. **Cons:** tents only; drinking water
isn't available off season. ⊠ *9 mi south of Estes Park on Rte. 7* ☎ *No
phone* ⚠ *26 tent sites* ⚐ *Flush toilets, pit toilets, drinking water (mid-
May–mid-Sept.), fire grates, ranger station* ⚐ *Reservations not accepted*
▭ *AE, D, MC, V.*

$$ ⚠**Moraine Park Campground.** This popular campground hosts ranger-led
★ campfire programs and is near hiking trails. You'll hear elk bugling if you
camp here in September or October. Sites accommodate RVs, tents, trailers,
and campers. Reservations are essential from mid-May to late September.
Pros: abundant shady trees; near many hiking trails; nice pine scent. **Con:**
no drinking water outside summer months. ⊠ *Drive south on Bear Lake*

Rd. from U.S. 36, ¾ mi to campground entrance ☎ *877/444–6777* ⚠ *245 tent/RV sites* ♿ *Flush toilets, pit toilets, dump station, drinking water (mid-May–mid-Sept.), fire grates, public telephone* ⊟ *AE, D, MC, V.*

$$ ⚠**Timber Creek Campground.** Anglers love this spot on the Colorado River, 10 mi from Grand Lake village. In the evening you can sit in on ranger-led campfire programs. All sites accommodate RVs, tents, trailers, or campers, and are limited to eight people. Firewood is sold here. Reservations are not accepted. **Pros:** great fishing spot by the Colorado River. **Cons:** mountain pine beetle has necessitated cutting of many mature Lodgepole Pines (but new growth is evident); no drinking water in the off season. ⊠ *Trail Ridge Rd. 1, 2 mi west of Alpine Visitor Center* ☎ *No phone* ⚠ *98 tent/RV sites* ♿ *Flush toilets, pit toilets, dump station, drinking water (mid-May to mid-Sept.), fire grates, public telephone* ♿ *Reservations not accepted* ⊟ *AE, D, MC, V.*

OUTSIDE THE PARK

ESTES PARK

$$$ 🛏**Boulder Brook.** Luxury suites at this secluded spot on the river are tucked in the pines, yet close to town and 1½ mi from Rocky Mountain National Park. Sleep regally on linens with at least 300-thread count. Three themed suites are furnished and appointed individually—stylishly and elegantly—and given fitting names like Cowboys & Indians or Shabby Chic. Suites have either a full kitchen or kitchenette, a private deck, a gas fireplace, and all but two have a jetted tub. **Pros:** scenic location, quiet area, attractive grounds. **Cons:** not within walking distance of attractions, no nearby dining. ⊠ *1900 Fall River Rd.* ☎ *970/586–0910 or 800/238–0910* ⊕ *www.boulderbrook.com* ⤙ *19 suites* ♿ *In-room: kitchen, DVD. In-hotel: parking* ⊟ *D, MC, V.*

$$$$ 🛏**C Lazy U Guest Ranch.** Secluded in a broad, verdant valley, this deluxe
☾ guest ranch attracts an international clientele, including Hollywood royalty and the real thing. Guests enjoy luxurious Western-style accommodations, fine meals, live entertainment, and any outdoor activity they can dream up—and their own personal horse. The instructors are top-notch, and the children's programs are unbeatable. The minimum stay is three days with arrival on Wednesday or Saturday in the summer, and two nights in winter. All meals are included. **Pros:** beautiful views. **Cons:** expensive. 🖂 *P.O. Box 379, Granby 80446* ⊹ *3½ mi north on CO Rte. 125 from U.S. Hwy. 40 junction* ☎ *970/887–3344* ⊕ *www.clazyu.com* ⤙ *40 rooms, 20 cabins* ♿ *In-room: no a/c, no phone, no TV. In-hotel: restaurant, bar, tennis courts, pool, gym, children's programs (ages 3–17)* ⊟ *AE, MC, V* ☾ *Closed early Sept.–mid-Dec. and mid-Feb.–Apr.* ⦿| *FAP.*

$ 🛏**Estes Park Center/YMCA of the Rockies.** This 890-acre, family-friendly
☾ property has a wealth of attractive and clean lodging options among its four lodges and many cabins. Sign up for a class and learn a skill like calligraphy, fly-fishing, or compass reading. A couple can rent a simple, rustic pine cabin, and newer cabins which have modern kitchen appliances and televisions accommodate 10–40 people. An extended family can reserve the Reunion Cabin that houses 40 people. Lodge rooms can be outfitted with queen beds or bunk beds for the kids. A meal plan is available for the all-you-can-eat buffet. There's a Frisbee-golf course, and a climbing wall to hone your rock-climbing skills. **Pros:** good value

THE GRAND DAYS OF THE SPA

Colorado's scenery has long attracted high-profile personalities like Teddy Roosevelt and Walt Whitman, but many early travelers were asthma, tuberculosis, and arthritis sufferers who came to the dry climate to convalesce. From the early to mid-20th century, healing spas and resorts like Hot Sulphur Springs and Eldorado Springs sprang up in the mountains of north central Colorado, serving as destinations for long-term visitors.

The list of rich or famous visitors is long: Robert Frost visited his daughter, Marjorie, in Boulder while she recuperated in the early 1930s; Dwight and Mamie Eisenhower honeymooned at Eldorado Springs.

This therapeutic tradition continues today. Refurbished hot springs and spas are regaining their popularity, and the National Jewish Medical and Research Center in Denver specializes in treatments for respiratory ailments.

for large groups and for longer stays, lots of family-oriented activities and amenities, stunningly scenic setting. **Cons:** very large, busy, and crowded property; fills fast; location requires vehicle to visit town or the national park. ✉ *2515 Tunnel Rd.* ☎ *970/586–3341, 303/448–1616, or 800/777–9622* ⊕ *www.ymcarockies.org* ⬳ *688 rooms, 220 cabins* ⬧ *In-room: no a/c, no TV. In-hotel: restaurant, tennis court, pool, children's programs (ages 3–18), parking* ▭ *MC, V* ⓘⓞⓘ *MAP.*

$$ ⌂ **Glacier Lodge.** Families are the specialty at this secluded, 19-acre guest ⓒ resort on the banks of the Big Thompson River. The kids will take home plenty of fun memories from the twice-weekly "soda saloons," nature walks, arts-and-crafts workshops, Tuesday evening campfire stories, and Thursday campfire sing-along. The whole family will enjoy the once-weekly "mountain breakfast" with omelets and flapjacks before a guided trail ride, some into Rocky Mountain National Park. You can stay in former Colorado governor James Peabody's (in office 1902–04) summer residence. There's a minimum stay of four nights. All bed and bath linens and kitchen utensils and dinnerware are provided. **Pros:** great place for families, attractive grounds on the river, on bus route. **Cons:** not within walking distance of attractions, along rather busy road. ✉ *2166 CO Hwy. 66, Estes Park* ☎ *970/586–4401 or 800/523–3920* ⊕ *www.glacierlodge.com* ⬳ *24 single-family cabins, 4 cabins for 12–30* ⬧ *In-room: no a/c, kitchen, DVD. In-hotel: pool, children's programs (ages 4–10), parking* ▭ *AE, D, MC, V.*

$$ ⌂ **Marys Lake Lodge and Resort.** This 1913 chalet-style lodge with brown siding, white trim, and a green roof overlooks peaceful Mary's Lake a couple of miles south of town. Original woodwork and some of the original antiques adorn the rooms; look for the Victorian floral lamps in the hallways. Some rooms still have claw-foot tubs, and others have Jacuzzi tubs. The elegant Grandmaison's Chalet Room ($$$–$$$$) serves such entrées as cioppino, bouillabaise, and Provimi veal chops and has an excellent wine list. Reservations are essential. The Tavern ($$) is more casual and has seating on the porch with expansive views. Popular dishes are the shepherd's pie and the lamb chops. The lodge also rents fully modern luxury condominiums. **Pros:** two excellent

32

on-site restaurants, beautiful views. **Cons:** not within walking distance of attractions or other dining; large, older hotel. ⊠ *2625 Mary's Lake Rd.* ☎ *970/586-5958 or 877/442-6279* ⊕ *www.maryslakelodge.com* 🛏 *16 rooms, 1 cabin, 40 condos* ⟨ *In-room: Wi-Fi. In-hotel: 2 restaurants, pool, spa, parking* ⊟ *AE, D, MC, V* ⦿*CP.*

$$$–$$$$
Fodor's Choice
★

The Stanley Hotel. Perched regally on a hill with a commanding view of the town, the Stanley is one of Colorado's great old hotels, impeccably maintained in its historic state, yet with all the modern conveniences. F. O. Stanley (the inventor of the Stanley Steamer) began construction in 1907, and when it opened in 1909 it was the first hotel in the world with electricity and the first in the U.S. with in-room telephones. Be sure to take one of the daily historical and ghost tours (The Stanley inspired Stephen King's novel *The Shining*). Many of the sunny rooms have mountain views and are decorated with antiques and period reproductions. **Pros:** many rooms have been updated recently; good restaurant; some rooms have mountain views. **Cons:** some rooms are small and tight; building is old; no air-conditioning. ⊠ *333 East Wonderview Ave., Estes Park* ☎ *970/586-3371 or 800/976-1377* ⊕ *www.stanleyhotel. com* 🛏 *138 rooms* ⟨ *In-room: no a/c, Wi-Fi. In-hotel: restaurant, bar, pool, spa* ⊟ *AE, D, DC, MC, V.*

$$$

Valhalla Resort. Away from the touristy bustle of Estes Park's main downtown area, this tucked-away resort allows you to relax in large cabins with modern amenities—in fact, the larger ones feel more like condos. Look out your window and it's quite likely you'll see an elk grazing. The resort is often booked in summer and early fall during the elk bugling, so be sure to reserve far in advance. All cabins have kitchen, living room, and deck or patio with a grill. Resort activities include shuffleboard, miniature golf, and horseshoes. There's also a lounge with video games and a hot tub. If you're 62 or older, you get a 10% discount. Also, prices drop in the shoulder season. **Pros:** cabins are remodeled and very well kept; lots of space; beautiful views. **Cons:** road into resort is very bumpy. ⊠ *2185 Eagle Cliff Rd., Estes Park* ☎ *970/586-3284 or 800/522-3284* ⊕ *www.valhallaresort.com* 🛏 *26 1- to 4-bedroom cabins* ⟨ *In-hotel: pool* ⊟ *AE, MC, V.*

CAMPING
$

National Recreation Reservation Service. West of Lyons and south of Estes Park, three campgrounds—Camp Dick, Olive Ridge, Peaceful Valley—are tucked away in quiet forests. Although reservations can be made, half of the sites in these campgrounds are not reservable and are filled on a first-come, first-served basis. Weekends are popular, so if you don't have a reservation, the rangers recommend arriving before noon on Friday. For campground details, see ⊕ *www.fs.fed.us\r2\arnf.* When making a reservation online only, you can pay by credit card (AE, D, MC, V). ☎ *877/444-6777* ⊕ *www.reserveusa.com.*

GRAND LAKE

$–$$
Fodor's Choice
★

The Historic Rapids Lodge & Restaurant. This 1915 lodgepole-pine structure on the Tonahutu River has seven lodge rooms—each with ceiling fan—done in the Rocky Mountain rustic style with a mix of antique furnishings, such as claw-foot tubs. The innkeepers also rent newer condos for large groups. The delightful Rapids Restaurant ($$$–$$$$; reservations advised) is Grand Lake's most romantic for fine dining, with stained glass and timber beams. The specialty is an 8-ounce filet mignon with artichokes and béarnaise sauce. **Pros:** in-house restaurant, condos are great for longer stays, quiet area of town. **Cons:** unpaved parking area, hotel rooms are above restaurant. ✉ *209 Rapids La., Grand Lake* ☎ *970/627–3707* ⊕ *www.rapidslodge.com* ⤡ *7 rooms, 8 suites, 5 cabins, 11 condos* ⚐ *In-room: no a/c, kitchen (some). In-hotel: restaurant, bar* ▭ *AE, MC, V* ⊘ *Closed Apr. and Nov.*

$–$$
★
⛭ **Mountain Lakes Lodge.** The scent of the pine forest welcomes you to these charming log cabins. All cabins have private decks and charcoal grills. Dogs are enthusiastically welcomed, and have their own private fenced yards. Cabins accommodate two to seven people. **Pros:** dog friendly, close to fishing, good value. **Cons:** dogs are the only pets allowed; two-day minimum year-round, three-day minimum for holidays and special events. ✉ *10480 U.S. 34, Grand Lake* ☎ *970/627–8448* ⊕ *www. mountainlakeslodge.com* ⤡ *11 cabins* ⚐ *In-room: no a/c, no phone, kitchen. In-hotel: some pets allowed (fee)* ▭ *MC, V.*

CAMPING
¢
⚠ **Arapaho National Recreation Area.** Five lakeside campgrounds—Stillwater, Cutthroat Bay, Green Ridge, Arapaho Bay, and Sunset Creek—keep you close to recreational activities. Stillwater has showers. **Pros:** campgrounds are well kept. **Cons:** some tree damage from pine beetle. ✉ *South of Grand Lake on U.S. 34* ☎ *970/887–0056 or 877/444–6777* ⊕ *www.reserveusa. com* ⚐ *Flush toilets, pit toilets, partial hookups (electric and water) dump station, drinking water, fire grates, picnic tables, public telephone* ⤡ *272 tent/RV sites (21 partial hook-ups with water and electricity), 29 tent sites, 3 group sites* ▭ *No credit cards* ⊘ *Closed Sept.–May.*

Saguaro
National Park

WORD OF MOUTH

"Don't miss Saguaro National Park, which has an east and a west part on either side of Tucson, and visit the Arizona Sonora Desert Museum while you are there."

—emalloy

WELCOME TO SAGUARO

TOP REASONS TO GO

★ **Saguaro sightseeing:** Hike, bike, or drive through dense saguaro stands for an up-close look at this king of all cacti.

★ **Wildlife watching:** Diverse wildlife roams through the park, including such ground dwellers as javelinas, coyotes, and rattlesnakes, and winged residents ranging from the migratory lesser long-nosed bat to the diminutive elf owl.

★ **Ancient artwork:** Get a glimpse into the past at the numerous rock-art sites where ancient peoples etched into the stones as far back as 5000 BC.

1 **Saguaro West: Tucson Mountain District.** This more-visited district makes up less than one-third of the park. Here you'll find a Native American video orientation to saguaros at the visitor center, hiking trails, an ancient Hohokam petroglyph site at Signal Hill, and a scenic drive through the park's densest desert growth.

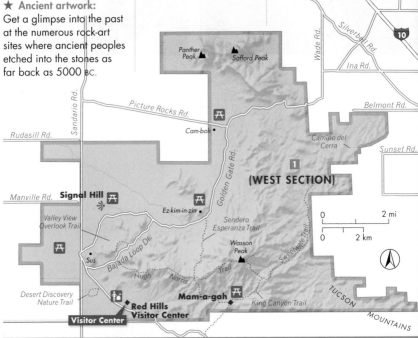

ARIZONA

33

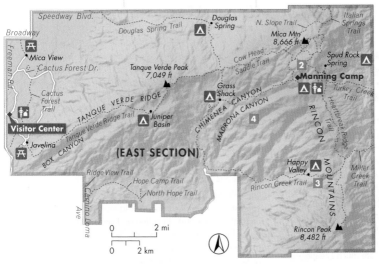

Speedway Blvd.
Broadway
Douglas Spring Trail
Douglas Spring ▲
N. Slope Trail
Italian Springs Trail
Mica Mtn 8,666 ft ▲
Freeman Rd.
Mica View
Cactus Forest Dr.
Cow Head Saddle Trail
Spud Rock Spring
Tanque Verde Peak 7,049 ft ▲
Grass Shack
Manning Camp
Turkey Creek Trail
Cactus Forest Trail
TANQUE VERDE RIDGE
CHIMENEA CANYON
MADRONA CANYON
RINCON
Visitor Center
Tanque Verde Ridge Trail
Juniper Basin
Javelina
BOX CANYON
(EAST SECTION)
Happy Valley
Miller Creek Trail
Ridge View Trail
Hope Camp Trail
North Hope Trail
Rincon Creek Trail
MOUNTAINS
Camino Loma Ave
0   2 mi
0   2 km
Rincon Peak 8,482 ft ▲

2 **Saguaro East: Rincon Mountain District.** In the Rincon Mountains, Saguaro East encompasses 57,930 acres of designated wilderness area, an easily accessible scenic loop drive, several easy and intermediate trails through the cactus forest, and opportunities for adventure and backcountry camping at six rustic campgrounds.

3 **Rincon Valley Area.** This 4,011-acre expansion along the southern border of Saguaro's Rincon Mountain District offers access to the riparian area along Rincon Creek.

4 **Saguaro Wilderness Area.** In the Rincon Mountain District, this backcountry area travels from desert scrublands at 3,000 feet to mixed conifer forests at 9,000 feet.

GETTING ORIENTED

Saguaro National Park preserves some of the densest stands of these massive cacti, which can live up to 200 years and weigh up to two tons. Today more than 90,000 acres include habitats stretching from the arid Sonoran Desert up to high mountain forests. The park is split into two sections, with Tucson, Arizona, sandwiched in the middle. The urban base proves useful, but the park is no less rugged. More than half of it is designated wilderness area.

KEY

🏠 Ranger Station
⛺ Campground
🌲 Picnic Area
🍴 Restaurant
🏨 Lodge
🥾 Trailhead
🚻 Restrooms
➹ Scenic Viewpoint
:::::: Walking/Hiking Trails

SAGUARO PLANNER

When to Go

Most people visit Saguaro in milder weather, October through April, though the park never gets crowded. December through February can be cool and is prone to gentle rain showers. The spring months from March through May offer bright, sunny days and desert wildflowers in bloom. Because of high temperatures, it's best to visit the park in the early morning or late afternoon from June through September. The intense summer heat puts off most hikers, at least at lower elevations, but lodging prices are much cheaper—rates at top resorts in Tucson drop by as much as 70%.

Cooler temperatures return in October and November, providing perfect weather for hiking and camping. In April, Hispanic culture and heritage are celebrated in the park during Fiesta de Saguaro.

AVG. HIGH/LOW TEMPS.

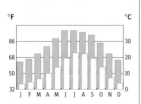

Flora and Fauna

More than 1,200 plant species, including 50 types of cactus, thrive in the park; among the most common are the prickly pear, barrel cactus, and teddy bear cholla—named so because it (falsely) appears cuddly—rangers suggest packing a comb to pull its barbed hooks from fingers.

For many of the desert fauna, the saguaro functions as a high-rise hotel. Each spring, the Gila woodpecker and gilded flicker create holes in the cactus and then nest there. When they give up their temporary digs, elf owls, cactus wrens, sparrow hawks, and other avians move in, as do dangerous Africanized honeybees.

The wildlife is most active in early morning and at dusk. Six species of rattlesnake and the Gila monster, a venomous lizard, inhabit the park. In spring and summer they are out and about but tend to keep a low profile during the midday heat. Look where you are walking and avoid sticking your hands or feet under rocks or into crevices. If you do get bitten, get to a clinic or hospital immediately. Not all snakes pass on venom; 50% of the time, the bite is "dry" (non-poisonous).

Getting Here and Around

Saguaro National Park's two distinct sections flank the city of Tucson and are each about a half-hour drive from the center of the city. To reach Tucson Mountain District (west section) from Interstate 10, take exit 242 or exit 257, then go west on Speedway Boulevard (the name will change to Gates Pass Road), follow it to Kinney Road, and turn right. To reach Rincon Mountain District (east section) from Interstate 10, take exit 275, then go north on Houghton Rd. for 10 miles. Turn right on Escalante and left onto Old Spanish Trail, and the Park will be on the right side. If you're coming from town, go east on Speedway Boulevard to Houghton Road. Turn right on Houghton and left onto Old Spanish Trail. In the western section, Bajada Loop Drive takes you through the park and to various trailheads; Cactus Forest Drive does the same for the eastern section. There is no public transportation to or within Saguaro.

33

Updated by
Mara Levin

Standing sentinel in the desert, the towering saguaro is perhaps the most familiar emblem of the Southwest. Known for their height (often 50 feet) and arms reaching out in weird configurations, these slow-growing giants can take 15 years to grow a foot high and up to 75 years to grow their first arm. They are found only in the Sonoran Desert, and the largest concentration is in Saguaro National Park. In late spring (usually May), the succulent's top is covered with tiny white blooms—the Arizona state flower.

PARK ESSENTIALS

ACCESSIBILITY
In the western section, the Red Hills Visitor Center and two nearby nature trails are wheelchair accessible. The eastern district's visitor center is accessible, as is the paved Desert Ecology Trail.

ADMISSION FEES AND PERMITS
Admission is $10 per vehicle and $5 for individuals on foot or bicycle; it is good for seven days from purchase. Annual passes cost $25. For backcountry camping, obtain a required permit for $6 nightly per campsite from the Saguaro East Visitor Center up to two months in advance.

ADMISSION HOURS
The park is open daily, 7 AM to sunset. It's in the mountain time zone.

ATMS/BANKS
The park has no ATMs, but banks are found throughout Tucson.

CELL-PHONE RECEPTION
Cell-phone reception is generally good in the eastern district but is unreliable in the western district. The visitor centers have pay phones.

PARK CONTACT INFORMATION
Saguaro National Park ⊠ 3693 S. Old Spanish Trail, Tucson AZ ☎ 520/733–5158 Saguaro West, 520/733–5153 Saguaro East ⊕ www.nps.gov/sagu.

SCENIC DRIVES

Unless you're ready for a long desert hike, the best way to see Saguaro is from the comfort of your car.

Bajada Loop Drive. This 6-mi unpaved and moderately bumpy drive winds through thick stands of saguaros and offers two picnic areas and a few short hikes, including one to a rock-art site. It's one way between Hugh Norris Trail and Golden Gate Road, so if you want to make the complete circuit, travel counterclockwise. The road is susceptible to flash floods during the monsoon season (July and August), so check road conditions at the visitor center before proceeding. ⊠ *Saguaro West.*

★ **Cactus Forest Drive.** This paved 8-mi drive provides a great overview of all Saguaro East has to offer. The one-way road, which circles clockwise, has several turnouts that make it easy to pull over and admire the scenery; you can also stop at two picnic areas and three easy nature trails. Repaved in 2006, Cactus Forest Drive now offers more scenic pullouts, new roadside displays, and wider bicycle lanes. This road is open from 7 AM to sunset daily. ⊠ *Saguaro East.*

WHAT TO SEE

HISTORIC SITE

Manning Camp. The summer home of Levi Manning, onetime Tucson mayor, was a popular gathering spot for the city's elite in the early 1900s. The cabin can be reached via one of several challenging high-country trails: Douglas Spring Trail to Cow Head Saddle Trail (12 mi), Turkey Creek Trail (7.5 mi), and Tanque Verde Ridge Trail (15.4 mi). The cabin itself is not open for viewing. ⊠ *Douglas Spring Trail (6 mi) to Cow Head Saddle Trail (6 mi).*

SCENIC STOP

☺ **Signal Hill.** An easy five-minute stroll from the signposted parking area takes you to one of the largest gatherings of rock carvings in the Southwest. You'll have a close-up view of the designs left by the Hohokam people between AD 900 and 1200, including large spirals some believe are astronomical markers. ⊠ *4½ mi north of visitor center on Bajada Loop Dr., Saguaro West.*

VISITOR CENTERS

The visitor centers in both districts have orientation slide shows and rangers who can answer your questions, as well as loads of books and maps. Neither has coffee, but they do sell bottled water and soda.

Red Hills Visitor Center. Take in gorgeous views of nearby mountains and the surrounding desert from the center's large windows and shaded outdoor terrace. A spacious gallery is filled with educational exhibits, and a lifelike display simulates the flora and fauna of the region. A 15-minute slide show, "Voices of a Desert," offers a poetic, Native American perspective of the saguaro. Park rangers and volunteers provide maps and suggest hikes to suit your interests. A nicely appointed gift shop and bookstore add to the experience. ⊠ *2700 N. Kinney Rd., Saguaro West* ☎ *520/733–5158* ☺ *Daily 9–5.*

SAGUARO IN ONE DAY

Before setting off, choose which section of the park to visit and pack a lunch. Also bring plenty of water so you don't get dehydrated in the dry climate (you can't depend on finding water in the park).

If you choose the western section, start out by watching the 15-minute slide show at the **Red Hills Visitor Center**, then stroll along the 0.5-mi-long **Desert Discovery Trail**. In the car, head north along Kinney Road, then turn right onto the graded dirt **Bajada Loop Drive**. Before long you'll soon see a turnoff for the **Hugh Norris Trail** on your right. Hike up and after about 45 minutes, you'll reach a perfect spot for a picnic. Hike back down and drive along the Bajada Loop Drive until you reach the turnoff for **Signal Hill**.

Alternatively, if you choose the eastern section, pick up a free map of the hiking trails at the **Saguaro East Visitor Center**. Drive south along the paved **Cactus Forest Drive** to the Javelina picnic area, where you'll see signs for the **Freeman Homestead Trail**, an easy 1-mi loop that winds through a stand of mesquite as interpretive signs describe early inhabitants in the Tucson basin. If you're reasonably fit you might want to tackle part of the **Tanque Verde Ridge Trail**, which affords excellent views of saguaro-studded hillsides.

Along the northern loop of the Cactus Forest Drive is **Cactus Forest Trail**, which branches off into several fairly level paths. You can easily spend the rest of the afternoon strolling among the saguaro.

33

Saguaro East Visitor Center. Stop here to pick up free maps and printed materials on various aspects of the park, including maps of hiking trails and backcountry camping permits (Red Hills Visitor Center, in Saguaro West, does not offer permits). Exhibits at the center are comprehensive, and a relief map of the park lays out the complexities of this protected landscape. A 15-minute "Home in the Desert" slide-show program gives the history of the region, and there is a short self-guided nature hike along the Cactus Garden Trail. A small, select variety of books and other gift items are sold here, too. ⊠ *3693 S. Old Spanish Trail, Saguaro East* ☎ *520/733–5153* ⊙ *Daily 9–5.*

SPORTS AND THE OUTDOORS

BIRD-WATCHING

To check out the more than 200 species of birds living or migrating through the park, begin by focusing your binoculars on the limbs of the saguaros, where many birds make their home. In general, early morning and early evening are the best times for sightings. In winter and spring, volunteer-led birding hikes begin at the visitor centers.

The finest areas to flock to in the Rincon Mountain District are the Desert Ecology Trail, where you may find rufous-winged sparrow, verdins, and Cooper's hawks along the washes, and the Javelina picnic area, where you will most likely spot canyon wrens and black-chinned sparrows. At the Tucson Mountain District, sit down on one of the visitor center benches and look for ash-throated flycatchers, Say's phoebes,

A saguaro grows under the protection of another tree, such as a palo verde or mesquite, before superseding it.

curve-billed thrashers, and Gila woodpeckers. During the cooler months keep a lookout for the wintering neotropical migrants such as hummingbirds, swallows, orioles, and warblers.

OUTFITTERS AND EXPEDITIONS
Run by the Tucson Audubon Society, **Audubon Nature Shop** (⊠ *300 E. University Blvd., Tucson* ☎ *520/629–0510 shop, 520/798–1005 recording*) carries field guides, binoculars, and other items of interest to birders. The shop can provide a list of local independent guides who will take you out birding. The society also operates a 24-hour recorded message about sightings of rare or interesting birds. **Borderlands** (⊠ *2550 W. Calle Padilla, Tucson* ☎ *520/882–7650*) conducts weeklong birding tours about three times yearly in southeastern Arizona, with trips originating in Tucson. **Wild Bird Store** (⊠ *3526 E. Grant Rd., Tucson* ☎ *520/322–9466*) is an excellent resource for bird-watching books, maps, and trail guides.

HIKING

The park has more than 100 mi of trails. The shorter hikes, such as the Desert Discovery and Desert Ecology trails are perfect for those looking to learn about the desert ecosystem without expending too much energy. Rattlesnakes are commonly seen on trails; so are coyotes, javelinas, roadrunners, Gambel's quail, and desert spiny lizards. Hikers should keep their distance from all wildlife.

EXPEDITIONS
The local branch of **Sierra Club** (⊠ *738 N. 5th Ave., Suite 214, Tucson* ☎ *520/620–6401*) sponsors weekend hikes around the area.

SAGUARO WEST

EASY **Desert Discovery Trail.** Learn about plants and animals native to the region on this paved path in Saguaro West. The 0.5-mi loop is wheelchair accessible and has resting benches and ramadas (wooden shelters that supply shade for your table). ⊠ *Trailhead 1 mi north of Red Hills Visitor Center, Saguaro West.*

MODERATE **Valley View Overlook Trail.** On clear days you can spot the distinctive slope of Picacho Peak from this 1.5-mi trail in Saguaro West. Even on an overcast day you'll be treated to splendid vistas of Avra Valley. ⊠ *Trailhead 3 mi north of Red Hills Visitor Center on Bajada Loop Dr., Saguaro West.*

DIFFICULT **Hugh Norris Trail.** This 10-mi trail
Fodor's Choice through the Tucson Mountains is one of the most impressive in the South-
★ west. It's full of switchbacks and some sections are moderately steep, but at the top of 4,687-foot Wasson Peak you'll enjoy views of the saguaro forest spread across the *bajada* (the gently rolling hills at the base of taller mountains). ⊠ *Trailhead 2½ mi north of Red Hills Visitor Center on Bajada Loop Dr., Saguaro West.*

SAGUARO EAST

EASY **Cactus Forest Trail.** This 2.5-mi one-way loop drive in the East district is open to pedestrians, bicyclists, and equestrians. It is an easy walk along a dirt path that passes historic lime kilns and a wide variety of Sonoran Desert vegetation. While walking this trail, keep in mind that it is the only off-road trail for bicyclists. ⊠ *Trailhead 1 mi southeast of Saguaro East Visitor Center on Cactus Forest Dr.*

Desert Ecology Trail. Exhibits on this 0.25-mi loop near the Mica View picnic area explain how local plants and animals subsist on a limited supply of water. ⊠ *Trailhead 2 mi north of Saguaro East Visitor Center.*

Freeman Homestead Trail. Learn a bit about the history of homesteading in the region on this 1-mi loop. Look for owls living in the cliffs above as you make your way through the lowland vegetation. ⊠ *Trailhead 2 mi south of Saguaro East Visitor Center at Javelina picnic area.*

MODERATE **Hope Camp Trail.** Well worth the 5.6-mi round-trip trek, this Rincon Valley
Fodor's Choice Area hike offers gorgeous views of the Tanque Verde Ridge and Rincon
★ Peak. ⊠ *Trail begins off Camino Loma Alta Trail ✤ From Saguaro East entrance, go south 7 mi on Old Spanish Trail, then east 2 mi on Camino Loma Alta to Camino Loma Alta trailhead, which connects to Hope Camp Trail.*

DIFFICULT **Tanque Verde Ridge Trail.** Be rewarded with spectacular scenery on this
★ 15.4-mi trail through desert scrub, oak, alligator juniper, and pinyon pine at the 6,000-foot peak, where views of the surrounding mountain

GOOD READS

■ The *Tucson Hiking Guide*, by Betty Leavengood, is a useful and entertaining book with day hikes in the park.

■ Books that give a general introduction to the park include *Saguaro National Park*, by Doris Evans, and *Sonoran Desert: The Story Behind the Scenery*, by Christopher L. Helms.

■ *All About Saguaros*, by Carle Hodge and published by Arizona Highways Books, includes fabulous color photos of the cactus.

33

ranges from both sides of the ridge delight. ⊠ *Trailhead 2 mi south of Saguaro East Visitor Center at Javelina picnic area.*

EDUCATIONAL OFFERINGS

🅒 **Junior Ranger Program.** Young visitors can pick up an activity pack any time of the year and complete it within an hour or two. Also, a special summer camp for kids 5 to 12, offered several times in June for two to three days at a time, includes daily hikes and workshops on pottery and petroglyphs. ⊠ *Saguaro East Visitor Center* ☎ *520/733–5153* ⊠ *Red Hills Visitor Center* ☎ *520/733–5158.*

Orientation Programs. Daily programs introduce visitors to the desert. You might find slide shows on bats, birds, or desert blooms, naturalist-led hikes (including moonlight hikes), and, in the summer only, films. ⊠ *Saguaro East Visitor Center* ☎ *520/733–5153* ⊠ *Red Hills Visitor Center* ☎ *520/733–5158* 🖅 *Free* ☉ *Daily.*

Ranger Talks. Hear about wildlife, geology, and archaeology at free presentations. For a schedule of upcoming talks, call the visitor centers or view online. ⊠ *Saguaro East Visitor Center* ☎ *520/733–5153* ⊠ *Red Hills Visitor Center, Saguaro West* ☎ *520/733–5158* 🖅 *Free* ☉ *Nov.–mid-Apr.*

WHAT'S NEARBY

Saguaro stands as a protected desert oasis, with metropolitan Tucson, Arizona's second-largest city, lying between the two park sections. Spread over 195 mi, and with a population of nearly a million, Tucson averages 340 days of sunshine a year.

NEARBY ATTRACTIONS

TUCSON ATTRACTIONS

🅒 **Arizona–Sonora Desert Museum.** The name "museum" is a bit mislead-
Fodor's Choice ing since this delightful site is actually a beautifully planned zoo and
★ botanical garden featuring the animals and plants of the Sonoran Desert. Hummingbirds, cactus wrens, rattlesnakes, scorpions, bighorn sheep, and prairie dogs all busy themselves in ingeniously designed habitats. An Earth Sciences Center has an artificial limestone cave and a hands-on meteor and mineral display. The coyote and javelina exhibits have "invisible" fencing that separates humans from animals, and the Riparian Corridor section affords great underwater views of otters and beavers. The restaurants and gift shop are outstanding. Admission is reduced in the summer. ⊠ *2021 N. Kinney Rd., Westside, Tucson* ☎ *520/883–2702* ⊕ *www.desertmuseum.org* 🖅 *$13* ☉ *Mar.–Sept., daily 7:30–5; Oct.–Feb., daily 8:30–5.*

🅒 **Old Tucson Studios.** This film studio/theme park, originally built for the 1940 motion picture *Arizona*, has been used to shoot countless movies, such as *Rio Bravo* (1959) and *The Quick and the Dead* (1994), and the TV shows *Gunsmoke, Bonanza,* and *Highway to Heaven.* Actors in western garb perform and roam the streets talking to visitors. Youngsters enjoy the simulated gunfights, rides, stunt shows, and petting farm, while adults might appreciate the screenings of old westerns and the little-bit-bawdy Grand Palace Hotel's Dance Hall Revue. Horseback riding is available for an additional charge. ✉ *Tucson Mountain Park, 201 S. Kinney Rd., Westside, Tucson* ☏ *520/883–0100* ⊕ *www. oldtucson.com* ✉ *$16.95* ☉ *Thurs.–Mon. 10–4; Tues.–Wed. call for limited tour hours and trail ride schedule.*

St. Augustine Cathedral. Although the imposing white-and-beige, late-19th-century, Spanish-style building was modeled after the Cathedral of Queretaro in Mexico, a number of its details reflect the desert setting: above the entryway, next to a bronze statue of St. Augustine, are carvings of local desert scenes with saguaro cacti, yucca, and prickly pears. Compared with the magnificent facade, the modernized interior is a bit disappointing. ■ **TIP➜ For a distinctly Southwestern experience, attend the mariachi mass celebrated Sunday at 8 AM.** ✉ *192 S. Stone Ave., downtown Tucson* ☏ *520/623–6351* ✉ *Free* ☉ *Daily 7–6.*

ATTRACTIONS OUTSIDE TUCSON

Colossal Cave Mountain Park. This limestone grotto 20 mi east of Tucson (take Broadway Boulevard or 22nd Street East, to Colossal Cave Road) is the largest dry cavern in the world. Guides discuss the fascinating crystal formations and relate the many romantic tales surrounding the cave, including the legend that an enormous sum of money stolen in a stagecoach robbery is hidden here. Forty-five-minute cave tours begin every 30 minutes and require a ½-mi walk and climbing 363 steps. The park includes a ranch area with trail rides ($27 per hour), a gemstone-sluicing area, a small museum, nature trails, a butterfly garden, a snack bar, and a gift shop. Parking is $5 per vehicle. ✉ *16721 E. Old Spanish Trail* ☏ *520/647–7275* ⊕ *www.colossalcave.com* ✉ *$8.50* ☉ *Oct.–mid-Mar., daily 9–5; mid-Mar.–Sept., daily 8–6.*

WHERE TO EAT AND STAY

ABOUT THE RESTAURANTS

At Saguaro, you won't find more than a Southwest sampling of jams, hot sauces, and candy bars at the two visitor centers' gift shops. Vending machines outside sell bottled water and soda, but pack some lunch for a picnic if you don't want to drive all the way back into town. Five picnic areas in the West district, and two in the East, offer scenery and shade. However, the city of Tucson, sandwiched neatly between the two park districts, offers some of the best Mexican cuisine in the country. It also has excellent upscale Southwestern cuisine, as well as good sushi, Thai, Italian, and Ethiopian food.

ABOUT THE HOTELS

While there are no hotels within the park, its immediate proximity to Tucson makes finding a place to stay easy. A couple of B&Bs are just a short drive from the park. Some ranches and smaller accommodations close during the hottest months of summer, but many inexpensive B&Bs and hotels are open year-round, and offer significantly lower rates from late May through August.

ABOUT THE CAMPGROUNDS

There's no drive-up camping in the park. All six primitive campgrounds are in the Eastern district and require a hike to reach—the shortest hikes are to Douglas Spring Campground (6 mi) and to Happy Valley (5 mi). All are open year-round. Pick up your backcountry camping permit ($6 per night) at the Saguaro East Visitor Center. Before choosing a camping destination, look over the relief map of hiking trails and the book of wilderness campground photos taken by park rangers. You can camp in the backcountry for a maximum of 14 days. Each site can accommodate up to six people. Reservations can be made via mail or in person up to two months in advance. Hikers are encouraged to set out before noon. If you haven't the time or the inclination to hike in, several more camping opportunities exist within a few miles of the park.

WHERE TO EAT

IN THE PARK

PICNIC AREAS   **Javelina.** You may not spot any javelinas, but there's a good chance some desert critters will come by begging for scraps at this popular picnic area. ⊠ *2 mi south of Saguaro East Visitor Center on Cactus Forest Dr.*

Mam-A-Gah. This is the most isolated picnic area in Saguaro West. It's on King Canyon Trail, a good area for birding and wildflower viewing. It's about a mile walk to reach the site, and the undeveloped trail is not wheelchair accessible. ⊠ *King Canyon Trail, 1 mi from Kinney Rd., Saguaro West.*

Mica View. Talk about truth in advertising: this picnic area gives you an eyeful of Mica Mountain, the park's highest peak. None of the tables are in the shade. ⊠ *2 mi north of Saguaro East Visitor Center on Cactus Forest Dr.*

Signal Hill. Because of the nearby petroglyphs, this is the park's most popular picnic site. Its many picnic tables, sprinkled around palo verde and mesquite trees, can accommodate large groups. ⊠ *4½ mi north of Red Hills Visitor Center on Bajada Loop Dr., Saguaro West.*

OUTSIDE THE PARK

¢   ✕ **Beyond Bread.** Twenty-seven varieties of bread are made at this bus-
CAFÉ   tling bakery with central and eastside locations, and highlights from the huge sandwich menu include Annie's Addiction (hummus, tomato, sprouts, red onion, and cucumber) and Brad's Beef (roast beef, provolone, onion, green chilies, and Russian dressing); soups and salads are equally scrumptious. Eat inside or on the patio, or order takeout sandwiches for a picnic, but be sure to splurge on one of the incredible desserts. ⊠ *3026 N. Campbell Ave., Central, Tucson* ☎ *520/322–9965* ⊠ *6260 E. Speedway Blvd., Eastside, Tucson* ☎ *520/747–7477* ⊕ *www. beyondbread.com* ▭ *AE, D, MC, V* ⊗ *No dinner Sun.*

$$$ ✕ **The Grill at Hacienda del Sol.** Tucked into the foothills and surrounded
SOUTHWESTERN   by flowering gardens, this special-occasion restaurant, a favorite among locals hosting out-of-town visitors, provides an alternative to the chili-laden dishes of most southwestern-nouvelle cuisine. Wild-mushroom bisque, grilled buffalo, and pan-seared sea bass are among the menu choices. Tapas (and most items on the full menu) can be enjoyed on the more casual outdoor patio, accented by live flamenco guitar music.

The lavish Sunday brunch buffet is worth a splurge. ⊠ *Hacienda del Sol Guest Ranch Resort, 5601 N. Hacienda del Sol Rd., Foothills, Tucson* ☎ *520/529–3500* ⊕ *www.haciendadelsol.com* ⊟ *AE, DC, MC, V.*

$ ✕ **Mi Nidito.** A perennial favorite among locals (be prepared to wait
MEXICAN   awhile), Mi Nidito—"My Little Nest"—has also hosted its share of visiting celebrities. Following President Clinton's lunch here, the rather hefty Presidential Plate (bean tostada, taco with barbecued meat, chiles rellenos, chicken enchilada, and beef tamale with rice and beans) was added to the menu. Top that off with the mango chimichangas for dessert, and you're talkin' executive privilege. ⊠ *1813 S. 4th Ave., South, Tucson* ☎ *520/622–5081* ⊕ *www.minidito.net* ⊟ *AE, DC, MC, V* ☾ *Closed Mon. and Tues.*

$$ ✕ **Vivace.** A nouvelle Italian bistro in the lovely St. Philip's Plaza, Vivace
ITALIAN   has long been a favorite with Tucsonans. Wild mushrooms and goat cheese in puff pastry is hard to resist as a starter. For a lighter alternative to such entrées as a rich osso buco, try the fettuccine with grilled salmon. For dessert, the molten chocolate cake with spumoni is worth the 20 minutes it takes to create. Patio seating is especially inviting on warm evenings. ⊠ *4310 N. Campbell Ave., Foothills, Tucson* ☎ *520/795–7221* ⊟ *AE, D, MC, V* ☾ *Closed Sun.*

$ ✕ **Zinburger.** Have a glass of wine or a cocktail with your gourmet burger
AMERICAN   and fries at this high-energy, somewhat noisy, and unquestionably hip new burger joint. Open until 11 PM on Friday and Saturday, late by Tucson standards, Zinburger delivers tempting burgers—try the Kobe beef with cheddar and wild mushrooms— and decadent milk shakes made of exotic combinations like dates and honey or melted chocolate with praline flakes. A few creative salads, including one with ahi tuna, round out the menu. ⊠ *1865 E. River Rd., Foothills, Tucson* ☎ *520/299–7799* ⊕ *www.foxrestaurantconcepts.com* ⊟ *AE, D, DC, MC, V.*

WHERE TO STAY

IN THE PARK

CAMPING   **Wilderness Camping Area.** All six campgrounds within the eastern district are backcountry, wilderness campsites and require a hike to reach them. None of them have any facilities. The cost is $6 for a stay up to 14 days, and a permit must be obtained through the Saguaro East visitor center (in person or by mail) before hiking in. **Pros:** some (such as Juniper Basin) have delightful views **Cons:** reached by challenging hikes. ☎ *No phone* ⚐ *21 tent sites* ☼ *Some have water, but it must be treated.*

OUTSIDE THE PARK

$–$$ ⊡ **Casa Tierra.** For a real desert experience, head to this B&B on 5 acres
Fodor'sChoice   near the Desert Museum and Saguaro National Park West. The last
★   1½ mi are on a dirt road. All rooms have private patio entrances and look out onto a lovely central courtyard. The southwestern-style furnishings include Mexican *equipales* (chairs with pigskin seats) and tile floors. A full vegetarian breakfast served on fine china is included, and there's a media room in case you need a break from the quiet. There's a minimum stay of two nights. **Pros:** peaceful; great Southwest character. **Cons:** very far from town. ⊠ *11155 W. Calle Pima, Westside, Tucson*

☎ *520/578–3058 or 866/254–0006* ⊕ *www.casatierratucson.com* ☟ *3 rooms, 1 suite* ♿ *In-room: refrigerator, Wi-Fi, no TV. In-hotel: gym* 🖃 *AE, D, MC, V* ☉ *Closed mid-June–mid-Aug.* ‖○‖ *BP.*

¢ 🏨 **Hotel Congress.** This hotel built in 1919 has been artfully restored to its original western version of art deco. The gangster John Dillinger was almost caught here in 1934 (apparently his luggage, filled with guns and ammo, was suspiciously heavy). Each room has a black-and-white tile bath and the original iron bed frames. The convenient location downtown means it can be noisy, so make sure you don't get a room over the popular Club Congress unless you plan to be up until the wee hours. A great place to stay for younger or more adventurous visitors, it's the center of Tucson's hippest scene. **Pros:** convenient location; good restaurant; funky and fun. **Cons:** no air-conditioning; noise from night-club. ⊠ *311 E. Congress St., Downtown, Tucson* ☎ *520/622–8848 or 800/722–8848* ⊕ *www.hotelcongress.com* ☟ *40 rooms* ♿ *In-room: no TV. In-hotel: restaurant, bar* 🖃 *AE, D, MC, V.*

$$$–$$$$ 🏨 **White Stallion Ranch.** A 3,000-acre working cattle ranch run by the hos-
Fodor'sChoice   pitable True family since 1965, this place is the real deal. You can ride up
★   to four times daily, hike in the mountains, enjoy a hayride cookout, and compete in team cattle penning. Most rooms retain their original western furniture, and newer deluxe rooms have whirlpool baths or fireplaces. A recently completed spa and fitness center bring even more comforts to this well-endowed but authentic setting. Rates include all meals, riding, and entertainment such as weekend rodeos, country line dancing, telescopic stargazing, and campfire sing-alongs. An airport shuttle is available. **Pros:** solid dude ranch experience; very charming hosts; satisfying for families as well as singles or couples. **Cons:** riding is very structured; no room TVs; closed in summer. ⊠ *9251 W. Twin Peaks Rd., Northwest, Tucson* ☎ *520/297–0252 or 888/977–2624* ⊕ *www.wsranch.com* ☟ *24 rooms, 17 suites* ♿ *In-room: no phone, no TV. In-hotel: bar, tennis courts, pool, gym* 🖃 *No credit cards* ☉ *Closed June–Aug.* ‖○‖ *FAP.*

CAMPING   ⚠ **Gilbert Ray Campground.** You can slumber amid saguaros at this
$–$$ campground about 15 mi west of town, just down the road from the Arizona–Sonora Desert Museum and Saguaro National Park's west unit. Open all year, this campground has drinking water, flush toilets (but no showers), and 130 sites with tables, grills, and electricity. Sites cost $20 with electric hookups, $10 without; no reservations are taken, and there is a seven-day stay limit. Cash or checks are the only payment options. **Pros:** very quiet; close to Saguaro West. **Cons:** setting is some-what isolated; no showers. ⊠ *8451 W. McCain Loop, Westside, Tucson* ☎ *520/883–4200* ⚠ *130 tent/RV sites* 🖃 *Flush toilets, full hookups, dump station, drinking water, grills, picnic tables, public telephone, ranger station staffed Jan.–Apr. only* 🖃 *No credit cards.*

Sequoia and Kings Canyon National Parks

WORD OF MOUTH

"We headed out to Crystal Cave, which is off the General's Highway, and up a narrow road. Gorgeous drive. The entrance to the cave is a ½ mile walk down a steep trail from the parking area. The trail passes a really nice waterfall and has some good views along the way. The cave itself is spectacular."

—J_Correa

WELCOME TO SEQUOIA AND KINGS CANYON

TOP REASONS TO GO

★ **Gentle giants:** You'll feel small—in a good way—walking among some of the world's largest living things in Sequoia's Giant Forest and Kings Canyon's Grant Grove.

★ **Because it's there:** You can't even glimpse it from the main part of Sequoia, but the sight of majestic Mount Whitney is worth the trek to the eastern face of the High Sierra.

★ **Underground exploration:** Far older even than the giant sequoias, the gleaming limestone formations in Crystal Cave will draw you along dark, marble passages.

★ **A grander-than-Grand Canyon:** Drive the twisting Kings Canyon Scenic Byway down into the jagged, granite Kings River Canyon, deeper in parts than the Grand Canyon.

★ **Regal solitude:** To spend a day or two hiking in a subalpine world of your own, pick one of the 11 trailheads at Mineral King.

1 **Giant Forest–Lodgepole Village.** The most heavily visited area of Sequoia lies at the base of the "thumb" portion of Kings Canyon National Park and contains major sights such as Giant Forest, General Sherman Tree, Crystal Cave, and Moro Rock.

2 **Grant Grove Village–Redwood Canyon.** The "thumb" of Kings Canyon National Park is its busiest section, where Grant Grove, General Grant Tree, Panoramic Point, and Big Stump are the main attractions.

3 **Cedar Grove.** Most visitors to the huge, high-country portion of Kings Canyon National Park don't go farther than Roads End, a few miles east of Cedar Grove on the canyon floor. Here, the river runs through Zumwalt Meadow, surrounded by magnificent granite formations.

4 **Mineral King.** In the southeast section of Sequoia, the highest road-accessible part of the park is a good place to hike, camp, and soak up the unspoiled grandeur of the Sierra Nevada.

5 **Mount Whitney.** The highest peak in the Lower 48 stands on the eastern edge of Sequoia; to get there from Giant Forest you must either backpack eight days through the mountains or drive nearly 400 mi around the park to its other side.

KEY

🛖	Ranger Station
⛺	Campground
🪑	Picnic Area
🍴	Restaurant
🏨	Lodge
🚶	Trailhead
🚻	Restrooms
⤳	Scenic Viewpoint
┄┄	Walking/Hiking Trails

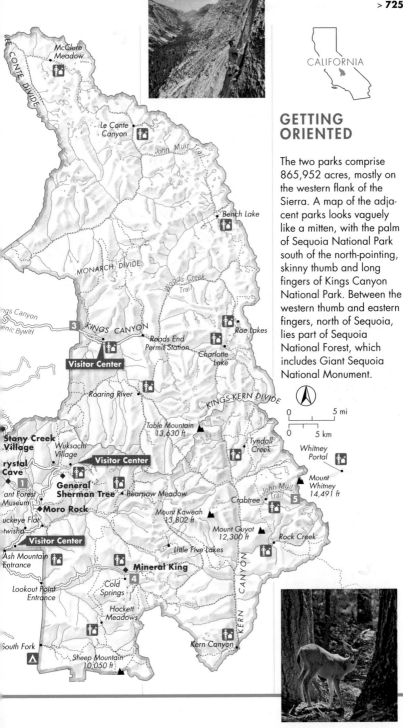

CALIFORNIA

GETTING ORIENTED

The two parks comprise 865,952 acres, mostly on the western flank of the Sierra. A map of the adjacent parks looks vaguely like a mitten, with the palm of Sequoia National Park south of the north-pointing, skinny thumb and long fingers of Kings Canyon National Park. Between the western thumb and eastern fingers, north of Sequoia, lies part of Sequoia National Forest, which includes Giant Sequoia National Monument.

McClure Meadow

Le Conte Canyon

John Muir Trail

LE CONTE DIVIDE

Bench Lake

MONARCH DIVIDE

Woods Creek Trail

ngs Canyon
enic Byway

3

KINGS CANYON

Roads End Permit Station

Rae Lakes

Visitor Center

Charlotte Lake

Roaring River

KINGS-KERN DIVIDE

0   5 mi
0   5 km

Table Mountain 13,630 ft

Tyndall Creek

Whitney Portal

Stony Creek Village

Wuksachi Village

Visitor Center

Mount Whitney 14,491 ft

rystal Cave

1

ant Forest Museum

General Sherman Tree

Bearpaw Meadow

John Muir Trail

Crabtree

5

uckeye Flat

Moro Rock

Mount Kaweah 13,802 ft

KERN CANYON

twisha

Mount Guyot 12,300 ft

Rock Creek

Visitor Center

Little Five Lakes

Ash Mountain Entrance

Mineral King

4

Lookout Point Entrance

Cold Springs

Hockett Meadows

South Fork

Kern Canyon

Sheep Mountain 10,050 ft

SEQUOIA AND KINGS CANYON PLANNER

When to Go

The best times to visit are late spring and early fall, when temperatures are moderate and crowds thin. Summertime can draw hoards of tourists to see the giant sequoias, and the few, narrow roads mean congestion at peak holiday times. If you must visit in summer, go during the week. By contrast, in wintertime you may feel as though you have the parks all to yourself. But because of heavy snows, sections of the main park roads can be closed without warning, and low-hanging clouds can move in and obscure mountains and valleys for days. Check road and weather conditions before venturing out mid-November to late April.

Temperatures in the chart below are for the mid-level elevations, generally between 4,000 and 7,000 feet.

AVG. HIGH/LOW TEMPS (°F)

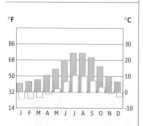

Flora and Fauna

The parks can be divided into three distinct zones. In the west (1,500–4,500 feet) are the rolling, lower elevation foothills, covered with shrubby chaparral vegetation or golden grasslands dotted with oaks. Chamise, red-barked manzanita, and the occasional yucca plant grow here. Fields of white popcorn flower cover the hillsides in spring, and the yellow fiddleneck flourishes. In summer, intense heat and absence of rain cause the hills to turn golden brown. Wildlife includes the California ground squirrel, noisy blue-and-gray scrub jay, black bears, coyotes, skunks, and gray fox.

At middle elevation (5,000–9,000 feet), where the giant sequoia belt resides, rock formations mix with meadows and huge stands of evergreens—red and white fir, incense cedar, and ponderosa pines, to name a few. Wildflowers like yellow blazing star and red Indian paintbrush, bloom in spring and summer. Mule deer, golden-mantled ground squirrels, Steller's jays, mule deer, and black bears (most active in fall) inhabit the area, as does the chickaree.

The high alpine section of the parks is extremely rugged, with a string of rocky peaks reaching above 13,000 feet to Mt. Whitney's 14,494 feet. Fierce weather and scarcity of soil make vegetation and wildlife sparse. Foxtail and whitebark pines have gnarled and twisted trunks, the result of high wind, heavy snowfall, and freezing temperatures. In summer you can see yellow-bellied marmots, pikas, weasels, mountain chickadees, and Clark's nutcrackers.

Getting Here and Around

Sequoia is 36 mi east of Visalia on Route 198; Kings Canyon is 53 mi east of Fresno on Route 180. There is no automobile entrance on the eastern side of the Sierra. Routes 180 and 198 are connected by Generals Highway, a paved two-lane road that sometimes sees delays at peak times due to ongoing improvements. The road is extremely narrow and steep from Route 198 to Giant Forest, so keep an eye on your engine temperature gauge, as the incline and congestion can cause vehicles to overheat; to avoid overheated brakes, use low gears on downgrades.

If you are traveling in an RV or with a trailer, study the restrictions on these vehicles. Do not travel beyond Potwisha Campground with an RV longer than 22 feet on Route 198; take straighter, easier Route 180 instead. Maximum vehicle length on Generals Highway is 40 feet, or 50 feet combined length for vehicles with trailers.

Generals Highway between Lodgepole and Grant Grove is sometimes closed by snow. The Mineral King Road from Route 198 into southern Sequoia National Park is closed 2 mi below Atwell Mill either on November 1 or after the first heavy snow. The Buckeye Flat–Middle Fork Trailhead Road is closed mid-October–mid-April when the Buckeye Flat Campground closes. The lower Crystal Cave Road is closed when the cave closes in November. Its upper 2 mi, as well as the Panoramic Point and Moro Rock–Crescent Meadow roads, are closed with the first heavy snow. Because of the danger of rockfall, the portion of Kings Canyon Scenic Byway east of Grant Grove closes in winter. For current conditions, call ☎ 559/565–3341 Ext. 4.

■TIP→ Snowstorms are common late October through April. Unless you have four-wheel drive with snow tires, carry chains and know how to apply them to the tires on the drive axle.

Festivals and Events

DEC. Annual Trek to the Tree. On the second Sunday, thousands of Christmas carolers gather at the base of General Grant Tree, the nation's official Christmas tree. ☎ 559/565–4307.

MAR. Blossom Days Festival. The first Saturday of March, communities along Fresno County's Blossom Trail celebrate the flowering the area's many orchards, citrus groves, and vineyards. ☎ 559/262–4271 ⊕ www.gofresnocounty.com.

APR. Jazzaffair. Held just south of the parks, a festival of mostly swing jazz takes place at several locations. The festival is usually the second weekend of the month. ☎ 559/561–4592 or 559/561–3105 ⊕ www.jazzaffair.info.

MAY Woodlake Rodeo. A weekend-long event thrown by the Woodlake Lions, this rodeo draws large crowds to Woodlake on Mother's Day weekend. ☎ 559/564–8555 ⊕ www.woodlakelionsrodeo.com.

SEPT. Celebrate Sequoias Festival. On the second Saturday of the month, rangers guide field trips to the lesser known groves of Sequoia National Park. ☎ 559/565–4307 Grant Grove Visitor Center.

OCT. Big Fresno Fair. The Fresno Fairgrounds come alive with an old-fashioned county fair. ☎ 559/650–3247.

34

Updated by
Reed Parsell

Although *Sequoiadendron giganteum* is the formal name for the redwoods that grow here, everyone outside the classroom calls them sequoias, big trees, or Sierra redwoods. Their monstrously thick trunks and branches, remarkably shallow root systems, and neck-craning heights are almost impossible to believe, as is the fact they can live for more than 2,500 years. Many of these towering marvels are in the Giant Forest stretch of Generals Highway, which connects Sequoia and Kings Canyon national parks.

Next to or a few miles off the 43-mi road Generals Highway are most of Sequoia National Park's main attractions and Grant Grove Village, the orientation hub for Kings Canyon National Park. The two parks share a boundary that runs west–east, from the foothills of the Central Valley to the Sierra Nevada's dramatic eastern ridges. Kings Canyon has two portions: the smaller is shaped like a bent finger and encompasses Grant Grove Village and Redwood Mountain Grove (the two parks' largest concentration of sequoias), and the larger is home to stunning Kings River Canyon, whose vast, unspoiled peaks and valleys are a backpacker's dream. Sequoia is in one piece and includes Mount Whitney, the highest point in the Lower 48 states (although it is impossible to see from the western part of the park and is a chore to ascend from either side).

PARK ESSENTIALS

ACCESSIBILITY

All of the visitor centers, the Giant Forest Museum, and Big Trees Trail are wheelchair-accessible, as are some short ranger-led walks and talks. General Sherman Tree can be reached via a paved, level trail near a parking area. None of the caves is accessible and wilderness areas must be reached by horseback or on foot. Some picnic tables are extended to accommodate wheelchairs. Many of the major sites are in the 6,000-foot range and thin air at high elevations can cause respiratory distress for people with breathing difficulties. Carry oxygen if necessary. Contact the park's main number for more information.

ADMISSION FEES AND PERMITS

The admission fee is $20 per vehicle and $10 for those who enter by bus, on foot, bicycle, motorcycle, or horse; it is valid for seven days in both parks. U.S. residents over the age of 62 pay $10 for a lifetime pass, and permanently disabled U.S. residents are admitted free.

If you plan to camp in the backcountry, you need a permit, which costs $15 for hikers or $30 for stock users (e.g., horseback riders). One permit covers the group. Availability of permits depends upon trailhead quotas. Advance reservations are accepted by mail, fax, or e-mail for a $15 processing fee, beginning March 1, and must be made at least three weeks in advance (⌂ *HCR 89, P.O. Box 60, Three Rivers, CA 93271* ☎ *559/575–3766* ⎙ *559/565–4239*). Without a reservation, you may still get a permit on a first-come, first-served basis starting at 1 PM the day before you plan to hike. For more information on backcountry camping or travel with pack animals (horses, mules, burros, or llamas), contact the Wilderness Permit Office (☎ *530/565–3761*).

ADMISSION HOURS

The parks are open 24/7 year-round. They are in the Pacific time zone

ATMS/BANKS

There are ATMs at the Grant Grove Gift Shop and the Lodgepole Market. The nearest banks are in Visalia and Three Rivers.

CELL-PHONE RECEPTION

Cell-phone reception is poor to nonexistent in the higher elevations, and spotty even on portions of Generals Highway, where you can (on rare clear days) see the Central Valley. Public telephones may be found at the park entrance stations, visitor centers, ranger stations, some trailheads, and at all restaurants and lodging facilities in the park.

PARK CONTACT INFORMATION

Sequoia and Kings Canyon National Parks ✉ *47050 Generals Hwy. (Rte. 198), Three Rivers, CA* ☎ *559/565–3341 or 559/565–3134* ⊕ *www.nps.gov/seki.*

SEQUOIA NATIONAL PARK

SCENIC DRIVES

★ **Generals Highway.** One of the most scenic drives in a state replete with them is this 43-mi road, the main asphalt artery between Sequoia and Kings Canyon national parks. Named after the landmark Grant and Sherman trees that leave so many visitors awestruck, it runs from the Foothills Visitor Center north to Grant Grove Village. Along the way, it passes the turnoff to Crystal Cave, the Giant Forest Museum, Lodgepole Village, and Sequoia National Park's other most popular attractions. The lower portion, from Hospital Rock to the Giant Forest, is especially steep and windy. If your vehicle is 22 feet or longer, avoid that stretch by entering the parks via Route 180 (from Fresno) rather than Route

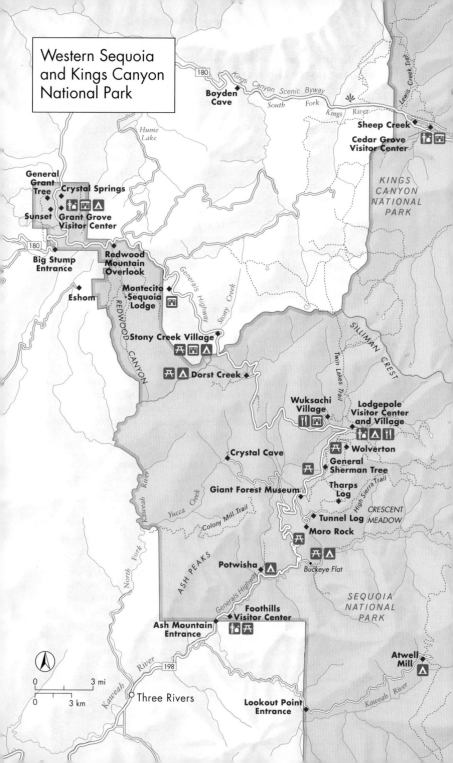

SEQUOIA IN ONE DAY

After spending the night in Visalia or Three Rivers—and provided your vehicle's length does not exceed 22 feet—shove off early on Route 198 to Sequoia National Park's **Ash Mountain entrance**. Pull over at the **Hospital Rock** picnic area to gaze up at the imposing granite formation of Moro Rock, which you later will climb. Heed signs that advise 10 MPH around tight turns as you climb 3,500 feet on **Generals Highway** to the **Giant Forest Museum**. Spend a half-hour there, then examine some firsthand by circling the lovely **Round Meadow** on the **Big Trees Trail**, which you must walk to from the museum or from its parking lot across the road.

Get back in your car and continue a few miles north on Generals Highway to see the jaw-dropping **General Sherman Tree**. Then set off on the **Congress Trail** so that you can be further awed by the

Senate and House big-tree clusters. Buy your lunch at the **Lodgepole** complex, 2 mi to the north, and take it—or what you packed the night before—to the nearby **Pinewood** picnic area. Now you're ready for the day's big exercise, the mounting of **Moro Rock**.

You can either drive there or, if it is summer, park at the museum lot and take the free shuttle. Count on spending at least an hour for the 350-step ascent and descent, with a pause on top to appreciate the 360-degree view. Get back in the car, or on the shuttle, and proceed past the **Auto Log** to Crescent Meadow. Spend a relaxing hour or two strolling on the trails that pass by, among other things, **Tharp's Log**. By now you've probably renewed your appetite; head to the **Wolverton Barbecue** (summer evenings only) or the highly regarded restaurant at **Wuksachi Lodge**.

34

198 (from Visalia). And take your time on this road—there's a lot to see, and wildlife can scamper across at any time.

Mineral King Road. Vehicles longer than 22 feet are prohibited on this side road into southern Sequoia National Park, and for good reason: It contains 589 twists and turns, according to one reputable source. Anticipating an average speed of 20 MPH is optimistic, considering all the potholes, blind curves, and narrow stretches. The scenery is splendid as you climb nearly 6,000 feet from Three Rivers to the Mineral King area . . . but be sure to focus on the road if you're driving. If you can, trade off with your spouse or companion on the return trip. Allow 90 minutes each way. Make sure you start off with a full tank, too, because gas is no longer sold at Silver City Resort. You can pick up a few snack items there, though, and the restaurant is pretty good. The road is usually closed from late October through late May.

WHAT TO SEE

Sequoia National Park is all about the trees, and to understand the scale of these giants you must walk among them. If you do nothing else, get out of the car for a short stroll through one of the groves. But there is much more to the park than the trees. Try to get up to one of the vista points that give you a panoramic view over the forested mountains. Whether you're driving south to north or north to south, Generals Highway (Route 198) will be your route to most of the park's sights. A few short spur roads lead off the highway to some sights, and Mineral King Road branches off Route 198 to enter the park at Lookout Point, winding east from there into the southernmost part of the park.

PARK PUBLICATIONS

The Guide: Sequoia and Kings Canyon National Parks is a free newspaper available at park entrance gates or by contacting the parks directly; ⊕ www.nps.gov/seki has current and back issues. For information on planning a backcountry hiking trip, download Backcountry Basics at ⊕ www.nps.gov/seki.

SCENIC STOPS

Auto Log. At one time, cars drove right on top of this giant fallen sequoia. Now it's a great place to pose for pictures. ⊠ Moro Rock–Crescent Meadow Rd., 1 mi south of Giant Forest.

Crescent Meadow. John Muir called this the "gem of the Sierra." Take an hour or two to walk around, and see if you agree. Wildflowers bloom here throughout the summer. ⊠ End of Moro Rock–Crescent Meadow Rd., 2.6 mi east off Generals Hwy.

★ **Crystal Cave.** One of more than 200 caves in Sequoia and Kings Canyon national parks, Crystal Cave is unusual in that it's composed largely of marble, the result of limestone being hardened under heat and pressure. It contains several impressive formations that will be easier to see once an environmentally sensitive relighting project is completed in the next few years. Unfortunately, some of the cave's formations have been damaged or destroyed by early 20th-century dynamite blasting. The standard tour will give you 45 minutes inside the cave. ⊠ Crystal Cave Rd., 6 mi west off Generals Hwy. ☎ 559/565–3759 ⊕ www.sequoiahistory.org ⊠ $11 ⊙ Mid-May–mid-Oct., daily 10–4.

★ **General Sherman Tree.** Neither the world's tallest nor oldest sequoia, General Sherman is nevertheless tops in volume—and it is still putting on weight, adding the equivalent of a 60-foot-tall tree every year to its 2.7 million-pound mass. ⊠ Generals Hwy. (Rte. 198), 2 mi south of Lodgepole Visitor Center.

Mineral King. This subalpine valley sits at 7,800 feet at the end of a steep, winding road. The trip from the park's entrance can take up to two hours. This is the highest point to which you can drive in the park. ⊠ End of Mineral King Rd., 25 mi east of Generals Hwy. (Rte. 198), east of Three Rivers.

★ **Moro Rock.** Sequoia National Park's best non-tree attraction offers panoramic views to those fit and determined enough to mount its 350-ish steps. In a case where the journey rivals the destination, Moro's stone stairway is so impressive in its twisty inventiveness that it's on the National Register of Historic Places. The rock's 6,725-foot summit overlooks the Middle Fork Canyon, sculpted by the Kaweah River and approaching the depth of Arizona's Grand Canyon. ⊠ Moro Rock–Crescent Meadow Rd., 2 mi east off Generals Hwy. (Rte. 198) to parking area.

Tunnel Log. It's been 40 years since you could drive through a standing sequoia—and that was in Yosemite National Park's Mariposa Grove, not here. This 275-foot tree fell in 1937, and soon a 17-foot-wide, 8-foot-high hole was cut through it for vehicular passage that continues today. Large vehicles take the nearby bypass. ⊠ *Moro Rock–Crescent Meadow Rd., 2 mi east of Generals Hwy. (Rte. 198).*

VISITOR CENTERS

Foothills Visitor Center. Exhibits focusing on the foothills and resource issues facing the parks are on display here. You can also pick up books, maps, and a list of ranger-led walks, and get wilderness permits. ⊠ *Generals Hwy. (Rte. 198), 1 mi north of the Ash Mountain entrance* ☎ *559/565–3135* ⊗ *Oct.–mid-May, daily 8–4:30; mid-May–Sept., daily 8–5.*

Lodgepole Visitor Center. Along with exhibits on the area's geologic history, wildlife, and longtime American Indian inhabitants, the center screens an outstanding 22-minute film about bears. You can also buy books and maps here. ⊠ *Generals Hwy. (Rte. 198), 21 mi north of Ash Mountain entrance* ☎ *559/565–4436* ⊗ *June–Oct., daily 7–6; Nov.–May, weekends 7–6.*

34

SPORTS AND THE OUTDOORS

The best way to see Sequoia is to take a hike. Unless you do so, you'll miss out on the up-close grandeur of mist wafting between deeply scored, red-orange tree trunks bigger than you've ever seen. If it's winter, put on some snowshoes or cross-country skis and plunge into the outscale woodland swaddled in snow. There are not too many other outdoor options: no off-road driving is allowed in the parks, and no special provisions have been made for bicycles. Boating, rafting, and snowmobiling are also prohibited.

BIRD-WATCHING

More than 200 species of birds inhabit Sequoia and Kings Canyon national parks. Not seen in most parts of the United States, the white-headed woodpecker and the pileated woodpecker are common in most mid-elevation areas here. There are also many hawks and owls, including the renowned spotted owl. Species are diverse in both parks due to the changes in elevation, and range from warblers, kingbirds, thrushes, and sparrows in the foothills to goshawk, blue grouse, red-breasted nuthatch, and brown creeper at the highest elevations. Ranger-led bird-watching tours are held on a sporadic basis. Call the park's main information number to find out more about these tours.

Contact the **Sequoia Natural History Association** (⬠ *HCR 89, P.O. Box 10, Three Rivers, CA 93271* ☎ *559/565–3759* ⊕ *www.sequoiahistory.org*) for information on bird-watching in the southern Sierra.

CROSS-COUNTRY SKIING

For a one-of-a-kind experience, cut through the groves of mammoth sequoias in Giant Forest. Some of the Crescent Meadow trails (⇨ *Hiking*) are suitable for skiing as well. None of the trails is groomed. You can park at Giant Forest. Note that roads can be precarious in bad weather. Some advanced trails begin at Wolverton.

Wuksachi Lodge. Rent skis here. Depending on snowfall amounts, instruction may also be available. Reservations are recommended. Marked trails cut through Giant Forest, just 5 mi south of the lodge. ☒ *Off Generals Hwy. (Rte. 198), 2 mi north of Lodgepole* ☎ *559/565–4070* ☒ *$15–$20 ski rental* ☉ *Nov.–May (unless no snow), daily 9–4.*

FISHING

There's limited trout fishing, bagging minimal hauls, in the creeks and rivers from late April to mid-November. The Kaweah River is a popular spot; check at visitor centers for open and closed waters. Some of the park's secluded backcountry lakes have good fishing. A California fishing license is $11.30 for one day, $17.60 for two days, $34.90 for 10 days (discounts are available for state residents) and is required for persons 16 and older. For park regulations, closures, and restrictions, call the parks at ☎ *559/565–3341* or stop at a park visitor center. Licenses and fishing tackle are usually available in Lodgepole. Among many other functions, the **California Department of Fish and Game** (☎ *916/653–7661* ⊕ *www.dfg.ca.gov*) supplies fishing licenses.

HIKING

The best way to see the park is to hike it. The grandeur and majesty of the Sierra is best seen up close. Carry a hiking map—available at any visitor center—and plenty of water. Check with rangers for current trail conditions, and be aware of rapidly changing weather. As a rule of thumb, plan on trekking 1 MPH.

EASY

Big Trees Trail. This one's a must, as it does not take long to stroll and the setting is spectacular: beautiful Round Meadow surrounded by many mature sequoias, with well-thought-out interpretive signs along the path that explain the ecology on display. From the handicapped parking lot off Generals Highway, the 0.7-mi Big Trees Trail is wheelchair-accessible. If you walk there from the Giant Museum, the total loop is 1.5 mi. ☒ *Trail begins off Generals Hwy. (Rte. 198), near the Giant Forest Museum.*

★ **Congress Trail.** This easy 2-mi trail is a paved loop that begins near General Sherman Tree and winds through the heart of the sequoia forest. You'll get close-up views of more big trees here than on any other Sequoia hike. Watch for the clusters known as the House and Senate. ☒ *Trail begins off Generals Hwy. (Rte. 198), 2 mi north of Giant Forest.*

★ **Crescent Meadow Trails.** John Muir reportedly called Crescent Meadow the "gem of the Sierra." Brilliant wildflowers bloom here by midsummer, and a 1.8-mi trail loops around the meadow. A 1.6-mi trail begins at Crescent Meadow and leads to Tharp's Log, a cabin built from a fire-hollowed sequoia. ☒ *Trail begins end of Moro Rock–Crescent Meadow Rd., 2.6 mi east off Generals Hwy. (Rte. 198).*

Muir Grove Trail. You will attain solitude—and possibly see a bear or two—on this unheralded gem of a hike, a fairly easy 4-mi round trip from the Dorst Creek Campground. The remote grove is small but indescribably lovely, its soundtrack provided solely by nature. The trailhead is very subtly marked; it is past the group campsite area, on the right. Use the

amphitheater parking lot. ⊠ *Trail begins in Dorst Creek Campground, Generals Hwy. (Rte. 198), 8 mi north of Lodgepole Visitor Center.*

MODERATE   **Little Baldy Trail.** Climbing 700 vertical feet in 1.75 mi of switchback-ing, this trail ends at a granite dome with a great view of the peaks of the Mineral King area and the Great Western Divide. The walk to the summit and back takes about four hours. ⊠ *Trail begins at Little Baldy Saddle, Generals Hwy. (Rte. 198), 11 mi north of Giant Forest.*

Tokopah Falls Trail. This moderate trail follows the Marble Fork of the Kaweah River for 1.75 mi one way and dead-ends below the impres-sive granite cliffs and cascading waterfall of Tokopah Canyon. It takes 2½ to 4 hours to make the 3.5-mi round-trip journey. The trail passes through a mixed-conifer forest. ⊠ *Trail begins off Generals Hwy. (Rte. 198), ¼ mi north of Lodgepole Campground.*

DIFFICULT   **Marble Falls Trail.** The 3.7-mi, moderately strenuous hike to Marble Falls crosses through the rugged foothills before reaching the cascading water. Plan on three to four hours one way. ⊠ *Trail begins off the dirt road across from the concrete ditch near site 17 at Potwisha Campground, off Generals Hwy. (Rte. 198).*

Mineral King Trails. Many trails to the high country begin at Mineral King. The two most popular day hikes are Eagle Lake and Timber Gap, both of which are somewhat strenuous. At 7,800 feet, this is the high-est point to which one can drive in either of the parks. Get a map and provisions, and check with rangers about conditions. ⊠ *Trailhead at end of Mineral King Rd., 25 mi east of Generals Hwy. (Rte. 198).*

HORSEBACK RIDING

Trips take you through redwood forests, flowering meadows, across the Sierra, or even up to Mt. Whitney. Costs per person range from $25 for a one-hour guided ride to around $200 per day for fully guided trips for which the packers do all the cooking and camp chores.

OUTFIT-   **Grant Grove Stables** *(⇨ Horseback Riding in Kings Canyon National*
TERS AND   *Park)* is the stable to choose if you want a short ride.
EXPEDITIONS

Horse Corral Pack Station. Hourly, half-day, full-day, or overnight trips through Sequoia are available for beginning and advanced riders. ⊠ *Off Big Meadows Rd., 12 mi east of Generals Hwy. (Rte. 198) between Sequoia and Kings Canyon national parks* ☎ *559/565–3404 in summer, 559/564–6429 in winter* ⊕ *www.horsecorralpackers.com* ☜ *$35–$145 day trips* ☉ *May–Sept.*

Mineral King Pack Station. Day and overnight tours in the high-mountain area around Mineral King are available here. ⊠ *End of Mineral King Rd., 25 mi east of East Fork entrance* ☎ *559/561–3039 in summer, 520/855–5885 in winter* ⊕ *mineralking.tripod.com* ☜ *$25–$75 day trips* ☉ *July–late Sept. or –early Oct.*

SLEDDING AND SNOWSHOEING

The Wolverton area, on Route 198 near Giant Forest, is a popular sled-ding spot, where sleds, inner tubes, and platters are allowed. You can buy sleds and saucers, starting at $8, at the Wuksachi Lodge (☎ *559/565–4070*), 2 mi north of Lodgepole.

You can rent snowshoes for $15–$20 at the Wuksachi Lodge (☎ *559/565–4070*), 2 mi north of Lodgepole. Naturalists lead snowshoe walks around Giant Forest and Wuksachi Lodge, conditions permitting, on Saturdays and holidays. Snowshoes are provided for a $1 donation. Make reservations and check schedules at Giant Forest Museum (☎ *559/565–4480*) or Wuksachi Lodge.

SWIMMING

Drowning is the number-one cause of death in both Sequoia and Kings Canyon parks. Though it is sometimes safe to swim in the parks' rivers in the late summer and early fall, it is extremely dangerous to do so in the spring and early summer, when the snowmelt from the high country causes swift currents and icy temperatures. Stand clear of the water when the rivers are running, and stay off wet rocks to avoid falling in. Check with rangers if you're unsure about conditions or to learn the safest locations to wade in the water.

EDUCATIONAL OFFERINGS

CLASSES AND SEMINARS

Evening Programs. In summer, the park shows documentary films and slide shows, and has evening lectures. Locations and times vary; pick up a schedule at any visitor center or check bulletin boards near ranger stations. ☎ *559/565–3341*.

★ **Seminars.** Expert naturalists lead seminars on a range of topics, including birds, wildflowers, geology, botany, photography, park history, backpacking, and pathfinding. Some courses offer transferable credits. Reserve in advance. For information and prices, pick up a course catalogue at any visitor center or contact the **Sequoia Natural History Association** (☎ *559/565–3759* ⊕ *www.sequoiahistory.org*).

Sequoia Sightseeing Tours. The only licensed tour operator in either park offers daily interpretive sightseeing tours in a 10-passenger van with a friendly, knowledgeable guide. Reservations are essential. They also offer private tours of Kings Canyon. ☎ *559/561–4489* ⊕ *www.sequoiatours.com*.

MUSEUMS AND NATURE CENTERS

★ **Beetle Rock Family Nature Center.** Across the road from Giant Forest Museum, the center has interactive exhibits and a children's bookstore. Beetle Rock Rollick, a ranger-led family program, is conducted at 2 PM daily. On the massive rock, children have lots of room to run around and climb on smooth and gentle slopes. ⊠ *Generals Hwy., 4 mi south of Lodgepole Visitor Center* ☎ *559/565–4251* ⊡ *Free* ⊙ *Early July–late Aug., daily 10–4.*

★ **Giant Forest Museum.** Well-imagined and interactive displays give you the basics about sequoias, of which there are 2,161 with diameters exceeding 10 feet in the 2,115-acre Giant Forest. The museum is entirely wheelchair-accessible. ⊠ *Generals Hwy., 4 mi south of Lodgepole Visitor Center* ☎ *559/565–4480* ⊡ *Free* ⊙ *Daily 8–5.*

☾ **Walter Fry Nature Center.** The hands-on nature exhibits here are designed primarily for children. The center is closed most of the year. ⊠ *Lodgepole*

Campground, ½ mi east of Lodgepole Visitor Center ☎ *559/565–4436* ✆ *Free* ⊙ *July–mid-Aug., weekends noon–5.*

RANGER PROGRAMS

Free Nature Programs. Almost any summer day, half-hour to 1½-hour ranger talks and walks explore subjects such as the life of the sequoia, the geology of the park, and the habits of bears. Giant Forest, Lodgepole Visitor Center, Wuksachi Village, and Dorst Creek Campground are frequent starting points. Check bulletin boards throughout the park for the week's offerings.

KINGS CANYON NATIONAL PARK

SCENIC DRIVES

★ **Kings Canyon Scenic Byway.** About 10 mi east of Grant Grove Village is Jackson View, where you'll first see Kings River Canyon. Near Yucca Point, it's thousands of feet deeper than the much more famous Grand Canyon. Continuing through Sequoia National Forest past Boyden Cavern, you'll enter the larger portion of Kings Canyon National Park and, eventually, Cedar Grove Village. Past there, the U-shaped canyon becomes broader. Be sure to allow an hour to walk through Zumwalt Meadow. Also, be sure to park and take the less-than-five-minute walks to the base of Grizzly Falls and Roaring River Falls. The drive dead-ends at a big parking lot, the launch point for many backpackers. Driving the byway takes about one hour each way (without stops).

WHAT TO SEE

Kings Canyon National Park consists of two sections that adjoin the northern boundary of Sequoia National Park. The western portion, covered with sequoia and pine forest, contains the park's most visited sights, such as Grant Grove. The vast eastern portion is remote high country, slashed across half its southern breadth by the deep, rugged Kings River Canyon. Separating the two is Sequoia National Forest, which encompasses Giant Sequoia National Monument. The Kings Canyon Scenic Byway (Route 180) links the major sights within and between the park's two sections.

HISTORIC SITES

★ **Fallen Monarch.** This Sequoia's hollow base was used in the second half of the 19th century as a home for settlers, a saloon, and even to stable U.S. Cavalry horses. As you walk through it (assuming entry is permitted, which has not always been the case in recent years), check out how little the wood has decayed, and imagine yourself tucked safely inside, sheltered from a storm or protected from the searing heat. ⊠ *Trailhead 1 mi north of Grant Grove Visitor Center.*

Gamlin Cabin. What you see is only borderline historical, despite its being on the National Register of Historic Places. This modest lodging that the Gamlin brothers built in 1872 has been moved and rebuilt several times, and a few brain-cramped visitors have carved their initials into its sides. This well-intentioned replica depicts what once served as U.S. Cavalry

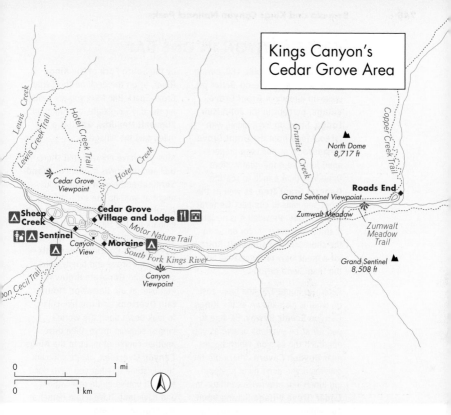

Kings Canyon's
Cedar Grove Area

Lewis Creek

Lewis Creek Trail

Hotel Creek Trail

Hotel Creek

Cedar Grove
Viewpoint

Sheep
Creek

Cedar Grove
Village and Lodge

Sentinel

Canyon
View

Moraine

Motor Nature Trail

South Fork Kings River

Canyon Cecil Trail

Canyon
Viewpoint

Granite Creek

Copper Creek Trail

North Dome
8,717 ft

Roads End

Grand Sentinel Viewpoint

Zumwalt Meadow

Zumwalt
Meadow
Trail

Grand Sentinel
8,508 ft

0   1 mi

0   1 km

storage space and, during the first decade of the 20th century, a ranger station. ⊠ *Trailhead 1 mi north of Grant Grove Visitor Center.*

SCENIC STOPS

Canyon View. There are many places along the scenic byway to pull over for sightseeing, but this special spot showcases evidence of the canyon's glacial history. Here, maybe more than anywhere else, you'll understand why John Muir compared Kings Canyon vistas with those in Yosemite. ⊠ *Kings Canyon Scenic Byway (Rte. 180), 1 mi east of the Cedar Grove turnoff.*

General Grant Tree. President Coolidge proclaimed this to be "the nation's Christmas tree," and 30 years later President Eisenhower designated it as a living shrine to all Americans who have died in wars. Bigger at its base than the General Sherman Tree, it tapers rather quickly and is estimated to be the world's second- or third-largest sequoia (by volume). ⊠ *Trailhead 1 mi north of Grant Grove Visitor Center.*

★ **Redwood Mountain Grove.** If you are serious about sequoias, you should consider visiting this, the world's largest big-tree grove. Within its 2,078 acres are 2,172 sequoias whose diameters exceed 10 feet. Your options range from the distant (pulling off the Generals Highway onto an overlook) to the intimate (taking a 6- to 10-mi hike down into its richest regions, which include two of the world's 25 heaviest trees). ⊠ *Drive*

KINGS CANYON IN ONE DAY

Enter the park via Route 180, having spent the night in Fresno. Better yet, wake up already in **Grant Grove Village**, perhaps in the **John Muir Lodge**. Stock up for a picnic with takeout food from the **Grant Grove Restaurant**, or purchase prepackaged food from the nearby store. Drive less than a mile to see the **General Grant Tree**, as well as the other sequoias in compact **General Grant Grove**. Provided it is no later than mid-morning, motor on up to the short trail at **Panoramic Point**, for a great view of Hume Lake and the High Sierra beyond.

Return to Route 180 and head east on what is also known as the **Kings Canyon Scenic Byway**. Be sure to pull off at an overlook or two as you approach the canyon, which begins near **Boyden Cavern**. Check out the caverns if you don't mind postponing lunch, but otherwise continue to **Cedar Grove Village** (having taken 10 minutes for a gander at **Grizzly Falls** along the way). Eat at a table

by the **South Fork of the Kings River**, or on the deck off the Cedar Grove Snack Bar. Now you are ready for the day's highlight, a stroll about **Zumwalt Meadow**, which is a few miles past the village.

After you have enjoyed that short trail and the views it offers of **Grand Sentinel** and **North Dome**, you might as well go the extra mile to **Road's End**, where backpackers embark for the High Sierra wilderness. Make the return trip—with a quick stop at **Roaring River Falls**—past Grant Grove and briefly onto southbound **Generals Highway**. Pull over at the **Redwood Mountain Overlook** and use binoculars to look down upon the world's largest sequoia grove, then drive another couple of miles to the **Kings Canyon Overlook**, where you can survey some of what you have done today. If you've made reservations and have time, have a late dinner at the **Wuksachi Lodge**.

5 mi south of Grant Grove on Generals Hwy. (Rte. 198), then turn right at Quail Flat; follow it 1½ mi to the Redwood Canyon trailhead.

VISITOR CENTERS

Cedar Grove Visitor Center. Off the main road and behind the Sentinel Campground, this small ranger station has books and maps, plus information about hikes and other things to do in the area. ⊠ *Kings Canyon Scenic Byway, 30 mi east of park entrance* ☎ *559/565–3793* ☉ *mid-May–late September, daily 9–5.*

Grant Grove Visitor Center. Acquaint yourself with the varied charms of this two-section national park by watching a 15-minute film and perusing the center's exhibits on the canyon, sequoias, and human history. Books, maps, and free wilderness permits are available, as are updates on the parks' weather and air-quality conditions. ⊠ *Generals Hwy. (Rte. 198), 3 mi northeast of Rte. 180, Big Stump entrance* ☎ *559/565–4307* ☉ *Summer, daily 8–6; mid-May–late Sept., daily 9–4:30; winter, daily 9:30–4:30.*

SPORTS AND THE OUTDOORS

The siren song of beauty, challenge, and relative solitude (by national parks standards) draws hard-core outdoors enthusiasts to the Kings River Canyon and the backcountry of the park's eastern section. Backpacking, rock-climbing, and extreme-kayaking opportunities get even the most experienced adrenal glands pumping, but the park also has day hikes for all ability levels. Winter brings sledding, skiing, and snowshoeing fun. No off-road driving or bicycling is allowed in the park, and snowmobiling is also prohibited.

CROSS-COUNTRY SKIING

Roads to Grant Grove are easily accessible during heavy snowfall, making the trails here a good choice over Sequoia's Giant Forest when harsh weather hits.

Grant Grove Ski Touring Center. The Grant Grove Market doubles as the ski-touring center, where you can rent cross-country skis in winter. This is a good starting point for a number of marked trails, including the Panoramic Point Trail and the General Grant Tree Trail *(⇨ Hiking). ⊠ Grant Grove Market, Generals Hwy. (Rte. 198), 3 mi northeast of Rte. 180, Big Stump entrance ☎ 559/335–2665 ⊠ $6–$11 ☉ Daily 9–6.*

FISHING

There is limited trout fishing in the park from late April to mid-November, and catches are minor. Still, Kings River is a popular spot. Some of the park's secluded backcountry lakes have good fishing. Licenses ($10.75 for two days, $29.40 for 10 days, less for state residents) are required for those over 16, and are available, along with fishing tackle, in Grant Grove and Cedar Grove. Only Grant Grove is open year-round. Fishing licenses are issued by the **California Department of Fish and Game** (☎ *916/653–7661* ⊕ *www.dfg.ca.gov*).

HIKING

You can enjoy many of Kings Canyon's sights from your car, but the giant gorge of the Kings River Canyon and the sweeping vistas of some of the highest mountains in the United States are best seen on foot. Carry a hiking map—available at any visitor center—and plenty of water. Check with rangers for current trail conditions, and be aware of rapidly changing weather.

If you're planning to hike the backcountry, you can pick up a permit and information on the backcountry at **Road's End Permit Station** (⊠ *5 mi east of Cedar Grove Visitor Center, at the end of Kings Canyon Scenic Byway* ☎ *No phone* ☉ *Late May–late Sept., daily 7–3:30*). You can also rent or buy bear canisters, a must for campers. When the station is closed, you can still complete a self-service permit form.

EASY

Big Stump Trail. From 1883 until 1890, logging was done here, complete with a mill. The 1-mi loop trail, whose unmarked beginning is a few yards west of the Big Stump entrance, passes by many enormous stumps. ⊠ *Trailhead near Rte. 180, Big Stump Entrance.*

General Grant Tree Trail. Though General Grant Grove is rather small, at 128 acres, it's a big deal. More than 120 sequoias here have a base

Mt. Whitney

At 14,494 feet, Mt. Whitney is the highest point in the contiguous United States and the crown jewel of Sequoia National Park's wild eastern side. The peak looms high above the tiny, high-mountain desert community of Lone Pine, where numerous Hollywood westerns have been filmed. The high mountain ranges, arid landscape, and scrubby brush of the Eastern Sierra are beautiful in their vastness and austerity.

Despite the mountain's scale, you can't see it from the more traveled west side of the park, because it is hidden behind the Great Western Divide. The only way to access Mt. Whitney from the main part of the park is to circumnavigate the Sierra Nevada via a 10-hour, nearly 400-mi drive outside the park (⇨ *Death Valley, chapter 16, for Mt. Whitney)*. No road ascends the peak; the best vantage point from which to catch a glimpse of the mountain is at the end of Whitney Portal Road. The 13 mi of winding road leads from U.S. 395

at Lone Pine to the trailhead for the hiking route to the top of the mountain. Whitney Portal Road is closed in winter.

The most popular route to the summit, the **Mt. Whitney Trail,** can be conquered by fit and moderately experienced hikers, unless there is snow on the mountain; then it is a challenge for expert mountaineers only. Day hikers must have a permit to hike the trail beyond Lone Pine Lake, about 2½ mi from the trailhead; all overnighters must have a permit. Reservations for climbing Mt. Whitney May through October are difficult to obtain because of a daily limit on the number of hikers allowed. You can apply for overnight and day permits by lottery each February. In May, if other hikers have canceled, a few permits become available. Contact the **Wilderness Permit Office of Inyo National Forest** (☎ *760/873–2485 wilderness information line, 760/873–2483 reservation line* ⊕ *www.fs.fed.us/r5/inyo).*

---

diameter that exceeds 10 feet, and the grove's signature tree is the world's second- or third-largest (by volume). Nearby, the vanquished Confederacy is represented by the Robert E. Lee Tree, recognized as the world's 11th-largest sequoia. ⊠ *Trailhead off Generals Hwy. (Rte. 198), 1 mi northwest of Grant Grove Visitor Center.*

Roaring River Falls Walk. Take a shady five-minute walk to this forceful waterfall that rushes through a narrow granite chute. The trail is paved and mostly accessible. ⊠ *Trailhead 3 mi east of Cedar Grove Village turnoff from Kings Canyon Scenic Byway.*

Fodor'sChoice ★ **Zumwalt Meadow Trail.** Rangers say this is the best (and most popular) day hike in the Cedar Grove area. Just 1.5 mi long, it offers three visual treats: the South Fork of the Kings River, the lush meadow, and the high granite walls above, including those of Grand Sentinel and North Dome. ⊠ *Trailhead 4½ mi east of Cedar Grove Village turnoff from Kings Canyon Scenic Byway.*

Hiking in the Sierra mountains is a thrilling experience, putting you amid some of the world's highest trees.

MODERATE

★ **Big Baldy.** This hike climbs 600 feet and 2 mi up to the 8,209-feet summit of Big Baldy. Your reward is the view of Redwood Canyon. The round-trip hike is 4 mi. ✉ *Trailhead 8 mi south of Grant Grove on Generals Hwy. (Rte. 198).*

Mist Falls Trail. This sandy trail follows the glaciated South Fork Canyon through forest and chaparral, past several rapids and cascades, to one of the largest waterfalls in the two parks. Nine miles round-trip, the hike is relatively flat, but climbs 600 feet in the last mile. It takes four to five hours to complete. ✉ *Trailhead at end of Kings Canyon Scenic Byway, 5½ mi east of Cedar Grove Village.*

Panoramic Point Trail. You'll get a nice view of whale-shaped Hume Lake from the top of this Grant Grove path, which is paved and only 300 feet long. It's fairly steep—strollers might work here, but not wheelchairs. Trailers and RVs are not permitted on the steep and narrow road that leads to the trailhead parking lot. ✉ *Trial begins at end of Panoramic Point Rd., 2.3 mi from Grant Grove Village.*

★ **Redwood Canyon Trail.** Avoid the hubbub of Giant Forest and its General Sherman Tree by hiking down to Redwood Canyon, the world's largest grove of sequoias. Opt for the trail toward Hart Tree, and you'll soon lose track of how many humongous trees you pass along the 6-mi loop. Count on spending four to six peaceful hours here—although some backpackers linger overnight (wilderness permit required). ✉ *Trail begins off Quail Flat ✢ Drive 5 mi south of Grant Grove on Generals Hwy. (Rte. 198), then turn right at Quail Flat; follow it 1½ mi to the Redwood Canyon trailhead.*

DIFFICULT

Buena Vista Peak. For a 360-degree view of Redwood Canyon and the High Sierra, make the 2-mi ascent to Buena Vista. ⊠ *Trailhead off Generals Hwy. (Rte. 198), south of Kings Canyon Overlook, 7 mi southeast of Grant Grove.*

Don Cecil Trail. This trail climbs the cool north-facing slope of the Kings River Canyon, passes Sheep Creek Cascade and provides several good views of the canyon and the 11,000-foot Monarch Divide. The trail leads to Lookout Peak, which affords an incredible panorama of the park's backcountry. It's a strenuous, all-day hike—13 mi round-trip—and climbs 4,000 feet. ⊠ *Trailhead off Kings Canyon Scenic Byway, across from parking lot, 0.2 mi west of Cedar Grove Village.*

★ **Hotel Creek Trail.** For gorgeous canyon views, take this trail from the canyon floor at Cedar Grove up a series of switchbacks until it splits. Follow the route left through chaparral to the forested ridge and rocky outcrop known as Cedar Grove Overlook, where you can see the Kings River Canyon stretching below. This strenuous 5-mi round-trip hike gains 1,200 feet and takes three to four hours to complete. For a longer hike, return via Lewis Creek Trail for an 8-mi loop. ⊠ *Trailhead at Cedar Grove pack station, 1 mi east of Cedar Grove Village.*

HORSEBACK RIDING

One-day destinations by horseback out of Cedar Grove include Mist Falls and Upper Bubb's Creek. In the backcountry, many equestrians head for Volcanic Lakes or Granite Basin, ascending trails that reach elevations of 10,000 feet. Costs per person range from $25 for a one-hour guided ride to around $200 per day for fully guided trips for which the packers do all the cooking and camp chores.

OUTFIT-
TERS AND
EXPEDITIONS
Take a day or overnight trip along the Kings River Canyon with **Cedar Grove Pack Station** (⊠ *Kings Canyon Scenic Byway, 1 mi east of Cedar Grove Village* ☎ *559/565–3464 in summer, 559/337–2314 off-season* 🖥 *Call for prices* ⊗ *May–Oct.*). Popular routes include the Rae Lakes Loop and Monarch Divide. A one- or two-hour trip through Grant Grove leaving from **Grant Grove Stables** (⊠ *Rte. 180, ½ mi north of Grant Grove Visitor Center* ☎ *559/335–9292 mid-June–Sept., 559/594–9307 Oct.–mid-June* 🖥 *$35–$50* ⊗ *June–Labor Day, daily 8–6*) is a good way to get a taste of horseback riding in Kings Canyon.

SLEDDING AND SNOWSHOEING

In winter, Kings Canyon has a few great places to play in the snow. Sleds, inner tubes, and platters are allowed at both the Azalea Campground area on Grant Tree Road, ¼ mi north of Grant Grove Visitor Center, and at the Big Stump picnic area, 2 mi north of the lower Route 180 entrance to the park.

Snowshoeing is good around Grant Grove, where you can take naturalist-guided snowshoe walks on Saturdays and holidays mid-December through mid-March as conditions permit.

OUTFITTER
Purchase sleds, saucers, snowshoes, and other snowplay gear at **Grant Grove Market** (⊠ *Generals Hwy. [Rte. 198], 3 mi northeast of Rte. 180, Big Stump entrance* ☎ *559/335–2665* ⊗ *Daily 9–6*). For a $1 donation, the **Grant Grove Visitor Center** (⊠ *Generals Hwy. [Rte. 198], 3 mi*

northeast of Rte. 180, Big Stump entrance ☎ *559/565–4307* ⊙ *Daily 9:30–4:30)* rents out snowshoes for ranger-led walks.

EDUCATIONAL OFFERINGS

There are no regularly scheduled tours of Kings Canyon. Grant Grove Visitor Center has maps of self-guided park tours. Ranger-led programs take place throughout the year in Grant Grove. Cedar Grove and Forest Service campgrounds have activities from Memorial Day to Labor Day. Check bulletin boards or visitor centers for schedules. *For information on programs and activities,* ⇨ *Educational Offerings in Sequoia National Park.*

34

WHAT'S NEARBY

The only way into Sequoia National Park is from the west on Route 198 or an offshoot, Mineral King Road. These are tortuously winding above Three Rivers, the only town within spitting distance of the park. Any way you look at it, Kings Canyon National Park is even a longer way from civilization. The only access is via a slow mountain highway, Route 180, at the Big Stump entrance, or through Sequoia on Generals Highway. The Kings River Canyon is even farther away from everything, and is entirely inaccessible in winter.

NEARBY TOWNS

In the foothills of the Sierra along the Kaweah River, **Three Rivers** is a leafy hamlet whose livelihood depends largely on tourism from Sequoia and Kings Canyon. Close to Sequoia's Ash Mountain and Lookout Point (Mineral King) entrances, this is a good spot to find a room when park lodgings are full. **Visalia,** a city of 93,000, lies 46 mi east of Sequoia and 55 mi west of Kings Canyon on the edge of the San Joaquin Valley. Its vibrant downtown contains several good restaurants and bed-and-breakfasts. Closest to Kings Canyon's Big Stump entrance, **Sanger** lies on the Kings River where it emerges from the foothills, about 40 minutes from the park. The agricultural community calls itself "the Nation's Christmas Tree City" and celebrates the holiday each year with a caravan to the General Grant Tree. **Fresno,** the main gateway to the Southern Sierra region, is about 55 mi west of Kings Canyon and about 65 mi southwest of Yosemite. California's sixth-largest city is sprawling and unglamorous, but it has all the amenities you'd expect of a major crossroads.

VISITOR INFORMATION
Fresno Convention & Visitors Bureau ⊠ *848 M St., Fresno* ☎ *559/445–8300* ⊕ *www.fresnocvb.org.* **Fresno County Office of Tourism** ⊠ *2220 Tulare St., Fresno* ☎ *559/262–4271* ⊕ *www.gofresnocounty.com.* **Sanger Chamber of Commerce** ⊠ *1789 Jensen Ave., Sanger* ☎ *559/875–4575* ⊕ *www.sanger.org.* **Sequoia Foothills Chamber of Commerce** ⊠ *42268 Sierra Dr., Three Rivers* ☎ *559/561–3300* ⊕ *www.threerivers.com.* **Visalia Chamber of Commerce & Visitors Bureau** ⊠ *220 N. Santa Fe Ave., Visalia* ☎ *559/734–5876 or 877/847–2542* ⊕ *www.visaliachamber.org.*

NEARBY ATTRACTIONS

FAMILY PICKS

White water Adventure. Conquer the the Kings or Kahweah rivers on a springtime rafting trip.

Forestiere Underground Gardens. Descend into another world here.

Uncle Harry's. Take a tastebud trip to Armenia at this eatery in Reedley.

Boyden Cavern. The Kings River runs through a canyon that's deeper than the Grand Canyon. The seepage of its waters has created many caves in this area, well below the surface of the ground. If you can't make it to Crystal Cave in Sequoia, Boyden is a reasonable substitute, but the operations here aren't on par with those at the former. Tours depart roughly every 45 minutes and start with a steep walk uphill. ✉ *74101 Kings Canyon Scenic Byway (Rte. 180), between Grant Grove and Cedar Grove, Sequoia National Forest* ☎ *209/736–2708 or 866/762–2837* 🌐 *www.caverntours.com/BoydenRt.htm* 🎫 *$14* ⏲ *Apr.–mid-May and mid-Sept.–Nov., daily 11–4; mid-May–mid-Sept., daily 10–5.*

★ **Forestiere Underground Gardens.** More than 10 acres of subterranean grottos, tunnels, and alcoves lie beneath a busy commercial strip. It took Sicilian immigrant Baldasare Forestiere 40 years, starting in 1906, to create this surreal complex of skylight-lighted fruit tree groves, a chapel, and living quarters 20 feet underground. The gardens are on the National Register of Historic Places. Access is by guided tour; reservations are recommended. ✉ *5021 W. Shaw Ave., 2 blocks east of Hwy. 99, Fresno* ☎ *559/271–0734* 🌐 *www.undergroundgardens.com* 🎫 *$12* ⏲ *Tours weekends at noon and 2; call for other times.*

Project Survival's Cat Haven. Take the rare opportunity to glimpse a Siberian lynx, a cloud leopard, a Bengal tiger, and other endangered wild cats at this conservation facility. A guided hour-long tour along a quarter-mile of walkway leads to fenced habitat areas shaded by trees and overlooking the Central Valley. ✉ *38257 E. Kings Canyon Rd. (Rte. 180), 15 mi west of Kings Canyon National Park, Dunlap* ☎ *559/338–3216* 🌐 *www.cathaven.com* 🎫 *$9* ⏲ *May–Sept., Wed.–Mon. 10–5; Oct.–Apr., Thurs.–Mon. 10–4. Last tour leaves 1 hr before closing.*

★ **Sequoia National Forest and Giant Sequoia National Monument.** Covering 1,139,500 acres, the monument is tucked north of Sequoia National Park between the two sections of Kings Canyon National Park. (The national forest encompasses the monument and both parks, plus more territory.) Of the world's sequoia groves, more than half are in the part of the forest that has been further protected as a national monument. Three National Recreation Trails and a section of the Pacific Crest Trail wind through the landscape. Four streams are designated National Wild and Scenic Rivers; some of the nation's liveliest white water is found on the Forks section of the Kern. Lake Isabella (11,000 acres) is one of the area's largest reservoirs. There's cross-country skiing and snowmobiling in winter, 900 mi of trail for hiking, camping, and picnicking. ✉ *Entrances: Forest Rd. off Generals Hwy. (Rte. 198), 7 mi southeast of Grant Grove; Hume Lake Rd. between Generals Hwy. (Rte. 198) and Kings Canyon Scenic Byway*

(Rte. 180); Kings Canyon Scenic Byway (Rte. 180) between Grant Grove and Cedar Grove ☎ 559/784–1500 ⊕ www.fs.fed.us/r5/sequoia.

AREA ACTIVITIES

SPORTS AND THE OUTDOORS
BOATING AND RAFTING

OUTFIT-TER AND EXPEDITIONS **Kaweah White Water Adventures** (☎ *559/561–1000 or 800/229–8658 ⊕ www. kaweah-whitewater.com*) guides two-hour and full-day rafting trips, with some Class III rapids; longer trips may include some Class IV. The Class III white water east of Fresno is the venue for one- and two-day trips led by **Kings River Expeditions** (☎ *559/233–4881 or 800/846–3674 ⊕ www. kingsriver.com*).

34

WHERE TO EAT AND STAY

ABOUT THE RESTAURANTS

In Sequoia and Kings Canyon national parks, you can treat yourself (and the family) to a high-quality meal in a wonderful setting in the Wuksachi Dining Room, but otherwise you should keep your expectations modest. One good strategy is to embrace outdoor eating. You can grab bread, spreads, drinks, and fresh produce at one of several small grocery stores, or get take-out food from the Grant Grove Restaurant, the Cedar Grove Snack Bar, or one of the two small Lodgepole eateries. The nightly Wolverton Barbecue is a hybrid experience between dining in and picnicking out; the all-you-can-eat feast is staged on a patio that overlooks a sublime meadow. Between the parks and just off Generals Highway, the Montecito Sequoia Lodge has a year-round buffet.

ABOUT THE HOTELS

Hotel accommodations in Sequoia and Kings Canyon are limited, and—although they are clean and comfortable—tend to lack much in-room character. Keep in mind, however, that the extra money you spend on lodging here is offset by the time you'll save by being inside the parks. You won't be faced with a 60- to 90-minute commute from the less-expensive motels in Three Rivers and Fresno. Reserve as far in advance as you can, especially for summertime stays.

ABOUT THE CAMPGROUNDS

Campgrounds in Sequoia and Kings Canyon are located in wonderful settings, with lots of shade and nearby hiking trails. But beware that party-loving "locals" from Fresno and other Central Valley cities swarm up here on Friday and Saturday nights. Only the Dorst Creek and Lodgepole campgrounds accept reservations (up to five months in advance), and none has RV hookups. Campgrounds around Lodgepole and Grant Grove get quite busy in summer with vacationing families. Permits are required for backcountry camping.

WHERE TO EAT

IN SEQUOIA

¢ ✕**Lodgepole Market and Snack Bar.** The choices here run the gamut from
CAFE   simple to very simple, with the three counters only a few strides apart
in a central eating complex. For hot food, venture into the snack bar.
The deli sells prepackaged sandwiches along with ice cream scooped
from tubs. You'll find other prepackaged foods in the market. ✉ *Next
to Lodgepole Visitor Center* ☎ *559/565–3301* ▭ *AE, D, DC, MC, V*
☾ *Closed early Sept.–mid-Apr.*

$ ✕**Wolverton Barbecue.** Weather permitting, diners congregate on a
BARBECUE   wooden porch that looks directly out onto a small but strikingly verdant meadow. In addition to the predictable meats such as ribs and
chicken, the all-you-can-eat buffet has sides that include baked beans,
corn on the cob, and potato salad. Following the meal, listen to a ranger
talk and clear your throat for a campfire sing-along. Purchase tickets at
Lodgepole Market, Wuksachi Lodge, or Wolverton Recreation Area's
office. ✉ *Wolverton Rd., 1½ mi northeast off Generals Hwy. (Rte. 198)*
☎ *559/565–4070 or 559/565–3301* ▭ *AE, D, DC, MC, V* ☾ *No lunch.
Closed Mon.–Thurs. and early Sept.–mid-June.*

$$–$$$ ✕**Wuksachi Village Dining Room.** Huge windows run the length of the high-
AMERICAN   ceilinged dining room, and a large fireplace on the far wall warms both
★   the body and the soul. The diverse dinner menu—by far the best in the
two parks—includes filet mignon, rainbow trout, and vegetarian pasta
dishes, in addition to the ever-present burgers. The children's menu is eco-
nomically priced. Breakfast and lunch also are served. ✉ *Wuksachi Village* ☎ *559/565–4070* ⚱ *Reservations essential* ▭ *AE, D, DC, MC, V.*

PICNIC AREAS   Take care to dispose of your food scraps properly (the bears might not
appreciate this short-term, but the practice helps ensure their long-term
survival).

Crescent Meadow. A mile or so past Moro Rock, this comparatively
remote picnic area has meadow views and, quite handily, is by a lovely
trail on which you can burn off those potato chips and cookies. Tables
are under the giant sequoias, off the parking area. There are restrooms
and drinking water. Fires are not allowed. ✉ *End of Moro Rock–
Crescent Rd., 2.6 mi east off Generals Hwy. (Rte. 198).*

Hospital Rock. American Indians once ground acorns into meal at this
site; outdoor exhibits tell the story. The picnic area's name, however,
stems from a Caucasian hunter/trapper who was treated for a leg wound
here in 1873. Look up and you'll see imposing Moro Rock up the road.
Grills, drinking water, and restrooms are available. ✉ *Generals Hwy.
(Rte. 198), 6 mi north of Ash Mountain entrance.*

Pinewood Picnic Area. Picnic in Giant Forest, in the vicinity of sequoias
if not actually under them. Drinking water, restrooms, grills, and
wheelchair-accessible spots are provided in this expansive, lovely setting
that is near Sequoia National Park's most popular attractions. ✉ *Generals Hwy. (Rte. 198), 2 mi north of Giant Forest Museum, halfway
between Giant Forest Museum and General Sherman Tree.*

Wolverton Meadow. At a major trailhead to the backcountry, this is a great
place to stop for lunch before a hike. The area sits in a mixed-conifer forest

adjacent to parking. Drinking water, grills, and restrooms are available. ✉ *Wolverton Rd., 1½ mi northeast off Generals Hwy. (Rte. 198).*

IN KINGS CANYON

¢–$ ✕ **Cedar Grove Restaurant.** For a small operation, the menu here is sur-
AMERICAN prisingly extensive, with dinner entrées such as pasta, pork chops, and steak. For breakfast, try the biscuits and gravy, French toast, pancakes, or cold cereal. Burgers (including vegetarian patties) and hot dogs dominate the lunch choices. Outside, a patio dining area overlooks the Kings River. ✉ *Cedar Grove Village* ☎ *559/565–0100* ▭ *AE, D, MC, V* ⊙ *Closed Oct.–May.*

$$–$$$ ✕ **Grant Grove Restaurant.** In a no-frills, open room, order basic Ameri-
AMERICAN can fare such as pancakes for breakfast or hot sandwiches and chicken for later meals. Vegetarians and vegans will have to content themselves with a simple salad. Take-out service is available. ✉ *Grant Grove Village* ☎ *559/335–5500* ▭ *AE, D, MC, V.*

PICNIC AREAS **Big Stump.** At the edge of a logged sequoia grove, some trees still stand at this site. Near the park's entrance, the area is paved and next to the road. It's the only picnic area in either park that is plowed in the wintertime. Restrooms, grills, and drinking water are available, and the area is entirely accessible. ✉ *Just inside Rte. 180, Big Stump entrance.*

Grizzly Falls. This little gem is worth a pull-over, if not a picnic. From the small parking lot, take a very short trek into the woods to picnic tables and to the base of the delightful, 100-foot-plus falls. An outhouse is on-site, but grills are not, and water is unavailable. ✉ *Off Rte. 180, 2½ mi west of Cedar Grove entrance.*

OUTSIDE THE PARKS

$$–$$$ ✕ **Gateway Restaurant and Lodge.** The patio of this raucous roadhouse over-
AMERICAN looks the roaring Kaweah River as it plunges out of the high country, and though the food is nothing special, the location makes up for it. Standouts include baby back ribs and eggplant parmigiana; there's also a cocktail lounge, and guest rooms are available for overnight visitors. Breakfast isn't served weekdays; dinner reservations are essential on weekends. ✉ *45978 Sierra Dr., Three Rivers* ☎ *559/561–4133* ▭ *AE, D, MC, V.*

1 MIDDLE ✕ **Uncle Harry's Classic Meals.** You can taste the Armenian heritage of the
EASTERN Fresno area at this local landmark about 10 mi southeast of Sanger. Shish kebab and *keyma* (seasoned raw beef or lamb with bulgur wheat) are two of the specialties that you can try in the casual dining room, on the patio, or to go. ✉ *1201 G St., Reedley* ☎ *559/638–5170* ⌲ *Reservations not accepted* ▭ *No credit cards.*

$$$–$$$$ ✕ **The Vintage Press.** The best restaurant in the Central Valley serves
NEW AMERICAN up California-French cuisine such as pistachio-crusted king salmon
★ and filet mignon with mustard and cognac. The homemade chocolate–Grand Marnier cake is a standout and the wine list has hundreds of selections. A brass-railed bar, Tiffany-style ceiling lamps, and wood paneling impart an adult but not stuffy tone. ✉ *216 N. Willis St., Visalia* ☎ *559/733–3033* ▭ *AE, DC, MC, V.*

34

WHERE TO STAY

IN SEQUOIA

$$–$$$

Silver City Mountain Resort. High on Mineral King Road, this privately owned resort has rustic cabins and Swiss-style chalets, all with at least a stove, refrigerator, and sink. While the more expensive chalets have full bathrooms and kitchens, the cabins share a central shower and bath. The spacious grounds contain several inviting hammocks and a babbling brook, and deer are likely to meander through at any time. Church services are conducted Sunday mornings on the patio, no alcohol is sold in the small store, and the generator is turned off before 10 PM—this is not a place that parties. **Pros:** lovely setting; friendly staff. **Cons:** no electricity except in the evenings. ⊠ *Mineral King Rd., 20 mi east of Hwy. 198* ☎ *559/561–3223 or 805/528–2730* ⊕ *www. silvercityresort.com* ⇨ *13 units, 8 with shared bath* ⚒ *In-room: no a/c, no phone (some), kitchen, refrigerator (some), no TV, Internet (some). In-hotel: restaurant* ⊟ *MC, V* ⊗ *Closed Nov.–May.*

$$$–$$$$
Fodor'sChoice
★

Wuksachi Lodge. The striking cedar-and-stone main building here is a fine example of how a man-made structure can blend effectively with lovely mountain scenery. Guest rooms, which have modern amenities, are in three buildings up the hill from the main lodge. You can usually see deer roaming around the spacious and hilly grounds, which are 7,200 feet above sea level. **Pros:** best place to stay in the parks, lots of wildlife. **Cons:** rooms can be small, main lodge is a few minutes' walk from guest rooms. ⊠ *Wuksachi Village* ☎ *559/565–4070 front desk, 559/253–2199, 888/252–5757 reservations* ⊕ *www.visitsequoia.com* ⇨ *102 rooms* ⚒ *In-room: no a/c, refrigerator, Internet, Wi-Fi. In-hotel: restaurant, bar* ⊟ *AE, D, DC, MC, V.*

CAMPING
$

Atwell Mill Campground. At 6,650 feet, this tents-only campground is just south of the Western Divide. There are telephones and a general store is ½ mi away at the Silver City Resort. Reservations are not accepted. **Pros:** peaceful; spacious; usually has spaces available. **Cons:** no frills; very remote. ⊠ *Mineral King Rd., 20 mi east of Hwy. 198* ☎ *559/565–3341* ⚠ *23 tent sites* ⚒ *Pit toilets, drinking water, showers, bear boxes, fire grates, picnic tables* ⊟ *No credit cards* ⊗ *Closed Nov.–Apr.*

$$

Dorst Creek Campground. This large campground is at 6,700 feet. Use the bear boxes: this is a popular area for the furry creatures to raid. Reservations, made by mail or through the Web site, are essential in summer. There are accessible sites here. **Pros:** centrally located; lots of wildlife sightings probable. **Cons:** so large it's impersonal; difficult to navigate; can be raucous Friday and Saturday nights. ⊠ *Generals Hwy. (Rte. 198), 8 mi north of Lodgepole Visitor Center, near Kings Canyon border* ☎ *301/722–1257 or 800/365–2267* ⚠ *204 tent/RV sites* ⚒ *Flush toilets, dump station, drinking water, bear boxes, fire grates, picnic tables, public telephone* ⊟ *D, MC, V* ⊗ *Closed after Labor Day–Memorial Day.*

$$

Lodgepole Campground. The largest Lodgepole-area campground is also the noisiest, though things do quiet down at night. Restrooms are nearby. Lodgepole and Dorst (a mile or so to the west) are the two campgrounds within Sequoia that accept reservations (essential up to five months in advance for stays between mid-May and mid-October). **Pros:** great central location; wonderful atmosphere for families. **Cons:**

spaces are rather small; reservations rather difficult to obtain. ⊠ *Off Generals Hwy. beyond Lodgepole Village* ☎ *559/565–3341 Ext. 2 for information, 800/365–2267 reservations* ⚠ *214 tent/RV sites* ⚑ *Flush toilets, dump station (summer only), drinking water, guest laundry (summer only), showers (summer only), bear boxes, fire grates, picnic tables, public telephone, general store* ☰ *D, MC, V.*

$$ ⚠ **Potwisha Campground.** On the Marble Fork of the Kaweah River, this midsize campground with attractive surroundings sits at 2,100 feet— which means it gets no snow in winter and can be hotter in summer than campgrounds at higher elevations. RVs up to 30 feet long can camp here. **Pros:** pretty setting; warm at night. **Cons:** you have a steep drive to get from here to the park's main attractions. ⊠ *Generals Hwy., 4 mi north of Foothills Visitor Center* ☎ *559/565–3341* ⚠ *42 tent/RV sites* ⚑ *Flush toilets, dump station, drinking water, bear boxes, fire grates, picnic tables, public telephone* ⚑ *Reservations not accepted* ☰ *No credit cards.*

¢–$ ⚠ **South Fork Campground.** At 3,600 feet, this tiny campground is at the southernmost corner of Sequoia. At the end of a dirt road, it best accommodates tent campers. **Pros:** rarely full; campers here aren't amateurs; quiet. **Cons:** so remote it might make you nervous; not near any of the parks' main attractions. ⊠ *End of South Fork Rd., 12 mi east of Generals Hwy. (Rte. 198)* ☎ *No phone* ⚠ *10 tent sites* ⚑ *Pit toilets, running water (non-potable), bear boxes, fire grates, picnic tables* ⚑ *Reservations not accepted* ☰ *No credit cards.*

IN KINGS CANYON

$$ ⛺ **Cedar Grove Lodge.** Backpackers like to stay here on the eve of long treks into the High Sierra wilderness, so bedtimes tend to be early and quiet. The lodge is not attractive (aside from the natural beauty that surrounds it), but it is the only indoor accommodation in this part of Kings Canyon National Park. Each room has two queen-size beds, and three have kitchenettes and patios. **Pros:** a definite step up from camping in terms of comfort. **Cons:** impersonal; not everybody agrees it's clean enough. ⊠ *Kings Canyon Scenic Byway* ⛺ *Sequoia Kings Canyon Park Services Co., 5755 E. Kings Canyon Rd., Suite 101, Fresno, CA 93727* ☎ *559/335–5500 or 866/522–6966* ⊕ *www.sequoia-kingscanyon.com* ⛺ *21 rooms* ⚑ *In-room: no phone, kitchen (some), no TV. In-hotel: laundry facilities* ☰ *AE, D, MC, V* ☾ *Closed mid-Oct.–mid-May.*

$–$$ ⛺ **Grant Grove Cabins.** Some of the wood-panel cabins here have heaters, electric lights, and private baths, but most have woodstoves, battery lamps, and shared baths. Those who don't mind roughing it might opt for the tent cabins. The Grant Grove Restaurant *(⇨ Where to Eat)*, a family-style coffee shop, serves American standards for breakfast, lunch, and dinner. In winter, only the cabins that have private baths remain open. **Pros:** warm, woodsy feel; clean. **Cons:** can be difficult to walk up to if you're not in decent physical shape; rather costly for what you get. ⊠ *Kings Canyon Scenic Byway in Grant Grove Village* ⛺ *Sequoia Kings Canyon Park Services Co., 5755 E. Kings Canyon Rd., Suite 101, Fresno, CA 93727* ☎ *559/335–5500 or 866/522–6966* ⊕ *www.sequoia-kingscanyon.com* ⛺ *36 cabins, 9 with bath; 19 tent cabins* ⚑ *In-room: no a/c, no phone, no TV. In-hotel: restaurant* ☰ *AE, D, MC, V.*

$$$ ⚏ **John Muir Lodge.** This modern, timber-sided lodge is nestled in a wooded area in the hills above Grant Grove Village and offers year-round accommodations. The rooms and suites all have queen-size beds and private baths, and there is a comfortable common room where you can play cards and board games, or peruse a loaner book. Look above the stone fireplace at a giant painting of Muir himself, shown relaxing on a rock by a meadow. **Pros:** common room stays warm; it's far enough from the main road to be quiet. **Cons:** check-in is down in the village. ⊠ *Kings Canyon Scenic Byway, ¼ mi north of Grant Grove Village* ⬒ *Sequoia Kings Canyon Park Services Co., 5755 E. Kings Canyon Rd., Suite 101, Fresno, CA 93727* ☎ *559/335–5500 or 866/522–6966* ⊕ *www.sequoia-kingscanyon.com* ⇱ *24 rooms, 6 suites* ⚂ *In-room: no a/c, no TV* ⊟ *AE, D, MC, V.*

CAMPING   ⚠ **Azalea Campground.** Of the three campgrounds in the Grant Grove area
¢–$ (the others are Sunset and Crystal Springs), Azalea is the only one open year-round. It sits at 6,500 feet amid giant sequoias, yet is close to restaurants, stores, and other facilities. Some sites at Azalea are wheelchair accessible. The campground can accommodate RVs up to 30 feet. **Pros:** open in wintertime; nice setting; good location. **Cons:** summer weekend reservations can be difficult to obtain. ⊠ *Kings Canyon Scenic Byway, ¼ mi north of Grant Grove Village* ☎ *559/565–3341* ⚠ *113 tent/RV sites* ⚂ *Flush toilets, drinking water, showers, bear boxes, fire grates, picnic tables, public telephone, general store* ⊟ *No credit cards.*

$$ ⚠ **Crystal Springs Campground.** Near the Grant Grove Village and the towering sequoias, this camp is at 6,500 feet. There are accessible sites here. **Pros:** good location; nicely tiered sites. **Cons:** weekend reservations are a challenge; curvy roads test RV maneuverability. ⊠ *Off Generals Hwy. (Rte. 198), ¼-mi north of Grant Grove Visitor Center* ☎ *No phone* ⚠ *62 tent/RV sites* ⚂ *Flush toilets, drinking water, bear boxes, fire grates, picnic tables, public telephone* ⚎ *Reservations not accepted* ⊟ *No credit cards* ⊘ *Closed after Labor Day–Memorial Day.*

$$ ⚠ **Sentinel Campground.** Of the four campgrounds in the Cedar Grove area, Sentinel is open the longest. At 4,600 feet and within walking distance of Cedar Grove Village, it fills up fast in the summer. Some sites are wheelchair accessible, and the campground can accommodate RVs up to 30 feet. Nearby, there are laundry facilities, a restaurant, a general store, and a ranger station. **Pros:** teeming with families; close to the village amenities. **Cons:** crowded; small spaces; flat. ⊠ *Kings Canyon Scenic Byway, ¼-mi west of Cedar Grove Village* ☎ *559/565–3341* ⚂ *Flush toilets, drinking water, bear boxes, fire grates, picnic tables, public telephone* ⚠ *82 tent/RV sites* ⚎ *Reservations not accepted* ⊟ *No credit cards* ⊘ *Closed Nov.–Apr.*

$$ ⚠ **Sheep Creek Campground.** Of the overflow campgrounds, this is one
Fodor'sChoice   of the prettiest. The camp, like the adjacent Cedar Grove, is at 4,600
★   feet along the Kings River. **Pros:** pretty setting; river sounds are soothing. **Cons:** a solid hike from the village; can be jam-packed. ⊠ *Off Kings Canyon Scenic Byway, 1 mi west of Cedar Grove Village* ☎ *No phone* ⚠ *111 tent/RV sites* ⚂ *Flush toilets, drinking water, bear boxes, fire grates, picnic tables, public telephone* ⚎ *Reservations not accepted* ⊟ *No credit cards* ⊘ *Closed Oct.–early May, as needed.*

$$ △ **Sunset Campground.** Many of the easiest trails through Grant Grove are adjacent to this large camp, near the giant sequoias at 6,500 feet. **Pros:** gorgeous setting; nicely imaged spacing of sites; good location. **Cons:** difficult to reserve on summer weekends; can be a bit noisy. ⊠ *Off Generals Hwy. (Rte. 198), near Grant Grove Visitor Center* ☎ *No phone* △ *200 tent/RV sites* ⚐ *Flush toilets, drinking water, bear boxes, fire grates, picnic tables, public telephone* ⚐ *Reservations not accepted* ⊟ *No credit cards* ☉ *Closed Oct.–Memorial Day.*

OUTSIDE THE PARKS

The only lodging immediately outside the parks is in Three Rivers. Numerous chain properties operate in Visalia or Fresno, about an hour from the south and north entrances, respectively.

$$–$$$ ⊞ **Ben Maddox House.** This homey B and B is in a tidy white 1876 house surrounded by trees and gardens. Interiors are rich with sequoia redwood woodwork; each guest room has a private bath and a plush bed. You can take breakfast on the sunny porch. **Pros:** short walk to downtown; beautiful landscaping; clean rooms. **Cons:** seems costly for the region; not so conveniently close to the parks. ⊠ *601 N. Encina St., Visalia* ☎ *559/732–0721 or 800/401–9800* ⊕ *www.benmaddoxhouse.com* ⤳ *5 rooms* ⚐ *In-room: Wi-Fi. In-hotel: pool* ⊟ *AE, D, MC, V* ⊙I *BP.*

$–$$ ⊞ **Buckeye Tree Lodge.** Every room at this two-story motel has a patio facing a sun-dappled grassy lawn, right on the banks of the Kaweah River. Accommodations are simple and well kept, and the lodge sits a mere quarter mile from the park gate. Book well in advance. **Pros:** near the park entrance; fantastic river views; friendly staff. **Cons:** can fill up quickly in the summer; could use a little updating. ⊠ *46000 Sierra Dr. (Hwy. 198), Three Rivers* ☎ *559/561–5900* ⊕ *www.buckeyetree.com* ⤳ *11 rooms, 1 cottage* ⚐ *In-hotel: pool, some pets allowed* ⊟ *AE, D, DC, MC, V* ⊙I *CP.*

$$$–$$$$ ⊞ **Montecito-Sequoia Lodge.** Outdoor activities are what this year-round family resort is all about, including many that are geared toward teenagers and small children. Off Generals Highway in Sequoia National Forest (between Sequoia National Park and the western portion of Kings Canyon National Park), it's also centrally located. The lodge rooms are spare but clean, and all have private baths. Cabins, which can sleep up to eight people, have electricity and contain wood-burning stoves, but bathrooms are in shared buildings. **Pros:** friendly staff; great for kids; lots of fresh air and planned activities. **Cons:** can be noisy with all the activity; could be cleaner. ⊠ *8000 Generals Hwy., 11 mi south of Grant Grove, Kings Canyon National Park* ☎ *559/565–3388, 800/227–9900 reservations* ⊕ *www.montecitosequoia.com* ⤳ *32 rooms, 13 cabins* ⚐ *In-room: no a/c, no phone, no TV. In-hotel: restaurant, tennis court, pool, bicycles, children's programs (ages 2–18)* ⊟ *AE, D, MC, V* ⊙I *FAP.*

$–$$ ⊞ **Sequoia Motel.** An old-fashioned single-story mom-and-pop motel, the Sequoia stands out with such extra touches as country-style quilts and mismatched Americana furnishings that lend a retro charm to the rooms. The on-site owners keep the rooms meticulously clean. There are also one- and two-bedroom cottages with full kitchens. **Pros:** clean; friendly; comparatively affordable. **Cons:** not especially modern; fills up quickly in the summer. ⊠ *43000 Sierra Dr. (Hwy. 198), P.O. Box 145,*

Three Rivers ☎ *559/561–4453* ⊕ *www.sequoiamotel.com* ↩ *11 rooms, 3 cottages* ☖ *In-room: no phone, kitchen (some), Wi-Fi. In-hotel: pool, laundry facilities* ▭ *AE, D, MC, V.*

CAMPING   △ **Hume Lake Campground.** Hume Lake is small and lovely, but gets busy
$ in summer, so reservations are essential. The campground has many
more sites for tents than RVs. It's set at 5,200 feet. RVs larger than 22
feet are not permitted. **Pros:** family atmosphere; gorgeous lake setting.
Cons: crowded in the summer; lots of screaming kids possible anytime.
⊠ *Hume Lake Rd., 3 mi south of Kings Canyon Scenic Byway (Rte. 180)*
☎ *877/444–6777* △ *60 tent sites, 14 RV sites* ☖ *Flush toilets, drinking
water, bear boxes, fire grates, picnic tables, public telephone, swimming
(lake)* ☖ *Reservations essential* ▭ *AE, D, MC, V* ☉ *Late May–Oct.*

Theodore Roosevelt National Park

WORD OF MOUTH

"I grow very fond of this place, and it certainly has a desolate, grim beauty of its own, that has a curious fascination for me."
—Theodore Roosevelt

WELCOME TO THEODORE ROOSEVELT

TOP REASONS TO GO

★ **The "Granddaddy Trail":** Hike the Maah Daah Hey Trail, which means "grandfather" or "been here long." It's one of the most popular and well-maintained trails in western North Dakota.

★ **Views from above:** Get an encompassing 360-degree view of the badlands from Buck Hill.

★ **History lessons from the frontier:** View Maltese Cross Ranch Cabin, which once belonged to Theodore Roosevelt.

★ **Badlands Broadway:** Come experience a theatrical tribute to the history and personalities that make up the Old West at the *Medora Musical.*

★ **Great clubbing—golf, that is:** Perfect your swing at Bully Pulpit Golf Course in Medora, one of America's best courses near the national park.

★ **Away from it all:** As this is one of the most isolated parks, you'll likely encounter more wild horses than people here.

1 North Unit. Visitors looking to enjoy the great outdoors should be sure to travel along the 14-mi scenic drive and stop at one of the many hiking trailheads along the way. These trailheads give easy access to the backcountry of the North Unit.

2 South Unit. Often considered the main unit of Theodore Roosevelt National Park and adjacent to the famous town of Medora, the South Unit is the home to some of the former president's personal artifacts and even his cabin.

3 Elkhorn Ranch. This area of the park is the actual location of one of T.R.'s ranches in the badlands. None of the ranch buildings are still standing, but signs show their former location.

GETTING ORIENTED

The Little Missouri River winds throughout this western North Dakota park, and plenty of bison, deer, antelope, coyote, prairie dogs, and bald eagles inhabit the land. Climb the peaks and you will get exceptional views of the canyons, caprocks, petrified forest, and other bizarre geological formations that make up the badlands.

KEY	
👫	Ranger Station
⛺	Campground
🛉	Picnic Area
🍴	Restaurant
🏨	Lodge
🚶	Trailhead
🚻	Restrooms
⇗	Scenic Viewpoint
⋯⋯	Walking/Hiking Trails

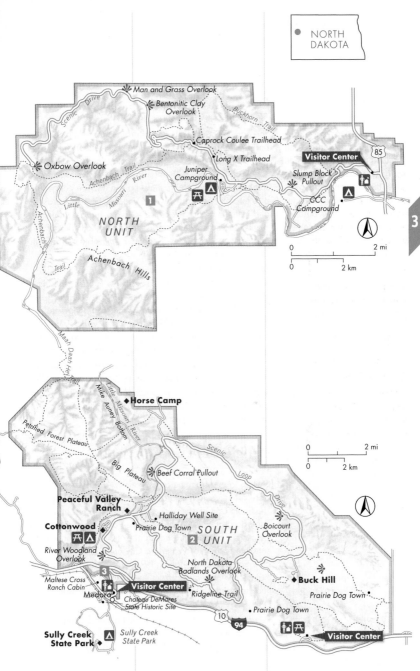

NORTH DAKOTA

Man and Grass Overlook
Bentonitic Clay Overlook
Scenic Drive
Buckhorn Trail
Caprock Coulee Trailhead
Long X Trailhead
Oxbow Overlook
Achenbach Trail
Little Missouri River
Juniper Campground
Slump Block Pullout
CCC Campground
Visitor Center
85

NORTH UNIT 1

Achenbach Trail
Achenbach Hills

0   2 mi
0   2 km

35

Maah Daah Hey Trail
Little Missouri River
Mike Auney Bottom
Horse Camp

Petrified Forest Plateau
Big Plateau
Beef Corral Pullout
Scenic Loop Drive

Peaceful Valley Ranch
Halliday Well Site
Prairie Dog Town
Boicourt Overlook

SOUTH UNIT 2

Cottonwood
River Woodland Overlook
North Dakota Badlands Overlook
Buck Hill
Prairie Dog Town

Maltese Cross Ranch Cabin
3
Medora
Visitor Center
Ridgeline Trail
Chateau DeMores State Historic Site
10
Prairie Dog Town
94
Visitor Center

Sully Creek State Park
Sully Creek State Park

0   2 mi
0   2 km

THEODORE ROOSEVELT PLANNER

When to Go

The park is open year-round, but North Dakota winters can be brutal—very cold, windy, and snowy. Portions of some roads close during winter months, depending on snowfall. Rangers discontinue their outdoor programs when autumn comes, and they recommend that only experienced hikers do any winter explorations.

Though July and August tend to be the busiest months, the park is rarely crowded. Fewer than 500,000 people visit each year, with the South Unit receiving the greater number of visitors. The best times to see wildlife and hike comfortably are May through October. The park is all but desolate December through February, but it's a beautiful time to see the wildlife—also, winter sunsets can be very vivid as the colors reflect off the snow and ice. The park gets an average of 30 inches of snow per year.

AVG. HIGH/LOW TEMPS.

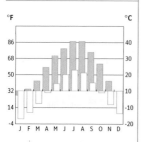

Flora and Fauna

The park's landscape is one of prairies marked by cliffs and rock chasms made of alternating layers of sandstone, siltstone, mudstone, and bentonite clay. In spring the prairies are awash with tall grasses, wildflowers, and shrubs including the ubiquitous poison ivy. The pesky plant also inhabits the forests, where you find box elders, ash, and junipers among the trees. To avoid the rash-inducing plant—and scrapes and bruises that may come from rocks and thick undergrowth—it's always advisable to hike with long pants and sturdy boots.

More than 500 American bison live in the park. These normally docile beasts look tame, but with a set of horns, up to a ton of weight and legs that will carry them at speeds in excess of 35 MPH, they could be the most dangerous animals within park boundaries. Rangers tell visitors repeatedly not to approach them. Some mountain lions also live in the park but are rarely seen. The same goes for prairie rattlers.

On the less-threatening side of the park's fauna, a herd of more than 900 elk live in the South Unit. As many as 150 feral horses are also in the South Unit. The North Unit has some longhorns, which are often found in the bison corral area, about 2½ mi west of the visitor center.

Getting Here and Around

Getting to and from the park is relatively easy due to its close proximity to Medora, as well as exceptional signage. The South Unit entrance and visitor center is just off I-94 in Medora at exits 24 and 27. The Painted Canyon Visitor Center is 7 mi east of Medora at exit 32. The North Unit entrance is south of Waterford City on U.S. 85. Bus transportation is available along I-94, with a stop in Medora that is only three blocks from the park entrance. Planes fly into the North Dakota towns of Bismarck, Dickinson, and Williston. Amtrak serves Williston.

There's ample parking space at all trailheads, and parking is free. Some roads are closed in winter. You may encounter buffalo and other wildlife on the roadway.

By T.D. Griffith Across the open plains of North Dakota, you can travel for miles without seeing a house or business. Then you spy craggy ravines, tablelands, and gorges, and know at once you're in the badlands. The terrain has remained virtually unchanged since Theodore Roosevelt stepped off the train here in 1883, eager to shoot his first bison. Within two weeks, the future 26th president purchased an open-range cattle ranch, and the following year he returned to establish a second, which is part of the 110-square-mi national park that bears his name.

35

PARK ESSENTIALS

ACCESSIBILITY
The visitor centers, campgrounds, and historic sites such as Roosevelt's cabin, are all wheelchair accessible, and films at the visitor centers are closed-captioned. The first part of the Little Mo Nature Trail in the North Unit and the ¼-mi Skyline Vista Trail in the South Unit are both paved.

ADMISSION FEES AND PERMITS
The entrance pass is $10 per vehicle, good for seven days. An annual pass is $20. A backcountry permit, free from the visitor centers, is required for overnight camping away from campgrounds.

ADMISSION HOURS
The park is open year-round. The North Unit is in the central time zone. The South Unit and the Painted Canyon Visitor Center are in the mountain time zone.

ATMS/BANKS
There are no ATMs in the park. The nearest bank is in Medora.

CELL-PHONE RECEPTION

Cell-phone reception occurs in some areas of the park, but most places receive no signal. Public telephones can be found at the South Unit's Cottonwood Campground, at the Painted Canyon Visitor Center, and at the North Unit Visitor Center.

PARK CONTACT INFORMATION

Theodore Roosevelt National Park ☏ *P.O. Box 7, Medora 58645* ☎ *701/842–2333 North Unit, 701/575–4020 Painted Canyon, 701/623–4466 South Unit* ⊕ *www.nps.gov/thro.*

SCENIC DRIVES

North Unit Scenic Drive. The 14-mi, two-way drive follows rugged terrain above spectacular views of the canyons, and is flanked by more than a dozen turnouts with interpretive signs. Notice the slump blocks, massive segments of rock that have slipped down the cliff walls over time. Farther along pass through badlands coulees, deep-water clefts that are now dry. There's a good chance of meeting bison, mule deer, and bighorn sheep along the way, also keep an eye out for longhorn steers, just like the ones you would see in Texas. ⊠ *From the unit entrance to the Oxbow Overlook, North Unit.*

★ **South Unit Scenic Loop Drive.** A 36-mi, two-way scenic loop takes you past prairie dog towns, coal veins, trailheads, and panoramic views of the badlands. Information on the park's natural history is posted at the various overlooks—stop at all of the interpretive signs to learn about the park's natural and historical phenomena. Some of the best views can be seen from Scoria Point Overlook, Boicourt Overlook, North Dakota Badlands Overlook, Skyline Vista, and Buck Hill. If you hit the road at dusk, be prepared to get caught in a buffalo traffic jam, as the huge creatures sometimes block the road and aren't in any hurry to move. Don't get out of your car or honk at them—they don't like it (think Pamplona with you in their path). ⊠ *Loop begins near Peaceful Valley Ranch, South Unit.*

WHAT TO SEE

HISTORIC SITES

Elkhorn Ranch. This unit of the park is composed of the 218 acres of ranchland where Theodore Roosevelt ran cattle on the open range. Today there are no buildings here, but foundation blocks outline the original structures. Check with of visitor center staff about road conditions before you go. ⊠ *35 mi north of the South Unit Visitor Center* ☎ *701/623–4466 South Unit.*

★ **Maltese Cross Ranch Cabin.** Seven mi from its original site in the river bottom sits the cabin Theodore Roosevelt commissioned to be built on his Dakota Territory property. Inside are Roosevelt's original writing table and rocking chair. Interpretive tours are held on the half hour every day June–September. ⊠ *South Unit entrance, exits 24 and 27 off I–94* ☎ *701/623–4466 South Unit.*

THEODORE ROOSEVELT IN ONE DAY

With just one day, focus on the South Unit. Arrive early at the **Painted Canyon Scenic Overlook,** near the visitor center, for a sweeping and colorful vista of the canyon's rock formations. Stay awhile to watch the effect of the sun's progress across the sky, or come back in the evening to witness the deepening colors and silhouettes in the fading sunlight.

Continue to the **South Unit Visitor Center** in Medora, spending about an hour here touring the Theodore Roosevelt exhibit and the Maltese Cross Ranch Cabin. Circle the 36-mi **Scenic Loop Drive** twice: once to stop and walk a few trails and visit the overlooks, and once at night to watch the wildlife. Your first time around, go counterclockwise. Stop at **Scoria Point Overlook** and hike 0.6 mi on **Ridgeline Nature Trail.**

Back on the drive, stop next at the North Dakota Badlands and Boicourt overlooks to gaze at the strange, ever-changing terrain. When you pass through Peaceful Valley, look for prairie dogs. Have a packed lunch at the **Cottonwood picnic area,** then use a couple of hours to hike Jones Creek Trail or Coal Vein Nature Trail—or sign up for a horseback ride at **Peaceful Valley Ranch.**

Return to your car at least an hour before sunset, and drive slowly around Scenic Loop Drive, clockwise this time, to view the wildlife. Plan to be at **Buck Hill** for one of the most spectacular sunsets you'll ever see. Bring a jacket, because it's a bit windy and it gets chilly as the sun sets. After dark, drive carefully out of the park—elk and other animals may still be on the road.

35

SCENIC STOPS

Fodor's Choice ★ **Buck Hill.** At 2,855 feet, this is one of the highest points in the park and provides a spectacular 360-degree view of the badlands. Come here for the sunset. ⊠ *17 mi east of the South Unit Visitor Center.*

Oxbow Overlook. The view from this spot at the end of the North Unit drive looks over the unit's westerly badlands and the Little Missouri River, where it takes a sharp turn south. This is the place to come for stargazing. ⊠ *14 mi west of the North Unit Visitor Center.*

Sperati Point. For an even better view of the Missouri River's 90-degree angle, than the OxBow Overlook, hike a 1½-mi round-trip trail to this spot 430 feet above the riverbed. ⊠ *14 mi west of the North Unit Visitor Center.*

★ **Painted Canyon Scenic Overlook.** Catch your first glimpse of badlands majesty here—the South Unit canyon's colors change dramatically with the movement of the sun across the sky. ⊠ *Exit 32 off I–94, South Unit.*

Petrified Forest. Although bits of petrified wood have been found all over the park, the densest collection is in the South Unit's west end, accessible on foot or horseback via the Petrified Forest Loop Trail from Peaceful Valley Ranch (10 mi round-trip) or from the park's west boundary (3 mi round-trip). ⊠ *Trailheads: Peaceful Valley Ranch (7 mi north of the South Unit Visitor Center); west boundary (10 mi north of exit 23 off I–94/U.S. 10, via an unpaved road).*

Don't let these bulky beasts fool you: even though a bison may weigh 2,000 pounds, it can run 40 MPH.

VISITOR CENTERS

North Unit Visitor Center. A bookstore, gift shop, and small auditorium where you can watch park films to acquaint you with the park. ⊠ *North Unit entrance, off U.S. 85, North Unit* ☎ *701/842–2333* ⊕ *www.nps. gov/thro* ⊙ *Daily 9–5:30.*

Painted Canyon Visitor Center. Easily reached off Interstate 94, this South Unit Visitor Center has a gift shop and bookstore, and exhibits. ⊠ *Exit 32 off I–94, South Unit* ☎ *701/575–4020* ⊕ *www.nps.gov/thro* ⊙ *Mid-June–Labor Day, daily 8–6; Apr.–mid-June and early Sept.–mid-Nov., daily 8:30–4:30.*

★ **South Unit Visitor Center.** Sometimes called the Medora Visitor Center, this building houses a large auditorium for films about the park, plus an excellent exhibit on Theodore Roosevelt's life. On display are artifacts such as the clothing Roosevelt wore while ranching in the Dakota Territory, his firearms, and several writings in his own hand reflecting his thoughts on the nation's environmental resources. A bookstore and public restrooms are available. ⊠ *South Unit entrance, exits 24 and 27 off I–94* ☎ *701/623–4466* ⊕ *www.nps.gov/thro* ⊙ *June–Sept., daily 8–8; Oct.–May, daily 8–4:30.*

SPORTS AND THE OUTDOORS

FISHING

Catfish, little suckers, northern pikes, and goldeyes are among the underwater inhabitants of the Little Missouri River. If you wish to fish in the park or elsewhere in the state and are over age 16, you must obtain a

North Dakota fishing license. For out-of-state residents, a three-day permit is $15, a ten-day permit is $25, and a one-year permit is $45. For in-state residents, a one-year permit is $10. The **Buffalo Gap Guest Ranch** (⌧ *3100 Buffalo Gap Rd., Medora* ☎ *701/623–4200*), 8 mi west of Medora, sells fishing licenses.

OUTFITTERS AND EXPEDITIONS
A champion of several regional and state fishing tournaments, the owner of **Greg Simonson Fishing Services** (⌧ *13892 U.S. 85 N, Alexander* ☎ *701/828–3425*) leads individuals or groups on expeditions through the park and the outlying grasslands.

HIKING

Particularly in the South Unit, there are numerous opportunities to jump on a trail right from the park road. The North and South units are connected by the 96-mi Maah Daah Hey Trail. Backcountry hiking is allowed, but you need a permit (free from any visitor center) to camp in the wild. Park maps are available at all three visitor centers. If you plan to camp overnight, let several people know about where you plan to pitch your tent, and inquire about river conditions, maps, regulations, trail updates, and additional water sources before setting out.

NORTH UNIT

EASY
Buckhorn Trail. A thriving prairie-dog town is just 1 mi from the trailhead of this 11-mi North Unit trail. It travels over level grasslands, then it loops back along the banks of Squaw Creek. If you're an experienced hiker, you'll complete the entire trail in about a half day. Novices or families might want to plan on a whole day, however. ⌧ *Begins at the Caprock Coulee Nature Trail, located 1½ mi west of the Juniper Campground.*

Little Mo Nature Trail. Flat and only 1.1-mi long, this trail in the North Unit passes through badlands and woodlands to the river's edge. The first 0.7 mi is wheelchair accessible. It's a great way to see the park's diverse terrain and wildlife, and because it shouldn't take you longer than an hour, it's a great trail for families with children. ⌧ *Begins at Juniper Campground in the North Unit.*

DIFFICULT
Upper Caprock Coulee Trail. This 4.3-mi round-trip trail follows a loop around the pockmarked lower-badlands coulees. There's a slow incline that takes you up 300 feet. Portions of the trail are slippery. Beginners should plan a half day for this hike. ⌧ *Begins 8 mi west of the North Unit Visitor Center.*

SOUTH UNIT

MODERATE
Fodor's Choice ★
Maah Daah Hey Trail. Hike, bike, or ride horseback on the 96-mi and growing Maah Daah Hey Trail, the most popular and well-maintained trail in western North Dakota. The U.S. Forest Service began a $220,000 expansion of the trail in 2007, adding 46 mi of new trail and 20 self-closing gates south of Interstate 90 and Medora in a project slated for completion in the summer of 2010. The expansion opens up new vistas

of the badlands and Little Missouri River breaks previously inaccessible to hikers and bikers of the Maah Daah Hey, a name which means "grandfather" or "been here long" in the Mandan language. The trail traverses both park units and the Little Missouri National Grasslands. Maps are available at the park visitor centers, from the U.S. Forest Service (☎ *701/225–5151*), and from the Maah Daah Hey Trail Association (☎ *701/628–2747* 🌐 *www.mdhta.com*). Walking the entire trail is a true wilderness adventure and will probably take you at least five days. If you want to do something shorter, such as a two- or three-hour hike, leave from the South Unit and walk an hour or hour and a half in one direction, and then return. (Note that you are not allowed to bike the portions of the trail that are within the national park.) ✉ *Begins at Sully Creek State Park, 3 mi south of the South Unit Visitor Center.*

HORSEBACK RIDING

The best way to see many of the park's sights is on horseback. You are allowed to bring your own horse to the park, or you can sign up for a guided trip. Horses are only allowed on backcountry trails or cross-country. Like campers, riders must obtain free backcountry-use permits. Riders taking multiday trips through the park must also have a permit and must camp in the Round-Up Group Horse Camp (☎ *701/623–4466*) or in the backcountry. Horses are not allowed on park roadways, in developed campgrounds, picnic areas, or on developed nature trails. Overnight parties in the backcountry are limited to a maximum of eight horses and eight riders per group. Horse must be tied down securely when not being ridden. Be sure to bring enough water for the animals.

OUTFITTERS AND EXPEDITIONS

Take a guided one-day, two-day, or weeklong horseback trip on the Maah Daah Hey Trail with the knowledgeable guides at Watford City-based **Little Knife Outfitters** (☎ *701/842–2631* ⏲ *May–Sept.*). Beginners are welcome. Experienced guides at **Peaceful Valley Ranch Horse Rides** (✉ *South Unit* ☎ *701/623–4568* ⏲ *Late May–Labor Day*) help you to see the park the way trappers, ranchers, and pioneers did a century ago. Rides are 90 minutes to five hours long.

EDUCATIONAL OFFERINGS

RANGER PROGRAMS

Evening Campfires. Rangers host hour-long presentations and discussions on such subjects as park history, archaeology, fires, and wildlife. Look for times and subjects posted at park campgrounds. ✉ *Cottonwood Campground, South Unit; Juniper Campground, North Unit* ⏲ *June–mid-Sept., daily.*

Ranger-Led Talks and Walks. Rangers take visitors on the trails of both units and through the backcountry and Elkhorn Ranch, discussing such subjects as geology, paleontology, wildlife, and natural history. Rangers also give talks at the South Unit Visitor Center on subjects such as cowboy clothing, seasonal changes in the park, and the history of cattle ranching. Check at campground entrances or at the visitor centers for times, topics, departure points, and destinations. ☎ *701/623–4466* 🎫 *Free* ⏲ *June–mid-Sept., daily.*

FESTIVALS AND EVENTS

JULY

Killdeer Mountain Roundup Rodeo. Begun in 1923, this is North Dakota's oldest rodeo sanctioned by the PRCA. The community goes all out, hosting a parade, petting zoo, street dance, barbecue, and fireworks display on July 4th. ☎ 701/764–5777.

The Medora Stampede. Recounting the heritage of the Wild West and rodeo in the badlands of the 1800s, the fast-paced rodeo, held in Medora's Ranch-O-Rama Arena on more than a dozen afternoons in July, has clowns and a shootout. ☎ 218/843–1162 ⊕ www.medorastampede.com 💰 $18.

AUGUST

Founder's Day. Each August 25th, activities commemorate the establishment of the National Park Service on that date in 1916. The visitor centers host special programs and serve cookies and lemonade ☎ 701/623–4466.

DECEMBER

Old-Fashioned Cowboy Christmas. Held the first full weekend in December in downtown Medora, the festivities begin with a wreath-hanging ceremony at the community center, followed by Christmas poetry readings, a holiday doll show, sleigh rides, and a dance. ☎ 701/623–4910.

35

FILM

T.R. Country. All three visitor centers show 13-minute film focusing on the unique beauty and breathtaking landscape of North Dakota's badlands, its wildlife, and its history, narrated with Roosevelt's own words. ⊠ *South Unit, North Unit, and Painted Canyon visitor centers* ☎ 701/623–4466 💰 *Free* ☉ *Daily, every half hr.*

ARTS AND ENTERTAINMENT

NIGHTLIFE

★ **Stargazing.** Without light pollution from nearby, the air at Theodore Roosevelt National Park has been officially certified to be at least 80% pure, making the park ideal for astronomical observation any cloudless night of the year. To enjoy the stars with others, come during an annual event when, on an early August weekend, the Northern Sky Astronomical Society sets up telescopes for an all-night star-watching party. ☎ *No phone* ⊕ *www.und.edu/org/nsas* 💰 *Free.*

WHAT'S NEARBY

NEARBY TOWNS

Medora, gateway to the park's South Unit, may only have a population of 96, but it is a walkable town with several museums, tiny shops, and plenty of restaurants and places to stay. Its Wild West history is reenacted in a madcap musical production each night in summer. To the east is **Dickinson** (pop. 17,700), the largest town near the national park. North of Dickinson and about 35 mi east of the park's North Unit, **Killdeer** (pop. about 700) is known for its Roundup Rodeo—North Dakota's oldest—and its gorgeous scenery. Killdeer is the place to fill your tank, since there isn't another gas station around for 40 mi. **Williston** (pop. about 13,000) is 60 mi north of the North Unit, just over the Missouri River. The Amtrak stop nearest to the national park is here.

VISITOR INFORMATION

Dickinson Convention and Visitors Bureau ☐ P.O. Box 181, 58601 ☎ 701/483–4988 or 800/279–7391 ⊕ www.dickinsonnd.com. **Killdeer City Hall** ☒ 214 Railroad St. 58640 ☎ 701/764–5295 ⊕ www.killdeer.com. **Medora Chamber of Commerce** ☒ 272 Pacific Ave. 58645 ☎ 701/623–4910 ⊕ www. medorand.com. **Williston Convention and Visitors Bureau** ☒ 10 Main St. 58801 ☎ 701/774–9041 or 800/615–9041 ⊕ www.willistonnd.com.

NEARBY ATTRACTIONS

Little Missouri State Park. Called *Mako Shika* or "Land Bad" by the Sioux, the unusual land formations here create the state's most awe-inspiring scenery. The beehive-shaped rock formations resulted from the erosion of sedimentary rock deposited millions of years ago by streams flowing from the Rocky Mountains. Undeveloped and rugged, this wilderness area has primitive and modern camping and 50 mi of horse trails. ☒ *Off Rte. 22, 18 mi north and 2 mi east of Killdeer* ☎ *701/764–5256 summer, 701/794–3731 winter* ⊕ *www.parkrec.nd.gov/parks/lmbsp.htm* ☒ *$5 per vehicle* ⊘ *Daily.*

★ **North Dakota Cowboy Hall of Fame.** Named North Dakota's Tourist Attraction of the Year shortly after it opened in 2007, this $3 million museum features six galleries and rotating exhibits (most recently Sitting Bull's headdress, Theodore Roosevelt's rifle, and Buffalo Bill Cody's six-shooter), hosts special events, and is dedicated to the horse culture of the plains. ☒ *250 Main St., Medora* ☎ *701/623–2000* ⊕ *www. northdakotacowboy.com* ☒ *$7.50* ⊘ *May–Sept., daily 10 AM–8 PM.*

AREA ACTIVITIES

SPORTS AND THE OUTDOORS
GOLF

Fodor's Choice **Bully Pulpit Golf Course.** This impressive golf course weaves its way
★ through the badlands buttes, giving players a truly breathtaking backdrop for a round of golf. In 2005, the course was voted the number-one affordable public golf course in the nation by *Golf Digest.* ☒ *East River Rd., Medora* ☎ *701/623–4653* ☒ *$79, includes cart* ⊘ *Mid-Apr.–Oct., daily dawn–dusk.*

ARTS AND ENTERTAINMENT

★ **Medora Musical.** Well worth your while in summer is this theatrical trib-
☺ ute to the Old West, its history, and its personalities. ☎ *701/623–4444 or 800/633–6721* ☒ *$36* ⊘ *Early June–Labor Day, daily 8:30 PM.*

WHERE TO EAT AND STAY

ABOUT THE RESTAURANTS

One does not visit Theodore Roosevelt National Park for the fine dining. In fact, the only venues within park are the picnic areas, and provided you've prepared, this can be a perfectly simple and satisfying way to experience the open spaces and natural wonder of the badlands. In the towns near the park you'll find casual, down-to-earth family establishments that largely cater to the locals. Expect steak and potatoes, and lots of them. Fortunately, the beef here is among the best in the country.

ROADSIDE ART

To see metal sculptures designed by a local artist, including a 51-foot Teddy Roosevelt, take a **self-guided 30-mi driving tour on Route 21** south of Dickinson. Sculptures include a grasshopper family, a 150-foot-long gaggle of geese, and a tin family with a 45-foot father, 44-foot mother, and 23-foot son. ⊠ *Exit 72 off I–94, Rte. 21 between Lefor and Regent* ☎ *701/483–4988 or 800/279–7391* ☁ *Free.*

35

ABOUT THE HOTELS

If you're set on sleeping within the park, be sure to pack your tent. Outside the park are mostly small chain hotels catering to interstate travelers—largely retired couples in RVs and young families in mini-vans. However, there are a handful of historic properties and working ranches that offer guests a truly Western experience. It's usually a good idea to book ahead during summer months.

ABOUT THE CAMPGROUNDS

For the adventurous traveler, camping in Theodore Roosevelt is well worth the effort. The unadulterated isolation, epic views, and relation-ship with nature afforded by the spartan campgrounds within the park create an experience you'll be hard-pressed to find elsewhere in the United States. Just remember that the park's campgrounds are relatively undeveloped—you'll need to pack in everything you need. If you pick a campsite in the surrounding wilderness, you'll need to obtain a back-country camping permit (available free) from a visitor center first.

Campgrounds outside the park are more developed, and typically attract an older and more laid-back crowd—usually retirees with massive RVs. These commercial operations also attract a fair number of young fami-lies, who prefer the few extra amenities. Reservations are usually not required, but are probably a wise choice in the summer months.

WHERE TO EAT

IN THE PARK

PICNIC AREAS **Cottonwood.** This is in a lovely valley near the river. There are fire pits, drinking water, restrooms, eight open tables, and eight covered tables. ⊠ *5½ mi north of South Unit Visitor Center.*

Juniper. This area has restrooms, grills, drinking water, and 28 tables (eight with shelter). ⊠ *5 mi west of North Unit Visitor Center.*

Painted Canyon Visitor Center. This area has eight covered tables, drinking water, restrooms, and a spectacular view. ⊠ *Exit 32 off I–94.*

OUTSIDE THE PARK

$–$$$
STEAK
★

✕ **Boots Bar and Grill.** Formerly the Iron Horse, this revamped watering hole is the same type of place your grandpa probably talked about. It's replete with a saloon, expanded upstairs dining room, patios, and seating for more than 200 patrons, plus live music, dancing, and microbrews. Diners feast on an eclectic menu offering rue bourbon burgers, *Fleischkuechle* (ground beef, pork, onions, and peppers encased in bread dough), elk, walleye, and a 14-ounce buffalo New York steak. ✉ *201 Main St., Medora* ☎ *701/623–2668* ⊟ *AE, D, MC.*

$–$$$
STEAK

✕ **Buckskin Bar and Grill.** This steak house, with saloon and dance hall, seats 350. Built in 1915, the building has rough wood walls, original wood floors, and tin ceilings. Stuffed critters are mounted on the walls in one room; the other rooms have photographs of local cowboy celebrities who dined here. Steak and seafood are the kitchen's focus, with prime rib a specialty. For dessert, the homemade peach and cherry cobbler is a must. There is a kids' menu and the premises are no-smoking. ✉ *416 Central Ave., Killdeer* ☎ *701/764–5321* ⊟ *MC, V.*

¢
AMERICAN

✕ **Cowboy Cafe.** This cozy, locally owned and operated café specializes in homemade soups, caramel rolls, and delicious roast beef specials. Be prepared for a (short) wait since the restaurant is popular with both locals and visitors. ✉ *215 4th St., Medora* ☎ *701/623–4343* ⊟ *No credit cards.*

$–$$
AMERICAN

✕ **Little Missouri Club.** Dine on pasta dishes, a 16-ounce T-bone with all the fixings, or go all out with steak and lobster in this 72-seat restaurant upstairs in this quaint establishment. Downstairs is a Victorian saloon, where on Friday and Saturday nights there's live music by local bands in the saloon. ✉ *440 3rd St., Medora* ☎ *701/623–4404* ⊟ *AE, D, MC, V* ☷ *Closed Sept.–May.*

$$–$$$$
Fodor's Choice
★

✕ **Theodore's.** Opened in the summer of 2009 after an extensive expansion and renovation, Theodore's offers the best fine dining in Medora and, perhaps, in western North Dakota. The lunch menu features salads, prime-rib sandwiches, and buffalo burgers, while dinner fare includes shrimp with pineapple dipping sauce, a crusted South American rib eye, and tenderloin with Gorgonzola cream sauce. The stained glass and wood paneling makes this restaurant inside the Rough Riders Hotel (⇨ *Where to Stay*) feel like a little hideaway for a quiet lunch or dinner. The fireplace was built from bricks taken from the North Dakota Capitol that burned in 1930. T.R.'s Tavern has a full-service bar. ✉ *301 3rd Ave., Medora* ☎ *701/623–4433* ⊟ *AE, D, MC, V.*

WHERE TO STAY

IN THE PARK

CAMPING
$
★

△ **Cottonwood Campground.** Nestled under juniper and cottonwood trees on the bank of the Little Missouri River, this is a wonderful place to watch buffalo, elk, and other wildlife drink from the river at sunrise and just before sunset. Flush toilets are only available May–September; pit toilets are available the remainder of the year. **Pros:** the best shade in the park; waterside sites; generally quiet. **Cons:** even with the shade and the river, this can be extremely hot and dry in summer; vehicle noise from highway at sites closest to road; off-season pit toilets. ✉ *5½ mi north of the South Unit Visitor Center* ☎ *701/623–4466* △ *78 sites*

♿ Flush toilets (May–Sept.), pit toilets, drinking water, grills, picnic tables ♿ Reservations not accepted ▭ No credit cards.

$ 🏕 **Juniper Campground.** The sites here are surrounded by junipers, hence the name. Don't be surprised if you see a bison herd wander through on its way to the Little Missouri River. Drinking water and flush toilets are only available May–September; pit toilets are available the remainder of the year. There are no RV hookups and reservations are not accepted. **Pros:** great rate; wilderness feel; well-tended facilities. **Cons:** lack of shade; summer sun can be stifling; no drinking water available early spring and late fall. ✉ 5 mi west of the North Unit Visitor Center ☎ 701/842–2333 🏕 50 sites ♿ Flush toilets (May–Sept.), pit toilets, drinking water, grills, picnic tables ▭ No credit cards.

OUTSIDE THE PARK

$$–$$$$ 🏨 **AmericInn Motel and Suites.** Polished wood accents, mounted animals, and western themes dominate the public areas of this contemporary hotel, while guests will find the rooms common yet clean. The two-story building is three blocks from downtown; restaurants and stores are nearby. Whirlpool suites are available. **Pros:** within close proximity to shops and restaurants; no charge for Wi-Fi; indoor pool; whirlpool suites ideal after long hikes in the park. **Cons:** right on the railroad tracks; no elevator to second-floor rooms; chain hotel. ✉ 75 E. River Rd. S, Medora ☎ 701/623–4800 or 800/634–3444 ⊕ www.americinn. com 🛏 56 rooms, 8 suites ♿ In-room: Wi-Fi. In-hotel: pool, laundry facilities, some pets allowed ▭ AE, D, DC, MC, V ⓧCP.

¢–$ 🏨 🏕 **Buffalo Gap Guest Ranch.** Perched on a bluff 8 mi west of Medora, this rustic property commands a premium view of the Dakota badlands and access to the Maah Daah Hey Trail. Its bar and steakhouse offer everything from burgers and buffalo to rib eyes and lobster, as well as takeaway lunches. The cabins have two queens and two single bunk beds and a full bath. A horse-boarding, hay, an arena, shuttle services, and 10 RV sites with hookups are available, as well as tons of space for tent camping. For some local color, talk to owner Mark "Olie" Golberg. Barbecue grills are available. **Pros:** great prices on lodging and food; exceptional view; large outdoor patio. **Cons:** bar can be smoky; 10 minutes from town; male hunters love it (hunting packages are available) but their wives probably won't. ✉ 3100 Buffalo Gap Rd., Exit 18 off Interstate 90, then 1.3 mi northwest on Buffalo Gap Rd., Medora ☎ 701/623–4200 ⊕ www.buffalogapguestranch.com 🛏 10 cabins, 10 RV sites ♿ In-hotel: restaurant, lounge. In-campground: partial hookups (electric and water) ▭ AE, D, MC, V.

$–$$ 🏨 **Days Hotel/Grand Dakota Lodge & Conference Center.** This newly remodeled three-story motel, across from the Prairie Hills Mall, is set to open in 2010. You can relax on couches before the fireplace in the huge lobby, where Wi-Fi is free. A mezzanine overlooks the pool. Guest rooms are decorated in golds and browns; western art adorns the walls. An airport shuttle is available. **Pros:** full-service restaurant on site; great customer service; no gambling on the premises. **Cons:** can be busy; pool can be quite popular, particularly in the summer. ✉ 532 15th St. W, Dickinson ☎ 701/483–5600 or 800/422–0949 ⊕ www.daysinn.com 🛏 106 rooms, 43 suites ♿ In-room: refrigerator (some). In-hotel: restaurant, room service, pool, laundry facilities, Wi-Fi, some pets allowed ▭ AE, D, MC, V.

35

$$$
Fodor's Choice
★

⛺ **Rough Riders Hotel.** Opening once again in May 2010 after a $12.5 million expansion, this hotel continues to be the cornerstone of Medora. Decor is warmly colored and decidedly posh, with pillow-top beds and flat-screen TVs, but still retains the Victorian red velvet chairs, antique armoires, and iron-rod and oak bed frames that have made this property a favorite for decades. Guest room shower tiles feature the three brands used by Theodore Roosevelt on his livestock during his time in the Dakota Badlands. Guests have pool privileges at a nearby motel. A 200-person conference center is on the grounds. **Pros:** all new; downtown Medora location; dining on the premises. **Cons:** relatively expensive; railroad noise. ✉ *301 3rd Ave., Medora* ☎ *701/623–4444 or 800/633–6721* ⊕ *www.medora.com/rough-riders/* ⇨ *76 rooms* ⚬ *In-room: Wi-Fi. In-hotel: restaurant, bar, Wi-Fi* ▭ *AE, D, MC, V.*

CAMPING
$$–$$$

⚠ **Red Trail Campground.** Live country music is performed every night from June through Labor Day in front of the store at this campground six blocks from downtown Medora. It was built especially for RVs. **Pros:** great rates; live music; only five blocks from the park entrance yet also close to downtown. **Cons:** railroad noise bothers some; limited trees. ✉ *250 E. River Rd. S, off Pacific Ave., Medora* ☎ *701/623–4317 or 800/621–4317* ⚠ *104 tent/RV sites (100 with hookups)* ⚬ *Flush toilets, full hookups, dump station, drinking water, guest laundry, showers, grills, picnic tables, electricity, public telephone, general store, play area* ▭ *MC, V* ☉ *May–Sept.*

¢

⚠ **Sully Creek State Campground.** On an 80-acre park at the head of the Maah Daah Hey Trail, this campground complete with horse corrals is perfect if you're planning a bike or horseback trip on the trail, or a canoe trip on the Little Missouri River. You'll find squeaky-clean pit toilets and solar-powered showers. Sites are first-come, first-served. **Pros:** clean; convenient to trail and to town; employs green technology. **Cons:** lack of hookups and modern facilities. ✉ *East River Rd., 3 mi south of Medora, Mandan* ☎ *701/623–2024* ⚠ *45 tent/RV sites* ⚬ *Pit toilets, showers, fire pits, picnic tables, swimming (river)* ▭ *No credit cards.*

Wind Cave
National Park

AND THE BLACK HILLS

WORD OF MOUTH

"Black Hills has so much to offer. I wouldn't miss either Wind Cave National Park or Jewell Cave; take one of the guided tours. We did Wind Cave, and the kids loved it so much that we went to Jewell Cave the next day (they're only about 45 minutes from each other)."
—dw732

WELCOME TO WIND CAVE

TOP REASONS TO GO

★ **Underground exploring:** Wind Cave offers visitors the chance to get their hands and feet dirty on a four-hour guided tour through one of American's longest and most complex caves.

★ **The call of the wild:** Wind Cave National Park boasts a wide variety of animals: bison, coyote, deer, antelope, elk, prairie dogs, and 215 species of birds, to name just a few.

★ **Education by candlelight:** Wind Cave offers numerous educational and interpretive programs, including the Candlelight Cave Tour, which allows guests to explore the cave only by candlelight.

★ **Noteworthy neighbors:** On the north border of Wind Cave sits Custer State Park, one of South Dakota's can't-miss areas. With its close proximity to numerous other national parks, state parks, and other monuments and memorials, Wind Cave is situated perfectly to explore some of American's greatest national treasures.

1 The Surface. Wind Cave lies at the confluence of western mountains and central plains, which blesses the park with a unique landscape. A series of established trails weaves in and out of forested hillsides and grassy meadows, providing treks of varying difficulty.

TO MOUNT RUSHMORE AND CUSTER STATE PARK 87

Rankin Ridge Trail

Centennial Tr.

336

◆ **Lookout Tower**

435

Rankin Ridge

Limestone

87

Centennial Trail

Curley Canyon

Canyon

385

Beaver

Point Trail

Creek

Prairie Dog Canyon

Elk Mountain Trail

Elk Mountain Campground

Creek Trail

Visitor Center 2

Wind Cave

Wind Cave Canyon

Canyon Trail

Elevator Building

Bison

Flats

East Bison Flats Trail

Cold Brook Canyon Trail

Cold Brook Canyon

Gobbler Ridge

385

2 The Cave. With an explored maze of caverns totaling 132 mi, Wind Cave is considered one of the longest caves in the world. Notably, scientists estimate that only 5% of the cave has been explored to date. It is also estimated that 95% of the world's boxwork formations are found in Wind Cave, which means that visitors here are treated to some of the rarest geological features on the planet.

SOUTH DAKOTA

GETTING ORIENTED

Bounded by Black Hills National Forest to the west and windswept prairie to the east, Wind Cave National Park, in southwestern South Dakota, encompasses the transition between two distinct ecosystems: mountain forest and mixed-grass prairie. Abundant wildlife, including bison and elk, roam the 28,295 acres of the park's diverse terrain. Underground, a year-round 53°F temperature gives summer visitors a cool oasis—and winter visitors a warm escape.

36

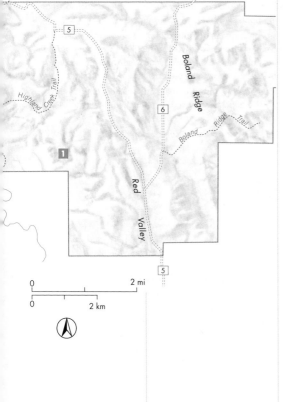

0   2 mi

0   2 km

KEY	
🏕	*Ranger Station*
🔺	*Campground*
🌲	*Picnic Area*
🍴	*Restaurant*
🏠	*Lodge*
🚶	*Trailhead*
🚻	*Restrooms*
➤	*Scenic Viewpoint*
⋯⋯	*Walking/Hiking Trails*

WIND CAVE PLANNER

When to Go

The biggest crowds come to Wind Cave from June to September, but the park and surrounding Black Hills are large enough to diffuse the masses. **Neither the cave nor grounds above are ever too packed.** Park officials contend it's actually less busy during the first full week in August, when the Sturgis Motorcycle Rally brings roughly a half-million bikers to the region, clogging highways for miles around. Most hotels within a 100-mi radius are booked up to a year in advance.

The colder months are the least crowded, though you can still explore underground, thanks to the cave's constant 53°F temperature. The shoulder seasons are also unpopular, though autumn is a perfect time to visit. The days are warm, the nights are cool, and in late September/early October the park's canyons and coulees display incredible colors.

Ave. High/Low Temps

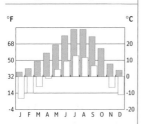

Flora and Fauna

About three-quarters of the park is grasslands. The rest is forested, mostly by the ponderosa pine. Poison ivy and poison oak are common in wetter, shadier areas, so wear long pants and boots when hiking.

The convergence of forest and prairies makes an attractive home for bison, elk, coyotes, pronghorn antelope, prairie dogs, and mule deer. Wild turkey and squirrels are less obvious, but commonly seen by the observant hiker.

Mountain lions also live in the park; although usually shy, they will attack if surprised or threatened. Make noise while hiking to prevent chance encounters.

Bison appear docile but can be dangerous. The largest land mammal in North America, they weigh up to a ton and run at speeds in excess of 35 MPH.

Getting Here and Around

Wind Cave is 56 mi from Rapid City, via U.S. 16 and Highway 87, which runs through the park, and 73 mi southwest of Badlands National Park. The nearest commercial airport is in Rapid City. Bus lines service Rapid City and Wall. **Gray Line of the Black Hills** (☎ *605/342–4461* ⊕ *www.blackhillsgrayline.com*) offers regional tours.

U.S. 385 and Highway 87 travel the length of the park on the west side. Additionally, two unpaved roads, NPS Roads 5 and 6, traverse the northeastern part of Wind Cave. NPS Road 5 joins Highway 87 at the park's north border.

By T.D. Griffith   If you don't get out of your car at Wind Cave, you haven't scratched the surface—literally. The park has more than 132 mi of underground passageways. Curious cave formations include 95% of the world's mineral boxwork, and gypsum beard so sensitive it reacts to the heat of a lamp. This underground wilderness is part of a giant limestome labyrinth beneath the Black Hills. Wind Cave ranks as fourth-longest cave in the world, but experts believe 95% of it has yet to be mapped.

36

PARK ESSENTIALS

ACCESSIBILITY
The visitor center is entirely wheelchair accessible, but only a few areas of the cave itself are navigable by those with limited mobility. Arrangements can be made in advance for a special ranger-assisted tour for a small fee.

ADMISSION FEES AND PERMITS
There's no fee to enter the park; cave tours cost $7–$23. The requisite backcountry camping and horseback riding permits are both free from the visitor center.

ADMISSION HOURS
The park is open year-round. It is in the mountain time zone.

ATMS/BANKS
There are no ATMs in the park. The nearest ATM and bank to the park is at the Wells Fargo Bank in Hot Springs.

CELL-PHONE RECEPTION
Cell-phone reception is hit-and-miss in the park, and western South Dakota is only serviced by Verizon Wireless and Alltel, so those with other carriers may be charged roaming fees. You won't find a public phone in the park.

WIND CAVE IN ONE DAY

Pack a picnic lunch, then head to the visitor center to purchase tickets for a morning tour of Wind Cave. Visit the exhibit rooms in the center afterward. Then drive or walk the quarter mile to the picnic area north of the visitor center. The refreshing air and deep emerald color of the pine woodlands will flavor your meal.

In the afternoon, take a leisurely drive through the parklands south of the visitor center, passing through Gobbler Pass and Bison Flats, for an archetypal view of the park and to look for wildlife. On the way back north, follow U.S. 385 east toward Wind Cave Canyon. If you enjoy bird-watching, park at a turnout and hike the 1.8-mi trail into the canyon, where you can spot swallows and

great horned owls in the cliffs and woodpeckers in the trees.

Next, get back on the highway going north, take a right on Highway 87, and continue a half mile to the turnout for Centennial Trail. Hike the trail about 2 mi to the junction with Lookout Point Trail, turn right and return to Highway 87. The whole loop is about 4.75 mi. As you continue driving north to the top of Rankin Ridge, a pull-out to the right serves as the starting point for 1.25-mi Rankin Ridge Trail. It loops around the ridge, past Lookout Tower—the park's highest point—and ends up back at the pull-out. This trail is an excellent opportunity to enjoy the fresh air, open spaces, and diversity of wildlife in the park.

PARK CONTACT INFORMATION
Wind Cave National Park ⊠ 26611 U.S. 385, Hot Springs, SD ☎ 605/745–4600 ⊕ www.nps.gov/wica.

SCENIC DRIVES

Bison Flats Drive (South Entrance). Entering the park from the south on U.S. 385 will take you past Gobbler Ridge and into the hills commonly found in the southern Black Hills region. After a couple of miles, the landscape gently levels onto the Bison Flats, one of the mixed-grass prairies on which the park prides itself. You might see a herd of grazing buffalo between here and the visitor center. You'll also catch panoramic views of the parklands, surrounding hills, and limestone bluffs.

★ **Rankin Ridge Drive (North Entrance).** Entering the park across the north border via Highway 87 is perhaps the most beautiful drive into the park. As you leave behind the grasslands and granite spires of Custer State Park and enter Wind Cave. You see the prairie, forest, and wetland habitats of the backcountry and some of the oldest rock in the Black Hills. The silvery twinkle of mica, quartz, and feldspar crystals dot Rankin Ridge east of Highway 87, and gradually give way to limestone and sandstone formations.

WHAT TO SEE

Rankin Ridge Lookout Tower. Some of the best panoramic views of the park and surrounding hills can be seen from this 5,013-foot tower, which is typically not staffed or open to the public. Hike the 1-mi Rankin Ridge loop to get there. ✉ *6 mi north of the visitor center on Hwy. 87.*

★ **Wind Cave.** Known to American Indians for centuries and named for the strong currents of air that alternately blow in and out of its entrance, Wind Cave was first documented by the Bingham brothers in 1881. The cave's winds are related to the difference in atmospheric pressure between the cave and the surface. When the atmospheric pressure is higher outside than inside the cave, the air blows in, and vice versa. With more than 130 mi of known passageway divided into three different levels, Wind Cave ranks the fourth longest worldwide. It's host to an incredibly diverse collection of geologic formations, including more boxwork than any other known cave, plus a series of underground lakes. The cave tours sponsored by the National Park Service allow you to see unusual and beautiful formations with names such as popcorn, frostwork, and boxwork. ✉ *U.S. 385 to Wind Cave Visitor Center.*

DID YOU KNOW? Theodore Roosevelt made Wind Cave one of the country's earliest national parks, and the first dedicated to preserving a cave resource, on January 3, 1903. It is one of the largest caves in the world, with 132 mi of explored passageways.

VISITOR CENTER

Wind Cave Visitor Center. The park's sole visitor center is the primary place to get general information. Located on top of the cave, it has three exhibit rooms, with displays on cave exploration, the Civilian Conservation Corps, park wildlife, and resource management. ■ TIP➔ There's no coffee here or elsewhere in the park, so if you need your morning caffeine fix, pick up your coffee before entering the park. ✉ *Off U.S. 385, 3 mi north of the park's southern border* ☎ 605/745–4600 ⊕ *www.nps.gov/wica* ✆ *Free* ✆ *Mid-Apr.–mid-Oct., daily 8–5; mid-Oct.–early Apr., daily 8–4:30.*

SPORTS AND THE OUTDOORS

Many visitors come to Wind Cave solely to descend into the park's underground passages. While there are great ranger-led tours for casual visitors—and more daring explorations for experienced cavers—the prairie and forest above the cave shouldn't be neglected.

BIRD-WATCHING

★ **Wind Cave Canyon.** Here's one of the best birding areas in the park. The limestone walls of the canyon are ideal nesting grounds for cliff swallows and great horned owls, while the standing dead trees on the canyon floor attract red-headed and Lewis woodpeckers. As you hike down the trail, the steep-sided canyon widens to a panoramic view east across the prairies. ✉ *About ½ mi east of the visitor center.*

Rankin Ridge. See large birds of prey here, including turkey vultures, hawks, and golden eagles. ✉ *6 mi north of the visitor center on Hwy. 87.*

36

GEAR UP!

On the way to the ski slopes in the northern Black Hills, **Edge Sports—Lead** (✉ 11380 Hwy. 14A, Lead ☎ 605/722–7547) maintains a good stock of winter sports equipment. It's open in the winter only. Rock climbers and hikers will find a good selection of equipment at **Edge Sports—Rapid City** (✉ 619 Main St., Rapid City ☎ 605/716–9912), while cavers will find a solid inventory of clothing and gear.

Several miles north of the park, **Granite Sports** (✉ 201 Main St., Hill City ☎ 605/574–2121) sells hiking boots, Gore-Tex jackets, packs, water bottles, and more. In the 100,000-square-foot Rushmore Crossing Mall, off I–90 at East-North Street or Lacrosse Street exits, **Scheels All Sport** (✉ 1225 Eglin St., Rapid City ☎ 605/342–9033) carries a wide selection of all-weather hiking clothes and binoculars.

HIKING

There are more than 30 mi of hiking trails within the boundaries of Wind Cave National Park, covering ponderosa forest and mixed-grass prairie. The landscape has changed little over the past century, so a hike through the park is as much a historical snapshot of pioneer life in the 1890s as it is exercise. Be sure to hit the Wind Cave Canyon Trail, where limestone cliffs attract birds like cliff swallows and great horned owls, and the Cold Brook Canyon Trail, a short but fun trip past a prairie-dog town to the park's edge. Besides birds and small animals such as squirrels, you're apt to see deer and pronghorn while hiking, and probably some bison.

Hiking into the wild, untouched backcountry is perfectly safe, provided you have a map (available from the visitor center) and a good sense of direction. Don't expect any developments, however; bathrooms are available only at the visitor center, and the trails are dirt or gravel. Since there are no easily accessible sources along the trails, and water from backcountry sources must be treated, pack your own.

EASY

★ **Wind Cave Canyon Trail.** This easy 1.8-mi trail follows Wind Cave Canyon to the park boundary fence. The canyon, with its steep limestone walls and dead trees, provides the best opportunity in the park for bird-watching. Be especially vigilant for cliff swallows, great horned owls, and red-headed and Lewis woodpeckers. Deer, least chipmunks, and other small animals also are attracted to the sheltered environment of the canyon. Even though you could probably do a round-trip tour of this trail in less than an hour and a half, be sure to spend more time here to observe the wildlife. This trail represents one of your best chances for seeing the park's animal inhabitants, and a little patience will almost certainly be rewarded. ✉ *Begins on the east side of Hwy. 385, 1 mi north of the southern access road to the visitor center.*

MODERATE

Centennial Trail. Constructed to celebrate South Dakota's 100th birthday, this trail bisects the Black Hills, covering 111 mi from north to south. Designed for bikers, hikers, and horses, the trail is rugged but accommodating (note, however, that bicycling on the trail is not allowed within park boundaries). It will take you at least a half day to cover the 6 mi of this trail that traverse the park. ⊠ *Begins off Hwy. 87, 2 mi north of the visitor center.*

☙ **Cold Brook Canyon Trail.** Starting on the west side of U.S. 385, 2 mi south of the visitor center, this 1.5-mi, mildly strenuous hike runs past a former prairie-dog town, the edge of an area burned by a controlled fire in 1986, and through Cold Brook Canyon to the park boundary fence. Experienced hikers will conquer this trail and return to the trailhead in an hour or less, but more leisurely

visitors will probably need more time. ⊠ *Begins on the west side of U.S. 385, 2 mi south of the visitor center.*

36

DIFFICULT

Boland Ridge Trail. Get away from the crowds for half a day via this strenuous, 2.5-mi round-trip hike. The panorama from the top is well worth it, especially at night. ⊠ *Trailhead off Forest Service Rd. 6, 1 mi north of the junction with Forest Service Rd. 5.*

Highland Creek Trail. This difficult, roughly 8.5-mi trail is the longest and most diverse trail within the park, traversing mixed-grass prairies, ponderosa pine forests, and the riparian habitats of Highland Creek, Beaver Creek, and Wind Cave Canyon. Even those in good shape will need a full day to cover this trail round-trip. ⊠ *Southern trailhead stems from Wind Cave Canyon trail 1 mi east of U.S. 385. Northern trailhead on Forest Service Rd. 5.*

SPELUNKING

★ You may not explore the depths of Wind Cave on your own, but you can choose from five ranger-led cave tours, available from June through August; the rest of the year, only one or two tours are available. On each tour you pass incredibly beautiful cave formations, including extremely well-developed boxwork. The least crowded times to visit in summer are mornings and weekends. The cave is 53°F year-round, so bring a sweater. Note that the uneven passages are often wet and slippery. Rangers discourage those with heart conditions and physical limitations from taking the organized tours. However, with some advance warning (and for a nominal fee) park rangers can arrange private, limited tours for those with physical disabilities. The park provides hard hats, knee pads, and gloves, and all cavers are required to have long pants, a long-sleeved shirt, and hiking boots or shoes with nonslip soles. If you prefer lighted passages and stairways to dark crawl spaces, a tour other than the Wild Caving Tour might appeal to you.

Tours depart from the visitor center. A schedule can be found online at
⊕ *www.nps.gov/wica.* To make a reservation, call ☎ *605/745–4600.*

EASY

Garden of Eden Cave Tour. You don't need to go far to see boxwork, popcorn, and flowstone formations. Just take the relatively easy, one-hour tour, which covers about 0.25 mi and 150 stairs. It's available four times daily, June through Labor Day, and three times daily, October to early June. (It is unavailable most of September.) The cost is $7.

Natural Entrance Cave Tour. This 1¼-hour tour takes you 0.5 mi into the cave, over 300 stairs (most heading down), and out an elevator exit. Along the way are some significant boxwork deposits on the middle level. The tour costs $9 and leaves 15 times daily from June through Labor Day, and seven times daily for the rest of September.

MODERATE

★ **Candlelight Cave Tour.** Available twice daily, early June through Labor Day, this tour goes into a section of the cave with no paved walks or lighting. Everyone on the tour carries a lantern similar to those used in expeditions in the 1890s. The $9 tour lasts two hours and covers 1 mi; reservations are essential. Children younger than 8 are not admitted.

Fairgrounds Cave Tour. View examples of nearly every type of calcite formation found in the cave on this 1½-hour tour, available eight times daily, June through Labor Day. There are some 450 steps, leading up and down; the cost is $9.

DIFFICULT

Fodor'sChoice **Wild Caving Tour.** For a serious caving experience, sign up for this chal-
★ lenging, extraordinary, four-hour tour. After some basic training in spelunking, you crawl and climb through fissures and corridors, most lined with gypsum needles, frostwork, and boxwork. Expect to get dirty. Wear shoes with good traction, long pants, and a long-sleeve shirt. The park provides knee pads, gloves, and hard hats with headlamps. You must be at least 16 to take this tour, and 16- and 17-year-olds must show signed consent from a parent or guardian. Tours cost $23 and are available at 1 PM daily, early June through mid-August, and at 1 PM weekends mid-August through Labor Day. Reservations are essential.

EDUCATIONAL OFFERINGS

RANGER PROGRAMS

Campfire Program. A park ranger lectures for about 45 minutes on topics such as wildlife, park management, and cave history. ✉ *Elk Mountain Campground amphitheater* ☉ *June–Labor Day, nightly at 8 or 9 PM; Sept., Tues., Thurs., Sat. at 7 PM.*

☺ **Junior Ranger Program.** Kids 12 and younger can earn a Junior Ranger badge by completing activities that teach them about the park's ecosystems, the cave, the animals, and protecting the environment. Pick up the Junior Ranger guidebook for $1.25 at the Wind Cave Visitor Center.

Prairie Hike. This two-hour exploration of parkland habitats begins with a short talk at the visitor center, then moves to a trailhead. ☉ *Early June–mid-Aug., daily at 9 AM.*

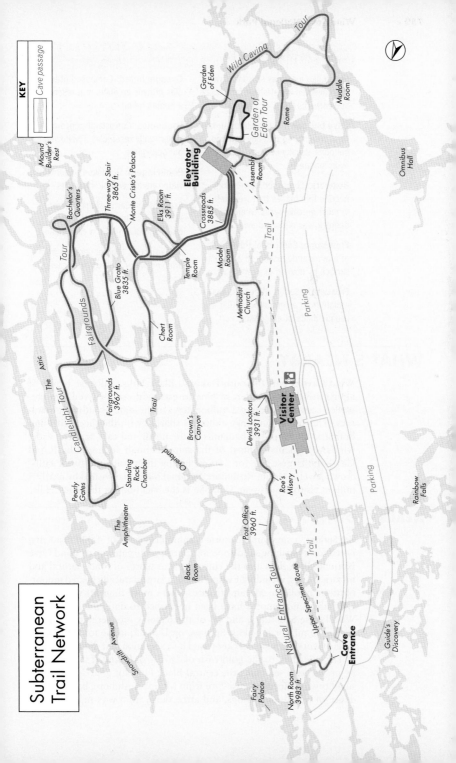

Subterranean Trail Network

KEY

Cave passage

Mound Builder's Rest

Wild Caving Tour

Garden of Eden

Garden of Eden Tour

Muddle Room

Rome

Omnibus Hall

Elevator Building

Assembly Room

Bachelor's Quarters

Three-way Stair 3865 ft.

Monte Cristo's Palace

Elks Room 3911 ft.

Crossroads 3885 ft.

Tour

Fairgrounds

Blue Grotto 3835 ft.

Temple Room

Model Room

Trail

The Attic

Candlelight Tour

Chert Room

Methodist Church

Parking

Fairgrounds 3967 ft.

Trail

Brown's Canyon

Devils Lookout 3931 ft.

Visitor Center

Standing Rock Chamber

Overland

Pearly Gates

The Amphitheater

Roe's Misery

Parking

Rainbow Falls

Snowcliff Avenue

Back Room

Post Office 3960 ft.

Trail

Natural Entrance Tour

Upper Specimen Route

Fairy Palace

North Room 3983 ft.

Cave Entrance

Guide's Discovery

CAVEMEN SPEAK

Sound like a serious spelunker with this cavemen cheat-sheet for various *speleothems* (cave formations).

Cave balloons: Thin-walled formations resembling partially deflated balloons, usually composed of hydromagnesite.

Boxwork: Composed of interconnecting thin blades that were left in relief on cave walls when the bedrock was dissolved away.

Flowstone: Consists of thin layers of a mineral deposited on a sloping surface by flowing or seeping water.

Frostwork: Sprays of needles that radiate from a central point that are usually made of aragonite.

Gypsum beard: Composed of bundles of gypsum fibers that resemble a human beard.

Logomites: Consists of popcorn and superficially resembles a hollowed-out stalagmite.

Pool Fingers: Deposited underneath water around organic filaments.

Stalactites: Carrot-shaped formations formed from dripping water that hang down from a cave ceiling.

Stalagmites: Mineral deposits from dripping water built up on a cave floor.

WHAT'S NEARBY

Wind Cave is part of South Dakota's Black Hills, a diverse region of alpine meadows, ponderosa pine forests, and creek-carved, granite-walled canyons covering 2 million acres in the state's southwest quadrant. This mountain range contrasts sharply with the sheer cliffs and dramatic buttes of the badlands to the north and east, and the wide, windswept plains of most of the state. Though anchored by Rapid City—the largest city for 350 mi in any direction—the Black Hills' crown jewel is Mount Rushmore National Memorial, visited by nearly 3 million visitors each year. U.S. 385 is the backbone of the Black Hills.

NEARBY TOWNS

Hot Springs, a small and historic community of about 4,000 residents, noted for its striking sandstone structures, is the gateway to Wind Cave National Park. It is also the entry point to scores of other natural and historical sites, including Evans Plunge, a large naturally heated indoor-outdoor pool; the Mammoth Site, where more than 50 woolly and Columbian mammoths have been unearthed to date; the Black Hills Wild Horse Sanctuary, and on of the region's premiere golf courses. About 30 mi north of Hot Springs, on U.S. 85, is the town of **Custer,** where George Armstrong Custer and his expedition first discovered gold in 1874, leading to the gold rush of 1875–76. Founded in the 1880s by prospectors searching the central Black Hills for gold deposits, the small town of **Keystone,** just 2 mi from Mount Rushmore, has an abundance of restaurants, shops, and attractions, from wax museums and miniature-golf courses to alpine slides and helicopter rides. To serve the millions of visitors passing through the area, there are 700 hotel rooms—more than twice the town's number of permanent residents. Because it's such a touristy town, we don't recommend it for your Black Hills base.

However, you may want to stay in the small, quiet mountain town

★ of **Hill City,** the gateway to Mount Rushmore. This town of 780 residents can claim no fewer than seven art galleries, a natural-history museum, a winery, a brewery, a vintage steam locomotive line, and a new visitor center on its eastern flank. Its brick-paved streets lined

★ with Victorian architecture, **Deadwood** owes its historical character to casinos. Gaming halls, restaurants, and hotels occupy virtually every storefront on Main Street, just as they did back in Deadwood's late-19th-century heyday. You can walk in the footsteps of Wild Bill Hickok and Calamity Jane, who swore she could outdrink, outspit, and outswear any man—and usually did. The central Black Hills is anchored by **Rapid City,** South Dakota's second-largest city (population 60,876) and the largest urban center in a 350-mi radius. The cultural, educational, medical, and economic hub of it is a good base from which to explore the treasures of the state's southwestern corner, including the badlands 70 mi to the east, Mount Rushmore and Wind Cave National Park 25 mi and 50 mi to the south, respectively.

36

> **PARK PUBLICATION**
>
> Wind Cave publishes a newspaper called *Passages.* Pick it up at the visitor center or at the chambers of commerce in Hot Springs, Custer, Keystone, and Rapid City. Call 605/745–4600 to have a copy mailed to you, and ask for the Southern Hills Visitor Guide as well.

VISITOR INFORMATION
Black Hills, Badlands & Lakes Association ✉ *1851 Discovery Circle, Rapid City* ☎ *605/355–3600* ⊕ *www.blackhillsbadlands.com.*

NEARBY ATTRACTIONS

CUSTER

★ **Crazy Horse Memorial.** Designed to be the world's largest sculpture (641 feet long by 563 feet high), this tribute to Crazy Horse, the legendary Lakota leader who defeated General Custer at Little Bighorn, is a work in progress. So far the warrior's head has been carved out of the mountain, and the head of his horse is starting to emerge; when work is underway you can expect to witness frequent blasting. Self-taught sculptor Korczak Ziolkowski conceived this memorial to American Indian heritage in 1948, and after his death in 1982 his family took on the project. The completion date is unknown, since activity is limited by weather and funding. Near the work site stands an exceptional orientation center, the Indian Museum of North America, Ziolkowski's studio/home and workshop, indoor and outdoor sculpture galleries, and a restaurant. ✉ *Along Hwy. 385, about 3 mi north of Custer* ☎ *605/673–4681* ⊕ *www.crazyhorsememorial.org* ⬛ *$10, carload of more than 2 adults $24* ⊙ *May–Sept., daily 7 AM–9 PM; Oct.–Apr., daily 8–4:30.*

★ **Custer State Park.** This 71,000-acre park is considered the crown jewel of South Dakota's state park system. Here, scenic backcountry is watered by clear trout streams. Elk, antelope, mountain goat, bighorn sheep, mountain lion, wild turkey, prairie dog, and the second-largest (behind the one in Yellowstone National Park) publicly owned herd of bison in the world roam this pristine landscape. Scenic drives roll past fingerlike granite spires and panoramic views (try the Needles Highway). Each year at the Buffalo Roundup and Arts Festival, thousands of spectators watch the park's 1,450 bison thunder through the hills at the start of a western-themed art and food expo. Take the 18-mi Wildlife Loop Road to see prairies teeming with animals. ⊠ *U.S. 16A, 4 mi east of Custer* ☎ *605/255-4515* ⊕ *www. sdgfp.info/parks/regions/custer* ☜ *$6-$28* ⊙ *24/7 year-round.*

★ **Jewel Cave National Monument.** Even though its 135 mi of surveyed passages make this cave the world's second largest (Kentucky's Mammoth Cave is the largest), it isn't the size of Jewel Cave that draws visitors, it's the rare crystalline formations that abound in the cave's vast passages. Wander the dark passageways, and you'll be rewarded with the sight of tiny crystal Christmas trees, hydromagnesite balloons that would pop if you touched them, and delicate calcite deposits dubbed "cave popcorn." Year-round, you can take ranger-led tours for a fee, from a simple half-hour walk to a lantern-light or wild caving tour. Surface trails and facilities are free. ⊠ *U.S. 16, 15 mi west of Custer* ☎ *605/673-2288* ⊕ *www.nps.gov/jeca* ☜ *$4-$27* ⊙ *Sept.-Apr., daily 8-4:30; May-Aug., daily 8-7.*

DEADWOOD

Adams Museum. Between the massive stone-block post office and the old railroad depot there are three floors of displays, including the first locomotive used in the area, photographs of the town's early days, and a reproduction of the largest gold nugget (7.75 troy ounces) ever discovered in the Black Hills. ⊠ *54 Sherman St., Deadwood* ☎ *605/578-1714* ⊕ *www.adamsmuseumandhouse.org* ☜ *Donations accepted* ⊙ *Late May-early Sept., Mon.-Sat. 9-7, Sun. noon-5; early Sept.-late May, Mon.-Sat. 10-4.*

Ⅽ **Broken Boot Gold Mine.** You can pan for gold and even if you don't find any, you'll leave with a souvenir stock certificate. ⊠ *U.S. 14A, Deadwood* ☎ *605/578-9997* ⊕ *www.brokenbootgoldmine.com* ☜ *Tour $5, gold panning $7* ⊙ *May-Aug., daily 8-5:30; mid-Sept., daily 9-4:30.*

HOT SPRINGS

★ **Black Hills Wild Horse Sanctuary.** Hundreds of wild mustangs inhabit this 11,000-acre preserve of rugged canyons, forests, and grasslands along the Cheyenne River. Take a guided tour or hike, and sign up for a chuck-wagon dinner. Drive 14 mi south of Hot Springs until you see signs off Route 71. ⊠ *12165 Highland Rd (Rte. 71), Hot Springs* ☎ *605/745-5955 or 800/252-6652* ⊕ *www.gwtc.net/~iram* ☜ *$50-$750* ⊙ *Memorial Day-Labor Day, Mon.-Sat. 9:30-5; tours at 10 and 1.*

Mammoth Site. During the construction of a housing development in the 1970s, earthmoving equipment uncovered this sinkhole where giant mammoths supposedly came to drink, got trapped, and died. Nearly 60 of the fossilized woolly beasts have been unearthed since digging began, and many can still be seen in situ. You can watch the excavation in progress and take guided tours. ⊠ *1800 Hwy. 18 Bypass/U.S. 18,*

In the fall, listen to elk bugling, a high-pitched, whistle-like sound the animals make as they mate.

15 mi south of Wind Cave National Park, Hot Springs ☎ 605/745–6017 ⊕ *www.mammothsite.com* ✉ *$8* ⊙ *Daily; hrs vary, call ahead.*

KEYSTONE

Beautiful Rushmore Cave. Stalagmites, stalactites, flowstone, ribbons, columns, helictites, and the "Big Room" are all part of the worthwhile tour into this cave. In 1876, miners found the opening to the cave while digging a flume into the mountainside to carry water to the gold mines below. The cave was opened to the public in 1927, just before the carving of Mount Rushmore began. ✉ *13622 Hwy. 40, Keystone* ☎ 605/255–4384 *or 605/255–4634* ⊕ *www.beautifulrushmorecave.com* ✉ *$12* ⊙ *June–Aug., daily 8–8; Sept. and Oct., daily 9–5.*

RAPID CITY

Ⓒ
Fodor's Choice
★
Bear Country U.S.A. Encounter black bears, elk, sheep, and wolves at this drive-through wildlife park. There's also a walk-through wildlife center. ✉ *13820 S. U.S. 16, Rapid City* ☎ 605/343–2290 ⊕ *www.bearcountryusa.com* ✉ *$15* ⊙ *May–Nov., daily 8–7.*

Black Hills Caverns. Frost crystal, amethyst, logomites, calcite crystals, and other specimens fill this cave, first discovered by pioneers in the late 1800s. Half-hour and hour tours are available. ✉ *2600 Cavern Rd., Rapid City* ☎ 605/343–0542 ⊕ *www.blackhillscaverns.com* ✉ *$9.75 per hour, $7.50 per half hour* ⊙ *May–mid-June and mid-Aug.–Sept., daily 8:30–6:30; mid-June–mid-Aug., daily 8–7.*

Ft. Hays *Dances with Wolves* Movie Set. Although it was released in the early 1990s, *Dances with Wolves* continues to generate interest in the Black Hills. View photos and a video of the making of the film. A chuck-wagon dinner show ($20) is held late May through Labor Day. ⊠ *Ft. Hays Dr. and U.S. 16, Rapid City* ☎ *605/394–9653* ⊕ *www.mountrushmoretours. com* ⊠ *Free* ☉ *Mid-May–mid-Sept., daily 7:30* AM–8 PM.

☧ **Reptile Gardens.** On the bottom of a valley between Rapid City and
★ Mount Rushmore is western South Dakota's answer to a zoo. In addition to the world's largest private reptile collection, the site also has a raptor rehabilitation center. No visit is complete without watching some alligator wrestling or letting the kids ride the giant tortoises. ⊠ *8955 S. U.S. 16, Rapid City* ☎ *605/342–5873* ⊕ *www.reptilegardens.com* ⊠ *$14* ☉ *Memorial Day–Labor Day, daily 8–7.*

South Dakota Air and Space Museum. See a model of a Stealth bomber that's 60% actual size. Also here are General Dwight D. Eisenhower's Mitchell B-25 bomber and more than two dozen other planes, and a once-operational missile silo. Tours are not available in winter. ⊠ *2890 Davis Dr., Box Elder* ☎ *605/385–5188* ⊕ *www.sdairandspacemuseum. com* ⊠ *Museum free, tour $5* ☉ *June–mid-Sept., daily 8:30–6; mid-Sept.–May, daily 8:30–4:30.*

SPEARFISH

☧ **High Plains Western Heritage Center.** Founded to honor the pioneers and American Indians of a region now covered by five states—the Dakotas, Wyoming, Montana, and Nebraska—the center features artifacts such as a Deadwood-Spearfish stagecoach. Outdoor exhibits include a sod home, a log cabin, a one-room schoolhouse, and in summer, an entire farm set up with antique equipment. Often on the calendar are cowboy poetry, live music, festivals, reenactments, and historical talks. ⊠ *825 Heritage Dr., Spearfish* ☎ *605/642–9378* ⊕ *www.westernheritagecenter. com* ⊠ *$7* ☉ *Daily 9–5.*

AREA ACTIVITIES

SPORTS AND THE OUTDOORS

The Black Hills are a haven for outdoor enthusiasts, and with good reason. The warmer temperatures of spring and summer make for excellent fishing, hiking, mountain climbing, mountain biking, camping, and horseback riding in the national forest. Autumn's cooler weather and changing colors brings out the leaf-peepers, and the hunters aren't far behind. Snow can fall as early as October, but the white stuff really starts coming down in December and January, when snowmobilers and skiers (both downhill and cross-country) come out to play. The northern Black Hills, where there are two ski areas, generally receive the highest accumulations, and have seen up to 180 inches of annual snowfall.

FISHING

The Black Hills are filled with tiny mountain creeks, especially on the wetter western and northern slopes, that are ideal for fly-fishing. Rapid Creek, which flows down from the Central Hills into Pactola Reservoir and finally into Rapid City, is a favorite fishing venue for the city's anglers, both because of its regularly stocked population of trout and for its easy accessibility. Besides the local chambers of commerce, **South Dakota Game, Fish, and Parks** (⊠ *523 E. Capitol Ave., Pierre*

☎ *605/773–3485* ⊕ *www.sdgfp.info*) is your best bet for updated information on regional fishing locations and their conditions.

WATER SPORTS

Angostura Reservoir State Recreation Area. Water-based recreation is the main draw at this park 10 mi south of Hot Springs. Besides the marina, you'll find a floating convenience store, a restaurant, campgrounds, and cabins. Boat and WaveRunner rentals are available. ⊠ *U.S. 385, off Rte. 79, Hot Springs* ☎ *605/745–6996* 🎫 *$5* ⊙ *Daily dawn–dusk.*

WINTER SPORTS

Heavy snowfalls and lovely views make the Black Hills prime cross-country skiing territory. Many trails are open to snowmobilers as well as skiers. Trade and travel magazines consistently rank the Black Hills among the top snowmobiling destinations in the country for two simple reasons: dramatic scenery and an abundance of snow.

Mystic Miner Ski Resort at Deer Mountain. This expanded resort has a massive beginner's area, tubing, snowboarding, sleigh rides, and the only night skiing in the Black Hills. ⊠ *11187 Deer Mt. Rd., 3 mi south of Lead on U.S. 85* ☎ *605/584–3230 or 888/410–3337* ⊕ *www.skimystic.com.*

Terry Peak Ski Area. Perched on the sides of a 7,076-foot mountain, Terry Peak claims the Balck Hills' second-highest mountain summit. The runs are challenging for novice and intermediate skiers and should keep the experts entertained. From the top, on a clear day, you can see into Wyoming, Montana, and North Dakota. ⊠ *2 mi south of Lead on U.S. 85* ☎ *800/456–0524* ⊕ *www.terrypeak.com.*

ARTS AND ENTERTAINMENT

THE ARTS

The **Rushmore Plaza Civic Center Fine Arts Theater** (⊠ *444 Mt. Rushmore Rd. N* ☎ *800/468–6463* ⊕ *www.gotmine.com*) hosts about a half-dozen touring Broadway shows in winter, and a brand new ice arena. It's also the venue for the Vucurevich Speaker Series, which has attracted prominent names such as the humorist Dave Barry, late astronomer Carl Sagan, and former Secretary of State Colin Powell.

ENTERTAINMENT

Fodor'sChoice

★

Billing itself as "the world's only museum with a bar," the **Old Style Saloon No. 10** (⊠ *657 Main St., Deadwood* ☎ *605/578–3346*) is where you want to come to drink, listen to music, and socialize. Thousands of artifacts, vintage photos, and a two-headed calf set the scene—plus the chair in which Wild Bill Hickok was supposedly shot. A reenactment of his murder takes place four times daily in the summer. For fine fare and the best wine and martini bar in the hills, head upstairs to the Deadwood Social Club.

SHOPPING

Fodor'sChoice

★

One of the world's top collections of Plains Indian artwork and crafts makes **Prairie Edge Trading Company and Galleries** (⊠ *6th and Main Sts., Rapid City* ☎ *605/342–3086 or 800/541–2388*) seem more like a museum than a store and gallery. The collection ranges from books and CDs to artifact

36

America's Shrine to Democracy

Abraham Lincoln was tall in real life—6 feet, 4 inches, though add a few more for his hat. But at one of the nation's most famous icons, Honest Abe, along with presidents George Washington, Thomas Jefferson, and Theodore Roosevelt, towers over the Black Hills in a 60-foot-high likeness. The four images looks especially spectacular at night, June through mid-September, when a lighting ceremony dramatically illuminates them.

THE MAKING OF THE SCULPTURE
Like most impressive undertakings, Mount Rushmore's path to realization was one of personalities and perseverance.

When Gutzon Borglum, a talented and patriotic sculptor, was invited to create a giant monument to Confederate soldiers in Georgia in 1915, he jumped at the chance. The son of Danish immigrants, Borglum was raised in California and trained in art in Paris, even studying under Auguste Rodin, who influenced his style. Georgia's Stone Mountain project was to be massive in scope—encompassing the rock face of an entire peak—and would give Borglum the opportunity to exercise his artistic vision on a grand scale.

But the relationship with the project backers and Borglum went sour, causing the sculptor to destroy his models and flee the state. South Dakota state officials had a vision for another mountain memorial, and Borglum was eager to jump on board. His passion and flamboyant personality were well matched to the project, which involved carving legends of the Wild West on a gigantic scale. In time, Borglum convinced officials to think larger, and the idea of carving a monument to U.S. presidents was born.

On a massive granite cliff, at an elevation of 5,725 feet, Borglum began carving Mount Rushmore in 1927 with the help of some 400 assistants. In consultation with U.S. Senator Peter Norbeck and State Historian Doane Robinson, Borglum chose the four presidents to signify the birth, growth, preservation, and development of the nation. In six and a half years of carving over a 14-year period, the sculptor and his crew drilled and dynamited a masterpiece, the largest work of art on earth. Borglum died in March, 1941, leaving his son, Lincoln, to complete the work only a few months later—in the wake of the gathering storm of World War II.

ATTRACTIONS
Follow the Presidential Trail through the forest to gain excellent views of the colossal sculpture, or stroll the Avenue of Flags for a different perspective. Also on-site are an impressive museum, indoor theaters where films are shown, an outdoor amphitheater for live performances, and concession facilities. The nightly ranger program and lighting of the

36

memorial is reportedly the most popular interpretive program in all of the national parks system.

Avenue of Flags. Running from the entrance of the memorial to the museum and amphitheater at the base of the mountain, the avenue represents each state, commonwealth, district, and territory of the U.S.

☾ **Lincoln Borglum Museum.** This giant granite-and-glass structure underneath the viewing platform has permanent exhibits on the carving of the mountain, its history, and its significance. There also are temporary exhibits, a bookstore, and an orientation film. Admission is free.

★ ☾ **Presidential Trail.** This easy hike along a boardwalk and down some stairs leads to the very base of the mountain. Although the trail is thickly forested, you'll have more than ample opportunity to look straight up the noses of the four giant heads. The trail is open year-round, so long as snow and/or ice don't present a safety hazard.

Sculptor's Studio. Built in 1939 as Gutzon Borglum's on-site workshop, it displays tools used by the mountain carvers, a model of the memorial, and a model depicting the unfinished Hall of Records. It's open May–September only; admission is free.

CONTACT INFORMATION
The **Mount Rushmore Information Center,** between the park entrance and the Avenue of Flags, has a small exhibit with photographs of the presidents' faces as they were being carved. There's also an information desk here, staffed by rangers who can answer questions about the memorial or the surrounding Black Hills. A nearly identical building across from the information center houses restrooms, telephones, soda machines, and an all-new audio tour offered by the nonprofit Mount Rushmore History Association. ⊠ *Beginning of Ave. of Flags, Keystone* ☎ *605/574–2523* ⊕ *www.nps.gov/moru* ✉ *Center free, parking $10* ☾ *May–Sept., daily 8 AM– 10 PM; Oct.–Apr., daily 8–5.*

FESTIVALS AND EVENTS

JUNE

Crazy Horse Volksmarch. This 6.2-mi hike up the mountain where the giant Crazy Horse Memorial is being carved is the largest event of its kind. It's held the first full weekend in June. ☎ 605/673–4681.

JULY

Gold Discovery Days. A parade, carnival, balloon rally, firemen's ball, and more are all part of the fun of this three-day event in late July in Custer. ☎ 800/992–9818.

Days of '76. This Deadwood festival has earned PRCA honors as Best Small Outdoor Rodeo numerous times. Rodeo performances, two parades with vintage carriages and coaches, street dances, and western arts and crafts make this five-day affair one of the best events in South Dakota. ☎ 800/999–1876.

SEPTEMBER/OCTOBER

Deadwood Jam. The Black Hills' premier two-day music event each September showcases the top in country, rock, and blues. ☎ 800/999–1876.

Custer State Park Buffalo Roundup. The nation's largest buffalo roundup is one of South Dakota's most exciting events. Early on a Monday morning in late September or early October, cowboys and park crews saddle up and corral the park's 1,400 head of bison so that they may later be vaccinated. ☎ 605/255–4515.

reproductions and artwork representing the Lakota, Crow, Cheyenne, Shoshone, Arapaho, and Assiniboin tribes of the Great Plains.

SCENIC DRIVES

★ **Peter Norbeck National Scenic Byway.** Even though the fastest way to get from Mount Rushmore to Crazy Horse Memorial and the southern Black Hills is along Highway 244 West and U.S. 16/U.S. 385 South, this scenic drive in the Black Hills is a more stunning route. Take U.S. 16A south into Custer State Park, where buffalo, bighorn sheep, elk, antelope, and burros roam free, then drive north on Highway 87 through the Needles, towering granite spires that rise above the forest. A short drive off the highway reaches 7,242-foot Harney Peak, the highest point in North America east of the Rockies. Highway 87 finally brings you to U.S. 16/U.S. 385, where you head south to the Crazy Horse Memorial. Because the scenic byway is a challenging drive (with one-lane tunnels and switchbacks) and because you'll likely want to stop a few times to admire the scenery, plan on spending two to three hours on this drive. Stretches of U.S. 16A and Highway 87 may close in winter.

★ **Spearfish Canyon Scenic Byway.** The easiest way to get from Deadwood to Rapid City and the central Black Hills is east through Boulder Canyon on U.S. 14A, which joins Interstate 90 in Sturgis. However, it's worth looping north and taking the long way around on this 20-mi scenic route past 1,000-foot limestone cliffs and some of the most breathtaking scenery in the region. Cascading waterfalls quench the thirst of quaking aspen, gnarled oaks, sweet-smelling spruce, and the ubiquitous ponderosa pine, which grow right off the edges of rocky precipices. The canyon is home to deer, mountain goats, porcupines, and bobcats. Near its middle is the old sawmill town of Savoy, a jumping-off point for scenic hikes to Spearfish Falls and Roughlock Falls.

WHERE TO EAT AND STAY

ABOUT THE RESTAURANTS

If you're determined to dine in Wind Cave National Park, be sure to pack your own meal, because the only dining venues inside park boundaries are the two picnic areas near the visitor center and Elk Mountain Campground. The towns beyond the park offer additional options. Deadwood claims some of the best-ranked restaurants in South Dakota. Buffalo, pheasant, and elk are relatively common ingredients in the Black Hills. No matter where you go, beef is king.

ABOUT THE HOTELS

While Wind Cave claims a singular campground, you'll have to look outside park boundaries if you want to bed down in something more substantial than a tent. New chain hotels with modern amenities are plentiful in the Black Hills, but when booking accommodations consider a stay at one of the area's historic properties. From grand brick downtown hotels to intimate Queen Anne homes converted to bed-and-breakfasts, historic lodgings are easy to locate. Other distinctive lodging choices include the region's mountain lodges and forest retreats.

It may be difficult to obtain quality accommodations during summer—and downright impossible during the Sturgis Motorcycle Rally, held the first full week of August every year—so plan ahead and make reservations (three or four months out is a good rule of thumb) if you're going to travel during peak season. To find the best value, choose a hotel far from Interstate 90.

ABOUT THE CAMPGROUNDS

Camping is one of this region's strengths. While there is only one primitive campground within the park, there are countless campgrounds in the Black Hills. The public campgrounds in the national forest are accessible by road but otherwise secluded and undeveloped; private campgrounds typically have more amenities. If you're up for a more adventurous experience, most of the public land within the Black Hills is open for backcountry camping, provided that you don't light any fires and that you obtain a permit (usually free) from the appropriate park or forest headquarters. Note that the Black Hills don't have any native bears, but there is a significant population of mountain lions.

WHERE TO EAT

IN THE PARK

PICNIC AREAS **Elk Mountain Campground Picnic Area.** You don't have to be a camper to use this well-developed picnic spot, with more than 70 tables, fire pits, and restrooms with water. Some of the tables are on the prairie, others are amidst the pines. ⊠ *½ mi north of the visitor center.*

36

Wind Cave Picnic Area. On the edge of a prairie and grove of ponderosa, this is a peaceful, pretty place. Small and simple, it's equipped with 12 tables and a potable-water pump. ⊠ *¼ mi north of the visitor center.*

OUTSIDE THE PARK

$$ ✕ **Blue Bell Lodge and Resort.** Feast on fresh trout or buffalo, which you
AMERICAN can have as a steak or a stew, in this rustic log building within the boundaries of Custer State Park. There's a kids' menu. On the property, hayrides and cookouts are part of the entertainment, and you can sign up for trail rides and overnight pack trips on old Indian trails with the nearby stable. ⊠ *About 6 mi south of U.S. 16A junction on Hwy. 87, in Custer State Park, Custer* ☎ *605/255–4531 or 800/658–3530* ⊟ *AE, D, MC, V* ☻ *Closed mid-Oct.–mid-May.*

$–$$ ✕ **Botticelli Ristorante Italiano.** With a wide selection of delectable veal and
ITALIAN chicken dishes as well as creamy pastas, this Italian eatery provides a
★ welcome respite from the traditional midwestern meat and potatoes. The artwork and traditional Italian music in the background give the place a European air. ⊠ *523 Main St., Rapid City* ☎ *605/348–0089* ⊟ *AE, MC, V.*

$–$$ ✕ **Branding Iron Steakhouse.** Within walking distance from the Mammoth
STEAK Site, this exceptional new and spacious restaurant is a hit among locals and visitors. Beef is king here with great rib eyes, New Yorks, and prime rib—but you'll find chicken and seafood on the menu as well. ⊠ *1648 US Hwy 18 Bypass, Hot Springs* ☎ *605/745–4545* ⊟ *D, DC, MC, V.*

¢–$ ✕ **Buffalo Dining Room.** The only restaurant within the bounds of the
AMERICAN Mount Rushmore Memorial affords commanding views of the memorial and the surrounding ponderosa pine forest, and exceptional food at a reasonable price. The menu includes New England pot roast, buffalo stew, and homemade rhubarb pie. It's open for breakfast, lunch, and dinner (spring–fall). ⊠ *Beginning of Ave. of Flags, Keystone* ☎ *605/574–2515* ⊟ *AE, D, MC, V* ☻ *No dinner mid-Oct.–early Mar.*

$–$$$ ✕ **Deadwood Social Club.** On the second floor of historic Saloon No. 10,
ITALIAN this warm restaurant surrounds you with wood and old-time photo-
Fodor'sChoice graphs of Deadwood's past. Light jazz and blues play over the sound
★ system. The decor is western, but the food is northern Italian, a juxtaposition that keeps patrons coming back. The menu stretches from wild-mushroom pasta-and-seafood nest with basil cream to chicken piccata (chicken served in a sauce containing lemon butter and spices), elk, buffalo, and melt-in-your-mouth Black Angus rib eyes. The wine list had nearly 200 selections at last count. Reservations are a good idea. ⊠ *657 Main St., Deadwood* ☎ *605/578–1533* ⊟ *AE, MC, V.*

$$–$$$ ✕ **Deadwood Thymes Bistro.** Located across from the historic courthouse,
CONTINENTAL away from the Main Street casinos, this has a quieter, more intimate
★ feel than other town restaurants—and the food is among the best. The menu changes frequently, but expect dishes like brioche French toast, salmon quiche, Parisian grilled ham and Swiss, Thai burrito with peanut sauce, and lamb chops marinated in white wine and mustard and served with parsley-gin sauce. The wine list features imports, and desserts are incredible. You might find raspberry cheesecake, chocolate angel food cake with a whiskey-bourbon sauce. ⊠ *87 Sherman St., Deadwood* ☎ *605/578–7566* ⊟ *MC, V.*

$$-$$$ ✕ **Jakes.** This restaurant owned by actor Kevin Costner is among South
ECLECTIC Dakota's classiest dining experiences. Cherrywood pillars inlaid with
★ etched-glass lights, white-brick fireplaces, and a pianist add to the elegance of the atrium dining room. Among the menu's eclectic offerings
are buffalo roulade, Cajun seafood tortellini, filet mignon, and fresh
fish. ✉ *677 Main St., Deadwood* ☎ *605/578–1555* ⊛ *Reservations
essential* ▭ *AE, D, DC, MC, V.*

$–$$ ✕ **Laughing Water Restaurant.** This airy pine restaurant with windows
AMERICAN facing the mountain sculpture is noted for its fry bread and buffalo
burgers. There's a soup-and-salad bar, but you'd do well to stick to
the American Indian offerings; try the Indian taco or "buffaloski" (a
Polish-style sausage made with Dakota buffalo). A kids' menu is available. ✉ *12151 Ave. of the Chiefs, Custer* ☎ *605/673–4681* ▭ *AE, D,
MC, V* ⊘ *Closed Nov.–Apr.*

¢–$$ ✕ **Woolly's Mammoth Family Fun.** Among the newest restaurants in the
AMERICAN southern Black Hills and operated by a friendly couple, this place caters
to families, with a modestly priced menu, video arcade, simulated golf,
and shooting games. It's tucked beside the new Holiday Inn Express
and close to the exceptional Southern Hills Golf Course. ✉ *1403 Hwy.
18 Bypass, Hot Springs* ☎ *605/745–6414* ▭ *AE, MC, V*

36

WHERE TO STAY

IN THE PARK

CAMPING ⛺ **Elk Mountain Campground.** If you prefer a relatively developed camp-
$ site and relative proximity to civilization, Elk Mountain is an excellent
★ choice. You can experience the peaceful pine forests and wild creatures
of the park without straying too far from the safety of the beaten path.
Most of the campers who stay here pitch tents, but there are 25 pull-
through sites for RVs, and sites 24 and 69 are reserved for campers with
disabilities. Note that water is shut off during winter. **Pros:** generally
not full; good mix of tents and RVs. **Cons:** remote; a long way to shop-
ping or restaurants. ✉ *½ mi north of the visitor center* ☎ *605/745–4600*
⛺ *75 sites* ⌂ *Flush toilets, running water (non-potable), fire grates,
public telephone* ▭ *No credit cards* ⊘ *Apr.–late Oct.*

OUTSIDE THE PARK

$$-$$$$ ⌂ **Audrie's Bed & Breakfast.** Victorian antiques and the hint of romance
Fodor'sChoice greet you at this out-of-the-way B and B, set in a thick woods 7 mi
★ west of Rapid City. Suites, cottages, and creek-side cabins sleeping two
come with old-world furnishings, fireplaces, private baths, hot tubs, and
big-screen TVs; cabins lack a/c and phones. Bicycles and fishing poles
can be obtained free from the office. Each room has a micowave. **Pros:**
great antiques; terrific treats; inspiring isolation. **Cons:** pricy lodging;
tough to get a unit due to popularity; no restaurant within walking distance. ✉ *23029 Thunderhead Falls Rd., Rapid City* ☎ *605/342–7788*
⊕ *www.audriesbb.com* ⇆ *2 suites, 7 cottages and cabins* ⌂ *In-room: no
a/c (some), no phone (some), refrigerator (some). In-hotel: bicycles, no
kids under 18* ▭ *No credit cards* ⫶⊙⫷ *BP.*

$$-$$$ ⌂ **Buffalo Rock Lodge B&B.** A large, native-rock fireplace surrounded by
hefty logs adds to the rustic quality of this lodge decorated with western

artifacts. There's an extensive view of Mount Rushmore from an oversize deck surrounded by a plush pine forest filled with wildflowers. **Pros:** quiet; exceptional furnishings. **Cons:** relatively pricy lodging option; drive to shopping and dining; no TVs. ⊠ *Playhouse Rd., P.O. Box 641, Keystone* ☎ *605/666–4781 or 888/564–5634* ⊕ *www.buffalorock.net* ⌁ *3 rooms* ⌂ *In-room: no TV. In-hotel: some pets allowed* ⊟ *DC, MC, V* ⊺⊙⎮ *CP.*

$–$$ ⌃ **Deadwood Gulch Gaming Resort.** Pine-clad hills, a little creek, and a deck from which to view the mountains are at your disposal at this family-style resort about a mile from downtown. A trolley stops here to take you to sites in Deadwood. The Creekside Restaurant (¢–$$) serves hearty breakfasts and some of the best burgers in town. The giant salads are also favorites, largely because of the side of sunflower bread and the homemade apricot dressing. In the lounge, check out the house specialties, including margaritas and martinis. **Pros:** away from downtown bustle; spacious; excellent staff. **Cons:** must take trolley downtown or to other restaurants; can be highly busy due to popularity with motor coaches. ⊠ *304 Cliff St., U.S. 85, Deadwood* ☎ *605/578–1294 or 800/695–1876* ⊕ *www.deadwoodgulch.com* ⌁ *88 rooms, 2 suites* ⌂ *In-room: Wi-Fi. In-hotel: restaurant, bar, some pets allowed* ⊟ *AE, D, DC, MC, V* ⊺⊙⎮ *BP.*

$$–$$$$ ⌃ **Franklin Hotel.** Built in 1903, this imposing hotel has housed many
Fodor's Choice   famous guests in its time, including John Wayne, Teddy Roosevelt, and
★   Babe Ruth. It still has its original banisters, ceilings, and fireplace. The guest rooms are Victorian style, with reproduction furniture, lace on hardwood tables, and flowery bedspreads. The second-floor veranda above the white-columned hotel entrance affords a great view down Main Street and the perfect hideaway for a quiet refreshment The fabled Franklin reopened in spring 2006 following a major face-lift on its main and lower levels. **Pros:** at the top of Main Street; spacious; historic. **Cons:** while great care and expense went into main-floor remodeling, guest rooms still need attention. ⊠ *700 Main St., Deadwood* ☎ *605/578–2241 or 800/688–1876* ⊕ *www.silveradofranklin.com* ⌁ *81 rooms* ⌂ *In-hotel: room service, bar* ⊟ *AE, D, DC, MC, V.*

$–$$ ⌃ **French Creek Ranch B&B.** Soak up views of the Needles formation while you sit on the porch of this luxurious B and B. On a 25-acre working horse ranch, French Creek is designed to meet the needs of the traveling horse owner: the stable has eight wooden box stalls each with its own run. Horses may be boarded for an additional fee. Facilities are also available for a horse trailer or camper hookup. The ranch is 1½ mi from Custer State Park. It is open year-round. **Pros:** privacy; away from highway noise. **Cons:** no restaurant within walking distance. ⊠ *25042 Kemp Dr. Custer* ☎ *605/673–4790 or 877/673–4790* ⊕ *www.frenchcreekranch.com* ⌁ *3 rooms* ⌂ *In-hotel: restaurant, tennis court, no kids under 13* ⊟ *D, MC, V* ⊺⊙⎮ *BP.*

$$–$$$ ⌃ **K Bar S Lodge.** This contemporary lodge on 45 lush, pine-clad acres
★   feels as if it's stood for a century. Quiet rooms decorated in subtle earth tones and native woods, windows that seemingly bring the surrounding forest into the guest accommodations, fine dining, and splendid meeting facilities make this a great place for an overnight stay. Breakfast is in the lodge's airy gazebo dining room. **Pros:** excellent staff; exceptional food; amid a wildlife preserve. **Cons:** quite a walk to shopping

or other dining options; pricey; always full. ✉ *434 Old Hill City Rd., Keystone* ☎ *866/522–7724 or 605/666–4545* ⊕ *www.kbarslodge.com* ⤶ *96 rooms* ♿ *In-room: Internet. In-hotel: restaurant, room service, bar, laundry facilities* ▤ *AE, D, MC, V* ❙◎❙ *BP.*

$$–$$$ ⛄ **Spearfish Canyon Lodge.** Located about midway between Spearfish and
★ Deadwood, near the bottom of Spearfish Canyon, this lodge-style hotel commands some of the best views in the Black Hills. Limestone cliffs rise nearly 1,000 feet in all directions. The rush of Spearfish Falls is only a 0.25-mi hike away, while the gentle flow of Roughlock Falls is a mile-long hike through pine, oak, and aspen from the lodge's front door. The rooms are furnished in natural woods, and fabrics are dark maroon and green. **Pros:** wonderful location; on-site snowmobile rentals in winter; bikes in summer; as pretty as it gets. **Cons:** remote; half-hour drive to Spearfish for other restaurants; standard rooms. ✉ *10619 Roughlock Falls Rd., Lead* ☎ *877/975–6343 or 605/584–3435* ⊕ *www.spfcanyon. com* ⤶ *54 rooms* ♿ *In-room: Wi-Fi. In-hotel: restaurant, bar, laundry facilities* ▤ *AE, D, MC, V.*

$–$$ ⛄ **Sylvan Lake Resort.** This spacious stone-and-wood lodge in Custer
☺ State Park affords fantastic views of pristine Sylvan Lake and Harney
★ Peak beyond. The rooms in the lodge are large and modern, and there are rustic cabins, some with fireplaces, scattered along the cliff and in the forest. The Lakota Dining Room ($–$$) has an exceptional view of the lake; its lovely veranda constructed of native stone is the perfect place to sip tea and watch the sunrise or enjoy an evening cocktail. On the menu are buffalo selections and rainbow trout. You can canoe, fish, and swim in the lake, and numerous hiking trails make this a great choice for active families. **Pros:** wonderful views in the midst of a forest; multitude of lodging options; alpine atmosphere: **Cons:** winding road to get there; limited dining options; can be pricy. ✉ *3389 U.S. Hwy. 16A, Custer* ⌂ *HC 83, P.O. Box 74, Custer 57730* ☎ *605/574–2561 or 800/658–3530* ⊕ *www.custerresorts.com* ⤶ *35 rooms, 31 cabins* ♿ *In-hotel: restaurant* ▤ *AE, D, MC, V* ⊘ *Closed Oct.–Mother's Day.*

CAMPING ⛺ **Happy Holiday RV Resort.** Outside of Rapid City on U.S. 16, this year-
$$ round campground has the advantage of easy access to Mount Rushmore and beautiful forest surroundings. There are also on-site cabins and motel rooms. You get 10% off on gas when you stay here. **Pros:** on the road to Rushmore; convenient to other attractions; camping or cabin options. **Cons:** big and busy with everything for everybody. ✉ *8990 U.S. 16 S, Rapid City* ☎ *605/342–7365* ⊕ *www.happyholidayrvresort.com* ⛺ *258 sites (170 with full hookups, 88 with partial hookups), 12 cabins, 31 motel units* ♿ *Flush toilets, full hookups, partial hookups (electric and water), dump station, drinking water, guest laundry, showers, fire grates, picnic tables, electricity, public telephone, general store, play area, service station, Wi-Fi, swimming (pool).*

$$–$$$$ ⛺ **Mount Rushmore KOA–Palmer Gulch Lodge.** This huge commercial camp-
☺ ground on Route 244 west of Mount Rushmore offers shuttles to the
Fodor'sChoice mountain, bus tours, horse rides, and car rentals. There are also large fur-
★ nished cabins and primitive camping cabins, as well as a new lodge shadowed by the massive granite ramparts of Harney Peak. With its pools, waterslide, outdoor activities, and kids' programs, this is a great place for

families, and parents will appreciate the three hot tubs. A shuttle takes you to Mount Rushmore and Crazy Horse for a nominal charge. **Pros:** idyllic setting; lots to do; great staff. **Cons:** large and busy; not for the wilderness camper ⌧ *12620 Hwy 244, Hill City* ☎ *605/574–2525* ⊕ *www.palmergulch.com* ⚠ *500 sites (130 with full hookups, 192 with partial hookups), 85 cabins* ♿ *In-cabin: kitchen (some), some pets allowed, no a/c, no phone (some). In-campground: Flush toilets, full hookups, partial hookups (electric and water), dump station, drinking water, guest laundry, showers, fire grates, picnic tables, food service, electricity, service station, play area, swimming (pool), Wi-Fi* ⊗ *May–Oct.*

$–$$ ⚠ **Whispering Pines Campground and Lodging.** Block party–style cookouts are followed by movies every night here as long as the weather is good. Located 16 mi west of Rapid City in Black Hills National Forest, the campground is exactly midway between Deadwood (22 mi to the north) and Mount Rushmore (22 mi to the south). In addition to RV and tent sites, cabins are available at a reasonable price. Reservations are essential. **Pros:** relatively quick trips to Deadwood or Rapid City; nice timber; pleasant spot. **Cons:** remote; a 20- to 30-minute drive to restaurants in Rapid City or Deadwood; some traffic noise. ⌧ *22700 Silver City Rd., Rapid City* ☎ *605/341–3667* ⊕ *www.blackhillscampresort.com* ⤸ *28 RV sites (26 full hookups, 2 partial hookups), 45 tent sites, 5 cabins* ♿ *Flush toilets, full hookups, partial hookups (electric and water), dump station, drinking water, guest laundry, showers, fire pits, picnic tables, food service, electricity, public telephone, general store, play area, swimming (lake)* ▭ *D, MC, V* ⊗ *May–Sept.*

Yellowstone National Park

WORD OF MOUTH

"Rarely do you find in one place the geological wonders and diversity Yellowstone has to offer. Add to that the diversity of the wildlife, and you've got almost the perfect picture of the totality of nature's collective handiwork in one location, and all in peaceful co-existence."

—dfr4848

WELCOME TO YELLOWSTONE

TOP REASONS TO GO

★ **Hot spots:** Thinner-than-normal crust depth and a huge magma chamber beneath the park explain Yellowstone's abundant geysers, steaming pools, hissing fumaroles, and bubbling mudpots.

★ **Bison:** They're just one of many species that roam freely here. Seemingly docile, the bison make your heart race if you catch them stampeding across Lamar Valley.

★ **Hiking:** Yellowstone has more than 1,000 mi of trails, along which you can summit a 10,000-foot peak, follow a trout-filled creek, or descend into the Grand Canyon of the Yellowstone.

★ **Yellowstone Lake:** Here you can fish, boat, kayak, stargaze, and bird-watch on black obsidian beaches—just don't stray too far into the frigid water.

★ **Canyon:** The Colorado River runs through the park, creating a deep yellow-colored canyon with two impressive waterfalls.

1 **Grant Village/West Thumb.** Named for President Ulysses S. Grant, Grant Village is on the western edge of Yellowstone Lake.

2 **Old Faithful area.** Famous for its regularity and awesome power, Old Faithful erupts every 94 minutes or so. The most important geyser site in the world is a full-service area with inns, restaurants, campsites, cabins, a visitor center, and general stores.

3 **Madison.** Here the Madison River is formed by the joining of the Gibbon and Firehole rivers. Fly fishermen will find healthy stocks of brown and rainbow trout and mountain whitefish.

4 **Norris.** The Norris area is the hottest and most changeable part of Yellowstone National Park. There are campsites here and a small information center.

5 **Mammoth Hot Springs.** This full-service fortlike area has an inn, restaurants, campsites, a visitor center, and general stores.

6 **Tower-Roosevelt.** This least-visited area of the park is the place to go for solitude, horseback riding, and animal sightings. There are a lodge, restaurant, and campsites here.

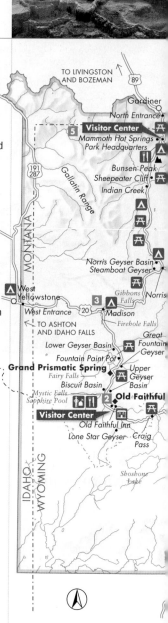

7 Canyon area. The Yellowstone River runs through here, and the yellow walls of the canyon lend the park its name. Two massive waterfalls highlight "downtown" Yellowstone, where cars, services and natural beauty all converge.

8 Lake area. The largest body of water within the park, Yellowstone Lake is believed to have once been 200 feet higher than it presently is. This is a full-service area with a hotel, lodge, restaurants, campsites, cabins, and general stores.

WYOMING

GETTING ORIENTED

At more than 2.2 million acres, Yellowstone National Park is considered one of America's most scenic and diverse national parks. The park has five entrances, each with its own attractions: the South has the Lewis River canyon; the East, Sylvan Pass; the West, the Madison River valley; the North, the beautiful Paradise Valley; and the Northeast, the spectacular Beartooth Pass.

37

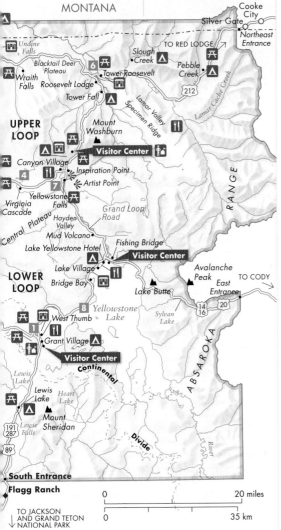

KEY	
👥	Ranger Station
△	Campground
⊼	Picnic Area
🍴	Restaurant
🏠	Lodge
🥾	Trailhead
🚻	Restrooms
⇒	Scenic Viewpoint
⋯⋯	Walking/Hiking Trails

YELLOWSTONE PLANNER

When to Go

There are two major seasons in Yellowstone: summer (May–October), the only time when most of the park's roads are open to cars; and winter (mid-December–February), when over-snow travel (snowmobiles, snow coaches, and skis) takes a fraction of the number of visitors to a frigid, bucolic sanctuary. Except for services at park headquarters at Mammoth Hot Springs, the park closes from October to mid-December and from March to late April or early May.

You'll find big crowds from mid-July to mid-August. There are fewer people in the park the month or two before and after this peak season, but there are also fewer facilities open. There's also more rain, especially at lower elevations. Except for holiday weekends, there are few visitors in winter. Snow is possible year-round at high elevations.

Flora and Fauna

Eighty percent of Yellowstone is forest, and the great majority of it is lodgepole pine. Miles and miles of the "telephone pole" pines burned in the massive 1988 fire that burned more than 35% of the park. The fire's heat created the ideal condition for the lodgepole pine's serotinous cones to release their seeds—which now provides a stark juxtaposition between 20-year-old and 100-year-old trees.

Yellowstone's scenery astonishes any time of day, though the play of light and shadow makes the park most appealing in early morning and late afternoon. That's exactly when you should be looking for wildlife, as most are active around dawn and dusk, moving out of the forest in search of food and water. May and June are the best months for seeing baby bison, moose, and other young arrivals. Look for glacier lilies among the spring wildflowers and goldenrod amidst the changing foliate of fall. Winter visitors see the park at its most magical, with steam billowing from geyser basins to wreath trees in ice, and elk foraging close to roads transformed into ski trails.

Bison, elk, and coyotes populate virtually all areas; elk and bison particularly like river valleys and the geyser basins. Moose like marshy areas along Yellowstone Lake and in the northeast corner of the park. Wolves are most common in the Lamar Valley and areas south of Mammoth; bears are most visible in the Pelican Valley–Fishing Bridge area, near Dunraven Pass, and near Mammoth. Watch for trumpeter swans along the Yellowstone River and for sandhill cranes near the Firehole River and in Madison Valley.

AVG. HIGH/LOW TEMPS

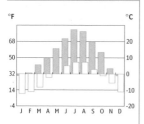

Getting Here and Around

Yellowstone National Park is served by airports in nearby communities, including Cody, Wyoming, one hour east; Jackson, Wyoming, one hour south; Bozeman, Montana, 90 minutes north; and West Yellowstone, Montana, just outside the park's west gate, which has only summer service. The best places to rent cars in the region are at airports in Cody, Jackson, Bozeman, and West Yellowstone. There is no commercial bus service to Yellowstone.

Yellowstone is well away from the interstates, so drivers make their way here on two-lane highways that are long on miles and scenery. From Interstate 80, take U.S. 191 north from Rock Springs; it's about 177 mi to Jackson, then another 60 mi north to Yellowstone. From Interstate 90, head south at Livingston, Montana, 80 mi to Gardiner and the park's North Entrance. From Bozeman travel south 90 mi to West Yellowstone.

Yellowstone has five primary entrances. Many visitors arrive through the South Entrance, north of Grand Teton National Park and Jackson, Wyoming. Other entrances are the East Entrance, with a main point of origin in Cody, Wyoming; the West Entrance at West Yellowstone, Montana and the North Entrance at Gardiner, Montana (these are the only two entrances open in winter); and the Northeast Entrance at Cooke City, Montana, which can be reached from either Cody, Wyoming, via the Chief Joseph Scenic Highway, or from Red Lodge, Montana, over the Beartooth Pass.

■TIP➔ The best way to keep your bearings in Yellowstone is to remember that the major roads form a figure eight, known as the Grand Loop, which all entrance roads feed into. It doesn't matter at which point you begin, as you can hit most of the major sights if you follow the entire route.

The 370 mi of public roads in the park used to be riddled with potholes and had narrow shoulders—a bit tight when a motor home was pulled over to the side to capture wildlife or scenery on film. But because of the park's efforts to upgrade its roads, most of them are now wide and smooth. Roadwork is likely every summer in some portion of the park—check the Yellowstone Today newspaper or ask a ranger. On holiday weekends, road construction usually halts so there are no construction delays for travelers. Remember, snow is possible any time of year in almost all areas of the park.

Where to Stay

There are a couple of factors to consider when deciding on which community to stay overnight in at the park. Some of these include deciding if you want to camp or if you want a hotel. But just as important is assessing your overnight accommodations based on the length of your trip. If you're only going to spend a day or two in the park, choose one location in the area that is most important for you to visit.

If you've never been to the park before and you only have a day or two, you'll probably want to choose Old Faithful, so you're near Yellowstone's most famous geyser. But if you're more interested in seeing the wildlife, you may want to choose the Canyon or Lake area so you're near Hayden and Pelican valleys.

On the other hand, if you're going to spend five days to a week or more in the park, you'll benefit from splitting your time between two or more regions of this huge park (such as Old Faithful and Canyon) so you aren't spending all of your time driving to the various communities. ⇨ *Where to Stay toward the back of the chapter for lodging reviews.*

37

Updated by
Steve Pastorino

A trip to Yellowstone has been a rich part of the American experience for five generations now. Though it's remote, we come, 3,000,000 strong year after year. When we arrive, we gasp at the incomparable combination of natural beauty, rugged wilderness, majestic peaks, and abundant wildlife. Indescribable geysers, mudpots, fumaroles, and hot springs make this magma-filled pressure cooker of a park unlike any place else on earth. If you're not here for the geysers, chances are that you've come to spot some of the teeming wildlife, from grazing bison to cruising trumpeter swans.

PARK ESSENTIALS

ACCESSIBILITY

Yellowstone has long been a National Park Service leader in providing for people with disabilities. Restrooms with sinks and flush toilets designed for those in wheelchairs are in all developed areas except Norris and West Thumb, where more rustic facilities are available. Accessible campsites and restrooms are at Bridge Bay, Canyon, Madison, Mammoth Hot Springs, and Grant Village campgrounds, while accessible campsites are found at both Lewis Lake and Slough Creek campgrounds. Ice Lake has an accessible backcountry campsite. An accessible fishing platform is about 3½ mi west of Madison at Mt. Haynes Overlook.

If you need a sign-language interpreter for NPS interpretive programs, arrange for it by calling ☎ 307/344–2251 three weeks in advance. For details, contact the accessibility coordinator at ☎ 307/344–2018 or pick up a free copy of *Visitor Guide to Accessible Features in Yellowstone National Park.*

ADMISSION FEES AND PERMITS

Entrance fees of $25 per car, $20 per motorcycle, and $12 per visitor (16 and older) arriving on a bus, motorcycle, or snowmobile provide visitors with access for seven days to both Yellowstone and Grand Teton. An annual pass to the two parks costs $50.

Fishing permits (available at ranger stations, visitor centers, and Yellowstone general stores) are required if you want to take advantage of Yellowstone's abundant lakes and streams. Live bait is not allowed, and for all native species of fish, a catch-and-release policy stands. Anglers 16 and older must purchase a $15 three-day permit, a $20 seven-day permit, or a $35 season permit; Those 12 to 15 need a free permit or must fish under the direct supervision of an adult with a permit; those 11 and under do not need a permit but must be supervised by an adult.

All camping outside of designated campgrounds requires a free back-country permit. Horseback riding also requires a free permit. All boats, motorized or nonmotorized, including float tubes, require a permit, which are $20 (annual) or $10 (seven days) for motorized boats and $10 (annual) or $5 (seven days) for nonmotorized vessels. Permits from Grand Teton National Park are valid in Yellowstone, but owners must register their vessel in Yellowstone.

ADMISSION HOURS

Depending on the weather, Yellowstone is generally open late April to November and mid-December to early March. In winter, only one road, going from the Northeast Entrance at Cooke City to the North Entrance at Gardiner, is open to wheeled vehicles; other roads are used by over-snow vehicles. The park is in the mountain time zone.

CELL-PHONE RECEPTION

A comprehensive cell-phone coverage plan is in process, but currently reception in the park is hit or miss and generally confined to developed areas like Old Faithful and Canyon. In general, don't count on it. Public telephones are near visitor centers and major park attractions.

■ TIP➔ Try to use inside phones rather than outside ones so your conversation doesn't distract you from being alert to wildlife that might approach you while you're on the phone.

RELIGIOUS SERVICES

Religious services are held at several park locations during the summer and on religious holidays. For times and locations of park services, check at visitor centers or lodging front desks.

SHOPS AND GROCERS

A dozen Yellowstone General Stores are located throughout the park. Each offers basic souvenirs and snacks, but several are destinations unto themselves. The 1950s-inspired Canyon General Store, the 100-year-old "Hamilton's Store" at Old Faithful and the Fishing Bridge store are three of the largest, combining architectural significance with a broad variety of groceries, books, apparel, outdoor needs, and soda-fountain-style food service.

Hours vary seasonally, but most stores are open 7:30 AM to 9:30 PM from late May to September; all except Mammoth General Store close for winter. All accept credit cards.

YELLOWSTONE IN ONE DAY

If you plan to spend just one full day in the park, your best approach would be to concentrate on one or two of the park's major areas, such as the two biggest attractions: the famous Old Faithful geyser and the Grand Canyon of the Yellowstone. En route between these attractions, you can see geothermal activity and most likely some wildlife.

Plan on at least two hours for Old Faithful, one of the most iconic landmarks in America. Eruptions are approximately 90 minutes apart, though they can be as close as 60 minutes apart. Before and after an eruption you can explore the surrounding geyser basin and Old Faithful Inn. To the north of Old Faithful, make Grand Prismatic Spring your can't-miss geothermal stop; farther north, near Madison, veer off the road to the west to do the short Firehole Canyon Drive to see the Firehole River cut a small canyon and waterfall (Firehole Falls).

If you're arriving from the east, start with sunrise at **Lake Butte, Fishing Bridge, and the wildlife-rich Hayden Valley** as you cross the park counter-clockwise to **Old Faithful**. To try and see wolves or bears, call ahead and ask when/if rangers will be stationed at roadside turnouts with spotting scopes. Alternatively, hike any trail in the park at least 2 mi—and remember that you're entering the domain of wild and sometimes dangerous animals, so be alert and don't hike alone.

If you're entering through the North or Northeast entrance, begin at dawn looking for wolves and other animals in Lamar Valley, then head to **Tower-Roosevelt** and take a horseback ride into the surrounding forest. After your ride, continue west to **Mammoth Hot Springs**, where you can hike the **Lower Terrace Interpretive Trail** past Liberty Cap and other strange, brightly colored limestone formations. If you drive 1½ mi south of the visitor center you will reach the **Upper Terrace Drive**, for close-ups of hot springs. In the late afternoon, drive south, keeping an eye out for wildlife as you go—you're almost certain to see elk, buffalo, and possibly even a bear. Alternatively, from Tower-Roosevelt you can head south to go through **Canyon Village** to see the north or south rim of the **Grand Canyon of the Yellowstone** and its waterfalls, and then head west through Norris and Madison.

When you reach **Old Faithful**, you can place the famous geyser into context by walking the 1½-mi **Geyser Hill Loop**. Watch the next eruption from the deck of the **Old Faithful Inn**.

PARK CONTACT INFORMATION
Yellowstone National Park ⌂ *P.O. Box 168, Mammoth, WY 82190-0168* ☎ *307/344–7381* ⊕ *www.nps.gov/yell*.

SCENIC DRIVES

Firehole Canyon Drive. The 2-mi narrow asphalt road twists through a deep canyon and passes the 40-foot Firehole Falls. In summer look for a sign marking a pullout and swimming hole. This is one of only two places in the park (Boiling River on the North Entrance Road is the other) where you can safely and legally swim in the park's thermally heated waters. Look carefully for osprey and other raptors. ⊠ *1 mi south of Madison junction off Grand Loop Rd.*

Firehole Lake Drive. This one-way, 3-mi-long road takes you past **Great Fountain Geyser,** which shoots out jets of water reaching as high as 200 feet about twice a day. Rangers' predictions have a two-hour window of opportunity. Should you witness it, however, you'll be rewarded with a view of waves of water cascading down the terraces that form the edges of the geyser. Watch for bison, particularly in the winter. ⊠ *Firehole Lake Dr., 8 mi north of Old Faithful Old Faithful.*

Hayden Valley on Grand Loop Road. Bison, bears, coyotes, wolves, and birds of prey all call Hayden Valley home almost year-round. Once part of Yellowstone Lake, the broad valley now features peaceful meadows, rolling hills, and the placid Yellowstone River. There are multiple turn-outs and picnic areas on the 16-mi drive, many with views of the river and valley. Ask a ranger about "Grizzly Overlook," an unofficial site where wildlife watchers, including NPS rangers with spotting scopes for the public to use, congregate in the summer. It's three turnouts north of Mud Volcano—there's no sign, so look for the timber railings. ⊠ *Between Canyon and Fishing Bridge on Grand Loop Rd.*

Fodor's Choice
★ **Northeast Entrance Road and Lamar Valley.** The 29-mi road features the richest diversity of landscape of the five entrance roads. Just after you enter the park, you cut between 10,928-foot Abiathar Peak and the 10,404-foot Barronette Peak. You pass the extinct geothermal cone called Soda Butte as well as the two nicest campgrounds in the park, Pebble Creek and Slough Creek. Lamar Valley is the melancholy home to hundreds of bison, while the rugged peaks and ridges adjacent to it are home to some of the park's most famous wolf packs (reintroduced in 1995). The main wolf-watching activities in the park occur here during early-morning and late-evening hours year-round. As you exit Lamar Valley, the road crosses the Yellowstone River before leading you to the rustic Roosevelt Lodge. ⊠ *From Northeast Entrance near Cooke City to junction with Grand Loop Rd. at Roosevelt Lodge.*

Northeastern Grand Loop. A 19-mi segment of Grand Loop Road climbs to nearly 9,000 feet as it passes some of the park's finest scenery, twisting beneath a series of leaning basalt towers 40 to 50 feet high. That behemoth to the east is 10,243-foot Mt. Washburn. ⊠ *Between Canyon Village and Roosevelt Falls.*

Upper Terrace Drive. Limber pines as old as 500 years line this 1½-mi loop near Mammoth Hot Springs, where a variety of mosses grow through white travertine, composed of lime deposited by the area's hot springs. ⊠ *Approximately 2 mi by car from Mammoth Hot Springs Hotel on Grand Loop Rd. Reachable by foot from Lower Terrace Dr.*

WHAT TO SEE

Along the park's main drive—the Grand Loop (also referred to as Yellowstone's Figure Eight)—are eight primary "communities," or developed areas. On the Western Yellowstone map are five of those

37

communities—Grant Village, Old Faithful, Madison, Norris, and Mammoth Hot Springs—with their respective sights, while the East Yellowstone map shows the remaining three—Tower-Roosevelt, Canyon, and Lake (for Yellowstone Lake area)—with their respective sights.

GRANT VILLAGE AND WEST THUMB

Along the western edge of Yellowstone Lake (called the West Thumb), Grant Village is the first community you encounter from the South Entrance. It has basic lodging and dining facilities.

SCENIC STOPS

West Thumb Geyser Basin. The primary Yellowstone caldera was created by one volcanic eruption, while West Thumb came about as the result of another, later volcanic eruption. This unique geyser basin is the only place to see active geothermal features in Yellowstone Lake. Two boardwalk loops are offered; take the longer one to see features like Fishing Cone, where fishermen used to catch fish, pivot, and drop their fish straight into boiling water for cooking without ever taking it off the hook. This area is particularly popular for winter visitors, who take advantage of the nearby warming hut and a stroll around the geyser basin before continuing their trip via snow coach or snowmobile. ⊠ *Grand Loop Rd., 22 mi north of South Entrance, West Thumb.*

VISITOR CENTER

Grant Village Visitor Center. Each visitor center in the park tells a small piece of the park's history. This one tells the story of fire in the park. A seminal moment in Yellowstone's historical record, the 1988 fire burned 36% of the total acreage of the park and forced multiple federal agencies to reevaluate their fire-control policies. Watch an informative video, purchase maps or books, and learn more about the 25,000 firefighters from across America who fought the 1988 fire. After a 2008 remodeling, bathrooms and a backcountry office are now housed here as well. ⊠ *Grant Village* ☎ *307/242–2650* ۞ *Late May–Sept. 30, daily 8–7.*

West Thumb Information Station. This historic log cabin houses a Yellowstone Association bookstore and doubles as a warming hut in the winter. There are restrooms in the parking area. Check for informal ranger-led discussions beneath the old sequoia tree in the summer. ⊠ *West Thumb* ۞ *Late May–late Sept., daily 9–5.*

OLD FAITHFUL

★ The world's most famous geyser is the centerpiece of this area, which has extensive boardwalks through the Upper Geyser Basin and equally extensive visitor services, including several choices in lodging and dining. In winter you can dine and stay in this area and cross-country ski or snowshoe through the Geyser Basin.

HISTORICAL SITES

Old Faithful Inn. It's hard to imagine how any work could be accomplished when snow and ice blanket the region, but this historic hotel was constructed over the course of a single winter in 1903. Serving as a lodging establishment since 1904, this massive log structure is an attraction in its own right. Even if you don't spend a night at the Old Faithful Inn, walk through or take the free 45-minute guided tour to admire its massive open-beam lobby and rock fireplace (where tours begin). There are

Fodor's Choice
★

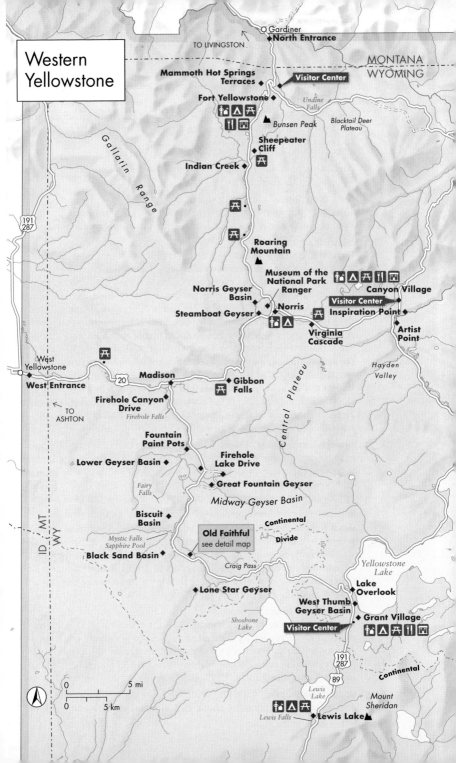

antique writing desks on the second-floor balcony, and during evening hours a pianist plays there as well. You can watch Old Faithful geyser from two second-floor outdoor decks. ⊠ *Old Faithful Bypass Rd., Old Faithful* ☏ *307/344–7901* ⊙ *May–mid-Oct.; tours daily, times vary.*

SCENIC STOPS

Biscuit Basin. North of Old Faithful, this basin is also the trailhead for the Mystic Falls Trail. The namesake "biscuit" formations were reduced to crumbs when Sapphire Pool erupted after the 1959 Hebgen Lake earthquake. Now, Sapphire is a calm, beautiful blue pool again, but that could change at any moment. ⊠ *3 mi north of Old Faithful on Grand Loop Rd., Old Faithful.*

Black Sand Basin. There are a dozen hot springs and geysers near the cloverleaf entrance from Grand Loop Road to Old Faithful. Emerald Pool is one of the prettiest. ⊠ *North of Old Faithful on Grand Loop Rd., Old Faithful.*

☺ **Geyser Hill Loop.** Along the 1.3-mi Geyser Hill Loop boardwalk you will see active thermal features such as violent Giantess Geyser. Normally erupting only a few times each year, Giantess spouts 100 to 250 feet in the air for five to eight minutes once or twice hourly for 12 to 43 hours. Nearby Doublet Pool's two adjacent springs have complex ledges and deep blue waters, which are highly photogenic. Starting as a gentle pool, Anemone Geyser overflows, bubbles, and finally erupts 10 feet or more, every three to eight minutes. The loop boardwalk brings you close to the action, making it especially appealing to children intrigued with the sights and sounds of the basin. Also keep a lookout for elk and buffalo in this area. To reach Geyser Hill, head counterclockwise around the Old Faithful boardwalk 0.3 mi from the visitor center, crossing the Firehole River and entering Upper Geyser Basin. ⊠ *Old Faithful, mi from Old Faithful Visitor Center, Old Faithful.*

★ **Grand Prismatic Spring.** This is Yellowstone's largest hot spring, 370 feet in diameter. It's in the Midway Geyser Basin, and you can reach it by following the boardwalk. The spring is deep blue in color, with yellow and orange rings formed by bacteria that give it the effect of a prism. For a stunning perspective, look down on in from the Fairy Falls Trail. ⊠ *Midway Geyser Basin, off Grand Loop Rd.*

Great Fountain Geyser. This geyser erupts twice a day; rangers predict when it will shoot some 200 feet into the air, but their prediction has a window of opportunity a couple of hours long. Should you see Great Fountain spew, however, you'll be rewarded with a view of waves of water cascading down the terraces that form the edges of the geyser. ⊠ *Firehole Lake Dr., north of Old Faithful.*

Lower Geyser Basin. Shooting more than 150 feet in the air, the Great Fountain Geyser is the most spectacular sight in this basin. Less impressive but more regular is White Dome Geyser, which shoots from a 20-foot-tall cone. You'll also find pink mudpots and blue pools at the basin's Fountain Paint Pots. ⊠ *Midway between Old Faithful and Madison on Grand Loop Rd.*

Upper Geyser Basin. With Old Faithful as its central attraction, this mile-square basin contains about 140 different geysers—one-fifth of

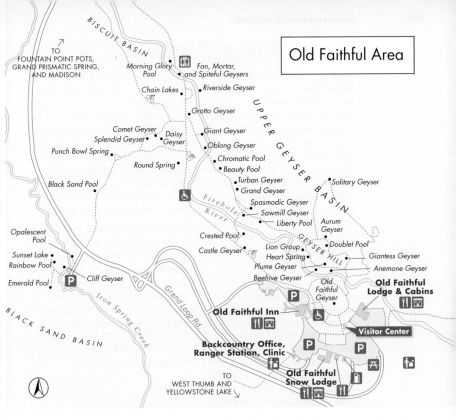

the known geysers in the world. It's an excellent place to spend a day or more exploring. You will find a complex system of boardwalks and trails—some of them used as bicycle trails—that take you to the basin's various attractions. ⊠ *Old Faithful.*

☺ **Old Faithful.** Almost every visitor includes the world's most famous gey-
Fodor's Choice ser on his or her itinerary. Yellowstone's most predictable big geyser—
★ although not its largest or most regular—sometimes reaches 180 feet, but it averages 130 feet. Sometimes it doesn't shoot as high, but in those cases the eruptions usually last longer. The mysterious plumbing of Yellowstone has lengthened Old Faithful's cycle somewhat in recent years, to every 94 minutes or so. To find out when Old Faithful is likely to erupt, check at the visitor center or at any of the lodging properties in the area. You can view the eruption from a bench just yards away, from the dining room at the lodge cafeteria, or the second-floor balcony of Old Faithful Inn. The 1-mi hike to Observation Point yields yet another view—from above—of the geyser and its surrounding basin. ⊠ *Southwest segment, Grand Loop Rd.*

Midway Geyser Basin. Called "Hell's Half Acre" by writer Rudyard Kipling, Midway Geyser Basin is a more interesting stop than Lower Geyser Basin. A series of boardwalks wind their way to the Excelsior Geyser, which deposits 4,000 gallons of vivid blue water per minute into the Firehole

A GOOD TOUR: OLD FAITHFUL

Begin your tour at **Old Faithful Visitor Center**, where you should pick up the Old Faithful area trail guide (50 cents) and check a board with the latest predictions for six geyser eruptions. You don't need to jostle for position on the boardwalk directly in front of the visitor's center to enjoy Old Faithful—any angle from the boardwalk surrounding the geyser is impressive—or view it from the deck of the **Old Faithful Inn**. And speaking of that famous, century-old inn, make time to stop in to check out its massive log-construction interior.

At Old Faithful Village you're in the heart of the **Upper Geyser Basin**, the densest concentration of geysers on Earth with about 140 geysers in a one square mile. The biggest attraction is where you should begin your tour: **Old Faithful** spouts 130 to 180 feet approximately every 94 minutes. Once you've watched Old Faithful erupt, explore the larger basin with a hike around **Geyser Hill**, where you

may see wildlife as well as thermal features. Follow the trail north to the **Morning Glory Pool**, with its unique flower shape. Along this trail are Castle, Grand, and Riverside geysers. Return to the village and continue by car to **Black Sand Basin** or **Biscuit Basin**. At Biscuit Basin, follow the boardwalks to the trailhead for the Mystic Falls Trail, where you can get views of the Upper Geyser Basin.

Take a break from geyser watching with a packed lunch at the Whiskey Flat picnic area. Afterward, continue your drive toward **Lower Geyser Basin**, with its colorful **Fountain Paint Pots**. Then, on the way back to Old Faithful, stop at **Midway Geyser Basin**, where steaming runoff from the colorful 370-foot **Grand Prismatic Spring** crash into the Firehole River each minute.

Relax and revisit your long day with dinner (advance reservations required!) at the Old Faithful Inn, or enjoy drinks on the second floor.

River. Just above Excelsior is Yellowstone's largest hot spring, Grand Prismatic Spring. Measuring 370 feet in diameter, it's deep blue in color with yellow and orange rings formed by bacteria that give it the effect of a prism. ⊠ *Between Old Faithful and Madison on Grand Loop Rd.*

Morning Glory Pool. Shaped somewhat like a morning glory flower, this pool once was a deep blue, but tourists dropping coins and other debris into it clogged the plumbing vent. As a result, the color is no longer as striking. To reach the pool, follow the boardwalk past Geyser Hill Loop and stately Castle Geyser, which has the biggest cone in Yellowstone. It erupts every 10 to 12 hours, to heights of 90 feet, for as much as an hour at a time. From Morning Glory Pool it's about 2 mi back to the Old Faithful visitor center. Morning Glory is the inspiration for popular children's author Jan Brett's story *Hedgie Blasts Off,* in which a hedge-hog goes to another planet to unclog a geyser damaged by space tourists' debris. ⊠ *At the north end of Upper Geyser Basin at Old Faithful.*

VISITOR CENTER
Old Faithful Visitor Center. A new LEED-certified visitor center is sched-uled to open here by August 2010, and plans indicate it will be one of the jewels of the entire national park system. This is the best place

to inquire about geyser eruption predictions. Backcountry and fishing permits are handled out of the ranger station adjacent to the Old Faithful Snow Lodge. ⊠ *Old Faithful Bypass Rd.* ☎ *307/545–2750* ◌ *Late May–late Sept., daily 8–7; late Dec.–early Mar., daily 9–6.*

MADISON

The area around the junction of the West Entrance Road and the Lower Loop is a good place to take a break as you travel through the park, because you will almost always see bison grazing along the Madison River, and often elk are in the area as well. Limited visitor services are here, including no dining facilities.

SCENIC STOPS

Gibbon Falls. Water rushes over the caldera rim in this 84-foot waterfall on the Gibbon River. You can see it on your right from the road as you're driving east from Madison to Canyon. ⊠ *4 mi east of Madison on Grand Loop Rd.*

VISITOR CENTER

Madison Information Center. In this National Historic Landmark, the ranger shares the space with a Yellowstone Association bookstore, which features high-quality books, guides, music, and learning aids. You may find spotting scopes set up for wildlife viewing out the rear window; if this is the case, look for eagles, swans, bison, elk, and more. Rangers will answer questions about the park, provide basic hiking information and maps, and issue permits for backcountry camping and fishing. Picnic tables, toilets, and an amphitheater for summer-evening ranger programs are shared with the nearby Madison campground. The park encourages Junior Rangers to start here. ⊠ *Grand Loop Rd. at West Entrance Rd.* ☎ *307/344–2821* ◌ *Late May–late Sept., daily 9–6.*

NORRIS

The area at the western junction of the Upper and Lower Loops has the most active geyser basin in the park. The underground plumbing occasionally reaches such high temperatures—the ground itself has heated up in areas to nearly 200°F—that a portion of the basin is periodically closed for safety reasons. There are limited visitor services: two museums, a bookstore, and a picnic area. ■TIP➔ Ask rangers at the Norris Geyser Basin Museum when different geysers are expected to erupt and to plan your walk accordingly.

SCENIC STOPS

Back Basin. The trail through Back Basin is a 1½-mi loop guiding you past dozens of features highlighted by Steamboat Geyser. When it erupts fully (most recently in 1985), it's the world's largest, climbing 400 feet above the basin. More often, Steamboat growls and spits constantly, sending clouds of steam high above the basin. Kids will love the Puff 'n' Stuff Geyser and the mysterious cave-like Green Dragon Spring. Ask the Norris ranger for an anticipated schedule of geyser eruptions—you might catch the Echinus Geyser, which erupts almost hourly. ⊠ *Grand Loop Rd. at Norris junction.*

◌ ★ **Norris Geyser Basin.** From the Norris Ranger Station, choose either Porcelain Basin or Back Basin, or both. These volatile thermal features are constantly changing, although you can expect to find a variety of geysers and springs here at any time. The area is accessible via an extensive system of boardwalks, some of them suitable for people with disabilities. The famous Steamboat Geyser is here. ⊠ *Grand Loop Rd. at Norris.*

Porcelain Basin. In the eastern portion of the Norris Geyser Basin this thermal area is reached by a ¾-mi, partially boardwalked loop from Norris Geyser Basin Museum. In this geothermal field of whitish geyserite stone, the earth bulges and belches from the underground pressure. You'll find bubbling pools, some milky white and others ringed in orange because of the minerals in the water, as well as small geysers such as extremely active Whirligig. ⊠ *Grand Loop Rd.*

MAMMOTH HOT SPRINGS

This northern community in the park is known for its massive natural terraces, where mineral water flows continuously, building an ever-changing display. (Note, however, that water levels can fluctuate, so if it's late in a particularly dry summer, you won't see the terraces in all their glory.) You will often see elk grazing here. In the early days of the park, it was the site of Fort Yellowstone, and the brick buildings constructed during that era are still used for various park activities.

HISTORICAL SITES

Fort Yellowstone. The oldest buildings at Mammoth Hot Springs served as Fort Yellowstone from 1886 to 1916, the period when the U.S. Army managed the park. The redbrick buildings cluster around an open area reminiscent of a frontier-era fort parade ground. You can pick up a self-guided tour map of the area to make your way around the historic fort structures. ⊠ *Mammoth Hot Springs.*

SCENIC STOPS

Ⓒ
★ **Mammoth Hot Springs Terraces.** Multicolor travertine terraces formed by slowly escaping hot mineral water mark this unusual geological formation. It constantly changes as a result of shifts in water flow. You can explore the terraces via an elaborate network of boardwalks. The best is the Lower Terrace Interpretive Trail. If you start at Liberty Cap, at the area's north end, and head uphill on the boardwalks, you'll pass bright and ornately terraced Minerva Spring. It's about an hour walk. Along the way you may spy elk, as they graze nearby. Alternatively, you can drive up to the Lower Terrace Overlook on Upper Terrace Drive and take the boardwalks down past New Blue Springs to the Lower Terrace. This route, which also take an hour, works especially well if you can park a second vehicle at the foot of Lower Terrace. ■TIP➔ There are lots of steps on the lower terrace boardwalks, so plan to take your time there. ⊠ *Northwest corner of Grand Loop Rd.*

VISITOR CENTER

Ⓒ **Albright Visitor Center.** Serving as bachelor quarters for cavalry officers from 1886 to 1918, this red-roof building now holds a museum with exhibits on the early inhabitants of the region and a theater showing films about the history of the park. There are original Thomas Moran paintings of the park on display here as well. Kids and taxidermists will love extensive displays of park wildlife, including bears and wolves. ⊠ *Mammoth Hot Springs* ☎ *307/344–2263* ☉ *Late May–Sept., daily 8–7; Oct.–late May, daily 9–6.*

TOWER-ROOSEVELT

The northeast region of Yellowstone is the least-visited part of the park, making it a great place to explore without running into as many people. Packs of wolves may be spotted in the Lamar Valley.

SCENIC STOPS

Petrified Tree. If you enjoy seeing bears in zoo pens, you'll get the same level of satisfaction as you look at this geological landmark surrounded on all four sides by high wrought-iron gates. Unfortunately, a century of vandalism has forced park officials to completely enclose this 45-million-year-old redwood tree—utterly ruining the experience. ⊠ *Grand Loop Rd., 1 mi west of Tower-Roosevelt.*

Tower Fall. This is one of the easiest waterfalls to see from the roadside (follow signs to the lookout point); you can also view volcanic pinnacles here. Tower Creek plunges 132 feet at this waterfall to join the Yellowstone River. A trail runs to the base of the falls, but it is closed at this writing (and for the foreseeable future) because of erosion several hundred yards above the bottom of the canyon; thus, there is no access to the base of Tower Fall from this trail at present. ⊠ *2 mi south of Roosevelt on Grand Loop Rd.*

CANYON

The Yellowstone River's source is in the Absaroka Mountains in the southeast corner of the park. It winds its way through the heart of the park, entering Yellowstone Lake then heading northward under Fishing Ridge through Hayden Valley. When it cuts through the multicolored Grand Canyon of the Yellowstone, it creates one of the most spectacular gorges in the world, enticing visitors with its steep canyon walls and waterfalls. All types of visitors' services are here, as well as lots of hiking opportunities.

37

SCENIC STOPS

★ **Artist Point.** An impressive view of the Lower Falls of the Yellowstone River is seen from this point, which has two different viewing levels, one of which is accessible to wheelchairs. The South Rim Trail goes right past this point, and there is a nearby parking area open in both summer and winter. ⊠ *East end of South Rim Rd.*

Fodor's Choice

★ **Grand Canyon of the Yellowstone.** This stunning canyon is 23 mi long, but there is only one trail from rim to base. As a result, a majority of Park visitors clog the north and south rims to see Upper and Lower Falls. The North Rim Road was rebuilt and widened in 2008 and its new one-way (south to north) traffic pattern enhances visitor flow and enjoyment. Unless you're up for the six-hour strenuous hike called Seven Mile Hole, you have no choice but to join the crowds on the rims to see this natural wonder. The red-and-ochre canyon walls are topped with emerald-green forest. It's a feast of color. Also look for ospreys, which nest in the canyon's spires and precarious trees. ⊠ *Canyon.*

Lookout Point. Midway on the North Rim Trail—or accessible via the one-way North Rim Drive—Lookout Point gives you a view of the Grand Canyon of the Yellowstone from above the falls. Follow the right-hand fork in the path to descend a steep trail (approximately 500-foot elevation change) for an "eye-to-eye" view of the falls from a half mile downstream.

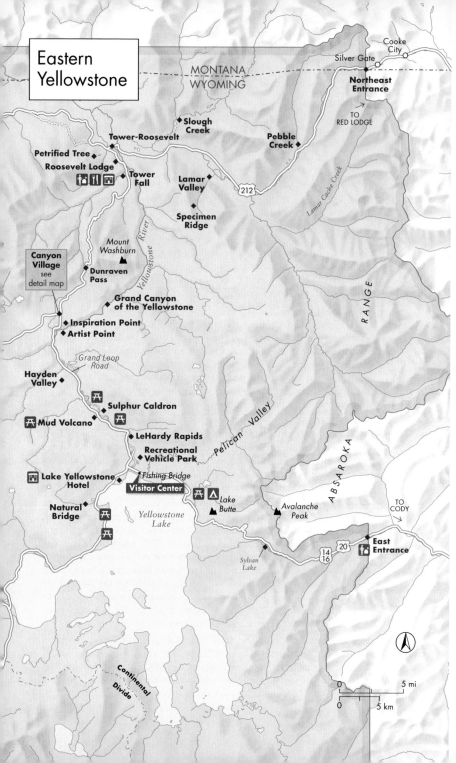

Eastern Yellowstone

Cooke City

Silver Gate

MONTANA
WYOMING

Northeast
Entrance

TO
RED LODGE

◆ Slough
Creek

Tower-Roosevelt

Pebble
Creek ◆

Petrified Tree ◆

Roosevelt Lodge

Tower
Fall

Lamar
Valley ◆

212

Specimen
Ridge ◆

Lamar Cache Creek

Mount
Washburn ▲

Canyon
Village
see
detail map

Dunraven
Pass ◆

Yellowstone River

R A N G E

◆ Grand Canyon
of the Yellowstone

◆ Inspiration Point
◆ Artist Point

Grand Loop
Road

Hayden
Valley ◆

Sulphur Caldron

Mud Volcano

◆ LeHardy Rapids

Recreational
Vehicle Park ◆

Pelican Valley

A B S A R O K A

Lake Yellowstone
Hotel

Fishing Bridge

Visitor Center

Natural
Bridge ◆

Lake
Butte ▲

Yellowstone
Lake

Avalanche
Peak ▲

TO
CODY

East
Entrance

14
20

16

Sylvan
Lake

Continental
Divide

0   5 mi

0   5 km

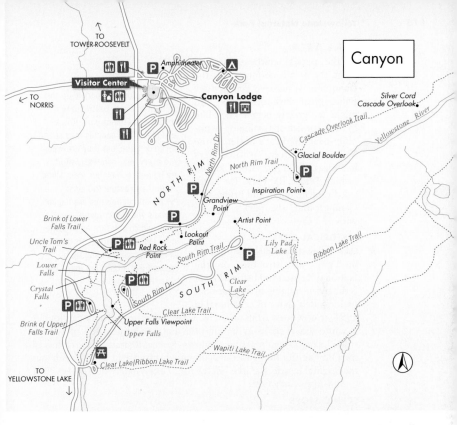

The best time to hike the trail is early morning, when sunlight reflects off the mist from the falls to create a rainbow. ⊠ *Off North Rim Dr.*

Upper Falls View. A spur road off Grand Loop Road south of Canyon gives you access to the west end of the North Rim Trail and takes you down a fairly steep trail for a view of Upper Falls from almost directly above. ⊠ *Off Grand Loop Rd., ¾ mi south of Canyon.*

VISITOR CENTER

☾ **Canyon Visitor Center.** This gleaming visitor center is the pride of the park
★ service with elaborate, interactive exhibits for adults and kids. The focus here is volcanoes and earthquakes, but there are also exhibits on Native Americans and park wildlife, including bison and wolves. The video titled *Land to Life* is a riveting look at the geo- and hydrothermal basis for the park. As at all visitor centers, you can obtain park information, backcountry camping permits, etc. The adjacent bookstore, operated by the Yellowstone Association, is the best in the park with guidebooks, trail maps, gifts, and hundreds of books on the park, its history, and the science surrounding it. ⊠ *Canyon Village* ☏ *307/242–2552* ☾ *Late May–late Sept., daily 8–8; early–mid-May, daily 9–5.*

LAKE AREA

In the park's southeastern segment, the area is permeated by the tranquility of massive Yellowstone Lake. Near Fishing Bridge you might see grizzly bears. They like to hunt for fish spawning or swimming near the lake's outlet to the Yellowstone River. Visitor centers include Lake Yellowstone Hotel, Fishing Bridge RV Park (for hardsided vehicles only), and Bridge Bay Campground, the park's largest, with 432 sites.

> ### CAUTION: A WILD PLACE
>
> As you explore the park keep this thought in mind: Yellowstone is not an amusement park. It is a wild place. The animals may seem docile or tame, but they are wild, and every year careless visitors are injured, sometimes even killed, when they venture too close. Particularly dangerous are female animals with their young, and bison, which can turn and charge in an instant. (Watch their tails: when they are standing up or crooked like a question mark, the bison is agitated.)

HISTORICAL SITES

★ **Lake Yellowstone Hotel.** Completed in 1891, this structure on the National Register of Historic Places is the oldest lodging in any national park. Spiffed up for its centennial in 1991, it now feels fresh and new. Casual daytime visitors can lounge in white wicker chairs in the sunroom and watch the waters of Yellowstone Lake through massive windows. Robert Reamer, the architect of the Old Faithful Inn, added its columned entrance in 1903 to enhance the original facade. ⊠ *Lake Village Rd., Lake Village* ☎ *307/344–7901* ☉ *Mid-May–early Oct.*

SCENIC STOPS

LeHardy Rapids. Witness one of nature's epic battles as cutthroat trout migrate upstream to spawn in spring by catapulting themselves out of the water to get by, over, and around rocks and rapids here on the Yellowstone River. The quarter-mile forested loop takes you to the river's edge. Also keep an eye out for waterfowl and bears, which feed on the trout. ⊠ *3 mi north of Fishing Bridge, Fishing Bridge.*

⟳ **Mud Volcano.** Gasses hiss from parking-lot vents underscoring the volatile nature of this area's geothermal features. The ¾-mi round-trip Mud Volcano Interpretive Trail loops gently around seething, sulfuric mudpots with names such as Black Dragon's Cauldron (which makes a noise like a dragon) and Sizzling Basin before making its way around Mud Volcano itself, a boiling pot of brown goo. ⊠ *10 mi south of Canyon; 4 mi north of Fishing Bridge on Grand Loop Rd., Fishing Bridge.*

Sulphur Caldron. You can smell the sulfur before you even leave your vehicle to walk to the overlook of Sulphur Caldron, where hissing steam escapes from a moonscape like surface as superheated bubbling mud. ⊠ *9½ mi south of Canyon; 4½ mi north of Fishing Bridge on Grand Loop Rd., Fishing Bridge.*

⟳ **Yellowstone Lake.** One of the world's largest alpine lakes, encompassing 132 Fodor's Choice square mi, Yellowstone Lake was formed when glaciers that once covered ★ the region melted into a caldera—a crater formed by a volcano. The lake has 141 mi of shoreline, less than one-third of it followed by the East

"On a cold and windy evening, walking along Yellowstone Lake, I came across this beautiful shot of a log engulfed by the flowing water." —photo by Brian Mosoff, Fodors.com member

Entrance Road and Grand Loop Road, along which you will often see moose, elk, waterfowl, and other wildlife. In winter you can sometimes see otters and coyotes stepping gingerly on the ice at the lake's edge. Many visitors head here for the excellent fishing—streams flowing into the lake give it an abundant supply of trout. ⊠ *Intersection of East Entrance Rd. and Grand Loop Rd., between Fishing Bridge and Grant Village.*

VISITOR CENTER

Fishing Bridge Visitor Center. This distinctive stone-and-log building, which was built in 1931, has been designated a National Historic Landmark. If you can't distinguish between a Clark's nut hatch and an ermine (note: one's a bird, the other a rodent), check out the extensive exhibits on park birds and other smaller wildlife. Step out the back door to find yourself on one of the beautiful black obsidian beaches of Yellowstone Lake. Adjacent is one of the park's larger amphitheaters. It features ranger presentations nightly in the summer. The Yellowstone Association bookstore here features books, guides, and other educational materials, but you can't buy coffee. ⊠ *East Entrance Rd., 1 mi from Grand Loop Rd.* ☎ *307/242–2450* ☉ *Memorial Day–late Sept., daily 8–7.*

SPORTS AND THE OUTDOORS

BOATING

Motorized boats are allowed only on Lewis Lake and Yellowstone Lake. Kayaking or canoeing is allowed on all park lakes except Sylvan Lake, Eleanor Lake, Twin Lakes, and Beach Springs Lagoon; however, most lakes are inaccessible by car, so accessing the park's lakes requires long portages. Boating is not allowed on any park river, except for the Lewis

River between Lewis Lake and Shoshone Lake, where nonmotorized boats are permitted.

You must purchase a seven-day, $5 permit for boats and floatables, or a $10 permit for motorized boats at Bridge Bay Ranger Station, South Entrance Ranger Station, Grant Village Backcountry Office, Lewis Lake Ranger Station (at the campground). Nonmotorized permits are available at the Northeast entrance, West Yellowstone Information Center; backcountry offices at Mammoth, Old Faithful, and Canyon; Bechler Ranger Station; and locations where motorized permits are sold. Annual permits are also available for $20.

Boat permits issued in Grand Teton National Park are honored in Yellowstone, but owners must register their vessel in Yellowstone and obtain a no-charge Yellowstone validation sticker from a permit issuing station.

OUTFITTERS AND EXPEDITIONS ☾ ★ Watercraft, from rowboats to powerboats, are available for trips on Yellowstone Lake at **Bridge Bay Marina** (⊠ *Grand Loop Rd., 2 mi south of Lake Village, Lake area* ☎ *307/344–7311* ⊠ *$76–$96/hr for guided cruisers for fishing or sightseeing; $9.75/hr for rowboat; $47/hr for small boat with outboard motor* ⊙ *Late May–early Sept., daily 8:30–8:30*). You also can rent 22- and 34-foot cabin cruisers with a guide. Daily rentals must be returned by 7 PM. Run by Xanterra Parks & Resorts, **Yellowstone Lake Scenic Cruises** (⊠ *Bridge Bay Marina, Lake area* ☎ *307/ 242–3876* ⊠ *Cruises $14.25* ⊙ *Late May–mid-Sept., daily 8:30 AM– 8:30 PM*), take visitors on one-hour cruises aboard the *Lake Queen II* throughout the day. The vessel makes its way from Bridge Bay to Stevenson Island and back. Reservations are strongly recommended.

FISHING

Anglers flock to Yellowstone beginning the Saturday of Memorial Day weekend, when fishing season begins. By the time the season ends in November, thousands have found a favorite spot along the park's rivers and streams. Native cutthroat trout are one of the prize catches, but four other varieties—brown, brook, lake, and rainbow—along with grayling and mountain whitefish inhabit Yellowstone's waters. Popular sportfishing opportunities include the Gardner and Yellowstone rivers as well as Soda Butte Creek, but the top fishing area in the region is Madison River, known to fly fishermen throughout the country.

Yellowstone fishing permits are required for people over age 16. Montana and Wyoming fishing permits are not valid in the park. Yellowstone fishing permits cost $15 for a three-day permit, $20 for a seven-day permit, or $35 for a season permit. Anglers ages 12 to 15 must have a (nonfee) permit or fish under direct supervision of an adult with a permit. Anglers younger than 12 don't need a permit but must be with an adult who knows the regulations. Permits are available at all ranger stations, visitor centers, and Yellowstone general stores.

HIKING

OLD FAITHFUL

Fountain Paint Pots Nature Trail. Take the easy ½-mi loop boardwalk of Fountain Paint Pot Nature Trail to see fumaroles (steam vents), blue pools, pink mudpots, and mini-geysers in this thermal area. It's popular in both summer and winter because it's right next to Grand Loop Road. ⊠ *Trail-head at Lower Geyser Basin, between Old Faithful and Madison.*

Ⓒ **Old Faithful Geyser Loop.** Old Faithful and its environs in the Upper
Fodor's Choice Geyser Basin are rich in short-walk options, starting with three con-
★ nected loops that depart from Old Faithful visitor center. The 0.75-mi loop simply circles the benches around Old Faithful, filled nearly all day long in summer with tourists. Currently erupting approximately every 94 minutes, Yellowstone's most frequently erupting big geyser—although not its largest or most regular—reaches heights of 100 to 180 feet, averaging 130 feet. ⊠ *Trailhead at Old Faithful Village, Old Faithful.*

MODERATE **Mystic Falls Trail.** From the Biscuit Basin boardwalk's west end, this trail
★ gently climbs 1 mi (3½ mi round-trip from Biscuit Basin parking area) through heavily burned forest to the lava-rock base of 70-foot Mystic Falls. It then switchbacks up Madison Plateau to a lookout with the park's least-crowded view of Old Faithful and the Upper Geyser Basin. ⊠ *Trailhead 3 mi north of Old Faithful Village off Grand Loop Rd., Old Faithful.*

MAMMOTH HOT SPRINGS

MODERATE **Bunsen Peak Trail.** Past the entrance to Bunsen Peak Road, the moderately difficult trail is a 4-mi, three-hour round-trip that climbs 1,300 feet to Bunsen Peak for a panoramic view of Blacktail Plateau, Swan Lake Flats, the Gallatin Mountains, and the Yellowstone River valley. (Use a topographical map to find these landmarks.) ⊠ *Trailhead at Grand Loop Rd., 1½ mi south of Mammoth Hot Springs.*

TOWER-ROOSEVELT

MODERATE **Slough Creek Trail.** Starting at Slough Creek Campground, this trail
Fodor's Choice climbs steeply along a historic wagon trail for the first 1½ mi before
★ reaching expansive meadows and prime fishing spots, where moose are common and grizzlies occasionally wander. From this point the trail, now mostly level, meanders another 9½ mi to the park's northern boundary. Anglers absolutely rave about this trail. ⊠ *Trailhead 7 mi east of Tower-Roosevelt off Northeast Entrance Rd.*

CANYON

MODERATE **Brink of the Lower Falls Trail.** Especially scenic, this trail branches off of
★ the North Rim Trail at the Brink of the Upper Falls parking area. The steep ½-mi one-way trail switchbacks 600 feet down to within a few yards of the top of the Yellowstone River's Lower Falls. ⊠ *Trailhead 300 yards east of Grand Loop Rd. on entrance to North Rim Drive, 1 mi south of Canyon.*

★ **North Rim Trail.** Offering great views of the Grand Canyon of the Yel-lowstone, the 3-mi North Rim Trail runs from Inspiration Point to Chittenden Bridge. You can wander along small sections of the trail or combine it with the South Rim Trail. Especially scenic is the 0.5-mi sec-tion of the North Rim Trail from the Brink of the Upper Falls parking area to Chittenden Bridge that hugs the rushing Yellowstone River as it approaches the canyon. This trail is paved and fully accessible between Lookout Point and Grand View. ⊠ *Trailhead 1 mi south of Canyon.*

Continued on page 829

GRAND HISSY FITS

By Brian Kevin

Steaming, bubbling,
and erupting
throughout the day
like giant teapots.

Yellowstone's geothermal features are constantly putting on a show. The 10,000 hot springs, mud pots, and fumaroles, plus 300 or so active geysers within the park comprise more than half the entire world's thermal features. You'd need to search two or three other continents for as many geysers as you can see during a single afternoon around Old Faithful.

HEATING UP

Past eruptions of cataclysmic volcanoes brought about the steaming, vaporous landscape of Yellowstone today. The heat from the magma (molten rock) under the Yellowstone Caldera, an active volcano, continues to fuel the park's geyser basins, such as the Upper Geyser Basin, where more than 200 spouters cram into less than two square miles; and Norris, where water 1,000 feet below ground is 450° F. The complex underground plumbing in these geyser basins is affected by earthquakes and other subterranean hijinks that geologists are only beginning to understand. Some spouters spring to life, while others fall dormant with little or no warning.

HOT SPOT TIPS

■ **Stay on trails and boardwalks.** In some areas, like in Norris, water boils at temperatures of more than 200°. If you want to venture into the back country, where there are no boardwalks, consult a ranger first.

■ **Leave the area if you feel sick or dizzy.** You might be feeling this way due to overexposure to various thermal gases.

■ **These hot springs aren't for bathing.** The pH levels of some of these features are extremely acidic.

■ **They also aren't wishing wells.** In the past people threw hundreds of coins into the bright blue Morning Glory Pool. The coins clogged the pool's natural water vents, causing it to change to a sickly green color.

(left) Old Faithful. (above) Punch Bowl Spring.

HOW DO GEYSERS WORK?

A few main ingredients make geysers possible: abundant water, a heat source, a certain kind of plumbing system, and rock strong enough to withstand some serious pressure. The layout of any one geyser's underground plumbing may vary, but we know that below each vent is a system of fissures and chambers, with constrictions here and there that prevent hot water from rising to the surface. As the underground water heats up, these constrictions and the cooler surface water "cap" the whole system, keeping it from boiling over and ratcheting up the underground pressure. When a few steam bubbles eventually fight their way through the constrictions, the result is like uncapping a shaken-up soda bottle, when the released pressure causes the soda to spray.

FUN FACTS

■ A cone geyser (like Lone Star Geyser in Yellowstone's backcountry) has a spout-like formation around its vent, formed by silica particles deposited during eruptions.

■ A fountain geyser (like Daisy Geyser in the Old Faithful area) erupts from a vent submerged in a hot spring-like pool. Eruptions tend to be smaller and more sporadic.

Yellowstone's tallest geyser is Steamboat, in Norris, shooting up to 350 feet high.

When they erupt, geysers sometimes create rainbows amid their spray.

❶ RECHARGE STAGE

Groundwater accumulates in plumbing and is heated by the volcano. Some hot water flashes to steam and bubbles try to rise toward surface.

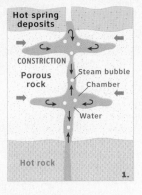

Hot spring deposits

CONSTRICTION

Porous rock — Steam bubble

Chamber

Water

Hot rock

1.

❷ PRELIMINARY ERUPTION STAGE

Pressure builds as steam bubbles clog at constriction. High pressure raises the boiling point, preventing superheated water from becoming steam.

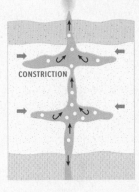

CONSTRICTION

❸ ERUPTION STAGE

Bubbles squeeze through constriction, displacing surface water and relieving pressure. Trapped water flashes to steam, forcing water out of the chambers and causing a chain reaction.

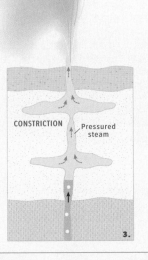

CONSTRICTION — Pressured steam

3.

❹ RECOVERY STAGE

Eruption ends when the chambers are emptied or the temperature falls below boiling. Chambers begin to refill with ground water and the process begins again.

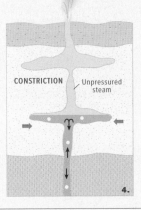

CONSTRICTION — Unpressured steam

4.

37

IN FOCUS GRAND HISSY FITS

(left) Lone Star Geyser.

HOW DO HOT SPRINGS WORK?

Essentially, what keeps a hot spring from becoming a geyser is a lack of constriction in its underground plumbing. Like their more explosive cousins, hot springs consist of water that seeps into the earth, only to simmer its way back up through fissures after it's heated by hot volcanic rocks. Unlike in constricted geysers, water in a hot spring can circulate by convection. Rising hot water displaces cooling surface water, which then sinks underground to be heated and eventually rise again. Thus the whole mixture keeps itself at a gurgly equilibrium. As it rises, superheated water dissolves some subterranean minerals, depositing them at the surface to form the sculptural terraces that surround many hot springs.

The vivid colors that characterize hot springs and their terraces can be attributed alternately to minerals like sulfur and iron or to thermophiles. Thermophiles are microorganisms that thrive in extremely high temperatures. Blooming in thick bacterial mats, they convert light to energy, like plants, and their bright photosynthetic pigments help give hot springs their rainbow hues. Scientists suppose only a small percentage of Yellowstone's thermophiles have been identified. Still, these microbes have had a big impact on science. In 1965, a microorganism called Thermus aquaticus, or Taq, was discovered in the Lower Geyser Basin. From it, scientists extracted an enzyme that revolutionized molecular biology, ultimately making possible both DNA fingerprinting and the mapping of the human genome. NASA is among those performing research in the park today, studying thermophiles to gain insight on extraterrestrial life.

WHAT'S THAT SMELL?

Most people think hot springs smell like rotten eggs; some even say "burnt gunpowder" and "paper mill smokestack." Whatever similie you settle on, there's no question that hot springs and other thermal features stink to high heaven. Sulphur gases escaping from the volcano produce distinctive smells. Other gases are reduced to the stinky chemical hydrogen sulfide, which bubbles up to the surface. In high concentration, hydrogen sulfide can actually kill you, but the small amounts released by thermals can only kill your appetite. It's because hydrogen sulfide is often present in volcanic areas that we associate brimstone (or sulfur) with the underworld.

DID YOU KNOW?

Grand Prismatic Spring (pictured here) is the world's third-largest hot spring, at more than 370 feet across. The pool's vivid red and orange colors drizzle down its runoff channels, but from the boardwalk you can only glimpse a portion of these psychedelic tentacles. Thank the little guys: heat-loving microorganisms (bacteria and algae) tint the Grand Prismatic Spring with a rainbow of colors.

THE INNER WORKINGS OF HOT SPRINGS

4 The water carries up dissolved minerals, which get deposited at the edges of the pool.

Hot Spring —— **3**

3 Heated water pools on the surface—it can be churning or quite calm.

POROUS ROCK

1 Water draining from the Earth's surface filters down through rock.

Groundwater

2 Water rises back up as it's heated geothermally.

A hot spring's inner plumbing isn't constricted, as in a geyser, so pressure doesn't reach an explosive point.

MAGMA

WHAT ARE FUMAROLES?

Take away the water from a hot spring and you're left with steam and other gas, forming a fumarole. Often called steam vents, these noisy thermals occur when available water boils away before reaching the surface. All that escapes the vent is heat, vapor, and the whisper-roar of a giant, menacing teakettle. Fumaroles are often found on high ground. The gases expelled from fumaroles might include carbon dioxide, sulfur dioxide, and hydrogen sulfide. Some hot spots, like Red Spouter in the Lower Geyser Basin, can exhibit different behaviors depending on the seasonal water table, so what's a fumarole today could be a hot spring in a few months.

FUN FACTS

■ The word fumarole comes from the Latin *fumus*, which means "smoke."

■ Fumaroles are also known as steam vents and solfataras, from *sulpha terra*, Latin for "land of sulfur."

■ Yellowstone's hottest fumarole is *Black Growler*, at Norris, which heats up to 280° F.Y

■ About 4,000 fumaroles are in Yellowstone.

IN FOCUS GRAND HISSY FITS

Fumarole

WHAT ARE MUD POTS?

Mud pots in Lower Geyser Basin.

Might as well say it up front: mud pots are great because their thick, bursting bubbles can sound like a chorus of rude noises or "greetings from the interior." That's why the few places they're found in Yellowstone are usually surrounded by gaggles of giggling visitors with video cameras rolling. A mud pot is basically just a hot spring where the water table results in a bubbling broth of water and clay. The acid gases react with surface rocks, breaking them down into silica and clay. As gases escape from below, bubbles swell and pop, flinging mud chunks onto the banks to form gloppy clay mounds. The mud's thickness varies with rainfall through the seasons.

FUN FACTS

■ Mud pots have been nicknamed "paint pots" due to iron and other metals tinting the mud.

■ The biggest cluster of mud pots in the park is in Pocket Basin in Lower Geyser Basin.

■ Before it exploded in 1872, Mud Volcano was 30 feet tall by 30 feet wide.

PHOTOGRAPHY TIPS

■ Set your alarm clock: generally, the best light for shooting the geothermal features is early in the morning. You'll avoid the thickest crowds then, too. The runner-up time is the late afternoon.

■ Breezy days are good for photographing geysers, since the steam will be blown away from the jetting water. But avoid standing downwind or your view can be clouded with steam.

■ If you get water from a thermal feature on your lens, dry it off as quickly as possible, because the water has a high mineral content that can damage your lens.

Thermal pool in the Rabbit Creek Thermal Area.

South Rim Trail. Partly paved and fairly flat, this 1¾-mi trail along the south rim of the Grand Canyon of the Yellowstone affords impressive views and photo opportunities of the canyon and falls of the Yellowstone River. It starts at Chittenden Bridge and ends at Artist Point. Along the way you can take a break for a snack or a picnic, but you'll need to sit on the ground, as there are no picnic tables. Beyond Artist Point, the trail gives way to a high plateau and high mountain meadows. Although popular with day hikers, technically, this is backcountry, and there were bear sightings in 2009, so prepare accordingly. ⊠ *Trailhead at Chittenden Bridge, off South Rim Dr., Canyon.*

ALTITUDE AWARENESS

Much of Yellowstone lies more than 7,500 feet above sea level—significantly higher than Denver. The most frequent incidents requiring medical attention in the park are respiratory problems, not animal attacks. So be aware of your physical limitations—as well as those of your young children or elderly companions if they are with you.

DIFFICULT **Uncle Tom's Trail.** Accessed by the South Rim Drive, the spectacular and strenuous 700-step trail ½ mi east of Chittenden Bridge descends 500 feet from the parking area to the roaring base of the Lower Falls of the Yellowstone. Much of this walk is on steel sheeting, which can have a film of ice on early summer mornings or anytime in spring and fall. ⊠ *Trailhead at South Rim Drive, 1 mi. east of Chittenden Bridge, 3 mi south of Canyon.*

LAKE

EASY **Storm Point Trail.** Well marked and mostly flat, this 1½-mi loop leaves the
☺ south side of the road for a perfect beginner's hike out to Yellowstone
★ Lake. The trail rounds the western edge of Indian Pond, then passes moose habitat on its way to Yellowstone Lake's Storm Point, named for its frequent afternoon windstorms and crashing waves. Heading west along the shore, you're likely to hear the shrill chirping of yellow-bellied marmots, rodents that grow as long as 2 feet. Also look for ducks, pelicans, and trumpeter swans. You will pass several small beaches where kids can explore on warm summer mornings. ⊠ *Trailhead 3 mi east of Lake Junction on East Entrance Rd., Fishing Bridge.*

DIFFICULT **Avalanche Peak Trail.** On a busy day in summer, maybe six parties will
Fodor'sChoice fill out the trail register at the Avalanche Peak trailhead, so you won't
★ have a lot of company on this hike. Yet many say it's one of the best-kept secrets in the park. Starting across from a parking area on the East Entrance Road, the difficult 4-mi, four-hour round-trip climbs 2,150 feet to the peak's 10,566-foot summit, from which you'll see the rugged Absaroka Mountains running north and south. Some of these peaks have patches of snow year-round. Look around the talus and tundra near the top of Avalanche Peak for alpine wildflowers and butterflies. Don't try this trail before late June or after early September—it may be covered in deep snow. Also, rangers discourage hikers from attempting this hike in September or October because of bear activity. Whenever you decide to go, carry a jacket: the winds at the top are strong. ⊠ *Trailhead 2 mi east of Sylvan Lake on north side of East Entrance Rd., Fishing Bridge.*

37

HORSEBACK RIDING

Xanterra Parks & Resorts offers horseback rides of one and two hours in length at Mammoth, Tower-Roosevelt, and Canyon. Advance reservations are recommended. Guides (and horses) catered to beginning riders (they estimate 90% of riders have not been on a horse in at least 10 years), but let them know if you're an experienced rider and would like a more challenging pace or ride.

> ### FAMILY PICKS
>
> ■ Old Faithful
>
> ■ Grand Canyon of the Yellowstone
>
> ■ Historic Yellow Bus Tours
>
> ■ Roosevelt Old West Cookout

Private stock can be brought into the park. Horses are not allowed in front-country campgrounds but are permitted in certain backcountry campsites. For information on planning a backcountry trip with stock, call the Backcountry Office (☎ 307/344–2160).

OUTFIT-
TER AND
EXPEDITIONS
☾

One- and two-hour horseback trail rides run by **Xanterra Parks & Resorts** (☎ 307/344–7311 ⊕ www.travelyellowstone.com ✉ $37–$56) leave from three sites in the park: Mammoth Hot Springs, Roosevelt Lodge, and Canyon Village. Children must be at least 8 years old and 48 inches tall; kids ages 8 to 11 must be accompanied by someone age 16 or older. In order not to spook horses or wildlife, guests are prohibited from bringing cameras or cell phones. Exclusively dedicated to trips inside Yellowstone National Park, **Yellowstone Wilderness Outfitters** (☎ 406/223–3300 ⊕ www.yellowstone.ws ✉ From $110 for half-day trips to $2,700 for multiday trips) employs musically inclined Jett Hitt as its multi-talented guide. Trips range from half- and full-day family rides to three- to 10-day pack trips in every area of the park. Trips may feature wildlife biologists and lecturers.

SKIING, SNOWSHOEING, AND SNOWMOBILING

Yellowstone can be the coldest place in the continental United States in winter, with temperatures of -30°F not uncommon. Still, winter-sports enthusiasts flock here when the park opens for its winter season the last week of December. Until early March, the park's roads teem with over-snow vehicles like snowmobiles and snow coaches. Its trails bristle with cross-country skiers and snowshoers.

Snowmobiling is an exhilarating way to experience Yellowstone. It's also controversial: there's heated debate about the pollution and disruption to animal habitats. The number of riders per day is limited, and you must have a reservation, a guide, and a four-stroke engine (which is less polluting than the more common two-stroke variety). About a dozen companies have been authorized to lead snowmobile excursions into the park from the North, West, South, and East entrances. Prices vary, as do itineraries and inclusions—be sure to ask about insurance, guides, taxes, park entrance fees, clothing, helmets, and meals. Regulations are subject to change.

At Mammoth Hot Springs Hotel and Old Faithful Snow Lodge, **Xanterra Parks & Resorts** (☎ 307/344–7901 ⊕ www.travelyellowstone.com) rents skis, snowmobiles, and snowshoes. Ski rentals (including skis, poles,

CLOSE UP | Yellowstone in Winter

To see a spectacularly different Yellowstone than that experienced by 90% of the park's visitors, come in winter. Rocky outcroppings are smoothed over. Waterfalls are transformed into jagged sheets of ice.

The best reason for a visit to Yellowstone between December and March is the opportunity to experience the park without the crowds. The first thing that strikes you during this season is the quiet. The gargantuan snowpack—as many as 200 inches annually at low elevation—seems to muffle the sounds of bison foraging in the geyser basins and of hot springs simmering. Yet even in the depths of a deep freeze, the park is never totally still: the mudpots bubble, geysers shoot skyward, and wind rustles the snow-covered pine trees. Above these sounds, the cry of a hawk, the yip of a coyote, or even on rare occasions the howl of a wolf may pierce the air.

Animals in Yellowstone head *down* when the thermometer falls. Herbivores like elk and bison head to the warmer, less snowy valleys to find vegetation; predators like wolves and cougars follow them. As a result, you're more likely to see these animals in the front country in winter. The snow also makes it easier to pick out animal tracks.

Snowmobiling is popular but is also controversial (critics site noise and pollution). At the time of this writing, guided trips with capped speed limits are offered in both Yellowstone and Grand Teton national parks. There are also the options of cross-country skiing and snowshoeing through geyser basins and along the canyon, both excellent ways to see the park. Dogsledding isn't permitted in the park, but outfitters in Jackson lead trips in the nearby national forests.

—Brian Kevin, excerpted from *Fodor's Compass American Guides Yellowstone and Grand Teton National Parks*

37

gloves, and gaiters) are $12 per half day, $18.50 per full day. Snowshoes rentals are $10 per half day, $15 per full day. Shuttle service is $14.50 from Snow Lodge, $15.50 from Mammoth. Group and private lessons are available. Skier shuttles run from Mammoth Hotel to Indian Creek and from Old Faithful Snow Lodge to Fairy Falls. Guided tours on snowmobiles start at $198/person. Guided snow-coach tours are available for $52.50 to $68). Both types of tours run from late December through early March. The **Yellowstone Association Institute** (☎ *307/344–2293* ⊕ *www.yellowstoneassociation.org*) offers everything from day-long cross-country skiing excursions to multiday Lodging and Learning trips geared around hiking, skiing, and snowshoeing treks. Expect to pay $200 to $500 for excursions; $500 to $1,000 or more for Lodging and Learning trips.

EDUCATIONAL OFFERINGS

CLASSES AND SEMINARS

Expedition: Yellowstone! Since 1985, this four- to five-day residential program for grades four through eight has taught kids about the natural and cultural history of Yellowstone, as well as the issues affecting its ecosystem. The curriculum includes hikes, discussions, journal keeping, and presentations. ⊠ *Lamar Buffalo Ranch facilities* ☎ *307/344–2658* ⊙ *Sept.–May.*

Yellowstone Institute. Stay in a log cabin in Lamar Valley while taking a course about the park's ecology, history, or wildlife. Search with a historian for the trail the Nez Perce Indians took in their flee a century ago from the U.S. Army, or get the perfect shot with tips from professional photographers. Facilities are fairly primitive—guests do their own cooking and camp during some of the courses—but prices are reasonable. Some programs are specifically designed for young people and families. ⊠ *North Park Rd., between Tower-Roosevelt and Northeast Entrance* ☎ *307/344–2294* ⊕ *www.yellowstoneassociation.org/institute* ⊙ *Year-round, programs vary with season.*

RANGER PROGRAMS

Yellowstone offers a busy schedule of guided hikes, talks, and campfire programs. For dates and times, check the park's *Yellowstone Today* newsletter, available at all entrances and visitor centers.

☾ ★ **Evening Programs.** Gather around to hear tales about Yellowstone's fascinating history, with hour-long programs on topics ranging from the return of the bison to 19th-century photographers. Every major area hosts programs, but check visitor centers or campground bulletin board for updates. Most programs begin at 9 or 9:30 PM, though there are earlier programs at Norris, Fishing Bridge, and Old Faithful. ⊙ *June–Aug., nightly at 9 and 9:30.*

☾ **Daytime Walks and Talks.** Ranger-led programs run during both the winter and summer seasons. Ranger Adventure Hikes are more strenuous and must be reserved in advance (the number of participants is limited), but anyone can join the regular ranger talks and ranger walks. Winter programs are held at West Yellowstone, Old Faithful, and Mammoth.

GOOD READS

- *The Yellowstone Story*, by Aubrey L. Haines, is a classic.

- *Yellowstone Place Names*, by Lee Whittlesey, tells the stories behind the names of many park destinations.

- *Yellowstone: The Official Guide to Touring America's First National Park*, published by Yellowstone Association, is a magazine-sized, full-color, glossy 80-page "yearbook."

- *Decade of the Wolf*, by Douglas Smith, is the most comprehensive and gripping account of the reintroduction of wolves into the park in the 1990s.

- *Yellowstone Trails, A Hiking Guide*, by Mark C. Marschall, will help you navigate the shortest and longest trails in the park.

- *Lost In My Own Backyard*, by Tim Cahill, is a hilarious account of one person's experience in the park.

- Explaining the park's geological processes are William R. Keefer's *The Geologic Story of Yellowstone National Park* and Robert B. Smith and Lee J. Siegel's *Windows into the Earth: The Geologic Story of Yellowstone and Grand Teton National Parks*.

- Alston Chase's controversial *Playing God in Yellowstone* chronicles a century of government mismanagement.

37

Junior Ranger Program. Children ages 5 to 12 are eligible to earn patches and become Junior Rangers. Pick up the Junior Ranger Newspaper at Madison, Canyon, or Old Faithful for $3 and start the fun, self-guided curriculum.

TOURS

Old Yellow Bus Tour. The historic 14-passenger yellow buses are originals built in 1937. Restored and reintroduced in 2007, the White Motors' vehicles are the most elegant way to learn about the park. Your driver, who narrates the trip, will roll back the soft-top convertible for you to bask under the sun (and look up to take in the sights!) if it's warm enough and not raining. More than a dozen itineraries range from one hour to all day, and will likely include wildlife sightings, photo opportunities, and some of the park's favorite landmarks. Yellow buses depart from various locations, including the Grey Wolf Inn in West Yellowstone and Canyon Lodge in Canyon. ☎ *866/439–7375* ⊕ *www. travelyellowstone.com* ✉ *$14.50–$92* ⊗ *June–Sept.*

WHAT'S NEARBY

Yellowstone National Park is a destination, not something to see as you pass through the area, and it covers a lot of ground; so if you plan on spending several days in the park, we suggest staying overnight in the park itself. If you don't mind the driving, however, or want to spend time outside the park, there are several upscale resorts in nearby towns as well as literally thousands of possible campsites for those looking to rough it.

Park Ranger Mary Wilson

For Yellowstone National Park Ranger Mary Wilson, every day is an adventure and, even after two decades of working in some of the nation's most pristine preserves, she never tires of assisting visitors who have come to explore America's natural treasures.

"Almost every day, I am approached by visitors who, in awe of the wonderful and exciting things they have experienced in the parks, tell me that these places are the most beautiful and inspiring places they have ever seen or been," she says. "Somehow, these places help foster memories and feelings that last a lifetime."

Visitors have left lasting impressions that Wilson has incorporated into her instruction of new park rangers. One of the most poignant occurred while she was working in the mid-1980s as an interpretive ranger at Grand Canyon National Park.

"I came across an elderly woman sitting near the south rim of the canyon who was just sobbing," Wilson recalls. "Thinking that she may have been hurt, sick, or missing someone, I approached and asked if I could help her. She told me she was fine, but that she was from New York City, had raised five kids, and that this was the first time she had ventured out of her home state. She told me that the one thing she had wanted to see more than anything else in the world in her entire life was the Grand Canyon. I told her it was so great that she was here now, to which she responded, 'Yes, but it makes me wonder how many other beautiful places I may have missed in my life...and will never get to see.' I sat down on the bench next to her and began to cry with her. It reminded me of the power these very special places we call national parks have on our lives; how they offer us a chance to reflect upon our relationship with nature, the importance of beauty and solitude, and how lucky we are to have them preserved for everyone to enjoy."

Wilson's passion for animals, combined with a love for the outdoors and helping people, turned her professional interests toward the National Park Service "Serving as a park ranger was a way to achieve a little of all of those worlds," says Wilson, who grew up in Muncie, IN, before earning her bachelor's and master's degrees from Purdue University.

After serving stints as a student volunteer in South Dakota's Custer State Park and Montana's Glacier National Park, working side by side with rangers, Wilson was hired by the National Park Service in Glacier. Since then, she's taken assignments at Rocky Mountain, Grand Canyon, and Sequoia/Kings Canyon national parks, and Montezuma Castle National Monument. At her job at Yellowstone she supervises other rangers as well as assists visitors.

RANGER WILSON'S TOP 10 TIPS

1. Before your trip, go online to get information from the park's official Web site, ⊕ *www.nps.gov/yell.*

2. Upon arrival at the park, stop at the nearest visitor center for information and updates.

3. Pack for all types of weather no matter what time of year.

4. Avoid the crowds by getting an early start to your day in the park.

5. Stay at least 75 feet away from wildlife (300 feet for bears).

6. Stay on geyser basin boardwalks to prevent serious thermal burns.

7. Drive defensively, and allow more time than you think you need.

8. Try to be to your destination before dark to avoid hitting wildlife on park roads.

9. Take a friend when you go hiking; it's safer and a lot more fun!

10. Don't try to see and do everything. You need two to three days just to visit the park highlights.

NEARBY TOWNS

Because of its airport and its proximity to both Grand Teton and Yellowstone national parks, **Jackson,** the closest town to Yellowstone's South Entrance, is the region's busiest community in the summer and has the widest selection of dining and lodging options. Meanwhile, the least well-known gateway, the little town of **Dubois,** southeast of the park, is far from the madding crowds and a good place to stop on the way in or out of the park if you want to visit the National Bighorn Sheep Interpretive Center.

The most popular gateway from Montana, particularly in winter, is **West Yellowstone,** near the park's West Entrance. This is where the open plains of southwestern Montana and northeastern Idaho come together along the Madison River Valley. Affectionately known among winter recreationists as the "snowmobile capital of the world," this town of 1,000 is also a good place to go for fishing, horseback riding, and downhill skiing. There's also plenty of culture, as this is where you'll find the Museum of the Yellowstone. There is also a small airport here.

As the only entrance to Yellowstone that's open the entire year, **Gardiner,** in Montana, is always bustling. The town's Roosevelt Arch has marked the park's North Entrance since 1903, when President Theodore Roosevelt dedicated it. The Yellowstone River slices through town, beckoning fishermen and rafters. The town of 800 has quaint shops and good restaurants. North of Gardiner, along Interstate 90, is **Livingston,** a town of 7,500 known for its charming historic district.

With both Yellowstone and the Absaroka-Beartooth Wilderness at its back door, the Montana village of **Cooke City,** at the park's Northeast Entrance, is a good place for hiking, horseback riding, mountain climbing, and other outdoor activities. Some 50 mi to the east of Cooke City and 60 mi southeast of Billings via U.S. 212 is the small resort town of **Red Lodge.** Nestled against the foot of the pine-draped Absaroka-Beartooth Wilderness and edged by the Limestone Palisades, Red Lodge

37

has a ski area, trout fishing, a golf course, horseback riding, and more options for dining and lodging than Cooke City. Driving along the Beartooth Scenic Byway between Red Lodge and Cooke City, you'll cross the southern tip of the Beartooth range, literally in the ramparts of the Rockies. From Cooke City, the drive into Yellowstone through the Lamar Valley is one of the prettiest routes in the park.

Named for Pony Express rider, army scout, and entertainer William F. "Buffalo Bill" Cody, the town of **Cody,** in Wyoming, sits near the park's East Entrance. It is a good base for hiking trips, horseback riding excursions, and white-water rafting on the North Fork of the Shoshone or the Clarks Fork of the Yellowstone. It also is home to dude ranches and, in season, the nightly rodeo.

VISITOR INFORMATION

Cody Country Chamber of Commerce ⊠ *836 Sheridan Ave., P.O. Box 2777, Cody, WY* ☎ *307/587–2297* ⊕ *www.codychamber.org.* Cooke City Chamber of Commerce ⊡ *P.O. Box 1071, Cooke City, MT 59020* ☎ *406/838–2495* ⊕ *www. cookecitychamber.org.* Dubois Chamber of Commerce ⊠ *616 W. Ramshorn, Dubois, WY 82513* ☎ *307/455–2556* ⊕ *www.duboiswyoming.org.* Gardiner Chamber of Commerce ⊠ *221 Park St., Gardiner, MT 59030* ☎ *406/848–7971* ⊕ *www. gardinerchamber.com.* Jackson Hole Chamber of Commerce ⊠ *990 W. Broadway, P.O. Box E, Jackson, WY 83001* ☎ *307/733–3316* ⊕ *www.jacksonholeinfo.com.* Livingston Chamber of Commerce ⊠ *208 W. Park St., Livingston, MT 59047* ☎ *406/ 222–0850* ⊕ *www.livingston-chamber.com.* Red Lodge Chamber of Commerce ⊠ *601 N. Broadway, Red Lodge, MT 59068* ☎ *406/446–1718* ⊕ *www.redlodge.com.* West Yellowstone Chamber of Commerce ⊠ *30 Yellowstone Ave., West Yellowstone, MT 59758* ☎ *406/646–7701* ⊕ *www.westyellowstonechamber.com.*

NEARBY ATTRACTIONS

CODY

★ **Buffalo Bill Historical Center.** This sprawling complex, sometimes called the Smithsonian of the West, contains the Buffalo Bill Museum, Whitney Gallery of Western Art, the Plains Indian Museum, the Cody Firearms Museum, the Draper Museum of Natural History, and the Harold McCracken Research Library. Plan to spend at least four hours here. ⊠ *720 Sheridan Ave.* ☎ *307/587–4771* ⊕ *www.bbhc.org* ⌨ *$15* ☉ *May–Sept., daily 8–8; Oct., daily 8–5; Nov.–Mar., Tues.–Sun. 10–3; Apr., daily 10–5.*

JACKSON

⇨ *See the Grand Teton National Park (chapter 19) for Jackson-area attractions.*

WEST YELLOWSTONE

☾ **Grizzly and Wolf Discovery Center.** Home to eight grizzlies and six wolves, the center gives visitors a fun, up-close experience with Yellowstone's two most feared predators. Accredited by the Associations of Zoos and Aquariums, the nonprofit center is also home to important scientific research. The animals were saved from injury and/or likely death in the United States and Canada and given a "second chance" here. ⊠ *201 S. Canyon* ☎ *406/646–7001 or 800/257–2570* ⌨ *$10.50* ☉ *Daily 8* AM–*dusk.*

FESTIVALS AND EVENTS

FEBRUARY

Buffalo Bill Birthday Ball. Hundreds of folks don their turn-of-the-20th-century attire and dance in Cody until the wee hours in this celebration of William F. Cody's birthday annually on the fourth Saturday in February. The ball is held at Cody Auditorium, which is dressed up as Wolfville Hall for the occasions. Tickets are $20–$25/person. ☎ *No phone* ⊕ *www.codykc.org/ball* ✉ *info@codykc.org.*

JULY

Cody Stampede Rodeo. The Rodeo Capital of the World's annual event around July 4 is affectionately known as "Cowboy Christmas." The event, held at Cody Stampede Park on Yellowstone Avenue, is one of the most important stops on the pro rodeo circuit. Tickets range from $18 to $24. If you're in town any night from Memorial Day to Labor Day, however, you can catch the Cody Night Rodeo ($8–$18). ☎ *307/587–5155* ⊕ *www.codystampederodeo.com.*

SEPTEMBER

Old Settler's Days. Celebrating Montana's pioneer history, this event in the center of Clyde Park (75 mi north of Yellowstone's North Entrance at Gardiner, MT) includes an art show, parade, 10K run, quilt display, and entertainment. This family-friendly event has a mix of free and paid activities. ☎ *406/222–0850.*

37

♻ **Yellowstone Historic Center.** Your time will likely be well spent at this 10-acre indoor/outdoor museum in West Yellowstone, Montana. The Union Pacific Depot, which was built in 1909, has been transformed into a museum dedicated to modes of travel—from trains to stagecoaches—to Yellowstone pre–World War II. Films provide insight on topics such as the 1988 Yellowstone fire that ravaged the park and how earthquakes affect the area's hydrothermal features. ✉ *104 Yellowstone Ave.* ☎ *406/446–1100* ⊕ *www.yellowstonehistoriccenter.org* ✉ *$6* ⊙ *Mid-May–mid-June and mid-Sept.–Oct., daily 9–6; mid-June–mid-Sept., daily 9–9; mid-Nov.–mid-Apr., weekdays 10–3.*

WHERE TO EAT AND STAY

ABOUT THE RESTAURANTS

When traveling in Yellowstone it's always a good idea to bring along a cooler—that way you can carry some snacks and lunch items for a picnic or break and not have to worry about making it to one of the more developed areas of the park, where all restaurants and cafeterias are managed by two competing companies (Xanterra and Delaware North). Generally you'll find burgers and sandwiches at cafeterias and full meals (as well as a kid's menu) at restaurants. There is a good selection of entrées, such as free-range beef and chicken; game meats such as elk, venison, and trout; plus organic vegetables. At the several delis and general stores in the park you can purchase picnic items, snacks, sandwiches, and desserts like fudge and ice cream. Considering you are in one of the most remote outposts of the United States, selection and quality are above average—but expect to pay more as well. Note that reservations are often needed for dinner at the dining rooms during the busy summer season.

ABOUT THE HOTELS

Park lodgings range from two of the national park system's magnificent old hotels to simple cabins to bland modern motels. Make reservations at least a year in advance for July and August for all park lodgings. Old Faithful Snow Lodge and Mammoth Hot Springs Hotel are the only accommodations open in winter; rates are the same as in summer. Ask about the size of beds, bathrooms, thickness of walls, and room location when you book, especially in the older hotels, where accommodations vary and upgrades are ongoing. Telephones have been put in some rooms, but there are no TVs. All park lodging is no smoking. There are no roll-away beds available.

ABOUT THE CAMPGROUNDS

Yellowstone has a dozen front-country campgrounds scattered around the park, in addition to more than 200 backcountry sites. Most campgrounds have flush toilets; some have coin-operated showers and laundry facilities. ■TIP➔ Fishing Bridge RV Park is the only campground offering water, sewer, and electrical hookups, and it is for hard-sided vehicles only (no tents or tent-trailers are allowed).

The seven small campgrounds operated by the National Park Service—Norris, Lewis Lake, Mammoth, Indian Creek, Tower Fall, Slough Creek, and Pebble Creek—are available on a first-come, first-served basis. Choice sites like those at Slough Creek fill up by 10 AM each day in the summer. To get a site in an NPS campground, arrive in the morning, pick out your site, pay (cash only, no change available) at a drop box near the campground host (look for a sign near the entrance to the campground), and leave your receipt and an inexpensive item (empty cooler, water jug, etc.) at the campsite. NPS limits campers to 14 days maximum at any one location in the summer.

The campgrounds run by Xanterra Parks & Resorts—Bridge Bay, Canyon, Fishing Bridge, Grant Village, and Madison—accept bookings in advance, although you'll pay about a $5 premium over the National Park Service campsites. These campgrounds are in great settings, but they are large—more than 250 sites each—and can feel very crowded. Tents and RVs coexist, although Xanterra designates certain areas as "tent only." Larger groups can reserve space in Bridge Bay, Grant, and Madison from late May through September. To reserve, call ☎ *307/344–7311.*

If you're prepared to carry your own water and other necessities, you could also consider a backcountry campsite. There are more than 300 backcountry sites in the park, located as little as 2 mi from parking lots and trailheads. Check availability and obtain the required (though free) permit at any ranger station, visitor center, or backcountry office; you may also pay $20 to reserve one of these sites in advance (the reservations open on April 1 each year). Talk to the park's accessibility coordinator about ADA-accessible backcountry sites. All backcountry campsites have restrictions on group size and length of stay. Boating is prohibited throughout the backcountry, and pit fires are prohibited at certain campsites.

WHERE TO EAT

IN THE PARK

¢–$
FAST FOOD
✕ **Bear Paw Deli.** You can grab a quick bite and not miss a geyser eruption at this snack shop located off the lobby in the Old Faithful Inn. Burgers, chicken sandwiches, and chili typify your choices for hot meals. If you're staying at the inn, this is also a good place to fill up your water bottles with cold water from the soda fountain. This is strictly a grab-and-go place, with no tables or bar seating. ⊠ *Old Faithful Village, Old Faithful* ☎ *307/344–7311* ▭ *AE, D, DC, MC, V* ⊗ *Closed early Oct.–late May.*

¢–$$
AMERICAN
✕ **Canyon Lodge Cafeteria.** This busy lunch spot serves such traditional and simple American fare, such as country-fried steak and hot turkey sandwiches. Grab a tray and get in line. It stays open for late diners and is open for early risers, too, with a full breakfast menu. ⊠ *Canyon Village* ☎ *307/344–7311* ▭ *AE, D, DC, MC, V* ⊗ *Closed mid-Sept.–early June.*

¢–$
FAST FOOD
✕ **Geyser Grill.** Location drives this busy grill where burgers, chicken nuggets, and hot dogs highlight the kids' menu; and Mom and Dad can squeak by on a sparse assortment of soup, salads, and sandwiches. Remember you're here for the geyser, not the grub. ⊠ *Inside Old Faithful Lodge at the south end of Old Faithful Village* ☎ *307/344–7311* ▭ *AE, D, DC, MC, V* ⊗ *Closed Nov.–mid-Dec. and early Jan.–mid-Apr. Closes at 5 PM in winter.*

$–$$$
AMERICAN
✕ **Grant Village Dining Room.** The floor-to-ceiling windows of this lakeshore restaurant provide views of Yellowstone Lake through the thick stand of pines. The most contemporary of the park's restaurants, it makes you feel at home with pine-beam ceilings and cedar-shake walls. You'll find dishes ranging from pasta to wild salmon to bison meatloaf; in late season you'll find a sandwich buffet on Sundays. ⊠ *About 2 mi south of West Thumb junction in Grant Village* ☎ *307/344–7311* ⌂ *Reservations essential* ▭ *AE, D, DC, MC, V* ⊗ *Closed late Sept.–late May.*

¢–$$
AMERICAN
✕ **Lake Lodge Cafeteria.** One of the park's most inspiring views overlooking the lake does not make up for this casual eatery's dreary cafeteria menu. Roast turkey breast, Stroganoff, and pot roast are typical fare. On the plus side, portions are hearty. It also has a full breakfast menu. ⊠ *At the end of Lake Village Rd., about 1 mi south of Fishing Bridge junction* ☎ *307/344–7311* ▭ *AE, D, DC, MC, V* ⊗ *Closed mid-Sept.–early June.*

$$–$$$$
AMERICAN
Fodor'sChoice
★
✕ **Lake Yellowstone Hotel Dining Room.** Opened in 1893 and renovated by Robert Reamer beginning in 1903, this double-colonnaded dining room off the hotel lobby is the most elegant dining experience in the park. It is an upgrade from Old Faithful Inn in every way—service, china, view, menu sophistication, and even the quality of the crisp salads. Arrive early and enjoy a beverage in the airy Reamer Lounge. The dinner menu includes attractive starters like an artisanal cheese plate and organic salads. Main courses feature elk, buffalo, steak, and at least one imaginative pasta, vegetarian, and fish entrée. The wine list focuses on wines from California, Oregon, and Washington—with prices as high as $125 for a bottle of Mondavi Reserve Cabernet. Reservations are not needed for breakfast or lunch but are essential for dinner; you can

37

make them up to a year in advance with your hotel room reservations; or 60 days in advance without a hotel reservation. ☒ *Approximately 1 mi south of Fishing Bridge Junction at Lake Village Rd., Lake Village* ☎ *307/344–7311* ⌂ *Reservations essential* 🖃 *AE, D, DC, MC, V* ⊙ *Closed early Oct.–mid-May.*

$–$$$

AMERICAN

✕ **Mammoth Hot Springs Dining Room.** A wall of windows overlooks an expanse of green that was once a military parade and drill field at Mammoth Hot Springs. The art-deco-style restaurant, decorated in shades of gray, green, and burgundy, has an airy feel with its bentwood chairs. Montana beef, bison, and fish are featured and there is always at least one pasta and vegetarian dish. ☒ *5 mi south of North Entrance in village of Mammoth Hot Springs* ☎ *307/344–7311* ⌂ *Reservations essential* 🖃 *AE, D, DC, MC, V* ⊙ *Closed mid-Oct.–mid-Dec. and mid-Mar.–mid-May.*

¢–$

FAST FOOD

✕ **Mammoth Terrace Grill.** Although the exterior looks rather elegant, this restaurant in Mammoth Hot Springs serves only fast food, ranging from biscuits and gravy for breakfast to hamburgers and veggie burgers for lunch and dinner. ☒ *Mammoth Springs Hotel, Mammoth Hot Springs, 5 mi south of North Entrance* ☎ *307/344–7311* 🖃 *AE, D, DC, MC, V* ⊙ *Closed late Sept.–mid-May.*

$$–$$$$

STEAK

FodorśChoice

★

✕ **Obsidian Dining Room.** From the wood-and-leather chairs etched with figures of park animals to the intricate lighting fixtures that resemble snowcapped trees, there's ample western atmosphere at this smaller dining room (capacity: 106 guests) inside the Old Faithful Snow Lodge. The huge windows give you a view of the Old Faithful area, and you can sometimes see the famous geyser as it erupts. Aside from Mammoth Hot Springs Dining Room, this is the only place in the park where you can enjoy a full dinner in winter. The French onion soup will warm you up on a chilly afternoon; among the main courses, look for prime rib, elk, beef, or salmon. ☒ *Old Faithful Snow Lodge, south end of Old Faithful Village* ☎ *307/344–7311* 🖃 *AE, D, DC, MC, V* ⊙ *Closed mid-Oct.–mid-Dec. and mid-Mar.–early May. No lunch.*

$$–$$$

AMERICAN

✕ **Old Faithful Inn Dining Room.** Just behind the lobby, the original dining room designed by Robert Reamer in 1903—and expanded by him in 1927—has lodgepole-pine walls and ceiling beams and a giant volcanic rock fireplace graced with a contemporary painting of Old Faithful by the late Paco Young. Note the etched glass panels featuring partying cartoon animals that separates the dining room from the Bear Pit Lounge. These are reproductions of oak panels commissioned by Reamer in 1933 to celebrate the end of Prohibition. A buffet offers quantity over quality: bison, chicken, shrimp, two salads, two soups, and a dessert. You're better off choosing from nearly a dozen entrees on the à la carte menu, including grilled salmon, baked chicken, prime rib, and bison rib eye. Expect at least one vegetarian entrée in addition to a choice of salads and soups (e.g., roasted red pepper and Gouda). Save room for a signature dessert such as the Caldera, a chocolate truffle torte with a molten middle. The most extensive wine list in the park offers more than 50 (all American) choices, including sparkling and nonalcoholic varieties (from $20 to $70 per bottle). For breakfast, there's a buffet as well as individual entrées. ☒ *Take first left off Old Faithful Bypass Road for the* *hotel parking lot; Old Faithful Village* ☎ *307/344–7311* ⌕ *Reservations essential* ▭ *AE, D, DC, MC, V* ⊙ *Closed late Oct.–early May.*

¢–$$
AMERICAN
✕ **Old Faithful Lodge Cafeteria.** As you navigate this noisy family-oriented eatery, remember that you came for the park, not the services. This cafeteria serves kid-friendly fare such as pizza and hamburgers. Its redeeming value is has some of the best views of Old Faithful, so you can watch it erupt while you eat. It is not open for breakfast, but the snack shop just outside is, offering a small selection of baked goods and cereal. ⊠ *At the end of Old Faithful Bypass Rd., less than 300 yards east of Old Faithful* ☎ *307/344–7311* ▭ *AE, D, DC, MC, V* ⊙ *Closed mid-Sept.–mid-May.*

$$–$$$
AMERICAN
✕ **Roosevelt Lodge Dining Room.** At this rustic log cabin in a pine forest, the menu ranges from barbecued ribs and baked beans to hamburgers and fries. Don't miss the killer cornbread muffins. Arrive early and watch horses and stagecoaches come and go from the front porch. For a real western adventure, call ahead to join the popular chuck-wagon cookout ($55; reservations essential) that includes an hour-long trail ride or a stagecoach ride. ⊠ *Tower-Roosevelt, immediately south of the junction of Northeast Entrance Rd. and Grand Loop Rd.* ☎ *307/344–7311* ▭ *AE, D, DC, MC, V* ⊙ *Closed early Sept.–early June.*

PICNIC AREAS
The 49 picnic areas in the park range from secluded spots with a couple of tables to more popular stops with a dozen or more tables and several amenities. Only nine areas—Snake River, Grant Village, Spring Creek, Nez Perce, Old Faithful East, Bridge Bay, Cascade Lake Trail, Norris Meadows, and Yellowstone River—have fire grates. Only gas stoves may be used in the other areas. None have running water; all but a few have pit toilets. You can stock up your cooler at any of the park's general stores. It is also possible to purchase box lunches that include drinks, snacks, sandwiches, and fruit, or vegetarian or cheese-and-crackers selections from some park restaurants.

■ **TIP**➔ Keep an eye out for wildlife; you never know when a herd of bison might decide to march through (if that happens, it's best to leave your food and move a safe distance away from them).

Firehole River. The Firehole River rolls past and you might see elk grazing along its banks. This picnic area has 12 tables and one pit toilet. ⊠ *Grand Loop Rd., 3 mi south of Madison.*

Gibbon Meadows. You are likely to see elk or buffalo along the Gibbon River from one of nine tables at this area, which has a wheelchair-accessible pit toilet. ⊠ *Grand Loop Rd., 3 mi south of Norris.*

Sedge Bay. On the northern end of this volcanic beach, look carefully for the large rock slabs pushed out of the lake bottom. Nearby trees offer shade and a table, or hop onto the level rocks for an ideal lakeside picnic. You may see bubbles rising from the clear water around the rocks—these indicate an active underwater thermal feature. The only company you may have here could be crickets, birds, and bison. ⊠ *East Entrance Rd., 8 mi east of Fishing Bridge Junction.*

37

OUTSIDE THE PARK

⇨ *See Grand Teton National Park (chapter 19) for more dining options.*

$$–$$$
STEAK
Fodor'sChoice
★

✕ **Proud Cut Saloon.** Locals say this is where the rodeo cowboys go for some of the best prime rib in northwest Wyoming. They're certainly represented in the decor, which includes historic photographs of cowboys working at the huge TA Ranch near Meeteetse. Owner Del Nose says he serves "kick-ass cowboy cuisine." Translation: steak, shrimp, crab legs, and ½-pound cheeseburgers. ⊠ *1227 Sheridan Ave., Cody, WY* ☎ *307/527–6905* ▭ *D, MC, V.*

¢–$$
AMERICAN
☺

✕ **Running Bear Pancake House.** You can get skillet breakfasts and eggs to order, plus pies, muffins, and cinnamon rolls made on-site. There are a lot of choices, but trust the name and go for the pancakes and enjoy the extremely friendly service. You can choose either buttermilk or buckwheat pancakes and have them topped with blueberries, coconut, strawberries, peaches, walnuts, or chocolate chips. There's also a basic lunch menu with sandwiches and salads and box lunches to go. ⊠ *538 Madison Ave., West Yellowstone, MT* ☎ *406/646–7703* ▭ *D, MC, V* ⊙ *Closed Nov.–late Dec. and mid-Mar.–May 1. No dinner.*

$$–$$$
ECLECTIC
★

✕ **Sydney's Bistro.** Since 2005, diners have competed for one of 10 tables inside Sydney's peaceful Canyon Street hideout—a welcome contrast to the teeming Dairy Queen next door. A table here entitles you to choose from West Yellowstone's most creative menu ranging from a porterhouse pork chop with blue-cheese–sage polenta to wild mushroom risotto with local morels. Owner Barrie Boulds keeps the menu fresh and uses exceptional local meats, herbs, and vegetables whenever possible. When it's warm enough, there are 10 more tables available outside. ⊠ *38 Canyon St., West Yellowstone, MT* ☎ *406/646–7660* ▭ *AE, MC.*

$
PIZZA
☺
★

✕ **Wild West Pizzeria.** Good pizza seems to taste better in mountain resort towns, and Wild West is no exception. Owners Aaron and Megan Hecht set out to make the best pizza in the West a decade ago. The combination of crisp crust, flavorful sauce, and "celebrities" from the frontier, works. The Sitting Bull pie features Italian pepperoni, sausage, salami, and Canadian bacon, while Calamity Jane offers white sauce, mushrooms, artichoke hearts, minced garlic, and fresh tomatoes. There are also sandwiches and pasta dishes. Wild West got bigger and better in 2009 when it incorporated the old Strozzi's Bar, added live music on weekends, a video-poker style gambling room for adults, and an expanded family area. ⊠ *14 Madison Ave., West Yellowstone, MT* ☎ *406/646–4400* ⊕ *www.wildwestpizza.com* ▭ *AE, D, MC, V.*

$–$$$
STEAK
☺

✕ **Yellowstone Mine.** Decorated with mining equipment such as picks and shovels, this is a place for casual family-style dining. Town residents come in for the steaks and seafood. The breakfast buffet is available in summer. ⊠ *U.S. 89, Gardiner, MT* ☎ *406/848–7336* ▭ *AE, D, MC, V* ⊙ *No lunch.*

WHERE TO STAY

IN THE PARK
CANYON

$–$$ ☷ **Canyon Cabins.** Unattractive and unassuming, these pine-frame cabins are mostly in clusters of four, six, and eight units. Thanks to an upgrade, they all now have private bathrooms, and higher-end cabins also have knotty-pine bed frames, hand sinks, and coffeemakers. Their popularity is based primarily on their location—you're in the heart of the park less than 30 minutes away from Lamar Valley, Hayden Valley, and Yellowstone Lake; Old Faithful is less than 45 minutes away. You also can park close to the door, so you don't have to schlep your luggage far. From the cabins there's a trail you can take down to the Grand View overlook of the canyon—it's through bear country, so make a lot of noise as you walk. Three restaurants and a bar are nearby. **Pros:** affordability; location; private baths. **Cons:** too much asphalt; too many neighbors; no central lodge/lobby area for hanging out. ✉ *North Rim Dr. at Grand Loop Rd., Canyon Village* ☎ *307/344–7901* ⊕ *www.travelyellowstone. com* ↩ *428 cabins* ⚵ *In-room: no a/c, no phone, no TV* ▤ *AE, D, DC, MC, V* ⊗ *Closed mid-Sept.–late May.*

$$$ ☷ **Cascade Lodge.** Pine wainscoting and brown carpets set the tone in this lodge built in 1992 in the trees above the Grand Canyon of the Yellowstone. The location is at the farthest edge of the Canyon Village, which means it's quite a hike to the nearest dining facilities—and you have to pass through rows upon rows of cabins, parking lots, and roads to get anywhere; the payoff is a quiet environment because it's away from the major traffic. **Pros:** the Canyon location is central; indoor lounge and outdoor patio can be a great place for a family card game. **Cons:** you'll mostly likely want to drive to restaurants. ✉ *North Rim Dr. at Grand Loop Rd., Canyon Village* ☎ *307/344–7901* ⊕ *www. travelyellowstone.com* ↩ *40 rooms* ⚵ *In-room: no a/c, no TV. In-hotel: bar* ▤ *AE, D, DC, MC, V* ⊗ *Closed mid-Sept.–late May.*

$$$ ☷ **Dunraven Lodge.** This dorm-style lodge is in the pine trees at the edge of the Grand Canyon of the Yellowstone, adjacent to the essentially identical Cascade Lodge. It's at the farthest edge of the Canyon Village, so it's a hike to the nearest dining facilities. **Pros:** canyon location. **Cons:** far from dining and other services; with children you'll need to drive to restaurants. ✉ *North Rim Dr., at Grand Loop Rd., Canyon Village* ☎ *307/344–7901* ⊕ *www.travelyellowstone.com* ↩ *41 rooms* ⚵ *In-room: no a/c, no TV. In-hotel: bar* ▤ *AE, D, DC, MC, V* ⊗ *Closed mid-Sept.–late May.*

CAMPING **$$** ⛺ **Canyon.** A massive campground with 250-plus sites, the Canyon campground accommodates everyone from hiker/biker tent campers to large RVs. The campground is accessible to Canyon's many short trails. Nearby Canyon Village offers every service—stores, laundry, ranger station, ice, etc.—which makes this campground a hit with families. The location is near laundry facilities and the visitor center. Generators are allowed from 8 AM to 8 PM. **Pros:** a great base in the middle of the park; all services close by. **Cons:** tents and RVs may share close quarters; not a very quiet campground; highest elevation (and therefore the coldest!) campground in the park. ✉ *North Rim Dr., ¼ mi east of Grand Loop*

37

Rd., Canyon Village ☎ *307/344–7311* ⊕ *www.travelyellowstone.com* ⚴ *Flush toilets, drinking water, guest laundry, showers, bear boxes, fire pits, picnic tables, public telephone, ranger station* ⚠ *272 sites* ▤ *AE, D, DC, MC, V* ☉ *Early June–early Sept.*

GRANT VILLAGE

CAMPING
$$

⚠ **Grant Village.** The park's second-largest campground, Grant Village has some sites with great views of Yellowstone Lake. Some of the sites are wheelchair accessible. The campground has a boat launch but no dock. Generators are allowed from 8 AM to 8 PM. **Pros:** group sites available; ease of access to Grand Teton National Park. **Cons:** huge campground means lots of engine noise, generators, and kid chatter in the evening; a long, long way from Mammoth Hot Springs and the wildlife-rich Lamar Valley. ⊠ *South Entrance Rd., 2 mi south of West Thumb* ☎ *307/344–7311* ⊕ *www.travelyellowstone.com* ⚴ *Flush toilets, dump station, drinking water, guest laundry, showers, bear boxes, picnic tables, public telephone, ranger station* ⚠ *425 sites* ▤ *AE, D, DC, MC, V* ☉ *Late June–late Sept.*

MADISON

CAMPING
$$

⚠ **Madison.** The largest National Park Service–operated campground, with no advance reservations are accepted, Madison has eight loops and nearly 300 sites. The outermost loop backs up to the Madison River, but other sites feel a bit claustrophobic. You can't beat the location, though, halfway between the Old Faithful village and the West Entrance, so you're minutes from five different geyser basins, Old Faithful, and three picturesque rivers (the Firehole, Madison, and Gibbon). The campground can accommodate trailers up to 45 feet. Generators are allowed from 8 AM to 8 PM. **Pros:** location; rivers; nearby geysers. **Cons:** no store for last-minute purchases; it's a busy junction (for both cars and buffalo). ⊠ *Grand Loop Rd., Madison* ☎ *307/344–7311* ⊕ *www. travelyellowstone.com* ⚴ *Flush toilets, dump station, drinking water, bear boxes, fire pits, picnic tables, public telephone, ranger station* ⚠ *277 tent/RV sites* ▤ *AE, D, DC, MC, V* ☉ *Closed late Sept.–early May.*

MAMMOTH HOT SPRINGS

$–$$

⌂ **Mammoth Hot Springs Hotel and Cabins.** Built in 1937, this hotel has a spacious art-deco lobby, where you'll find an espresso cart after 4 PM. The rooms are smaller and less elegant than those at the park's other two historic hotels, but the Mammoth Hot Springs Hotel is less expensive and usually less crowded. In summer the rooms can get hot, but you can open the windows, and there are fans. More than half the rooms do not have their own bathrooms; shared baths are down the hall. The cabins, set amid lush lawns, are the nicest inside the park, but most do not have private bathrooms, and only two very expensive suites have TVs. This is one of only two lodging facilities open in winter. Some cabins have hot tubs, a nice amenity after a day of cross-country skiing or snowshoeing. **Pros:** great rates for a historic property; terrific place to watch elk in the fall. **Cons:** those elk grazing on the lawn can create traffic jams; many hotel rooms and cabins are without private bathrooms; rooms can get hot during the day. ⊠ *Mammoth Hot Springs* ☎ *307/344–7901* ⊕ *www.travelyellowstone.com* ⚲ *97 rooms, 67 with bath; 2 suites; 115 cabins, 76 with bath* ⚴ *In-room: no a/c, no phones* (some), no TV. In-hotel: restaurant, bar ▭ AE, D, DC, MC, V ⊗ Closed early Oct.–late-Dec. and mid-Mar.–early May.

CAMPING
$
🏕️ **Indian Creek.** In a picturesque setting next to a creek, this campground is in the middle of a prime wildlife-viewing area. There are some combination sites that can accommodate trailers up to 40 feet. **Pros:** tree-covered creek-side sites are some of the park's most tranquil places to rest; nice spot to watch wildlife. **Cons:** pit toilets only. ⊠ 8 mi south of Mammoth Hot Springs on Grand Loop Rd. ☎ 828/497–4361 ⚒ Pit toilets, bear boxes, fire pits, picnic tables 🏕️ 75 tent/RV sites ▭ No credit cards ⊗ Closed mid-Sept.–mid-June.

NORRIS

CAMPING
$
🏕️ **Norris.** Straddling the Gibbon River, this is a quiet, popular campground. A few of its "walk-in" sites are among the best in the park. Anglers love catching brook trout and grayling here. The campground can accommodate trailers up to 45 feet. Generators are allowed from 8 AM to 8 PM. **Pros:** a fisherman's dream; some sites are especially secluded. **Cons:** the secret is out—this campsite fills up quickly. ⊠ Grand Loop Rd., Norris ☎ 307/344–2177 ⚒ Flush toilets, drinking water, bear boxes, fire pits, picnic tables, ranger station 🏕️ 116 tent/RV sites ▭ No credit cards ⊗ Closed late Sept.–mid-May.

OLD FAITHFUL AREA

$$$–$$$$
♨
Fodor's Choice
★
🏨 **Old Faithful Inn.** This Robert Reamer signature building is deserving of its National Historic Landmark status—and has been a favorite of five generations of park visitors. The so-called Old House was originally built in 1904 and is worth a visit regardless of whether you are staying the night. The lobby has a 76-foot-high, eight-sided fireplace; bright red iron-clad doors, and two balconies as well as a fantasy-like "tree house" of platforms, ladders, and dormer windows high above the foyer. You can stay in 1904-era rooms with thick wood timber walls and ceilings for less than $100 if you are willing to forsake a private bathroom. Rooms with bathrooms in either the Old House or the "modern" wings (built in 1913 and 1927) rent for as high as $200-plus. There's no insulation, so it's closed in the winter. **Pros:** a one-of-a-kind property, Old House rooms are truly memorable with pine-pine walls and ceilings. **Cons:** thin walls; waves of tourists in the lobby; shared baths make you recall college dorm days. ⊠ Old Faithful Village ✛ Take the first left off of the Bypass Road to the hotel parking lot and miss the busy geyser parking area, Old Faithful ☎ 307/344–7901 ⊕ www.travelyellowstone. com ➥ 324 rooms, 246 with bath; 6 suites ⚒ In-room: no a/c, no phone (some), no TV. In-hotel: restaurant, bar ▭ AE, D, DC, MC, V ⊗ Closed mid-Oct.–early May.

¢–$$
🏨 **Old Faithful Lodge Cabins.** There are no rooms inside the Old Faithful Lodge, though there are 97 cabins sitting at the northeast end of the village. Typical of cabins throughout the park, these are very basic—lacking most amenities (including bathrooms in about one-third of the cabins), views, or character. However, the location can't be beat—cabins are almost as close to the geyser as Old Faithful Inn. If you plan to spend a day or three exploring the geyser basins or the central area of the park, this is a great budget-conscious option to lay down your head since you'll be out and about most of the time anyway. **Pros:** considering its

37

location, price can't be beat; a stone's throw from Old Faithful Geyser, all area services are within walking distance. **Cons:** some cabins lack private bathrooms; pretty basic. ⊠ *South end of Old Faithful Bypass Rd.* ☎ *307/344–7901* ⊕ *www.travelyellowstone.com* ⤶ *96 cabins, 60 with bath* ⚴ *In-room: no a/c, no phone, no TV. In-hotel: restaurant* ☰ *AE, D, DC, MC, V* ⊘ *Closed mid-Sept.–mid-May.*

$$$ ⌘ **Old Faithful Snow Lodge.** Built in 1998, this massive structure brings back the grand tradition of park lodges by making good use of heavy timber beams and wrought-iron accents in a distinctive facade. Inside you'll find soaring ceilings, natural lighting, and a spacious lobby with a stone fireplace. Nearby is a long sitting room, where writing desks and overstuffed chairs invite you to linger. Guest rooms combine traditional style with modern amenities. This is one of only two lodging facilities in the park that are open in winter, when the only way to get here is on over-snow vehicles. **Pros:** the most modern hotel in the park; the lobby and adjacent breezeway are great for relaxing; the only property on the interior of the park open in winter. **Cons:** pricey, but you're paying for location and some modern conveniences. ⊠ *Far end of Old Faithful Bypass Rd., Old Faithful* ☎ *307/344–7901* ⊕ *www. travelyellowstone.com* ⤶ *100 rooms* ⚴ *In-room: no a/c, no TV. In-hotel: restaurant, bicycles* ☰ *AE, D, DC, MC, V* ⊘ *Closed mid-Oct.– mid-Dec. and mid-Mar.–early May.*

$–$$ ⌘ **Old Faithful Snow Lodge Cabins.** The massive 1988 fires claimed some of the cabins just yards from Old Faithful, but like the park's foliage, new ones have sprung up. Western cabins feature brighter interiors, newer furnishings and modern motel ambience. Frontier cabins resemble barracks, but the simple pine structures offer a roof, warmth, and shelter during cool summer nights. **Pros:** price and proximity to America's iconic geyser. **Cons:** expect no amenities beyond the basics of a bathroom, double beds, a roof, and a radiator. ⊠ *Far end of Old Faithful Bypass Rd., Old Faithful* ☎ *307/344–7901* ⊕ *www.travelyellowstone. com* ⤶ *100 rooms* ⚴ *In-room: no a/c, no TV. In-hotel: restaurant, bicycles* ☰ *AE, D, DC, MC, V* ⊘ *Closed mid-Oct.–early May.*

TOWER-ROOSEVELT

¢–$$ ⌘ **Roosevelt Lodge Cabins.** Near the beautiful Lamar Valley in the park's northeast corner, this simple lodge dating from the 1920s surpasses some of the more expensive options. All lodging is in rustic cabins set around a pine forest. Some cabins have bathrooms, but most do not, though there is a bathhouse nearby. Roughrider cabins may have woodstoves as the only heating system. You can make arrangements here for horseback and stagecoach rides. **Pros:** closest cabins to Lamar Valley and its world-famous wildlife; authentic western ranch feel; Roughrider cabins are the most inexpensive in the park. **Cons:** cabins are very close together; many lack private bathrooms; you may have to draw straws to stoke the fire at 3 AM if your Roughrider cabin has only a woodstove for heat. ⊠ *Tower-Roosevelt Junction on Grand Loop Rd., Tower-Roosevelt* ☎ *307/344–7901* ⊕ *www.travelyellowstone.com* ⤶ *80 cabins, 14 with bath* ⚴ *In-room: no a/c, no TV. In-hotel: restaurant* ☰ *AE, D, DC, MC, V* ⊘ *Closed early Sept.–early June.*

CAMPING
$
★
🏕 **Pebble Creek.** Beneath multiple 10,000-foot peaks (Thunderer, Barronnette Peak, and Mt. Norris) this easternmost campground in the park is set creek-side in a forested canopy. Pebble Creek is a babbling stream here, but hike a few yards north of the canyon to see the small canyon the river has carved. Great fishing, hikes, and wildlife abound in the vicinity. Along with nearby Slough Creek, this is the best campground in the park. Because of its small size, it fills up by 10 AM on busy days. It's also smaller than most, which means it tends to be a little quieter. Sites can accommodate trailers up to 45 feet. Charming campground hosts Ray and Darlene Rathmell have been here for more than a decade. **Pros:** a small wilderness camping experience in one of the busiest national parks in the world; unparalleled setting. **Cons:** no services for miles. ⊠ *Northeast Entrance Rd., 22 mi east of Tower-Roosevelt Junction* ☎ *no phone* ⚏ *Pit toilets, bear boxes, fire pits, picnic tables* 🏕 *32 tent/RV sites* ⊟ *No credit cards* ⊙ *Closed late Sept.–mid-June.*

$
★
🏕 **Slough Creek.** Down the most rewarding 2 mi of dirt road in the park, Slough Creek is a gem. Nearly every site is adjacent to the creek, which is prized by anglers. The campground sits at the edge of the wildlife-rich Lamar Valley, and one of the famous wolf packs introduced in 1995 has taken residence several miles up the river and bears the name Slough Creek Pack. Listen carefully for grunting bison, howling wolves, and bugling elk. If you want to stay here in the summer, make this your first stop in the morning—on many days it fills up by 10 AM. **Pros:** one of the last campgrounds to close annually; lower elevation often means warmer temps. **Cons:** there are fewer than three-dozen sites here, so you'll be hard-pressed to get a site in the summer if you're not here first thing in the morning to grab your spot. ⊠ *Northeast Entrance Rd., 10 mi east of Tower-Roosevelt Junction* ☎ *no phone* ⚏ *Pit toilets, bear boxes, fire pits, picnic tables* 🏕 *29 tent/RV sites* ⊟ *No credit cards* ⊙ *Closed late Oct.–late May.*

$
🏕 **Tower Fall.** It's within hiking distance of the roaring waterfall, so this modest-size campground gets a lot of foot traffic. It can accommodate shorter trailers. Hot water and flush toilets are at Tower Store restrooms nearby. **Pros:** can't beat the price for a spot so close to the waterfall; easy to navigate; you can go for the ice cream at nearby Tower store. **Cons:** feels cramped and crowded. ⊠ *3 mi southeast of Tower-Roosevelt on Grand Loop Rd.* ☎ *no phone* 🏕 *32 tent/RV sites* ⚏ *Pit toilets, bear boxes, fire pits, picnic tables* ⊟ *No credit cards* ⊙ *Closed late Sept.–mid-May.*

YELLOWSTONE LAKE AREA

$$–$$$$
★
🏨 **Lake Yellowstone Hotel.** More Kennebunkport than western, this distinguished hotel is the park's oldest. Dating from 1891, the white-and-pastel-color hotel has maintained an air of refinement that Old Faithful Inn can't because of its constant tour buses full of visitors. Just off the lobby, a spacious sunroom offers priceless views of Yellowstone Lake at sunrise or sunset. It's also a great place to play cards, catch up on a newspaper from the gift shop, or just soak in the grandeur of a 117-year-old National Historic Landmark. Note the tile-mantel fireplace, the etched windows of the gift shop, and the beautiful bay windows. Rooms have white wicker furnishings, which give them a light, airy feeling; some

37

have views of the water. There is one two-room suite with lake views that has been used as accommodations for U.S. presidents. The least expensive rooms are in an annex, not the original building. **Pros:** an oasis of elegance in the park, with the best views of any park lodging. **Cons:** the most expensive property in the park; restaurant is expensive; not particularly kid-friendly. ⊠ *Lake Village Rd., Lake Village, about 1 mi south of Fishing Bridge* ☎ *307/344–7901* ⊕ *www.travelyellowstone. com* ⤳ *194 rooms* ⌂ *In-room: no a/c, no TV. In-hotel: restaurant, bar* ☐ *AE, D, DC, MC, V* ☉ *Closed early Oct.–mid-May.*

¢–$$ 🏨 **Lake Lodge Cabins.** Just beyond the Lake Yellowstone Hotel lies one
☼   of the park's hidden treasures: Lake Lodge, built in 1920. The 140-foot lobby and porch offer one of the best views of sunrise in the park. The lodge itself no longer offers rooms. Rather, check in at the lobby (make a note to return to enjoy the two fireplaces, a visiting speaker, or a meal), and then head for your cabin, which is just north of the lodge. The accommodations are basic Yellowstone no-frills style—clean, with one to three beds, and a sink (some also have a shower/tub). There are views of the lake from the lodge but not from the rooms. **Pros:** the best front porch at a Yellowstone lodge and a great lobby; affordability; good for families. **Cons:** no frills of any kind; sound of dribbling basketballs in the employee gym can ruin the lobby atmosphere. ⊠ *Lake Village Rd., Lake Village, about 1 mi south of Fishing Bridge* ☎ *307/344–7901* ⊕ *www.travelyellowstone.com* ⤳ *186 rooms, 100 with bath* ⌂ *In-room: no a/c, no phones, no TV. In-hotel: restaurant, bar* ☐ *AE, D, DC, MC, V* ☉ *Closed mid-Sept.–early June.*

CAMPING   ⚠ **Bridge Bay.** The park's largest campground, Bridge Bay rests in a
$$ wooded grove above Yellowstone Lake and adjacent to the park's major
★   marina. Ask for one of the few sites with a lake view. Xanterra tries to keep tent and RV campers separate—make sure you ask if you have a preference. If you end up on one of the inner loops, you may find yourself surrounded. You can rent boats at the nearby marina, take guided walks, or listen to rangers lecture about the history of the park. Don't expect solitude, as there are more than 400 campsites. Generators are allowed from 8 AM to 8 PM. Hot showers and laundry are 4 mi north at Fishing Bridge. **Pros:** the best spot for boaters to wake up, rev their outboard motor, and head out on the lake. **Cons:** the campground's size precludes this from being a wilderness camping experience. ⊠ *3 mi southwest of Lake Village on Grand Loop Rd., Bridge Bay* ☎ *307/344–7311* ⊕ *www.travelyellowstone.com* ⌂ *Flush toilets, dump station, drinking water, showers, bear boxes, fire pits, picnic tables, public telephone, ranger station* ⚠ *432 tent/RV sites* ☐ *AE, D, DC, MC, V* ☉ *Closed mid-Sept.–late May.*

$$ ⚠ **Fishing Bridge RV Park.** Fishing Bridge is the only facility in the park that caters exclusively to recreational vehicles. It's more of a parking lot than a campground, but RV services like tank filling/emptying and plug-ins are available. Because of bear activity in the area, only hard-sided campers are allowed. Liquid propane is available. Generators are allowed from 8 AM to 8 PM. No boat access here (put in at Bridge Bay Marina, 4 mi away). Note that the nearby Fishing Bridge service station offers RV-specific services, including engine, mechanical,

and "living space" repairs, as well as diesel gasoline and parts. **Pros:** Fishing Bridge general store has ample supplies and groceries. **Cons:** this is active bear country, so safeguard your food, children, and pets. ✉ *East Entrance Rd. at Grand Loop Rd.* ☎ *307/344–7311* ⊕ *www. travelyellowstone.com* ⚠ *344 RV sites* ⚒ *Flush toilets, full hookups, dump station, drinking water, guest laundry, showers, bear boxes, picnic tables, public telephone, ranger station* ▭ *AE, D, DC, MC, V* ⊗ *Closed late Sept.–mid-May.*

OUTSIDE THE PARK

⇨ *Grand Teton National Park (chapter 19) for more area hotels and campgrounds.*

$$$$ 🏨 **The Cody.** Since 2008, this all-suites hotel has incorporated western themes into a thoroughly modern and eco-friendly property. Exposed timber, tile accents, the sunset-and-ochre color scheme, and a creek connect you to the land. Meanwhile, a flat-screen TV, iPod docking station, and wireless Internet keep you in touch with the rest of the world. Green features include reclaimed wood trim from old structures inside Yellowstone National Park, natural bamboo fiber covers, recycled-materials doors, and energy-efficient utilities and amenities such as organic soaps and shampoos. Some rooms have Jacuzzis and fireplaces. **Pros:** a hybrid-fuel SUV shuttles guests to airport and downtown attractions; deluxe continental breakfast included. **Cons:** luxury has its price: these are the most expensive rooms in town. ✉ *232 W. Yellowstone Ave., Cody, WY* ☎ *307/587–5915* ⊕ *www.thecody.com* ⌐ *75 suites* ⚒ *In-room: safe, refrigerator, DVD, Wi-Fi. In-hotel: pool, gym, spa, bicycles, Wi-Fi, some pets allowed* ▭ *AE, D, MC, V* ⊚ *CP.*

$$–$$$ 🏨 **Pahaska Tepee Resort.** Just 2 mi from Yellowstone's East Entrance, these cabins in a pine forest are a good base for recreation both inside and outside the park. This was Buffalo Bill's original getaway in the high country and is a National Historic Landmark. The cabins, some of which stand alone and some of which are grouped together, have two, four, or six bedrooms. A trailhead for an extensive cross-country-ski-trail network is at Pahaska, as are a gas station and a place for horseback rides. **Pros:** historic property adjacent to East entrance of the park on a scenic highway. **Cons:** few services between Cody and Fishing Bridge. ✉ *183 Yellowstone Hwy., Cody, WY* ☎ *307/527–7701 or 800/628–7791* ⊕ *www.pahaska.com* ⌐ *48 cabins, 1 lodge* ⚒ *In-room: no a/c, kitchen (some), no TV, Wi-Fi. In-hotel: restaurant, bar, Wi-Fi, some pets allowed* ▭ *D, MC, V.*

$$–$$$$ 🏨 **Pollard Hotel.** They say guns have been banned in the hotel ever since Harry Longbaugh, *aka* the Sundance Kid, brandished one when he robbed a bank on the corner of the property. Other legendary characters from the West, including Buffalo Bill and Calamity Jane, have stayed at this 1893 landmark in the heart of Red Lodge's historic district. Common areas include a balcony that overlooks the gallery and fireplace, plus oak-paneled parlors that are perfect for a drink or a book. Rooms range from historic (i.e., tiny!) to comfortable suites; some have mountain views, claw-foot tubs, and/or balconies. **Pros:** full breakfast included; a truly historical property. **Cons:** front desk service can be erratic. ✉ *2 N. Broadway, Red Lodge, MT* ☎ *406/446–0001 or*

37

800/765–5273 🖨 *406/446–0002* ⊕ *www.thepollard.com* 🖙 *34 rooms, 4 suites* ⚘ *In-room: refrigerator (some), Wi-Fi. In-hotel: restaurant, bar, gym, Wi-Fi* ▭ *AE, D, MC, V* ⏐❍⏐ *BP.*

CAMPING

$$–$$$

△ **Wagon Wheel Campground and Cabins.** Located a few blocks west of the park, this campground has tent and RV sites along with cozy one-, two-, and three-bedroom cabins with porches, barbecue grills, and cable TV. The forested setting and location make up for some confusing policies. Pets are allowed on the RV sites. Some cabins may be open year-round, but call/e-mail in the winter since Wagon Wheel may be closed if there are no reservations. There's no smoking in the cabins. ✉ *408 Gibbon Ave., West Yellowstone, MT* ☎ *406/646–7872* ⊕ *www. wagonwheelrv.com* △ *8 tent sites, 40 RV sites, 9 cabins* ⚘ *Flush toilets, full hookups, drinking water, guest laundry, showers, public telephone* ▭ *No credit cards* ⊙ *Closed mid-Sept.–late May.*

Yosemite National Park

WORD OF MOUTH

"I tried cross country skiing for the first time in Yosemite. An avid downhill skier, I quickly learned that cross country is more physically demanding, slower going, but scenically spectacular. I chose to use the time to find the perfect shot of Half Dome."

—photo by Sarah Corley, Fodors.com member

WELCOME TO YOSEMITE

TOP REASONS TO GO

★ **Feel the earth move:** An easy stroll brings you to the base of Yosemite Falls, America's highest, where thundering springtime waters shake the ground.

★ **Tunnel to heaven:** Winding down into Yosemite Valley, Wawona Road passes through a mountainside and emerges before one of the park's most heart-stopping vistas.

★ **Touch the sky:** Watch clouds scudding across the bright blue dome that arches above the High Sierra's Tuolumne Meadows, a wide-open alpine valley ringed by 10,000-foot granite peaks.

★ **Walk away from it all:** Early or late in the day, leave the crowds behind and take a forest hike on a few of Yosemite's 800 mi of trails.

★ **Powder your nose:** Winter's hush floats into Yosemite on snowflakes. Wade into a fluffy drift, lift your face to the sky, and listen to the trees.

1 Yosemite Valley. At an elevation of 4,000 feet, in roughly the center of the park, beats Yosemite's heart. This is where you'll find the park's most famous sights and biggest crowds.

2 Wawona and Mariposa Grove. The park's southeastern tip holds Wawona, with its grand old hotel and pioneer history center, and the Mariposa Grove of Big Trees, filled with giant sequoias. These are closest to the South Entrance, 35 mi (a 1-hour drive) south of Yosemite Village.

3 Tuolumne Meadows. The highlight of east-central Yosemite is this wildflower-strewn valley with hiking trails, nestled among sharp, rocky peaks. It's a two-hour drive northeast of Yosemite Valley along Tioga Road (closed mid-October–late May).

4 Hetch Hetchy. The most remote, least-visited part of Yosemite accessible by automobile, this glacial valley is dominated by a reservoir and veined with wilderness trails. It's near the park's western boundary, about a half-hour drive north of Big Oak Flat Entrance.

CALIFORNIA

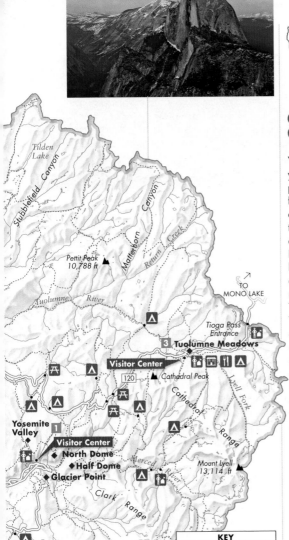

GETTING ORIENTED

Yosemite is so large that you can think of it as five parks. Yosemite Valley, famous for waterfalls and cliffs, and Wawona, where the giant sequoias stand, are open all year. Hetch Hetchy, home of less-used backcountry trails, closes after the first big snow and reopens in May or June. The subalpine high country, Tuolumne Meadows, is open for summer hiking and camping; in winter it's accessible only via cross-country skis or snowshoes. Badger Pass Ski Area is open in winter only. Most visitors spend their time along the park's south-western border, between Wawona and Big Oak Flat Entrance; a bit farther east in Yosemite Valley and Badger Pass Ski Area; and along the east–west corridor of Tioga Road, which spans the park north of Yosemite Valley and bisects Tuolumne Meadows.

38

KEY

🧍 Ranger Station
🔺 Campground
🎋 Picnic Area
🍴 Restaurant
🖼 Lodge
🚶 Trailhead
🚻 Restrooms
⚜ Scenic Viewpoint
⋯ Walking/Hiking Trails

YOSEMITE PLANNER

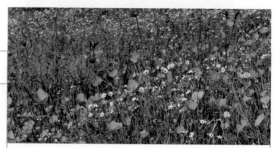

When to Go

During extremely busy periods—like the 4th of July—you may experience delays at the entrance gates. **For less crowds, visit midweek.** Or come mid-April through Memorial Day or mid-September through October, when the park is only a bit busy and the days are usually sunny and clear.

Summer rainfall is rare. In winter, heavy snows occasionally cause road closures, and tire chains or four-wheel drive may be required on the roads that remain open. The road to Glacier Point beyond the turnoff for Badger Pass is closed after the first major snowfall; Tioga Road is closed from late October through May or mid-June. Mariposa Grove Road is typically closed for a shorter period in winter.

The temperature chart below is for Yosemite Valley. In the high country, it's cooler.

AVG HIGH/LOW TEMPS

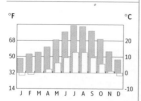

Flora and Fauna

Dense stands of incense cedar and Douglas fir—as well as ponderosa, Jeffrey, lodgepole, and sugar pines—cover much of the park, but the stellar standout, quite literally, is the *Sequoia sempervirens*, the giant sequoia. Sequoias grow only along the west slope of the Sierra Nevada between 4,500 and 7,000 feet in elevation. Starting from a seed the size of a rolled-oat flake, each of these ancient monuments assumes remarkable proportions in adulthood; you can see them in the Mariposa Grove of Big Trees. In late May the Valley's dogwood trees bloom with white, star-like flowers. Wildflowers, such as black-eyed Susan, bull thistle, cow parsnip, lupine, and meadow goldenrod, peak in June in the Valley and in July at higher elevations.

The most visible animals in the park—aside from the omnipresent western gray squirrel—are the mule deer. Though sightings of bighorn sheep are infrequent in the park itself, you can sometimes see them on the eastern side of the Sierra Crest, just off Route 120 in Lee Vining Canyon. You may also see the American black bear, which often has a brown, cinnamon, or blond coat. The Sierra Nevada is home to thousands of bears, and you should take all necessary precautions to keep yourself—and the bears—safe. For one, do not feed the bears. Bears that acquire a taste for human food can become very aggressive and destructive and often must be destroyed by rangers.

Watch for the blue Steller's jay along trails, near public buildings, and in campgrounds, and look for Golden eagles soaring over Tioga Road.

Getting Here and Around

Roughly 200 mi from San Francisco, 300 mi from Los Angeles, and 500 mi from Las Vegas, Yosemite takes awhile to reach—and its many sites and attractions merit much more time than what rangers say is the average visit: four hours. Most people arrive via automobile or tour bus, but public transportation (courtesy of Amtrak and the regional YARTS bus system) also can get you to the Valley efficiently.

Of the park's four entrances, Arch Rock is the closest to Yosemite Valley. The road that goes through it, Route 140 from Merced and Mariposa, is a scenic western approach that snakes alongside the boulder-packed Merced River. Route 41, through Wawona, is the way to come from Los Angeles (or Fresno, if you've flown in and rented a car). Route 120, through Crane Flat, is the most direct route from San Francisco. The only way in from the east is Tioga Road, which may be the best route in terms of scenery—though due to snow accumulation it's open for a frustratingly short amount of time each year (typically early June through mid-October).

However you get to the Valley, once you're there you can take advantage of the free shuttle buses, which operate on low emissions, have 21 stops, and run every 10 minutes or so from 9 AM to 6 PM year-round; a separate (but also free) summer-only shuttle runs out to El Capitan. Also during the summer, from Yosemite Valley you can pay to take the morning "hikers' bus" to Tuolumne or the bus up to Glacier Point. Bus service from Wawona is geared for people who are staying there and want to spend the day in Yosemite Valley. Free and frequent shuttles transport people between the Wawona Hotel and Mariposa Grove. During the snow season, buses run regularly between Yosemite Valley and Badger Pass Ski Area. For more information on shuttles within the park, visit ⊕ *www.nps.gov/yose/planyourvisit/ bus.htm* or call ☎ *209/372–1240*.

There are few gas stations within Yosemite (Crane Flat, Tuolumne Meadows, and Wawona; none in the Valley), so fuel up before you reach the park. From late fall until early spring, the weather is unpredictable, and driving can be treacherous. You should carry chains. For road condition updates, call ☎ *800/427–7623 or 209/372–0200* from within California or go to ⊕ *www.dot.ca.gov*.

Good Reads

■ *The Photographer's Guide to Yosemite*, by Michael Frye, is an insider's guide to the park, with maps for shutterbugs looking to capture perfect images.

■ John Muir penned his observations of the park he long advocated for in *The Yosemite*.

■ *Yosemite and the High Sierra*, edited by Andrea G. Stillman and John Szarkowski, features beautiful reproductions of landmark photographs by Ansel Adams, accompanied by excerpts from the photographer's journals written when Adams traveled in Yosemite National Park in the early 20th century.

■ An insightful collection of essays accompany the museum-quality artworks in *Yosemite: Art of an American Icon*, by Amy Scott.

■ Perfect for beginning wildlife watchers, *Sierra Nevada Wildflowers*, by Karen Wiese, indentifies more than 230 kinds of flora growing in the Sierra Nevada region.

38

By Reed
Parsell

By merely standing in Yosemite Valley and turning in a circle, you can see more natural wonders in a minute than you could in a full day pretty much anywhere else. Half Dome, Yosemite Falls, El Capitan, Bridalveil Fall, the meadows, Sentinel Dome, the Merced River, white-flowering dogwood trees, maybe even bears ripping into the bark of fallen trees or sticking their snouts into beehives—it's all in the Valley.

In the mid-1800s, when tourists were arriving to the area, the Valley's special geologic qualities, and the giant sequoias of Mariposa Grove 30 mi to the south, so impressed a group of influential Californians that they persuaded President Abraham Lincoln to grant those two areas to the state for protection. On Oct. 1, 1890—thanks largely to lobbying efforts by naturalist John Muir and Robert Underwood Johnson, the editor of *Century Magazine*—Congress set aside 1,500 square mi for Yosemite National Park.

PARK ESSENTIALS

ACCESSIBILITY

Yosemite's facilities are continually being upgraded to make them more accessible. Many of the Valley floor trails—particularly at Lower Yosemite Falls, Bridalveil Fall, and Mirror Lake—are wheelchair accessible, though some assistance may be required. The Valley Visitor Center is fully accessible, as are the park shuttle buses. A sign-language interpreter is available for ranger programs if you call ahead. For details, pick up the park's accessibility brochure at any visitor center or entrance, read it at ⊕ *www.nps.gov/yose/planyourvisit/accessibility.htm*, or call the public information office at ☎ 209/372–0200. Visitors with respiratory difficulties should take note of the park's high elevations—the Valley floor is approximately 4,000 feet above sea level, but Tuolumne Meadows and parts of the high country hover around 10,000 feet.

ADMISSION FEES AND PERMITS

The admission fee, valid for seven days, is $20 per vehicle or $10 per individual.

If you plan to camp in the backcountry, you must have a wilderness permit. Availability of permits, which are free, depends upon trailhead quotas. It's best to make a reservation, especially if you will be visiting May through September. You can reserve two days to 24 weeks in advance by phone, mail, or fax (⬡ *P.O. Box 545, Yosemite, CA 95389* ☎ *209/372–0740* ⬡ *209/372–0739*); a $5 per person processing fee is charged if and when your reservations are confirmed. Requests must include your name, address, daytime phone, the number of people in your party, trip date, alternative dates, starting and ending trailheads, and a brief itinerary. Without a reservation, you may still get a free permit on a first-come, first-served basis at wilderness permit offices at Big Oak Flat, Hetch Hetchy, Tuolumne, Wawona, the Wilderness Center (in Yosemite Village), and Yosemite Valley in summer; fall through spring, visit the Valley Visitor Center.

ADMISSION HOURS

The park is open 24/7 year-round. All entrances are open at all hours, except for Hetch Hetchy Entrance, which is open roughly dawn to dusk. Yosemite is in the Pacific time zone.

ATMS/BANKS

There are ATMs inside the stores at Yosemite Village, Curry Village, Wawona, and Tuolumne Meadows, as well as in the lobby of Yosemite Lodge, and outside the Art Activity Center. Banks are in surrounding communities.

CELL-PHONE RECEPTION

Cell phone reception usually works just fine in the valley, but is hit-or-miss elsewhere in the park. There are public telephones at park entrance stations, visitor centers, all restaurants and lodging facilities in the park, gas stations, and in Yosemite Village.

PARK CONTACT INFORMATION

Yosemite National Park ⬡ *Information Office, P.O. Box 577, Yosemite National Park, CA 95389* ☎ *209/372–0200* ⊕ *www.nps.gov/yose.*

SCENIC DRIVES

Tioga Road. Few mountain drives anywhere can compare visually with this 59-mi seasonal road, especially its eastern half between Lee Vining and Olmstead Point. As you climb 3,200 feet up to the 9,945-foot summit of Tioga Pass (Yosemite's sole eastern entrance for automobiles), you'll encounter broad vistas of the granite-splotched High Sierra and its craggy but hearty trees and shrubs. Past the bustling scene at Tuolumne Meadows, you'll see picturesque Tenaya Lake and then Olmstead Point, where you'll get your first peak at Half Dome. Driving Tioga Road one-way takes approximately 1½ hours. Wildflowers bloom here in July and August. By November, the high-altitude road will have closed for the winter; it sometimes doesn't reopen again until as late as early June.

YOSEMITE IN ONE DAY

Begin at the **Valley Visitor Center**, where you can watch the inspiring documentary *Spirit of Yosemite*. A minute's stroll from there is the **Indian village of Ahwahneechee**, which depicting American Indian life circa 1870. Take another 20 minutes to see the **Yosemite Museum**. Then, take the free shuttle to the Yosemite Falls and hike the **Lower Yosemite Falls Trail** to the base of the falls. Then proceed via shuttle or a 20-minute walk to **Yosemite Lodge**.

Next choose one of three things: leisurely exploring **Curry Village**—perhaps going for a swim or ice skating, shopping, renting a bike, or having a beer on the deck; checking out **Happy Isles Nature Center** and the adjacent nature trail, then enjoying an ice-cream treat while walking back to Curry Village; or hiking up the **Mist Trail** to the Vernal Fall footbridge to admire the view.

Hop back on the shuttle, then disembark at the **Ahwahnee Hotel**. Step into the Great Lounge, which has a magnificent fireplace and Indian artwork, and sneak a peek into the Dining Room, if you're up for a splurge. Get back on the shuttle, and head to **Yosemite Village**, where you can stop by the **Ansel Adams Gallery**. Get back in your car and drive to the **El Capitan picnic area** and enjoy an outdoor evening meal. At this time of day, "El Cap" should be sun-splashed. (You will have gotten several good looks at world-famous **Half Dome** throughout the day.) Any sunlight left? If so, continue driving on around to see **Bridalveil Fall**.

WHAT TO SEE

HISTORIC SITES

★ **Ahwahnee Hotel.** Gilbert Stanley Underwood, the architect for Grand Canyon Lodge on the North Rim in Arizona, also designed the Ahwahnee. Opened in 1927, it is generally considered to be his best work. The Great Lounge, 77 feet long with magnificent 24-foot-high ceilings and all manner of Indian artwork on display, is the most special interior space in Yosemite. You can stay here (for $450 a night), or simply explore the first-floor shops and perhaps have breakfast or lunch in the lovely Dining Room. ⊠ *Ahwahnee Rd., about ¾ mi east of Yosemite Valley Visitor Center, Yosemite Village* ☎ *209/372–1489.*

Ahwahneechee Village. This solemn smattering of re-created structures, accessed by a short loop trail, is an imagination of what Indian life might have resembled here in the 1870s. One interpretive sign points out that Miwok referred to the 19th century newcomers as "Yohemite" or "Yohometuk," which have been translated as "some of them are killers." ⊠ *Northside Dr., Yosemite Village* 🖀 *Free* ☉ *Daily sunrise–sunset.*

Pioneer Yosemite History Center. Some of Yosemite's first structures—those not occupied by American Indians, that is—were relocated from various parts of the park and placed here in the 1950s and 1960s. You can spend a pleasurable and informative half-hour walking about them and reading the signs, perhaps springing for a self-guided-tour pamphlet (50¢) to further enhance the history lesson. Wednesdays through

Yosemite's Valley Floor

KEY

- 🏛 Ranger Station
- ⛺ Campground
- 🪵 Picnic Area
- 🍴 Restaurant
- 🏨 Lodge
- 🥾 Trailhead
- 🚻 Restrooms
- ✳ Scenic Viewpoint
- ⋯ Walking/Hiking Trails
- ⋯ John Muir Trail
- – – Bicycle Path
- Valley Floor

Half Dome
8,836 ft

Liberty Cap

Nevada Falls

Emerald Pools

Vernal Falls

Mist Trail

Footbridge

John Muir Trail

Clark Point

Mirror Lake

Washington Column

Royal Arch Cascade

Royal Arches

Grizzly Peak

Sierra Point

John Muir Trail

Illilouette Gorge

Panorama Cliff

Road open only to bicycles and Shuttlebuses

bicycle path

North Pines

Upper Pines

Clarks Bridge

Happy Isles Bridge

Nature Center at Happy Isles

Lower Pines

CURRY VILLAGE

Road open only to bicycles and Shuttlebuses

Glacier Point
7,214 ft

Panorama Trail

The Ahwahnee Hotel

bicycle path

Curry Village Store

Staircase Falls

Glacier Point Road

Pohono Trail

Village Store

Auto Repair

Medical Clinic

P.O.

LeConte Memorial Lodge

Moran Point

Four Mile Trail

YOSEMITE VILLAGE

Yosemite Museum

Ansel Adams Gallery

Valley Visitor Center

Chapel

Union Point

Merced River

Sentinel Rock

Lower Yosemite Falls

Yosemite Lodge

bicycle path

Road open only to bicycles and Shuttlebuses

Sentinel Falls

Four Mile Trail

0 — 1/2 mi
0 — 1/2 km

"This is us taking a break before conquering the top of Lembert Dome, while enjoying the beautiful view over Yosemite's high country." —photo by Rebalyn, Fodors.com member

Sundays in the summer, costumed docents conduct free blacksmithing and "wet-plate" photography demonstrations, and for a small fee you can take a stagecoach ride. ⊠ *Rte. 41, Wawona* ☎ *209/375–9531 or 209/379–2646* 🎫 *Free* ⏱ *Building interiors are open mid-June–Labor Day, Wed. 2–5, Thurs.–Sun. 10–1 and 2–5.*

★ **Wawona Hotel.** One can imagine an older Mark Twain relaxing in a rocking chair on one of the broad verandas of Yosemite's first lodge, a whitewashed series of two-story buildings from the Victorian era. Across the road is a somewhat odd sight: Yosemite's only golf course, one of the few links in the world that does not employ fertilizers or other chemicals. The Wawona is an excellent place to stay or to stop for lunch, but be aware that the hotel is closed in January. ⊠ *Rte. 41, Wawona* ☎ *209/375–1425.*

SCENIC STOPS

★ **El Capitan.** Rising 3,593 feet—more than 350 stories—above the Valley, El Capitan is the largest exposed-granite monolith in the world. Since 1958, people have been climbing its entire face, including the famous "nose." You can spot adventurers with your binoculars by scanning the smooth and nearly vertical cliff for specks of color. ⊠ *Off Northside Dr., about 4 mi west of the Valley Visitor Center.*

Fodor'sChoice
★
Glacier Point. If you lack the time, desire, or stamina to hike more than 3,200 feet up to Glacier Point from the Yosemite Valley floor, you can drive here—or take a bus from the Valley—for a bird's-eye view. You are likely to encounter a lot of day-trippers on the short, paved trail that leads from the parking lot to the main overlook. Take a moment to veer off a few yards to the Geology Hut, which succinctly explains and

illustrates how the Valley looked like 10 million, 3 million, and 20,000 years ago. For details about the summer-only buses, call ☎ 209/372–1240. ⊠ *Glacier Point Rd., 16 mi northeast of Rte. 41.*

★ **Half Dome.** Visitors' eyes are continually drawn to this remarkable granite formation that tops out at more than 4,700 feet above the Valley floor. Despite its name, the dome is actually about three-quarters "intact." You can hike to the top of Half Dome on an 8.5-mi (one-way) trail whose last 400 feet must be ascended while holding onto a steel cable. To see Half Dome reflected in the Merced River, view it from Sentinel Bridge just before sundown. But stay for sunset, when the setting sun casts a brilliant orange light onto Half Dome, a stunning sight.

Hetch Hetchy Reservoir. When Congress green-lighted the O'Shaughnessy Dam in 1913, pragmatism triumphed over aestheticism. Some 2.4 million residents of the San Francisco Bay Area continue to get their water from this 117-billion-gallon reservoir, although spirited efforts are being made to restore the Hetch Hetchy Valley to its former, pristine glory. Eight miles long, the reservoir is Yosemite's largest body of water, and one that can be seen up close from several trails. ⊠ *Hetch Hetchy Rd., about 15 mi north of the Big Oak Flat entrance station.*

High Country. The above-tree-line, high-alpine region east of the Valley—a land of alpenglow and top-of-the-world vistas—is often missed by crowds who come to gawk at the Valley's more publicized splendors. Summer wildflowers, which usually spring up mid-July through August, carpet the meadows and mountainsides with pink, purple, blue, red, yellow, and orange. On foot or on horseback are the only ways to get here. For information on trails and backcountry permits, check with the visitor center.

38

★ **Mariposa Grove of Big Trees.** Of Yosemite National Parks' three sequoia groves—the others being Merced and Tuolumne, both near Crane Flat well to the north—Mariposa is by far the largest and easiest to walk around. Grizzly Giant, whose base measures 96 feet around, has been estimated to be the world's 25th largest tree by volume. Perhaps more astoundingly, it's about 2,700 years old. On up the hill, you'll find many more sequoias, a small museum, and fewer people. Summer weekends are especially crowded here. Consider taking the free shuttle from Wawona. ⊠ *Rte. 41, 2 mi north of the South Entrance station.*

Sentinel Dome. The view from here is similar to that from Glacier Point, except you can't see the Valley floor. A moderately steep 1.1-mi path climbs to the viewpoint from the parking lot. Topping out at an elevation of 8,122 feet, Sentinel is more than 900 feet higher than Glacier Point. ⊠ *Glacier Point Rd., off Rte. 41.*

★ **Tuolumne Meadows.** The largest subalpine meadow in the Sierra (at 8,600 feet) is a popular way station for backpack trips along the Pacific Crest and John Muir trails. The setting is not as dramatic as Yosemite Valley, 56 mi away, but the almost perfectly flat basin, about 2½ mi long, is intriguing, and in July it's resplendent with wildflowers. The most popular day hike is up Lembert Dome, atop which you'll have breathtaking views of the basin below. Keep in mind that Tioga Road rarely opens sooner than June and usually closes by mid-October. ⊠ *Tioga Rd. (Rte. 120), about 8 mi west of the Tioga Pass entrance station.*

WATERFALLS

Yosemite's waterfalls are at their most spectacular in May and June. When the snow starts to melt (usually peaking in May), almost every rocky lip or narrow gorge becomes a spillway for streaming snowmelt churning down to meet the Merced River. By summer's end, some falls, including the mighty Yosemite Falls, dry up. They begin flowing again in late fall, and in winter they may be hung dramatically with ice. Even in drier months, the waterfalls can be breathtaking. If you choose to hike any of the trails to or up the falls, be sure to wear shoes with good, no-slip soles; the rocks can be extremely slick. Stay on trails at all times.

■TIP→ Visit the park during a full moon, and you can stroll in the evening without a flashlight and still make out the ribbons of falling water, as well as silhouettes of the giant granite monoliths.

Bridalveil Fall. The filmy waterfall of 620 feet is often diverted as much as 20 feet one way or the other by the breeze. It is the first marvelous view of Yosemite Valley you will see if you come in via Route 41. ⊠ *Yosemite Valley, access from parking area off Wawona Rd.*

Nevada Fall. Climb Mist Trail from Happy Isles for an up-close view of this 594-foot cascading beauty, the first major fall as the Merced River plunges out of the high country toward the eastern end of Yosemite Valley. If you don't want to hike, you can see it—distantly—from Glacier Point. ⊠ *Yosemite Valley, access via Mist Trail from Nature Center at Happy Isles.*

Ribbon Fall. At 1,612 feet, this is the highest single fall in North America. It's also the first valley waterfall to dry up in summer; the rainwater and melted snow that create the slender fall evaporate quickly at this height. Look just west of El Capitan from the Valley floor for the best view of the fall from the base of Bridalveil Fall. ⊠ *Yosemite Valley, west of El Capitan Meadow.*

Vernal Fall. Fern-covered black rocks frame this 317-foot fall, and rainbows play in the spray at its base. You can get a distance view from Glacier Point, or hike to see it close up. ⊠ *Yosemite Valley, access via Mist Trail from Nature Center at Happy Isles.*

Fodor'sChoice
★

Yosemite Falls. Actually three falls, they together constitute the highest waterfall in North America and the fifth-highest in the world. The water from the top descends a total of 2,425 feet, and when the falls run hard, you can hear them thunder all across the Valley. When they dry up—usually in late summer—the Valley seems naked without the wavering tower of spray. ■TIP→ If you hike the mile-long loop trail (partially paved) to the base of the Lower Falls during the peak water flow in May, expect to get soaked. You can get a view of of the falls from the lawn of Yosemite Chapel, off Southside Drive. ⊠ *Yosemite Valley, access from Yosemite Lodge or trail parking area.*

VISITOR CENTERS

Le Conte Memorial Lodge. This small but striking National Historic Landmark, with its granite walls and steeply pitched shingle roof, is Yosemite's first permanent public information center. Step inside to see the cathedral-like interior, which contains a library and environmental exhibits. To find out about evening programs, check the kiosk out front,

look in the park's newspaper, or visit ⊕ *www.sierraclub.org.* ⊠ *Southside Dr., about ½ mi west of Curry Village* ☉ *Memorial Day–Labor Day, Wed.–Sun. 10–4.*

Valley Visitor Center. At this center—which was overhauled in 2007—you can learn how Yosemite Valley was formed and about its vegetation, animals, and human inhabitants. Don't leave without watching the superb *Spirit of Yosemite,* a 23-minute introductory film that runs every half-hour in the theater behind the visitor center. ⊠ *Yosemite Village* ☎ *209/372–0299* ☉ *Late May–early Sept., daily 8–6; early Sept.–late May, daily 9–5.*

SPORTS AND THE OUTDOORS

BICYCLING

There may be no more enjoyable way to see Yosemite Valley than to ride a bike beneath its lofty granite monoliths. The eastern valley has 12 mi of paved, flat bicycle paths across meadows and through woods, with bike racks at convenient stopping points. For a greater challenge, you can ride on 196 mi of paved park roads—but bicycles are not allowed on hiking trails or in the backcountry. Kids under 18 must wear a helmet.

OUTFITTERS AND EXPEDITIONS You can get **Yosemite bike rentals** (⊠ *Yosemite Lodge or Curry Village* ☎ *209/372–1208* ⊕ *www.yosemitepark.com* ☞ *$9.50/hour, $25.50/day* ☉ *Apr.–Oct.*) from either Yosemite Lodge or Curry Village bike stands. Bikes with child trailers, baby-jogger strollers, and wheelchairs are available.

BIRD-WATCHING

Nearly 250 bird species have been spotted in the park, including the sage sparrow, pygmy owl, blue grouse, and mountain bluebird. Park rangers lead free bird-watching walks in Yosemite Valley one day each week in summer; check at a visitor center or information station for times and locations. Binoculars are sometimes available for loan.

OUTFITTERS AND EXPEDITIONS The Yosemite Association sponsors one- to four-day **birding seminars** (☎ *209/379–2321* ⊕ *www.yosemite.org* ☞ *$82–$254* ☉ *Apr.–Aug.*) for beginner and intermediate birders.

FISHING

The waters in Yosemite are not stocked; trout, mostly brown and rainbow, live here but are not plentiful. Yosemite's fishing season begins on the last Saturday in April and ends on November 15. Some waterways are off-limits at certain times; be sure to inquire at the visitor center about regulations.

A California fishing license is required; licenses run $12.60 for one day, $19.45 for two days, and $38.85 for 10 days. Full season licenses cost $38.85 for state residents, and a whopping $104.20 for nonresidents. Buy your license in season at **Yosemite Village Sport Shop** (☎ *209/372–1286*) or at the **Wawona Store** (☎ *209/375–6574*). Obtain a license in advance of your trip by contacting the **California Department of Fish and Game** (⊠ *3211 S St., Sacramento CA 95814* ☎ *916/227–2245* ⊕ *www.dfg.ca.gov*).

HIKING

OUTFITTERS
AND
EXPEDITIONS

The staff at the **Wilderness Center** (☎ 209/372–0740), in Yosemite Village, provides free wilderness permits, which are required for overnight camping (advance reservations are available for $5 and are highly recommended for popular trailheads from May through September and on weekends). The staff here also provide maps and advice to hikers heading into the backcountry. From April through November, **Yosemite Mountaineering School and Guide Service** (✉ *Yosemite Mountain Shop, Curry Village* ☎ 209/372–8344) leads two-hour to full-day treks.

EASY

"A Changing Yosemite" Interpretive Trail. Take this 1-mi, wheelchair-accessible, looped path about Cook's Meadow to see and learn the basics about Yosemite Valley's past, present, and future. A self-guiding trail guide (50¢) explains the differences among oaks, cedars, and pines; how fires help keeping the Valley floor healthy; and how human factors such as pollution pose significant challenges to the park's inhabitants. ✉ *Trailhead across from the Valley Visitor Center.*

★ **Yosemite Falls Trail.** This is the highest waterfall in North America. The upper fall (1,430 feet), the middle cascades (675 feet), and the lower fall (320 feet) combine for a total of 2,425 feet and, when viewed from the valley, appear as a single waterfall. The ¼-mi trail leads from the parking lot to the base of the falls. Upper Yosemite Fall Trail, a strenuous 3½-mi climb rising 2,700 feet, takes you above the top of the falls. ✉ *Trailhead off Camp 4, north of Northside Dr.*

MODERATE

★ **Mist Trail.** More visitors take this trail (or portions of it) than any other in the park other than Lower Yosemite Falls. The trek up to and back from Vernal Fall is 3 mi. Add another 4 mi total by continuing up to 594-foot Nevada Fall; the trail becomes quite steep and slippery in its final stages. The elevation gain to Vernal Fall is 1,000 feet, and to Nevada Fall an additional 1,000 feet. Merced River tumbles down both falls on its way to a tranquil flow through the Valley. ✉ *Trailhead at Happy Isles.*

★ **Panorama Trail.** Few hikes come with the visual punch that this 8½-mi trail provides. The star attraction is Half Dome, visible from many intriguing angles, but you also see three waterfalls up close and walk through a manzanita grove. Before you begin, look down on Yosemite Valley from Glacier Point, a special experience in itself. ✉ *Trailhead at Glacier Point.*

DIFFICULT

Chilnualna Falls Trail. This Wawona-area trail runs 4 mi one way to the top of the falls, then leads into the backcountry, connecting with miles of other trails. This is one of the park's most inspiring and secluded—albeit strenuous—trails. Past the tumbling cascade, and up through forests, you'll emerge before a panoramic vista at the top. ✉ *Trailhead at Chilnualna Falls Rd., off Rte. 41, Wawona.*

Fodor's Choice
★

John Muir Trail to Half Dome. Ardent and courageous trekkers can continue on from the top of Nevada Fall, off Mist Trail, to the top of Half Dome. Some hikers attempt this entire 10- to 12-hour, 16¾-mi round-trip trek from Happy Isles in one day; if you're planning to do this, remember that the 4,800-foot elevation gain and the 8,842-foot altitude will cause

38

shortness of breath. Another option is to hike to a campground in Little Yosemite Valley near the top of Nevada Fall the first day, then climb to the top of Half Dome and hike out the next day; it's highly recommended that you get your wilderness permit reservations at least a month in advance. Be sure to wear hiking boots and bring gloves. The last pitch up the back of Half Dome is very steep—the only way to climb this sheer rock face is to pull yourself up using the steel cable handrails, which are in place only from late spring to early fall. Those who brave the ascent will be rewarded with an unbeatable view of Yosemite Valley below and the high country beyond. ⊠ *Trailhead at Happy Isles.*

HORSEBACK RIDING

Reservations for guided trail rides must be made in advance at the hotel tour desks or by phone. For overnight saddle trips, which use mules, call ☎ 559/253–5673 on or after September 15 to request a lottery application for the following year. Scenic trail rides range from two hours to a full day; six-day High Sierra saddle trips are also available.

OUTFITTERS AND EXPEDITIONS **Tuolumne Meadows Stables** (⊠ *Off Tioga Rd., 2 mi east of Tuolumne Meadows Visitor Center* ☎ *209/372–8427* ⊕ *www.yosemitepark.com*) runs two-, four-, and eight-hour trips—which cost $53, $69, and $96, respectively—and High Sierra four- to six-day camping treks on mules, beginning at $625. Reservations are essential. **Wawona Stables** (⊠ *Rte. 41, Wawona* ☎ *209/375–6502*) has two- and five-hour rides, starting at $53. Reservations are essential. You can tour the valley and the start of the high country on two-hour, four-hour, and all-day rides at **Yosemite Valley Stables** (⊠ *At entrance to North Pines Campground, 100 yards northeast of Curry Village* ☎ *209/372–8348* ⊕ *www.yosemitepark.com*). Reservations are required for the $53, $69, and $96 trips.

RAFTING

Rafting is permitted only on designated areas of the Middle and South Forks of the Merced River. Check with the Valley Visitor Center for closures and other restrictions.

OUTFITTERS AND EXPEDITIONS The per-person rental fee at **Curry Village raft stand** (⊠ *South side of Southside Dr., Curry Village* ☎ *209/372–8319* ⊕ *www.yosemitepark.com* ⊠ *$20.50* ⊙ *Late May–July*) covers the four- to six-person raft, two paddles, and life jackets, plus a shuttle to the launch point on Sentinel Beach.

ROCK CLIMBING

Fodor'sChoice
★ The granite canyon walls of Yosemite Valley are world-renowned for rock climbing. El Capitan, with its 3,593-foot vertical face, is the most famous and difficult, but there are many other options here for all skill levels.

OUTFITTERS AND EXPEDITIONS The one-day basic lesson at **Yosemite Mountaineering School and Guide Service** (⊠ *Yosemite Mountain Shop, Curry Village* ☎ *209/372–8344* ⊕ *www. yosemitepark.com* ⊠ *$80–$190* ⊙ *Apr.–Nov.*) includes some bouldering and rappelling, and three or four 60-foot climbs. Climbers must be at least 10 (kids under 12 must be accompanied by a parent or guardian) and in reasonably good physical condition. Intermediate and advanced classes include instruction in belays, self-rescue, summer snow climbing, and free climbing.

WINTER SPORTS

The beauty of Yosemite under a blanket of snow has long inspired poets and artists, as well as ordinary folks. Skiing and snowshoeing activities in the park center on Badger Pass Ski Area, California's oldest snow-sports resort, which is about 40 minutes away from the valley on Glacier Point Road. Here you can rent equipment, take a lesson, have lunch, join a guided excursion, and take the free shuttle back to the valley after a drink in the lounge.

ICE-SKATING

Curry Village ice-skating rink. Winter visitors have skated at this outdoor rink for decades, and there's no mystery why: it's a kick to glide across the ice while soaking up views of Half Dome and Glacier Point. ⊠ *South side of Southside Dr., Curry Village* ☎ *209/372–8319* ⚏ *$8 per 2 hrs, $3 skate rental* ☉ *Mid-Nov.–mid-Mar. afternoons and evenings daily, morning sessions weekends (hrs vary).*

SKIING AND SNOWSHOEING

Badger Pass Ski Area. California's first ski resort has five lifts and 10 downhill runs, as well as 90 mi of groomed cross-country trails. Free shuttle buses from Yosemite Valley operate during ski season (December through early April, weather permitting). Lift tickets are $38, downhill equipment rents for $24, and snowboard rental with boots is $35. The gentle slopes of Badger Pass make **Yosemite Ski School** (☎ *209/372–8430*) an ideal spot for children and beginners to learn downhill skiing or snowboarding for as little as $28 for a group lesson. The highlight of Yosemite's cross-country skiing center is a 21-mi loop from Badger Pass to Glacier Point. You can rent cross-country skis for $21.50 per day at the **Cross-Country Ski School** (☎ *209/372–8444*), which also rents snowshoes ($19.50 per day), telemarking equipment ($29), and skate-skis ($24). **Yosemite Mountaineering School** (⊠ *Badger Pass Ski Area* ☎ *209/372–8344* ⊕ *www.yosemitepark.com*) conducts snowshoeing, cross-country skiing, telemarking, and skate-skiing classes starting at $30. ⊠ *Badger Pass Rd., off Glacier Point Rd., 18 mi from Yosemite Valley* ☎ *209/372–8430.*

SWIMMING

The pools at **Curry Village** (☎ *209/372–8324* ⊕ *www.yosemitepark.com*) and **Yosemite Lodge** (☎ *209/372–1250* ⊕ *www.yosemitepark.com*) are open to nonguests for $5, late May through early or mid-September. Additionally, several swimming holes with small sandy beaches can be found in midsummer along the Merced River at the eastern end of Yosemite Valley. Find gentle waters to swim; currents are often stronger than they appear, and temperatures are chilling. To conserve riparian habitats, step into the river at sandy beaches and other obvious entry points. ⚠ **Do not attempt to swim above or near waterfalls or rapids; fatalities have occurred.**

EDUCATIONAL OFFERINGS

CLASSES AND SEMINARS

Art Classes. Professional artists conduct workshops in watercolor, etching, drawing, and other mediums. Bring your own materials or purchase the basics at the Art Activity Center, next to the Village Store. Call to verify scheduling. ☒ *Art Activity Center, Yosemite Village* ☎ *209/372–1442* ⊕ *www.yosemitepark.com* ✉ *Free* ⊗ *Early Apr.–early Oct., Mon.–Sat., 10 AM–2 PM.*

Yosemite Outdoor Adventures. Naturalists, scientists, and park rangers lead multi-hour to multiday educational outings on topics from woodpeckers to fire management to pastel painting. Most sessions take place spring through fall, but a few focus on winter phenomena. ☒ *Various locations* ☎ *209/379–2321* ⊕ *www.yosemite.org* ✉ *$82–$465.*

MUSEUMS

Nature Center at Happy Isles. Designed for children, this small museum could use some updating. One of its dioramas has several stuffed animals, including a baby bear. Taxidermy hardly promotes a spirit of conservation and respect for living creatures; carvings and synthetics, like the ones you'll find at the Valley Visitor Center, are better alternatives these days. The Nature Center at Happy Isles also has a small gift shop, with coloring books, T-shirts, and water bottles. ☒ *Off Southside Dr., about ¾ mi east of Curry Village* ✉ *Free* ⊗ *Mid-May–Oct., 10–noon and 12:30–4.*

Yosemite Museum. This small museum consists of a permanent exhibit room and an adjacent gallery that promotes contemporary Yosemite art. An American Indian is sometimes on hand to demonstrate the ancient techniques of beadwork and basket weaving, as well as answer your questions. ☒ *Yosemite Village* ☎ *209/372–0299* ✉ *Free* ⊗ *Daily 9–noon and 1–4:30.*

38

RANGER PROGRAMS

Junior Ranger Program. Children ages 3 to 13 can participate in the informal, self-guided Little Cub and Junior Ranger programs. A park activity handbook ($8) is available at the Valley Visitor Center or the Nature Center at Happy Isles; once your child has completed the book, a ranger will present him or her with a certificate and a badge. ☒ *Valley Visitor Center or the Nature Center at Happy Isles* ☎ *209/372–0299.*

Ranger-Led Programs. Rangers lead walks and hikes and give informative and entertaining talks on a range of topics at different locations several times a day from spring through fall. The schedule is reduced in winter, but most days you can usually find a ranger program somewhere in the park. In the evenings at Yosemite Lodge and Curry Village, lectures by rangers, slide shows, and documentary films present unique perspectives on Yosemite. On summer weekends, Camp Curry and Tuolumne Meadows Campground host sing-along campfire programs. There's usually at least one ranger-led activity each night in the Valley; schedules and locations are posted on bulletin boards throughout the park and published in the *Yosemite Guide* you receive when you enter the park.

Q & A with Ranger Scott Gediman

What's your favorite thing to do in the park?

I really enjoy hiking in Yosemite; in my opinion there's no better way to see the park. My favorite is the classic hike up the Mist Trail to Vernal Fall. I've done it literally hundreds of times—I've got family photos of my folks pushing me up the trail in a stroller. If you can only take one hike in Yosemite, do this one, especially in spring and summer.

Which time of year is best for visiting Yosemite?

The spring is wonderful, with the waterfalls going full blast and the meadows so green. The fall colors are beautiful, too. But in winter, the weather is great. The most stunning time in the valley is when a winter storm clears and there are incredible blue skies above the granite rocks, and the snow. There's a feeling you get seeing Half Dome with snow on it, or doing a winter hike on the Four-Mile Trail, Yosemite Falls Trail, or the Glacier Point trails.

What's there to do here in winter?

There's the ice-skating rink at Curry Village, and up at Badger Pass there's a wonderful ski school that specializes in teaching kids. There's cross-country skiing on groomed tracks along Glacier Point Road. Snowshoeing is really catching on. It's fun, it's easy, families can do it. You don't need special skills or a bunch of gear to go hiking through the snow; just put some snowshoes on your sneakers or hiking boots, and you're off. Every morning from about mid-December to mid-March, park rangers lead free snowshoe walks from Badger Pass. We talk about winter ecology and adaptations animals make, or we

hike up to the old Badger Summit for some fantastic views.

What about summer?

There's a misperception that the crowds are unmanageable, but it's not true. It's very easy to get away from the crowds in the Valley. One easy way is to hike the Valley Loop Trail, which a lot of people don't even know about. It goes all around the valley perimeter. Five minutes from Yosemite Lodge, and you won't see anybody.

How crowded does the Valley really get?

At the busiest time, probably Memorial Day Weekend, there can be as many as 25,000 people in the park at one time, many of them in the Valley. The biggest mistake people make in summer is to drive everywhere. It's frustrating because of the traffic, and it takes longer even than walking. Park your car in the day-use lot or leave it at your hotel, and take the free shuttle around. The shuttle goes to all the popular spots in the Valley.

TOURS

★ **Ansel Adams Photo Walks.** Photography enthusiasts shouldn't miss these two-hour guided camera walks that are offered three mornings each week—Tuesday, Thursday, and Saturday—by professional photographers. Some walks are hosted by the Ansel Adams Gallery, others by Delaware North; meeting points vary. All are free, but participation is limited to 15 people. Reservations are essential. To reserve a spot, call up to 10 days in advance or visit the gallery. ☎ *209/372–4413 or 800/568–7398* ⊕ *www.anseladams.com* ✉ *Free.*

Big Trees Tram Tour. This open-air tram tour of the Mariposa Grove of Big Trees departs from the parking lot every half-hour, covers 7 mi, and takes 75 minutes. As an alternative to driving here, consider parking at the Wawona Hotel and taking the free shuttle; the ride takes about 15 minutes. ☎ *209/372–1240* ✉ *$25.50* ☯ *Usually June–Oct., depending on snowfall.*

Glacier Point Tour. This four-hour trip takes you from Yosemite Valley (you're picked up from your lodging site) to the Glacier Point vista, 3,214 feet above the Valley floor. ☎ *209/372–1240* ✉ *$41* ⚓ *Reservations essential* ☯ *June–Oct.*

Grand Tour. For a full-day tour of the Mariposa Grove and Glacier Point, try the Grand Tour. The tour stops for lunch at the historic Wawona Hotel, but the meal is not included in the tour price. ☎ *209/372–1240* ✉ *$82 ($10 additional for lunch)* ⚓ *Reservations essential* ☯ *June–Thanksgiving.*

Tuolumne Meadows Tour. For a full day's outing to the high country, opt for this ride up Tioga Road to Tuolumne Meadows. You'll stop at several overlooks, and you can connect with another shuttle at Tuolumne Lodge. This service is mostly for hikers and backpackers who want to reach high-country trailheads, but anyone can ride. ☎ *209/372–1240* ✉ *$23* ⚓ *Reservations essential* ☯ *July–Labor Day.*

Valley Floor Tour. Take a 26-mi, two-hour tour of the Valley's highlights, with narration on area history, geology, and plant and animal life. Tour vehicles are either trams or enclosed motor coaches, depending on weather conditions. Tours run year-round. **Moonlight Tour,** a late-evening version of the Valley Floor Tour, takes place on moonlit nights, depending on weather conditions. ☎ *209/372–1240* ✉ *$25, $66 for a family of four* ☯ *Apr.–Sept.*

☾ **Wee Wild Ones.** Designed for kids 6 and under, this 45-minute program includes animal-theme games, songs, stories, and craft activities. The event is held outdoors before the regular Yosemite Lodge or Curry Village evening programs in summer and fall; children gather in daytime before the Ahwahnee's big fireplace in winter and spring. All children must be accompanied by an adult. ☎ *209/372–1240* ✉ *Free.*

38

Ansel Adams's Black and White Yosemite

What John Muir did for Yosemite with words, Ansel Adams did with photographs. His photographs have inspired millions of people to visit Yosemite, and his persistent activism has helped to ensure the park's conservation.

Born in 1902, Adams first came to the valley when he was 14, photographing it with a Box Brownie camera. He later said his first visit "was a culmination of experience so intense as to be almost painful. From that day in 1916 my life has been colored and modulated by the great earth gesture of the Sierra." By 1919 he was working in the valley, as custodian of LeConte Memorial Lodge, the Sierra Club headquarters in Yosemite National Park.

Adams had harbored dreams of a career as a concert pianist, but the park sealed his fate as a photographer in 1928, the day he shot *Monolith: The Face of Half Dome*, which remains one of his most famous works. Adams also married Virginia Best in 1928, in her father's studio in the valley (now the Ansel Adams Gallery).

As Adams's photographic career took off, Yosemite began to sear itself into the American consciousness. David Brower, first executive director of the Sierra Club, later said of Adams' impact, "That Ansel Adams came to be recognized as one of the great photographers of this century is a tribute to the places that informed him."

In 1934 Adams was elected to the Sierra Club's board of directors; he would serve until 1971. As a representative of the conservation group, he combined his work with the club's mission, showing his photographs of the Sierra to influential officials such as Secretary of the Interior Harold L.

Ickes, who showed them to President Franklin Delano Roosevelt. The images were a key factor in the establishment of Kings Canyon National Park.

In 1968, the Department of the Interior granted Adams its highest honor, the Conservation Service Award, and in 1980 he received the Presidential Medal of Freedom in recognition of his conservation work. Until his death in 1984, Adams continued not only to record Yosemite's majesty on film but to urge the federal government and park managers to do right by the park.

In one of his many public pleas on behalf of Yosemite, Adams said, "Yosemite Valley itself is one of the great shrines of the world and—belonging to all our people—must be both protected and appropriately accessible." As an artist and an activist, Adams never gave up on his dream of keeping Yosemite wild yet within reach of every visitor who wants to experience that wildness.

ARTS AND ENTERTAINMENT

Vintage Music of Yosemite. From spring through fall, a pianist-singer performs four hours of live old-time music at the Wawona Hotel (call for schedule). ⊠ *Wawona Hotel, Rte. 41, Wawona* ☎ *209/375–1425* ✉ *Free* ⊙ *Shows May–Oct. at 5:30.*

Yosemite Theatre. Theatrical and musical presentations are held at various times throughout the year. One of the best loved is Lee Stetson's portrayal of John Muir in *Conversation with a Tramp, John Muir Is Back—And Boy Is He Ticked Off!,* and *The Spirit of John Muir.* Tickets should be purchased in advance at the Valley Visitor Center. Unsold seats are available at the door at performance time, 8 PM. ⊠ *Valley Visitor Center auditorium* ☎ *209/372–0299* ✉ *$8–$10.*

SHOPPING

The Ahwahnee Gift Shop. This shop sells comparatively upscale items, such as American Indian crafts, photographic prints, nice photo frames, handmade bowls, and jewelry. Look too at the book selection, which includes writings by John Muir. ⊠ *Ahwahnee Hotel* ☎ *209/372–1409.*

Ansel Adams Gallery. Here you can purchase gorgeous prints by the nature photographer, from posters that cost about $30 apiece to more expensive framed images. Contemporary photographers' works are sold here, too, along with American Indian jewelry and handicrafts. The gallery's elegant camera shop conducts photography workshops and sometimes holds private showings of fine prints on Saturdays. ⊠ *Northside Dr., Yosemite Village* ☎ *209/372–4413 or 888/361–7622 or 800/568–7398* ⊙ *Apr.–Oct., daily 9–6; Nov.–Mar., daily 10–5.*

38

WHAT'S NEARBY

NEARBY TOWNS

Marking the southern end of the Sierra's gold-bearing mother lode, **Mariposa** is the last moderate-sized town before you enter Yosemite on Route 140. In addition to a mining museum, Mariposa has numerous shops, restaurants, and service stations. Motels and restaurants dot both sides of Route 41 as it cuts through the town of **Oakhurst,** a boomtown during the Gold Rush that is now a magnet for fast-food restaurants and chain stores. Oakhurst has a population of about 13,000 and sits 15 mi south of the park. The gracious **Sonora,** 70 mi west of the park via Routes 120 and 49, retains evidence of its own vibrant, Gold Rush history. Stroll Washington Street and see Old West storefronts with second-story porches and 19th-century hotels. The tiny town of **Lee Vining,** near the park's eastern entrance, is home to the eerily beautiful, salty Mono Lake, where millions of migratory birds nest. Visit **Mammoth Lakes,** about 40 mi southeast of Yosemite's Tioga Pass entrance, for excellent skiing and snowboarding in winter, with fishing, mountain biking, hiking, and horseback riding in summer. Nine deep-blue lakes form the Mammoth Lakes Basin, and another hundred dot the surrounding countryside. Devils Postpile National Monument sits at the base of Mammoth Mountain.

VISITOR INFORMATION
Lee Vining Office and Information Center ⬚ *P.O. Box 29, Lee Vining, CA 93541* ☎ *760/647-6595* ⊕ *www.leevining.com.* **Mammoth Lakes Visitors Bureau** ⬚ *Along Rte. 203 (Main St.), near Sawmill Cutoff Rd., Mammoth Lakes 93546* ☎ *760/934-2712 or 888/466-2666* ⊕ *www.visitmammoth. com.* **Mariposa County Visitors Bureau** ⬚ *5158 Rte. 140, Mariposa 95338* ☎ *209/966-7082 or 888/554-9013* ⊕ *www.homeofyosemite.com.* **Tuolumne County Visitors Bureau** ⬚ *P.O. Box 4020, Sonora, CA 95370* ☎ *209/533-4420 or 800/446-1333* ⊕ *www.thegreatunfenced.com.* **Yosemite Sierra Visitors Bureau** ⬚ *41969 Rte. 41, Oakhurst 93644* ☎ *559/683-4636* ⊕ *www. yosemitethisyear.com.*

NEARBY ATTRACTIONS

★ **Bodie Ghost Town.** Old shacks and shops, abandoned mine shafts, a Methodist church, the mining village of Rattlesnake Gulch, and the remains of a small Chinatown are among the sights at this fascinating ghost town turned state historic park, which sits at an elevation of 8,200 feet. The town boomed from about 1878 to 1881, but by the late 1940s, all its residents had departed. A state park was established here in 1962, with a mandate to preserve the town in a state of "arrested decay," but not to restore it. Evidence of Bodie's wild past survives at an excellent museum, and you can tour an old stamp mill (where ore was stamped into fine powder to extract gold and silver) and a ridge that contains many mine sites. No food, drink, or lodging is available in Bodie; the nearest picnic area is ½ mi away. The town is 23 mi from Lee Vining, north on U.S. 395, then east on Route 270; the last 3 mi are unpaved. Snow may close Route 270 late fall through early spring, but you can ski the 13 mi from the highway to the park. ⬚ *Main and Green Sts., Bodie* ☎ *760/647-6445* ⊕ *www.parks.ca.gov* 🎫 *Park $2, museum free* ☉ *Park: Memorial Day–Labor Day, daily 8–7; early Sept.– late May, daily 8–4. Museum: Memorial Day–Labor Day, daily 9–6; early Sept.–late May, hrs vary.*

Devils Postpile National Monument. East of Mammoth Lakes lies this rock formation of smooth, vertical basalt columns sculpted by volcanic and glacial forces. A short, steep trail winds to the top of the 60-foot cliff for a bird's-eye view of the columns. Follow Route 203 west from U.S. 395 to Mammoth Mountain Ski Area to board the shuttle bus to the monument, which you must take if you are a day-use visitor entering the monument between 7:30 AM and 5:30 PM, mid-June through early September. A 2-mi hike past Devils Postpile leads to the monument's second scenic wonder, **Rainbow Falls,** where a branch of the San Joaquin River plunges more than 100 feet over a lava ledge. When the water hits the pool below, sunlight turns the resulting mist into a spray of color. Scenic picnic spots dot the banks of the river. ⬚ *Minaret Rd., Mammoth Lakes* ☎ *760/934-2289, 760/934-0606 shuttle* ⊕ *www.nps. gov/depo* 🎫 *$7* ☉ *Mid-June–Oct., 24 hrs.*

FESTIVALS AND EVENTS

NOVEMBER–DECEMBER

Vintners' Holidays. Free two- and three-day seminars by California's most prestigious vintners are held midweek in the Great Room of the Ahwahnee Hotel in Yosemite Village and culminate in an elegant—albeit pricey—banquet dinner. Arrive early for seats in the free seminars; book early for lodging and dining packages. ☎ 559/253–5641
⊕ www.yosemitepark.com.

DECEMBER

The Bracebridge Dinner. Held at the Ahwahnee Hotel in Yosemite Village every Christmas since 1928, this 17th-century-themed madrigal dinner is so popular that you must book in mid-May to secure a seat. ☎ 559/252–4848
⊕ www.yosemitepark.com.

JANUARY–FEBRUARY

Chefs' Holidays. Celebrated chefs present cooking demonstrations and five-course meals at the Ahwahnee Hotel in Yosemite Village on weekends from early January through early February. Special lodging packages are available; space is limited. ☎ 559/253–5641
⊕ www.yosemitepark.com.

MAY

Fireman's Muster. North of Sonora in the old mining town of Columbia, history springs to life at this festival of antique fire engines, with hose-spraying contests and a parade of the old pumpers. ☎ 209/536–1672.

Mother Lode Roundup Parade and Rodeo. On Mother's Day weekend the town of Sonora celebrates its gold-mining, agricultural, and lumbering heritage with a parade, rodeo, entertainment, and food. ☎ 209/532–7428 or 800/446–1333.

JULY

Mammoth Lakes Jazz Jubilee. This festival, founded in 1989, is hosted by the local Temple of Folly Jazz Band and takes place in 10 venues, most with dance floors. ☎ 760/934–2478 or 800/367–6572
⊕ www.mammothjazz.org.

AUGUST

Bluesapalooza. For one long weekend every summer, Mammoth Lakes hosts a blues and beer festival—with an emphasis on the beer tasting. ☎ 760/934–0606 or 800/367–6572
⊕ www.mammothmountain.com.

OCTOBER

Sierra Art Trails. The work of more than 100 artists is on display in studios and galleries throughout eastern Madera and Mariposa counties. Purchase the catalog of locations and hours at area shops. ☎ 559/658–8844
⊕ www.sierraarttrails.org.

Oakhurst Fall Chocolate and Wine Festival. Dessert judging, vendor booths, a beauty pageant, and more celebrate the glories of the world's most beloved sweet. ☎ 559/683–1993
⊕ www.wildwonderfulwomen.net.

38

Hot Creek Geologic Site. Forged by an ancient volcanic eruption, the Hot Creek Geologic Site is a landscape of boiling hot springs, fumaroles, and geysers about 10 mi southeast of the town of Mammoth Lakes. You can walk along boardwalks through the canyon to view the steaming volcanic features. Fly-fishing for trout is popular upstream from the springs. En route to Hot Creek Geologic Site is the **Hot Creek Fish Hatchery** (⊠ *Hot*

Creek Hatchery Rd. east of U.S. 395, Mammoth Lakes ☎ *760/934–2664* ✉ *Free* ☉ *June–Oct., daily 8–4, depending on snowfall)*, the breeding ponds for most of the fish (3–5 million annually) the state uses to stock eastern Sierra lakes and rivers. ✉ *Hot Creek Hatchery Rd. east of U.S. 395, Mammoth Lakes* ☎ *760/924–5500* ✉ *Free* ☉ *Daily sunrise–sunset.*

★ **Mono Lake.** Since the 1940s the city of Los Angeles has diverted water from the streams that feed this lake, lowering its water level and exposing striking towers of tufa, or calcium carbonate. Court victories by environmentalists have forced a reduction of the diversions, and the lake is rising again. Millions of migratory birds nest in and around Mono Lake. If you join the naturalist-guided **South Tufa Walk,** bring your binoculars. Tours depart the South Tufa parking lot 5 mi east of U.S. 395 on Route 120 and last about 1½ hours. ✉ *South of Lee Vining on U.S. 395* ☎ *760/647–3044* ⊕ *www.monolake.org* ✉ *$3* ☉ *Walks weekends at 1* PM.

Yosemite Mountain–Sugar Pine Railroad. Travel back to a time when powerful locomotives hauled massive log trains through the Sierra. This 4-mi, narrow-gauge, steam-powered railroad excursion takes you near Yosemite's south gate; there's also a moonlight special, with dinner and entertainment. Take Route 41 south from Yosemite about 8 mi to the departure point. ✉ *56001 Rte. 41, Fish Camp* ☎ *559/683–7273* ⊕ *www.ymsprr.com* ✉ *$13–$46* ☉ *Mar.–Oct., daily; hrs vary.*

AREA ACTIVITIES

SPORTS AND THE OUTDOORS
BOATING AND RAFTING

OUTFITTERS AND EXPEDITIONS **Zephyr Whitewater Expeditions** (☎ *800/431–3636* ⊕ *www.zrafting.com*), in Columbia, conducts half-day to three-day white-water trips on the Tuolumne, Merced, and American rivers for paddlers of all experience levels.

SKIING

★ **Mammoth Mountain** (✉ *Rte. 203, off U.S. 395, Mammoth Lakes* ☎ *800/626–6684* ⊕ *www.mammothmountain.com*), one of the nation's premier ski resorts, offers more than 3,500 acres of skiable boulevards, canyons, and bowls, and a 3,100-foot vertical drop. Ski season starts in November and can run through June. There's a ski school, cross-country trails, snowboarding, snowmobiling, and dogsledding. You can rent or buy equipment. The resort has extensive lodging, dining, and shopping options in the Village at Mammoth.

WHERE TO EAT AND STAY

ABOUT THE RESTAURANTS

Yosemite National Park has a couple of moderately priced restaurants in lovely (which almost goes without saying) settings: the Mountain Room at Yosemite Lodge and Wawona Hotel's dining room. And the Ahwahnee Hotel provides one of the finest dining experiences in the country.

Otherwise, food service is geared toward satisfying the masses as efficiently as possible. Yosemite Lodge's food court and Curry Village Pavilion's buffet (breakfast and dinner only) are the Valley's best lower-cost, hot-food options. In Valley Village, the Village Grill whips up burgers and fries, Degnan's Deli has $5–$7 made-to-order sandwiches, and Loft Pizzeria has a chaletlike open dining area in which you can enjoy pizza, salads, and desserts until 9 PM. The White Wolf Lodge and Tuolumne Meadows Lodge—both off Tioga Road and therefore guaranteed open only from early June through September—have small restaurants where meals are competently prepared. Tuolumne Meadows also has a grill, as does the store at Glacier Point, and Sliders Grab-N-Go serves fast food during the ski season at Badger Pass, off Glacier Point Road.

ABOUT THE HOTELS

Indoor lodging options inside the park are perhaps a bit more expensive than initially seems warranted, but that small premium pays off big-time in terms the time you'll save—unless you are bunking within a few miles of a Yosemite entrance, you will face really long commutes to the park when you stay outside it's borders (though the Yosemite View Lodge, on Route 140, is within a reasonable hour's drive of Yosemite Valley). If you can, book something appropriate to your needs and your bank balance in the Valley.

38

Because of Yosemite National Park's immense popularity—not just with tourists from around the world but with Northern Californians who make weekend trips here—reservations are all but mandatory.

Delaware North Companies Parks and Resorts (*6771 N. Palm Ave., Fresno, CA 93704* ☎ *559/252–4848* ⊕ *www.yosemitepark.com*), which handles most in-park reservations, takes reservations beginning one year plus one day in advance of your proposed stay. Or, you can roll the dice by showing up at the front desk and asking if there have been any cancellations.

ABOUT THE CAMPGROUNDS

It should come as no surprise that the 464 campsites within Yosemite Valley are the park's most tightly spaced and, along with the 304-site campground at Tuolumne Meadows, the most difficult to secure on anything approaching short notice—say, less than three months. If you are going to concentrate solely on Valley sites and activities, you should endeavor to stay in one of the three "Pines" campgrounds, which are clustered near Curry Village and within an easy stroll from that busy complex's many facilities (buffet, shops, pool, bike rentals, etc.). For a more primitive and quiet experience, and to be near many backcountry hikes, try one of the Tioga Road campgrounds, a few of which are several miles off that seasonal road and therefore quite remote. From the

CAMPING IN BEAR COUNTRY

The national parks' campgrounds and some campgrounds outside the parks provide food-storage boxes that can keep bears from pilfering your edibles (portable canisters for backpackers can be rented in most park stores). It's imperative that you move all food, coolers, and items with a scent (including toiletries, toothpaste, chewing gum, and air fresheners) from your car (including the trunk) to the storage box at your campsite; day-trippers should lock food in bear boxes provided at parking lots. If you don't, a bear may break into your car by literally peeling off the door or ripping open the trunk, or it may ransack your tent. The familiar tactic of hanging your food from high tree limbs is not an effective deterrent, as bears can easily scale trees. In the Southern Sierra, bear canisters are the only effective and proven method for preventing bears from getting human food.

Wawona Campground, you will have fewer hiking options (although they are good ones), but will be close to the Mariposa Grove of Giant Sequoias, Yosemite's most popular attraction outside of the Valley.

All sites come with picnic tables, fire pits or grills, and a food locker to keep bears from ruining your day. At Valley campgrounds, shower and laundry facilities are nearby. Off the beaten path, at Porcupine Flat, Tamarack Flat, and Yosemite Creek, pit toilets are as good as it gets bathroom-wise, there's no water, and RVs longer than 24 feet are not recommended. No sites in the park have RV hookups.

The park's backcountry and the surrounding wilderness have some unforgettable campsites that can be reached only via long and often difficult hikes or horseback rides. Delaware North operates five High Sierra Camps with comfortable, furnished tent cabins in the remote reaches of Yosemite; rates include breakfast and dinner service. The park concessionaire books the extremely popular backcountry camps by lottery; applications are due by late November for the following summer season. Phone ☎ *801/559–4909* for more information, or check for current availability by navigating from ⊕ *www.yosemitepark.com* to the High Sierra Camps pages.

To camp in a High Sierra campground such as Glen Aulin near Tuolumne Meadows and the centrally placed Merced Lake, you must obtain a wilderness permit. Make reservations up to 24 weeks in advance first by visiting the park's Web site (⊕ *www.nps.gov/yose/planyourvisit/ backpacking.htm*) and checking availability. For a $5 nonrefundable fee, you can make reservations by phone (☎ *209/372–0740*) or by mail (✉ *P.O. Box 545, Yosemite, CA 95389*; make checks payable to "Yosemite Association").

Reservations are required at most of Yosemite's campgrounds, especially in summer. You can reserve a site up to five months in advance; bookings made more than 21 days in advance require prepayment. Unless otherwise noted, book your site through the central **National Park Service Reservations Office** (✉ *P.O. Box 1600, Cumberland, MD 21502* ☎ *800/436–7275* ⊕ *www.recreation.gov* ⊟ D, MC, V ☉ *Daily 7–7.*

WHERE TO EAT

IN THE PARK

In addition to the dining options listed here, you'll find fast-food grills and cafeterias, plus temporary snack bars, hamburger stands, and pizza joints lining park roads in summer. Many dining facilities in the park are open summer only.

$$$–$$$$
CONTINENTAL
Fodor'sChoice
★
✕ **Ahwahnee Hotel Dining Room.** Rave reviews about the dining room's appearance are fully justified—it features floor-to-ceiling windows, a 34-foot-high ceiling with interlaced sugar-pine beams, and massive chandeliers. Although many continue to applaud the food, others have reported that they sense a recent dip in the quality both in the service and what is being served. Diners must spend a lot of money here, so perhaps that inflates the expectations and amplifies the disappointments. In any event, the Sunday brunch ($40) is consistently praised. Reservations are always advised, and for dinner, the attire is "resort casual." ✉ *Ahwahnee Hotel, Ahwahnee Rd., about ¾ mi east of Yosemite Valley Visitor Center, Yosemite Village* ☎ *209/372–1489* ⌚ *Reservations essential* ▭ *AE, D, DC, MC, V.*

¢–$$
AMERICAN
✕ **Food Court at Yosemite Lodge.** Fast and convenient (if outdated), this food court serves simple fare, ranging from hamburgers and pizzas to pastas, carved roasted meats, and salads at lunch and dinner. There's also a selection of beer and wine. At breakfast, you can get pancakes and eggs made any way you like. An espresso and smoothie bar near the entrance keeps longer hours. ✉ *Yosemite Lodge, about ¾ mi west of the visitor center, Yosemite Village* ☎ *209/372–1265* ▭ *AE, D, DC, MC, V.*

$$–$$$
AMERICAN
★
✕ **Mountain Room.** Though good, the food becomes secondary when you see Yosemite Falls through this dining room's wall of windows—almost every table has a view. The chef makes a point of using locally sourced, organic ingredients, so you can be assured of fresh greens and veggies here. The Mountain Room Lounge, a few steps away in the Yosemite Lodge complex, has a broad bar with about 10 beers on tap. ✉ *Yosemite Lodge, Northside Dr. about ¾ mi west of the visitor center, Yosemite Village* ☎ *209/372–1281* ▭ *AE, D, DC, MC, V* ⊘ *No lunch.*

$–$$
AMERICAN
✕ **Pavillion Buffet.** Come to this bustling Curry Village restaurant for a hot, cafeteria-style meal. Bring your tray outside to the deck, and take in the views of the Valley's granite walls. ✉ *Curry Village* ☎ *209/372–8303* ▭ *AE, D, DC, MC, V* ⊘ *Closed mid-Oct.–mid-Apr. No lunch.*

¢–$
FAST FOOD
✕ **Tuolumne Meadows Grill.** Serving continuously throughout the day until 5 or 6 PM, this fast-food grill cooks up breakfast, lunch, and snacks. Stop in for a quick meal before exploring the Meadows. ✉ *Tioga Rd. (Rte. 120), 1½ mi east of Tuolumne Meadows Visitor Center* ☎ *209/372–8426* ▭ *AE, D, DC, MC, V* ⊘ *Closed Oct.–Memorial Day.*

$$–$$$
AMERICAN
✕ **Tuolumne Meadows Lodge.** At the back of a small building that contains the lodge's front desk and small gift shop, this restaurant serves hearty American fare at breakfast and dinner. Let the front desk know in advance if you have any dietary restrictions, and the cooks will not let you down. ✉ *Tioga Rd. (Rte. 120)* ☎ *209/372–8413* ⌚ *Reservations essential* ▭ *AE, D, DC, MC, V* ⊘ *Closed late Sept.–Memorial Day. No lunch.*

38

¢–$ ✕**The Village Grill.** For that burger-joint fix you may be missing from
FAST FOOD life at lower elevations, this family-friendly eatery in Yosemite Village
serves grilled sandwiches from a counter until 6 PM daily. Take your tray
out to the deck and enjoy your meal under the trees. ⊠ *100 yards east
of Yosemite Valley Visitor Center, Yosemite Village* ☎ *209/372–1207*
⊟ *AE, D, DC, MC, V* ⊘ *Closed Oct.–May. No dinner after 6 PM.*

$$–$$$$ ✕**Wawona Hotel Dining Room.** Watch deer graze on the meadow while you
AMERICAN dine in the romantic, candlelit dining room of the whitewashed Wawona
★ Hotel, which dates from the late 1800s. The American-style cuisine favors
fresh California ingredients and flavors; trout is a menu staple. There's
also a Sunday brunch Easter through Thanksgiving, and a barbeque on
the lawn Saturday evenings in summer. A jacket is required at dinner.
⊠ *Wawona Hotel, Rte. 41, Wawona* ☎ *209/375–1425* ⚲ *Reservations
essential* ⊟ *AE, D, DC, MC, V* ⊘ *Closed Jan. and Feb.*

$$$ ✕**White Wolf Lodge.** This high-country historic lodge's casual, rustic dining
AMERICAN room is small enough that every meal requires four seating times. Break-
fast and dinners (no lunch) are all-you-can-eat affairs, served family style
with vegetarian options. ⊠ *Tioga Rd. (Rte. 120), 25 mi west of Tuolumne
Meadows and 15 mi east of Crane Flat* ☎ *209/372–8416* ⚲ *Reservations
essential* ⊟ *AE, D, DC, MC, V* ⊘ *Closed late Sept.–June. No lunch.*

PICNIC AREAS Considering how large the park is and how many visitors come here—
some 3.5 million people every year, most of them just for the day—it
is somewhat surprising that Yosemite has so few formal picnic areas,
though in many places you can find a smooth rock to sit on and enjoy
breathtaking views along with your lunch. The convenience stores all
sell picnic supplies, and prepackaged sandwiches and salads are widely
available. Those options can come in especially handy during the middle
of day, when you might not want to spend precious daylight hours in
such a spectacular setting sitting in a restaurant for a formal meal.
None of the below options has drinking water available; most have
some type of toilet.

Cathedral Beach. You may have some solitude picnicking here, as this
spot usually has fewer people than picnic areas at the eastern end of the
valley. ⊠ *On Southside Dr. underneath spire-like Cathedral Rocks.*

Church Bowl. Tucked behind the Ahwahnee Hotel, this picnic area nearly
abuts the granite walls below the Royal Arches. If you're walking from
the village with your supplies, this is the shortest trek to a picnic area.
⊠ *Behind the Ahwahnee Hotel, Yosemite Valley.*

Swinging Bridge. This picnic area is just before the little wooden footbridge that crosses the Merced River, which babbles pleasantly by.
⊠ *East of Sentinel Beach on Southside Dr.*

Yellow Pine. This shady spot is named for the towering trees that cluster
on the banks of the Merced River. There are no toilets here. ⊠ *Right
next to Sentinel Beach on Southside Dr.*

OUTSIDE THE PARK

$–$$ ✕**Banny's Café and Wine Bar.** A calm, pleasant environment and hearty
ECLECTIC yet refined dishes make Banny's an attractive alternative to Sonora's
noisier eateries. Try the grilled salmon fillet with scallion rice and
ginger-wasabi aioli, or have a great burger. ⊠ *83 S. Stewart St., Sonora*
☎ *209/533–4709* ⊟ *D, MC, V* ⊘ *No lunch Sun.*

$$$$
CONTINENTAL
Fodor's Choice
★
✕ **Erna's Elderberry House.** Erna Kubin, the grande dame of Château du Sureau (⇨ *Where to Stay*), has created a culinary oasis, stunning for its understated elegance, gorgeous setting, and impeccable service. Red walls and dark beams accent the dining room's high ceilings, and arched windows reflect the glow of candles. The seasonal six-course prix-fixe dinner can be paired with superb wines. When the waitstaff places all the plates on the table in perfect synchronicity, you'll know this will be a meal to remember. A small bistro menu is also served in the former wine cellar. ⊠ *48688 Victoria La., Oakhurst* ☎ *559/683–6800* ⬧ *Reservations essential* ⊟ *AE, D, MC, V* ⊘ *No lunch Mon.–Sat.*

$$-$$$$
STEAK
✕ **The Mogul.** The Mogul has been around for a long time. It's the place to go when you want a straightforward steak and salad bar. The only catch is that the waiters cook your steak—and the result depends on the waiter's experience. But generally you can't go wrong. And kids love it. The knotty-pine-panel walls lend a woodsy touch and suggest Mammoth Mountain before all the development there. ⊠ *1528 Mammoth Tavern Rd., off Old Mammoth Rd., Mammoth Lakes* ☎ *760/934–3039* ⊟ *AE, D, MC, V* ⊘ *No lunch.*

$-$$
AMERICAN
✕ **Nicely's.** For-sale artworks decorate the walls of this vintage-1965 diner. The country cooking isn't fancy—think blueberry pancakes for breakfast and chicken-fried steak for dinner—but it's a good spot for families with kids and unfussy eaters looking for a square meal, the kind of place where the waitress walks up with a pot of coffee and asks, "Ya want a warm-up, hon?" ⊠ *U.S. 395 and 4th St., Lee Vining* ☎ *760/647–6477* ⊟ *MC, V* ⊘ *Closed Wed., Dec.–Mar.*

$-$$
AMERICAN
★
✕ **Tioga Gas Mart & Whoa Nelli Deli.** This might be the only gas station in the United States that serves cocktails, but its appeal goes way beyond novelty. The mahimahi tacos are succulent, the gourmet pizzas tasty, and the herb-crusted pork loin with berry glaze elegant. Order at the counter and grab a seat inside or out. ⊠ *Rte. 120 and U.S. 395, Lee Vining* ☎ *760/647–1088* ⊟ *AE, MC, V* ⊘ *Closed mid-Nov.–mid-Apr.*

38

WHERE TO STAY

IN THE PARK

■ TIP➜ Reserve your room or cabin in Yosemite as far in advance as possible. You can make a reservation up to a year before your arrival (within minutes after the reservation office makes a date available, the Ahwahnee, Yosemite Lodge, and Wawona Hotel often sell out their weekends, holiday periods, and all days between May and September).

$$$$
Fodor's Choice
★
🏨 **The Ahwahnee.** A National Historic Landmark, the hotel is constructed primarily of concrete and sugar-pine logs. Guest rooms have American Indian design motifs; public spaces are decorated with art deco detailing, oriental rugs, and elaborate iron- and woodwork. Some luxury hotel amenities, including turndown service and guest bathrobes, are standard here. The Dining Room is by far the most impressive restaurant in the park and one of the most beautiful rooms in California. If you stay in a cottage room, be aware that each cottage has multiple guest rooms, though all have an en-suite bath. Even if you cannot afford to stay here, take the time to stroll about the main floor. Reservations are made through Delaware North Companies Parks and Resorts. **Pros:**

best lodge in Yosemite (if not all of California); concierge. **Cons:** expensive; some reports that service has slipped in recent years. ✉ *Ahwahnee Rd., about ¾ mi east of Yosemite Valley Visitor Center, Yosemite Village* 🏠 *1 Ahwahnee Rd., Yosemite National Park 95389* ☎ *559/252–4848* 🌐 *www.yosemitepark.com* ⤳ *99 lodge rooms, 4 suites, 24 cottage rooms* ♿ *In-room: no a/c (some), refrigerator, Wi-Fi. In-hotel: restaurant, room service, bar, tennis court, pool* ▭ *AE, D, DC, MC, V.*

$–$$ 🍴 **Curry Village.** Opened in 1899 as a place where travelers could enjoy the beauty of Yosemite for a modest price, Curry Village has plain accommodations: standard motel rooms, cabins, and tent cabins, which have rough wood frames, canvas walls, and roofs. The tent cabins are a step up from camping, with linens and blankets provided (maid service upon request); some even have heat. The guest lounge and reservations buildings underwent a multimillion-dollar renovation during the winter of 2008–2009. Happy Isles and the popular Mist Trail are a few minutes' walk away. Reservations are made through Delaware North Companies Parks and Resorts. **Pros:** comparatively economical; family-friendly atmosphere. **Cons:** can be crowded; sometimes a bit noisy. ✉ *South side of Southside Dr., Yosemite Valley* ☎ *559/252–4848* 🌐 *www.yosemitepark.com* ⤳ *18 rooms, 390 cabins* ♿ *In-room: no a/c, no phone, no TV. In-hotel: 3 restaurants, bar, pool, bicycles* ▭ *AE, D, DC, MC, V.*

$$$–$$$$ 🍴 **Redwoods Guest Cottages.** The only lodging in the park not operated by Delaware North, this collection of individually owned cabins and homes in the Wawona area is a great alternative to the overcrowded Valley. Fully furnished cabins range from small, romantic one-bedroom units to bright, resortlike, six-bedroom houses with decks overlooking the river. Most have fireplaces, TVs, and phones. The property rarely fills up, even in summer, so it's a good choice for last-minute lodging; there's a two-night minimum in the off-season and a three-night minimum in summer. **Pros:** staying in private homes can be very nice; peaceful setting; some rooms have a VCR. **Cons:** remote from the Valley; some rooms have no TV. ✉ *8038 Chilnualna Falls Rd., off Rte. 41, Wawona* ☎ *209/375–6666* 🌐 *www.redwoodsinyosemite.com* ⤳ *130 units* ♿ *In-room: no a/c (some), no phone (some), kitchen, no TV (some). In-hotel: some pets allowed* ▭ *AE, D, MC, V.*

$$–$$$ 🍴 **Wawona Hotel.** This 1879 National Historic Landmark sits at Yosemite's southern end, a 15-minute drive (or free shuttle bus ride) from the Mariposa Grove of Big Trees. It's an old-fashioned New England–style estate, with whitewashed buildings, wraparound verandas, and pleasant, no-frills rooms decorated with period pieces. About half the rooms share bathrooms; those that do come equipped with robes. The romantic, candlelit dining room ($$–$$$$) lies across the lobby from the cozy Victorian parlor, which has a fireplace, board games, and a piano, where a pianist plays ragtime most evenings. Reservations are made through Delaware North Companies Parks and Resorts. **Pros:** lovely; peaceful atmosphere; close to Mariposa Grove. **Cons:** few modern in-room amenities. ✉ *Hwy. 41, Wawona* ☎ *559/252–4848* 🌐 *www.yosemitepark.com* ⤳ *104 rooms, 50 with bath* ♿ *In-room: no a/c, no phone, no TV. In-hotel: restaurant, bar, golf course, tennis court, pool* ▭ *AE, D, DC, MC, V* ⊗ *Closed Jan. and Feb.*

$-$$ White Wolf Lodge. Set in a subalpine meadow, White Wolf offers rustic accommodations in tent cabins. This is an excellent base camp for hiking the backcountry. Breakfast and dinner are served home-style in the snug main building. Keep in mind that you will be seated in one of four time slots, so you might eat earlier or later than you would prefer if you do not reserve well in advance. Reservations are made through Delaware North Companies Parks and Resorts. **Pros:** quiet; convenient for hikers; good restaurant. **Cons:** far from the Valley; not much to do here other than hiking. ⊠ *Off Tioga Rd. (Rte. 120), 25 mi west of Tuolumne Meadows and 15 mi east of Crane Flat* ☎ *559/252–4848* ⤵ *24 tent cabins, 4 cabins* ♿ *In-room: no a/c, no phone, no TV. In-hotel: restaurant* ☰ *AE, D, DC, MC, V* ☯ *Closed mid-Sept.–early June.*

$$-$$$ Yosemite Lodge at the Falls. This lodge near Yosemite Falls, which dates from 1915, looks like a 1960s motel-resort complex, with numerous brown, two-story buildings tucked beneath the trees, surrounded by large parking lots. Motel-style rooms have two double beds; larger rooms also have dressing areas and patios or balconies. A few have views of the falls. Of the lodge's eateries, the Mountain Room Restaurant is the most formal. The cafeteria-style Food Court serves three meals a day. Many park tours depart from the main building. **Pros:** centrally located; dependably clean rooms; lots of tours leave from out front. **Cons:** can feel impersonal; appearance is little dated. Reservations are made through Delaware North Companies Parks and Resorts. ⊠ *Northside Dr. about ¾ mi west of the visitor center, Yosemite Village* ☎ *559/252–4848* ⊕ *www.yosemitepark.com* ⤵ *245 rooms* ♿ *In-room: no a/c, Wi-Fi. In-hotel: restaurant, bar, pool, bicycles* ☰ *AE, D, DC, MC, V.*

CAMPING   Bridalveil Creek. This campground sits among lodgepole pines at
$ 7,200 feet, above the valley on Glacier Point Road. From here, you can easily drive to Glacier Point's magnificent valley views. Fall evenings can be quite cold. **Pros:** quiet; you have a good chance of getting a spot here last-minute. **Cons:** no frills; comparatively remote; reservations not accepted. ⊠ *From Hwy. 41 in Wawona, go north to Glacier Point Rd. and turn right; entrance to campground is 25 mi ahead on right side* ☎ *no phone* ⊕ *www.nps.gov/yose* ⛺ *74 tent/RV sites* ♿ *Flush toilets, drinking water, bear boxes, grills, picnic tables, public telephone* ♿ *Reservations not accepted* ☰ *AE, D, MC, V* ☯ *Closed early Sept.–June.*

¢   Camp 4. Formerly known as Sunnyside Walk-In, this is the only valley campground available on a first-come, first-served basis—and the only one west of Yosemite Lodge. Open year-round, it is a favorite for rock climbers and solo campers; it fills quickly and is typically sold out by 9 AM daily spring through fall. This is a tents-only campground. **Pros:** people tend to go to bed early here, so it's quiet at night; centrally located. **Cons:** if you're not a climber, you may feel out of place; it's close to the main loop road. ⊠ *Base of Yosemite Falls Trail, just west of Yosemite Lodge on Northside Dr., Yosemite Village* ☎ *209/372–8502* ⊕ *www.nps.gov/yose* ⛺ *35 tent sites* ♿ *Flush toilets, drinking water, showers, bear boxes, fire grates, picnic tables, public telephone, ranger station* ☰ *AE, D, MC, V.*

38

$$ ⚠ **Crane Flat.** This camp on Yosemite's western boundary, south of Hodgdon Meadow, is just 17 mi from the valley but far from its bustle. A small grove of sequoias is nearby. **Pros:** for a large campground, it doesn't feel crowded; good spot strategically if you're dividing your time among Hetch Hetchy, Yosemite Valley, and Tioga Road attractions. **Cons:** not itself close to anything particularly interesting. ✉ *From Big Oak Flat entrance on Hwy. 120, drive 10 mi east to campground entrance on right* 🕿 *800/436–7275 or 209/372–0265* ⚠ *166 tent/RV sites* ⚐ *Flush toilets, drinking water, bear boxes, fire pits, picnic tables, general store, ranger station* ⚑ *Reservations essential* ▭ *AE, D, MC, V* ☉ *Closed Oct.–May.*

$$ ⚠ **Hodgdon Meadow.** On the park's western boundary, at an elevation of about 4,900 feet, the vegetation here is similar to that in the valley—but there's no river and no development. Reservations are essential May through September. **Pros:** relatively low-key campground; good access to Hetch Hetchy and Tioga Road. **Cons:** nothing exceptionally interesting is nearby; lacks a good view. ✉ *From Big Oak Flat entrance on Hwy. 120, immediately turn left to campground* 🕿 *209/379–2123* ⊕ *reservations.nps.gov* ⚠ *105 tent/RV sites* ⚐ *Flush toilets, drinking water, bear boxes, grills, picnic tables, ranger station* ▭ *AE, D, MC, V.*

$$$$ ⚠ **Housekeeping Camp.** Composed of three walls (usually concrete) and covered with two layers of canvas, each unit has an open-ended fourth side that can be closed off with a heavy, white canvas curtain. Inside, typically, are bunk beds and a full-size bed (dirty mattresses included); outside is a covered patio, fire ring, picnic table, and bear box. You rent "bedpacks," consisting of blankets, sheets, and other comforts in the main building, which also has a small grocery. Lots of guests take advantage of the adjacent Merced River and sun on its rocks or drop inflatable rafts onto its gentle surface. Showers ($5 a pop) and a laundry area are on premises. **Pros:** generally has a friendly, family vibe; good spots next to the river; centrally located. **Cons:** rather cramped; three-sided enclosures can seem strange; restrooms can be a hassle to walk to, especially at night. ✉ *Southside Dr., ½ mi west of Curry Village* ⚐ *Delaware North, 6771 N. Palm Ave., Fresno, CA 93704* 🕿 *209/372–8338, 559/252–4848 reservations* ⊕ *www.yosemitepark.com* ⚠ *266 units* ⚐ *Flush toilets, drinking water, bear boxes, fire pits, picnic tables, general store, guest laundry* ▭ *AE, D, DC, MC, V* ☉ *Closed early Oct.–late Apr.*

$$ ⚠ **Lower Pines.** This moderate-size campground sits directly along the Merced River; it's a short walk to the trailheads for the Mirror Lake and Mist trails. Expect small sites and lots of people. **Pros:** flat, smooth ground for tents; close to family attractions such as Mist Trail and Happy Isles; closes Pines campground to Curry Village. **Cons:** crowded during the summer; small lots; impersonal. ✉ *At east end of valley* 🕿 *209/372–8502* ⚠ *60 tent/RV sites* ⚐ *Flush toilets, drinking water, bear boxes, fire grates, picnic tables, public telephone, ranger station, swimming (river)* ⚑ *Reservations essential* ▭ *AE, D, MC, V* ☉ *Closed Nov.–Feb.*

$ ⚠ **Porcupine Flat.** Sixteen miles west of Tuolumne Meadows, this campground sits at 8,100 feet. Sites are close together, but if you want to be in the high country and Tuolumne Meadows is full, this is a good bet. There is no water available. RVs over 35 are prohibited. **Pros:** lovely clean air; several really spacious sites; can luck out here last-minute. **Cons:** far from the valley; can get very cold at night; no reservations. ⊠ *16 mi west of Tuolumne Meadows on Hwy. 120* ☎ *209/372–0265* ⊕ *www.nps.gov/yose* ⚲ *52 tent/RV sites* ⚿ *Pit toilets, bear boxes, fire pits, picnic tables* ⚲ *Reservations not accepted* ⊟ *AE, D, MC, V* ⊙ *Closed mid-Oct.–July.*

$$ ⚲ **Tuolumne Meadows.** In a wooded area at 8,600 feet, just south of its
Fodor'sChoice namesake meadow, this is one of the most spectacular and sought-after
★ campgrounds in Yosemite. Hot showers can be used at the Tuolumne Meadows Lodge—though only at certain strictly regulated times. Half the sites are first-come, first-served, so arrive early or make reservations. The campground is open July–September. **Pros:** lovely setting; good access to services; lively campfire activities. **Cons:** short season; difficult to reserve; far from the valley. ⊠ *Hwy. 120, 46 mi east of Big Oak Flat entrance station* ☎ *209/379–2123* ⚲ *314 tent/RV sites* ⚿ *Flush toilets, dump station, drinking water, bear boxes, fire grates, picnic tables, public telephone, general store, ranger station* ⊟ *AE, D, MC, V* ⊙ *Closed Oct.–May.*

$$ ⚲ **Upper Pines.** This is the valley's largest campground, and the closest one to the trailheads. Expect large crowds in the summer—and little privacy. **Pros:** convenient to Happy Isles and the Mist Trail; cheaper than Curry Village. **Cons:** large and impersonal; could use more restrooms. ⊠ *At east end of valley, near Curry Village* ☎ *no phone* ⊕ *www. recreation.gov* ⚲ *238 tent/RV sites* ⚿ *Flush toilets, dump station, drinking water, showers, bear boxes, fire grates, picnic tables, public telephone, ranger station, swimming (river)* ⚲ *Reservations essential* ⊟ *AE, D, MC, V.*

$$ ⚲ **Wawona.** Near the Mariposa Grove, just downstream from a popular fishing spot, this year-round campground (reservations essential May–September) has larger, less densely packed sites than campgrounds in the valley, located right by the river. The downside is that it's an hour's drive to the valley's major attractions. **Pros:** spots are comparatively spacious; river's sound is soothing. **Cons:** a lot of people get up early here to go fishing; far from the valley. ⊠ *Hwy. 41, 1 mi north of Wawona* ☎ *800/436–7275* ⊕ *www.recreation.gov* ⚲ *93 tent/RV sites* ⚿ *Flush toilets, dump station, drinking water, bear boxes, fire grates, picnic tables, ranger station, swimming (river)* ⊟ *AE, D, MC, V.*

$ ⚲ **White Wolf.** Set in the beautiful high country at 8,000 feet, this is a
★ prime spot for hikers. RVs up to 27 feet long are permitted. **Pros:** wonderful mountain air; quiet; trails near here are less-crowded and lovely. **Cons:** you may need luck to get a spot, especially on weekends; far from the valley; no reservations. ⊠ *From Big Oak Flat entrance, go 15 mi east on Tioga Road (Hwy. 120); campground is on right* ☎ *209/372–0265* ⊕ *www.nps.gov/yose* ⚲ *87 tent/RV sites* ⚿ *Flush toilets, drinking water, bear boxes, fire grates, picnic tables, public telephone, ranger station* ⊟ *No credit cards* ⊙ *Closed early Sept.–June.*

38

OUTSIDE THE PARK

$$–$$$ ⛱ **Best Western Yosemite Gateway Inn.** Oakhurst's best motel has carefully
☺ tended landscaping and rooms with attractive dark-wood American
colonial–style furniture and slightly kitsch hand-painted wall murals
of Yosemite. Kids love choosing between the two pools. **Pros:** pretty
close to Yosemite; clean; comfortable. **Cons:** chain property; some
walls may seem thin. ⊠ *40530 Hwy. 41, Oakhurst* 🕾 *559/683–2378
or 800/545–5462* ⊕ *www.yosemitegatewayinn.com* ⟳ *122 rooms, 12
suites* ⟵ *In-room: refrigerator, Internet. In-hotel: restaurant, bar, pools,
laundry facilities* ⊟ *AE, D, MC, V.*

$$$$ ⛱ **Château du Sureau.** This romantic inn, adjacent to Erna's Elderberry
Fodor'sChoice House, is straight out of a children's book. From the moment you drive
★ through the wrought-iron gates and up to the fairy-tale castle, you feel
pampered. Every room is impeccably styled with European antiques,
sumptuous fabrics, fresh-cut flowers, and oversize soaking tubs. Fall
asleep by the glow of a crackling fire amid goose-down pillows and
Italian linens, then awaken to a hearty European breakfast in the dining room. Afterward, relax with a game of chess in the piano room
beneath an exquisite ceiling mural. Cable TV is available by request
only. **Pros:** luxurious; you'll feel pampered; great views. **Cons:** debili-
tatingly expensive; if you're not really into spas, it might not be worth
your while. ⊠ *48688 Victoria La., Oakhurst* 🕾 *559/683–6860* ⊕ *www.
elderberryhouse.com* ⟳ *10 rooms, 1 villa* ⟵ *In-room: refrigerator, Internet, Wi-Fi. In-hotel: restaurant, bar, pool, laundry service, no kids under
12* ⊟ *AE, MC, V* ⫧⊙ *BP* ⊗ *Closed two weeks early Jan.–mid-Jan.*

$$–$$$$☺ ⛱ **Evergreen Lodge.** The perfect blend of rustic charm and modern com-
★ fort, the cabins here have sumptuous beds, comfy armchairs, candy-
cane-striped pull-out sofas, and tree-stump end tables. The terrific
roadhouse-style restaurant ($$) serves bean burgers and meaty dishes
like broiled elk tenderloin. The long bar has a friendly feel, perhaps
owing to the reggae music that plays here often). After dinner, you can
shoot pool in the bar, play Ping-Pong outside, melt s'mores, attend a
lecture or film, or play Scrabble by the fire in the barnlike recreation
center. Multi-night stays are required from April through October, as
well as on holidays. **Pros:** rustic setting is romantic; staff is very friendly;
lots of things to do. **Cons:** far from Yosemite Valley (though close to
Hetch Hetchy). ⊠ *33160 Evergreen Rd., 25 mi east of Groveland, 23 mi
north of Yosemite Valley, Groveland* 🕾 *209/379–2606 or 800/935–
6343* ⊕ *www.evergreenlodge.com* ⟳ *90 cabins* ⟵ *In-room: no a/c, no
phone, refrigerator, no TV. In-hotel: restaurant, bar, bicycles, children's
programs (ages 5–12), Internet terminal, Wi-Fi* ⊟ *AE, D, DC, MC, V*
⊗ *Closed Jan.*

$$–$$$$ ⛱ **Homestead Cottages.** Serenity is the order of the day at this secluded
★ getaway in Ahwahnee, 6 mi west of Oakhurst. Set on 160 acres of
rolling hills that once held a Miwok village, the cottages here have gas
fireplaces, living rooms, fully equipped kitchens, and queen-size beds;
the largest sleeps six. Hand-built by the owners out of real adobe bricks,
the cottages are also stocked with soft robes, oversize towels, and paper-
back books. **Pros:** remote; quiet; friendly owners. **Cons:** remote; some
urbanites might find it a little *too* quiet. ⊠ *41110 Rd. 600, 2½ mi*

off Hwy. 49, Ahwahnee ☎ *559/683–0495 or 800/483–0495* ⊕ *www. homesteadcottages.com* ⇨ *5 cottages, 1 loft* ♿ *In-room: no phone, kitchen* ⊟ *AE, D, MC, V.*

$$-$$$ 📺 **Little Valley Inn.** Historical photos and old mining tools recall Mariposa's heritage at this modern B and B. A suite that sleeps five people includes a full kitchen. All rooms have private entrances, baths, and decks. The large grounds include a creek where you can pan for gold. **Pros:** quiet; comfortable; about halfway between Yosemite's western entrances. **Cons:** still about 40 minutes outside the park. ⊠ *3483 Brooks Rd., off Rte. 49, Mariposa* ☎ *209/742–6204 or 800/889–5444* ⊕ *www. littlevalley.com* ⇨ *4 rooms, 1 suite, 1 cabin* ♿ *In-room: no phone, refrigerator* ⊟ *MC, V* ⦿ *CP.*

$$-$$$$ 📺 **Narrow Gauge Inn.** All of the rooms at this well-tended, family-owned
  ★   property have balconies (some shared) and great views of the surrounding woods and mountains. For maximum atmosphere, book a room overlooking the brook; for quiet, choose a lower-level room on the edge of the forest. All of the rooms are comfortably furnished with old-fashioned accents. Reserve way ahead. The restaurant ($$$, open Wednesday–Sunday, April–October), which is festooned with moose, bison, and other wildlife trophies, specializes in steaks and American fare, and merits a special trip. **Pros:** close to Yosemite's South Entrance; well-appointed; wonderful balconies. **Cons:** rooms can feel a bit dark; dining options are limited (especially for vegetarians). ⊠ *48571 Hwy. 41, Fish Camp* ☎ *559/683–7720 or 888/644–9050* ⊕ *www.narrowgaugeinn. com* ⇨ *25 rooms, 1 suite* ♿ *In-room: no a/c (some), Wi-Fi. In-hotel: restaurant, bar, pool, some pets allowed* ⊟ *D, MC, V* ⦿ *CP.*

$$-$$$$ 📺 **Tamarack Lodge Resort.** Tucked away on the edge of the John Muir
  ★   Wilderness Area, where cross-country ski trails loop through the woods, this 1924 lodge looks like something out of a snow globe; the lake it borders is serenely beautiful. Rooms in the charming main lodge have spartan furnishings, and, in old-fashioned style, some share a bathroom. For more privacy, opt for one of the cabins, which range from rustic to downright cushy; many have fireplaces, kitchens, or wood-burning stoves. In warm months, fishing, canoeing, hiking, and mountain biking are right outside. The small, romantic Lakefront Restaurant ($$$) serves outstanding contemporary French-inspired dinners—with an emphasis on game—in a candlelit dining room. Reservations are essential. **Pros:** rustic but not run-down; tons of nearby outdoor activities. **Cons:** thin walls; some main lodge rooms have shared bathrooms. ⊠ *Lake Mary Rd., off Rte. 203, Mammoth Lakes* ☎ *760/934–2442 or 800/237–6879* ⊕ *www.tamaracklodge.com* ⇨ *11 rooms, 34 cabins* ♿ *In-room: no a/c, kitchen (some), no TV. In-hotel: restaurant, bar, some pets allowed* ⊟ *AE, MC, V.*

$-$$ 📺 **Tioga Lodge.** This lodge, across the highway from the lake, centers around a 19th-century building that has been by turns a store, a saloon, a tollbooth, and a boardinghouse. Surrounding the rustic lodge are modest, attached, weathered-wooden cottages, tucked beneath towering cottonwoods on a grassy hillside. The simple, country-cute rooms have cozy furnishings that—thank heaven—manage not to be tacky. **Pros:** nine-table Hammond Station Restaurant is quite pleasant. **Cons:** close to the

38

road. ⊠ *54411 U.S. 395, Lee Vining* ☎ *760/647–6423 or 888/647–6423* ⊕ *www.tiogalodge.com* ➥ *13 rooms* ⚬ *In-room: no a/c, no phone, no TV. In-hotel: restaurant, bar, some pets allowed* ☲ *AE, D, MC, V.*

$$$–$$$$ ▦ **Yosemite View Lodge.** This clean, thoroughly modern property—just 2 mi outside the park's Arch Rock entrance on Route 140—is the most convenient place to spend the night if you are unable to secure lodgings in the Valley. All rooms have good views, but the ones with balconies that overlook the Merced River are the best. You have your choice of four pools here, one of which is indoors. The restaurant cooks up an impressive breakfast buffet, and there also is a pizza joint on-site. The lodge's gift shop and small grocery store are open until 11 PM. **Pros:** great location; good views; lots of on-site amenities. **Cons:** can be pricey for what you get. ⊠ *11136 Hwy. 140, El Portal* ☎ *209/379–2681 or 888/742–4371* ⊕ *www.yosemite-motels.com* ➥ *279 rooms* ⚬ *In-room: kitchen (some). In-hotel: restaurant, bar, pools, laundry facilities, some pets allowed* ☲ *MC, V.*

Zion National Park

WORD OF MOUTH

"I took this hiking the Narrows through the Virgin River."
      —photo by John Vaccarelli, Fodors.com member

"We just returned from a 9-day trip to Zion and loved every minute of it. Zion provides a perfect retreat."

      —Elnap29

WELCOME TO ZION

TOP REASONS TO GO

★ **Varicolored cliffs:** Take the Angels Landing Trail, which culminates in one of the park's many astounding viewpoints full of pink, orange, and crimson rock formations.

★ **Auto immunity:** During the busy summer season, cars are no longer allowed in Zion Canyon, allowing for a relaxing and scenic shuttle bus ride.

★ **Botanical wonderland:** Zion Canyon is home to approximately 900 species of plants, more than anywhere else in Utah.

★ **Animal tracks:** Zion has expansive hinterlands where furry, scaly, and feathered residents are common. Hike long enough and you'll encounter deer, elk, rare lizards, birds of prey, and other zoological treats.

★ **Unforgettable canyoneering:** Zion's array of rugged slot canyons is the richest place on earth for scrambling, rappelling, climbing, and descending.

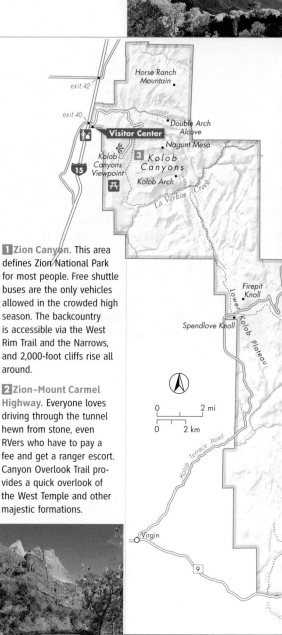

1 Zion Canyon. This area defines Zion National Park for most people. Free shuttle buses are the only vehicles allowed in the crowded high season. The backcountry is accessible via the West Rim Trail and the Narrows, and 2,000-foot cliffs rise all around.

2 Zion–Mount Carmel Highway. Everyone loves driving through the tunnel hewn from stone, even RVers who have to pay a fee and get a ranger escort. Canyon Overlook Trail provides a quick overlook of the West Temple and other majestic formations.

3 **Kolob Canyons.** The quiet northwest corner of Zion has its own park entrance and offers many rewarding attractions, such as the West Temple, without the crowds. Kolob Arch is easily reached via a relatively short trail.

UTAH

GETTING ORIENTED

The heart of Zion National Park is Zion Canyon, which follows the North Fork of the Virgin River for 6½ mi beneath cliffs that rise 2,000 feet from the river bottom. The Kolob area is considered by some to be superior in beauty, and because it's isolated from the rest of the park, you aren't likely to run into any crowds here. Both sections hint at the extensive backcountry beyond, open for those with the stamina, time, and the courage to go off the beaten paths of the park.

4 **Lava Point.** Infrequently visited, this area has a primitive campground and two nearby reservoirs that provide the only significant fishing opportunities in Zion National Park. Lava Point Overlook provides a view of Zion Canyon from the north.

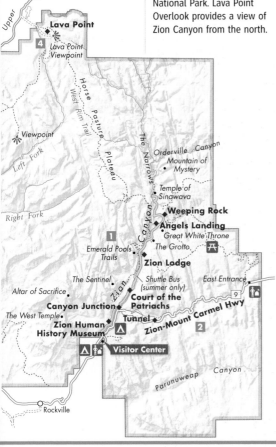

39

KEY
🧍 *Ranger Station*
⚠ *Campground*
🎪 *Picnic Area*
🍴 *Restaurant*
🖼 *Lodge*
🏃 *Trailhead*
🚻 *Restrooms*
🔻 *Scenic Viewpoint*
⋯⋯ *Walking/Hiking Trails*

ZION PLANNER

When to Go

Zion is the most heavily visited national park in Utah, receiving nearly 2.5 million visitors each year. **Most visitors come between April and October.**

Summer in the park is hot and dry punctuated with sudden cloudbursts, which can create flash flooding and spectacular waterfalls. Expect afternoon thunderstorms between July and September. In the summer sun, wear sunscreen and drink lots of water, even if you aren't exerting yourself.

Winters are mild at lower desert elevations. You can expect to encounter winter driving conditions November through March, and although most park programs are suspended, winter is a wonderful and solitary time to see the canyons.

⚠ **Extreme highs in Zion can often exceed 100°F in July and August.**

AVG. HIGH/LOW TEMPS.

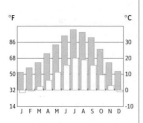

Flora and Fauna

Zion Canyon's unique geography—the park is on the Colorado Plateau and bordered by the Great Basin and Mojave Desert provinces—supports more than 900 species of plants in environments that range from desert to hanging garden to high plateau. (Those so inclined can pick up a plant identification guide at the Zion Canyon Visitor Center.) And yes, poison ivy is among the plant species; if you're not sure how to recognize it, take a quick lesson from a ranger prior to your first hike.

You are more likely to see wildlife in off-seasons as the flow of visitors dips. The introduction of the park shuttle, and the exit of public automobile traffic, has led to many animals returning to the park's interior, so even in high season you can spot mule deer wandering in shady glens as you ride through the park, especially in early morning and near dusk.

The best opportunity for viewing wildlife is on the hiking trails. You'll see a large variety of lizards and you may be surprised by a Gambel's quail. Mountain lions and ringtail cats (which are not cats but are similar to a raccoons) prowl the park, but you're more likely to spot their tracks than the elusive animals themselves. Black bear are rare, and when they do stumble into park boundaries, it is in the remote high country. All animals, from the smallest chipmunk to the biggest elk, should be given plenty of space.

Getting Here and Around

In southwestern Utah, not far from the Nevada border, Zion National Park is closer to Las Vegas (158 mi) than to Salt Lake City (310 mi). The nearest commercial airport is 46 mi away in St. George, Utah. Off Route 9, the park is 21 mi east of Interstate 15 and 24 mi west of U.S. 89.

Zion used to be considered an accessibility nightmare, with only 400 parking spaces that had to be shared among the 5,000 or so cars that entered the park every day. But no more. In May 2000 the National Park Service banned all private vehicles inside the park from April through October and simultaneously introduced the free shuttle bus system that loops from the parking lot at the Zion Canyon Visitor Center through the park and into nearby Springdale. You can drive into the park November through March.

The Zion Canyon Visitor Center parking lot fills up quickly. You can avoid parking heartburn by leaving your car in town and riding the shuttle to the park entrance. Town shuttle stops are at Eagle's Nest, Driftwood Lodge, Bit & Spur Restaurant, Best Western Zion Park Inn, Bumbleberry Inn, Zion Pizza & Noodle Co., Watchman Cafe, Flanigan's Inn, and Zion Canyon Giant Screen Theatre. The shuttle service starts at 5:30 AM and rolls through 10:30 PM; they come often enough that you won't likely wait more than 15 minutes at any stop before you see one.

If you enter or exit Zion via the east entrance you will have the privilege of driving a gorgeous, twisting 24-mi stretch of the Zion–Mount Carmel Highway (Route 9). Two tunnels, including the highway's famous 1.1-mi tunnel, lie between the east park entrance and Zion Canyon. Oversize vehicles have to buy a $15 escort permit at the park entrance to cover the extra safety precautions the rangers have to take for your tunnel transit. West of the tunnels the highway meets Zion Canyon Scenic Drive at Canyon Junction, about 1 mi north of the Zion Canyon Visitor Center.

Festivals and Events

JAN. St. George Winter Bird Festival. Numerous free birding field trips are the highlight of this three-day festival that includes a number of activities geared for kids. ☎ 435/634–5948.

MAR. Hurricane Easter Car Show. Classic cars from all over the West descend on Hurricane for this event, which attracts about 10,000 people each year. On Easter Sunday there's a slow Rod Run through Zion National Park. ☎ 435/635–5720.

APR. Dixie Downs Horse Races. For more than 25 years, St. George Lions Club has hosted two spring weekends of quarter horse racing to prepare horses for the larger tracks in summer. ☎ 435/673–5553.

AUG. Western Legends Roundup. This nostalgic festival is for anyone with a love of all things cowboys and Indians. For three days the small town of Kanab plays host to cowboy poets, musicians, and character actors from Old West TV series of yesteryear. Arts-and-crafts vendors, American Indian dancers and weavers, wagon trains, quilt shows, and a parade are all part of the fun. ☎ 435/644–3444.

SEPT. Dixie Roundup. Sponsored by the St. George Lions Club, the Dixie Roundup rodeo has been a tradition for decades. It's held on the green grass of Sun Bowl Stadium. ☎ 435/634–5479.

39

Updated by
Swain Scheps

The walls of Zion Canyon soar more than 2,000 feet above the valley below, but it's the character, not the size, of the sandstone forms that defines the park's splendor. Throughout the park stratigraphic evidence points to the distant past, with fantastically colored bands of limestone, sandstone, and lava. Stripes and spots of greenery high in the cliff walls create a "hanging garden" effect, and invariably indicate the presence of a water seepage or spring. Erosion has left behind a collection of domes, fins, and blocky massifs bearing the names and likenesses of cathedrals and temples, prophets and angels.

Trails lead deep into side canyons and up narrow ledges to waterfalls, serene spring-fed pools, and shaded spots of solitude. So diverse is this place that 85% of Utah's flora and fauna species are found here. Some, like the tiny Zion snail, appear nowhere else in the world.

The Colorado River helped create the Grand Canyon, while the Virgin River—the Colorado's muddy progeny—carved Zion's features. Because of the park's unique topography, distant storms and spring runoff can transform a tranquil slot canyon into a sluice.

PARK ESSENTIALS

ACCESSIBILITY

Both visitor centers, all shuttle buses, and Zion Lodge are fully accessible to people in wheelchairs. Several campsites (sites A24 and A25 at Watchman Campground and sites 103, 114, and 115 at South Campground) are reserved for people with disabilities, and two trails—Riverside Walk and Pa'rus Trail—are accessible with some assistance.

ADMISSION FEES AND PERMITS

Entrance to Zion National Park is $25 per vehicle for a seven-day pass. People entering on foot or by bicycle or motorcycle pay $12 per person (not to exceed $25 per family) for a seven-day pass. Entrance to the Kolob Canyons section of the park costs only $10, and you receive credit for this entrance fee when you pay to enter Zion Canyon.

Permits are required for backcountry camping and overnight hikes. You'll also need a permit for a through-hike of the Narrows and Kolob Creek, or if you're taking the Left Fork of the North Creek to the Subway slot canyon. Climbing and canyoneering parties will also need a permit before using technical equipment.

Zion National Park limits the total number of overnight and canyoneering permits issued per day and has a reservation system with an online lottery to apportion permits fairly. Permits to the Subway, Mystery Canyon, the Narrows through-hikes, and West Rim are in short supply during high season. The maximum size of a group hiking into the backcountry is 12 people. The cost for a permit for one to two people is $10; three to seven people, $15; and 8 to 12 people, $20. Permits and hiking information are available at either visitor center. For more information, visit ⊕ *www.nps.gov/zion* prior to your trip to the park.

ADMISSION HOURS

The park is open daily year-round, 24 hours a day. The park is in the mountain time zone.

ATMS/BANKS

The park has no ATM. The nearest bank and ATM is in Springdale.

CELL-PHONE RECEPTION

Cell-phone reception is decent in Springdale but spotty in Zion Canyon itself. Public telephones may be found at South Campground, Watchman Campground, Zion Canyon Visitor Center, Zion Lodge, and Zion Human History Museum.

RELIGIOUS SERVICES

Interdenominational services are held in the summer at Zion Lodge and South Campground. Catholic and Mormon services are also available. Check bulletin boards at the Zion Canyon Visitor Center for times.

PARK CONTACT INFORMATION

Zion National Park ⊠ *Springdale, UT 84767* ☎ *435/772–3256* ⊕ *www.nps.gov/zion.*

SCENIC DRIVES

Zion Canyon's grandeur is best experienced on foot whenever possible, but there is something to be said for covering a lot of ground in the car—and indeed, there is a lot to see if you've only a short amount of time in the area. Driving is the only way to easily access Kolob Canyon, for example, and from November through March, driving your own vehicle is the only way to access the Zion Canyon scenic drive.

★ **Kolob Canyons Road.** From Interstate 15 you get no hint of the beauty that awaits you on this 5-mi road. Most visitors gasp audibly when they get their first glimpse of the red canyon walls that rise suddenly and spectacularly out of the earth. The scenic drive winds its way to

ZION IN ONE DAY

Begin your visit at the **Zion Canyon Visitor Center**, where outdoor exhibits inform you about the park's geology, wildlife, history, and trails. Catch the shuttle or drive—depending on the season—into Zion Canyon. On your way in, make a quick stop at the **Zion Human History Museum** to watch a 22-minute park orientation program and to see exhibits chronicling the human history of the area. Board the shuttle and travel to the **Court of the Patriarchs** viewpoint to take photos and walk the short path. Then pick up the next bus headed into the canyon. Stop at Zion Lodge and cross the road to the **Emerald Pools** trailhead, and take the short hike up to the pools themselves.

Before reboarding the shuttle, grab lunch in the snack shop or dining room at **Zion Lodge**. Take the shuttle as far as **Weeping Rock** trailhead for a brief, cool walk up to the dripping, spring-fed cascade.

Ride the next shuttle to the end of the road, where you can walk to the gateway of the canyon's narrows on the paved, accessible **Riverside Walk**.

Reboard the shuttle to return to the Zion Canyon Visitor Center to pick up your car. Head out onto the beautiful **Zion–Mount Carmel Highway**, with its long, curving tunnels, making sure your camera is loaded and ready for stops at viewpoints along the road. Once you reach the park's east entrance, turn around, and on your return trip stop to take the short hike up to **Canyon Overlook**. Now you're ready to rest your feet at a screening of *Zion Canyon: Treasure of the Gods* on the giant screen of the **Zion Canyon Theatre**. In the evening, you might want to attend a **ranger program** at one of the campground amphitheaters or at Zion Lodge. Or you can follow a relaxing dinner in **Springdale** with a stroll downtown.

a viewpoint that overlooks the whole Kolob region of Zion National Park. The shortest hike in this part of the park is the Middle Fork of Taylor Creek Trail (⇨ *Hiking, in Sports and the Outdoors*), which is 2.7 mi one way to Double Arch Alcove, and gets fairly rugged toward the end. During heavy snowfall Kolob Canyons Road may be closed. ⊠ *Kolob Canyons Rd. east of I–15, Exit 40.*

★ **Zion–Mount Carmel Highway and Tunnels.** Two narrow tunnels as old as the park itself lie between the east entrance and Zion Canyon on this breathtaking 24-mi stretch of Route 9. One was once the longest manmade tunnel in the world. As you travel the (1.1 mi) passage through solid rock, five arched portals along one side provide fleeting glimpses "outside" of cliffs and canyons. When you emerge into the daylight again, you'll find that the landscape has changed dramatically. Before taking this route, take note of the tunnels' safety policies. For example, large vehicles (those over 7'10" wide or 11'4" tall) can travel through the tunnel only during certain hours and require a $15 permit (this covers two tunnel transits over a seven-day period), available at the park entrance. The 0.5-mi Canyon Overlook Trail starts from a parking area between the two tunnels. The road is open April through October. ⊠ *Zion–Mount Carmel Rte. 9, about 5 mi east of Canyon Junction.*

WHAT TO SEE

The park comprises two distinct sections—Zion Canyon, and the Kolob Plateau and Canyons. Most people restrict their visit to the better-known Zion Canyon, especially if they have only one day to explore, but the Kolob area has much to offer and should not be missed if time allows. Though there's little evidence of Kolob's beauty from the entrance point off Interstate 15, once you negotiate the first switchback on the park road, you are hit with a vision of red rock cliffs shooting out of the earth. As you climb in elevation you are treated first to a journey through these canyons, then with a view into the chasm.

■TIP➔ You have to exit the park to get between Zion Canyon with Kolob Canyon, so it is not feasible to explore both sections in one day.

HISTORIC SITES

★ **Zion Human History Museum.** Enrich your visit with a stop here, where you'll get a complete overview of the park with special attention to human history. Exhibits explain how settlers interacted with the geology, wildlife, plants, and unpredictable weather in the canyon from prehistory to the present. Temporary art exhibits also come and go. A 22-minute film plays throughout the day. ⊠ *Zion Canyon Scenic Dr., 1 mi north of south entrance* ☎ *435/772-3256* ⊠ *Free* ☉ *May–early Sept., daily 8–7, ; Mar.–May and Sept.–Oct., daily 10–5.*

Zion Lodge. The Union Pacific Railroad opened the first Zion National Park Lodge in 1925. A fire destroyed the original building, but it was rebuilt to recapture some of the look and feel of the first building. The original western-style cabins are still in use today. Among giant cottonwoods across the road from the Emerald Pools trailhead, the lodge houses a restaurant, snack bar, and gift shop. ⊠ *Zion Canyon Scenic Dr., about 3 mi north of Canyon Junction* ☎ *435/772-7700.*

SCENIC STOPS

Checkerboard Mesa. The distinctive waffle patterns on this huge, white mound of sandstone was created by a combination of vertical fractures created through eons of freeze/thaw cycles, and the exposure of horizontal bedding planes by erosion. Regardless of its origins, the crosshatch effect is stunning and is worth stopping at the pull-out for a long gaze. ⊠ *Zion–Mount Carmel Hwy., 1 mi west of the east entrance.*

★ **Court of the Patriarchs.** This trio of peaks bears the names of, from left to right, Abraham, Isaac, and Jacob. Mount Moroni is the reddish peak on the far right, which partially blocks your view of Jacob. Hike the trail that leaves from the Court of the Patriarchs Viewpoint to get a much better view of the sandstone prophets; you may catch a glimpse of rock climbers camming their way up Isaac's sheer face. ⊠ *Zion Canyon Scenic Dr., 1½ mi north of Canyon Junction.*

Great White Throne. Dominating the Grotto picnic area near Zion Lodge is this massive Navajo sandstone peak, which juts 2,000 feet above the valley floor. The Throne was for decades the most popular formation in the park; today Zion's arches are what draw visitors in droves. ⊠ *Zion Canyon Scenic Dr., about 3 mi north of Canyon Junction.*

39

"There were great contrasts between the Narrows' red rock, green trees, and cool, clear water. This spot was an ideal swimming hole." —photo by Brad Campbell, Fodors.com member

Fodor's Choice ★ **The Narrows.** This sinuous 16-mi crack in the earth where the Virgin River flows over gravel and boulders is one of the most stunning gorges in the world. If you hike through it (⇨ *Hiking)*, you'll find yourself surrounded—and sometimes, nearly closed in by—smooth walls stretching high into the heavens. You also will get wet, as the river still flows through here. ⊠ *Begins at Riverside Walk.*

★ **Weeping Rock.** Surface water from the Echo Canyon rim spends several thousand years seeping down through the porous sandstone before exiting at this picturesque alcove. A hike to see it won't take nearly that long; a paved walkway climbs a quarter mile to this flowing rock face, where wildflowers and delicate ferns grow. In fall, the maples and cottonwoods along the trail riot with color. It's too steep and slippery for wheelchairs. ⊠ *Weeping Rock shuttle bus stop; parking lot on Canyon Scenic Dr., 4½ mi north of Canyon Junction.*

VISITOR CENTERS

The visitor center should be the first stop on your itinerary regardless of how deep into the bush you plan to go. Because access to Kolob Canyon is separate from the rest of the park, Zion has a dedicated visitor center in that section of the park in addition to the main facility at the south entrance of the park. Both centers are open year-round, with longer operating hours during the summer high season. Plan to get snacks, lunch, or coffee at the lodge.

Kolob Canyons Visitor Center. At the origin of Kolob Canyons Road, this park office has books and maps, a small gift shop, and helpful rangers to answer questions about Kolob Canyons exploration. Clean public restrooms can also be found here. ⊠ *Exit 40 off I–15, 17 mi south of*

Cedar City ☎ *435/586–9548* ⊕ *www.nps.gov/zion* ☉ *June–early Sept.,*
daily 8–6; early Sept.–May, daily 8–4:30.

Zion Canyon Visitor Center. Unlike most national park visitor centers,
which are filled with indoor displays, Zion's presents most of its
information in an appealing outdoor exhibit next to a gurgling run-
nel shaded by cottonwood trees. These displays help you plan your
stay and introduce you to the area's geology, flora, and fauna. Inside,
a large bookstore operated by the Zion Natural History Association
sells field guides and other publications. **Ranger-guided shuttle tours**
of Zion Canyon depart from the parking lot and travel to the Temple
of Sinawava, with several photo-op stops along the way. The tour
schedule and free tour tickets are available inside. ⊠ *At south entrance,*
Springdale ☎ *435/772–3256* ⊕ *www.nps.gov/zion* ☉ *June–early Sept.,*
daily 8–8; early Sept.–May, daily 8–6.

SPORTS AND THE OUTDOORS

Hiking is by far the most popular activity at Zion, with a panoply of
trails leading to rewarding destinations in the hinterlands: extreme slot
canyons, gorgeous overlooks, verdant meadows, and dripping springs.
Some sections of the Virgin River are ideal for canoeing (inner tubes
are not allowed). In the winter, hiking boots can be exchanged for
snowshoes and cross-country skis, but check with a ranger to determine
backcountry snow conditions.

AIR TOURS

OUTFIT-
TERS AND
EXPEDITIONS
Bryce Canyon Airlines & Helicopters. For a once-in-a-lifetime view of Zion
National Park, join professional pilots and guides for an airplane ride
over the park (and Bryce Canyon National Park during the same flight).
Flights depart from Ruby's Inn Heliport near Bryce Canyon National
Park. ☎ *435/834–5341* ⊕ *www.rubysinn.com/bryce-canyon-airlines.*
html ⚏ *$75.*

BICYCLING

Starting with the introduction of the park shuttle in 2000, Zion National
Park has taken steps to become much more bicycle-friendly, including
having bike racks at some of the facilities and on the shuttle buses
themselves. Buses and bikes are not allowed to pass each other on park
roads; if you're pedaling in front of a shuttle bus you're expected to pull
completely off the road to allow the bus to pass.

Within the park proper, bicycles are only allowed on established park
roads and on the 3½-mi Pa'rus Trail, which winds along the Virgin
River in Zion Canyon. You cannot ride your bicycle through the Zion–
Mount Carmel Tunnels; the only way to get your bike past this stretch
of the highway is to transport it by motor vehicle.

OUTFIT-
TERS AND
EXPEDITIONS
A treasure trove of information on mountain biking in southern Utah,
Bicycles Unlimited (⊠ *90 S. 100 East, St. George* ☎ *888/673–4492* ⊕ *www.*
bicyclesunlimited.com) rents bikes and sell parts, accessories, and guidebooks. **Springdale Cycles** (⊠ *1458 Zion Park Blvd., Springdale* ☎ *435/772–*
0575 or 800/776–2099 ⊕ *www.springdalecycles.com*) rents bikes, car
racks, and trailers, and gives tips on the local trails. The outfitter also

39

GOOD READS

■ *Towers of Stone*, by J.L. Crawford, summarizes the essence of Zion National Park, its landscape, plants, animals, and human history.

■ *Wildflowers of Zion National Park*, by Dr. Stanley L. Welsh, is always helpful during wildflower season.

■ *An Introduction to the Geology of Zion*, by Al Warneke, is a good pick for information on Zion's geology.

■ *The Zion Tunnel, from Slickrock to Switchback*, by Donald T. Garate, tells the fascinating story of the construction of the mile-long Zion Tunnel in the 1920s.

■ *Zion National Park: Sanctuary in the Desert*, by Nicky Leach, gives you a photographic overview and a narrative journey through the park.

offers one-day and multiday tours for both mountain bikers and road-biking enthusiasts. ■TIP➜ If you prefer to explore on your own, ask them about the best area trails.

BIRD-WATCHING

More than 200 bird species call Zion Canyon home, and dozens more occasionally pass through the park. Some species, such as the white-throated swift and ospreys, make their home in the towering cliff walls. Red-tailed- and Cooper's hawks are abundant. Closer to the ground you'll doubtless see the bold Steller's jay and scrub jay rustling around the pinyon thickets. Wild turkeys are not only common, but some aren't very wild, venturing up to visitors looking for a handout. Five species of hummingbirds are residents of the park, with black-chinned variety being the most common. The Park Service says four other species of hummers may zip by you on their way to some nectar-filled destination, but these birds are just tourists here like you. The luckiest bird-watchers might see two of the park's rarest species: the Mexican spotted owl and the enormous California condor. ■TIP➜ Ask for a bird checklist at the visitor center.

HIKING

The best way to experience Zion Canyon is to walk beneath, between and, if you can bear it (and have good balance!), along its towering cliffs. Trails vary, from paved and flat river strolls to precarious cliff-side scrambles. Whether you're heading out for a day of rock-hopping or an hour of meandering, plan on packing and consuming plenty of drinking water throughout your hike to counteract the effects of a high-altitude workout in the arid climate.

■TIP➜ It can't be said enough: bring water and wear a hat. Keeping the sun at bay is a real challenge at Zion National Park; put on sunscreen before you set out, and re-apply at regular intervals. Because the park's hikes usually include uneven surfaces and elevation changes, wear sturdy shoes or hiking boots. A lot of veteran hikers carry good walking sticks, too, as they're invaluable along trails that ford or follow the Virgin River or its tributaries.

It can be hard to envision just how alone you'll be on some of the less-traveled trails. The park service discourages solo treks, because getting

lost or injured can quickly become life threatening in this environment. If that's not motivation enough, consider that on the rare occasions when mountain lions and humans cross paths, attacks are much less likely if there's more than one person. Above all, plan ahead and be honest with yourself about your capabilities. If you want to do a back-country hike, make a reservation.

■ TIP➔ Park rangers warn hikers to remain on alert for flash floods; these walls of water can appear out of nowhere, even when the sky above you is clear.

EASY

Emerald Pools Trail. Two small waterfalls cascade (or drip, in dry weather) into algae-filled pools along this trail. The path leading to the lower pool is paved and appropriate for strollers and wheelchairs. If you've got any gas left, keep going past the lower pool. The quarter-mile from there to the middle pool gets rocky and steep but offers increasingly scenic views. A less crowded and exceptionally enjoyable return route follows the Kayenta Trail connecting on to the Grotto Trail. Allow 50 minutes round-trip to the lower pool and 2½ hours round-trip to the middle and upper pools. ⊠ *Trailhead at Zion Canyon Scenic Dr., about 3 mi north of Canyon Junction.*

Grotto Trail. This flat and very easy trail takes you from Zion Lodge to the Grotto picnic area, traveling for the most part along the park road. Allow 20 minutes or less for the walk. If you are up for a longer hike, and have two to three hours, connect with the Kayenta Trail after you cross the footbridge, and head for the Emerald Pools. You will begin gaining elevation, and it's a steady, steep climb to the pools. ⊠ *Trailhead at Zion Canyon Scenic Dr., about 3 mi north of Canyon Junction.*

Pa'rus Trail. This 2-mi relatively flat walking and biking path parallels and occasionally crosses the Virgin River, starting at South Campground and proceeding north along the river to the beginning of Zion Canyon Scenic Drive. It's paved and gives you great views of the Watchman, the Sentinel, the East and West Temples, and Towers of the Virgin. Dogs are allowed on this trail as long as they are leashed. Cyclists must follow traffic rules on this heavily used trail. ⊠ *Trailhead at Canyon Junction, ½ mi north of south entrance.*

Riverside Walk. Beginning at the Temple of Sinawava shuttle stop at the end of Zion Canyon Scenic Drive, this easy 1-mi round-trip shadows the Virgin River. The river gurgles by on one side of the trail; on the other, wildflowers bloom out of the canyon wall in fascinating hanging gardens. This is the park's most trekked trail; it is paved and suitable for strollers and for wheelchairs. A round-trip walk takes between one and two hours. The end of the trail marks the beginning of the Narrows Trail. ⊠ *Trailhead at Zion Canyon Scenic Dr., 5 mi north of Canyon Junction.*

MODERATE

Fodor's Choice **Canyon Overlook Trail.** It's a little tough to locate this trailhead, but you'll
★   find it if you watch for the parking area just east of Zion–Mount Carmel tunnel. The trail is moderately steep but only 1 mi round-trip; allow an hour to hike it. The overlook at trail's end gives you views of the West and East Temples, Towers of the Virgin, the Streaked Wall, and

other Zion Canyon cliffs and peaks. The elevation change is 160 feet. ⊠ *Trailhead at Rte. 9, east of Zion–Mount Carmel Tunnel.*

Taylor Creek Trail. In the Kolob Canyons area of the park, this trail immediately descends parallel to Taylor Creek, sometimes crossing it, sometimes shortcutting benches beside it. The historic Larsen Cabin precedes the entrance to the canyon of the Middle Fork, where the trail becomes rougher. After the old Fife Cabin, the canyon bends to the right and delivers you into Double Arch Alcove, a large, colorful grotto with a high arch towering above. The distance one way to Double Arch is 2¾ mi. Allow about four hours round-trip for this hike. The elevation change on this trail is 440 feet. ⊠ *Trailhead at Kolob Canyons Rd., about 1½ mi east of Kolob Canyons Visitor Center.*

Watchman Trail. For a view of the town of Springdale and a look at lower Zion Creek Canyon and the Towers of the Virgin, take the strenuous hike that begins on a service road east of Watchman Campground. Some springs seep out of the sandstone to nourish hanging gardens and attract wildlife here. There are a few sheer cliff edges on this route, so children should be supervised carefully. Plan on two hours for this 3-mi hike with a 380-foot elevation change. ⊠ *Trailhead east of Rte. 9 (main park road), on access road inside south entrance.*

DIFFICULT

Fodor's Choice ★ **Angels Landing Trail.** As much a trial as it is a trail, this hike beneath the Great White Throne is one of the most challenging in the park—but rewarding! Leave your acrophobia at home as you work your way through Walter's Wiggles, a series of 21 switchbacks built out of sandstone blocks. From here you traverse sheer cliffs with chains bolted into the rock face to serve as handrails in some places. In spite of its hair-raising nature, this trail attracts many people. Allow 2½ hours round-trip if you stop at Scout's Lookout, and four hours if you keep going to where the angels (and birds of prey) play. The trail is not appropriate for children; you'll get the heebie-jeebies every time there's a handrail-free drop-off. ⊠ *Trailhead at Zion Canyon Scenic Dr., about 4½ mi north of Canyon Junction.*

★ **Narrows Trail.** After leaving the paved ease of the Gateway to the Narrows trail behind, the real fun begins. This route does not follow a trail or path; rather, you are walking on the riverbed itself. In places you'll find a pebbly shingle or dry sandbar footpath, but eventually the walls of the canyon close in on you and you'll be forced into the chilly waters of the Virgin River itself, walking against the current (tack back and forth, don't fight it head-on). The hike is a stunning and unique nature experience, but it's no picnic. The riverbed is uneven, rocky, and slippery. You must walk deliberately and slowly using a walking stick. Be prepared to swim, as chest-deep holes may occur even when water levels are low. Like any narrow desert canyon, this one is famous for sudden flash flooding even when skies are clear. ■ TIP➔ Before attempting to hike into the Narrows, check with park rangers about the likelihood of flash floods. A day trip up the lower section of the Narrows is 6 mi one way to the turnaround point. Allow at least five hours round-trip. ⊠ *Trailhead at the end of Riverside Walk.*

39

View stunning vistas on Angels Landing Trail, but take note that it's not for those with acrophobia.

HORSEBACK RIDING

OUTFIT-
TERS AND
EXPEDITIONS

Canyon Trail Rides. Grab your hat and boots and see Zion Canyon the way the pioneers did—on the back of a horse or mule. Easygoing, one-hour and half-day guided rides along the Virgin River are available, with a minimum age of 7 and 10 years, respectively. Maximum weight on either trip is 220 pounds. These friendly folks have been around for years, and they are the only outfitter for trail rides inside the park. Reservations are recommended. ⊠ *Across the road from Zion Lodge* ☎ *435/679–8665* ⊕ *www.canyonrides.com* 🖃 *$40–$75 per person* 🕙 *Late Mar.–Oct.*

SWIMMING

Swimming is allowed in the Virgin River, but be careful of cold water, slippery rock bottoms, and the occasional flash floods whenever it rains. Swimming is not allowed in the Emerald Pools, and the use of inner tubes is prohibited within park boundaries.

WINTER SPORTS

Cross-country skiing and snowshoeing are best experienced in the park's higher elevations during the winter, where snow stays on the ground longer. Inquire at the Zion Canyon Visitor Center for backcountry conditions. Snowmobiling is only allowed for residential access.

EDUCATIONAL OFFERINGS

CLASSES AND SEMINARS

Zion Canyon Field Institute. The educational arm of the Zion Natural History Association offers one- and two-day workshops on the park's natural and cultural history with an expert instructor. Each session includes classroom time plus a hike into the field to apply what you've learned. Take a deep dive into subjects like edible plants, bat biology, river geology, photography, adobe-brick making, or general-interest offerings, like Zion 101, Zion geology, and bird-watching. Classes are limited to small groups; reserve ahead to assure placement. There also are ongoing park projects visitors can volunteering to help out with, giving them a behind-the-scenes glimpse at Zion's inner workings. ☎ *435/772–3264 or 800/635–3959* ⊕ *www.zionpark.org* ✆ *$25–$80 per day.*

RANGER PROGRAMS

Expert Talks. These informal lectures take place throughout the day on the Zion Human History Museum patio or the Zion Lodge lawn. Recent session titles are typical: "Pioneer Glimpses," a discussion of the park's early residents; "Animal Icons," a look at Zion's diverse wildlife; and "Windows Into the Past," a lecture on the park's 100-year history. There are no reservations; you can come and go as you please. Talks are usually scheduled for 30 minutes, but some topics may run longer. Park bulletin boards and publications will have an updated schedule. ☎ *435/772–3256.*

Evening Programs. Held each evening in campground amphitheaters and in the Zion Lodge auditorium, these entertaining ranger-led discussions give you the Zion slant on geology, biology, and history topics. You may learn about the bats that swoop through the canyons at night, the surreptitious ways of the mountain lion, or how plants and animals adapt to life in the desert. Programs may include a slide show or audience participation. ☎ *435/772–3256.*

♻ **Junior Ranger Program.** The park offers an array of worthy educational activities aimed at indoctrinating kids in eco-awareness and piquing their interest in Zion facts. Parents can drop off kids, ages 6 to 12, for the 2½-hour Junior Ranger Explorer program, where they learn about plants, animals, geology, and archaeology through hands-on activities, games, and hikes. The Junior Ranger Discovery session is designed for kids to take part in with a parent. All programs are held at the nature center. There are also self-directed programs in the form of an activity booklet available at park visitor centers. At the end of each session, youngsters earn a patch, pin, or decal. Sign up for Junior Ranger sessions half an hour before they begin. ✉ *Zion Nature Center, near South Campground entrance, ½ mi north of south entrance* ☎ *435/772–3256* ✆ *Free* ☉ *Daily at 9:30 and 1.*

Ranger-Led Hikes. These guided hikes are perfect for Zion explorers who crave more knowledge about the sites and sounds of the trail, but who don't have the time to get a degree in botany or zoology prior to the trip. Itineraries vary between easy 1-mi strolls to strenuous five-hour-long tribulations. Inquire at the Zion Canyon Visitor Center or check park bulletin boards for locations and times. Wear sturdy footgear and bring a hat, sunglasses, sunscreen, and water.

39

Ride with a Ranger Shuttle Tours. To learn about the geology, ecology, and history of Zion Canyon, join a park ranger for a two-hour narrated tour by shuttle bus. Tours depart from the Zion Canyon Visitor Center and travel to Temple of Sinawava. Along the way there are several stops so you can take photographs and hear park interpretation from the ranger. Tour times are posted at the Zion Canyon Visitor Center, which is also where you can pick up your free but mandatory tour tickets. ⊠ *Zion Canyon Visitor Center* ☎ *435/772–3256* ⊠ *Free* ☉ *May–Sept., daily at 9* AM *and 6:30* PM.

WHAT'S NEARBY

NEARBY TOWNS

☾ Hotels, restaurants, and shops keep popping up in **Springdale,** population 457, on the southern boundary of Zion National Park, yet the town still manages to maintain its small-town charm—and oh, the view! There are a surprising number of wonderful places to stay and eat, and if you take the time to stroll the main drag, or make use of frequent shuttle stops, you'll find some great shops and galleries. On Route 9 between St. George and Zion stands the small town of **Hurricane,** population 8,250. Pronounced *hur*-ah-ken, this community on the Virgin River has experienced enormous growth, probably owing to the boom in nearby St. George. Hurricane is home to one of Utah's most scenic 18-hole golf courses and is a less expensive and less crowded base for exploring Zion National Park. On Route 9, 13 mi to the east of the park is **Mount Carmel Junction,** an intersection offering some funky small-town lodging and the don't-miss studio of American West artist Maynard Dixon. Other nearby towns, much smaller in size, include Virgin, La Verkin, and the ghost town of **Grafton,** where there's only a stone school and dusty cemetery. It has starred in films such as *Butch Cassidy and the Sundance Kid.*

VISITOR INFORMATION
Color Country Travel Region (Hurricane) ⊠ *906 N. 1400 W, St. George* ☎ *800/233–8824.* **Kane County Office of Tourism (Mount Carmel)** ⊠ *78 S. 100 E, Kanab* ☎ *800/733–5263* ⊕ *www.kaneutah.com.* **Zion Canyon Visitors Bureau (Springdale)** ⊕ *P.O. Box 331, Springdale 84767* ☎ *888/518–7070* ⊕ *www.zionpark.com.*

NEARBY ATTRACTIONS

Coral Pink Sand Dunes State Park. This sweeping expanse of pink sand comes from eroding sandstone. Funneled through a notch in the rock, wind picks up speed and carries grains of sand into the area. Once the wind slows down, the sand is deposited, creating this giant playground for dune buggies, ATVs—called OHVs in Utah (off-highway vehicles), and dirt motorcycles. A small area is fenced off for walking, but the sound of wheeled toys is always with you. Children love to play in the sand, but before you let them loose, check the surface temperature; it can become very hot. ⊠ *Yellowjacket and Hancock Rds., 12 mi off U.S. 89, near Kanab* ☎ *435/648–2800* ⊕ *www.stateparks.utah.gov* ⊠ *$6 day use* ☉ *Daily.*

★ **Snow Canyon State Park.** Named not for winter weather but after a pair of pioneering Utahans named Snow, this overlooked gem of a state park is filled with natural wonders. Hiking trails lead to lava cones, sand dunes, cactus gardens, and high-contrast vistas. From the campground you can scramble up huge sandstone mounds and overlook the entire valley. About an hour from Zion, this state park is near St. George. ⊠ *1002 Snow Canyon Dr., Ivins* ☏ *435/628–2255* ⊕ *www.stateparks. utah.gov* ⊠ *$5 per vehicle* ⊙ *Daily 6* AM–10 PM.

AREA ACTIVITIES

SPORTS AND THE OUTDOORS
GOLF
★ Hurricane has **Sky Mountain** (⊠ *1030 N. 2600 West St.* ☏ *888/345– 5551*), a scenic 18-hole public course. Many fairways are framed by red-rock outcroppings; the course has a front-tee view of the nearby 10,000-foot Pine Valley Mountains. There's also a snack bar, pro shop, and driving range on the premises. Peak season at this course is February through April. Greens fees are from $10 to walk nine hols in the off-season to $65 for 18 holes with a cart during peak season.

ARTS AND ENTERTAINMENT
ART GALLERIES
Worthington Gallery. Opened in 1980 by a single potter in a pioneer-era home near the mouth of Zion Canyon, Worthington Gallery now features more than 20 artists who create in clay, metal, glass, paint, and more. ⊠ *789 Zion Park Blvd., Springdale* ☏ *800/626–9973 or 435/772– 3446* ☏ *www.worthingtongallery.com* ⊙ *Daily 9–9.*

NIGHTLIFE
Bit & Spur Restaurant and Saloon. As good as the Mexican food is, this place is best known as the premier place to see live music in southern Utah. Many touring rock, blues, and reggae bands go out of their way to play here. ⊠ *1212 Zion Park Blvd., Springdale* ☏ *435/772–3498.*

WHERE TO EAT AND STAY

ABOUT THE RESTAURANTS
There is only one full-service restaurant in Zion National Park. Springdale has the greatest number and diversity of dining options. Because this is conservative Utah, don't presume a restaurant serves beer, much less wine or cocktails, especially in the smaller towns. Most restaurants are family friendly, and dress tends to be casual. Prices are reasonable, though they inch higher in and near the national park.

ABOUT THE HOTELS
The Zion Canyon Lodge is rustic but comfortable. Nearby Springdale has many lodging options to choose from, from quaint smaller motels and bed-and-breakfasts, to upscale hotels with modern amenities and riverside rooms. If you're looking for the least expensive options short of camping, look in the villages an hour or more away from the park entrance. You'll get same-day reservations in some cases and dirt-cheap

room rates. Panguitch and Hurricane have some particularly good options for budget and last-minute travelers.

ABOUT THE CAMPGROUNDS

The two campgrounds within Zion National Park—Watchman and South campgrounds—are family friendly, convenient, and quite pleasant, but in the high season they do fill up fast. Outside the park you'll find a number of private campgrounds. Backpackers looking to camp in the backcountry need to get a permit at the visitor center.

WHERE TO EAT

IN THE PARK

¢   ✕ **Castle Dome Café & Snack Bar.** Right next to the Zion Lodge shuttle stop

AMERICAN   and adjoining the gift shop, this small fast-food restaurant is all about convenience. Hikers on the go can grab a banana or a sandwich here, or you can while away an hour with ice cream on the sunny patio. ⊠ *Zion Canyon Scenic Dr., 3¼ mi north of Canyon Junction* ☎ *435/772–7700* ⊕ *www.zionlodge.com* ▭ *AE, D, DC, MC, V.*

$–$$$ ✕ **Red Rock Grill at Zion Lodge.** This restaurant's monopoly on in-park

AMERICAN   pseudo-gourmet dining has not made them complacent. The menu won't have you doing back flips, but the solid American fare with a southwestern twang is serviceable. The restaurant is adorned with historic photos dating back to the early days of the lodge. You take in the scenery while you eat from the grill's comfortable patio. A good selection of steak, fish, and poultry is offered for dinner as well as decent vegetarian options and an expansive dessert menu. The lunch menu consists of simpler plates (burgers, sandwiches, salads, etc.); breakfast is also served. ⊠ *Zion Canyon Scenic Dr., 3¼ mi north of Canyon Junction* ☎ *435/772–7760* ⊕ *www.zionlodge.com* ᕳ *Reservations essential* ▭ *AE, D, DC, MC, V.*

PICNIC AREAS   **The Grotto.** Get your food to go at the Zion Lodge, take a short walk to
☾   this lunch retreat, and dine beneath a shady Gambel oak. There are lots of amenities—drinking water, fire grates, picnic tables, and restrooms. A trail leads to the Emerald Pools from here if you want to walk off your lunchtime calories. ⊠ *Zion Canyon Scenic Dr., 3½ mi north of Canyon Junction.*

Kolob Canyons Viewpoint. Take in a shaded meal with a view at this charming picnic site 100 yards down the Timber Creek trail. ⊠ *At the end of Kolob Canyons Rd., 5 mi from Kolob Canyons Visitor Center.*

☾   **Zion Nature Center.** On your way to or from the Junior Ranger Program feed your kids at the nature center picnic area. When the nature center is closed, you can use the restrooms in South Campground. ⊠ *Near the entrance to South Campground ½ mi north of the south entrance* ☎ *435/772–3256.*

OUTSIDE THE PARK

$$–$$$ ✕ **Bit & Spur Restaurant and Saloon.** This restaurant has been a legend in

SOUTHWESTERN   Utah for 20 years. The seasonal menu lists familiar Mexican dishes like

Fodor'sChoice   tamales, but the kitchen also gets creative. Try the chili-rubbed *bistek*
★   *asado* (roasted steak) or chipotle shrimp pasta. When the weather is nice, arrive early so you can eat outside and enjoy the lovely grounds and views. ⊠ *1212 Zion Park Blvd., Springdale* ☎ *435/772–3498* ⊕ *www.bitandspur.com* ▭ *AE, D, MC, V* ☻ *No lunch.*

39

¢   × **Main Street Café.** One of the best cups of coffee in Dixie is poured in
AMERICAN   Hurricane. A full espresso bar will satisfy "caffiends," while vegetarians
and others can choose from salads, sandwiches, breakfast burritos, and
desserts. Also come here for the excellent home-baked goods. Sit inside
to admire the works of local artists, or share the patio with the hummingbirds. ⊠ *138 S. Main St., Hurricane* ☎ *435/635–9080* ▭ *No credit
cards* ⊘ *Closed Sun. No dinner.*

$–$$ × **Scaldoni's Grill.** At this local favorite you can't go wrong if you're
ITALIAN   hankering for Italian fusion food in an upscale atmosphere. The grill
also serves a variety of steaks and seafood. The lounge has tapas and
over-the-top cocktails. ⊠ *1183 E 100 S, St. George* ☎ *435/674–1300*
⊕ *www.scaldonis.com* ▭ *AE, D, MC, V* ⊘ *Closed Sun.*

¢–$ × **Sol Foods Market and Deli.** Stop here for a quick burger, sandwich, or
AMERICAN   vegetarian snack; or stock up on camping staples from their attached
supermarket. Daily specials include freshly made wraps and sandwiches.
They can also prepare picnic baskets or box lunches for your day in
the park. The patio seating is near the Virgin River, with views into
the park. ⊠ *95 Zion Park Blvd., Springdale* ☎ *435/772–0277* ⊕ *www.
solfoods.com* ▭ *MC, V.*

$$–$$$ × **Sullivan's Rococo Steakhouse & Inn.** Specializing in beef and seafood, this
STEAK   St. George restaurant is known for its prime rib and diverse salad options.
It sits atop a hill overlooking town, so you can enjoy spectacular views
right from your table. ⊠ *511 Airport Rd., St. George* ☎ *435/628–3671*
⊕ *www.rococo.net/steakhouse.html* ▭ *AE, D, DC, MC, V.*

$–$$ × **Zion Pizza & Noodle Co.** It may look like a church, but the only thing
PIZZA   being worshipped here is beer. The Cholesterol Hiker and Good for You
pizzas put some pizzazz into the menu; you can also order pasta dishes
like linguine with peanuts and grilled chicken and spaghetti with homemade marinara sauce. A selection of Utah microbrews is also served.
You can dine indoors or in the beer garden. The restaurant opens at
4 PM. ⊠ *868 Zion Park Blvd., Springdale* ☎ *435/772–3815* ⊕ *www.zion-
pizzanoodle.com* ▭ *No credit cards* ⊘ *No lunch. Closed Dec.–Feb.*

WHERE TO STAY

IN THE PARK

$$$ 🏠 **Zion Lodge.** Knotty pine woodwork and log and wicker furnishings
accent the lobby. Lodge rooms are modern but not fancy, and the his-
toric western-style cabins have gas-log fireplaces. This is a place of quiet
retreat, so there are no TVs—kids can amuse themselves outdoors on
the abundant grassy lawns. The lodge is within easy walking distance
of trailheads, horseback riding, and the shuttle stop, all of which are
less than ½ mi away. Make reservations at least six months in advance.
Note that this is not the original lodge. The first Zion Lodge burned
down in 1966; however, the rebuilt structure convincingly re-creates the
classic look of the old inn. **Pros:** guests can drive their cars all the way
up to the lodge, even during shuttle-only season; beautifully recreated
lodge; gets nice and dark at night. **Cons:** no in-room coffee; bring a
flashlight to make your way to your cabin; staff seems overwhelmed at
busiest times. ⊠ *Zion Canyon Scenic Dr., 3¼ mi north of Canyon Junc-
tion* ☎ *888/297–2757* ⊕ *www.zionlodge.com* ⤳ *75 rooms, 6 suites, 40*

cabins ⚠ In-room: Wi-Fi, no TV. In-hotel: restaurant, Internet terminal ▤ *AE, D, DC, MC, V.*

CAMPING ⛺ **South Campground.** All the sites here are under big cottonwood trees,
$ providing some relief from the summer sun. The campground operates on a first-come, first-served basis, and sites are usually filled before noon each day during high season. **Pros:** campsites have more space in between them, and seem to be farther away from the parking lot as opposed to Watchman. **Cons:** showers require a shuttle ride; closed in the off-season; no hookups; no reservations. ✉ *Rte. 9, ½ mi north of south entrance* ☎ *435/772–3256* ⛺ *126 tent/RV sites* ⚠ *Flush toilets, dump station, drinking water, fire grates, picnic tables* ▤ *No credit cards* ⊙ *Mid-Mar.–Oct.*

$-$$ ⛺ **Watchman Campground.** This large campground on the Virgin River
★ operates on a reservation system between April and October (⊕ *www. recreation.gov*), but you do not get to choose your own site. **Pros:** the only campground in the park open year-round; right by the south entrance. **Cons:** some campsites feel stacked on top of each other; the closest showers require a ride on the park shuttle. ✉ *Access road off Zion Canyon Visitor Center parking lot* ☎ *435/772–3256, 800/365– 2267 reservations* ⛺ *160 tent/RV sites, 91 with hookups* ⚠ *Flush toilets, partial hookups (electric), dump station, drinking water, fire grates, picnic tables* ▤ *D, MC, V.*

OUTSIDE THE PARK

$$-$$$ 🏨 **Cliffrose Lodge and Gardens.** Comfortable rooms border on plush at
★ this friendly, charming lodge. Long after your hike is over you can continue to enjoy views of the towering, colorful cliffs from your balcony or the lodge's riverside beach. Flowers adorn the 5-acre grounds, and the Virgin River runs right along the property. It's within walking distance of the Zion Canyon Visitor Center and shuttle stop. **Pros:** excellent pool area; you could throw a rock and hit the south entrance to the park; bedding and linens are absolutely top-notch; responsive and caring management team. **Cons:** the grounds outshine the appearance of the rooms; walls of some rooms are thin. ✉ *281 Zion Park Blvd., Springdale* ☎ *435/772–3234 or 800/243–8824* ⊕ *www.cliffroselodge. com* ⇥ *40 rooms* ⚠ *In-room: kitchen, Wi-Fi. In-hotel: pool, laundry facilities* ▤ *AE, D, MC, V.*

$$-$$$ 🏨 **Desert Pearl Inn.** You're not exactly roughing it at the Desert Pearl.
Fodor'sChoice Every room has vaulted ceilings and thick carpets, plus cushy throw
★ pillows, Roman shades, oversize windows, bidets, sleeper sofas, and tiled showers with deep tubs. The pool area is exceptionally well landscaped and fully equipped, with a double-size hot tub and a shower-and-restroom block. A 1,000-square-foot suite with a full kitchen is also available. **Pros:** vanity/sink separate from the bathroom; the rooms facing the Virgin River have balconies or terraces with majestic views. **Cons:** bedding is plush but decor is Euro-minimalist; walls are thin (so the wrong neighbor can spoil your quiet retreat). ✉ *707 Zion Park Blvd., Springdale* ☎ *435/772–8888 or 888/828–0898* ⊕ *www.desertpearl.com* ⇥ *61 rooms* ⚠ *In-room: safe, kitchen, refrigerator, DVD (some), Wi-Fi. In-hotel: pool* ▤ *AE, D, MC, V.*

39

¢ ⌗ **Golden Hills Motel.** Don't judge a book by its cover. This is not a beautiful resort, but the rooms are comfortable and inexpensive—where else can you get a two-room suite for under $100? This no-frills lodging option is right at Mount Carmel Junction. Its funky pink-and-blue roadside diner serves good, basic country-style fare like country-fried steak, liver and onions, and homemade breads and pies. **Pros:** clean; simple; affordable. **Cons:** tour groups flock to the Golden Hills like moths to a flame, which means rooms sell out early, and it can be crowded. ⊠ *125 East State, at the junction of U.S. 89 and Rte. 9, Mount Carmel Junction* ☎ *435/648–2268 or 800/648–2268* ⊕ *www.goldenhillsmotel. com* ⋈ *30 rooms* ᣮ *In-room: refrigerator, DVD, Wi-Fi. In-hotel: restaurant, pool, laundry facilities, Internet terminal, some pets allowed* ▭ *AE, D, MC, V.*

CAMPING ⚠ **Zion Canyon Campground & RV Park.** In Springdale about a half mile from
$$ the south entrance to the park, this campground is surrounded on three sides by the canyon's rock formations. Many of the sites are on the river. **Pros:** staff has developed a sterling reputation as helpful and friendly. **Cons:** the heat can be stifling in July and August because of the topography. ⊠ *479 Zion Park Blvd., Springdale* ☎ *435/772–3237* ⊕ *www. zioncamp.com/rv_park.html* ⚠ *110 RV sites, 110 tent sites* ᣮ *Flush toilets, full hookups, dump station, drinking water, guest laundry, showers, fire grates, picnic tables, food service, electricity, public telephone, general store, play area, swimming (river), Wi-Fi (some)* ▭ *D, MC, V.*

CAMPGROUNDS
AT A GLANCE

CAMPGROUNDS AT A GLANCE

CAMPGROUND NAME	Total # of sites	# of RV sites	# of hook-ups	Drive-to sites	Hike-to sites	Flush toilets	Pit toilets	Drinking water	Showers	Fire grates/pits	Swimming	Boat access	Playground	Dump station	Ranger station	Public telephone	Reservations possible	Daily fee per site	Dates open
ARCHES																			
★ Devils Garden	52	52	0	Y		Y	Y	Y		Y						Y	Y	$20	Y/R
BADLANDS																			
★ Cedar Pass Campground	96	96	0	Y		Y	Y	Y						Y	Y			$10	Apr.–Oct.
Sage Creek Primitive	ULP	ULP	0		Y		Y											Free	Y/R
BANFF																			
Castle Mountain	43	43	0	Y		Y		Y		Y				Y				$21	May–Sept.
Johnston Canyon	132	132	0	Y		Y		Y	Y	Y				Y	Y			$27	June–Sept.
★ Lake Louise	409	189	189	Y		Y		Y	Y	Y				Y	Y	Y	Y	$28–$32	Y/R
Mosquito Creek	32	32	0	Y			Y			Y								$18	Y/R
Protection Mountain	89	89	0	Y		Y		Y		Y				Y				$21	June–Sept.
Rampart Creek	50	50	0	Y			Y			Y								$16	June–Sept.
★ Tunnel Mountain Trailer Court	321	321	321	Y		Y		Y	Y	Y				Y	Y		Y	$38	May–Oct.
★ Tunnel Mountain Village 1	618	618	0	Y		Y		Y	Y	Y				Y	Y	Y	Y	$27	May–Oct.
★ Tunnel Mountain Village 2	188	188	188	Y		Y		Y	Y	Y				Y	Y	Y	Y	$32	Y/R
Two Jack Main	380	380	0	Y		Y		Y		Y				Y	Y			$21	May–Sept.
Two Jack Lakeside	74	0	0	Y		Y		Y	Y	Y	Y			Y				$27	May–Sept.
Waterfowl Lakes	116	116	0	Y		Y		Y		Y	Y			Y				$21	June–Sept.
BIG BEND																			
Chisos Basin	60			Y	Y	Y		Y		Y				Y	Y		Y	$14	Y/R
★ Rio Grande Village	100			Y	Y	Y		Y		Y	Y			Y	Y			$14	Y/R
Rio Grande RV	25	25	25	Y			Y	Y	Y	Y	Y			Y	Y	Y	Y	$27	Y/R
Cottonwood	31			Y	Y		Y	Y		Y				Y	Y			$14	Y/R

	Sites															Fee	Season
BLACK CANYON																	
East Portal	15	0		Y						Y	Y			Y	Y	$12	late May–Sept.
North Rim	13	13	0		Y					Y	Y			Y	Y	$12	May–Oct.
★ South Rim	65	23	23*		Y				Y	Y	Y			Y	Y	$12, $18	Y/R
BRYCE CANYON																	
North	103	47	0		Y		Y		Y	Y	Y			Y	Y	$15	Y/R
Sunset	96	49	0		Y				Y	Y	Y			Y	Y	$15	May–Oct.
CANYONLANDS																	
Needles Outpost	23	0	0		Y		Y		Y	Y	Y		Y		Y	$20	March–Nov.
★ Squaw Flat	26	26	0		Y		Y	Y	Y							$15	Y/R
Willow Flat	12	2	0		Y		Y		Y		Y					$10	Y/R
CAPITOL REEF																	
Cathedral Valley Campground	6	0	0		Y		Y		Y	Y						free	Y/R
Cedar Mesa Campground	5	0	0		Y		Y		Y	Y	Y			Y		free	Y/R
★ Fruita Campground	71	71	0		Y		Y		Y	Y						$10	Y/R
CARLSBAD CAVERNS																	
Wilderness Camping Only																	
CHANNEL ISLANDS																	
Del Norte	4	0	0				Y		Y	Y				Y		$15	Y/R
East Anacapa	7	0	0				Y		Y	Y	Y		Y	Y		$15	Y/R
★ Santa Cruz	40	0	0				Y	Y	Y					Y		$15	Y/R
San Miguel	9	0	0				Y		Y	Y			Y	Y		$15	Y/R
Santa Barbara	10	0	0				Y		Y	Y			Y	Y		$15	Y/R
Santa Rosa	15	0	0			Y	Y		Y	Y				Y		$15	Y/R

Key:
ULP: Unlimited Primitive
Y/R: Year-round
* Partial hookups

CAMPGROUNDS AT A GLANCE

CAMPGROUND NAME	Total # of sites	# of RV sites	# of hook-ups	Drive-to sites	Hike-to sites	Flush toilets	Pit toilets	Drinking water	Showers	Fire grates/pits	Swimming	Boat access	playground	Dump station	Ranger station	Public telephone	Reservations possible	Daily fee per site	Dates open
CRATER LAKE																			
Mazama	212	212	0	Y		Y		Y	Y					Y	Y	Y		$21–$30	June–Oct.
Lost Creek	16	0	0	Y		Y		Y	Y	Y					Y			$10	July–Sept.
DEATH VALLEY																			
Furnace Creek	136	136	0	Y		Y		Y	Y	Y				Y	Y	Y		$18	Y/R
★ Mahogany Flat	13	0	0				Y		Y									Free	Mar.–Nov.
Mesquite Springs	30	30	0	Y		Y		Y		Y				Y				$12	Y/R
Panamint Springs Resort	67	41	41	Y		Y		Y	Y	Y	Y			Y	Y			$15–$30	Y/R
Stovepipe Wells Village	204	14	14	Y		Y		Y	Y	Y	Y			Y	Y	Y		$12–$23	Oct. 15–Apr. 15
Sunset	750	750	0	Y		Y		Y		Y				Y	Y			$12	Oct. 15–Apr. 15
★ Texas Spring	92	92	0	Y		Y		Y		Y		Y		Y	Y			$14	Oct. 15–Apr. 15
Thorndike	6	6	0	Y			Y		Y	Y								Free	Mar.–Nov.
Wildrose	30	30	0	Y			Y		Y	Y								Free	Oct. 15–Apr. 15
GLACIER & WATERTON																			
Glacier																			
Apgar	194	25	0		Y	Y		Y		Y				Y	Y			$15	May–Oct.
Avalanche Creek	87	50	0	Y		Y		Y		Y	Y			Y	Y			$15	June–Sept.
Bowman Lake	48	0	0		Y	Y		Y		Y	Y			Y				$12	May–Sept.
Fish Creek	178	18	0	Y		Y		Y		Y				Y		Y		$17	June–Oct.
Kintla Lake	13	0	0		Y		Y			Y								$12	May–Sept.
★ Many Glacier	110	13	0	Y		Y		Y		Y				Y	Y			$15	May–Sept.
Rising Sun	83	3	0	Y		Y		Y		Y				Y				$15	May–Sept.
Sprague Creek	25	0	0	Y		Y		Y		Y								$15	May–Sept.

Campground	Sites	RV Sites	Hookups	Fee	Open
St. Mary	148	25	0	$17	May–Sept.
Two Medicine	99	13	0	$15	May–Sept.
Waterton Lakes					
Waterton Townsite	238	208	95	$24–$33	Apr.–Oct.
Belly River	24	24	0	$14	May–Oct.
Crandell Mountain	129	129	0	$19	May–Oct.
GRAND CANYON					
Bright Angel	32	0	0	Free	Y/R
Cottonwood	12	0	0		
Desert View	50	50	0	$12	mid-May–mid-Oct.
Indian Garden	15	0	0	Free	
★ Mather	308	308	0	$15	Y/R
North Rim	83	83	0	$15–$20	May–Oct.
Trailer Village	79	79	79	$28	Y/R
GRAND TETON					
★ Colter Bay	350	238	0	$19	May–Sept.
Colter Bay Trailer Village	112	112	112	$48–$54	May–Sept.
Gros Ventre	360	360	0	$19	May–Oct.
★ Jenny Lake	49	0	0	$19	May–Sept.
Lizard Creek	60	60	0	$18	June–Sept.
Signal Mountain	86	86	0	$20	May–Oct.
GREAT BASIN					
Baker Creek	34	0	0	$12	mid-May–Sept.
Lower Lehman Creek	11	limited	0	$12	Y/R
Upper Lehman Creek	22	0	0	$12	mid-May–Sept.
★ Wheeler Peak	37	0	0	$12	June–Sept.

Key:
Y/R: Year-round
** Summer only

CAMPGROUNDS AT A GLANCE

	Campground Name	Total # of sites	# of RV sites	# of hook-ups	Drive-to sites	Hike-to sites	Flush toilets	Pit toilets	Drinking water	Showers	Fire grates/pits	Swimming	Boat access	Playground	Dump station	Ranger station	Public telephone	Reservations possible	Daily fee per site	Dates open
GREAT SAND DUNES																				
	Pinyon Flats Campground	88	88	0	Y		Y		Y		Y			Y	Y	Y			$14	Y/R
GUADALUPE MOUNTAINS																				
	Dog Canyon	13	4	0	Y		Y		Y						Y	Y			$8	Y/R
	Pine Springs	38	18	0	Y		Y		Y						Y	Y	Y		$8	Y/R
JASPER																				
	Columbia Icefield	33	0	0		Y		Y	Y										$14	May–Oct.
	Honeymoon Lake	35	35	0	Y			Y	Y		Y	Y				Y			$14	June–Sept.
	Jonas Creek	25	25	0	Y	Y		Y	Y		Y					Y			$14	May–Sept.
	Mt. Kerkeslin	42	42	0	Y	Y		Y	Y		Y					Y			$14	June–Sept.
	Pocahontas	140	130	0	Y	Y	Y		Y		Y					Y	Y		$19	May–Oct.
	Snaring River	66	48	0		Y		Y	Y		Y								$14	May–Sept.
❀	Wabasso	228	228	0	Y	Y	Y		Y		Y		Y	Y		Y	Y		$19	June–Sept.
	Wapiti	362	362	40	Y		Y		Y	Y	Y			Y		Y	Y		$24–$28	June–Sept.
❀	Whistlers	781	781	177	Y		Y		Y	Y	Y		Y	Y		Y	Y		$21–$33	May–Oct.
	Wilcox Creek	46	46	0	Y			Y	Y		Y			Y		Y			$14	June–Sept.
JOSHUA TREE																				
	Belle	18	0	0	Y			Y			Y								$10	Y/R
★	Black Rock Canyon	100	100	0	Y		Y		Y		Y			Y	Y	Y	Y		$15	Y/R
	Cottonwood	62	62	0	Y		Y		Y		Y			Y	Y	Y			$15	Y/R
	Hidden Valley	45	45	0	Y			Y			Y								$10	Y/R
	Indian Cove	101	101	0	Y			Y			Y								$15	Y/R
	Jumbo Rocks	125	125	0	Y			Y			Y						Y		$10	Y/R

Campground	Total sites	RV sites	Group sites											Fee	Dates open
Ryan	31	31	0	Y					Y	Y				$10	Y/R
White Tank	15	0	0	Y					Y	Y				$10	Y/R
LASSEN VOLCANIC															
★ Manzanita Lake	179	148	0	Y		Y		Y**	Y	Y	Y			$18	May–Oct.
Summit Lake North	46	46	0	Y		Y		Y	Y	Y				$18	June–Sept.
Juniper Lake	18	0	0	Y			Y		Y	Y	Y			$10	July–Sept.
Southwest Walk-In	21	0	0		Y	Y		Y**	Y	Y				$14	Y/R
Summit Lake South	48	48	0	Y		Y		Y	Y	Y				$16	June–Oct.
Warner Valley	18	0	0	Y		Y		Y	Y	Y				$14	June–Oct.
MESA VERDE															
★ Morefield Campground	380	15	15	380		Y		Y	Y	Y	Y	Y	Y	$20–$30	Late Apr.–mid-Oct.
MOUNT RAINIER															
★ Cougar Rock	173	173	0	Y		Y		Y	Y	Y	Y	Y	Y	$12–$15	May–Oct.
Ipsut	30	0	0	Y			Y		Y	Y	Y			$8	Y/R
★ Mowich Lake	30	0	0		Y							Y		Free	July–Oct.
★ Ohanapecosh	188	188	0	Y		Y		Y	Y	Y	Y	Y	Y	$12–$15	May–Oct.
Sunshine Point	18	18	0	Y		Y		Y	Y	Y	Y	Y		$10	Y/R
White River	112	112	0	Y		Y		Y	Y	Y	Y	Y		$10	June–Sept.
NORTH CASCADES															
Colonial Creek	162	32	0	Y		Y		Y	Y	Y	Y	Y		$12	May–Sept.
Goodell Creek	21	0	0	Y		Y		Y**	Y	Y				$10**	Y/R
Newhalem Creek	111	111	0	Y			Y	Y	Y	Y	Y	Y	Y	$12	May–Oct.
Lake Chelan National Recreation Area	63	0	0		Y			Y	Y					Free	Y/R

Key:
Y/R: Year-round
** Summer only

CAMPGROUNDS AT A GLANCE

OLYMPIC

CAMPGROUND NAME	Total # of sites	# of RV sites	# of hook-ups	Drive-to sites	Hike-to sites	Flush toilets	Pit toilets	Drinking water	Showers	Fire grates/pits	Swimming	Boat access	playground	Dump station	Ranger station	Public telephone	Reservations possible	Daily fee per site	Dates open
Altaire	30	30	0	Y		Y		Y		Y								$12	Apr.–Oct.
Deer Park	14	0	0	Y			Y	Y		Y								$10	May–Sept.
Dosewallips	30	0	0	Y			Y			Y								$10	May–Oct.
Elwha	40	40	0	Y			Y			Y				Y	Y			$12	Y/R
★ Fairholme	88	88	0	Y		Y		Y		Y	Y	Y	Y		Y			$12	Apr.–Oct.
Graves Creek	30	30	0	Y		Y		Y		Y				Y	Y			$12	Apr.–Oct.
Heart o' the Hills	105	105	0	Y		Y		Y		Y	Y			Y	Y			$12	Y/R
Hoh	88	88	0	Y		Y		Y		Y				Y	Y			$12	Y/R
July Creek	28	0	0		Y		Y	Y		Y								$10	Apr.–Oct.
Kalaloch	175	175	0	Y		Y		Y		Y				Y	Y	Y		$14–$18	Y/R
Lake Quinault Resort Village	31	31	31	Y		Y		Y	Y	Y					Y	Y	Y	$22	Apr.–Oct.
★ Mora	94	93	0	Y		Y		Y		Y			Y	Y	Y			$12	Y/R
North Fork	7	0	0	Y			Y			Y				Y				$10	May–Sept.
Ozette	15	15	0	Y			Y			Y	Y			Y				$12	May–Oct.
Queets	20	0	0	Y			Y			Y				Y				$10	Apr.–Oct.
Sol Duc	82	82	0	Y		Y		Y		Y	Y		Y	Y	Y			$14	May–Oct.
South Beach	50	50	0	Y						Y								$10	May–Oct.
Staircase	56	56	0	Y		Y		Y		Y				Y	Y			$12	Apr.–Oct.

PETRIFIED FOREST

CAMPGROUND NAME	Total # of sites	# of RV sites	# of hook-ups	Drive-to sites	Hike-to sites	Flush toilets	Pit toilets	Drinking water	Showers	Fire grates/pits	Swimming	Boat access	playground	Dump station	Ranger station	Public telephone	Reservations possible	Daily fee per site	Dates open
Wilderness Camping Only					Y													Free	

	Sites			1	2	3	4	5	6	7	8	Fee	Season
REDWOOD													
DeMartin	10	0	0				Y		Y			Free	Y/R
Elk Prairie	75	75	0	Y		Y	Y		Y	Y	Y**	$20	Y/R
Flint Ridge	10	0	0		Y		Y	Y				Free	Y/R
★ Gold Bluffs Beach	26	26	0	Y		Y	Y		Y	Y	Y**	$15	Y/R
Jedediah Smith	86	86	0	Y		Y	Y	Y	Y	Y	Y**	$20	mid-May–mid Nov.
Little Bald Hills	5	0	0			Y		Y				Free	May–LD
Mill Creek	145	145	0	Y		Y	Y		Y	Y	Y**	$20	May–LD
Nickel Creek	5	0	0		Y		Y	Y				Free	Y/R
ROCKY MOUNTAIN													
Aspenglen	54	19	0	Y	Y**	Y**	Y	Y	Y	Y		$20	mid-May–late Sept.
Glacier Basin	150	39	0	Y	Y**	Y**	Y	Y	Y	Y	Y	$20	late May–early Sept.
Longs Peak	26	0	0	Y	Y**	Y**	Y	Y	Y			$20	Y/R
★ Moraine Park	245	245	0	Y	Y**	Y**	Y	Y	Y	Y**	Y	$20	Y/R
Timber Creek	98	70	0	Y	Y**	Y**	Y	Y	Y	Y	Y	$20	Y/R
SAGUARO													
Douglas Spring	3	0				Y		Y			Y	$6	Y/R
Grass Shack	3	0	0			Y		Y			Y	$6	Y/R
Happy Valley	3	0	0			Y		Y			Y	$6	Y/R
Juniper Basin	3	0	0			Y		Y				$6	Y/R
Manning Camp	6	0	0			Y		Y				$6	Y/R
Spud Rock Spring	3	0	0			Y		Y				$6	Y/R

Key:
Y/R: Year-round
** Summer only
LD: Labor Day

CAMPGROUNDS AT A GLANCE

CAMPGROUND NAME	Total # of sites	# of RV sites	# of hook-ups	Drive-to sites	Hike-to sites	Flush toilets	Pit toilets	Drinking water	Showers	Fire grates/pits	Swimming	Boat access	Playground	Dump station	Ranger station	Public telephone	Reservations possible	Daily fee per site	Dates open
SEQUOIA/KINGS CANYON																			
Sequoia																			
Atwell Mill	23	0	0	Y			Y			Y								$12	May–Oct.
Buckeye Flat	28	0	0	Y		Y		Y		Y								$18	Apr.–Sept.
Dorst Creek	204	204	0	Y		Y		Y		Y					Y			$20	MD–LD
Lodgepole	214	214	0	Y		Y		Y**		Y			Y**		Y	Y	Y	$20	Y/R
Potwisha	42	42	0	Y		Y				Y			Y		Y	Y		$18	Y/R
South Fork	10	0	0	Y			Y			Y								$12**	Y/R
Kings Canyon																			
Azalea	113	113	0	Y		Y		Y		Y					Y			$18	Y/R
Canyon View	37	0	0		Y	Y				Y					Y			$18	MD–Sept.
Crystal Springs	67	67	0	Y		Y				Y					Y			$18	MD–LD
Sentinel	82	82	0	Y		Y		Y		Y					Y			$18	May–Oct.
★ Sheep Creek	111	111	0	Y		Y				Y					Y			$18	May–Oct.
Sunset	200	200	0	Y		Y				Y					Y			$18	MD–Sept.
THEODORE ROOSEVELT																			
★ Cottonwood	78	30	0	Y		Y**	Y			Y				Y				$10	Y/R
Juniper	50	25	0	Y		Y**	Y			Y				Y				$10	Y/R
Round-Up Group Horse Camp	10	0	0		Y		Y			Y						Y		$20	May–Sept.
WIND CAVE																			
★ Elk Mountain Campground	75	75	0	Y						Y					Y	Y		$12	Y/R

YELLOWSTONE																			
Bridge Bay	432	432	0	Y		Y		Y		Y		Y		Y	Y	Y	Y**	$19	May–Sept.
Canyon	272	272	0	Y		Y		Y	Y	Y					Y	Y	Y	$19	June–Sept.
Fishing Bridge RV Park	344	344	344	Y		Y		Y	Y					Y	Y	Y	Y	$35	May–Sept.
Grant Village	425	425	0	Y		Y		Y	Y	Y		Y		Y	Y	Y	Y	$19	June–Sept.
Indian Creek	75	75	0	Y			Y			Y								$12	June–Sept.
Lewis Lake	85	85	0	Y			Y	Y		Y		Y			Y			$12	June–Oct.
Madison	277	277	0	Y		Y		Y						Y	Y	Y	Y	$19	May–Sept.
Mammoth Hot Springs	85	85	0	Y		Y		Y		Y					Y	Y		$14	Y/R
Norris	116	116	0	Y		Y		Y							Y	Y		$14	May–Sept.
Pebble Creek	32	32	0	Y			Y			Y								$12	June–Sept.
Slough Creek	29	29	0	Y			Y			Y								$12	May–Oct.
Tower Fall	32	32	0	Y			Y			Y								$12	May–Sept.
YOSEMITE																			
Bridalveil Creek	74	74	0	Y		Y		Y		Y						Y	Y	$14	July–Sept.
Camp 4	35	0	0		Y	Y		Y	Y	Y					Y	Y		$5	Y/R
Crane Flat	166	166	0	Y		Y		Y		Y					Y	Y	Y	$20	June–Sept.
Hodgdon Meadow	105	105	0	Y		Y		Y							Y		Y	$20	Y/R
Housekeeping Camp	266	266	0	Y		Y		Y	Y	Y	Y						Y	$72	May–Oct.
Lower Pines	60	60	0	Y		Y		Y		Y	Y				Y	Y	Y	$20	Mar.–Oct.
North Pines	80	80	0	Y		Y		Y	Y	Y	Y				Y	Y	Y	$20	Y/R
Porcupine Flat	52	52	0	Y			Y			Y								$10	July–Oct.
Tamarack Flat	52	52	0	Y			Y			Y								$10	July–Sept.

Key:
Y/R: Year-round
*** Summer only*
MD: Memorial Day
LD: Labor Day

CAMPGROUND NAME	Total # of sites	# of RV sites	# of hook-ups	Drive-to sites	Hike-to sites	Flush toilets	Pit toilets	Drinking water	Showers	Fire grates/pits	Swimming	Boat access	Playground	Dump station	Ranger station	Public telephone	Reservations possible	Daily fee per site	Dates open
★ Tuolumne Meadows	314	314	0	Y		Y		Y						Y	Y	Y	Y	$20	July–Sept.
Upper Pines	238	238	0	Y		Y		Y		Y				Y	Y	Y	Y	$20	Y/R
Wawona	93	93	0	Y		Y		Y	Y	Y				Y	Y	Y		$20	Y/R
★ White Wolf	87	87	0	Y		Y		Y						Y	Y			$14	July–Sept.
Yosemite Creek	75	75	0	Y			Y								Y			$10	July–Sept.
ZION																			
South	126	126	0	Y		Y		Y					Y		Y			$16	Apr.–Sept.
★ Watchman	160	91	91	Y		Y		Y					Y		Y	Y	Y	$16–20	Y/R

Key:
Y/R: Year-round

INDEX

A

A & A Mesa Verde RV Park and Campground ⚠, *588*
Abyss, The, *400*
Accessibility concerns, *46, 69*
Adams, Ansel, *874*
Adams Museum, *784*
Affordable Adventures Badlands Tour, *142*
Agate Bridge, *658*
Agate House, *657, 659*
Agua Canyon, *227*
Ahwahnee, The ✕▦ , *18, 860, 881, 885–886*
Ahwahneechee Village, *860*
Akamina Parkway, *377*
Alamosa, CO, *495*
Alamosa National Wildlife Refuge, *495*
Albright Visitor Center, *812*
Albuquerque, *102*
Alexander's Country Inn & Restaurant ✕▦ , *606, 608*
Alluvial Fan, *690–691*
Alpine, TX, *194, 195*
Alpine Visitor Center, *691*
Altitude sickness, *68*
Amangani ▦ , *469*
Anacapa Island, *307–308*
Anasazi Heritage Center, *582*
Anasazi State Park, *278*
Ancient Bristlecone Pine Forest, *351–352*
Andy's Bistro ✕ , *528*
Angels Landing Trail, *907*
Animal bites, *68*
Ansel Adams Gallery, *875*
Ansel Adams Photo Walks, *873*
Antelope Flats Road, *443*
Antonito, CO, *495*
Apgar Discovery Cabin, *366*
Apgar Visitor Center, *367*
Arcata, CA, *677*
Arches National Park, *32, 103–130*
dining, *123, 124–126*
educational offerings, *118–119*
essential info, *107–108*
exploring, *108–110*
festivals and events, *120*
flora and fauna, *106*
getting oriented, *104–105*
lodging, *123–124, 127–130*
nearby attractions, *119, 121–123*
scenic drives, *96, 108–109, 123*

sports and the outdoors, *110–116, 118, 121–122*
top reasons to go, *104*
visitor centers, *110*
when to go, *106*
Arizona-Sonora Desert Museum, *718*
Artist Point, *813*
Artist's Drive, *341*
Artist's Palette, *342*
Ashford, WA, *601*
Ashland, OR, *330, 331*
Athabasca Falls, *157, 519*
Athabasca Glacier, *157*
Audrie's Bed & Breakfast ▦ , *793*
Auto Log, *732*
Avalanche Peak Trail, *829*
Avenue of the Flags, *789*

B

Back Basin, *811*
Badger House Community, *575*
Badlands Loop Road, *136*
Badlands National Park, *32, 131–148*
dining, *144–145, 146–147*
educational offerings, *141–142*
essential info, *135–136*
exploring, *136–139*
festivals and events, *143*
flora and fauna, *134*
getting oriented, *132–133*
lodging, *145–146, 147–148*
nearby attractions, *142–144*
scenic drives, *88, 136*
sports and the outdoors, *139–141*
top reasons to go, *132*
tours, *139, 142*
visitor centers, *138–139*
when to go, *134*
Badlands Wilderness Area, *138*
Badwater, *343*
Bajada Loop Drive, *714*
Baker, NV, *482*
Baker Creek Road, *478*
Balanced Rock, *109*
Balcony House, *575*
Bald Eagles, *52*
Ballarat Ghost Town, *352*
Bamboo Garden Restaurant ✕ , *299*
Banff Centre, *168*
Banff Gondola, *159*

Banff National Park, *32, 149–180*
dining, *171–175*
educational offerings, *168*
essential info, *153, 154–155*
exploring, *155, 156–157, 158–160*
family picks, *153*
festivals and events, *169*
flora and fauna, *152*
getting oriented, *150–151*
lodging, *171, 175–180*
nearby attractions, *168–170*
scenic drives, *82–83, 155*
sports and the outdoors, *160–166, 168, 170*
top reasons to go, *150*
visitor centers, *160*
when to go, *152*
Banff Park Museum, *158*
Banff Upper Hot Springs, *158*
Bar J Chuckwagon ✕ , *464*
Barker Ranch, *352*
Barton Warnock Environmental Education Center, *195*
Battery Point Lighthouse, *677*
Bats, *296*
Beachcombing, *638*
Bear Country U.S.A., *785*
Bear Lake, *691, 694, 695*
Bear Lake Road, *689*
Bear's Hump Trail, *379*
Beatty, NV, *351*
Beautiful Rushmore Cave, *785*
Beaver Meadows Visitor Center, *691*
Beetle Rock Family Nature Center, *737*
Behunin Cabin, *270*
Belton Chalet Grill Dining Room ✕ , *385*
Ben Reifel Visitor Center, *138*
Best Western Grand ▦ , *240–241*
Best Western Grand Canyon Squire Inn ▦ , *435*
Best Western Ruby's Inn ▦ , *241*
Best Western Ruby's Inn Campground and RV Park ⚠ , *242*
Best Western Stevens Inn ▦ , *300*
Bicknell, CO, *277*
Bidwell House ▦ , *568*
Big Badlands Overlook, *138*
Big Baldy, *743*
Big Bend National Park, *33, 181–202*
border crossings, *197, 198*

PHOTO CREDITS

1, Evan Spiler, Fodors.com member. 2, Christina Collucci, Fodors.com member. 5, Jeff Vanuga. **Chapter 1: Welcome to the Parks:** 10-11, Jeff Vanuga. 12, Christopher Byczko, Fodors.com member. 14 (top), Eric Foltz/iStockphoto. 14 (bottom), NPS (National Park Service). 15 (left), Eric Foltz/iStockphoto. 15 (right), Bill Pofahl, Fodors.com member. 16, Nancy A. Hann, Fodors.com member. 17 (top left), Erica

L. Wainer, Fodors.com member. 17 (top right), Natalia Eliason, Fodors.com member. 17 (bottom), Pete Souza/wikipedia.org. 18 (left and right), Library of Congress Prints and Photographs Division. 19, texasbookworm, Fodors.com member. 20 (left), Erica L. Wainer, Fodors.com member. 20 (top center), Gene Zdonek, Fodors.com member. 20 (top right), Art_man/Shutterstock. 20 (bottom right), Stephen Fadem, Fodors.com member. 21 (left), Alan Gleichman/Shutterstock. 21 (top center), Roger Bravo, Fodors.com member. 21 (top right), David Davis/Shutterstock. 21 (bottom right), Debbie Bowles, Fodors.com member. 22 (left), Heather A. Craig/Shutterstock. 22 (top center), Dan King, Fodors.com member. 22 (top right), Mark Yarchoan/Shutterstock. 22 (bottom right), BostonGal, Fodors.com member. 23 (top left), Dan King, Fodors.com member. 23 (bottom left), Blue Ice/Shutterstock. 23 (top center), Alan Scheer/Shutterstock. 23 (bottom center), Eric Gevaert/Shutterstock. 23 (right), Bill Perry/Shutterstock. 24, Xanterra Parks & Resorts. 25, Jill Fromer/iStockphoto. 26 (top), Danita Delimont/Alamy. 26 (bottom), Library of Congress Prints and Photographs Division. 27 (top and bottom), Xanterra Parks & Resorts. 28 (top), Roberto Soncin Gerometta/Alamy. 28 (bottom), Danita Delimont/Alamy. 29 (top), Travel Alberta. 29 (bottom), Carmen Sorvillo/Shutterstock. **Chapter 2: Choosing a Park:** 30-31, Daniel McFadden, Fodors.com member. 32, Jonmikel Pardo, Fodors.com member. 33 (left), William A. McConnell, Fodors.com member. 33 (right), travlingdude, Fodors.com member. 34, travlingdude, Fodors.com member. 35 (left), Jaan-Martin Kuusmann/Shutterstock. 35 (right), hpeabody, Fodors.com member. 36, Victor Sutan, Fodors.com member. 37 (left), Christine Ferreira, Fodors.com member. 37 (right), John H. Kim, Fodors.com member. 38, NPS. 39 (left), CAN BALCIOGLU/Shutterstock. 39 (right), Jina A Miller, Fodors.com member. 40, prplab, Fodors.com member. 41 (left), Kimberly Jozwiak, Fodors.com member. 41 (right), annieak, Fodors.com member. 42, David Boxer, Fodors.com member. 43 (left), Jennifer Petoff, Fodors.com member. 43 (right), freq_wonder, Fodors.com member. 44, Keith Jorgensen, Fodors.com member. 45 (left), Debra Becker, Fodors.com member. 45 (right), Brad Campbell, Fodors.com member. 47 (left), DebitNM, Fodors.com member. 47 (right), Jennifer Petoff, Fodors.com member. 48, Sandy Rubinstein, Fodors.com member. 49 (left), Dan King, Fodors.com member. 49 (right), Rebalyn, Fodors.com member. 50, Luca Moi/Shutterstock. 51 (left), Kimberly Jozwiak, Fodors.com member. 51 (right), cyndyq, Fodors.com member. 52, Evan Spiler, Fodors.com member. **Chapter 3: Planning Your Visit:** 54-55, Lura Smith, Fodors.com member. 56, NPS. 57, Diego Cervo/Shutterstock. 58, Jim Lopes/Shutterstock. 59, David Restivo/Glacier National Park/NPS. 60, Kevin Inman, Fodors.com member. 61 (left), Keith Jorgensen, Fodors.com member. 61 (right), David Restivo/Glacier National Park/NPS. 62, Jeffrey Kramer, Fodors.com member. 64, Vitalii Nesterchuk/Shutterstock. 65 (left), Michael Svoboda/Shutterstock. 65 (right), Inc/Shutterstock. 66, Erica L. Wainer, Fodors.com member. 67, carolv, Fodors.com member. 68, David Davis/Shutterstock. 69, Diana Lundin/Shutterstock. 70 (left), NPS. 70 (top center), Public Domain. 70 (top right), Nevada Commission on Tourism. 70 (bottom right), worldwidetraveler, Fodors.com member. 71 (left), Joe Rossi/NPS. 71 (top center and top right), NPS. 71 (bottom right), Jacom Stephens/Avid Creative, Inc./iStockphoto. 73 (left), NPS. 73 (right), Public Domain. 74, Loic Bernard/iStockphoto. 75 (left), Larry Carver/viestiphoto.com. 75 (right), Bill Garber, Fodors.com member. **Chapter 4: Driving Tours:** 76-77, Som Vembar, Fodors.com member. 78, Jan Paul/iStockphoto. 83, Bart Edson, Fodors.com member. 96, CarlB9090, Fodors.com member. **Chapter 5: Arches National Park:** 103, Evan Spiler, Fodors.com member. 104 (all), NPS. 107, David Noton/age fotostock. 117, mlgb, Fodors.com member. **Chapter 6: Badlands National Park:** 131, Andrew Mace, Fodors.com member. 132 (top and bottom) and 133, South Dakota Tourism. 135, Jim W. Parkin/iStockphoto. **Chapter 7: Banff National Park:** 149, Mayskyphoto/Shutterstock. 150-54, Travel Alberta. 158, Artifan/Shutterstock. 167, Travel Alberta. 173, Mayskyphoto/Shutterstock. **Chapter 8: Big Bend National Park:** 181, Eric Foltz/iStockphoto. 182 (top), Kenny Braun/Texas Tourism. 182 (bottom), Jim Woodard/NPS. 184, John Kamaras/NPS. 185, Eric Foltz/iStockphoto. 188, Mike Norton/Shutterstock. **Chapter 9: Black Canyon of the Gunnison National Park:** 203, Tom Till/Alamy. 204, iStockphoto. 205, Tom Stillo/CTO. 206, iStockphoto. 207, Lisa Lynch/NPS. 211, Jim Parkin/Shutterstock. **Chapter 10: Bryce Canyon National Park:** 221, Chris Christensen, Fodors.com member. 222 (all), Public Domain. 225, Ron Yue/Alamy. 228, Pete Foley, Fodors.com member. 233, Inc/Shutterstock. **Chapter 11: Canyonlands National Park:** 243, Bryan Brazil/Shutterstock. 244-45, NPS. 247, rollie rodriguez/Alamy. 254-55, Doug Lemke/Shutterstock. **Chapter 12: Capitol Reef National Park:** 265, Luca Moi/Shutterstock. 266 (top), Jacom Stephens/Avid Creative, Inc./iStockphoto. 266 (center and bottom), Frank Jensen/Utah Office of Tourism. 268, Jacom Stephens/Avid Creative, Inc./iStockphoto. 269, imagebroker/Alamy. 276, Kerrick James. Anton Foltin/Shutterstock. **Chapter 13: Carlsbad Caverns National Park:** 285, W.P. Fleming/viestiphoto.com. 286 and 287, Peter Jones/NPS. 289, Craig Lovell/viestiphoto.com. 299, John Cancalosi/Alamy. **Chapter 14: Channel Islands National Park:** 301, Christopher Russell/iStockphoto. 302 (top), Yenwen Lu/iStockphoto. 302 (bottom), NatalieJean/Shutterstock. 303 and 306, ZanyZeus/Shutterstock. 304, hpeabody, Fodors.com

ABOUT OUR WRITERS

Writer John Blodgett has moved to Utah three times since 1996. He's explored almost every corner of the Beehive State but has a particular passion for the southern swath, with its glorious national parks. It was in these silent canyons and wide-open lands of sage brush and juniper that John discovered a new muse. Currently editor of *Utah CEO*, he has written for *Utah Business, Digital IQ, Salt Lake Magazine, Utah Homes & Garden, Salt Lake City Weekly,* and *Catalyst*; and is a former newspaper reporter and photojournalist.

A big fan of the National Park System, Denver resident Barbara Colligan has made numerous trips to Rocky Mountain National Park and the surrounding areas, often going with her twin daughters and the family dog.

Native Californian Cheryl Crabtree has worked as a freelance writer since 1987 and has contributed to *Fodor's California* since 2003. Cheryl is editor of *Montecito Magazine*. She currently lives in Santa Barbara with her husband, two sons, and Jack Russell terrier.

The author of nine novels and eight nonfiction books, Patrick Dearen is a recognized authority on the history and legends of the Pecos River and Big Bend regions of Texas. He garnered nine national and state journalism awards as a reporter for two West Texas dailies and has been honored by Western Writers of America, West Texas Historical Association, and Permian Historical Association. He makes his home in Midland, Texas, with his wife Mary and their son Wesley.

Jennifer Edwards is an author and a journalist based in St. Augustine, Florida. Her stories have appeared in dozens of newspapers, including the *Dallas Morning News, Houston Chronicle, New York Sun,* and *International Herald Tribune*. She was the features editor for the *Odessa American* and assistant lifestyle editor for the *Midland Reporter Telegram*. Each year she eagerly awaits her annual Western park fix and the cowboy coffee she brews up at her campsite.

Jane Gendron stopped in Park City on what was meant to be a cross-country trek and never left. Like any good resort worker, she dabbled in everything from waiting tables to heading up public relations for a non-profit organization before abandoning the office for her underused skis, loyal golden retriever, neglected husband, and smiling baby boy (not necessarily in that order). She's written for *Park City Magazine, Wasatch Journal, Utah Business, Las Vegas Life,* and *Estates West* magazines.

Carrie Frasure, who currently splits her time between Arizona and Alaska, has wandered the wilds of the Southwest for more than a decade. She has written hundreds of travel articles and is a regular contributor to *Arizona Highways*.

A Phoenix-based freelance writer and editor, Cara LaBrie left her native Arizona to report for newspapers across the country. She quickly learned that no place had Mexican food like the Valley, and eventually found the way back to her favorite salsas and enchiladas. She also appreciates the striking desert sunsets and loves to take out-of-state visitors on a tour of her favorite restaurants.

Fodor's Arizona writer Mara Levin divides her time between travel writing, social work, and her role as a mother of two daughters. A native of California, Mara now lives in Tucson, Ariz., where the grass may not always be greener, but the mountains, tranquility, and slower place of desert life have their own appeal.

Tom Griffith, who's penned articles for such publications as *The New York Times*, the *Chicago Tribune, Denver Post,* and the *Houston Chronicle,* lives with his wife, Nyla, in Deadwood, S.D. He's written or co-authored more than 50 books, including *Fodor's Compass American Guides South Dakota* and *America's Shrine of Democracy,* with a foreword by President Ronald Reagan. He helped found the Mount Rushmore Preservation Fund, which raised $25 million for the mountain memorial.

Brian Kevin has covered adventure travel and the outdoors for *Outside* and *Away. com*, and has written about books, music, and culture for publications like *Mother Jones, Paste,* and *High Country News.* Author of *Fodor's Compass American Guides Yellowstone and Grand Teton,* Brian lives in Missoula, Montana.

There is no place freelance writer Debbie Olsen would rather be than hiking a beautiful mountain trail. This veteran Fodor's contributor spends much of her time exploring national parks with her husband and four children. Her travel adventures appear regularly in the *Red Deer Advocate* and the *Calgary Herald.*

Steve Pastorino is a Salt Lake City-based sports executive who loves to travel and write in his rare spare time. His has written previously for Fodor's about Yellowstone, Zion, and Bryce Canyon national parks, and updated Yellowstone for this edition. A regular contributor to the *Salt Lake Tribune,* Steve also maintains a blog titled "Not Just a Hat Rack." He and his wife, Teri, have three children: Lucca, Declan, and Sophia.

Nebraska native Gary Peterson is the editor of AAA's *Home & Away* magazine. His love of history and nature came together in his piece about the Roosevelts and their contributions to the National Park Service.

Marge Peterson, an Omaha, Nebraska-based travel journalist, is the former executive editor of *Home & Away* magazine. She has traveled extensively to the national parks of the West.

A Northern California resident for 15 years, Reed Parsell has traveled extensively throughout the region and written hundreds of newspaper travel stories based on this experiences. A part-time copy editor and travel writer for the *Sacramento Bee,* Parsell also writes a "going green"

column for *Sacramento* magazine as was the primary writer for *Fodor's InFocus Yosemite, Sequoia and Kings Canyon National Parks.*

Martha Schindler Connors is a freelance writer in Evergreen, Colo., where she lives with her husband, two step-daughters and three dogs. She enjoys hiking and skiing.

Native Texan Swain Scheps is an author and IT professional who's contributed to *Fodor's Las Vegas* and *Fodor's Essential USA.* In terms of favorites, Swain thinks that any national park with gigantic trees is a good one. He lives with his wife in Dallas, the home base for his ongoing quest to locate the best salsa in the Southwest.

Seattle-based writer and editor Holly S. Smith has written often for Fodor's, covering the Pacific Northwest among other destinations. She is the author of such titles as *Aceh: Art & Culture* and *Adventuring in Indonesia.* Holly also is the proud mother of three adventurers, who often accompany her on the road.

Freelance writer Christine Vovakes has also contributed to *Fodor's California* and *Fodor's Essential USA.* Her travel articles and photographs have also appeared in many other publications, including *The Washington Post, The Christian Science Monitor, The Sacramento Bee* and the *San Francisco Chronicle.*

Bobbi Zane grew up in Southern California, watching the region grow from its mostly rural roots into one of the most exciting places in the world. Her articles on Palm Springs have appeared in the *Orange County Register* and *Westways* magazine. A lifelong Californian, Bobbi has visited every corner of the state on behalf of Fodor's. She recently contributed to *Fodor's California, Fodor's San Diego,* and *Fodor's Escape to Nature Without Roughing It.*